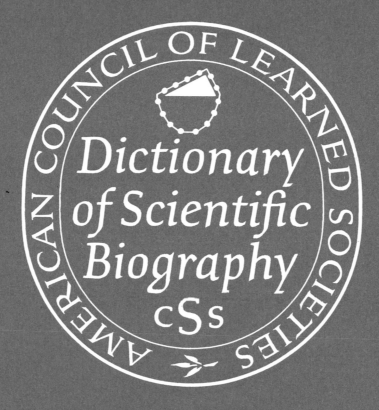

AMERICAN COUNCIL OF LEARNED SOCIETIES

Dictionary
of Scientific
Biography

cSs

DICTIONARY
OF
SCIENTIFIC BIOGRAPHY

PUBLISHED UNDER THE AUSPICES OF
THE AMERICAN COUNCIL OF LEARNED SOCIETIES

The American Council of Learned Societies, organized in 1919 for the purpose of advancing the study of the humanities and of the humanistic aspects of the social sciences, is a nonprofit federation comprising forty national scholarly groups. The Council represents the humanities in the United States in the International Union of Academies, provides fellowships and grants-in-aid, supports research-and-planning conferences and symposia, and sponsors special projects and scholarly publications.

MEMBER ORGANIZATIONS

AMERICAN PHILOSOPHICAL SOCIETY, 1743
AMERICAN ACADEMY OF ARTS AND SCIENCES, 1780
AMERICAN ANTIQUARIAN SOCIETY, 1812
AMERICAN ORIENTAL SOCIETY, 1842
AMERICAN NUMISMATIC SOCIETY, 1858
AMERICAN PHILOLOGICAL ASSOCIATION, 1869
ARCHAEOLOGICAL INSTITUTE OF AMERICA, 1879
SOCIETY OF BIBLICAL LITERATURE, 1880
MODERN LANGUAGE ASSOCIATION OF AMERICA, 1883
AMERICAN HISTORICAL ASSOCIATION, 1884
AMERICAN ECONOMIC ASSOCIATION, 1885
AMERICAN FOLKLORE SOCIETY, 1888
AMERICAN DIALECT SOCIETY, 1889
AMERICAN PSYCHOLOGICAL ASSOCIATION, 1892
ASSOCIATION OF AMERICAN LAW SCHOOLS, 1900
AMERICAN PHILOSOPHICAL ASSOCIATION, 1901
AMERICAN ANTHROPOLOGICAL ASSOCIATION, 1902
AMERICAN POLITICAL SCIENCE ASSOCIATION, 1903
BIBLIOGRAPHICAL SOCIETY OF AMERICA, 1904
ASSOCIATION OF AMERICAN GEOGRAPHERS, 1904
THE HISPANIC SOCIETY OF AMERICA, 1904
AMERICAN SOCIOLOGICAL ASSOCIATION, 1905
AMERICAN SOCIETY OF INTERNATIONAL LAW, 1906
ORGANIZATION OF AMERICAN HISTORIANS, 1907
COLLEGE ART ASSOCIATION OF AMERICA, 1912
HISTORY OF SCIENCE SOCIETY, 1924
LINGUISTIC SOCIETY OF AMERICA, 1924
MEDIAEVAL ACADEMY OF AMERICA, 1925
AMERICAN MUSICOLOGICAL SOCIETY, 1934
SOCIETY OF ARCHITECTURAL HISTORIANS, 1940
ECONOMIC HISTORY ASSOCIATION, 1940
ASSOCIATION FOR ASIAN STUDIES, 1941
AMERICAN SOCIETY FOR AESTHETICS, 1942
METAPHYSICAL SOCIETY OF AMERICA, 1950
AMERICAN STUDIES ASSOCIATION, 1950
RENAISSANCE SOCIETY OF AMERICA, 1954
SOCIETY FOR ETHNOMUSICOLOGY, 1955
AMERICAN SOCIETY FOR LEGAL HISTORY, 1956
SOCIETY FOR THE HISTORY OF TECHNOLOGY, 1958
AMERICAN COMPARATIVE LITERATURE ASSOCIATION, 1960

DICTIONARY

OF

SCIENTIFIC BIOGRAPHY

CHARLES COULSTON GILLISPIE

Princeton University

EDITOR IN CHIEF

Volume X

S. G. NAVASHIN – W. PISO

CHARLES SCRIBNER'S SONS · NEW YORK

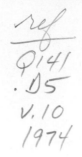
COPYRIGHT © 1974 AMERICAN COUNCIL OF LEARNED SOCIETIES

This book published simultaneously in the
United States of America and in Canada—
Copyright under the Berne Convention

All rights reserved. No part of this book
may be reproduced in any form without the
permission of Charles Scribner's Sons.

1 3 5 7 9 11 13 15 17 19 MD/C 20 18 16 14 12 10 8 6 4 2

Printed in the United States of America
Library of Congress Catalog Card Number 69-18090
ISBN 0–684–10121–1

Editorial Board

Editorial Staff

MARSHALL DE BRUHL, *MANAGING EDITOR*

SARAH FERRELL, *Assistant Managing Editor*

LOUISE BILEBOF KETZ, *Administrative Editor*

FREDERIC C. BEIL III, *Assistant Editor*

LYLE CHURCHILL, *Assistant Editor*

ROSE MOSELLE, *Editorial Assistant*

MARY GREENBERG, *Editorial Assistant*

ELIZABETH I. WILSON, *Copy Editor*

JOEL HONIG, *Copy Editor*

DORIS ANNE SULLIVAN, *Proofreader*

MICHAEL KNIBBS, *Proofreader*

Panel of Consultants

Contributors to Volume X

The following are the contributors to Volume X. Each author's name is followed by the institutional affiliation at the time of publication and the names of the articles written for this volume. The symbol † means that an author is deceased.

GIORGIO ABETTI
Istituto Nazionale di Ottica
ODIERNA; PIAZZI

LUÍS DE ALBUQUERQUE
University of Coimbra
D. P. PEREIRA; PIRES

MICHELE L. ALDRICH
Smithsonian Institution
NEWBERRY

GARLAND E. ALLEN
Washington University
PAINTER

TORSTEN ALTHIN
Royal Institute of Technology, Stockholm
NOBEL

G. C. AMSTUTZ
University of Heidelberg
NIGGLI; OCHSENIUS

IRINA V. BATYUSHKOVA
Academy of Sciences of the U.S.S.R.
NIKITIN; A. P. PAVLOV

ROBERT P. BECKINSALE
University of Oxford
A. PENCK; W. PHILLIPS

WHITFIELD J. BELL, JR.
American Philosophical Society Library
C. W. PEALE

LUIGI BELLONI
University of Milan
ODDI; PACCHIONI

RICHARD BERENDZEN
Boston University
H. A. NEWTON; PARKHURST; PEASE;
PERRINE

ALEX BERMAN
University of Cincinnati
PARMENTIER; P.-J. PELLETIER; PELOUZE;
PERSONNE; PERSOZ

KURT-R. BIERMANN
Akademie der Wissenschaften der DDR
NETTO

P. W. BISHOP
Smithsonian Institution
OSMOND

ASIT K. BISWAS
Department of Environment, Ottawa
PALISSY; P. PERRAULT

MARGARET R. BISWAS
Department of Environment, Ottawa
PALISSY; P. PERRAULT

J. MORTON BRIGGS, JR.
University of Rhode Island
PARENT

JAMES E. BRITTAIN
Georgia Institute of Technology
PACINOTTI

W. H. BROCK
University of Leicester
ODLING; PENNY

HARCOURT BROWN
PEIRESC

JED Z. BUCHWALD
Harvard University
NOBILI

K. E. BULLEN
University of Sidney
R. D. OLDHAM; OMORI

VERN L. BULLOUGH
California State University, Northridge
PANDER

IVOR BULMER-THOMAS
Oenopides of Chios; Pappus of Alexandria; Perseus

JOHN G. BURKE
University of California, Los Angeles
F. E. NEUMANN

JEROME J. BYLEBYL
University of Chicago
PICCOLOMINI

KENNETH L. CANEVA
University of Utah
OHM

CARLO CASTELLANI
PERRONCITO

MARÍA ASUNCIÓN CATALÁ
University of Barcelona
ORTEGA

PIERRE CHABBERT
Hôpitaux de Castres
PINEL

JOHN CHALLINOR
University College of Wales
E. T. NEWTON; G. OWEN

M. C. CHANG
Worcester Foundation for Experimental Biology
PINCUS

RICHARD CHORLEY
University of Cambridge
W. PENCK

MARSHALL CLAGETT
Institute for Advanced Study, Princeton
ORESME

EDWIN CLARKE
Wellcome Institute of the History of Medicine
NEWPORT; PHILIP

I. BERNARD COHEN
Harvard University
I. NEWTON

EDWIN H. COLBERT
Museum of Northern Arizona, Flagstaff
OSBORN

RUNAR COLLANDER †
OVERTON

PIERRE COSTABEL
École Pratique des Hautes Études
PARDIES; PÉRÈS

GLYN DANIEL
University of Cambridge
PETRIE; PIETTE

KARL H. DANNENFELDT
Arizona State University
OLYMPIODORUS

G. E. R. DEACON
National Institute of Oceanography, U.K.
PETTERSSON

S. DEMIDOV
Academy of Sciences of the U.S.S.R.
PETROVSKY

CLAUDE E. DOLMAN
University of British Columbia
NOGUCHI; PETTENKOFER

M. A. DONK
Rijksherbarium, Leiden
PERSOON

HAROLD DORN
Stevens Institute of Technology
NEWCOMEN

SIGALIA DOSTROVSKY
Barnard College
PÉROT

A. G. DRACHMANN
Philo of Byzantium

SIDNEY EDELSTEIN
Dexter Chemical Corporation
W. H. PERKIN

J. M. EDMONDS
University Museum, Oxford
J. PHILLIPS

CONTRIBUTORS TO VOLUME X

FRANK N. EGERTON III
University of Wisconsin-Parkside
PETTY

CAROLYN EISELE
Hunter College, City University of New York
B. PEIRCE; B. O. PEIRCE II; C. S. PEIRCE

CHURCHILL EISENHART
National Bureau of Standards
K. PEARSON

ANN MARIE ERDMAN
Florida State University
PEKELHARING

VASILIY A. ESAKOV
Academy of Sciences of the U.S.S.R.
PALLAS

JOSEPH EWAN
Tulane University
ORTON

JOAN M. EYLES
T. OLDHAM

W. V. FARRAR
University of Manchester
NERI; NIEUWLAND; PAYEN; W. H. PERKIN, JR.

LUCIENNE FÉLIX
PAINLEVÉ; C. É. PICARD

KONRADIN FERRARI D'OCCHIEPPO
University of Vienna
OPPENHEIM; OPPOLZER; PALISA

MARTIN FICHMAN
York University
P. PETIT

M. FIERZ
Federal Institute of Technology, Zurich
PAULI

KARIN FIGALA
Deutsches Museum
PAULLI

BERNARD S. FINN
Smithsonian Institution
PELTIER

PAUL FORMAN
Smithsonian Institution
ORNSTEIN; PASCHEN

ROBERT FOX
University of Lancaster
A. T. PETIT; M.-A. PICTET

PIETRO FRANCESCHINI
University of Florence
PACINI

EUGENE FRANKEL
NICOL

H.-CHRIST. FREIESLEBEN
C. A. F. PETERS; C. F. W. PETERS

RICHARD D. FRENCH
Privy Council Office, Government of Canada
OLIVER

HANS FREUDENTHAL
Rijksuniversiteit, Utrecht
NIEUWENTIJT

KURT VON FRITZ
University of Munich
PHILOLAUS OF CROTONA

GERALD L. GEISON
Princeton University
PASTEUR

PATSY A. GERSTNER
Howard Dittrick Museum of Historical Medicine
J. PARKINSON

PAUL GLEES
University of Göttingen
NISSL

A. GOUGENHEIM
Académie des Sciences de l'Institut de France
G. PERRIER

EDWARD GRANT
Indiana University, Bloomington
PETER PEREGRINUS

FRANK GREENAWAY
Science Museum, London
PERCY

A. T. GRIGORIAN
Academy of Sciences of the U.S.S.R.
NEKRASOV; PETERSON; N. P. PETROV

N. A. GRIGORIAN
Academy of Sciences of the U.S.S.R.
ORBELI; I. P. PAVLOV

A. RUPERT HALL
Imperial College of Science and Technology
OLDENBURG

WALLACE B. HAMBY, M.D.
PARÉ

RICHARD HART
Boston University
PEASE

HAROLD HARTLEY †
PARTINGTON

JOHN L. HEILBRON
University of California, Berkeley
NOLLET

DIETER B. HERRMANN
Archenhold Observatory, Berlin
NICOLAI

PIERRE HUARD
René Descartes University
PECQUET; PEYER

KARL HUFBAUER
University of California, Irvine
C. NEUMANN

MARIE-JOSÉ IMBAULT-HUARD
René Descartes University
PECQUET; PEYER

JEAN ITARD
Lycée Henri IV
OCAGNE

S. A. JAYAWARDENE
Science Museum, London
PACIOLI

BØRGE JESSEN
University of Copenhagen
PETERSEN

PAUL JOVET
Centre National de Floristique
PÉRON

GEORGE B. KAUFFMAN
California State University, Fresno
PFEIFFER

ALEX G. KELLER
University of Leicester
D'ORTA; C. PERRAULT

SUZANNE KELLY, O.S.B.
Stonehill College
NORMAN

HUBERT C. KENNEDY
Providence College
PADOA; PARSEVAL DES CHÊNES; PEANO; PIERI

MILTON KERKER
Clarkson College of Technology
PAMBOUR

DANIEL J. KEVLES
California Institute of Technology
NICHOLS

PEARL KIBRE
Hunter College, City University of New York
PETRUS BONUS

GEORGE KISH
University of Michigan
A. E. NORDENSKIÖLD

MARC KLEIN
Louis Pasteur University
OKEN

ZDENĚK KOPAL
University of Manchester
E. AND N. PIGOTT

ELAINE KOPPELMAN
Goucher College
PEACOCK

HANS GÜNTHER KÖRBER
Zentralbibliothek des Meteorologischen Dienstes der DDR, Potsdam
OLSZEWSKI; C. W. W. OSTWALD

T. W. KORZYBSKI
Polish Academy of Sciences
PARNAS

CONTRIBUTORS TO VOLUME X

EDNA E. KRAMER
Polytechnic Institute of New York
A. E. NOETHER; M. NOETHER

FRIDOLF KUDLIEN
University of Kiel
ORIBASIUS; PHILINUS OF COS

P. G. KULIKOVSKY
Moscow University
NEUYMIN; NUMEROV; A. Y. ORLOV;
S. V. ORLOV; PARENAGO

LOUIS I. KUSLAN
Southern Connecticut State College
NORTON

BENGT-OLOF LANDIN
University of Lund
PAYKULL

GEORGE H. M. LAWRENCE
Hunt Institute for Botanical Documentation
F. NYLANDER; W. NYLANDER

JACQUES R. LÉVY
Paris Observatory
PERROTIN

O. A. LEZHNEVA
Academy of Sciences of the U.S.S.R.
V. V. PETROV

JOHN H. LIENHARD
University of Kentucky
NUSSELT

C. LIMOGES
University of Montreal
E. PERRIER

DAVID C. LINDBERG
University of Wisconsin
PECHAM

STEN LINDROTH
University of Uppsala
N. E. NORDENSKIÖLD; OLAUS MAGNUS

JAMES LONGRIGG
University of Newcastle Upon Tyne
NICOLAUS OF DAMASCUS

J. M. LÓPEZ DE AZCONA
Comisión Nacional de Geología, Madrid
NUÑEZ SALACIENSE

AVERIL M. LYSAGHT
S. PARKINSON

RUSSELL McCORMMACH
Johns Hopkins University
J. W. NICHOLSON

MARVIN W. McFARLAND
Library of Congress
PICCARD

ROBERT McKEON
Babson College
NAVIER

PATRICIA P. MacLACHLAN
College of DuPage
PAPIN

ROGERS McVAUGH
University of Michigan
PALMER

EDWARD P. MAHONEY
Duke University
NIFO

MICHAEL S. MAHONEY
Princeton University
NICERON

J. C. MALLET
Centre National de Floristique
PÉRON

BRIAN G. MARSDEN
Smithsonian Astrophysical Observatory
NEWCOMB; W. H. PICKERING

OTTO MAYR
Smithsonian Institution
PERRONET; R.-P. PICTET

A. J. MEADOWS
University of Leicester
NEWALL

JEAN MESNARD
University of Paris
NOEL

S. R. MIKULINSKY
Academy of Sciences of the U.S.S.R.
PIROGOV

MARCEL MINNAERT †
PANNEKOEK

A. M. MONNIER
University of Paris
PEZARD

ERNEST A. MOODY
OCKHAM

LETTIE S. MULTHAUF
NIESTEN; NORWOOD; OLBERS

ARNE MÜNTZING
University of Lund
NILSSON-EHLE

G. NAUMOV
Academy of Sciences of the U.S.S.R.
OBRUCHE

AXEL V. NIELSEN †
OLUFSEN

WŁODZIMIERZ NIEMIERKO
Nencki Institute of Experimental Biology
NENCKI

CALVERT E. NOLAND
San Diego State University
PACKARD

J. D. NORTH
University of Oxford
PARSONS; T. E. R. PHILLIPS

H. OETTEL
NIELSEN

C. D. O'MALLEY †
NEMESIUS

JANE M. OPPENHEIMER
Bryn Mawr College
NICHOLAS

WALTER PAGEL
Wellcome Institute of the History of Medicine
PARACELSUS

JOHN PARASCANDOLA
University of Wisconsin-Madison
NOVY

FRANKLIN PARKER
West Virginia University
PEARL

LINUS PAULING
Institute of Orthomolecular Medicine
A. A. NOYES

OLAF PEDERSEN
University of Aarhus
ORTELIUS; PETER PHILOMENA OF DACIA

RUDOLF PEIERLS
University of Oxford
OPPENHEIMER

J. PELSENEER
University of Brussels
NEUBERG

VICENTE R. PILAPIL
California State University, Los Angeles
PÉREZ DE VARGAS

DAVID PINGREE
Brown University
NĪLAKAṆṬHA; PARAMEŚVARA; PAULIŚA; PAUL OF ALEXANDRIA; PETOSIRIS

LUCIEN PLANTEFOL
University of Paris
NICOT; PEYSSONNEL

HOWARD PLOTKIN
University of Western Ontario
E. C. PICKERING

JESSIE POESCH
Newcomb College, Tulane University
T. R. PEALE

JOHANNES PROSKAUER †
NEES VON ESENBECK

SAMUEL X. RADBILL
College of Physicians of Philadelphia
OTT

GLORIA ROBINSON
Yale University
PAULY; PFEFFER

JOEL M. RODNEY
Widener College
PALEY

COLIN A. RONAN
Journal of the British Astronomical Association
PARSONS; PINGRÉ

PAUL LAWRENCE ROSE
New York University
B. PEREIRA

xi

CONTRIBUTORS TO VOLUME X

EDWARD ROSEN
City College, City University of New York
NOSTRADAMUS; NOVARA; OSIANDER

K. E. ROTHSCHUH
Universität Münster/Westphalia
PFLÜGER

A. I. SABRA
Harvard University
AL-NAYRĪZĪ

WILLIAM L. SCHAAF
Brooklyn College
OZANAM

H. SCHADEWALDT
University of Düsseldorf
NEISSER

CHARLES B. SCHMITT
Warburg Institute
PATRIZI

IVO SCHNEIDER
University of Munich
NEANDER

E. L. SCOTT
Stamford High School, Lincolnshire
NEWLANDS; G. PEARSON

J. F. SCOTT †
OUGHTRED

T. K. SCOTT, JR.
Purdue University
PAUL OF VENICE

DANIEL SEELEY
Boston University
PERRINE

A. SEIDENBERG
University of California, Berkeley
PASCH

E. M. SENCHENKOVA
Academy of Sciences of the U.S.S.R.
NAVASHIN; PALLADIN

W. A. SMEATON
University College London
B. PELLETIER; PILATRE DE ROZIER

ROBERT SOULARD
Musée du Conservatoire National des Arts et Métiers
NIEPCE

HAROLD SPEERT
Columbia University
PAPANICOLAOU

ERNEST G. SPITTLER, S.J.
John Carroll University
PANETH

NILS SPJELDNAES
University of Aarhus
NIEBUHR

ROGER H. STUEWER
University of Minnesota
PERRIN

CHARLES SÜSSKIND
University of California, Berkeley
PIERCE

FERENC SZABADVÁRY
Technical University, Budapest
NODDACK; PÉAN DE SAINT-GILLES

LEONARDO TARÁN
Columbia University
NICOMACHUS OF GERASA; PARMENIDES OF ELEA

JULIETTE TATON
PEZENAS; J. PICARD

RENÉ TATON
École Pratique des Hautes Études
B. PASCAL; É. PASCAL; J. PICARD

KENNETH L. TAYLOR
University of Oklahoma
NECKER

SEVIM TEKELI
Ankara University
PIRĪ RAIS

ARNOLD THACKRAY
University of Pennsylvania
W. NICHOLSON

PHILLIP DRENNON THOMAS
Wichita State University
NUTTALL; PAUL OF AEGINA

V. V. TIKHOMIROV
Academy of Sciences of the U.S.S.R.
OZERSKY

RONALD TOBEY
University of California, Riverside
OMALIUS D'HALLOY

HEINZ TOBIEN
University of Mainz
NEHRING; NEUMAYR; OPPEL; D'ORBIGNY

G. J. TOOMER
Brown University
NICOMEDES

F. G. TRICOMI
Academia delle Scienze de Torino
PINCHERLE

G. L'E. TURNER
University of Oxford
NOBERT

CAROL URNESS
University of Minnesota
PENNANT

PETER W. VAN DER PAS
South Pasadena, Calif.
OUDEMANS; PISO

GERALD R. VAN HECKE
Harvey Mudd College
W. A. NOYES

J. J. VERDONK
PELETIER

HUBERT BRADFORD VICKERY
Connecticut Agricultural Experiment Station
OSBORNE

P. J. WALLIS
University of Newcastle Upon Tyne
PELL

J. L. WALSH †
OSGOOD

DEBORAH JEAN WARNER
Smithsonian Institution
S. B. NICHOLSON; OUTHIER; C. H. F. PETERS

RACHEL HORWITZ WESTBROOK
NEEDHAM

RICHARD S. WESTFALL
Indiana University
PEMBERTON

GEORGE W. WHITE
University of Illinois
D. D. OWEN

L. PEARCE WILLIAMS
Cornell University
OERSTED

WESLEY C. WILLIAMS
Case Western Reserve University
R. OWEN

M. L. WOLFROM †
NEF

H. WUSSING
Karl Marx University
C. G. NEUMANN; PFAFF

A. P. YOUSCHKEVITCH
Academy of Sciences of the U.S.S.R.
OSTROGRADSKY; PETERSON

BRUNO ZANOBIO
University of Pavia
NEGRI

DICTIONARY
OF
SCIENTIFIC BIOGRAPHY

DICTIONARY OF
SCIENTIFIC BIOGRAPHY

NAVASHIN— PISO

NAVASHIN, SERGEY GAVRILOVICH (*b.* Tsarevshin, Saratov guberniya, Russia, 14 December 1857; *d.* Detskoye Selo [now Pushkin], U.S.S.R., 10 December 1930), *biology, plant cytology, plant embryology.*

The son of a physician, Navashin graduated from the Saratov Gymnasium in 1874 and entered the St. Petersburg Academy of Medicine and Surgery although medicine did not especially interest him. His courses in chemistry with Borodin led to a strong interest in the subject. After four years Navashin transferred to the University of Moscow and entered second-year courses in the natural sciences section of the department of physics and mathematics. He was especially enthusiastic about his courses in chemistry with Markovnikov and in botany with Timiryazev. After his graduation from the university, Markovnikov offered Navashin an assistantship, first at Moscow University (1881) and then at the Petrov Academy (1884). After he passed his master's examination in 1887 Navashin began to teach courses: "Introduction to the Taxonomy of Fungi" at the university and plant pathology at the Petrov Academy. After the dissolution of the Petrov Academy in 1888, he became Borodin's assistant at the University of St. Petersburg. His interest in mycology drew Navashin to the mycologist Voronin, who suggested a study of the fungus *Sclerotinia betulae* (*Woroninaceae*), a parasite of the birch tree, for the subject of his master's thesis, which he defended in 1894 at St. Petersburg. After receiving the master's degree in botany, Navashin became professor of botany at the University of Kiev, where he accomplished his most fruitful scientific research and teaching. In 1915 serious illness obliged him to leave Kiev for the warmer climate of Tbilisi, where he devoted much energy to the university. Invited to Moscow in 1923 to organize the K. A. Timiryazev Institute of Plant Physiology, he was its director until 1929, the year before his death.

Navashin's basic research was devoted to the morphology and taxonomy of mosses and parasitic fungi. The study of the development of *Sclerotinia* in the ovaries of birches (1894) led him in 1895 to the discovery of chalazogamy in birches and, in 1899, in alders, elms, and other trees. Chalazogamy is a process of fertilization in which the pollen tubes penetrate to the embryo sac not through the micropyle but through its base, the chalaza. The phenomenon had previously been observed in the beefwood (*Casuarina*), only by Melchior Treub (1891), who considered it a distinguishing feature of these flowering plants. Navashin's observations introduced a correction into Treub's division of angiosperms into chalaziferous and porogamic.

Navashin's embryological research led him to the important discovery in 1898 of double fertilization in angiosperms. Observing fertilization in the Turk's-cap lily (*Lilium martagon*) and *Fritillaria tenella*, he was the first to note that this process involves not one but two sperm, which form in the pollen tube. One of them merges with the ovicell; the other, with the nucleus of the embryo sac, so that both the embryo and the endosperm develop as a result of the sexual process. On 24 August 1898 Navashin communicated this discovery to the Tenth Congress of Natural Scientists and Physicians, held in Kiev; later that year a description of the phenomenon appeared in print. The important discovery of double fertilization immediately attracted international attention; several scientists had already observed this phenomenon but had not given it proper attention. The presence of double fertilization made possible discovery of the fact that the endosperms of angiosperms and gymnosperms are not homologous formations but are completely distinct in nature and origin, despite the external similarity caused by their identical functions.

The last period of Navashin's life was dedicated to research in karyology. His work contributed to the comparative karyological trend in cytology, which was especially intensively developed in the Soviet Union. The success of Navashin's research was determined in substantial measure by his outstanding abilities as a microscope technician and observer.

1

For his research in embryology and plant cytology Navashin was made a corresponding member (1901) and an academician (1918) of the Russian Academy of Sciences, and an active member of the Ukrainian S.S.R. Academy of Sciences (1924). In 1929 he was awarded the title of Honored Scientist of the R.S.F.S.R.

BIBLIOGRAPHY

I. ORIGINAL WORKS. Navashin's collected works were published as *Izbrannye trudy* (Moscow–Leningrad, 1951). His writings include "Sklerotinia berezy (*Sclerotinia betulae Woroninaceae*)" ("Sclerotinia of Birches"), in *Trudy Sankt-Peterburskago obshchestva estestvoispytatelei*, Otd. botanichesky, **23** (1893), 56–64; "Ein neues Beispiel der Chalazogamie," in *Botanisches Zentralblatt*, **63**, no. 12 (1895), 353–357; "Resultate einer Revision der Befruchtungsvorgänge bei *Lilium martagon* und *Fritillaria tenella*," in *Mélanges biologiques tirés du Bulletin de l'Académie des sciences de Pétersbourg*, **9**, no. 9 (Nov. 1898), 377–382; "Neue Beobachtungen über Befruchtung bei *Fritillaria tenella* und *Lilium martagon*," in *Botanisches Zentralblatt*, **77** (1899), 62; and "Getero- i idiokhromozomy rastitelnogo yadra kak prichina dimorfizma nekotorykh vidov rastenii" ("Hetero- and Idiochromosomes in the Plant Nucleus as the Reason for Dimorphism in Certain Plant Species"), in *Izvestiya Akademii nauk*, no. 17 (1915), 1812–1834.

II. SECONDARY LITERATURE. On Navashin and his work, see his autobiography, in *Izbrannye trudy*, 13–20, with illustrations and portrait; V. V. Finn, "K 50-letiyu otkrytia S. G. Navashinym dvoynogo oplodotvorenia y pokrytosemennykh rastenii" ("On the Fiftieth Anniversary of Navashin's Discovery of Double Fertilization in Angiosperms"), in *Priroda*, no. 9 (1948), 80–81; and D. A. Granovsky, *Sergey Gavrilovich Navashin* (Moscow, 1947), with illustrations, portrait, and bibliography of nineteen works on Navashin.

E. M. SENCHENKOVA

NAVIER, CLAUDE-LOUIS-MARIE-HENRI (*b.* Dijon, France, 10 February 1785; *d.* Paris, France, 21 August 1836), *engineering, mechanics.*

During the French Revolution, Navier's father was a lawyer to the Legislative Assembly at Paris and his mother's uncle, the engineer Emiland Gauthey, worked in the head office of the Corps des Ponts et Chaussées at Paris. After her husband's death in 1793, Navier's mother moved back to Chalon-sur-Saône and left her son in Paris, under the tutelage of her uncle. In 1802, after receiving preparation from his granduncle, Navier entered the École Polytechnique near the bottom of the list; but he did so well during his first year that he was one of ten students sent to work in the field at Boulogne instead of spending their second year in Paris. Navier's first year at the École Polytechnique had critical significance for the formation of his scientific style, which reflects that of Fourier because the latter was briefly his professor of analysis. He subsequently became Fourier's protégé and friend.

In 1804 Navier entered the École des Ponts et Chaussées, from which he graduated in 1806 near the top of his class. After spending a few months in the field, he was brought to Paris to edit the works of his granduncle, who had just died and who had become France's leading engineer. Navier, who seems to have been insecure financially, lived for the rest of his life in the St.-Germain-des-Prés quarter of Paris. His wife, Marie Charlot, whom he married around 1812, came from a family of small landowners in Burgundy.

Navier was a member of the Société Philomatique (1819) and of the Académie des Sciences (1824). In 1831 he became *Chevalier* of the Legion of Honor. From 1819 he taught and had complete charge of the courses in applied mechanics at the École des Ponts et Chaussées but did not become titular professor until 1830, when A.-J. Eisenmann died. In 1831 Navier replaced Cauchy at the École Polytechnique. Navier participated in Saint-Simonianism and the positivist movements. He had Auguste Comte appointed to be one of his assistants at the École Polytechnique and participated actively in Raucourt de Charleville's Institut de la Morale Universelle.

Navier sought to complete the publishing project of his granduncle Gauthey. The administration of the Corps des Ponts et Chaussées, which looked with favor on this project, had him brought back to Paris in 1807 to publish Gauthey's manuscripts. This convergence of interests turned Navier into a theoretician who wrote textbooks for practicing engineers. His taste for scholarship and his background of higher analysis at the École Polytechnique and of practical engineering learned from his granduncle gave him the ideal preparation to make significant contributions to engineering science. During the period 1807–1820 he made mathematical analysis a fundamental tool of the civil engineer and codified the nascent concept of mechanical work for the science of machines.

Navier contributed only a few notes, of little scientific interest, to the first volume of Gauthey's works, which appeared in 1809. But during the next three years (1809–1812) he did a great deal of research in analytical mechanics and its application to the strength of materials as preparation for the second volume of Gauthey's works and for the revised edition of Bélidor's *Science des ingénieurs*, both of which appeared in 1813. The traditional engineering approach as exemplified by Gauthey studied experimentally the materials used in construction. These materials—primarily stone and wood—possess poor resistance to bending and were used rigidly. They also have widely varying properties that depend on their type and origin. In the traditional approach the engineer designed to avoid rupture and gave no thought to bending. He used large safety factors to compensate for the widely varying properties of the materials, which he viewed as rigid bodies subjected only to extension and to compression. On the other hand, the analytical tradition, which belonged to mathematical physics and did not form part of an engineer's training until after the creation of the École Polytechnique, studied idealized flexible bodies that can vibrate, such as strings, thin bars, and thin columns. In the derivation of analytical expressions these bodies were assumed to be subjected uniquely to pure bending; compression and tension were, therefore, ignored.

Navier, who had received training in both traditions, united them when he considered iron, which was just beginning to be used for bridges. He used a sort of principle of superposition: two sets of independent forces developed when bodies were bent—those resisting compression and extension and those resisting bending. He drew on the traditional engineering approach for the study of the first set of forces and on the analytical one for the second set. The first set follows Hooke's law that stress is proportional to strain. For the second set Navier used the relationship that the resistance varies as the angle of contingency (one divided by the radius of curvature), for which he referred to Euler's *Methodus inveniendi lineas curvas maximi minimive proprietate gaudentes* (1744).

Navier found an expression for the static moment of the resistance of any given fiber and then integrated it to find the total resisting moment, which he equated with the total moment of the applied forces. He concluded that for simple cases the moment of elasticity varies as the thickness squared, which quantity measures the resistance to extension, and as the thickness cubed times the length, which measures the resistance to bending. In his later study on the bending of an elastic plane (1820), Navier used the same general approach, which, however, led to fourth-order partial differential equations that had already been set down by Lagrange and Poisson. He showed how these can be solved in certain cases by applying methods that Fourier had used in an unpublished study.

In the 1813 editions of Bélidor and of Gauthey, Navier added notes which drew on the research of Coulomb and on the experimental tradition of eighteenth-century physics that had given him data for tables of the strength of stone and of wood. He appealed for further experiments on the strength of materials so that they could be used well in construction.

Navier's success as editior of Bélidor's *Science des ingénieurs* and of Gauthey's works led their publisher, Firmin Didot, to invite him to prepare a revised edition of Bélidor's *Architecture hydraulique*. Navier sought to correct the errors found in this work and to give it a mathematical sophistication that would make it useful to the graduates of the École Polytechnique. One item needed particular attention—the study of machines, for which Navier sought a quantitative criterion that would facilitate the selection of the best machines and motors. Research on this topic, conducted during 1814–1818, led him to the concept of quantity of action, which Coriolis shortly afterward transformed into that of mechanical work. A body animated by a force, Navier argued, can produce an effect observable to our senses only if this body covers a distance and at the same time exerts a pressure against an obstacle. Thus, for any interval of time, we can measure the effect of an acting force by the integral of $F\,dx$, where F designates the acting force and x the distance through which it acts. Navier, who drew on Lazare Carnot, then equated this to half the *vis viva* (mv^2) acquired by the moving body during the same interval, less that lost through sudden changes of speed. Because he thought that the above relation applied only to cases for which the various parts of a system are linked by expressions independent of time, he did not achieve a full concept of the conservation of mechanical work as did G.-G. Coriolis. Navier called the action of a force over a distance "quantity of action," an expression taken from Coulomb, and related this to the quantity of work (in a nontechnical sense) used to run the machine. Citing Montgolfier, who said that it was the quantity of action which pays, Navier called the quantity of action a mechanical form of money. In Navier's writings the march of the argument leads to the concept of work, whereas in those of J.-V. Poncelet and of Coriolis it flows from this concept. It took an embryonic form in the writings of Lazare Carnot, found its birth in those of A.-T. Petit, Poncelet, and Navier, and achieved the status of a general principle of applied mechanics in those of Coriolis. In Navier's revision of *Architecture hydraulique*, the engineer found this concept so defined as to give a measure of the usefulness of motors and a criterion that permitted rational design of motors and machines.

Editing the works of Gauthey and Bélidor in the years between 1809 and 1819 led Navier to make significant contributions to engineering science and placed him in a position to institute a new era in the teaching of engineering. His courses, the style of which was influential for well over a half a century, built on the creative physics of his generation, liberally applied analytical mechanics, and thus gave to the civil engineer tools adapted to an industrializing age.

During the years 1820–1829 Navier's research moved in two directions. In practical engineering he designed a suspension bridge that spanned the Seine in front of the Invalides, where today the Pont Alexandre III stands. Just as his bridge was in the final stages of construction, a sewer broke and the resultant flooding caused the bridge to list. This accident, which, in the view of the Corps des Ponts et Chaussées, could have been easily repaired, gave to the Municipal Council of Paris, which had opposed Navier's project, the opportunity to put pressure on the government to order the bridge torn down, to Navier's great chagrin.

In theoretical science Navier studied the motion of solid and liquid bodies, deriving partial differential equations to which he applied Fourier's methods to find particular solutions. This theoretical research led him to formulate the well-known equation identified with his name and that of Stokes. Navier viewed bodies as made up of particles which are close to each other and which act on each other by means of two opposing forces—one of attraction and one of repulsion—which, when in a state of equilibrium, cancel each other out. The repelling force resulted from the caloric that a body possessed. When equilibrium is disturbed in a solid, a restoring force acts which is proportional to the change in distance between the particles. In a liquid this force becomes proportional to the difference in speed of the particles. For both cases Navier derived equations that proved to have the same mathematical form. Although he had no concept of shear and used a concept of inter-molecular forces that is unacceptable today, he achieved results of which the expressions remain valid because he carefully summed moments of forces about orthogonal axes. This guaranteed that he did not overlook any forces that were acting even though he did not possess an efficient formulation for them.

Following the July Revolution, Navier became an active technical consultant to the state. He reported on the policy that should be adopted for policing the road transportation of heavy loads, for bidding to obtain government contracts, for constructing roads, and for laying out a national railway system. His reports exhibit Navier's high engineering ability and his continuing commitment to the Saint-Simonian and positivist movements.

BIBLIOGRAPHY

I. ORIGINAL WORKS. A. Barré de Saint-Venant, in C. Navier, *Résumé des leçons données à l'École des ponts et chaussées . . . première partie . . . première section. De la résistance des corps solides*, 3rd ed. (Paris, 1864), I, lv–lxxxiii, lists Navier's major works. The *Catalogue des manuscrits de la Bibliothèque de l'École des ponts et chaussées* (Paris, 1886) details Navier's extant scientific MSS. Autograph copies of Navier's "Mémoire sur la flexion des plans élastiques" (1820) are at the New York City Public Library and at the Archives Nationales, Paris, in $F^{14}2289^1$, dossier Navier. Navier's debate with Poisson concerning the molecular structure of matter is recorded in *Annales de chimie et de physique*, 2nd ser., **38** (1828), 304–314, 435–440; **39** (1828), 145–151, 204–211; **40** (1829), 99–110. Navier wrote a preface to J. B. Fourier, *Analyse des équations déterminées* (Paris, 1831). Navier's views on determinism are in *Comptes rendus . . . de l'Académie des sciences*, **2** (1836), 382. At the Archives Nationales, Paris, the following are of interest: $F^{14}2289^1$, dossier Navier, contains many autograph letters; $F^{14}11057$ contains reports by Navier on the École des Ponts et Chaussées and on the teaching of applied mechanics; $F^{14}11139$ documents Navier's bridge-building activities. The library of the Institut de France, Paris, has a few letters by Navier.

II. SECONDARY LITERATURE. A. Barré de Saint-Venant, *op cit.*, pp. xxxix–liv, lists obituaries by P. S. Girard, by C. H. Emmery de Sept-Fontaines, and by G. C. Prony, who errs in Navier's date of birth; in the library of the École des Ponts et Chaussées a MS biography of Navier contains obituaries by Coriolis and by Raucourt, the latter from *Éducateur, journal de l'Institut de la morale universelle . . .*, **1**, no. 5 (Sept.–Oct. 1836), 38–39; there is also a notice by Fayolle in *Biographie universelle*, LXXV (Paris, 1844), 314–317. Navier's standing as a student at the École des Ponts et Chaussées is detailed in Archives nationales, Paris, $F^{14}2148$, $F^{14}11054$, $F^{14}11055$ (which also contains remarks about Navier's course).

A. Barré de Saint-Venant, *op. cit.*, pp. xc–cccxi, gives a comprehensive history of the strength of materials and locates Navier's work within it; S. Timoshenko, in *History of Strength of Materials* (New York, 1953), 70–80; and I. Todhunter, in *A History of the Theory of Elasticity and of the Strength of Materials*, I (repr. New York, 1960), 133–146, cover the same ground. F. Stüssi, "Baustatik vor 100 Jahren—die Baustatik Naviers," in *Schweizerische Bauzeitung*, **116**, no. 18 (2 Nov. 1940), 201–205, discusses Navier's ill-fated bridge and the correctness of his research on the strength of materials.

For Navier's contribution to mechanics consult M. R. Rühlmann, *Geschichte der technischen Mechanik* (Leipzig, 1885); and R. Dugas, *Histoire de la mécanique* (Neuchâtel, 1950), 393–401. Navier's views on *vis viva* and on the composition of matter are discussed in W. L. Scott, *The Conflict Between Atomism and Conservation Theory 1644 to 1860* (London, 1970), 104–135, 155–182; and C. C. Gillispie, *Lazare Carnot Savant* (Princeton, 1971), 111–115. Navier's contribution to thermodynamics is mentioned in D. S. L. Cardwell, *From Watt to Clausius . . .* (Ithaca, N.Y., 1971), 167–169. F. Klemm, "Die Rolle der Mathematik in der Technik des 19. Jahrhunderts," in *Technikgeschichte*, **33** (1966), 72–90, devotes a few pages to Navier.

The official *Moniteur universel* (24 Feb. 1828), 251–252, defends Navier's bridge, which Balzac ridicules in his *Oeuvres*, M. Boutreron and H. Longnon, eds., XXV (Paris, 1922), 196, and notes on 299–302. G. Le Franc, "The French Railroads 1823–1842," in *Journal of Economic and Business History*, **2** (1929–1930), 299–333, gives the background that enables one to situate Navier's writings on railway systems.

Navier's association with positivism may be traced through *Journal du génie civil . . .*, *Éducateur, journal de l'Institut de la morale universelle* (Bibliothèque Nationale, Paris, cote R7368), and through the archives of the École Polytechnique, Paris, "Registres du Conseil d'instruction," **7bis**, 30 Oct. 1833 and 31 Oct. 1834.

At the archives of the École Polytechnique, the "Registre matricule des élèves" describes Navier; the cartons for 1802 and for 1803 give Navier's standing; that for 1831 contains the letter appointing Navier professor; the "Registre du Conseil d'instruction," **7bis**, 18 Dec. 1830 and 29 Jan., 18 Feb., 4 Mar., and 18 Mar. 1831, details Navier's election to his professorship at the École Polytechnique; the same vol. reveals the conflict between Navier and Poisson concerning the teaching of Fourier's theory of heat (see 20 July 1831, 29 May 1832); on this conflict also see the "Registre du Conseil de perfectionnement," **6**, 54.

Also consult the following works by R. McKeon: "A Study in the History of Nineteenth Century Science and Technology: Engineering Science in the Works of Navier," in *Proceedings of the XIIIth International Congress of the History of Science*, section 11, history of technology; "Profile chronologique de Navier," deposited at the Centre Alexandre Koyré, Paris, on 23 Nov. 1970; and "Navier éditeur de *l'Architecture hydraulique* de Bélidor," unpublished report read at the Congrès de l'Association française pour l'avancement des sciences, Chambéry, France, 8 July 1971, of which an extract is in *Sciences*, **3** (1972), 256–257.

ROBERT M. MCKEON

AL-NAYRĪZĪ, ABU'L-'ABBĀS AL-FAḌL IBN ḤĀTIM (*fl.* Baghdad, *ca.* 897; *d. ca.* 922), *geometry, astronomy.*

As his name indicates, al-Nayrīzī's origins were in Nayrīz, a small town southeast of Shīrāz, Fārs, Iran. For at least part of his active life he lived in Baghdad, where he probably served the 'Abbāsid caliph al-Mu'taḍid (892–902), for whom he wrote an extant treatise on meteorological phenomena (*Risāla fī aḥdāth al-jaww*) and a surviving work on instruments for determining the distances of objects.

The tenth-century bibliographer Ibn al-Nadīm refers to al-Nayrīzī as a distinguished astronomer; Ibn al-Qifṭī (*d.* 1248) states that he excelled in geometry and astronomy; and the Egyptian astronomer Ibn Yūnus (*d.* 1009) takes exception to some of al-Nayrīzī's astronomical views but shows respect for him as an accomplished geometer.

Of the eight titles attributed to al-Nayrīzī by Ibn al-Nadīm and Ibn al-Qifṭī, two are commentaries on Ptolemy's *Almagest* and *Tetrabiblos* and two are astronomical handbooks (*zījes*). Ibn al-Qifṭī indicates that the larger handbook (*Kitāb al-zīj al-kabīr*) was based on the *Sindhind*. None of these works has survived, but the commentary on the *Almagest* and one (or both?) of the handbooks were known to al-Bīrūnī. Ibn Yūnus cites, critically, a certain *zīj* in which, he states, al-Nayrīzī adopted the mean motion of the sun as determined in the *Mumtaḥan zīj*, which was prepared under the direction of Yaḥyā ibn Abī Manṣūr in the time of al-Ma'mūn (813–833). Ibn Yūnus wonders at al-Nayrīzī's adoption of this "erroneous" determination without further examination and, continuing his criticism of the "excellent geometer," refers further to oversights and errors, particularly in connection with the theory of Mercury, the eclipse of the moon, and parallax.

Al-Nayrīzī has been known mainly as the author of a commentary on Euclid's *Elements* that was based on the second of two Arabic translations of Euclid's text, both of which were prepared by al-Ḥajjāj ibn Yūsuf ibn Maṭar (see *Dictionary of Scientific Biography*, IV, 438–439). The commentary survives in a unique Arabic manuscript at Leiden (bks. I–VI) and in a Latin version (bks. I–X), made in the twelfth century by Gerard of Cremona. (The Arabic manuscript lacks the comments on definitions 1–23 of book I, but these are preserved in the Latin translation.) In the course of his own comments al-Nayrīzī quotes extensively from two commentaries on the *Elements* by Hero of Alexandria and Simplicius, neither of which has survived in the original Greek.

The first of these must have covered at least the first eight books (Hero's last comment cited by al-Nayrīzī deals with Euclid VIII.27), whereas the second, entitled "A Commentary on the Premises [*ṣadr, muṣādara, muṣādarāt*] of Euclid's *Elements*," was concerned solely with the definitions, postulates, and axioms at the beginning of book I of the *Elements*.

Simplicius' *Commentary*, almost entirely reproduced by al-Nayrīzī, played a significant part in arousing the interest of Islamic mathematicians in methodological problems. It further quotes verbatim a full proof of Euclid's postulate 5, the parallels postulate, by "the philosopher Aghānīs." The proof, which is based on the definition of parallel lines as equidistant lines and which makes use of the "Eudoxus-Archimedes" axiom, has left its mark on many subsequent attempts to prove the postulate, particularly in Islam.

Aghānīs is no longer identified with Geminus, as Heiberg and others once thought because of a similarity between their views on parallels. He almost certainly lived in the same period as Simplicius; and Simplicius' reference to him in the *Commentary* as "our associate [or colleague] Aghānīs," or, simply, "our Aghānīs" (*Aghānīsu, ṣāḥibunā*, rendered by Gerard as *socius noster Aganis*) strongly suggests that the two philosophers belonged to the same school. There is an anonymous fifteenth-century Arabic manuscript that aims to prove Euclid's parallels postulate and refers in this connection to Simplicius and Aghānīs, but spells the latter's name "Aghānyūs," thus supplying a vowel that can only be conjectured in the form "Aghānīs." Given that the Arabic "gh" undoubtedly stood for the letter γ, "Aghānyūs" may very easily have been a mistranscription of the recognizable Greek name "Agapius." Reading "Aghānyūs" for "Aghābyūs" (Arabic has no "p") may well have resulted from misplacing a single diacritical point, thereby transforming the "b" (that is, "p") into an "n." This hypothesis is the more plausible since we know that diacritical points were often omitted in Arabic manuscripts. It therefore seems reasonable to assume that Aghānīs-Aghānyūs was no other than the Athenian philosopher Agapius, a pupil of Proclus and Marinus who lectured on the philosophy of Plato and Aristotle about A.D. 511 and whose versatility was praised by Simplicius' teacher, Damascius. Agapius' name, place, date, affiliation, and interests agree remarkably with the reference in Simplicius' *Commentary*.

In his commentary on the *Elements*, al-Nayrīzī followed a conception of ratio and proportion that had previously been adopted by al-Māhānī (see *Dictionary of Scientific Biography*, IX, 21–22). Al-Nayrīzī's treatise "On the Direction of the *qibla*" (*Risāla fī samt al-qibla*) shows that he knew and utilized the equivalent of the tangent function. But in this, too, he is now known to have been preceded, for example, by Ḥabash (see *Dictionary of Scientific Biography*, V, 612).

Again, his unpublished treatise "On the Demonstration of the Well-Known Postulate of Euclid" (Paris,

Bibliothèque Nationale, arabe 2467, fols. 89r–90r) clearly depends on Aghānīs. In it al-Nayrīzī argues that, because equality is "naturally prior" to inequality, it follows that straight lines that maintain the same distance between them are prior to those that do not, since the former are the standard for estimating the latter. From this reasoning he concludes the existence of equidistant lines, accepting as a "primary proposition" that equidistant lines do not meet, however extended. His proof consists of four propositions, of which the first three state that: (1) the distance (that is, shortest line) between any two equidistant lines is perpendicular to both lines; (2) if a straight line drawn across two straight lines is perpendicular to both of them, then the two lines are equidistant; and (3) a line falling on two equidistant lines makes the interior angles on one side together equal to two right angles. These three propositions correspond to Aghānīs's propositions 1–3, while the fourth is the same as Euclid's postulate 5: If a straight line falling on two straight lines makes the interior angles on one side together less than two right angles, then the two lines will meet on that side. The proof closely follows Aghānīs.

Al-Nayrīzī, however, claims originality for the theorems that he proves in the extant but unpublished treatise for al-Muʿtaḍid—"On the Knowledge of Instruments by Means of Which We May Know the Distances of Objects Raised in the Air or Set Up on the Ground and the Depths of Valleys and Wells, and the Widths of Rivers." Al-Bīrūnī also states that al-Nayrīzī, in his commentary on the *Almagest*, was the only writer known to him who had provided a method for computing "a date for a certain time, the known parts of which are various *species* that do not belong to one and the same *genus*. There is, *e.g.*, a day the date of which within a Greek, Arabic, or Persian month is known; but the name of this month is unknown, whilst you know the name of another month that corresponds with it. Further, you know an era, to which, however, these two months do *not* belong, or such an era, of which the name of the month in question is not known" (*Chronology*, p. 139).

Al-Nayrīzī's work on the construction and use of the spherical astrolabe (*Fi 'l-asṭurlāb al-kurī*), in four *maqālas*, is considered the most complete treatment of the subject in Arabic.

BIBLIOGRAPHY

I. ORIGINAL WORKS. The Arabic text of al-Nayrīzī's commentary on the *Elements* (bks. I–VI and a few lines from bk. VII) was published as *Codex Leidensis* 399,

I. *Euclidis Elementa ex interpretatione al-Hadschdschadschii cum commentariis al-Narizii*, R. O. Besthorn and J. L. Heiberg, eds. (Copenhagen, 1893–1932). This ed. is in three pts., each comprising two fascicules, of which pt. III, fasc. II (bks. V–VI), is edited by G. Junge, J. Raeder and W. Thomson. Gerard of Cremona's Latin trans. is *Anaritii in decem libros priores Elementorum Euclidis commentarii . . . in codice Cracoviensi 569 servata*, Maximilianus Curtze, ed. (Leipzig, 1899), in Euclid's *Opera omnia*, J. L. Heiberg and H. Menge, eds., supp. (Suter mentions the probable existence of another MS of Gerard's trans. in "Nachträge," p. 164).

A German trans. and discussion of al–Nayrīzī's treatise on the direction of the *qibla* (*Risāla fī samt al-qibla*) is C. Schoy, "Abhandlung von al-Faḍl b. Ḥātim an Nairîzî: Über die Rechtung der Qibla," in *Sitzungsberichte der Bayerischen Akademie der Wissenschaften zu München*, Mathematisch-physikalische Klasse (1922), 55–68.

A short "chapter" (perhaps drawn from a longer work by al Nayrīzī) on the hemispherical sundial was published as *Faṣl fī takhṭīṭ al-sā'āt al-zamāniyya fī kull qubba aw fī qubba tusta'mal lahā* ("On Drawing the Lines of Temporal [that is, unequal] Hours in Any Hemisphere or in a Hemisphere Used for That Purpose"); see *al-Rasā'il al-mutafarriqa fi 'l-hay'a l 'l-mutaqaddimīn wa-mu'āṣiri 'l-Bīrūnī* (Hyderabad, 1947).

II. Secondary Literature. MSS of al-Nayrīzī's works are in C. Brockelmann, *Geschichte der arabischen Literatur*, supp. vol. I (Leiden, 1937), 386–387; 2nd ed., I, (Leiden, 1943), 245; H. Suter, "Die Mathematiker und Astronomen der Araber und ihre Werke," in *Abhandlungen zur Geschichte der mathematischen Wissenschaften mit Einschluss ihrer Anwendungen*, 10 (1900), no. 88, 45; and "Nachträge und Berichtigungen zu 'Die Mathematiker . . . ,'" *ibid.*, 14 (1902), 164; and H. P. J. Renaud, "Additions et corrections à Suter 'Die Mathematiker . . . ,'" in *Isis*, 18 (1932), 171.

The little information that we have of al-Nayrīzī's activities and a list of his works are in Ibn al-Nadīm, *al-Fihrist*, G. Flügel, ed., I (Leipzig, 1871), 265, 268, 279; and Ibn al-Qifṭī, *Ta'rīkh al-ḥukamā'*, J. Lippert, ed. (Leipzig, 1930), 64, 97, 98, 254.

For the references to al-Nayrīzī's *zīj* in Ibn Yūnus' Ḥākimite *zīj*, see *Notices et extraits des manuscrits de la Bibliothèque nationale . . .*, VII (Paris, 1803), 61, 65, 69, 71, 73, 121, 161, 165. Al-Bīrūnī refers to al-Nayrīzī in *Rasā'il*, 2 (Hyderabad, 1948), 39, 51, and in *The Chronology of Ancient Nations*, C. E. Sachau, trans. (London, 1879), 139. See also E. S. Kennedy, "A Survey of Islamic Astronomical Tables," in *Transactions of the American Philosophical Society*, n.s. 46, pt. 2 (1956), nos. 46, 63, 75.

For a description of the contents and character of Hero's commentary on the *Elements* as preserved by al-Nayrīzī, see T. L. Heath, *The Thirteen Books of Euclid's Elements*, 2nd ed. (Cambridge–New York, 1956), 21–24.

Simplicius' commentary on the *Elements*, including a proof of Euclid's parallels postulate that seems to have been omitted from the text quoted by al-Nayrīzī, is discussed by A. I. Sabra in "Simplicius's Proof of Euclid's Parallels Postulate," in *Journal of the Warburg and Courtauld Institutes*, 32 (1969), 1–24.

For a detailed description of al-Nayrīzī's work on the spherical astrolabe, see Hugo Seemann and T. Mittelberger, "Das kugelförmige Astrolab nach den Mitteilungen von Alfonso X. von Kastilien und den vorhandenen arabischen Quellen," in *Abhandlungen zur Geschichte der Naturwissenschaften und der Medizin*, 8 (1925), 32–40.

For a discussion of al-Nayrīzī's concept of ratio, see E. B. Plooij, *Euclid's Conception of Ratio and His Definition of Proportional Magnitudes as Criticized by Arabian Commentators* (Rotterdam, 1950), 51–52, 61; and J. E. Murdoch, "The Medieval Language of Proportions," in A. C. Crombie, ed., *Scientific Change* (London, 1963), 237–271, esp. 240–242, 253–255.

The identity of Aghānīs is discussed in Paul Tannery, "Le philosophe Aganis est-il identique à Géminus?" in *Bibliotheca mathematica*, 3rd ser., 2 (1901), 9–11, reprinted in *Mémoires scientifiques*, III (Toulouse–Paris, 1915), 37–41; Sir Thomas Heath, *A History of Greek Mathematics*, II (Oxford, 1921), 224; *The Thirteen Books of Euclid's Elements*, I (Cambridge–New York, 1956), 27–28; A. I. Sabra, "Thābit ibn Qurra on Euclid's Parallels Postulate," in *Journal of the Warburg and Courtauld Institutes*, 31 (1968), 13. The information on Agapius is summarized in Pauly-Wissowa, *Real-Encyclopädie der classischen Altertumswissenschaft*, 1st ser., I (Stuttgart, 1894), 735.

See also the notice on al-Nayrīzī in Sarton's *Introduction*, I (Baltimore, 1927), 598–599.

A. I. Sabra

NEANDER, MICHAEL (*b.* Joachimsthal, Bohemia, 3 April 1529; *d.* Jena, Germany, 23 October 1581), *mathematics, medicine.*

The assessment of Neander and his work is complicated by confusion with another Michael Neander (1525–1595), who came from Sorau and was a school principal in Ilfeld. The achievements of each have been credited to the other, and to date no library has correctly cataloged their respective writings. Neander from Joachimsthal, like his namesake, studied at the Protestant university in Wittenberg, where he earned his baccalaureate degree in 1549 and his master's degree in 1550; he was eighth among fifty candidates. Beginning in 1551, he taught mathematics and Greek at the Hohe Schule in Jena. In 1558, when this school became a new Protestant university, Neander obtained the doctor of medicine degree with a work on baths, *De thermis*. In 1560 he advanced from professor at the faculty of arts to the more lucrative position of professor of medicine at Jena, which post he held until his death.

Neander's scholarly reputation was based on textbooks written primarily for students at the faculty of arts. He considered the writings of the ancients, especially Galen, absolutely authoritative. In the introduction to his *Methodorum in omni genere artium . . .* (1556), he based his exposition on Galen's opinion that the best kind of demonstration is mathematical. Neander distinguished the analytic and synthetic methods and introduced proof by contradiction as a third independent possibility.

In opposition to his contemporary Petrus Ramus, Neander contended that, even from a pedagogical point of view, Euclid's *Elements* contained the essence of a satisfactory synthetic demonstration. Neander's account of the metrology of the Greeks and Romans seems to have served for a time as a sort of reference work. His *Elementa sphaericae doctrinae* (1561), which includes an appendix on calendrical computation, endorsed Melanchthon's rejection of the Copernican view of the universe. The *Elementa* influenced one of Neander's colleagues at Jena, Victorinus Strigelius, whose *Epitome doctrinae de primo motu* (1564) also placed the earth at rest in the center of the universe.

Although Neander typified the close connection between mathematics and medicine frequently seen in the sixteenth century, this link appears only indirectly in his writings.

BIBLIOGRAPHY

I. ORIGINAL WORKS. Neander's major works are Σύνοψις *mensurarum et ponderum, ponderationisque mensurabilium secundum Romanos, Athenienses . . . Accesserunt etiam quae apud Galenum hactenus extabant de ponderum et mensurarum ratione* (Basel, 1555); *Methodorum in omni genere artium brevis et succincta* ὑφήγησις (Basel, 1556); *Gnomologia graecolatina, hoc est . . . Sententiae . . . ex magno anthologio Joannis Stobaei excerptae . . . Accessit praeterea* Ὄνειρος vel Ἀλεκτρυὼν, *id est somnium vel Gallus, dialogus Luciani . . . graece et latine . . .* (Basel, 1557); and *Elementa sphaericae doctrinae, seu de primo motu: in usum studiosae iuventutis methodicé et perspicué conscripta. Accessit praecipua computi astronomici materia, ubi temporis pleraeque differentiae explicantur* (Basel, 1561).

Biographisches Lexikon hervorragender Ärzte, IV (Berlin–Vienna, 1932), 331–332, lists a work entitled *De thermis* (Jena, 1558), but the author has been unable to verify this title in any library.

II. SECONDARY LITERATURE. Works on Neander and his work (in chronological order) are Heinrich Pantaleon, *Prosopographiae heroum atque illustrium virorum totius Germaniae* (Basel, 1566), 553; also in *Teutscher Nation Heldenbuch . . .* (Basel, 1578), 515; Paul Freher, *Theatrum virorum eruditione clarorum* (Nuremberg, 1688), 1279; Johann Caspar Zeumer, *Vitae professorum theologiae omnium Jenensium* (Jena, 1711), 14; *Hamburgische vermischte Bibliothek*, pt. 1 (Hamburg, 1743), 695–701;

Christian Gottlieb Jöcher, ed., *Allgemeines Gelehrten-Lexicon*, III (Leipzig, 1751), 840; Johannes Günther, *Lebensskizzen der Professoren der Universität Jena von 1558 bis 1858* (Jena, 1858); *Allgemeine deutsche Biographie*, XXIII (Leipzig, 1886), 340; and Otto Knopf, *Die Astronomie an der Universität Jena von der Gründung der Universität im Jahre 1558 bis zur Entpflichtung des Verfassers im Jahre 1927* (Jena, 1937), 1–6.

IVO SCHNEIDER

NECKER, LOUIS-ALBERT, known as **NECKER DE SAUSSURE** (*b*. Geneva, Switzerland, 10 April 1786; *d*. Portree, Skye, Scotland, 20 November 1861), *geology, mineralogy, zoology.*

The name Necker de Saussure represents the union of two illustrious Swiss families. Louis-Albert's father, Jacques Necker, was professor of botany and a magistrate at Geneva, and the nephew of Louis XVI's director general of finance (and thus first cousin of Mme de Staël). His mother, Albertine de Saussure, was the daughter of Horace-Bénédict de Saussure, the eminent geologist and naturalist.

The eldest of four children, Necker studied at the Academy of Geneva, then went to Edinburgh in 1806 to pursue university studies. Already versed in mineralogy and geology, in Scotland he was exposed to both Huttonian and Wernerian geological doctrines and became personally acquainted with Playfair, Hall, and other Edinburgh intellectuals. After visiting many parts of Scotland, with special attention to geological features, Necker returned to Geneva, where he became a professor of mineralogy and geology at the Academy in 1810. He retained a chair there for over two decades. During these years he traveled widely, sometimes conducting excursions with his students, and undertook geological investigations, especially in the Alps, concentrating particularly on the eastern and western extremities of the Alpine ranges.

During the 1830's Necker lived restlessly in Edinburgh, London, and Paris, as well as Geneva. He suffered increasingly from depressions that may have stemmed from declining health. Following his mother's death in 1841, he settled at Portree, Skye. He passed most of his remaining years there as a recluse.

Necker's scientific work was marked by a deep concern with the special methods and procedures that distinguished geology and mineralogy from other sciences. He emphasized the dependence of mineralogists and geologists upon real characteristics of actual objects, as opposed to abstractions. In mineralogical classification, one of his most serious concerns, he opposed the use of chemical composition as a major taxonomic criterion, viewing chemical entities as fundamentally abstract. A suitable organizational scheme for minerals, he believed, ought to depend on the characteristics that the observer perceives directly in mineral objects. The integrant molecule, in his opinion an abstract conception without real existence, could not define the "individual" that gives meaning to mineral species, whereas the crystal could. Together with zoology and botany, the other branches of natural history, mineralogy was "positive and descriptive," not speculative. As a member of the tradition of the natural method of classification, Necker claimed inspiration from Augustin-Pyramus de Candolle and Cuvier.

A strong advocate of field observation in geology, Necker presented the first geological map of the whole of Scotland to the Geological Society of London in 1808. Although he resisted committing himself completely to the theoretical schemes of either the Huttonians or the Wernerians, in Scotland Necker did become convinced of the igneous origin of granite. His fieldwork included studies of the volcanoes of Italy; the geological features of parts of Savoy, Carniola, Carinthia, Istria, and Illyria; and the Arran dike swarms. He also investigated the origins of mineral deposits and concluded that metalliferous veins are formed by sublimation from igneous intrusions. In 1832 he gave the Royal Society of Edinburgh an improved "clinometrical compass" of his own design for rapid determination of the positions of strata. As his geological outlook matured, he showed an increasing tendency to favor a uniformitarian approach.

Necker disdained artificial boundaries of scientific specialization. Notable among his publications are studies of birds and of meteorological optical phenomena, including the aurora borealis and parhelia. He was inclined to see links between phenomena conventionally regarded as unrelated, as in his endeavor to establish relationships among temperature, stratigraphic configuration, and magnetic intensity in various geographic locations.

BIBLIOGRAPHY

I. ORIGINAL WORKS. Necker's major works include *Voyage en Écosse et aux Îles Hébrides*, 3 vols. (Geneva, 1821), an appreciative account of Scotland and the character and accomplishments of its inhabitants, with some geological observations; *Le règne minéral ramené aux méthodes de l'histoire naturelle*, 2 vols. (Paris–Strasbourg, 1835), an expansion of the ideas found in "On Mineralogy Considered as a Branch of Natural History, and Outlines of an Arrangement of Minerals Founded on the Principles

of the Natural Method of Classification," in *Edinburgh New Philosophical Journal*, **12** (1832), 209–265; and *Études géologiques dans les Alpes* (Paris–Strasbourg, 1841), dealing with the geology of the environs of Geneva. Later volumes, intended to present results of Necker's investigations in the eastern Alps and along the southern flank of the Alps, were never published. Much of his research, in fact, was never published, and what did appear in print was sometimes delayed. Partial listings of Necker's works are given in the Candolle obituary notice, *Mémoires*, pp. 455–456, or *Verhandlungen*, pp. 276–278; by Eyles, pp. 125–126; and in the Royal Society's *Catalogue of Scientific Papers*, IV (1870), 581–582, and X (1894), 904.

II. SECONDARY LITERATURE. A useful recent account is V. A. Eyles, "Louis Albert Necker, of Geneva, and His Geological Map of Scotland," in *Transactions of the Edinburgh Geological Society*, **14** (1952), 93–127. Among contemporary biographical sketches the fullest is James David Forbes, "Biographical Account of Professor Louis Albert Necker," in *Proceedings of the Royal Society of Edinburgh*, **5** (1862–1866), 53–76. Others include Henri de Saussure, "Nécrologie de M. Louis Necker," in *Revue et magasin de zoologie . . .*, 2nd ser., **13** (1861), 553–555; and an obituary notice by Alphonse de Candolle, in *Mémoires de la Société de physique et d'histoire naturelle de Genève*, **16** (1862), 452–456, also in *Verhandlungen der Schweizerischen naturforschenden Gesellschaft*, **46** (1862), 272–278. Forbes's account served as the basis for a "notice biographique" in a republication of Necker's *Mémoire sur les oiseaux des environs de Genève* (Geneva–Paris, 1864), pp. 5–45.

KENNETH L. TAYLOR

NEEDHAM, JOHN TURBERVILLE (*b.* London, England, 10 September 1713; *d.* Brussels, Belgium, 30 December 1781), *biology*, *microscopy*.

Needham's most important contributions to science were early observations of plant pollen and the milt vessels of the squid, a forward-looking theory of reproduction (1750), and a classic experiment for determining whether spontaneous generation occurs on the microscopic level (1748).

The son of recusants, John Needham and Margaret Lucas, Needham received a religious education in French Flanders, which prepared him for the intellectual life of the Continent. Ordained a secular priest in 1738, he supported himself first by teaching, and then by accompanying young English Catholic noblemen on the grand tour, until he settled in Brussels in 1768 as director of what was to become the Royal Academy of Belgium. His scientific interests were motivated largely by a desire to defend religion in an age when biological question had serious theological and philosophical meanings for many. Needham's extrascientific activities made him equally well known throughout educated Europe; in these he also defended the faith. He was particularly notable for his dispute with Voltaire over miracles and for a linguistic theory of the biblical chronology based on a supposedly Egyptian statue.

Needham was elected a fellow of the Royal Society (1747) and of the Society of Antiquaries of London (1761), as Buffon's correspondent for the Académie des Sciences (1768), a member of the Royal Basque Society of Amis de la Patrie, and first director of the Royal Academy of Belgium (1773), where he did much to disseminate advanced laboratory techniques. A genus of Australian plants, *Needhama*, was named for him.

Until cell theory reconciled both aspects of the problem of reproduction, explanations emphasized either the preformed nature of the primordia out of which new organisms came into being (were generated) or the gradual differentiation of growing tissue apparent in the embryo. During Needham's lifetime iatromechanists insisted on preformation, since known mechanical principles could not account for extensive differentiation; vitalists, led by Buffon, accounted for extensive differentiation through chance combining of genetic factors brought together by hypothetical natural principles that were peculiar to living things but that contemporary science had yet to discover.

In 1748, at Buffon's invitation, Needham examined fluids extracted from the reproductive organs of animals and infusions of plant and animal tissue. Given the weak, indistinct magnifying power of instruments then available, it is not surprising that the two men observed globules under their microscopes. For Buffon these were genetic factors, which he termed "organic molecules."

The second volume of Buffon's *Histoire naturelle* (1749) based proof of the "organic molecules" largely on these experiments, which in turn rested on Needham's skill and reknown as an empirical scientist. Thus Needham found himself at the focal point of the controversy over generation.

Buffon never claimed to have observed the microscopic joining of molecules that he speculated took place, but Needham thought he actually did see new organisms taking shape out of disorganized material. This was his famous experiment with boiled mutton gravy (1748). Foreshadowing recapitulation theory, he "saw" certain species of microscopic creatures giving birth to other species of animalcules and imagined that in embryonic development of higher organisms a similar phenomenon must occur. Needham's own theory of generation (1750) placed him in the vitalist camp through its reliance on principles peculiar to living things and its assignment of self-patterning powers to matter. It differed from

Buffon's in its denial of chance combinations of mathematically countable genetic traits.

In Needham's view God would not allow chance to play a role in reproduction. The embryo was not preformed but predetermined. Two kinds of physical force were the building blocks of all matter. In each embryo a specific combination of these elements was contributed by each parent. This combination produced a unique vibratory motion which simultaneously molded the growing embryonic tissue into new shapes and changed their chemistry. Thus Needham considered the organism on physical, chemical, and biological levels, an approach through which the mechanist-vitalist controversy was later transcended. In his correspondence Needham, in the tradition of Aristotle and Descartes, referred to "my system of spontaneous generation and epigenesis."

The many attempts to refute Needham's claim were based either on logic or on inconclusive experiments until 1765, when Spallanzani boiled hermetically sealed mutton gravy and, upon opening the flasks, found nothing there where Needham claimed to have found animalcules. For Needham's sterilization techniques had in fact been faulty. While the iatromechanists sided with Spallanzani, the matter was not settled until Pasteur replied to Needham's contention (in footnotes to Spallanzani's *Nouvelles recherches*, 1769) that through using a longer boiling period Spallanzani had destroyed something in the air responsible for sustaining life.

BIBLIOGRAPHY

I. ORIGINAL WORKS. For further references and a bibliography of Needham's works consult *Dictionary of National Biography*, XIV (1967–1968), 157–159; *Bibliographical Dictionary of the English Catholics*.

On early observations and the spontaneous generation controversy, see Needham's *An Account of Some New Microscopical Discoveries Founded on an Examination of the Calamary and Its Wonderful Milt-Vessels* (London, 1745); "A Summary of Some Late Observations Upon the Generation, Composition, and Decomposition of Animal and Vegetable Substances," in *Philosophical Transactions of the Royal Society*, **45**, no. 490 (1748), 615–666; and *Nouvelles observations microscopiques, avec des découvertes intéressantes sur la composition et la décomposition des corps organisés* (Paris, 1750).

Correspondence between Needham and Charles Bonnet and a rare pamphlet, *Idées républicaines, par un membre d'un corps, M.D.V.*, published anonymously (Geneva, 1766), are in the Bibliothèque Publique et Universitaire, Geneva; *Mémoire sur la maladie contagieuse des bêtes à cornes* (Brussels, 1770) is in the Belgian National Library (Bibliothèque Royale Albert 1er); and a portrait of

Needham (by Henry Edridge after Reynolds) is in the Holburne of Menstrie Museum, Great Pulteney St., Bath, England.

II. SECONDARY LITERATURE. Lazzaro Spallanzani's works on spontaneous generation are *Saggio de observazione microscopiche concernante il systema della generazione de Needham et Buffon* (Modena, 1765); *Nouvelles recherches sur les découvertes microscopiques et la génération des corps organisés* (London–Paris, 1769); and *Opuscoli de fisica animale et vegetabile* (Modena, 1776).

See also Silvio Curto, "Storia di un falso celebre," in *Bollettino della Società piemontese d'archeologia e belle arti* (1962–1963), 5–15, with four plates; Elizabeth Gasking, *Investigations Into Generation 1651–1828* (Baltimore, 1967); Stephen F. Milliken, "Buffon and the British" (doctoral diss., Columbia University, 1965); Jacques Roger, *Les sciences de la vie dans la pensée française du XVIIIe siècle* (Paris, 1963); Jean Rostand, *La genèse de la vie* (Paris, 1943) and *Les origines de la biologie expérimentale et l'abbé Spallanzani* (Paris, 1951); and Rachel Westbrook, "John Turberville Needham and His Impact on the French Enlightenment" (diss. in progress, Columbia University).

RACHEL HORWITZ WESTBROOK

NEES VON ESENBECK, CHRISTIAN GOTTFRIED (DANIEL) (b. Reichenberg Castle, near Erbach, Hesse, 14 February 1776; d. Breslau, Silesia [now Wrocław, Poland], 16 March 1858), *botany.*

Nees's father, estate administrator for the count of Erbach, had as official residence a castle in the Odenwald. There Nees was born and raised. He received a highly liberal education at home, and in 1792 he entered the humanistic high school in Darmstadt. From 1796 to 1799 he attended the University of Jena, studying medicine and natural history under Batsch, and philosophy under Schelling. In this period Nees was drawn into the nearby Weimar circle. His personal friendship with Goethe, which led to years of correspondence, greatly influenced his career. After receiving a doctorate from Giessen in 1800, Nees practiced medicine in the Odenwald (according to his autobiography; some others state Frankfurt) and experimented with Mesmerian magnetic techniques. Financially his practice was a failure—he cared only for sick patients. His wife of one year died in childbirth, and in 1802 Nees retired to a small estate—Sickershausen, near Kitzingen, Bavaria—which she had left him. A move to the University of Jena, encouraged by Goethe, was prevented by war in 1806. At Sickershausen he lived the life of a country gentleman, happily married to his second wife, née von Mettingh. Nees acquired a working knowledge of the major European languages except the Slavic ones. (He was coauthor of a book on modern Greek history and poetry in translation, pub-

lished in 1825.) He also assembled natural history collections, some of them with his younger brother, Friedrich, and wrote scientific papers and reviews. By 1818 the estate was in such bad shape that he had to get a job.

Thus Nees's career proper started when he was forty-two. He assumed the professorship of botany at Erlangen, as Scheber's belated successor; but in the same year the Prussian minister of education, Karl von Stein zum Altenstein, Nees's protector, appointed him to the chair of botany at the newly founded University of Bonn.[1] With zest he established a botanical garden, aided by his brother, whom he appointed inspector. Goethe helped even here, by contributing seeds.[2] In 1830, ostensibly at his request, Nees was allowed to exchange professorships with Treviranus at Breslau, where he started by reorganizing the botanical garden. As professor of botany he was progressively less successful. Presumably his lectures were too full of obscurantist *Naturphilosophie*, and the students turned to his colleague Goeppert. But Nees made a name for himself in courses on speculative philosophy and social ethics. Having, at Altenstein's request, drafted the requirements for the high school teaching certificate in natural science, he became the first examiner in the field at Breslau (1839). He was promptly relieved of this post when Altenstein died and was replaced, in 1840, by the reactionary Eichhorn. In 1852 Nees provided a textbook for the teachers of natural science, dealing with the study of form in nature. But natural history teaching in the schools faltered after charges that it was conducive to agnosticism.

At Breslau, Nees played an active role in civic affairs. It started with the organization of public scientific lectures and gradually broadened. He was cofounder of a successful health insurance scheme. In 1845 he became the beloved leader ("Father Nees") of a community of "Christian Catholics" following J. Ronge. This radical movement soon aroused the active opposition of the state. Nees freely expressed his deeply devout views in articles and tracts, such as his 1845 publication on matrimony in an intelligent society, and its relation to state and church. He practiced what he preached. His third marriage, to a weaver's daughter from Warmbrunn, in the Riesengebirge, was without state or church sanction but was reputedly a model marriage.

As a boy Nees had been deeply impressed by the French Revolution. The Napoleonic era brought disillusionment. He became a fervent and conspiratorial supporter of German unity, placing his hope in enlightened Prussian leadership, but was in turn disillusioned by the conservatism of the crown. Thus the way was opened to his becoming an active radical democrat, a liberal intellectual. (Other professors at Breslau were also politically active, but as conservatives or moderates.) Nees stood alone then—a German botanist, a member of a group not renowned for liberalism. In 1848 he helped found the Breslau Workers' Club. He was elected a deputy from Breslau to the Prussian National Assembly meeting at Berlin in 1848. Even the other members of Waldeck's left group —striving, like Nees, for an English-style constitutional monarchy—shuddered at his speeches and at the "extremism" of the draft constitution he presented. Apparently the most hair-raising article of that document was "The people is sovereign, and the concept 'subject' is struck from the life of the state for all time." Nees presided over the Berlin Workers' Congress and also founded (in Berlin) the German Workers' Brotherhood. In January 1849 he was banished from Berlin for life "because of dangerous socialistic tendencies."

Back in Breslau, Nees's house was subject to constant police search. In 1851 he was suspended from his professorship; in June 1852, at the age of seventy-six, he was dismissed without pension. The official charge was moral turpitude; specifically, concubinage. (In the Roman law of Germany that was the term for the "common law" marriage of Germanic Anglo-Saxon law; it was a "bad thing" if it caused "public annoyance.") The real reason, his political activity, apparently was sufficiently protected. Nees had no money; it had all been spent subsidizing scientific publications and on charity.

Pitiful advertisements announced the sale of his herbarium, containing some 80,000 specimens or 40,000 species.[3] His library also was sold. He moved to a garret. When he died, at the age of eighty-two, an immense crowd (reputedly 10,000) of mourners, mainly artisans and students, accompanied him to his grave.

Nees had many children. I have found information on only one: Carl Nees von Esenbeck was inspector of the Breslau Botanical Garden from 1853 to 1880. Friedrich Nees von Esenbeck, a Christian Catholic writer, was probably another. He even left some minor children; the Leopoldina contributed 100 copies of an engraved portrait of him for sale by their guardian.[4]

Nees's greatest contribution to science has not yet been mentioned. The venerable *Academia Caesarea Leopoldina-Carolina Naturae Curiosorum*, the Imperial German Academy of Natural Science (or Leopoldina), in Erlangen, had fallen on bad times during the Napoleonic era. Nees was elected a member in 1816, with the cognomen Aristoteles, and in the same year he became an officer. On 3 August 1818 he was elected president. To German science he would remain "Herr President" until his death. The Leopoldina, however,

was not viable. When he was invited to move from Erlangen to Bonn, Nees suggested to the Prussian chancellor K. A. von Hardenberg and to Altenstein that he should bring the Leopoldina with him from Bavaria to Prussia. The two gentlemen were not only enlightened, but as politicians they were quick to recognize a splendid propaganda stroke. They gladly accepted and guaranteed financial support.[5] Outlasting even the privileges of the house of Thurn und Taxis (the last hereditary postmaster generalship was lost in 1918), the Leopoldina is the only surviving institution of the Holy Roman Empire. The proposal by Nees and D. G. Kieser, addressed to the abortive Frankfurt Parliament in 1848, to make an expanded Leopoldina the center of German cultural life, was bound to fail. The officers of the Leopoldina insisted on Nees's remaining in his unpaid presidency even when he had been stripped of his professorship; and the Prussian government continued its subsidies, for the Hapsburgs were only too anxious to regain the Leopoldina.[6] Nees commented that he was "dead to the Prussian state, but lives still for the Academy."[7] Nees personally edited forty-seven volumes of the *Nova acta Academiae Caesareae Leopoldino Carolinae germanicae naturae curiosorum*, the high quality of which was partly the result of his bringing the artist Aimé Henry to Bonn. His last direct contribution was the preface to *Nova acta*, **26**, Abt. 2, dated 1 February 1858. Nees spared no money, including the last of his own, on publications. He apologized for the overdraft he had incurred.[8] His successor was not amused, but he was left a flourishing and proud academy.[9]

A logical outgrowth of the rebirth of the Leopoldina was the invention of the "annual meeting" by L. Oken in 1822. This type of gathering, which almost immediately assumed the detailed form so familiar to the present-day American scientist, was a major force in the blossoming of German science. It was copied by the British Association (1831) and the American Association for the Advancement of Science (1848). It is incomprehensible that the visionary Nees (perhaps in uncharacteristic jealousy) bungled the request to have it made an official practice of the Leopoldina,[10] although its adoption became inevitable.

Nees's primary services to German science were, in order of importance, as an organizer; as an editor, not only of the *Nova acta* but also of a vast body of additional material; and as a transmitter of outstanding foreign publications. In the last field the item of greatest impact was the five-volume edition of Robert Brown's botanical works, . . . *vermischte botanische Schriften* (Nuremberg, 1825–1834). Volume III is the original publication of the second edition of the *Prodromus florae Novae hollandiae* in Latin; the bulk of the remaining volumes consists of German translations, largely by Nees himself, with his occasional notes and additions. Nees was highly conscious of the antiquated Linnaean flavor persisting in much of German botany; and one of the avowed aims of his two-volume *Handbuch der Botanik* (1821–1822) was to stress the modern structural work, including that done in France (he leaned heavily on Mirbel) and by Robert Brown in England, and even the inclusion of what now are called physiological aspects. The work seems to be Nees's most dismal failure, although Cohn (1858) reported that it acted as a major stimulus. It is permeated not only by *Naturphilosophie* but also by an attempt to apply Goethe's theory of metamorphosis (the work is dedicated to him). The books consist of a series of aphorisms that to an unsympathetic reviewer appear to be outpourings from a strange dream world. If his lectures were similar, that would explain Nees's failure as a botany professor. But he did keep trying. As late as 1850 he asked Cohn to give a demonstration of microscopy to his students, but the only decent microscope available was, shamefully, Cohn's private one. In his later writings Nees managed to disentangle his botany and *Naturphilosophie*, and they both became "pure"—the latter in his book *Naturphilosophie* (1841).

Finally there are Nees's direct scientific contributions; they are far-reaching, even if the medical ones are excluded. In zoology there are major contributions to the taxonomy of ichneumon flies. His earliest botanical monograph (1814) dealt with freshwater algae. This was followed by a systematic treatment of the fungi, *System der Pilze und Schwämme* (1816).

A digression is required here. Nees's younger brother, Theodor Friedrich Ludwig Nees von Esenbeck (1787–1837), progressed from being his admirer to coauthor of numerous botanical works, especially during their joint period at Bonn. In 1805 he became an apprentice in the Martius pharmacy in Erlangen. (This led to his connection with Martius and Brazilian plants, for he interested Carl von Martius in botany.) In 1817 he was appointed inspector at the botanical garden in Leiden (hence the link to C. F. Blume and Javanese plants). Friedrich's brother brought him to the new Bonn garden in 1819, and at Bonn he became professor of pharmacy. Some confusion in the literature needs disentangling: It was Friedrich who made the contributions to the development of the mosses and to the discovery of spermatozoids in plants (in *Sphagnum*). The genus *Neesia* Blume is dedicated to him, while the genus *Esenbeckia* Humboldt et Bonpland ex Kunth commemorates C. G. Nees. The most important joint works by the brothers deal with cinnamon and with mycological subjects.

Most of Nees's botanical work is in the form of taxonomic monographs, initially dealing with the German flora: his treatment of the genus *Rubus* and of the Astereae, and the moss flora *Bryologica germanica*, written with Hornschuch and Sturm. (Volume I of the latter [1823] contains a superb Neesian history of the field.) In keeping with the age of discovery, he became a world expert on certain groups; their diversity is spectacular. In the flowering plants the main ones are the Lauraceae, Acanthaceae, Solanaceae, Restionaceae, Juncaceae, Cyperaceae, and Gramineae, which Nees treated variously for the Brazilian (Martius), Indian, Australian, and South African floras, or for worldwide works (Acanthaceae in A. de Candolle's *Prodromus, XI*).

Of major interest are Nees's contributions to the study of liverworts. He wrote monographs on two tropical floras, those of Java (1830) and Brazil (1833, for Martius). His four-volume account of the European liverworts, *Naturgeschichte der europäischen Lebermoose* (1833–1838), is regarded as his botanical masterpiece. It constitutes the only published part of a projected series of reminiscences from the Riesengebirge, the mountains in which Nees spent his spare time on excursions, accompanied by a local amateur botanist, J. von Flotow. The work begins with a superb introduction to the subject. The main body presents a completely new level of detail, with the recognition of innumerable subspecific variation and growth forms and a wealth of information on substrate and habitat. The final volume ends, characteristically, with a German translation, by Flotow, of Mirbel's studies on *Marchantia*, annotated by Nees. In 1841 Nees published an annotated reprint of G. Raddi's important but overlooked *Jungermanniografia etrusca* (1818). Nees's system of the world's liverworts was originally contributed to the second edition of J. Lindley's *Natural System of Botany* in 1836—Nees used Lindley's system in arranging his own general herbarium.[11] It was refined for the *Synopsis hepaticarum*. This work, still a standard reference volume, deals with all the liverworts then known. It was organized by Lehmann, principal of the Hamburg classical high school. Nees's coauthors were C. M. Gottsche, who practiced medicine in Altona and became the greatest hepaticologist of the century, and J. B. W. Lindenberg, Lübeck-Hamburgian administrator of Bergedorf. Nees's talent is perhaps most concisely displayed in his review of Corda's *Deutschlands Jungermannien* and in some notes on liverworts published in 1833.[12] The latter range from a pungent attack on chauvinism to the publication of a revolutionary report by Flotow on the culturing of liverworts in his room and the results obtained.

NOTES

1. *Flora*, **1** (1818), 137, 411, 518.
2. *Ibid.*, **2** (1819), 406.
3. *Ibid.*, **34** (1851), 559; **35** (1852), 347; *Bonplandia*, **2** (1854), 161–162.
4. *Leopoldina*, **2** (1861), 75.
5. For documents see *Nova acta*, **10** (1820), vii–xii; **11** (1823), 1x–x.
6. Cf. *Bonplandia*, **1** (1852), 24–26; **6** (1858), 1–2; *Nova acta*, **24**, Abt. 1 (1854), lii–lviii, lxxxviii–lxxxix.
7. *Ibid.*, **23**, Abt. 1 (1851), xxiii.
8. *Bonplandia*, **6** (1858), 152.
9. *Nova acta*, **27** (1860), xciv.
10. Cf. *Verhandlungen Gesellschaft deutscher Naturforscher und Ärzte*, **10** (1832), 4, 6; *Nova acta*, **24**, Abt. 1 (1854), xi ff.
11. See *Flora*, **35** (1852), 347.
12. *Ibid.*, **18** (1835), "Literaturberichte," 145–165; **14** (1833), 385–412.

BIBLIOGRAPHY

I. ORIGINAL WORKS. No proper Nees bibliography has been published, but it would comprise some 1,500 entries. Listings of his major works are available in the following standard volumes: *British Museum General Catalogue of Printed Books*, CLXIX (1963), 477–478, including nonscientific publications; *Catalogue of the Library of the British Museum (Natural History)*, III (1910), 1407–1408; and the Royal Society *Catalogue of Scientific Papers*, IV, 583–585, which lists 72 of his major papers. The magnitude becomes clear from the general index to *Flora*, **1** (1818)–**25** (1842), which lists more than 300 items by Nees.

Nees's insect collection is at the University of Bonn, his remaining private papers in the municipal archives at Wrocław, and the liverwort section of his herbarium at the University of Strasbourg.

II. SECONDARY LITERATURE. Abundant contemporary information is found in the journals *Bonplandia* and *Flora*, and in the introductory material to volumes of the *Nova acta Academiae Caesareae Leopoldino Carolinae germanicae naturae curiosorum*. Some of this has been cited in the notes. A one-page leaflet issued by Nees on 1 Feb. 1851, entitled *Erklärung* and dealing with his suspension from his professorship, is tipped into the copy of his *Handbuch der Botanik*, I, in the library of the German Society of Philadelphia. The MS of a full biography by H. Winkler, obviously unpublishable during Nazi times, came into the hands of an unidentified West German free church organization (*Nova acta*, 2nd ser., **15** [1952], 41). There is also a personal communication from the late Professor R. Zaunick of the Leopoldina, 17 Nov. 1956. For a charming photograph of Nees's head taken from the Weigelt photograph, a copy of which Nees presented to Humboldt, see *Bonplandia*, **6** (1858), 144 (an unsatisfactory engraving from this photograph is in F. Cohn [1858]).

Other works of value are the unsigned "Nees von Esenbeck, 1," in *Der grosse Brockhaus*, XIII (Leipzig, 1932), 250; F. T. Bratranek, *Neue Mittheilungen aus Johann Wolfgang von Goethe's handschriftlichem Nachlasse*, II (Leipzig, 1874), Nees-Goethe correspondence, pp. 13–

180; F. Cohn, "Christian Gottfried Daniel Nees von Esenbeck," in *Illustrirte Zeitung* (Leipzig), **30**, no. 778 (29 May 1858), 345–347, published anonymously; P. Cohn, *Ferdinand Cohn*, 2nd ed. (Breslau, 1901); G. Kaufmann, ed., *Festschrift zur Feier des hundertjährigen Bestehens der Universität Breslau*, 2 vols. (Breslau, 1911); D. G. Kieser, "Lebensbeschreibung des . . . Dr. Christian Gottfried Daniel Nees von Esenbeck," in *Nova acta Academiae Caesareae Leopoldino Carolinae germanicae naturae curiosorum*, **27** (1860), lxxxv–xcii, which includes Nees's autobiography, written in 1836; C. Nissen, *Die botanische Buchillustration*, I (Stuttgart, 1966), 217–218, for the relationship of A. Henry to Nees and the Leopoldina; G. Schmid, *Goethe und die Naturwissenschaften* (Halle, 1940); B. Seemann and W. E. G. Seemann, eds., "Christian Gottfried Daniel Nees von Esenbeck," in *Bonplandia*, **6** (1858), 145–152, which includes a list of the more than 70 scientific societies to which Nees belonged, an account of the funeral, an obituary by a Dr. M. Elsner originally published in a Breslau newspaper, a description of Nees's final illness by his physician, and his official "testament" explaining the overdraft for which he was responsible to the officers of the Leopoldina; H. Winkler, "Christian Gottfried Nees von Esenbeck als Naturforscher und Mensch," in *Naturwissenschaftliche Wochenschrift*, **36** (1921), 337–346; and "Christian Gottfried Nees von Esenbeck," in Historische Kommission für Schlesien, *Schlesische Lebensbilder*, II (Breslau, 1926), 203–208; and E. Wunschmann, "Christian Gottfried Daniel Nees von Esenbeck," in *Allgemeine deutsche Biographie*, XXIII (Leipzig, 1886), 368–376; and "Theodor Friedrich Ludwig Nees von Esenbeck," *ibid.*, pp. 376–380.

JOHANNES PROSKAUER

NEF, JOHN ULRIC (*b*. Herisau, Switzerland, 14 June 1862; *d*. Carmel, California, 13 August 1915), *chemistry*.

Nef, a pioneer in the transfer of the German university traditions in organic chemistry to the United States, immigrated with his parents to Housatonic, Massachusetts, in 1866. He graduated from Harvard University with honors, in 1884, and received from the university a traveling fellowship that enabled him to obtain the Ph.D. under Adolf von Baeyer at Munich in 1886. He remained as a postdoctoral student for one year and later was instrumental in establishing postdoctoral fellowship study in the United States. He held academic positions at Purdue (1887–1889), Clark (1889–1892), and Chicago (1892–1915) universities.

Nef was a great experimentalist and, as a pioneer in theoretical organic chemistry, contributed new methods to synthetic organic chemistry, in which three separate reactions are termed "Nef reactions." He studied the apparently bivalent carbon compounds and their dissociation. His theoretical work clearly contains the germs of the present concepts of free radicals, transition states, and polymerization. He was concerned with all products formed in an organic reaction and not just with the desired end product.

The later work of Nef and his students at Chicago was concerned with the action of alkali and alkaline oxidizing agents on the sugars. They isolated and characterized various types of saccharinic acids and used enolization and subsequent carbonyl migrations to interpret the alkaline transformations and degradations of the sugars. They discovered the two types of aldonolactones.

Nef's students helped to establish graduate research in organic chemistry in the universities of the American Middle West. An intense individual, Nef impressed his personality and aims on his students, who strove to continue and extend his work.

BIBLIOGRAPHY

A listing of Nef's writings is in Poggendorff, IV, 1060–1061, and V, 896; see also the biography by Wolfrom (1960).

Two biographies, both by M. L. Wolfrom, are in Eduard Farber, ed., *Great Chemists* (New York, 1931); and *Biographical Memoirs. National Academy of Sciences*, **34** (1960), 204–227.

M. L. WOLFROM

NEGRI, ADELCHI (*b.* Perugia, Italy, 2 August 1876; *d.* Pavia, Italy, 19 February 1912), *pathology.*

Negri studied medicine and surgery at Pavia University, where, as a resident student, he worked in the pathology laboratory directed by Camillo Golgi. After graduating with honors in 1900, he became Golgi's assistant. He was named lecturer in general pathology in 1905 and in 1909 was appointed to teach bacteriology, thus becoming the first official teacher of that subject at Pavia. In 1906 he married his colleague Lina Luzzani and six years later, at the age of thirty-five, died of tuberculosis.

Trained in Golgi's school, Negri conducted research in histology, hematology, cytology, protozoology, and hygiene. His fundamental scientific contribution was the discovery, announced to the Pavia Medical Society on 27 March 1903, of the rabies corpuscles, now known as "Negri bodies." During histological research undertaken to clarify the etiology of rabies and performed on Golgi's advice, Negri found that in animals suffering from rabies, certain cells of the nervous system, especially the pyramidal cells of the horn of Ammon, contain endocellular bodies with an internal structure so evident and regular as to constitute a characteristic feature. These bodies consist of single or multiple eosinophile, spherical, ovoid, or pyriform endocytoplasmic (never endonuclear) formations with a well-defined outline, varying in size from two to more than twenty microns (apparently in proportion to the size of the animal) and containing minute basophil granules having a diameter of 0.2–0.5 micron.

This cytological phenomenon proved to be almost constant and was found typically and abundantly in the histological material from living victims of advanced spontaneous rabies (street virus) or from those who had died of it. On the other hand, it was absent or very rare in cases of infection following inoculation of fixed virus. Rabbits and dogs infected experimentally with the street virus, dogs dead from spontaneous rabies, a cat infected experimentally by subdural injection, and one human case (a woman of sixty-four who had died of rabies after being bitten by a rabid dog) furnished the material on which Negri gave the first demonstrations of his discovery.

From the beginning Negri believed that the endocellular bodies he had observed in the nerve cells were the pathogenic agents of rabies and that they were forms belonging to the developmental cycle of a protozoan, the systematic position of which he could not define. This opinion, which Negri never abandoned, immediately became the object of scientific discussion. Some months after Negri's discovery, Alfonso Di Vestea in Naples, and Paul Remlinger and Riffat Bey in Constantinople, showed that the etiological agent of rabies is a filterable virus; and the argument about the significance of Negri's bodies became wider and more intense, with eminent parasitologists taking conflicting positions. Even today, despite research with the electron microscope, the significance of Negri's bodies has not been definitively clarified. Thus, as Luigi Bianchi wrote, it is still possible to accept Emilio Veratti's opinion that Negri's bodies are to be interpreted as specific formations closely linked to the virus and not as products of the cell containing it, without thereby assuming that they constitute the sole, infallible manifestation of the virus.

The specificity of Negri's bodies and their importance for diagnosis are universally recognized; the search for them, however, has absolute probative value in diagnosis only when there is a positive result. Negri himself indicated the rules to be observed in identifying the bodies for diagnostic purposes in animals suspected of rabies. The bodies, in material simply fixed for eighteen to twenty-four hours in Zenker's fluid and delicately pulped between cover glass and slide in a drop of glycinerinated water, appear under small enlargement as light yellow, glassy formations in the cytoplasm of the pyramidal cells; at enlargements of 400–600 diameters they reveal their characteristic internal structure.

BIBLIOGRAPHY

I. ORIGINAL WORKS. Negri produced some thirty publications, some of them joint works, which appeared in Italian and foreign journals between 1899 and 1911. They are listed in Veratti's article (see below) and in *Archives de parasitologie*, **16** (1913), 166. Documentary material concerning Negri is kept in the Museum of University History, Pavia.

II. SECONDARY LITERATURE. See Luigi Bianchi, "Rabbia," in Paolo Introzzi, ed., *Trattato italiano di medicina interna*, pt. 4, *Malattie infettive e parassitarie*, II (Bologna, 1965), 1351–1364; and *I corpi del Negri nello sviluppo della microbiologia all'Università di Pavia* (Pavia, 1967); and Emilio Veratti, "Adelchi Negri. La vita e l'opera scientifica," in *Rivista di biologia*, **16**, no. 3 (1934), 577–601.

BRUNO ZANOBIO

NEHRING, ALFRED (*b.* Gandersheim, Germany, 29 January 1845; *d.* Berlin, Germany, 29 September 1904), *paleontology, zoology.*

After graduating from the Gymnasium, Nehring studied natural sciences, especially zoology, from 1863 to 1867 at the universities of Göttingen and Halle, receiving his doctorate from Halle in 1867. He then taught biology at the Gymnasiums in Wesel and Wolfenbüttel. In 1881, on the strength of his scientific achievements, he was appointed professor of zoology at the Agricultural College in Berlin, where he later also became curator of the zoological collections. He held these posts until his death. Nehring never recovered from the psychological effects of a gas explosion in 1902 under the museum of the Agricultural College; this accident, which destroyed or damaged one portion of the collections and disrupted another, also weakened his health during his last years.

Nehring's scientific works covered Recent, postglacial, and Pleistocene vertebrates, particularly domestic animals; their domestication; their history; their relations in the wild; and the zoology of untamed game animals. His publications on Pleistocene mammals are of major importance. Nehring's works on Recent zoology concern the distribution of *Mus rattus* and *Mus decumanus*; canine teeth in horses, wild swine, Saiga antelopes, and various species of deer; the skeleton and systematic position of the seal *Halichoerus*; dog skulls with abnormal dentition; the craniological differences between the lion and the tiger; the origin, descent, and hybridizations of the South American rodent *Cavia cobaya*; the distribution and agricultural importance of the hamster *Cricetus cricetus* in Germany; various genera and species of Cricetidae; the origin of the duck *Anas moschata*; the distribution of the snake *Coronella austriaca* and of the freshwater fish *Pelecus*; and the presence of the snail *Helix candicans* in Pomerania.

Nehring's investigations of postglacial and domesticated animals concerned dwarf swine from Pomerania; primitive domesticated dogs near Berlin; the influence of domestication on the size of an animal's body; lake-dwelling fauna of East Prussia; the remains of *Bos primigenius* and *Alces* in the regions around Berlin; Herberstain's woodcuts (1557) of *Bison priscus* and *Bos primigenius*; Inca dogs from Peru; ancient Egyptian animal mummies; and the descent of domestic sheep.

The largest portion of Nehring's work consists of writings on Pleistocene mammals and birds, especially small mammals. In them he treated the morphology, taxonomy, and biogeographic distribution of many Pleistocene species; he also compared them in these respects with living representatives and relatives. He covered such rodents as lemmings and other Arvicolidae, including the genus *Dolomys*, which Nehring himself established, and members of other rodent families. He also dealt with the dog and cat families; the bear; several species of deer, ox, goat, sheep, and antelope; *Bison priscus*, camels, wild asses, horses, and the mammoth; and such birds as *Tetrao* (wood grouse), *Lyrurus* (black grouse), *Lagopus* (ptarmigan), *Nyctea scandiaca* (snowy owl), and *Scolopax rusticola* (woodcock). Most of Nehring's material was of German origin; but it also came from Europe (as far east as Russia and as far west as Portugal and England), Lebanon, and China.

Besides these individual descriptions Nehring wrote many accounts of the Pleistocene fauna: a survey of twenty-four central European Quaternary local faunas; the Quaternary local faunas of Thiede and Westeregeln near Brunswick; micromammals from the caves of Upper Franconia; diluvial vertebrates from Pösneck, Thuringia; the local fauna of a Pleistocene cave near Schaffhausen, Switzerland; diluvial animal remains from the Seveckenberg near Quedlinburg; and mammal remains from a Pleistocene peatbog near Cottbus.

Nehring not only studied the morphological, taxonomic, and phylogenetic relationships of the Pleistocene mammals but also treated some of the ecological problems involved. He wrote at length on these matters in *Über Tundren und Steppen der Jetzt- und Vorzeit* (1890), after having already treated them in several shorter papers. Following a description of the tundra (arctic steppes) in northern Russia and Siberia, as well as of the steppes of southern Russia and southwest Siberia, and their characteristic mammals, Nehring showed that regions of tundra and steppe, with their corresponding fauna, had existed in the later Pleistocene in central and western Europe. This study, filled with numerous and exact data, is still among the most important foundations of the paleoecology and paleobiogeography of the later Pleistocene in central and western Europe. Nehring also was interested in the fossil remains of man and his implements, and he participated vigorously in the discussions on the *Pithecanthropus erectus* of Java at the end of the nineteenth century.

Nehring's painstaking and thorough works still provide useful and much-employed data for research on Pleistocene mammals.

BIBLIOGRAPHY

I. ORIGINAL WORKS. A nearly complete bibliography is in A. S. Romer, N. E. Wright, T. Edinger, and R. van Frank, *Bibliography of Fossil Vertebrates Exclusive of North America, 1509–1927*, II, *L–Z*, Geological Society of America Memoir no. 87 (New York, 1962), 978–985. Nehring's writings include "Länge und Lage der Schneidezahnalveolen bei den wichtigsten Nagethieren," in *Zeitschrift für Naturwissenschaften*, **45** (1875), 217–239; "Beiträge zur Kenntniss der Diluvialfauna," *ibid.*, **47** (1876), 1–68; "Beiträge zur Kenntniss der Diluvialfauna (Fortsetzung)," *ibid.*, **48** (1876), 177–236; "Die quaternären Faunen von Thiede und Westeregeln nebst Spuren des vorgeschichtlichen Menschen," in *Archiv für Anthropologie*, **10** (1878), 359–398; "Fortsetzung und Schluss," *ibid.*, **11** (1879), 1–24; "Übersicht über vierundzwanzig mitteleuropäische Quartärfaunen," in *Zeitschrift der Deutschen geologischen Gesellschaft*, **32** (1880), 478–509; "Über die Abstammung unserer Hausthiere," in *Jahresberichte und Abhandlungen des Naturwissenschaftlichen Vereins in Magdeburg* for 1885–1886 (1886), 129–144; *Über Tundren und Steppen der Jetzt- und Vorzeit, mit besonderer Berücksichtigung ihrer Faunen* (Berlin, 1890); "Die geographische Verbreitung der Säugethiere in dem Tschernosem-Gebiete des rechten Wolga-Ufers," in *Zeitschrift der Gesellschaft für Erdkunde zu Berlin*, **26** (1891), 297–351; "Über einen Molar aus dem Diluvium von Taubach," in *Zeitschrift für Ethnologie*, **27** (1895), 573–577; "Die kleineren Wirbeltiere aus dem Schweizersbild bei Schaffhausen," in J. Nüesch *et al.*, "Das Schweizersbild, eine Niederlassung aus paläolithischer und neolithischer Zeit," in *Neue Denkschriften der Allgemeinen schweizerischen Gesellschaft für die gesamten Naturwissenschaften*, **35** (1902), 159–198.

II. SECONDARY LITERATURE. See the following, listed chronologically: J. V. Zelizko, "Alfred Nehring. Črta Životopisná," in *Pravěk*, **2** (1904), 150–155, with portrait; E. Friedel, "Alfred Nehring als Erforscher unserer Heimat," in *Brandenburgia*, **13** (1905), 289–301, with partial bibliography; and G. Tornier, "Rückblick auf Anatomie und Zoologie," in *Sitzungsberichte der Gesellschaft naturforschender Freunde zu Berlin* (1923), 12–71, see 43–44; and "Rückblick auf die Paläontologie," *ibid.* (1925), 72–106, titles of many of Nehring's paleontological papers, 101–103.

HEINZ TOBIEN

NEISSER, ALBERT LUDWIG SIGESMUND (*b.* Schweidnitz, Germany [now Swidnica, Poland], 22 January 1855; *d.* Breslau, Germany [now Wrocław, Poland], 30 July 1916), *dermatology.*

Neisser's father was a highly respected physician; his mother died before he was a year old, and he was raised by his stepmother. Neisser attended the Volksschule in Münsterberg, then entered the St. Maria Magdalena Humanistic Gymnasium in Breslau, where Paul Ehrlich was a classmate. In 1872 he began his medical studies, which, with the exception of one semester of clinical work in Erlangen, were carried out entirely in Breslau. His studies were not outstanding—in fact, he had to repeat the chemistry test—but he passed the state examination and received the medical degree in 1877 with a thesis on echinococcosis, prepared under the direction of the internist Anton Biermer. His other teachers included Rudolf Heidenhain, Julius Cohnheim, Carl Weigert, and C. J. Salomonsen. Neisser originally planned to become a specialist in internal medicine, but there were no openings for assistants in Biermer's clinic. It was therefore purely by chance that he turned to dermatology, becoming an assistant in Oskar Simon's clinic, where he worked for two years. It was there that in 1879 Neisser discovered the gonococcus.

Neisser's discovery occurred in the wake of the rapid development of the new field of bacteriology. It was made possible in large part by his close association with the botanist Ferdinand Cohn, who taught him Koch's smear tests for the identification of bacteria, and with Cohnheim and Weigert, who taught him staining techniques, including those with methylene blue. Neisser was further able to make use of a new Zeiss microscope that incorporated Abbe's innovative condenser and oil-immersion system. He at first called the microorganisms that he thus observed "micrococcus"; they were then given the name "gonococcus" by Ehrlich. Neisser's paper "Über eine der Gonorrhoe eigenthümliche Micrococcenform," published in 1879, was a milestone in elucidating the etiology of venereal diseases.

Neisser made a research trip to Norway in the same year. He was able to examine more than 100 patients with leprosy in Trondheim, Molde, and Bergen, and to take secretion smears back to Germany to study. In examining the smears he found, in almost all cases, "bacilli as small, thin rods, whose length amounts to about half the diameter of a human red blood corpuscle and whose width I estimate at one-fourth the length." These results embroiled him in a priority dispute with the Norwegian bacteriologist G. H. A. Hansen, who had found similar microorganisms in leprosy secretions as early as 1873; when Neisser published his findings in 1880, Hansen responded with a paper, published in four languages, in which he stated his earlier claim. It is clear, however, that while Hansen first discovered the leprosy bacillus, Neisser was the first to identify it as the etiological agent of the disease. The etiology, diagnosis, and prophylaxis of leprosy occupied him for much of his subsequent career.

His early publications made Neisser's name well known. On his return to Breslau, he was able to qualify as a lecturer in dermatology on the university medical faculty, and he was named *Privatdozent* on 6 August 1880. In 1882 Simon died suddenly, and Neisser was appointed his successor in the chair of dermatology and as director of the clinic. His promotion at the age of twenty-seven was sponsored by Friedrich Althoff, the Prussian councillor for education and cultural affairs. In the following year Neisser married Toni Kauffmann, who assisted him in his investigations and accompanied him on research trips. At about the same time he became involved in planning a new dermatological clinic, which, built to his design, was opened in 1892 and became an internationally famous research center.

Neisser's work with leprosy led him to study another infectious skin disease, lupus. He early suspected a connection between lupus and tuberculosis and went on to distinguish non-tubercular forms of the disease, including lupus erythematosus, lupus pernio, and sarcoidosis of the skin. His attempts to cure lupus with tuberculin came to nothing, however; he remained particularly concerned in alleviating the lot of those scarred by lupus. His servant, Hein, was so afflicted, and Neisser often used him as an object lesson in what might be done toward rehabilitation.

Neisser also devoted intensive study to syphilis, although his therapeutic suggestions are of little significance. His attempt to discover the cause of the disease through a series of inoculation experiments were unfortunate; he was accused of having "maliciously inoculated innocent children with syphilis poison," and a scandal resulted. Neisser was misled by drawing an analogy with the serum therapy that Behring had used against diphtheria and tetanus; the supposed serum with which he inoculated young prostitutes was probably highly infectious in itself.

In 1903 Metchnikoff and Roux demonstrated that syphilis could be communicated to apes, and Neisser immediately repeated their experiments and confirmed their findings. He made two trips to Java, in 1905 and 1906, to obtain ape specimens and to continue his research toward determining the cause of the disease. On 16 May 1905, however, he heard of Schaudinn and Hoffmann's discovery of the syphilis spirochete; the news must have been disappointing to him, and he at first was disinclined to accept that the spirochete was actually the causative agent. In a letter of June 1905, he wrote, "We are still toiling with the syphilis spirilla. Here and there we find something positive, but on the whole we are more convinced than ever that these spirilla . . . are not really the syphilis spirilla." By the time of his second Java trip he was convinced, however, and he turned to the investigation of the transmission of syphilis among both apes and men—the temporary stationing of Dutch sailors in Java supplied him with the human syphilis patients formerly lacking on that island. His observations yielded valuable data concerning reinfection and superinfection.

Neisser encouraged Wassermann to study seroreaction in syphilis in 1906. With him and with Carl Bruck, he developed the serological test, now named for Wassermann. He also worked in testing therapeutically the arsenic preparations, especially arsenophenylglycine, with which Ehrlich provided him. He found these to be effective but dangerous as remedies for syphilis. He also contributed to Ehrlich's introduction of Salvarsan (1910).

Neisser's work with venereal diseases brought him into the field of public health. He propagandized widely for better prophylactic measures and for more public education about these diseases; he was active in founding the Deutschen Gesellschaft zur Bekämpfung der Geschlechtskrankheiten and served as its president in 1901. He strongly supported stricter regulation of prostitution, and favored increased sanitary measures rather than police action. He also supported the establishment of a central board of health but objected to the obligation to inform the police and advocated the confidentiality of the doctor-patient relationship.

In 1907 Neisser was named full-time professor of dermatology at Breslau. He trained a number of eminent dermatologists, and conducted research on lichen infestations and urticaria. He experimentally explored the emergence of weals in the latter condition, and contributed substantially to Heidenhain's conclusion that the weal is a vasodilatory edema. As early as 1894 he described vitiligo with lichenoid eruptions, and he published a number of other findings about skin tumors, infectious diseases (including anthrax, actinomycosis, glanders, blastomycosis, and skin diphtheria), psoriasis, mycosis fungoids, and various forms of pemphigus. His work received wide official recognition.

The death of his wife, in 1913, affected Neisser deeply. His own health began to fail rapidly in 1916, and he died shortly after he was named a member of the Imperial Health Council. In 1920 his house was made a museum; in 1933 it was confiscated by the Nazis and turned into a guesthouse. Neisser's papers were salvaged by a Schweinfurt physician named Brock and form the basis for recent works about him.

BIBLIOGRAPHY

I. ORIGINAL WORKS. A full list of Neisser's publications may be found in the biography by Sigrid Schmitz, cited below. His most important works include "Über eine der Gonorrhoe eigenthümliche Micrococcenform," in *Centralblatt für die medizinischen Wissenschaften*, **28** (1879), 497–500; "Über die Aetiologie des Aussatzes," in *Jahresbericht der Schlesischen Gesellschaft für vaterländische Kultur*, **57** (1880), 65–72; "Weitere Beiträge zur Aetiologie der Lepra," in *Archiv für pathologische Anatomie und Physiologie*, **84** (1881), 514–542; "Die Mikrokokken der Gonorrhoe," in *Deutsche medizinische Wochenschrift*, **8** (1882), 279–283; "Die chronischen Infektionskrankheiten der Haut," in H. W. von Ziemssen, ed., *Handbuch der speciellen Pathologie und Therapie*, XIV (Leipzig, 1883), 560–723; "Über das Leukoderma syphiliticum," in *Vierteljahrsschrift für Dermatologie und Syphilis*, **15** (1883), 491–508; "Über die Mängel der zur Zeit üblichen Prostituiertenuntersuchungen," in *Deutsche medizinische Wochenschrift*, **16** (1890), 834–837; "Pathologie des Ekzems," in *Archiv für Dermatologie und Syphilis*, **1** (1892), suppl., 116–161; "Über den gegenwärtigen Stand der Lichenfrage," *ibid.*, **28** (1894), 75–99; and "Über Vitiligo mit lichenoiden Eruptionen," in *Verhandlungen der Deutschen Dermatologischen Gesellschaft. IV. Kongress zu Breslau* (Vienna-Leipzig, 1894), 435–439.

See also "Syphilis maligne," in *Journal des maladies cutanées et syphilitiques*, **9** (1896), 210–213; "Was wissen wir von einer Serumtherapie der Syphilis und was haben wir von ihr zu hoffen?," in *Archiv für Dermatologie und Syphilis*, **44** (1898), 431–439; "Über Versuche, Syphilis auf Schweine zu übertragen," *ibid.*, **59** (1902), 163–170; "Meine Versuche zur Übertragung der Syphilis auf Affen," in *Deutsche medizinische Wochenschrift*, **30** (1904), 1369–1373, 1431–1434; "Weitere Mitteilungen über den Nachweis spezifischer luetischer Substanzen durch Komplement-bindung," in *Zeitschrift für Hygiene und Infektionskrankheiten*, **55** (1906), 451–477, written with A. Wassermann, C. Bruck, and A. Schucht; *Über die Bedeutung der Lupuskrankheit und die Notwendigkeit ihrer Bekämpfung* (Leipzig, 1908); "Über das neue Ehrlich'sche Mittel," in *Deutsche medizinische Wochenschrift*, **36** (1910), 1212–1213; "Beiträge zur Pathologie und Therapie der Syphilis," in *Arbeiten aus dem Kaiserlichen Gesundheitsamt*, **37** (1911), 1–624; *Syphilis und Salvarsan* (Berlin, 1913); "Ist es wirklich ganz unmöglich, die Prostitution gesundheitlich unschädlich zu machen?," in *Deutsche medizinische Wochenschrift*, **41** (1915), 1385–1388; "Über das urtikarielle Ekzem," in *Archiv für Dermatologie und Syphilis*, **121** (1916), 579–612; and *Die Geschlechtskrankheiten und ihre Bekämpfung* (Berlin, 1916).

II. SECONDARY LITERATURE. In addition to obituary notices in a number of medical journals, see K. Bochmann, "Albert Neisser," in *Heilberufe*, **7** (1955), 179; E. Czaplewski, "Albert Neisser und die Entdeckung des Leprabazillus," in *Archiv für Dermatologie und Syphilis*, **124** (1917), 513–530; G. L. Flite and H. W. Wade, "The Contribution of Neisser to the Establishment of the Hansen Bacillus as the Etiologic Agent of Leprosy and the So-called Hansen-Neisser Controversy," in *International Journal of Leprosy*, **23** (1955), 418–428; J. Jadassohn, "Albert Neisser," in F. Andreae, ed., *Schlesische Lebensbilder*, I (Breslau, 1922), 111–115; J. Schäffer, *Albert Neisser* (Berlin-Vienna, 1917); W. Schönfeld, "In Memoriam Albert Neisser zum 100. Geburtstag," in *Hautarzt*, **6** (1955), 94–96; A. Stühmer, "Albert Neisser," in *Dermatologische Wochenschrift*, **131** (1955), 214–216; and T. M. Vogelsang, "The Hansen-Neisser Controversy, 1879–1880," in *International Journal of Leprosy*, **31** (1963), 74–80, and **32** (1964), 330–331.

The best and most comprehensive biography, which draws upon Neisser's posthumous papers and other previously unpublished sources, is Sigrid Schmitz, "Albert Neisser. Leben und Werk auf Grund neuer, unveröffentlicher Quellen," in H. Schadewaldt, ed., *Düsseldorfer Arbeiten zur Geschichte der Medizin*, XXIX (Düsseldorf, 1968).

H. SCHADEWALDT

NEKRASOV, ALEKSANDR IVANOVICH (*b.* Moscow, Russia, 9 December 1883; *d.* Moscow, 21 May 1957), *mechanics, mathematics.*

Nekrasov graduated from the Fifth Moscow Gymnasium in 1901 with a gold medal and entered the mathematical section of the Faculty of Physics and Mathematics at Moscow University. In 1906 he graduated with a first-class diploma and received a gold medal for "Teoria sputnikov Yupitera" ("Theory of the Satellites of Jupiter"). Nekrasov remained at the university to prepare for a professorship. At the same time he taught in several secondary schools in Moscow. In 1909–1911 Nekrasov passed his master's examinations in two specialties, astronomy and mechanics. In 1912 he became assistant professor in the department of astronomy and geodesy of the Faculty of Physics and Mathematics at the university, and in 1913 he was appointed to the same post in the department of applied mathematics (theoretical mechanics) of the same faculty. From 1917 until his death Nekrasov taught and conducted research at Moscow University, the Higher Technical School, the Central Aerohydrodynamics Institute, the Sergo Orjonikidze Aviation Institute, and the Institute of Mechanics of the Academy of Sciences of the U.S.S.R.

In 1922 Nekrasov was awarded the N. E. Zhukovsky Prize for "O volnakh ustanovivshegosya vida na poverkhnosti tyazheloy zhidkosti" ("On Smooth-Form Waves on the Surface of a Heavy Liquid"). For his distinguished scientific services he was elected corresponding member of the Academy of Sciences of the U.S.S.R. in 1932 and an active member in 1946. He was awarded the title Honored Worker in Science and Technology in 1947 for his services in the development of aviation technology. Nekrasov was a brilliant representative of the trend in the development of precise mathematical methods in hydromechanics and aeromechanics that is associated with Zhukovsky and S. A. Chaplygin. He published basic works on the theory of waves, the theory of whirlpools, the theory of jet streams, and gas dynamics.

Nekrasov's Tochnaya teoria voln ustanovivshegosya vida na poverkhnosti tyazheloy zhidkosti ("A Precise Theory of Smooth-Form Waves on the Surface of a Heavy Liquid"), on classical problems of hydromechanics, was awarded the State Prize of the U.S.S.R. in 1951. In an extensive monograph on aerodynamics, Teoria kryla v nestatsionarnom potoke ("Theory of the Wing in a Nonstationary Current"; 1947), he presented a systematic and detailed account of all the basic scientific works dealing with the theory of the unsmooth motion of a wing in the air without allowing for its compressibility. He not only systematized material published earlier but also analyzed and compared it, in a number of cases providing a new mathematical treatment of the subject. Other important works in aerodynamics are Primenenie teorii integralnykh uravneny k opredeleniyu kriticheskoy skorosti flattera kryla samoleta ("Application of the Theory of Integral Equations to the Determination of the Critical Velocity of the Flutter of an Airplane Wing"; 1947) and Obtekanie profilya Zhukovskogo pri nalichii na profile istochnika i stoka ("Flow on a Zhukovsky Cross Section in the Presence of a Cross Section of the Source and Outflow"). Besides his work on aerohydrodynamics Nekrasov published an excellent two-volume textbook on theoretical vector mechanics (1945–1946).

Nekrasov's works also enriched mathematics. Among his contributions are the first fruitful investigations of nonlinear integral equations with symmetrical nuclei, the books O nelineynikh integralnykh uravneniakh s postoyannymi predelami ("On Nonlinear Integral Equations With Constant Limits"; 1922) and Ob odnom klasse lineynykh integro-differentsialnykh uravneny ("On One Class of Linear Integral-Differential Equations"; 1934), and many investigations in an important area of aerohydrodynamics. The extremely varied mathematical apparatus that he used contains many original details developed by Nekrasov himself.

Nekrasov translated into Russian É. Goursat's Cours d'analyse mathématique as Kurs matematicheskogo analiza. To a substantial degree this project made possible Nekrasov's assimilation of the mathematical methods that he later applied so skillfully to the solution of concrete problems in aerodynamics.

A fully worthy disciple of and successor to Zhukovsky, Nekrasov enriched Soviet science with his scientific works and, through his work in education, aided the development of many scientists and engineers.

BIBLIOGRAPHY

Many of Nekrasov's writings are in his Sobranie sochineny ("Collected Works"), 2 vols. (Moscow, 1961–1962).

Secondary literature includes Aleksandr Ivanovich Nekrasov (Moscow–Leningrad, 1950); and Y. I. Sekerzh-Zenkovich, "Aleksandr Ivanovich Nekrasov," in Uspekhi matematicheskikh nauk, 15, no. 1 (1960).

A. T. GRIGORIAN

NEMESIUS (fl. Emesa [now Homs], Syria, A.D. 390–400), medicine.

Nemesius, possibly although not certainly a provincial governor of Cappadocia, is believed to have been converted to Christianity about 390, and sometime thereafter he became bishop of Emesa. During these final years of the fourth century he composed his treatise Περὶ φύσεως ἀνθρώπου ("On the Nature of Man"), which is essentially concerned with the reconciliation of Platonic doctrines on the soul with Christian philosophy and also, importantly, with the interpretation of Greek scientific knowledge of the human body from the standpoint of Christian doctrine. For a time the work was attributed to Gregory of Nyssa; and it was not until the seventh century that there was any ascription of it to Nemesius, of whom almost nothing is known except for such self-revelations as are to be found in his text. From these it is apparent that he was well-read in the writings of Galen and may even have had some medical training.

Although Nemesius' book contains many passages dealing with Galenic anatomy and physiology, the most important contribution of the work was to establish the idea that the mental faculties were localized in the ventricles of the brain, a belief that was generally accepted and retained as late as the sixteenth century. Actually the belief in such localization had been advanced even earlier in the fourth century by the Greek physician Posidonius, to whom Nemesius referred; but because only fragments of Posidonius' writings survived, the doctrine of ventricular localization gained prominence only through the later treatise.

According to Nemesius' doctrine, all sensory perceptions were received in the anterior—now called lateral—ventricles of the brain. Later this area came to be designated the "sensus communis," that is, the region where all the sensory perceptions were held in common by a force known as the faculty of imagination. The middle or, as it is now called, third ventricle was the region of the faculty of intellect, which controlled the "judging, approving, refuting, and assaying" of the sensory perceptions gathered in the lateral ventricles. The third faculty was that of memory, the storehouse of sensory perceptions after they had been judged by the faculty of intellect. Memory was located by Nemesius in the cerebellum but, according to succeeding interpretations, in the fourth ventricle. Moreover, later writers extended Nemesius' doctrine by causing the intellectual or rational faculty to draw upon memory in the making of decisions. The faculties operated through the agency of the animal spirit, the very refined spirit which, according to Galen, was produced from vital spirit after it had been carried through the supposititious network of arteries, called the *rete mirabile*, at the base of the brain. Nemesius was convinced of the correctness of his doctrine of the ventricular localization of the mental faculties, since in his opinion injury to those areas of the brain caused the loss of the faculties.

After its composition Nemesius' book seems to have gone through a period of disregard, to be rediscovered only after the passage of several centuries. It was cited by John of Damascus in the eighth century, by Timothy I, the Nestorian *catholicos*, and by the Phrygian monk and physician Meletius. Possibly it was from one of these sources that ventricular localization came to be accepted and described as early as the late ninth and early tenth centuries by Quṣṭā ibn Lūqā and by al-Rāzī, the latter of whom was important in the diffusion of the doctrine.

The first extensive and medically important treatment of Nemesius' book was that by Alphanus, a monk of the Benedictine abbey of Monte Cassino and later archbishop (1058–1085) of Salerno. Alphanus translated it into Latin under the title of *Premnon physicon* ("Tree of Nature") and thus made the medical portions available to the Salernian medical school, although there is no clear evidence of their influence upon Salernian medicine. The work was again translated in 1155 by Burgundio of Pisa; neither translator appears to have been aware of the identity of the author. These Latin translations were definitely effective in promotion of the idea of the localization of the mental faculties in the ventricles—the former, for example, on Albertus Magnus and the latter on Thomas Aquinas. Localization began to be described with some frequency in the twelfth and thirteenth centuries. It was also illustrated by drawings of the head in which the lateral ventricles were often identified by circular figures, frequently called "cellulae" and specified as the area of "imaginatio," "phantasia," or "sensus communis"; a further circle representing the third ventricle was commonly designated as the area of "aestimativa" or "cogitativa," and the circle of the fourth ventricle was most often labeled "memoria."

The first translation of Nemesius' work to be printed (Strasbourg, 1512) was that by John Cono of Nuremberg, and the first printed edition of the Greek text was published under the editorship of Nicasius Ellebodius by the Plantin Press of Antwerp in 1565.

The idea of ventricular localization of the mental faculties in the form presented by Nemesius was first attacked in 1521 by Berengario da Carpi, who grouped the three faculties in three separate areas of the lateral ventricles. Vesalius delivered the coup de grace to the entire theory in 1543, when he denied any role to the ventricles except the collection of fluid and declared that in some manner the mind was in the brain at large. Although Vesalius did not elaborate upon this point, his theme was picked up by Costanzo Varolio, who in 1573 asserted more clearly that there was a single mental faculty in the brain as a whole and that the ventricles served merely to collect and drain off superfluous fluid.

BIBLIOGRAPHY

There is an English trans. of Περὶ φύσεως ἀνθρώπου by William Telfer in *Cyril of Jerusalem and Nemesius of Emesa*, W. Telfer, ed., vol. IV in Library of Christian Classics (London, 1955). It includes references to all the pertinent literature on Nemesius and eds. of his work.

C. D. O'MALLEY

NEMORE, JORDANUS DE. See **Jordanus de Nemore.**

NENCKI, MARCELI (*b*. Boczki, near Kielce, Russia [now Poland], 15 January 1847; *d*. St. Petersburg, Russia, 14 December 1901), *biochemistry*.

Nencki was the son of Wilhelm Nencki, a landowner, and the former Katarzyna Serwaczyńska. In 1863 he graduated from a classical secondary school in Piotrków Trybunalski; active participation in the Polish uprising made his situation uncertain and forced him to emigrate. For about a year Nencki studied philosophy and ancient languages at the University of Berlin before transferring to the Medical Faculty of the same university, where he studied the chemistry of living organisms. To increase his knowledge of inorganic and organic chemistry, Nencki worked during two years of his medical studies under the direction of Baeyer in his laboratory at the Gewerbeinstitut.

While still a university student Nencki published, with his friend O. Schultzen, a paper dealing with precursors of urea in mammals. He received the M.D. in 1870 with a dissertation on the oxidation of aromatic compounds in the body. In 1871 Nencki published a paper related to the chemistry of uric acid and similar compounds. These three subjects were the center of his interest throughout his life.

Nencki's initial publications appeared to be of such value that shortly after receiving the M.D. he was engaged as an assistant at the University of Bern, where his scientific career developed swiftly. Within a few years he was appointed to a professorship and became head of the department of biochemistry. A pioneer of a chemical approach to microorganisms, he also lectured on pharmacology and bacteriology. Nencki became an internationally recognized authority on biochemistry and theoretical medicine, attracting students from all parts of Europe and America.

In 1890 Nencki left Switzerland for St. Petersburg, to help organize a new institute of experimental medicine. As head of the department of chemistry and biochemistry he began work in a new building specially constructed and equipped according to his plans. Partly in collaboration with Pavlov, who was head of the department of physiology, Nencki started to reinvestigate the method and site of formation of urea in the body. These fundamental and beautiful experiments showed that urea is formed chiefly, if not exclusively, in the liver. According to Nencki, urea was synthesized from amino groups of amino acids and from carbon dioxide and did not preexist in the protein molecule, as was then quite generally believed. This important idea anticipated modern views of the utilization of carbon dioxide in certain synthetic processes that occur in the animal body. Speculating on the various possibilities of biosynthesis, especially of fatty acids, Nencki proposed a hypothesis according to which a gradual condensation of some active two-carbon-atom fragments takes place; a splitting-off of these fragments may occur during oxidation. This hypothesis, together with the results of Nencki's earlier investigation on the oxidation of aromatic compounds in the animal body, formed a basis for Knoop's β oxidation theory. Nencki supposed that the active two-carbon-unit compound was acetaldehyde and hence, in principle, he was not far from the modern view of the role of acetyl coenzyme A.

Nencki's best-known investigations concerned hemoglobin. Using original methods he systematically studied for many years the degradation products of this blood pigment. Somewhat later Marchlewski, working first in England and later in Cracow, performed similar studies on chlorophyll. It soon appeared that some of the degradation products of these two pigments resembled each other. Nencki and Marchlewski thus initiated a peculiar art of collaboration at a distance. They exchanged and carefully investigated the particular degradation products of the pigments and finally obtained, both from hemoglobin and from chlorophyll, the same substance, hemopyrrole.

On the basis of these results Nencki put forward a hypothesis concerning the chemical relationship between the animal and plant kingdoms. He planned vast investigations in the field, which now would be called evolutionary biochemistry. Unfortunately these plans were not realized; at the end of 1901 Nencki died of stomach cancer.

Nencki's work is unusually impressive for its magnitude, as well as for the variety of the problems he investigated, the ingenuity and the precision of his experiments, and his perseverance in achieving his aims. His chief interest was biochemistry; but some of his papers deal with analytical and organic chemistry, bacteriology, pharmacology, pharmacy, hygiene, and practical medicine.

All of Nencki's scientific life took place outside Poland, but he was always in contact with his motherland: he published many of his papers in Polish scientific journals, held an honarary doctorate from the University of Cracow, was a member of several Polish scientific societies, and often participated in Polish congresses. In accordance with his wishes, he was buried in Warsaw.

Shortly after Nencki's death it was suggested that a scientific institute be built and named for him. This idea was not realized until 1918, with the creation of the Nencki Intstiute of Experimental Biology, devoted chiefly to biochemistry and physiology, in Warsaw.

BIBLIOGRAPHY

Marceli Nencki. Opera omnia. Gesammelte Arbeiten von Prof. M. Nencki, Nadine Sieber and J. Zaleski, eds., (Brunswick, 1904), contains Nencki's 150 papers and 450 papers by his colleagues at Bern and St. Petersburg.

Fifty Years of Activity of the M. Nencki Institute of Experimental Biology (1918–1968) (Warsaw, 1968), in Polish with English summaries, contains articles on the history of the Nencki Institute (W. Niemierko), the investigations of the physiology of the brain (J. Konorski), biochemistry (W. Niemierko), neurochemistry (Stella Niemierko), biology (S. Dryl), hydrobiology (R. Klekowski), data concerning the library of the Institute (H. Adler), and a complete list of workers there (1918–1968). *Marceli Nencki, Materiały biograficzne i bibliograficzne*, Aniela Szwejcerowa and Jadwiga Groszyńska, eds. (Warsaw, 1956), contains a full bibliography of Nencki's works and of works on him, his correspondence with Marchlewski, some of his letters to his family, a biographical article by W. Niemierko, some other biographical articles, photographs, and documents. See also M. H. Bickel, *Marceli Nencki, 1847–1901* (Bern–Stuttgart–Vienna, 1972).

WŁODZIMIERZ NIEMIERKO

NERI, ANTONIO (*b.* Florence, Italy, 29 February 1576; *d.* Pisa or Florence, *ca.* 1614), *chemical technology.*

Almost nothing is known with certainty about Neri, except that his father, Jacopo, was a physician; that Neri was ordained a priest before 1601; and that he led a wandering life. He appears to have learned the art of glassmaking at Murano, near Venice, and to have continued his studies of this and other chemical arts in the Low Countries. From about 1604 to 1611 he was at Antwerp, lodging in the house of Emanuel Ximenes, a Portuguese; he published his book and spent the last years of his life in northern Italy. The evidence for the date of his death is very scanty.

Neri is remembered only for *L'arte vetraria* (1612), a little book in which many, although by no means all, of the closely guarded secrets of glassmaking were printed for the first time. He recommended that glass be made from *rocchetta* (a fairly pure sodium sesquicarbonate from the Near East) and *tarso*, which he described as a kind of marble but which must have been some form of silica. He did not indicate the source of the necessary proportion of lime. The main part of the text deals with the coloring of glass with metallic oxides to give not only clear and uniform colors but also various veined effects. There are chapters on making lead glass of high refractive index and enamel (opaque) glass by the addition of tin oxide.

There are no illustrations, and the operations are not described in much detail. The proportions of ingredients are often left to the experience of the operator. It is difficult to believe that the book could have been of great value to a practical glassmaker, but it served as a nucleus for the observations of later writers.

BIBLIOGRAPHY

I. ORIGINAL WORKS. The full title of Neri's book is *L'arte vetraria distinta in libri sette, ne quali si scoprone, effetti maravigliosi, & insegnano segreti bellissimi del vetro nel fuoco & altre cose curiose* (Florence, 1612). Later Italian eds. appeared at Florence (1661), Venice (1663, 1678), and Milan (1817). The book and its various eds. and trans. are discussed by Luigi Zecchin in "Il libro di prete Neri," in *Vetro e silicati*, **7** (1963), 17–20.

An English version was prepared by C. M. (Christopher Merrett) for the Royal Society as part of its plan for "histories" of trades, and published as *The Art of Glass . . . With Observations on the Author* (London, 1662). The "observations" are a collection of explanations, additions, and emendations which double the length of the text. The British Museum copy is heavily annotated, perhaps by Merrett, clearly in preparation for a drastically rev. 2nd ed., which never appeared.

Merrett's version and notes were trans. into Latin as *Ars vitraria . . .* by Andreas Frisius (Amsterdam, 1668). It was also trans. into German by Friedrich Geissler (1678) and appeared as part of Johann Kunckel's *Ars vitraria experimentalis* (Frankfurt–Leipzig, 1679, 1689). A French version by M. D. (Baron d'Holbach), entitled *Art de la verrerie* (Paris, 1752), incorporated the additions of Merrett, Kunckel, and d'Holbach himself. *De l'Art de la Verrerie*, by Haudicquer de Blancourt (Paris, 1697), is a French version, without acknowledgment, of the Neri-Merrett text, expanded by redundant verbiage to nearly twice the original length.

An "alchemical" MS by Neri is mentioned by G. F. Rodwell in "On the Theory of Phlogiston," in *Philosophical Magazine*, **35** (1868), 10, without any indication of its location.

II. SECONDARY LITERATURE. The lack of information about Neri has resulted in his omission from most works of reference, but he is mentioned in J. Ferguson, *Bibliotheca chemica*, II (Glasgow, 1906), 135. Luigi Zecchin, in "Lettere a prete Neri," in *Vetro e silicati*, **8** (1964), 17–20, discovered the record of Neri's baptism in Florence and 28 letters from Ximenes to Neri, most of them dated between 1601 and 1603. The Neri-Merrett text is discussed by

W. E. S. Turner, "A Notable British Seventeenth-Century Contribution to the Literature of Glassmaking," in *Glass Technology*, **3** (1962), 201–213.

W. V. FARRAR

NERNST, HERMANN WALTHER (*b*. Briesen, Prussia [now Wąbrzeżno, Poland], 25 June 1864; *d*. Bad Muskau, Prussia [now German Democratic Republic], 18 November 1941), *chemistry*.

For a detailed study of his life and work, see Supplement.

NETTESHEIM. See **Agrippa, Heinrich Cornelius.**

NETTO, EUGEN (*b*. Halle, Germany, 30 June 1848; *d*. Giessen, Germany, 13 May 1919), *mathematics*.

Netto was the grandson of a Protestant clergyman and the son of an official of the "Franckeschen Stiftungen," Heinrich Netto, and his wife, Sophie Neumann. He attended elementary school in Halle and at the age of ten entered the Gymnasium in Berlin. There he was a pupil of Karl Heinrich Schellbach, who had been Eisenstein's teacher; this famous educator aroused his interest in mathematics. In 1866, following his graduation from the Gymnasium, Netto enrolled at the University of Berlin, where he was influenced mainly by Kronecker, Kummer, and Weierstrass. In 1870 he graduated with honors from Berlin with the dissertation *De transformatione aequationis* $y^n = R(x)$, *designante* $R(x)$ *functionem integram rationalem variabilis* x, *in aequationem* $\eta^2 = R_1(\xi)$ (Weierstrass was chief referee). After teaching at a Gymnasium in Berlin, he became an associate professor at the University of Strasbourg in 1879.

In 1882, on Weierstrass' recommendation, Netto was appointed associate professor at the University of Berlin. Besides the introductory lectures for first-semester students, he gave those on higher algebra, the calculus of variations, Fourier series, and theoretical mechanics; he also lectured on synthetic geometry. His textbook *Substitutionentheorie und ihre Anwendung auf die Algebra* (Berlin, 1882) is a milestone in the development of abstract group theory. In it two historical roots of abstract group theory are united—the theory of permutation groups and that of implicit group-theoretical thinking in number theory. Even though Netto did not yet include transformation groups in his concept of groups, he nevertheless clearly recognized the far-reaching importance of the theory of composition in a group and its significance for future developments.

In 1888 Netto became professor at the University of Giessen, where he remained until his retirement in 1913. He contributed to the dissemination of group theory in further papers; and in *Lehrbuch der Combinatorik* (Leipzig, 1901; 2nd ed., enlarged by T. Skolem and Viggo Brun, 1927) he skillfully gathered the scattered literature in this area. His *Die Determinanten* (Leipzig, 1910) was translated into Russian in 1911. Netto was a clever, persuasive, and witty teacher who demonstrated his educational abilities and productivity through additional textbooks and other publications on algebra.

BIBLIOGRAPHY

Netto's works are listed in Poggendorff, III, 962; IV, 1064; and V, 897–898.

On Netto or his work see Wilhelm Lorey, "Die Mathematiker an der Universität Giessen vom Beginn des 19. Jahrhunderts bis 1914," in *Nachrichten der Giessener Hochschulgesellschaft*, **11** (1937), 54–97; Egon Ullrich, "Die Naturwissenschaftliche Fakultät," in *Ludwigs-Universität–Justus-Liebig-Hochschule. 1607–1957. Festschrift zur 350-Jahrfeier* (Giessen, 1957), 267–287; Hans Wussing, "Zum historischen Verhältnis von Intension und Extension des Begriffes Gruppe im Herausbildungsprozess des abstrakten Gruppenbegriffes," in *NTM—Schriftenreihe für Geschichte der Naturwissenschaften, Technik und Medizin*, **4** (1967), 23–34; and Kurt-R. Biermann, "Die Mathematik und ihre Dozenten an der Berliner Universität 1810–1920" (Berlin, 1973).

KURT-R. BIERMANN

NEUBERG, JOSEPH (*b*. Luxembourg City, Luxembourg, 30 October 1840; *d*. Liège, Belgium, 22 March 1926), *geometry*.

Neuberg was one of the founders of the modern geometry of the triangle. The considerable body of his work is scattered among a large number of articles for journals; in it the influence of A. Möbius is clear. In general, his contribution to mathematics lies in the discovery of new details, rather than in any large contribution to the development of his subject.

Neuberg was educated at the Athénée de Luxembourg, and later at the Normal School of Sciences, which was then a part of the Faculty of Sciences of the University of Ghent. From 1884 to 1910 he was a professor at the University of Liège. He was a naturalized citizen of Belgium and was a member of the sciences section (which he headed in 1911) of the Belgian Royal Academy. From 1874 to 1880 Neuberg, with Catalán and Mansion, published the *Nouvelle correspondance mathématique*; subsequently he collaborated with Mansion in publishing *Mathesis*.

BIBLIOGRAPHY

A portrait of Neuberg and a notice with a complete bibliography of his work by A. Mineur may be found in *Annuaire de l'Académie royale de Belgique*, **98** (1932), 135–192; see also L. Godeaux, in *Biographie nationale publiée par l'Académie royale de Belgique*, XXX (1958), cols. 635–637; and in *Liber Memorialis. L'Université de Liège de 1867 à 1935*, II (Liège, 1936), 162–175.

J. PELSENEER

NEUMANN, CARL GOTTFRIED (*b.* Königsberg, Prussia [now Kaliningrad, R.S.F.S.R.], 7 May 1832; *d.* Leipzig, Germany, 27 March 1925), *mathematics, theoretical physics.*

Neumann's father, Franz Ernst Neumann, was professor of physics and mineralogy at Königsberg; his mother, Luise Florentine Hagen, was a sister-in-law of the astronomer F. W. Bessel. Neumann received his primary and secondary education in Königsberg, attended the university, and formed particularly close friendships with the analyst F. J. Richelot and the geometer L. O. Hesse. After passing the examination for secondary school teaching he obtained his doctorate in 1855; in 1858 he qualified for lecturing in mathematics at Halle, where he became *Privatdozent* and, in 1863, assistant professor. In the latter year he was called to Basel, and in 1865 to Tübingen. From the autumn of 1868 until his retirement in 1911 he was at the University of Leipzig. In 1864 he married Hermine Mathilde Elise Kloss; she died in 1875.

Neumann, who led a quiet life, was a successful university teacher and a productive researcher. More than two generations of future Gymnasium teachers received their basic mathematical education from him. As a researcher he was especially prominent in the field of potential theory. His investigations into boundary value problems resulted in pioneering achievements; in 1870 he began to develop the method of the arithmetical mean for their solution. He also coined the term "logarithmic potential." The second boundary value problem of potential theory still bears his name; a generalization of it was later provided by H. Poincaré.

Neumann was a member of the Berlin Academy, and the Societies of Göttingen, Munich, and Leipzig. He performed a valuable service in founding and editing the important German mathematics periodical *Mathematische Annalen*.

BIBLIOGRAPHY

I. ORIGINAL WORKS. Neumann's writings include *Vorlesungen über Riemanns Theorie der Abelschen Integrale* (Leipzig, 1865); *Untersuchungen über das logarithmische und Newtonsche Potential* (Leipzig, 1877); and *Über die nach Kreis-, Kugel- und Zylinderfunktionen fortschreitenden Entwicklungen* (Leipzig, 1881).

II. SECONDARY LITERATURE. See H. Liebmann, "Zur Erinnerung an Carl Neumann," in *Jahresberichte der Deutschen Mathematikervereinigung*, **36** (1927), 175–178; and H. Salié, "Carl Neumann," in *Bedeutende Gelehrte in Leipzig*, II, G. Harig, ed. (Leipzig, 1965), 13–23.

H. WUSSING

NEUMANN, CASPAR (*b.* Züllichau, Germany [now Sulechów, Poland], 11 July 1683; *d.* Berlin, Germany, 20 October 1737), *chemistry.*

The first child of a merchant-musician, Caspar Neumann was intended for the clergy. He learned music from his father and studied at the local Latin school. But, orphaned at the age of twelve, he had to go into pharmacy as an apprentice to his godfather. He showed such aptitude that three years later his guardian put him in charge of an apothecary shop, brewery, and distillery in nearby Unruhstadt. Neumann remained there until 1704, when the Great Northern War forced him to flee to Berlin. In the Prussian capital he soon became an assistant to the traveling pharmacist of Frederick I. As part of the royal entourage, he played the clavier for the king, he traveled throughout Germany and Holland, and he pursued a growing interest in science and medicine.

Neumann's serious scientific education began in 1711, when, apparently at the urging of the renowned royal physician F. Hoffmann, he was sent abroad to study chemistry. He first visited the Harz mining towns, where he learned assaying and smelting, and then went to Holland, where he inspected large chemical works and studied with Boerhaave. In 1713 he went to London, where he was stranded because of the recent death of his royal patron. He found employment as a laboratory assistant to the wealthy Dutch surgeon A. Cyprian, who spent £1,000 annually on chemical experiments. In his free time, Neumann gave private courses on chemistry and participated in the scientific life of London. After three years there he returned to Berlin to collect his belongings. Stahl, who had recently been made royal physician, persuaded Neumann to reenter Prussian service by obtaining a continuation of his travel stipend and promising him a position in the court apothecary shop. On his second tour Neumann first visited his friends in London. Then he proceeded to Paris, where he attended courses on chemistry and botany; taught a course of his own on chemistry; experimented two afternoons weekly with C. J. and E. F. Geoffroy; and made the acquaintance of all the leading scientists. In 1719 he returned to Berlin by way of Rome.

Upon his return, Neumann as court apothecary took on the demanding job of running one of Europe's busiest pharmacies. Nevertheless, he managed to find time for other activities. In 1721 he began active membership in Berlin's Society of Sciences, and in 1724 he became a member of the chief Prussian medical board and began teaching in the new Medical-Surgical College as professor of practical (experimental) chemistry. He remained in all these positions until his death in 1737 at the age of fifty-four.

In the mid-1720's, after more than a decade of serious work in chemistry, Neumann began his short yet prolific career as an author with a series of articles in the *Philosophical Transactions*. After his death his collected lectures appeared in two German versions and, partially at least, in English, Dutch, and French translations.

Though Neumann was not a highly original chemist, he did influence the development of chemistry in a variety of ways. First, during his *Wanderjahre*, he conveyed knowledge of German techniques and theories to chemists in London and Paris. Second, as master pharmacist and as professor, he gave the young Marggraf his initial instruction in chemistry. It may well have been Neumann's exhortations that inspired Marggraf to develop "wet" analysis. Third, as an author he contributed significantly to the establishment of Stahlian chemistry, especially in Germany but also abroad. Like Stahl's other main disciples—Pott, Henckel, and Juncker—Neumann distinguished clearly between pure and applied chemistry and insisted that the chemical approach to nature was vastly superior to the mechanical philosophy. He envisioned many levels of chemical aggregation and invoked the phlogiston theory to explain combustion and calcination-reduction. Unlike Stahl's other main disciples, Neumann concentrated on pharmaceutical chemistry, thereby reaching and inspiring a generation of pharmacists which included Scheele and Klaproth.

BIBLIOGRAPHY

I. ORIGINAL WORKS. See *Praelectiones chemicae seu chemia medico-pharmaceutica experimentalis & rationalis, oder gründlicher Unterricht der Chemie . . .* (Berlin, 1740), edited on the basis of student notes by J. C. Zimmermann with the assistance of J. H. Pott, with portrait. Zimmermann republished this ed. with minor changes under his

own name in 1755. Neumann's nephew C. H. Kessel put out a different ed. which was based on Neumann's own notes, *Chymiae medicae dogmatico-experimentalis . . . oder der gründlichen und mit Experimenten erwiesenen Medicinischen Chymie . . .*, 4 vols. (Züllichau, 1749–1755; partial reprint, 1755–1756). W. Lewis' English ed. appeared in 1759 and 1773, the Dutch ed. in 1766, and Roux's French ed. in 1781. A complete bibliography of Neumann's works which mentions many reviews appears in Exner's biography, cited below, and an annotated partial bibliography in J. R. Partington, *A History of Chemistry*, II (London–New York, 1961), 702–706.

II. SECONDARY LITERATURE. The best biography is Alfred Exner, *Der Hofapotheker Caspar Neumann (1683–1737)* (Berlin, 1938). Exner begins with an annotated trans. of A. P. Queitsch's Latin biography (1737) and then, relying heavily on Kessel's ed. of the lectures, he assesses Neumann's role in chemistry and pharmacy. Some additional materials are in Herbert Lehmann, *Das Collegium medico-chirurgicum in Berlin als Lehrstätte der Botanik und der Pharmazie* (Berlin, 1936).

KARL HUFBAUER

NEUMANN, FRANZ ERNST (*b.* Joachimsthal, Germany [now Jachymov, Czechoslovakia], 11 September 1798; *d.* Königsberg, Germany [now Kaliningrad, R.S.F.S.R.], 23 May 1895), *mineralogy, physics, mathematics.*

Neumann extended the Dulong-Petit law—that the specific heats of the elements vary inversely as their atomic weights—to include compounds having similar chemical constitutions. His work in optics contributed to the establishment of the dynamical theory of light, and he formulated mathematically the laws of induction of electric currents. He also aided in developing the theory of spherical harmonics. Neumann was a highly influential teacher; many of his students became outstanding scientists, and he inaugurated the mathematical science seminar at German universities.

Neumann's mother was a divorced countess whose family prevented her marrying his father, a farmer who later became an estate agent, because he was not of noble birth. Neumann was therefore raised by his paternal grandparents. He attended the Berlin Gymnasium, where he displayed an early talent for mathematics. His education was interrupted in 1814, when he became a volunteer in the Prussian army to fight against Napoleon. He was seriously wounded on 16 June 1815 at the battle of Ligny, the prelude to Waterloo. After recovering in a Düsseldorf hospital, he rejoined his company and was mustered out of the army in February 1816.

Because his father had lost all of his resources in a fire, Neumann pursued his education under severe financial difficulties. He completed his studies at the Gymnasium and in 1817 entered the University of Berlin, studying theology in accordance with his father's wishes. In April 1818 he left Berlin for Jena, where he began his scientific studies and was particularly attracted to mineralogy. In 1819 Neumann returned to Berlin to study mineralogy and crystallography under Christian S. Weiss, who became his close friend as well as his mentor. Weiss made the financial arrangements for Neumann to take a three-month geological field trip in Silesia during the summer of 1820, and Neumann was planning other trips for 1822 and 1823 when his father died. Thereafter Neumann and his mother became very close; his concern for her health and financial independence caused him to leave the university during 1822–1823 and manage her farm. Nevertheless, in 1823 he published his first work, *Beiträge zur Kristallonomie*, which was highly regarded in Germany; and on Weiss's recommendation he was appointed curator of the mineral cabinet at the University of Berlin in November 1823.

Neumann received the doctorate at Berlin in November 1825; and in May 1826, together with Jacobi and Dove, he became a *Privatdozent* at the University of Königsberg. Dove and Neumann were destined to assume the physics and mineralogy courses, respectively, of Karl G. Hagen, who had been teaching botany, zoology, mineralogy, chemistry, and physics. In 1828 Neumann was advanced to the rank of lecturer, and in 1829 he was named professor of mineralogy and physics. He married Hagen's daughter, Luise Florentine, in 1830; they had five children before her death in 1838. He married Wilhelmina Hagen, her first cousin, in 1843.

Neumann's early scientific works, published between 1823 and 1830, concerned crystallography; in these he introduced the method of spherical projection and extended Weiss's work on the law of zones (law of rational intercepts). At Königsberg, however, he was influenced by Bessel, Dove, and Jacobi; and he began to concentrate on mathematical physics. His first two important papers were published in Poggendorff's *Annalen der Physik und Chemie* (**23** [1831], 1–39 and 40–53); the first was entitled "Untersuchung über die specifische Wärme der Mineralien" and the second "Bestimmung der specifischen Wärme des Wassers in der Nähe des Siedpunctes gegen Wasser von niedriger Temperatur." In the first article Neumann investigated the specific heats of minerals and extended the Dulong-Petit law to include compound substances having similar chemical constitutions. He arrived at what has been termed Neumann's law, that the molecular heat of a compound is equal to the sum of the atomic heats of its constituents. In the second paper Neumann considered the specific heat of water. In earlier investigations physicists had noticed that when equal quantities of hot and cold water are mixed the temperature of the mixture is lower than the arithmetic mean of the temperatures of the original quantities. This result was generally interpreted as being due to a progressive decrease in the specific heat of water from the point of fusion to that of vaporization, a conclusion that appears to be validated by a number of experiments. Neumann disclosed errors in these experiments and concluded instead that the specific heat of water increases as its temperature increases. He failed to determine, however, that an increase occurs over only a portion of the temperature range from fusion to vaporization.

In 1832 Neumann published another important paper, again in Poggendorff's *Annalen*, "Theorie der doppelten Strahlenbrechung abgeleitet aus der Gleichungen der Mechanik." Many physicists and mathematicians of the period were concerned with determining the conditions under which waves are propagated in ordinary elastic bodies so that they might develop a model which could serve as the optical medium; that is, they wished to evolve an elastic-solid theory of the ether in order to promote the undulatory theory of light. In his article Neumann reported obtaining a wave surface identical with that determined earlier by Augustin Cauchy, and he succeeded in deducing laws of double refraction agreeing with those of Fresnel except in the case of biaxial crystals.

Neumann encountered difficulty in explaining the passage of light from one medium to another. He attempted to overcome this obstacle in an article entitled "Theoretische Untersuchungen der Gesetze, nach welchen das Licht an der Grenze zweier vollkommen durchsichtigen Medien reflectirt und gebrochen wird," published in *Abhandlungen der Preussischen Akademie der Wissenschaften*, mathematische Klasse ([1835], 1–160). In this paper Neumann raised the question of the mathematical expression of the conditions which must hold at the surface separating the two crystalline media, and he adopted the view that the density of the ether must be identical in all media.

Neumann and his contemporary Wilhelm Weber were the founders of the electrodynamic school in Germany, which later included, among others, Riemann, Betti, Carl Neumann, and Lorenz. The investigations and analyses of this group were guided by the assumption, held originally by Ampère, that electromagnetic phenomena resulted from direct action at a distance rather than through the mediation of a field. Neumann's major contributions were contained in two papers published in 1845 and 1848, in which he established mathematically the laws of induction of electric currents. The papers, transmitted to the Berlin Academy, were entitled "Allgemeine Gesetze der inducirten elektrischen Ströme" and "Über ein allgemeines Princip der mathematischen Theorie inducirter elektrischer Ströme."

As a starting point Neumann took the proposition, formulated in 1834 by F. E. Lenz after Faraday's discovery of induction, that the current induced in a conductor moving in the vicinity of a galvanic current or a magnet will flow in the direction that tends to oppose the motion. In his mathematical analysis Neumann arrived at the formula $E \cdot Ds = -\epsilon v \, C \cdot Ds$, where Ds is an element of the moving conductor, $E \cdot Ds$ is the elementary induced electromotive force, v is the velocity of the motion, $C \cdot Ds$ is the component of the inducing current, and ϵ is a constant coefficient. With this formula Neumann was able to calculate the induced current in numerous particular instances. At present a common formulation is $E = -dN/dt$, where E is the electromotive force generated in the circuit through which the number of magnetic lines of force is changing at the rate of dN/dt.

Continuing his analysis Neumann noticed a way in which the treatment of currents induced in closed circuits moving in what is now termed a magnetic field might be generalized. He saw that the induced current depends only on the alteration, caused by the motion, in the value of a particular function. Considering Ampère's equations for a closed circuit, Neumann arrived at what is known as the mutual potential of two circuits, that is, the amount of mechanical work that must be performed against the electromagnetic forces in order to separate the two circuits to an infinite distance apart, when the current strengths are maintained unchanged. In modern notation the potential function, Vii', is written:

$$Vii' = -ii' \iint \frac{\mathbf{ds} \cdot \mathbf{ds}'}{r},$$

$\mathbf{ds} \cdot \mathbf{ds}'$ is the scalar product of the two vectors $\mathbf{ds}$ and $\mathbf{ds}'$, and r their distance apart. If a fixed element $\mathbf{ds}'$ is taken and integrated with respect to $\mathbf{ds}$, the vector potential of the first circuit at the point occupied by $\mathbf{ds}$ is obtained. Maxwell arrived at the concept of vector potentials by another method and interpreted them as analytical measures of Faraday's electrotonic state.

According to his contemporaries, only a small portion of Neumann's original scientific work was published. But he was an extremely effective teacher, and he made known many of his discoveries in heat, optics, electrodynamics, and capillarity during his lectures, thinking that priority of discovery extended equally to lectures and publications. Thus he made numerous contributions to the theory of heat without receiving credit; on occasion he thought about raising questions concerning priority but never did.

In 1833, with Jacobi, Neumann inaugurated the German *mathematisch-physikalische* seminar, employing such sessions to supplement his lectures and to introduce his students to research methodology. Gustav Kirchhoff attended these seminars from 1843 to 1846; his first papers on the distribution of electrical conductors, and H. Weld's development of the photometer and polarimeter, were among the direct results of Neumann's seminars. Neumann pleaded continually for the construction of a physics laboratory at Königsberg, but his hopes were thwarted during his tenure as professor; a physics institute was not completed at Königsberg until 1885. In 1847, however, the inheritance from the estate of the parents of his second wife enabled Neumann to build a physics laboratory next to his home, the facilities of which he shared with his students. He retired as professor in 1873, although he continued his seminar for the next three years. He maintained his good health by making frequent walking tours throughout Germany and Austria, and he was still climbing mountains at the age of eighty.

Throughout his life Neumann was an ardent Prussian patriot. He aided in keeping peace in Königsberg during the uprisings of 1848. He pleaded continually for the unification of Germany under the leadership of Prussia, and in the early 1860's he made numerous political speeches supporting Bismarck and the war against Austria. At the fiftieth anniversary of his doctorate in 1876, he was congratulated by the crown prince, later Wilhelm II; and he received honors from Bismarck in 1892 as a veteran of the campaign of 1815. Neumann was a corresponding member of every major European academy of science; he received the Copley Medal of the Royal Society in 1887.

BIBLIOGRAPHY

I. ORIGINAL WORKS. Three of Neumann's most important works were published in Ostwalds Klassiker der Exakten Wissenschaften: *Die mathematischen Gesetze der inducirten elektrischen Ströme*, no. 10 (Leipzig, 1889); *Über ein allgemeines Princip der mathematischen Theorie inducirter elektrischer Ströme*, no. 36 (Leipzig, 1892); and *Theorie der doppelten Strahlenbrechung*, no. 76 (Leipzig, 1896). Other books are *Beiträge zur Kristallonomie* (Berlin–Posen, 1823); *Über den Einfluss der Krystallflächen bei der Reflexion des Lichtes und über die Intensität des gewöhnlichen und ungewöhnlichen Strahls* (Berlin, 1837); and *Beiträge zur Theorie der Kugelfunktionen* (Leipzig, 1878). Some of his lectures were published in *Vorlesung über mathematischen Physik gehalten an der Universität Königsberg von Franz Neumann*, Carl Neumann, C. Pape, Carl Vondermühll, and E. Dorn, eds., 5 vols. (Leipzig, 1881–1887). His collected works were published as *Franz Neumanns Gesammelte Werke*, 3 vols. (Leipzig, 1906–1928).

II. Secondary Literature. See C. Voit, "Nekrolog auf Franz Ernst Neumann," in *Sitzungsberichte der Akademie München*, **26** (1896), 338–343; Luise Neumann, *Franz Neumann: Erinnerungsblätter* (Tübingen–Leipzig, 1904); W. Voigt, "Gedächtnissrede auf Franz Neumann," in *Franz Neumanns Gesammelte Werke*, I (Leipzig, 1906), 1–19; and Paul Volkmann, *Franz Neumann . . . den Andenken an dem Altmeister der mathematischen Physik gewidmete Blätter* (Leipzig, 1896).

See also James Clerk Maxwell, *A Treatise on Electricity and Magnetism*, 3rd ed. (Oxford, 1891), art. 542; and Sir Edmund Whittaker, *A History of the Theories of Aether and Electricity*, I (London, 1951), 137–138, 166–167, 198–200.

JOHN G. BURKE

NEUMAYR, MELCHIOR (*b*. Munich, Germany, 24 October 1845; *d*. Vienna, Austria, 29 January 1890), *paleontology, geology.*

Neumayr was the son of Max von Neumayr, a Bavarian government minister. He attended secondary schools in Stuttgart and in Munich, where he also studied law. Under the influence of Oppel, he soon turned to paleontology and geology and received the doctorate in Munich in 1867. The following year he moved to Vienna and joined the Imperial Austrian Geological Survey. In 1872 he became *Privatdozent* in paleontology and stratigraphy at the University of Heidelberg. He returned to Vienna in 1873 to fill the new professorship of paleontology that had been created for him at the university and held this post until his death from a heart ailment. On 2 April 1879 he married Paula Suess, the daughter of his colleague Eduard Suess; they had three daughters.

Neumayr's first scientific work was his geological mapping of southern Germany, the Carpathians, and the eastern Alps. His subsequent paleontological and stratigraphical investigations of the Jurassic period (1870–1871, 1874) soon established him as an expert on this period and its fauna. In studies of the Upper Tertiary freshwater mollusks of Yugoslavia, work that he began in 1869, he showed the gradual transformation of the shell morphology in the various horizons. A follower of Darwin from his student days, Neumayr

was the first to give a concise demonstration of the Darwinian theory of variation and evolution of species in invertebrate fossils (1875).

Neumayr's geological and paleontological investigations in Greece and in the Aegean Islands (1874–1876) made fundamental contributions to the knowledge of the geological structure of this region. In the Upper Tertiary of the island of Cos he found an even finer example of the evolution of freshwater snails (1880). A result of his studies in the Aegean was the first geological history of the eastern Mediterranean, in which methodological principles of paleogeography were demonstrated (1882).

Continuing his studies of the ammonites, Neumayr then turned his attention to the Cretaceous species, dividing them into new genera, as Suess had done for the Triassic and Jurassic forms. He clarified the relationships of the straightened forms to the parent curled genera and discussed the Cretaceous ammonites in relation to those of the Jurassic and Triassic periods. By extending his paleobiogeographic research to the Jurassic and Cretaceous periods he created the foundations of the present conceptions of the faunal regions in the Jurassic seas (1885). He also studied climatic differentiation during the Jurassic and Cretaceous periods (1883).

During his last years, Neumayr was occupied with writing comprehensive surveys and in his *Erdgeschichte* he produced a popular synthesis with strictly scientific methods. His unfinished *Die Stämme des Thierreiches* was Darwinian in approach and showed the close relationship between zoology and paleontology. He thereby raised paleontology—previously considered simply a study of index fossils—to the level of a basic biological science.

BIBLIOGRAPHY

I. Original Works. Neumayr's writings include "Jura-studien," in *Jahrbuch der Geologischen Bundesanstalt*, **20** (1870), 549–558; **21** (1871), 297–379; "Die Fauna der Schichten mit Aspidoceras acanthicum," in *Abhandlungen der Geologischen Bundesanstalt*, **5** (1874), 141–257; "Die Congerien- und Paludinenschichten Slavoniens und deren Fauna," *ibid.*, **7**, no. 3 (1875), written with C. M. Paul; "Über den geologischen Bau der Insel Kos und die Gliederung der jungtertiären Binnenablagerungen im Archipel," in *Denkschriften der Akademie der Wissenschaften*, **40** (1880), 213–240; *Zur Geschichte des östlichen Mittelmeerbeckens* (Berlin, 1882); "Ueber klimatische Zonen während der Kreide- und Jurazeit," in *Denkschriften der Akademie der Wissenschaften*, **47** (1883), 277–310; "Die geographische Verbreitung der Jura-formation," *ibid.*, **50** (1885), 57–145; *Erdgeschichte,*

2 vols. (Leipzig, 1886–1887); and the unfinished, posthumously published *Die Stämme des Thierreiches. Wirbellose Thiere* (Vienna–Prague, 1889).

II. SECONDARY LITERATURE. See W. T. Blanford's obituary in *Quarterly Journal of the Geological Society of London*, **46** (1890), 54–56; F. Toula, "Zur Erinnerung an Melchior Neumayr," in *Annales géologiques de la Péninsule balkanique*, **3** (1891), 1–9, with bibliography of 30 titles covering Neumayr's work in the Balkans; V. Uhlig, "Melchior Neumayr. Sein Leben und Wirken," in *Jahrbuch der Geologischen Bundesanstalt*, **40** (1891), 1–20, with complete bibliography of 133 works; K. Lambrecht and W. and A. Quenstedt, "Palaeontologi. Catalogus bio-bibliographicus," in *Fossilium Catalogus I: Animalia,* **72**(1938), 311; and F. Steininger and E. Thenius: "Die Ära Melchior Neumayr (1873–1890)," in *100 Jahre Paläontologisches Institut der Universität Wien, 1873–1973* (Vienna, 1973), 14–17, with portrait.

HEINZ TOBIEN

NEUYMIN, GRIGORY NIKOLAEVICH (*b.* Tiflis, Georgia [now Tbilisi, Georgian S.S.R.], 3 January 1886; *d.* Leningrad, U.S.S.R., 17 December 1946), *astronomy.*

Neuymin was the son of a military oculist-physician. In 1904 he graduated with a gold medal from the Second Tiflis Gymnasium and entered the Faculty of Physics and Mathematics at St. Petersburg University. Among his teachers were the astronomers A. A. Ivanov and S. P. Glazenap, and the mathematician V. A. Steklov. He graduated with a first-class diploma in 1910 and remained in the department of astronomy to prepare for a scientific career. From 1908 he was an assistant at the Pulkovo Observatory, where he was directed by F. F. Renz (astrometry) and A. A. Belopolsky (astrospectroscopy). Under their direction Neuymin conducted his first scientific research and mastered the techniques of astronomical observation. His first published works dealt with the determination of the radial velocity of the star α Cygni (Deneb) and the photographic observations of the annular eclipse of 12 April 1912. In June 1910 Neuymin became supernumerary astronomer at Pulkovo Observatory. After working on stellar spectroscopy in the astrophysical laboratory he participated in the processing of observations with the great transit instrument and began to observe comets and double stars on the thirty-eight-centimeter refractor.

In December 1912 Neuymin was sent as an adjunct astronomer to the recently created southern section of Pulkovo Observatory, at Simeiz, in the Crimea. Almost all his subsequent scientific work was associated with the Simeiz Observatory. In 1922 he returned for three years to Pulkovo, where he made observations with the seventy-six-centimeter refractor and made extensive computations of the final orbit of the comet Neuymin II, discovered by him in 1916. In 1924 the Scientific Council of Pulkovo Observatory elected him senior astronomer. The following year he returned to Simeiz as director of the observatory. In 1935 Neuymin was awarded a doctorate in the physical and mathematical sciences.

At Simeiz, Neuymin developed a broad program for the systematic search and photographic observation of comets and asteroids. With the help of a very modest 125-millimeter double astrograph the observatory soon held second place for the number of asteroids discovered there. Neuymin discovered sixty-three of the 110 numbered asteroids (those for which enough observations had been collected for the orbit to be calculated). About 400 others discovered at Simeiz were not numbered at that time. Widely known as the "comet hunter," Neuymin discovered six comets, five of which were periodic, with periods from 5.4 to 17.9 years. The comet Neuymin II was especially interesting. Having computed its orbit and calculated the planetary perturbations, Neuymin obtained very precise ephemerides, with which the comet was rediscovered in 1927. Neuymin developed a special method of calculating higher-order terms for use in computing perturbations.

Neuymin discovered thirteen variable stars, including the bright variable X Trianguli, and developed a method for discovering short-period variables on photographic plates.

Neuymin's work at Pulkovo included his measurements of double stars, micrometric measurements of the satellites of Neptune, and the determination of the proper motions of seventeen stars.

In connection with compiling a catalog of faint stars he selected and tested galaxies in order to attach the fundamental stars of the catalog to them.

In the fall of 1941, when the Simeiz Observatory was evacuated, Neuymin saved some of the valuable equipment and the archive of astronegatives. At Kitab, to which some of the observatory workers were sent, he continued his work on asteroids and his study of the comet Neuymin II. One of the asteroids he discovered was named Uzbekistan.

In 1944 Neuymin was named director of the Pulkovo Observatory, then in ruins. Charged with the difficult task of restoring and reorganizing the institution, he did not live to complete it. On 17 December 1946, exhausted by the evacuation and by the hard conditions of Central Asia, he died after a brief illness. Asteroid 1129 and a crater on the moon were named after him. In 1945 Neuymin was awarded the order of the Red Banner of Labor. His discoveries of comets were recognized by three prizes of the Russian Astronomical Society and six medals from the Astronomical Society of the Pacific.

BIBLIOGRAPHY

I. ORIGINAL WORKS. Neuymin's writings include "Sur les éléments et le prochain retour de la comète Neujmin (1916 a)," in *Astronomie*, **35** (1921), 160–162; "Mikrometrennye izmerenia dvoynykh zvezd v Pulkove" ("Micrometric Measurements of Double Stars at Pulkovo"), in *Izvestiya Glavnoi astronomicheskoi observatorii v Pulkove*, **9**, pt. 1, no. 88 (1923), 1–84; and "Vyvod sobstvennykh dvizhenii 17 zvezd" ("Definition of the Proper Motions of Seventeen Stars"), *ibid.*, **10**, pt. 3, no. 96 (1925), 305–314.

On his research on the orbit of the comet Neuymin II see "Definitive Bahnbestimmung des periodischen Kometen 1916 II (Neujmin) aus der Erscheinung in Jahre 1916," in *Izvestiya Glavnoi astronomicheskoi observatorii v Pulkove*, **10**, pt. 6, no. 99 (1927), 531–584; "Svyaz poyavlenia komety v 1916 i 1926 gg. (1916 II–1927 I)" ("Relations of the Appearance of the Comet in 1916 and 1926 [1916 II–1927 I]"), in *Tsirkulyar Glavnoi astronomicheskoi observatorii v Pulkove* (1941), no. 32, 25–61; and "Issledovanie orbity komety Neuymina II" ("Research on the Orbit of the Comet Neuymin II"), in *Izvestiya Glavnoi astronomicheskoi observatorii v Pulkove*, **17**, pt. 6, no. 141 (1948), 6–23.

See also "On a Method of Discovering Short-Period Variables With Rapid-Changes in Brightness," in *Tsirkulyar Glavnoi astronomicheskoi observatorii v Pulkove* (1932), no. 4, 22–24; "Rabochii katalog vnegalakticheskikh tumannostey dlya privyazki Kataloga slabykh zvezd" ("Working Catalog of Extragalactic Nebulae for Attachment to the Catalog of Faint Stars"), in *Uchyenye zapiski Kazanskogo gosudarstvennogo universiteta*, **100**, bk. 4 (1940), 116–127; "Simeizskoe otdelenie Pulkovskoy observatorii za 25 let (1908–1933)" ("Simeiz Section of Pulkovo Observatory for 25 Years"), in *Astronomicheskii Kalendar na 1934 god* ("Astronomical Calendar for 1934"; Nizhny Novgorod, 1934), 115–137; "Ob uchete vozmushcheny vysshikh poryadkov pri vychislenii spetsialnykh vozmushcheny" ("On Taking Into Account Perturbations of Higher Orders in Calculating Special Perturbations"), in *Astronomicheskii zhurnal*, **11**, pt. 2 (1934), 140–143; "Prostoy obiektivny mikrofotometr" ("Simple Objective Microphotometer"), in *Optiko-mekhanicheskaya promyshlennost* (1936), no. 9, 22–23; and "Periodicheskaya kometa Neuymina II i ee predstoyashchee vozvrashchenie k perigeliyu v 1943 godu" ("Periodic Comet Neuymin II and Its Forthcoming Return to Perihelion in 1943"), in *Astronomicheskii zhurnal*, **20**, pt. 1 (1943), 34–40.

II. SECONDARY LITERATURE. See the unsigned obituary, "Grigory Nikolaevich Neuymin," in *Izvestiya Glavnoi astronomicheskoi observatorii v Pulkove*, **17**, pt. 6, no. 141 (1948), 1–3; N. I. Idelson, "Pamyati Grigoria Nikolaevicha Neuymina" ("Memories of . . . Neuymin"), in *Astronomicheskii Kalendar na 1948 god* ("Astronomical Calendar for 1948"; Gorky, 1947), 138–142; B. Yu. Levin, "G. N. Neuymin," in *Priroda* (1948), no. 3, 86–87; and G. A. Shayn, "G. N. Neuymin," in *Izvestiya Krymskoi astrofizicheskoi observatorii*, **2** (1948), 136–138, with portrait.

P. G. KULIKOVSKY

NEWALL, HUGH FRANK (*b.* Gateshead, England, 21 June 1857; *d.* Cambridge, England, 22 February 1944), *astrophysics.*

Newall was the son of R. S. Newall, a wealthy manufacturer and a fellow of the Royal Society. During the 1860's Thomas Cooke of York constructed a twenty-five-inch refracting telescope—for a short time the largest in the world—for the father, who installed it at his home. Newall was not then interested in astronomy; he read mathematics as an undergraduate at Cambridge and subsequently worked under J. J. Thomson in the Cavendish Laboratory. In 1889, only weeks before his death, Newall's father offered his refractor to Cambridge University, with the request that it be used primarily for work in stellar physics. Certain financial problems arose, however, which were resolved when Newall offered the university a sum of money in addition to his own services as an unpaid observer. Throughout the early 1890's he concentrated on putting the telescope into service and providing it with appropriate instrumentation. He continued to be interested in the design of instrumentation throughout his life.

From the mid-1890's Newall's interest focused increasingly on the sun. He took part in four eclipse expeditions between 1898 and 1905, studying the flash and coronal spectra and the polarization of the corona. As the result of a substantial bequest of money by Frank McClean in 1905, Newall was able to construct a horizontal solar telescope at Cambridge and to begin a program of solar observations there. He concerned himself primarily with sunspot spectra and the rotation of the sun. His time was much occupied, however, by the transfer of Sir William Huggins' instrumentation to Cambridge in 1908, followed by the transfer of the Solar Physics Observatory (formerly under the direction of Sir Norman Lockyer) from South Kensington in 1911.

Newall was appointed professor of astrophysics in 1909 and held this post until his retirement in 1928. He published less than many of his contemporaries; partly, perhaps, because he was a perfectionist and partly because, being financially independent, he was under no pressure. His influence in the astronomical community was felt mainly through his local, national, and international organizational work.

BIBLIOGRAPHY

Some of Newall's MS diaries are preserved at the Cambridge Observatories. The majority of his published astronomical work appeared in the *Monthly Notices of the Royal Astronomical Society* between 1892 and 1927.

There is a detailed obituary of Newall by E. A. Milne in *Obituary Notices of Fellows of the Royal Society of London*, **4** (1944), 717–732. Additional details, especially concerning instrumentation, can be found in *Annals of the Solar Physics Observatory* (Cambridge), **1** (1949).

A. J. MEADOWS

NEWBERRY, JOHN STRONG (*b.* Windsor, Connecticut, 22 December 1822; *d.* New Haven, Connecticut, 7 December 1892), *paleontology, geology.*

Newberry was the son of Elizabeth Strong Newberry and Henry Newberry, an entrepreneur who prospered in the development of the Western Reserve lands in Ohio. When James Hall studied the geology of Ohio in 1841, he met young Newberry and encouraged his interest in the fossils of nearby coal fields. Newberry graduated from Western Reserve College in 1846 and from Cleveland Medical School as an M.D. in 1848. In 1849 and 1850 he attended scientific lectures by Adolphe Brongniart, Charles Robin, and Louis Cordier at the Jardin des Plantes in Paris. He returned to practice medicine in Cleveland from 1851 to 1855. Newberry married Sarah Brownell Gaylord of Cleveland; they had five sons and a daughter. From 1861 to 1865 he served as a doctor and executive with the United States Sanitary Commission.

Newberry served as physician-naturalist for several important army exploring expeditions in the trans-Mississippi West. He was with the Pacific Railroad Survey group led by Lieut. R. S. Williamson, which explored the northern Pacific coast in 1855 and 1856. He then joined the party under Lieut. Joseph C. Ives, which surveyed the Colorado River in 1857 and 1858. In 1859 he accompanied Capt. John N. Macomb on the survey of the area around Santa Fe. Newberry was professor of geology at the Columbia University School of Mines from 1866 to his death, and he is credited with making that part of the university a first-rate scientific institution. He worked as a paleobotanist for the Hayden and Powell Surveys in the 1870's and directed the Ohio State Geological Survey from 1869 to 1874. Newberry was a charter member of the National Academy of Sciences (1863) and of the Geological Society of America (1888), and in 1867 he presided over the American Association for the Advancement of Science. He helped revitalize the Lyceum of Natural History of New York City, which

became, with his guidance, the New York Academy of Sciences.

As his appointments suggest, Newberry was a field scientist; when he needed a petrographic sample studied under the microscope or a chemical analysis done, he usually asked a colleague or student to do it. Although he contributed to nearly every branch of geology, he concentrated on paleobotany, especially on the stratigraphic relations and the fossil flora of American coal beds. Beginning in 1859, he argued for a Cretaceous age for the Western lignites, opposing Lesquereux, who thought they were Tertiary, and Marcou, who said they were Jurassic.[1] Lester Frank Ward's work (1885) on the Laramie flora convinced Newberry that there were several distinct beds of both Tertiary and Cretaceous age.[2] Newberry also wrote on glacial phenomena in the Great Lakes and Midwest area, but he was unaware that more than one stage of glaciation affected the region. Newberry was a staunch uniformitarian in geological philosophy. For example, his theory of cycles of deposition (1873), which fits American rocks into sequence by texture and by the nature of organic contents, was based on an analogy to shores, continental shelves, and ocean bottoms.[3] He is best known for his accurate description (1861) of the Grand Canyon as erosion on a large scale, an explanation he buttressed with analogies to present-day erosion patterns in the Colorado River Basin.[4]

NOTES

1. See Newberry's letter in Ferdinand Hayden and Fielding Meek, "On the So-Called Triassic Rocks of Kansas and Nebraska," in *American Journal of Science*, 2nd ser., **27** (1859), 33; and Newberry, "Explorations in New Mexico," *ibid.*, **28** (1859), 298–299.
2. Ward, "Synopsis of the Flora of the Laramie Group," in *Report of the United States Geological Survey* (Washington, 1885), 399–557. Newberry's rather grudging admission appeared in his article, "The Laramie Group," in *Bulletin of the Geological Society of America*, **1** (1890), 524–541.
3. "Circles of Deposition in American Sedimentary Rocks," in *Proceedings of the American Association for the Advancement of Science*, **22** (1873), 185–196.
4. "Geological Report," in Joseph C. Ives, *Report Upon the Colorado River of the West, Explored in 1857 and 1858*, U.S., Congress, Senate, Executive Document (1861), pp. 25, 32, 41–48, 103.

BIBLIOGRAPHY

I. ORIGINAL WORKS. For a bibliography of Newberry's writings see Charles A. White, "Biographical Memoir of John Strong Newberry," in *Memoirs of the National Academy of Sciences*, **6** (1909), 1–24. White's list is full but not exhaustive. For other publications by Newberry, see Max Meisel, *A Bibliography of American Natural History:*

The Pioneer Century, 1769–1865, 3 vols. (Brooklyn, N. Y., 1924–1929); and Lawrence Schmeckebier, *Catalogue and Index of the Hayden, King, Powell, and Wheeler Surveys*, in *Bulletin of the United States Geological Survey*, **222** (Washington, 1904). The citations in White are casual and must be checked against the sources. White occasionally paraphrased titles, omitted page numbers, or failed to indicate whether the item was an abstract rather than the full piece. White's list is especially inaccurate for government documents.

Newberry's frequent articles (1880–1889) in the *Columbia University School of Mines Quarterly* appear to be written versions of his classroom lectures. Newberry's MS notes from the lectures at Paris are at the New York Botanical Garden.

II. SECONDARY LITERATURE. White's memoir is a convenient and adequate account of Newberry's life. For citations to other biographies, see George P. Merrill's article on Newberry in *Dictionary of American Biography;* and Meisel, I, 214. Merrill has a useful ch. on the lignite controversy in *The First One Hundred Years of American Geology* (New Haven, 1924), 579–593. William H. Goetzmann reevaluates Newberry's work in the American West, esp. his Grand Canyon monograph, in *Army Exploration in the American West 1803–1863* (New Haven, 1959), 317 ff., and in *Exploration and Empire: The Explorer and the Scientist in the Winning of the American West* (New York, 1966), 307 ff.

MICHELE L. ALDRICH

NEWCOMB, SIMON (*b.* Wallace, Nova Scotia, Canada, 12 March 1835; *d.* Washington, D.C., 11 July 1909), *astronomy.*

Simon Newcomb was the most honored American scientist of his time. During his lifetime his influence on professional astronomers and laymen was unparalleled, and it is still widely felt today. Having revolutionized the observational methods of the United States Naval Observatory, he reformed the entire theoretical and computational basis of the *American Ephemeris*. The planetary theories and astronomical constants that he derived are either still in official use or have been superseded only recently. Newcomb's discovery of the departure of the moon from its predicted position led to the investigations on the variations in the rate of rotation of the earth. These inquiries dominated dynamical astronomy during the first half of the twentieth century.

Though almost wholly of New England ancestry, Newcomb was born in Canada, the elder son of John Burton Newcomb, an itinerant country schoolteacher, and Emily Prince, daughter of a New Brunswick magistrate. Newcomb's early years were spent in various villages in Nova Scotia and Prince Edward Island. At the age of sixteen he was apprenticed to one

Dr. Foshay, on the understanding that in return for schooling in "medical botany" he would serve as general assistant for five years. Dr. Foshay was a quack, and Newcomb ran away empty-handed, after serving two years. He walked most of the 120 miles to Calais, Maine, where he was befriended by a sea captain who agreed to let him work his passage to Salem, Massachusetts. There he was met by his father and they journeyed together to Maryland.

Newcomb obtained a teaching post at a country school at Massey's Cross Roads, Kent County, and a year later he moved to a school in nearby Sudlersville. In his spare time he taught himself mathematics, studying in particular Newton's *Principia*. In 1856 Newcomb became a private tutor nearer Washington and frequently traveled to the capital; he visited the library of the Smithsonian Institution and secured secretary Joseph Henry's permission to borrow the first volume of Bowditch's translation of Laplace's *Mécanique céleste*—a work that proved then to be somewhat beyond his mathematical powers. Soon afterward he met Henry, who suggested he seek employment at the Coast Survey. He was in turn recommended to the Nautical Almanac Office, then located in Cambridge, Massachusetts. Newcomb arrived there at the beginning of 1857 and a few weeks later was given a trial appointment as an astronomical computer. He also took the opportunity of studying mathematics under Benjamin Peirce at the Lawrence Scientific School of Harvard University and graduated the following year.

The outbreak of the Civil War in 1861 brought the resignations of several of the professors of mathematics attached to the United States Navy, and Newcomb was invited to fill a vacancy at the Naval Observatory. He was assigned to assist in observing the right ascensions of stars with the transit circle. He deplored the random observation of stars, as was customary, and was dismayed that there was no concerted action with the person observing declinations with the mural circle. In 1863 he was placed in charge of the mural circle, and he proposed to Superintendent Gilliss a plan, based largely on the practice at European observatories, whereby the right ascension and declination observations would be conducted more systematically. When a new transit circle was acquired in 1865 Newcomb initiated a four-year program of fundamental observations of stellar positions, involving both day and night measurements.

Newcomb had great respect, but no particular love, for observational work. While in Cambridge he had put the principles of the *Mécanique céleste* to good use and studied the secular variations in the motions of some of the minor planets. He showed that their orbits did not intersect and that there was no reason for accepting the then prevalent hypothesis that the minor planets were fragments of a larger planet that had exploded or been shattered by a collision.

After moving to Washington, Newcomb became especially interested in the motion of the moon and in the accuracy of Hansen's lunar tables. It soon became clear that the moon was starting to deviate from its predicted position. Hansen had fitted his theory to observations back to 1750, and in order to study the deviation it was desirable to make use of even earlier observations. Surmising that older records of occultations of stars by the moon existed in the archives of the Paris Observatory, Newcomb visited Paris during the siege of 1871 (departing only three weeks before the observatory found itself in the line of retreat of the Commune) and located a wealth of high-quality observations extending back to 1672. His analysis of these and other observations revealed that Hansen's tables were considerably in error prior to 1750. He suspected that the discrepancy was due to variations in the rate of rotation of the earth—and thus in the astronomical reckoning of time—but his attempt to verify this from observations of transits of Mercury was inconclusive (1882). Newcomb again took up the problem of the "fluctuation" in the motion of the moon during the final years of his life, and his exhaustive discussion of lunar observations from 720 B.C. to A.D. 1908 was completed only a month before his death. It remained for Brown, Innes, Spencer Jones, de Sitter, and others to prove that the cause of the fluctuation is indeed the irregular rotation of the earth.

In 1875 Newcomb was offered the directorship of the Harvard College Observatory, which he declined. In 1877 he was appointed superintendent of the Nautical Almanac Office, which had by then been transferred to Washington. After improving the efficiency with which the calculations for the *American Ephemeris* were made, he embarked on two ambitious projects: discussing the observations of the sun, moon, and planets obtained since 1750 at thirteen of the leading observatories throughout the world, and developing new theories and tables for the motions of these bodies. (He had published preliminary theories and tables for Uranus and Neptune several years earlier.) The project was clearly too much for one individual; and Newcomb thus went to considerable pains to obtain the best possible assistance. The most difficult part of the work, that of constructing the theories of Jupiter and Saturn, was entrusted to G. W. Hill. For these, Hansen's method was employed, and Newcomb subsequently regretted that he had not

used the same method for the other planets; the use of Encke's method, although much more straightforward, introduced problems into the determination of the orbital constants that Newcomb was not able to solve. Most of the work was completed by 1895, although it was left for E. W. Brown to construct the lunar theory.

In the course of his work on planetary theory Newcomb devised a useful procedure for developing the "disturbing function" that gives the perturbative action of one planet on another. In the case of circular orbits it is usual to develop the reciprocal of the distance between the planets as a cosine series in multiples of the longitude difference between the planets, each term being multiplied by a "Laplace coefficient." Newcomb showed that the process could easily be extended to elliptical orbits by the introduction of quantities dependent upon the multiple of the mean longitude difference and differential operators that act on the Laplace coefficients. He tabulated these quantities, now commonly known as "Newcomb operators," out to those corresponding to the eighth power of the orbital eccentricities, although some of the final ones have been found to be incorrect.

During his early years at the Naval Observatory, Newcomb made an investigation of the solar parallax, principally from observations of Mars at its 1862 opposition. In 1870 he proposed the establishment of a committee to plan observations of the 1874 and 1882 transits of Venus, with a view to obtaining a more precise value of the solar parallax. The committee became the Transit of Venus Commission, and Newcomb was appointed secretary. The results from the 1874 transit were disappointing; and although he was very much in the minority, Newcomb seriously questioned the wisdom of dispatching expeditions to observe the 1882 transit. (He did, however, conduct an expedition to South Africa in 1882.) He felt that a better value of the parallax could be obtained from the velocity of light and the constant of aberration. Newcomb's investigation of the velocity of light, using mirrors at the Naval Observatory, the Washington Monument, and Fort Myer, Virginia, was essentially a refinement of Foucault's method. The value obtained was long the astronomical standard.

Newcomb's study of the transits of Mercury confirmed Leverrier's conclusion that the perihelion of Mercury is subject to an anomalous advance (now known to be due to relativity), and he sought vainly for an explanation. In the course of his work on the transits of Venus of 1761 and 1769 he resolved the doubts surrounding the 1769 observations of Maximilian Hell. The value for the mass of Jupiter which he determined from the observations of Polyhymnia has still not been significantly improved. Newcomb also established that the retrograde motion of the line of apsides of Saturn's satellite Hyperion is due to the resonant influence of Titan. He was able to show that the fourteen-month period found by Chandler in the variation of latitude is due to some lack of rigidity of the earth. He studied the zodiacal light, the distribution and motions of the stars, and solar radiation.

Around 1880 Newcomb founded the *Astronomical Papers Prepared for the Use of the American Ephemeris and Nautical Almanac*, and the greater part of the above-mentioned researches was printed in the first seven volumes of this series. He also published a short account of his work on astronomical constants under the title *The Elements of the Four Inner Planets and the Fundamental Constants of Astronomy* (1895). At an international conference in Paris in 1896, it was agreed that from 1901 onwards, these constants (with only minor modifications) should be used in all the national ephemerides of the world. Newcomb was also charged with completing a catalogue of the positions and motions of the brighter stars and with making a new determination of the constant of precession. Completion of this work was complicated by his automatic retirement on his sixty-second birthday (1897), but arrangements were made for him to continue on a consulting basis.

Newcomb was instrumental in securing from Alvan Clark and Sons a twenty-six-inch refractor for the Naval Observatory, and with it he made measurements of the satellites of Uranus and Neptune. He was also prominently involved in negotiations with the Clarks for a thirty-inch refractor for the Pulkovo Observatory and in the establishment of the Lick Observatory.

In addition to his many scientific papers Newcomb wrote *A Compendium of Spherical Astronomy* (1906). It was intended to be the first of a series of texts, and it is regrettable that he never produced any further volumes. He wrote popular works on astronomy as well as three novels, some mathematical texts, several papers on economics, psychical research, and rainmaking, and one on the "flying machine" (in which his gift of foresight completely failed him: his view that man would never fly brought him into direct conflict with the astrophysicist Samuel Pierpont Langley).

Newcomb was a member or foreign associate of the national academies or astronomical societies of seventeen countries, and he received honorary degrees from as many universities. He was one of the first lecturers at the Johns Hopkins University and became a professor there in 1884; he was awarded the Sylvester prize in 1901. Among his other awards were the Copley Medal of the Royal Society, the Gold Medal of the Royal Astronomical Society, and the (first) Bruce Medal of the Astronomical Society of the Pacific. In 1863 he married Mary Caroline Hassler. He retired from the navy with the rank of captain and was promoted to rear admiral (retired) in 1906. Newcomb was buried with military honors in Arlington National Cemetery; President Taft and the representatives of several foreign governments attended the funeral.

BIBLIOGRAPHY

I. ORIGINAL WORKS. An exhaustive bibliography of Newcomb, compiled by R. C. Archibald, is contained in *Biographical Memoirs. National Academy of Sciences,* **17** (1924), 19–69. The best single source of biographical information is Newcomb's autobiography, *The Reminiscences of an Astronomer* (Boston–New York, 1903). Most of Newcomb's important writings are contained in *Astronomical Papers Prepared for the Use of the American Ephemeris and Nautical Almanac,* **1–9** (1879–1913).

Among other astronomical writings, in addition to those cited in the text, are "On the Secular Variations and Mutual Relations of the Orbits of the Asteroids," in *Memoirs of the American Academy of Arts and Sciences,* n.s. **5** (1860), 123–152; "An Investigation of the Distance of the Sun and of the Elements Which Depend Upon It," in *Washington Observations for 1865* (1867), app. 2; "Researches on the Motion of the Moon. Part I: Reduction and Discussion of Observations of the Moon Before 1750," in *Washington Observations for 1875* (1878), app. 2; *Popular Astronomy* (New York, 1878); *The Stars* (New York, 1901); *Astronomy for Everybody* (New York, 1902); "On the Position of the Galactic and Other Principal Planes Toward Which the Stars Tend to Crowd," which is *Carnegie Institute of Washington Contributions to Stellar Statistics,* no. 10 (1904); "An Observation of the Zodiacal Light to the North of the Sun," in *Astrophysical Journal,* **22** (1905), 209–212; *Sidelights on Astronomy* (New York–London, 1906); "A Search for Fluctuations in the Sun's Thermal Radiation Through Their Influence on Terrestrial Temperature," in *Transactions of the American Philosophical Society,* n.s. **21** (1908), 309–387.

Among his mathematical works are "A Generalized Theory of the Combination of Observations so as to Obtain the Best Result," in *American Journal of Mathematics,* **8** (1886), 343–366; "The Philosophy of Hyperspace," in *Science,* **7** (1898), 1–7.

Newcomb's works on economics include *The ABC of Finance* (New York, 1877); *Principles of Political Economy* (New York, 1886); *A Plain Man's Talk on the Labor Question* (New York, 1886).

II. SECONDARY LITERATURE. Among the many accounts of Newcomb's life and work are G. W. Hill, "Simon Newcomb as an Astronomer," in *Science,* **30** (1909), 353–357; T. J. J. See, "An Outline of the Career of Professor

Newcomb," in *Popular Astronomy*, **17** (1909), 465–481; E. W. Brown, "Simon Newcomb," in *Bulletin of the American Mathematical Society*, **16** (1910), 341–355; an obituary notice by H. H. Turner in *Monthly Notices of the Royal Astronomical Society*, **70** (1910), 304–310; W. W. Campbell, "Simon Newcomb," in *Biographical Memoirs. National Academy of Sciences*, **17** (1916), 1–18.

For recent work on astronomical constants, see W. de Sitter (and D. Brouwer), "On the System of Astronomical Constants," in *Bulletin of the Astronomical Institutes of the Netherlands*, **8** (1938), 213–231; G. M. Clemence, "On the System of Astronomical Constants," in *Astronomical Journal*, **53** (1948), 169–179; "Colloque International sur les Constants Fondamentales de l'Astronomie," in A. Danjon, ed., *Bulletin astronomique*, **15** (1950), 163–292; *International Astronomical Union Symposium No. 21: On the System of Astronomical Constants*, in J. Kovalevsky, ed., *Bulletin astronomique*, **25** (1965), 1–324; *International Astronomical Union Colloquium No. 9: The IAU System of Astronomical Constants*, in B. Emerson and G. A. Wilkins, eds., *Celestial Mechanics*, IV (1971), 128–280.

For material on the rotation of the earth, see W. de Sitter, "On the Secular Accelerations and the Fluctuations of the Longitudes of the Moon, Sun, Mercury, and Venus," in *Bulletin of the Astronomical Institutes of the Netherlands*, **4** (1927), 21–38; H. Spencer Jones, "The Rotation of the Earth, and the Secular Accelerations of the Sun, Moon, and Planets," in *Monthly Notices of the Royal Astronomical Society*, **99** (1939), 541–558. For further calculations of the Newcomb operators, see Sh. G. Sharaf, "Teoriya dvizheniya Plutona" ("Theory of the Motion of Pluto"), in *Trudy Instituta Teoreticheskoi astronomii. Akademiya nauk SSSR*, **4** (1955); I. G. Izsak *et al.*, "Construction of Newcomb Operators on a Digital Computer," which is *Smithsonian Astrophysical Observatory Special Report*, no. 140 (1964).

BRIAN G. MARSDEN

NEWCOMEN, THOMAS (*b.* Dartmouth, England; christened 24 February 1663; *d.* London, England, 5 August 1729), *steam technology*.

Newcomen is renowned as the inventor of the steam engine. He was descended from an aristocratic family that had lost its property during the reign of Henry VIII. His grandfather and father were merchants and nonconformists, and Newcomen followed them in both respects. During the 1680's he became an ironmonger in partnership with John Calley, an artisan and fellow Baptist who later collaborated with him on the development of the steam engine. Newcomen became a leader of the local Baptists and often preached to their congregations. His formal education appears to have been rudimentary, and he published nothing. Few details are known of his personal life or of the circumstances that surrounded his invention.

Newcomen's first successful engine, which was erected in the Midlands in 1712, was the reward of years of trials and tinkering. The increasingly troublesome problem of removing water from mines had already provided the stimulus for attempts by Newcomen and others to design an improved machine to serve either as a pump or as an engine to drive a pump. In 1698 Thomas Savery (also of Devon) invented a steam pump which he protected with a broad patent that covered all "vessells or engines for raiseing water or occasioning motion to any sort of millworks by the impellent force of fire." Because of the scope of Savery's patent, Newcomen was later prevented from patenting his own engine and was required to build his engines under license from Savery, although his work was entirely independent of Savery's and his engine was totally different from Savery's pump.

Newcomen's engine was an ingenious combination of familiar elements: piston and cylinder, pumps, levers, valves, and the process of producing low pressure by the condensation of steam in a vessel. The key invention, which was the injection of cold water directly into the cylinder, was hit upon accidentally in the course of experiments that used cold water jackets to produce condensation. Later James Watt significantly increased the efficiency of the engine through his invention of the separate condenser (1765), which avoided the necessity of alternately heating and cooling the cylinder. Nevertheless, unmodified Newcomen engines continued to be used long after Watt's improvement, but because of their low efficiency, they were confined largely to collieries, where coal was cheap.

At the end of the eighteenth century John Robison propagated the belief that Newcomen's achievement somehow depended upon the application of scientific principles gained through an alleged correspondence between Newcomen and Robert Hooke. (Robison advanced a similar claim for the derivation of Watt's separate condenser from Joseph Black's theory of latent heat.) Robison's allegation has been discredited; the records reveal no contact whatever between Newcomen and his contemporaries in science. His invention was the product of a familiarity with technical operations and needs in the mining industry, a close knowledge of contemporary craftsmanship, repeated trials and improvements, and a stroke of luck.

BIBLIOGRAPHY

For a full biography, see L. T. C. Rolt, *Thomas Newcomen: The Prehistory of the Steam Engine* (London, 1963); this work modifies some of the views presented in

H. W. Dickinson, *A Short History of the Steam Engine* (London, 1938, 1963), ch. 3. An important contemporary account of Newcomen's work, which is based apparently on firsthand knowledge, is Mårten Triewald, *Beskrifning om eld- och luftmachin vid Dannemora grufvor* (Stockholm, 1734), trans. as *A Short Description of the Fire- and Air-Machine at the Dannemora Mines*, and published by the Newcomen Society as *Mårten Triewald's Short Description of the Atmospheric Engine*, Extra Publication no. 1 (London, 1928). On the question of the influence of science on Newcomen's work, see Rhys Jenkins, "The Heat Engine Idea in the Seventeenth Century," in *Transactions of the Newcomen Society*, **17** (1936–1937), 1–11.

HAROLD DORN

NEWLANDS, JOHN ALEXANDER REINA (*b.* London, England, 26 November 1837; *d.* London, 29 July 1898), *chemistry.*

Newlands was one of the precursors of Mendeleev in the formulation of the concept of periodicity in the properties of the chemical elements. He was the second son of a Presbyterian minister, William Newlands, from whom he received his general education. In 1856 he entered the Royal College of Chemistry, where he studied for a year under A. W. Hofmann. He then became assistant to J. T. Way, chemist to the Royal Agricultural Society. He stayed with Way until 1864, except for a short interlude in 1860, when he served as a volunteer with Garibaldi in Italy. Newlands' mother, Mary Sarah Reina, was of Italian descent.

In 1864 he set up practice as an analytical chemist and supplemented his income by teaching chemistry. He seems to have made a special study of sugar chemistry and in 1868 became chief chemist in a refinery belonging to James Duncan, with whom he developed a new system of cleaning sugar and introduced a number of improvements in processing. The business declined as a result of foreign competition, and in 1886 he left the refinery and again set up as an analyst, this time in partnership with his brother, B. E. R. Newlands. The brothers collaborated with C. G. W. Lock, one of the previous authors, in the revision of an established treatise on sugar growing and refining. Newlands died of influenza in 1898; he was survived by his wife, a daughter, and a son.

Newlands' early papers on organic compounds, the first suggesting a new nomenclature, the second proposing the drawing up of tables to show the relationships between compounds, were vitiated by the absence at that time of clear ideas regarding structure and valency; but they are interesting because they show the cast of his mind toward systematization. His first communication (*Chemical News*, 7 February 1863) on the numerical relationships existing between the atomic weights of similar elements was a summing-up, with some of his own observations, of what had been pointed out by others (of whom he mentioned only Dumas). Two main phenomena had been observed: (*a*) there existed "triads" (first noticed by Döbereiner), groups of three elements of similar properties, the atomic weight of one being the numerical mean of the others, and (*b*) it was also found that the difference between the atomic weights of analogous elements seemed often to be a multiple of eight.

Like many of his contemporaries, Newlands at first used the terms "equivalent" and "atomic weight" without distinction of meaning, and in this first paper he employed the values accepted by his predecessors. In a July 1864 letter he used A. W. Williamson's values,[1] which were based on Cannizzaro's system. The letter contains a table of the sixty-one known elements in the order of their "new" atomic weights. In a second table he grouped thirty-seven elements into ten classes, most of which contained one or more triads. The incompleteness of the table was attributed to uncertainty regarding the properties of some of the more recently discovered elements and also to the possible existence of undiscovered elements. He considered silicon (atomic weight 28) and tin (atomic weight 118) to be the extremities of a triad, the middle term of which was unknown; thus his later claim to having predicted the existence of germanium (atomic weight 73) before Mendeleev is valid.

About a month later he said that if the elements were numbered in the order of their atomic weights (giving the same number to any two with the same weight) it was observed "that elements having consecutive numbers frequently either belong to the same group or occupy similar positions in other groups." The following table[2] was given in illustration:

TABLE I

Group	No.		No.		No.		No.		No.	
a	N	6	P	13	As	26	Sb	40	Bi	54
b	O	7	S	14	Se	27	Te	42	Os	50
c	F	8	Cl	15	Br	28	I	41	—	—
d	Na	9	K	16	Rb	29	Cs	43	Tl	52
e	Mg	10	Ca	17	Sr	30	Ba	44	Pb	53

The difference between the number of the lowest member of a group and that immediately above it was seven: "in other words, the eighth element starting from a given one is a kind of repetition of the first, like the eighth note in an octave of music." One or two transpositions had been made to give an acceptable grouping; the element omitted (no. 51) would have been mercury, which clearly could not be grouped with the halogens.

Newlands was groping toward an important discovery, although it excited little comment. A year later (August 1865) he again drew attention to the difference of seven (or a multiple thereof) between the ordinal numbers of elements in the same horizontal group: "This peculiar relationship I propose to provisionally term the 'Law of Octaves.'" This time he put all sixty-two elements (he included the newly discovered indium) in his table[3]:

TABLE II

No.	No.	No.	No.	No.	No.	No.	No.
H 1	F 8	Cl 15	Co, Ni 22	Br 29	Pd 36	I 42	Pt, Ir 50
Li 2	Na 9	K 16	Cu 23	Rb 30	Ag 37	Cs 44	Tl 53
Be 3	Mg 10	Ca 17	Zn 25	Sr 31	Cd 38	Ba, V 45	Pb 54
B 4	Al 11	Cr 19	Y 24	Ce, La 33	U 40	Ta 46	Th 56
C 5	Si 12	Ti 18	In 26	Zr 32	Sn 39	W 47	Hg 52
N 6	P 13	Mn 20	As 27	Di, Mo 34	Sb 41	Nb 48	Bi 55
O 7	S 14	Fe 21	Se 28	Rh, Ru 35	Te 43	Au 49	Os 51

But this forcing of the elements into too rigid a framework weakened his case. It seemed to preclude (a conclusion that he subsequently denied) the possibility of gaps in the sequence which, when filled, would lead to a more acceptable grouping. The resulting anomalies were seized upon by his critics, when on 1 March 1866 he read a paper to the Chemical Society presenting the same table—except that the elements in the last column now appeared in numerical order. The facetious inquiry of G. C. Foster, professor of physics at University College, London, as to whether Newlands had ever examined the elements when placed in alphabetical order, has often been quoted; but Foster also made the cogent criticism that no system of classification could be accepted which separated chromium from manganese and iron from cobalt and nickel.[4]

The hostile reception of his paper and the disinclination of the Society to publish it (on the grounds of its purely theoretical nature) seem to have discouraged Newlands from following up his ideas until after the publication of Mendeleev's table in 1869. After that table appeared, Newlands continued to seek numerical relationships among atomic weights, while attempting, in a series of letters to *Chemical News*, to establish his priority. He set out his claims more specifically in December 1882, on hearing of the award of the Davy Medal of the Royal Society to Mendeleev and Lothar Meyer. His persistence was eventually rewarded in 1887, when the medal was awarded to him.

NOTES

1. A. W. Williamson, "On the Classification of the Elements in Relation to Their Atomicities," in *Journal of the Chemical Society*, **17** (1864), 211–222.
2. *Chemical News* (20 Aug. 1864), 94; *On the Discovery of the Periodic Law*, 11.
3. *Chemical News* (18 Aug. 1865), 83; *On the Discovery of the Periodic Law*, 14. A few symbols have been altered to conform with modern usage (Di = "didymium," shown in 1885 to be a mixture of neodymium and praseodymium).
4. For a report of the meeting see *Chemical News*, **13** (1866), 113–114. There was no hint of both a "vertical" and a "horizontal" relationship between elements prior to the publication of Mendeleev's table.

BIBLIOGRAPHY

I. ORIGINAL WORKS. Newlands' writings on periodicity were republished in a small book, *On the Discovery of the Periodic Law* (London, 1884); those published after the appearance of Mendeleev's table, with some additional notes, are in the appendix. *Sugar: A Handbook for Planters and Refiners* (London–New York, 1888), written with C. G. W. Lock and B. E. R. Newlands, was based on C. G. W. Lock, G. W. Wigner, and R. H. Harland, *Sugar Growing and Refining* (London–New York, 1882); a further rev. ed. by "the late J. A. R. Newlands and B. E. R. Newlands," with no mention of a third author, was published in 1909.

An incomplete list of Newlands' papers is in the Royal Society *Catalogue of Scientific Papers*, IV (London, 1870), 600; VIII (London, 1879), 494; X (London, 1894), 916–917; and XVII (Cambridge, 1921), 506. Those particularly mentioned in the text are "On Relations Among the Equivalents," in *Chemical News*, **7** (1863), 70–72; "Relations Between Equivalents," *ibid.*, **10** (1864), 59–60, 94–95; "On the Law of Octaves," *ibid.*, **12** (1865), 83; a reply to his critics at the Chemical Society meeting is *ibid.*, **13** (1866), 130; "On the Discovery of the Periodic Law," *ibid.*, **46** (1882), 278–279, is the most detailed of Newlands' claims for priority over Mendeleev. All of the above papers, except the last, are reprinted in *On the Discovery of the Periodic Law*.

II. SECONDARY LITERATURE. Most of the biographical details stem from the obituary by W. A. Tilden, in *Nature*, **58** (1898), 395–396; another obituary is W. Smith, in *Journal of the Society of Chemical Industry*, **17** (1898), 743.

W. A. Smeaton, "Centenary of the Law of Octaves," in *Journal of the Royal Institute of Chemistry*, **88** (1964), 271–274, reproduces the more important of Newlands' tables and gives a useful summary of the relevant work of others, particularly W. Odling.

See also J. A. Cameron, "J. A. R. Newlands (1837–1898), A Pioneer Whom the Chemists Ridiculed," in *Chemical Age*, **59** (1948), 354–356; W. H. Taylor, "J. A. R. Newlands: A Pioneer in Atomic Numbers," in *Journal of*

Chemical Education, **26** (1949), 491–496; J. W. van Spronsen, "One Hundred Years of the 'Law of Octaves,'" in *Chymia,* **11** (1966), 125–137.

For a detailed history of the periodic table see J. W. van Spronsen, *The Periodic System of Chemical Elements* (Amsterdam–London–New York, 1969). An earlier and less comprehensive work, but giving a good summary of Newlands' work, is A. E. Garrett, *The Periodic Law* (London, 1909). See also H. Cassebaum and G. B. Kaufman, "The Periodic System of the Chemical Elements: the Search for Its Discoverer," in *Isis,* **62** (1971), 314–317.

E. L. SCOTT

NEWPORT, GEORGE (*b.* 4 July 1803, Canterbury, England; *d.* 7 April 1854, London, England), *entomology, natural history.*

Newport was the son of a wheelwright and after receiving a simple schooling, he became an apprentice to his father's trade at age fourteen. During the next nine years he read widely in many subjects and by dint of tireless application extended his scanty education. From an early age he had been interested in insect life, and now he began serious entomological studies that were to continue throughout his life. He took advantage of the Canterbury Philosophical and Literary Institution and made liberal use of its library, lectures, and natural history collections. In 1825 and 1826 he gave lectures there on mechanics, and in 1826 he became general exhibitor of the museum when the institution's new building was opened. Among his various activities were lectures and demonstrations on entomology, and he donated many specimens of British insects, which he himself had preserved.

During the two-year tenure of this post, Newport became acquainted with William Henry Weekes, a surgeon of Sandwich, and in 1828 he began an apprenticeship with him. Throughout his early life he suffered great privations and was at times dependent upon friends for financial support, debts which he in later life honorably liquidated. After his apprenticeship Newport enrolled in the University of London (now University College, London), on 16 January 1832. In 1835 he was admitted a licentiate of the Society of Apothecaries of London and a member of the Royal College of Surgeons of England, which at that time was the usual combination of diplomas for medical practice. Newport held the post of house surgeon to the Chichester Infirmary until January 1837, when he established himself in practice at 30 Southwick Street, London. He was more interested in scientific pursuits so that his practice gradually declined; and when in 1847 he was awarded a pension from the civil list of £100 per annum for his contributions to natural history, he was able to devote all his time to research.

Newport never married, and as his habits were of the most frugal kind he was able to subsist on this limited income. His extensive researches were rewarded with several honors. On 11 December 1843 he was elected a fellow of the Royal College of Surgeons of England, of which he was one of the original 300 fellows, and from 1844 to 1845 he was president of the Entomological Society. On 26 March 1846 he became a fellow of the Royal Society, and at the time of his death he was a Member of Council. He was also a fellow of the Linnean Society and of several foreign natural history societies. He contracted an illness—from which he died—in the marshy ground west of London while collecting research material.

Newport was a man of the strictest honesty, both in his scientific studies and in his dealings with the world. He had a nervous temperament and a morbid sensitivity to criticism which caused him to make enemies readily. He possessed unwearied patience and remarkable digital dexterity, evidenced in his dissections, demonstrations, and insect preparations; he could draw equally well with either hand; and his powers of observation were acute. He was exceedingly zealous and industrious and was interested only in the advancement of science. His services were commemorated in a public monument in Kensal Green Cemetery, erected by fellows of the Royal Society and of the Linnean Society.

Newport's contributions to biology lay mostly within the field of entomology and the embryology of the Insecta and Amphibia. His first papers—sufficiently important and original to appear in the *Philosophical Transactions*—were on the bumblebee, butterflies, and moths; and he investigated the nervous system, respiration, and temperature of these and other insects. He also published many subsequent papers on insect structure, which included an important survey of Insecta (1839). For his essay on the turnip fly (1838) he was awarded a medal by the Agricultural Society of Saffron Walden. Newport's most outstanding contribution to biology was his discovery that during fertilization in higher animals impregnation of the ovum by the spermatozoon is by penetration and not just by contact as previously thought. For this work on the frog (1851) he was awarded the Royal Medal of the Royal Society. He was also the first to observe the coincidence between the first plane of cleavage in the egg made by the spermatozoon at its place of entry and the median plane of the body of the embryo and thus of the adult body (1854).

BIBLIOGRAPHY

I. ORIGINAL WORKS. A list of Newport's writings (thirty-five items produced during a period of twenty-two years) is in *Proceedings of the Royal Society*, **7** (1855), 281–283. They were published mainly in periodicals; his excellent article on Insecta appeared in Robert B. Todd, ed., *The Cyclopaedia of Anatomy and Physiology*, II (London, 1836–1839), 835–994, and his prize essay on the turnip fly was a monograph, *Observations on the Anatomy, Habits, and Economy of "Athalia centrifoliae," the Saw-fly of the Turnip, and on the Means Adopted for the Prevention of Its Ravages* (London, 1838). His *Catalogue of the Myriapoda in the British Museum* (London, 1856) appeared posthumously. Of Newport's earlier papers those on *Sphinx* are outstanding; "On the Nervous System of the *Sphinx Ligustri*," in *Philosophical Transactions of the Royal Society*, pt. 2 (1832), 383–398; and "On the Nervous System of the *Sphinx* During the Latter Stages of Its Pupa and Imago States," *ibid.*, pt. 2 (1834), 389–423.

Newport's classic papers on embryology are "On the Impregnation of the Ovum in Amphibia," in *Philosophical Transactions of the Royal Society*, 1st ser., **141** (1851), 169–242; "On the Impregnation of the Ovum in Amphibia (2nd Series Revised), and on the Direct Agency of the Spermatozoon," *ibid.*, **143** (1853), 233–290; and "Researches on the Impregnation of the Ovum in the Amphibia," *ibid.*, **144** (1854), 229–244; this article contains material selected and arranged by G. V. Ellis from the author's MSS after his death.

II. SECONDARY LITERATURE. There are only a few brief biographical notices on Newport; the best are *Proceedings of the Linnean Society of London*, **2** (1855), 309–312; *Dictionary of National Biography*, **14** (1844), 357–358; *Gentleman's Magazine* (June 1854), 660–661; *Medical Times and Gazette* (London), n.s. **8** (1854), 392–393; *Proceedings of the Royal Society*, **7** (1855), 278–285; and *Plarr's Lives of the Fellows of the Royal College of Surgeons of England*, **2** (1930), 95–96. An account of his epitaph is in *Lancet* (1855), **2**, 554.

Newport's embryological investigations are discussed in F. J. Cole, *Early Theories of Sexual Generation* (Oxford, 1930), 193–196, and in A. W. Meyer, *The Rise of Embryology* (Stanford, 1939), 188–190.

EDWIN CLARKE

NEWTON, EDWIN TULLEY (*b.* Islington, London, England, May 1840; *d.* Canonbury, London, 28 January 1930), *paleontology.*

Newton began his scientific career as a student at the Royal School of Mines. In 1865 he became assistant naturalist under T. H. Huxley at the Geological Survey Museum. He was appointed paleontologist and curator of fossils in 1882; he retired in 1905. Newton took an active part in the work of the Geological Society: he was vice-president from 1903 to 1905 and again from 1916 to 1918, and was awarded the Lyell Medal in 1893. In the same year (1893) he was elected a fellow of the Royal Society. He was president of the Paleontographical Society from 1921 to 1928 and president of the Geologists' Association in 1896–1898. He also served on committees of the Zoological Society.

Newton's work was always thorough, and he showed remarkable patience and skill in performing delicate manipulations. His beautiful model of the brain of a cockroach, constructed by means of serial sections, is displayed in the museum of the Royal College of Surgeons (London). He began his research by inventing a new method for making microsections of coal. A number of these sections, as well as many skeletons prepared by him, are in the British Museum. In his official work Newton studied a wide variety of fossils, but he is noted for his original investigations in vertebrate paleontology. He first studied the Cretaceous fishes, and later made observations on the bones of birds and the remains of man, but he devoted his chief energies to studying the vertebrate fragments from the Pleistocene and Pliocene deposits in England. His most important monographs are probably those on the brain of the Jurassic flying reptile, the pterodactyl (1888), and on the reptilian remains from the Permotriassic rocks at Elgin, Scotland (1893 and 1894). In the latter research Newton lacked the actual bones to work with; he had only their cavities in sandstone, from which, after great labor, he obtained and fitted together casts of gutta-percha. He discovered dicynodonts and pareiasaurs for the first time in Europe, showing how closely they resembled the descriptions of those found in the Karroo Formation of South Africa.

All of Newton's published work was descriptive. He was a realist and thought that although the search back in evolutionary forms might end in so-called fish forms, such retrospection should not lead away "from scientific facts to a slough of unscientific imagination."

BIBLIOGRAPHY

I. ORIGINAL WORKS. Among Newton's important works are *The Chimaeroid Fishes of the British Cretaceous Rocks* (London, 1878); *The Vertebrata of the Forest-Bed Series of Norfolk and Suffolk* (London, 1882); "On the Skull, Brain, and Auditory Organ of a New Species of Pterosaurian From the Upper Lias Near Whitby, Yorkshire," in *Philosophical Transactions of the Royal Society*, ser. B, **179** (1888), 503–537; "Notes on Pterodactyls," in *Proceedings of the Geologists' Association*, **10** (1888), 406–424; *The Vertebrata of the Pliocene Deposits of Britain* (London,

1891); "Reptiles From the Elgin Sandstone," in *Philosophical Transactions of the Royal Society*, ser. B, **184** (1893), 431–503, and **185** (1894), 573–607; and "The [Pleistocene] Vertebrate Fauna Collected by Mr. Lewis Abbott From the Fissure Near Ightham, Kent," in *Quarterly Journal of the Geological Society of London*, **50** (1894), 188–211.

II. SECONDARY LITERATURE. For an article on Newton's work, see *Journal of Microscopical Science* (1879), p. 340. Obituary notices include *Geological Magazine*, **67** (1930), 286–287; A. S. Woodward, in *Quarterly Journal of the Geological Society of London*, **86** (1930), lix–lxii; and A. S. W[oodward], in *Obituary Notices of the Fellows of the Royal Society*, **1** (1932), 5–7.

JOHN CHALLINOR

NEWTON, HUBERT ANSON (*b.* Sherburne, New York, 19 March 1830; *d.* New Haven, Connecticut, 12 August 1896), *astronomy, mathematics.*

Hubert was one of eleven children of William and Lois Butler Newton, both of whom were descendants of the first Puritan settlers in New England. After attending public schools in Sherburne, Newton entered Yale at age sixteen. He was an outstanding student; he won election to the Phi Beta Kappa Society and first prize for the solution of mathematics problems.

Following his graduation in 1850, Newton studied mathematics for two and a half years at his home and in New Haven. He became tutor at Yale in 1853, and almost immediately thereafter, on the death of A. D. Stanley, he was asked to chair the mathematics department. Two years later Newton was elected professor and at age twenty-five was one of the youngest persons ever to have reached that rank at Yale.

The professorship included a year's leave of absence, which he took at the Sorbonne with the geometer Chasles. That experience clearly influenced Newton, who subsequently published several important papers on mathematics.

Even though mathematics constituted his education and vocation, his principal efforts began to shift to astronomy and meteorology. His interest in those subjects was sparked by the spectacular meteor shower of 13 November 1833. Although Newton was too young to remember it, others in New Haven, like Edward C. Herrick, Alexander C. Twining, and Denison Olmsted (his undergraduate teacher in astronomy), had written about the event and had checked the records of earlier showers. Thus by 1860 rudimentary data on meteors existed and tentative hypotheses about their orbits were being proffered.

Newton's first papers on the subject (1860–1862) dealt primarily with the orbits and velocities of fireballs. In 1861 the Connecticut Academy of Arts and Sciences established a committee to obtain systematic sightings from diverse observers of the meteor showers of August and November. As one of the leaders of that group, Newton soon accumulated vast amounts of information.

From a careful study of all extant records of the shower of November 1861 Newton in 1864 published his important finding that the shower had occurred thirteen times since A.D. 902, in a cycle of 33.25 years. He reasoned that the phenomenon was caused by a swarm of meteoroids orbiting the sun and concluded that the number of revolutions they must make in one year would be $2 \pm 1/33.25$ or $1 \pm 1/33.25$ or $1/33.25$. These frequencies correspond to periods of 180.0, 185.4, 354.6, and 375.5 days and 33.25 years. Using these five values, the position of the radiant point, and the knowledge that the meteoroids' heliocentric motion is retrograde, Newton calculated five possible orbits.

He noted that the real orbit could be distinguished from the others by calculating the secular motion of the node that was due to planetary perturbations for each of the hypothetical orbits. J. C. Adams, who undertook those calculations, found that the four short periods were not compatible with the observations; the period of 33.25 years, however, corresponds to an elliptical orbit, which extends past Uranus and is subject to perturbations by Uranus and Saturn. Since Adams' determination of the effect of perturbations agreed with Newton's data for the Leonids, these meteoroids were proved to be in such an orbit with a period of 33.25 years.

The Leonids' dramatic reappearance in 1866 spurred meteoroid research and added credence to Newton's calculations; moreover, the reappearance led to the positive identification of the swarm with a comet. By 1865 Newton in the United States and Schiaparelli in Italy had independently concluded that the mean velocities of meteoroids are nearly parabolic and resemble those of comets. When it was found in 1866 that a comet and the Leonids had virtually identical orbits, their relationship was firmly established.

From about 1863 to 1866 Newton amassed and published extensive statistics from observations of sporadic meteors. From this information, he derived the paths and the numbers of meteors, plus the spatial density of meteoroids near the earth's orbit and their velocity about the sun.

Newton's next major contribution to meteor studies came in the mid-1870's when he compared the statistical distribution of known cometary orbits with the hypothetical distributions that would result from two currently leading theories for the origin of the solar system—those of Kant and Laplace. According to Kant, comets formed as part of the primeval solar nebula, while according to Laplace they originated independently from the solar system. Newton found that the distribution of comets' aphelia and inclinations agrees better with the latter theory, although he noted that the problem was unsettled.

These calculations included considerations of the effect of large planetary perturbations on the distribution of cometary orbits; such studies culminated in 1891 in his most famous paper on perturbations. During the 1870's and 1880's Newton accumulated statistical data that indicated that long period comets could be captured by Jupiter, shortening their periods.

Newton devoted the last decade of his research to Biela's comet and meteor shower, to fireballs, and to meteorites. At his death he was probably the foremost American pioneer in the study of meteors.

Besides his scientific research, Newton was active in teaching and educational reform, especially about the metric system. He was a founder of the American Metrological Society, and he persuaded many manufacturers of scientific instruments and publishers of school arithmetic texts to adopt the system.

In 1868 the University of Michigan awarded Newton an honorary LL.D. After joining the American Association for the Advancement of Science in 1850, he served as the vice-president of its Section A in 1875, and as president of the Association in 1885. He was a president of the Connecticut Academy of Arts and Sciences, a member of the American Philosophical Society, and one of the original members of the National Academy of Sciences. In 1888 the National Academy awarded him its J. Lawrence Smith Gold Medal in recognition of his research on meteoroids. At his death he was the vice-president of the American Mathematical Society and an associate editor of the *American Journal of Science*.

Aside from societies in the United States, he was elected in 1860 corresponding member of the British Association for the Advancement of Science, in 1872 associate of the Royal Astronomical Society of London, in 1886 foreign honorary fellow of the Royal Philosophical Society of Edinburgh, and in 1892 foreign member of the Royal Society of London.

Newton's association with Yale and New Haven was long and rich. He directed the Yale mathematics department and also the observatory, which he helped organize in 1882, and he helped build the extensive collection of meteorites in the Peabody Museum. He also provided considerable assistance to poor students who wanted to attend Yale. For a time he was the only Democrat on the Yale faculty and became alderman in the strongly Republican first ward of New Haven.

BIBLIOGRAPHY

I. ORIGINAL WORKS. Newton published approximately seventy papers, an extensive bibliography of which is included in the memoir by Gibbs that is cited below. Newton's most significant writings included the following: "Explanation of the Motion of the Gyroscope," in *American Journal of Science*, **24** (1857), 253–254; "On the Geometrical Construction of Certain Curves by Points," in *Mathematics Monthly*, **3** (1861), 235–244, 268–279; "On November Star-Showers," in *American Journal of Science*, **37** (1864), 377–389; **38** (1864), 53–61; "On Shooting Stars," in *Memoirs of the National Academy of Sciences*, **1** (1866), 291–312; *The Metric System of Weights and Measures* (Washington, 1868); "On the Transcendental Curves Whose Equation Is $\sin y \sin my = a \sin x \sin nx + b$," in *Transactions of the Connecticut Academy of Arts and Sciences*, **3** (1875), 97–107, written with A. W. Phillips; "On the Origin of Comets," in *American Journal of Science*, **16** (1878), 165–179; "The Story of Biela's Comet," *ibid.*, **31** (1886), 81–94; and "On the Capture of Comets by Planets, Especially Their Capture by Jupiter," in *Memoirs of the National Academy of Sciences*, **6** (1891), 7–23.

II. SECONDARY LITERATURE. An article on meteors that gives a critique of Newton's work is M. Faye, in *Comptes rendus hebdomadaires des séances de l'Académie des sciences*, **64** (1867), 550. Biographical sketches, which were written about the time of Newton's becoming president of the American Association for the Advancement of Science, are in *Science*, **6** (1885), 161–162; in *Popular Science Monthly*, **27** (1885), 840–843; and in James Grant Wilson and John Fisk, eds., *Appleton's Cyclopedia of American Biography*, IV (New York, 1888), 506–507.

Obituaries on Newton are William L. Elkin, in *Astronomische Nachrichten*, **141** (1896), 407; unsigned writers, in *Popular Astronomy*, **4** (1896), 236–240; in *Monthly Notices of the Royal Astronomical Society*, **57** (1897), 227–231; and in *New York Times* (13 Aug. 1896), 5. Biographical articles that were written after his death were J. Willard Gibbs, in *Biographical Memoirs. National Academy of Sciences*, **4** (1902), 99–124, which includes a bibliography; Anson Phelps Stokes, in *Memorials of Eminent Yale Men* (New Haven, 1914), 48–54; and David Eugene Smith, in Dumas Malone, ed., *Dictionary of American Biography*, XIII (New York, 1934), 470–471.

RICHARD BERENDZEN

NEWTON, ISAAC (*b.* Woolsthorpe, England, 25 December 1642; *d.* London, England, 20 March 1727), *mathematics, dynamics, celestial mechanics, astronomy, optics, natural philosophy.*

Isaac Newton was born a posthumous child, his father having been buried the preceding 6 October.

Newton was descended from yeomen on both sides: there is no record of any notable ancestor. He was born prematurely, and there was considerable concern for his survival. He later said that he could have fitted into a quart mug at birth. He grew up in his father's house, which still stands in the hamlet of Woolsthorpe, near Grantham in Lincolnshire.

Newton's mother, Hannah (née Ayscough), remarried, and left her three-year-old son in the care of his aged maternal grandmother. His stepfather, the Reverend Barnabas Smith, died in 1653; and Newton's mother returned to Woolsthorpe with her three younger children, a son and two daughters. Their surviving children, Newton's four nephews and four nieces, were his heirs. One niece, Catherine, kept house for Newton in the London years and married John Conduitt, who succeeded Newton as master of the Mint.

Newton's personality was no doubt influenced by his never having known his father. That he was, moreover, resentful of his mother's second marriage and jealous of her second husband may be documented by at least one entry in a youthful catalogue of sins, written in shorthand in 1662, which records "Threatning my father and mother Smith to burne them and the house over them."[1]

In his youth Newton was interested in mechanical contrivances. He is reported to have constructed a model of a mill (powered by a mouse), clocks, "lanthorns," and fiery kites, which he sent aloft to the fright of his neighbors, being inspired by John Bate's *Mysteries of Nature and Art*.[2] He scratched diagrams and an architectural drawing (now revealed and preserved) on the walls and window edges of the Woolsthorpe house, and made many other drawings of birds, animals, men, ships, and plants. His early education was in the dame schools at Skillington and Stoke, beginning perhaps when he was five. He then attended the King's School in Grantham, but his mother withdrew him from school upon her return to Woolsthorpe, intending to make him a farmer. He was, however, uninterested in farm chores, and absent-minded and lackadaisical. With the encouragement of John Stokes, master of the Grantham school, and William Ayscough, Newton's uncle and rector of Burton Coggles, it was therefore decided to prepare the youth for the university. He was admitted a member of Trinity College, Cambridge, on 5 June 1661 as a subsizar, and became scholar in 1664 and Bachelor of Arts in 1665.

Among the books that Newton studied while an undergraduate was Kepler's "optics" (presumably the *Dioptrice*, reprinted in London in 1653). He also began Euclid, which he reportedly found "trifling," throwing it aside for Schooten's second Latin edition of Descartes's *Géométrie*.[3] Somewhat later, on the occasion of his election as scholar, Newton was reportedly found deficient in Euclid when examined by Barrow.[4] He read Descartes's *Géométrie* in a borrowed copy of the Latin version (Amsterdam, 1659–1661) with commentary by Frans van Schooten, in which there were also letters and tracts by de Beaune, Hudde, Heuraet, de Witt, and Schooten himself. Other books that he studied at this time included Oughtred's *Clavis*, Wallis' *Arithmetica infinitorum*, Walter Charleton's compendium of Epicurus and Gassendi, Digby's *Two Essays*, Descartes's *Principia philosophiae* (as well as the Latin edition of his letters), Galileo's *Dialogo* (in Salusbury's English version)—but not, apparently, the *Discorsi*—Magirus' compendium of Scholastic philosophy, Wing and Streete on astronomy, and some writings of Henry More (himself a native of Grantham), with whom Newton became acquainted in Cambridge. Somewhat later, Newton read and annotated Sprat's *History of the Royal Society*, the early *Philosophical Transactions*, and Hooke's *Micrographia*.

Notebooks that survive from Newton's years at Trinity include an early one[5] containing notes in Greek on Aristotle's *Organon* and *Ethics*, with a supplement based on the commentaries by Daniel Stahl, Eustachius, and Gerard Vossius. This, together with his reading of Magirus and others, gives evidence of Newton's grounding in Scholastic rhetoric and syllogistic logic. His own reading in the moderns was organized into a collection of "Questiones quaedam philosophicae,"[6] which further indicate that he had also read Charleton and Digby. He was familiar with the works of Glanville and Boyle, and no doubt studied Gassendi's epitome of Copernican astronomy, which was then published together with Galileo's *Sidereus nuncius* and Kepler's *Dioptrice*.[7]

Little is known of Newton's friends during his college days other than his roommate and onetime amanuensis Wickins. The rooms he occupied are not known for certain; and we have no knowledge as to the subject of his thesis for the B.A., or where he stood academically among the group who were graduated with him. He himself did record what were no doubt unusual events in his undergraduate career: "Lost at cards twice" and "At the Taverne twice."

For eighteen months, after June 1665, Newton is supposed to have been in Lincolnshire, while the University was closed because of the plague. During this time he laid the foundations of his work in mathematics, optics, and astronomy or celestial mechanics. It was formerly believed that all of these discoveries were made while Newton remained in seclusion at Woolsthorpe, with only an occasional excursion into nearby Boothby. During these "two plague years of 1665 & 1666," Newton later said, "I was in the prime of my age for invention & minded Mathematicks & Philosophy more then at any time since." In fact, however, Newton was back in Cambridge on at least one visit between March and June 1666.[8] He appears to have written out his mathematical discoveries at Trinity, where he had access to the college and University libraries, and then to have returned to Lincolnshire to revise and polish these results. It is possible that even the prism experiments on refraction and dispersion were made in his rooms at Trinity, rather than in the country, although while at Woolsthorpe he may have made pendulum experiments to determine the gravitational pull of the earth. The episode of the falling of the apple, which Newton himself said "occasioned" the "notion of gravitation," must have occurred at either Boothby or Woolsthorpe.[9]

Lucasian Professor. On 1 October 1667, some two years after his graduation, Newton was elected minor fellow of Trinity, and on 16 March 1668 he was admitted major fellow. He was created M.A. on 7 July 1668 and on 29 October 1669, at the age of twenty-six, he was appointed Lucasian professor. He succeeded Isaac Barrow, first incumbent of the chair, and it is generally believed that Barrow resigned his professorship so that Newton might have it.[10]

University statutes required that the Lucasian professor give at least one lecture a week in every term. He was then ordered to put in finished form his ten (or more) annual lectures for deposit in the University Library. During Newton's tenure of the professorship, he accordingly deposited manuscripts of his lectures on optics (1670–1672), arithmetic and algebra (1673–1683), most of book I of the *Principia* (1684–1685), and "The System of the World" (1687). There is, however, no record of what lectures, if any, he gave in 1686, or from 1688 until he removed to London early in 1696. In the 1670's Newton attempted unsuccessfully to publish his annotations on Kinckhuysen's algebra and his own treatise on fluxions. In 1672 he did succeed in publishing an improved or corrected edition of Varenius' *Geographia generalis*, apparently intended for the use of his students.

During the years in which Newton was writing the *Principia*, according to Humphrey Newton's recollection,[11] "he seldom left his chamber except at term time, when he read in the schools as being Lucasianus Professor, where so few went to hear him, and fewer that understood him, that ofttimes he did in a manner,

for want of hearers, read to the walls." When he lectured he "usually staid about half an hour; when he had no auditors, he commonly returned in a 4th part of that time or less." He occasionally received foreigners "with a great deal of freedom, candour, and respect." He "ate sparingly," and often "forgot to eat at all," rarely dining "in the hall, except on some public days," when he was apt to appear "with shoes down at heels, stockings untied, surplice on, and his head scarcely combed." He "seldom went to the chapel," but very often "went to St Mary's church, especially in the forenoon."[12]

From time to time Newton went to London, where he attended meetings of the Royal Society (of which he had been a fellow since 1672). He contributed £40 toward the building of the new college library (1676), as well as giving it various books. He corresponded, both directly and indirectly (often through Henry Oldenburg as intermediary), with scientists in England and on the Continent, including Boyle, Collins, Flamsteed, David Gregory, Halley, Hooke, Huygens, Leibniz, and Wallis. He was often busy with chemical experiments, both before and after writing the *Principia*, and in the mid-1670's he contemplated a publication on optics.[13] During the 1690's, Newton was further engaged in revising the *Principia* for a second edition; he then contemplated introducing into book III some selections from Lucretius and references to an ancient tradition of wisdom. A major research at this time was the effect of solar perturbations on the motions of the moon. He also worked on mathematical problems more or less continually throughout these years.

Among the students with whom Newton had friendly relations, the most significant for his life and career was Charles Montague, a fellow-commoner of Trinity and grandson of the Earl of Manchester; he "was one of the small band of students who assisted Newton in forming the Philosophical Society of Cambridge"[14] (the attempt to create this society was unsuccessful). Newton was also on familiar terms with Henry More, Edward Paget (whom he recommended for a post in mathematics at Christ's Hospital), Francis Aston, John Ellis (later master of Caius), and J. F. Vigani, first professor of chemistry at Cambridge, who is said to have eventually been banished from Newton's presence for having told him "a loose story about a nun." Newton was active in defending the rights of the university when the Catholic monarch James II tried to mandate the admission of the Benedictine monk Alban Francis. In 1689, he was elected by the university constituency to serve as Member of the Convention Parliament.

While in London as M.P., Newton renewed contact

with Montague and with the Royal Society, and met Huygens and others, including Locke, with whom he thereafter corresponded on theological and biblical questions. Richard Bentley sought Newton's advice and assistance in preparing the inaugural Boyle Lectures (or sermons), entitled "The Confutation of Atheism" and based in part on the Newtonian system of the world.

Newton also came to know two other scientists, each of whom wanted to prepare a second edition of the *Principia*. One was David Gregory, a professor at Edinburgh, whom Newton helped to obtain a chair at Oxford, and who recorded his conversations with Newton while Newton was revising the *Principia* in the 1690's. The other was a refugee from Switzerland, Nicolas Fatio de Duillier, advocate of a mechanical explanation of gravitation which was at one time viewed kindly by Newton. Fatio soon became perhaps the most intimate of any of Newton's friends. In the early autumn of 1693, Newton apparently suffered a severe attack of depression and made fantastic accusations against Locke and Pepys and was said to have lost his reason.[15]

In the post-*Principia* years of the 1690's, Newton apparently became bored with Cambridge and his scientific professorship. He hoped to get a post that would take him elsewhere. An attempt to make him master of the Charterhouse "did not appeal to him"[16] but eventually Montague (whose star had risen with the Whigs' return to power in Parliament) was successful in obtaining for Newton (in March 1696) the post of warden of the mint. Newton appointed William Whiston as his deputy in the professorship. He did not resign officially until 10 December 1701, shortly after his second election as M.P. for the university.[17]

Mathematics. Any summary of Newton's contributions to mathematics must take account not only of his fundamental work in the calculus and other aspects of analysis—including infinite series (and most notably the general binomial expansion)—but also his activity in algebra and number theory, classical and analytic geometry, finite differences, the classification of curves, methods of computation and approximation, and even probability.

For three centuries, many of Newton's writings on mathematics have lain buried, chiefly in the Portsmouth Collection of his manuscripts. The major parts are now being published and scholars will shortly be able to trace the evolution of Newton's mathematics in detail.[18] It will be possible here only to indicate highlights, while maintaining a distinction among four levels of dissemination of his work: (1) writings printed in his lifetime, (2) writings

circulated in manuscript, (3) writings hinted at or summarized in correspondence, and (4) writings that were published only much later. In his own day and afterward, Newton influenced mathematics "following his own wish," by "his creation of the fluxional calculus and the theory of infinite series," the "two strands of mathematical technique which he bound inseparably together in his 'analytick' method."[19] The following account therefore emphasizes these two topics.

Newton appears to have had no contact with higher mathematics until 1664 when—at the age of twenty-one—his dormant mathematical genius was awakened by Schooten's "Miscellanies" and his edition of Descartes's *Géométrie*, and by Wallis' *Arithmetica infinitorum* (and possibly others of his works). Schooten's edition introduced him to the mathematical contributions of Heuraet, de Witt, Hudde, De Beaune, and others; Newton also read in Viète, Oughtred, and Huygens. He had further compensated for his early neglect of Euclid by careful study of both the *Elements* and *Data* in Barrow's edition.

In recent years[20] scholars have come to recognize Descartes and Wallis as the two "great formative influences" on Newton in the two major areas of his mathematical achievement: the calculus, and analytic geometry and algebra. Newton's own copy of the *Géométrie* has lately turned up in the Trinity College Library; and his marginal comments are now seen to be something quite different from the general devaluation of Descartes's book previously supposed. Rather than the all-inclusive "Error. Error. Non est geom." reported by Conduitt and Brewster, Newton merely indicated an "Error" here and there, while the occasional marginal entry "non geom." was used to note such things as that the Cartesian classification of curves is not really geometry so much as it is algebra. Other of Newton's youthful annotations document what he learned from Wallis, chiefly the method of "indivisibles."[21]

In addition to studying the works cited, Newton encountered the concepts and methods of Fermat and James Gregory. Although Newton was apparently present when Barrow "read his Lectures about motion," and noted[22] that they "might put me upon taking these things into consideration," Barrow's influence on Newton's mathematical thought was probably not of such importance as is often supposed.

A major first step in Newton's creative mathematical life was his discovery of the general binomial theorem, or expansion of $(a + b)^n$, concerning which he wrote, "In the beginning of the year 1665 I found the Method of approximating series & the Rule for reducing any dignity [power] of any Binomial into such a series. . . ."[23] He further stated that:

> In the winter between the years 1664 & 1665 upon reading Dr Wallis's *Arithmetica Infinitorum* & trying to interpole his progressions for squaring the circle [that is, finding the area or evaluating $_0\!\int^1 (1 - x^2)^{\frac{1}{2}} dx$], I found out another infinite series for squaring the circle & then another infinite series for squaring the Hyperbola. . . .[24]

On 13 June 1676, Newton sent Oldenburg the "Epistola prior" for transmission to Leibniz. In this communication he wrote that fractions "are reduced to infinite series by division; and radical quantities by extraction of roots," the latter

. . . much shortened by this theorem,

$$\overline{P + PQ}^{\frac{m}{n}} = P^{\frac{m}{n}} + \frac{m}{n} AQ + \frac{m-n}{2n} BQ$$

$$+ \frac{m-2n}{3n} CQ + \frac{m-3n}{4n} DQ + \cdots \&c.$$

where $P + PQ$ signifies the quantity whose root or even any power, or the root of a power, is to be found; P signifies the first term of that quantity, Q the remaining terms divided by the first, and m/n the numerical index of the power of $P + PQ$, whether that power is integral or (so to speak) fractional, whether positive or negative.[25]

A sample given by Newton is the expansion

$$\sqrt{(c^2 + x^2)} \quad \text{or} \quad (c^2 + x^2)^{\frac{1}{2}} = c + \frac{x^2}{2c} - \frac{x^4}{8c^3}$$

$$+ \frac{x^6}{16c^5} - \frac{5x^8}{128c^7} + \frac{7x^{10}}{256c^9} + \text{etc.}$$

where

$$P = c^2, \quad Q = x^2/c^2, \quad m = 1, \quad n = 2, \quad \text{and}$$

$$A = P^{\frac{m}{n}} = (c^2)^{\frac{1}{2}} = c, \quad B = (m/n) AQ = x^2/2c,$$

$$C = \frac{m-n}{2n} BQ = -x^4/8c^3,$$

and so on.
Other examples include

$$(y^3 - a^2y)^{-\frac{1}{3}}$$

$$(c^5 + c^4x - x^5)^{\frac{1}{5}},$$

$$(d + e)^{-\frac{3}{5}}.$$

What is perhaps the most important general statement made by Newton in this letter is that in dealing with infinite series all operations are carried out "in the symbols just as they are commonly carried out in decimal numbers."

Wallis had obtained the quadratures of certain curves (that is, the areas under the curves), by a technique of indivisibles yielding $_0\!\int^1 (1 - x^2)^n dx$ for certain positive integral values of n (0, 1, 2, 3); in attempting to find the quadrature of a circle of unit radius, he had sought to evaluate the integral $_0\!\int^1 (1 - x^2)^{\frac{1}{2}} dx$ by interpolation. He showed that

$$\frac{4}{\pi} = \frac{1}{_0\!\int^1 (1 - x^2)^{\frac{1}{2}} dx} = \frac{3 \cdot 3 \cdot 5 \cdot 5 \cdot 7 \cdot 7 \cdots}{2 \cdot 4 \cdot 4 \cdot 6 \cdot 6 \cdot 8 \cdots}.$$

Newton read Wallis and was stimulated to go considerably further, freeing the upper bound and then deriving the infinite series expressing the area of a quadrant of a circle of radius x:

$$x - \frac{\frac{1}{2}x^3}{3} - \frac{\frac{1}{8}x^5}{5} - \frac{\frac{1}{16}x^7}{7} - \frac{\frac{5}{128}x^9}{9} - \cdots.$$

In so freeing the upper bound, he was led to recognize that the terms, identified by their powers of x, displayed the binomial coefficients. Thus, the factors $\frac{1}{2}$, $\frac{1}{8}$, $\frac{1}{16}$, $\frac{5}{128}$, . . . stand out plainly as $\binom{q}{1}$, $\binom{q}{2}$, $\binom{q}{3}$, $\binom{q}{4}$, . . . , in the special case $q = \frac{1}{2}$ in the generalization

$$\int_0^x (1 - x^2)^q dx = X - \binom{q}{1} \cdot \frac{1}{3} X^3 + \binom{q}{2} \cdot \frac{1}{5} X^5$$

$$- \binom{q}{3} \cdot \frac{1}{7} X^7 + \frac{q}{5} \cdot \frac{1}{9} X^9 + \cdots,$$

where

$$\binom{q}{n} = \frac{q(q - 1) \cdots (q - n + 1)}{n!}.$$

In this way, according to D. T. Whiteside, Newton could begin with the indefinite integral and, "by differentiation in a Wallisian manner," proceed to a straightforward derivation of the "series-expansion of the binomial $(1 - x^p)^q$ . . . virtually in its modern form," with "$| x^p |$ implicitly less than unity for convergence." As a check on the validity of this general series expansion, he "compared its particular expansions with the results of algebraic division and square-root extraction ($q = \frac{1}{2}$)." This work, which was done in the winter of 1664–1665, was later presented in modified form at the beginning of Newton's *De analysi*.

He correctly summarized the stages of development of his method in the "Epistola posterior" of 24 October 1676, which—as before—he wrote for Oldenburg to transmit to Leibniz:

At the beginning of my mathematical studies, when I had met with the works of our celebrated Wallis, on considering the series, by the intercalation of which he himself exhibits the area of the circle and the hyperbola, the fact that in the series of curves whose common base or axis is x and the ordinates

$$(1-x^2)^{\frac{0}{2}}, (1-x^2)^{\frac{1}{2}}, (1-x^2)^{\frac{2}{2}}, (1-x^2)^{\frac{3}{2}}, (1-x^2)^{\frac{4}{2}}, (1-x^2)^{\frac{5}{2}},$$

etc., if the areas of every other of them, namely

$$x, x-\tfrac{1}{3}x^3, x-\tfrac{2}{3}x^3+\tfrac{1}{5}x^5, x-\tfrac{3}{3}x^3+\tfrac{3}{5}x^5-\tfrac{1}{7}x^7, \quad \text{etc.}$$

could be interpolated, we would have the areas of the intermediate ones, of which the first $(1-x^2)^{\frac{1}{2}}$ is the circle. . . .[26]

The importance of changing Wallis' fixed upper boundary to a free variable x has been called "the crux of Newton's breakthrough," since the "various powers of x order the numerical coefficients and reveal for the first time the binomial character of the sequence."[27]

In about 1665, Newton found the power series (that is, actually determined the sequence of the coefficients) for

$$\sin^{-1} x = x + \tfrac{1}{6}x^3 + \tfrac{3}{40}x^5 + \cdots,$$

and—most important of all—the logarithmic series. He also squared the hyperbola $y(1 + x) = 1$, by tabulating

$$\int_0^x (1 + t)^r \, dt$$

for $r = 0, 1, 2, \cdots$ in powers of x and then interpolating

$$\int_0^x (1 + t)^{-1} \, dt.[28]$$

From his table, he found the square of the hyperbola in the series

$$x - \frac{x^2}{2} + \frac{x^3}{3} - \frac{x^4}{4} + \frac{x^5}{5} - \frac{x^6}{6} + \frac{x^7}{7}$$
$$- \frac{x^8}{8} + \frac{x^9}{9} - \frac{x^{10}}{10} + \cdots,$$

which is the series for the natural logarithm of $1 + x$. Newton wrote that having "found the method of infinite series," in the winter of 1664–1665, "in summer 1665 being forced from Cambridge by the Plague I computed the area of the Hyperbola at Boothby . . . to two & fifty figures by the same method."[29]

At about the same time Newton devised "a completely general differentiation procedure founded on the concept of an indefinitely small and ultimately vanishing element o of a variable, say, x." He first used the notation of a "little zero" in September 1664, in notes based on Descartes's *Géométrie*, then extended it to various kinds of mathematical investigations. From the derivative of an algebraic function $f(x)$ conceived ("essentially") as

$$\operatorname*{Lim}_{o \to \text{zero}} \frac{1}{0} [f(x + 0) - f(x)]$$

he developed general rules of differentiation.

The next year, in Lincolnshire and separated from books, Newton developed a new theoretical basis for his techniques of the calculus. Whiteside has summarized this stage as follows:

> [Newton rejected] as his foundation the concept of the indefinitely small, discrete increment in favor of that of the "fluxion" of a variable, a finite instantaneous speed defined with respect to an independent, conventional dimension of time and on the geometrical model of the line-segment: in modern language, the fluxion of the variable x with regard to independent time-variable t is the "speed" dx/dt.[30]

Prior to 1691, when he introduced the more familiar dot notation ($\dot{x}$ for dx/dt, $\dot{y}$ for dy/dt, $\dot{z}$ for dz/dt; then $\ddot{x}$ for d^2x/dt^2, $\ddot{y}$ for d^2y/dt^2, $\ddot{z}$ for d^2z/dt^2), Newton generally used the letters p, q, r for the first derivatives (Leibnizian dx/dt, dy/dt, dz/dt) of variable quantities x, y, z, with respect to some independent variable t. In this scheme, the "little zero" o was "an arbitrary increment of time,"[31] and op, oq, or were the corresponding "moments," or increments of the variables x, y, z (later these would, of course, become $o\dot{x}$, $o\dot{y}$, $o\dot{z}$).[32] Hence, in the limit ($o \to$ zero), in the modern Leibnizian terminology

$$q/p = dy/dx \qquad r/p = dz/dx,$$

where "we may think of the increment o as absorbed into the limit ratios." When, as was often done for the sake of simplicity, x itself was taken for the independent time variable, since $x = t$, then $p = \dot{x} = dx/dx = 1$, $q = dy/dx$, and $r = dz/dx$.

In May 1665, Newton invented a "true partial-derivative symbolism," and he "widely used the notation $\ddot{p}$ and $\dot{p}$ for the respective homogenized derivatives $x(dp/dx)$ and $x^2(d^2p/dx^2)$," in particular to express the total derivative of the function

$$\sum_i (p_i y^i) = 0$$

before "breaking through . . . to the first recorded use of a true partial-derivative symbolism." Armed with this tool, he constructed "the five first and second order partial derivatives of a two-valued function" and composed the fluxional tract of October 1666.[33]

Extracts were published by James Wilson in 1761, although the work as a whole remained in manuscript until recently.[34] Whiteside epitomizes Newton's work during this period as follows:

> In two short years (summer 1664–October 1666) Newton the mathematician was born, and in a sense the rest of his creative life was largely the working out, in calculus as in his mathematical thought in general, of the mass of burgeoning ideas which sprouted in his mind on the threshold of intellectual maturity. There followed two mathematically dull years.[35]

From 1664 to 1669, Newton advanced to "more general considerations," namely that the derivatives and integrals of functions might themselves be expressed as expansions in infinite series, specifically power series. But he had no general method for determining the "limits of convergence of individual series," nor had he found any "valid tests for such convergence."[36] Then, in mid-1669, he came upon Nicolaus Mercator's *Logarithmotechnica*, published in September 1668, of which "Mr Collins a few months after sent a copy . . . to Dr Barrow," as Newton later recorded.[37] Barrow, according to Newton, "replied that the Method of Series was invented & made general by me about two years before the publication of" the *Logarithmotechnica* and "at the same time," July 1669, Barrow sent back to Collins Newton's tract *De analysi*.

We may easily imagine Newton's concern for his priority on reading Mercator's book, for here he found in print "for all the world to read . . . his [own] reduction of $\log(1 + a)$ to an infinite series by continued division of $1 + a$ into 1 and successive integration of the quotient term by term."[38] Mercator had presented, among other numerical examples, that of $\log(1.1)$ calculated to forty-four decimal places, and he had no doubt calculated other logarithms over which Newton had spent untold hours. Newton might privately have been satisfied that Mercator's exposition was "cumbrous and inadequate" when compared to his own, but he must have been immeasurably anxious lest Mercator generalize a particular case (if indeed he had not already done so) and come upon Newton's discovery of "the extraction of roots in such series and indeed upon his cherished binomial expansion."[39] To make matters worse, Newton may have heard the depressing news (as Collins wrote to James Gregory, on 2 February 1668/1669) that "the Lord Brouncker asserts he can turne the square roote into an infinite Series."

To protect his priority, Newton hastily set to work to write up the results of his early researches into the properties of the binomial expansion and his methods for resolving "affected" equations, revising and amplifying his results in the course of composition. He submitted the tract, *De analysi per aequationes infinitas*, to Barrow, who sent it, as previously mentioned, to Collins.

Collins communicated Newton's results to James Gregory, Sluse, Bertet, Borelli, Vernon, and Strode, among others.[40] Newton was at that time unwilling to commit the tract to print; a year later, he incorporated its main parts into another manuscript, the *Methodus fluxionum et serierum infinitarum*. The original Latin text of the tract was not printed until long afterward.[41] Among those who saw the manuscript of *De analysi* was Leibniz, while on his second visit to London in October 1676; he read Collins' copy, and transcribed portions. Whiteside concurs with "the previously expressed opinions of the two eminent Leibniz scholars, Gerhardt and Hofmann," that Leibniz did not then "annex for his own purposes the fluxional method briefly exposed there," but "was interested only in Newton's series expansions."[42]

The *Methodus fluxionum* provides a better display of Newton's methods for the fluxional calculus in its generality than does the *De analysi*. In the preface to his English version of the *Methodus fluxionum*, John Colson wrote:

> The chief Principle, upon which the Method of Fluxions is here built, is this very simple one, taken from the Rational Mechanicks; which is, That Mathematical Quantity, particularly Extension, may be conceived as generated by continued local Motion; and that all Quantities whatever, at least by analogy and accommodation, may be conceived as generated after a like manner. Consequently there must be comparative Velocities of increase and decrease, during such generations, whose Relations are fixt and determinable, and may therefore (problematically) be proposed to be found.[43]

Among the problems solved are the differentiation of any algebraic function $f(x)$; the "method of quadratures," or the integration of such a function by the inverse process; and, more generally, the "inverse method of tangents," or the solution of a first-order differential equation.

As an example, the "moments" $\dot{x}o$ and $\dot{y}o$ are "the infinitely little accessions of the flowing quantities [variables] x and y": that is, their increase in "infinitely small portions of time." Hence, after "any infinitely small interval of time" (designated by o), x and y become $x + \dot{x}o$ and $y + \dot{y}o$. If one substitutes these for x and y in any given equation, for instance

$$x^3 - ax^2 + axy - y^3 = 0,$$

"there will arise"

$$x^3 + 3\dot{x}ox^2 + 3\dot{x}^2oox + \dot{x}^3o^3$$

$$- ax^2 - 2a\dot{x}ox - a\dot{x}^2oo$$

$$+ axy + a\dot{x}oy + a\dot{y}ox + a\dot{x}\dot{y}oo$$

$$- y^3 - 3\dot{y}oy^2 - 3\dot{y}^2ooy - \dot{y}^3o^3 = 0.$$

The terms $x^3 - ax^2 + axy - y^3$ (of which "by supposition" the sum $= 0$) may be cast out; the remaining terms are divided by o, to get

$$3\dot{x}x^2 + 3\dot{x}^2ox + \dot{x}^3oo - 2ax\dot{x} - a\dot{x}^2o + a\dot{x}y$$

$$+ a\dot{y}x + a\dot{x}\dot{y}o - 3\dot{y}y^2 - 3\dot{y}^2oy - \dot{y}^3oo = 0.$$

"But whereas o is suppos'd to be infinitely little, that it may represent the moments of quantities, consequently the terms that are multiplied by it will be nothing in respect of the rest."[44] These terms are therefore "rejected," and there remains

$$3x^2\dot{x} - 2a\dot{x}x + a\dot{x}y + a\dot{y}x - 3\dot{y}y^2 = 0.$$

It is then easy to group by $\dot{x}$ and $\dot{y}$ to get

$$\dot{x}(3x^2 - 2ax + ay) + \dot{y}(ax - 3y^2) = 0$$

or

$$\frac{\dot{y}}{\dot{x}} = - \frac{3x^2 - 2ax + ay}{ax - 3y^2},$$

which is the same result as finding dy/dx after differentiating

$$x^3 - ax^2 + axy - y^3 = 0.[45]$$

Problem II then reverses the process, with

$$3\dot{x}x^2 - 2a\dot{x}x + a\dot{x}y + a\dot{y}x - 3\dot{y}y^2 = 0$$

being given. Newton then integrates term by term to get $x^3 - ax^2 + axy - y^3 = 0$, the validity of which he may then test by differentiation.

In an example given, o is an "infinitely small quantity" representing an increment in "time," whereas, in the earlier *De analysi*, o was an increment x (although again infinitely small). In the manuscript, as Whiteside points out, Newton canceled "the less precise equivalent 'indefinitè' (indefinitely)" in favor of "infinitely."[46] Certainly the most significant feature is Newton's general and detailed treatment of "the converse operations of differentiation and integration (in Newton's terminology, constructing the 'fluxions' of given 'fluent' quantities, and vice versa)," and "the novelty of Newton's . . . reformulation of the calculus of continuous increase."[47]

Other illustrations given by Newton of his method are determining maxima and minima and drawing tangents to curves at any point. In dealing with maxima and minima, as applied to the foregoing equation, Newton invoked the rule (Problem III):

When a quantity is the greatest or the least that it can be, at that moment it neither flows backwards nor forwards: for if it flows forwards or increases it was less, and will presently be greater than it is; and on the contrary if it flows backwards or decreases, then it was greater, and will presently be less than it is.

In an example Newton sought the "greatest value of x" in the equation

$$x^3 - ax^2 + axy - y^3 = 0.$$

Having already found "the relation of the fluxions of x and y," he set $\dot{x} = o$. Thus, $\dot{y}(ax - 3y^2) = 0$, or $3y^2 = ax$, gives the desired result since this relation may be used to "exterminate either x or y out of the primary equation; and by the resulting equation you may determine the other, and then both of them by $-3y^2 + ax = 0$." Newton showed how "that famous Rule of *Huddenius*" may be derived from his own general method, but he did not refer to Fermat's earlier method of maxima and minima. Newton also found the greatest value of y in the equation

$$x^3 - ay^2 + \frac{by^3}{a + y} - xx \sqrt{ay + xx} = 0$$

and then indicated that his method led to the solution of a number of specified maximum-minimum problems.

Newton's shift from a "loosely justified conceptual model of the 'velocity' of a 'moveing body' . . ." to the postulation of "a basic, uniformly 'fluent' variable of 'time' as a measure of the 'fluxions' (instantaneous 'speeds' of flow) of a set of dependent variables which continuously alter their magnitude" may have been due, in part, to Barrow.[48] This concept of a uniformly flowing time long remained a favorite of Newton's; it was to appear again in the *Principia*, in the scholium following the definitions, as "mathematical time" (which "of itself, and from its own nature, flows equably without relation to anything external"), and in lemma 2, book II (see below), in which he introduced quantities "variable and indetermined, and increasing or decreasing, as it were, by a continual motion or flux." He later explained his position in a draft review of the *Commercium epistolicum* (1712),

I consider time as flowing or increasing by continual flux & other quantities as increasing continually in time & from the fluxion of time I give the name of fluxions to the velocitys with which all other quantities increase. Also from the moments of time I give the name of moments to the parts of any other quantities generated in moments of time. I expose time by any quantity flowing uniformly & represent its fluxion by an unit, & the fluxions of other quantities I represent by any other fit symbols & the fluxions of their fluxions by other fit symbols & the fluxions of those fluxions by others, & their moments generated by those fluxions I represent by the symbols of the fluxions drawn into the letter o & its powers o^2, o^3, &c: vizt their first moments by their first fluxions drawn into the letter o, their second moments by their second fluxions into o^2, & so on. And when I am investigating a truth or the solution of a Probleme I use all sorts of approximations & neglect to write down the letter o, but when I am demonstrating a Proposition I always write down the letter o & proceed exactly by the rules of Geometry without admitting any approximations. And I found the method not upon summs & differences, but upon the solution of this probleme: *By knowing the Quantities generated in time to find their fluxions.* And this is done by finding not prima momenta but primas momentorum nascentium rationes.

In an addendum (published only in 1969) to the 1671 *Methodus fluxionum*,[49] Newton developed an alternative geometrical theory of "first and last" ratios of lines and curves. This was later partially subsumed into the 1687 edition of the *Principia*, section 1, book I, and in the introduction to the *Tractatus de quadratura curvarum* (published by Newton in 1704 as one of the two mathematical appendixes to the *Opticks*). Newton had intended to issue a version of his *De quadratura* with the *Principia* on several occasions, both before and after the 1713 second edition, because, as he once wrote, "by the help of this method of Quadratures I found the Demonstration of Kepler's Propositions that the Planets revolve in Ellipses describing . . . areas proportional to the times," and again, "By the inverse Method of fluxions I found in the year 1677 the demonstration of Kepler's Astronomical Proposition. . . ."[50]

Newton began *De quadratura* with the statement that he did not use infinitesimals, "in this Place," considering "mathematical Quantities . . . not as consisting of very small Parts; but as describ'd by a continued Motion."[51] Thus lines are generated "not by the Apposition of Parts, but by the continued Motion of Points," areas by the motion of lines, solids by the motion of surfaces, angles by the rotation of the sides, and "Portions of Time by a continual Flux." Recognizing that there are different rates of increase and decrease, he called the "Velocities of the Motions or Increments *Fluxions*, and the generated

Quantities *Fluents*," adding that "Fluxions are very nearly as the Augments of the Fluents generated in equal but very small Particles of Time, and, to speak accurately, they are in the *first Ratio* of the nascent Augments; but they may be expounded in any Lines which are proportional to them."

As an example, consider that (as in Fig. 1) areas *ABC*, *ABDG* are described by the uniform motion of

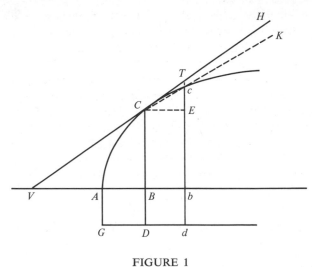

FIGURE 1

the ordinates *BC*, *BD* moving along the base in the direction *AB*. Suppose *BC* to advance to any new position *bc*, complete the parallelogram *BCEb*, draw the straight line *VTH* "touching the Curve in *C*, and meeting the two lines *bc* and *BA* [produced] in *T* and *V*." The "augments" generated will be: *Bb*, by *AB*; *Ec*, by *BC*; and *Cc*, by "the Curve Line *ACc*." Hence, "the Sides of the Triangle *CET* are in the *first Ratio* of these Augments considered as nascent." The "Fluxions of *AB*, *BC* and *AC*" are therefore "as the Sides *CE*, *ET* and *CT* of that Triangle *CET*" and "may be expounded" by those sides, or by the sides of the triangle *VBC*, which is similar to the triangle *CET*.

Contrariwise, one can "take the Fluxions in the *ultimate Ratio* of the evanescent Parts." Draw the straight line *Cc*; produce it to *K*. Now let *bc* return to its original position *BC*; when "*C* and *c* coalesce," the line *CK* will coincide with the tangent *CH*; then, "the evanescent Triangle *CEc* in its ultimate Form will become similar to the Triangle *CET*, and its evanescent Sides *CE*, *Ec*, and *Cc* will be *ultimately* among themselves as the sides *CE*, *ET* and *CT* of the other Triangle *CET*, are, and therefore the Fluxions of the Lines *AB*, *BC* and *AC* are in this same Ratio."

Newton concluded with an admonition that for the line *CK* not to be "distant from the Tangent *CH* by a small Distance," it is necessary that the points *C* and c not be separated "by any small Distance." If the points C and c do not "coalesce and exactly coincide," the lines CK and CH will not coincide, and "the ultimate Ratios in the Lines CE, Ec, and Cc" cannot be found. In short, "The very smallest Errors in mathematical Matters are not to be neglected."[52]

This same topic appears in the mathematical introduction (section 1, book I) to the *Principia*, in which Newton stated a set of lemmas on limits of geometrical ratios, making a distinction between the limit of a ratio and the ratio of limits (for example, as $x \to 0$, lim. $x^n/x \to 0$; but lim. $x^n/$lim. $x \to 0/0$, which is indeterminate).

The connection of fluxions with infinite series was first publicly stated in a scholium to proposition 11 of *De quadratura*, which Newton added for the 1704 printing, "We said formerly that there were first, second, third, fourth, &c. Fluxions of flowing Quantities. These Fluxions are as the Terms of an infinite converging series." As an example, he considered z^n to "be the flowing Quantity" and "by flowing" to become $(z + o)^n$; he then demonstrated that the successive terms of the expansion are the successive fluxions: "The first Term of this Series z^n will be that flowing Quantity; the second will be the first Increment or Difference, to which consider'd as nascent, its first Fluxion is proportional . . . and so on *in infinitum*." This clearly exemplifies the theorem formally stated by Brook Taylor in 1715; Newton himself explicitly derived it in an unpublished first version of *De quadratura* in 1691.[53] It should be noted that Newton here showed himself to be aware of the importance of convergence as a necessary condition for expansion in an infinite series.

In describing his method of quadrature by "first and last ratios," Newton said:

> Now to institute an Analysis after this manner in finite Quantities and investigate the *prime* or *ultimate* Ratios of these finite Quantities when in their nascent or evanescent State, is consonant to the Geometry of the Ancients: and I was willing [that is, desirous] to show that, in the Method of Fluxions, there is no necessity of introducing Figures infinitely small into Geometry.[54]

Newton's statement on the geometry of the ancients is typical of his lifelong philosophy. In mathematics and in mathematical physics, he believed that the results of analysis—the way in which things were discovered—should ideally be presented synthetically, in the form of a demonstration. Thus, in his review of the *Commercium epistolicum* (published anonymously), he wrote of the methods he had developed in *De quadratura* and other works as follows:

> By the help of the new *Analysis* Mr. *Newton* found out most of the Propositions in his *Principia Philosophiae*: but because the Ancients for making things certain admitted nothing into Geometry before it was demonstrated synthetically, he demonstrated the Propositions synthetically, that the Systeme of the Heavens might be founded upon good Geometry. And this makes it now difficult for unskilful Men to see the Analysis by which those Propositions were found out.[55]

As to analysis itself, David Gregory recorded that Newton once said "Algebra is the Analysis of the Bunglers in Mathematicks."[56] No doubt! Newton did, nevertheless, devote his main professorial lectures of 1673–1683 to algebra,[57] and these lectures were printed a number of times both during his lifetime and after.[58] This algebraical work includes, among other things, what H. W. Turnbull has described as a general method (given without proof) for discovering "the rational factors, if any, of a polynomial in one unknown and with integral coefficients"; he adds that the "most remarkable passage in the book" is Newton's rule for discovering the imaginary roots of such a polynomial.[59] (There is also developed a set of formulas for "the sums of the powers of the roots of a polynomial equation.")[60]

Newton's preference for geometric methods over purely analytical ones is further evident in his statement that "Equations are Expressions of Arithmetical Computation and properly have no place in Geometry." But such assertions must not be read out of context, as if they were pronouncements about algebra in general, since Newton was actually discussing various points of view or standards concerning what was proper to geometry. He included the positions of Pappus and Archimedes on whether to admit into geometry the conchoid for the problem of trisection and those of the "new generation of geometers" who "welcome" into geometry many curves, conics among them.[61]

Newton's concern was with the limits to be set in geometry, and in particular he took up the question of the legitimacy of the conic sections in solid geometry (that is, as solid constructions) as opposed to their illegitimacy in plane geometry (since they cannot be generated in a plane by a purely geometric construction). He wished to divorce synthetic geometric considerations from their "analytic" algebraic counterparts. Synthesis would make the ellipse the simplest of conic sections other than the circle; analysis would award this place to the parabola. "Simplicity in figures," he wrote, "is dependent on the simplicity of their genesis and conception, and it is not its equation but its description (whether geometrical or mechanical) by which a figure is generated and rendered easy to conceive."[62]

The "written record of [Newton's] first researches in the interlocking structures of Cartesian coordinate geometry and infinitesimal analysis"[63] shows him to have been establishing "the foundations of his mature work in mathematics" and reveals "for the first time the true magnitude of his genius."[64] And in fact Newton did contribute significantly to analytic geometry. In his 1671 *Methodis fluxionum*, he devoted "Prob. 4: To draw tangents to curves" to a study of the different ways in which tangents may be drawn "according to the various relationships of curves to straight lines," that is, according to the "modes" or coordinate systems in which the curve is specified.[65]

Newton proceeded "by considering the ratios of limit-increments of the co-ordinate variables (which are those of their fluxions)."[66] His "Mode 3" consists of using what are now known as standard bipolar coordinates, which Newton applied to Cartesian ovals as follows: Let x, y be the distances from a pair of fixed points (two "poles"); the equation $a \pm (e/d)x - y = 0$ for Descartes's "second-order ovals" will then yield the fluxional relation $\pm(e/d)\dot{x} - \dot{y} = 0$ (in dot notation) or $\pm em/d - n = 0$ (in the notation of the original manuscript, in which m, n are used for the fluxions $\dot{x}$, $\dot{y}$ of x, y). When $d = e$, "the curve turns out to be a conic." In "Mode 7," Newton introduced polar coordinates for the construction of spirals; "the equation of an Archimedean spiral" in these coordinates becomes $(a/b)x = y$, where y is the radius vector (now usually designated r or ρ) and x the angle (ϑ or ϕ).

Newton constructed equations for the transformation of coordinates (as, for example, from polar to Cartesian), and found formulas in both polar and rectangular coordinates for the curvature of a variety of curves, including conics and spirals. On the basis of these results Boyer has quite properly referred to Newton as "an originator of polar coordinates."[67]

Further geometrical results may be found in *Enumeratio linearum tertii ordinis*, first written in 1667 or 1668, and then redone and published, together with *De quadratura*, as an appendix to the *Opticks* (1704).[68] Newton devoted the bulk of the tract to classifying cubic curves into seventy-two "*Classes, Genders, or Orders,* according to the Number of the Dimensions of an Equation, expressing the relation between the *Ordinates* and the *Abscissae*; or which is much at one [that is, the same thing], according to the Number of Points in which they may be cut by a Right Line."

In a brief fifth section, Newton dealt with "The Generation of Curves by Shadows," or the theory of projections, by which he considered the shadows produced "by a luminous point" as projections "on an infinite plane." He showed that the "shadows" (or projections) of conic sections are themselves conic sections, while "those of curves of the second genus will always be curves of the second genus; those of the third genus will always be curves of the third genus; and so on *ad infinitum*." Furthermore, "in the same manner as the circle, projecting its shadow, generates all the conic sections, so the five divergent parabolae, by their shadows, generate all the other curves of the second genus." As C. R. M. Talbot observed, this presentation is "substantially the same as that which is discussed at greater length in the twenty-second lemma [book III, section 5] of the *Principia*, in which it is proposed to 'transmute' any rectilinear or curvilinear figure into another of the same analytical order by means of the method of projections."[69]

The work ends with a brief supplement on "The Organical Description of Curves," leading to the "Description of the Conick-Section by Five Given Points" and including the clear statement, "*The Use of Curves in Geometry is, that by their Intersections Problems may be solved*" (with an example of an equation of the ninth degree). Newton in this tract laid "the foundation for the study of Higher Plane Curves, bringing out the importance of asymptotes, nodes, cusps," according to Turnbull, while Boyer has asserted that it "is the earliest instance of a work devoted solely to graphs of higher plane curves in algebra," and has called attention to the systematic use of two axes and the lack of "hesitation about negative coordinates."[70]

Newton's major mathematical activity had come to a halt by 1696, when he left Cambridge for London. The *Principia*, composed in the 1680's, marked the last great exertion of his mathematical genius, although in the early 1690's he worked on porisms and began a "Liber geometriae," never completed, of which David Gregory gave a good description of the planned whole.[71] For the most part, Newton spent the rest of his mathematical life revising earlier works.

Newton's other chief mathematical activity during the London years lay in furthering his own position against Leibniz in the dispute over priority and originality in the invention of the calculus. But he did respond elegantly to a pair of challenge problems set by Johann [I] Bernoulli in June 1696. The first of these problems was "mechanico-geometrical," to find the curve of swiftest descent. Newton's answer was brief: the "brachistochrone" is a cycloid. The second problem was to find a curve with the following property, "that the two segments [of a right line drawn from a given point through the curve], being

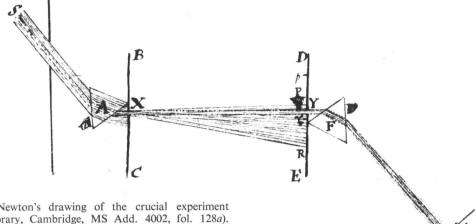

FIGURE 2. Newton's drawing of the crucial experiment (University Library, Cambridge, MS Add. 4002, fol. 128a). Newton himself was a careful draftsman, but the diagrams have become so corrupt in later editions as to violate the fundamental laws of optics.

raised to any given power, and taken together, may make everywhere the same sum."[72]

Newton's analytic solution of the curve of least descent is of particular interest as an early example of what became the calculus of variations. Newton had long been concerned with such problems, and in the *Principia* had included (without proof) his findings concerning the solid of least resistance. When David Gregory asked him how he had found such a solid, Newton sent him an analytic demonstration (using dotted fluxions), of which a version was published as an appendix to the second volume of Motte's English translation of the *Principia*.[73]

Optics. The study of Newton's work in optics has to date generally been limited to his published letters relating to light and color (in *Philosophical Transactions*, beginning in February 1672), his invention of a reflecting telescope and "sextant," and his published *Opticks* of 1704 and later editions (in Latin and English). There has never been an adequate edition or a full translation of the *Lectiones opticae*. Nor, indeed, have Newton's optical manuscripts as yet been thoroughly studied.[74]

Newton's optical work first came to the attention of the Royal Society when a telescope made by him was exhibited there. Newton was elected a fellow shortly thereafter, on 11 January 1672, and responded by offering the Society an account of the discovery that had led him to his invention. It was, he proudly alleged, "the oddest if not the most considerable detection yet made in the operations of nature": the analysis of dispersion and the composition of white light.

In the published account Newton related that in 1666 ("at which time I applied myself to the grinding of Optick glasses of other figures than *Spherical*") he procured a triangular glass prism, "to try therewith

the celebrated *Phaenomena of Colours.*" Light from a tiny hole in a shutter passed through the prism; the multicolored image—to Newton's purported surprise—was of "an *oblong* form," whereas "according to the received laws of Refraction, I expected [it] should have been *circular*." To account for this unexpected appearance, Newton looked into a number of possibilities, among them that "the Rays, after their trajection through the Prisme did not move in curve lines," and was thereby led to the famous "experimentum crucis."[75] In this experiment Newton used two prisms: the first was employed to produce a spectrum on an opaque board (*BC*) into which a small hole had been drilled; a beam of light could thus pass through the hole to a second board (*DE*) with a similar aperture; in this way a narrow beam of light of a single color would be directed to a second prism, and the beam emerging from the second prism would project an image on another board (Fig. 2). Thus, all light reaching the final board had been twice subjected to prismatic dispersion. By rotating the first prism "to and fro slowly about its Axis," Newton allowed different portions of the dispersed light to reach the second prism.

Newton found that the second prism did not produce any further dispersion of the "homogeneal" light (that is, of light of about the same color); he therefore concluded that "Light it self is a *Heterogeneous mixture of differently refrangible Rays*"; and asserted an exact correspondence between color and "degree of Refrangibility" (the least refrangible rays being "disposed to exhibit a *Red* colour," while those of greatest refrangibility are a deep violet). Hence, colors "are not *Qualifications* of Light, derived from Refractions, or Reflections of natural Bodies," as commonly believed, but "*Original* and *connate* properties," differing in the different sorts of rays.[76]

The same experiment led Newton to two further conclusions, both of real consequence. First, he gave up any hope of "the perfection of Telescopes" based on combinations of lenses and turned to the principle of the reflector; second, he held it to be no longer a subject of dispute "whether Light be a Body." Observing, however, that it "is not so easie" to determine specifically "what Light is," he concluded, "I shall not mingle conjectures with certainties."[77]

Newton's letter was, as promised, read at the Royal Society on 6 February 1672. A week later Hooke delivered a report in which he criticized Newton for asserting a conclusion that did not seem to Hooke to follow necessarily from the experiments described, which—in any event—Hooke thought too few. Hooke had his own theory which, he claimed, could equally well explain Newton's experimental results.

In the controversy that followed with Hooke, Huygens, and others, Newton quickly discovered that he had not produced a convincing demonstration of the validity and significance of the conclusions he had drawn from his experiments. The objection was made that Newton had not explored the possibility that theories of color other than the one he had proposed might explain the phenomena. He was further criticized for having favored a corporeal hypothesis of light, and it was even said that his experimental results could not be reproduced.

In reply, Newton attacked the arguments about the "hypothesis" that he was said to have advanced about the nature of light, since he did not consider this issue to be fundamental to his interpretation of the "experimentum crucis." As he explained in reply to Pardies[78] he was not proposing "an hypothesis," but rather "properties of light" which could easily "be proved" and which, had he not held them to be true, he would "rather have . . . rejected as vain and empty speculation, than acknowledged even as an hypothesis." Hooke, however, persisted in the argument. Newton was led to state that he had deliberately declined all hypotheses so as "to speak of *Light* in *general* terms, considering it abstractly, as something or other propagated every way in straight lines from luminous bodies, without determining what that Thing is." But Newton's original communication did assert, "These things being so, it can be no longer disputed, whether there be colours in the dark, nor . . . perhaps, whether Light be a Body." In response to his critics, he emphasized his use of the word "perhaps" as evidence that he was not committed to one or another hypothesis on the nature of light itself.[79]

One consequence of the debate, which was carried on over a period of four years in the pages of the *Philosophical Transactions* and at meetings of the Royal Society, was that Newton wrote out a lengthy "Hypothesis Explaining the Properties of Light Discoursed of in my Several Papers,"[80] in which he supposed that light "is something or other capable of exciting vibrations in the aether," assuming that "there is an aetherial medium much of the same constitution with air, but far rarer, subtler, and more strongly elastic." He suggested the possibility that "muscles are contracted and dilated to cause animal motion," by the action of an "aethereal animal spirit," then went on to offer ether vibration as an explanation of refraction and reflection, of transparency and opacity, of the production of colors, and of diffraction phenomena (including Newton's rings). Even "the gravitating attraction of the earth," he supposed, might "be caused by the continual condensation of some other such like aethereal spirit," which need not be "the main body of phlegmatic aether, but . . . something very thinly and subtilly diffused through it."[81]

The "Hypothesis" was one of two enclosures that Newton sent to Oldenburg, in his capacity of secretary of the Royal Society, together with a letter dated 7 December 1675. The other was a "Discourse of Observations," in which Newton set out "such observations as conduce to further discoveries for completing his theory of light and colours, especially as to the constitution of natural bodies, on which their colours or transparency depend." It also contained Newton's account of his discovery of the "rings" produced by light passing through a thin wedge or layer of air between two pieces of glass. He had based his experiments on earlier ones of a similar kind that had been recorded by Hooke in his *Micrographia* (observation 9). In particular Hooke had described the phenomena occurring when the "lamina," or space between the two glasses, was "*double concave*, that is, thinner in the middle then at the edge"; he had observed "various coloured rings or lines, with differing consecutions or orders of Colours."

When Newton's "Discourse" was read at the Royal Society on 20 January 1676, it contained a paragraph (proposition 3) in which Newton referred to Hooke and the *Micrographia*, "in which book he hath also largely discoursed of this . . . and delivered many other excellent things concerning the colours of thin plates, and other natural bodies, which I have not scrupled to make use of so far as they were for my purpose."[82] In recasting the "Discourse" as parts 1, 2, and 3 of book II of the *Opticks*, however, Newton omitted this statement. It may be assumed that he had carried these experiments so much further than Hooke, introducing careful measurements and quantitative analysis, that he believed them to be his own. Hooke, on the other hand, understandably thought that he deserved more credit for his own contributions —including hypothesis-based explanations—than Newton was willing to allow him.[83] Newton ended the resulting correspondence on a conciliatory note when he wrote in a letter of 5 February 1676, "What Des-Cartes did was a good step. You have added much in several ways, and especially in taking the colours of thin plates into philosophical consideration. If I have seen further it is by standing on the shoulders of Giants."[84]

The opening of Newton's original letter on optics suggests that he began his prism experiments in 1666, presumably in his rooms in Trinity, but was interrupted by the plague at Cambridge, returning to this topic only two years later. Thus the famous eighteen months supposedly spent in Lincolnshire would mark a hiatus in his optical researches, rather than being the period in which he made his major discoveries concerning light and color. As noted earlier, the many pages of optical material in Newton's manuscripts[85] and notebooks have not yet been sufficiently analyzed to provide a precise record of the development of his experiments, concepts, and theories.

The lectures on optics that Newton gave on the assumption of the Lucasian chair likewise remain only incompletely studied. These exist as two complete, but very different, treatises, each with carefully drawn figures. One was deposited in the University Library, as required by the statutes of his professorship, and was almost certainly written out by his roommate, John Wickins,[86] while the other is in Newton's own hand and remained in his possession.[87] These two versions differ notably in their textual content, and also in their division into "lectures," allegedly given on specified dates. A Latin and an English version, both based on the deposited manuscript although differing in textual detail and completeness, were published after Newton's death. The English version, called *Optical Lectures*, was published in 1728, a year before the Latin. The second part of Newton's Latin text was not translated, since, according to the preface, it was "imperfect" and "has since been published in the *Opticks* by Sir Isaac himself with great improvements." The preface further states that the final two sections of this part are composed "in a manner purely Geometrical," and as such they differ markedly from the *Opticks*. The opening lecture (or section 1) pays tribute to Barrow and mentions telescopes, before getting down to the hard business of Newton's discovery "that . . . Rays [of light] in respect to the Quantity of Refraction differ from one another." To show the reader that he had not set forth "Fables instead of Truth," Newton at once gave

"the Reasons and Experiments on which these things are founded." This account, unlike the later letter in the *Philosophical Transactions*, is not autobiographical; nor does it proceed by definitions, axioms, and propositions (proved "by Experiment"), as does the still later *Opticks*.[88]

R. S. Westfall has discussed the two versions of the later of the *Lectiones opticae*, which were first published in 1729;[89] he suggests that Newton eliminated from the *Lectiones* those "parts not immediately relevant to the central concern, the experimental demonstration of his theory of colors." Mathematical portions of the *Lectiones* have been analyzed by D. T. Whiteside, in Newton's *Mathematical Papers*, while J. A. Lohne and Zev Bechler have made major studies of Newton's manuscripts on optics. The formation of Newton's optical concepts and theories has been ably presented by A. I. Sabra; an edition of the *Opticks* is presently being prepared by Henry Guerlac.

Lohne finds great difficulty in repeating Newton's "experimentum crucis,"[90] but more important, he has traced the influence of Descartes, Hooke, and Boyle on Newton's work in optics.[91] He has further found that Newton used a prism in optical experiments much earlier than hitherto suspected—certainly before 1666, and probably before 1665—and has shown that very early in his optical research Newton was explaining his experiments by "the corpuscular hypothesis." In "Questiones philosophicae," Newton wrote: "Blue rays are reflected more than red rays, because they are slower. Each colour is caused by uniformly moving globuli. The uniform motion which gives the sensation of one colour is different from the motion which gives the sensation of any other colour."[92]

Accordingly, Lohne shows how difficult it is to accept the historical narrative proposed by Newton at the beginning of the letter read to the Royal Society on 8 February 1672 and published in the *Philosophical Transactions*. He asks why Newton should have been surprised to find the spectrum oblong, since his "note-books represent the sunbeam as a stream of slower and faster globules occasioning different refrangibility of the different colours?" Newton must, according to Lohne, have "found it opportune to let his theory of colours appear as a Baconian induction from experiments, although it primarily was deduced from speculations." Sabra, in his analysis of Newton's narrative, concludes that not even "the 'fortunate Newton' could have been fortunate enough to have achieved this result in such a smooth manner." Thus one of the most famous examples of the scientific method in operation now seems to have been devised as a sort of scenario by which Newton attempted to convey the impression of a logical train of discovery based on deductions from experiment. The historical record, however, shows that Newton's great leap forward was actually a consequence of implications drawn from profound scientific speculation and insight.[93]

In any event, Newton himself did not publish the *Lectiones opticae*, nor did he produce his planned annotated edition of at least some (and maybe all) of his letters on light and color published in the *Philosophical Transactions*.[94] He completed his English *Opticks*, however, and after repeated requests that he do so, allowed it to be printed in 1704, although he withheld his name, save on the title page of one known copy. It has often been alleged that Newton released the *Opticks* for publication only after Hooke —the last of the original objectors to his theory of light and colors—had died. David Gregory, however, recorded another reason for the publication of the *Opticks* in 1704: Newton, Gregory wrote, had been "provoked" by the appearance, in 1703, of George Cheyne's *Fluxionum methoda inversa* "to publish his [own tract on] Quadratures, and with it, his Light & Colours, &c."[95]

In the *Opticks*, Newton presented his main discoveries and theories concerning light and color in logical order, beginning with eight definitions and eight axioms.[96] Definition 1 of book I reads: "By the Rays of Light I understand its least Parts, and those as well Successive in the same Lines, as Contemporary in several Lines." Eight propositions follow, the first stating that "Lights which differ in Colour, differ also in Degrees of Refrangibility." In appended experiments Newton discussed the appearance of a paper colored half red and half blue when viewed through a prism and showed that a given lens produces red and blue images, respectively, at different distances. The second proposition incorporates a variety of prism experiments as proof that "The Light of the Sun consists of Rays differently refrangible."

The figure given with experiment 10 of this series illustrates "two Prisms tied together in the form of a Parallelopiped" (Fig. 3). Under specified conditions, sunlight entering a darkened room through a small hole *F* in the shutter would not be refracted by the parallelopiped and would emerge parallel to the incident beam *FM*, from which it would pass by refraction through a third prism *IKH*, which would by refraction "cast the usual Colours of the Prism upon the opposite Wall." Turning the parallelopiped about its axis, Newton found that the rays producing the several colors were successively "taken out of the transmitted Light" by "total Reflexion"; first "the

Rays which in the third Prism had suffered the greatest Refraction and painted [the wall] with violet and blew were . . . taken out of the transmitted Light, the rest remaining," then the rays producing green, yellow, orange, and red were "taken out" as the parallelopiped was rotated yet further. Newton thus experimentally confirmed the "experimentum crucis," showing that the light emerging from the two prisms "is compounded of Rays differently Refrangible, seeing [that] the more Refrangible Rays may be taken out while the less Refrangible remain." The arrangement of prisms is the basis of the important discovery reported in book II, part 1, observation 1.

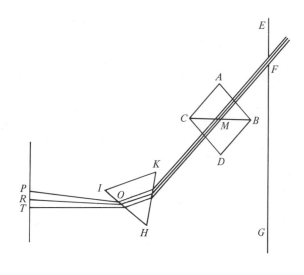

FIGURE 3

In proposition 6 Newton showed that, contrary to the opinions of previous writers, the sine law actually holds for each single color. The first part of book I ends with Newton's remarks on the impossibility of improving telescopes by the use of color-corrected lenses and his discussion of his consequent invention of the reflecting telescope (Fig. 4).

In the second part of book I, Newton dealt with colors produced by reflection and refraction (or transmission), and with the appearance of colored objects in relation to the color of the light illuminating them. He discussed colored pigments and their mixture and geometrically constructed a color wheel, drawing an analogy between the primary colors in a compound color and the "seven Musical Tones or Intervals of the eight Sounds, *Sol, la, fa, sol, la, mi, fa, sol*. . . ."[97]

Proposition 9, "Prob. IV. By the discovered Properties of Light to explain the Colours of the Rain-bow," is devoted to the theory of the rainbow. Descartes had developed a geometrical theory, but had

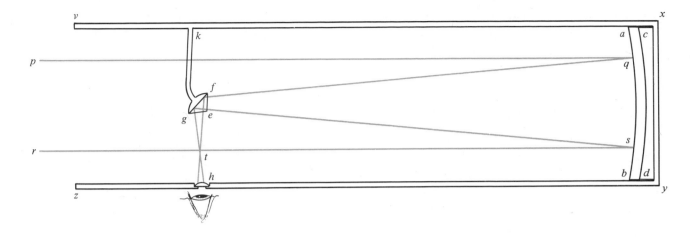

FIGURE 4. Newton's method "To shorten Telescopes": *efg* represents the prism, *abcd* the speculum, and *h* the lens.

used a single index of refraction (250:187) in his computation of the path of light through each raindrop.[98] Newton's discovery of the difference in refrangibility of the different colors composing white light, and their separation or dispersion as a consequence of refraction, on the other hand, permitted him to compute the radii of the bows for the separate colors. He used 108:81 as the index of refraction for red and 109:81 for violet, and further took into consideration that the light of the sun does not proceed from a single point. He determined the widths of the primary and secondary bows to be 2°15′ and 3°40′, respectively, and gave a formula for computing the radii of bows of any order *n* (and hence for orders of the rainbow greater than 2) for any given index of refraction.[99] Significant as Newton's achievement was, however, he gave only what can be considered a "first approximation to the solution of the problem," since a full explanation, particularly of the supernumerary or spurious bows, must require the general principle of interference and the "rigorous application of the wave theory."

Book II, which constitutes approximately one third of the *Opticks*, is devoted largely to what would later be called interference effects, growing out of the topics Newton first published in his 1675 letter to the Royal Society. Newton's discoveries in this regard would seem to have had their origin in the first experiment that he describes (book II, part 1, observation 1); he had, he reported, compressed "two Prisms hard together that their sides (which by chance were a very little convex) might somewhere touch one another" (as in the figure provided for experiment 10 of book I, part 1). He found "the place in which they touched" to be "absolutely transparent," as if there had been one "continued piece of Glass," even though there was

total reflection from the rest of the surface; but "it appeared like a black or dark spot, by reason that little or no sensible light was reflected from thence, as from other places." When "looked through," it seemed like "a hole in that Air which was formed into a thin Plate, by being compress'd between the Glasses." Newton also found that this transparent spot "would become much broader than otherwise" when he pressed the two prisms "very hard together."

Rotating the two prisms around their common axis (observation 2) produced "many slender Arcs of Colours" which, the prisms being rotated further, "were compleated into Circles or Rings." In observation 4 Newton wrote that

> To observe more nicely the order of the Colours . . . I took two Object-glasses, the one a Plano-convex for a fourteen Foot Telescope, and the other a large double Convex for one of about fifty Foot; and upon this, laying the other with its plane side downwards, I pressed them slowly together, to make the Colours successively emerge in the middle of the Circles, and then slowly lifted the upper Glass from the lower to make them successively vanish again in the same place.

It was thus evident that there was a direct correlation between particular colors of rings and the thickness of the layer of the entrapped air. In this way, as Mach observed, "Newton acquired a complete insight into the whole phenomenon, and at the same time the possibility of determining the thickness of the air gap from the known radius of curvature of the glass."[100]

Newton varied the experiment by using different lenses, and by wetting them, so that the gap or layer was composed of water rather than air. He also studied the rings that were produced by light of a single color, separated out of a prismatic spectrum; he found that in a darkened room the rings from a single color extended to the very edge of the lens. Furthermore, as he noted in observation 13, "the Circles which the red Light made" were "manifestly bigger than those which were made by the blue and violet"; he found it "very pleasant to see them gradually swell or contract accordingly as the Colour of the Light was changed." He concluded that the rings visible in white light represented a superimposition of the rings of the several colors, and that the alternation of light and dark rings for each color must indicate a succession of regions of reflection and transmission of light, produced by the thin layer of air between the two glasses. He set down the latter conclusion in observation 15: "And from thence the origin of these Rings is manifest; namely that the Air between the Glasses, according to its various thickness, is disposed in some places to reflect, and in others to transmit the Light

of any one Colour (as you may see represented . . .) and in the same place to reflect that of one Colour where it transmits that of another" (Fig. 5).

Book II, part 2, of the *Opticks* has a nomogram in which Newton summarized his measures and computations and demonstrated the agreement of his analysis of the ring phenomenon with his earlier conclusions drawn from his prism experiments—"that whiteness is a dissimilar mixture of all Colours, and that Light is a mixture of Rays endued with all those Colours." The experiments of book II further confirmed Newton's earlier findings "that every Ray have its proper and constant degree of Refrangibility connate with it, according to which its refraction is ever justly and regularly perform'd," from which he argued that "it follows, that the colorifick Dispositions of Rays are also connate with them, and immutable." The colors of the physical universe are thus derived "only from the various Mixtures or Separations of

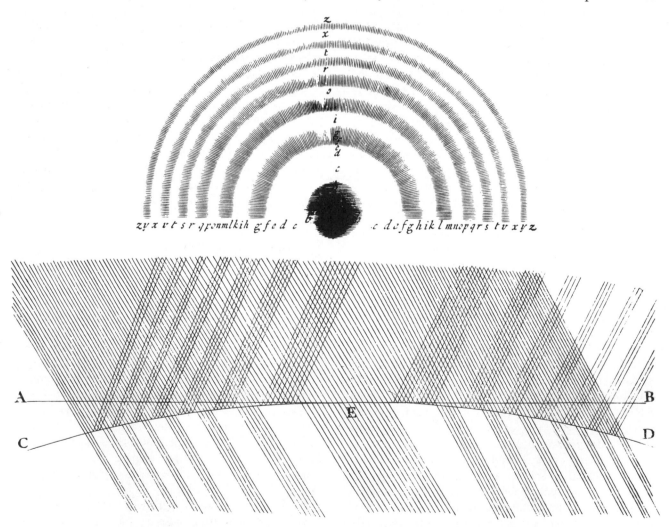

FIGURE 5. Two drawings from book II, part 1, plate 1 of the 1704 edition of the *Opticks*, illustrating Newton's studies of what are now called Newton's rings.

Rays, by virtue of their different Refrangibility or Reflexibility"; the study of color thus becomes "a Speculation as truly mathematical as any other part of Opticks."[101]

In part 3 of book II, Newton analyzed "the permanent Colours of natural Bodies, and the Analogy between them and the Colours of thin transparent Plates." He concluded that the smallest possible subdivisions of matter must be transparent, and their dimensions optically determinable. A table accompanying proposition 10 gives the refractive powers of a variety of substances "in respect of . . . Densities." Proposition 12 contains Newton's conception of "fits":

> Every Ray of Light in its passage through any refracting Surface is put into a certain transient Constitution or State, which in the progress of the Ray returns at equal Intervals, and disposes the Ray at every return to be easily transmitted through the next refracting Surface, and between the returns to be easily reflected by it.

The succeeding definition is more specific: "The returns of the disposition of any Ray to be reflected I will call its *Fits of easy Reflection*, and those of its disposition to be transmitted its *Fits of easy Transmission*, and the space it passes between every return and the next return, the *Interval of its Fits*."

The "fits" of easy reflection and of easy refraction could thus be described as a numerical sequence; if reflection occurs at distances 0, 2, 4, 6, 8, $\cdots$, from some central point, then refraction (or transmission) must occur at distances 1, 3, 5, 7, 9, $\cdots$. Newton did not attempt to explain this periodicity, stating that "I do not here enquire" into the question of "what kind of action or disposition this is." He declined to speculate "whether it consists in a circulating or a vibrating motion of the Ray, or of the Medium, or something else," contenting himself "with the bare Discovery, that the Rays of Light are by some cause or other alternately disposed to be reflected or refracted for many vicissitudes."

Newton thus integrated the periodicity of light into his theoretical work (it had played only a marginal part in Hooke's theory). His work was, moreover, based upon extraordinarily accurate measurements—so much so that when Thomas Young devised an explanation of Newton's rings based on the revived wave theory of light and the new principle of interference, he used Newton's own data to compute the wavelengths and wave numbers of the principal colors in the visible spectrum and attained results that are in close agreement with those generally accepted today.

In part 4 of book II, Newton addressed himself to "the Reflexions and Colours of thick transparent polish'd Plates." This book ends with an analysis of halos around the sun and moon and the computation of their size, based on the assumption that they are produced by clouds of water or by hail. This led him to the series of eleven observations that begin the third and final book, "concerning the Inflexions of the Rays of Light, and the Colours made thereby," in which Newton took up the class of optical phenomena previously studied by Grimaldi,[102] in which "fringes" are produced at the edges of the shadows of objects illuminated by light "let into a dark Room through a very small hole." Newton discussed such fringes surrounding the projected shadows of a hair, the edge of a knife, and a narrow slit.

Newton concluded the first edition of the *Opticks* (1704) with a set of sixteen queries, introduced "in order to a further search to be made by others." He had at one time hoped he might carry the investigations further, but was "interrupted," and wrote that he could not "now think of taking these things into farther Consideration." In the eighteenth century and after, these queries were considered the most important feature of the *Opticks*—particularly the later ones, which were added in two stages, in the Latin *Optice* of 1706 and in the second English edition of 1717–1718.

The original sixteen queries at once go beyond mere experiments on diffraction phenomena. In query 1, Newton suggested that bodies act on light at a distance to bend the rays; and in queries 2 and 3, he attempted to link differences in refrangibility with differences in "flexibility" and the bending that may produce color fringes. In query 4, he inquired into a single principle that, by "acting variously in various Circumstances," may produce reflection, refraction, and inflection, suggesting that the bending (in reflection and refraction) begins before the rays "arrive at the Bodies." Query 5 concerns the mutual interaction of bodies and light, the heat of bodies being said to consist of having "their parts [put] into a vibrating motion"; while in query 6 Newton proposed a reason why black bodies "conceive heat more easily from Light than those of other Colours." He then discussed the action between light and "sulphureous" bodies, the causes of heat in friction, percussion, putrefaction, and so forth, and defined fire (in query 9) and flame (in query 10), discussing various chemical operations. In query 11, he extended his speculations on heat and vapors to sun and stars. The last four queries (12 to 16) of the original set deal with vision, associated with "Vibrations" (excited by "the Rays of Light") which cause sight by "being propagated along the solid Fibres of the optick Nerves into the Brain." In query 13 specific wavelengths are associated with each of several colors. In query 15 Newton discussed binocular vision, along with other aspects of seeing, while in query 16 he took up the phenomenon of persistence of vision.

Newton has been much criticized for believing dispersion to be independent of the material of the prism and for positing a constant relation between deviation and dispersion in all refractive substances. He thus dismissed the possibility of correcting for chromatic aberration in lenses, and directed attention from refraction to reflecting telescopes.[103]

Newton is often considered to be the chief advocate of the corpuscular or emission theory of light. Lohne has shown that Newton originally did believe in a simple corpuscular theory, an aspect of Newton's science also forcibly brought out by Sabra. Challenged by Hooke, Newton proposed a hypothesis of ether waves associated with (or caused by) these corpuscles, one of the strongest arguments for waves probably being his own discovery of periodicity in "Newton's rings." Unlike either Hooke or Huygens, who is usually held to be the founder of the wave theory but who denied periodicity to waves of light, Newton postulated periodicity as a fundamental property of waves of (or associated with) light, at the same time that he suggested that a particular wavelength characterizes the light producing each color. Indeed, in the queries, he even suggested that vision might be the result of the propagation of waves in the optic nerves. But despite this dual theory, Newton always preferred the corpuscle concept, whereby he might easily explain both rectilinear propagation and polarization, or "sides." The corpuscle concept lent itself further to an analysis by forces (as in section 14 of book I of the *Principia*), thus establishing a universal analogy between the action of gross bodies (of the atoms or corpuscles composing such bodies), and of light. These latter topics are discussed below in connection with the later queries of the *Opticks*.

Dynamics, Astronomy, and the Birth of the "Principia." Newton recorded his early thoughts on motion in various student notebooks and documents.[104] While still an undergraduate, he would certainly have studied the Aristotelian (or neo-Aristotelian) theory of motion and he is known to have read Magirus' *Physiologiae peripateticae libri sex*; his notes include a "Cap:4. De Motu" (wherein "Motus" is said to be the Aristotelian ἐντελέχεια). Extracts from Magirus occur in a notebook begun by Newton in 1661;[105] it is a repository of jottings from his student years on a variety of physical and non-physical topics. In it Newton recorded, among other extracts, Kepler's third law, "that the mean distances of the primary Planets from the Sunne are in

sesquialter proportion to the periods of their revolutions in time."[106] This and other astronomical material, including a method of finding planetary positions by approximation, comes from Thomas Streete's *Astronomia Carolina.*

Here, too, Newton set down a note on Horrox' observations, and an expression of concern about the vacuum and the gravity of bodies; he recorded, from "Galilaeus," that "an iron ball" falls freely through "100 braces Florentine or cubits [or 49.01 ells, perhaps 66 yards] in 5″ of an hower." Notes of a later date—on matter, motion, gravity, and levity—give evidence of Newton's having read Charleton (on Gassendi), Digby (on Galileo), Descartes, and Henry More.

In addition to acquiring this miscellany of information, making tables of various kinds of observations, and supplementing his reading in Streete by Wing (and, probably, by Galileo's *Sidereus nuncius* and Gassendi's epitome of Copernican astronomy), Newton was developing his own revisions of the principles of motion. Here the major influence on his thought was Descartes (especially the *Principia philosophiae* and the Latin edition of the correspondence, both of which Newton cited in early writings), and Galileo (whose *Dialogue* he knew in the Salusbury version, and whose ideas he would have encountered in works by Henry More, by Charleton and Wallis, and in Digby's *Two Essays*).

An entry in Newton's Waste Book,[107] dated 20 January 1664, shows a quantitative approach to problems of inelastic collision. It was not long before Newton went beyond Descartes's law of conservation, correcting it by algebraically taking into account direction of motion rather than numerical products of size and speed of bodies. In a series of axioms he declared a principle of inertia (in "Axiomes" 1 and 2); he then asserted a relation between "force" and change of motion; and he gave a set of rules for elastic collision.[108] In "Axiome" 22, he had begun to approach the idea of centrifugal force by considering the pressure exerted by a sphere rolling around the inside surface of a cylinder. On the first page of the Waste Book, Newton had quantitated the centrifugal force by conceiving of a body moving along a square inscribed in a circle, and then adding up the shocks at each "reflection." As the number of sides were increased, the body in the limiting case would be "reflected by the sides of an equilateral circumscribed polygon of an infinite number of sides (i.e. by the circle it selfe)." Herivel has pointed out the near equivalence of such results to the early proof mentioned by Newton at the end of the scholium to proposition 4, book I, of the

Principia. Evidently Newton learned the law of centrifugal force almost a decade before Huygens, who published a similar result in 1673. One early passage of the Waste Book also contains an entry on Newton's theory of conical pendulums.[109]

According to Newton himself, the "notion of gravitation" came to his mind "as he sat in a contemplative mood," and "was occasioned by the fall of an apple."[110] He postulated that, since the moon is sixty times as far away from the center of the earth as the apple, by an inverse-square relation it would accordingly have an acceleration of free fall $1/(60)^2 = 1/3600$ that of the apple. This "moon test" proved the inverse-square law of force which Newton said he "deduced" from combining "Kepler's Rule of the periodical times of the Planets being in a sesquialterate proportion of their distances from the Centers of the Orbs"—that is, by Kepler's third law, that $R^3/T^2 =$ constant, combined with the law of central (centrifugal) force. Clearly if $F \propto V^2/R$ for a force F acting on a body moving with speed V in a circle of radius R (with period T), it follows simply and at once that

$$F \propto V^2/R = 4\pi^2 R^2/T^2 R = 4\pi^2/R^2 \times (R^3/T^2).$$

Since R^3/T^2 is a constant, $F \propto 1/R^2$.

An account by Whiston states that Newton took an incorrect value for the radius of the earth and so got a poor agreement between theory and observation, "which made Sir *Isaac* suspect that this Power was partly that of Gravity, and partly that of *Cartesius*'s Vortices," whereupon "he threw aside the Paper of his Calculation, and went to other Studies." Pemberton's narration is in agreement as to the poor value taken for the radius of the earth, but omits the reference to Cartesian vortices. Newton himself said (later) only that he made the two calculations and "found them [to] answer pretty nearly."[111] In other words, he calculated the falling of the moon and the falling of a terrestrial object, and found the two to be (only) approximately equal.

A whole tradition has grown up (originated by Adams and Glaisher, and most fully expounded by Cajori)[112] that Newton was put off not so much by taking a poor value for the radius of the earth as by his inability then to prove that a sphere made up of uniform concentric shells acts gravitationally on an external point mass as if all its mass were concentrated at its center (proposition 71, book I, book III, of the *Principia*). No firm evidence has ever been found that would support Cajori's conclusion that the lack of this theorem was responsible for the supposed twenty-year delay in Newton's announcement of his "discovery"

of the inverse-square law of gravitation. Nor is there evidence that Newton ever attempted to compute the attraction of a sphere until summer 1685, when he was actually writing the *Principia.*

An existing document does suggest that Newton may have made just such calculations as Whiston and Pemberton described, calculations in which Newton appears to have used a figure for the radius of the Earth that he found in Salusbury's version of Galileo's *Dialogue*, 3,500 Italian miles *(milliaria)*, in which one mile equals 5,000, rather than 5,280, feet.[113] Here, some time before 1669, Newton stated, to quote him in translation, "Finally, among the primary planets, since the cubes of their distances from the Sun are reciprocally as the squared numbers of their periods in a given time, their endeavours of recess from the Sun will be reciprocally as the squares of their distances from the Sun," and he then gave numerical examples from each of the six primary planets. A. R. Hall has shown that this manuscript is the paper referred to by Newton in his letter to Halley of 20 June 1686, defending his claim to priority of discovery of the inverse-square law against Hooke's claims. It would have been this paper, too, that David Gregory saw and described in 1694, when Newton let him glance over a manuscript earlier than "the year 1669."

This document, however important it may be in enabling us to define Newton's values for the size of the earth, does not contain an actual calculation of the moon test, nor does it refer anywhere to other than centrifugal "endeavours" from the sun. But it does show that when Newton wrote it he had not found firm and convincing grounds on which to assert what Whiteside has called a perfect "balance between (apparent) planetary centrifugal force and that of solar gravity."[114]

By the end of the 1660's Newton had studied the Cartesian principles of motion and had taken a critical stand with regard to them. His comments occur in an essay of the 1670's or late 1660's, beginning "De gravitatione et aequipondio fluidorum,"[115] in which he discussed extensively Descartes's *Principia* and also referred to a letter that formed part of the correspondence with Mersenne. Newton further set up a series of definitions and axioms, then ventured "to dispose of his [Descartes's] fictions." A large part of the essay deals with space and extension; for example, Newton criticized Descartes's view "that extension is not infinite but rather indefinite." In this essay Newton also defined force ("the causal principle of motion and rest"), conatus (or "endeavour"), impetus, inertia, and gravity. Then, in the traditional manner, he reckoned "the quantity of these powers" in "a double way: that is, according to intension or extension." He defined bodies, in the later medieval language of the intension and remission of forms, as "denser when their inertia is more intense, and rarer when it is more remiss."

In a final set of "Propositions on Non-Elastic Fluids" (in which there are two axioms and two propositions), axiom 2, "Bodies in contact press each other equally," suggests that the eventual third law of motion (*Principia*, axiom 3: "To every action is always opposed an equal and opposite reaction") may have arisen in application to fluids as well as to the impact of bodies. The latter topic occurs in another early manuscript, "The Lawes of Motion," written about 1666 and almost certainly antedating the essay on Descartes and his *Principia*.[116] Here Newton developed some rules for the impact of "bodyes which are absolutely hard," and then tempered them for application to "bodyes here amongst us," characterized by "a relenting softnesse & springynesse," which "makes their contact be for some time in more points than one."

Newton's attention to the problems of elastic and inelastic impact is manifest throughout his early writings on dynamics. In the *Principia* it is demonstrated by the emphasis he there gave the concept of force as an "impulse," and by a second law of motion (Lex II, in all editions of the *Principia*) in which he set forth the proportionality of such an impulse (acting instantaneously) to the change in momentum it produces.[117] In the scholium to the laws of motion Newton further discussed elastic and inelastic impact, referring to papers of the late 1660's by Wallis, Wren, and Huygens. He meanwhile developed his concept of a continuously acting force as the limit of a series of impulses occurring at briefer and briefer intervals *in infinitum*.[118]

Indeed, it was not until 1679, or some time between 1680 and 1684, following an exchange with Hooke, that Newton achieved his mature grasp of dynamical principles, recognizing the significance of Kepler's area law, which he had apparently just encountered. Only during the years 1684–1686, when, stimulated by Halley, he wrote out the various versions of the tract *De motu* and its successors and went on to compose the *Principia*, did Newton achieve full command of his insight into mathematical dynamics and celestial mechanics. At that time he clarified the distinction between mass and weight, and saw how these two quantities were related under a variety of circumstances.

Newton's exchange with Hooke occurred when the latter, newly appointed secretary of the Royal Society, wrote to Newton to suggest a private philosophical correspondence. In particular, Hooke asked Newton for his "objections against any hypothesis or opinion of mine," particularly "that of compounding the celestiall motions of the planetts of a direct motion by the tangent & an attractive motion towards the centrall body. . . ." Newton received the letter in November, some months after the death of his mother, and evidently did not wish to take up the problem. He introduced, instead, "a fancy of my own about discovering the Earth's diurnal motion, a spiral path that a freely falling body would follow as it supposedly fell to Earth, moved through the Earth's surface into the interior without material resistance, and eventually spiralled to (or very near to) the Earth's centre, after a few revolutions."[119]

Hooke responded that such a path would not be a spiral. He said that, according to "my theory of circular motion," in the absence of resistance, the body would not move in a spiral but in "a kind [of] Elleptueid," and its path would "resemble an Ellipse." This conclusion was based, said Hooke, on "my Theory of Circular Motions [being] compounded by a Direct [that is, tangential] motion and an attractive one to a Centre." Newton could not ignore this direct contradiction of his own expressed opinion. Accordingly, on 13 December 1679, he wrote Hooke that "I agree with you that . . . if its gravity be supposed uniform [the body would] not descend in a spiral to the very centre but circulate with an alternate descent & ascent." The cause was "its *vis centrifuga* & gravity alternately overballancing one another." This conception was very like Borelli's, and Newton imagined that "the body will not describe an Ellipsoeid," but a quite different figure. Newton here refused to accept the notion of an ellipse produced by gravitation decreasing as some power of the distance—although he had long before proved that for circular motion a combination of Kepler's third law and the rule for centrifugal force would yield a law of centrifugal force in the inverse square of the distance. There is no record of whether his reluctance was due to the poor agreement of the earlier moon test or to some other cause.

Fortunately for the advancement of science, Hooke kept pressing Newton. In a letter of 6 January 1680 he wrote ". . . But my supposition is that the Attraction always is in a duplicate proportion to the Distance from the Centre Reciprocall, and Consequently that the Velocity will be in a subduplicate proportion to the Attraction, and Consequently as Kepler Supposes Reciprocall to the Distance." We shall see below that this statement, often cited to support Hooke's claim to priority over Newton in the discovery of the inverse-square law, actually shows that Hooke was not a very good mathematician. As Newton proved, the force law here proposed contradicts the alleged velocity relation.

Hooke also claimed that this conception "doth very Intelligibly and truly make out all the Appearances of the Heavens," and that "the finding out the proprietys of a Curve made by two principles will be of great Concerne to Mankind, because the Invention of the Longitude by the Heavens is a necessary Consequence of it." After a few days, Hooke went on to challenge Newton directly:

> . . . It now remains to know the proprietys of a curve Line (not circular nor concentricall) made by a centrall attractive power which makes the velocitys of Descent from the tangent Line or equall straight motion at all Distances in a Duplicate proportion to the Distances Reciprocally taken. I doubt not but that by your excellent method you will easily find out what that Curve must be, and its proprietys, and suggest a physicall Reason of this proportion.[120]

Newton did not reply, but he later recorded his next steps:

> I found now that whatsoever was the law of the forces which kept the Planets in their Orbs, the areas described by a Radius drawn from them to the Sun would be proportional to the times in which they were described. And . . . that their Orbs would be such Ellipses as Kepler had described [when] the forces which kept them in their Orbs about the Sun were as the squares of their . . . distances from the Sun reciprocally.[121]

Newton's account seems to be reliable; the proof he devised must have been that written out by him later in his "De motu corporum in gyrum."[122]

Newton's solution is based on his method of limits, and on the use of infinitesimals.[123] He considered the motion along an ellipse from one point to another during an indefinitely small interval of time, and evaluated the deflection from the tangent during that interval, assuming the deflection to be proportional to the inverse square of the distance from a focus. As one of the two points on the ellipse approaches the other, Newton found that the area law supplies the essential condition in the limit.[124] In short, Newton showed that if the area law holds, then the elliptical shape of an orbit implies that any force directed to a focus must vary inversely as the square of the distance.

But it was also incumbent upon Newton to show the significance of the area law itself; he therefore proved that the area law is a necessary and sufficient condition that the force on a moving body be directed to a center. Thus, for the first time, the true significance of Kepler's first two laws of planetary

motion was revealed: that the area condition was equivalent to the action of a central force, and that the occurrence of the ellipse under this condition demonstrates that the force is as the inverse square of the distance. Newton further showed the law of areas to be only another aspect of the law of inertia, since in linear inertial motion, in the absence of external forces, equal areas are swept out in equal times by a line from the moving body directed toward any point not on the line of motion.[125]

Newton was thus quite correct in comparing Hooke's claim and Kepler's, as he wrote to Halley on 20 June 1686:

> But grant I received it [the hypothesis of the inverse-square relation] afterwards [that is, after he had come upon it by himself, and independently of Hooke] from Mr Hook, yet have I as great a right to it as to the Ellipsis. For as Kepler knew the Orb to be not circular but oval & guest it to be Elliptical, so Mr Hook without knowing what I have found out since his letters to me, can know no more but that the proportion was duplicate *quam proximè* at great distances from the center, & only guest it to be so accurately & guest amiss in extending that proportion down to the very center, whereas Kepler guest right at the Ellipsis. And so Mr Hook found less of the Proportion than Kepler of the Ellipsis.[126]

What Newton "found out" after his correspondence with Hooke in 1679 was the proof that a homogeneous sphere (or a sphere composed of homogeneous spherical shells) will gravitate as if all its mass were concentrated at its geometric center.

Newton refrained from pointing out that Hooke's lack of mathematical ability prevented him (and many of those who have supported his claim) from seeing that the "approximate" law of speed ($v \propto 1/r$) is

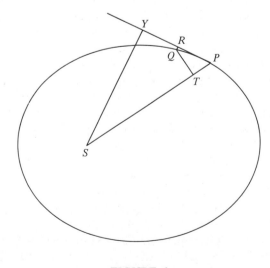

FIGURE 6

inconsistent with the true area law and does not accord with a force law of the form $f \propto 1/r^2$. Newton proved (Fig. 6: *Principia*, book I, proposition 16), that the speed at any point in an elliptical orbit is inversely proportional to the perpendicular dropped from the sun (focus) to the tangent drawn to the ellipse at that point, rather than being inversely proportional to the simple distance as Hooke and others had supposed; these two quantities being, of course, the same at the apsides. In the second edition of the *Principia* (1713) Newton shifted the corollaries to propositions 1 and 2, introducing a new set of corollaries to proposition 1, with the result that a prominent place was given to the true speed law.

Newton therefore deserves sole credit for recognizing the significance of the area law, a matter of some importance between 1679 and 1684. Following the exchange with Hooke in the earlier year, however, Newton did not at once go on to complete his work in celestial mechanics, although he did become interested in comets, corresponding with Flamsteed about their motion. He was converted from a belief in the straight-line motion of comets to a belief in parabolic paths, and thereafter attributed the motions of comets (in conic sections) to the action of the inverse-square law of the gravitation of the sun. He was particularly concerned with the comet of 1680, and in book III of the *Principia* devoted much space to its path.

In 1684, Halley visited Newton to ask about the path a planet would follow under the action of an inverse-square force: Wren, Hooke, and he had all been unsuccessful in satisfactorily resolving the matter, although Hooke had asserted (vainly) that he could do it. When Newton said to Hooke that he himself had "calculated" the result and that it was "an Ellipsis," Halley pressed him "for his calculation," but Newton could not find it among his papers and had to send it to Halley at a later date, in November. Halley then went back to Cambridge, where he saw "a curious treatise, *De Motu*." He obtained Newton's promise to send it "to the [Royal] Society to be entered upon their Register,"[127] and Newton, thus encouraged, wrote out a *De motu corporum*, of which the first section largely corresponds to book I of the *Principia* (together with an earnest of what was to become book II), while the second represents a popular account of what was later presented in book III.

Texts of both parts were deposited in the University Library, as if they were Newton's professorial lectures for 1684, 1685, and 1687; the second was published posthumously in both Latin and English, with the introduction of a new and misleading title of *De mundi*

systemate, or *The System of the World*. (This misnomer has ever since caused the second part of *De motu* to be confused with book III of the *Principia*, which is subtitled "De mundi systemate.")

Newton composed the *Principia* in a surprisingly short time.[128] The manuscript of book I was presented on 28 April 1686 to the Royal Society, which ordered it to be printed, although in the event Halley paid the costs and saw the work through the press. Halley's job was not an easy one; when Hooke demanded credit in print for his share in the inverse-square law, Newton demurred and even threatened to suppress book III. Halley fortunately dissuaded Newton from so mutilating his great treatise.

On 1 March 1687 Newton wrote to Halley that book II had been sent to him "by the Coach." The following 5 April Halley reported to Newton that he had received book III, "the last part of your divine Treatise." The printing was completed on 5 July 1687. The first edition included a short preface by Newton and an introductory ode to Newton by Halley—but book III ended abruptly, in the midst of a discussion of comets. Newton had originally drafted a "Conclusio" dealing with general aspects of natural philosophy and the theory of matter,[129] but he suppressed it. The famous conclusion, the "Scholium Generale," was first published some twenty-six years later, in 1713, in the second edition.

The development of Newton's views on comets may be traced through his correspondence with Flamsteed[130] and with Halley, and by comparing the first and second editions of the *Principia*. From Flamsteed he obtained information not only on comets, but also on the distances and periods of the satellites of Jupiter (which data appear in the beginning of book III of the *Principia* as a primary instance of Kepler's third law), and on the possible influence of Jupiter on the motion of Saturn. When Newton at first believed the great comet observed November 1680–March 1681 to be a pair of comets moving (as Kepler proposed) in straight lines, although in opposite directions, it was Flamsteed who convinced him that there was only one, observed coming and going, and that it must have turned about the sun.[131] Newton worked out a parabolic path for the comet of 1680 that was consistent with the observations of Flamsteed and others, the details of which occupy a great part of book III of the *Principia*. Such a parabolic path had been shown in book I to result from the inverse-square law under certain initial conditions, differing from those producing ellipses and hyperbolas.

In 1695, Halley postulated that the path of the comet of 1680 was an elongated ellipse—a path not very distinguishable from a parabola in the region of the sun, but significantly different in that the ellipse implies periodic returns of the comet—and worked out the details with Newton. In the second and third editions of the *Principia*, Newton gave tables for both the parabolic and elliptical orbits; he asserted unequivocally that Halley had found "a remarkable comet" appearing every seventy-five years or so, and added that Halley had "computed the motions of the comet in this elliptic orbit." Nevertheless, Newton himself remained primarily concerned with parabolic orbits. In the conclusion to the example following proposition 41 (on the comet of 1680), Newton said that "comets are a sort of planets revolved in very eccentric orbits about the sun." Even so, the proposition itself states (in all editions): "From three given observations to determine the orbit of a comet moving in a parabola."

Mathematics in the "Principia." The *Philosophiae naturalis principia mathematica* is, as its title suggests, an exposition of a natural philosophy conceived in terms of new principles based on Newton's own innovations in mathematics. It is too often described as a treatise in the style of Greek geometry, since on superficial examination it appears to have been written in a synthetic geometrical style.[132] But a close examination shows that this external Euclidean form masks the true and novel mathematical character of Newton's treatise, which was recognized even in his own day. (L'Hospital, for example—to Newton's delight—observed in the preface to his 1696 *Analyse des infiniment petits*, the first textbook on the infinitesimal calculus, that Newton's "excellent Livre intitulé *Philosophiae Naturalis principia Mathematica* . . . est presque tout de ce calcul.") Indeed, the most superficial reading of the *Principia* must show that, proposition by proposition and lemma by lemma, Newton usually proceeded by establishing geometrical conditions and their corresponding ratios and then at once introducing some carefully defined limiting process. This manner of proof or "invention," in marked distinction to the style of the classical Greek geometers, is based on a set of general principles of limits, or of prime and ultimate ratios, posited by Newton so as to deal with nascent or evanescent quantities or ratios of such quantities.

The doctrine of limits occurs in the *Principia* in a set of eleven lemmas that constitute section 1 of book I. These lemmas justify Newton in dealing with areas as limits of sums of inscribed or circumscribed rectangles (whose breadth → 0, or whose number → ∞), and in assuming the equality, in the limit, of arc, chord, and tangent (lemma 7), based on the proportionality of "homologous sides of similar figures, whether curvilinear or rectilinear" (lemma 5),

whose "areas are as the squares of the homologous sides." Newton's mathematical principles are founded on a concept of limit disclosed at the very beginning of lemma 1, "Quantities, and the ratios of quantities, which in any finite time converge continually to equality, and before the end of that time approach nearer to each other than by any given difference, become ultimately equal."

Newton further devoted the concluding scholium of section 1 to his concept of limit, and his method of taking limits, stating the guiding principle thus: "These lemmas are premised to avoid the tediousness of deducing involved demonstrations *ad absurdum*, according to the method of the ancient geometers." While he could have produced shorter ("more contracted") demonstrations by the "method of indivisibles," he judged the "hypothesis of indivisibles "to be "somewhat harsh" and not geometrical:

I chose rather to reduce the demonstrations of the following propositions to the first and last sums and ratios of nascent and evanescent quantities, that is, to the limits of those sums and ratios; and so to premise, as short as I could, the demonstrations of those limits. For hereby the same thing is performed as by the method of indivisibles; and now those principles being demonstrated, we may use them with greater safety. Therefore if hereafter I should happen to consider quantities as made up of particles, or should use little curved lines for right ones, I would not be understood to mean indivisibles, but evanescent divisible quantities; not the sums and ratios of determinate parts, but always the limits of sums and ratios; and that the force of such demonstrations always depends on the method laid down in the foregoing Lemmas.

Newton was aware that his principles were open to criticism on the ground "that there is no ultimate proportion of evanescent quantities; because the proportion, before the quantities have vanished, is not the ultimate, and when they are vanished, is none"; and he anticipated any possible unfavorable reaction by insisting that "the ultimate ratio of evanescent quantities" is to be understood to mean "the ratio of the quantities not before they vanish, nor afterwards, but [that] with which they vanish." In a "like manner, the first ratio of nascent quantities is that with which they begin to be," and "the first or last sum is that with which they begin and cease to be (or to be augmented or diminished)." Comparing such ratios and sums to velocities (for "it may be alleged, that a body arriving at a certain place, and there stopping, has no ultimate velocity; because the velocity, before the body comes to the place, is not its ultimate velocity; when it has arrived, there is none"), he imagined the existence of "a limit which the velocity at the end of the motion may attain, but not exceed," which limit is "the ultimate velocity," or "that velocity with which the body arrives at its last place, and with which the motion ceases." By analogy, he argued, "there is the like limit in all quantities and proportions that begin and cease to be," and "such limits are certain and definite." Hence, "to determine the same is a problem strictly geometrical," and thus may be used legitimately "in determining and demonstrating any other thing that is also geometrical."

In short, Newton wished to make a clear distinction between the ratios of ultimate quantities and "those ultimate ratios with which quantities vanish," the latter being "limits towards which the ratios of quantities decreasing without limit do always converge. . . ." He pointed out that this distinction may be seen most clearly in the case in which two quantities become infinitely great; then their "ultimate ratio" may be "given, namely, the ratio of equality," even though "it does not from thence follow, that the ultimate or greatest quantities themselves, whose ratio that is, will be given."

Section 1 of book I is unambiguous in its statement that the treatise to follow is based on theorems of which the truth and demonstration almost always depend on the taking of limits. Of course, the occasional analytical intrusions in book I and the explicit use of the fluxional method in book II (notably in section 2) show the mathematical character of the book as a whole, as does the occasional but characteristic introduction of the methods of expansion in infinite series. A careful reading of almost any proof in book I will, moreover, demonstrate the truly limital or infinitesimal character of the work as a whole. But nowhere in the *Principia* (or in any other generally accessible manuscript) did Newton write any of the equations of dynamics as fluxions, as Maclaurin did later on. This continuous form is effectively that published by Varignon in the *Mémoires* of the Paris Academy in 1700; Newton's second law was written as a differential equation in J. Hermann's *Phoronomia* (1716).

The similarity of section 1, book I, to the introductory portion of the later *De quadratura* should not be taken to mean that in the *Principia* Newton developed his principles of natural philosophy on the basis of first and last ratios exclusively, since in the *Principia* Newton presented not one, but rather three modes of presentation of his fluxional or infinitesimal calculus. A second approach to the calculus occurs in section 2, book II, notably in lemma 2, in which Newton introduced the concept and method of moments. This represents the first printed statement (in the first edition of 1687) by Newton himself of

his new mathematics, apart from its application to physics (with which the opening discussion of limits in section 1, book I is concerned). In a scholium to lemma 2, Newton wrote that this lemma contains the "foundation" of "a general method," one

> . . . which extends itself, without any troublesome calculation, not only to the drawing of tangents to any curve lines . . ., but also to the resolving other abstruser kinds of problems about the crookedness, areas, lengths, centres of gravity of curves, &c.; nor is it . . . limited to equations which are free from surd quantities. This method I have interwoven with that other of working in equations, by reducing them to infinite series.

He added that the "last words relate to a treatise I composed on that subject in the year 1671,"[133] and that the paragraph quoted above came from a letter he had written to Collins on 10 December 1672, describing "a method of tangents."

The lemma itself reads: "The moment of any *genitum* is equal to the moments of each of the generating sides multiplied by the indices of the powers of those sides, and by their coefficients continually."[134] It may be illustrated by Newton's first example: Let AB be a rectangle with sides A, B, diminished by $\frac{1}{2}a$, $\frac{1}{2}b$, respectively. The diminished area is $(A - \frac{1}{2}a)(B - \frac{1}{2}b) = AB - \frac{1}{2}aB - \frac{1}{2}bA + \frac{1}{4}ab$. Now, by a "continual flux," let the sides be augmented by $\frac{1}{2}a$, $\frac{1}{2}b$, respectively; the area ("rectangle") will then become $(A + \frac{1}{2}a)(B + \frac{1}{2}b) = AB + \frac{1}{2}aB + \frac{1}{2}bA + \frac{1}{4}ab$ (Fig. 7). Subtract one from the other, "and there will

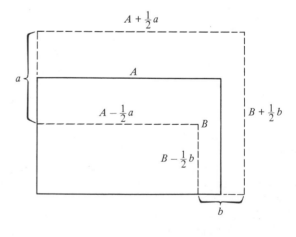

FIGURE 7

remain the excess $aB + bA$." Newton concluded, "Therefore with the whole increments a and b of the sides, the increment $aB + bA$ of the rectangle is generated." Here a and b are the moments of A and B, respectively, and Newton has shown that the moment of AB, corresponding to the moments a and b of A and B, respectively, is $aB + bA$. And, for the special case of $A = B$, the moment of A^2 is determined as $2aA$.

In order to extend the result from "area" to "content" or ("bulk"), from AB to ABC, Newton set $AB = G$ and then used the prior result for AB twice, once for AB, and again for GC, so as to get the moment of ABC to be $cAB + bCA + aBC$; whence, by setting $A = B = C$, the moment of A^3 is determined as $3aA^2$. And, in general, the moment of A^n is shown to be naA^{n-1} for n as a positive integer.

The result is readily extended to negative integral powers and even to all products $A^m B^n$, "whether the indices m and n of the powers be whole numbers or fractions, affirmative or negative." Whiteside has pointed out that by using the decrements $\frac{1}{2}a$, $\frac{1}{2}b$ and the increments $\frac{1}{2}a$, $\frac{1}{2}b$, rather than the increments a, b, "Newton . . . deluded himself into believing" he had "contrived an approach which avoids the comparatively messy appeal to the limit-value of $(A + a)/(B + b) - AB$ as the increments a, b vanish." The result is what is now seen as a "celebrated *non-sequitur*."[135]

In discussing lemma 2, Newton defined moments as the "momentary increments or decrements" of "variable and indetermined" quantities, which might be "products, quotients, roots, rectangles, squares, cubes, square and cubic sides, and the like." He called these "quantities" *genitae*, because he conceived them to be "generated or produced in arithmetic by the multiplication, division, or extraction of the root of any terms whatsoever; in geometry by the finding of contents and sides, or of the extremes and means of proportionals." So much is clear. But Newton warned his readers not "to look upon finite particles as such [moments]," for finite particles "are not moments, but the very quantities generated by the moments. We are to conceive them as the just nascent principles of finite magnitudes." And, in fact, it is not "the magnitude of the moments, but their first proportion [which is to be regarded] as nascent."

Boyer has called attention to the difficulty of conceiving "the limit of a ratio in determining the moment of AB."[136] The moment of AB is not really a product of two independent variables A and B, implying a problem in partial differentiation, but rather a product of two functions of the single independent variable time. Newton himself said, "It will be the same thing, if, instead of moments, we use either the velocities of the increments and decrements (which may also be called the motions, mutations, and fluxions of quantities), or any finite quantities proportional to those velocities."

Newton thus shifted the conceptual base of his procedure from infinitely small quantities or moments —which are not finite, and clearly not zero—to the "first proportion," or ratio of moments (rather than "the magnitude of the moments") "as nascent." This nascent ratio is generally not infinitesimal but finite, and Newton thus suggested that the ratio of finite quantities may be substituted for the ratio of infinitesimals, with the same result, using in fact the velocities of the increments or decrements instead of the moments, or "any finite quantities proportional to those velocities," which are also the "fluxions of the quantities." Boyer summarized this succinctly:

> Newton thus offered in the *Principia* three modes of interpretation of the new analysis: that in terms of infinitesimals (used in his *De analysi . . .*); that in terms of prime and ultimate ratios or limits (given particularly in *De quadratura*, and the view which he seems to have considered most rigorous); and that in terms of fluxions (given in his *Methodus fluxionum*, and one which appears to have appealed most strongly to his imagination).[137]

From the point of view of mathematics, proposition 10, book II, may particularly attract our attention. Here Newton boldly displayed his methods of using the terms of a converging series to solve problems and his method of second differences. Expansions are given with respect to "the indefinite quantity o," but there are no references to (nor uses of) moments, as in the preceding lemma 2, and, of course, there is no use made of dotted or "pricked" letters.

The proposition is of particular interest for at least two reasons. First, its proof and exposition (or exemplification) are highly analytic and not geometric (or synthetic), as are most proofs in the *Principia*. Second, an error in the first edition and in the original printed pages of the second edition was discovered by Johann [I] Bernoulli and called to Newton's attention by Nikolaus [I] Bernoulli, who visited England in September or October 1712. As a result, Newton had Cotes reprint a whole signature and an additional leaf of the already printed text of the second edition; these pages thus appear as cancels in every copy of this edition of the *Principia* that has been recorded. The corrected proposition, analyzed by Whiteside, illustrates "the power of Newton's infinitesimal techniques in the *Principia*," and may thus confute the opinion that "Newton did not (at least in principle, and in his own algorithm) know how 'to formulate and resolve problems through the integration of differential equations.'"[138]

From at least 1712 onward, Newton attempted to impose upon the *Principia* a mode of composition that could lend support to his position in the priority dispute with Leibniz: he wished to demonstrate that he had actually composed the *Principia* by analysis and had rewritten the work synthetically. He affirmed this claim, in and after 1713, in several manuscript versions of prefaces to planned new editions of the *Principia* (both with or without *De quadratura* as a supplement). It is indeed plausible to argue that much of the *Principia* was based upon an infinitesimal analysis, veiled by the traditional form of Greek synthetic geometry, but the question remains whether Newton drew upon working papers in which (in extreme form) he gave solutions in dotted fluxions to problems that he later presented geometrically. But, additionally, there is no evidence that Newton used an analytic method of ordinary fluxional form to discover the propositions he presented synthetically.

All evidence indicates that Newton had actually found the propositions in the *Principia* in essentially the way in which he there presented them to his readers. He did, however, use algebraic methods to determine the solid of least resistance. But in this case, he did not make the discovery by analysis and then recast it as an example of synthesis; he simply stated his result without proof.[139]

It has already been mentioned that Newton did make explicit use of the infinitesimal calculus in section 2, book II, of the *Principia*, and that in that work he often employed his favored method of infinite series.[140] But this claim is very different indeed from such a statement of Newton's as: "... At length in 1685 and part of 1686 by the aid of this method and the help of the book on Quadratures I wrote the first two books of the mathematical Principles of Philosophy. And therefore I have subjoined a Book on Quadratures to the Book of Principles."[141] This "method" refers to fluxions, or the method of differential calculus. But it is true, as mentioned earlier, that Newton stated in the *Principia* that certain theorems depended upon the "quadrature" (or integration) of "certain curves"; he did need, for this purpose, the inverse method of fluxions, or the integral calculus. And proposition 41 of book I is, moreover, an obvious exercise in the calculus.

Newton himself never did bring out an edition of the *Principia* together with a version of *De quadratura*.[142] In the review that he published of the *Commercium epistolicum*,[143] Newton did announce in print, although anonymously, that he had "found out most of the Propositions in his *Principia*" by using "the new *Analysis*," and had then reworked the material and had "demonstrated the Propositions synthetically." (This claim cannot, however, be substantiated by documentary evidence.)

Apart from questions of the priority of Newton's method, the *Principia* contains some problems of notable mathematical interest. Sections 4 and 5 of book I deal with conic sections, and section 6 with Kepler's problem; Newton here introduced the method of solution by successive iteration. Lemma 5 of book III treats of a locus through a given number of points, an example of Newton's widely used method of interpolating a function. Proposition 71, book I, contains Newton's important solution to a major problem of integration, the attraction of a sphere, called by Turnbull "the crown of all." Newton's proof that two spheres will mutually attract each other as if the whole of their masses were concentrated at their respective centers is posited on the condition that, however the mass or density may vary within each sphere as a function of that radius, the density at any given radius is everywhere the same (or is constant throughout any concentric shell).

The "Principia": General Plan. Newton's masterwork was worked up and put into its final form in an incredibly short time. His strategy was to develop the subject of general dynamics from a mathematical point of view in book I, then to apply his most important results to solving astronomical and physical problems in book III. Book II, introduced at some point between Newton's first conception of the treatise and the completion of the printer's manuscript, is almost independent, and appears extraneous.

Book I opens with a series of definitions and axioms, followed by a set of mathematical principles and procedural rules for the use of limits; book III begins with general precepts concerning empirical science and a presentation of the phenomenological bases of celestial mechanics, based on observation.

It is clear to any careful reader that Newton was, in book I, developing mathematical principles of motion chiefly so that he might apply them to the physical conditions of experiment and observation in book III, on the system of the world. Newton maintained that even though he had, in book I, used such apparently physical concepts as "force" and "attraction," he did so in a purely mathematical sense. In fact, in book I (as in book II), he tended to follow his inspiration to whatever aspect of any topic might prove of mathematical interest, often going far beyond any possible physical application. Only in an occasional scholium in books I and II did he raise the question of whether the mathematical propositions might indeed be properly applied to the physical circumstances that the use of such words as "force" and "attraction" would seem to imply.

Newton's method of composition led to a certain amount of repetition, since many topics are discussed twice—in book I, with mathematical proofs, to illustrate the general principles of the motions of bodies, then again in book III, in application to the motions of planets and their satellites or of comets. While this mode of presentation makes the *Principia* more difficult for the reader, it does have the decided advantage of separating the Newtonian principles as they apply to the physical universe from the details of the mathematics from which they derive.

As an example of this separation, proposition 1 of book III states that the satellites of Jupiter are "continually drawn off from rectilinear motions, and are retained in their proper orbits" by forces that "tend to Jupiter's centre" and that these forces vary inversely as the square of their distances from that center. The proof given in this proposition is short and direct; the centripetal force itself follows from "Phen. I [of book III], and Prop. II or III, Book I." The phenomenon cited is a statement, based upon "astronomical observations," that a radius drawn from the center of Jupiter to any satellite sweeps out areas "proportional to the times of descriptions"; propositions 2 and 3 of book I prove by mathematics that under these circumstances the force about which such areas are described must be centripetal and proportional to the times. The inverse-square property of this force is derived from the second part of the phenomenon, which states that the distances from Jupiter's center are as the $\frac{3}{2}$th power of their periods of revolution, and from corollary 6 to proposition 4 of book I, in which it is proved that centripetal force in uniform circular motion must be as the inverse square of the distance from the center.

Newton's practice of introducing a particular instance repeatedly, with what may seem to be only minor variations, may render the *Principia* difficult for the modern reader. But the main hurdle for any would-be student of the treatise lies elsewhere, in the essential mathematical difficulty of the main subject matter, celestial mechanics, however presented. A further obstacle is that Newton's mathematical vocabulary became archaic soon after the *Principia* was published, as dynamics in general and celestial mechanics in particular came to be written in the language of differentials and integrals still used today. The reader is thus required almost to translate for himself Newton's geometrical-limit mode of proof and statement into the characters of the analytic algorithms of the calculus. Even so, dynamics was taught directly from the *Principia* at Cambridge until well into the twentieth century.

In his "Mathematical Principles" Whiteside describes the *Principia* as "slipshod, its level of verbal fluency none too high, its arguments unnecessarily diffuse and repetitive, and its content on occasion markedly irrelevant to its professed theme: the theory of bodies moving under impressed forces." This view is somewhat extreme. Nevertheless, the work might have been easier to read today had Newton chosen to rely to a greater extent on general algorithms.

The *Principia* is often described as if it were a "synthesis," notably of Kepler's three laws of planetary motion and Galileo's laws of falling bodies and projectile motion; but in fact it denies the validity of both these sets of basic laws unless they be modified. For instance, Newton showed for the first time the dynamical significance of Kepler's so-called laws of planetary motion; but in so doing he proved that in the form originally stated by Kepler they apply exactly only to the highly artificial condition of a point mass moving about a mathematical center of force, unaffected by any other stationary or moving masses. In the real universe, these laws or planetary "hypotheses" are true only to the limits of ordinary observation, which may very well have been the reason that Newton called them "Hypotheses" in the first edition. Later, in the second and third editions, he referred to these relations as "Phaenomena," by which it may be assumed that he now meant that they were not simply true as stated (that is, not strictly deducible from the definitions and axioms), but were rather valid only to the limit of (or within the limits of) observation, or were phenomenologically true. In other words, these statements were to be regarded as not necessarily true, but only contingently (phenomenologically) so.

In the *Principia*, Newton proved that Kepler's planetary hypotheses must be modified by at least two factors: (1) the mutual attraction of each of any pair of bodies, and (2) the perturbation of a moving body by any and all neighboring bodies. He also showed that the rate of free fall of bodies is not constant, as Galileo had supposed, but varies with distance from the center of the earth and with latitude along the surface of the earth.[144] In a scholium at the end of section 2, book I, Newton further pointed out that it is only in a limiting case, not really achieved on earth, that projectiles (even *in vacuo*) move in Galilean parabolic trajectories, as Galileo himself knew full well. Thus, as Karl Popper has pointed out, although "Newton's dynamics achieved a unification of Galileo's terrestrial and Kepler's celestial physics," it appears that "from a logical point of view, Newton's theory, strictly speaking, contradicts both Galileo's and Kepler's."[145]

The "Principia": Definitions and Axioms. The *Principia* opens with two preliminary presentations: the "Definitions" and the "Axioms, or Laws of

Motion." The first two entities defined are "quantity of matter," or "mass," and "quantity of motion." The former is said to be the measure of matter proportional to bulk and density conjunctively. "Mass" is, in addition, given as being generally known by its weight, to which it is proportional at any given place, as shown by Newton's experiments with pendulums, of which the results are more exact than Galileo's for freely falling bodies. Newton's "quantity of motion" is the entity now known as momentum; it is said to be measured by the velocity and mass of a body, conjunctively.

Definition 3 introduces *vis insita* (probably best translated as "inherent force"), a concept of which the actual definition and explanation are both so difficult to understand that much scholarly debate has been expended on them.[146] Newton wrote that the *vis insita* may be known by "a most significant name, *vis inertiae*." But this "force" is not like the "impressed forces" of definition 4, which change the state of rest or uniform rectilinear motion of a body; the *vis inertiae* merely maintains any new state acquired by a body, and it may cause a body to "resist" any change in state.[147]

Newton then defined "centripetal force" (*vis centripeta*), a concept he had invented and named to complement the *vis centrifuga* of Christiaan Huygens.[148] In definitions 6 through 8, Newton gave three "measures" of centripetal force, of which the most important for the purposes of the *Principia* is that one "proportional to the velocity which it generates in a given time" (for point masses, unit masses, or for comparing equal masses). There follows the famous scholium on space and time, in which Newton opted for concepts of absolute space and absolute time, although recognizing that both are usually reckoned by "sensible measures"; time, especially, is usually "relative, apparent, and common." Newton's belief in absolute space led him to hold that absolute motion is sensible or detectable, notably in rotation, although contemporaries as different in their outlooks as Huygens and Berkeley demurred from this view.

The "Axioms" or "Laws of Motion" are three in number: the law of inertia, a form of what is today known as the second law, and finally the law that "To every action there is always opposed an equal and opposite reaction." There is much puzzlement over the second law, which Newton stated as a proportionality between "change in motion" (in momentum) and "the motive force impressed" (a change "made in the direction . . ., in which that force is impressed"); he did not specify "per unit time" or "in some given time." The second law thus seems clearly to be stated for

an impulse, but throughout the *Principia* (and, in a special case, in the antecedent definition 8), Newton used the law for continuous forces, including gravitation, taking account of time. For Newton, in fact, the concepts of impulse and continuous force were infinitesimally equivalent, and represented conditions of action "altogether and at once" or "by degrees and successively."[149] There are thus two conditions of "force" in the second law; accordingly, this Newtonian law may be written in the two forms $f \propto d(mv)$ and $f \propto d(mv)/dt$, in which both concepts of force are taken account of by means of two different constants of proportionality. The two forms of the law can be considered equivalent through Newton's concept of a uniformly flowing time, which makes dt a kind of secondary constant, which can arbitrarily be absorbed in the constant of proportionality.

There may be some doubt as to whether or not Newton himself was unclear in his own mind about these matters. His use of such expressions as "vis impressa" shows an abiding influence of older physics, while his continued reference to a "vis" or a "force" needed to maintain bodies in a state of motion raises the question of whether such usage is one of a number of possibly misleading "artifacts left behind in the historical development of his [Newton's] dynamics."[150] It must be remembered, of course, that throughout the seventeenth and much of the eighteenth century the word "force" could be used in a number of ways. Most notably, it served to indicate the concept now called "momentum," although it could also even mean energy. In Newton's time there were no categories of strict formalistic logic that required a unitary one-to-one correspondence between names and concepts, and neither Newton nor his contemporaries (or, for that matter, his successors) were always precise in making such distinctions.

The careful reader of books I–III should not be confused by such language, however, nor by the preliminary intrusion of such concepts. Even the idea of force as a measure of motion or of change of motion (or of change *per se*, or rate of change) is not troublesome in practice, once Newton's own formulation is accepted and the infinitesimal level of his discourse (which is not always explicitly stated) understood. In short, Newton's dynamical and mathematical elaboration of the three books of the *Principia* is free of the errors and ambiguities implicit in his less successful attempt to give a logically simple and coherent set of definitions and axioms for dynamics. (It is even possible that the definitions and axioms may represent an independent later exercise, since there are, for example, varying sets of definitions and axioms for the same system of dynamics.) One of the most important consequences of Newton's analysis is that it must be one and the same law of force that operates in the centrally directed acceleration of the planetary bodies (toward the sun) and of satellites (toward planets), and that controls the linear downward acceleration of freely falling bodies. This force of universal gravitation is also shown to be the cause of the tides, through the action of the sun and the moon on the seas.

Book I of the "Principia." Book I of the *Principia* contains the first of the two parts of *De motu corporum*. It is a mathematical treatment of motion under the action of impressed forces in free spaces—that is, spaces devoid of resistance. (Although Newton discussed elastic and inelastic impact in the scholium to the laws, he did not reintroduce this topic in book I.) For the most part, the subject of Newton's inquiries is the motion of unit or point masses, usually having some initial inertial motion and being acted upon by a centripetal force. Newton thus tended to use the change in velocity produced in a given time (the "accelerative measure") of such forces, rather than the change in momentum produced in a given time (their "motive" measure).[151] He generally compared the effects of different forces or conditions of force on one and the same body, rather than on different bodies, preferring to consider a mass point or unit mass to computing actual magnitudes. Eventually, however, when the properties and actions of force had been displayed by an investigation of their "accelerative" and "motive" measures, Newton was able to approach the problem of their "absolute" measure. Later in the book he considered the attraction of spherical shells and spheres and of nonsymmetrical bodies.

Sections 2 and 3 are devoted to aspects of motion according to Kepler's laws. In proposition 1 Newton proceeded by four stages. He first showed that in a purely uniform linear (or purely inertial) motion, a radius vector drawn from the moving body to any point not in the line of motion sweeps out equal areas in equal times. The reason for this is clearly shown in

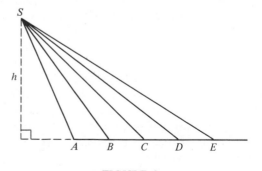

FIGURE 8

Figure 8, in which in equal times the body will move through the equal distances $AB, BC, CD, DE, \cdots$. If a radius vector is drawn from a point PS, then triangles $ABS, BCS, CDS, DES, \cdots$ have equal bases and a common altitude h, and their areas are equal. In the second stage, Newton assumed the moving object to receive an impulsive force when it reaches point B. A component of motion toward S is thereby added to its motion toward C; its actual path is thus along the diagonal Bc of a parallelogram (Figure 9).

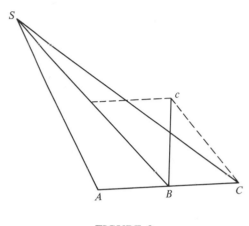

FIGURE 9

Newton then showed by simple geometry that the area of the triangle SBc is the same as the area of the triangle SBC, so that area is still conserved. He repeated the procedure in the third stage, with the body receiving a new impetus toward S at point C, and so on. In this way, the path is converted from a straight line into a series of joined line segments, traversed in equal intervals of time, which determine triangles of equal areas, with S as a common vertex.

In Newton's final development of the problem, the number of triangles is increased "and their breadth diminished *in infinitum*"; in the limit the "ultimate perimeter" will be a curve, the centripetal force "will act continually," and "any described areas" will be proportional to the times. Newton thus showed that inertial motion of and by itself implies an area-conservation law, and that if a centripetal force is directed to "an immovable centre" when a body has such inertial motion initially, area is still conserved as determined by a radius vector drawn from the moving body to the immovable center of force. (A critical examination of Newton's proof reveals the use of second-order infinitesimals.)[152] The most significant aspect of this proposition (and its converse, proposition 2) may be its demonstration of the hitherto wholly unsuspected logical connection, in the case of planetary motion, between Descartes's law of inertia and Kepler's law of areas (generalized to hold for an arbitrary central orbit).

Combining proposition 1 and proposition 2, Newton showed the physical significance of the law of areas as a necessary and sufficient condition for a central force (supposing that such forces exist; the "reality" of accelerative and motive forces of attraction is discussed in book III). In proposition 3, Newton dealt with the case of a body moving around a moving, rather than a stationary, center. Proposition 4 is concerned with uniform circular motion, in which the forces (F, f) are shown not only to be directed to the centers of the circles, but also to be to each other "as the squares of the arcs $[S, s]$ described in equal times divided respectively by the radii $[R, r]$ of the circles" $(F : f = S/R^2 : s/r^2)$. A series of corollaries demonstrate that $F : f = V^2/R : v^2r = R/T^2 : r/t^2$, where V, v are the tangential velocities, and so on; and that, universally, T being the period of revolution, if $T \propto R^n$, $V \propto 1/R^{n-1}$, then $F \propto 1/R^{2n-1}$, and conversely. A special case of the last condition (corollary 6) is $T \propto R^{3/2}$, yielding $F \propto 1/R^2$, a condition (according to a scholium) obtaining "in the celestial bodies," as Wren, Hooke, and Halley "have severally observed." Newton further referred to Huygens' derivation, in *De horologio oscillatorio*, of the magnitude of "the centrifugal force of revolving bodies" and introduced his own independent method for determining the centrifugal force in uniform circular motion. In proposition 6 he went on to a general concept of instantaneous measure of a force, for a body revolving in any curve about a fixed center of force. He then applied this measure, developed as a limit in several forms, in a number of major examples, among them proposition 11.

The last propositions of section 2 were altered in successive editions. In them Newton discussed the laws of force related to motion in a given circle and equiangular (logarithmic) spiral. In proposition 10 Newton took up elliptical motion in which the force tends toward the center of the ellipse. A necessary and sufficient cause of this motion is that "the force is as the distance." Hence if the center is "removed to an infinite distance," the ellipse "degenerates into a parabola," and the force will be constant, yielding "Galileo's theorem" concerning projectile motion.

Section 3 of book I opens with proposition 11, "If a body revolves in an ellipse; it is required to find the law of the centripetal force tending to the focus of the ellipse." The law is: "the centripetal force is inversely . . . as the square of the distance." Propositions 12 and 13 show that a hyperbolic and a parabolic orbit imply the same law of force to a

focus. It is obvious that the converse condition, that the centripetal force varies inversely as the square of the distance, does not by itself specify which conic section will constitute the orbit. Proposition 15 demonstrates that in ellipses "the periodic times are as the 3/2th power of their greater axes" (Kepler's third law). Hence the periodic times in all ellipses with equal major axes are equal to one another, and equal to the periodic time in a circle of which the diameter is equal to the greater axis of each ellipse. In proposition 17, Newton supposed a centripetal force "inversely proportional to the squares of the distances" and exhibited the conditions for an orbit in the shape of an ellipse, parabola, or hyperbola. Sections 4 and 5, on conic sections, are purely mathematical.

In section 6, Newton discussed Kepler's problem, introducing methods of approximation to find the future position of a body on an ellipse, according to the law of areas; it is here that one finds the method of successive iteration. In section 7, Newton found the rectilinear distance through which a body falls freely in any given time under the action of a "centripetal force . . . inversely proportional to the square of the distance . . . from the centre." Having found the times of descent of such a body, he then applied his results to the problem of parabolic motion and the motion of "a body projected upwards or downwards," under conditions in which "the centripetal force is proportional to the . . . distance." Eventually, in proposition 39, Newton postulated "a centripetal force of any kind" and found both the velocity at any point to which any body may ascend or descend in a straight line and the time it would take the body to get there. In this proposition, as in many in section 8, he added the condition of "granting the quadratures of curvilinear figures," referring to his then unpublished methods of integration (printed for the first time in the *De quadratura* of 1704).

In section 8, Newton often assumed such quadrature. In proposition 41 he postulated "a centripetal force of any kind"; that is, as he added in proposition 42, he supposed "the centripetal force to vary in its recess from the center according to some law, which anyone may imagine at pleasure, but [which] at equal distances from the centre [is taken] to be everywhere the same." Under these general conditions, Newton determined both "the curves in which bodies will move" and "the times of their motions in the curves found." In other words, Newton presented to his readers a truly general resolution of the inverse problem of finding the orbit from a given law of force. He extended this problem into a dynamics far beyond that commonly associated with the *Principia*. In the ancillary proposition 40, for example, Newton (again under the most general conditions of force) had sought the velocity at a point on an orbit, finding a result that is the equivalent of an integral, which (in E. J. Aiton's words) in "modern terms . . . expresses the invariance of the sum of the kinetic and gravitational potential energies in an orbit."[153]

In section 11, Newton reached a level of mathematical analysis of celestial motions that fully distinguishes the *Principia* from any of its predecessors. Until this point, he there explained, he had been "treating of the attractions of bodies towards an immovable centre; though very probably there is no such thing existent in nature." He then outlined a plan to deal with nature herself, although in a "purely mathematical" way, "laying aside all physical considerations"—such as the nature of the gravitating force. "Attractions" are to be treated here as originating in bodies and acting toward other bodies; in a two-body system, therefore, "neither the attracted nor the attracting body is truly at rest, but both . . . being as it were mutually attracted, revolve about a common centre of gravity." In general, for any system of bodies that mutually attract one another, "their common centre of gravity will either be at rest, or move uniformly" in a straight line. Under these conditions, both members of a pair of mutually attractive bodies will describe "similar figures about their common centre of gravity, and about each other mutually" (proposition 57).

By studying such systems, rather than a single body attracted toward a point-center of force, Newton proved that Kepler's laws (or "planetary hypotheses") cannot be true within this context, and hence need modification when applied to the real system of the world. Thus, in proposition 59, Newton stated that Kepler's third law should not be written $T_1{}^2 : T_2{}^2 = a_1{}^3 : a_2{}^3$, as Kepler, Hooke, and everybody else had supposed, but must be modified.

A corollary that may be drawn from the proposition is that the law might be written as $(M + m_1)T_1{}^2 : (M + m_2)T_2{}^2 : a_1{}^3 : a_2{}^3$, where m_1, m_2 are any two planetary masses and M is the mass of the sun. (Newton's expression of this new relation may be reduced at once to the more familiar form in which we use this law today.) Clearly, it follows from Newton's analysis and formulation that Kepler's own third law may safely be used as an approximation in most astronomical calculations only because m_1, m_2 are very small in relation to M. Newton's modification of Kepler's third law fails to take account of any possible interplanetary perturbations. The chief

function of proposition 59 thus appears to be not to reach the utmost generalization of that law, but rather to reach a result that will be useful in the problems that follow, most notably proposition 60 (on the orbits described when each of two bodies attracts the other with a force proportional to the square of the distance, each body "revolving about the common centre of gravity").

From proposition 59 onward, Newton almost at once advanced to various motions of mutually attractive bodies "let fall from given places" (in proposition 62), "going off from given places in given directions with given velocities" (proposition 63), or even when the attractive forces "increase in a simple ratio of their [that is, the bodies'] distances from the centres" (proposition 64). This led him to examine Kepler's first two laws for real "bodies," those "whose forces decrease as the square of their distances from their centres." Newton demonstrated in proposition 65 that in general it is not "possible that bodies attracting each other according to the law supposed in this proposition should move exactly in ellipses," because of interplanetary perturbations, and discussed cases in astronomy in which "the orbits will not much differ from ellipses." He added that the areas described will be only "very nearly proportional to the times."

Proposition 66 presents the restricted three-body problem, developed in a series of twenty-two corollaries. Here Newton attempted to apply the law of mutual gravitational attraction to a body like the sun to determine how it might perturb the motion of a moonlike body around an earthlike body. Newton examined the motion in longitude and in latitude, the annual equation, the evection, the change of the inclination of the orbit of the body resembling the moon, and the motion on the line of apsides. He considered the tides and explained, in corollary 22, that the internal "constitution of the globe" (of the earth) can be known "from the motion of the nodes." He further demonstrated that the shape of the globe can be derived from the precession constant (precession being caused, in the case of the earth, by the pull of the moon on the equatorial bulge of the spinning earth). He thus established, for the first time, a physical theory, elaborated in mathematical expression, from which some of the "inequalities" of the motion of the moon could be deduced; and he added some hitherto unknown "inequalities" that he had found. Previous to Newton's work, the study of the irregularities in the motion of the moon had been posited on the elaboration of geometric models, in an attempt to make predicted positions agree with actual observations.[154]

Section 12 of book I contains Newton's results on the attractions of spheres, or of spherical shells. He dealt first with homogeneous, then nonhomogeneous spheres, the latter being composed of uniform and concentric spherical shells so that the density is the same at any single given distance from the center. In proposition 71 he proved that a "corpuscle" situated outside such a nonhomogeneous sphere is "attracted towards the centre of the sphere with a force inversely proportional to the square of its distance from the centre." In proposition 75, he reached the general conclusion that any two such spheres will gravitationally attract one another as if their masses were concentrated at their respective centers—or, in other words, that the distance required for the inverse-square law is measured from their centers. A series of elegant and purely mathematical theorems follow, including one designed to find the force with which a corpuscle placed inside a sphere may be "attracted toward any segment of that sphere whatsoever." In section 13, Newton, with a brilliant display of mathematics (which he did not fully reveal for the benefit of the reader) discussed the "attractive forces" of nonspherical solids of revolution, concluding with a solution in the form of an infinite series for the attraction of a body "towards a given plane."[155]

Book I concludes with section 14, on the "motion of very small bodies" acted on by "centripetal forces tending to the several parts of any very great body." Here Newton used the concept of "centripetal forces" that act under very special conditions to produce motions of corpuscles that simulate the phenomena of light—including reflection and refraction (according to the laws of Snell and Descartes), the inflection of light (as discovered by Grimaldi), and even the action of lenses. In a scholium, Newton noted that these "attractions bear a great resemblance to the reflections and refractions of light," and so

> ... because of the analogy there is between the propagation of the rays of light and the motion of bodies, I thought it not amiss to add the following Propositions for optical uses; not at all considering the nature of the rays of light, or inquiring whether they are bodies or not; but only determining the curves of [the paths of] bodies which are extremely like the curves of the rays.

A similar viewpoint with respect to mathematical analyses (or models and analogies) and physical phenomena is generally sustained throughout books I and II of the *Principia*.

Newton's general plan in book I may thus be seen as one in which he began with the simplest conditions and added complexities step by step. In sections 2 and 3, for example, he dealt with a mass-point moving under the action of a centripetal force directed toward a stationary or moving point, by which the dynamical significance of each of Kepler's three laws of planetary motion is demonstrated. In section 6, Newton developed methods to compute Keplerian motion (along an ellipse, according to the law of areas), which leads to "regular ascent and descent" of bodies when the force is not uniform (as in Galilean free fall) but varies, primarily as the inverse square of the distance, as in Keplerian orbital motion. In section 8 Newton considered the general case of "orbits in which bodies will revolve, being acted upon by any sort of centripetal force." From stationary orbits he went on, in section 9, to "movable orbits; and the motion of the apsides" and to a mathematical treatment of two (and then three) mutually attractive bodies. In section 10 he dealt with motion along surfaces of bodies acted upon by centripetal force; in section 12, the problems of bodies that are not mere points or point-masses and the question of the "attractive forces of spherical bodies"; and in section 13, "the attractive forces of bodies that are not spherical."

Book II of the "Principia." Book II, on the motion of bodies in resisting mediums, is very different from book I. It was an afterthought to the original treatise, which was conceived as consisting of only two books, of which one underwent more or less serious modifications to become book I as it exists today, while the other, a more popular version of the "system of the world," was wholly transformed so as to become what is now book III. At first the question of motion in resisting mediums had been relegated to some theorems at the end of the original book I; Newton had also dealt with this topic in a somewhat similar manner at the end of his earlier tract *De motu*. The latter parts of the published book II were added only at the final redaction of the *Principia*.

Book II is perhaps of greater mathematical than physical interest. To the extent that Newton proceeded by setting up a sequence of mathematical conditions and then exploring their consequences, book II resembles book I. But there is a world of difference between the style of the two books. In book I Newton made it plain that the gravitational force exists in the universe, varying inversely as the square of the distance, and that this force accordingly merits our particular attention. In book II, however, the reader is never certain as to which of the many conditions of resistance that Newton considers may actually occur in nature.[156]

Book II enabled Newton to display his mathematical ingenuity and some of his new discoveries. Occasionally, as in the static model that he proposed to explain the elasticity and compressibility of gases according to Boyle's law, he could explore what he believed might be actual physical reality. But he nonetheless reminded his readers (as in the scholium at the end of section 1) that the condition of resistance that he was discussing was "more a mathematical hypothesis than a physical one." Even in his final argument against Cartesian vortices (section 9), he admitted the implausibility of the proposed hypothesis that "the resistance . . . is, other things being equal, proportional to the velocity." Although a scholium to proposition 52 states that "it is in truth probable that the resistance is in a less ratio than that of the velocity," Newton in fact never explored the consequences of this probable assumption in detail. Such a procedure is in marked contrast to book I, in which Newton examined a variety of conditions of attractive and centripetal forces, but so concentrated on the inverse-square force as to leave the reader in no doubt that this is the chief force acting (insofar as weight is concerned) on the sun, the planets, the satellites, the seas, and all terrestrial objects.

Book II differs further from book I in having a separate section devoted to each of the imagined conditions of resistance. In section 1, resistance to the motions of bodies is said to be as "the ratio of the velocity"; in section 2, it is as "the square of their velocities"; and in section 3, it is given as "partly in the ratio of the velocities and partly as the square of the same ratio." Then, in section 4, Newton introduced the orbital "motion of bodies in resisting mediums," under the mathematical condition that "the density of a medium" may vary inversely as the distance from "an immovable centre"; the "centripetal force" is said in proposition 15 to be as the square of the said density, but is thereafter arbitrary. In a very short scholium, Newton added that these conditions of varying density apply only to the motions of very small bodies. He supposed the resistance of a medium, "other things being equal," to be proportional to its "density."

In section 5, Newton went on to discuss some general principles of hydrostatics, including properties of the density and compression of fluids. Historically, the most significant proposition of section 5 is proposition 23, in which Newton supposed "a fluid [to] be composed of particles fleeing from each other," and then showed that Boyle's law ("the density" of a gas varying directly as "the compression") is a necessary and a sufficient condition for the centrifugal forces to "be inversely proportional to distances of their [that is, the particles'] centers."

Then, in the scholium to this proposition, Newton generalized the results, showing that for the com-

pressing forces to "be as the cube roots of the power E^{n+2}," where E is "the density of the compressed fluid," it is both a necessary and sufficient condition that the centrifugal forces be "inversely as any power D^n of the distance [between particles]." He made it explicit that the "centrifugal forces" of particles must "terminate in those particles that are next [to] them, or are diffused not much farther," and drew upon the example of magnetic bodies. Having set such a model, however, Newton concluded that it would be "a physical question" as to "whether elastic fluids [gases] do really consist of particles so repelling each other," and stated that he had limited himself to demonstrating "mathematically the property of fluids consisting of particles of this kind, that hence philosophers may take occasion to discuss that question."[157]

Section 6 introduces the "motion and resistance of pendulous bodies." The opening proposition (24) relates the quantity of matter in the bob to its weight, the length of the pendulum, and the time of oscillation in a vacuum. Because, as corollary 5 states, "in general, the quantity of matter in the pendulous body is directly as the weight and the square of the time, and inversely as the length of the pendulum," a method is at hand for using pendulum experiments to compare directly "the quantity of matter" in bodies, and to prove that the mass of bodies is proportional "to their weight." Newton added that he had tested this proposition experimentally, then further stated, in corollary 7, that the same experiment may be used for "comparing the weights of the same body in different places, to know the variation of its gravity."[158] This is the first clear recognition that "mass" determines both weight (the amount of gravitational action) and inertia (the measure of resistance to acceleration)—the two properties of which the "equivalence" can, in classical physics, be determined only by experiment.

In section 6 Newton also considered the motion of pendulums in resisting mediums, especially oscillations in a cycloid, and gave methods for finding "the resistance of mediums by pendulums oscillating therein." An account of such experiments makes up the "General Scholium" with which section 6 concludes.[159] Among them is an experiment Newton described from memory, designed to confute "the opinion of some that there is a certain aethereal medium, extremely rare and subtile, which freely pervades the pores of all bodies."

Section 7 introduces the "motion of fluids," and "the resistance made to projected bodies," and section 8 deals with wave motion. Proposition 42 asserts that "All motion propagated through a fluid diverges from a rectilinear progress into the unmoved spaces"; while proposition 50 gives a method of finding "the distances of the pulses," or the wavelength. In a scholium, Newton stated that the previous propositions "respect the motions of light and sound" and asserted that "since light is propagated in right lines, it is certain that it cannot consist in action alone (by Prop. XLI and XLII)"; there can be no doubt that sounds are "nothing else but pulses of the air" which "arise from tremulous bodies." This section concludes with various mathematical theorems concerning the velocity of waves or pulses, and their relation to the "density and elastic force of a medium."

In section 9, Newton showed that in wave motion a disturbance moves forward, but the parts (particles) of the medium in which the disturbance occurs only vibrate about a fixed position; he thereby established the relation between wavelength, frequency, and velocity of undulations. Proposition 47 (proposition 48 in the first edition) analyzes undulatory motion in a fluid; Newton disclosed that the parts (or particles) of an undulating fluid have the same oscillation as the bob of a simple pendulum. Proposition 48 (proposition 47 in the first edition) exhibits the proportionality of the velocity of waves to the square root of the elastic force divided by the density of an elastic fluid (one whose pressure is proportional to the density). The final scholium (much rewritten for the second edition) shows that Newton's propositions yield a velocity of sound in air of 979 feet per second, whereas experiment gives a value of 1,142 feet per second under the same conditions. Newton offered an ingenious explanation (including the supposition, in the interest of simplicity, that air particles might be rigid spheres separated from one another by a distance of some nine times their diameter), but it remained for Laplace to resolve the problem in 1816.[160]

Section 9, the last of book II, is on vortices, or "the circular motion of fluids." In all editions of the *Principia*, this section begins with a clearly labeled "hypothesis" concerning the "resistance arising from the want of lubricity in the parts of a fluid . . . other things being equal, [being] proportional to the velocity with which the parts of the fluid are separated from one another." Newton used this hypothesis as the basis for investigating the physics of vortices and their mathematical properties, culminating in a lengthy proposition 52 and eleven corollaries, followed by a scholium in which he said that he has attempted "to investigate the properties of vortices" so that he might find out "whether the celestial phenomena can be explained by them." The chief "phenomenon" with which Newton was here concerned is Kepler's third (or harmonic) law for the motion of the satellites of Jupiter about that planet, and for the primary "planets that revolve about the Sun"—although Newton did not refer to Kepler by name. He found "the periodic times of the parts of the vortex" to be "as the squares of their distances." Hence, he concluded, "Let philosophers then see how that phenomenon of the 3/2th power can be accounted for by vortices."

Newton ended book II with proposition 53, also on vortices, and a scholium, in which he showed that "it is manifest that the planets are not carried round in corporeal vortices." He was there dealing with Kepler's second or area law (although again without naming Kepler), in application to elliptic orbits. He concluded "that the hypothesis of vortices is utterly irreconcilable with astronomical phenomena, and rather serves to perplex than to explain the heavenly motions." Newton himself noted that his demonstration was based on "an hypothesis," proposed "for the sake of demonstration . . . at the beginning of this Section," but went on to add that "it is in truth probable that the resistance is in a less ratio than that of the velocity." Hence "the periodic times of the parts of the vortex will be in a greater ratio than the square of the distances from its centre." But it must be noted that it is in fact probable that the resistance would be in a greater "ratio than that of the velocity," not a lesser, since almost all fluids give rise to a resistance proportional to the square (or higher powers) of the velocity.[161]

Book III, "The System of the World." In the Newtonian system of the world, the motions of planets and their satellites, the motions of comets, and the phenomena of tides are all comprehended under a single mode of explanation. Newton stated that the force that causes the observed celestial motions and the tides and the force that causes weight are one and the same; for this reason he gave the name "gravity" to the centripetal force of universal attraction. In book III he showed that the earth must be an oblate spheroid, and he computed the magnitude of the equatorial bulge in relation to the pull of the moon so as to produce the long-known constant of precession; he also gave an explanation of variation in weight (as shown by the change in the period of a seconds pendulum) as a function of latitude on such a rotating non-spherical earth. But above all, in book III Newton stated the law of universal gravitation. He showed that planetary motion must be subject to interplanetary perturbation —most apparent in the most massive planets, Jupiter and Saturn, when they are in near conjunction—and he explored the perturbing action of the sun on the motion of the moon.

Book III opens with a preface in which Newton

stated that in books I and II he had set forth principles of mathematical philosophy, which he would now apply to the system of the world. The preface refers to an earlier, more popular version,[162] of which Newton had recast the substance "into the form of Propositions (in the mathematical way)."

A set of four "rules of reasoning in [natural] philosophy" follows the preface. Rule 1 is to admit no more causes than are "true and sufficient to explain" phenomena, while rule 2 is to "assign the same causes" insofar as possible to "the same natural effects." In the first edition, rules 1 and 2 were called "hypotheses," and they were followed by hypothesis 3, on the possibility of the transformation of every body "into a body of any other kind," in the course of which it "can take on successively all the intermediate grades of qualities." This "hypothesis" was deleted by the time of the second edition.[163]

A second group of the original "hypotheses" (5 through 9) were transformed into "phenomena" 1 and 3 through 6. The first states (with phenomenological evidence) the area law and Kepler's third law for the system of Jupiter's satellites (again Kepler is not named as the discoverer of the law). Phenomenon 2, which was introduced in the second edition, does the same for the satellites of Saturn (just discovered as the *Principia* was being written, and not mentioned in the first edition, where reference is made only to the first [Huygenian] satellite discovered). Phenomena 3 through 6 (originally hypotheses 6 through 9) assert, within the limits of observation: the validity of the Copernican system (phenomenon 3); the third law of Kepler for the five primary planets and the earth— here for the first time in the *Principia* mentioning Kepler by name and thus providing the only reference to him in relation to the laws or hypotheses of planetary motion (phenomenon 4); the area law for the "primary planets," although without significant evidence (phenomenon 5); and the area law for the moon, again with only weak evidence and coupled with the statement that the law does not apply exactly since "the motion of the moon is a little disturbed by the action of the sun" (phenomenon 6).

It has been mentioned that Newton probably called these statements "phenomena" because he knew that they are valid only to the limits of observation. In this sense, Newton had originally conceived Kepler's laws as planetary "hypotheses," as he had also done for the phenomena and laws of planetary satellites.[164]

The first six propositions given in book III display deductions from these "phenomena," using the mathematical results that Newton had set out in book I. Thus, in proposition 1, the forces "by which the circumjovial planets are continually drawn off from rectilinear motions, and retained in their proper orbits" are shown (on the basis of the area law discussed in propositions 2 and 3, book I, and in phenomenon 1) to be directed toward Jupiter's center. On the basis of Kepler's third law (and corollary 6, proposition 4, book I) these forces must vary inversely as the square of the distance; propositions 2 and 3 deal similarly with the primary planets and our moon.

By proposition 5, Newton was able to conclude (in corollary 1) that there "is . . . a power of gravity tending to all the planets" and that the planets "gravitate" toward their satellites, and the sun "towards all the primary planets." This "force of gravity" varies (corollary 2) as the inverse square of the distance; corollary 3 states that "all the planets do mutually gravitate towards one another." Hence, "near their conjunction," Jupiter and Saturn, since their masses are so great, "sensibly disturb each other's motions," while the sun "disturbs" the motion of the moon and together both sun and moon "disturb our sea, as we shall hereafter explain."

In a scholium, Newton said that the force keeping celestial bodies in their orbits "has been hitherto called centripetal force"; since it is now "plain" that it is "a gravitating force" he will "hereafter call it gravity." In proposition 6 he asserted that "all bodies gravitate towards every planet"; while at equal distances from the center of any planet "the weight" of any body toward that planet is proportional to its "quantity of matter." He provided experimental proof, using a pair of eleven-foot pendulums, each weighted with a round wooden box (for equal air resistance), into the center of which he placed seriatim equal weights of wood and gold, having experimented as well with silver, lead, glass, sand, common salt, water, and wheat. According to proposition 24, corollaries 1 and 6, book II, any variation in the ratio of mass to weight would have appeared as a variation in the period; Newton reported that through these experiments he could have discovered a difference as small as less than one part in a thousand in this ratio, had there been any.[165]

Newton was thus led to the law of universal gravitation, proposition 7: "That there is a power of gravity tending to all bodies, proportional to the several quantities of matter which they contain." He had shown this power to vary inversely as the square of the distance; it is by this law that bodies (according to the third law of motion) act mutually upon one another.

From these general results, Newton turned to practical problems of astronomy. Proposition 8 deals with gravitating spheres and the relative masses and densities of the planets (the numerical calculations in this proposition were much altered for the second edition). In proposition 9, Newton estimated the force of gravity within a planet and, in proposition 10, demonstrated the long-term stability of the solar system. A general "Hypothesis I" (in the second and third editions; "Hypothesis IV" in the first) holds the "centre of the system of the world" to be "immovable," which center is given as the center of gravity of the solar system in proposition 11; the sun is in constant motion, but never "recedes" far from that center of gravity (proposition 12).

It is often asserted that Newton attained his results by neglecting the interplanetary attractions, and dealing exclusively with the mutual gravitational attractions of the planets and our sun. But this is not the case, since the most fully explored example of perturbation in the *Principia* is indeed that of the sun-earth-moon system. Thus Newton determined (proposition 25) the "forces with which the sun disturbs the motions of the moon," and (proposition 26) the action of those forces in producing an inequality ("horary increment") of the area described by the moon (although "in a circular orbit").

The stated intention of proposition 29 is to "find the variation of the moon," the inequality thus being sought being due "partly to the elliptic figure of the Moon's orbit, partly to the inequality of the moments of the area which the Moon by a radius drawn to the Earth describes." (Newton dealt with this topic more fully in the second edition.) Then Newton studied the "horary motion of the nodes of the moon," first (proposition 30) "in a circular orbit," and then (proposition 31) "in an elliptic orbit." In proposition 32, he found "the mean motion of the nodes," and, in proposition 33, their "true motion." (In the third edition, following proposition 33, Newton inserted two propositions and a scholium on the motion of the nodes, written by John Machin.) Propositions 34 and 35, on the inclination of the orbit of the moon to the ecliptic plane, are followed by a scholium, considerably expanded and rewritten for the second edition, in which Newton discussed yet other "inequalities" in the motion of the moon and developed the practical aspects of computing the elements of that body's motion and position.

Propositions 36 and 37 deal at length and in a quantitative fashion with the tide-producing forces of the sun and of the moon, yielding, in proposition 38, an explanation of the spheroidal shape of the moon and the reason that (librations apart) the same face of it is always visible. A series of three lemmas introduces the subject of precession and a fourth lemma (transformed into hypothesis 2 in the second and third editions) treats the precession of a ring. Proposition 39 represents an outstanding example of the high level of mathematical natural science that Newton reached in the *Principia*. In it he showed the manner in which the shape of the earth, in relation to the pull of the moon, acts on its axis of rotation so as to produce the observed precession, a presentation that he augmented and improved for the second edition. Newton here employed the result he had previously obtained (in propositions 20 and 21, book III) concerning the shape of the earth, and joined it to both the facts and theory of precession and yet another aspect of the perturbing force of the moon on the motion of the earth. He thus inaugurated a major aspect of celestial mechanics, the study of a three-body system.

Lemma 4, book III initiates a section on comets, proving that comets are "higher" than the moon, move through the solar system, and (corollary 1) shine by reflecting sunlight; their motion shows (corollary 3) that "the celestial spaces are void of resistance." Comets move in conic sections (proposition 40) having the sun as a focus, according to the law of areas. Those comets that return move in elliptic orbits (corollary 1) and follow Kepler's third law, but (corollary 2) "their orbits will be so near to parabolas, that parabolas may be used for them without sensible error."

Almost immediately following publication of the *Principia*, Halley, in a letter of 5 July 1687, urged Newton to go on with his work on lunar theory.[166] Newton later remarked that his head so ached from studying this problem that it often "kept him awake" and "he would think of it no more." But he also said that if he lived long enough for Halley to complete enough additional observations, he "would have. another stroke at the moon." In the 1690's Newton had depended on Flamsteed for observations of the moon, promising Flamsteed (in a letter of 16 February 1695) not to communicate any of his observations, "much less publish them, without your consent." But Newton and Flamsteed disagreed on the value of theory, which Newton held to be useful as "a demonstration" of the "exactness" of observations, while Flamsteed believed that "theories do not command observations; but are to be tried by them," since "theories are . . . only probable" (even "when they agree with exact and indubitable observations"). At about this same time Newton was drawing up a set of propositions on the motion of the moon for a proposed new edition of the *Principia*, for which he requested from Flamsteed such planetary observations "as tend to [be useful for] perfecting the theory of the planets," to serve Newton in the preparation of a second edition of his book.

Revision of the "Opticks" (the Later Queries); Chemistry and Theory of Matter. Newton's *Opticks*, published in 1704, concluded with a Third Book, consisting of eleven "Observations" and sixteen queries, occupying a bare five pages of print. A Latin translation, undertaken at Newton's behest by Samuel Clarke, appeared in 1706, and included as its most notable feature the expansion of the original sixteen queries into twenty-three. The new queries 17 through 23 correspond to the final queries 25–31 of the later editions. In a series of "Errata, Corrigenda, & Addenda," at the beginning of the Latin volume, lengthy additions are provided to be inserted at the end of query 8 and of query 11; there is also a short insertion for query 14.

In a second English edition (London, 1717) the number of queries was increased to thirty-one. The queries appearing for the first time are numbered 17 to 24, and they have no counterparts in the 1706 Latin version. Newton's own copy of the 1717 English edition, in the Babson Institute Library, contains a number of emendations and corrections in Newton's hand, some of which were incorporated into the third edition (London 1721), as was a postscript to the end of the last sentence, referring to Noah and his sons.

The queries new to the 1717 edition cover a wide range of topics. Query 17 introduces the possibility that waves or vibrations may be excited in the eye by light and that vibrations of this sort may occur in the medium in which light travels. Query 18 suggests that radiant heat may be transmitted by vibrations of a medium subtler than air that pervades all bodies and expands by its elastic force throughout the heavenly spaces—the same medium by which light is put into "fits" of "easy" reflection and refraction, thus producing "Newton's rings." In queries 19 and 20, variations in the density of this medium are given as the possible cause of refraction and of the "inflection" (diffraction) of light rays. Query 21 would have the medium be rarer within celestial bodies than in empty celestial spaces, which may "impel Bodies from the denser parts of the Medium towards the rarer"; its elasticity may be estimated by the ratio of the speed of light to the speed of sound. Although he referred in this query to the mutually repulsive "particles" of ether as being "exceedingly smaller than those of Air, or even those of Light," Newton confessed that he does "not know what this *Aether* is."

In query 22, the resistance of the ether is said to be inconsiderable; the exhalations emitted by "electrick" bodies and magnetic "effluvia" are offered as other instances of such rareness. The subject of vision is introduced in query 23. Here vision is again said to be chiefly the effect of vibrations of the medium, propagated through the "optick Nerves"; an analogy is made to hearing and the other senses. Animal motion (query 24) is considered as a result of vibrations in the medium propagated from the brain through the nerves to the muscles.

Queries 25 to 31 are the English recasting of queries 17 to 23 of the Latin edition. Query 25 contains a discussion of double refraction in calcite (Iceland spar) and a geometrical construction of both the ordinary ray and (fallaciously) the extraordinary ray; query 26 concludes that double refraction may be caused by the two "sides" of rays of light. Then, in query 27, Newton attacked as erroneous all hypotheses explaining optical phenomena by new modifications of rays, since such phenomena depend upon original unalterable properties.

Query 28 questions "all Hypotheses" in which light is supposed to be a "Pression or Motion, propagated through a fluid Medium." Newton showed that Huygens' wave theory of double refraction would fail to account for the heating of bodies and the rectilinear propagation of light. Those who would fill "the Heavens with fluid Mediums" come under attack, while Newton praised the ancient philosophers who "made a *Vacuum*, and Atoms, and the Gravity of Atoms, the first Principles of their Philosophy." He added that "the main Business of natural Philosophy is to argue from Phaenomena without feigning Hypotheses"; we are to "deduce Causes from Effects, till we come to the very first Cause, which certainly is not mechanical," since nature exhibits design and purpose.

In query 29, Newton suggested that rays of light are composed of "very small Bodies emitted from shining Substances," since rays could not have a permanent virtue in two of their sides (as demonstrated by the double refraction of Iceland spar) unless they be bodies. This query also contains Newton's famous theory that rays of light could be put into "Fits of easy Reflexion and easy Transmission" if they were "small Bodies which by their attractive Powers, or some other Force, stir up Vibrations in what they act upon." These vibrations would move more swiftly than the rays themselves, would "overtake them successively," and by agitating them "so as by turns to increase and decrease their Velocities" would put them into those "fits."[167] Newton further argued that if light were to consist of waves in an ethereal medium, then in order to have the fits of easy reflection and easy transmission, a second ether would be required, in which there would be waves (of higher velocity) to put the waves of the first ether into the necessary fits. He had, however, already argued in query 28 that it would be inconceivable for two ethers to be "diffused through all

Space, one of which acts upon the other, and by consequence is re-acted upon, without retarding, shattering, dispersing and compounding one another's Motions."

In query 30, Newton discussed the convertibility of gross bodies and light, with examples showing that nature delights in transmutations. In illustration, he cited Boyle's assertion that frequent distillations had turned water into earth. In query 31, he discussed questions ranging from the forces that hold particles of matter together to the impact of bodies on one another; also causes of motion, fermentation, the circulation of the blood and animal heat, putrefaction, the force of inertia, and occult qualities. He stated a general philosophy and concluded with the pious hope that the perfection of natural philosophy will enlarge the "Bounds of Moral Philosophy."

Newton's queries, particularly the later ones, thus go far beyond any simple questions of physical or geometrical optics. In them he even proposed tentative explanations of phenomena, although explanations that are perhaps not as fully worked out, or as fully supported by experimental evidence, as he might have wished. (Some queries even propose what is, by Newton's own definition, a hypothesis.) In each case, Newton's own position is made clear; and especially in the queries added in the Latin version of 1706 (and presented again in the English version of 1717/1718), his supporting evidence is apt to be a short essay.

One notable development of the later queries is the emphasis on an "Aethereal Medium" as an explanation for phenomena. In his first papers on optics, in the 1670's, Newton had combined his cherished conception of corpuscular or globular light with the possibly Cartesian notion of a space-filling ether, elastic and varying in density. Although Newton had introduced this ether to permit wave phenomena to exist as concomitants of the rays of light, he also suggested other possible functions for it—including causing sensation and animal motion, transmitting radiant heat, and even causing gravitation. His speculations on the ether were incorporated in the "Hypothesis" that he sent to the Royal Society (read at their meetings in 1675 and 1676) and in a letter to Boyle of 28 February 1679.[168]

In the second English edition of the Opticks (1717/1718) Newton made additions which "embodied arguments for the existence of an elastic, tenuous, aetherial medium." The new queries in the Latin version of 1706 did not deal with an ether, however, and by the time of the Principia, Newton may have "rejected the Cartesian dense aether" as well as "his own youthful aetherial speculations."[169]

Newton thus did not propose a new version of the ether until possibly the 1710's; he then suggested, in the general scholium at the conclusion of the second edition of the Principia (1713), that a most subtle "spiritus" ("which pervades and lies hid in all gross bodies") might produce just such effects as his earlier ether (or the later ethereal medium of queries 18 through 24). In the general scholium of the Principia, however, Newton omitted gravitation from the list of effects that the "spiritus" may produce. There is evidence that Newton conceived of this "spiritus" as electrical, and may well have been a precursor of the ether or ethereal medium of the 1717/1718 queries.[170] In a manuscript intended for the revised second English edition of the Opticks,[171] Newton wrote the heading, "The Third Book of Opticks. Part II. Observations concerning the Medium through which Light passes, & the Agent which emits it," a title that would thus seem to link the ethereal medium with the emission of electrical effluvia. It would further appear that Newton used both the earlier and later concepts of the ether to explain, however hypothetically, results he had already obtained; and that the concept of the ether was never the basis for significant new experiments or theoretical results. In a general scholium to book II, Newton described from memory an experiment that he had performed which seemed to him to prove the nonexistence of an ether; since Newton's original notes have never been found, this experiment, which was presumably an important element in the decline of his belief in an ether, cannot be dated.

The later queries also develop a concept of matter, further expounded by Newton in his often reprinted De natura acidorum (of which there appear to have been several versions in circulation).[172] Newton here, as a true disciple of Boyle, began with the traditional "mechanical philosophy" but added "the assumption that particles move mainly under the influence of what he at first called sociability and later called attraction."[173] Although Newton also considered a principle of repulsion, especially in gases, in discussing chemical reactions he seems to have preferred to use a concept of "sociability" (as, for example, to explain how substances dissolve).

He was equally concerned with the "aggregation" of particles (in queries 28 and 31 as well as at the end of De natura acidorum) and even suggested a means of "differentiating between reaction and transmutation."[174] Another major concern was the way in which aqua regia dissolves gold but not silver, while aqua fortis dissolves silver but not gold,[175] a phenomenon Newton explained by a combination of the attraction of particles and the relation between the size of the acid particles and the "pores" between the particles of metal. He did not, however, have a sound operational definition of acid, but referred to acids theoretically, in *De natura acidorum*, as those substances "endued with a great Attractive Force; in which Force their Activity consists." He maintained this definition in query 31, in which he further called attention to the way in which metals may replace one another in acid solutions and even "went so far as to list the six common metals in the order in which they would displace one another from a solution of aqua fortis (strong nitric acid)."[176]

Alchemy, Prophecy, and Theology. Chronology and History. Newton is often alleged to have been a mystic. That he was highly interested in alchemy has been embarrassing to many students of his life and work, while others delight in finding traces of hermeticism in the father of the "age of reason." The entries in the *Catalogue of the Portsmouth Collection* give no idea of the extent of the documents in Newton's hand dealing with alchemy; these were listed in the catalogue, but not then presented to Cambridge University. Such information became generally available only when the alchemical writings were dispersed in 1936, in the Sotheby sale. The catalogue of that sale gives the only full printed guide to these materials, and estimates their bulk at some 650,000 words, almost all in Newton's hand.

A major problem in assessing Newton's alchemical "writings" is that they are not, for the most part, original compositions, nor even critical essays on his readings (in the sense that the early "De gravitatione et aequipondio fluidorum" is an essay based on his reading in Descartes's *Principia*). It would be necessary to know the whole corpus of the alchemical literature to be able to declare that any paper in Newton's hand is an original composition, rather than a series of extracts or summaries.[177]

In a famous letter to Oldenburg (26 April 1676), Newton offered an explanation of Boyle's presentations of the "incalescence" of gold and mercury (*Philosophical Transactions*, **9**, no. 122 [1675], 515–533), and presented an explanation based on the size of the particles of matter and their mechanical action. Newton particularly commended Boyle for having concealed some major steps, since here was possibly "an inlet into something more noble, and not to be communicated without immense dammage to the world if there be any verity in the Hermetick writers." He also gave some cautionary advice about alchemists, even referring to a "true Hermetic Philosopher, whose judgment (if there be any such)" might be of interest and highly regarded, "there being other things beside the transmutation of metals (if those pretenders

bragg not) which none but they understand." The apparently positive declarations in Newton's letter thus conflict with the doubts expressed in the two parenthetical expressions.

Newton's studies of prophecy may possibly provide a key to the method of his alchemical studies. His major work on the subject is *Observations upon the Prophecies of Daniel, and the Apocalypse of St. John* (London, 1733). Here Newton was concerned with "a figurative language" used by the prophets, which he sought to decipher. Newton's text is a historical exegesis, unmarked by any mystical short-circuiting of the rational process or direct communication from the godhead. He assumed an "analogy between the world natural, and an empire or kingdom considered as a world politic," and concluded, for example, that Daniel's prophecy of an "image composed of four metals" and a stone that broke "the four metals into pieces" referred to the four nations successively ruling the earth ("*viz.* the peoples of Babylonia, the Persians, the Greeks, and the Romans"). The four nations are represented again in the "four beasts."

"The folly of interpreters," Newton wrote, has been "to foretell times and things by this Prophecy, as if God designed to make them Prophets." This is, however, far from God's intent, for God meant the prophecies "not to gratify men's curiosities by enabling them to foreknow things" but rather to stand as witnesses to His providence when "after they were fulfilled, they might be interpreted by events." Surely, Newton added, "the event of things predicted many ages before, will then be a convincing argument that the world is governed by providence." (It may be noted that this book also provided Newton with occasion to refer to his favorite themes of "the corruption of scripture" and the "corruption of Christianity.")

The catalogue of the Sotheby sale states that Newton's manuscript remains include some 1,300,000 words on biblical and theological subjects. These are not particularly relevant to his scientific work and— for the most part—might have been written by any ordinary divinity student of that period, save for the extent to which they show Newton's convinced anti-Trinitarian monotheism or Unitarian Arianism. (His tract *Two Notable Corruptions of Scripture*, for example, uses historical analysis to attack Trinitarian doctrine.) "It is the temper of the hot and superstitious part of mankind in matters of religion," Newton wrote, "ever to be fond of mysteries, and for that reason to like best what they understand least."[178]

Typical of Newton's theological exercises is his "Queries regarding the word *homoousios*." The first query asks "Whether Christ sent his apostles to preach metaphysics to the unlearned common people, and to their wives and children?" Other queries in this set are also historical; in the seventh Newton marshaled his historico-philological acumen in the matter of the Latin rendering *unius substantiae*, which he considered to have been imposed on the Western churches instead of *consubstantialis* by "Hosius (or whoever translated that [Nicene] Creed into Latin)." Another manuscript entitled "Paradoxical Questions" turns out to be less a theological inquiry than a carefully reasoned proof of what Lord Keynes called "the dishonesty and falsification of records for which St Athanasius [and his followers] were responsible." In it Newton cited, as an example, the spreading of the story that Arius died in a house of prostitution.

In a Keynes manuscript (in King's College, Cambridge), "The First Book Concerning the Language of the Prophets," Newton explained his method:

> He that would understand a book written in a strange language must first learn the language. . . . Such a language was that wherein the Prophets wrote, and the want of sufficient skill in that language is the reason why they are so little understood. John . . ., Daniel . . ., Isaiah . . . all write in one and the same mystical language . . . [which] so far as I can find, was as certain and definite in its signification as is the vulgar language of any nation. . . .

Having established this basic premise, Newton went on: "It is only through want of skill therein that Interpreters so frequently turn the Prophetic types and phrases to signify whatever their fancies and hypotheses lead them to." Then, in a manner reminiscent of the rules at the beginning of book III of the *Principia*, he added:

> The rule I have followed has been to compare the several mystical places of scripture where the same prophetic phrase or type is used, and to fix such a signification to that phrase as agrees best with all the places: . . . and when I had found the necessary significations, to reject all others as the offspring of luxuriant fancy, for no more significations are to be admitted for true ones than can be proved.

Newton's alchemical manuscripts show that he sometimes used a similar method, drawing up comparative tables of symbols and of symbolic names used by alchemists, no doubt in the conviction that a key to their common language might be found thereby. His careful discrimination among the alchemical writers may be seen in two manuscripts in the Keynes Collection, one a three-page classified list of alchemical writers and the other a two-page selection of "authores optimi," by whom Newton perhaps meant authorities who described processes that might be repeated and verified. The Babson Collection of Newtoniana contains a two-page autograph manuscript listing 113 writers on alchemy arranged by nationalities and another seven-page manuscript of "chemical authors and their writings" in which Newton commented on the more important ones. At least two other such bibliographical works by Newton are known. An "Index Chemicus," an elaborate subject index to the literature of alchemy with page references to a number of different works (described as containing more than 20,000 words on 113 pages), is one of at least five such indexes, all in autograph manuscripts.[179]

It must be emphasized that Newton's study of alchemy was not a wholly rational pursuit, guided by a strict code of linguistic and historical investigative procedures. To so consider it would be to put it on the same plane as his chronological inquiries.[180] The chronological studies are, to a considerable degree, the result of the application of sound principles of astronomical dating to poor historical evidence—for which his *Chronology of Ancient Kingdoms Amended* was quite properly criticized by the French antiquarians of his day—while his alchemical works show that he drew upon esoterical and even mystical authors, far beyond the confines of an ordinary rational science.

It is difficult to determine whether to consider Newton's alchemy as an irrational vagary of an otherwise rational mind, or whether to give his hermeticism a significant role as a developmental force in his rational science. It is tempting, furthermore, to link his concern for alchemy with his belief in a secret tradition of ancient learning. He believed that he had traced this *prisca sapientia* to the ancient Greeks (notably Pythagoras) and to the Chaldean philosophers or magicians; he concluded that these ancients had known even the inverse-square law of gravitation. Cohen, McGuire, and Rattansi have shown that in the 1690's, when Newton was preparing a revised edition of the *Principia*, he thought of including references to such an ancient tradition in a series of new scholia for the propositions at the beginning of book III of the *Principia*, along with a considerable selection of verses from Lucretius' *De natura rerum*. All of this was to be an addendum to an already created *Principia*, which Newton was revising for a new edition.

There is not a shred of real evidence, however, that Newton ever had such concerns primarily in mind in those earlier years when he was writing the *Principia* or initially developing the principles of dynamics and of mathematics on which the *Principia* was ultimately to be based. In Newton's record of alchemical experiments (University Library, Cambridge, MS Add. 3975), the experiments dated 23 May [1684] are immediately followed by an entry dated 26 April 1686. The former ends in the middle of a page, and the latter starts on the very next line; there is no lacuna, and no possibility that a page—which chronologically might concern experiments made while the *Principia* was being written—might be missing from the notebook.[181]

The overtones of alchemy are on occasion discernible in Newton's purely scientific writings. In query 30 of the *Opticks* (first published in the Latin version, then in the second English edition), Newton said that "Nature . . . seems delighted with Transmutations," although he was not referring specifically to changing metals from one to another. (It must be remembered in fact that "transmutation" would not necessarily hold an exclusively chemical or alchemical meaning for Newton; it might, rather, signify not only transformations in general, but also particular transformations of a purely mathematical sort, as in lemma 22 of book I of the *Principia*.) This is a far cry, indeed, from Newton's extracts from the mystical Count Michael Maier and kindred authors. P. M. Rattansi particularly calls attention to the alchemist's "universal spirit," and observes: "It is difficult to understand how, without a conviction of deep and hidden truths concealed in alchemy, Newton should have attached much significance to such ideas."[182]

Notable instances of the conflation of alchemical inspiration and science occur in Newton's letter to Boyle (1679) and in the hypothesis he presented to explain those properties of light of which he wrote in his papers in the *Philosophical Transactions*. While it is not difficult to discover alchemical images in Newton's presentation, and to find even specific alchemical doctrines in undisguised form and language, the problem of evaluating the influence of alchemy on Newton's true science is only thereby compounded, since there is no firm indication of the role of such speculations in the development of Newton's physical science. The result is, at best, one mystery explained by another, like the alchemist's confusing doctrine of *ignotum per ignotius*. Rattansi further suggests that alchemy may have served as a guiding principle in the formulation of Newton's views on fermentation and the nourishment of the vegetation of the earth by fluids attracted from the tails of comets. He would even have us believe that alchemical influences may have influenced "the revival of aetherical notions in the last period of Newton's life."[183] This may be so; but what, if any, creative effect such "aetherical notions" then had on Newton's thought would seem to be a matter of pure hypothesis.

Scholars do not agree whether Newton's association with some "Hermetic tradition" may have been a creative force in his science, or whether it is legitimate to separate his alleged hermeticism from his positive science. Apart from the level of general inspiration, it must be concluded that, excluding some aspects of the theory of matter and chemistry, notably fermentation, and possibly the ether hypotheses, the real creative influence of alchemy or hermeticism on Newton's mathematics and his work in optics, dynamics, and astronomy (save for the role of the tails of comets in the economy of nature) must today be evaluated in terms of the Scottish verdict, "not proven." Investigations of this topic may provide valuable insights into the whole man, Newton, and into the complexities of his scientific inspiration. His concern for alchemy and theology should not be cast aside as irrelevant aberrations of senility or the product of a mental breakdown. Yet it remains a fact beyond dispute that such early manuscripts as the Waste Book—in which Newton worked out and recorded his purely scientific discoveries and innovations—are free from the tinges of alchemy and hermeticism.

The London Years: the Mint, the Royal Society, Quarrels with Flamsteed and with Leibniz. On 19 March 1696, Newton received a letter from Charles Montagu informing him that he had been appointed warden of the mint. He set up William Whiston as his deputy in the Lucasian professorship, to receive "the full profits of the place." On 10 December 1701 he resigned his professorship, and soon afterward his fellowship. He was designated an *associé étranger* of the Paris Académie des Sciences in February 1699, chosen a member of the Council of the Royal Society on the following 30 November, and on 30 November 1703 was made president of the Royal Society, an office he held until his death. He was elected M.P. for Cambridge University, for the second time, on 26 November 1701, Parliament being prorogued on 25 May 1702. Queen Anne knighted Newton at Trinity College on 16 April 1705; on the following 17 May he was defeated in his third contest for the university's seat in Parliament.

At the mint, Newton applied his knowledge of chemistry and of laboratory technique to assaying, but he apparently did not introduce any innovations in the art of coinage. His role was administrative and his duties were largely the supervision of the recoinage and (curious to contemplate) the capture, interrogation, and prosecution of counterfeiters. Newton used the patronage of the mint to benefit fellow scientists. Halley entered the service in 1696 as comptroller of the Chester mint, and in 1707 David

Gregory was appointed (at a fee of £250) as general supervisor of the conversion of the Scottish coinage to British.

Newton ruled over the Royal Society with an iron hand. When Whiston was proposed as a fellow in 1720, Newton said that if Whiston were chosen, he "would not be president." At Newton's urging, the council brought the society from the verge of bankruptcy to solvency by obtaining regular contributions from fellows. When a dispute arose between Woodward and Sloane, Newton had Woodward ejected from the council. Of Newton's chairmanship of meetings, Stukeley reported, "Everything was transacted with great attention and solemnity and dignity," for "his presence created a natural awe in the assembly"; there was never a sign of "levity or indecorum." As England's foremost scientist, president of the Royal Society, and civil servant, Newton appeared before Parliament in Spring 1714, to give advice about a prize for a method of finding longitude.

When Newton moved from Cambridge to London in the 1690's to take up the wardenship of the mint, he continued to work on the motion of the moon. He became impatient for Flamsteed's latest observations and they soon had a falling-out, no doubt aggravated by the strong enmity which had grown up between Halley and Flamsteed. Newton fanned the flames by the growing arrogance of his letters: "I want not your calculations but your observations only." And when in 1699 Flamsteed let it be known that Newton was working to perfect lunar theory, Newton sent Flamsteed a letter insisting that on this occasion he not "be brought upon the stage," since "I do not love to be printed upon every occasion much less to be dunned & teezed by foreigners about Mathematical things or to be thought by our own people to be trifling away my time about them when I should be about the King's business." Newton and Halley published Flamsteed's observations in an unauthorized printing in 1712, probably in the conviction that his work had been supported by the government and was therefore public property. Flamsteed had the bitter joy of burning most of the spurious edition; and he then started printing his own *Historia coelestis Brittanica*.

A more intense quarrel arose with Leibniz. This took two forms: a disagreement over philosophy or theology in relation to science (carried out through Samuel Clarke as intermediary), and an attempt on Newton's part to prove that Leibniz had no claim to originality in the calculus. The initial charge of plagiarism against Leibniz came from Fatio de Duillier, but before long Keill and other Newtonians were involved and Leibniz began to rally his own supporters. Newton held that not only had Leibniz

stolen the calculus from him, but that he had also composed three tracts for publication in the *Acta eruditorum* claiming some of the main truths of the *Principia* as independent discoveries, with the sole original addition of some mistakes. Today it appears that Newton was wrong; no doubt Leibniz had (as he said) seen the "epitome" or lengthy review of the *Principia* in the *Acta eruditorum* of June 1688, and not the book, when (to use his own words) "Newton's work stimulated me" to write out some earlier thoughts on "the causes of the motions of the heavenly bodies" as well as on the "resistance of a medium" and motion in a medium.[184] Newton stated, however, that even if Leibniz "had not seen the book itself, he ought nevertheless to have seen it before he published his own thoughts concerning these matters."[185]

That Newton should have connived at declaring Leibniz a plagiarist gives witness to his intense possessiveness concerning his discoveries or inventions; hence his consequent feeling of violation or robbery when Leibniz seemed to be publishing them. Newton was also aware that Leibniz must have seen one or more of his manuscript tracts then in circulation; and Leibniz had actually done so on one of his visits, when, however, he copied out some material on series expansions, not on fluxions.[186]

No one today seriously questions Leibniz' originality and true mathematical genius, nor his independence—to the degree that any two creative mathematicians living in the same world of mathematical thought can be independent—in the formulation of the calculus. Moreover, the algorithm in general use nowadays is the Leibnizian rather than the Newtonian. But by any normal standards, the behavior of both men was astonishing. When Leibniz appealed to the Royal Society for a fair hearing, Newton appointed a committee of good Newtonians. It has only recently become known that Newton himself wrote the committee's report, the famous *Commercium epistolicum*,[187] which he presented as if it were a set of impartial findings in his own favor.

Newton was not, however, content to stop there; following publication of the report there appeared an anonymous review, or summary, of it in the *Philosophical Transactions*. This, too, was Newton's work. When the *Commercium epistolicum* was reprinted, this review was included, in Latin translation, as a kind of introduction, together with an anonymous new preface "To the Reader," which was also written by Newton. This episode must be an incomparable display of thoroughness in destroying an enemy, and Whiston reported that he had heard directly that Newton had "once pleasantly" said to Samuel Clarke that "He had broke Leibnitz's Heart with his Reply to him."

Newton's later London years were marked by creative scientific efforts. During this time he published the *Opticks*, with the two mathematical tracts, and added new queries for its later editions. He also produced, with Roger Cotes's aid, a second edition of the *Principia*, including the noteworthy general scholium, and, with assistance from Henry Pemberton, a third edition. In the last, however, Newton altered the scholium to lemma 2, book II, to prevent its being read as if Leibniz were entitled to a share of credit for the calculus—although Leibniz had been dead for nearly twelve years.

Newton died on Monday, 20 March 1727,[188] at the age of eighty-five, having been ill with gout and inflamed lungs for some time. He was buried in Westminster Abbey.

Newton's Philosophy: The Rules of Philosophizing, the General Scholium, the Queries of the "Opticks." Like others of his day, Newton believed that the study of natural philosophy would provide evidence for the existence of God the Creator in the regularities of the solar system. In the general scholium at the end of book III of the *Principia*, he said "it is not to be conceived that mere mechanical causes could give birth to so many regular motions," then concluded his discussion with observations about God, "to discourse of whom from phenomena does certainly belong to Natural Philosophy" ("Experimental Philosophy" in the second edition). He then went on to point out that he had "explained the phenomena of the heavens and of our sea, by the power of Gravity" but had not yet "assigned the cause of this power," alleging that "it is enough that Gravity does really exist, and act according to the laws which we have explained" and that its action "abundantly serves to account for all the motions of the celestial bodies, and of our sea." The reader was thus to accept the facts of the *Principia*, even though Newton had not "been able to discover the cause of those properties of gravity from phenomena." Newton here stated his philosophy, "Hypotheses non fingo."[189]

Clearly, Newton was referring here only to "feigning" a hypothesis about the cause of gravitation, and never intended that his statement should be applied on all levels of scientific discourse, or to all meanings of the word "hypothesis." Indeed, in each of the three editions of the *Principia*, there is a "hypothesis" stated in book II. In the second and third editions there are a "Hypothesis I" and a "Hypothesis II" in book III. The "phaenomena" at the beginning of book III, in the second and third editions, were largely the "hypotheses" of the first

edition. It may be that Newton used these two designations to imply that these particular statements concerning planetary motions are not mathematically true (as he proved), but could be only approximately "true," on the level of (or to the limits of) phenomena.

Newton believed that his science was based upon a philosophy of induction. In the third edition of the *Principia*, he introduced rule 4, so that "the argument of induction may not be evaded by hypotheses." Here he said that one may look upon the results of "general induction from phenomena as accurately or very nearly true," even though many contrary hypotheses might be imagined, until such time as the inductive result may "either be made more accurate or liable to exceptions" by new phenomena. In rule 3, in the second and third editions, he stated his philosophical basis for establishing general properties of matter by means of phenomena.

Newton's philosophical ideas are even more fully developed in query 31, the final query of the later editions of the *Opticks*, in which he argued for both the philosophy of induction and the method of analysis and composition (or synthesis). In both mathematics and natural philosophy, he said, the "Investigation of difficult Things by the method of Analysis, ought ever to precede the Method of Composition." Such "Analysis consists in making Experiments and Observations, and in drawing general Conclusions from them by Induction, and admitting of no Objections against the Conclusions, but such as are taken from Experiments, or other certain Truths."

In both the *Principia* and the *Opticks*, Newton tried to maintain a distinction among his speculations, his experimental results (and the inductions based upon them), and his mathematical derivations from certain assumed conditions. In the *Principia* in particular, he was always careful to separate any mathematical hypotheses or assumed conditions from those results that were "derived" in some way from experiments and observations. Often, too, when he suggested, as in various scholiums, the applicability of mathematical or hypothetical conditions to physical nature, he stated that he had not proved whether his result really so applies. His treatment of the motion of small corpuscles, in book I, section 14, and his static model of a gas composed of mutually repulsive particles, in book II, proposition 23, exemplify Newton's use of mathematical models of physical reality for which he lacked experimental evidence sufficient for an unequivocal statement.

Perhaps the best expression of Newton's general philosophy of nature occurs in a letter to Cotes (28 March 1713), written during the preparation of the second edition of the *Principia*, in which he referred to the laws of motion as "the first Principles or Axiomes" and said that they "are deduced from Phaenomena & made general by Induction"; this "is the highest evidence that a Proposition can have in this philosophy." Declaring that "the mutual & mutually equal attraction of bodies is a branch of the third Law of motion," Newton pointed out to Cotes "how this branch is deduced from Phaenomena," referring him to the "end of the Corollaries of the Laws of Motion." Shortly thereafter, in a manuscript bearing upon the Leibniz controversy, he wrote, "To make an exception upon a mere Hypothesis is to feign an exception. It is to reject the argument from Induction, & turn Philosophy into a heap of Hypotheses, which are no other than a chimerical Romance."[190] That is a statement with which few would disagree.

NOTES

1. See R. S. Westfall, "Short-writing and the State of Newton's Conscience, 1662," in *Notes and Records. Royal Society of London*, **18** (1963), 10–16. L. T. More, in *Isaac Newton* (New York, 1934), p. 16, drew attention to the necessary "mental suffering" of a boy of Newton's physical weakness, living in a lonely "farmhouse situated in a countryside only slowly recovering from the terrors of a protracted and bitter civil war," with "no protection from the frights of his imagination except that of his grandmother and such unreliable labourers as could be hired."

   F. E. Manuel, in *A Portrait of Isaac Newton* (Cambridge, Mass., 1968), has subjected Newton's life to a kind of psychoanalytic scrutiny. He draws the conclusion (pp. 54–59) that the "scrupulosity, punitiveness, austerity, discipline, industriousness, and fear associated with a repressive morality" were apparent in Newton's character at an early age, and finds that notebooks bear witness to "the fear, anxiety, distrust, sadness, withdrawal, self-belittlement, and generally depressive state of the young Newton."

   For an examination of Manuel's portrait of Newton, see J. E. McGuire, "Newton and the Demonic Furies: Some Current Problems and Approaches in the History of Science," in *History of Science*, **11** (1973), 36–46; see also the review in *Times Literary Supplement* (1 June 1973), 615–616, with letters by Manuel (8 June 1973), 644–645; D. T. Whiteside (15 June 1973), 692, and (6 July 1973), 779; and G. S. Rousseau (29 June 1973), 749.

2. See E. N. da C. Andrade, "Newton's Early Notebook," in *Nature*, **135** (1935), 360; and G. L. Huxley, "Two Newtonian Studies: I. Newton's Boyhood Interests," in *Harvard Library Bulletin*, **13** (1959), 348–354, in which Andrade has first called attention to the importance of Bate's collection, an argument amplified by Huxley.

3. Newton apparently came to realize that he had been hasty in discarding Euclid, since Pemberton later heard him "even censure himself for not following them [that is, 'the ancients' in their 'taste, and form of demonstration'] yet more closely than he did; and speak with regret of his mistake at the beginning of his mathematical studies, in applying himself to the works of Des Cartes and other algebraic writers, before he had considered the elements of Euclide with that attention, which so excellent a writer

deserves" (*View of Sir Isaac Newton's Philosophy* [London, 1728], preface).

4. Newton's college tutor was not (and indeed by statute could not have been) the Lucasian professor, Barrow, but was Benjamin Pulleyn.

5. University Library, Cambridge, MS Add. 3996, discussed by A. R. Hall in "Sir Isaac Newton's Notebook, 1661–1665," in *Cambridge Historical Journal*, **9** (1948), 239–250.

6. *Ibid.*; also partially analyzed by R. S. Westfall, in "The Foundations of Newton's Philosophy of Nature," in *British Journal for the History of Science*, **1** (1962), 171–182. Westfall has attempted a reconstruction of Newton's philosophy of nature, and his growing allegiance to the "mechanical philosophy," in ch. 7 of his *Force in Newton's Physics* (London, 1971).

7. On Newton's entrance into the domains of mathematics higher than arithmetic, see the account by A. De Moivre (in the Newton MSS presented by the late J. H. Schaffner to the University of Chicago) and the recollections of Newton assembled by John Conduitt, now mainly in the Keynes Collection, King's College, Cambridge.

8. See D. T. Whiteside, "Newton's Marvellous Year. 1666 and All That," in *Notes and Records. Royal Society of London*, **21** (1966), 37–38.

9. See A. H. White, ed., William Stukeley, *Memoirs of Sir Isaac Newton's Life* (London, 1936). Written in 1752, this records a conversation with Newton about his discovery of universal gravitation (the apple story), pp. 19–20.

10. In November 1669 John Collins wrote to James Gregory that "Mr Barrow hath resigned his Lecturers place to one Mr Newton of Cambridge" (in the Royal Society ed. of Newton's *Correspondence*, I, 15). Newton himself may have been referring to Barrow in an autobiographical note (*ca.* 1716) that stated, "Upon account of my progress in these matters he procured for me a fellowship . . . in the year 1667 & the Mathematick Professorship two years later"—see University Library, Cambridge, MS Add. 3968, §41, fol. 117, and I. B. Cohen, *Introduction to Newton's Principia*, supp. III, p. 303, n. 14.

11. Among the biographical memoirs assembled by Conduitt (Keynes Collection, King's College, Cambridge). Humphrey Newton's memoir is in L. T. More, *Isaac Newton*, pp. 246, 381, and 389.

12. According to J. Edleston (p. xlv in his ed. of *Correspondence of Sir Isaac Newton and Professor Cotes . . .*; see also pp. xlix–1), in 1675 (or March 1674, OS), "Newton obtained a Royal Patent allowing the Professor to remain Fellow of a College without being obliged to go into orders." See also L. T. More, *Isaac Newton*, p. 169.

13. This work might have been an early version of the *Lectiones opticae*, his professorial lectures of 1670–1672; or perhaps an annotated version of his letters and communications to Oldenburg, which were read at the Royal Society and published in major part in its *Philosophical Transactions* from 1672 onward.

14. Quoted in L. T. More, *Isaac Newton*, p. 217.

15. It has been erroneously thought that Newton's "breakdown" may in part have been caused by the death of his mother. But her death occurred in 1679, and she was buried on 4 June. "Her will was proved 11 June 1679 by Isaac Newton, the executor, who was the residuary legatee"; see *Correspondence*, II, 303. n. 2. David Brewster, in *Memoirs . . .*, II, 123, suggested that Newton's "ailment may have arisen from the disappointment he experienced in the application of his friends for a permanent situation for him." On these events and on contemporaneous discussion and gossip about Newton's state of mind, see L. T. More, *Isaac Newton*, pp. 387–388, and F. E. Manuel, *A Portrait of Isaac Newton*, pp. 220–223. Newton himself, in a letter to Locke of 5 October 1693, blamed his "distemper" and insomnia on "sleeping too often by my fire."

16. L. T. More, *Isaac Newton*, p. 368.

17. See J. Edleston, ed., *Correspondence . . . Newton and . . . Cotes*, pp. xxxvi, esp. n. 142.

18. *Mathematical Papers of Isaac Newton*, D. T. Whiteside, ed., in progress, to be completed in 8 vols. (Cambridge, 1967–   ); these will contain edited versions of Newton's mathematical writings with translations and explanatory notes, as well as introductions and commentaries that constitute a guide to Newton's mathematics and scientific life, and to the main currents in the mathematics of the seventeenth century. Five volumes have been published (1973).

19. See D. T. Whiteside, "Newton's Discovery of the General Binomial Theorem," in *Mathematical Gazette*, **45** (1961), 175.

20. Especially because of Whiteside's researches.

21. Whiteside, ed., *Mathematical Papers*, I, 1–142. Whiteside concludes: "By and large Newton took his arithmetical symbolisms from Oughtred and his algebraical from Descartes, and onto them . . . he grafted new modifications of his own" (I, 11).

22. Ca. 1714; see University Library, Cambridge, MS Add. 3968, fol. 21. On this often debated point, see D. T. Whiteside, "Isaac Newton: Birth of a Mathematician," in *Notes and Records. Royal Society of London*, **19** (1964), n. 25; but compare n. 48, below.

23. University Library, Cambridge, MS Add. 3968. 41, fol. 85. This sentence occurs in a passage canceled by Newton.

24. *Ibid.*, fol. 72. This accords with De Moivre's later statement (in the Newton manuscripts recently bequeathed the University of Chicago by J. H. Schaffner) that after reading Wallis' book, Newton "on the occasion of a certain interpolation for the quadrature of the circle, found that admirable theorem for raising a Binomial to a power given."

25. Translated from the Latin in the Royal Society ed. of the *Correspondence*, II, 20 ff. and 32 ff.; see the comments by Whiteside in *Mathematical Papers*, IV, 666 ff. In the second term, A stands for $P^{m/n}$ (the first term), while in the third term B stands for $(m/n)AQ$ (the second term), and so on. This letter and its sequel came into Wallis' hands and he twice published summaries of them, the second time with Newton's own emendations and grudging approval. Newton listed some results of series expansion—coupled with quadratures as needed—for $z = r \sin^{-1}[x/r]$ and the inverse $x = r \sin[z/r]$; the versed sine $r(1 - \cos[z/r])$; and $x = e^{z/b} - 1$, the inverse of $z = b \log(1 + x)$, the Mercator series (see Whiteside, ed., *Mathematical Papers*, IV, 668).

26. Translated from the Latin in the Royal Society ed. of the *Correspondence*, II, 110 ff., 130 ff.; see the comments by Whiteside in *Mathematical Papers*, IV, 672 ff.

27. See Whiteside, *Mathematical Papers*, I, 106.

28. *Ibid.*, I, 112 and n. 81.

29. The Boothby referred to may be presumed to be Boothby Pagnell (about three miles northeast of Woolsthorpe), whose rector, H. Babington, was senior fellow of Trinity and had a good library. See further Whiteside, *Mathematical Papers*, I, 8, n. 21; and n. 8, above.

30. *The Mathematical Works of Isaac Newton*, I, x.

31. *Ibid.*, I, xi.

32. Here the "little zero" o is not, as formerly, the "indefinitely small" increment in the variable t, which "ultimately vanishes." In the *Principia*, bk. II, sec. 2, Newton used an alternative system of notation in which $a, b, c, \cdots$ are the "moments of any quantities A, B, C, &c.," increasing by a continual flux or "the velocities of the mutations which are proportional" to those moments, that is, their fluxions.

33. See Whiteside, *Mathematical Works*, I, x.

34. See A. R. and M. B. Hall, eds., *Unpublished Scientific Papers of Isaac Newton* (Cambridge, 1962).

35. *Mathematical Works*, I, xi.

36. *Ibid.*, xii.

37. University Library, Cambridge, MS Add. 3968.41, fol. 86, v.

38. Whiteside, *Mathematical Papers*, II, 166.

39. *Ibid.*, 166–167.

40. *Ibid.*, I, 11, n. 27. where Whiteside lists those "known to have seen substantial portions of Newton's mathematical papers during his lifetime" as including Collins, John Craig, Fatio de Duillier, Raphson, Halley, De Moivre, David Gregory, and William Jones, "but not, significantly, John Wallis," who did, however, see the "Epistola prior" and "Epistola posterior" (see n. 25, above); and II, 168. Isaac Barrow "probably saw only the *De analysi*."

41. The *Methodus fluxionum* also contained an amplified version of the tract of October 1666; it was published in English in 1736, translated by John Colson, but was not properly printed in its original Latin until 1779, when Horsley brought out *Analysis per quantitatum series, fluxiones, ac differentias*, incorporating William Jones's transcript, which he collated with an autograph manuscript by Newton. Various MS copies of the *Methodus fluxionum* had, however, been in circulation many years before 1693, when David Gregory wrote out an abridged version. Buffon translated it into French (1740) and Castillon used Colson's English version as the basis of a retranslation into Latin (*Opuscula mathematica*, I, 295 ff.). In all these versions, Newton's equivalent notation was transcribed into dotted letters. Horsley (*Opera*, I) entitled his version *Artis analyticae specimina vel geometria analytica*. The full text was first printed by Whiteside in *Mathematical Papers*, vol. III.

42. *Mathematical Papers*, II, 170.

43. P. xi; and see n. 41, above.

44. The reader may observe the confusion inherent in using both "indefinitely small portions of time" and "infinitely little" in relation to o; the use of index notation for powers (x^3, x^2, o^2) together with the doubling of letters (oo) in the same equation occurs in the original. These quotations are from the anonymous English version of 1737, reproduced in facsimile in Whiteside, ed., *Mathematical Works*. See n. 46.

45. In this example, I have (following the tradition of more than two centuries) introduced $\dot{x}$ and $\dot{y}$ where Newton in his MS used m and n. In his notation, too, r stood for the later $\dot{z}$.

46. *Mathematical Papers*, III, 80, n. 96. In the anonymous English version of 1737, as in Colson's translation of 1736, the word "indefinitely" appears; Castillon followed these (see n. 41). Horsley first introduced "*infinité*."

47. *Ibid.*, pp. 16–17.

48. See Whiteside, *ibid.*, p. 17; on Barrow's influence, see further pp. 71–74, notes 81, 82, 84.

49. *Ibid.*, pp. 328–352. On p. 329, n. 1, Whiteside agrees with a brief note by Alexander Witting (1911), in which the "source of the celebrated 'fluxional' Lemma II of the second Book of Newton's *Principia*" was accurately found in the first theorem of this addendum; see also p. 331, n. 11, and p. 334, n. 16.

50. On this topic, see the collection of statements by Newton assembled in supp. I to I. B. Cohen, *Introduction to Newton's Principia*.

51. This and the following quotations of the *De quadratura* are from John Stewart's translation of 1745.

52. As C. B. Boyer points out, in *Concepts of the Calculus*, p. 201, Newton was thus showing that one should not reach the conclusion "by simply neglecting infinitely small terms, but by finding the ultimate ratio as these terms become evanescent." Newton unfortunately compounded the confusion, however, by not wholly abjuring infinitesimals thereafter; in bk. II, lemma 2, of the *Principia* he warned the reader that his "moments" were not finite

quantities. In the eighteenth century, many English mathematicians, according to Boyer, "began to associate fluxions with the infinitely small differentials of Leibniz."

53. University Library, Cambridge, MS Add. 3960, fol. 177. Newton, however, was not the first mathematician to anticipate the Taylor series.

54. Introduction to *De quadratura*, in John Stewart, trans., *Two Treatises of the Quadrature of Curves, and Analysis by Equations of an Infinite Number of Terms* . . . (London, 1745), p. 4.

55. *Philosophical Transactions*, no. 342 (1715), 206.

56. Attributed to Newton, May 1708, in W. G. Hiscock, ed., *David Gregory, Isaac Newton and Their Circle* (Oxford, 1937), p. 42.

57. Henry Pemberton recorded, in his preface to his *View of . . . Newton's Philosophy* (London, 1728), that "I have often heard him censure the handling [of] geometrical subjects by algebraic calculations; and his book of Algebra he called by the name of Universal Arithmetic, in opposition to the injudicious title of Geometry, which Des Cartes had given to the treatise wherein he shews, how the geometer may assist his invention by such kind of computations."

58. There were five Latin eds. between 1707 and 1761, of which one was supervised by Newton, and three English eds. between 1720 and 1769.

59. For details, see Turnbull, *The Mathematical Discoveries of Newton*, pp. 49-50.

60. See C. B. Boyer, *History of Mathematics*, p. 450.

61. *Arithmetica universalis*, English ed. (London, 1728), p. 247; see Whiteside, *Mathematical Papers*, V, 428–429, 470–471.

62. *Arithmetica universalis*, in Whiteside's translation, *Mathematical Papers*, V, 477.

63. Published by Whiteside, *Mathematical Papers*, I, pp. 145 ff.

64. See especially *ibid.*, pp. 298 ff., pt. 2, sec. 5, "The Calculus Becomes an Algorithm."

65. *Ibid.*, III, pp. 120 ff.

66. *Ibid.*

67. In "Newton as an Originator of Polar Coördinates," in *American Mathematical Monthly*, **56** (1949), 73–78.

68. Made available in English translation (perhaps supervised by Newton himself) in John Harris, *Lexicon technicum*, vol. II (London, 1710); reprinted in facsimile (New York, 1966). The essay entitled "Curves" is reprinted in Whiteside, *Mathematical Papers*, II.

69. C. R. M. Talbot, ed. and trans., *Enumeration of Lines of the Third Order* (London, 1860), p. 72.

70. On other aspects of Newton's mathematics see Whiteside, *Mathematical Papers*, specifically III, 50–52, on the development of infinite series; II, 218–232, on an iterative procedure for finding approximate solutions to equations; and I, 519, and V, 360, on "Newton's identities" for finding the sums of the powers of the roots in any polynomial equation. See, additionally, for Newton's contributions in porisms, solid loci, number theory, trigonometry, and interpolation, among other topics, Whiteside, *Mathematical Papers*, *passim*, and Turnbull, *Mathematical Discoveries*.

71. See Whiteside, *Mathematical Works*, I, XV, and Boyer, *History of Mathematics*, p. 448. Drafts of the "Liber geometria" are University Library, Cambridge, MS Add. 3963 *passim* and MS Add. 4004, fols. 129–159. Gregory's comprehensive statement of Newton's plans as of summer 1694 is in Edinburgh University Library, David Gregory MS C42; an English version in Newton's *Correspondence*, III, 384–386, is not entirely satisfactory.

72. Newton's laconic statement of his solution, published anonymously in *Philosophical Transactions*, no. 224 (1697), p. 384, elicited from Bernoulli the reply "Ex ungue, Leonem" (the claw was sufficient to reveal the lion); see *Histoire des ouvrages des savans* (1697), 454–455.

73. See I. B. Cohen, "Isaac Newton, John Craig, and the Design of Ships," in *Boston Studies for the Philosophy of Science* (in press).

74. Even the variants in the eds. of the *Opticks* have never been fully documented in print (although Horsley's ed. gives such information for the Queries), nor have the differences between the Latin and English versions been fully analyzed. Zev Bechler is in the process of publishing four studies based on a perceptive and extensive examination of Newton's optical MSS. Henry Guerlac is presently engaged in preparing a new ed. of the *Opticks* itself.

75. The expression "experimentum crucis" is often attributed to Bacon, but Newton in fact encountered it in Hooke's account of his optical experiments as given in *Micrographia* (observation 9), where Hooke referred to an experiment that "will prove such a one as our *thrice excellent Verulam* [that is, Francis Bacon] calls *Experimentum crucis.*" While many investigators before Newton— Dietrich von Freiberg, Marci, Descartes, and Grimaldi among them—had observed the oval dispersion of a circular beam of light passing through a prism, they all tended to assign the cause of the phenomenon to the consideration that the light source was not a point, but a physical object, so that light from opposite limbs of the sun would differ in angle of inclination by as much as half a degree. Newton's measurements led him from this initial supposition to the conclusion that the effect—a spectrum some five times longer than its width—was too great for the given cause, and therefore the prism must refract some rays to a considerable degree more than others.

76. This account of the experiment is greatly simplified, as was Newton's own account, presented in his letter to Oldenburg and published in *Philosophical Transactions*. See J. A. Lohne, "Experimentum Crucis," in *Notes and Records. Royal Society of London*, **23** (1968), 169-199; Lohne has traced the variations introduced into both the later diagrams and descriptions of the experiment. Newton's doctrine of the separation of white light into its component colors, each corresponding to a unique and fixed index of refraction, had been anticipated by Johannes Marcus Marci de Kronland in his *Thaumantias, liber de arcu coelesti* (Prague, 1648). An important analysis of Newton's experiment is in A. I. Sabra, *Theories of Light*.

77. See R. S. Westfall, "The Development of Newton's Theory of Color," in *Isis*, **53** (1962), 339–358; and A. R. Hall, "Newton's Notebook," pp. 245–250.

78. Dated 13 April 1672, in *Philosophical Transactions*, no. 84.

79. See R. S. Westfall, "Newton's Reply to Hooke and the Theory of Colors," in *Isis*, **54** (1963), 82–96; an edited text of the "Hypothesis" is in *Correspondence*, I, 362–386.

80. Published in Birch's *History of the Royal Society* and in I. B. Cohen, ed., *Newton's Papers and Letters*.

81. R. S. Westfall has further sketched Newton's changing views in relation to corpuscles and the ether, and, in "Isaac Newton's Coloured Circles Twixt Two Contiguous Glasses," in *Archive for History of Exact Sciences*, **2** (1965), 190, has concluded that "When Newton composed the *Opticks*, he had ceased to believe in an aether; the pulses of earlier years became 'fits of easy reflection and transmission,' offered as observed phenomena without explanation." Westfall discusses Newton's abandonment of the ether in "Uneasily Fitful Reflections on Fits of Easy Transmission [and of Easy Reflection]," in Robert Palter, ed., *The Annus Mirabilis of Sir Isaac Newton 1666–1966*, pp. 88–104; he emphasizes the pendulum experiment that Newton reported from memory in the *Principia* (bk. II, scholium at the end of sec. 7, in the first ed., or of sec. 6, in the 2nd and 3rd eds.). Henry Guerlac has discussed Newton's return to a modified concept of the ether in a series of studies (see Bibliography, sec. 8).

82. Birch, *History of the Royal Society*, III, 299; the early text of the "Discourse" is III, 247–305, but Newton had

already published it, with major revisions, as book II of the *Opticks*. Both the "Hypothesis" and the "Discourse" are reprinted in Newton's *Papers and Letters*, 177–235. Newton's original notes on Hooke's *Micrographia* have been published by A. R. and M. B. Hall, *Unpublished Scientific Papers of Isaac Newton*, 400 ff., especially sec. 48, in which he refers to "coloured rings" of "8 or 9 such circuits" in this "order (white perhaps in the midst) blew, purple, scarlet, yellow, greene, blew. . . ."

83. Newton's notes on Hooke were first published by Geoffrey Keynes in *Bibliography of Robert Hooke* (Oxford, 1960), pp. 97–108. Hooke claimed in particular that Newton's "Hypothesis" was largely taken from the *Micrographia*; see Newton's letters to Oldenburg, 21 December 1675 and 10 January 1676, in *Correspondence*, I, 404 ff. Hooke then wrote to Newton in a more kindly vein on 20 January 1676, provoking Newton's famous reply.

84. In this presentation, attention has been directed only to certain gross differences that exist between the texts of Newton's "Discourse of Observations" of 1675 and bk. II of the *Opticks*. The elaboration of Newton's view may be traced through certain notebooks and an early essay "On Colours" to his optical lectures and communications to the Royal Society. In particular, R. S. Westfall has explored certain relations between the essay and the later *Opticks*. See also his discussion on Newton's experiments cited in n. 81, above.

85. Chiefly in University Library, Cambridge, MS Add. 3970; but see n. 76.

86. University Library, Cambridge, MS Dd. 9.67.

87. Now part of the Portsmouth Collection, University Library, Cambridge, MS Add. 4002. This MS has been reproduced in facsimile, with an introduction by Whiteside, as *The Unpublished First Version of Isaac Newton's Cambridge Lectures on Optics* (Cambridge, 1973).

88. The development of the *Opticks* can be traced to some degree through a study of Newton's correspondence, notebooks, and optical MSS, chiefly University Library, Cambridge, MS Add. 3970, of which the first 233 pages contain the autograph MS used for printing the 1704 ed., although the final query 16 is lacking. An early draft, without the preliminary definitions and axioms, begins on fol. 304; the first version of prop. 1, book I, here reads, "The light of one natural body is more refrangible than that of another." There are many drafts and versions of the later queries, and a number of miscellaneous items, including the explanation of animal motion and sensation by the action of an "electric" and "elastic" spirit and the attribution of an "electric force" to all living bodies. A draft of a proposed "fourth Book" contains, on fol. 336, a "Conclusion" altered to "Hypoth. 1. The particles of bodies have certain spheres of activity with in which they attract or shun one another . . ."; in a subsequent version, a form of this is inserted between props. 16 and 17, while a later prop. 18 is converted into "Hypoth. 2," which is followed shortly by hypotheses 3 to 5. It may thus be seen that Newton did not, in the 1690's, fully disdain speculative hypotheses. On fol. 409 there begins a tract, written before the *Opticks*, entitled "Fundamentum Opticae," which is similar to the *Opticks* in form and content. The three major notebooks in which Newton entered notes on his optical reading and his early thoughts and experiments on light, color, vision, the rainbow, and astronomical refraction are MSS Add. 3975, 3996, and 4000.

89. In "Newton's Reply to Hooke and the Theory of Colors," in *Isis*, **54** (1963), 82–96; an analysis of the two versions of Newton's lectures on optics is given in I. B. Cohen, *Introduction to Newton's 'Principia,'* supp. III.

90. See "Experimentum Crucis," in *Notes and Records. Royal Society of London*, **23** (1968), 169–199.

91. See, notably, "Isaac Newton: The Rise of a Scientist 1661–1671," in *Notes and Records. Royal Society of London*, **20** (1965), 125–139.

92. University Library, Cambridge, MS Add. 3996.

93. See Sabra, *Theories of Light*; also Westfall, "The Development of Newton's Theory of Color," in *Isis*, **53** (1962), 339–358. A major source for the development of Newton's optical concepts is, of course, the series of articles by Lohne, esp. those cited in nn. 90 and 91.

94. The surviving pages of this abortive ed. are reproduced in I. B. Cohen, "Versions of Isaac Newton's First Published Paper, With Remarks on the Question of Whether Newton Planned to Publish an Edition of His Early Papers on Light and Color," in *Archives internationales d'histoire des sciences*, **11** (1958), 357–375, 8 plates. See also A. R. Hall, "Newton's First Book," in *Archives internationales d'histoire des sciences*, **13** (1960), 39–61.

95. In W. C. Hiscock, ed., *David Gregory*, p. 15. The preface to the first ed. of the *Opticks* is signed "I.N."

96. See the "Analytical Table of Contents" prepared by Duane H. D. Roller for the Dover ed. of the *Opticks* (New York, 1952) for the contents of the entire work.

97. *Opticks*, book I, part 2, proposition 6. Newton's first statement of a musical analogy to color occurs in his "Hypothesis" of 1675; for an analysis of Newton's musical theory, see *Correspondence*, I, 388, n. 14, which includes a significant contribution by J. E. Bullard.

98. As Boyer has pointed out, "In the Cartesian geometrical theory [of the rainbow] it matters little what light is, or how it is transmitted, so long as propagation is rectilinear and the laws of reflection and refraction are satisfied"; see *The Rainbow from Myth to Mathematics* (New York, 1959), ch. 9.

99. Although Newton had worked out the formula at the time of his optical lectures of 1669-1671, he published no statement of it until the *Opticks*. In the meantime Halley and Johann [I] Bernoulli had reached this formula independently and had published it; see Boyer, *The Rainbow*, pp. 247 ff. In the *Opticks*, Newton offered the formula without proof, observing merely that "The Truth of all this Mathematicians will easily examine." His analysis is, however, given in detail in the *Lectiones opticae*, part 1, section 4, propositions 35 and 36, as a note informs the reader of the 1730 ed. of the *Opticks*.

For a detailed analysis of the topic, see Whiteside, *Mathematical Papers*, III, 500–509.

100. Ernst Mach, *The Principles of Physical Optics*, John S. Anderson and A. F. A. Young, trans. (London, 1926), 139.

101. This final sentence of book II, part 2, is a variant of a sentiment expressed a few paragraphs earlier: "Now as all these things follow from properties of Light by a mathematical way of reasoning, so the truth of them may be manifested by Experiments."

102. The word "diffraction" appears to have been introduced into optical discourse by Grimaldi, in his *Physico-mathesis de lumine, coloribus, et iride* (Bologna, 1665), in which the opening proposition reads: "Lumen propagatur seu diffunditur non solùm Directè, Refractè, ac Reflexè, sed etiam alio quodam Quarto modo, DIFFRACTÈ." Although Newton mentioned Grimaldi by name (calling him "Grimaldo") and referred to his experiments, he did not use the term "diffraction," but rather "inflexion," a usage the more curious in that it had been introduced into optics by none other than Hooke (*Micrographia*, "Obs. LVIII. Of a new Property in the Air and several other transparent *Mediums* nam'd *Inflection* . . ."). Newton may thus have been making a public acknowledgment of his debt to Hooke; see n. 83.

103. Newton's alleged denial of the possibility of correcting chromatic aberration has been greatly misunderstood. See the analysis of Newton's essay "Of Refractions" in Whiteside, *Mathematical Papers*, I, 549–550 and 559–576,

esp. the notes on the theory of compound lenses, pp. 575–576, and notes 60 and 61. This topic has also been studied by Zev Bechler; see " 'A Less Agreeable Matter'— Newton and Achromatic Refraction" (in press).

104. Many of these are available in two collections: A. R. and M. B. Hall, eds., *Unpublished Scientific Papers;* and John Herivel, *The Background to Newton's Principia.* See also the Royal Society's ed. of the *Correspondence.*

105. University Library, Cambridge, MS Add. 3996, first analyzed by A. R. Hall in 1948.

106. *Ibid.,* fol. 29. See also R. S. Westfall, *Force in Newton's Physics.* Newton's entry concerning the third law was first published by Whiteside in 1964; see n. 114.

107. University Library, Cambridge, MS Add. 4004; Herivel also gives the dynamical portions, with commentaries.

108. Def. 4; see Herivel, *Background,* p. 137.

109. *Ibid.,* p. 141.

110. See William Stukeley, *Memoirs of Sir Isaac Newton's Life,* p. 20; see also Douglas McKie and G. R. de Beer, "Newton's Apple," in *Notes and Records. Royal Society of London,* **9** (1952), 46–54, 333–335.

111. Various nearly contemporary accounts are given by W. W. Rouse Ball, *An Essay on Newton's "Principia,"* ch. 1.

112. See F. Cajori, "Newton's Twenty Years' Delay in Announcing the Law of Gravitation," in F. E. Brasch, ed., *Sir Isaac Newton,* pp. 127–188.

113. This document, a tract on "circular motion," University Library, Cambridge, MS Add. 3958.5, fol. 87, was in major part published for the first time by A. R. Hall in 1957. It has since been republished, with translation, in *Correspondence,* I, 297–300, and by Herivel in *Background,* pp. 192 ff.

114. In "Newton's Early Thoughts on Planetary Motion: A Fresh Look," in *British Journal for the History of Science,* **2** (1964), 120, n. 13.

115. In A. R. and M. B. Hall, *Unpublished Papers,* pp. 89 ff.

116. University Library, Cambridge, MS Add. 3958, fols. 81–83; also in Turnbull, *Correspondence,* III, 60–64.

117. Newton's concept of force has been traced, in its historical context, by Westfall, *Force in Newton's Physics;* see also Herivel, *Background,* and see I. B. Cohen, "Newton's Second Law and the Concept of Force in the *Principia,*" in R. Palter, ed., *Annus Mirabilis,* pp. 143–185.

118. In the scholium to the Laws of Motion, Newton mentioned that Wren, Wallis, and Huygens at "about the same time" communicated their "discoveries to the Royal Society"; they agreed "exactly among themselves" as to "the rules of the congress and reflexion of hard bodies."

119. Almost all discussions of Newton's spiral are based on a poor version of Newton's diagram; see J. A. Lohne, "The Increasing Corruption of Newton's Diagrams," in *History of Science,* **6** (1967), 69–89, esp. pp. 72–76.

120. Whiteside, "Newton's Early Thoughts," p. 135, has paraphrased Hooke's challenge as "Does the central force which, directed to a focus, deflects a body uniformly travelling in a straight line into an elliptical path vary as the inverse-square of its instantaneous distance from that focus ?"

121. University Library, Cambridge, MS Add. 3968.41, fol. 85r, first printed in *Catalogue of the Portsmouth Collection,* p. xviii; it is in fact part of a draft of a letter to Des Maizeaux, written in summer 1718, when Des Maizeaux was composing his *Recueil.* In a famous MS memorandum (University Library, Cambridge, MS Add. 3968, fol. 101), Newton recalled the occasion of his correspondence with Hooke concerning his use of Kepler's area law in relation to elliptic orbits; see I. B. Cohen, *Introduction to Newton's Principia,* supp. I, sec. 2.

122. University Library, Cambridge, MS Add. 3965.7, fols. 55r-62(bis)r; printed versions appear in A. R. and M. B. Hall, *Unpublished Papers*; J. Herivel, *Background*; and W. W. Rouse Ball, *Essay.*

123. See Whiteside, "Newton's Early Thoughts," pp. 135–136; and see I. B. Cohen, "Newton's Second Law and the Concept of Force in the *Principia,*" in R. Palter, ed., *Annus Mirabilis,* pp. 143–185.

124. Analysis shows that great care is necessary in dealing with the limit process in even the simplest of Newton's examples, as in his early derivation of the Huygenian rule for centrifugal force (in the Waste Book, and referred to in the scholium to prop. 4, bk. I, in the *Principia*), or in the proof (props. 1–2, bk. I) that the law of areas is a necessary and sufficient condition for a central force. Whiteside has analyzed these and other propositions in "Newtonian Dynamics," pp. 109–111, and "Mathematical Principles," pp. 11 ff., and has shown the logical pitfalls that await the credulous reader, most notably the implied use by Newton of infinitesimals of an order higher than one (chiefly those of the second, and occasionally those of the third, order).

125. See the *Principia,* props. 1–3, bk. I, and the various versions of *De motu* printed by A. R. and M. B. Hall, J. Herivel, and W. W. Rouse Ball.

126. In *Correspondence,* II, 436–437. This letter unambiguously shows that Newton did not have the solution to the problem of the attraction of a sphere until considerably later than 1679, and declaredly not "until last summer [1685]."

127. There is considerable uncertainty about what "curious treatise, *De Motu*" Halley saw; see I. B. Cohen, *Introduction,* ch. 3, sec. 2.

128. *Ibid.,* sec. 6.

129. First published by A. R. and M. B. Hall, *Unpublished Papers.*

130. Newton at first corresponded with Flamsteed indirectly, beginning in December 1680, through the agency of James Crompton.

131. In 1681, Newton still thought that the "comets" seen in November and December 1680 were "two different ones" (Newton to Crompton for Flamsteed, 28 February 1681, in *Correspondence,* II, 342); in a letter to Flamsteed of 16 April 1681 (*ibid.,* p. 364), Newton restated his doubts that "the Comets of November & December [were] but one." In a letter of 5 January 1685 (*ibid.,* p. 408), Flamsteed hazarded a "guess" at Newton's "designe": to define the curve that the comet of 1680 "described in the aether" from a general "Theory of motion," while on 19 September 1685 (*ibid.,* p. 419), Newton at last admitted to Flamsteed that "it seems very probable that those of November & December were the same comet." Flamsteed noted in the margin of the last letter that Newton "would not grant it before," adding, "see his letter of 1681." In the *Arithmetica universalis* of 1707, Newton, in problem 52, explored the "uniform rectilinear motion" of a comet, "supposing the 'Copernican hypothesis' "; see Whiteside, *Mathematical Papers,* V, 299, n. 400, and esp. pp. 524 ff.

132. As far as actual Greek geometry goes, Newton barely makes use of Archimedes, Apollonius, or even Pappus (mentioned in passing in the preface to the 1st ed. of the *Principia*); see Whiteside, "Mathematical Principles," p. 7.

133. This is the tract "De methodis serierum et fluxionum," printed with translation in Whiteside, ed., *Mathematical Papers,* III, 32 ff.

134. Motte has standardized the use of the neuter *genitum* in his English translation, although Newton actually wrote: "Momentum Genitae aequatur . . .," and then said "Genitam voco quantitatem omnem quae . . .," where *quantitas genita* (or "generated quantity") is, of course, feminine.

135. Whiteside, *Mathematical Papers,* IV, 523, note 6.

136. *Concepts,* p. 200.

137. *Ibid.;* on Newton's use of infinitesimals in the *Principia,* see also A. De Morgan, "On the Early History of Infinitesimals in England," in *Philosophical Magazine,* **4** (1852), 321–330, in which he notes especially some changes in

Newton's usage from the 1687 to the 1713 eds. See further F. Cajori, *A History of the Conceptions of Limits*, pp. 2–32.

138. Whiteside, "Mathematical Principles," pp. 20 ff.

139. Newton's method, contained in University Library, Cambridge, MS Add. 3965.10, fols. 107v and 134v, will be published for the first time in Whiteside, *Mathematical Papers*, VI.

140. Halley refers to this specifically in the first paragraph of his review of the *Principia*, in *Philosophical Transactions of the Royal Society*, no. 186 (1687), p. 291.

141. Translated from University Library, Cambridge, MS Add. 3968, fol. 112.

142. *De quadratura* was printed, together with the other tracts in the collection published by W. Jones in 1711, as a supp. to the second reprint of the 2nd ed. of the *Principia* (1723).

143. In *Philosophical Transactions of the Royal Society* (1715), p. 206.

144. Newton was aware that a shift in latitude causes a variation in rotational speed, since $v = 2r/T \times \cos \varphi$, where v is the linear tangential speed at latitude φ; r, T being the average values of the radius of the earth and the period of rotation. The distance from the center of the earth is also affected by latitude, since the earth is an oblate spheroid. These two factors appear in the variation with latitude in the length of a seconds pendulum.

145. "The Aim of Science," in *Ratio*, **1** (1957), 24–35; repr. in Karl Popper, *Objective Knowledge* (Oxford, 1972), 191–205.

146. See, for example, R. S. Westfall, *Force in Newton's Physics*. See also Alan Gabbey, "Force and Inertia in 17th-century Dynamics," in *Studies in History and Philosophy of Science*, **2** (1971), 1–67; Gabbey contests Westfall's point of view concerning the *vis insita*, in *Science*, **176** (1972), 157–159.

147. This would no longer even be called a force; some present translations, among them F. Cajori's version of Motte, anachronistically render Newton's *vis inertiae* as simple "inertia."

148. University Library, Cambridge, MS Add. 3968, fol. 415; published in A. Koyré and I. B. Cohen, "Newton and the Leibniz-Clarke Correspondence," in *Archives internationales d'histoire des sciences*, **15** (1962), 122–123.

149. See I. B. Cohen, "Newton's Second Law and the Concept of Force in the *Principia*," in R. Palter, ed., *Annus Mirabilis*, pp. 143–185.

150. R. S. Westfall, *Force*, p. 490. It is with this point of view in particular that Gabbey takes issue; see n. 146. See further E. J. Aiton, "The Concept of Force," in A. C. Crombie and M. A. Hoskin, eds., *History of Science*, X (Cambridge, 1971), 88–102.

151. In prop. 7, bk. III (referring to prop. 69, bk. I, and its corollaries), Newton argued from "accelerative" measures of forces to "absolute" forces, in specific cases of attraction.

152. See D. T. Whiteside, in *History of Science*, V (Cambridge, 1966), 110.

153. E. J. Aiton, "The Inverse Problem of Central Forces," in *Annals of Science*, **20** (1964), 82.

154. This position of the *Principia* was greatly altered between the 1st and 2nd eds.; Newton's intermediate results were summarized in a set of procedural rules for making up lunar tables and were published in a Latin version in David Gregory's treatise on astronomy (1702). Several separate English versions were later published; these are reprinted in facsimile in I. B. Cohen, *Newton's Theory of the Moon* (London, 1974).

155. W. W. Rouse Ball gives a useful paraphrase in *Essay*, p. 92.

156. See the analyses by Clifford Truesdell, listed in the bibliography to this article.

157. In his review of the *Principia*, in *Philosophical Transactions* (1687), p. 295, Halley referred specifically to this proposition, "which being rather a Physical than Mathematical Inquiry, our Author forbears to discuss."

158. This problem had gained prominence through the independent discovery by Halley and Richer that the length of a pendulum clock must be adjusted for changes in latitude.

159. This "General Scholium" should not be confused with the general scholium that ends the *Principia*. It was revised and expanded for the 2nd ed., where it appears at the end of sec. 6; in the 1st ed. it appears at the end of sec. 7.

160. In *Mécanique céleste*, V, bk. XII, ch. 3, sec. 7. Newton failed to take into account the changes in elasticity due to the "heat of compression and cold of rarefaction"; Laplace corrected Newton's formula ($v = k \sqrt{p/d}$), replacing it with his own ($v = k \sqrt{1.41 p/d}$, where p is the air pressure and d the density of the air).

Laplace, who had first published his own results in 1816, later said that Newton's studies on the velocity of sound in the atmosphere were the most important application yet made of the equations of motion in elastic fluids: "sa théorie, quoique imparfaite, est un monument de son génie" (*Mécanique céleste*, V, bk. XII, ch. 1, pp. 95–96). Lord Rayleigh pointed out that Newton's investigations "established that the velocity of sound should be independent of the amplitude of the vibration, and also of the pitch."

161. The confutation of Descartes's vortex theory was thought by men of Newton's century to be one of the major aims of bk. II. Huygens, for one, accepted Newton's conclusion that the Cartesian vortices must be cast out of physics, and wrote to Leibniz to find out whether he would be able to continue to believe in them after reading the *Principia*. In "my view," Huygens wrote, "these vortices are superfluous if one accepts the system of Mr. Newton."

162. On the earlier tract in relation to bk. III of the *Principia*, see the preface to the repr. (London, 1969) and I. B. Cohen, *Introduction*, supp. VI.

163. At one time, according to a manuscript note, Newton was unequivocal that hypothesis 3 expressed the belief of Aristotle, Descartes, and unspecified "others." It was originally followed by a hypothesis 4, which in the 2nd and 3rd eds. was moved to a later part of bk. III. For details, see I. B. Cohen, "Hypotheses in Newton's Philosophy," in *Physis*, **8** (1966), 163–184.

164. See *De motu* in A. R. and M. B. Hall, *Unpublished Papers*, and J. Herivel, *Background*.

165. Newton apparently never made the experiment of comparing mass and weight of different quantities of the same material.

166. There has been little research on the general subject of Newton's lunar theory; even the methods he used to obtain the results given in a short scholium to prop. 35, bk. I, in the 1st ed., are not known. W. W. Rouse Ball, in *Essay*, p. 109, discusses Newton's formula for "the mean hourly motion of the moon's apogee," and says, "The investigation on this point is not entirely satisfactory, and from the alterations made in the MS. Newton evidently felt doubts about the correctness of the coefficient $\frac{11}{2}$ which occurs in this formula. From this, however, he deduces quite correctly that the mean annual motion of the apogee resulting would amount to 38°51′51″, whereas the annual motion" is known to be 40°41′30″. His discussion is based upon the statement, presumably by J. C. Adams, in the preface to the *Catalogue of the Portsmouth Collection* (Cambridge, 1888), pp. xii–xiii. Newton's MSS on the motion of the moon—chiefly University Library, Cambridge, MS Add. 3966—are one of the major unanalyzed collections of his work. For further documents concerning this topic, and a scholarly analysis by A. R. Hall of some aspects of Newton's researches on the motion of the moon, see *Correspondence*, V (in press), and I. B. Cohen, intro. to a facsimile repr. of Newton's pamphlet on the motion of the moon (London, in press).

167. Although Newton had suspected the association of color with wavelength of vibration as early as his "Hypothesis" of 1675, he did not go on from his experiments on rings, which suggested a periodicity in optical phenomena, to a true wave theory—no doubt because, as A. I. Sabra has suggested, his a priori "conception of the rays as discrete entities or corpuscles" effectively "prevented him from envisaging the possibility of an undulatory interpretation in which the ray, as something distinguished from the waves, would be redundant" (*Theories of Light*, p. 341).

168. Both printed in facsimile in I. B. Cohen, ed., *Isaac Newton's Papers and Letters on Natural Philosophy*. They were published and studied in the eighteenth century and had a significant influence on the development of the concept of electric fluid (or fluids) and caloric. This topic is explored in some detail in I. B. Cohen, *Franklin and Newton* (Philadelphia, 1956; Cambridge, 1966; rev. ed. in press), esp. chs. 6 and 7.

169. Henry Guerlac has studied the development of the queries themselves, and in particular the decline of Newton's use of the ether until its reappearance in a new form in the queries of the 2nd English ed. He has also noted that the concept of the ether is conspicuously absent from the Latin ed. of 1706. See especially his "Newton's Optical Aether," in *Notes and Records. Royal Society of London*, **22** (1967), 45–57. See, further, Joan L. Hawes, "Newton's Revival of the Aether Hypothesis . . .," *ibid.*, **23** (1968), 200–212.

170. A. R. and M. B. Hall have found evidence that Newton thought of this "spiritus" as electrical in nature; see *Unpublished Papers*, pp. 231 ff., 348 ff. Guerlac has shown that Newton was fascinated by Hauksbee's electrical experiments and by certain experiments of Desaguliers; see bibliography for this series of articles.

171. University Library, Cambridge, MS Add. 3970, sec. 9, fols. 623 ff.

172. These works, especially queries 28 and 31, have been studied in conjunction with Newton's MSS (particularly his notebooks) by A. R. and M. B. Hall, D. McKie, J. R. Partington, R. Kargon, J. E. McGuire, A. Thackray, and others, in their elucidations of a Newtonian doctrine of chemistry or theory of matter. *De natura acidorum* has been printed from an autograph MS, with notes by Pitcairne and transcripts by David Gregory, in *Correspondence*, III, 205–214. The first printing, in both Latin and English, is reproduced in I. B. Cohen, ed., *Newton's Papers and Letters*, pp. 255–258.

173. According to M. B. Hall, "Newton's Chemical Papers," in *Newton's Papers and Letters*, p. 244.

174. *Ibid.*, p. 245.

175. Discussed by T. S. Kuhn, "Newton's '31st Query' and the Degradation of Gold," in *Isis*, **42** (1951), 296–298.

176. M. B. Hall, "Newton's Chemical Papers," p. 245; she continues that there we may find a "forerunner of the tables of affinity" developed in the eighteenth century, by means of which "chemists tried to predict the course of a reaction."

177. In "Newton's Chemical Experiments," in *Archives internationales d'histoire des sciences*, **11** (1958), 113–152—a study of Newton's chemical notes and papers—A. R. and M. B. Hall have tried to show that Newton's primary concern in these matters was the chemistry of metals, and that the writings of alchemists were a major source of information on every aspect of metals. Humphrey Newton wrote up a confusing account of Newton's alchemical experiments, in which he said that Newton's guide was the *De re metallica* of Agricola; this work, however, is largely free of alchemical overtones and concentrates on mining and metallurgy.

178. R. S. Westfall, in *Science and Religion in Seventeenth-Century England*, ch. 8, draws upon such expressions by Newton to prove that "Newton was a religious rationalist who remained blind to the mystic's spiritual communion with the divine."

179. These MSS are described in the Sotheby sale catalog and by F. Sherwood Taylor, in "An Alchemical Work of Sir Isaac Newton," in *Ambix*, **5** (1956), 59–84.

180. These have been the subject of a considerable study by Frank E. Manuel, *Isaac Newton, Historian* (Cambridge, Mass., 1964).

181. Newton's interest in alchemy mirrors all the bewildering aspects of that subject, ranging from the manipulative chemistry of metals, mineral acids, and salts, to esoteric and symbolic (often sexual) illustrations and mysticism of a religious or philosophical kind. His interest in alchemy persisted through his days at the mint, although there is no indication that he at that time still seriously believed that pure metallic gold might be produced from baser metals—if, indeed, he had ever so believed. The extent of his notes on his reading indicate the seriousness of Newton's interest in the general subject, but it is impossible to ascertain to what degree, if any, his alchemical concerns may have influenced his science, beyond his vague and general commitment to "transmutations" as a mode for the operations of nature. But even this belief would not imply a commitment to the entire hermetic tradition, and it is not necessary to seek a unity of the diverse interests and intellectual concerns in a mind as complex as Newton's.

182. P. M. Rattansi, "Newton's Alchemical Studies," in Allen Debus, ed., *Science, Medicine and Society in the Renaissance*, II (New York, 1972), 174.

183. The first suggestion that Newton's concept of the ether might be linked to his alchemical concerns was made by Taylor; see n. 179, above.

184. Leibniz, *Tentamen* . . . ("An Essay on the Cause of the Motions of the Heavenly Bodies"), in *Acta eruditorum* (Feb. 1689), 82–96, English trans. by E. J. Collins. Leibniz' marked copy of the 1st ed. of the *Principia*, presumably the one sent to him by Fatio de Duillier at Newton's direction, is now in the possession of E. A. Fellmann of Basel, who has discussed Leibniz' annotations in "Die Marginalnoten von Leibniz in Newtons Principia Mathematica 1687," in *Humanismus und Technik*, **2** (1972), 110–129; Fellmann's critical ed., G. W. Leibniz, *Marginalia in Newtoni Principia Mathematica 1687* (Paris, 1973), includes facsimiles of the annotated pages.

185. Translated from some MS comments on Leibniz' essay, first printed in Edleston, *Correspondence*, pp. 307–314.

186. Leibniz' excepts from Newton's *De analysi*, made in 1676 from a transcript by John Collins, have been published from the Hannover MS by Whiteside, in *Mathematical Papers*, II, 248–258. Whiteside thus demonstrates that Leibniz was "clearly interested only in its algebraic portions: fluxional sections are ignored."

187. Several MS versions in his hand survive in University Library, Cambridge, MS Add. 3968.

188. At this period the year in England officially began on Lady Day, 25 March. Hence Newton died on 20 March 1726 old style, or in 1726/7 (to use the form then current for dates in January, February, and the first part of March).

189. In the 2-vol. ed. of the *Principia* with variant readings edited by A. Koyré, I. B. Cohen, and Anne Whitman; Koyré has shown that in the English *Opticks* Newton used the word "feign" in relation to hypotheses, in the sense of "fingo" in the slogan, a usage confirmed by example in Newton's MSS. Motte renders the phrase as "I frame no hypotheses." Newton himself in MSS used both "feign" and "frame" in relation to hypotheses in this regard; see I. B. Cohen, "The First English Version of Newton's *Hypotheses non fingo*," in *Isis*, **53** (1962), 379–388.

190. University Library, Cambridge, MS Add. 3968, fol. 437.

BIBLIOGRAPHY

This bibliography is divided into four major sections. The last, by A. P. Youschkevitch, is concerned with Soviet studies on Newton and is independent of the text.

ORIGINAL WORKS (numbered I–IV): Newton's major writings, together with collected works and editions, bibliographies, manuscript collections, and catalogues.

SECONDARY LITERATURE (numbered V–VI): including general works and specific writings about Newton and his life.

SOURCES (numbered 1–11): the chief works used in the preparation of this biography; the subdivisions of this section are correlated to the subdivisions of the biography itself.

SOVIET LITERATURE: a special section devoted to Newtonian scholarship in the Soviet Union.

The first three sections of the bibliography contain a number of cross-references; a parenthetical number refers the reader to the section of the bibliography in which a complete citation may be found.

ORIGINAL WORKS

I. MAJOR WORKS. Newton's first publications were on optics and appeared in the *Philosophical Transactions of the Royal Society* (1672–1676); repr. in facs., with intro. by T. S. Kuhn, in I. B. Cohen, ed., *Isaac Newton's Papers & Letters on Natural Philosophy* (Cambridge, Mass., 1958; 2nd ed., in press). His *Opticks* (London, 1704; enl. versions in Latin [London, 1706], and in English [London, 1717 or 1718]) contained two supps.: his *Enumeratio linearum tertii ordinis* and *Tractatus de quadratura curvarum*, his first published works in pure mathematics. The 1704 ed. has been repr. in facs. (Brussels, 1966) and (optical part only) in type (London, 1931); also repr. with an analytical table of contents prepared by D. H. D. Roller (New York, 1952). French trans. are by P. Coste (Amsterdam, 1720; rev. ed. 1722; facs. repr., with intro. by M. Solovine, Paris, 1955); a German ed. is W. Abendroth, 2 vols. (Leipzig, 1898); and a Rumanian trans. is Victor Marian (Bucharest, 1970). A new ed. is currently being prepared by Henry Guerlac.

The *Philosophiae naturalis principia mathematica* (London, 1687; rev. eds., Cambridge, 1713 [repr. Amsterdam, 1714, 1723], and London, 1726) is available in an ed. with variant readings (based on the three printed eds., the MS for the 1st ed. and Newton's annotations in his own copies of the 1st and 2nd eds.) prepared by A. Koyré, I. B. Cohen, and Anne Whitman: *Isaac Newton's Philosophiae naturalis principia mathematica, the Third Edition (1726) With Variant Readings*, 2 vols. (Cambridge, Mass.–Cambridge, England, 1972). Translations and excerpts have appeared in Dutch, English, French, German, Italian, Japanese, Rumanian, Russian, and Swedish, and are listed in app. VIII, vol. II, of the Koyré, Cohen, and Whitman ed., together with an account of reprs. of the whole treatise. The 1st ed. has been printed twice in facs. (London, 1954[?]; Brussels, 1965).

William Jones published Newton's *De analysi* in his ed. of *Analysis per quantitatum series, fluxiones, ac differentias . . .* (London, 1711), repr. in the Royal Society's *Commercium epistolicum D. Johannis Collins, et aliorum de analysi promota . . .* (London, 1712–1713; enl. version, 1722; "variorum" ed. by J.-B. Biot and F. Lefort, Paris, 1856), and as an appendix to the 1723 Amsterdam printing of the *Principia*. Newton's *Arithmetica universalis* was published from the MS of Newton's lectures by W. Whiston (Cambridge, 1707); an amended ed. followed, supervised by Newton himself (London, 1722). For bibliographical notes on these and some other mathematical writings (and indications of other eds. and translations), see the introductions by D. T. Whiteside to the facs. repr. of *The Mathematical Works of Isaac Newton*, 2 vols. (New York–London, 1964–1967). Newton's *Arithmetica universalis* was translated into Russian with notes and commentaries by A. P. Youschkevitch (Moscow, 1948); English eds. were published in London in 1720, 1728, and 1769.

After Newton's death the early version of what became bk. III of the *Principia* was published in English as *A Treatise of the System of the World* (London, 1728; rev. London, 1731, facs. repr., with intro. by I. B. Cohen, London, 1969) and in Latin as *De mundi systemate liber* (London, 1728). An Italian trans. is by Marcella Renzoni (Turin, 1959; 1969). The first part of the *Lectiones opticae* was translated and published as *Optical Lectures* (London, 1728) before the full Latin ed. was printed (1729); both are imperfect and incomplete. The only modern ed. is in Russian, *Lektsii po optike* (Leningrad, 1946), with commentary by S. I. Vavilov.

For Newton's nonscientific works (theology, biblical studies, chronology), and for other scientific writings, see the various sections below.

II. COLLECTED WORKS OR EDITIONS. The only attempt ever made to produce a general ed. of Newton was S. Horsley, *Isaaci Newtoni opera quae exstant omnia*, 5 vols. (London, 1779–1785; photo repr. Stuttgart–Bad Cannstatt, 1964), which barely takes account of Newton's available MS writings but has the virtue of including (vol. I) the published mathematical tracts; (vols. II–III) the *Principia* and *De mundi systemate*, *Theoria lunae*, and *Lectiones opticae*; (vol. IV) letters from the *Philosophical Transactions* on light and color, the letter to Boyle on the ether, *De problematis Bernoullianis*, the letters to Bentley, and the *Commercium epistolicum*; (vol. V) the *Chronology*, the *Prophecies*, and the *Corruptions of Scripture*. An earlier and more modest collection was the 3-vol. *Opuscula mathematica, philosophica, et philologica*, Giovanni Francesco Salvemini (known as Johann Castillon), ed. (Lausanne–Geneva, 1744); it contains only works then in print.

A major collection of letters and documents, edited in the most exemplary manner, is Edleston (1); Rigaud's *Essay* (5) is also valuable. S. P. Rigaud's *Correspondence of Scientific Men of the Seventeenth Century . . . in the collection of . . . the Earl of Macclesfield*, 2 vols. (Oxford, 1841; rev., with table of contents and index, 1862) is of special importance because the Macclesfield collection is not at present open to scholars.

Four vols. of the Royal Society's ed. of Newton's *Correspondence* (Cambridge, 1959–) have (as of 1974) been published, vols. I–III edited by H. W. Turnbull, vol. IV by J. F. Scott; A. R. Hall has been appointed editor of the succeeding volumes. The *Correspondence* is not limited to letters but contains scientific documents of primary importance. A recent major collection is A. R. and M. B. Hall, eds., *Unpublished Scientific Papers of Isaac Newton, a Selection From the Portsmouth Collection in the University Library, Cambridge* (Cambridge, 1964). Other presentations of MSS are given in the ed. of the *Principia* with variant readings (1972, cited above), Herivel's *Background* (5), and in D. T. Whiteside's ed. of Newton's *Mathematical Papers* (3).

III. BIBLIOGRAPHIES. There are three bibliographies of Newton's writings, none complete or free of major error. One is George J. Gray, *A Bibliography of the Works of Sir Isaac Newton, Together With a List of Books Illustrating His Works*, 2nd ed., rev. and enl. (Cambridge, 1907; repr. London, 1966); H. Zeitlinger, "A Newton Bibliography," pp. 148–170 of the volume ed. by W. J. Greenstreet (VI); and *A Descriptive Catalogue of the Grace K. Babson Collection of the Works of Sir Isaac Newton . . .* (New York, 1950), plus *A Supplement . . .* compiled by Henry P. Macomber (Babson Park, Mass., 1955), which lists some secondary materials from journals as well as books.

IV. MANUSCRIPT COLLECTIONS AND CATALOGUES. The Portsmouth Collection (University Library, Cambridge) was roughly catalogued by a syndicate consisting of H. R. Luard, G. G. Stokes, J. C. Adams, and G. D. Liveing, who produced *A Catalogue of the Portsmouth Collection of Books and Papers Written by or Belonging to Sir Isaac Newton . . .* (Cambridge, 1888); the bare descriptions do not always identify the major MSS or give the catalogue numbers (*e.g.*, the Waste Book, U.L.C. MS Add. 4004, the major repository of Newton's early work in dynamics and in mathematics, appears as "A common-place book, written originally by B. Smith, D.D., with calculations by Newton written in the blank spaces. This contains Newton's first idea of Fluxions"). There is no adequate catalogue or printed guide to the Newton MSS in the libraries of Trinity College (Cambridge), the Royal Society of London, or the British Museum. The Keynes Collection (in the library of King's College, Cambridge) is almost entirely based on the Sotheby sale and is inventoried in the form of a marked copy of the sale catalogue, available in the library; see A. N. L. Munby, "The Keynes Collection of the Works of Sir Isaac Newton at King's College, Cambridge," in *Notes and Records. Royal Society of London*, **10** (1952), 40–50. The "scientific portion" of the Portsmouth Collection was given to Cambridge University in the 1870's; the remainder was dispersed at public auction in 1936. See Sotheby's *Catalogue of the Newton Papers, Sold by Order of the Viscount Lymington, to Whom They Have Descended From Catherine Conduitt, Viscountess Lymington, Great-niece of Sir Isaac Newton* (London, 1936). No catalogue has ever been made available of the Macclesfield Collection (rich in Newton MSS), based originally on the papers of John Collins and William Jones,

for which see S. P. Rigaud's 2-vol. *Correspondence . . .* (I). Further information concerning MS sources is given in Whiteside, *Mathematical Papers*, I, xxiv–xxxiii (3).

Many books from Newton's library are in the Trinity College Library (Cambridge); others are in public and private collections all over the world. R. de Villamil, *Newton: The Man* (London, 1931[?]; repr., with intro. by I. B. Cohen, New York, 1972), contains a catalogue (imperfect and incomplete) of books in Newton's library at the time of his death; an inventory with present locations of Newton's books is greatly to be desired. See P. E. Spargo, "Newton's Library," in *Endeavour*, **31** (1972), 29–33, with short but valuable list of references. See also *Library of Sir Isaac Newton. Presentation by the Pilgrim Trust to Trinity College Cambridge 30 October 1943* (Cambridge, 1944), described on pp. 5–7 of *Thirteenth Annual Report of the Pilgrim Trust* (Harlech, 1943).

SECONDARY LITERATURE

V. GUIDES TO THE SECONDARY LITERATURE. For guides to the literature concerning Newton, see . . . *Catalogue . . . Babson Collection . . .* (III); and scholarly eds., such as *Mathematical Papers* (3), *Principia* (I), and *Correspondence* (II). A most valuable year-by-year list of articles and books has been prepared and published by Clelia Pighetti: "Cinquant'anni di studi newtoniani (1908–1959)," in *Rivista critica di storia della filosofia*, **20** (1960), 181–203, 295–318. See also Magda Whitrow, ed., *ISIS Cumulative Bibliography . . . 1913–65*, II (London, 1971), 221–232. Two fairly recent surveys of the literature are I. B. Cohen, "Newton in the Light of Recent Scholarship," in *Isis*, **51** (1960), 489–514; and D. T. Whiteside, "The Expanding World of Newtonian Research," in *History of Science*, **1** (1962), 16–29.

VI. GENERAL WORKS. Biographies (*e.g.*, by Stukeley, Brewster, More, Manuel) are listed below (1). Some major interpretative works and collections of studies on Newton are Ferd. Rosenberger, *Isaac Newton und seine physikalischen Principien* (Leipzig, 1895); Léon Bloch, *La philosophie de Newton* (Paris, 1908); S. I. Vavilov, *Isaak Nyuton; nauchnaya biografia i stati*, 3rd ed. (Moscow, 1961), German trans. by Josef Grün as *Isaac Newton* (Vienna, 1948), 2nd ed., rev., German trans. by Franz Boncourt (Berlin, 1951); Alexandre Koyré, *Newtonian Studies* (London–Cambridge, Mass., 1965) which, posthumously published, contains a number of errors—a more correct version is the French trans., *Études newtoniennes* (Paris, 1968), with an *avertissement* by Yvon Belaval; and Alberto Pala, *Isaac Newton, scienza e filosofia* (Turin, 1969).

Major collections of Newtonian studies include W. J. Greenstreet, ed., *Isaac Newton 1642–1727* (London, 1927); F. E. Brasch, ed., *Sir Isaac Newton 1727–1927* (Baltimore, 1928); S. I. Vavilov, ed., *Isaak Nyuton 1643*[n.s.]*–1727*, a symposium in Russian (Moscow–Leningrad, 1943); Royal Society, *Newton Tercentenary Celebrations, 15–19 July 1946* (Cambridge, 1947); and Robert Palter, ed., *The Annus Mirabilis of Sir Isaac Newton 1666–1966* (Cambridge, Mass., 1970), based on an earlier version in *The Texas Quarterly*, **10**, no. 3 (autumn 1967).

On Newton's reputation and influence (notably in the eighteenth century), see Hélène Metzger, *Newton, Stahl, Boerhaave et la doctrine chimique* (Paris, 1930), and *Attraction universelle et religion naturelle chez quelques commentateurs anglais de Newton* (Paris, 1938); Pierre Brunet, *L'introduction des théories de Newton en France au XVIIIe siècle*, I, *Avant 1738* (Paris, 1931); Marjorie Hope Nicolson, *Newton Demands the Muse, Newton's Opticks and the Eighteenth Century Poets* (Princeton, 1946); I. B. Cohen, *Franklin and Newton, an Inquiry Into Speculative Newtonian Experimental Science . . .* (Philadelphia, 1956; Cambridge, Mass., 1966; rev. repr. 1974); Henry Guerlac, "Where the Statue Stood: Divergent Loyalties to Newton in the Eighteenth Century," in Earl R. Wasserman, ed., *Aspects of the Eighteenth Century* (Baltimore, 1965), pp. 317–334; R. E. Schofield, *Mechanism and Materialism, British Natural Philosophy in an Age of Reason* (Princeton, 1970); Paolo Casini, *L'universo-macchina, origini della filosofia newtoniana* (Bari, 1969); and Arnold Thackray, *Atoms and Powers, an Essay in Newtonian Matter-Theory and the Development of Chemistry* (Cambridge, Mass., 1970). Still of value today are three major eighteenth-century expositions of the Newtonian natural philosophy, by Henry Pemberton, Voltaire, and Colin Maclaurin.

Whoever studies any of Newton's mathematical or scientific writings would be well advised to consult J. A. Lohne, "The Increasing Corruption of Newton's Diagrams," in *History of Science*, **6** (1967), 69–89.

Newton's MSS comprise some 20–25 million words; most of them have never been studied fully, and some are currently "lost," having been dispersed at the Sotheby sale in 1936. Among the areas in which there is a great need for editing of MSS and research are Newton's studies of lunar motions (chiefly U.L.C. MS Add. 3966); his work in optics (chiefly U.L.C. MS Add. 3970; plus other MSS such as notebooks, etc.); and the technical innovations he proposed for the *Principia* in the 1690's (chiefly U.L.C. MS Add. 3965); see (4), (7). It would be further valuable to have full annotated editions of his early notebooks and of some major alchemical notes and writings.

Some recent Newtonian publications include Valentin Boss, *Newton and Russia, the Early Influence 1698–1796* (Cambridge, Mass., 1972); Klaus-Dietwardt Buchholtz, *Isaac Newton als Theologe* (Wittenburg, 1965); Mary S. Churchill, "The Seven Chapters With Explanatory Notes," in *Chymia*, **12** (1967), 27–57, the first publication of one of Newton's complete alchemical MS; J. E. Hofmann, "Neue Newtoniana," in *Studia Leibnitiana*, **2** (1970), 140–145, a review of recent literature; D. Kubrin, "Newton and the Cyclical Cosmos," in *Journal of the History of Ideas*, **28** (1967), 325–346; J. E. McGuire, "The Origin of Newton's Doctrine of Essential Qualities," in *Centaurus*, **12** (1968), 233–260; and L. Trengrove, "Newton's Theological Views," in *Annals of Science*, **22** (1966), 277–294.

SOURCES

1. *Early Life and Education.* The major biographies of Newton are David Brewster, *Memoirs of the Life, Writings, and Discoveries of Isaac Newton*, 2 vols. (Edinburgh, 1855; 2nd ed., 1860; repr. New York, 1965), the best biography of Newton, despite its stuffiness; for a corrective, see Augustus De Morgan, *Essays on the Life and Work of Newton* (Chicago–London, 1914); Louis Trenchard More, *Isaac Newton* (New York–London, 1934; repr. New York, 1962); and Frank E. Manuel, *A Portrait of Isaac Newton* (Cambridge, Mass., 1968). Of the greatest value is the "synoptical view" of Newton's life, pp. xxi–lxxxi, with supplementary documents, in J. Edleston, ed., *Correspondence of Sir Isaac Newton and Professor Cotes . . .* (London, 1850; repr. London, 1969). Supplementary information concerning Newton's youthful studies is given in D. T. Whiteside, "Isaac Newton: Birth of a Mathematician," in *Notes and Records. Royal Society of London*, **19** (1964), 53–62, and "Newton's Marvellous Year: 1666 and All That," *ibid.*, **21** (1966), 32–41.

John Conduitt assembled recollections of Newton by Humphrey Newton, William Stukeley, William Derham, A. De Moivre, and others, which are now mainly in the Keynes Collection, King's College, Cambridge. Many of these documents have been printed in Edmund Turnor, *Collections for the History of the Town and Soke of Grantham* (London, 1806). William Stukeley's *Memoirs of Sir Isaac Newton's Life* (1752) was edited by A. Hastings White (London, 1936).

On Newton's family and origins, see C. W. Foster, "Sir Isaac Newton's Family," in *Reports and Papers of the Architectural Societies of the County of Lincoln, County of York, Archdeaconries of Northampton and Oakham, and County of Leicester*, **39** (1928–1929), 1–62. Newton's early notebooks are in Cambridge in the University Library, the Fitzwilliam Museum, and Trinity College Library; and in New York City in the Morgan Library. For the latter, see David Eugene Smith, "Two Unpublished Documents of Sir Isaac Newton," in W. J. Greenstreet, ed., *Isaac Newton 1642–1727* (London, 1927), pp. 16 ff. Also, E. N. da C. Andrade, "Newton's Early Notebook," in *Nature*, **135** (1935), 360; George L. Huxley: "Two Newtonian Studies: I. Newton's Boyhood Interests," in *Harvard Library Bulletin*, **13** (1959), 348–354; and A. R. Hall, "Sir Isaac Newton's Notebook, 1661–1665," in *Cambridge Historical Journal*, **9** (1948), 239–250. Elsewhere, Andrade has shown that Newton did not write the poem, attributed to him, concerning Charles II, a conclusion supported by William Stukeley's 1752 *Memoirs of Sir Isaac Newton's Life*, A. Hastings White, ed. (London, 1936).

On Newton's early diagrams and his sundial, see Charles Turnor, "An Account of the Newtonian Dial Presented to the Royal Society," in *Proceedings of the Royal Society*, **5** (1851), 513 (13 June 1844); and H. W. Robinson, "Note on Some Recently Discovered Geometrical Drawings in the Stonework of Woolsthorpe Manor House," in *Notes and Records. Royal Society of London*, **5** (1947), 35–36. For Newton's catalogue of "sins," see R. S. Westfall, "Short-writing and the State of Newton's Conscience, 1662," in *Notes and Records. Royal Society of London*, **18** (1963), 10–16.

On Newton's early reading, see R. S. Westfall, "The

Foundations of Newton's Philosophy of Nature," *British Journal for the History of Science*, **1** (1962), 171–182, which is repr. in somewhat amplified form in his *Force in Newton's Physics*. On Newton's reading, see further I. B. Cohen, *Introduction to Newton's Principia* (7) and vol. I of Whiteside's ed. of Newton's *Mathematical Papers* (3). And, of course, a major source of biographical information is the Royal Society's edition of Newton's *Correspondence* (II).

2. *Lucasian Professor*. For the major sources concerning this period of Newton's life, see (1) above, notably Brewster, Cohen (*Introduction*), Edleston, Manuel, More, Whiteside (*Mathematical Papers*), and *Correspondence*.

Edleston (pp. xci–xcviii) gives a "Table of Newton's Lectures as Lucasian Professor," with the dates and corresponding pages of the deposited MSS and the published ed. for the lectures on optics (U.L.C. MS Dd. 9.67, deposited 1674; printed London, 1729); lectures on arithmetic and algebra (U.L.C. MS Dd. 9.68; first published by Whiston, Cambridge, 1707); lectures *De motu corporum* (U.L.C. MS Dd. 9.46), corresponding *grosso modo* to bk. I of the *Principia* through prop. 54; and finally *De motu corporum liber secundus* (U.L.C. MS Dd. 9.67); of which a more complete version was printed as *De mundi systemate liber* (London, 1728)—see below.

Except for the last two, the deposited lectures are final copies, complete with numbered illustrations, as if ready for the press or for any reader who might have access to these MSS. The *Lectiones opticae* exist in two MS versions, an earlier one, which Newton kept (U.L.C. MS Add. 4002, in Newton's hand), having a division by dates quite different from that of the deposited lectures; this has been printed in facs., with an intro. by D. T. Whiteside as *The Unpublished First Version of Isaac Newton's Cambridge Lectures on Optics 1670–1672* (Cambridge, 1973). See I. B. Cohen, *Introduction*, supp. III, "Newton's Professorial Lectures," esp. pp. 303–306.

The deposited MS *De motu corporum* consists of leaves corresponding to different states of composition of bk. I of the *Principia*; the second state (in the hand of Humphrey Newton, with additions and emendations by Isaac Newton) is all but the equivalent of the corresponding part of the MS of the *Principia* sent to the printer, but the earlier state is notably different and more primitive. See I. B. Cohen, *Introduction*, supp. IV, pp. 310–321.

Edleston did not list the deposited copy of the lectures for 1687, a fair copy of only the first portion of *De motu corporum liber secundus* (corresponding to the first 27 sections, roughly half of Newton's own copy of the whole work, U.L.C. MS Add. 3990); he referred to a copy of the deposited lectures made by Cotes (Trinity College Library, MS R.19.39), in which the remainder of the text was added from a copy of the whole MS belonging to Charles Morgan. See I. B. Cohen, *Introduction*, supp. III, pp. 306–308, and supp. VI, pp. 327–335. This MS, an early version of what was to be rewritten as *Liber tertius: De mundi systemate* of the *Principia*, was published in English (London, 1728) and in Latin (London, 1728); see I. B. Cohen, "Newton's *System of the World*," in *Physis*,

11 (1969), 152–166; and intro. to repr. of the English *System of the World* (London, 1969).

The statutes of the Lucasian professorship (dated 19 Dec. 1663) are printed in the appendix to William Whiston's *An Account of . . .* [His] *Prosecution at, and Banishment From, the University of Cambridge* (London, 1718) and are printed again by D. T. Whiteside in Newton's *Mathematical Papers*, III, xx–xxvii.

It is often supposed, probably mistakenly, that Newton actually read the lectures that he deposited, or that the deposited lectures are evidence of the state of his knowledge or his formulation of a given subject at the time of giving a particular lecture, because the deposited MSS may be divided into dated lectures; but the statutes required that the lectures be rewritten after they had been read.

The MSS of Humphrey Newton's memoranda are in the Keynes Collection, King's College, Cambridge (K. MS 135) and are printed in David Brewster, *Memoirs*, II, 91–98, and again in L. T. More, *Isaac Newton*, pp. 246–251.

The evidence for Newton's plan to publish an ed. of his early optical papers, including the letters in the *Philosophical Transactions*, is in a set of printed pages (possibly printed proofs) forming part of such an annotated printing of these letters, discovered by D. J. de S. Price. See I. B. Cohen, "Versions of Isaac Newton's First Published Paper With Remarks on . . . an Edition of His Early Papers on Light and Color," in *Archives internationales d'histoire des sciences*, **11** (1958), 357–375; D. J. de S. Price, "Newton in a Church Tower: The Discovery of an Unknown Book by Isaac Newton," in *Yale University Library Gazette*, **34** (1960), 124–126; A. R. Hall, "Newton's First Book," in *Archives internationales d'histoire des sciences*, **13** (1960), 39–61. On 5 Mar. 1677, Collins wrote to Newton that David Loggan "informs me that he hath drawn your effigies in order to [produce] a sculpture thereof to be prefixed to a book of Light [&] Colours [&] Dioptricks which you intend to publish."

The most recent and detailed analysis of the Newton-Fatio relationship is given in Frank E. Manuel, *A Portrait of Isaac Newton*, ch. 9, "The Ape of Newton: Fatio de Duillier," and ch. 10, "The Black Year 1693." For factual details, see Newton, *Correspondence*, III. The late Charles A. Domson completed a doctoral dissertation, "Nicolas Fatio de Duillier and the Prophets of London: An Essay in the Historical Interaction of Natural Philosophy and Millennial Belief in the Age of Newton" (Yale, 1972).

Newton's gifts to the Trinity College Library are listed in an old MS catalogue of the library; see I. B. Cohen: "Newton's Attribution of the First Two Laws of Motion to Galileo," in *Atti del Symposium internazionale di storia, metodologia, logica e filosofia della scienza: "Galileo nella storia e nella filosofia della scienza"* (Florence, 1967), pp. xxii–xlii, esp. pp. xxvii–xxviii and n. 22.

3. *Mathematics*. The primary work for the study of Newton's mathematics is the ed. (to be completed in 8 vols.) by D. T. Whiteside: *Mathematical Papers of Isaac Newton* (Cambridge, 1967–   ). Whiteside has also provided a valuable pair of introductions to a facs. repr. of early translations of a number of Newton's tracts, *The Mathe-*

matical Works of Isaac Newton, 2 vols. (New York–London, 1964–1967); these introductions give an admirable and concise summary of the development of Newton's mathematical thought and contain bibliographical notes on the printings and translations of the tracts reprinted, embracing De analysi; De quadratura; Methodus fluxionum et serierum infinitarum; Arithmetica universalis (based on his professorial lectures, deposited in the University Library); Enumeratio linearum tertii ordinis; and Methodus differentialis ("Newton's Interpolation Formulas"). Attention may also be directed to several other of Whiteside's publications: "Isaac Newton: Birth of a Mathematician," in Notes and Records. Royal Society of London, 19 (1964), 53–62; "Newton's Marvellous Year: 1666 and All That," ibid., 21 (1966), 32–41; "Newton's Discovery of the General Binomial Theorem," in Mathematical Gazette, 45 (1961), 175–180. (See other articles of his cited in (6), (7), (8) below.)

Further information concerning the eds. and translations of Newton's mathematical writings may be gleaned from the bibliographies (Gray, Zeitlinger, Babson) cited above (III). Various Newtonian tracts appeared in Johann Castillon's Opuscula . . . (II), I, supplemented by a two-volume ed. (Amsterdam, 1761) of Arithmetica universalis. The naturalist Buffon translated the Methodus fluxionum . . . (Paris, 1740), and James Wilson replied to Buffon's preface in an appendix to vol. II (1761) of his own ed. of Benjamin Robins' Mathematical Tracts; these two works give a real insight into "what an interested student could then know of Newton's private thoughts." See also Pierre Brunet, "La notion d'infini mathématique chez Buffon," in Archeion, 13 (1931), 24–39; and Lesley Hanks, Buffon avant l'"Histoire naturelle" (Paris, 1966), pt. 2, ch. 4 and app. 4. Horsley's ed. of Newton's Opera (II) contains some of Newton's mathematical tracts. A modern version of the Arithmetica universalis, with extended notes and commentary, has been published by A. P. Youschkevitch (Moscow, 1948). A. Rupert Hall and Marie Boas Hall have published Newton's October 1666 tract, "to resolve problems by motion" (U.L.C. MS Add. 3458, fols. 49–63) in their Unpublished Scientific Papers (II); see also H. W. Turnbull, "The Discovery of the Infinitesimal Calculus," in Nature, 167 (1951), 1048–1050.

Newton's Correspondence (II) contains letters and other documents relating to mathematics, with valuable annotations by H. W. Turnbull and J. F. Scott. See, further, Turnbull's The Mathematical Discoveries of Newton (London–Glasgow, 1945), produced before he started to edit the Correspondence and thus presenting a view not wholly borne out by later research. Carl B. Boyer has dealt with Newton in Concepts of the Calculus (New York, 1939; repr. 1949, 1959), ch. 5; "Newton as an Originator of Polar Coordinates," in American Mathematical Monthly, 56 (1949), 73–78; History of Analytic Geometry (New York, 1956), ch. 7; and A History of Mathematics (New York, 1968), ch. 19.

Other secondary works are W. W. Rouse Ball, A Short Account of the History of Mathematics, 4th ed. (London, 1908), ch. 16—even more useful is his A History of the Study of Mathematics at Cambridge (Cambridge, 1889), chs. 4–6; J. F. Scott, A History of Mathematics (London, 1958), chs. 10, 11; and Margaret E. Baron, The Origins of the Infinitesimal Calculus (Oxford–London–New York, 1969).

Some specialized studies of value are D. T. Whiteside, "Patterns of Mathematical Thought in the Later Seventeenth Century," in Archive for History of Exact Sciences, 1 (1961), 179–388; W. W. Rouse Ball, "On Newton's Classification of Cubic Curves," in Proceedings of the London Mathematical Society, 22 (1891), 104–143, summarized in Bibliotheca mathematica, n.s. 5 (1891), 35–40; Florian Cajori, "Fourier's Improvement of the Newton-Raphson Method of Approximation Anticipated by Mourraile," in Bibliotheca mathematica, 11 (1910–1911), 132–137; "Historical Note on the Newton-Raphson Method of Approximation," in American Mathematical Monthly, 18 (1911), 29–32; and A History of the Conceptions of Limits and Fluxions in Great Britain From Newton to Woodhouse (Chicago–London, 1919); W. J. Greenstreet, ed., Isaac Newton 1642–1727 (London, 1927), including D. C. Fraser, "Newton and Interpolation"; A. R. Forsyth, "Newton's Problem of the Solid of Least Resistance"; J. J. Milne, "Newton's Contribution to the Geometry of Conics"; H. Hilton, "Newton on Plane Cubic Curves"; and J. M. Child, "Newton and the Art of Discovery"; Duncan C. Fraser, Newton's Interpolation Formulas (London, 1927), repr. from Journal of the Institute of Actuaries, 51 (1918–1919), 77–106, 211–232, and 58 (1927), 53–95; C. R. M. Talbot, Sir Isaac Newton's Enumeration of Lines of the Third Order, Generation of Curves by Shadows, Organic Description of Curves, and Construction of Equations by Curves, trans. from the Latin, with notes and examples (London, 1860); Florence N. David, "Mr. Newton, Mr. Pepys and Dyse," in Annals of Science, 13 (1957), 137–147, on dice-throwing and probability; Jean Pelseneer, "Une lettre inédite de Newton à Pepys (23 décembre 1693)," in Osiris, 1 (1936), 497–499, on probabilities; J. M. Keynes, "A Mathematical Analysis by Newton of a Problem in College Administration," in Isis, 49 (1958), 174–176; Maximilian Miller, "Newton, Aufzahlung der Linien dritter Ordnung," in Wissenschaftliche Zeitschrift der Hochschule für Verkehrswesen, Dresden, 1, no. 1 (1953), 5–32; "Newtons Differenzmethode," ibid., 2, no. 1 (1954), 1–13; and "Über die Analysis mit Hilfe unendlicher Reihen," ibid., no. 2 (1954), 1–16; Oskar Bolza, "Bemerkungen zu Newtons Beweis seines Satzes über den Rotationskörper kleinsten Widerstandes," in Bibliotheca mathematica, 3rd ser., 13 (1912–1913), 146–149.

Other works relating to Newton's mathematics are cited in (6) and (for the quarrel with Leibniz over priority in the calculus) (10).

4. Optics. The eds. of the Opticks and Lectiones opticae are mentioned above (I); the two MS versions of the latter are U.L.C. MS Add. 4002, MS Dd.9.67. An annotated copy of the 1st ed. of the Opticks, used by the printer for the composition of the 2nd ed. still exists (U.L.C. MS Adv.b.39.3—formerly MS Add. 4001). For information Cohen, Introduction to Newton's Principia (7), p. 34;

and R. S. Westfall, "Newton's Reply," pp. 83–84—extracts are printed with commentary in D. T. Whiteside's ed. of Newton's *Mathematical Papers* (3). At one time Newton began to write a *Fundamentum opticae*, the text of which is readily reconstructible from the MSS and which is a necessary tool for a complete analysis of bk. I of the *Opticks*, into which its contents were later incorporated; for pagination, see *Mathematical Papers* (3), III, 552. This work is barely known to Newton scholars. Most of Newton's optical MSS are assembled in the University Library, Cambridge, as MS Add. 3970, but other MS writings appear in the Waste Book, correspondence, and various notebooks.

Among the older literature, F. Rosenberger's book (VI) may still be studied with profit, and there is much to be learned from Joseph Priestley's 18th-century presentation of the development and current state of concepts and theories of light and vision. See also Ernst Mach, *The Principles of Physical Optics: An Historical and Philosophical Treatment*, trans. by John S. Anderson and A. F. A. Young (London, 1926; repr. New York, 1953); and Vasco Ronchi, *The Nature of Light: An Historical Survey*, trans. by V. Barocas (Cambridge, Mass., 1970)—also 2 eds. in Italian and a French translation by Juliette Taton.

Newton's MSS have been used in A. R. Hall, "Newton's Notebook" (1), pp. 239–250; and in J. A. Lohne, "Newton's 'Proof' of the Sine Law," in *Archive for History of Exact Sciences*, 1 (1961), 389–405; "Isaac Newton: The Rise of a Scientist 1661–1671," in *Notes and Records. Royal Society of London*, 20 (1965), 125–139; and "Experimentum crucis," *ibid.*, 23 (1968), 169–199. See also J. A. Lohne and Bernhard Sticker, *Newtons Theorie der Prismenfarben, mit Übersetzung und Erläuterung der Abhandlung von 1672* (Munich, 1969); and R. S. Westfall, "The Development of Newton's Theory of Color," in *Isis*, 53 (1962), 339–358; "Newton and his Critics on the Nature of Colors," in *Archives internationales d'histoire des sciences*, 15 (1962), 47–58; "Newton's Reply to Hooke and the Theory of Colors," in *Isis*, 54 (1963), 82–96; "Isaac Newton's Coloured Circles Twixt Two Contiguous Glasses," in *Archive for History of Exact Sciences*, 2 (1965), 181–196; and "Uneasily Fitful Reflections on Fits of Easy Transmission [and of easy reflection]," in Robert Palter, ed., *The Annus Mirabilis* (VI), pp. 88–104.

Newton's optical papers (from the *Philosophical Transactions* and T. Birch's *History of the Royal Society*) are repr. in facs. in *Newton's Papers and Letters* (I), with an intro. by T. S. Kuhn. See also I. B. Cohen, "I prismi del Newton e i prismi dell'Algarotti," in *Atti della Fondazione "Giorgio Ronchi"* (Florence), 12 (1957), 1–11; Vasco Ronchi, "I 'prismi del Newton' del Museo Civico di Treviso," *ibid.*, 12–28; and N. R. Hanson, "Waves, Particles, and Newton's 'Fits,' " in *Journal of the History of Ideas*, 21 (1960), 370–391. On Newton's work on color, see George Biernson, "Why did Newton see Indigo in the Spectrum?," in *American Journal of Physics*, 40 (1972), 526–533; and Torger Holtzmark, "Newton's *Experimentum Crucis* Reconsidered," *ibid.*, 38 (1970), 1229–1235.

An able account of Newton's work in optics, set against the background of his century, is A. I. Sabra, *Theories of Light From Descartes to Newton* (London, 1967), ch. 9–13. An important series of studies, based on extensive examination of the MSS, are Zev Bechler, "Newton's 1672 Optical Controversies: A Study in the Grammar of Scientific Dissent," in Y. Elkana, ed., *Some Aspects of the Interaction Between Science and Philosophy* (New York, in press); "Newton's Search for a Mechanistic Model of Color Dispersion: A Suggested Interpretation," in *Archive for History of Exact Sciences*, 11 (1973), 1–37; and an analysis of Newton's work on chromatic aberration in lenses (in press). On the last topic, see also D. T. Whiteside, *Mathematical Papers*, III, pt. 3, esp. pp. 442–443, 512–513 (n. 61), 533 (n. 13), and 555–556 (nn. 5–6).

5. *Dynamics, Astronomy, and the Birth of the "Principia."* The primary documents for the study of Newton's dynamics have been assembled by A. R. and M. B. Hall (II) and by J. Herivel, *The Background to Newton's Principia* (Oxford, 1965); other major documents are printed (with historical and critical essays) in the Royal Society's ed. of Newton's *Correspondence* (II); S. P. Rigaud, *Historical Essay on the First Publication of Sir Isaac Newton's Principia* (Oxford, 1838; repr., with intro. by I. B. Cohen, New York, 1972); W. W. Rouse Ball, *An Essay on Newton's Principia* (London, 1893; repr. with intro. by I. B. Cohen, New York, 1972); and I. B. Cohen, *Introduction* (7).

The development of Newton's concepts of dynamics is discussed by Herivel (in *Background*, and in a series of articles summarized in that work), in Rouse Ball's *Essay*, I. B. Cohen's *Introduction*, and in R. S. Westfall's *Force in Newton's Physics* (London–New York, 1971). On the concept of inertia and the laws of motion, see I. B. Cohen, *Transformations of Scientific Ideas: Variations on Newtonian Themes in the History of Science*, the Wiles Lectures (Cambridge, in press), ch. 2; and "Newton's Second Law and the Concept of Force in the *Principia*," in R. Palter ed., *Annus mirabilis* (VI), pp. 143–185; Alan Gabbey, "Force and Inertia in Seventeenth-Century Dynamics," in *Studies in History and Philosophy of Science*, 2 (1971),1–68; E. J. Aiton, *The Vortex Theory of Planetary Motions* (London–New York, 1972); and A. R. Hall, "Newton on the Calculation of Central Forces," in *Annals of Science*, 13 (1957), 62–71. Newton's encounter with Hooke in 1679 and his progress from the Ward-Bullialdus approximation to the area law are studied in J. A. Lohne, "Hooke Versus Newton, an Analysis of the Documents in the Case of Free Fall and Planetary Motion," in *Centaurus*, 7 (1960), 6–52; D. T. Whiteside, "Newton's Early Thoughts on Planetary Motion: A Fresh Look," in *British Journal for the History of Science*, 2 (1964), 117–137, "Newtonian Dynamics," in *History of Science*, 5 (1966), 104–117, and "Before the *Principia*: The Maturing of Newton's Thoughts on Dynamical Astronomy, 1664–84," in *Journal for the History of Astronomy*, 1 (1970), 5–19; A. Koyré, "An Unpublished Letter of Robert Hooke to Isaac Newton," in *Isis*, 43 (1952), 312–337, repr. in Koyré's *Newtonian Studies* (VI); and R. S. Westfall, "Hooke and the Law of Universal Gravitation," in *British Journal for the History of Science*, **3** (1967), 245–261. "The Background and Early Development of Newton's Theory of Comets" is the title of a Ph.D. thesis by James Alan Ruffner (Indiana Univ., May 1966).

6. *Mathematics in the Principia*. The references for this section will be few, since works dealing with Newton's preparation for the *Principia* are listed under (5), and additional sources for the *Principia* itself are given under (7). See, further, Yasukatsu Maeyama, *Hypothesen zur Planetentheorie des 17. Jahrhunderts* (Frankfurt, 1971), and Curtis A. Wilson, "From Kepler's Laws, So-called, to Universal Gravitation: Empirical Factors," in *Archive for History of Exact Sciences*, **6** (1970), 89–170.

Two scholarly studies may especially commend our attention: H. W. Turnbull, *Mathematical Discoveries* (3), of which chs. 7 and 12 deal specifically with the *Principia*; D. T. Whiteside, "The Mathematical Principles Underlying Newton's *Principia Mathematica*," in *Journal for the History of Astronomy*, **1** (1970), 116–138, of which a version with less annotation was published in pamphlet form by the University of Glasgow (1970). See also C. B. Boyer, *Concepts of Calculus* and *History* (3), and J. F. Scott, *History* (3), ch. 11. Valuable documents and commentaries also appear in the Royal Society's ed. of Newton's *Correspondence*, J. Herivel's *Background* (5) and various articles, and D. T. Whiteside, *Mathematical Papers* (3). Especially valuable are three commentaries: J. M. F. Wright, *A Commentary on Newton's Principia*, 2 vols. (London, 1833; repr., with intro. by I. B. Cohen, New York, 1972); Henry Lord Brougham and E. J. Routh, *Analytical View of Sir Isaac Newton's Principia* (London, 1855; repr., with intro. by I. B. Cohen, New York, 1972); and Percival Frost, *Newton's Principia, First Book, Sections I., II., III., With Notes and Illustrations* (Cambridge, 1854; 5th ed., London–New York, 1900). On a post-*Principia* MS on dynamics, using fluxions, see W. W. Rouse Ball, "A Newtonian Fragment Relating to Centripetal Forces," in *Proceedings of the London Mathematical Society*, **23** (1892), 226–231; A. R. and M. B. Hall, *Unpublished Papers* (II), pp. 65–68; and commentary by D. T. Whiteside, in *History of Science*, **2** (1963), 129, n. 4.

7. *The Principia*. Many of the major sources for studying the *Principia* have already been given, in (5), (6), including works by A. R. Hall and M. B. Hall, J. Herivel, R. S. Westfall, and D. T. Whiteside. Information on the writing of the *Principia* and the evolution of the text is given in I. B. Cohen, *Introduction to Newton's Principia* (Cambridge, 1971) and the 2-vol. ed. of the *Principia* with variant readings, ed. by A. Koyré, I. B. Cohen, and Anne Whitman (I). Some additional works are R. S. Westfall, "Newton and Absolute Space," in *Archives internationales d'histoire des sciences*, **17** (1964), 121–132; Clifford Truesdell, "A Program Toward Rediscovering the Rational Mechanics of the Age of Reason," in *Archive for History of Exact Sciences*, **1** (1960), 3–36, and "Reactions of Late Baroque Mechanics to Success, Conjecture, Error, and Failure in Newton's *Principia*," in Robert Palter, ed., *The Annus Mirabilis* (VI), pp. 192–232—both articles by

Truesdell are repr. in his *Essays in the History of Mechanics* (New York–Berlin, 1968); E. J. Aiton, "The Inverse Problem of Central Forces," in *Annals of Science*, **20** (1964), 81–99; J. A. Lohne, "The Increasing Corruption" (VI), esp. "5. The Planetary Ellipse of the *Principia*"; and Thomas L. Hankins, "The Reception of Newton's Second Law of Motion in the Eighteenth Century," in *Archives internationales d'histoire des sciences*, **20** (1967), 43–65. Highly recommended is L. Rosenfeld, "Newton and the Law of Gravitation," in *Archive for History of Exact Sciences*, **2** (1965), 365–386: see also E. J. Aiton, "Newton's Aether-Stream Hypothesis and the Inverse-Square Law of Gravitation," in *Annals of Science*, **25** (1969), 255–260; and L. Rosenfeld, "Newton's Views on Aether and Gravitation," in *Archive for History of Exact Sciences*, **6** (1969), 29–37.

I. B. Cohen has discussed some further aspects of *Principia* questions in the Wiles Lectures (5) and a study of "Newton's Second Law" (5); and in "Isaac Newton's *Principia*, the Scriptures and the Divine Providence", in S. Morgenbesser, P. Suppes, and M. White, eds., *Essays in Honor of Ernest Nagel* (New York, 1969), pp. 523–548, esp. pp. 537 ff.; and "New Light on the Form of Definitions I–II–VI–VIII," where Newton's concept of "measure" is explored. On the incompatibility of Newton's dynamics and Galileo's and Kepler's laws, see Karl R. Popper, "The Aim of Science," in *Ratio*, **1** (1957), 24–35; and I. B. Cohen, "Newton's Theories vs. Kepler's Theory," in Y. Elkana, ed., *Some Aspects of the Interaction Between Science and Philosophy* (New York, in press).

8. *Revision of the Opticks* (*The Later Queries*); *Chemistry, and Theory of Matter*. The doctrine of the later queries has been studied by F. Rosenberger, *Newton und seine physikalischen Principien* (VI), and by Philip E. B. Jourdain, in a series of articles entitled "Newton's Hypothesis of Ether and of Gravitation. . . ," in *The Monist*, **25** (1915), 79–106, 233–254, 418–440; and by I. B. Cohen in *Franklin and Newton* (VI).

In addition to his studies of the queries, Henry Guerlac has analyzed Newton's philosophy of matter, suggesting an influence of Hauksbee's electrical experiments on the formation of Newton's later concept of ether. See his *Newton et Epicure* (Paris, 1963); "Francis Hauksbee: Expérimentateur au profit de Newton," in *Archives internationales d'histoire des sciences*, **17** (1963), 113–128; "Sir Isaac and the Ingenious Mr. Hauksbee," in *Mélanges Alexandre Koyré: L'aventure de la science* (Paris, 1964), pp. 228–253; and "Newton's Optical Aether," in *Notes and Records. Royal Society of London*, **22** (1967), 45–57. See also Joan L. Hawes, "Newton and the 'Electrical Attraction Unexcited,' " in *Annals of Science*, **24** (1968), 121–130; "Newton's Revival of the Aether Hypothesis and the Explanation of Gravitational Attraction," in *Notes and Records. Royal Society of London*, **23** (1968), 200–212; and the studies by Bechler listed above (4).

The electrical character of Newton's concept of "spiritus" in the final paragraph of the General Scholium has been disclosed by A. R. and M. B. Hall, in *Unpublished Papers* (II). On Newton's theory of matter, see Marie Boas [Hall],

"Newton's Chemical Papers," in *Newton's Papers and Letters* (I), pp. 241–248; and A. R. Hall and M. B. Hall, "Newton's Chemical Experiments," in *Archives internationales d'histoire des sciences*, **11** (1958), 113–152; "Newton's Mechanical Principles," in *Journal of the History of Ideas*, **20** (1959), 167–178; "Newton's Theory of Matter," in *Isis*, **51** (1960), 131–144; and "Newton and the Theory of Matter," in Robert Palter, ed., *The Annus Mirabilis* (VI), pp. 54–68.

On Newton's chemistry and theory of matter, see additionally R. Kargon, *Atomism in England From Hariot to Newton* (Oxford, 1966); A. Koyré, "Les Queries de l'Optique," in *Archives internationales d'histoire des sciences*, **13** (1960), 15–29; T. S. Kuhn, "Newton's 31st Query and the Degradation of Gold," in *Isis*, **42** (1951), 296–298, with discussion *ibid.*, **43** (1952), 123–124; J. E. McGuire, "Body and Void . . .," in *Archive for History of Exact Sciences*, **3** (1966), 206–248; "Transmutation and Immutability," in *Ambix*, **14** (1967), 69–95; and other papers; D. McKie, "Some Notes on Newton's Chemical Philosophy," in *Philosophical Magazine*, **33** (1942), 847–870; and J. R. Partington, *A History of Chemistry*, II (London, 1961), 468–477, 482–485.

For Newton's theories of chemistry and matter, and their influence, see the books by Hélène Metzger (VI), R. E. Schofield (VI), and A. Thackray (VI).

Geoffroy's summary ("extrait") of the *Opticks*, presented at meetings of the Paris Academy of Sciences, is discussed in I. B. Cohen, "Isaac Newton, Hans Sloane, and the Académie Royale des Sciences," in *Mélanges Alexandre Koyré*, I, *L'aventure de la science* (Paris, 1964), 61–116; on the general agreement by Newtonians that the queries were not so much asking questions as stating answers to such questions (and on the rhetorical form of the queries), see I. B. Cohen, *Franklin and Newton* (VI), ch. 6.

9. *Alchemy, Theology, and Prophecy. Chronology and History.* Newton published no essays or books on alchemy. His *Chronology of Ancient Kingdoms Amended* (London, 1728) also appeared in an abridged version (London, 1728). His major study of prophecy is *Observations Upon the Prophecies of Daniel, and the Apocalypse of St. John* (London, 1733). A selection of *Theological Manuscripts* was edited by H. McLachlan (Liverpool, 1950).

For details concerning Newton's theological MSS, and MSS relating to chronology, see secs. VII–VIII of the catalogue of the Sotheby sale of the Newton papers (IV); for other eds. of the *Chronology* and the *Observations*, see the Gray bibliography and the catalogue of the Babson Collection (III). There is no analysis of Newton's theological writings based on a thorough analysis of the MSS; see R. S. Westfall, *Science and Religion in Seventeenth-Century England* (New Haven, 1958), ch. 8; F. E. Manuel, *The Eighteenth Century Confronts the Gods* (Cambridge, 1959), ch. 3; and George S. Brett, "Newton's Place in the History of Religious Thought," in F. E. Brasch, ed., *Sir Isaac Newton* (VI), pp. 259–273. For Newton's chronological and allied studies, see F. E. Manuel, *Isaac Newton, Historian* (Cambridge, 1963).

On alchemy, the catalogue of the Sotheby sale is most illuminating. Important MSS and annotated alchemical books are to be found in the Keynes Collection (King's College, Cambridge) and in the Burndy Library and the University of Wisconsin, M.I.T., and the Babson Institute. A major scholarly study of Newton's alchemy and hermeticism, based on an extensive study of Newton's MSS, is P. M. Rattansi, "Newton's Alchemical Studies," in Allen G. Debus, ed., *Science, Medicine and Society in the Renaissance: Essays to Honor Walter Pagel*, II (New York, 1972), 167–182; see also R. S. Westfall, "Newton and the Hermetic Tradition," *ibid.*, pp. 183–198.

On Newton and the tradition of the ancients, and the intended inclusion in the *Principia* of references to an ancient tradition of wisdom, see I. B. Cohen, " 'Quantum in se est': Newton's Concept of Inertia in Relation to Descartes and Lucretius," in *Notes and Records. Royal Society of London*, **19** (1964), 131–155; and esp. J. E. McGuire and P. M. Rattansi, "Newton and the 'Pipes of Pan'," *ibid.*, **21** (1966), 108–143; also J. E. McGuire, "Transmutation and Immutability," in *Ambix*, **14** (1967), 69–95. On alchemy, see R. J. Forbes, "Was Newton an Alchemist?," in *Chymia*, **2** (1949), 27–36; F. Sherwood Taylor, "An Alchemical Work of Sir Isaac Newton," in *Ambix*, **5** (1956), 59–84; E. D. Geoghegan, "Some Indications of Newton's Attitude Towards Alchemy," *ibid.*, **6** (1957), 102–106; and A. R. and M. B. Hall, "Newton's Chemical Experiments," in *Archives internationales d'histoire des sciences*, **11** (1958), 113–152.

A salutary point of view is expressed by Mary Hesse, "Hermeticism and Historiography: An Apology for the Internal History of Science," in Roger H. Stuewer, ed., *Historical and Philosophical Perspectives of Science*, vol. V of Minnesota Studies in the Philosophy of Science (Minneapolis, 1970), 134–162. But see also P. M. Rattansi, "Some Evaluations of Reason in Sixteenth- and Seventeenth-Century Natural Philosophy," in Mikuláš Teich and Robert Young, eds., *Changing Perspectives in the History of Science, Essays in Honour of Joseph Needham* (London, 1973), pp. 148–166.

10. *The London Years: the Mint, the Royal Society, Quarrels With Flamsteed and With Leibniz.* On Newton's life in London and the affairs of the mint, see the biographies by More and Brewster (1), supplemented by Manuel's *Portrait* (1). Of special interest are Augustus De Morgan, *Newton: His Friend: and His Niece* (London, 1885); and Sir John Craig, *Newton at the Mint* (Cambridge, 1946). On the quarrel with Flamsteed, see Francis Baily, *An Account of the Rev^d. John Flamsteed* (London, 1835; supp., 1837; repr. London, 1966); the above-mentioned biographies of Newton; and Newton's *Correspondence* (II). On the controversy with Leibniz, see the *Commercium epistolicum* (I). Newton's MSS on this controversy (U.L.C. MS Add. 3968) have never been fully analyzed; but see Augustus De Morgan, "On the Additions Made to the Second Edition of the *Commercium epistolicum*," in *Philosophical Magazine*, 3rd ser., **32** (1848), 446–456; and "On the Authorship of the Account of the *Commercium epistolicum*, Published in the *Philosophical Transactions*," *ibid.*, 4th ser., **3** (1852), 440–444. The most recent ed. of

The Leibniz-Clarke Correspondence was edited by H. G. Alexander (Manchester, 1956).

11. *Newton's Philosophy: The Rules of Philosophizing, the General Scholium, the Queries of the Opticks.* Among the many books and articles on Newton's philosophy, those of Rosenberger, Bloch, and Koyré (VI) are highly recommended. On the evolution of the General Scholium, see A. R. and M. B. Hall, *Unpublished Papers* (II), pt. IV, intro. and sec. 8; and I. B. Cohen, *Transformations of Scientific Ideas* (the Wiles Lectures, in press) (5) and "Hypotheses in Newton's Philosophy," in *Physis*, **8** (1966), 163–184.

The other studies of Newton's philosophy are far too numerous to list here; authors include Gerd Buchdahl, Ernst Cassirer, A. C. Crombie, N. R. Hanson, Ernst Mach, Jürgen Mittelstrass, John Herman Randall, Jr., Dudley Shapere, Howard Stein, and E. W. Strong.

I. B. COHEN

SOVIET LITERATURE ON NEWTON

A profound and manifold study of Newton's life and work began in Russia at the beginning of the twentieth century; for earlier works see the article by T. P. Kravets, cited below.

The foundation of Soviet studies on Newton was laid by A. N. Krylov, who in 1915–1916 published the complete *Principia* in Russian, with more than 200 notes and supplements of a historical, philological, and mathematical nature. More than a third of the volume is devoted to supplements that present a complete, modern analytic exposition of various theorems and proofs of the original text, the clear understanding of which is often too difficult for the modern reader: "Matematicheskie nachala naturalnoy estestvennoy filosofii" ("The Mathematical Principles of Natural Philosophy"), in *Izvestiya Nikolaevskoi morskoi akademii*, **4–5** (1915–1916); 2nd ed. in *Sobranie trudov akademika A. N. Krylova* ("Collected Works of Academician A. N. Krylov"), VII (Moscow–Leningrad, 1936). Krylov devoted special attention to certain of Newton's methods and demonstrated that after suitable modification and development they could still be of use. Works on this subject include "Besedy o sposobakh opredelenia orbit komet i planet po malomu chislu nabludenii" ("Discourse on Methods of Determining Planetary and Cometary Orbits Based on a Limited Number of Observations"), *ibid.*, VI, 1–149; a series of papers, *ibid.*, V, 227–298; and "Nyutonova teoria astronomicheskoy refraktsii" ("Newton's Theory of Astronomical Refraction"), *ibid.*, V, 151–225; see also his "On a Theorem of Sir Isaac Newton," in *Monthly Notices of the Royal Astronomical Society*, **84** (1924), 392–395. On Krylov's work, see A. T. Grigorian, "Les études Newtoniennes de A. N. Krylov," in I. B. Cohen and R. Taton, eds., *Mélanges Alexandre Koyré*, II (Paris, 1964), 198–207.

A Russian translation of Newton's *Observations on the Prophecies . . . of Daniel and the Apocalypse of St. John* was published simultaneously with the first Russian edition of *Principia* as *Zamechania na knigu Prorok Daniil i Apokalipsis sv. Ioanna* (Petrograd, 1916); the translator's name is not given.

An elaborately annotated translation of Newton's works on optics is S. I. Vavilov, ed., *Optika ili traktat ob otrazheniakh, prelomleniakh, izgibaniakh i tsvetakh sveta* ("Optics"; Moscow–Leningrad, 1927; 2nd ed., Moscow, 1954). Vavilov also published Russian translations of two of Newton's essays, "Novaya teoria sveta i tsvetov" ("A New Theory of Light and Colors") and "Odna gipotesa, obyasnyayushchaya svoystva sveta, izlozhennaya v neskolkikh moikh statyakh" ("A Hypothesis Explaining the Properties of Light Presented in Several of My Papers"), in *Uspekhi fizicheskikh nauk*, **2** (1927), 121–163; and *Lektsii po optike* ("Lectiones opticae"; Leningrad, 1946). Vavilov was the first to study thoroughly the significance of the last work in the development of physics.

Newton's mathematical works published by Castillon in vol. I of *Opuscula mathematica* (1744) were translated by D. D. Mordukhay-Boltovskoy as *Matematicheskie raboty* ("Mathematical Works"; Moscow–Leningrad, 1937); the editor's 336 notes constitute nearly a third of the volume. *Arithmetica universalis* was translated by A. P. Youschkevitch with commentary as *Vseobshchaya arifmetika ili kniga ob arifmeticheskikh sintese i analise* (Moscow, 1948).

Many works dedicated to various aspects of Newton's scientific activity and to his role in the development of science were included in the tercentenary volumes *Isaak Nyuton. 1643–1727. Sbornik statey k trekhsotletiyu so dnya rozhdenia*, S. I. Vavilov, ed. (Moscow–Leningrad, 1943); and *Moskovsky universitet—pamyati Nyutona—sbornik statey* (Moscow, 1946). These works are cited below as *Symposium I* and *Symposium II*, respectively.

Z. A. Zeitlin, in *Nauka i gipotesa* ("Science and Hypothesis"; Moscow–Leningrad, 1926), studied the problem of Newton's methodology, particularly the roles of Bentley and Cotes in preparing the 2nd ed. of the *Principia*, and emphasized that both scientists had falsified Newtonian methods; the majority of other authors did not share his viewpoint. In "Efir, svet i veshchestvo v fisike Nyutona" ("Ether, Light, and Matter in Newton's Physics"), in *Symposium I*, 33–52, S. I. Vavilov traced the evolution of Newton's views on the hypothesis of the ether, the theory of light, and the structure of matter. Vavilov also dealt with Newton's methods and the role of hypothesis in ch. 10 of his biography *Isaak Nyuton* (Moscow–Leningrad, 1943; 2nd ed., rev. and enl., 1945; 3rd ed., 1961). The 3rd ed. of this work appeared in vol. III of Vavilov's *Sobranie sochinenii* ("Selected Works"; Moscow, 1956), which contains all of Vavilov's papers on Newton. The biography also appeared in German trans. (Vienna, 1948; Berlin, 1951).

B. M. Hessen in *Sotsialno-ekonomicheskie korni mekhaniki Nyutona* ("The Socioeconomic Roots of Newton's Mechanics"), presented to the Second International Congress of the History of Science and Technology held in London in 1931 (Moscow–Leningrad, 1933), attempted to analyze the origin and development of Newton's work in Marxist terms. Hessen examined the *Principia* in the light of contemporary economic and technological problems and in the context of the political, philosophical, and religious views which reflected the social conflict occurring during the period of revolution in England. His essay appeared in English as *Science at the Crossroads* (London, 1931), which is reprinted in facsimile with a foreword by Joseph Needham and an introduction by P. G. Werskey (London, 1971) and with a foreword by Robert S. Cohen (New York, 1971).

In his report on Newton's atomism, "Newton on the Atomic Theory," in Royal Society, *Newton Tercentenary Celebrations: 15–19 July, 1946* (Cambridge, 1947), Vavilov compared Newtonian chemical ideas with the development of chemistry in the nineteenth and twentieth centuries and, in particular, with the work of Mendeleev. The latter topic was also discussed in T. I. Raynov, "Nyuton i russkoe estestvoznanie" ("Newton and Russian Natural Science"), in *Symposium I*, 329–344, which also examined Lomonosov's attitude toward Newton. See also P. S. Kudriavtsev, "Lomonosov i Nyuton," in *Trudy Instituta istorii estestvoznaniya i tekhniki. Akademiya nauk SSSR*, 5 (1955), 33–51. On Newton's role in the development of chemistry see also N. I. Flerov, "Vlianie Nyutona na razvitie khimii" ("Newton's Influence on the Development of Chemistry"), in *Symposium II*, 101–106.

For detailed comments on some important problems of the *Principia*, see L. N. Sretensky, "Nyutonova teoria prilivov i figury zemli" ("Newton's Theory of Tides and of the Figure of the Earth"), in *Symposium I*, 211–234; and A. D. Dubyago, "Komety i ikh znachenie v obshchey sisteme Nyutonovykh Nachal ("Comets and Their Significance in the General System of Newton's *Principia*"), *ibid.*, 235–263. N. I. Idelson dealt with the history of the theory of lunar motion and presented a detailed study of the St. Petersburg competition of 1751, through which the theory of universal gravitation received lasting recognition, in "Zakon vsemirnogo tyagotenia i teoria dvizhenia luny" ("The Law of Universal Gravitation and the Theory of Lunar Motion"), *ibid.*, 161–210. See also Idelson's paper "Volter i Nyuton," in *Volter 1694–1778. Stati i materialy* (Moscow–Leningrad, 1948), 215–241; and A. D. Lyublinskaya's paper on the discussions between the Newtonians and the Cartesians, "K voprosu o vlianii Nyutona na frantsuzkuyu nauku" ("On the Problem of Newton's Influence on French Science"), in *Symposium I*, 361–391. On Newton's physics, see V. G. Fridman, "Ob uchenii Nyutona o masse" ("Newton's Doctrine of Mass"), in *Uspekhi fizicheskikh nauk*, 61, no. 3 (1957), 451–460.

On Newton's optics, apart from the fundamental studies of Krylov and Vavilov, see G. G. Slyusarev, "Raboty Nyutona po geometricheskoy optike" ("Newton's Works in Geometrical Optics"), in *Symposium I*, 127–141; I. A. Khvostikov, "Nyuton i razvitie uchenia o refraktsii sveta v zemnoy atmosfere" ("Newton and the Development of Studies of the Refraction of Light in the Earth's Atmosphere"), *ibid.*, 142–160; and L. I. Mandelshtam, "Opticheskie raboty Nyutona" ("Newton's Works in Optics"), in *Uspekhi fizicheskikh nauk*, 28, no. 1 (1946), 103–129.

P. S. Kudriavtsev treated Newtonian mechanics and physics in his *Istoria fiziki* ("History of Physics"), 2nd ed. (Moscow, 1956), I, 200–258; and also published a biography, *Isaak Nyuton* (Moscow, 1943; 2nd ed., 1955). The basic ideas of Newton's mechanics are described in A. T. Grigorian and I. B. Pogrebyssky, eds., *Istoria mekhaniki s drevneyshikh vremen do kontsa 18 veka* ("The History of Mechanics from Antiquity to the End of the 18th Century"; Moscow, 1971).

Many works on Newton as mathematician were devoted to an analysis of his views on the foundations of infinitesimal calculus and, in particular, of his conceptions of the limiting process and of moment. S. Gouriev dealt with this question in "Kratkoe izlozhenie razlichnykh sposobov izyasnyat differentsialnoe ischislenie" ("A Brief Account of Various Methods of Explaining the Differential Calculus"), in *Umozritelnye issledovanie SPb. Akademii nauk*, 4 (1815), 159–212. Gouriev's conception was subsequently reinterpreted—occasionally with disagreement—in the commentaries of Krylov and Mordukhay-Boltovskoy (see above); and in the papers of S. A. Yanovskaya related to the publication of the mathematical MSS of Karl Marx, "O matematicheskikh rukopisyakh Marksa" ("On Marx's Mathematical Manuscripts"), in *Marksism i estestvoznanie* (Moscow, 1933), 136–180. See also K. Marx, *Matematicheskie rukopisi* ("Mathematical Manuscripts"; Moscow, 1968), 573–576; S. A. Bogomolov, *Aktualnaya beskonechnost* ("Actual Infinity"; Leningrad–Moscow, 1934); N. N. Luzin, "Nyutonova teoria predelov" ("Newton's Theory of Limits"), in *Symposium I*, 53–74; S. Y. Lurie, "Predshestvenniki Nyutona v filosofii beskonechno malykh" ("Newton's Predecessors in the Philosophy of Infinitesimal Calculus"), *ibid.*, 75–98; A. N. Kolmogorov, "Nyuton i sovremennoe matematicheskoe myshlenie" ("Newton and Modern Mathematical Thought"), *ibid.*, II, 27–42; and F. D. Kramar, "Voprosy obosnovania analisa v trudakh Vallisa i Nyutona" ("The Problems of the Foundation of the Calculus in the Works of Wallis and Newton"), in *Istoriko-matematicheskie issledovaniya*, 3 (1950), 486–508.

K. A. Rybnikov studied the role of infinite series as a universal algorithm in Newton's method of fluxions in "O roli algoritmov v istorii obosnovania matematicheskogo analisa" ("On the Role of Algorithms in the History of the Origin of the Calculus"), in *Trudy Instituta istorii estestvoznaniya i tekhniki. Akademiya nauk SSSR*, 17 (1957), 267–299. The history of Newton's parallelogram and its applications was discussed in N. G. Chebotaryov, "Mnogougolnik Nyutona i ego rol v sovremennom razvitii matematiki" ("Newton's Polygon and his Role in the Modern Development of Mathematics"), in *Symposium I*, 99–126. I. G. Bashmakova examined the research of Newton and Waring on the problem of reducibility of algebraic equations in "Ob odnom voprose teorii algebraicheskikh uravneny v trudakh I. Nyutona i E. Varinga" ("On a Problem of the Theory of Algebraic Equations in the Works of I. Newton and E. Waring"), in *Istoriko-matematicheskie issledovaniya*, 12 (1959), 431–456. Newton's use of asymptotic series was discussed in M. V.

Chirikov, "Iz istorii asimptoticheskikh ryadov" ("On the History of Asymptotic Series"), *ibid.*, **13** (1960), 441–472. On Newton's calculations equivalent to the use of multiple integrals, see V. I. Antropova, "O geometricheskom metode 'Matematicheskikh nachal naturalnoy filosofii' I. Nyutona" ("On the Geometrical Method in Newton's *Philosophiae naturalis mathematica principia*"), *ibid.*, **17** (1966), 208–228; and "O roli Isaaka Nyutona v razvitii teorii potentsiala" ("On Isaac Newton's Role in the Development of Potential Theory"), in *Uchenye zapiski Tulskogo gosudarstvennogo pedagogicheskogo instituta*, Mat. kafedr, **3** (1970), 3–56. N. I. Glagolev described Newton's geometrical ideas in "Nyuton kak geometr" ("Newton as Geometer"), in *Symposium II*, 71–80; and his mathematical discoveries were summarized in vols. II and III of A. P. Youschkevitch, ed., *Istoria matematiki s drevneyshikh vremen do nachala XIX stoletia* ("A History of Mathematics From Antiquity to the Beginning of the Nineteenth Century"; Moscow, 1970–1972).

See also two papers on Newton as historian of antiquity: S. Y. Lurie, "Nyuton—istorik drevnosti" ("Newton—Historian of Antiquity"), in *Symposium I*, 271–311; and E. C. Skrzhinskaya, "Kembridgsky universitet i Nyuton" ("Cambridge University and Newton"), *ibid.*, 392–421.

On Soviet studies of Newton, see T. P. Kravets, "Nyuton i izuchenie ego trudov v Rossii" ("Newton and the Study of His Works in Russia"), *ibid.*, 312–328; A. P. Youschkevitch, "Sovetskaya yubileynaya literatura o Nyutone" ("Soviet Jubilee Literature on Newton"), in *Trudy Instituta istorii estestvoznaniya. Akademiya nauk SSSR*, **1**, 440–455; and *Istoria estestvoznaniya. Bibliografichesk11y ukazatel. Literatura, opublikovannaya v SSSR (1917–1948)* ("History of Natural Science. Bibliography. Literature Published in the U.S.S.R. 1917–1948"; Moscow–Leningrad, 1949).

A. P. YOUSCHKEVITCH

NICERON, JEAN-FRANÇOIS (*b.* Paris, France, 1613; *d.* Aix-en-Provence, France, 22 September 1646), *geometrical optics.*

Niceron was the eldest child of Claude Niceron and Renée Barbière. He studied under Mersenne at the Collège de Nevers in Paris and then entered the Order of Minims, where he took his second name to distinguish him from a paternal uncle, also named Jean. In 1639 Niceron was appointed professor of mathematics at Trinità dei Monti, the order's convent in Rome. From 1640 he also served as auxiliary visitor for Minim monasteries. The frequent travels required by the latter post weakened his already frail health, and he died at the age of thirty-three while visiting Aix.

Having been a student of Mersenne, Niceron shared his mentor's broad interest in natural philosophy as well as his penchant for gathering and disseminating news of the latest developments. Niceron's journeys to Rome brought him into contact with many Italian scientists, to whom he communicated the results of French investigations and whose work he in turn forwarded to Paris. In 1639 Niceron informed Cavalieri of the work of Fermat, Descartes, and Roberval on the quadrature and cubature of curves of the form $y = x^n$ and on the properties of the cycloid. Niceron's revelations concerning the cycloid angered Roberval, who apparently wished to keep his results secret until he could publish them or use them in the triennial defense of his chair at the Collège Royal. Not knowing the true source of Cavalieri's information, Roberval accused Beaugrand of having betrayed confidences. The affair seems to have become something of a *cause célèbre* until Cavalieri clarified matters in 1643 (see Cavalieri's letters in *Correspondance de Mersenne*, C. de Waard *et al.*, eds., XII [Paris, 1972], *passim*). In 1640 Niceron returned to Paris with the first copies of Cavalieri's *Geometria indivisibilibus . . . promota.*

While in Italy in 1639–1640, Niceron measured the declination of the magnetic compass in Ligurno, Rome, and Florence. From 1643 to 1645 he collaborated with a group of scientists in Rome (including Magiotti, Baliani, Kircher, Ricci, and Maignan) in conducting experiments suggested by the work of Galileo. It was from Niceron that Mersenne first heard of Galileo's death (see Niceron to Mersenne, 2 Feb. 1642, *Correspondance de Mersenne*, XI, 30–34).

Niceron's major work, however, dealt with perspective and geometrical optics. His *Perspective curieuse* (1638) defines the range and nature of the problems he addressed; later editions of the work simply provide more detail. Although aware of the latest theoretical developments, Niceron concentrated primarily on the practical applications of perspective, catoptrics, and dioptrics, and on the illusory effects of optics then traditionally associated with natural magic. The work is divided into four books, of which the first presents briefly the fundamental geometrical theorems that are necessary for what follows; it then develops a general method of perspective collineation, borrowing heavily from Alberti and Dürer. Book II, which is addressed to the problem of establishing perspective for paintings executed on curved or irregular surfaces (for example, vaults and niches), presents a general technique of anamorphosis; that is, the determination of the surface distortions necessary to bring a picture into perspective when viewed from a given point. Niceron showed, for example, how to construct on the interior surface of a cone a distorted image which, when viewed end on through the base, appears in proper proportion.

Book III discusses the anamorphosis of figures that are viewed by reflection from plane, cylindrical, and conical mirrors. He explained how to draw on a plane surface a distorted figure which, when viewed by means of a cylindrical mirror standing perpendicular to the plane, appears in normal proportion. Book IV deals with the distortions created by refraction. Here Niceron abandoned any effort at general treatment and concentrated instead on constructing an optical device consisting of a polyhedral lens that gathers elements of one figure and unites them into another, totally different figure. The discussion contains perhaps the first published reference to Descartes's derivation of the law of refraction (1638) and thus gains some historical significance.

Later editions of Niceron's work, particularly the Latin version of 1646, do not differ from the 1638 edition in their basic content. Although clearly a capable mathematician, Niceron was interested more in practice than in theory. Sympathetic to the natural magic still current in his time, he tended to view optics as the art of illusion rather than the science of light.

BIBLIOGRAPHY

I. ORIGINAL WORKS. Niceron's major works are *La perspective curieuse, ou magie artificielle des effets merveilleux de l'optique, par la vision directe; la catoptrique, par la réflexion des miroirs plats, cylindriques et coniques; la dioptrique, par la réfraction des crystaux* . . . (Paris, 1638; expanded Latin version of I and II under title *Thaumaturgus opticus, seu admiranda optics . . . catoptrices . . . dioptrices . . .*, Paris, 1646; 3rd ed., heavily edited by Roberval, together with Mersenne's *L'optique et la catoptrique*, Paris, 1651; 4th ed., in Latin and French, Paris, 1663); and *L'interprétation des chiffres, ou règle pour bien entendre et expliquer facilement toutes sortes de chiffres simples, tirée de l'italien d'Antonio Maria Cospi, augmentée et accommodée particulièrement à l'usage des langues française et espagnole* (Paris, 1641). Of Niceron's correspondence, only two letters survive, both written to Mersenne and published in *Correspondance de Mersenne*, Cornelis de Waard, *et al.*, eds. (Paris, 1932–), X, 811–814 (8 Dec. 1641); XI, 30–34 (2 Feb. 1642).

II. SECONDARY LITERATURE. See Maria Luisa Bonelli, "Una lettera di Evangelista Torricelli a Jean François Niceron," in *Convegno di studi Torricelliani* (Faenza, 1959), 37–41; Robert Lenoble, "Roberval 'éditeur' de Mersenne et du P. Niceron," in *Revue d'histoire des sciences et de leurs applications*, **10** (1957), 235–254, and *Mersenne, ou la naissance du méchanisme* (Paris, 1943), *passim*; and *Correspondance de Mersenne*, VIII–XII, *passim*, with a short biography in X, 811.

MICHAEL S. MAHONEY

NICHOLAS CHUQUET. See Chuquet, Nicolas.

NICHOLAS OF CUSA. See Cusa, Nicholas.

NICHOLAS OF DAMASCUS. See Nicolaus of Damascus.

NICHOLAS, JOHN SPANGLER (*b.* Allegheny, Pennsylvania, 10 March 1895; *d.* New Haven, Connecticut, 11 September 1963), *biology.*

Nicholas was a descendant of two old Pennsylvania families. His father, Samuel Trauger Nicholas, was a Lutheran minister; his mother, formerly Elizabeth Spangler, had been trained as a teacher before her marriage. An only child, Nicholas was educated at Pennsylvania (now Gettysburg) College (B.S., 1916; M.S., 1917). He entered Yale as a graduate student in the autumn of 1917 but in 1918 interrupted his work there to enlist in the Army Medical Corps. Nicholas was assigned to the vaccine department of the Army Medical School in Washington, D.C., where he worked on methods of improving typhoid vaccine until his discharge in 1919. He then returned to Yale, where he received a Ph.D. in zoology in 1921. In the same year he married Helen Benton Brown.

After teaching for six years in the department of anatomy at the University of Pittsburgh, Nicholas returned to Yale in 1926 to teach zoology and remained there until his retirement in 1963. He became Sterling professor of zoology in 1939 and was chairman of the department of zoology from 1946 to 1956 and Master of Trumbull College from 1945 until his retirement. Nicholas performed many other administrative duties, at Yale and elsewhere. He served as editor of a number of biological journals, most notably the *Journal of Experimental Zoology*. He held office in a number of professional societies, including the American Philosophical Society and the National Academy of Sciences. As adviser to government agencies he was particularly influential as a consultant to the National Research Council on the effective use of scientific manpower during World War II.

Nicholas' primary interest, however, was in embryology; and within this area his activities were quite varied. He studied experimentally the development of fishes, amphibians, and mammals; worked in endocrinology, reproductive physiology, and neurology; and conducted original and pioneering investigations so numerous and diverse that only the most important will be mentioned here.

Nicholas began his experimental work by studying various aspects of the development of asymmetry in the amphibian limb. Ross Harrison had previously shown, through grafting experiments on salamander larvae, that whether a limb will become a left or a right limb depends on the orientation of the limb bud with respect to its surroundings in the embryo at certain specified periods in development. That is, by rotating only a narrow ring of tissue surrounding the limb bud, Nicholas demonstrated that this ring contains the factors that interact with the limb bud to determine its asymmetry. Nicholas also performed experiments on amphibian embryos and larvae to elucidate the development of the nervous system. His vital staining experiments on amphibian eggs showed that extensive movements take place in the endoderm before gastrulation; previously it had been believed that such movements begin only at gastrulation.

Nicholas made an important contribution to the study of teleost development by being the first to improvise a method for removing the horny covering of the egg, thereby making it possible to apply the modern methods of experimental embryology to the eggs of these fishes. He also applied the new methods of experimental embryology to the study of mammalian eggs—this was his most important scientific contribution. Although not the first to attempt mammalian experimental embryology, Nicholas was the first to carry out an intensive program in this field. He studied young rat eggs, or young rat embryos or their parts, both in tissue culture and in grafts implanted at a number of sites in adult rats—and even on the chick chorioallantois. His most noteworthy experiments along this line demonstrated that single blastomeres, isolated at the two-cell stage and then transplanted into the uterus of foster mothers, could develop to the egg cylinder stage. This was the first experiment to demonstrate the flexible nature of mammalian development and to prove that the important embryological principles of induction and progressive differentiation are applicable to higher as well as to lower vertebrates.

BIBLIOGRAPHY

The most detailed biography of Nicholas, with a complete bibliography of his articles, is Jane M. Oppenheimer, "John Spangler Nicholas 1895–1963," in *Biographical Memoirs. National Academy of Sciences*, **40** (1969), 239–289.

Nicholas' professional correspondence is in the Archives Collection of the Sterling Library, Yale University.

Jane Oppenheimer

NICHOLAS ORESME. See **Oresme, Nicole.**

NICHOLS, ERNEST FOX (*b.* Leavenworth, Kansas, 1 June 1869; *d.* Washington, D.C., 29 April 1924), *physics.*

The son of Alonzo Curtis Nichols, a photographer, and Sophronia Fox, Nichols was orphaned at an early age and raised in Manhattan, Kansas, by his aunt and uncle, General and Mrs. S. M. Fox. Having inherited some money for his education, Nichols graduated from Kansas State College of Agriculture in 1888 and did graduate work at Cornell University from 1888 to 1892. While holding an associate professorship at Colgate University from 1892 to 1898, he married Katharine W. West, the daughter of a prominent family in Hamilton, New York (1894); did further graduate work in the laboratory of Emil Warburg at Berlin (1894 to 1896); and received his D.Sc. from Cornell (1897).

A professor of physics at Dartmouth College from 1898 to 1903 and at Columbia University from 1903 to 1909, Nichols was president of Dartmouth from 1909 to 1916. While serving on the physics faculty at Yale from 1916 to 1920 he did war work for the National Research Council and the ordnance department of the U.S. Navy. The president of M.I.T. for some months in 1920, Nichols was director of research in pure science at the laboratories of the National Electric Light Association in Cleveland, Ohio, from 1921 until his death. Nichols was awarded the Rumford Medal in 1904, was coeditor of the *Physical Review* from 1913 to 1916, and was elected to the National Academy of Sciences, the American Academy of Arts and Sciences, and the American Philosophical Society.

As a research scientist Nichols' reputation rested on his development and use of the Nichols radiometer. While in Berlin, with the help of Ernst Pringsheim he constructed a radiometer far more sensitive than any other then in existence. In his new model he made the moving parts as light as possible, reduced the torsional moment, employed a delicate suspension fiber, and set the gas pressure for maximum operational effectiveness. Free of the chief disturbances suffered by thermoelements and the bolometer, Nichols' device was superior to those instruments for measurements in the infrared range. With his radiometer Nichols successfully explored the reflection and transmission of infrared rays, measured the relative heats of fixed stars, and, independently of Peter Lebedev, quantitatively confirmed the existence of the pressure of light predicted by Maxwell's laws. Near the end of his life Nichols used a resonant form of the radiometer to close the final gap between the radiations produced by thermal and electric means. He was reporting his results at a meeting of the National Academy when, in mid-sentence, he collapsed and died of heart failure.

BIBLIOGRAPHY

Leigh Page, "Ernest Fox Nichols," in *Dictionary of American Biography*, XIII, 491–494, is an authoritative introduction to Nichols' life and work. It may be supplemented by Edward L. Nichols, "Ernest Fox Nichols," in *Biographical Memoirs. National Academy of Sciences*, **12** (1929), 97–131, which contains a complete bibliography of Nichols' scientific writings. In the archives of Colgate University are eight Nichols items: six letters from Joseph Larmor and two books of notes on Larmor's lectures at Cambridge University, all from 1904–1905, when Nichols spent a sabbatical year in England.

DANIEL J. KEVLES

NICHOLSON, JOHN WILLIAM (*b*. Darlington, England, 1 November 1881; *d*. Oxford, England, 10 October 1955), *mathematical physics, astrophysics*.

The eldest son of John William Nicholson and Alice Emily Kirton, Nicholson received his early education at Middlesbrough High School. He studied mathematics and physical science at the University of Manchester from 1898 to 1901. He went on to Trinity College, Cambridge, where he took the mathematical tripos in 1904. At Cambridge he was Isaac Newton student in 1906, Smith's prizeman in 1907, and Adam's prizeman in 1913 and again in 1917. He lectured at the Cavendish Laboratory, Cambridge, and later at the Queen's University, Belfast, before being appointed professor of mathematics at King's College, London, in 1912. In 1921 he became fellow and director of studies in mathematics at Balliol College, Oxford, retiring in 1930 because of bad health. In 1922 he married Dorothy Wrinch, fellow of Girton College, Cambridge; they had one daughter. Their marriage was dissolved in 1938.

Nicholson became fellow of the Royal Astronomical Society in 1911 and fellow of the Royal Society in 1917. He was vice-president of the London Physical Society, president of the Röntgen Society, and member of the London Mathematical Society and the Société de Physique. He received the M.A. from the universities of Oxford and Cambridge, the D.Sc. from the University of London, and the M.Sc. from the University of Manchester.

Nicholson's most original work was his atomic theory of coronal and nebular spectra, which he published in a series of papers, beginning in November 1911, in the *Monthly Notices of the Royal Astronomical Society*. The spectra of the solar corona and galactic nebulae contained lines of unknown origin, which Nicholson, following a common astrophysical speculation at the time, supposed were produced by elements that were primary in an evolutionary sense to terrestrial elements. The presumed simplicity of the primary elements opened the possibility of their exact dynamical treatment. Adapting an atomic model of J. J. Thomson, Nicholson viewed an atom of a primary element as a single, planetary ring of electrons rotating about a small, massive, positively charged nucleus. Associating the frequencies of the unidentified spectral lines with those of the transverse modes of oscillation of the electrons about their equilibrium path, he accounted for most coronal and nebular lines with impressive numerical accuracy, even predicting a new nebular line that was soon observed.

In his first two papers on celestial spectra, Nicholson had no theoretical means for fully specifying his atomic systems, having to fix empirically the radius and angular velocity of the electron rings from observed spectral frequencies. In his third paper (June 1912) he rectified the incompleteness of his theory by introducing the Planck constant, h. He did so by observing that the angular momentum of primary atoms was a multiple of $h/2\pi$. Niels Bohr read Nicholson's papers in the *Monthly Notices* in late 1912, at the time he was working out his own early thoughts on the relation of the Planck constant to the structure of atoms and molecules. Impressed by the unprecedented spectral capability of Nicholson's theory, Bohr sought its relation to his own theory. In so doing Bohr came to a deeper understanding of his own atomic model, in particular of his need to attribute excited states to it. After Bohr published his theory in 1913, Nicholson challenged it and extended his own theory. But it was Bohr's theory and not his that led to a full understanding of spectra and beyond that to a new quantum atomic physics. The significance of Nicholson's theory for the development of twentieth-century atomic physics lies chiefly in the early impetus it gave Bohr for exploring the spectral implications of his very different quantum theory.

BIBLIOGRAPHY

I. ORIGINAL WORKS. Nicholson's active career spanned the years 1905–1925, during which he published roughly seventy-five papers. His most important papers on coronal and nebular spectra are "The Spectrum of Nebulium," in *Monthly Notices of the Royal Astronomical Society*, **72** (1911), 49–64; and "The Constitution of the Solar Corona," *ibid.*, 139–150; *ibid.* (1912), 677–692, 729–739. In addition to his astrophysical papers, Nicholson published on a wide range of topics that included electric and elastic vibrations, electron theory of metals, electron structure, atomic structure and spectra of terrestrial elements, relativity principle, and special mathematical functions.

Although Nicholson wrote no books, he contributed to Arthur Dendy, ed., *Problems of Modern Science. A Series of Lectures Delivered at King's College—University of London* (London, 1922). He collaborated with Arthur Schuster in revising and enlarging the third ed. of the latter's *An Introduction to the Theory of Optics* (London, 1924); and with Joseph Larmor *et al.* he edited the *Scientific Papers of S. B. McLaren* (Cambridge, 1925).

II. SECONDARY LITERATURE. Nicholson's contribution to modern atomic theory has been recently assessed by John L. Heilbron and Thomas S. Kuhn, "The Genesis of the Bohr Atom," in *Historical Studies in the Physical Sciences*, **1** (1969), 211–290; T. Hirosige and S. Nisio, "Formation of Bohr's Theory of Atomic Constitution," in *Japanese Studies in the History of Science*, no. 3 (1964), 6–28; and Russell McCormmach, "The Atomic Theory of John William Nicholson," in *Archives for History of Exact Sciences*, **3** (1966), 160–184.

In his introduction to Niels Bohr, *On the Constitution of Atoms and Molecules* (Copenhagen, 1963), xi–liii, Léon Rosenfeld has, in addition to discussing Nicholson's theory, published and analyzed letters by Bohr in 1912 and 1913 that bear on his reading of the theory. An older historical discussion of Nicholson's theory is Edmund Whittaker, *A History of the Theories of Aether and Electricity. The Modern Theories 1900–1926* (London, 1953), 107. A contemporary scientific account of Nicholson's theory is W. D. Harkens and E. D. Wilson, "Recent Work on the Structure of the Atom," in *Journal of the American Chemical Society*, **37** (1915), 1396–1421.

For biographical information, see William Wilson, "John William Nicholson 1881–1955," in *Biographical Memoirs of Fellows of the Royal Society*, **2** (1956), 209–214.

RUSSELL MCCORMMACH

NICHOLSON, SETH BARNES (*b.* Springfield, Illinois, 12 November 1891; *d.* Los Angeles, California, 2 July 1963), *observational astronomy.*

Nicholson spent his youth in rural communities in Illinois, where his father, a somewhat trained geologist, alternated between farming and teaching in elementary and high schools. At Drake University, Nicholson's career choice was influenced by the professor of astronomy, D. W. Morehouse, who was well-known for his discovery in 1908 of a particularly bright comet. In 1912 Nicholson and Alma Stotts, a classmate at Drake whom he soon married, enrolled as graduate students in astronomy at Berkeley; from then on, they were part of the West Coast astronomical community.

Nicholson's most noted astronomical work was his discovery of four faint moons of Jupiter. In 1914, while at Lick Observatory photographing Jupiter VIII, which had been found by P. Melotte a few years before, Nicholson discovered Jupiter IX. This small satellite was at the limit of detectability of the thirty-six-inch telescope and the then available photographic plates, and for many years other astronomers had to take Nicholson's word for its existence. Nicholson's Ph.D. dissertation concerned the discovery of Jupiter IX and calculations of its orbit. After receiving his doctorate Nicholson was appointed to the staff at the Mt. Wilson Observatory, where he found Jupiter X and Jupiter XI in 1938, and Jupiter XII in 1951.

In addition to his work on the minor bodies of the solar system, Nicholson tackled several astrophysical problems. He made long-term and detailed observations of the surface features and spectrum of the sun. With Edison Pettit he used a vacuum thermocouple to measure the temperatures of stars, planets, and the eclipsed moon. He charted the profiles of spectral lines in Cepheid stars, and from spectrograms of Venus he derived a value for the solar parallax and a verification of the absence of oxygen and water vapor from the Venusian atmosphere.

A mentor to numerous young astronomers, Nicholson was an active member of the Astronomical Society of the Pacific and several other astronomical and civic organizations. He received the Catherine Bruce Gold Medal of the Astronomical Society of the Pacific (1963) and was elected to membership in the National Academy of Sciences (1937).

BIBLIOGRAPHY

For biography and bibliography see Paul Herget, "Seth Barnes Nicholson," in *Biographical Memoirs. National Academy of Sciences*, **42** (1971), 201–227. See also R. M. Petrie, "Award of the Bruce Gold Medal to Seth B. Nicholson," in *Publications of the Astronomical Society of the Pacific*, **75** (1963), 305–307.

DEBORAH JEAN WARNER

NICHOLSON, WILLIAM (*b.* London, England, 1753; *d.* London, 21 May 1815), *chemistry, technology.*

As is characteristic of minor scientific figures of the British industrial revolution, only fragmentary information survives on William Nicholson's variegated activities. Many of these endeavors were of considerable significance within the rapidly developing and changing scientific world of his day. Nicholson was successively a servant of the East India Company, a European commercial agent of Josiah Wedgwood, the potter, master of a London mathematical school, patent agent, and water engineer. He also found time to translate foreign scientific works, compile a chemical dictionary, perfect a number of inventions, devise new instruments, act as secretary of the General Chamber of Manufacturers of Great Britain, undertake significant original research and, for sixteen years, edit and promote the monthly scientific journal for which he is most often remembered. Despite—or possibly because of—advanced scientific knowledge and practical ingenuity, "he lived in trouble and died poor."

The son of a London solicitor, Nicholson was educated in North Yorkshire, before entering the service of the East India Company in 1769. In 1776 he returned home from India. He then spent time in Amsterdam, as Dutch sales agent for Wedgwood. By 1780 he apparently had settled in London with the proceeds of his foreign ventures and had begun to find his métier as inventor, translator, and scientific projector. It was presumably about this time that he married Catherine, daughter of Peter Boullie of London and remote descendant of Edward III. Nothing is known of their family life, save that at least one son reached maturity.

On arriving in London, Nicholson seems to have intended an assault on its literary world. Initially he lodged with the dramatist Thomas Holcroft, with whom he collaborated on at least one novel. The burgeoning scientific life of the capital soon captured his fancy, although a taste for literary and historical works remained with him. Nicholson appears to have run a mathematical school for some years, until other pursuits crowded it out. Reestablished in 1799, the school again experienced its earlier fate. Pedagogic concerns were certainly paramount in Nicholson's first scientific publication, *An Introduction to Natural Philosophy* (1781), which enjoyed some success as a Newtonian text.

In December 1783 Nicholson's serious scientific interests were recognized in his election to the Chapter Coffee House Society, or Philosophical Society. This ephemeral research club flourished throughout the 1780's and Nicholson soon became its secretary. Among its twenty-five participants the club numbered J. H. de Magellan, Richard Kirwan, and Tiberius Cavallo; Joseph Priestley and Thomas Percival figured among its provincial honorary members. Association with the group no doubt prompted Nicholson's interest in the intellectual and commercial possibilities of the new French chemistry, then generating intense debate. His translation of A. F. de Fourcroy's *Élémens d'histoire naturelle et de chimie* appeared in 1788; that of the French rebuttal of Richard Kirwan's *Essay on Phlogiston*, in 1789; and

that of J. A. C. Chaptal's *Élémens de chimie*, in 1791. A natural consequence of this activity was the publication of Nicholson's *First Principles of Chemistry* in 1790 and of a weighty, competent, but pedestrian *Dictionary of Chemistry* in 1795. At a slightly later date he translated Fourcroy's *Tableaux synoptiques de chimie* and also his authoritative eleven-volume *Système des connaissances chimiques*, as well as Chaptal's four-volume *Chimie appliquée aux arts.*

Just as this cluster of works is indicative of growing British concern with chemistry, so the success accorded Nicholson's decision to found a monthly journal of scientific news and commentary reflects the quickening of British interest across a wider range of natural knowledge. The *Journal of Natural Philosophy, Chemistry and the Arts* began publication in April 1797. Its success invited emulation. Alexander Tilloch's *Philosophical Magazine* appeared in June 1798 and offered a continuing threat to the less worldly Nicholson. When in 1813 the field was crowded still further by Thomas Thomson's *Annals of Philosophy*, Nicholson, already ill, withdrew. His *Journal* was merged with Tilloch's, which throughout had shown greater commercial if less scientific acumen, and which continues to flourish (having also ingested Thomson's *Annals*).

The reception accorded Nicholson's *Journal* reveals the growing number of cultivators of science to be found in the urbanizing and industrializing culture of late-Georgian Britain. Reliable news of scientific discoveries, technical processes, instruments, books, translations, and meetings met an evident demand. The medium itself also created a fresh audience and new possibilities for scientific controversy and intellectual fashion. In July 1800 Nicholson's *Journal* enjoyed its greatest coup, when it gave the first report of its proprietor's sensational electrolysis of water, in collaboration with Anthony Carlisle. The *Journal* immediately became the accepted vehicle and the powerful reinforcer of the resulting scientific fashion for electrolysis, a fashion which Humphry Davy effectively exploited in his own brilliant demonstration of the newly possible art of scientific careerism. Another illustration of the changes wrought by this fresh medium of scientific communication may be seen in the work of John Dalton. He used the monthly journals to engage critics of his theory of mixed gases and thereby was encouraged to persevere in the work which finally led to his chemical atomic theory.

Nicholson's real genius was that of a projector. As a researcher he was competent but uninspired; as an entrepreneur, persistent but empty-handed. The range of his inventions was wide, running from hydrometers to machinery for manufacturing files. All were as commercially unrewarding as they were technically excellent. His plans for a new Middlesex waterworks, for supplying Southwark, and for piping water to Portsmouth were important and practical pieces of urban engineering from which he drew little reward. Indeed, Nicholson's financial problems were such that he spent time in debtors' prison, deliberately sold his name to the proprietors of the six-volume *British Encyclopaedia* in 1809, and died in poverty after a lingering illness. He neither became a fellow of the Royal Society nor did he enjoy other public recognition. If his activities illustrate the widening scientific opportunities of a new age, they also show that energy, imagination, and expert knowledge provided no infallible route to personal fortune or social reward.

BIBLIOGRAPHY

I. ORIGINAL WORKS. There is no bibliography of Nicholson's works, many of which are now very rare. The following list is necessarily tentative, not definitive. Scientific books are *An Introduction to Natural Philosophy*, 2 vols. (London, 1781; 5th ed., 1805); *First Principles of Chemistry* (London, 1790; 3rd ed., 1796); and *A Dictionary of Chemistry*, 2 vols. (London, 1795), rev. as *A Dictionary of Practical and Theoretical Chemistry* (London, 1808). Other books are *The History of Ayder Ali Khan, Nabob Buhader; or New Memoirs Concerning the East Indies, With Historical Notes*, 2 vols. (London, 1783); *The Navigator's Assistant* (London, 1784); and *Abstract of Such Acts of Parliament as Are Now in Force for Preventing the Exportation of Wool* (London, 1786).

Nicholson's editions and translations of works by others are *Ralph's Critical Review of the Public Buildings, Statues and Ornaments in and About London and Westminster . . . With Additions* (London, 1783); Fourcroy's *Elements of Natural History and Chemistry*, 4 vols. (London, 1788) plus *Supplement* (London, 1789); the French reply to Kirwan's *Essay on Phlogiston, and the Constitution of Acids . . . With Additional Remarks . . .* (London, 1789); *Memoirs and Travels of the Count de Benyowsky*, 2 vols. (London, 1789); Chaptal's *Elements of Chemistry*, 3 vols. (London, 1791; 4th ed., 1803); Pajot des Charmes's *The Art of Bleaching Piece Goods, Cottons, and Threads . . . by . . . Oxygenated Muriatic Acid* (London, 1799); G. B. Venturi's *Experimental Enquiries Concerning . . . Motion in Fluids* (London, 1799); Fourcroy's *Synoptic Tables of Chemistry* (London, 1801); Fourcroy's *General System of Chemical Knowledge*, 11 vols. (London, 1804); and Chaptal's *Chemistry Applied to Arts and Manufactures*, 4 vols. (London, 1807).

Scientific papers by Nicholson include "Description of a New Instrument for Measuring the Specific Gravity of Bodies," in *Memoirs of the Manchester Literary and Philosophical Society*, **2** (1785), 386–396; "The Principles

and Illustration of an Advantageous Method of Arranging the Differences of Logarithms, on Lines Graduated for the Purpose of Computation," in *Philosophical Transactions of the Royal Society*, **77** (1787), 246–252; "Experiments and Observations on Electricity," *ibid.*, **79** (1789), 265–287; "Account of the New Electrical or Galvanic Apparatus of Sig. Alex. Volta, and Experiments Performed With the Same," in *Journal of Natural Philosophy, Chemistry and the Arts*, **4** (1800), 179–187, written with A. Carlisle; and numerous other contributions (many anonymous) to his own journal. A list of 62 papers is in the Royal Society *Catalogue of Scientific Papers*, IV, 610–612.

II. SECONDARY LITERATURE. The best obituary of Nicholson is that in *New Monthly Magazine*, **3** (1815), 569; **4** (1816), 76–77, on which the *Dictionary of National Biography* leans heavily. There is some additional information in *Gentlemen's Magazine*, **85** (1815), 570. His mechanical inventions are treated briefly in Samuel Smiles, *Men of Invention and Industry* (London, 1884), 164, 177, 194, 202; his chemical work is mentioned in J. R. Partington, *A History of Chemistry*, IV (London, 1964), 19–20. S. Lilley, "Nicholson's Journal (1797–1813)," in *Annals of Science*, **6**, (1948), 78–101, discusses the content and significance of the *Journal*. Nicholson's other publications are exhaustively examined in R. S. Woolner, "Life and Scientific Work of William Nicholson" (M.Sc. diss., University College, London, 1959). Some further information, and reference to a manuscript biography by his son, are in R. W. Corlass, "A Philosophical Society of a Century Ago," in *Reliquary*, **18** (1878), 209–211. The MS minute book of the Chapter Coffee House Society, to which Corlass refers, is now in the Museum of the History of Science, Oxford (MS Gunter 4).

ARNOLD THACKRAY

NICOL, WILLIAM (*b.* 1768; *d.* Edinburgh, Scotland, 2 September 1851), *optics, petrology, paleontology.*

Although he achieved fame in physics as the inventor of the first polarizer, the Nicol prism, Nicol was primarily a geologist who made important but unappreciated contributions to petrology and paleontology.

Little is known about Nicol's early career at the University of Edinburgh, where he lectured in natural philosophy, for he did not publish until he was fifty-eight. His first known scientific research dealt with the structure of crystals, and it was undoubtedly in connection with this work that he invented the prism. Nicol constructed his device by splitting a parallelepiped of calcite spar along its shorter diagonal and then cementing the halves together with Canada balsam, a substance with an index of refraction intermediate to the two indices of the doubly refracting calcite spar. The balsam allows the extraordinary ray to pass almost undeviated through the prism while it reflects the ordinary beam (see Figure 1). The two beams emerging from the prism are so widely separated they can be used independently. When it was invented (1828) Nicol's device was the most convenient means of producing polarized light, and it became an important tool in physical optics and petrography.

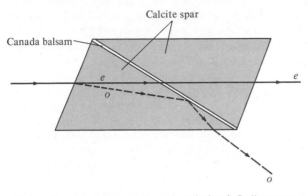

Calcite spar

Canada balsam

e   *e*

o

o

Extraordinary ray, *e,* passes through undeviated. Ordinary ray, *o,* reflected by first Canada balsam surface.

FIGURE 1

Nicol's inventive talents were equally well displayed in geology, although he received less credit than he deserved for his work in this field. To aid his early studies of crystals and rocks, he developed a technique for preparing transparent slivers for viewing directly through a microscope. Previous microscopic studies of minerals had been done with reflected light, which could reveal only surface qualities. Nicol's technique was to cement the mineral in question to a glass plate and then grind it down to extreme thinness, thereby making possible for the first time direct microscopic investigation of the innermost structure of rocks and crystals.

Unfortunately, the potential of Nicol's new method was not realized in petrology for more than forty years after its invention, in or around 1815. Nicol himself was partly to blame for this, since he never published any structural studies of his slide specimens (indeed he may never have made any such studies), except for two papers on fluid cavities in crystals. Furthermore, the first printed account of his technique did not appear until 1831, and then in a book on fossil woods (Witham's *Observations on Fossil Vegetables*), which few petrologists were likely to read. Thus, it is not altogether surprising that this promising new method was not incorporated into the science of petrology until 1853, when Henry Sorby obtained Nicol's slides and showed how they could divulge the secrets of mineral structure.

Nicol had far more success in the field of paleontology. He found that the same slidemaking technique could be used in the study of fossil woods in order to obtain a view of the minute cell structure with a microscope. Knowledge of the cell pattern thus obtained could be used as a basis for classifying and identifying the specimens being examined. Nicol made these identifications for a large number of fossil woods and displayed the arrangement of the cells in Witham's *Observations*. Yet he seems not to have been accorded full recognition for this important work either.

BIBLIOGRAPHY

Nicol's articles include "Observations on the Fluids Contained in Crystallized Minerals," in *Edinburgh New Philosophical Journal*, **5** (1828), 94–96; "On a Method of So Far Increasing the Divergency of the Two Rays in Calcareous Spar That Only One Image May Be Seen at a Time," *ibid.*, **6** (1829), 83–84; "On the Cavities Containing Fluids in Rock Salt," *ibid.*, **7** (1829), 111–113; *ibid.*, **10** (1831), 361–364; *ibid.*, **14** (1833), 153–158; "On the Anatomical Structure of Recent and Fossil Woods," in *British Association for the Advancement of Science Report* (1834), 660–666; *Edinburgh New Philosophical Journal*, **18** (1835), 335–339; and "Observations on the Structure of Recent and Fossil Coniferae," *ibid.*, **29** (1840), 175.

The only biographical material on Nicol is in Poggendorff, II, 151. The account of his mounting technique is in H. T. M. Witham, *Observations on Fossil Vegetables* (Edinburgh, 1831).

EUGENE FRANKEL

NICOLAI, FRIEDRICH BERNHARD GOTTFRIED (*b.* Brunswick, Germany, 25 October 1793; *d.* Mannheim, Germany, 4 July 1846), *astronomy.*

After Nicolai had begun to study theology in Göttingen, he started to attend Gauss's mathematics lectures. In 1813 he became an assistant at the observatory at Seeberg near Gotha, which was then under the direction of Lindenau. When Schumacher left the observatory at Mannheim, Nicolai succeeded him as director, a position he held until his death.

Nicolai spent most of his career observing comets and planets. He made preliminary calculations of lunar occultations which were important in astronomical geography. In particular he pointed out the distorting influence of the profile of the moon.

Of greater influence were Nicolai's works on the determination of differences of longitude from lunar observations. He modified a method devised in the first third of the eighteenth century, in which the right ascension of the moon could be determined by culmination observations. From this information, and with the aid of the ephemerides, the true time at the place of observation could be derived. Nicolai proposed that instead of measuring the culmination of the moon, what should be measured is the time between the transit of the rim of the moon through the local meridian and that of several nearby fixed stars of similar declination. The defective reduction to the center of the moon thereby became unnecessary, while at the same time the lesser error introduced by setting up the meridian telescope was not of great importance.

In pure mathematics, Nicolai worked on series expansions and integral functions. He improved the uncertain values of the mass of Jupiter by employing Gauss's perturbation equations of the planetoid Juno.

BIBLIOGRAPHY

I. ORIGINAL LITERATURE. See "Berechnung der Meridiandifferenz zweier Orte, aus correspondirenden Mondsculminationen," in *Astronomische Nachrichten*, **2** (1824), cols. 17–24. About eighty additional works that Nicolai published in *Astronomischen Nachrichten* are listed in H. Kobold, ed., *Generalregister der Bände 1–40 der Astronomischen Nachrichten Nr. 1–960 (1821–1855)* (Kiel, 1936), cols. 78–79.

II. SECONDARY LITERATURE. See the article by S. Gunther, in *Allgemeine Deutsche Biographie*, XXIII (Leipzig, 1886), 590–591. On the Mannheim Observatory and Nicolai's activity there see G. Klare, "Ein Jahrhundert wechselvoller Geschichte der Mannheimer Sternwarte 1783–1883," in *Sterne und Weltraum*, **9** (1970), 148–150. On his correspondence with Gauss, see W. Valentiner, ed., *Briefe von C. F. Gauss an B. Nicolai* (Karlsruhe, 1877).

DIETER B. HERRMANN

NICOLAUS OF DAMASCUS (*b*. Damascus, 64 B.C.), *botany*.

Nicolaus was the son of wealthy parents, whose names, Antipater and Stratonice, suggest that they were of Macedonian origin. He received an expensive liberal education, probably from Greek tutors, and became so distinguished a scholar that he attracted the attention of Herod the Great, king of Judaea. He subsequently spent his life in the service of Herod, accompanying him twice to Rome during the last ten years of his rule (14–4 B.C.). Nicolaus served the king as secretary, adviser, and court historian and, in Rome, endeavored to explain Herod's anti-Nabataean politics to the Roman Senate. After Herod's death he sought to retire but was obliged to represent Herod's son, Archelaus, and to travel again to Rome to undertake the latter's defense against complaints

by the Jews. In spite of Nicolaus' efforts, Archelaus was banished by Augustus to Vienne and died there. It is not known what happened subsequently to Nicolaus.

Besides dramatic compositions, an autobiography, a panegyrical biography of Augustus' youth, a *Universal History* in 144 books from the earliest times to the death of Herod, and a collection of writings on the manners and customs of some fifty nations (Παραδόξων ἐθῶν συναγωγή), Nicolaus wrote commentaries on Aristotle, now largely lost, and also an extant treatise on plants in two books; the latter were written in Peripatetic style and dealt with the generalities of plant life. Indeed, so Peripatetic in style and structure are these books that they were believed to have been the work of Aristotle himself.

The first book is divided into seven chapters, in which are discussed the nature of plant life; sex in plants; the parts, structure, classification, composition, and products of plants; their methods of propagation and fertilization; and their changes and variations. Book II contains ten chapters, which describe the origins of plant life; the material of plants; the effects of external conditions and climate; water and rock plants; effects of topography upon plants; parasitism; the production of fruits and leaves; the colors and shapes of plants; and fruits and their flavors.

The original Greek text of the *De plantis* has been lost. It was, however, translated into Syriac in the ninth century; and a few scattered fragments have survived in Cambridge MS. Gg. 2.14 (fifteenth–sixteenth century), together with the translation of Nicolaus' Περὶ τῆς τοῦ Ἀριστοτέλους φιλοσοφίας. It has been suggested by Hemmerdinger, but denied by Drossaart Lulofs, that this Syriac translation was made by Ḥunayn ibn Isḥāq, court physician at Baghdad. The fragments of the Syriac translation of the *De plantis* consist of a series of dislocated sentences from the first book. Bar-Hebraeus possessed a copy of it and preserved a brief but valuable excerpt of book I in Syriac in his *Candelabrum Sanctorum*. The Syriac version was subsequently translated into Arabic by Isḥāq ibn Ḥunayn about 900. This Arabic translation is badly preserved and four pages toward the end are missing. In 1893 Steinschneider discovered a Hebrew translation made verbatim from the Arabic by the Provençal Kalonymus ben Kalonymus in 1314. The Arabic text was also translated into Latin by Alfred of Sareshel (first half of the thirteenth century), and during the Middle Ages it exercised a wide influence, as is attested by numerous manuscripts and several commentaries. The Latin translation, however, was superseded by the clumsy thirteenth-century translation of the Latin into Greek by Maximus

Planudes, which has been printed in Bekker's edition of Aristotle (815A–830B).

The *De plantis*, apart from the herbals deriving from Dioscorides and pseudo-Apuleius, became the most important single source for later medieval botany. As has been seen above, its two volumes were long credited to Aristotle himself and were included in his *Opera*. Scaliger actually devoted a commentary to these books, entitled "In libros duos qui inscribuntur *De plantis*, Aristotele autore" (Paris, 1556). He subsequently corrected his mistake in the heading of his Preface to "In libros De plantis falso Aristoteli attributos," but it may be assumed that the majority of Renaissance botanists were ready to accept uncritically Aristotle's authority upon the basis of these two incorrectly attributed volumes.

It was not only in botany that Nicolaus' work was influential. So great was his prestige as an Aristotelian commentator that Porphyry and even Simplicius used to appeal to his authority. The following titles of treatises written by him on Aristotelian philosophy have survived: $\Pi\epsilon\rho\grave{\iota}\ \tau\hat{\eta}\varsigma\ \tauο\hat{\upsilon}\ \text{'}Aριστοτέλους\ φιλοσοφίας$, $\Pi\epsilon\rho\grave{\iota}\ \theta\epsilon\hat{\omega}\nu$, $\Pi\epsilon\rho\grave{\iota}\ \tau\hat{\omega}\nu\ \grave{\epsilon}\nu\ \tauο\hat{\iota}\varsigma\ \pi\rho\alpha\kappa\tau\iota\kappao\hat{\iota}\varsigma\ \kappa\alpha\lambda\hat{\omega}\nu$ and, possibly, $\Pi\epsilon\rho\grave{\iota}\ \tauο\hat{\upsilon}\ \pi\alpha\nu\tauός$. The first of these works, and the sole survivor, is preserved only in the Syriac abridgment described above (Cantab. MS Gg. 2.14). Although Nicolaus was eclipsed by other commentators in Greek, notably Alexander and Simplicius, it is clear from the Islamic bibliographers that his commentaries were read and studied in the East.

BIBLIOGRAPHY

For the Latin medieval translation see E. H. F. Meyer, *Nicolai Damasceni "De plantis" libri duo Aristoteli vulgo adscripti* (Leipzig, 1841). For the Greek text (which is a retranslation from the Latin) see I. Bekker, *Aristote is Opera*, II (Berlin, 1831), 815A–830B. There is an English translation by E. S. Foster in *The Works of Aristotle Translated into English*, VI (Oxford, 1913), 815A–830B, and by W. S. Hett in his Loeb volume, *Aristotle, Minor Works* (London–Cambridge, Mass., 1936).

Secondary literature includes A. J. Arberry, "An Early Arabic Translation from the Greek," in *Bulletin of the Faculty of Arts* (Cairo University), **1** (1933), 48 ff., and **2** (1934), 72 ff.; R. P. Bouyges, "Sur le *De plantis* d'Aristote-Nicolas à propos d'un manuscrit arabe de Constantinople," in *Mélanges de la Faculté orientale, Université St.-Joseph* (Beirut), **9**, no. 2 (1932), 71–89; H. J. Drossaart Lulofs, "Aristotle's $\Pi EPI\ \Phi YT\Omega N$," in *Journal of Hellenic Studies*, **77**, 1 (1957), 75–80; and *Nicolaus Damascenus on the Philosophy of Aristotle*, Philosophia Antiqua, XIII (Leiden, 1965); B. Hemmerdinger, "Le *De Plantis*, de Nicolas de Damas à Planude," in *Philologus*, **111** (1967), 56–65; E. H. F. Meyer, *Geschichte der Botanik* (Königsberg, 1854); and G. Sarton, *The Appreciation of Ancient and*

Medieval Science During the Renaissance (Philadelphia, 1955), 63 ff.

James Longrigg

NICOLLE, CHARLES JULES HENRI (*b.* Rouen, France, 21 September 1866; *d.* Tunis, 28 February 1936), *bacteriology*.

For a detailed study of his life and work, see Supplement.

NICOMACHUS OF GERASA (*fl. ca.* A.D. 100), *mathematics, harmonics*.

That Nicomachus was from Gerasa, probably the city in Palestine, is known from Lucian (*Philopatris*, 12), from scholia to his commentator Philoponus, and from some manuscripts that contain Nicomachus' works. The period of his activity is determined by inference. In his *Manual of Harmonics* Nicomachus mentions Thrasyllus, who died in A.D. 36; Apuleius, born about A.D. 125, is said to have translated the *Introduction to Arithmetic* into Latin; and a character in Lucian's *Philopatris* says, "You calculate like Nicomachus," which shows that Lucian, born about A.D. 120, considered Nicomachus a famous man.[1] Porphyry mentions him, together with Moderatus and others, as a prominent member of the Pythagorean school, and this connection may also be seen in his writings.[2] Only two of his works are extant, *Manual of Harmonics* and *Introduction to Arithmetic*. He also wrote a *Theologumena arithmeticae*, dealing with the mystic properties of numbers, and a larger work on music, some extracts of which have survived.[3] Other works are ascribed to him, but it is not certain that he wrote any of them.[4]

In the *Manual of Harmonics*, after an introductory chapter, Nicomachus deals with the musical note in chapters 2–4 and devotes the next five chapters to the octave. Chapter 10 deals with tuning principles based on the stretched string; chapter 11, with the extension of the octave to the two-octave range of the Greater Perfect System in the diatonic genus; and the work ends with a chapter in which, after restating the definitions of note, interval, and system, Nicomachus gives a survey of the Immutable System in the three genera: diatonic, chromatic, and enharmonic. He deals with notes, intervals, systems, and genera, the first four of the seven subdivisions of harmonics recognized by the ancients, but not with keys, modulation, or melodic composition. The treatise exhibits characteristics of both the Aristoxenian and the Pythagorean schools of music. To the influence of the latter must be ascribed Nicomachus' assignment of number and numerical ratios to notes and intervals, his recognition of the indivisibility of the octave and the whole tone, and his notion that the musical consonances are in either multiple or superparticular ratios. But unlike Euclid, who attempts to prove musical propositions through mathematical theorems, Nicomachus seeks to show their validity by measurement of the lengths of strings. Hence his treatment of consonances and of musical genera, as well as his definition of the note, are Aristoxenian.

The *Introduction to Arithmetic* is in two books. After six preliminary chapters devoted to the philosophical importance of mathematics, Nicomachus deals with number per se, relative number, plane and solid numbers, and proportions. He enunciates several definitions of number and then discusses its division into even and odd. He states the theorem that any integer is equal to half the sum of the two integers on each side of it and proceeds to give the classification of even numbers (even times even, odd times even, and even times odd), followed by that of odd numbers (prime, composite, and relative prime).[5] The fundamental relations of number are equality and inequality, and the latter is divided into the greater and the less. The ratios of the greater are multiples, superparticulars, superpartients, multiple superparticulars, and multiple superpartients; those of the less are the reciprocal ratios of these. Book I concludes with a general principle whereby all forms of inequality of ratio may be generated from a series of three equal terms.[6] At the beginning of the second book the reverse principle is given. It is followed by detailed treatments of squares, cubes, and polygonal numbers. Nicomachus divides proportions into disjunct and continuous, and describes ten types. He presents no abstract proofs (as are found in Euclid's *Elements*, VII–IX), and he limits himself for the most part to the enunciation of principles followed by examples with specific numbers.[7] On one occasion this method leads to a serious mistake,[8] but there are many other mistakes which are independent of the method of exposition—for example, his inclusion of composite numbers, a class which belongs to all numbers, as a species of the odd. Yet despite its notorious shortcomings, the treatise was influential until the sixteenth century and gave its author the undeserved reputation of being a great mathematician.

NOTES

1. For references to modern discussions, see Tarán, *Asclepius on Nicomachus*, p. 5, n. 3. J. M. Dillon, "A Date for the Death of Nicomachus of Gerasa?" in *Classical Review*, n.s. **19** (1969), 274–275, conjectures that Nicomachus died in A.D. 196, because Proclus, who was born in A.D. 412, is said by Marinus, *Vita Procli*, 28, to have believed that he was a reincarnation of Nicomachus, and because some

Pythagoreans believed that reincarnations occur at intervals of 216 years. But Dillon fails to cite any passage in which Proclus would attach particular importance to the number 216 and, significantly enough, this number is not mentioned in Proclus' commentary on the creation of the soul in Plato's *Timaeus*, a passage where one would have expected this number to occur had Dillon's conjecture been a probable one.

2. In Eusebius of Caesarea, *Historia ecclesiastica*, VI, xix, 8.

3. Some of the contents of the *Theologumena* can be recovered from the summary of it given by Photius, *Bibliotheca*, codex 187, and from the quotations from it in the extant *Theologumena arithmeticae* ascribed to Iamblichus.

  In his *Manual of Harmonics*, I, 2, Nicomachus promises to write a longer and complete work on the subject; and the extracts in some MSS, published by Jan in *Musici scriptores Graeci*, pp. 266–282, probably are from this work. They can hardly belong to a second book of the *Manual*, because Nicomachus' words at the end of this work indicate that it concluded with chapter 12. Eutocius seems to refer to the first book of the larger work on music; see *Eutocii Commentarii in libros De sphaera et cylindro*, in *Archimedis Opera omnia*, J. L. Heiberg, ed., III (Leipzig, 1915), 120, ll. 20–21.

4. In his *Introduction to Arithmetic*, II, 6, 1, Nicomachus refers to an *Introduction to Geometry*. Some scholars attribute to him a *Life of Pythagoras* on the grounds that Nicomachus is quoted by both Porphyry and Iamblichus in their biographies of Pythagoras. It is also conjectured that he wrote a work on astronomy because Simplicius, *In Aristotelis De caelo*, Heiberg ed., p. 507, ll. 12–14, says that Nicomachus, followed by Iamblichus, attributed the hypothesis of eccentric circles to the Pythagoreans. A work by Nicomachus with the title *On Egyptian Festivals* is cited by Athenaeus and by Lydus, but the identity of this Nicomachus with Nicomachus of Gerasa is not established. Finally, the "Nicomachus the Elder" said by Apollinaris Sidonius to have written a life of Apollonius of Tyana in which he drew from that of Philostratus cannot be the author of the *Manual*, since Philostratus was born *ca.* A.D. 170.

5. Nicomachus considers prime numbers a class of the odd, because for him 1 and 2 are not really numbers. For a criticism of this and of Nicomachus' classifications of even and odd numbers, see Heath, *A History of Greek Mathematics*, I, 70–74. In I, 13, Nicomachus describes Eratosthenes' "sieve," a device for finding prime numbers.

6. This principle is designed to show that equality is the root and mother of all forms of inequality.

7. Euclid represents numbers by lines with letters attached, a system that makes it possible for him to deal with numbers in general, whereas Nicomachus represents numbers by letters having specific values.

8. See *Introduction to Arithmetic*, II, 28, 3, where he infers a characteristic of the subcontrary proportion from what is true only of the particular example (3, 5, 6) that he chose to illustrate this proportion. See Tarán, *Asclepius on Nicomachus*, p. 81 with references.

BIBLIOGRAPHY

I. ORIGINAL WORKS. The best, but not critical, ed. of the *Introduction to Arithmetic* is *Nicomachi Geraseni Pythagorei Introductionis arithmeticae libri II*, R. Hoche, ed. (Leipzig, 1866), also in English with notes and excellent introductory essays as *Nicomachus of Gerasa, Introduction to Arithmetic*, trans. by M. L. D'Ooge, with studies in Greek arithmetic by F. E. Robbins and L. C. Karpinski (New York, 1926); Boethius' Latin trans. and adaptation is *Anicii Manlii Torquati Severini Boetii De institutione arithmeticae libri duo*, G. Friedlein, ed. (Leipzig, 1867).

The *Manual of Harmonics* is in Carolus Jan, *Musici scriptores Graeci* (Leipzig, 1895), 235–265; an English trans. and commentary is F. R. Levin, "Nicomachus of Gerasa, Manual of Harmonics: Translation and Commentary" (diss., Columbia University, 1967).

II. Secondary Literature. Ancient commentaries are an anonymous "Prolegomena" in P. Tannery, ed., *Diophanti Opera omnia*, II (Leipzig, 1895), 73–76; Iamblichus' commentary, *Iamblichi in Nicomachi Arithmeticam introductionem liber*, H. Pistelli, ed. (Leipzig, 1894); Philoponus' commentary, R. Hoche, ed., 3 fascs. (Wesel, 1864, 1865; Berlin, 1867); another recension of this commentary in Hoche (Wesel, 1865), pp. ii–xiv, for the variants corresponding to the first book, and in A. Delatte, *Anecdota Atheniensia et alia*, II (Paris, 1939), 129–187, for those corresponding to the second book; Asclepius' commentary, "Asclepius of Tralles, Commentary to Nicomachus' Introduction to Arithmetic," edited with an intro. and notes by L. Tarán, *Transactions of the American Philosophical Society*, n.s., **59**, pt. 4 (1969); there is an anonymous commentary, still unpublished, probably by a Byzantine scholar—see Tarán, *op. cit.*, pp. 6, 7–8, 18–20.

For an exposition of the mathematical contents of Nicomachus' treatise and a criticism of it, see T. Heath, *A History of Greek Mathematics*, I (Oxford, 1921), 97–112.

Leonardo Tarán

NICOMEDES (*fl. ca.* 250 B.C. [?]), *mathematics.*

Nothing is known of the life of Nicomedes. His period of activity can be only approximately inferred

from the facts that he criticized the solution of Eratosthenes (*fl.* 250 B.C.) to the problem of doubling the cube and that Apollonius (*fl.* 200 B.C.) named a curve "sister of the cochlioid," presumably as a compliment to Nicomedes, who had discovered the curve known as cochlioid, cochloid, or conchoid.[1] The second inference is far from secure, but what we know of Nicomedes' mathematical investigations fits well into the period of Archimedes (*d.* 212 B.C.).

The work for which Nicomedes became famous was called *On Conchoid Lines* (Περὶ κογχοειδῶν γραμμῶν).[2] We know it only through secondhand references. In it Nicomedes described the generation of a curve, which he called the "first conchoid," as follows (see Figure 1): Given a fixed straight line *AB* (the "canon") and a fixed point *E* (the "pole"), draw *EDG* perpendicular to *AB*, cutting it at *D*, and make *DG* a fixed length (the "interval"); then let *GDE* move about *E* in such a way that *D* is always on *AB* (thus when *D* reaches *H*, *G* will have reached *T*). *G* will then describe a curve, *LGTM*, the first conchoid. The advantages of this curve are that it is very easy to construct (Nicomedes described a mechanical instrument for drawing it)[3] and that it can be used to solve a variety of problems, including the "classical" problems of doubling the cube and trisecting the angle. These are all soluble by means of the auxiliary construction which we may call the "lemma of Nicomedes": Given two straight lines, *X*, *Y*, meeting in a given angle and a point *P* outside the angle, it is possible to draw a line through *P* cutting *X* and *Y* so

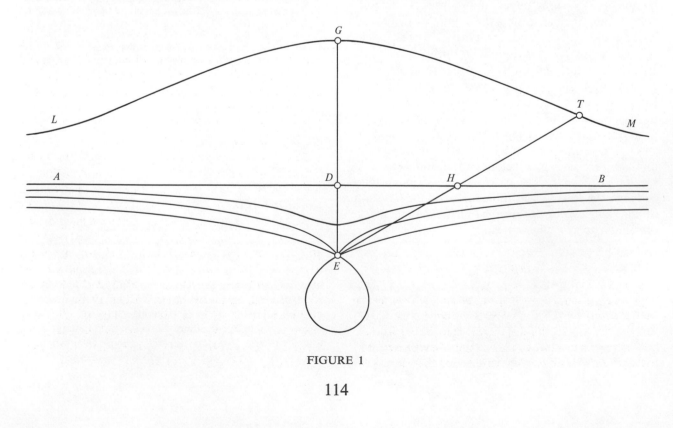

FIGURE 1

that a given length, *l*, is intercepted between *X* and *Y*. This is done by constructing a conchoid with "canon" *X*, "pole" *P*, and "interval" *l*; the intersection of this conchoid and *Y* gives the solution.

Nicomedes solved the problem of finding two mean proportionals (to which earlier Greek mathematicians had reduced the problem of doubling the cube) as shown in Figure 2.

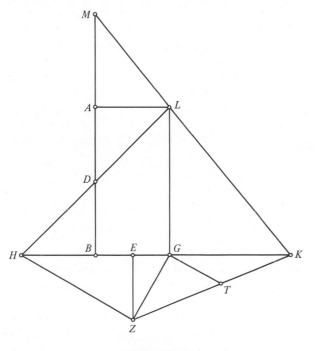

FIGURE 2

Given two straight lines *AB*, *BG*, between which it is required to find two mean proportionals. Complete the rectangle *ABGL*. Bisect *AB*, *BG* in *D* and *E*, respectively. Join *LD* and produce it to meet *GB* produced in *H*. Draw *EZ* perpendicular to *EG*, of length such that *GZ = AD*. Join *HZ*, and draw *GT* parallel to it. Then draw *ZTK*, meeting *BG* produced in *K*, so that *TK = AD* (this is possible by the "lemma of Nicomedes"). Join *KL* and produce it to meet *BA* produced in *M*. Then

$$\frac{AB}{GK} = \frac{GK}{MA} = \frac{MA}{BG},$$

and *GK*, *MA* are the required mean proportionals.[4]

Nicomedes also showed how to trisect the angle by means of his lemma and proved that the "first conchoid" is asymptotic to its "canon."[5] In addition he described what he called the "second, third, and fourth conchoids" and their uses. The ancient sources tell us nothing about them beyond their names, but it has been plausibly conjectured that they are to be

identified with the other branch of the curve in its three possible forms. In modern terms the curve is a quartic whose equation is, in polar coordinates,

$$\rho = \frac{a}{\cos \theta} \pm l,$$

or, in Cartesian coordinates,

$$(x - a)^2 (x^2 + y^2) - l^2 x^2 = 0.$$

This curve has two branches, both asymptotic to the line *x = a*. The lower branch (see Figure 1, in the lower part of which the three forms are depicted) has a double point at the pole *E*, which is either a node, a cusp, or an isolated point according as $l \gtreqless a$ (here *l* corresponds to the interval, *a* to the distance from the pole to the canon). This second branch can be constructed in the same way that Nicomedes constructed the first, with the sole difference that the interval is taken on the same side of the canon *AB* as the pole *E*.[6]

As far as is known, all applications of the conchoid made in antiquity were developed by Nicomedes himself. It was not until the late sixteenth century, when the works of Pappus and Eutocius describing the curve became generally known, that interest in it revived and new applications and properties were discovered. Viète used the "lemma of Nicomedes" as a postulate in his *Supplementum geometriae* (1593) to solve a number of problems leading to equations of the third and fourth degrees, including the construction of the regular heptagon. Johann Molther, in his little-known but remarkable *Problema deliacum* (1619), used the same lemma for an elegant reworking of the old problem of finding two mean proportionals. The conchoid attracted the attention of some of the best mathematicians of the seventeenth century. Descartes discussed the construction of tangents to it (in his *Géométrie* of 1637); Fermat and Roberval treated the same problem with respect to both branches. Huygens discovered a neat construction of the point of inflection (1653). Newton discussed the curve more than once, and in his *Arithmetica universalis* he recommended its use as an auxiliary in geometry because of the ease of its construction (it is in fact sufficient to solve any problem involving equations of the third and fourth degrees). In the appendix to the *Arithmetica*, on the linear construction of equations, he makes extensive use of the "lemma of Nicomedes." The seventeenth century also saw the first generalization of the conchoid, produced by taking a circle instead of a straight line for canon: this generates Pascal's limaçon.

NOTES

1. Eutocius, *Commentary on Archimedes' Sphere and Cylinder*, in *Archimedis Opera omnia*, J. L. Heiberg, ed., III, 98; Simplicius, *Commentary on Aristotle's Categories*, Kalbfleisch, ed., p. 192.
2. Eutocius, *loc. cit.* It is uncertain whether Nicomedes called the curve κοχλοειδής, κοχλιοειδής, or κογχοειδής (all three are found in our sources). The first two mean "snail-shaped"; the third, "mussel-shaped."
3. *Ibid.*
4. For a proof see Pappus, *Synagoge*, bk. 4, sec. 43, Hultsch, ed., I, 248–250, repro. in Heath, *History of Greek Mathematics*, I, 260–262. In fact all of the construction after the determination of point K is superfluous, for $ZT = MA$ and therefore GK, ZT are the required mean proportionals. As D. T. Whiteside pointed out to me, this was realized by Molther (*Problema deliacum*, pp. 55–58), and by Newton (*Mathematical Papers*, II, prob. 15, pp. 460–461).
5. On trisection of the angle see Pappus, *Synagoge*, bk. 4, sec. 62, Hultsch, ed., I, 274–276; see also Proclus, *Commentary on Euclid I*, Friedlein, ed., p. 272. On the "first conchoid" being asymptotic to its "canon," see Eutocius, *op. cit.*, in *Archimedis Opera omnia*, J. L. Heiberg, ed., III, 100–102.
6. I do not know who first proposed this identification of Nicomedes' "second, third, and fourth conchoids," but a probable guess is either Fermat or Roberval. In a letter to Roberval of 1636, Fermat (*Oeuvres*, II, 94) mentions the "second conchoid of Nicomedes." Roberval refers to the two branches as "conchoide de dessus" and "conchoide de dessous," respectively ("Composition des mouvemens," in *Ouvrages de mathématique* [1731], p. 28).

BIBLIOGRAPHY

The principal ancient passages concerning Nicomedes are Pappus, *Synagoge*, F. Hultsch, ed., I (Berlin, 1875), bk. 3, sec. 21, p. 56; bk. 4, secs. 39–45, pp. 242–252, and secs. 62–64, pp. 274–276; Eutocius, *Commentary on Archimedes' Sphere and Cylinder*, in *Archimedis Opera omnia*, J. L. Heiberg, ed., 2nd ed., III (Leipzig, 1915), 98–106; Proclus, *Commentary on Euclid I*, G. Friedlein, ed. (Leipzig, 1873), 272; and Simplicius, *Commentary on Aristotle's Categories*, K. Kalbfleisch, ed., which is Commentaria in Aristotelem Graeca, VIII (Berlin, 1907), 192. The best modern account of Nicomedes is Gino Loria, *Le scienze esatte nell'antica Grecia*, 2nd ed. (Milan, 1914), 404–410. See also T. L. Heath, *A History of Greek Mathematics* (Oxford, 1921), I, 238–240, 260–262, and II, 199. There is no adequate account of the treatment of the conchoid in the sixteenth and seventeenth centuries. The best available is Gino Loria, *Spezielle algebraische und transzendente ebene Kurven*, 2nd ed. (Leipzig–Berlin, 1910), I, 136–142, which also gives a good description of the mathematical properties of the curve; see also F. Gomes Teixeira, *Traité des courbes spéciales remarquables*, I, which is vol. IV of his *Obras sobre matematica* (Coimbra, 1908), 259–268.

On generalizations of the conchoid see Loria, *Spezielle . . . Kurven*, pp. 143–152. Viète's *Supplementum geometriae* is printed in his *Opera mathematica*, F. van Schooten, ed. (Leiden, 1646; repr. Hildesheim, 1970), 240–257. Johann Molther's extremely rare opuscule, *Problema deliacum de cubi duplicatione*, was printed at Frankfurt in 1619. For Descartes's treatment of the conchoid see *The Geometry of René Descartes*, trans. by D. E. Smith and M. L. Latham (Chicago–London, 1925), 113–114. The discussions of Fermat and Roberval are printed in Pierre de Fermat, *Oeuvres*, P. Tannery and C. H. Henry, eds., II (Paris, 1894), 72, 82, 86–87. See also Roberval, *Ouvrages de mathématique* (The Hague, 1731), 28–32 (on Pascal's limaçon, see p. 35). Huygens' solution is printed in *Oeuvres complètes de Christiaan Huygens*, XII (The Hague, 1910), 83–86. For Newton's treatment see *The Mathematical Papers of Isaac Newton*, D. T. Whiteside, ed., II (Cambridge, 1968), prob. 15, pp. 460–461, and especially the app. to his "Universal Arithmetick," printed in *The Mathematical Works of Isaac Newton*, D. T. Whiteside, ed., II (New York–London, 1967), 118–134.

G. J. TOOMER

NICOT, JEAN (*b.* Nîmes, France, *ca.* 1530; *d.* Paris, France, 10 May 1604), *philology, botany.*

Any dictionary of scientific biography would be incomplete without an entry for Jean Nicot. His name designates in French "the nicotian plant, admirably suited to curing all wounds, sores, cankers, scurfs, and other such misfortunes of the human body" (*Thresor*, p. 429); it is preserved in the Linnaean designation *Nicotiana tabacum*, which to a certain extent renders Nicot a botanist.

The son of a court clerk, he studied letters at Nîmes, his native city, then at Paris, where he became a friend of the poet Ronsard. He was admitted to the king's household and took charge of charters. As councillor to the king he was sent on a diplomatic mission to Portugal, from which in 1560 he sent to Queen Mother Marie de' Medici seeds and leaves of "petun" (the Indian name for tobacco), pointing out the therapeutic value of the plant. Its cultivation later spread from France.

After two years of diplomatic service, Nicot began to dedicate himself to historical and literary study in his vast library at Brie-Comte Robert, near Paris. In 1568 he published *Historiae francorum lib. IV* of Aimonius (960–1010); in 1573 he supervised the publication of a new edition of the *Dictionnaire francois latin* of Robert Estienne, then began his own magnum opus, *Thresor de la langue francoyse*, published posthumously in 1606. This new French-Latin dictionary was enriched with a commentary in French that facilitated the compilation of subsequent French dictionaries. Although not strictly a scientist, Nicot was concerned in this work with animals and plants—the above citation is the prime example. He also left an unpublished treatise on nautical subjects.

BIBLIOGRAPHY

Nicot's works are *Aimonii monachi . . . Historiae francorum libri IV* (Paris, 1568) and *Thresor de la langue francoyse tant ancienne que moderne* (Paris, 1606).

On Nicot and his work, see Maxime Lanusse, *De Joanne Nicotio philologo* (Paris, 1893).

L. PLANTEFOL

NIEBUHR, CARSTEN (*b.* Altendorf, Holstein, 17 March 1733; *d.* Meldorf, Holstein, 26 April 1815), *cartography, exploration.*

The son of a farmer, Niebuhr did not attend school until he was eighteen. After inheriting some money he began training to be a surveyor by studying mathematics and astronomy at the University of Göttingen, but he never obtained a degree. In 1758 he was hired as a cartographer for a Danish expedition to Arabia that lasted from 1761 to 1767. During the expedition he made very exact determinations of longitude and latitude of localities in the eastern Mediterranean, made maps of cities, and mapped the Middle East, especially Arabia and Yemen. These maps were the best available for a long time. All the other members of the expedition died, and after having returned most of the scientific collections by ship from Bombay to Denmark, Niebuhr returned overland through Persia, Palestine, and Constantinople. During this trip he continued his geographic observations and made exact copies of the cuneiform inscriptions at Persepolis. The interpretation of the cuneiform alphabet by R. C. Rask and others was based on these copies, which were the best and most complete available. After the expedition Niebuhr declined several offers of high positions and became registrar at Meldorf, near his birthplace. The real value of his contributions was discovered later, partly because of the advanced and not always accepted mathematical methods used in his calculations and partly because he shunned publicity. Niebuhr's success as an explorer was based on his ability to make exact observations under highly adverse conditions and his ability to win the acceptance and cooperation of the local population. He preferred to write and speak in low German, published his papers in German, and regarded himself as Danish. (Holstein was then under the Danish crown.)

BIBLIOGRAPHY

I. ORIGINAL WORKS. Niebuhr's writings are *Beschreibung von Arabien* (Copenhagen, 1772), the first, preliminary account of the results of the expedition; *Reisebeschreibung nach Arabien und andern umliegenden Ländern*, 2 vols. (Copenhagen, 1774–1778), vol. III, edited posthumously by J. N. Gloyer and J. Olshausen (Hamburg, 1837).

II. SECONDARY LITERATURE. There are few biographical papers on Niebuhr, the most important being a short biography by his son, B. G. Niebuhr, "Carsten Niebuhrs Leben," in *Kieler Blätter*, **3** (1816), 1–86. A semipopular narrative of the expedition and Niebuhr's life, which became a best seller in Denmark, is Thorkild Hansen, *Det lykkelige Arabien* (Copenhagen, 1962).

NILS SPJELDNAES

NIELSEN, NIELS (*b.* Ørslev, Denmark, 2 December 1865; *d.* Copenhagen, Denmark, 16 September 1931), *mathematics.*

Nielsen's father was a small farmer, and his family lived in modest circumstances. He originally wished to attend the polytechnical institute, but he was early attracted to pure science. In 1885 he began his studies at the University of Copenhagen, where he passed the government examination in 1891 and received his doctorate in 1895. He had been teaching in the secondary schools since 1887, and in 1900 he began to give preparatory courses for the polytechnic institute. From 1903 to 1906 he belonged to the University Inspectorate for secondary schools. In 1905 he became *Dozent* and in 1909 he succeeded Julius Petersen as full professor of mathematics at the University of Copenhagen.

He became a member of the Leopoldina of Halle in 1906 and an honorary member of the Wiskundig Genootschap of Amsterdam in 1907. Nielsen's principal achievements were his many textbooks, which dealt with various classes of special functions. Before he prepared these books he wrote numerous papers. His textbooks on cylindrical functions (1904) and on the gamma function (1906) were widely used.

Nielsen developed no new ideas and did not even present any fundamental theorems, but he possessed great knowledge and the ability to generalize existing formalisms. Moreover, he did make an important contribution to the theory of gamma function and factorial series. The theory originated with W. V. Jensen; Nielsen gave it further impetus, and Nörlund provided its definitive clarification. Nielsen's abilities were thus very restricted. He was a master in the treatment of unmethodical calculations and came up with a multitude of particular points. He playfully conceived new things that were not always in a completed form, and he was a significant influence on his students.

In 1917 Nielsen suffered a breakdown. He never fully recovered but his powers were not perceptibly diminished. He turned his attention to number theory (Bernoulli's numbers, Fermat's equation), which he treated unsystematically. In the history of mathematics he occupied himself primarily with accounts of personalities and the historical development of specific mathematical problems. Two books on Danish mathematicians and two on French mathematicians are the fruits of his work in this area.

BIBLIOGRAPHY

I. ORIGINAL WORKS. Nielsen's works include the following: *Handbuch der Theorie der Zylinderfunktionen* (Leipzig, 1904), which contains sixteen pp. of bibliography; *Theorie der Integrallogarithmus und verwandter Transzendenten* (Leipzig, 1906), which has ten pp. of bibliography, tables, and applications; *Handbuch der Theorie der Gammafunktion* (Leipzig, 1906), which represents twenty years of work and is the first comprehensive treatment of the gamma function since Legendre's *Traité;* and *Lehrbuch der unendlichen Reihen; Vorlesung gehalten an der Universität Kopenhagen* (Leipzig, 1908), an elementary treatment without the use of calculus.

See also *Laeren on Graensvaerdier som indledning til analysen* (Copenhagen, 1910); *Mathematiken i Danmark*, 1528–1800, I; 1801–1908, II (Copenhagen–Oslo, 1910), which contains data on his life and a compilation of his published works; *Elemente der Funktionentheorie Vorlesung gehalten an der Universität Kopenhagen* (Leipzig, 1911); *Géomètres français sous la révolution* (Copenhagen, 1929), treats of seventy-six mathematicians; and *Géomètres français du dix-huitième siècle*, Niels Nörlund, ed. (Copenhagen–Paris, 1929), which is a posthumous work and treats of 153 mathematicians.

II. SECONDARY LITERATURE. Nielsen also published about 100 articles in twenty-one different Danish and foreign periodicals. For further information see Harald Bohr, "Niels Nielsen 2 December 1865–16 September 1931," in *Matematisk Tidsskrift*, 41–45; and Poggendorff, IV, 1073; V, 905; VI, 1855.

H. OETTEL

NIEPCE, JOSEPH (later **NICÉPHORE**) (*b.* Chalon-sur-Saône, France, 1765; *d.* St. Loup de Varenne, France, 5 July 1833), *photography.*

In 1789 Niepce was a professor at an Oratorian *collège* in Angers; he then took up a military career, eventually becoming a staff officer with the French army in Italy. In 1794 he left the army to settle in Nice, where he married. He was appointed administrator of the district of Nice at the beginning of 1795, but resigned after a few months; his elder brother Claude, who had also retired from the army, came to join him, and together they pursued their common interest in research.

By 3 August 1807, the date upon which they patented their "pyréolophore," the brothers had left Nice for their paternal home at Chalon-sur-Saône and their country estate of St. Loup de Varenne. The "pyréolophore" was an internal combustion engine fueled by lycopodium powder. It was sufficiently powerful to move a boat, and trials of it were conducted on a pond at St. Loup de Varenne and on the Saône. The tests were reported favorably to the Académie des Sciences by Berthollet and Lazare Carnot, but the invention never became practical, although the Niepce brothers attempted to render it more economical by substituting first pulverized coal, then petroleum, for the expensive lycopodium powder. A further invention of the same year, a sort of hydraulic ram, devised in response to a government competition to replace the apparatus formerly used to supply Versailles with water from the Seine, won them only an encouraging letter from Carnot.

The brothers next turned to agricultural research. In 1813 the government offered a prize for a woad that could replace indigo, which was then totally unavailable because of the Continental Blockade. The Niepces investigated a variety of materials, but did not succeed in extracting a suitable dye. They also tried to derive sugar from beets and starch from pumpkins, and examined plants that might yield fibers for textiles. Their only rewards were flattering letters from the government.

By 1813 Nicéphore Niepce had taken up the then fashionable occupation of lithography. The development of his researches during the next few years is not known, but it would seem probable that having himself tried to sketch some simple subjects for lithographic reproduction, he next tried to copy engravings automatically by rendering them transparent for transfer to the stone. He thus may have reached the idea of reproducing nature itself. Claude Niepce assisted him in this work. At the same time, the brothers tried to recoup their finances, depleted since the failure of the "pyréolophore," by searching their neighborhood for a supply of stone suitable for being made into lithographic tablets. Although they were unsuccessful in this effort, Nicéphore Niepce was in 1817 recompensed for his attempt by the Société d'Encouragement pour l'Industrie Nationale.

In the meantime, Claude Niepce had, in March 1816, gone first to Paris and then to England to conduct further tests and solicit support for the "pyréolophore." The brothers remained in constant correspondence, and their letters document Nicéphore Niepce's subsequent invention of photography. The latter continued in his efforts to reproduce nature directly on a specially prepared surface; a letter to

Claude of 5 May 1816 refers to a photographic apparatus that produced a negative image. A letter of the following 28 May adds, "I am hurrying to get these four new prints to you . . ." It is thus clear that Nicéphore had succeeded in fixing the images.

Nicéphore Niepce then began work on the chambers, diaphragms, and shutters that constituted his camera. In his 1816 experiments he used paper impregnated with silver chloride fixed with nitric acid; in March 1817 he began to use the Judean bitumen process of reproduction, making use of a light-sensitive lithographer's asphalt. By 1821, he was using this method to produce images on both glass and metal, notably tin. In 1822 he recorded the first fixed positive image, which he called a "point de vue," to distinguish it from transparency-copied engravings. In January 1826 Nicéphore Niepce received from Daguerre, then unknown to him, a letter of inquiry about his work, which he answered courteously but uninformatively. A year later, Daguerre wrote a second letter, which prompted Nicéphore Niepce to make inquiries about him; in June 1827 he relented, and offered Daguerre a helio-graph. The two men met when Nicéphore Niepce, alarmed by news about his brother, passed through Paris on his way to London.

In London Nicéphore Niepce discovered that his brother had been out of his senses for several years, and that the inventions about which Claude had written him—and for which he had in fact ruined himself financially—were mere follies. Disappointed, he returned to France at the beginning of 1828. His brother died a few days after his departure. Although Nicéphore Niepce was old, tired, and in debt, he still hesitated to reveal his secrets to Daguerre; it was only in October 1829 that he offered to "cooperate" with the latter, and an agreement was signed on 14 December of the same year. Little is known of the development of this association, save that in 1831 Daguerre suggested to Niepce that he experiment with silver iodide. Niepce was struck by apoplexy on 3 July 1833, and died two days later.

BIBLIOGRAPHY

I. ORIGINAL WORKS. Niepce's only writings, apart from the patent for the pyréolophore (No. 405 at the Institut National de la Propriété Industrielle), are his letters, some of which are preserved together with some of his devices at the Conservatoire National des Arts et Métiers. Others are at the Musée de Chalons and at the Academy of Sciences of the U.S.S.R.

II. SECONDARY LITERATURE. See Raymond Lécuyer, *Histoire de la photographie* (Paris, 1945); Georges Potonniée, *Histoire de la découverte de la photographie* (Paris, 1925); and B. Newhall, *Image* (New York, 1967).

The Berthollet and Carnot "Rapports sur une nouvelle machine inventée par MM. Niepce et nommée par eux pyréolophore," are in *Mémoires de la classe de sciences mathématiques et physiques de l'Institut*, **8** (1807), 146–153.

ROBERT SOULARD

NIESTEN, JEAN LOUIS NICOLAS (*b.* Visé, Liège, Belgium, 4 July 1844; *d.* Laeken, Brussels, Belgium, 27 December 1920), *astronomy*.

Niesten initially made a career in the military, where he served as a captain in the artillery. He wrote two textbooks on military science: *Artillerie. Passage des rivières* (Brussels, 1876) and *Précis des connaissances exigées des officiers sortis des cadres et des sous-officiers de l'artillerie par les programmes de 1876*. In 1877 he resigned from the service, and Jean Charles Houzeau, director of the Brussels observatory, appointed him assistant astronomer. In 1878 he was promoted to full astronomer, and he became *chef de service* in 1884.

Niesten was particularly interested in planetary astronomy, and in 1882 he was appointed chief of the Belgian mission to Santiago, Chile, to observe the transit of Venus. Houzeau himself directed another mission to Texas. (This was the first time Belgium officially participated in an international astronomical expedition.) In contrast with the mission to Texas, Niesten had favorable weather and was able to make useful observations. His report on the expedition was published in 1884. In 1887 he traveled to Yurievets, Russia, to observe the total solar eclipse. Niesten was a systematic observer, and many of his articles were concerned with the physical aspects of the planets: the "canals" on Mars (he claimed also to have seen rivers) and the red spot on Jupiter. He also subscribed to the now discredited theory of the daily nutation of the earth. Most of his astronomical observations appeared in the various publications of the Brussels observatory between 1878 and 1900. Niesten was one of the founders of the journal *Ciel et terre*, which first appeared in 1880; he contributed more than seventy articles, all of a semipopular nature, between 1880 and 1899.

BIBLIOGRAPHY

A complete bibliography of Niesten's works has been compiled by A. Collard, in *Ciel et terre*, **38** (1922), 330–338, 400–406; **39** (1923), 21–23, 41–44, 62–68, 86–89.

Niesten's report on the 1882 expedition is "Passage de Venus du 6 décembre 1882," in *Annuaire de l'observatoire de Bruxelles*, **51** (1884).

LETTIE S. MULTHAUF

NIEUWENTIJT, BERNARD (*b*. Westgraftdijk, North Holland, 10 August 1654; *d*. Purmerend, North Holland, 30 May 1718), *mathematics, philosophy.*

Bernard was the son of Emmanuel Nieuwentijt, minister at Westgraftdijk, and Sara d'Imbleville. Although he was expected to enter the ministry, he chose instead to study natural sciences. On 28 February 1675 he was enrolled as a student in medicine at Leiden University; later in the year he was also enrolled at Utrecht University, where he studied law and defended his medical thesis in 1676 [1]. He then settled as a medical practitioner in Purmerend. On 12 November 1684 he married Eva Moens, the widow of Philips Munnik, a naval captain in the service of the Dutch States-General. He was elected a member of the city council and became a burgomaster of Purmerend. As a youth Nieuwentijt was influenced by Cartesianism and he acquired a thorough knowledge of mathematics and natural philosophy. In 1695–1700 he was engaged in a controversy with Leibniz and his school on the foundations of calculus. On 12 March 1699 he married his second wife, Elisabeth Lams, the daughter of Willem Lams, burgomaster of Wormer.

Nieuwentijt became famous in his home country and abroad because of the publication of two lengthy works. One [6] was originally published in Dutch in 1714; according to [12] it was reedited in 1717, 1720, 1725, 1741, and 1759; editions with other dates are incidentally found in various libraries (1715, 1718, 1730; see [13]). The work was translated into English by J. Chamberlayne in 1718 [6a]; a fourth edition (1730) is mentioned. It was also translated into French by P. Noguez [6b]; this translation was published in 1725 (Paris), 1727 (Amsterdam), and 1760 (Amsterdam–Leipzig). A German translation by W. C. Baumann appeared in 1732 and another by J. A. von Segner in 1747 [6c]. The second of his two works [8] was posthumously published in Dutch in 1720; it was published again in 1741 and 1754; and was translated into French (1725) and English (1760). Nieuwentijt's portrait, painted by D. Valkenburg, is in the University of Amsterdam; the portrait in his 1714 publication [6] was engraved by P. van Gunst.

The title of Nieuwentijt's *Analysis infinitorum* [3] reminds the historian of the title of Leibniz' article of 1686, "De geometria recondita et analysi indivisibilium atque infinitorum." Nieuwentijt's [3] was the first comprehensive book on "analysis infinitorum." By L. Euler's *Introductio in analysin infinitorum*, analysis became the name of a mathematical discipline. To this field Nieuwentijt contributed little more than the name. What is surprising, however, is the erudite scholarship of a small-town physician who, except for limited university study, does not seem to have cultivated many learned colleagues. Nieuwentijt's work reveals his full acquaintance with the mathematics of his period and a remarkable self-reliance.

Nieuwentijt rejected Leibniz' approach to analysis. He did not admit infinitesimals of higher order. Nieuwentijt's method consists, in modern terms, in adjoining to the real field an element e with $e^2 = 0$. Leibniz' answer [9] to Nieuwentijt's objections [2] (see also [4]) was not convincing. Nieuwentijt's objections, however, may have contributed to improving the insight into higher-order differentials. It is disappointing that he did not sufficiently appreciate Leibniz' integral calculus.

His 1714 publication [6], of about 1,000 pages, was intended to demonstrate the existence of God by teleological arguments. Never before had this been tried on such a scale, and none among Nieuwentijt's numerous imitators equaled his completeness. It is not clear, however, whether or to what degree he depended on William Derham, whose *Physico-Theology* [10] (see also [11]) appeared almost simultaneously. Nieuwentijt may have known of Derham's lectures of 1711–1712, which were the nucleus for the work.

It is an old idea that nature, by its purposiveness, betrays the existence of a creator; Nieuwentijt, however, was one of the first who, rather than relying on a few examples, reviewed the whole of natural sciences to show in detail how marvelously things fitted in the world. His work [6] looks like a manual of up-to-date science and as such it may have contributed to the propagation of knowledge. On the other hand, by the abundance of its argumentation, it is tiring reading and full of platitudes. Its fundamental shortcoming is its static world picture and its lack of any trace of the oncoming evolutionary ideas. Its background philosophy, however, is remarkably sound. Nieuwentijt opposed both chance and necessity as explanatory principles of nature. He preferred empiricist above rationalist arguments. Natural laws have, according to Nieuwentijt, factual rather than rational truth, and as such they must have been ordained by a lawgiver.

Nieuwentijt felt that rationalism led to Spinozism and other kinds of atheism. A more methodical struggle against rationalism was fought in his second major work [8]. This is, indeed, a methodology of science which surprises by a seemingly modern view.

In fact it is nothing but a philosophy of common sense, and this explains why it fell into oblivion amid more sophisticated philosophies. In this work [8] Nieuwentijt arrived at a clear distinction between what he called ideal and factual mathematics, and at the insight that both avail themselves of the same formal methods, that all ideal statements are conditional, and that the ultimate criterion for factual statements is corroboration by experience. Nieuwentijt distinguished himself from the British empiricists by his closeness to mathematics and exact sciences. Although his influence in philosophy was negligible, his position as a methodologist was unique up to modern times.

BIBLIOGRAPHY

1. *Disputatio medica inauguralis de obstructionibus,* 8 Feb. 1676, Ultraiecti.

2. *Considerationes circa analyseos ad quantitates infinitè parvas applicatae principia, et calculi differentialis usum in resolvendis problematibus geometricis* (Amsterdam, 1694).

3. *Analysis infinitorum, seu curvilineorum proprietates ex polygonorum natura deductae* (Amsterdam, 1695).

4. *Considerationes secundae circa calculi differentialis principia; et responsio ad virum nobilissimum C. G. Leibnitium* (Amsterdam, 1696).

5. "Nouvel usage des tables des sinus au moyen de s'en servir sans qu'il soit nécessaire de multiplier et de diviser," in *Journal litéraire,* **5** (1714), 166–174.

6. *Het regt gebruik der wereltbeschouwingen ter overtuiginge van ongodisten en ongelovigen, aangetoont door . . .* (Amsterdam, 1714).

6a. *The Religious Philosopher, or the Right Use of Contemplating the Works of the Creator*: (I) *In the Wonderful Structure of Animal Bodies,* (II) *In the Formation of the Elements,* (III) *In the Structure of the Heavens, Designed for the Conviction of Atheists,* trans. by J. Chamberlayne, 3 vols. (London, 1718).

6b. *L'existence de Dieu démontrée par les merveilles de la nature, en trois parties, où l'on traite de la structure des corps de l'homme, des élémens, des astres et de leurs divers effets,* trans. by P. Noguez (Paris, 1725).

6c. *Rechter Gebrauch der Weltbetrachtung zur Erkenntnis der Macht, Weisheit und Güte Gottes, auch Überzeugung der Atheisten und Ungläubigen,* trans. by J. A. v. Segner (Jena, 1747).

7. "Brief aen den Heer J. Bernard, zynde een antwoord op de Aenmerkingen van den Heer Bernard, omtrent de werelt-beschouwingen, in de Nouv. de la Repub. 1716, 252," in *Maandelijke Uittreksels, of Boekrael der Geleerde Werelt* (1716), 673–690.

8. *Gronden van zekerheid of de regte betoogwyze der wiskundigen so in het denkbeeldige als in het zakelijke: ter weerlegging van Spinosaas denkbeeldig samenstel; en ter aanleiding van eene sekere sakelyke wysbegeerte, aangetoont door . . .* (Amsterdam, 1720).

9. G. G. L. [Leibniz], "Responsio ad nonnullas difficultates, a Dn. Bernardo Nieuwentijt circa methodum differentialem seu infinitesimalem motas," in *Acta eruditorum* 1695, pp. 310–316.

10. William Derham, *Physico-Theology, or a Demonstration of the Being and Attributes of God From His Works of Creation* (London, 1713).

11. William Derham, *Astro-Theology, or a Demonstration of the Being and Attributes of God From a Survey of the Heavens* (London, 1715).

12. *Nieuw Nederlandsch Biographisch Woordenboek,* **6** (1924), 1062–1063.

13. A. J. J. Van der Velde, "Bijdrage tot de bio-bibliographie van Bernard Nieuwentyt (1654–1718)," in *Bijdragen en Mededelingen Koninklijke Vlaamsche Academie van Taal- en Letterkunde 1926,* 709–718.

14. E. W. Beth, "Nieuwentyt's Significance for the Philosophy of Science," in *Synthese,* **9** (1955), 447–453.

15. H. Freudenthal, "Nieuwentijt und der teleologische Gottesbeweis," in *Synthese,* **9** (1955), 454–464.

16. J. Vercruysse, "La fortune de Bernard Nieuwentyd en France au 18e siècle et les notes marginales de Voltaire," in *Studies on Voltaire and the 18th Century,* **30** (1964), 223–246.

17. J. Vercruysse, "Frans onthaal voor een Nederlandse apologeet: Bernard Nieuwentyd—1654–1718," in *Tijdschrift van de Vrije Universiteit te Brussel,* **11** (1968–1969), 97–120.

HANS FREUDENTHAL

NIEUWLAND, JULIUS ARTHUR (b. Hansbeke, Belgium, 14 February 1878; d. Washington, D.C., 11 June 1936), *organic chemistry.*

Nieuwland was the son of poor Flemings who in 1880 immigrated to South Bend, Indiana, where they joined a settlement of Flemish speakers from the Ghent region. Nieuwland was educated in a German school. He graduated from Notre Dame University in 1899, and studied for the priesthood at the Congregation of the Holy Cross in South Bend and then at Holy Cross College of the Catholic University of America in Washington, D.C. He was ordained in 1903. Meanwhile, he studied botany and chemistry at the Catholic University, gaining a Ph.D. in 1904 with a thesis—which contained the germ of much of his later work—on the reactions of acetylene. His discovery of the reaction between acetylene and arsenic trichloride (which he did not pursue because of the noxious nature of the product) led to the development of the poison gas and vesicant lewisite (named after W. Lee Lewis) in World War I.

For several years Nieuwland almost abandoned chemistry and taught botany at Notre Dame, an interest which he maintained throughout his life. Botanical excursions were one of his favorite relaxations, and he published many papers on the subject—although none of them seem to be of importance. In 1909 Nieuwland founded the journal *American Midland Naturalist*; he edited it until near the end of his life.

In 1918 Nieuwland became professor of organic chemistry at Notre Dame and, with a series of junior collaborators, resumed his work on acetylene. He was able to polymerize acetylene under controlled conditions, using a cuprous chloride–ammonium chloride catalyst, to give a mixture of which the main constituent was divinyl-acetylene (hex-1,5-diene 3-yne). In 1925 a chance encounter at a scientific meeting led to the collaboration of Nieuwland with the firm of Du Pont, which was interested in this reaction. The Du Pont chemists modified the polymerization to produce good yields of vinyl-acetylene (but-1-ene 3-yne), which on treatment with hydrogen chloride formed 2-chlorobutadiene ("Chloroprene"). This in turn could be polymerized to the first really successful synthetic rubber, which Du Pont marketed in the early 1930's as "Duprene" or neoprene.

Nieuwland died suddenly of a heart attack while visiting his old university in Washington.

BIBLIOGRAPHY

I. ORIGINAL WORKS. A complete list of Nieuwland's papers is given in *American Midland Naturalist*, **17**, no. 4 (1936), vii–xv. There are ninety-seven biological articles, eighty-eight articles on chemistry, including, in addition to his acetylene studies, much pioneer work on the catalytic properties of boron trifluoride. His most important paper, "A New Synthetic Rubber: Chloroprene and Its Polymers," in *Journal of the American Chemical Society*, **53** (1931), 4198, was followed by a companion paper from the Du Pont team, *ibid.*, 4203. See also *The Chemistry of Acetylene* (New York, 1945), written with R. R. Vogt, which has a portrait as frontispiece.

II. SECONDARY LITERATURE. Nieuwland is noticed in *Dictionary of American Biography*, supp. 2 (1958), 488–489, and in *National Cyclopedia of American Biography* XXVI. The best account of his life and work is in a memorial ed. of the Notre Dame house journal, *Catalyzer* (February 1937), 39–44.

W. V. FARRAR

NIFO, AGOSTINO (*b*. Sessa Aurunca, Italy, *ca*. 1469–1470; *d*. Sessa Aurunca, 18 January 1538), *medicine, natural philosophy, psychology.*

The son of Giacomo Nifo and Francesco Gallione, Nifo received his early education at Naples before attending the University of Padua. After receiving his degree around 1490, he taught at Padua from about 1492 until 1499, when he returned to his native city. He was involved in controversies at Padua with his teacher, Nicoletto Vernia, as well as with his life-long rival, Pietro Pomponazzi, and the Franciscan theologian Antonio Trombetta. In the south he became a member of the circle of the famed humanist Giovanni Pontano, and he himself wrote and published humanistic treatises. He had learned Greek by 1503. Nifo appears to have been professor of philosophy at Naples and at Salerno during the first decade of the sixteenth century and also to have practiced medicine. He served as physician to Gonsalvo Hernández de Córdoba in 1504–1505.

Subsequently, Leo X invited him to teach at the University of Rome, where he was ordinary professor of philosophy in 1514. In 1520 Leo made Nifo a count palatine, granted him the right to use the Medici name, and authorized him to grant degrees in his own name. Nifo had openly attacked Pomponazzi in his *De immortalitate animae* (1518), which was dedicated to Leo. He served as ordinary professor of philosophy at the University of Pisa from 1519 until 1522. He then departed for Salerno, where he appears to have taught from 1522 until 1535, except for the academic year 1531–1532, when he taught philosophy and medicine at Naples. Although the Florentines attempted to lure him back to Pisa in 1525 and Paul III asked him to return to Rome to teach natural philosophy in 1535, Nifo declined both invitations. He was elected mayor of Sessa and extended the formal welcome to Emperor Charles V during his visit there on 24 March 1536.

Nifo wrote commentaries on almost all the works of Aristotle, usually providing his own translation. In some cases he wrote a second, revised commentary. While he held to the doctrine of Averroës (Ibn Rushd) of the unity of the intellect in two early works, the commentary on Averroës' *Destructio destructionum* and the early commentary on the *De anima*, he rejected this as the true interpretation of Aristotle in his *De intellectu*, published in 1503. In later works he emphasized that the true interpretation of Aristotle is reached through reading the Greek text. Nifo also came to prefer the Greek commentators over Averroës. This shift is especially noticeable in his psychological and logical writings. He did not, however, give up his interest in establishing the true interpretation of Averroës himself.

In his early commentary on the *Physics*, book I, t.c. 4 (Venice, 1508; fols. 7v–8), Nifo held that through a *negotiatio* the intellect could grasp the cause of an effect and thus formulate a *propter quid* demonstration in natural philosophy, whereas in his posthumously published *Recognitiones* on the *Physics*, after having studied Aristotle and the Greek commentators more carefully, he rejected the notion of a *negotiatio* (see Venice ed., 1569, pp. 13–14) and proposed instead that the cause of an effect is learned through a merely hypothetical syllogism *(syllogismus coniecturalis)*. To the possible objection that natural science would then cease to be science, he replied that while it is not science *simpliciter*, like mathematics, it is still a science *propter quid*, but one that remains conjectural, insofar as in it the knowledge of the cause can never be as certain as the knowledge of the effect, since the latter is based on sense experience. Although Nifo allowed in his commentary on the *Posterior Analytics* (1526), book I, t.c. 21, that there could be *demonstratio simpliciter* in natural science, he gave no examples of such a demonstration. The other form of demonstration, that "from hypothesis," was now called *demonstratio coniecturalis* and appeared to dominate in science.

Nifo also attempted in his early commentary on the *Physics*, book VIII, t.c. 81 (fols. 236–236v), to reconcile Aristotle with the impetus theory by making the impetus the principal mover, and the medium and its properties only auxiliary causes or passive dispositions. Later, in his commentary on the *De caelo*, book III, t.c. 28 (Naples, 1517; fols. 22v–23), he added the interesting refinement that a *vis impressa* is communicated not only to the projectile but also to the air or medium. Nifo developed Averroës' doctrine of natural minima by further refining the notion of qualitative minima, which explain qualitative changes, and by using the theory of minima to explain physical structure and chemical reactions. His medical interests are clearly evident in his *De ratione medendi* and his unpublished commentary on Hippocrates' *Aphorisms*. They are also occasionally reflected in remarks found in his *De pulchro et amore*, in which he proposed a sexual theory of love, and in his commentaries on the *Parva naturalia* and the *De animalibus*.

BIBLIOGRAPHY

I. ORIGINAL WORKS. There is no collected ed. of Nifo's works. His commentaries on Aristotle, some of which contain a commentary on Ibn Rushd, include *Super tres libros De anima* (Venice, 1503), repr. with rev. commentary (Venice, 1522, 1523, 1544, 1549, 1552, 1553, 1554, 1559); *Aristotelis De generatione et corruptione liber Augustino Nipho philosopho suessano interprete et expositore* (Venice, 1506), repr. with *Recognitiones* and *Quaestio de infinitate*

primi motoris (Venice, 1526, 1543, 1550, 1557, 1577); *Aristotelis Physicarum acroasum hoc est naturalium auscultationum liber interprete atque expositore Eutyco Augustino Nypho phylotheo suessano* (Venice, 1508, 1519), to which *Recognitiones* was later added (Venice, 1540, 1543, 1549, 1552, 1558, 1559, 1569); *In quattuor libros De caelo et mundo et Aristotelis et Averrois expositio* (Naples, 1517); *Parva naturalia Augustini Niphi Medices philosophi suessani* (Venice, 1523); *Suessanus super posteriora cum tabula, Eutychi Augustini Nyphi Medices philosophi suessani commentaria in libris posteriorum Aristotelis* (Venice, 1526, 1538, 1539, 1544, 1548, 1552, 1553, 1554, 1565; Paris, 1540); and *Expositiones in omnes Aristotelis libros De historia animalium, De partibus animalium et earum causis, ac De generatione animalium* (Venice, 1546), which was completed in 1534 and published posthumously.

Besides his comments on Ibn Rushd in these works, Nifo wrote commentaries on Ibn Rushd's *Destructio destructionum* (Venice, 1497); *De animae beatitudine* (Venice, 1508); *De substantia orbis* (Venice, 1508); and a short opusculum, *Averrois de mixtione defensio* (Venice, 1505). There is also a commentary on Ptolemy, *Ad Apotelesmata Ptolemaei eruditiones* (Naples, 1513); and one on the *Aphorisms* of Hippocrates, Biblioteca Lancisiana, Rome, Codex 158, fols. 55 ff. Other works of interest are his *De demonibus*, printed with his *De intellectu* (Venice, 1503); *De diebus criticis* (Venice, 1504); *De nostrarum calamitatum causis liber* (Venice, 1505); *De immortalitate animae* (Venice, 1518); *De falsa diluvii prognosticatione* (Naples, 1519); *De figuris stellarum helionoricis* (Naples, 1526); *De pulchro et amore* (Rome, 1531); and *De ratione medendi* (Naples, 1551), which was completed in 1528.

II. SECONDARY LITERATURE. See Leopoldo Cassese, "Agostino Nifo a Salerno," in *Atti del Centro di studi di medicina medioevale*, **3** (1958), app. to *Rassegna storica salernitana*, **19** (1958), 3–17; Angelo Crescini, *Le origini del metodo analitico, Il Cinquecento* (Trieste, 1965), 141–144, 181, 187; E. J. Dijksterhuis, *The Mechanization of the World Picture*, C. Dikshoorn, trans. (Oxford, 1961), 236–237, 278; Giovanni di Napoli, *L'immortalità dell'anima nel Rinascimento* (Turin, 1963), 203–217, 309–314; Pierre Duhem, *Études sur Léonard de Vinci*, III (Paris, 1955), 115–120; Eugenio Garin, *La cultura filosofica del Rinascimento italiano* (Florence, 1961), 114–118, 295–303; and *Storia della filosofia italiana*, II (Turin, 1966), 523–527, 535–538, 572–573; Michele Giorgiantonio, "Un nostro filosofo dimenticato del'400 (Luca Prassicio e Agostino Nifo)," in *Sophia* (Naples), **16** (1948), 212–214, 303–312; Gustav Hellmann, *Beiträge zur Geschichte der Meteorologie*, I, Nr. 1 (Berlin, 1914), 40–44, 79–83; Edward P. Mahoney, "Agostino Nifo's *De sensu agente*," in *Archiv für Geschichte der Philosophie*, **53** (1971), 119–142; "Agostino Nifo's Early Views on Immortality," in *Journal of the History of Philosophy*, **8** (1970), 451–460; "A Note on Agostino Nifo," in *Philological Quarterly*, **50** (1971), 125–132; "Nicoletto Vernia and Agostino Nifo on Alexander of Aphrodisias: An Unnoticed Dispute," in *Rivista critica di storia della filosofia*, **23** (1968), 268–296; "Pier Nicola Castellani and Agostino Nifo on Averroës' Doctrine of the Agent Intellect," *ibid.*, **25** (1970), 387–409; and Anneliese Maier, *Zwei Grundprobleme der scholastischen Naturphilosophie*, 2nd ed. (Rome, 1951), 61, 295–297.

See also Bruno Nardi, *Saggi sull'aristotelismo padovano dal secolo XIV al XVI* (Florence, 1958); and *Sigieri di Brabante nel pensiero del Rinascimento italiano* (Rome, 1945), *passim*; Antonino Poppi, *Causalità e infinità nella scuola padovana dal 1480 al 1513* (Padua, 1966), 222–236; and *Saggi sul pensiero inedito di Pietro Pomponazzi* (Padua, 1970), 97–101, 121–144; John Herman Randall, *The School of Padua and the Rise of Modern Science* (Padua, 1961), 42–47, 57 ff., 74 ff.; Wilhelm Risse, *Die Logik der Neuzeit*, I (Stuttgart, 1964), 218–229; Lynn Thorndike, *A History of Magic and Experimental Science*, V (New York, 1941), 69–98, 162 ff., 182–188; Giuseppe Tommasino, *Tra umanisti e filosofi* (Maddaloni, 1921), pt. I, 123–147; Pasquale Tuozzi, "Agostino Nifo e le sue opere," in *Atti e memorie della R. Accademia di scienze, lettere ed arti* (Padua), n.s. **20** (1904), 63–86; Andreas G. M. van Melsen, *From Atomos to Atom: The History of the Concept "Atom"* (Pittsburgh, 1952), 64–76; and William A. Wallace, *Causality and Scientific Explanation*, I (Ann Arbor, 1972), 139–153.

EDWARD P. MAHONEY

NIGGLI, PAUL (*b.* Zofingen, Switzerland, 26 June 1888; *d.* Zurich, Switzerland, 13 January 1953), *crystallography, mineralogy, petrology, geology, chemistry.*

Niggli's father was a teacher and principal of the technical high school at Zofingen. Both his father and his Gymnasium teacher Fritz Mühlberg sparked his lifelong enthusiasm for the natural sciences and for geological-mineralogical problems in particular. As early as his high school years he participated in the mapping of his home canton; and at the age of nineteen he wrote his first scientific paper, "Die geologische Karte von Zofingen" (1913).

In the fall of 1907 Niggli enrolled in the Section for Natural Science Teachers at the Eidgenössische Technische Hochschule in Zurich. His early interest in both the descriptive and the analytic aspects of research prompted him to choose a petrologic topic for his M.S. thesis under Ulrich Grubenmann. In 1911 he received his teacher's diploma and, after a brief stay in the department of physical chemistry of the Technical University at Karlsruhe, received his Ph.D. in 1912 at the University of Zurich. His thesis, which became famous, was entitled *Die Chloritoidschiefer des nordöstlichen Gotthardmassivs.* It showed the traits of Niggli's style of research, the combination of a fundamentalist approach with a strong trend toward the integration of broad aspects.

Shortly after receiving his doctorate, Niggli qualified as a lecturer; and in 1913 he was at the Geophysical Laboratory of the Carnegie Institution in Washington, D.C., where he worked with Norman L. Bowen on phase diagrams of petrology, especially those with a volatile component. From the end of 1915 to 1918 he was a professor at Friedrich Rinne's Institute at Leipzig; he then taught for two years at Tübingen. In 1920 Niggli succeeded Grubenmann as professor of mineralogy and petrography at the University of Zurich and the Swiss Federal Institute of Technology. He held these positions until his death, receiving but declining offers from well-known foreign universities.

Niggli's influence is still felt in virtually all fields of applied and pure crystallography, mineralogy, and petrology. To those who did not know him Niggli appeared at times to be dry or even unfriendly; this was a result of his intense dedication to his work and his modest, simple, and direct way of dealing with people. To a majority of his students, co-workers, and friends he was by no means authoritative or despotic; he was warm and interested in their scientific problems and education and in their more personal affairs. His terms as rector of the Eidgenössische Technische Hochschule (1927–1931) and the University of Zurich (1940–1942) are proof of his talent for organization and his interest in public affairs. Nevertheless, the intensity of his scientific disputes, particularly over transformism, spilled over to affect personal relationships and the careers of two generations of Swiss geologists.

Niggli took a great and continuing interest in his teaching. During his thirty-two years at Zurich he constantly sought to improve all aspects of instruction in his field, in order to offer the students a well-rounded education. His courses were rather condensed and often hard to follow because of the wealth of material presented in a short time. The advanced student or co-worker could, however, gain much from taking the "same" course a second time, not only because of the density and breadth of material but also because Niggli hardly ever gave the same lecture in the same way or with the same content.

Although Niggli was mainly interested in theory, he devoted considerable time to the field and to the field training of his students. The excursions were always well prepared; and Niggli attempted to offer a balanced program covering igneous, metamorphic, sedimentary, and applied petrology.

Niggli's significant accomplishments range from theoretical considerations of crystal lattices through many facets of petrology and geochemistry to the very practical problems of avalanche prevention through snow petrology and mineralogy. His crystallographic accomplishments were summarized by P. P. Ewald:

> Crystallographers will remember him as the author of *Geometrische Kristallographie des Diskontinuums* (1919) in which he transformed the theory of space groups from the mathematical skeleton left by Schoenflies (1891), E. S. Fedorov (1891), and Harold Hilton (1903), to a helpful friend and advisor of the modern crystallographer. This first of Niggli's books testifies well to his aim of achieving convergence of previously separate fields. Once this was accomplished, he stopped; he never made an all-out attempt at structure determination, the details of which he may have felt likely to divert him from his main course. He kept, however, a profound interest in extending morphological methods to account for the inner structure of crystals. His two papers "Atombau und Kristallstruktur" (1921) contain a detailed survey of atomic and ionic volumes in the solid state throughout the periodic system and discuss the importance of similarity of volumes for the crystallographic properties of salts. His book *Kristallographische und Strukturtheoretische Grundbegriffe* (1928) is an attempt to arrive at a more refined classification of the translation lattices of structures and to connect to it the external morphology of the crystals. His papers "Topologische Strukturanalyse" and "Stereochemie der Kristallverbindungen" (1928–1933) serve as preliminary study for his book *Grundlagen der Stereochemie* (1945), which, by its treatment of the internal morphology of crystals, is a counterpart to his textbook *Spezielle Mineralogie* (1924). Niggli's urge for unifying, condensing and classifying knowledge so as to make it applicable to ever wider fields also stands out in papers on "Charaktertafeln" (1950–1951) in which a method is developed for symbolizing each space group so as to make any further reference to tables unnecessary.
>
> Even in view of the infiltration of detailed wave-mechanical bond theory into the realm of crystallography Niggli remained convinced of the lasting power of morphological methods. Morphology was the central theme of his interest and philosophy and his last large book *Probleme der Naturwissenschaften erläutert am Begriffe der Mineralart* (1949) is, in this sense, his testament ["Paul Niggli," p. 240].

During the twenty years Niggli edited the *Zeitschrift für Kristallographie*, the journal acquired an international reputation. During these two first decades of X-ray analysis he strove to maintain a reasonable unified system of crystallographic terminology. It is also characteristic of his analytical mind that as early as 1919 Niggli recognized, in his *Geometrische Kristallographie des Diskontinuums*, the difference between "real" and "ideal" crystals, at that time speaking of the "pathology of crystals." In 1934

Zeitschrift für Kristallographie published, at his urging, a double issue on ideal and real crystals. Niggli published over sixty papers on crystal structures and summarized this field in the two-volume *Lehrbuch der Mineralogie und Kristallchemie* (1941–1944); a third volume (dealing with crystal chemistry) was destroyed by fire in Berlin during the last months of World War II. These three volumes were actually the third edition of his *Lehrbuch der Mineralogie* (1920). Significantly, volume I contains the foundation of a statistical morphological science, the principles of which, largely original with Niggli, have only recently begun to find application. In his last years Niggli showed that even the wave-mechanical approach to crystal physics required the assistance of morphological concepts, and he presented papers and lectures on the vibration symmetries and degrees of freedom of vibrations of atomic complexes.

In petrography and petrology Niggli also tended to be the integrating, unifying spirit. Almost a century of work had to be pulled together. It should be stressed that throughout his career Niggli used and emphasized the importance of physical chemistry and that phase diagrams formed an essential part of his courses on petrology and mineral deposits. But he did not mistake bare experimental results for proof of natural processes; rather, he was aware that experiments are bound to be oversimplifications, which are designed by man and may miss some essential factors present in natural processes. When experimental results did not match observations of nature, he suggested the possibility of misdirection or of missing parameters in the experiment.

Soon after his stay at the Geophysical Laboratory of the Carnegie Institution, Niggli recognized that his métier was integrating available experimental results instead of duplicating or adding to them. He accomplished this task in long, close teamwork with Bowen at the Geophysical Laboratory, A. Smits at Amsterdam, and especially with colleagues at the Eidgenössische Technische Hochschule and the University of Zurich.

Niggli applied the theory of phase equilibria for the first time to the role of volatile fractions in magmas, as also to problems of metamorphic petrology. The experimental criteria acquired during his work at the Geophysical Laboratory were soon applied to an understanding of the pneumatolytic and autohydrothermal alterations of the Eibenstock granite near Dresden, work done in cooperation with F. Rinne. The result was his first book, *Die leichtflüchtigen Bestandteile im Magma* (1920), which received an award from the Fürstlich Jablonowitsche Gesellschaft in Leipzig and became a standard work.

The 1937 book *Das Magma und seine Produkte* (*mit besonderer Berücksichtigung der leichtflüchtigen Bestandteile*) can be considered the second edition of the 1920 work.

Niggli and his students undertook the gigantic task of petrographic classification and interpretation of the chemical analyses of the world's rocks. The original CIPW-norm procedures proved to be inadequate for the project, so he modified them, creating "molecular values," which soon were used throughout the world and were known as Niggli values. These two fundamentally new principles inherent in these "values" calculated from the weight percentages of metal oxides are (1) conversion to atomic percentages instead of weight percentages, which blur the crystal-chemical relationships, and (2) the immediate juxtaposition of the atomic abundance of the basic oxides (aluminum, iron, magnesium, manganese, calcium, sodium, and potassium) with that of silicon dioxide since most of these elements are contained in silicates. This allows the rapid calculation of the possible mineralogical composition of a rock.

Combined with variation diagrams and normative calculation schemes designed by Niggli and his co-workers (1922–1945), the new methods proved far superior to any others. Some of the basic ideas which he developed are (1) the principle of magmatic crystallization and the influence of the volatile fraction; (2) the principle of gravitative crystallization differentiation in magmas; (3) the principle of petrographic-geochemical provinces; and (4) the importance of a calculation and a comparison of the normative and the modal composition of rocks. His principal works on the mineralogical composition of rocks were "Das Magma und seine Produkte" (*Naturwissenschaften*, **9** [1921], also published as a book in 1937); *Gesteins- und Mineralprovinzen* (1923); "Die komplexe gravitative Kristallisationsdifferentiation" (*Schweizerische mineralogische und petrographische Mitteilungen*, **18** [1938]); "Die Magmentypen," written with A. H. Stutz (*ibid.*, **16** [1936]); and, with C. Burri, the two-volume *Die jungen Eruptivgesteine des mediterranen Orogens* (1945–1948). A late but important work was "Gesteinschemismus und Magmenlehre."

Niggli's 1948 book *Gesteine und Minerallagerstätten* summarized his previous work. In it he developed petrologic science from the level of the crystal structure (including the role of trace elements in petrology) to the mineral, the rock specimen as the mineral aggregate, the outcrop, the regional, and the global levels, in a synthesis of geochemical and geometric problems. The set of rock fabric patterns in this book illustrates his knowledge of petrographic-petrologic processes and fabric possibilities.

Niggli also applied his molecular values and norm calculations to metamorphic and sedimentary rocks to show that extreme transformist or relatively migrationist interpretations were oversimplifications. Extreme migrationist views were challenged about 1970–1972, when new global comparisons showed the average composition of sediments to be basaltic rather than granitic. This revived a differentiation concept of anatexis, similar to that proposed by Niggli. The principles of metamorphic transformation were well known to him; but extensions of local processes to a regional scale were unacceptable to his critical mind.

Niggli insisted on the application of physico-chemical principles, as is exemplified in all of his work on metamorphic rocks starting in 1913–1914 (some papers with J. Johnston) and in the *Gesteinsmetamorphose* (1924), prepared with Grubenmann.

Niggli's work is sometimes considered to be that of an "extreme orthodox magmatist." On examination it is obvious that he was aware of the importance of exchange reactions in metamorphism. Nevertheless, before invoking a deus ex machina for the majority of igneous rocks, he insisted that the physicochemical aspects of the development of both igneous and metamorphic processes had to be understood. He was aware that his theory of magmatic processes and provinces was not the final answer to all problems of field petrology and that additional work was needed. This is perhaps best expressed in a statement from his 1952 paper "Gesteinschemismus und Magmenlehre," in which he explicitly states that there may be various ways of interpreting regional variations.

Niggli's interest in sedimentary rocks led to original papers on clastic sediments, especially the morphological aspects of grains. His classification of shapes, developed with dal Vesco, is probably still the most widely used one. The general principles of Niggli's petrology-petrography, especially the close ties with his crystallographic interests, are summarized in volume I of *Gesteine und Minerallagerstätten* (1948), and he offered as complete a summary on sedimentary rocks in volume II. His papers on snow research, which had a profound impact in the field, also concern sedimentation, diagenesis, and metamorphism.

Niggli exerted a strong influence on applied petrology, especially through his work on rock weathering and other aspects of building stone petrology, most of it done with F. de Quervain, who headed the Geotechnische Prüfstelle and the Geotechnische Kommission, both created at Niggli's suggestion. Although never directly active in consulting work—he was too dedicated to fundamental science—Niggli nevertheless was in constant touch with applied fields of his science. He knew very well how often new "pure" aspects emerge from technological applications, and he also realized that most of his students had to prepare for work in applied fields. Also in this vein he promoted the publication of the geotechnical map of Switzerland and was active in the foundation of the Schweizerische Mineralogische und Petrographische Gesellschaft, of which he was president from 1928 to 1930.

Niggli wrote several papers and one booklet on ore deposits. Here his main point of departure was the accumulation of metals during the gravitative crystallization differentiation and the accumulation of volatiles in later magmatic stages. His booklet *Versuch einer natürlichen Klassifikation der im weiteren Sinne magmatischen Lagerstätten* (1925) is a classic synopsis of magmatic ore deposits. In this work Niggli devoted less space to experimental problems and to direct observations of ore deposits, being more concerned to classify synopses of the published results and observations. This approach proved to be generally acceptable in crystallography, mineralogy, and petrology but rather negative with regard to ore deposits, the descriptive terminology of which was filled with preconceived genetic concepts. He did, however, recognize many physicochemical relationships within magmatic and hydrothermal ore deposits for the first time, especially the role of the volatile fraction in the accumulation of metals in a magma. His booklet was internationally quoted and used, especially the English translation.

BIBLIOGRAPHY

I. ORIGINAL WORKS. A summary of Niggli's works can be found in R. L. Parker, "Memorial of Paul Niggli" (see below); a complete list of all publications is given by J. Marquard and I. Schroeter, in *Schweizerische mineralogische und petrographische Mitteilungen*, 33 (1953), 9–20.

Niggli's major works include *Die Chloritoidschiefer des nordöstlichen Gotthardmassivs* (diss., University of Zurich; Bern, 1912); *Geometrische Kristallographie des Diskontinuums* (Leipzig, 1918–1919); *Lehrbuch der Mineralogie* (Berlin, 1920), 2nd ed., 2 vols. (Berlin, 1924–1926), 3rd ed., entitled *Lehrbuch der Mineralogie und Kristallchemie*, 3 vols. (Berlin, 1941–1944), vol. III destroyed by fire; "Das Magma und seine Produkte," in *Naturwissenschaften*, 9 (1921), 463–471; *Gesteins- und Mineralprovinzen* (Berlin, 1923), written with P. I. Beger; *Die Gesteinsmetamorphose* (Berlin, 1924), written with U. Grubenmann; *Versuch einer natürlichen Klassifikation der im weiteren Sinne magmatischen Lagerstätten* (Halle, 1925), trans. by Thomas Murby as *Ore Deposits of Magmatic Origin. Their Genesis and Natural Classification* (London, 1929); *Tabellen zur allgemeinen und speziellen Mineralogie* (Berlin, 1927); *Kristallographische und strukturtheoretische Grundbegriffe,* which is *Handbuch der Experimentalphysik*, VII, pt. 1 (Leipzig, 1928); "Chemismus schweizerischer Gesteine," which is *Beiträge zur geologischen Karte der Schweiz*, Geotechnische Reihe, 8, no. 14 (1930), written with F. de Quervain and R. U. Winterhalter; *Geotechnische Karte der Schweiz 1:200 000*, 4 sheets (Bern, 1934–1938), prepared with F. de Quervain, M. Gschwind, and R. U. Winterhalter; *Internationale Tabellen zur Bestimmung von Kristallstrukturen* (Berlin, 1935), written with E. Brandenberger; and "Die Magmentypen," in *Schweizerische mineralogische und petrographische Mitteilungen*, 16 (1936), 335–399, written with A. H. Stutz.

Also see *Das Magma und seine Produkte (mit besonderer Berücksichtigung der leichtflüchtigen Bestandteile)*, (Leipzig, 1937), which is the 2nd ed. of *Die leichtflüchtigen Bestandteile im Magma* (Leipzig, 1920); "Die komplexe gravitative Kristallisationsdifferentiation," in *Schweizerische mineralogische und petrographische Mitteilungen*, 18 (1938), 610–664; *La loi des phases en minéralogie et pétrographie* (Paris, 1938); *Die Mineralien der Schweizeralpen*, 2 vols. (Basel, 1940), written with J. Koenigsberger and R. L. Parker; *Grundlagen der Stereochemie* (Basel, 1945); *Schulung und Naturerkenntnis* (Erlenbach–Zurich, 1945); *Die jungen Eruptivgesteine des mediterranen Orogens*, 2 vols. (Zurich, 1945–1948), written with C. Burri; "Krystallogia von J. H. Hottinger (1698)," in *Veröffentlichungen der Schweizerischen Gesellschaft für Geschichte der Medizin und der Naturwissenschaften*, no. 14 (1946); *Gesteine und Minerallagerstätten*, 2 vols. (Basel, 1948–1952), written with E. Niggli; *Probleme der Naturwissenschaften erläutert am Begriff der Mineralart* (Basel, 1949); "Gesteinschemismus und Magmenlehre," in *Geologische Rundschau*, 39 (1951), 8–32; and *International Tables for X-ray Crystallography* (Birmingham, 1952), written with E. Brandenberger.

II. SECONDARY LITERATURE. See E. Brandenberger, "Paul Niggli (1888–1953). Seine Verdienste um die Lehre des festen Körpers," in *Zeitschrift für angewandte Mathematik und Physik*, 4 (1953), 415–418; P. P. Ewald, "Paul Niggli," in *Acta crystallographica*, 6 (Mar. 1953), 225–226; P. Karrer and E. Brandenberger, *Prof. Dr. Paul Niggli. Ansprachen zu seinem Gedenken* (Zurich, 1953); F. Laves, "Paul Niggli," in *Experientia*, 9 (1953), 197–202; F. Laves and A. Niggli, "In Memoriam: Paul Niggli's Crystallographic Oeuvre," in *Zeitschrift für Kristallographie und Mineralogie*, 120 (1964), 212–215; H. O'Daniel, K. H. Scheumann, and H. Schneiderhöhn, "Paul Niggli," in *Neues Jahrbuch für Mineralogie* (1953), 51–67; R. L. Parker, "Memorial of Paul Niggli," in *American Mineralogist*, 39 (1954), 280–283; F. de Quervain, "Prof. Dr. Paul Niggli," in *Schweizerische mineralogische und petrographische Mitteilungen*, 33 (1953), 1–20; K. H. Scheumann, "Paul Niggli und sein Werk," in *Geologie*, 2 (1953), 124–130; and A. Streckeisen, "Paul Niggli," in *Mitteilungen der Naturforschenden Gesellschaft in Bern*, n.s. 11 (1954), 109–113.

G. C. AMSTUTZ

NIKITIN, SERGEY NIKOLAEVICH (*b.* Moscow, Russia, 4 February 1851; *d.* St. Petersburg, Russia, 18 November 1909), *geology.*

Nikitin's father was a dissector in the department of anatomy at Moscow University. While still a Gymnasium student the boy was attracted to the natural sciences, especially botany and geology. In 1867 he entered the natural sciences section of the Faculty of Physics and Mathematics at Moscow University. After graduating in 1871, Nikitin taught botany and geography in secondary schools. He was one of the organizers of the Moscow Natural History Courses for Women, where he lectured in mineralogy and geology. At the same time he studied Paleozoic and Mesozoic deposits of the Russian platforms. In 1878 Nikitin was awarded the master's degree for work on the ammonites.

In 1882, when the Russian Geological Survey was founded, he was elected its senior geologist. Concerned with the stratigraphy of the Russian platform, he investigated the coal deposits in the Moscow Basin and the Permian deposits of the Ural foothills. He suggested the name "Tatar layer" for the Upper Permian horizons; divided Jurassic deposits, according to the ammonites, into seven paleontological zones; and established a phylogenetic series of Kelloveyskikh and Oxford ammonites. Nikitin was a Darwinian who introduced evolutionary theory into invertebrate paleontology. He compiled a stratigraphic scheme of the Russian Upper Cretaceous deposits, comparing them with corresponding deposits in Western Europe, and determined the northern limit of the distribution of the Upper Cretaceous remains. Nikitin assigned great importance to the study of Quaternary deposits, distinguishing ten sorts of regions in Russia according to geological types of glacial deposits. Regarding the origin of loess he advocated the eolian hypothesis.

Nikitin laid the foundation for systematic hydrogeological and hydrological research in Russia. Participating in the expeditions organized by the Geological Survey to study the southern arid regions through investigations of the sources of Russian rivers, he generalized the material obtained and published several works. These investigations were of great importance for the development of agriculture. He studied the conditions of occurrence of underground water in the Moscow region and showed the possibility of using artesian wells for supplying the capital. From 1907 through 1909 he was president of the Hydrological Committee. He presented his conclusions on the conditions for artesian water supply to cities and on the hydrogeological conditions for railroad regions.

From 1905 through 1907 Nikitin headed an expedition that studied the geological structure of the Mugodzhar Hills. During the last years of his life, at the request of the imperial mining department, he was concerned with ways to prevent the flooding of the salt mines in the Urals. Nikitin was well acquainted with the geological literature and published a bibliographical guide, *Russkaya geologicheskaya biblioteka* ("Russian Geological Library," 1886–1900), and surveys of Russian and general geology.

In 1883 the St. Petersburg Academy of Sciences awarded Nikitin the Helmersen Prize for his paleontological works, and in 1894 the Russian Geographical Society awarded him the Medal of Constantine. In 1902 he was elected a corresponding member of the St. Petersburg Academy of Sciences.

BIBLIOGRAPHY

I. ORIGINAL WORKS. Nikitin's most important writings are "Ammonity gruppy *Amaltheus funiferus*" ("Ammonites of the Group *Amaltheus funiferus*"), in *Bulletin de la Société impériale des naturalistes de Moscou,* n.s. **3** (1878), 81–160; "Darvinizm i vopros o vide v oblasti sovremennoy paleontologii" ("Darwinism and the Question of Form in Contemporary Paleontology"), in *Mysl* (St. Petersburg), no. 8 (1881), 144–170; no. 9 (1881), 229–245; "Yurskie obrazovania mezhdu Rybinskom, Mologoy i Myshkinym" ("Jurassic Formations Between Rybinsk, Mologa and Myshkin"), in *Materialy dlya geologii Rossii,* **10** (1881), 199–331; "Posletretichnye otlozhenia Germanii v ikh otnoshenii k sootvetstvennym obrazovaniam Rossii" ("Post-Tertiary Deposits of Germany In Their Relations to the Corresponding Formations of Russia"), in *Izvestiya Geologicheskago komiteta,* **5,** no. 3–4 (1886), 133–185; "Sledy melovogo perioda v Tsentralnoy Rossii" ("Traces of the Cretaceous Period in Central Russia"), in *Trudy Geologischeskago komiteta,* **5,** no. 2 (1888), 1–205; and "Ukazatel literatury po burovym na vodu skvazhinam v Rossii" ("A Guide to Literature on Wells Drilled for Water in Russia"), supp. to *Izvestiya Geologicheskago komiteta,* **29** (1911).

II. SECONDARY LITERATURE. See F. N. Chernyshev, "Sergey Nikolaevich Nikitin," in *Izvestiya Imperatorskoi akademii nauk,* 6th ser., **3,** no. 18 (1909), 1171–1173; F. N. Chernyshev, A. A. Borisyak, N. N. Tikhonovich, and M. M. Prigorovsky, "Pamyati Sergeya Nikolaevicha Nikitina" ("Recollections of . . . Nikitin"), in *Izvestiya Geologicheskago komiteta,* **28,** no. 10 (1909), 1–51; and N. N. Karlov, "S. N. Nikitin i znachenie ego rabot dlya razvitia otechestvennykh geologicheskikh nauk" ("S. N. Nikitin and the Importance of His Work for the Development of Native Geological Sciences"), in *Ocherki po istorii geologicheskikh znany,* no. 1 (1953), 157–180.

IRINA V. BATYUSHKOVA

NĪLAKAŅTHA (*b.* Tṛ-k-kaṇṭiyūr [Kuṇḍapura], Kerala, *ca.* 14 June 1444; *d.* after 1501), *astronomy*.

Nīlakaņṭha, a Nampūtiri Brahman, was born in the house *(illam)* called Keḷallūr (Keralasadgrāma), which is said to be identical with the present Eṭamana *illam* in Tṛ-k-kaṇṭiyūr, a village near Tirur, Kerala. His father was named Jātavedas, and the family belonged to the Gārgyagotra and followed the Āśvalāyanasūtra of the *Ṛgveda*; Nīlakaņṭha was a Somasutvān (performer of the Soma sacrifice). He studied Vedānta and some astronomy under Ravi, but his principal instructor in *jyotiḥśāstra* was Dāmodara (*fl.* 1417), the son of the famous Parameśvara (*ca.* 1380–1460), whom he also met at the Dāmodara house in Ālattūr (Aśvatthagrāma), Kerala. His younger brother, Śaṅkara, studied astronomy under his tutelage and in turn professed that science. It is possible, but not certain, that Nīlakaņṭha is identical with the father of the Rāma who wrote a *Laghurāmāyaṇa* in Malayālam.

Nīlakaņṭha was a follower of Parameśvara's *dṛggaṇita* system (see essay in Supplement), although he gives various parameters in his several works (see D. Pingree, in *Journal of the Oriental Institute, Baroda* 21 [1971–1972], 146–148). These works include the following:

1. The *Golasāra*, in fifty-six verses, gives the parameters of his planetary system, a description of the celestial spheres, and a description of the principles of computation used in Indian mathematical astronomy. It was edited by K. V. Sarma (Hoshiarpur, 1970).

2. The *Siddhāntadarpaṇa*, in thirty-two verses, gives another set of parameters and a description of (impossible) planetary models. It also was edited by K. V. Sarma (Madras, 1955). Nīlakaņṭha's commentary *(vyākhyā)* on the *Siddhāntadarpaṇa* has not been published.

3. The *Candracchāyāgaṇita* describes, in thirty-one verses, the computation of the moon's zenith distance. Neither it nor Nīlakaņṭha's commentary *(vyākhyā)* has been published.

4. The *Tantrasaṅgraha* is an elaborate treatise on *dṛggaṇita* astronomy, composed in 1501. It consists of eight chapters:

a. On the mean motions of the planets.

b. On the true longitudes of the planets.

c. On the three questions relating to the diurnal rotation of the sun.

d. On lunar and solar eclipses.

e. Particulars of solar eclipses.

f. On the *pātas* of the sun and moon.

g. On the first visibilities of the moon and planets.

h. On the horns of the moon.

The *Tantrasaṅgraha* was edited with the commentary, *Laghuvṛtti*, of Śaṅkara Vāriyar (*fl.* 1556) by S. K. Pillai (Trivandrum, 1958).

5. The *Āryabhaṭīyabhāṣya* is an extensive and important commentary on the *Āryabhaṭīya* composed by Āryabhaṭa I in 499. Nīlakaņṭha's patron for this work was the religious head of the Nampūtiri Brahmans, Netranārāyaṇa. In his commentary on Kālakriyā 12–15 he states that he observed a total eclipse of the sun on 6 March 1467 (Oppolzer no. 6358) and an annular eclipse at Anantakṣetra on 28 July 1501 (not in Oppolzer). The *Āryabhaṭīyabhāṣya* was published in three volumes by K. S. Sastri (volumes I and II) and S. K. Pillai (volume III), (Trivandrum 1930–1957).

6 and 7. In the *Āryabhaṭīyabhāṣya*, Nīlakaņṭha refers to his *Grahanirṇaya* on eclipses and to his *Sundararājapraśnottara*, in which he answers questions posed by Sundararāja, the author of a commentary on the *Vākyakaraṇa*. Neither of these works is extant.

8. An untitled prose work on eclipses by Nīlakaņṭha is included in a manuscript of the *Siddhāntadarpaṇavyākhyā*; it refers to the *Āryabhaṭīyabhāṣya*, and thus is his last known work.

BIBLIOGRAPHY

Nīlakaņṭha's method of computing π is discussed by K. M. Marar and C. T. Rajagopal, "On the Hindu Quadrature of the Circle," in *Journal of the Bombay Branch of the Royal Asiatic Society*, n.s. **20** (1944), 65–82. A general survey of his life and works (now superseded by the introductions to Sarma's latest eds.) is given by K. V. Sarma, "Gārgya-Kerala Nīlakaņṭha Somayājin: The Bhāṣyakāra of the Āryabhaṭīya (1443–1545)," in *Journal of Oriental Research* (Madras), **26** (1956–1957), 24–39; and by K. K. Raja, "Astronomy and Mathematics in Kerala," in *Brahmavidyā*, **27** (1963), 118–167, esp. 143–152.

DAVID PINGREE

NILSSON-EHLE, HERMAN (*b.* Skurup, Sweden, 12 February 1873; *d.* Lund, Sweden, 29 December 1949), *genetics*, *plant breeding*.

Nilsson-Ehle was the son of Nils Nilsson, a farmer, and his wife, Elin. After first studying in Malmö, he enrolled in 1891 at the University of Lund, where he received the candidate's degree in 1894, the licentiate degree in 1901, and the Ph.D. in 1909. He began his scientific research in 1894, at first concentrating on plant taxonomy and plant physiology. In 1900 he became an assistant at the Swedish Seed Association in Svalöf (near Lund), and thereafter devoted himself to the new science of genetics and its practical applications in plant breeding.

Nilsson-Ehle realized the fundamental importance of Mendel's principles of heredity, which had just been rediscovered, and he was especially impressed by Mendel's clarification of the mechanism of genetic recombination. Nilsson-Ehle was the first to demonstrate that economically important properties in cultivated plants are inherited according to Mendel's laws and may be recombined in a specific way. In a now-classic paper of 1906 he recommended artificial crosses as the best method of obtaining a recombination of various desirable properties. He cited a series of examples from his own experience and pointed out that part of the offspring of experimentally produced hybrids combined the valuable properties of the parents. At the same time he obtained, as expected, other offspring which represented a combination of the undesirable properties of the parents.

In three papers published in 1908–1911 Nilsson-Ehle demonstrated that quantitative characters (size, earliness, resistance to disease) are inherited in the same Mendelian way as the qualitative characters (differences in flower color, etc.) with which Mendel and the early Mendelists had been working. As a rule, however, the quantitative characters were found to be conditioned by a relatively high number of polymeric (or multiple) genes. After recombination these genes may give rise to numerous quantitative gradations of the characters involved in the crosses. This finding was a very important contribution to the development of basic genetics and a solid basis for its practical application to plant breeding.

In 1915 Nilsson-Ehle was appointed to the chair of physiological botany at the University of Lund. Two years later he moved to the chair of genetics. From 1925 until his retirement in 1939 Nilsson-Ehle was director of the Swedish Seed Association. During this period as an active administrator, he encouraged the development of new fields of research and in 1931 organized a new department for chromosome investigations and the production of new types of polyploid cultivated plants. He realized that induced mutations would be important in plant breeding, and advocated mutation research.

As professor emeritus, Nilsson-Ehle became actively interested in forestry and horticulture, and he was helpful in the founding and development of organizations which sought to improve the stock for forests and orchards through breeding.

Nilsson-Ehle was a member of many academies and received several honorary doctorates. His life was marked by a cyclical mental state: periods of ill health, extraordinary activity, deep depression, and great optimism. He was a fascinating combination of creative fantasy and sober realism; and he combined a farmer's intimate practical knowledge of soil and crops with the theoretical education and logical acumen of a university professor. Moreover, he was talented musically and often entertained himself and his guests at the piano. He was married and had a daughter and two sons.

BIBLIOGRAPHY

I. ORIGINAL WORKS. Among Nilsson-Ehle's numerous publications the following ones are of especial importance: "Einige Ergebnisse von Kreuzungen bei Hafer und Weizen," in *Botaniska notiser* (1908), 257–294; "Kreuzungsuntersuchungen an Hafer und Weizen," in *Acta Universitatis lundensis*, n.s. 2, **5**, no. 2 (1909), 1–122; **7**, no. 6 (1911), 1–84; and "Mendélisme et acclimatation," in *IVe Conférence international génétique Paris* (Paris, 1911), 1–22.

II. SECONDARY LITERATURE. See A. Müntzing, "Lebensbeschreibung von H. Nilsson-Ehle," in *Zeitschrift für Pflanzenzüchtung*, **29**, no. 1 (1950), 110–114. In *Sveriges utsädesförenings tidskrift* (1950), no.1, there are articles in Swedish about Nilsson-Ehle and his importance for the development of genetics and plant breeding. See also A. Müntzing, "Minnesteckning över Professor H. Nilsson-Ehle," in *Kungliga Fysiografiska Sällskapets förhandlingar*, **20** (1950), 1–7; Å. Gustafsson, "Herman Nilsson-Ehle, minnesteckning," in *Levnadsteckningar över Kungliga Svenska Vetenskapsakademiens ledamöter*, **175** (1971), 279–293; A. Müntzing, "Om aktualiteten av Herman Nilsson-Ehles teoretiska forskning," in *Sveriges Utsädesförenings tidskrift* (1973), no. 2–3, 159–168; and E. Åkerberg, "Om aktualiteten i Herman Nilsson-Ehles insatser i växtförädling och jordbruksforskning," *ibid.*, 169–178.

ARNE MÜNTZING

NISSL, FRANZ (*b.* Frankenthal, Germany, 9 September 1860; *d.* Munich, Germany, 11 August 1919), *psychiatry, neuropathology.*

Nissl was the son of Theodor Nissl and Maria Haas. He is known for the discovery of a granular basophilic substance, now called Nissl's bodies, that is found in the nerve cell body and the dendrites. In connection with this discovery he classified changes in the distribution and number of these granules following disease or the severing of the axon; coined the term *nervöses grau*, or gray nerve network, a misleading concept of a diffuse interconnection of all nerve processes; and, both alone and with Alois Alzheimer, made a detailed study of dementia paralytica, paying special attention to the behavior of microglia (rod cells).

Nissl's father, who taught Latin in a Catholic school, intended his son to become a priest but, against his parents' wishes, Nissl studied medicine at Munich University. His interest in the nervous system was firmly established by his first scientific effort. He entered a competition for a prize in neurology offered by the Medical Faculty at Munich. The judge was Bernard von Gudden, a scientist and psychiatrist. Gudden was so impressed by Nissl's work on the pathological changes of cortical neurons that he offered him an assistantship in 1884. Gudden drowned in the lake of Starnberg with his patient, King Ludwig of Bavaria, in 1886, and Nissl then became an assistant at the psychiatric hospital in Frankfurt. There he met the comparative neurologist Ludwig Edinger and the neuropathologist Carl Weigert. Nissl worked for seven years with Alzheimer, a psychiatrist and an outstanding neuropathologist. Together they edited the *Histologische und Histopathologische Arbeiten über die Grosshirnrinde* (1904–1921). In 1895 Nissl moved to the University of Heidelberg, becoming university lecturer in 1896, associate professor of psychiatry in 1901, and full professor and director of the department of psychiatry in 1904.

The burden of teaching and administration, combined with poor research facilities, forced Nissl to leave many scientific projects unfinished. He also suffered from a kidney disease. World War I proved to be an even greater burden for he was commissioned to administer a large military hospital as well. In 1918 Nissl moved to Munich to take a research position at the Deutsche Forschungsanstalt für Psychiatrie. He died a year later, before deriving any benefit from these new opportunities.

The present stage of development of neurohistological techniques, including electron microscopy, makes possible an appraisal of Nissl's real scientific achievements. The granular basophilic Nissl's substance is an important ultrastructure of nerve cells, composed of ribosomes and the membranes of the endoplasmic reticulum. The Nissl bodies, in reacting to injury and toxins, mirror the life cycle of a neuron very closely, and the importance Nissl attached to them was fully justified. The gray nerve network, however, proved to be untenable and demonstrates that the use of only one technique leads to faulty interpretation. Nissl and his contemporaries fought for recognition of their respective views. His only monograph, *Die Neuronenlehre und ihre Anhänger* (1903), is a sad and depressing account of a speculative mind incapable of listening to other scientists'

arguments. His attitude was rigid, and his stature in German neurology was one of the reasons that after the magnificent start given to German neuropathology by the studies of Nissl, W. Spielmeyer, Alzheimer, Weigert, and others, no real advances were made by fully experimental methods. Such studies would have early revealed that many observations of cellular changes or of the gray nerve network resulted from bad fixation and application of only one technique.

Nevertheless, Nissl's arguments against the neuron doctrine, which is based on areas of contact between neurons, survived in many quarters until recent times, when electron microscopy amply confirmed the early observations of his contemporary Ramón y Cajal, which Nissl had rejected in vitriolic terms. While Nissl's studies on dementia paralytica are still valid, his admirable attempt to discover a neuropathological cause for mental diseases failed. This is not to detract from Nissl, however, for the cause of these mainly functional diseases is neurobiochemical, not morphological.

BIBLIOGRAPHY

I. ORIGINAL WORKS. Nissl's writings include "Resultate und Erfahrungen bei der Untersuchung der pathologischen Veränderungen der Nervenzellen in der Grosshirnrinde" his diss. (unpublished) (1884); "Über die Veränderungen der Ganglienzellen am Facialiskern des Kaninchens nach Ausreissung des Nerven," in *Versammlungen des Südwestdeutschen Psychiatervereins in Karlsruhe*, **22** (1890); "Über experimentell erzeugte Veränderungen an den Vorderhornzellen des Rückenmarkes bei Kaninchen," in *Zeitschrift für Neurologie*, **48** (1892), 675–682; "Über die sogenannten Granula der Nervenzellen," in *Neurologisches Zentralblatt*, **13** (1894), 676–685, 781–789, 810–814; "Die Beziehungen der Nervenzellsubstanzen zu den tätigen, ruhenden und ermüdeten Zellzuständen," in *Allgemeine Zeitschrift für Psychiatrie*, **52** (1896), 1147–1154; "Mitteilungen zur pathologischen Anatomie der Dementia paralytica," in *Archiv für Psychiatrie*, **28** (1896), 987–992; "Über die Veränderungen der Nervenzellen nach experimentell erzeugter Vergiftung. Autoreferat," in *Neurologisches Zentralblatt*, **15** (1896); "Über einige Beziehungen zwischen Nervenzellerkrankungen und gliösen Erscheinungen bei verschiedenen Psychosen," in *Archiv für Psychiatrie*, **32** (1899), 656–676; *Die Neuronenlehre und ihre Anhänger* (Jena, 1903); "Zur Histopathologie der paralytischen Rindenerkrankung," in *Histologische und histopathologische Arbeiten über die Grosshirnrinde*, **1** (Jena, 1904); "Diskussionsbemerkung zu Alzheimer: Die syphilitischen Geistesstörrungen," in *Neurologisches Zentralblatt*, **32** (1909), 680; and "Zur Lehre der Lokalisation in der Grosshirnrinde des Kaninchens," in *Sitzungsberichte der*

Heidelberger Akademie der Wissenschaften, Math.-natur-wiss. Kl. (1911).

II. SECONDARY LITERATURE. Biographies are A. Jakob, "Franz Nissl," in *Deutsche medizinische Wochenschrift,* XLV, (1919), 1087; E. Kraepelin, "Franz Nissl," in *Münchener medizinische Wochenschrift* (1919); and "Lebensschicksale deutscher Forscher," *ibid.* (1920); H. Marcus, "Franz Nissl," in *Minnesood i Svenska läkaresällskapet* (1919); P. Schröder, "Franz Nissl," in *Monatsschrift für Psychiatrie . . .,* **46** (1919), 294; H. Spatz, "Franz Nissl," in *Berliner klinische Wochenschrift* (1919), 1006; and "Nissl und die theoretische Hirnanatomie," in *Archiv für Psychiatrie und Nervenkrankheiten,* **87** (1929), 100–125; and W. Spielmeyer, "Franz Nissl," in *Kirchhoffs deutsche Irrenärzte,* **2** (1924), 288.

Specialized works are J. E. C. Bywater and P. Glees, *Der Einfluss der Fixationsart und des Intervalles zwischen Tod und Fixation auf die Struktur der Motoneurone des Affen* (Zurich, 1959), offprint from *Verhandlungen der Anatomischen Gesellschaft* (Jena), **55** (1959), 194–200; P. Glees, "Ludwig Edinger," in *Journal of Neurophysiology,* **15** (1952), 251–255; and "Neuere Ergebnisse auf dem Gebiet der Neurohistologie: Nissl-Substanz, corticale Synapsen, Neuroglia und intercellulärer Raum," in *Deutsche Zeitschrift für Nervenheilkunde,* **184** (1963), 607–631; P. Glees and J. E. C. Bywater, "The Effect of the Mode of Fixation and the Interval Between Death and Fixation on Monkeys' Motoneurones," in *Proceedings of the Physiology Society Journal of Physiology,* **149** (1959), 3–4P; and P. Glees and K. Meller, "The Finer Structure of Synapses and Neurones. A Review of Recent Electron-microscopical Studies," in *Paraplegia,* **2,** no. 2 (1964), 77–95.

PAUL GLEES

NOBEL, ALFRED BERNHARD (*b.* Stockholm, Sweden, 21 October 1833; *d.* San Remo, Italy, 10 December 1896), *chemistry.*

Nobel's father, Immanuel Nobel the younger, was a builder, industrialist, and inventor; his great-great-great-grandfather, Olof Rudbeck, was one of the most important Swedish scientists of the seventeenth century. His mother was Andrietta Ahlsell.

Nobel attended St. Jakob's Higher Apologist School in Stockholm in 1841–1842. The family then moved to St. Petersburg, where he and his brothers were tutored privately from 1843 to 1850 by Russian and Swedish tutors. They were also encouraged to be inventive by their energetic father.

After a two-year study trip to Germany, France, Italy, and North America, Nobel had improved his knowledge in chemistry and was an excellent linguist, with a mastery of German, English, French, Swedish, and Russian. During the Crimean War (1853–1856) Nobel worked in St. Petersburg in his father's firm,

which produced large quantities of war matériel. After the war the new Russian government canceled all delivery agreements; Immanuel Nobel had to declare bankruptcy, and he returned to Sweden in 1859.

Immanuel had long experimented with powder-charged mines, and his attention had been drawn by Nikolai Zinin and Yuli Trapp to the explosive substance nitroglycerin. Both he and Alfred worked with it independently, using different methods. In 1862 Immanuel was the first to demonstrate a comparatively simple way of producing nitroglycerin on a factory scale, using Ascano Sobrero's method with some modifications.

In 1863 Alfred Nobel, back in Sweden, developed his first important invention, the Nobel patent detonator, constructed so that detonation of the liquid nitroglycerin explosive charge was effected by a smaller charge placed in a metal cap charged with detonating mercury (mercury fulminate). The "initial ignition principle," using a strong shock rather than heating, was thus introduced into the technique of blasting.

In 1865 the world's first true factory for producing nitroglycerin was put into operation by the Nobel company, Nitroglycerin Ltd., in an isolated area outside Stockholm. Young Alfred Nobel was not only managing director but also works engineer, correspondent, traveling salesman, advertising manager, and treasurer. This responsibility marked the beginning of his life as an inventor and industrialist and led to the establishment of many factories throughout the world and to the development of new production methods. Accidents in factories and in the handling of nitroglycerin made Nobel aware of the danger of fluid nitroglycerin. After a long period of experimentation, in 1867 he patented dynamite in Sweden, England, and the United States. It was an easily handled, solid, and ductile explosive that consisted of nitroglycerin absorbed by kieselguhr, a very porous diatomite. The invention aroused great interest among users of explosives. Nitroglycerin, the fundamental discovery of Sobrero (1847), had been transformed into a useful explosive. A worldwide industry was built up by Alfred Nobel himself.

Guhr dynamite, as it was known, had certain technical weaknesses. Continuing his research, Nobel in 1875 created blasting gelatin, a colloidal solution of nitrocellulose (guncotton) in nitroglycerin which in many respects proved to be an ideal explosive. Its force was somewhat greater than that of pure nitroglycerin, it was less sensitive to shock, and it was strongly resistant to moisture and water. It was called Nobel's Extra Dynamite, Express Dynamite, Blasting Gelatin,

Saxonite, and Gelignite. As early as 1875 it was put into production in most of Nobel's dynamite factories.

The problem of improving blasting powder had quite early occupied the Nobels. In 1879 Alfred Nobel was working on less smoky military explosive charges for artillery missiles, torpedoes, and ammunition. In 1887 he produced a nearly smokeless blasting powder —Ballistite, or Nobel's blasting powder—a mixture of nitroglycerin and nitrocellulose plus 10 percent camphor, which upon ignition burned with almost mathematical precision in concentric layers.

Nobel's last discovery in the realm of explosives was progressive smokeless powder (Swedish primary patent no. 7552, in 1896). A further product of Ballistite for special purposes, it was developed in his laboratory at San Remo during the last years of his life.

Nobel's interests as an inventor were by no means confined to explosives; his later work covered electrochemistry, optics, biology, and physiology. The list of his patents runs to no fewer than 355 in different countries. His pioneer work helped later inventors solve many problems in the manufacture of artificial rubber, leather, and silk, of semiprecious and precious stones from fused alumina, and of other products.

Through his skill as an industrialist and his fundamental patents on explosives, Nobel became a multimillionaire. By his last will and testament, dated Paris, 27 November 1895, he left his total fortune, over 33 million Swedish crowns (over two million pounds sterling), to a foundation that would award prizes "to those who, during the preceding year, shall have conferred the greatest benefit on mankind." The prize-awarding institutions are the Royal Swedish Academy of Science (physics, chemistry), the Royal Caroline Medical Institute (medicine, physiology), the Swedish Academy (literature), and a committee of the Norwegian Parliament (peace). The prize for economic sciences is a separate entity established by the Swedish Riksbank.

BIBLIOGRAPHY

Nobel's only writing is *On Modern Blasting Agents* (Glasgow, 1875).

The three main biographies are *Alfred Nobel och hans släkt* (Stockholm, 1926); E. Bergengren, *Alfred Nobel, the Man and His Work* (London–New York, 1962), with a supp. on the Nobel Institutions and the Nobel prizes by N. K. Ståhle; and H. Schück and R. Sohlman, *The Life of Alfred Nobel* (London, 1929).

Other works to be consulted are *The Book of High Explosives* (Birmingham, 1908); A. P. Gelder and H. Schlatter, *History of the Explosives Industry in America* (New York, 1927); *The History of Nobel's Explosives Co. Ltd. and Nobel Industries Ltd. 1871–1926*, which is vol. I of *Imperial Chemical Industries Ltd. and Its Founding Companies* (Birmingham, 1938); F. D. Miles, *A History of Research in the Nobel Division of ICI* (Birmingham, 1955); R. Moe, *Le Prix Nobel de la paix et l'Institut Nobel norvégien* (Oslo, 1932); H. de Mosenthal, "The Inventor of Dynamite," in *Nineteenth Century*, no. 260 (Oct. 1898), 567–581; H. Schück *et al.*, *Nobel, the Man and His Prizes* (Amsterdam, 1962), a discussion of the role of the Nobel prizes in the development of the prize fields during the first sixty years by eminent representatives of the five prize sections, with a biographical sketch of Nobel by H. Schück and a sketch of Nobel and the Nobel Foundation by R. Sohlman; and B. von Suttner, *Memoirs* (Stuttgart–Leipzig, 1909).

TORSTEN ALTHIN

NOBERT, FRIEDRICH ADOLPH (*b.* Barth, Pomerania [now German Democratic Republic], 17 January 1806; *d.* Barth, 21 February 1881), *clockmaking, optical instruments.*

Nobert was the elder son of Johann Friedrich Nobert, a clockmaker. After a scanty education he took up his father's occupation. In 1827, at a Berlin trade exhibition, Nobert entered a pocket chronometer that was commended and brought him to the attention of the astronomer Johann Encke. To check the going of his timepieces Nobert constructed a telescope and, with Encke's encouragement, made a number of astronomical measurements. In the spring of 1833, realizing that his ambitions would never be achieved without further education, he applied for a scholarship to study at the Technical Institute at Charlottenburg in Berlin. During the academic year 1833–1834 Nobert learned dividing methods and made a circle-dividing engine. This was most probably the machine with which he later ruled diffraction gratings, test objects, and micrometers; marked out scales for optical instruments; and cut chronometer gears. In 1835 Nobert was appointed *Universitätsmechaniker* at the University of Greifswald. During the 1840's he began to develop the fine ruling techniques that brought him some measure of fame. Not long after his father's death in 1846 Nobert returned to the family house in Barth, where he remained, working alone, until his death.

The key to Nobert's production of scientific instruments is his use of the circle-dividing engine. The art of dividing straight lines, arcs, and circles into various numbers of equal parts is the most important and difficult aspect of the work of the mathematical instrument maker. At the end of a paper on improvements in dividing the circle (1845), Nobert described his newly discovered technique for using the dividing engine in ruling parallel lines on glass that was to be used in micrometers by microscopists. In 1846 he described an extension of the technique to the production of a resolution test plate for the microscope. At this time the optical microscope was undergoing rapid improvements in the design of the objective lens systems, and a standard physical test was needed for judging improvements in resolution. Nobert's first test plate consisted of ten bands, each comprising a number of lines a definite distance apart, the first and tenth bands being ruled to a spacing of 2.25 and 0.56 microns respectively. Whenever the finest band on one of the test plates had been resolved by improved objectives, Nobert made another plate containing even finer bands; in all he made a series of seven different test plates between 1845 and 1873. The last plate in the series contained bands ruled to a spacing of 0.11 micron, well below the resolution limit of the optical microscope. Plates of this type were sold in London in 1880 for £15 apiece.

Nobert used his circle-dividing engine to produce rulings on glass for other purposes. The most important of these were the diffraction gratings made for V. S. M. van der Willigen in Haarlem and Ångström in Uppsala. For his celebrated measurements of the wavelengths of the elements in the spectrum of the sun, Ångström used four gratings made by Nobert. Other devices made by ruling were a micrometer for the astronomical telescope and a "spectrum plate" designed to prove that the velocity of light is greater in air than in glass. Nobert also made compound microscopes and objective lenses.

BIBLIOGRAPHY

I. ORIGINAL WORKS. Nobert's writings include "Ueber Kreistheilung im Allegemeinen und über einige, bei einer Kreistheilmaschine angewendete, verfahren zur Erzielung einer grossen Vollkommenheit der Theilung derselben," in *Verhandlungen des Vereins zur Beförderung des Gewerbfleisses in Preussen* (1845), 202–212; "Ueber die Prüfung und Vollkommenheit unserer jetzigen Mikroskope," in *Annalen der Physik und Chemie*, **67** (1846), 173–185; "Ueber Glas-Skalen von Herren Universitäts-Mechanicus Nobert in Greifswalde," in *Ergänzungs-Heft zu den Astronomischen Nachrichten* (Altona, 1849), cols. 93–96; "Ueber eine Glasplatte mit Theilungen zur Bestimmung der Wellenlänge und relativen Geschwindigkeit des Lichts in der Luft und im Glase," in *Annalen der Physik und Chemie*, **85** (1852), 83–92; "Ein Ocularmikrometer mit leuchtenden farbigen Linien im dunkel Gesichtsfelde," *ibid.*, 93–97; "Die höchste Leistung des heutigen Mikroskops, und seine Prüfung durch künstliche und natürliche Objekte," in *Mittheilungen aus dem naturwissenschaftlichen Vereine von Neu-Vorpommern und Rügen in Greifswald*, **13** (1882), 92–105. For a list of papers on astronomical observations and other matters see the Royal Society's *Catalogue of Scientific Papers*, IV, 628.

Some letters from Nobert to Ernst Abbe, as well as two microscopes made by Nobert, are in the optical museum of VEB Carl Zeiss, Jena, German Democratic Republic. Nobert's circle-dividing engine is preserved in the Smithsonian Institution, Washington, D.C.

II. SECONDARY LITERATURE. See W. Rollman, "Friedrich Adolph Nobert," in *Mittheilungen aus dem naturwissenschaftlichen Vereine von Neu-Vorpommern und Rügen in Greifswald*, **15** (1884), 38–58; G. L'E. Turner, "The Microscope as a Technical Frontier in Science," in *Historical Aspects of Microscopy*, S. Bradbury and G. L'E. Turner, eds. (Cambridge, 1967), 175–199; "The Contributions to Science of Friedrich Adolph Nobert," in *Bulletin of the Institute of Physics and the Physical Society*, **18** (1967), 338–348; and "F. A. Nobert's Invention of Artificial Resolution Tests for the Optical Microscope," in *Actes du XIᵉ Congrès international d'histoire des sciences*, III (Warsaw, 1968), 435–440; and G. L'E. Turner and S. Bradbury, "An Electron Microscopical Examination of Nobert's Finest Test-Plate of Twenty Bands," in *Journal of the Royal Microscopical Society*, **85** (1966), 435–447.

G. L'E. TURNER

NOBILI, LEOPOLDO (*b*. Trassilico, Italy, 1784; *d*. Florence, Italy, 5 August 1835), *physics*.

Although Nobili received a university training, he did not immediately become a physicist. He passed the first years of his adult life as an artillery captain in Modena and Brescia. He resigned from the military to become a professor of physics at Florence, where he conducted most of his experimental and theoretical work.

Nobili was primarily interested in the electrical current. His education in the school of Ampère had taught him to view currents as phenomena that could be analyzed by supposing the existence of a central, action-at-a-distance force between their parts. Ampère had never given a precise definition of what the current was or how it was connected with the electrical fluid of Coulomb and Poisson. This imprecision troubled Nobili, and his earliest papers attempted to clarify the nature of electrical currents (1, 2).

Nobili was impressed by the existence of what seemed to be two distinct types of electrical current. Those currents that occur whenever there is a temperature gradient across a conductor he termed "thermoelectric currents." The currents that are generated in processes involving wet conductors, as in a Voltaic apparatus, he called "hydroelectric currents." Although both currents exerted forces on magnets and on other current-bearing conductors in the same manner, in accordance with Ampère's law, Ampère gave no explanation of how currents originating in two seemingly distinct fashions could produce the same range of effects. Nobili resolved this dichotomy by deciding that there was actually only one type of current: thermoelectric. He believed that the currents produced with wet conductors did not result from direct chemical action, as Volta's followers thought, but were created by the heat generated in the chemical action.

Once Nobili became convinced that all currents resulted from the release of heat, he thought that the conjunction of heat flux and electrical current was more than coincidental; he concluded that the current is a flow of heat or caloric. Nobili firmly believed in his identification of caloric flow as electrical current, and it was this belief that led him to oppose the contemporary theory of the Voltaic decomposition of water (3).

By the 1820's and 1830's Volta's successors thought that Voltaic decomposition of water depended on the generation of electromotive force produced by the contact of dissimilar metals. If a strip of zinc is joined end to end to a strip of copper, and the ends of the compound strip are placed in a vessel of water (see Figure 1), then the water is decomposed into oxygen and hydrogen, and the zinc is oxidized. Volta's group held that there were two successive processes involved here. First the contact of the zinc and the copper produced a potential difference between the zinc and copper terminals of the compound strip. Since the strip was not closed, the electrical potential could not be neutralized. A state of electrostatic tension thus resulted between the ends of the strip, in which the zinc became positively electrified and the copper became negatively electrified. Since water is composed of two elements, one of which bears negative electrical fluid (oxygen) and the other positive fluid (hydrogen),

the water particles will line up between the submerged ends of the copper-zinc strip.

This configuration produces a constant stress on the water particles and induces some of them to dissociate into electronegative and electropositive components. This dissociation initiates the second stage, in which the dissociated components are attracted to the electrified zinc and copper terminals where they are held, thereby neutralizing the potential for electrical contact which occurred when the zinc and copper were joined. It is this neutralization, a quasi-static relaxation of tension in the copper-zinc strip, that is the electrical current conceptualized by Volta's disciples.

The Voltaic explanation was rejected by Nobili and indeed by every follower of Ampère. They believed that the forces of currents were unrelated to the forces of statical electricity; the Ampèrean forces pertained uniquely to the electrical current that was thought of as an entity distinct from the statical fluid of Coulomb. Nobili believed, furthermore, that the current was a flow of caloric, not a relaxation of statical tension; and he felt called upon to explain Voltaic decomposition in Ampèrean terms. He began by criticizing the Voltaic schema.

He reasoned that the current in the strip, according to Volta, occurred as a result of the neutralizing process of oxidation; it should therefore follow, and not precede, the commencement of oxidation. But in fact the current preceded oxidation. Nobili reasoned that when the ends of the copper-zinc strip were submerged in water, a true electrical current or caloric flow was immediately engendered between the submerged ends. As Ampère had shown, the adjacent parts of any electrical current repel one another; that is why, for example, a closed conducting loop bearing a current tends to expand. Nobili suspected that this principle was operative in the Voltaic apparatus. He thought that the current, while attempting to increase in length because of the self-repulsion of its parts, exerted a powerful force at the zinc and copper terminals between which it occurs. It was this force that wrenched the water particles apart. Nobili thus concluded that the generation of current by Voltaic means was not due to the release of statical electricity by electrochemical decomposition; rather, the release was itself the result of the presence of an electrical current.

Nobili's explanation of the Voltaic apparatus was influential in eliminating the assumption of any direct connection between statical electricity and the electrical current. His conclusion was also essential to the ultimate acceptance of Maxwellian electrodynamics and, more significantly on the Continent, to the

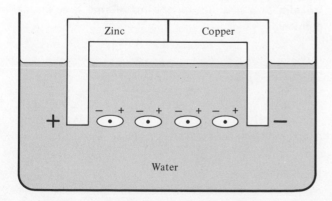

FIGURE 1

ability of Weber and his group to concentrate their attention on the electrical forces necessary to explain the phenomena discovered by Faraday.

BIBLIOGRAPHY

Works by Nobili referred to above are:

1. "Sur une nouvelle classe de phénomènes électrochimiques," in *Annales de chimie*, **34** (1827), 280–297.

2. "Sur la nature des courans électriques," in *Bibliothèque universelle*, **37** (1828), 118–144, 180–184.

3. "De la distribution et des effets des courans électriques dans les masses conductrices," *ibid.*, **49** (1835), 263–281, 416–436.

JED Z. BUCHWALD

NODDACK, WALTER (*b*. Berlin, Germany, 17 August 1893; *d*. Bamberg, West Germany, 7 December 1960), *chemistry*.

Noddack attended the secondary school in his native city and then entered the University of Berlin in 1912 to study chemistry, physics, and mathematics. World War I interrupted his studies and he therefore did not receive his doctorate until 1920. His dissertation, completed under the direction of W. Nernst, examined Einstein's law of photochemical equivalence. Noddack then worked for two years with Nernst at the Physical Chemistry Institute of the University of Berlin, and in 1922 he became director of the chemical laboratory of the Physikalisch-Technische Reichsanstalt under Nernst.

In 1927 Noddack became director at the newly founded Photochemistry Laboratory in Berlin, but he subsequently accepted an offer from the University of Freiburg to become chairman of the department of physical chemistry (1935). In 1941 he became director of both the physical chemistry department and the Research Institute for Photochemistry at the University of Strasbourg. Following World War II, Noddack offered his services to the Philosophisch-Theologische Hochschule in Bamberg, where instruction in chemistry was being introduced. From 1956 to 1960 he directed the newly established research institute for geochemistry in Bamberg.

Noddack's principal achievement was the discovery of element seventy-five of the periodic table, which he called rhenium (after the Rhine). He conducted this research in Berlin with his co-worker, Ida Tacke, whom he married in 1926. (Their joint research continued until his death.) They discovered rhenium

by X-ray spectroscopy in columbite that had been systematically enriched (*Naturwissenschaften*, **13** [1925], 567). O. Berg also assisted in the discovery. Although they succeeded in obtaining two milligrams of rhenium from various ores, it was not until 1926, when they produced the first gram of rhenium, that they were able to examine the chemical properties of the new element.

Simultaneously with this discovery, the Noddacks claimed that they had discovered a second new element, element forty-three of the periodic table, which they named masurium. This element was discussed for years in the literature until E. Segrè and C. Perrie discovered that it could be produced only artificially; they named the element technetium.

In the field of geochemistry Noddack studied the abundance of individual elements in the crust of the earth and in the universe. This research was based on the evaluation of 1,600 mineral assays. Noddack believed that every element was present in every mineral, but could not be detected in its existing concentrations with the analytic methods then available. He thought that for each element there was a threshold concentration, beyond which the element could be recognized in all minerals; he named this *Allgegenwartskonzentration* ("omnipresent concentration") and calculated it for various elements. Noddack also took considerable interest in theoretical and practical questions concerning the rare earths and their separation.

Noddack's second major field of research was photochemistry. In 1920 he found, on a photographic plate, that under suitable conditions an absorbed quantum $h\nu$ of blue or ultraviolet radiation corresponds to a silver atom. He then investigated the photographic quantum sensitivity of X and α radiation. In his studies on photographic sensitizing Noddack gave particular attention to the physical properties of the sensitizing coloring substances, and his treatment of photochemical problems in the human eye led him to a new demonstration of the three visual pigments.

BIBLIOGRAPHY

I. ORIGINAL WORKS. Noddack and his wife published approximately 100 papers in various periodicals. Their major work is *Das Rhenium* (Leipzig, 1933).

II. SECONDARY LITERATURE. H. Meier and E. Ruda, "Zum Tode von Walter Noddack," in *Zeitschrift für Chemie*, **2** (1962), 33; and O. Bayer *et al.*, "Walter Noddack," in *Chemische Berichte*, **96** (1963), xxvii.

FERENC SZABADVÁRY

NOEL, ÉTIENNE (*b*. Bassigny, Haute-Marne, France, 29 September 1581; *d*. La Flèche, France, 16 October 1659), *physics*.

Noel entered the Society of Jesus in 1599. He taught in several colleges, although principally at La Flèche, where he was *répétiteur* of philosophy when the young Descartes was studying there prior to 1612; he later became rector of the college. He served as vice-provincial of the Society in 1645–1646. At the end of 1646, when he became rector of the Collège de Clermont in Paris, Noel sent to Descartes his first two published works: *Aphorismi physici* (1646) and *Sol flamma* (1646). The double perspective that characterized all of Noel's later work is already present: adherence to Aristotelian physics and receptiveness to new ideas.

Well disposed towards Descartes, Noel had several disputes with Pascal, a more radically modern physicist than Descartes. In 1646 Pascal took part in the first performance of Torricelli's experiment in France. It raised a problem: what remained above the mercury? The traditional philosophers, opposed to the existence of a vacuum, suggested that it was either air or vapors of mercury, while Descartes, also a partisan of the Aristotelian universe, proposed the idea of a subtle matter. When Pascal published *Expériences nouvelles touchant le vide* (1647), in which he disputed the Aristotelian concept of a full universe, Noel sent the young scientist a letter containing his objections. He asserted, in particular, that the upper portion of Torricelli's barometer was not empty, but was filled with a refined air that had entered through the pores in the glass—a notion similar to Descartes's. Pascal's reply was a lesson in method, which exposed the lack of rigor in Noel's principles and arguments. Noel made a few concessions, but refused to admit the existence of a vacuum. He attacked this idea in a work with the baroque title *Le plein du vide* (1648), which provoked new criticisms from Pascal in *Lettre à Le Pailleur*.

Noel remained unembittered toward Pascal and the following summer, in *Gravitas comparata*, honored Pascal for his role in developing an experiment to produce a vacuum within a vacuum. Noel left Paris a short time later and returned to La Flèche, where he published several further works of minor importance.

BIBLIOGRAPHY

A bibliography of Noel's writings is given in Sommervogel, ed., *Bibliothèque de la Compagnie de Jésus*, V (Brussels–Paris, 1894), cols. 1789–1790. The Noel–Descartes correspondence is found in Descartes's *Oeuvres de Descartes*, C. Adam and P. Tannery, eds., IV (Paris, 1901), 498, 567, 584–586; V (1903), 101, 117–118, 119–120, 549–552; XII (1910), 556; and Descartes's *Correspondance*, C. Adam and G. Milhaud, eds., I (Paris, 1936), 374–375; II (1939), 29–30; VII (1960), 171, 221, 238–240, 411; VIII (1963), 7.

For a discussion of Noel or his work see *Oeuvres de Descartes*, C. Adam and P. Tannery, eds., I (Paris, 1897), 382–384, 454–456; Dupont-Ferrier, *Du collège de Clermont au lycée Louis-le-Grand*, III (Paris, 1925), 7; Pascal, *Oeuvres*, Brunschvicg and Boutroux, eds., II (Paris, 1908), 77–125, 158, 174–214, 253–282, 291–294, and *Oeuvres complètes*, J. Mesnard, ed., II (Paris, 1971), 509–540, 556–576, 584–602, 633–639; C. de Waard, *L'expérience barométrique, ses antécédents et ses applications* (Thouars, 1936); and J. Lewis, "Pascal's Physical Science," unpub. diss. (Princeton, 1968).

JEAN MESNARD

NOETHER, AMALIE EMMY (*b*. Erlangen, Germany, 23 March 1882; *d*. Bryn Mawr, Pennsylvania, 14 April 1935), *mathematics*.

Emmy Noether, generally considered the greatest of all female mathematicians up to her time, was the eldest child of Max Noether, research mathematician and professor at the University of Erlangen, and Ida Amalia Kaufmann. Two of Emmy's three brothers were also scientists. Alfred, her junior by a year, earned a doctorate in chemistry at Erlangen. Fritz, two and a half years younger, became a distinguished physicist; and his son, Gottfried, became a mathematician.

At first Emmy Noether had planned to be a teacher of English and French. From 1900 to 1902 she studied mathematics and foreign languages at Erlangen, then in 1903 she started her specialization in mathematics at the University of Göttingen. At both universities she was a nonmatriculated auditor at lectures, since at the turn of the century girls could not be admitted as regular students. In 1904 she was permitted to matriculate at the University of Erlangen, which granted her the Ph.D., *summa cum laude,* in 1907. Her sponsor, the algebraist Gordan, strongly influenced her doctoral dissertation on algebraic invariants. Her divergence from Gordan's viewpoint and her progress in the direction of the "new" algebra first began when she was exposed to the ideas of Ernst Fischer, who came to Erlangen in 1911.

In 1915 Hilbert invited Emmy Noether to Göttingen. There she lectured at courses that were given under his name and applied her profound invariant-theoretic knowledge to the resolution of problems which he and Felix Klein were considering. In this connection she was able to provide an elegant pure mathematical formulation for several concepts of Einstein's general theory of relativity. Hilbert repeatedly tried to obtain her appointment as *Privatdozent*, but the strong prejudice against women prevented her "habilitation" until 1919. In 1922 she was named a *nichtbeamteter ausserordentlicher Professor* ("unofficial associate professor"), a purely honorary position. Subsequently, a modest salary was provided through a *Lehrauftrag* ("teaching appointment") in algebra. Thus she taught at Göttingen (1922–1933), interrupted only by visiting professorships at Moscow (1928–1929) and at Frankfurt (summer of 1930).

In April 1933 she and other Jewish professors at Göttingen were summarily dismissed. In 1934 Nazi political pressures caused her brother Fritz to resign from his position at Breslau and to take up duties at the research institute in Tomsk, Siberia. Through the efforts of Hermann Weyl, Emmy Noether was offered a visiting professorship at Bryn Mawr College; she departed for the United States in October 1933. Thereafter she lectured and did research at Bryn Mawr and at the Institute for Advanced Study, Princeton, but those activities were cut short by her sudden death from complications following surgery.

Emmy Noether's most important contributions to mathematics were in the area of abstract algebra, which is completely different from the early algebra of equation solving in that it studies not so much the results of algebraic operations (addition, multiplication, etc.) but rather their formal properties, such as associativity, commutativity, distributivity; and it investigates the generalized systems that arise if one or more of these properties is not assumed. Thus, in classical algebra it is postulated that the rational, the real, or the complex numbers should constitute a "field" with respect to addition and multiplication, operations assumed to be associative and commutative, the latter being distributive with respect to the former. One of the traditional postulates, namely the commutative law of multiplication, was relinquished in the earliest example of a generalized algebraic structure (William Rowan Hamilton's "quaternion algebra" of 1843) and also in many of the 1844 Grassmann algebras. The entities in such systems and in some of the research of Emmy Noether after 1927 are still termed numbers, albeit hypercomplex numbers. In further generalization the elements of an algebraic system are abstractions that are not necessarily capable of interpretation as numbers, and the binary operations are not literally addition and multiplication, but merely laws of composition that have properties akin to the traditional operations.

If Hamilton and Grassmann inspired Emmy Noether's later work, it was Dedekind who influenced the abstract axiomatic "theory of ideals" which

Noether developed from 1920 to 1926. The Dedekind ideals—which are not numbers but sets of numbers—were devised in order to reinstate the Euclidean theorem on unique decomposition into prime factors, a law which breaks down in algebraic number fields. Two of the generalized structures which Noether related to the ideals are the "group" and the "ring."

A group is more general than a field because it involves only a single operation (either an "addition" or a "multiplication") which need not be commutative. It is, then, a system $\{S, \bigcirc\}$ where S is a set of elements, $\bigcirc$ is a closed associative binary operation, and S contains a unit element or identity as well as a unique inverse for every element. A ring is a system $\{S, \oplus, \otimes\}$ which is a commutative group with respect to $\oplus$, an "addition," and which is closed under a "multiplication," that is, a second binary associative operation $\otimes$, which is distributive with respect to the first operation. Finally, a subset of a ring with a commutative multiplication $\otimes$ is called an "ideal" if it is a subgroup of the additive group of the ring—for this it is sufficient that the difference of any two elements of the subset belong to that set—and if it contains all products of subset elements by arbitrary elements of the ring. In a ring with a noncommutative multiplication, there are left ideals and right ideals.

Emmy Noether showed that the ascending chain condition is important for ideal theory. A ring satisfies that condition if every sequence of ideals C_1, C_2, C_3, $\cdots$, in the ring—such that each ideal is a proper part of its successor—has only a finite number of terms. Noether demonstrated that for a commutative ring with a unit element the requirement is equivalent to each of two other requirements: namely, that every ideal in the ring have a finite basis, that is, that the ideal consist of the set of all elements

$$x_1 a_1 + x_2 a_2 + \cdots + x_n a_n,$$

where the a_i are fixed elements of the ring and the x_i are any elements whatsoever in the ring, and that, given any nonempty set of ideals in the ring, there be at least one ideal which is "maximal" in that set.

Having formulated the concept of primary ideals—a generalization of Dedekind's prime ideals—Noether used the ascending chain condition in order to prove that an ideal in a commutative ring can be represented as the intersection of primary ideals. Then she studied the necessary and sufficient conditions for such an ideal to be the product of "prime power ideals." A somewhat different aspect of ideal theory was her use of polynomial ideals to rigorize, generalize, and give modern pure mathematical form to the concepts and methods of algebraic geometry as they had first been developed by her father and subsequently by the Italian school of geometers.

In another area Emmy Noether investigated the noncommutative rings in linear algebras like the Hamilton and Grassmann systems. An "algebra" is a ring in which the two binary operations are supplemented by a unary operation, an external or scalar multiplication, that is, a multiplication by the elements (scalars) of a specified field. From 1927 to 1929 Emmy Noether contributed notably to the theory of representations, the object of which is to provide realizations of noncommutative rings (or algebras) by means of matrices or linear transformations in such a way that all relations which involve the ring addition and/or multiplication are preserved; in other words, to study the homomorphisms of a given ring into a ring of matrices. From 1932 to 1934 she was able to probe profoundly into the structure of noncommutative algebras by means of her concept of the *verschränktes* ("cross") product. In a 1932 paper that was written jointly with Richard Brauer and Helmut Hasse, she proved that every "simple" algebra over an ordinary algebraic number field is cyclic; Weyl called this theorem "a high water mark in the history of algebra."

Emmy Noether wrote some forty-five research papers and was an inspiration to Max Deuring, Hans Fitting, W. Krull, Chiungtze Tsen, and Olga Taussky Todd, among others. The so-called Noether school included such algebraists as Hasse and W. Schmeidler, with whom she exchanged ideas and whom she converted to her own special point of view. She was particularly influential in the work of B. L. van der Waerden, who continued to promote her ideas after her death and to indicate the many concepts for which he was indebted to her.

BIBLIOGRAPHY

I. ORIGINAL WORKS. Among Emmy Noether's many papers are "Invarianten beliebiger Differentialausdrücke," in *Nachrichten von der Gesellschaft der Wissenschaften zu Göttingen* (1918), 37–44; "Moduln in nichtkommutativen Bereichen, insbesondere aus Differential- und Differenzenausdrücken," in *Mathematische Zeitschrift*, **8** (1920), 1–35, written with W. Schmeidler; "Idealtheorie in Ringbereichen," in *Mathematische Annalen*, **83** (1921), 24–66; "Abstrakter Aufbau der Idealtheorie in algebraischen Zahlund Funktionenkörpern," *ibid.*, **96** (1927), 26–61; "Über minimale Zerfällungskörper irreduzibler Darstellungen," in *Sitzungsberichte der Preussischen Akademie der Wissenschaften zu Berlin* (1927), 221–228, written with R. Brauer; "Hyperkomplexe Grössen und Darstellungstheorie," in *Mathematische Zeitschrift*, **30** (1929), 641–692;

"Beweis eines Hauptsatzes in der Theorie der Algebren," in *Journal für die reine und angewandte Mathematik*, **167** (1932), 399–404, written with R. Brauer and H. Hasse; and "Nichtkommutative Algebren," in *Mathematische Zeitschrift*, **37** (1933), 514–541.

II. SECONDARY LITERATURE. For further information about Noether and her work, see A. Dick, "Emmy Noether," in *Revue de mathématiques élémentaires*, supp. 13 (1970); C. H. Kimberling, "Emmy Noether," in *American Mathematical Monthly*, **79** (1972), 136–149; E. E. Kramer, *The Nature and Growth of Modern Mathematics* (New York, 1970), 656–672; B. L. van der Waerden, "Nachruf auf Emmy Noether," in *Mathematische Annalen*, **111** (1935), 469–476; and H. Weyl, "Emmy Noether," in *Scripta mathematica*, **3** (1935), 201–220.

EDNA E. KRAMER

NOETHER, MAX (*b.* Mannheim, Germany, 24 September 1844; *d.* Erlangen, Germany, 13 December 1921), *mathematics*.

Max Noether was the third of the five children of Hermann Noether and Amalia Würzburger. Noether's father was a wholesaler in the hardware business—a family tradition until 1937 when it was "Aryanized" by the Nazis. Max attended schools in Mannheim until an attack of polio at age fourteen made him unable to walk for two years and left him with a permanent handicap. Instruction at home enabled him to complete the Gymnasium curriculum; then, unassisted, he studied university-level mathematics.

After a brief period at the Mannheim observatory, he went to Heidelberg University in 1865. There he earned the doctorate in 1868 and served as *Privatdozent* (1870–1874) and as associate professor (*extraordinarius*) from 1874 to 1875. Then he became affiliated with Erlangen as associate professor until 1888, as full professor (*ordinarius*) from 1888 to 1919, and as professor emeritus thereafter. In 1880 he married Ida Amalia Kaufmann of Cologne. She died in 1915. Three of their four children became scientists, including Emmy Noether, the mathematician.

Noether was one of the guiding spirits of nineteenth-century algebraic geometry. That subject was motivated in part by problems that arose in Abel's and Riemann's treatment of algebraic functions and their integrals. The purely geometric origins are to be found in the work of Plücker, Cayley, and Clebsch, all of whom developed the theory of algebraic curves—their multiple points, bitangents, and inflections. Cremona also influenced Noether, who in turn inspired the great Italian geometers who followed him—Segre, Severi, Enriques, and Castelnuovo. In another direction Emmy Noether and her disciple B. L. van der Waerden made algebraic geometry rigorous and more general. Lefschetz, Weil, Zariski, and others later used topological and abstract algebraic concepts to provide further generalization.

In both the old and the new algebraic geometry, the central object of investigation is the algebraic variety, which, in n-dimensional space, is the set of all points $(x_1, x_2, \cdots, x_n)$ satisfying a finite set of polynomial equations,

$$f_i(x_1, x_2, \cdots, x_n) = 0, \quad i = 1, 2, \cdots, r$$

with $r \leqslant n$ and coefficients in the real (or complex) field or, in modern algebraic geometry, an arbitrary field. Thus, in the plane, the possible varieties are curves and finite sets of points; in space there are surfaces, curves, and finite point sets; for $n > 3$ there are hypersurfaces and their intersections.

Following Cremona, Noether studied the invariant properties of an algebraic variety subjected to birational transformations; that is, one-to-one rational transformations with rational inverses, those of lowest degree being the collineations or projective transformations. Next in order of degree come the quadratic transformations, for which Noether obtained a number of important theorems. For example, any irreducible plane algebraic curve with singularities can be transformed by a finite succession of standard quadratic transformations into a curve whose multiple points are all "ordinary" in the sense that the curve has multiple but distinct tangents at such points.

In 1873 Noether proved what came to be his most famous theorem: Given two algebraic curves

$$\Phi(x, y) = 0, \quad \Psi(x, y) = 0$$

which intersect in a finite number of isolated points, then the equation of an algebraic curve which passes through all those points of intersection can be expressed in the form $A\Phi + B\Psi = 0$ (where A and B are polynomials in x and y) if and only if certain conditions (today called "Noetherian conditions") are satisfied. If the intersections are nonsingular points of both curves, the desired form can readily be achieved. The essence of Noether's theorem, however, is that it provides necessary and sufficient conditions for the case where the curves have common multiple points with contact of any degree of complexity.

Although Noether asserted that his results could be extended to surfaces and hypersurfaces, it was not until 1903 that the Hungarian Julius König actually generalized the Noether theorem to n dimen-

sions by providing necessary and sufficient conditions for the

$$A_1 f_1 + A_2 f_2 + \cdots + A_n f_n = 0$$

form to be possible for the equation of the surface or hypersurface through the finite set of points of intersection of n surfaces ($n = 3$) or n hypersurfaces ($n > 3$),

$$f_1(x_1, x_2, \cdots, x_n) = 0, \cdots, f_n(x_1, x_2, \cdots, x_n) = 0.$$

Noether himself derived a theorem that gives conditions for the equation of a surface passing through the curve of intersection of the surfaces $\Phi(x, y, z) = 0$ and $\Psi(x, y, z) = 0$ to have the form $A\Phi + B\Psi = 0$. Generalization turned out to be complicated and difficult, but Emanuel Lasker, the chess champion, saw that the issue could be simplified by the use of the theory of polynomial ideals which he and Emmy Noether had developed. Thus he was able to derive Noetherian conditions for the

$$A_1 f_1 + \cdots + A_r f_r = 0$$

form to be possible for a hypersurface through the intersection of

$$f_1(x_1, x_2, \cdots, x_n) = 0, \cdots, f_r(x_1, x_2, \cdots, x_n) = 0$$

with $n > 3$, $r < n$, in which case the intersection will, in general, be a curve or a surface or a hypersurface.

The Noether, König, and Lasker theorems all start with a set of polynomial equations that defines a variety the nature of which varies in the different propositions. The objective in every case is the same, namely to see under what conditions a polynomial that vanishes at all points of the given variety can be expressed as a linear combination of the polynomials originally given. Since those polynomials play a basic role, it is especially significant that the representation of a variety as the intersection of other varieties, that is, by a set of polynomial equations, is not unique. Thus a circle in space might be described as the intersection of two spheres, or as the intersection of a cylinder and a plane, or as the intersection of a cone and a plane, and so forth. Hence, in general, the only impartial way to represent a given variety

$$f_i(x_1, x_2, \cdots, x_n) = 0, \quad i = 1, 2, \cdots, r$$

where $r \leqslant n$ and the f_i are polynomials with real or complex coefficients, is not by this one system of equations, but rather in terms of all polynomial equations which points on the variety satisfy. Now if $f(x_1, x_2, \cdots, x_n)$ and $g(x_1, x_2, \cdots, x_n)$ are any two polynomials that vanish at all points of the given variety, then the difference of the polynomials also vanishes at those points, as does the product of either polynomial by an arbitrary polynomial, $A(x_1, x_2, \cdots, x_n)$. By the definition of an ideal, these two facts are sufficient for the set of all polynomials that vanish at every point of the variety to be a polynomial ideal in the ring of polynomials with real (complex) coefficients, and it is that ideal which is considered to represent the variety. The linear combinations $A_1f_1 + A_2f_2 + \cdots + A_rf_r$ obviously vanish at all points of the given variety and hence belong to the representative polynomial ideal. These are the linear combinations that were the subject of the special criteria developed in the Noether, König, and Lasker theorems. Other important results related to the representative polynomial ideal are contained in a famous proposition of Hilbert, namely his basis theorem.

BIBLIOGRAPHY

I. ORIGINAL WORKS. Noether's most important papers include "Zur Theorie des eindeutigen Entsprechens algebraischer Gebilde von beliebig vielen Dimensionen," in *Mathematische Annalen*, **2** (1870), 293–316; "Über einen Satz aus der Theorie der algebraischen Functionen," *ibid.*, **6** (1873), 351–359; "Über die algebraische Functionen und ihre Anwendung in der Geometrie," *ibid.*, **7** (1874), 269–310, written with A. W. von Brill; and "Die Entwicklung der Theorie der algebraischen Functionen in älterer und neurer Zeit," in *Jahresbericht der Deutschen Mathematiker-vereinigung*, **3** (1894), 107–566, written with A. W. von Brill.

II. SECONDARY LITERATURE. On Noether and his work, see A. W. von Brill, "Max Noether," in *Jahresbericht der Deutschen Mathematiker-vereinigung*, **32** (1923), 211–233; A. Dick, "Emmy Noether," in *Revue de mathématiques élémentaires*, supp. 13 (1970), 4–8, 19, 53–56, 67–68; W. Fulton, *Algebraic Curves, an Introduction to Algebraic Geometry* (New York–Amsterdam, 1969), 119–129; J. König, *Einleitung in die Allgemeine Theorie der Algebraischen Grössen* (Leipzig, 1903), 385–398; E. Lasker, "Zur Theorie der Moduln und Ideale," in *Mathematische Annalen*, **60** (1905), 44–46, 51–54; F. S. Macaulay, "Max Noether," in *Proceedings of the London Mathematical Society*, 2nd ser., **21** (1920–1923), 37–42; and C. A. Scott, "A Proof of Noether's Fundamental Theorem," in *Mathematische Annalen*, **52** (1899), 593–597.

See also J. G. Semple and L. Roth, *Introduction to Algebraic Geometry* (Oxford, 1949), 94–99, 391; R. J. Walker, *Algebraic Curves* (Princeton, 1950), 120–124; H. Wieleitner, *Algebraische Kurven*, II (Berlin–Leipzig, 1919), 18–20, 45, 88; and the editors of *Mathematische Annalen*, "Max Noether," in *Mathematische Annalen*, **85** (1922), i–iii.

EDNA E. KRAMER

NOGUCHI, (SEISAKU) HIDEYO (*b.* Sanjogata, Okinashima-mura, Fukushima, Honshu, Japan, 24 November 1876; *d.* Accra, Gold Coast, 21 May 1928), *microbiology.*

Despite humble origins and a physical handicap, Noguchi attained extraordinary fame during his lifetime. He discovered *Treponema pallidum* in the brain of general paralytics, and he proved that either Oroya fever or verruga peruana might be produced by *Bartonella bacilliformis*. But his technique and conclusions were often faulty, and his work on *Leptospira icteroides* as the causal agent of yellow fever was gravely misleading.

Noguchi was the second child and only son of Sayosuke, a thriftless peasant, and his illiterate but industrious wife, Shika; he was given the name Seisaku. As an infant he was burned by an indoor brazier, and his left hand was seriously injured. After rapid elementary schooling, he attended secondary school at Inawashiro, a distance of three miles from his home, and graduated with honors at age seventeen. While working as dispenser to a local surgeon (who restored partial function to his crippled hand) and as janitor at a dental college, he studied medicine from borrowed books. Helped financially by friends, he briefly attended a proprietary medical school in Tokyo, receiving his practitioner's diploma in 1897.

Various temporary appointments then followed, including an assistantship at S. Kitasato's Institute for Infectious Diseases, where advancement was slow. Noguchi then replaced the name Seisaku by Hideyo ("to excel in the world"). When Simon Flexner visited the Institute in 1899, leading a medical commission from the Johns Hopkins University, Noguchi expressed a desire to study pathology and bacteriology in the United States. Flexner cautiously endorsed the wish. In December 1900, having borrowed passage money, Noguchi arrived unannounced and penniless at the University of Pennsylvania, where Flexner had become professor of pathology. With Weir Mitchell's modest support, Noguchi began snake venom investigations under Flexner's tutelage.

Noguchi amassed data for a dozen papers, and grants were forthcoming. In 1903 the Carnegie Institution appointed Noguchi research assistant and awarded him a one-year fellowship at the Statens Seruminstitut, Copenhagen. He was befriended by Thorvald Madsen, who stressed quantitative accuracy and physicochemical concepts in their immunologic studies, mainly of venoms and potent antivenins. Late in 1904 Noguchi began an assistantship at the Rockefeller Institute for Medical Research, inaugurated under Flexner's direction. He and Flexner were the first scientists in America to confirm F. Schaudinn's discovery of *Spirochaeta pallida* (1905). Following A. Wassermann's publication of his complement-fixation test (1906), Noguchi became preoccupied with problems of syphilis and produced twenty papers and a book on serodiagnostic methods. Between 1909 and 1913 he cultured *Sp. pallida* and various other spirochetes in artificial media, described specific cutaneous reactions in latent and tertiary syphilitics after intradermal injection of emulsified spirochetes ("luetin"), and detected *Sp. pallida* in the brain of paretics—the sole enduring accomplishment of this prolific period. He also reported on cultivable bodies as probable causal agents of poliomyelitis, rabies, and trachoma. Late in 1913 his lecture-demonstrations were received triumphantly in European medical centers. His promotion to membership in the Institute ensued from these researches.

In 1915 Noguchi visited his ailing mother in Japan and received the Order of the Rising Sun and an Imperial Prize. He also learned of *Spirochaeta icterohaemorrhagiae*, recently identified by R. Inada and Y. Ido as the causative agent of hemorrhagic jaundice (Weil's disease). Noguchi made extensive studies of this microorganism, whose generic name he revised to *Leptospira*. Soon after reaching Guayaquil in 1918 with the Rockefeller Foundation yellow fever commission to Ecuador, he isolated an organism resembling *Leptospira icterohaemorrhagiae* from several allegedly classic cases of yellow fever. Convalescent patients' serums showed positive "Pfeiffer reactions" (specific bacteriolysis) with this organism, which he named *Leptospira icteroides*; outbreaks of the disease in Yucatan, Peru, and Brazil yielded similar evidence. Guinea pigs injected with *L. icteroides* developed lesions like those of yellow fever. Numerous reports from Noguchi implicating *L. icteroides* as the causative agent of yellow fever appeared between 1919 and 1922, in the *Journal of Experimental Medicine*, then under Flexner's editorship. Yellow fever prophylactic vaccine and therapeutic antiserum were prepared from this organism and distributed experimentally by the Rockefeller Institute until 1926. Noguchi's inconclusive experimental data had been superimposed on the fallacious presumptions that leptospiral jaundice and yellow fever were distinguishable by regional physicians and were caused by kindred agents. Criticism was silenced initially by overenthusiasm, but in 1924, at a Jamaican conference on tropical medicine, the leptospiral theory was disputed on various grounds. By then, yellow fever had practically vanished from the Western Hemisphere, and further tests therefore awaited transfer of the campaign to West Africa.

Noguchi had meanwhile solved the long-standing enigma concerning the relationship between Oroya fever (Carrión's disease) and verruga peruana. Using his special *Leptospira* medium, he isolated *Bartonella bacilliformis* (previously uncultivated) from an Oroya fever patient's blood, and also from verruga nodules. This microorganism, administered intravenously to macaques, provoked an acute febrile anemia, whereas intradermal inoculations caused local verruga formation. Thus the etiologic unity of these diseases was established. He simultaneously resumed enquiries into trachoma among Arizona Indians and isolated *Bacterium granulosis*, which induced progressive granular conjunctivitis when injected into the conjunctiva of monkeys and chimpanzees. Notwithstanding his stimulating monograph on trachoma (1928), this bacillus gained little credence.

In 1927 the leptospiral theory was finally discredited by careful reports that *L. icteroides* and *L. icterohaemorrhagiae* were indistinguishable, and by investigations sponsored by the Rockefeller Foundation International Health Board in Nigeria since late 1925. After negative bacteriologic findings in sixty-seven typical cases, a filterable virus was implicated, undetected by guinea pigs, but producing characteristic fatal lesions in rhesus monkeys. Convalescent human serums protected such animals, but *L. icteroides* vaccine and antiserum did not. In September 1927, before these results were published, the senior author, Adrian Stokes, died from yellow fever. Noguchi sailed for Africa in October. He established himself at Accra, Gold Coast, in the Medical Research Institute; the director, W. A. Young, collaborated closely with Noguchi. By frenzied, often solitary work, day and night, Noguchi apparently confirmed the viral findings, but also isolated a banal bacillus that he considered significant. When about to depart for New York, after six unhappy months, he fell ill and in nine days died of yellow fever. One week later, the same fate befell Young. A marble memorial to their joint research was erected in the Institute's compound at Accra. Noguchi's tomb, surmounted by natural rock, is in Woodlawn Cemetery, New York.

Speculation centered upon the manner of Noguchi's fatal infection. To some, increasing despondency and ill health suggested that he courted infection, fulfilling a youthful motto, "Success or suicide"; others, particularly in Japan, viewed his death as martyrdom, worthy of veneration. Noguchi's quick perceptivity and remarkable energy often permitted him to correct or amplify the more original discoveries of others. Unfortunately, he applied bacteriologic techniques to many viral diseases. In the laboratory he was deft and ingenious, but disorderly and extravagant; at Accra, for example, he accumulated over 500 monkeys. These qualities were magnified by his propensity for working alone upon multiple projects. His small stature, fine head, and oriental manners could be very appealing, despite his frequent unpredictability and moodiness. An unannounced, childless marriage to Mary Dardis in 1912 moderated a tempestuous life.

Noguchi's spoken English was difficult to follow, and his writings needed editing; but he understood many languages. Various universities conferred honorary doctorates, and several countries granted honors and decorations. He was awarded the John Scott Medal (1920) and the Kober Medal (1925). Noguchi's tragedy lay not in lack of recognition, but arose from insatiable ambition, reckless industry, and shrewd intelligence so overlaid with disarming modesty and charm that mentors and benefactors in Japan and America minimized his faults and overestimated his capabilities. He owed an incalculable debt to the Rockefeller Institute for Medical Research, which fostered his activities for a quarter-century. In its library stands a striking bronze bust of Noguchi done in his last year of life.

BIBLIOGRAPHY

I. ORIGINAL WORKS. A list of Noguchi's publications, comprising 186 titles, was prepared and bound with 81 collected reprints by the Rockefeller Institute for Medical Research (now the Rockefeller University). In 1935 some 20 sets of this bibliography were distributed to selected libraries in the United States, Japan, and Europe. The list has minor inaccuracies and omissions. Most of his writings are in English, but a few appear only in German, French, or Spanish. Many articles had multiple publication, sometimes in two or more foreign-language journals.

Noguchi's books are *Snake Venoms* (Washington, 1909); *Serum Diagnosis of Syphilis and the Butyric Acid Test for Syphilis* (Philadelphia, 1910; 2nd ed., 1911; 3rd ed., 1912); and *Laboratory Diagnosis of Syphilis* (New York, 1923). He also contributed chapters to various texts, of which the more noteworthy are "Snake Venoms," in W. Osler and T. McCrae, eds., *System of Medicine*, I (London, 1907), 247–265; "Serodiagnostic de la syphilis," in A. Gilbert and M. Weinberg, eds., *Traité du sang* (Paris, 1921); "Yellow Fever," in R. L. F. Cecil, ed., *Textbook of Medicine* (Philadelphia, 1927); and "The Spirochetes," in E. O. Jordan and I. S. Falk, eds., *The Newer Knowledge of Bacteriology and Immunology* (Chicago, 1928), 452–497.

His early contributions to the knowledge of snake venoms and antivenins and of hemolysins, include "Snake Venom in Relation to Haemolysis, Bacteriolysis, and Toxicity," in *Journal of Experimental Medicine*, 6 (1902), 277–301, and "On the Plurality of Cytolysins in Snake Venom," in *Journal of Pathology and Bacteriology*, 10 (1905), 111–124, both written with S. Flexner; "The

Photodynamic Action of Eosin and Erythrosin Upon Snake Venom," in *Journal of Experimental Medicine*, 8 (1906), 252–267; "The Influence of Temperature Upon the Rate of Reaction (Haemolysis, Agglutination, Precipitation)," *ibid.*, 337–364, written with T. Madsen and L. Walbum; and "Toxins and Antitoxins—Snake Venoms and Antivenins," *ibid.*, 9 (1907), 18–50, written with T. Madsen.

Among his reports on the serodiagnosis of syphilis are "The Relation of Protein, Lipoids and Salts to the Wassermann Reaction," *ibid.*, 11 (1909), 84–99; "A New and Simple Method for the Serum Diagnosis of Syphilis," *ibid.*, 392–401; "The Present Status of the Noguchi System of Serodiagnosis of Syphilis," in *Interstate Medical Journal*, 18 (1911), 11–25; "Biochemical Studies on So-called Syphilis Antigen," in *Journal of Experimental Medicine*, 13 (1911), 43–68, and "The Comparative Merits of Various Complements and Amboceptors in the Serum Diagnosis of Syphilis," *ibid.*, 78–91, both written with J. Bronfenbrenner; "A Cutaneous Reaction in Syphilis," *ibid.*, 14 (1911), 557–568; "Experimental Research in Syphilis, With Especial Reference to Spirochaeta pallida (Treponema pallidum)," in *Journal of the American Medical Association*, 58 (1912), 1163–1172, the Fenger-Senn Memorial Address; "A Homohemolytic System for the Serum Diagnosis of Syphilis," in *Journal of Experimental Medicine*, 28 (1918), 43–67.

His wide-ranging studies of spirochetes include "On the Occurrence of *Spirochaeta pallida*, Schaudinn, in Syphilis," in *Medical News*, 86 (1905), 1145, written with S. Flexner; "A Method for the Pure Cultivation of Pathogenic Treponema pallidum (Spirochaeta pallida)," in *Journal of Experimental Medicine*, 14 (1911), 99–108; "The Pure Cultivation of Spirochaeta duttoni, Spirochaeta kochi, Spirochaeta obermeieri, and Spirochaeta novyi," *ibid.*, 16 (1912), 199–210; "A Demonstration of Treponema pallidum in the Brain in Cases of General Paralysis," *ibid.*, 17 (1913), 232–238, written with J. W. Moore; "Spirochaetes," in *Journal of Laboratory and Clinical Medicine*, 2 (1917), 365–400, 472–499, the Harvey lecture; "Spirochaeta icterohaemorrhagiae in American Wild Rats and Its Relation to the Japanese and European Strains," in *Journal of Experimental Medicine*, 25 (1917), 755–763; "Morphological Characteristics and Nomenclature of Leptospira (Spirochaeta) icterohaemorrhagiae (Inada and Ido)," *ibid.*, 27 (1918), 575–592; and "The Survival of Leptospira (Spirochaeta) icterohaemorrhagiae in Nature; Observations Concerning Microchemical Reactions and Intermediary Hosts," *ibid.*, 609–625.

Noguchi's fallacious claims respecting yellow fever involve over 30 papers. The laboratory data, embodied mainly in a series of 18 reports in the *Journal of Experimental Medicine*, include "Etiology of Yellow Fever. I. Symptomatology and Pathological Findings of the Yellow Fever Prevalent in Guayaquil," in *Journal of Experimental Medicine*, 29 (1919), 547–564; "II. Transmission Experiments on Yellow Fever," *ibid.*, 565–584; "III. Symptomatology and Pathological Findings in Animals Experimentally Infected," *ibid.*, 585–596; "VI.

Cultivation, Morphology, Virulence, and Biological Properties of Leptospira icteroides," *ibid.*, **30** (1919), 13–29; "VII. Demonstration of Leptospira icteroides in the Blood, Tissues, and Urine of Yellow Fever Patients and of Animals Experimentally Infected With the Organism," *ibid.*, 87–93; "IX. Mosquitoes in Relation to Yellow Fever," *ibid.*, 401–410; and "X. Comparative Immunological Studies in Leptospira icteroides and Leptospira icterohaemorrhagiae," *ibid.*, **31** (1920), 135–158. Among four papers written with I. J. Kligler are "Immunological Studies With a Strain of Leptospira Isolated From a Case of Yellow Fever in Mérida, Yucatan," *ibid.*, **32** (1920), 627–637, and "Experimental Studies on Yellow Fever in Northern Peru," *ibid.*, **33** (1921), 239–252.

Other key publications are "Prophylactic Inoculation Against Yellow Fever," in *Journal of the American Medical Association*, **76** (1921), 96–99, written with W. Pareja; "Prophylaxis and Serum Therapy of Yellow Fever," *ibid.*, **77** (1921), 181–185; *Experimental Studies of Yellow Fever in Northern Brazil*, Monograph no. 20, Rockefeller Institute for Medical Research (New York, 1924), written with H. R. Muller and others; "The Pfeiffer Reaction in Yellow Fever," in *American Journal of Tropical Medicine*, **4** (1924), 131–138; and "Yellow Fever Research, 1918–1924: A Summary," in *Journal of Tropical Medicine and Hygiene*, **28** (1925), 185–193.

Noguchi's earliest searches for the causal agent of trachoma appeared as "The Relationship of the So-called Trachoma Bodies to Conjunctival Affections," in *Archives of Ophthalmology*, **40** (1911), 1–9, and culminated in his monograph "The Etiology of Trachoma," in *Journal of Experimental Medicine*, **48** (1928), supp. no. 2. Misleading reports on the causal agents of rabies and poliomyelitis are "Contribution to the Cultivation of the Parasite of Rabies," in *Journal of Experimental Medicine*, **18** (1913), 314–316; "Experiments on the Cultivation of the Microorganism Causing Epidemic Poliomyelitis," *ibid.*, 461–485, written with S. Flexner; and "Concerning Survival and Virulence of the Microorganism Cultivated From Poliomyelitis Tissues," *ibid.*, **21** (1915), 91–102, written with S. Flexner and H. L. Amoss.

Characteristic papers on miscellaneous researches include "Pure Cultivation in Vivo of Vaccine Virus Free From Bacteria," *ibid.*, 539–570; "Bacteriological and Clinical Studies of an Epidemic of Koch-Weeks Bacillus Conjunctivitis Associated With Cell Inclusion Conjunctivitis," *ibid.*, **22** (1915), 304–318, written with M. Cohen; "Immunity Studies of Rocky Mountain Spotted Fever. II. Prophylactic Inoculation in Animals," *ibid.*, **38** (1923), 605–626; "The Isolation and Maintenance of Leishmania on the Medium Employed for the Cultivation of Organisms of the Leptospira Group of Spirochetes," in *American Journal of Tropical Medicine*, **5** (1925), 63–69, written with A. Lindenberg; and "Comparative Studies of Herpetomonads and Leishmanias. I. Cultivation of Herpetomonads From Insects and Plants," in *Journal of Experimental Medicine*, **44** (1926), 307–325, written with E. B. Tilden.

Noguchi's last series of publications, on the causal agent of Oroya fever and verruga peruana, comprises 17 reports in the *Journal of Experimental Medicine*, of which three appeared posthumously in 1929. The more important are "Etiology of Oroya Fever. I. Cultivation of Bartonella bacilliformis," *ibid.*, **43** (1926), 851–864, written with T. S. Battistini; "III. The Behaviour of Bartonella moniliformis in Macacus rhesus," *ibid.*, **44** (1926), 697–713; "The Etiology of Verruga Peruana," *ibid.*, **45** (1927), 175–189; "VIII. Experiments on Cross-Immunity Between Oroya Fever and Verruga Peruana," *ibid.*, 781–786; and "XIV. The Insect Vectors of Carrión's Disease," *ibid.*, **49** (1929), 993–1008, written with R. C. Shannon *et al.*

Correspondence with Flexner and others is in the Simon Flexner Papers at the American Philosophical Society Library, Philadelphia. Relevant material is also among the Philip S. Hench Collection, Walter Reed Yellow Fever Archive, at the Alderman Library, University of Virginia.

II. SECONDARY LITERATURE. Memorial addresses delivered at the New York Academy of Medicine on 20 December 1928 are T. Smith, "Hideyo Noguchi, 1876–1928," in *Bulletin of the New York Academy of Medicine*, 2nd ser., **5** (1929), 877–884; and W. Welch, *ibid.*, 884–886. The chief obituary is S. Flexner, "Hideyo Noguchi. A Biographical Sketch," in *Science*, **69** (1929), 653–660, repr. with portrait in *Report of the Smithsonian Institution* (1929), pp. 595–608. G. Eckstein, *Noguchi* (New York–London, 1931), a vivid but awkward biography, lacks an index and authenticating details.

Other references to Noguchi's life and work are S. Benison, *Tom Rivers. Reflections on a Life in Medicine and Science* (Cambridge, Mass., 1967), pp. 93–98; A. R. Burr, *Weir Mitchell. His Life and Letters* (New York, 1929), pp. 293–296; P. F. Clark, "Hideyo Noguchi, 1876–1928," in *Bulletin of the History of Medicine*, **33** (1959), 1–20, with portrait; H. Hanson, *The Pied Piper of Peru* (Jacksonville, Fla., 1961), pp. 83–85; P. de Kruif, *The Sweeping Wind* (New York, 1962), pp. 17–18; K. Morishita, "Dr. Noguchi's Last Photo," in *Tokyo-iji-shinski*, no. 3143 (1939), 1920–1921, in Japanese; W. A. Sawyer, "A History of the Activities of the Rockefeller Foundation in the Investigation and Control of Yellow Fever," in *American Journal of Tropical Medicine*, **17** (1937), 35–50; M. G. Schultz, "A History of Bartonellosis (Carrión's disease)," in *American Journal of Tropical Medicine and Hygiene*, **17** (1968), 503–515; A. Takahashi, ed., *Hideyo Noguchi, November 9, 1876–May 21, 1928* (Tokyo, 1961), a booklet published by the Doctor Noguchi Memorial Association; and G. Williams, *The Plague Killers* (New York, 1969), pp. 215–249.

Crucial reports that finally discredited *L. icteroides* include A. Agramonte, "Some Observations Upon Yellow Fever Prophylaxis," in *Proceedings of the International Conference on Health Problems in Tropical America, Held at Kingston, Jamaica, July 22–August 1, 1924* (Boston, 1924), 201–227; W. Schüffner and A. Mochtar, "Gelbfieber und Weilsche Krankheit," in *Archiv für Schiffs- u. Tropen-Hygiene*, **31** (1927), 149–165; A. W. Sellards, "The Pfeiffer Reaction With Leptospira in Yellow Fever," in *American Journal of Tropical Medicine*, **7** (1927), 71–95; A. Stokes *et al.*, "Experimental Transmission of Yellow Fever to Laboratory Animals," *ibid.*, **8** (1928), 103–164; and M. Theiler and A. W. Sellards, "The Immunological Relationship of Yellow Fever as it Occurs in West Africa and in South America," in *Annals of Tropical Medicine and Parasitology*, **22** (1928), 449–460.

CLAUDE E. DOLMAN

NOLLET, JEAN-ANTOINE (*b.* Pimprez, near Noyon, France, 19 November 1700; *d.* Paris, France, 24 April 1770), *physics*.

Nollet's rise from the semiliterate peasantry to the top of the aristocratic Paris Academy of Sciences was a *chef d'oeuvre* of the Age of Reason. His village curé had recognized his intelligence and recommended him for the Church; his father, a stranger to learning, reluctantly consented; Jean-Antoine, having completed the humanities course in the provincial *collège* of Clermont, went to Paris to study theology. The capital opened his mind. The range of commodities, industries, and techniques particularly took his fancy; and soon he was devoting more time to the processes later pictured in the *Encyclopédie* of Diderot than to the system of St. Thomas. He supported himself by tutoring while inertia carried him to a master's degree in theology (1724) and the diaconate (*ca.* 1728); but there he suspended his clerical career, withdrew with the equivocal title "abbé," and cast about for a livelihood in the unpromising borderland between science and art.

Nollet had become acquainted with a few like-minded individuals who, with the financial backing of the Comte de Clermont, had constituted themselves a Société des Arts dedicated to bringing science to the artisan. In 1728 Nollet joined this group, which included Clairaut, La Condamine, and Grandjean de Fouchy—all of whom were to be his colleagues in the Academy—and Pierre Polinière, a public lecturer on natural philosophy, who was to leave him an example and an audience. The Société des Arts disbanded in the early 1730's, partly because of the disparity between its purpose and its purse and partly because of the opposition of the Academy of Sciences. The short-lived association, however, probably decided Nollet's future, for it was doubtless through contacts made there that he came to the attention of two leading academicians, C. F. Dufay and R. A. F. de Réaumur. From 1731 or 1732 to about 1735 Nollet assisted them in investigations of extraordinary range, touching the anatomy of insects, the fertilization of frogs, thermometry, pneumatics, phosphorescence, magnetism, and what was to become Nollet's special subject, electricity. From his masters the abbé learned

—besides an ocean of facts—the best contemporary laboratory technique and a useful, moderate Cartesian approach to physical theory. Moreover, through them, especially Dufay, who took him on a *Gelehrtenreise* to England and Holland, Nollet came to know a number of men of science, including the two most successful expositors of Newton, J. T. Desaguliers and W. J. 'sGravesande.

On returning from Holland in 1735, Nollet decided to take up the calling of Polinière, who had died the preceding year, and to follow the methods, if not the theories, of the expositors of Newton. But he found the requisite apparatus so expensive that he could finance it only by building and selling duplicates. "I wielded the file and scissors myself [he wrote of that time]; I trained and hired workmen; I aroused the curiosity of some gentlemen, who placed my products in their studies; I levied a kind of voluntary tribute; in a word (I will not hide it) I have often made two or three instruments of the same kind in order to keep one for myself."[1] By 1738 Nollet could handle an order from Voltaire for instruments costing over 10,000 livres, equivalent to about as many dollars today.[2]

Nollet's *cours de physique* was perhaps the most popular exhibition of its kind ever given.[3] With carefully orchestrated demonstrations performed on some 350 different instruments, the abbé entertained his enthusiastic auditors as, in the spirit of the Enlightenment, he undertook to dispel their "vulgar errors, extravagant fears and faith in the marvelous."[4] These were not mere shows, as one sees from their expanded syllabus, the famous *Leçons de physique*, which appeared in six volumes between 1743 and 1748 and was often reprinted. The presentations are lively, comprehensive, and up-to-date, with full directions for realizing the effects under study and excellent illustrations of apparatus. Nollet strove ceaselessly to perfect his technique; and his last work, *L'art des expériences* (1770), offers the "amateur of physics" the distillation of forty years of attention to the "choice, construction, and use of instruments." The establishment as well as the literate and leisured public rewarded the abbé. In 1739 he entered the Academy as "adjunct mechanician" and went to Turin to instruct the heir to the kingdom of Sardinia; in 1741 the Académie Royale de Bordeaux invited him to lecture before it, and three years later he enlightened the dauphin and the queen at Versailles. Eventually Nollet collected the newly created chair of physics at the Collège de Navarre (the first such post at the University of Paris), an annual lectureship at the technical schools of La Fère and Mézières (where Coulomb attended his course), the succession to

Réaumur as pensionary in the Academy's class of "mechanics," and appointment as preceptor to the royal family.

Nollet's repertoire always included electricity. Until 1745 the electrical demonstrations offered nothing beyond the results of Hauksbee, Stephen Gray, and Dufay, while the accompanying patter probably referred the phenomena to the vague vortical theories of Dufay and Fontenelle. In February of that year, however, word reached Nollet of the first fundamentally new experiments since those of his master: the antics of G. M. Bose and ignition of spirits by sparks. These colorful effects interested Nollet both as showman and as physicist; he threw himself into their study, from which he emerged, three months later, with the elements of the ill-fated theory of simultaneous effluence and affluence.

The theory is a compound of Cartesian common sense, bits and pieces of earlier hypotheses, the results of the Germans, and immediate experience. From the last—the sparks, pricklings, hissings, snappings, and smells surrounding a working electric—Nollet inferred, as had most electricians before him, that electricity consists in the action of a particular matter in motion. From the German experiments he deduced that, contrary to the opinion of Dufay, the matters of electricity and light are fundamentally the same and that, consequently, one can safely infer from the appearance of the brush discharge that the electrical matter leaves a charged body in divergent conical jets. Such jets, in their entirety, make up the body's "effluence." In answer to it, as suggested by the earlier theories of Cabeo, Hauksbee, and Privat de Molières, environing objects and even the air return an "affluence" to the body. According to Nollet the two currents, which differ only in direction, not in kind, nearly or exactly balance, so that a body can never be emptied of its electrical matter. Finally, in accordance with the principles of Descartes, Nollet insisted that all "attractions" and "repulsions" arise from the direct impact of the electrical matter in motion: "mechanical explanations are the only ones capable of advancing experimental physics."[5] Since the effluent flow is divergent and the affluent roughly homogeneous, one understands that local imbalances always exist; and, if one can accept certain ancillary hypotheses about the distribution of the imbalances, one may perceive why Bose, Musschenbroek, and many other physicists agreed that (in the words of Réaumur) "a more probable and natural explanation [of electrical phenomena] can scarcely be expected."[6] Nollet immediately became the chief of the European electricians. In the late 1740's he consolidated his position with several papers and two books—which,

among other things, tried to apply the theory to the Leyden jar—and with a trip across the Alps, undertaken at the request of his colleagues and at the expense of his government, to examine electrical cures advertised by Italian physicians. His expert, tactful, decisive debunking of these claims won him a kind word from Benjamin Franklin.

Shortly after his return from Italy, at the height of his reputation, Nollet found himself the quarry of Buffon, who was promoting the translation of a book by an unknown printer from Philadelphia. The abbé at first believed this American to be a fabrication of his enemies, and in this he was not far wrong; for Buffon, whose raging feud with Réaumur had reached a new stage of ferocity with the publication of the first volumes of the *Histoire naturelle* (1749), pushed Franklin in an effort to embarrass his enemy's favorite and most successful disciple. The plot worked far better than Buffon could have hoped. In the spring of 1752 his henchman, the naturalist Dalibard, issued the translation, prefaced by a "short history of electricity" that found space for third-rate contributors and none for Nollet; and while contemporaries puzzled over the slap, the plotters announced that Franklin's views about lightning had been proved by experiments they had set up in Marly-la-Ville, a small town outside Paris where Dalibard had earlier botched a geologizing errand for Buffon. No one remembered that in the fourth volume of his *Leçons* (1748) Nollet had stressed the analogy between electricity and lightning. Franklin's name was on everyone's lips. "The abbé Nollet," Buffon wrote in evident satisfaction, "is dying of chagrin from it all."[7] Worst of all, from Nollet's point of view, the apparent success of the lightning experiment lent support to the truly menacing aspects of Franklin's scheme, with which in fact it had nothing to do.

The first menace was the Philadelphia theory of the Leyden jar, which unfortunately for Nollet had been discovered just after the system of effluence and affluence. The new theory required the novel assumption that glass was impermeable to the electrical matter, a proposition in manifest disagreement with the patent fact that a feather in a sealed bottle can be drawn by an external electrified object. Franklin, concerned to elucidate the Leyden jar, accepted impenetrability and with it macroscopic action at a distance; Nollet, eager to retain the standard theory of electrical motions, insisted on transparency and mechanical action. The second threat was the doctrine that electricity (but not the electrical matter) came in two qualitatively different, opposite, and mutually destructive types. In Nollet's system only quantitative differences can obtain; it could never handle the disappearance of electricity in the discharge of the Leyden jar.

Nollet recognized these menaces and replied in an amusing set of *Lettres sur l'électricité* (1753), containing a wealth of counterexamples which drew their strength from Franklin's occasional obscurities, imprecisions, exaggerations, and inappropriate appeals to traditional effluvial models. Buffon's group was unable to respond and seized with relief the reply of Franklin's first European paladin, Giambatista Beccaria, which they issued in French before they left the field. Within the Academy, Franklin found a supporter in J. B. Le Roy, who had learned electricity from Nollet. But Le Roy was not a match for his mentor, whose tireless ingenuity, expressed in seven memoirs and two more volumes of *Lettres*, kept the Academy bamboozled until his death in 1770.

France had no electrician of stature again before Coulomb. One must not conclude, however, that Nollet's attack on Franklinists had no positive results. Under prodding from Paris the Philadelphia system was progressively refined into classical electrostatics. In particular, the need to come to terms with Nollet colored the reforms of Aepinus (1759); and Nollet himself, by spreading the dualistic theory of Robert Symmer in Italy, set in train developments that culminated in the invention of the electrophorus (1775), which in turn forced the excision of the last vestiges of the traditional theories (the "electrical atmospheres") from Franklin's system.

For the rest Nollet was by no means the ignorant and friendless recluse of Franklinist mythology. Among his important work outside electricity and pedagogy are his discovery and clear explanation of osmotic pressure (1748) and his account of the hatmaking trade (1765). Among his immediate disciples were M. J. Brisson and J. A. Sigaud de la Fond, and, among his correspondents, Bergman, Bose, Musschenbroek, William Watson, and Benjamin Wilson. His friends included Réaumur, the permanent secretary of the Academy, Grandjean de Fouchy, and the portrait painter Quentin de La Tour. He was one of the few people acceptable at both Cirey and Versailles. Despite his success he retained close ties with his family, whom he often helped financially. "No one [according to Grandjean] ever saw him lose his composure or his unfailing consideration; he only became excited when he talked about physics."[8]

NOTES

1. *Programme ou idée générale d'un cours de physique expérimentale* (Paris, 1738), xviii–xix.

2. Estimated from letters from Voltaire to B. Moussinot, June and July 1738, in Voltaire, *Correspondance*, 107 vols., T. Besteman, ed. (Geneva, 1953–1965), VII, *passim*.
3. It attracted some 500 auditors in 1760. Bengt Ferrner, *Resa i Europa 1758-1762*, S. G. Lindroth, ed. (Uppsala, 1956), xliii.
4. *Programme*, pp. xxxv–xxxvi.
5. Nollet to Bergman, 20 September 1766, in *Torbern Bergman's Foreign Correspondence*, G. Carlid and J. Nordström, eds., I (Stockholm, 1965), 285.
6. Réaumur to J. F. Séguier, 25 May 1747, in *Lettres inédites de Réaumur*, G. Musset, ed. (La Rochelle, 1886), 60.
7. Buffon to de Ruffey, 22 July 1752, in *Correspondance de Buffon de 1729 à 1788*, N. de Buffon, ed., 2nd ed., 2 vols., I (Paris, 1885), 84.
8. *Histoire de l'Académie . . . des sciences* (1770), 135. Bošković also testified to Nollet's wisdom and kindness; see Elizabeth Hill, in L. L. Whyte, ed., *Roger Joseph Boscovich* (London, 1961), 61.

BIBLIOGRAPHY

I. ORIGINAL WORKS. Nollet's chief works are *Programme ou idée générale d'un cours de physique expérimentale* (Paris, 1738); *Leçons de physique expérimentale*, 6 vols. (Paris, 1743–1748), often repr. and once trans. into Spanish (Madrid, 1757); "Conjectures sur les causes de l'électricité des corps," in *Mémoires de l'Académie des sciences* for 1745, 107–151; *Essai sur l'électricité des corps* (Paris, 1746; 4th ed., 1764); "Recherches sur les causes du bouillonnement des liquides," in *Mémoires de l'Académie des sciences* for 1748, 57–109; *Recherches sur les causes particulières des phénomènes électriques* (Paris, 1749; 2nd ed., 1754); *Lettres sur l'électricité*, 3 vols. (Paris, 1753–1767); "Nouvelles expériences d'électricité faites à l'occasion d'un ouvrage publié depuis peu en Angleterre, par M. Robert Symmer," in *Mémoires de l'Académie des sciences* for 1761, 244–258; *L'art de faire les chapeaux* (Paris, 1765); and *L'art des expériences ou avis aux amateurs de la physique*, 3 vols. (Paris, 1770; 3rd ed., 1784). Nollet published a great many papers in the volumes of the Paris Academy; the content of most of them appears in his books, the chief exception being the reports of his Italian trip published in the Academy's *Mémoires* for 1749 and 1750.

The best bibliography of both Nollet's works and secondary literature is in J. Torlais, *Un physicien au siècle des lumières, l'abbé Nollet 1700–1770* (Paris, 1954), 251–262. Less complete is the entry in *Nouvelle table des articles contenus dans les volumes de l'Académie royale des sciences de Paris depuis 1666 jusqu'en 1770* (Paris, 1775); Poggendorff is quite inadequate.

The most important MS remains are letters to Étienne-François Dutour (1711–1789), a corresponding member of the Academy and Nollet's staunchest supporter; the correspondence, which covers 25 years and includes drafts of Dutour's replies, is preserved at the Burndy Library, Norwalk, Connecticut. The MS of Nollet's Italian travel diary is in the Bibliothèque Municipale, Soissons.

II. SECONDARY LITERATURE. Information about Nollet's career may be collected from his books, from his dossier at the Académie des Sciences, from the *éloge* by Grandjean de Fouchy in *Histoire de l'Académie . . . des sciences* for 1770 (1771), 121–137, and from the published correspondence of Bergman, Buffon, Mme du Châtelet, Franklin, Montesquieu, Réaumur, and Voltaire. The best biography is the work of Torlais cited above; see also his "Une grande controverse scientifique au xviiie siècle, l'abbé Nollet et Benjamin Franklin," in *Revue d'histoire des sciences*, **9** (1953), 339–349; "Une rivalité célèbre, Réaumur et Buffon," in *Presse médicale*, **66**, no. 2 (1958), 1057–1058; and *Un esprit encyclopédique en dehors de "l'Encyclopédie."* *Réaumur d'après les documents inédits*, 2nd ed. (Paris, 1961). Important additional data is given by R. Hahn, *The Anatomy of a Scientific Institution, The Paris Academy of Sciences, 1666–1803* (Berkeley, 1971), esp. 108–110; V. Lecot, *L'abbé Nollet de Pimprez* (Noyon, 1856); and G. H. Quignon, *L'abbé Nollet, physicien. Son voyage en Piémont et en Italie* (Amiens, 1905). For details about Nollet's physics see the works of Torlais; J. A. Sigaud de la Fond, *Précis historique et expérimental des phénomènes électriques* (Paris, 1781); J. C. Poggendorff, "Über die Entdeckung der Diffusion tropfbarer Flüssigkeiten," in *Annalen der Physik*, **139** (1884), 350–351; and the unfriendly Franklinist histories, such as J. Priestley, *The History and Present State of Electricity*, 3rd ed., rev. (London, 1775); and I. B. Cohen, *Franklin and Newton* (Philadelphia, 1956).

JOHN L. HEILBRON

NORDENSKIÖLD, (NILS) ADOLF ERIK (*b.* Helsinki, Finland, 18 November 1832; *d.* Dalbyö, Sweden, 12 August 1901), *geography, geology, mineralogy, history of cartography.*

Nordenskiöld came from a distinguished family of soldiers, administrators, and scientists who, originally Swedish, had long been settled in southern Finland. He was educated at the University of Helsinki, where his outspoken liberalism brought him into conflict with the Russian administration of the country; he was therefore compelled to leave Finland shortly after his graduation. In 1858 he departed for Sweden, where a reputation based upon his first publications in mineralogy had preceded him. In the same year, at the age of twenty-six, he was appointed chief of the mineralogy division of Sweden's National Museum, a post that he held for the rest of his life.

Nordenskiöld's career as an Arctic explorer had begun even earlier. In 1857 he made his first Arctic voyage, accompanying Otto Torrell to Spitsbergen. He either participated in or led four more voyages to Spitsbergen in the course of the next fifteen years, as well as leading eight other expeditions between 1864 and 1886. His explorations culminated in the voyage of the *Vega*; this expedition, carried out under his command in 1878–1879, penetrated the seas north of Asia to reach the Pacific, thus achieving the long-sought northeastern passage to the Orient. (For this accomplishment, King Oscar of Sweden created Nordenskiöld a baron.)

Nordenskiöld was responsible for making scientific work an integral part of Arctic exploration. The expeditions that he conducted were distinguished by careful planning; scientific equipment was meticulously prepared and a well-qualified staff selected to aid in the collection of data and observations. Nordenskiöld himself contributed to the extensive series of papers that resulted from these voyages; that of the *Vega* was reported in five volumes that dealt with the zoological, botanical, geodetic, geomagnetic, geophysical, oceanographic, and anthropological aspects of the regions investigated. These volumes marked the beginning of serious polar studies.

Nordenskiöld also wrote on a wide range of subjects within his chief fields of interest, geology and mineralogy. Many of his descriptive publications remain valuable but, for the most part, his theoretical contributions are now of only historical interest. He did more important work in the history of science. He was interested in Swedish science of the eighteenth century from an early age, and the preparations for his Arctic voyages led him to study historic maps. He published a fundamental work on Scheele, then the two magnificent folio volumes, published simultaneously in Swedish and English, that laid the foundations of the history of cartography. These were *Facsimile-atlas to the Early History of Cartography* (1889) and *Periplus—An Essay on the Early History of Charts and Sailing Directions* (1897).

The *Facsimile-atlas* is a survey of map making, from the Alexandrine cartographer Ptolemy to the beginnings of scientific surveying and mapping in the seventeenth century. *Periplus*, its companion piece, offered a collection of historically important charts and documents, assembled for the first time. While there had been attempts to compose histories of cartography earlier in the nineteenth century—most notably the works of Santarém and Jomard—they had not met the criteria of careful, truly scientific inquiry; it was Nordenskiöld who first applied the critical approach of the historian to this field of study.

Nordenskiöld exerted considerable influence on two generations of Scandinavian natural scientists, offering them ample field experience and generous support. He helped to establish the study of the earth sciences and promoted polar research in northern Europe, and was persuasive in urging others to report their findings in these fields.

BIBLIOGRAPHY

The basic bibliography of Nordenskiöld's complete works was published in *Ymer*, **21**, no. 2 (1902), 277–302. The same issue contains extensive accounts of Nordenskiöld's life and statements on his work as a polar explorer, geologist, mineralogist, and historian of geography and cartography. His successor at the Swedish National Museum, H. Sjögren, published a detailed memorial of Nordenskiöld's scientific accomplishments in *Geologiska Föreningens i Stockholm Förhandlingar*, **34** (1912), 45–100. Popular biographies were published by Sven Hedin, *Adolf Erik Nordenskiöld—en levnadsbeskrivning* (Stockholm, 1926); and Henrik Ramsay, *Nordenskiöld Sjöfararen* (Stockholm, 1950). An extensive biography in English is George Kish, *Northeast Passage: Adolf Erik Nordenskiöld, His Life and Times* (Amsterdam, 1973).

GEORGE KISH

NORDENSKIÖLD, NILS ERIK (*b.* Frugård, Nyland [now Uusimaa], Finland, 23 November 1872; *d.* Stockholm, Sweden, 28 April 1933), *zoology, history of biology.*

Nordenskiöld belonged to a well-known Swedish-Finnish family which had for generations produced outstanding government officials, military men, and scientists. He grew up on the family estate in southern Finland and in the 1890's studied biology at the University of Helsinki. He did graduate work at Padua and Leipzig and in 1899 was appointed lecturer in zoology at Helsinki, where he taught invertebrate anatomy until 1915. His zoological studies, some of which were done at foreign universities and marine biological stations, were devoted almost entirely to the systematics, anatomy, histology, and spermatogenesis of the Acarina (especially hydrachnids and ticks).

Nordenskiöld's most important contribution were in the history of biology. His series of lectures at the University of Helsinki (1916–1917) constituted an extensive survey of the development of biology and was published in Swedish in three volumes as *Biologiens historia* (1921–1924). This work, which was soon translated into German and English, received great international acclaim. Grounded on basic studies in the botanical and zoological sources, it shows as a rule sound judgment in its final analyses, though Nordenskiöld shows, by treating Darwin's theory of natural selection as obsolete and discredited, that he was dependent on the general evaluation of the biologists of his generation. Throughout his work he always considers the relation of biological theories to philosophy and general cultural development.

In 1917 Nordenskiöld moved to Sweden and became a citizen. In 1926 he was appointed lecturer in the history of zoology at the University of Stockholm. He became a member of the Finnish Academy of Science and Letters in 1908.

BIBLIOGRAPHY

Nordenskiöld's *Biologiens historia* was published in German (Jena, 1926) and in English as *The History of Biology* (New York, 1928; new ed., 1935; London, 1929).

A secondary source is Tor Carpelan and L. O. T. Tudeer, *Helsingfors universitet. Lärare och tjänstemän från år 1828*, II (Helsinki, 1925), 669–670, and supp. II (Helsinki, 1940), 586–587.

STEN LINDROTH

NORMAN, ROBERT (*fl.* England, late sixteenth century), *navigation, magnetism.*

Little is known of Norman, an English instrument maker of the late sixteenth century, other than that he was for a considerable time a sailor and later had a house at Radcliffe, where he sold navigational instruments. At a time when sailing and the construction of good compasses were of primary importance, Norman established his reputation not only as a maker of superior instruments but also as one interested in their irregularities.

In making magnetic compasses, Norman noticed that the needle did not remain parallel to the earth's surface but that the north-seeking pole dipped toward the earth. He constructed his compasses with a wax counterbalance on the south-seeking pole to counteract this dip; when, by accident, he found that the attached wax did not serve as an equalizer if the needle was shortened, he became interested in the theory of the phenomenon.

In *The Newe Attractive* (1581), a treatise on the lodestone, Norman discussed the known properties of the magnet; suggested that the orientation of the compass was due to its turning toward, rather than its being attracted to, a certain point; and related his newly discovered deviation of the needle from the horizontal. He measured this deviation to be 71°50′ at London and was interested in finding its value at other points on the earth's surface.

This work appears to have been well known and was one of the few writings on magnetism favorably referred to by William Gilbert. In *De magnete* (1600), Gilbert credited Norman with the discovery of the dip of the magnetic needle and suggested that this property could be used to measure latitude on the earth's surface.

Norman also published *The Safegarde of Saylers* (1590), a book of sailing directions which he translated from Dutch.

BIBLIOGRAPHY

Norman's writings are *The Newe Attractive, Containing a Short Discourse of the Magnes or Lodestone, and Amongst Other His Vertues, of a Newe Discovered Secret and Subtill Properties, Concerning the Declinying of the Needle Touched Therewith Under the Plaine of the Horizon* (London, 1581); and *The Safegarde of Saylers* (London, 1590).

SUZANNE KELLY

NORTON, JOHN PITKIN (*b*. Albany, New York, 19 July 1822; *d*. Farmington, Connecticut, 5 September 1852), *agriculture, agricultural chemistry.*

Norton was encouraged by his father, John Treadwell Norton, a wealthy Connecticut farmer, to study "scientific" farming. To this end, Norton attended the lectures given by Benjamin Silliman, Sr., Denison Olmsted, and other faculty members at Yale College from 1840 to 1842, although he never formally matriculated. In addition he learned experimental chemistry and mineralogy in Benjamin Silliman, Jr.'s private laboratory. In 1842 and 1843 Norton enrolled for lectures at the Harvard Law School and attended many scientific lectures in Boston. From 1843 to 1844 he again enrolled in the younger Silliman's laboratory, where his progress was so rapid and his interest in "scientific" agriculture so great that the Sillimans arranged for him to spend two years, from 1844 to 1846, in Scotland with James F. W. Johnston, whose work in agricultural chemistry was well known in the United States. While in Scotland, Norton won a prize of £50 from the Highland Agricultural Society of Scotland for his essay on the chemical constitution of oats.

Together with the two Sillimans, Norton devised a plan for professorships in agricultural and practical chemistry at Yale College. After initial reluctance from the Yale Corporation, this plan was approved on 19 August 1846, although formal instruction in these sciences did not begin until 1 November 1847. These professorships, in what was known informally as the Yale School of Applied Chemistry, evolved into the Sheffield Scientific School. Norton, named professor of agricultural chemistry, was probably the first in the United States to hold such a special position. He was also awarded an honorary M.A. by Yale College at this time, his only academic degree. Following his election to this professorship, Norton spent the winter of 1846 and the spring of 1847 in Gerardus Johannes Mulder's chemistry laboratory in Utrecht, analyzing plant proteins.

In addition to his full schedule of lectures and laboratory instruction at Yale College, Norton campaigned vigorously throughout the Northeast for a new scientific approach to agriculture and agricultural education. In keeping with this emphasis he organized laboratory instruction at the School of Applied Chemistry around analytical chemistry, believing that accurate soil analysis was essential to improved farming.

Norton was a well-trained chemist capable of research of high quality, as his work in Scotland and Utrecht showed. He is chiefly remembered for his inspirational leadership of the scientific farming movement in the United States, for his part in founding a leading American scientific institution, and for an excellent textbook on scientific farming. Many of his students made substantial contributions to scientific teaching and research, although only a handful remained in scientific agriculture. Of these the best-known were Samuel W. Johnson and William H. Brewer, both of whom later joined the faculty of the Sheffield Scientific School. Johnson became director of the Connecticut Agricultural Experiment Station (the first of its kind in the nation), and Brewer taught agricultural sciences.

BIBLIOGRAPHY

I. ORIGINAL WORKS. Norton's most important publication was *Elements of Scientific Agriculture* (Albany, 1850). He wrote a series of articles for *Cultivator*, n.s. **1–9** (1844–1852), as well as for *American Agriculturist* (1844–1846). His major research papers were "On the Analysis of the Oat," in *American Journal of Science*, 2nd ser., **3** (1847), 222–236, 318–333; "Account of Some Researches on the Protein Bodies of Peas and Almonds, and a Body of a Somewhat Similar Nature Existing in Oats," *ibid.*, **5** (1848), 22–33; "On the Value of Soil Analysis, and the Points to Which Special Attention Should Be Directed," in *Proceedings of the American Association for the Advancement of Science* (1850), 199–206, written with William J. Craw.

The Yale Memorabilia Room in the Sterling Memorial Library at Yale University holds a sizable collection of Norton MS and printed material, including unpublished diaries and letters.

II. SECONDARY LITERATURE. There is an extensive, although short and fragmentary, literature on Norton. One of the most recent accounts is Louis I. Kuslan, "The Founding of the Yale School of Applied Chemistry," in

Journal of the History of Medicine and Allied Sciences, **24**, no. 4 (1969), 430–451. See also *Memorials of John Pitkin Norton* (Albany, 1853), a collection of contemporary periodical accounts of his work, which particularly stresses his deep religious faith; and Russell H. Chittenden, *History of the Sheffield Scientific School of Yale University*, I (New Haven, 1928), ch. 2. Margaret W. Rossiter, "Justus Liebig and the Americans" (Ph.D. dissertation, Yale University, 1971), will also be useful.

LOUIS I. KUSLAN

NORWOOD, RICHARD (*b.* Stevenage, Hertfordshire, England, 1590; *d.* Bermuda, 1665), *mathematics, surveying, navigation.*

Norwood's family were gentlefolk who apparently had fallen upon hard times; he attended grammar school, but at the age of fifteen was apprenticed to a London fishmonger. The many seamen he met in London aroused his interest in learning navigation and seeing the world. Eventually he was able to switch his apprenticeship to a coaster plying between London and Newcastle. He tells in his *Journal* how, while forced to lay over for three weeks at Yarmouth, he went through Robert Record's treatise on arithmetic, *The Ground of Arts*. So involved was he in studying mathematics that he almost forgot to eat and caught "a spice of the scurvy." During the following years Norwood made several voyages to the Mediterranean and on his first trip was fortunate to find a fellow passenger with an extensive mathematical library, among which was Leonard Digges's *Pantometria*. On following trips Norwood himself took along mathematical books, including Euclid's *Elements* and Clavius' *Algebra*.

To retrieve a piece of ordnance that had fallen into the harbor at Lymington, Norwood devised a kind of diving bell, descended in it to the bottom, and was able to attach a rope to the lost piece. This exploit brought him to the attention of the Bermuda Adventurers, a company that planned to finance its colonization of Bermuda by exploiting the oyster beds that supposedly surrounded the islands. In 1616 Norwood joined them and sailed for Bermuda. It soon became evident that very few pearls were to be found, and Norwood was then offered the task of surveying the islands. He made several surveys between 1614 and 1617, and upon their completion he returned to London. In 1622 he married Rachel Boughton, and in the same year his map of Bermuda was published by Nathaniel Newbery. No copy of this map is now known to exist, but in 1624–1625 Samuel Purchas reprinted the Newbery version.

Upon his return to London, Norwood taught mathematics and wrote a number of books on mathematics and navigation, which went through many editions. His *Trigonometrie, or, The Doctrine of Triangles* (1631), based on the logarithms of Napier and Briggs as well as on works by Wright and Gunter, was intended essentially as a navigational aid to seamen. In it Norwood explained the common logarithms, the trigonometrical functions, the spherical triangles, and their applications to the problems confronting the navigator. He posed practical problems of increasing complexity; his explanations were clear; and he enabled the navigator to determine his course with the aid of a plane or Mercator chart and the logarithmic and trigonometric formulas. He emphasized great circle navigation by giving the formulas involved and thus facilitated the calculations. In his *The Seaman's Practice* (1637), he set out a great circle course between the Lizard (the southernmost point in Great Britain) and Bermuda.

Norwood was the first to use consistently the trigonometric abbreviations s for sine, t for tangent, sc for sine complement, tc for tangent complement, and sec for secant.

The Seaman's Practice was especially concerned with the length of a degree and improvements in the log line. In 1635 Norwood measured the length of a degree along the meridian between London and York. His degree was 367,167 English feet, a surprisingly good measurement in view of the crude tools he used. Based on this volume, he reknotted the log line, putting a knot every fifty feet. Running this with a half-minute glass gave sixty sea miles to a degree.

Norwood was a convinced nonconformist, and because of Archbishop Laud's oppressive actions he decided to leave England. He returned to Bermuda in 1638 and established himself as a schoolmaster; planted olive trees and shipped olive oil to London; and made a new survey in 1663. He also corresponded with the newly founded Royal Society.

BIBLIOGRAPHY

I. ORIGINAL WORKS. The British Museum has a copy of Norwood's chart of Bermuda, which, together with his *Description of the Sommer Islands*, was repr. in John Speed, *A Prospect of the Most Famous Parts of the World* (London, 1631). His other works include *Trigonometrie, or, The Doctrine of Triangles* (London, 1631); *The Seaman's Practice; Containing a Fundamental Problem in Navigation, Experimentally Verified* (London, 1637); *Fortification, or Architecture Military* (London, 1639); *Table of the Sun's True Place, Right Ascension, Declination, etc.* (London, 1657); and *A Triangular Canon Logarithmicall* (London, 1665[?]). *The Journal of Richard Norwood, Surveyor of Bermuda; With Introductions by Wesley F. Craven and*

Walter B. Hayward (New York, 1945). Norwood wrote this account of his early life when he was 49 years old, but it ends with the year 1620. It is concerned with his religious conversion. The intros. are excellent and the book also contains a biblio. of Norwood's writings (pp. lix–lxiv).

II. SECONDARY LITERATURE. Norwood's contributions to mathematics and navigation are extensively discussed in E. G. R. Taylor, *The Mathematical Practitioners of Tudor and Stuart England* (Cambridge, 1954); and David W. Waters, *The Art of Navigation in England in Elizabethan and Early Stuart Times* (London, 1958).

LETTIE S. MULTHAUF

NOSTRADAMUS, MICHAEL (latinized form of **NOSTREDAME, MICHEL DE**) (*b*. Saint-Rémy, France, 14 December 1503; *d*. Salon, France, 2 July 1566), *medicine, astrology.*

More than any other writer in modern times Nostradamus knew how to titillate the deep-seated craving, felt by potentate and plebeian alike, to foresee the future, near and remote.

After receiving his early education in the liberal arts at the University of Avignon, he proceeded to the University of Montpellier to study medicine. When a plague broke out in southern France, many of the local licensed physicians cravenly fled from the epidemic, whereas the student Nostradamus courageously enlisted in the struggle to combat it. After traveling about for four years in this intensive and dangerous effort, he returned to Montpellier when the pestilence abated and was officially matriculated on 23 October 1529. He was, however, labeled an apothecary, accused of having slandered doctors, and was struck from the list of students by Guillaume Rondelet, who was the procurator of students during that year.[1] Nevertheless, the jealous and hostile faculty was coerced into co-opting Nostradamus by strong pressure from a grateful populace and a student body eager to learn from his experience. Yet at this stage of his life he was not satisfied to settle down in the humdrum routine of a university professor of medicine, surrounded by unfriendly colleagues. In 1532 Nostradamus left Montpellier with no definite destination in mind.

During the course of his travels he was invited by a prominent intellectual, Julius Caesar Scaliger, to join his circle in Agen.[2] There Nostradamus married and became the father of two children. But when the Inquisition came to Agen, he deemed it prudent to leave. After the uproar subsided, he returned to Agen, only to have a recurrence of the plague wipe out the three members of his family.

Once more alone in the world, Nostradamus resumed the life of the wandering physician. When the plague again ravaged Aix-en-Provence, that stricken city persuaded him in 1546 to help fight the dread disease and, in gratitude for his labors, awarded him a pension for life. The following year he settled in Salon, a small town halfway between Avignon and Marseilles. On 11 November 1547 he married a wealthy widow, who bore him six children, of whom the eldest, César (perhaps named after Scaliger), became the first local historian of Provence. In the Salon cadastral survey of 1552 Nostradamus acknowledged acquisition of a house after his marriage.[3] The marked improvement in his financial situation freed him from the necessity of continuing his medical practice for the sake of the income. Nevertheless, on 23 September 1555 he was consulted at Salon by Felix Platter and some German fellow students from Montpellier, and on 20 October 1559 he gave medical advice to Bishop Laurent Strozzi at Béziers.[4] But for years he had devoted his major energies to an entirely different pursuit.

Wrapping himself in the mantle of the ancient Hebrew prophets, to whose religion his ancestors had adhered until his grandfather's compulsory conversion to Roman Catholicism,[5] and claiming divine inspiration for his astrological forecasts, Nostradamus dedicated the first edition of his *Prophecies* to his infant son César on 1 March 1555. This opening salvo also contained the first three centuries, or groups of 100 quatrains of rhyming iambic pentameters, plus century IV, quatrains 1–53. The numerous allusions to heavily veiled persons, places, and events were strewn about in no discernible arrangement, either chronological or geographical. These deliberately vague forebodings, promulgated in a France trembling on the verge of a religious civil war, were an instantaneous success. Nostradamus was promptly summoned to the capital in 1556 to cast the horoscopes of the royal children. Encouraged by such favorable responses and ignoring his harsh critics, Nostradamus published his first seven centuries in 1557 (I–VI and VII, 1–40), and on 27 June 1558 dedicated to King Henry II centuries VIII–X (issued posthumously in 1568).

In 1560 Pierre de Ronsard (1524–1585), prince of poets and poet of princes, aligned himself with Nostradamus:

> By the ambiguous words of his prophetic voice,
> Like an ancient oracle, he has for many years
> Predicted the greatest part of our destiny.
> I would not have believed him, had not Heaven,
> Which separates good from evil for humans,
> Been on his side.[6]

On 17 October 1564 the young King Charles IX sought out the seer at Salon. But the rationalistic philosopher Pierre Gassendi examined a horoscope cast by Nostradamus, his fellow Provençal, for the father of a personal friend and showed it to have been totally wrong in numerous details.[7]

By the same token, the adversaries and supporters of Nostradamus have continued until our time respectively to denounce him as a charlatan and to predict retrospectively such portentous crises as the French Revolution and World War II.

NOTES

1. Marcel Gouron, "Documents inédits sur l'Université de médecine de Montpellier (1495–1559)," in *Montpellier médical*, 3rd ser., **50** (1956), 374–375; and Gouron, ed., *Matricule de l'Université de médecine de Montpellier 1503–1599*, Travaux d'Humanisme et Renaissance, XXV (Geneva, 1957), 58.
2. Vernon Hall, "Life of Julius Caesar Scaliger," in *Transactions of the American Philosophical Society*, **40** (1950), 117.
3. Edgar Leroy, "Nostradamus, médecin de la Faculté de médecine de Montpellier," in *Histoire de la médecine*, **4** (Mar. 1954), 10, with a facs. of Nostradamus' oath of allegiance to the University of Montpellier on p. 7.
4. *Beloved Son Felix, the Journal of Felix Platter*, Seán Jennett, trans. (London, 1961), 107; Gouron, "Documents," pp. 375–377.
5. Paul Masson, *Dictionnaire biographique*, which is *Les Bouches-du-Rhône Encyclopédie départementale*, IV, pt. 2 (Paris–Marseilles, 1931), 357.
6. Pierre de Ronsard, *Oeuvres* (Paris, 1560), III, *Poèmes*, bk. V, "Élégie à Guillaume des Autels," ll. 184–188; repr. in Ronsard's *Oeuvres complètes*, Paul Laumonier, ed., 2nd ed., X (Paris, 1939), 359.
7. Pierre Gassendi, *Syntagma philosophicum*, pt. 2 (physics), sec. 2, bk. 6, ch. 5, in Gassendi's *Opera omnia* (Lyons, 1658; repr. Stuttgart–Bad Cannstatt, 1964), I, 745–746. The relevant passage was trans. into English in P. Gassendus, *The Vanity of Judiciary Astrology* (London, 1659), 139–141.

BIBLIOGRAPHY

See Edgar Leoni, *Nostradamus: Life and Literature* (New York, 1961), 77–89 for the original works and 89–101 for the secondary literature. See also H. Noll-Husum, "Nostradamus und die Astronomie," in *Vierteljahrsschrift der astronomischen Gesellschaft*, **71** (1936), 242–249; Nostradamus, *Interprétation des hiéroglyphes de Horapollo*, Pierre Rollet, ed. (Aix-en-Provence, 1968); Michel Chomarat, *Nostradamus entre Rhône et Saône* (Lyons, 1971); and Pierre Guérin, *Le véritable secret de Nostradamus* (Paris, 1971).

EDWARD ROSEN

NOVARA, DOMENICO MARIA (*b.* Ferrara, Italy, 1454; *d.* Bologna, Italy, 1504), *astronomy.*

As is indicated by Novara's surname (Novara or da Novara), that city in northwestern Italy had been the home of his ancestors. One of them, however, had been invited to move eastward to Ferrara, where Domenico Maria was born.[1] Hence he was variously known as Maria (as Kepler always cited him), Novara (or da Novara), and Ferrariensis (of Ferrara).[2] In his own publications he usually called himself Domenico Maria da Novara of Ferrara.

In his publications Novara described himself as holding two academic degrees, Doctor of Arts and Doctor of Medicine. It is not yet known when and where he pursued these studies, but from 1483 to 1504 he taught at Bologna University.[3] As professor of astronomy,[4] he was, in addition to his teaching duties, required to publish a prognostication for every year. Such a slender and ephemeral forecast, of which only a relatively small number of copies was printed, has often perished without a trace. In Novara's case, however, his writings were available as late as 1619.[5] At present twelve of his twenty-one prognostications still survive.[6]

After the return of Columbus' crew from his first voyage to America, the outbreak of syphilis in southern Europe stimulated widespread discussion. According to a contemporary Bolognese writer, "The astrologers assert that the cause of this disease was the conjunction of Jupiter and Saturn on 9 November 1484, and they base this [date] on the very accurate observation of Professor Domenico Maria of Ferrara, this being the city where he was born but he has become a citizen of Bologna by virtue of his accomplishments and work."[7] The foregoing statement has been misunderstood to mean "The astrologers, particularly Dominicus Maria of Ferrara, attributed this new disease to the conjunction of 1484."[8] What the astrologers took from the professor of astronomy, however, was the date of the conjunction, not the etiology of syphilis.

In his prognostication published in 1489, Novara declared that the latitude of Cádiz and of places in Italy was found in his own time to exceed by 1°10′ the corresponding latitude reported in Ptolemy's *Geography*. Since this discrepancy occurred too often to be attributed to scribal error, Novara concluded that northern latitudes in general had been increasing imperceptibly since antiquity. This systematic displacement he ascribed to a gradual shift of the terrestrial north pole toward the zenith in a slow motion requiring 395,000 years to complete the circuit. Novara's thesis was quoted in Giovanni Antonio Magini's widely consulted planetary tables, from which it was repeated by William Gilbert, Willebrord Snel, Pierre Gassendi, and Giovanni Battista Riccioli.[9] While Novara's greatest pupil, Copernicus, did not accept his teacher's argument that the terrestrial pole had changed its direction, that mistaken view may nevertheless have encouraged him to doubt the traditionally asserted absolute immobility of the earth.[10]

Novara's tombstone was erected by one of the two heirs to whom he had bequeathed all his modest worldly goods in the absence of a wife, children, and servants.[11]

NOTES

1. Lorenzo Barotti, ed., *Memorie istoriche di letterati ferraresi*, II (Ferrara, 1793), 26–27.
2. Johannes Kepler, *Gesammelte Werke* (Munich, 1937–), II, 135:29–30; VII, 147:12; XIII, 114:63; XIV, 16:347, 26:191, 27:219, 55:515, 347:218, 352:389; XV, 308:94; XVII, 339:13, 353:82; Kepler, *Opera omnia*, Christian Frisch, ed., VIII (Frankfurt–Erlangen, 1871), 235:25. The "Ferrariensis" who is cited three times in Galileo's student papers is someone other than Domenico Maria Novara of Ferrara, whom Galileo discussed in a marginal note in his copy of William Gilbert's *Magnet*: Galileo Galilei, *Opere*, nat. ed. (Florence, 1890–1909; repr. 1968), I, 32:6, 76:33, 105:27; VIII, 625.
3. Umberto Dallari, ed., *I rotuli dei lettori legisti e artisti dello studio bolognese dal 1384 al 1799*, I (Bologna, 1888), 121–185.
4. Not astrology, as in Lynn Thorndike, *A History of Magic and Experimental Science*, V (New York, 1941), 234. The name of the regular course was changed from astrology to astronomy a decade before Novara was born: Dallari, I, 18, 21; with the single exception of 1463–1464, see I, 64.
5. Kepler, *Gesammelte Werke*, XVII, 339:9–12.
6. Gustav Hellmann, "Versuch einer Geschichte der Wettervorhersage im XVI. Jahrhundert," in *Abhandlungen der Preussischen Akademie der Wissenschaften*, Phys.-math. Kl. (1924), no. 1, 34.
7. Bartholomeus Cocles, *Chyromantie ac physionomie anastasis* (Bologna, 1504), bk. VI, ch. 248, sig. T2r.
8. Thorndike, *op. cit.*, V, 62–63.
9. More recently by Curtze, "Ueber . . . Schriften . . . Ferrara," 519–520; by Boncompagni, "Sopra alcuni scritti . . . Ferrara," 146–148; and by Antonio Favaro, ed., *Carteggio inedito di Ticone Brahe, Giovanni Keplero . . . con Giovanni Antonio Magini* (Bologna, 1886), 80–81.
10. Edward Rosen, *Three Copernican Treatises*, 3rd ed. (New York, 1971), 323.
11. The tombstone no longer survives, and a transcription of it inadvertently postponed Novara's death by 10 years in Roman numerals, an error corrected by Silvestro Gherardi, *Di alcuni materiali per la storia della facoltà matematica nell'antica Università di Bologna* (Bologna, 1846), 37–38, offprinted from R. Accademia delle scienze dell'Istituto di Bologna, *Nuovi annali delle scienze naturali*, 2nd ser., 5 (1846), 161–187, 244–268, 321–356, 401–436, and trans. into German by Maximilian Curtze, in *Archiv der Mathematik und Physik*, 52 (1871), 106–107. According to the transcription of the tombstone, Novara died on 1 Sept., whereas the university's payroll records report his death on 17 Aug. and on 20 Aug.—Carlo Malagola, *Della vita e delle opere di Antonio Urceo* (Bologna, 1878), 350–351. The inventory of Novara's bequeathed property was found and published by Lino Sighinolfi, "Domenico Maria Novara e Nicolò Copernico allo Studio di Bologna," in *Studi e memorie per la storia dell'Università di Bologna*, 5 (1920), 213–215, 235.

BIBLIOGRAPHY

Novara's writings are listed and discussed in the following (presented in chronological order): Maximilian Curtze, "Ueber einige bis jetzt unbekannte gedruckte Schriften des Domenico Maria Novara da Ferrara," in *Altpreussische Monatsschrift*, 7 (1870), 515–521; Baldassarre Boncompagni, "Sopra alcuni scritti stampati, finora non conosciuti, di Domenico Maria Novara da Ferrara," in *Bullettino di bibliografia e di storia delle scienze matematiche e fisiche*, 4 (1871), 140–149, 340–341; Domenico Berti, *Copernico- e le vicende del sistema copernicano in Italia* (Rome, 1876), 34–42, 179–184; Gustav Hellmann, *Beiträge zur Geschichte der Meteorologie*, in Veröffentlichungen des K. Preussischen Meteorologischen Instituts no. 296 (Berlin, 1917), 217; and Pietro Riccardi, *Biblioteca matematica italiana*, enl. ed., II (Milan, 1952), 205–207.

See also Luigi Napoleone Cittadella, "Domenico Maria Novara," in *Buonarroti*, 11 (1876), 157–163; Ferdinando Jacoli, "Intorno alla determinazione di Domenico Maria Novara dell'obliquità dell'eclittica," in *Bullettino di bibliografia e di storia delle scienze matematiche e fisiche*, 10 (1877), 75–88; Paul J. Melchior, "Sur une observation faite par Copernic et Dominique Maria," in *Bulletin de l'Académie r. de Belgique. Classe des sciences*, 5th ser., 40 (1954), 416–417; and Edward Rosen, "Copernicus and His Relation to Italian Science," forthcoming under the auspices of the Accademia dei Lincei.

EDWARD ROSEN

NOVY, FREDERICK GEORGE (*b.* Chicago, Illinois, 9 December 1864; *d.* Ann Arbor, Michigan, 8 August 1957), *microbiology.*

Novy's father, a tailor, and his mother, a milliner, emigrated from Bohemia to the United States in 1864. A high school teacher stimulated Novy's interest in chemistry, and he received a bachelor's degree in that subject from the University of Michigan in 1886. Following graduation he remained at Michigan— where he was to spend his entire career—to work as an assistant to the organic chemist Albert Prescott and to pursue graduate studies. He received a master's degree in 1887 for his research on cocaine and its derivatives. In that year the direction of his interests began to shift from organic chemistry to physiological chemistry and bacteriology when he accepted an instructorship in the department of hygiene and physiological chemistry, headed by Victor Vaughan. He continued his graduate work, receiving the D.Sc. in 1890 and a medical degree in 1891. He was promoted to assistant professor in the latter year and to junior professor in 1893. In 1902 he became professor and chairman of the newly founded department of bacteriology, a post that he held until his retirement in 1935. He also served as dean of the medical school from 1933 to 1935.

Novy's strong commitment to truth and to meticulous scientific work was immortalized in the person of Max Gottlieb in Sinclair Lewis' novel *Arrowsmith*. Paul de Kruif, one of Novy's students, served as a technical advisor to Lewis on the book and helped to create the character of Gottlieb, the dedicated scientist, who represented a blend of Novy and Jacques Loeb. Honors received by Novy during his lifetime included membership in the National Academy of Sciences and the American Philosophical Society and honorary degrees from the University of Cincinnati and the University of Michigan. He was married in 1891 and was the father of five children.

Novy was one of the pioneers in bacteriology in the United States. He and Vaughan spent their vacation in 1888 at Robert Koch's Berlin laboratory, learning the techniques and concepts of the new science of bacteriology. In January 1889 they instituted at Michigan a course that may well have been the first systematic laboratory instruction in bacteriology offered at an American medical school, although lectures and occasional experiments in the subject had apparently entered the medical curriculum of some American universities by that time. The course, which consisted of three months of intensive laboratory work, was so successful that it was made a required part of the medical curriculum in 1890. Novy was also one of the charter members of the Society of American Bacteriologists, founded in 1899, and served as its president in 1904.

Novy's early work in microbiology dealt with the toxic products produced by bacteria. In 1888 he collaborated with Vaughan on a book on this subject which expressed the view that pathogenic bacteria cause disease by decomposing complex substances in the body to produce poisonous alkaloids. By the fourth edition of the work (1902), the authors had adopted a view more in accord with current thought: that the bacterial toxins involved in disease are usually complex proteins which are synthesized by the microorganisms. They still overemphasized, however, the importance of toxins in infectious diseases. For example, the symptoms of anthrax and pneumonia were assumed to be due to toxins produced by the bacteria involved, whereas the ability of these and many other bacteria to produce disease actually appears to be due to their invasiveness (their ability to invade tissues and spread and multiply).

Novy devoted a significant amount of attention to anaerobic bacteria and developed apparatus for the cultivation and study of these organisms, such as the Novy jar, an anaerobic culture method in which the air in the jar is removed by a vacuum pump and replaced by an inert gas such as nitrogen. In 1894 he discovered and isolated the organism now known as *Clostridium novyi*, a species of gas gangrene bacillus.

Novy is probably best known for his extensive studies on trypanosomes and spirochetes, and he was apparently the first to cultivate a pathogenic protozoan (the trypanosome) in an artifical culture medium. *Spirochaeta novyi*, the organism that causes the American variety of relapsing fever, was discovered in his laboratory in 1906.

Among Novy's other research contributions were his studies in microbial respiration (especially on the respiration of the tubercle bacillus) and his investigation of anaphylaxis.

BIBLIOGRAPHY

I. ORIGINAL WORKS. For bibliographies of Novy's publications, see Esmond Long, "Frederick George Novy," in *Biographical Memoirs. National Academy of Sciences*, **33** (1959), 342–350; and S. E. Gould, "Frederick George Novy, Microbiologist," in *American Journal of Clinical Pathology*, **29** (1958), 305–309. For his views on bacterial toxins, see *Ptomaines and Leucomaines, or the Putrefactive and Physiological Alkaloids* (Philadelphia, 1888), written with V. C. Vaughan. The 4th ed., which was considerably revised, is entitled *Cellular Toxins, or the Chemical Factors in the Causation of Disease* (Philadelphia–New York, 1902). For a review of his work on trypanosomes, see his "On Trypanosomes," *Harvey Lectures*, **1** (1905–1906), 33–72. On spirochetes, see "Relapsing Fever and Spirochetes," in *Transactions of the Association of American Physicians*, **21** (1906), 456–464, written with R. E. Knapp. His most important studies on anaphylaxis were reported in a series of papers in *Journal of Infectious Diseases*, **20** (1917). Two important papers entitled "Microbic Respiration" appeared *ibid.*, **36** (1925), 109–232.

II. SECONDARY LITERATURE. Two substantial biographical articles about Novy have been cited above: Long, pp. 326–350; and Gould, pp. 297–309. There is list of eight biographical sketches in Genevieve Miller, ed., *Bibliography of the History of Medicine of the United States and Canada, 1939–1960* (Baltimore, 1964), 80–81. See also Thomas Francis, Jr., "Frederick George Novy, 1864–1957," in *Transactions of the Association of American Physicians*, **71** (1958), 35–37; and the article on Novy in *National Cyclopedia of American Biography*, XVI (1918), 93. Paul de Kruif, *The Sweeping Wind: A Memoir* (New York, 1962), makes several references to Novy—including pp. 93–94, 96, 102–103, 109—and discusses the aspects of Novy's character that were portrayed in the person of Max Gottlieb in Sinclair Lewis' *Arrowsmith*.

JOHN PARASCANDOLA

NOYES, ARTHUR AMOS (*b.* Newburyport, Massachusetts, 13 September 1866; *d.* Pasadena, California, 3 June 1936), *chemistry*.

Noyes's father, Amos Noyes, was an able and scholarly lawyer. One of his forebears, Nicolas Noyes, had come from England in 1633 and had settled in the town (then called Newbury) in 1635. Noyes's mother, Anna Page Andrews Noyes, was interested in literature, especially poetry. After her husband's death in 1896 she became a close companion to her son, who never married.

As a boy Noyes carried out chemical experiments at home. When he graduated from high school he found that he could not attend the Massachusetts Institute of Technology because of lack of money. At home he studied all of the first-year subjects except drawing and was able to enter the sophomore class at M.I.T. the following year, when he was granted the Wheelright Scholarship, which had been established for Newburyport students. He received his bachelor's degree in 1886, with a thesis on the action of heat on ethylene. He continued his research in organic chemistry, and after receiving the M.S. in 1887 he was appointed assistant in analytical chemistry. During this period he became a close friend of one of his students, George Ellery Hale, who was later to play an important part in his life.

In the summer of 1888 Noyes, accompanied by two other M.I.T. graduates in chemistry, went to Europe for advanced study in organic chemistry under Adolf von Baeyer at Munich. On their arrival in Rotterdam they received word that there would be no space for them in Baeyer's laboratory, and Noyes elected Leipzig as the alternative. There Wilhelm Ostwald had just begun to present lectures in the new subject of physical chemistry, and Noyes became interested in this field. He carried out an investigation of deviations from van't Hoff's laws of perfect solutions, for which he received his doctorate in 1890. On his return to M.I.T. he was for a number of years engaged in teaching analytical chemistry, organic chemistry, and physical chemistry. Noyes wrote a book on each of these subjects: *A Detailed Course of Qualitative Chemical Analysis* (1895), following a preliminary edition, *Notes on Qualitative Analysis* (1892); *Laboratory Experiments on the Class Reactions and Identification of Organic Substances* (1898), written with S. P. Mulliken; and *The General Principles of Physical Science* (1902). His textbook on qualitative analysis, which has gone through many editions, was widely used and of great importance in introducing concepts of physical chemistry into that field. His first book on physical chemistry was later expanded, with the collaboration of Miles Sherrill, into a textbook,

at first entitled *The General Principles of Chemistry* and in later editions *A Course of Study in Chemical Principles*, which has been of much value in bringing precision into the teaching of this subject in the United States. A characteristic of *Chemical Principles* was the use of problems so phrased as to lead the student to derive the basic equations. These two books have been described as revolutionizing the teaching of analytical chemistry and physical chemistry in America.

One of Noyes's important contributions to chemistry, carried out with many collaborators, was his thorough study of the chemical properties of the rarer elements and the development of a complete system of chemical analysis including these elements. This work, which extended over a period of twenty-five years, was summarized in *A System of Qualitative Analysis for the Rare Elements* (1927), written with W. C. Bray.

Noyes was one of the first chemists to surmise that the large deviations from unity of the activity coefficients of ions might be ascribed to the interaction of the electric charges of the ions. He carried out extensive studies of the properties of solutions of electrolytes, over a wide range of temperatures and pressures. Around 1920 this work culminated in the testing of the theory of electrostatic interactions of ions that was proposed by S. R. Milner in 1911 and by P. Debye and E. Hückel in 1923.

In 1903 Noyes became director of the Research Laboratory of Physical Chemistry at M.I.T., which was set up under a provision that half of the support would be provided by Noyes himself. He was director of this laboratory for sixteen years. He also served as acting president of M.I.T. for two years, beginning in 1907.

In 1913, at the request of George Ellery Hale, Noyes became associated on a part-time basis with the California Institute of Technology (then called Throop College of Technology), and in 1919 he resigned his post at M.I.T. and moved to California. During the remaining years of his life he devoted himself to developing the California institution into a great center of education and research in science and engineering. He and Hale, who was a member of the board of trustees, succeeded in bringing the physicist Robert Andrews Millikan from Chicago to Pasadena to develop the physics program and to serve as chief administrative officer of the Institute.

Noyes was a very good chemist. He diligently carried on research throughout his life and made some significant discoveries. But he was a great teacher of chemistry, and it is as a teacher of chemistry that he will be long remembered. He believed that students of chemistry should be introduced to research as early as possible. He was always on the watch for "carefully selected seeds," and he was a good judge of young people. In Boston he had been fond of sailing, and he made trips on his yacht with young friends. In Pasadena this interest was largely replaced by camping. He had a large touring car, and he liked to drive with the top down. It was his custom in the 1920's to invite new graduate students in chemistry to go with him on a camping trip to the desert, or to stay for a day with him in his beach house. These trips gave him an opportunity to size them up. The time was spent partly in enjoying nature and partly in discussions of scientific interest. In the evening he would often recite poetry at length, with evident pleasure and enthusiasm. He was also fond of tennis.

Noyes's personality was reserved, but he was not at all withdrawn from the general activities of the California Institute of Technology nor of American scientists as a whole. He never sought publicity and was rarely mentioned publicly in connection with innovations or changes in policy that led to the progress of the California Institute of Technology, although he was often the one who was responsible for the policies. It seems likely that Noyes was primarily responsible for the emphasis on pure rather than applied science, the limitation of the number of undergraduate students to 160 (later 180) per annual class, and the emphasis on the humanities and on undergraduate, graduate, and postdoctorate research.

In 1895 Noyes founded a journal, *Review of American Chemical Research*, which in 1907 became *Chemical Abstracts*. He was president of the American Chemical Society in 1904—the youngest man ever to hold office. During World War I he served as chairman of the National Research Council, an organization set up through the efforts of Noyes, Hale, and Millikan to aid the National Academy of Sciences in advising the government on scientific questions. He was president of the American Association for the Advancement of Science in 1927; and he was awarded the Humphry Davy Medal by the Royal Society in 1927, the Willard Gibbs Medal by the Chicago Section of the American Chemical Society in 1915, and the Theodore William Richards Medal by the Northeastern Section of the American Chemical Society in 1932 (first recipient). He was a member of a number of scientific societies.

Despite his reserved personality, which was perhaps due to shyness, Noyes had a great influence on students. He inspired them by his own unselfish devotion to science, his high principles, and his idealism, which was sometimes expressed in poetic selections that he read in class. He believed in the importance of a broad basic education. He strove to discover the most talented among his students as early as possible, and to encourage them by the provision of special instruction and other opportunities for rapid growth, such as scholarships permitting summer travel in Europe. His estate was left to the California Institute of Technology for the support of research in chemistry.

The qualities of Noyes that impressed themselves most strongly on his associates were his gentlemanliness, integrity, and unselfishness. His effectiveness in his work is attested by the great number of able scientists who came under his influence and received part of their training from him.

BIBLIOGRAPHY

A bibliography of Noyes's writings is given in Linus Pauling, "Arthur Amos Noyes, a Biographical Memoir," in *Biographical Memoirs. National Academy of Sciences*, **31** (1958), 322–346.

Other biographical notices are Frederick G. Keyes, "Arthur Amos Noyes," in *Nucleus* (Boston) (Oct. 1936), 28–33; R. A. Millikan, "Arthur Amos Noyes," in *Science*, **83** (1936), 613; and Miles S. Sherrill, "American Contemporaries: Arthur Amos Noyes," in *Industrial and Engineering Chemistry*, **23** (Apr. 1931), 443; and "Arthur Amos Noyes (1866–1936)," in *Proceedings of the American Academy of Arts and Sciences*, **74** (1940), 150–155.

LINUS PAULING

NOYES, WILLIAM ALBERT (*b.* Independence, Iowa, 6 November 1857; *d.* Urbana, Illinois, 24 October 1941), *chemistry*.

The youngest son of Spencer W. and Mary Packard Noyes, William Albert grew up in a farm environment, which did not lend itself to the study of chemistry. Although he enrolled at Grinnell College in classical studies, he read chemistry on the side and earned both the A.B. and B.S. degrees in 1879. He continued at Grinnell, teaching and studying analytical chemistry until January 1881, when he entered Johns Hopkins to study with Ira Remsen. In June 1882 he received not only the Ph.D. from Johns Hopkins, for work on benzene oxidation with chromic acid, but also an A.M. from Grinnell.

Noyes spent a year at Minnesota as an instructor and then, in 1883, went to the University of Tennessee as professor of chemistry. He married Flora Collier in December 1884. The couple had three children— Ethel and Helen, who both died in early childhood, and William Albert, Jr. His first wife died, and in 1902 Noyes married Mattie Elwell; they had one son,

Charles Edward. In 1886 Noyes began a seventeen-year career at the Rose Polytechnic Institute, Terre Haute, Indiana, where most of his work on camphor derivatives, especially camphoric acid, was performed. In 1889 he spent several months in Munich at the laboratory of Adolf von Baeyer.

In 1903 Noyes left the Institute to become chief chemist at the National Bureau of Standards, where he was engaged in atomic weight determinations. Burning hydrogen over palladium in pure oxygen and weighing the resultant water, he obtained a value of 1.00787:16 for the critical hydrogen:oxygen weight ratio, which still stands as one of the most precise chemical determinations ever made.

In 1907 Noyes became director of the chemical laboratories at the University of Illinois. He held this post until his retirement in 1926. Noyes married his third wife, Katherine Macy, in 1915; they had two sons, Richard Macy and Henry Pierre.

Besides his determination of the hydrogen:oxygen ratio, Noyes studied the structure of camphor and its derivatives and conducted early applications of the valence theory.

Noyes published his own numerous works and edited the papers of his colleagues while serving as editor of the *Journal of the American Chemical Society* from 1902 to 1917. He was the first editor of the following publications: *Chemical Abstracts* (1907–1910), *Chemical Reviews* (1924–1926), and the *American Chemical Society Scientific Monographs* (1919–1941).

BIBLIOGRAPHY

I. ORIGINAL WORKS. The majority of Noyes's papers appeared in *Journal of the American Chemical Society* between 1900 and 1941; his earlier works appeared in *American Chemistry Journal*. A key paper illustrating his researches in camphor chemistry is "Confirmation of Bredt's Formula. Some Derivatives of Inactive Camphoric Acid," in *American Chemistry Journal*, **27** (1902), 425, written with A. Patterson. His more important books are *Elements of Qualitative Analysis* (first published privately in 1887; 5th ed., 1926); *A Textbook of Organic Chemistry* (New York, 1913); and *Modern Alchemy* (Springfield, 1932), written with W. A. Noyes, Jr.

II. SECONDARY WORKS. Two excellent biographical sketches are Austin M. Patterson, "William Albert Noyes," in *Science*, **94** (1941), 477–479; and B. S. Hopkins, "William Albert Noyes," in *Journal of the American Chemical Society*, **66** (1944), 1045–1056, which includes a bibliography.

GERALD R. VAN HECKE

NUMEROV, BORIS VASILIEVICH (*b.* Novgorod, Russia, 17 January 1891; *d.* 19 March 1943), *astronomy, gravimetry.*

Numerov graduated in 1909 from the Novgorod Gymnasium and entered the faculty of physics and mathematics at St. Petersburg University. On graduating in 1913 he remained in the department of astronomy to prepare for a scientific career. In 1913–1915 he was a supernumerary astronomer at Pulkovo Observatory, where he observed on the zenith telescope. From 1915 to 1925 Numerov was astronomer-observer at the University's astronomical observatory. In 1924 he was appointed professor of practical astronomy, higher geodesy, and the technology of computation at the university and professor of mathematics at the Mining Institute.

In 1919 Numerov organized the Computation Bureau, the aim of which was to compile an astronomical yearbook. The following year a subdivision was established, the State Computation Institute (in 1924 renamed the Leningrad Astronomical Institute and now the Institute of Theoretical Astronomy of the Soviet Academy of Sciences). From 1920 through 1936 Numerov directed the Institute. In 1926–1928 he was also director of the Leningrad geophysical observatory. From 1931 to 1935 he also headed the section of applied mathematics of the State Optical Institute. In 1929 he was elected corresponding member of the USSR Academy of Sciences. In 1934 he received a doctorate in physical and mathematical sciences.

In 1930–1934 Numerov headed the Astronomical Committee of the People's Commissariat of Education, created to plan and organize astronomical institutions in the Soviet Union and to coordinate their work. Its successor was the Astronomical Council of the USSR Academy of Sciences. In connection with the work of the committee, Numerov traveled to Holland, France, England, Germany, and the United States, visiting astronomical observatories and observing geophysical methods of prospecting for useful minerals. In 1920–1926 Numerov was president of the Russian Astronomical Society.

Numerov's scientific career was devoted to practical astronomy and astrometry, celestial mechanics, and gravimetry. He was notable in Soviet astronomy for having organized the construction and manufacture of gravimetric and astronomical instruments and equipment. For this purpose in 1928 he created a mechanical workshop at the Leningrad Astronomical Institute and, later, a construction bureau that produced a number of new and improved gravimeters and the first Soviet telescope—a reflector with a thirty-two-centimeter mirror installed at the first mountain astronomical observatory in the Soviet Union, at Abastumani (now the Abastumani Astrophysical Observatory of the Academy of Sciences of the Georgian S.S.R.). In 1931, under the presidency of Numerov, the Commission of Astronomical Instruments was created in the All-Union Cooperative of Optical-Mechanical Production. It laid the foundation for the industrial manufacture of large astronomical instruments.

Numerov's new program and method (1916) of analyzing zenith telescope observations was used in determining variations in latitude and was later adopted at Pulkovo. He developed a complete theory of the zenith telescope and introduced formulas for the influence of instrumental errors, proposed a new method of studying the forms of pivots of transit instruments, and developed a theory of universal and photographic transit instruments. At the beginning of the 1920's Numerov organized the compilation and publication of astronomical yearbooks, necessary for the observatories and numerous expeditions; later the Astronomical Institute also compiled and published *Morskoi ezhegodnik* ("Marine Yearbook") and *Aviatsionny ezhegodnik* ("Aviation Yearbook"). In the astronomy of ephemerides, Numerov developed useful tables and charts for computing geographical and Gauss-Kruger rectangular coordinates.

Numerov's new method of computing planetary perturbation was widely used in compiling the annual reference book founded by Numerov, *Efemeridi malykh planet* ("Ephemerides of Asteroids"), which acquired an international reputation. In 1923, for large-scale computation and improvements in the calculation of the orbits of asteroids, he proposed an original and effective method of integrating differential equations of celestial mechanics (the method of extrapolation). The application of this method allowed the computation in 1930 of a new and very precise ephemerides of the eighth satellite of Jupiter. After 1923 the satellite was not sighted again until it was rediscovered on 22 November 1930 by astronomers at the Lick Observatory in California.

Numerov gave a theoretical basis to the analysis of star catalogs by means of observational data on asteroids, and he proposed an original plan for international cooperation in determining the constants that characterize star catalogs. This plan was approved by the International Astronomical Union in 1935 and is now used in working the catalog of faint stars.

Numerov introduced into practice the pendulum gravimeter and the variograph for studying the upper layers of the earth's crust in geological prospecting. He participated in about ten gravimetrical expeditions to the Urals, the Donets Basin, the Kazakh S.S.R., and other areas, testing the new instruments developed under his direction: a light quarter-second pendulum apparatus, a half-second pendulum apparatus, a gravitation torsion balance with three levers, and many others. Numerov's plan for a general gravimetrical survey of the Soviet Union provided extremely valuable results.

BIBLIOGRAPHY

I. ORIGINAL WORKS. Numerov's earlier works include "Nouveau programme pour le zénith-télescope," in *Izvestiya Pulkovskoi observatorii*, **7**, no. 1 (1916), 1–20; "Teoria universalnogo instrumenta" ("Theory of the Universal Instrument"), in *Astronomichesky ezhegodnik na 1923* ("Astronomical Yearbook for 1923"; Petrograd, 1923), app. 3, 239–272; "Novy metod opredelenia orbit i vychislenia efemerid s uchetom vozmushcheny" ("A New Method for Determining Orbits and Computing Ephemerides That Takes Into Account Perturbations"), in *Trudy Glavnoi rossiiskoi astrofizicheskoi observatorii*, **2** (1923), 188–288; "A Method of Extrapolation of Perturbations," in *Monthly Notices of the Royal Astronomical Society*, **84** (1924), 592–601; "Chislennoe integrirovanie uravneny nevozmushchennogo dvizhenia v polyarnykh koordinatakh" ("Numerical Integration of Equations of Unperturbed Motion in Polar Coordinates"), in *Byulleten Astronomicheskogo Instituta*, no. 2 (1924), 7–107; "Résultats du calcul des éphémérides et des perturbations approchées des coordonnées rectangulaires de 99 planètes pour l'époque 1921–1925," in *Izvestiya Glavnoi astronomicheskoi observatorii v Pulkove*, **10**, no. 94 (1924), 58–155; "Teoreticheskie osnovania primenenia gravimetricheskogo metoda v geologii" ("Theoretical Bases of the Application of the Gravimetric Method in Geology"), in *Izvestiya Geologicheskogo komiteta*, **14**, no. 3 (1925), 331–347; "Calcul des éphémérides pour une excentricité arbitraire," in *Journal des Observateurs*, **7** (1926), 125–130; "Berechnung der gestörten Ephemeriden nach der Extrapolationsmethode," in *Byulleten Astronomicheskogo Instituta*, no. 12 (1926), 109–120; "Hilfstafeln zur Bahnbestimmung und gestörten Ephemeridenrechnung nach der Extrapolationsmethode," *ibid.*, no. 13 (1926), 121–152; *Programma sposoba Talkotta dlya opredelenia shiroty* ("Program of the Talcott Method for Determining Latitude"; Leningrad, 1927); and "Zavisimost mezhdu mestnymi anomaliami sily tyazhesti i proizvodnymi ot potentsiala" ("The Relation Between the Local Anomalies in the Force of Gravitation and the Derivatives of Potential"), in *Doklady Akademii nauk SSSR*, ser. A (1929), 101–105, and in *Zeitschrift für Geophysik*, **5**, no. 2 (1929), 58–62.

Later works include "Gravitatsionny variometr s tremya rychagami" ("A Gravitational Torsion Balance With Three Levers"), in *Byulleten Astronomicheskogo Instituta*, no. 30 (1931), 103–108; "K voprosu opredelenia sistematicheskikh oshibok skloneny fundamentalnykh zvezd" ("On the Problem of Determining Systematic Errors in the Declination of Fundamental Stars"), *ibid.*, no. 32 (1932), 139–147; "Konstruirovanie i izgotovlenie astronomicheskikh priborov" ("The Construction and Manufacture of Astronomical Instruments"), in *Astronomia* ("Nauka v SSSR za 15 let") "Astronomy" ("Science in the USSR During 15 Years"); (Moscow–Leningrad, 1932), 207–215; "Svetosilny fotografichesky meridianny krug" ("An Efficient Photographic Meridian Circle"), in *Astronomichesky zhurnal*, **12** (1935), 349–355, and in *Doklady Akademii nauk SSSR*, **3** (1935), 201–204; "Primenenie metoda ekstrapolirovania k tochnomy vychisleniyu vozmushchennogo dvizhenia malykh planet" ("The Use of the Method of Extrapolation for the Exact Computation of the Perturbational Motion of Asteroids"), in *Astronomichesky zhurnal*, **12** (1935), 455–475; "K voprosu o sovmestnom opredelenii popravok elementov planety i Zemli" ("On the Problem of the Simultaneous Correction of the Elements of a Planet and of the Earth"), in *Astronomichesky zhurnal*, **12** (1935), 584–593, and in *Astronomical Journal*, **45**, no. 12 (1936), 105–111; "K voprosu ob opredelenii geoida na osnovanii gravitatsionnykh nablyudeny" ("On the Problem of Determining the Geoid on the Basis of Gravitational Observations"), in *Astronomichesky zhurnal*, **12**, no. 1 (1935), 47–59; "K voprosu opredelenia sistematicheskikh oshibok zvezdnykh polozheny" ("On the Problem of Determining Systematic Errors in Stellar Positions"), in *Doklady Akademii nauk SSR*, **2** no. 7 (1935), 451–457, in *Astronomichesky zhurnal*, **12**, no. 4 (1935), 339–348, and in *Journal des Observateurs*, **18**, no. 4 (1935), 57–64, in French; "K voprosu o postroenii fundamental'nogo kataloga slabykh zvezd" ("On the Problem of Compiling a Fundamental Catalog of Faint Stars"), in *Doklady Akademii nauk SSSR*, **12** (1936), 261–263, and in *Astronomische Nachrichten*, **260** (1936), 305–322; "Ob opredelenii figury geoida na osnovanii nablyudeny sily tyazhesti" ("On Determining the Figure of the Geoid on the Basis of Observations of the Force of Gravity"), in *Doklady Akademii nauk SSSR*, **12** (1936), 265–268, written with D. N. Khramov; "On the Problem of the Stability of the Motion of Trojans," in *Byulleten Astronomicheskogo Instituta*, no. 41 (1936), 1–4; and "Absolute Perturbations of Polar Coordinates of Asteroids From Outer Planets," *ibid.*, no. 42 (1937), 37–57, in English and Russian.

II. SECONDARY LITERATURE. On Numerov and his work, see S. I. Seleshnikov, in *Astronomichesky kalendar* for 1966 (Moscow, 1965), 211–214; and N. S. Yakhontova, "Boris Vasilievich Numerov, 1891–1943," in *Byulleten Instituta teoreticheskoi astronomii*, **9**, no. 3 (1963), 213–215, with portrait.

P. G. KULIKOVSKY

NUÑEZ SALACIENSE, PEDRO (*b.* Alcácer do Sol, Portugal, 1502; *d.* Coimbra, Portugal, 11 August 1578), *mathematics, cosmography.*

Nuñez's parents are believed to have been Jewish, since he was registered as a "new Christian." He was married at Salamanca in 1523 to Giomar de Arias,

daughter of a Spanish Christian, Pedro Fernández de Arias; they had six children. The earliest information on his education places him as an independent student at the University of Salamanca in 1521 and 1522. He moved to Lisbon in 1524 or 1525, at which time he received a bachelor's degree in medicine while simultaneously extending his knowledge of mathematics and studying astrology. This excellent preparation served as a basis for his appointment as royal cosmographer on 16 November 1529. In recognition of his abilities as a practical researcher, he was named on 4 December 1529 to the professorship of moral philosophy at the University of Lisbon, then to the chair of logic (15 January 1530); during 1531 and 1532 he also held the chair of metaphysics. At the same time Nuñez was pursuing his own studies, and on 16 February 1532 he graduated as licentiate in medicine from the University of Lisbon.

The professorship of mathematics at Lisbon was moved to Coimbra in 1537; and on 16 October 1544 Nuñez was named to the post, which he occupied until his retirement on 4 February 1562. On 22 December 1547 he was named chief royal cosmographer and fulfilled the duties of the office until his death.

Nuñez was called to court on 11 September 1572 by his former student Sebastian, grandson of John III. He remained in Lisbon for two years as adviser for the projected reform of weights and measures, which was promulgated in 1575. He was also appointed professor of mathematics for the instruction of pilots, navigators, and cartographers. After the reform of weights and measures he returned to Coimbra, where he remained until his death.

Considered the greatest of Portuguese mathematicians, Nuñez reveals in his discoveries, theories, and publications that he was a first-rate geographer, physicist, cosmologist, geometer, and algebraist. In addition to works in Portuguese (*Tratado da sphera*), he wrote and published several works in Latin so that his discoveries might be utilized by educated people of other nations. His writings are rigorously scientific and usually contain a profusion of drawings and figures so that they may be understood more easily.

Among Nuñez's students in Lisbon were the brothers of John III, Louis and Henry, the latter the future king and cardinal. While at Coimbra he taught Clavius, known as the sixteenth–century Euclid. Also among his outstanding students were Nicolas Coelho de Amaral, who succeeded Nuñez in his professorship; Manuel de Figueredo, who became chief royal cosmographer; and João de Castro, viceroy of India, and one of the greatest Portuguese navigators.

Nuñez made important contributions in the design of instruments. In astronomical observations the impossibility of precisely measuring small portions of an arc was an impediment, and to overcome this difficulty he conceived the idea of the nonius. In its original form this instrument, consisting of forty-four concentric auxiliary circles, was attached to an astrolabe for measuring fractions of a degree. Upon each circle and upon their quadrants were equal divisions, ranging from eighty-nine on the circle of greatest diameter to forty-six on the circle of least diameter. Each circle had one division less than the one outside it and one division more than the one inside, making it possible to take a reading from the circle that gave the most accurate approximation.

This instrument has not been modified during the four centuries since it was devised, but it has been refined. In 1593 Clavius reduced the auxiliary circles to one divided into sixty-one parts and divided the limb of the astrolabe into sixty; and in 1631 Pierre Vernier let the auxiliary arc move freely by attaching it to the alidade of the astrolabe. (The latter variation is called a vernier in some countries.) With the nonius exceedingly small measures may be read on any scale or system of division, either circular or rectilinear.

As a navigator Nuñez made a significant discovery based on observations reported to him in 1533 by Admiral Martim Afonso de Sousa. They relate to rhumb line sailing and to great circle sailing. The former is the course of the ship while sailing on a single bearing (always oblique to the meridian in the direction of one and the same point of the compass), subsequently (1624) called "loxodrome" by Willebrord Snell. The latter, which is the shortest distance between any two terrestrial points, has been called "orthodrome"; in it the bearing varies. Until that time pilots had considered them equivalent; but Nuñez demonstrated their dissimilarity, an important discovery that exerted great influence on the making of charts for navigation. For this purpose he conceived and drew curved rhumb lines (1534–1537), several years before Mercator made a loxodromic terrestrial globe with rhumb lines for eight sea routes in each quadrant, drawn from various points in different latitudes (1541).

Another of Nuñez's contributions to navigation was his technique for determining latitude by means of two readings of the sun's altitude and the azimuth, with solutions that were quite interesting and ingenious but of little practical use on shipboard; they relate more to the concerns of a scientist in the observatory than to the needs of a practical navigator and therefore have fallen into disuse.

In physics and seamanship Nuñez wrote a commentary on Aristotle's mechanical problem of propulsion by oars. It is a contribution to the geometry of motion —an attempt to determine, at each moment and in every circumstance, the deviation of the boat in relation to the oars.

Nuñez's cosmological theories relating to solar and lunar motions are important, as are his inquiries into the duration of day and night, the transformation of astronomical coordinates, and other problems concerning the motions of celestial bodies. He commented on the planetary theories of Georg Peurbach; worked on the problem of determining the duration of twilight; and solved the problem of afterglow or second twilight.

Nuñez also exhibited mathematical ability in geometry with his original solutions to the problems of spherical triangles. He demonstrated the errors made by Oronce Fine, professor at the Collège de France, in his attempt to solve three problems by means of ruler and compass: trisecting an angle, doubling a cube, and squaring a circle.

Finally, Nuñez was a poet; his highly regarded sonnets were collected and published by Joaquín Ignacio de Fraitas (Coimbra, 1826).

BIBLIOGRAPHY

I. ORIGINAL WORKS. *Tratado da sphera* (Lisbon, 1537) consists of three parts: (1) annotated translations by Nuñez from Sacrobosco's *Tractatus de sphaera*, writings on the theory of the sun and moon by Georg Peurbach, and the first book of Ptolemy's *Geography*; (2) two writings by Nuñez, a treatise on certain difficulties in navigation and a treatise in defense of his navigation chart and tables of the movements of the sun and its declination; (3) an epigram in Latin written to Nuñez by Jorge Coelho. The first part of this work was reprinted at Lisbon in 1911 and 1912, the second part in 1913, and a facs. ed. was published at Munich in 1915. There is an ed. of a French trans. prior to 1562, published in France. The Latin version, *Opera quae complectuntur*, *primum duos libros . . .* , was published at Basel in 1566 and in subsequent, much improved, eds. in 1573 and 1592. It is in this work that the theory of loxodromic curves is first set forth.

Other works are *De crepusculis liber unus* (Lisbon, 1542; 2nd ed., Coimbra, 1571), which treats the afterglow and the nonius; *Astronomici introductorii De Sphaera epitome* (n.p., n.d. [1543?]), with 12 folios thought to be an introduction to *Tratado da sphera*; *De erratis Promtii Finoei, regii mathematicarum Lutetice professoris* (Coimbra, 1546; 2nd ed. 1571); and *Libro de álgebra en arithmética y geometría* (Antwerp, 1567).

In *De crepusculis*, Nuñez mentions MS treatises, now believed lost, on the geometry of spherical triangles, on the astrolabe, on the geometrical representation of the sphere on a plane surface, on proportions in measurement, and on the method of delineating a globe for the use of navigators. Another MS mentioned is a work on the sea routes to Brazil. In catalog no. 508, item no. 15, of Maggs Bros. bookstore in London, there is a reference to "Codice de circa 1560 de Nunes (Pedro) y Vaz Fraguoso (Pedro)," containing the elements of navigation and routes to the East, which is believed to have been compiled by Vaz Fraguoso.

II. SECONDARY LITERATURE. See the following, listed chronologically: *Diccionario enciclopédico hispano-americano*, XIII (Barcelona, 1813), 1190–1198; Rodolfo Guimaräes, *Sur la vie et l'oeuvre de Pedro Nunes* (Coimbra, 1915); Luciano Pereira da Silva, *As obras de Pedro Nunes, sua cronologia bibliográfica* (Coimbra, 1925); and A. Fontoura da Costa, *Pedro Nunes (1502–1578)* (Lisbon, 1938); and *Quarto centenârio da publicaçao de Tratado de sphera de Pedro Nunes* (Lisbon, 1938).

J. M. LóPEZ DE AZCONA

NUSSELT, ERNST KRAFT WILHELM (*b.* Nuremberg, Germany, 25 November 1882; *d.* Munich, Germany, 1 September 1957), *heat transfer, thermodynamics.*

Nusselt was the first significant contributor to the subject of analytical convective heat transfer. He completed his schooling at a time when the problems of heating and cooling in the increasingly high-performance power equipment of the early twentieth century finally demanded accurate analysis. For a century Fourier's mathematical theory of heat conduction in rigid media had provided the only analytical attack on the problem, but it was inadequate to predict the heat flux in a flowing fluid. In 1915 Nusselt cut the Gordian knot. Although analytical solutions to the appropriate fluid-flow equations were so intrinsically complicated that they had to await the more fundamental work of others, Nusselt used dimensional analysis to show, in a single stroke, the functional form that such solutions would have to take. He thus made it possible to generalize limited experimental data.

Nusselt was the son of Johannes Nusselt, a factory owner, and Pauline Fuchs Nusselt. He completed his early education in Nuremberg in 1900 and then enrolled at the Technische Hochschule in Munich to study mechanical engineering. After six semesters he transferred to the Technische Hochschule of Charlottenburg, in Berlin, where he completed his studies. He then returned to Munich and passed his mechanical engineering diploma examination there.

Nusselt began his studies toward a doctorate in mechanical engineering in Munich, and from 1906 through 1907 he served as an assistant to Oskar Knoblauch, who was also the teacher of another early heat transfer luminary, Ernst Schmidt. He completed the degree in August 1907, and from then until 1925 he moved about Germany from post to post. From September 1907 to June 1909 he was assistant to the well-known thermodynamicist Richard Mollier at the Technische Hochschule in Dresden. He then worked in the heat technology division of the Sulzer brothers' firm in Switzerland (1909–1911). He returned to the mechanical laboratory in Dresden in 1913 and held indefinite teaching appointments until 1917. From January 1918 through March 1919 he returned to industry and worked at the Badische Anilin- und Soda-Fabrik in Ludwigshafen. In April 1920 he was appointed professor at the Technische Hochschule in Karlsruhe. In 1925, Nusselt was named to the chair in theoretical mechanics at the Technische Hochschule in Munich. He retired from this post in 1952 and was succeeded by Schmidt.

Two of Nusselt's most important works were completed during his years in Dresden. His paper on the similitude of convective heat transfer, "The Basic Law of Heat Transfer" (1915), followed his earlier work on the thermal conductivity of insulating materials and some work with heat convection coefficients. The scope of his 1915 paper, however, was far broader; in this work he set up the dimensionless functional equations for both natural and forced convection. He thus reduced the large number of physical variables that appear in the boundary layer equations to the familiar dimensionless groups that today bear the names "Nusselt number," "Reynolds number," "Prandtl number," and "Grashof number." He also noted additional groups that are needed when physical properties vary or when the full equations of motion are used to define natural convection. It was thus possible for experimentalists to reduce limited data into these few parameters and to form simple empirical equations among them. Such correlations have, in most cases, preceded heat transfer theory down to the present day.

His other major contribution during this period was a paper entitled "The Film Condensation of Steam" (1916), in which he provided a clear-headed and simple description of the film condensation of any liquid by linearizing the temperature profile and ignoring inertia in the liquid. Subsequent efforts to refine this heat transfer prediction have failed to alter his numerical results, except for liquid metals and the most extreme heat fluxes.

Nusselt's later works branched into radiant heat transfer, combustion, and a variety of applications of heat transfer and thermodynamics to power equipment. In 1930 he provided an important description of the similarity between heat and mass transfer, and

162

in 1934 and 1944 he published the first and second volumes, respectively, of a book on technical thermodynamics.

Nusselt was married on December 12, 1917, while teaching at Dresden, to Susanne Thurmer. The couple had two daughters and one son. Nusselt was an energetic man, strongly inner-directed, soft-spoken, and self-contained. He was an avid mountain climber throughout his life, and he appears to have equated the methodical assault of a mountain to the kind of assault a man should make on the problems that beset him. He brought this same kind of energy and concentration to his technical work. He was, however, circumspect and, perhaps, even cautious.

During the 1930's and 1940's German scientists made great advances in heat transfer. But Nusselt did not wield great influence within the peer group that controlled this field. It was probably not in his makeup to do so, and he is known to have suffered from a chronic internal ailment during these years. Although he was an exacting taskmaster with his students, he apparently lacked charisma and he was not a good lecturer.

In 1947 Nusselt's son, Dietrich, also a mountaineer, fell to his death on the east wall of the Riffelkopf in the Wetterstein Gebirge. Nusselt did little more in his remaining years, and upon his retirement he left the university completely and lived out his life in relative seclusion.

BIBLIOGRAPHY

I. ORIGINAL WORKS. G. Lück and G. Kling (see below) both provide a bibliography of over 50 major works. Nusselt's most important writings include "Das Grundgesetz des Wärmeüberganges," in *Gesundheits Ingenieur*, **38** (1915), 872; "Die Oberflächenkondensation des Wasserdampfes," in *Zeitschrift des Vereines deutscher Ingenieure*, **60** (1916), 541, 569; "Wärmeübergang, Diffusion und Verdunstung," in *Zeitschrift für angewandte Mathematik und Physik*, **10** (1930), 105; and *Technische Thermodynamik*, 2 vols. (Berlin, 1934, 1944). Nusselt's autobiographical deposition for the American occupation force after World War II provides a wealth of personal detail.

II. SECONDARY LITERATURE. Poggendorff, VIIa, 455, lists several biographical articles; the most extensive is G. Kling in *Chemie-Ingenieur-Technik*, **24** (1952), 597–608, which includes a bibliography of works by both Nusselt and his co-workers. G. Lück's article on Nusselt's retirement in *Gesundheits Ingenieur*, **74** (1953), 7–8, also provides a similar bibliography. *Allgemeine Warmetechnik*, **3** (1952), 161–163, includes a bibliography and a list of Nusselt's doctoral students and their theses.

JOHN H. LIENHARD

NUTTALL, THOMAS (*b.* Long Preston, near Settle, Yorkshire, England, 5 January 1786; *d.* Nut Grove Hall, near St. Helens, Lancashire, England, 10 September 1859), *botany, ornithology, natural history.*

Very little is known of the early life of Nuttall. A bachelor throughout his life, he was extremely reticent about his personal affairs. Through careful frugality while in America, he was able to make numerous field trips collecting botanical specimens.

His father, James Nuttall, married Mary Hardacre in January 1785. He died before Thomas was twelve years old, and his profession is unknown. The family was not prosperous, and at the age of fourteen Thomas was apprenticed to an uncle to learn the printing trade. At the conclusion of his apprenticeship, he sought other employment. In 1808 he sailed for Philadelphia, and shortly after his arrival in America, he became a friend of and plant collector for Benjamin Smith Barton.

With Barton's encouragement Nuttall began to take a serious interest in American flora, teaching himself the principles of botany. In 1809 he made two field trips, collecting botanical specimens for Barton. The next year Barton outlined and financed a more ambitious collecting program, which was designed to take Nuttall through hazardous Indian country into Canada. Unable to complete Barton's itinerary, Nuttall joined an expedition of John Jacob Astor's Pacific Fur Company. The English botanist John Bradbury was also a member of this party. Traveling up the Missouri River, the two Englishmen collected new species of plants from lands that were botanically unexplored. At the conclusion of the expedition, Nuttall sailed for England in the fall of 1811. The War of 1812 prevented his return to America until 1815.

Nuttall published the results of his first western trip in *The Genera of North American Plants, and a Catalogue of the Species, to the Year 1817* (1818). As the first comprehensive study of American flora, this work established his reputation as a botanist. Although he classified his plants by the Linnaean system, Nuttall nevertheless discussed the natural relationships of the different genera he described. He thus provided American naturalists with an introduction to the merits of A. L. de Jussieu's natural system of classification. *Genera* described many western species new to botany and helped to stimulate an interest in the study of the plant life of the western United States.

From 1818 to 1820 Nuttall journeyed west again, collecting plants on the Arkansas River in Indian territory. In May 1820 he presented a paper describing the geology and fossils of the Mississippi Valley to the Academy of Natural Sciences of Philadelphia. His memoir anticipated modern geological techniques of stratigraphical correlations by suggesting a similarity between the geological formations of America and Europe.

In late 1822 Nuttall received his first professional appointment when he was named curator of the botanic garden at Cambridge, Massachusetts, and lecturer in natural history at Harvard. He remained at Harvard for eleven years, occasionally absenting himself for collecting trips. For the use of his students, he published *An Introduction to Systematic and Physiological Botany* (1827). The second edition of this work introduced new materials on plant physiology; and in its descriptions of the cellular composition of plants, Nuttall partially anticipated Schleiden's cell theory. While in Cambridge, Nuttall developed an interest in ornithology and began to gather data for a guide to North American birds. Between 1832 and 1834 he published his only major ornithological study, *A Manual of the Ornithology of the United States and Canada*. This inexpensively priced study demonstrated Nuttall's intimate familiarity with the literature on the subject and his personal observations of birds in their natural habitats. One of the most original features of this work was his careful attempt to describe the songs of birds through syllabic patterns.

Claiming that he was "vegetating at Harvard," Nuttall desired to return to the virgin flora of the West. His discovery of many new species of plants on his Arkansas trip convinced him that the study of western plant life was still in its initial stages. Resigning his position at Harvard, he won a chance to go west once more when he joined Nathaniel Jarvis Wyeth's second expedition to Oregon in 1834. Nuttall invited the young ornithologist John Kirk Townsend to accompany this party. Arriving safely in Oregon, Nuttall was the first experienced botanist to have traveled across the continent collecting specimens. On the Pacific coast he gathered not only plants but also mollusks and crustaceans. After spending two winters in Hawaii collecting, he returned to Boston in September 1836.

Nuttall's remaining years in America (1836–1841) were spent primarily in Philadelphia, where he began to work up the recently acquired western specimens. He included some of his data on western plants in his contribution to Torrey and Gray's *Flora of North America*. His last major activity in America was the preparation of a three-volume appendix for a new edition of François André Michaux's *North American Sylva*. This appendix, which was also published

separately, contained extensive information on the sylva of the western United States.

In 1842 Nuttall returned to England; and except for a six-month visit to America in 1847–1848, he remained there until his death in 1859. His last years in England were not notable for any major botanical studies and were not scientifically productive. He did become interested in the rhododendrons of Assam, but published only a brief paper on the subject.

Nuttall's greatest scientific strength was his meticulous skill as a fieldworker and his detailed knowledge of plants in their native habitats. His taxonomy was at times marred by use of the Linnaean system of classification. Since he was forced by the circumstances of wilderness travel to collect specimens at random seasons, his data about the seasonal development of plants were often insufficient for correct taxonomic determination. Nuttall willingly shared specimens that he obtained on his expeditions with more skilled and specialized co-workers in other fields of natural history. He provided materials for further study to Audubon, Say, Pursh, Gambel, Torrey, Gray, and John Bachman. Nevertheless, Nuttall was the preeminent figure in the discovery of the flora of the American West.

BIBLIOGRAPHY

I. ORIGINAL WORKS. In addition to papers in *Transactions of the American Philosophical Society* and *Journal of the Academy of Natural Sciences of Philadelphia*, Nuttall published the following works: *The Genera of North American Plants, and a Catalogue of the Species, to the Year 1817* (Philadelphia, 1818); *An Introduction to Systematic and Physiological Botany* (Cambridge, Mass., 1827; 2nd ed., enl., 1830); *A Journal of Travels Into the Arkansa Territory, During the Year 1819* (Philadelphia, 1821), repr. as vol. XIII of Reuben G. Thwaites, ed., *Early Western Travels, 1748–1846* (Cleveland, 1905); *A Manual of the Ornithology of the United States and Canada: The Land Birds* (Cambridge, Mass., 1832) and *The Water Birds* (Boston, 1834); and *The North American Sylva*, 3 vols. (Philadelphia, 1842–1849).

II. SECONDARY WORKS. The only extensive study of Nuttall's life and career is Jeannette E. Graustein, *Thomas Nuttall Naturalist, Explorations in America 1808–1841* (Cambridge, Mass., 1967). Carefully documented, this volume contains numerous references to Nuttall's correspondence and scientific papers as well as contemporary biographical notices. Additional information is in Richard G. Beidleman, "Some Biographical Sidelights of Thomas Nuttall, 1786–1859," in *Proceedings of the American Philosophical Society*, **104**, no. 1 (Feb. 1960), 86–100; Jeannette E. Graustein, "Nuttall's Travels Into the Old Northwest, an Unpublished 1810 Diary," in *Chronica* *botanica*, **14**, nos. 1–2 (1950–1951), 1–85; and Francis W. Pennell, "Travels and Scientific Collections of Thomas Nuttall," in *Bartonia*, **18** (1936), 1–51.

PHILLIP DRENNON THOMAS

NYLANDER, FREDRIK (*b.* Uleåborg [now Oulu], Russia [now Finland], 9 September 1820; *d.* Contrexéville, Vosges, France, 2 October 1880), *botany, medicine*.

Nylander was the son of Anders Nylander, a merchant, and the former Margareta Magdalena Fahlander, and the great-grandson of Johan Nylander, bishop of Borgå (now Porvoo) and of Åbo (now Turku). In 1853 he married Ida Babette Hummel, of Frankfurt.

Nylander received his secondary education at the Gymnasium in Åbo and graduated in 1836. He matriculated at the University of Helsinki in the same year and was awarded a master's degree in 1840; he remained at the university to specialize in botany and medicine, taking his examination and receiving his candidate's degree in medicine in 1843. He was lecturer in botany at the University of Helsinki from 1843 to 1853. In 1844 he received his doctorate in botany. He spent 1843–1846 at the St. Petersburg Botanic Garden, during which time he became fluent in Russian. On his return he studied for several months at the University of Uppsala. In 1853 he received the M.D. from the University of Helsinki and was then appointed assistant to the municipal physician of Uleåborg. He became the municipal physician there in 1865, holding that post until his death.

Nylander was the first to study the flora of Finland critically. He made many botanical expeditions and published five important papers on the Finnish-Russian flora. He pioneered in the botanical exploration of the then almost unknown Kola Peninsula. With Johan Ångström (1813–1879) he explored eastern Finland, Russian Karelia to the White Sea, and Russian Lapland in the summer of 1843. The following summer they explored Russian and Norwegian Lapland.

Nylander later abandoned botanical pursuits to concentrate on medicine. In addition to administering health services in Uleåborg, he was active in the political life of Finland, being elected by the Socialist party to the House of Burghers of Uleåborg and representing the party in the Diet convened in 1872. Throughout his later life Nylander was a staunch promoter of the Finnish language for all official use and a strong partisan of Finnish autonomy. Reports of his appointment as professor by the city of Uleåborg in 1877 are unclear; the title must have been honorary, since the University of Oulu was not founded until 1959.

BIBLIOGRAPHY

Biographical notices include A. Oswald Kairamo, "Fredrik Nylander," in *Kansallinen Elamakerrasto*, IV (Porvoo, 1927), 251; Sextus Otto Lindberg, "Fredrik Nylander, 1820–1880," in *Meddelanden af Societas pro fauna et flora fennica*, **6** (1881), 260; N. J. S[cheutz], "Fredrik Nylander," in *Botaniska notiser* (1880), no. 6, 199; and Theodor Saelan, "Nylander, Fredrik," in *Acta Societatis pro fauna et flora fennica*, **43** (1928), 354–355, which contains a bibliography.

GEORGE H. M. LAWRENCE

NYLANDER, WILLIAM (*b.* Uleåborg [now Oulu], Russia [now Finland], 3 January 1822; *d.* Paris, France, 29 March 1899), *botany*.

Nylander, brother of Fredrik Nylander, was the son of Anders Nylander, a merchant, and Margareta Magdalena Fahlander. He never married. For much of his life he was a world authority on the identification of lichens.

Nylander graduated from the gymnasium in Åbo (now Turku) in 1839 and matriculated at the University of Helsinki the same year. He passed examinations as a candidate in philosophy in 1843 and continued his studies at the university, where he received the M.D. in 1847. He never established medical practice, and his interests thereafter were limited to natural history.

An ardent naturalist, Nylander traveled throughout Finland in 1847 and 1848, collecting plant and insect specimens. His early publications dealt with entomology, especially with the identification of Finnish ants and bees. In 1848 Nylander went to Paris, where he studied lichens at the Muséum d'Histoire Naturelle, under Charles Tuslane. During most of the following decade he published much about lichens, primarily their classification and identification, and his work was acclaimed in Europe and America.

In 1857 Nylander became the first professor of botany at the University of Helsinki. Unhappy with his treatment there, he resigned in 1863 and emigrated permanently to France, where he had neither academic affiliation nor gainful employment.

Through his abundant, if often trivial, publications Nylander became known as the one who had acquired the reputation of being able to identify lichens from any part of the world. Specimens that he identified became his personal property, and he subsequently amassed the world's richest and largest private lichen herbarium. In 1868 the French government awarded Nylander the Prix des Mazières for his contributions to lichenology. Somewhat earlier the Portuguese had conferred on him the Ordre du Christ. He was elected to honorary membership in learned societies and stood at the pinnacle of his career.

The decade following 1868 witnessed revolutionary discoveries about the origin and biology of lichens, concepts accepted internationally by leading scientists.

Nylander held to the earlier theory that the green cells in lichens were primitive prototypes of algae. In 1867 Schwendener proposed that the green cells were themselves true algae, parasitized and imprisoned by fungal hyphae, and that the two separate and unrelated organisms lived together by obligative symbiosis. This was proved by Rees in England (1871), by Bornet in France (1872), and by du Bary in Germany (1873). Summarily dismissing the new ideas, Nylander became one of a shrinking handful who held to the earlier but scientifically untenable view. His vitriolic abuse of fellow botanists in France and elsewhere closed the doors of many institutions, including the Muséum d'Histoire Naturelle, to Nylander. Most editors then denied him access to publication in their journals. He became a paranoid recluse who considered all who disagreed with him to be his enemies.

About 1879, in poor financial circumstances, Nylander made an agreement with the University of Helsinki whereby, in return for a lifetime annual pension of 1,200 francs, he would bequeath it his lichen herbarium, library, notebooks, and papers.

Nylander's full bibliography contains 314 papers. Less than a score of them, published before 1875, continue to be recognized as major contributions to botanical science; but so great was the impact he made during the first fifteen years of his professional life that he will always be counted as the dominant lichenologist of the mid-nineteenth century.

BIBLIOGRAPHY

I. Original Works. Nylander's major scientific works include *Conspectus florae Helsingforsiensis* (Helsinki, 1852); "Essai d'une classification des lichens. I–II," in *Mémoires de la Société impériale académique des sciences naturelles de Cherbourg* (1854), 5–16 and (1855), 161–202; "Énumération générale des lichens, avec l'indication sommaire de leur distribution géographique," *ibid.* (1857), 85–146, 332–339; "Prodromus lichenographie Galliae et Algeriae," in *Actes de la Société linnéenne de Bordeaux*, **21** (1857), 249–467, also pub. as a separate vol. with the same title (Bordeaux, 1857); *Synopsis methodica lichenum omnium hucusque cognitorum, praemissa introductione lingua gallica*

tracta, 2 vols. (I, Paris, 1858–1860; II, Paris [1861], 1869), never completed; "Lichenes Scandinaviae," in *Notiser ur sällskapets pro fauna et flora fennica förhandlingar*, **5** (1861), 1–312; and "Lichenes Lapponiae orientalis," *ibid.*, n.s. **8** (1882), 101–192—a few preprints correctly dated 1866 are known.

II. Secondary Literature. Biographical notices include Alphonse Boistel, "Le Professeur William Nylander," in *Revue générale de botanique*, **11** (1899), 218–237, with partial bibliography; Auguste Hue, "William Nylander," in *Bulletin. Société botanique de France*, **47** (1899), 152–165, with portrait; Thorgny Krok, "Nylander, William," in *Bibliotheca botanica suecana* (Uppsala–Stockholm, 1925), 559–560; and Theodor Saelan, "Nylander, William," in *Acta Societatis pro fauna et flora fennica*, **43** (1928), 355–379, with complete bibliography.

George H. M. Lawrence

OBRUCHEV, VLADIMIR AFANASIEVICH (*b.* Klepenino, Rzhev district, Tver [now Kalinin] guberniya, Russia, 10 October 1863; *d.* Moscow, U.S.S.R., 19 June 1956), *geology, geography.*

Obruchev was the son of Afanasy Aleksandrovich Obruchev, a personnel officer in the Russian army, and Paulina Hertner, the daughter of a German pastor. After attending elementary school in Brest, he graduated from the technical high school in Vilna (now Vilnyus), where he showed a special interest in geography and the natural sciences, especially chemistry. In 1881 he won admission to the St. Petersburg Mining Institute, from which he graduated in 1886. It was there that he first became strongly interested in geology.

Obruchev showed outstanding abilities during his first Transcaspian expedition (1886–1888). He was assigned the task of studying the Transcaspian depression, discovering the conditions of the mobility of quicksand in the regions where railroads were being constructed, seeking water-bearing levels in the sands, and making observations of the Tedzhen and Murgab rivers and the ancient Amu-Darya river bed. His study of the action of the wind as a geological agent inspired a lifelong interest in wind processes, particularly in the production of loess. Obruchev's interest in dynamic geology also dates from this expedition.

Contrary to the then prevalent opinion that the Transcaspian sands were of exclusively oceanic origin, Obruchev discovered convincing evidence that they were of triple origin—marine, continental, and fluviatile. Explaining the conditions under which immobile or slightly mobile sands become mobile, he suggested practical measures that were subsequently implemented for combating migrating sands.

In 1888 Obruchev accepted Mushketov's offer to go to eastern Siberia as staff geologist of the Irkutsk Administration of Mines, with supervision of a vast territory that comprised part of Irkutsk and Yenisey provinces, and the Yakutsk and Transbaikal regions. The geology of Siberia subsequently remained his main scientific topic. Obruchev's area of responsibility included the study of the geological structure of the area and distribution of useful minerals, especially gold, which was mined in the Olekma-Vitim district and the area surrounding Lake Baikal.

In 1889 Obruchev completed an expedition across the Pribaikal Mountains, studied mica deposits on the Slyudyanka River, looked for lapsis lazuli and lazurite in the Khamar-Daban range and graphite on the Baikal island of Olkhon, investigated mineral springs in the Nilova Desert, and prospected for brown coal on the banks of the Oka River (a tributary of the Angara). In 1890 and 1891 he inspected in detail the goldfields in the Olekma-Vitim basins. Goldfields in these districts—in contrast to those in other areas of Siberia—were generally covered with a coating of loose glacial deposits to a depth of 60–180 feet. These layers prevented the gold-bearing ones from rewashing and preserved their extraordinary richness.

Having confirmed Kropotkin's views on the pre-glacial history of the gold-bearing layers, Obruchev explained their origin not by the erosion of thick quartz lodes, as had been asserted, but from the gold disseminated in thin quartz veins and in pyrite, dispersed through certain layers of bedrock. The destruction of this rock *in situ*, at the bottom of valleys under river beds, endowed these deposits with their unique structure and enriched their gold, which was chemically extracted from pyrite. This explanation of the origin of gold deposits, given by Obruchev in 1900, has retained its importance.

Summarizing his predecessors' results in "Geologichesky ocherk Irkutskoy gubernii" ("A Geological Sketch of Irkutsky Province," 1890), Obruchev expressed his own views on the current question of the origin of the depression of Lake Baikal.

When one stands on an elevation at the edge of the majestic depression of Baikal, it is impossible to agree with Chersky's opinion that this depression is the result of the combination of prolonged erosion and slow crustal folding. It is too deep and wide, and its slopes are too steep and precipitous. Such a depression could have been created only by faulting, and comparatively recently; otherwise its steep slopes would have been smoothed by erosion and the lake would have been filled with its products [*Moi puteshestvia po Sibiri* ("My Travels Through Siberia"; 1948), p. 35].

Obruchev's views on the origin of the Baikal depression were supported by Suess. Obruchev published more than thirty works during his four years with the mining administration. During the winters he worked in the eastern Siberian section of the Russian Geographical Society as director of affairs and curator of its museum.

From 1892 to 1895 Obruchev traveled through Mongolia and China as a member of the central Asian expedition. His work gained him a worldwide reputation as an explorer and geologist: the Russian Geographical Society awarded him the Przhevalsky Prize and the Great Medal of Constantine, and the Paris Academy of Sciences honored him for his contributions. His research was based on Suess's synthetic work on the geology of central Asia. From Kyakhta to Kuldja, Obruchev investigated the steppe, the Gobi Desert, and the quicksands of the Ordos Desert; traveled throughout the loess area of northern China; spent time in the Alashan range; investigated the Nan Shan and eastern Kunlun ranges; visited the shores of Lake Koko Nor; traveled through all the oases of Kansu Province; traced the course of the Edsin Gol River; crossed the mountainous south-western region of the Gobi and central Mongolia; and thus extended Richthofen's research deep into central Asia to the north, northwest, and west. From along the eastern Tien Shan Mountains he came out into Kuldja. His two-volume diary of the expedition (1900–1901) has remained the only source material on certain areas of central Asia.

Through his work with the expedition Obruchev disproved Richthofen's ideas about the Tertiary Lake Khanka in central Asia, showing that the multicolored deposits of the Khanka suite are continental. In addition he noted that continental conditions had prevailed there since the Mesozoic Era. He introduced significant corrections and additions into Richthofen's theory of the formation and distribution of loess in China and central Asia. Contrary to Richthofen's views, Obruchev asserted that there is no loess in those depressions of central Asia that are part of the area of weathering and wind erosion. Obruchev considered that it was precisely from this area that the loess was carried by wind to the borders of central Asia, mainly into northern China, where it was deposited, preserving and smoothing the forms of the ancient topography.

Returning to Irkutsk in 1895 as head of a special mining party, Obruchev spent the next three years studying the geology of Selenga Dauria (western Transbaikalia) along the route of the main line of the Trans-Siberian railway, then under construction. The material gathered on this expedition formed the basis for the conclusions presented in his *Orografi-chesky i geologichesky ocherk Yugo-Zapadnogo Zabay-kalya* ("Orographical and Geological Sketch of Southwestern Transbaikalia"), for which the Russian Academy of Sciences awarded him the Helmersen Prize.

Advancing new ideas about the tectonics of Siberia, Obruchev believed that the Transbaikal, composed of huge stretches of granites and crystalline slates, was part of the oldest dry land of Eurasia, "of the ancient shield of Asia." Around this skeletal nucleus, he believed, further growth of the continent had occurred in more recent periods, from the Paleozoic to the Quaternary. The concept of the "ancient shield of Asia," raised in the works of Ivan Chersky and Obruchev, was accepted by Suess. Obruchev continued to develop it throughout his life.

Obruchev also developed the idea of the origin of a series of large depressions of the Transbaikal, filled with Mesozoic and Cenozoic deposits. In his opinion these depressions are grabens, which appeared as a result of faulting of the rigid blocks of the ancient shield of Asia, and they are similar to the depressions of Lake Baikal. Obruchev subsequently developed a concept of the prime role of faulting in the formation of the surface and geological structure of Siberia.

From 1898 to 1901 Obruchev worked in St. Petersburg on the material from his expeditions to central Asia and Transbaikalia. In 1899 he studied geology in Germany, Switzerland, and Austria, where he became acquainted with Suess; and in 1900 he participated in the Eighth International Geological Congress in Paris. In 1901 he again returned to Siberia, to study the goldfields on the Bodaybo River.

In 1901, on Mushketov's recommendation, Obruchev was invited to the Tomsk Technological Institute to organize a department of mining and to teach general geology. An outstanding teacher (1902–1912), he also founded the Siberian school of geology.

Continuing his research expeditions, Obruchev traveled to the border regions of Dzungaria in the summers of 1905, 1906, and 1909, with the aim of clarifying the interplay of the Altay and Tien Shan mountain systems. In his opinion the distinguishing feature of the topography is that the mountain heights are remains of an ancient plateau, broken by faults. The flat peaks are horsts (tectonically raised blocks), while the hollows dividing them—the grabens—are zones of tectonic sinking along faults, filled in by large amounts of lake alluvium. Obruchev discovered traces in the mountains of two glaciations and established the presence of vertical zonation of vegetation.

After retiring from Tomsk in 1912, Obruchev

settled in Moscow, continued writing up the results of his previous research, and conducted geological fieldwork by contract with private firms. In 1914 he traveled through the Russian Altay, and the following year his *Altayskie etyudy* ("Altay Studies") appeared; the second sketch, "O tektonike Russkogo Altaya" ("On the Tectonics of the Russian Altay"), is of special interest for his analysis of the views of previous investigators, notably Helmersen, P. A. Chikhachev, G. E. Shchurovsky, Karl Ritter, Cotta, Chersky, and Suess.

In Suess's presentation the Altay are folded mountains convex to the south, formed by tangential stresses of the earth's crust. Obruchev, however, after studying the adjoining Dzungaria, concluded that the recent topography was primarily the result of faulting:

> It was not ancient folds that caused this topography; they have long since been worn down and reduced to almost a plain. It was, rather, faults that turned the entire area into a combination of horsts and grabens. Such land cannot be called plicate; it was such in Paleozoic times but has long since lost its characteristic peculiarities; what now dominate here are more or less extensive stepped plateaux, broad plains, frequently arranged inconsistently with a stretch of Paleozoic sedimentary rock, of which the planed-off ends come to the surface [*Izbrannye trudy*, V (Moscow, 1963), 34].

On his trips through the Altay, Obruchev was especially concerned with relating the topography to the geological structure. He established the existence of a severe discrepancy in orographical maps in relation to the actual position of mountain ranges. In describing the topography, Obruchev counted three mountain chains: "The Russian Altay in its topography has little similarity to the system of narrow and long mountain chains of folded origin. It is, rather, an ancient plateau, a highland, broken down by faulting into more or less broad and long parts, frequently consisting of two or more ledges of different heights and divided by deep and wide fault valleys" (*ibid.*, p. 43).

Obruchev was close to the truth; according to the latest data the mountainous Altay is a complex block-fault structure, formed as a result of an arched uplift, faulting, and uneven vertical displacements of separate blocks of an ancient peneplained surface of folded Paleozoic formations. The uplift occurred at the end of the Tertiary and was especially forceful in the mid- and upper Tertiary periods. The raised parts of the peneplain form mountain systems; the lowered parts are the hollows between mountains. Obruchev's original treatment of the geomorphology of the Altay and Siberia was subsequently developed as an independent branch of science—neotectonics.

At the request of the Higher Council of National Economy, in 1918 Obruchev went to the Donets Basin to prospect for fire-clays and marls. Cut off from central Russia by the civil war, he was obliged to accept the post of professor of geology at the University of the Crimea, in Simferopol. In 1920 he returned to Moscow and the following year was appointed to the chair of applied geology at the Moscow Mining Academy. For the next eight years he taught advanced courses on ore deposits and field geology; his lecture material formed the basis for the texts *Polevaya geologia* ("Field Geology") and *Rudnye mestorozhdenia* ("Ore Deposits"). The former is the best-known Soviet handbook for beginning geologists and covers the entire work cycle of the geologist-prospector.

In 1928 Obruchev reported on Chinese loess to the All-Union Geological Congress in Tashkent, of which he was also president. Elected a member of the Soviet Academy of Sciences in 1929, he subsequently headed its Geological Institute and Committee for the Study of Permafrost. Working with materials gathered in China and Dzungaria, he began the compilation of the five-volume *Istoria geologicheskogo issledovania Sibiri* ("History of Geological Research in Siberia").

Obruchev retained a lifelong interest in the geography of Siberia, especially in the former glaciation of the northern region, already suggested by Kropotkin after the expedition of 1866. The formation of the topography of Siberia also occupied an important place in Obruchev's geographical works. Defending the necessity of the geomorphological regionalization of Siberia, Obruchev wrote in the first volume of *Geologia Sibiri* ("The Geology of Siberia," 1935) that earlier characterizations of its regions, given by Kropotkin, Chersky, and Suess, had become outdated and required "certain more or less essential changes and additions on the basis of new data." His delineation and characterizations of ten geomorphological regions have retained their importance.

Referring to the research of Hans Stille and W. H. Bucher, Obruchev wrote in "Molodost relefa Sibiri" ("The Youth Stage of the Topography of Siberia"), "At present, on the basis of the numerous investigations of the past decade, it is possible to assert with full justification that the topography not only of the ancient shield but of almost all Siberia is young and was formed by movements during the Tertiary and post-Tertiary periods that attained in places quite a substantial amplitude."

Obruchev also investigated the conditions of the origin and development of permafrost, its geographical distribution, and its influence on agriculture. For many years he was head of the Institute of Permafrost Management of the Soviet Academy of Sciences.

In 1937 Obruchev was head of the Soviet delegation to the Seventeenth International Geological Congress in Moscow, and in 1939 he became editor of the geological series of *Izvestiya Akademii nauk SSSR*. During World War II he was secretary of the Geological Sciences Section of the Soviet Academy of Sciences. A recipient of many Soviet medals and awards, he was corresponding member of the Royal Geographical Society and a member of the Russian Geographical Society, the American Geological and Geographical Societies, the Geological Society of China, the Hungarian Geographical Society, and the Deutsche Geophysikalische Gesellschaft.

A volcano in Transbaikalia, a glacier in the Mongolian Altay, a peak in the Russian Altay, and a steppe between the Murgab and Amu-Darya rivers are named for him. In 1941 a prize in his name was established for work on the geology of Siberia.

BIBLIOGRAPHY

I. Original Works. Obruchev's published work comprises more than 2,000 pages of scientific works and more than 3,000 reviews for foreign journals, as well as teaching materials, classical works on geology and mining, and several science fiction novels. Only the basic works reflecting his scientific activity are given here.

His selected works were published as *Izbrannye trudy*, 6 vols. (Moscow, 1958–1964). His account of his journey completed at the request of the Imperial Russian Geographical Society was published as *Tsentralnaya Azia, Severny Kitay i Nan-Shian* ("Central Asia, Northern China, and the Nan Shan"), 2 vols. (St. Petersburg, 1901). Subsequent fundamental works include *Rudnye mestorozhdenia* ("Ore Deposits"), 2 vols. (Moscow–Leningrad, 1928–1929); *Istoria geologicheskogo issledovania Sibiri* ("History of Geological Research on Siberia"), 5 pts. (Moscow–Leningrad, 1931–1949); *Polevaya geologia* ("Field Geology"), 2 vols. (Moscow–Leningrad, 1927; 4th ed., 1932); and *Izbrannye raboty po geografii Azii* ("Selected Works on the Geography of Asia"), 3 vols. (Moscow, 1951). *V staroy Sibiri* ("In Old Siberia"; Irkutsk, 1958), contains articles, recollections, and letters from 1888 to 1955.

His science fiction works include *Plutonia. Neobychaynoe puteshestvie v nedra Zemli* ("Plutonia. An Extraordinary Journey to the Depths of the Earth"; Leningrad, 1924; repr., Moscow, 1958); *V debryakh Tsentralnoy Azii. Zapiski kladoiskatelya* ("In the Depths of Central Asia. Notes of a Treasure Hunter"), 3rd ed. (Moscow, 1955); and *Zemlya Sannikova ili poslednie onkilony* ("The Land of Sannikov or the Last Onkilons"; Moscow, 1958).

II. Secondary Literature. On Obruchev and his work, see *V. A. Obruchev* (Moscow–Leningrad, 1946), materials for a bibliography published by the Soviet Academy of Sciences; and the notice in *Bolshaya sovetskaya entsiklopedia* ("Great Soviet Encyclopedia"), 2nd ed., XXX, 390–392. See also A. N. Granina, "Deyatelnost V. A. Obrucheva v Vostochno-Sibirskom otdele Geograficheskogo obshchestva SSSR" ("The Career of V. A. Obruchev in the Eastern Siberian Section of the Geographical Society of the U.S.S.R."), in *Izvestiya Vsesoyuznogo geograficheskogo obshchestva*, **89**, no. 2 (1957), 123–130; L. G. Kamanin and B. A. Fedorovich, "V. A. Obruchev—issledovatel Sredney i Tsentralnoy Azii i Sibiri" ("V. A. Obruchev—Investigator of Middle and Central Asia and Siberia"), in *Voprosy geomorfologii i paleogeografii Azii* ("Questions of Asian Geomorphology and Paleogeography"; Moscow, 1955); E. M. Murzaev *et al.*, *Vladimir Afanasevich Obruchev. Zhizn i deyatelnost* (Moscow, 1959), on his life and work; and V. V. Obruchev and G. N. Finashina, *Vladimir Afanasevich Obruchev* (Moscow, 1965), with bibliography.

G. V. Naumov

OCAGNE, PHILBERT MAURICE D' (*b.* Paris, France, 25 March 1862; *d.* Le Havre, France, 23 September 1938), *mathematics, applied mathematics, history of mathematics.*

D'Ocagne was a student and then *répétiteur* at the École Polytechnique. He then became a civil engineer and a professor at the École des Ponts et Chaussées. In 1912 he was appointed professor of geometry at the École Polytechnique. He was elected to the Académie des Sciences on 30 January 1922.

Active both as researcher and teacher, d'Ocagne published a great many articles, mostly on geometry, in mathematical journals and in the *Comptes rendus . . . de l'Académie des sciences*. His name, however, remains linked especially with graphical calculation procedures and with the systematization he gave to that field under the name of nomography. Graphical calculation consists in the execution of graphs employing straight-line segments representing the numbers to be found. This discipline was reduced to an autonomous body of principles chiefly through the work of Junius Massau (1852–1909). Nomography, on the other hand, consists in the construction of graduated graphic tables, nomograms, or charts, representing formulas or equations to be solved, the solutions of which were provided by inspection of the tables.

The overwhelming majority of formulas and equations encountered in practice can be represented graphically by three systems of converging straight lines. By making a dual transformation on the nomograms d'Ocagne obtained nomograms on which the relationship among the variables consisted in the alignment of numbered points. Hence this type of nomogram is called an aligned-point nomogram.

In a pamphlet published in 1891 d'Ocagne presented the first outline of a rationally ordered discipline embracing all the individual procedures of nomographic calculation then known. Pursuing this subject, he succeeded in defining and classifying the most general modes of representation applicable to equations with an arbitrary number of variables. The results of all these investigations, along with a considerable number of applications, were set forth in *Traité de nomographie* (1899), which was followed by other more or less developed expositions. This material appeared in fifty-nine partial or entire translations in fourteen languages.

D'Ocagne retained a lifelong interest in the history of science and published many articles on the subject, some of which were collected.

BIBLIOGRAPHY

D'Ocagne published many articles in *Comptes rendus . . . de l'Académie des sciences, Revue de mathématiques spéciales, Nouvelles annales de mathématiques, Annales des ponts et chaussées, Bulletin de la Société mathématique de France, Enseignement mathématique, Mathésis,* and other journals. His books include *Nomographie, les calculs usuels effectués au moyen des abaques* (Paris, 1891); *Le calcul simplifié par les procédés mécaniques et graphiques* (Paris, 1893; 2nd ed., 1905; 3rd ed., 1928); *Traité de nomographie. Théorie des abaques, applications pratiques* (Paris, 1899; 2nd ed., 1921); *Calcul graphique et nomographie* (Paris, 1908; 2nd ed., 1914); *Souvenirs et causeries* (Paris, 1928); *Hommes et choses de science,* 3 vols. (Paris, 1930–1932); and *Histoire abrégée des sciences mathématiques,* René Dugas, ed. (Paris, 1955).

Jean Itard

OCHSENIUS, CARL (*b.* Kassel, Germany, 9 March 1830; *d.* Marburg, Germany, 9 December 1906), *geology, sedimentology.*

The son of an administrator at the court of Hessen-Kassel, Ochsenius attended the Gymnasium and the Polytechnische Schule in Kassel, where he studied mining engineering and geology. In 1851 he accompanied his professor, Rudolf Amandus Philippi, on an expedition to Chile, where he remained for twenty years. During his stay in South America, Ochsenius investigated coal, salt, guano, and sulfur deposits; served in various administrative and directorial positions; and traveled widely as a German consul.

In 1879 he married Rau von Holzhausen; they had four children. After 1871 Ochsenius settled in Marburg, where he was a private scientist and promoter of potash mining near Hannover. He began to publish reports on the observations made during his twenty years abroad. In 1884 the University of Marburg awarded him an honorary doctorate.

Ochsenius is best known for his book *Die Bildung der Steinsalzlager und ihrer Mutterlaugensalze* (1877). This work was outstanding for the great amount of direct observations reported, for the accuracy with which the depositional sequence of salt formation was presented, and for the vigor with which a relatively new idea on the origin of salt deposits was presented (Bischof had offered some preliminary ideas pointing in this direction in the second edition of his *Lehrbuch der chemischen und physikalischen Geologie* [1863–1871]). This new idea, the "bar theory" to explain thick deposits of salt, gypsum, and other evaporites, assumes lagoons separated by bars from the ocean proper. As water is lost by evaporation, evaporites precipitate in the lagoon and additional seawater is fed into the lagoon from the open ocean. With increasing evaporation, the salinity in the almost closed basin increases to the point where gypsum, rock salt, and other evaporites are deposited. The best examples, in Ochsenius' opinion, are the basins of Kara-Bogaz-Gol and Adzhi Darya on the eastern rim of the Caspian Sea. The Stassfurt sequence of the German Zechstein also appeared to confirm his theory. The physicochemical results of van't Hoff's work were welcomed by Ochsenius as confirmations of his observations in nature.

The bar theory was opposed by Johannes Walther, whose "desert theory" proposed a formation of salt basins as closed evaporation basins. Both theories were confirmed by observation of present-day processes, but the bar theory was preferred by more geoscientists. Ochsenius published his last revision of this theory in 1906, the year of his death.

Ochsenius contributed other models and theories to the earth sciences, but none was as successful as his bar theory. Of his theory on petroleum formation only the close association of petroleum and salt provinces has remained confirmed. Equally well confirmed was his theory on partial uplift zones of continents, which was based on numerous observations on the Pacific coast of South America. On the other hand, his theory on coal formation was based on a too restricted observation and, consequently, today applies only to local, special modes of origin. He had tried to apply his bar theory to coal genesis in an attempt to explain the facies change coal / sandstone or coal / claystone in soft-water basins.

Ochsenius' contributions to science are based on an enormous wealth of keenly remembered and recorded observations and on his independent, undogmatic approach. If a theory appeared to be confirmed by observations, he was not afraid to stand alone in its defense.

BIBLIOGRAPHY

I. ORIGINAL WORKS. Ochsenius' writings include *Die Bildung der Steinsalzlager und ihrer Mutterlaugensalze unter besonderer Berücksichtigung der Flöze von Douglashall in der Egelnschen Mulde* (Halle, 1877); *Chile, Land und Leute* (Leipzig, 1884); "Bedeutung des orographischen Elementes 'Barre' in Hinsicht auf Bildungen und Veränderungen von Lagerstätten und Gesteinen," in *Zeitschrift für praktische Geologie*, **1** (1893), 189–201, 217–233; and "Theorien über die Entstehung der Salzlager," in *Deutschlands Kaliindustrie*, supp. to the newspaper *Industrie*, 2nd ed. (1906), 1–8.

II. SECONDARY LITERATURE. See the unsigned "Dr. Carl Ochsenius, der Forscher und Mensch," in *Festschrift zum 100 jährigen Geburtstage* (Chemnitz, 1931), pp. 67–161; Kurt Ochsenius, "Zum 100. Geburtstag von Dr. Carl Christian Ochsenius," in *Zeitschrift Kali und verwandte Salze*, **24**, no. 5 (1930), 68–70; and W. Weissermel, "Zum 100. Geburtstag von Carl Ochsenius," in *Zeitschrift der Deutschen geologischen Gesellschaft*, **82**, no. 4 (1930), 229–236.

G. C. AMSTUTZ

OCKENFUSS, LORENZ. See **Oken, Lorenz.**

OCKHAM, WILLIAM OF (*b.* Ockham, near London, England, *ca.* 1285; *d.* Munich, Germany, 1349), *philosophy, theology, political theory.*

Traditionally regarded as the initiator of the movement called nominalism, which dominated the universities of northern Europe in the fourteenth and fifteenth centuries and played a significant role in shaping the directions of modern thought, William of Ockham ranks, with Thomas Aquinas and Duns Scotus, as one of the three most influential Scholastic philosophers. Of his early life nothing is known; but it is supposed that he was born in the village of Ockham, Surrey, between 1280 and 1290 and that he became a Franciscan friar at an early age. He entered Oxford around 1310 as a student of theology and completed his formal requirements for the degree by lecturing on Peter Lombard's *Sentences* in the years 1318–1319, thereby becoming a *baccalaureus formatus*, or *inceptor*. During the next four years, while awaiting the teaching license which would have made him a *magister actu regens*, or doctor of theology, Ockham took part in quodlibetal disputations, revised his lectures on the first book of the *Sentences* for public circulation, and wrote some philosophical and theological treatises.

In this period his teachings, recognized for their power and originality, became a center of controversy and aroused opposition from partisans of Duns Scotus, whose doctrines Ockham criticized, as well as from most of the Dominican masters and some of the secular teachers. In 1323 one of the latter, John Lutterell, went to the papal court at Avignon to press charges of heretical teaching against Ockham, who was summoned to Avignon to answer these accusations early in 1324. Because his academic career was cut short by these events, so that he never received his license to teach, he came to be known as "the venerable inceptor"—that is, candidate who never received the doctoral degree he had earned.

At Avignon, Ockham stayed at the Franciscan convent while awaiting the outcome of the process against him; and during this period he probably wrote several of his theological and philosophical works. A commission of six theologians was appointed by Pope John XXII to examine the charges against his teaching; and although this commission drew up two lists of suspect doctrines, no action appears to have been taken on the charges. Meanwhile Ockham became actively involved in the dispute then raging between Michael of Cesena, general of the Franciscan order, and Pope John XXII over the question of evangelical poverty; and he gave his support to Cesena.

When, in May 1328, it became apparent that the pope was about to issue an official condemnation of their position, Cesena, Ockham, and two other Franciscan leaders fled by night from Avignon and sought the protection of the German emperor, Louis of Bavaria. Louis, whose claim to the imperial crown was contested by Pope John, welcomed the support of Ockham in his cause, as well as that of Marsilius of Padua. The pope, enraged by this defection, excommunicated Ockham and his companions, not for heretical doctrines but for disobedience to his authority. During the ensuing years Ockham remained at Munich and devoted his energies to writing a series of treatises and polemical works directed against John XXII, some of which contained carefully argued discussions of the powers and functions of the papal office, the church, and the imperial or civil authority. When Louis of Bavaria died in 1347, the contest with the Avignon papacy became a lost cause; and there is some evidence that Ockham sought to reconcile himself with the Franciscan faction that had remained loyal to the pope. It is thought that he died in 1349, a victim of the Black Plague, and that he was buried in the Franciscan church at Munich.

Ockham's writings, as preserved, fall into three main groups: philosophical, theological, and political. The philosophical works include commentaries and sets of questions on Aristotle's *Physics* and commentaries on Porphyry's *Predicables* and Aristotle's *Categoriae*, *De interpretatione*, and *De sophisticis elenchis*. Ockham wrote an independent work on logic, entitled *Summa logicae*, that gave full expression to his own philosophy of language and logical doctrines. An incomplete treatise, published under the title *Philosophia naturalis*, dealt with the concepts of motion, place, and time in an original and independent manner. Of his theological writings the most important is the set of questions on book I of the *Sentences*, edited by Ockham for publication and therefore known as his *ordinatio*, along with the questions on the other three books, which are in the form of *reportata* (stenographic versions of the lectures as actually delivered). The *Quodlibeta septem*, containing 172 questions on theological and philosophical topics divided among seven quodlibetal disputations, are of great value as an expression of Ockham's distinctive philosophical positions.

Of logical as well as theological interest are the treatise *De praedestinatione et de praescientia dei et de futuris contingentibus* and the work known as *De sacramento altaris*, which seems to consist of two distinct treatises and which is devoted chiefly to arguing that the doctrine of transubstantiation does not require the assumption that quantity is an entity distinct from substances or qualities. One other theological work, the authenticity of which has been questioned, is the *Centiloquium theologicum*, consisting of 100 conclusions directed mainly to showing that doctrines of natural theology cannot be proved by evident reason or experience.

The third group of Ockham's writings is made up of the polemical and political works written in his Munich period. Many of these are of interest only in connection with the historical events of the time; but some of them contain important discussions of moral, legal, and political concepts and issues developed in connection with the controversies over the powers of pope and emperor, of church and state. Such are the lengthy *Dialogus inter magistrum et discipulum de imperatorum et pontificum potestate*, the *Octo quaestiones super potestate et dignitate papali*, and the shorter but eloquent *Tractatus de imperatorum et pontificum potestate*, written in 1347. Modern critical editions of the political works are well under way; but editions of the philosophical and theological writings are very much needed, since the early printed editions are both rare and not fully reliable, while some important works (those on Aristotle's *Physics*) have never been printed at all.

Ockham was a thinker of profound originality, independence, and critical power. Although he had scarcely any acknowledged disciples, and did not found a school in the sense of having followers committed to defense of his teachings (as did Thomas Aquinas and Duns Scotus), the actual influence exerted by Ockham's thought, in his own time and into the seventeenth century, was of a significance and breadth that may well have surpassed that of Aquinas or Scotus. This influence is clearly discernible in the empiricist doctrines of Locke and Hume, in the controversies concerning faith and merit associated with the Reformation, and in the political theories that found expression in the Conciliar Movement and in seventeenth-century constitutional liberalism. Although some historians have portrayed Ockham as an innovator who revolted against the traditional values and standards of medieval Christendom, it is nearer the truth to say that he was very much a product of the medieval culture and educational system, who sought to resolve problems that were generated by that culture and that had reached critical dimensions in his own time.

The condemnations of strict Aristotelianism that took place in 1277 were symptomatic of a crisis in the Scholastic effort to harmonize Greek metaphysics with the Christian creed; while the conflict between Philip the Fair and Boniface VIII, followed by the controversy between Louis of Bavaria and John XXII, brought to the surface issues concerning the sources of political and ecclesiastical authority that were becoming acute with the decline of the feudal system. It was to save the values threatened by these conflicts, rather than to destroy them, that Ockham subjected the prevailing Scholastic positions to criticism, and sought more adequate and powerful principles of analysis. His chief contributions to philosophy, lying in the areas of philosophy of language, metaphysics, and theory of knowledge, were the direct result of his effort, as a theologian, to meet the twofold commitment to reason and experience, on the one hand, and to the articles of the faith, on the other.

This dual commitment to faith and reason finds expression in two maxims that are constantly invoked in Ockham's writings. The first is that God can bring about anything whose accomplishment does not involve a contradiction. Although this principle is accepted on the basis of the Christian creed, it is equivalent to the philosophical principle that whatever is not self-contradictory is possible, so that what is actually the case cannot be established on a priori grounds but must be ascertained by experience. The second maxim, known as Ockham's Razor because of his frequent use of it, is the methodological principle of economy in explanation, frequently expressed in the formula "What can be accounted for by fewer assumptions is explained in vain by more." Ockham often expressed it, however, in this longer form: "Nothing is to be assumed as evident, unless it is known per se, or is evident by experience, or is proved by the authority of Scripture" (*Sentences* I, d. 30, qu. 1).

These maxims are equivalent in force and constitute the unifying principle of Ockham's doctrine, whether viewed in its theological or philosophical aspect. They determine a view of the universe as radically contingent in its being, a theory of knowledge that is thoroughly empiricist, and a rejection of all realist doctrines of common natures and necessary relations in things—all of which constitute what is called Ockham's nominalism. They also eliminate every form of determinism in Ockham's metaphysics and psychology, by associating the principle of divine omnipotence with that of divine liberty and freedom of choice and by making the liberty of the human will basic to moral and legal theory.

A first consequence of these principles is the elimination of various metaphysical "distinctions" that played a dominant role in late thirteenth-century Scholasticism and that derived in large measure from the interpretation of Aristotle made by the Islamic philosopher Ibn Sīnā. The real distinction between essence and existence, held to be a doctrine of St. Thomas Aquinas, supposed that in an existing thing its essence or nature, although not separable from its existence, is nevertheless really distinct from it. Ockham argued that if essence and existence are distinct realities, then it is not self-contradictory for one to exist without the other; but since it is self-contradictory to suppose that an essence exists without existence, it follows that there cannot be a real distinction between the two. By a similar argument it is shown that there cannot be a real distinction between individuals and their natures, as the theory of common natures existing in individuals supposes.

Ockham directed his main critique against the Scotist theory that the common nature differs from the individuating principle by a formal distinction that is less than a real distinction but more than a distinction of reason. To show that this involves a contradiction, Ockham argued as follows: Let the common nature be indicated by the letter *a* and the individuating difference by the letter *b*. Then, according to Duns Scotus, *a* is formally distinct from *b*. But Scotus must concede that *a* is not formally distinct from *a*. Yet,

Ockham argued, wherever contradictory predicates are verified of two things, those two things must be really distinct. Hence *b* and *a* cannot be really identical if they are formally distinct, as Scotus claimed; and by the same argument it can be shown that if they are really identical, they cannot be formally distinct.

The notion of a common nature in individuals, really or formally distinct from them, is therefore self-contradictory; and it remains that universality is a property of terms, or of concepts expressed by general nouns, and is simply their capacity to be used to signify or denote many individuals. In denying that there is any universality in things, Ockham does not deny that the basis for universal predication of general terms is objectively present in individual things; he only denies that the fact that Socrates and Plato, for example, are similar in that each is a man entails that there is some entity common to both and distinct from each. Ockham's nominalism is not to be construed as a doctrine that denies any foundation in things for the generality of terms, and his theory of human cognition rests squarely on the assumption that direct experience of existing things gives rise to concepts of universal character that directly signify things as they are or can be.

Since whatever exists is individual, Ockham holds that our knowledge of things is based on a direct and immediate awareness of what is present to our senses and intellect, which he calls intuitive cognition. He defines this type of awareness as one which enables us to form an evident judgment of contingent fact— that is, that the object apprehended exists, or that it is qualified in a certain way, or is next to another object, and so forth. Such cognition gives rise only to singular contingent propositions that are evident; hence it does not yield scientific knowledge in Aristotle's sense, in which premises and conclusions must be of universal character. Every intuitive cognition, however, can give rise to an abstractive cognition of the same object, which Ockham defines as the cognition of an object which does not suffice for an evident judgment concerning the existence of the object or concerning a contingent fact about the object. Thus, while I am observing Socrates and hearing him talk, I can judge evidently that Socrates exists and that he is talking; but if I depart from the spot and then form the proposition that Socrates exists, or that he is talking, my statement is not evident and may in fact be false.

But Ockham insists that there is no distinction between intuitive and abstractive cognition with respect to objects cognized, but only with respect to their capacity to yield evident judgments of existence and contingent fact. In the natural course of events, every abstractive cognition presupposes an intuitive cognition of an object understood by it; but Ockham says that since the cognitions are distinct from each other and from their objects, it is logically possible for God to cause an intuitive cognition of an object which is not present or not presently existing. In such a case, Ockham says, the intuitive cognition will yield a judgment that the object is not present or that it does not exist; for it would be self-contradictory to hold that one can have an evident judgment that an object exists, if it does not exist.

The general propositions which serve as premises of scientific knowledge, in the strict sense, are established by inductive generalization from singular judgments evident by experience. But Ockham holds that such scientific statements, being formed from abstractive cognitions of their objects, cannot have absolute evidence, or necessary truth, as categorical propositions; they must be construed as necessary propositions concerning the possible, or as conditional statements. Except for premises of mathematics, which are known per se by the meanings of the terms, the principles of the natural sciences are held by Ockham to be evident by experience but not as necessary in the absolute sense, although they may be said to be necessary in the conditional sense of presupposing the common course of nature without divine interference.

Ockham's empirical theory of knowledge and his nominalist doctrine of the relation of discourse to reality are reinforced by a remarkably original and thoroughgoing use of the *logica moderna* of the arts faculties, with its theory of the supposition of terms, which takes the form of a fully developed philosophy of language. Ockham's *Summa logicae* gives the most complete expression to this semantically oriented logic.

Ockham's treatment of theology is consistent with his treatment of philosophy and natural science, in the sense that absolute evidence for theological propositions cannot be had in this life and only a positive theology based on acceptance of the testimony of Christ and the saints is possible. The order established by God and revealed in the laws of the church, which Ockham ascribes to God's *potentia ordinata*, is freely established by divine choice but is not necessary, since God, by his absolute power, could have ordained a different order. In moral and political philosophy Ockham applies these same criteria of divine freedom and omnipotence to refute the claims of pope and emperor alike to absolute power and dominion over members of the church or citizens of the state. The dignity of man is found in his freedom of choice; and Ockham reiterates that the law of God is a law of liberty, not to be degraded and corrupted into absolutism and coercive tyranny.

BIBLIOGRAPHY

I. ORIGINAL WORKS. Individual works include *Quodlibeta septem* (Paris, 1487; Strasbourg, 1491); *Summa logicae* (Paris–Bologna, 1498; Venice, 1508, 1522, 1591; Oxford, 1675), modern ed. of *Pars prima* and *Pars IIa et tertiae prima*, P. Boehner, ed., 2 vols. (St. Bonaventure, N.Y., 1951–1954); *De sacramento altaris et De corpore christi* (Strasbourg, 1491), with *Quodlibeta*, new ed. by T. B. Birch, with English trans., *The De sacramento altaris of William of Ockham* (Burlington, Iowa, 1930); *Summulae in libros Physicorum* (Bologna, 1494; Venice, 1506; Rome, 1637), also known as *Philosophia naturalis; Super quatuor libros Sententiarum . . . quaestiones* (Lyons, 1495), with *Centiloquium theologicum*, modern critical ed. of *Sentences* I, *Prologus* and *Dist.* I, Gedeon Gal, O.F.M., ed. (St. Bonaventure, N.Y., 1967); *Expositio aurea . . . super artem veterem* (Bologna, 1496), modern ed. of the *Proemium* and *Expositio super librium Porphyrii*, Ernest A. Moody, ed. (St. Bonaventure, N.Y., 1965); *Tractatus de praedestinatione et de praescientia Dei et de futuris contingentibus*, P. Boehner, ed. (St. Bonaventure, N.Y., 1945), English trans. by Marilyn McCord Adams and Norman Kretzmann (New York, 1969); *Dialogus inter magistrum et discipulum* (Lyons, 1495); and *The De imperatorum et pontificum potestate of William of Ockham*, C. K. Brampton, ed. (Oxford, 1927).

Collections are *Guillelmi de Ockham Opera politica*, vol. I, J. G. Sikes, ed. (Manchester, 1940), vol. III, H. S. Offler, ed. (Manchester, 1956), other vols. in preparation or in course of publication; and *Ockham: Philosophical Writings*, P. Boehner, ed. (Edinburgh, 1957), selections with English trans.

II. SECONDARY LITERATURE. On Ockham and his work see Nicola Abbagnano, *Guglielmo di Ockham* (Lanciano, 1931); Léon Baudry, *Le Tractatus de principiis theologiae attribué à G. d'Occam* (Paris, 1936); *Guillaume d'Occam*, I, *L'homme et les oeuvres* (Paris, 1950), with an excellent bibliography; and *Lexique philosophique de Guillaume d'Occam* (Paris, 1958); P. Boehner, *Collected Articles on Ockham* (St. Bonaventure, N.Y., 1956); Franz Federhofer, *Die Erkenntnislehre des Wilhelm von Ockham* (Munich, 1924); Martin Gottfried, *Wilhelm von Ockham* (Berlin, 1949); Robert Guelluy, *Philosophie et théologie chez Guillaume d'Occam* (Louvain–Paris, 1947); Erich Hochstetter, *Studien zur Metaphysik und Erkenntnislehre Wilhelms von Ockham* (Berlin, 1927); Georges de Lagarde, *La naissance de l'esprit laïque au déclin du moyen âge*, IV–VI (Paris, 1942–1946); Ernest A. Moody, *The Logic of William of Ockham* (New York–London, 1935); Simon Moser, *Grundbegriffe der Naturphilosophie bei Wilhelm von Ockham* (Innsbruck, 1932); Richard Scholz, *Wilhelm von Ockham als politischer Denker und sein Breviloquium de principatu tyrannico* (Leipzig, 1944); Herman Shapiro, *Motion, Time and Place According to William Ockham* (St. Bonaventure, N.Y., 1957); Cesare Vasoli, *Guglielmo d'Occam* (Florence, 1953), which contains a good bibliography; Paul Vignaux, *Justification et prédestination au XIVe siècle* (Paris, 1934); *Le nominalisme au XIVe siècle* (Montreal, 1948); and "Nominalisme" and "Occam," in *Dictionnaire de théologie catholique*, 15 vols. (Paris, 1903–1950), XI, cols. 733–789, 864–904; Damascene Webering, *The Theory of Demonstration According to William Ockham* (St. Bonaventure, N.Y., 1953); and Sytse Zuidema, *De Philosophie van Occam in zijn Commentaar op de Sententien*, 2 vols. (Hilversum, 1936).

ERNEST A. MOODY

ODDI, RUGGERO (*b.* Perugia, Italy, 20 July 1864; *d.* Tunis, Tunisia, 22 March 1913), *medicine.*

The son of Filippo Oddi and Zelinda Pampaglini, Oddi spent four years at the University of Perugia, one at Bologna, and one at Florence, where he graduated in medicine and surgery on 2 July 1889. He remained as an assistant at the Physiology Institute in Florence (directed by L. Luciani) and made a study trip to the Experimental Pharmacological Institute at the University of Strasbourg (directed by Oswald Schmiedeberg), during which he isolated chondroitin sulfate from the amyloid substance. In January 1894 Oddi was appointed head of the Physiology Institute at the University of Genoa, from which he resigned on 1 April 1900 as the result of a complex series of events (reconstructed in 1965 by L. Belloni). This was followed by a short period as physician in the Belgian Congo, during which time his mental condition became more unbalanced, partly as a result of his using narcotics.

Oddi's main contribution is the discovery of the sphincter of the choledochus, made at Perugia as a fourth-year medical student (1886–1887). Intent on studying *in vivo* the action of bile on the digestion, he had the idea of obtaining an uninterrupted flow of bile into the duodenum by removing the reservoir. In a dog that had been cholecystectomized some time before, he was surprised to observe a marked dilatation of the bile ducts, which led him to suppose "that at the outlet of the choledochus into the duodenum there was a special device which allowed the flow of bile only at certain times, preventing it at others, so that the bile, no longer accumulating in the gallbladder, but compelled to create a space in the larger bile ducts, thus caused their enormous dilatation."

A subsequent series of refined morphological researches in various animal species allowed him to demonstrate, both at the outlet of the choledochus and at the outlet of Wirsüng's duct, that there is a special sphincteral device that is largely independent of the muscular layers of the intestine.

Oddi also measured the tone of the sphincter of the choledochus by perfecting an experimental device substantially identical with that used today for the intraoperative manometry of the biliary ducts.

BIBLIOGRAPHY

I. ORIGINAL WORKS. Oddi's writings include "Di una speciale disposizione a sfintere allo sbocco del coledoco," in *Annali dell'Università Libera di Perugia*, **2** (1886–1887), vol. I, Facoltà medico-chirurgica, 249–264 and pl. IX; "Effetti dell'estirpazione della cistifellea," in *Bullettino delle scienze mediche*, 6th ser., **21** (1888), 194–202; "Sulla tonicità dello sfintere del coledoco," in *Archivio per le scienze mediche*, **12** (1888), 333–339; "Sul centro spinale dello sfintere del coledoco," in *Lo Sperimentale*, sec. biologica, **48** (1894), 180–191; "Sulla esistenza di speciali gangli nervosi in prossimità dello sfintere del coledoco," in *Monitore zoologico italiano*, **5** (1894), 216–219 and pl. IV; "Ueber das Vorkommen von Chondroïtinschwefelsäure in der Amyloidleber," in *Archiv für experimentelle Pathologie und Pharmakologie*, **33** (1894), 376–388; "Sulla fisio-patologia delle vie biliari," in *Conferenze cliniche italiane dirette dal Prof. Achille de Giovanni . . .*, 1st ser., I (Milan, n.d.), 77–124; *L'inibizione dal punto di vista fisio-patologico, psicologico e sociale* (Turin, 1898); and *Gli alimenti e la loro funzione nella economia dell'organismo individuale e sociale* (Turin, 1902). For other publications by Oddi, see the works by L. Belloni below.

II. SECONDARY LITERATURE. See Luigi Belloni, "Sulla vita e sull'opera di Ruggero Oddi (1864–1913)," in *Rendiconti dell'Istituto lombardo di scienze e lettere*, Classe di scienze (B), **99** (1965), 35–50; and "Über Leben und Werk von Ruggero Oddi (1864–1913), dem Entdecker des Schliessmuskels des Hauptgallenganges," in *Medizinhistorisches Journal*, **1** (1966), 96–109.

LUIGI BELLONI

ODIERNA (or **Hodierna**), **GIOANBATISTA** (*b.* Ragusa, Sicily, 13 April 1597; *d.* Palma di Montechiaro, Sicily, 6 April 1660), *astronomy, meteorology, natural history*.

A self-taught scholar, Odierna was born into a modest artisan family, and, apart from a journey to Rome and Loreto, spent all his life in Sicily. He taught mathematics and astronomy at the school in Ragusa and later studied theology at Palermo. He observed the three comets of 1618–1619, which spurred the famous polemic resolved in 1623 by Galileo in his *Saggiatore*. Odierna's observations were published many years later, when he was at the peak of his career.

After having read Galileo's *Sidereus nuncius*, Odierna wrote an enthusiastic appraisal of it, in which he mentions that Galileo had presented him with a telescope of moderate focal distance. He served the barons of Montechiaro as chaplain and parish priest of their newly founded town of Palma di Montechiaro, in the province of Agrigento. They gave him an apartment on a high floor of their palace for his astronomical observations and later named him archpriest and court mathematician.

Odierna's observations were aimed principally at determining the period of revolution of the four satellites of Jupiter. Like Galileo he tried to predict their eclipses, which would have helped to solve the long-standing, important problem of determining longitudes at sea; lacking sufficient knowledge of celestial mechanics, neither he nor Galileo was successful. Odierna's pamphlet on the subject, *Medicaeorum ephemerides* (1656), was dedicated to Grand Duke Ferdinand II of Tuscany.

With Galileo's telescope, Odierna made careful observations of Saturn but did not comprehend the true shape of its ring. In 1656 he published a pamphlet on it, *Protei caelestis seu Saturni systema*, and sent it to Huygens, the discoverer of the nature of the ring, Huygens replied, encouraging him to continue his useful observations, and sent him a drawing of his pendulum clock to assist him in his research.

After studying the passage of light through prisms Odierna offered a vague explanation of the rainbow and of the spectrum. His *Thaumantia Junonis nuntia praeconium pulchritudinis* (1647), on the nature of the iris and its colors, was followed in 1652 by *Thaumantiae miraculum*.

Odierna's interest in meteorology resulted in some research on cyclones. In natural history his explanation of the structure and function of the retractile poison fangs of vipers anticipated the work of Redi. In his studies on the eyes of flies and of other insects, he used a microscope and a camera obscura.

Odierna's numerous works were almost all published at Palermo and are now in the Municipal Library of Palermo and in the University Library of Catania. Although they cannot be said to be of real scientific value, Odierna must be considered among the pioneers of the experimental method.

BIBLIOGRAPHY

Odierna's "L'occhio della mosca" was repub. with a commentary by C. Pighetti, in *Physis*, **3** (1961), 309–335, with a complete bibliography.

See also G. Abetti, "Don Giovanni Battista Odierna," in *Celebrazioni siciliane* (Urbino, 1939), 3–28, and "Onoranze a D. Gioanbatista Hodierna della città di Ragusa in Sicilia," in *Physis*, **3** (1961), 177–179.

GIORGIO ABETTI

ODINGTON. See **Walter of Odington.**

ODLING, WILLIAM (*b.* Southwark, London, England, 5 September 1829; *d.* Oxford, England, 17 February 1921), *chemistry.*

Before Odling became Waynflete professor of chemistry at Oxford, where he was a conscientious teacher but personally uninterested in the emergence of a research school, he had been (with A. W. Williamson, B. C. Brodie, and E. Frankland) one of England's leading theoretical chemists during the exciting renaissance of British chemistry between 1850 and 1870. The only son of George Odling, a London doctor with a long family tradition of medicine, he received his elementary schooling at Stockwell and then at the interesting Nesbit's Chemical Academy and Agricultural College, where he gave his first public lecture in 1844.[1] He entered Guy's Hospital at the age of sixteen and was one of the hospital's first students to take the London University M.D. in 1851.

Although Odling attended A. W. Hofmann's course at the Royal College of Chemistry for a semester in 1848, his principal chemistry teacher, who initially biased him toward toxicological studies, was Alfred Swaine Taylor (1806–1880), the Guy's lecturer in chemistry and medical jurisprudence. Odling held several teaching positions at Guy's while he was medical officer of health for Lambeth from 1856 to 1862. From 1863 to 1870 he taught chemistry at St. Bartholomew's Hospital and, on Faraday's death in 1867, became Fullerian professor of chemistry at the Royal Institution, whereupon he abandoned applied medicine except for remunerative work on water analysis. On succeeding Brodie at Oxford in 1872 he married Elizabeth Mary Smee; they had three sons. He retired in 1912 but remained active until the end of his life.

Through his long and influential association with the Chemical Society, which he joined in 1848, Odling became a close friend and overmodest "follower" of Brodie and of the older and authoritative Williamson. Through the latter he met Kekulé during his *Wanderjahre* in London (1854–1855). All these men had been stimulated by the revolutionary French chemistry of C. Gerhardt and A. Laurent. On the latter's death in 1853 Williamson recommended Odling to Biot (Laurent's editor) as the English translator of Laurent's posthumous masterpiece, *Méthode de chimie.* The few months Odling spent in Paris with Gerhardt in 1854 completed his chemical education. Thereafter he and Williamson became the

formidable British spokesmen for the type theory and for two-volume formulas (such as H_2O for water instead of the prevailing confusion of HO or H_4O_2).

Laurent and Gerhardt also induced Odling's lifelong interest in the problems of classifying chemical compounds and of exploiting their analogies. Unlike Williamson, however, who believed in the existence of atoms, Odling was sufficiently influenced by Brodie's skepticism to remain uncommitted to atomism per se. Like Gerhardt he preferred to regard formulas as heuristic devices, and he had only harsh words for the pictorial "fancies" involved in the graphic formulas of A. Crum Brown and Frankland. The radical theories of J. J. Berzelius—and more recently those of H. Kolbe and Frankland—were irrational, Odling believed, because they involved the real existence of hypothetical components; on the other hand, Gerhardt's two-volume types (hydrogen, hydrogen chloride, water, and ammonia) merely used chemical analogies that were based upon facts which did not involve a commitment to unattainable absolute structures.

This positivism was prominent in Odling's first paper to the Chemical Society in 1853.[2] In it he extended Williamson's use of the multiple water type (which classified compounds as substitution products in a double water molecule) and showed how all salts, however complex, could be reduced to "the types of one or more atoms of water." ("Atom" was here being used in a conventionalist sense.) For example, the problematic phosphoric acids were construed as

$$\left.\begin{array}{c}2H' \\ 2H'\end{array}\right\}2O'' \qquad \left.\begin{array}{c}PO''' \\ H'\end{array}\right\}2O'' \quad \text{metaphosphoric acid}$$

$$\left.\begin{array}{c}3H' \\ 3H'\end{array}\right\}3O'' \qquad \left.\begin{array}{c}PO''' \\ 3H'\end{array}\right\}3O'' \quad \text{orthophosphoric acid}$$

while alum was a quadruple water type:

$$\left.\begin{array}{c}2SO_2'' \\ KAl_2'''\end{array}\right\}4O''$$

Superscript single, double, and triple vertical lines were introduced by Odling to indicate the equivalence, or "replaceable value," of the element or group within the type formula compared with hydrogen. (He recognized, and allowed for, elements with variable equivalence, such as Fe' in ferrous and Fe''' in ferric salts; CO'' in carbonic and CO' in oxalic acid.) This useful notation was rapidly adopted by other chemists, and by the 1860's the vertical lines were recognized as denoting the valence of particular atoms. Odling also introduced "mixed types" for molecules like sodium thiosulfate:

$$\left.\begin{matrix} H \\ H \\ H \\ H \end{matrix}\right\rbrace \begin{matrix} O'' \\ \\ O'' \end{matrix} \qquad \left.\begin{matrix} Na' \\ SO_2'' \\ Na' \end{matrix}\right\rbrace \begin{matrix} O'' \\ \\ S'' \end{matrix}$$

Such types were later used extensively by Kekulé.

In an important lecture on hydrocarbons in 1853, Odling extended these ideas and argued, against the radical school, that in hydrogen compounds, such as the hydrocarbons, there were as many potential radicals as there were parts of hydrogen.[3] Thus

1 HCl

2 $H \cdot OH$ H^2O

3 $H \cdot NH^2$ $H^2 \cdot NH$ H^3N

4 $H \cdot CH^3$ $H^2 \cdot CH^2$ $H^3 \cdot CH$ H^4C methane

The methane example was made famous by Kekulé in 1857 as the "marsh gas type." But unlike Kekulé, who possessed an offprint of the lecture, Odling failed to extend the type to several carbon compounds and thus failed to exploit the unifying possibilities implicit in his own notation, $C^{iv}H^4$: the quadrivalence of carbon. Here the historical problem of Odling's precise influence on Kekulé, as opposed to Gerhardt's, is particularly puzzling.

Odling was one of the secretaries at the international conference on a rational system of combining or atomic weights held at Karlsruhe in 1860. Between 1853 and 1863 he was an enthusiastic propagandist for Gerhardt's partial revision of atomic weights,[4] and although he did not immediately see the need for Cannizzaro's more sweeping revision, he accepted and publicized them beginning in 1864. Like Laurent, Odling had a passion for learned, and often impracticable, neologisms. In 1864 he introduced the terms "monad," "dyad," and "tetrad" for variable units of valence, and "artiads" and "perissads" for elements with even and odd valences, respectively. The terms were used widely in British textbooks and examinations until about 1900.

Odling's interest in classification inevitably led him to examine the natural relationships between chemical elements and to publish several prescient schemes between 1857 and 1865. He was perhaps unique among Mendeleev's many predecessors in placing more emphasis on the physical and chemical analogies between elements and their compounds, rather than indulging in numerical speculations about the atomic weights of the elements.

NOTES

1. His lecture on chemical affinity was reported extensively in *Maidstone and South Eastern Gazette* (June 1844), quoted in entirety by Freeman, pp. 190–202.
2. "On the Constitution of Acids and Salts as Substitution Products Formed on the Water Type," in *Quarterly Journal of the Chemical Society*, **7** (1855), 1–21 (read 7 Nov. 1853 and probably extensively revised).
3. "On the Constitution of the Hydrocarbons," in *Proceedings of the Royal Institution of Great Britain*, **2** (1854–1858), 63–66 (read 16 Mar. 1855).
4. "On the Atomic Weights of Oxygen and Water," in *Quarterly Journal of the Chemical Society*, **11** (1859), 107–129; and "On the Molecule of Water," in *Chemical News*, **8** (1863), 147–152.

BIBLIOGRAPHY

I. ORIGINAL WORKS. An unpublished bibliography of 150 publications is given by P. J. Freeman in "The Life and Times of William Odling (1829–1921), Waynflete Professor of Chemistry, 1872–1912" (B.Sc. thesis, Oxford, 1963). This supplements the published bibliography by John L. Thornton and Anna Wiles, "William Odling, 1829–1921," in *Annals of Science*, **12** (1956), 288–295. To their lists, the following significant items should be added: "On the Basis of Chemical Notation," in *Nature*, **1** (1869–1870), 600–602; "On the Unit Weight and Mode of Constitution of Compounds," in *Chemical News*, **45** (1882), 63–65; and "The Whole Duty of a Chemist," in *Nature*, **33** (1885–1886), 99, a reply to an editorial attack (*ibid.*, 73–77) on Odling's presidential address to the Royal Institute of Chemistry.

Odling's textbooks, which are easily confused, are *A Course of Practical Chemistry, Arranged for the Use of Medical Students* (London, 1854; 2nd ed., 2 pts., 1863–1865; 3rd ed., 1865 [*sic*], trans. into Russian by R. Savtschenkoff [St. Petersburg, 1867] and read by Mendeleev; 4th ed., 1869; 5th ed., 1876, trans. into French by A. Naquet [1876]); *A Manual of Chemistry, Descriptive and Theoretical*, pt. I (London, 1861)—pt. II never appeared, but see MSS—trans. into Russian (St. Petersburg, 1863), German (Erlangen, 1865), and French (Paris, 1868)—for the O_3 formula for ozone, see 1861 ed., pp. 93–94; *Tables of Chemical Formulae* (London, 1864), 8 leaves, the first list of Cannizzaro's atomic weights in English; *Lectures on Animal Chemistry, Delivered at the Royal College of Physicians* (London, 1866), also trans. into Russian (St. Petersburg, 1867); *A Course of Six Lectures on the Chemical Changes of Carbon*, W. Crookes, ed. (London, 1869), also trans. into French (Paris, 1870); *Outlines of Chemistry, or Brief Notes of Chemical Facts* (London, 1870 [published Nov. 1869]), for the influential bleaching powder formula, see p. 24; and *Science Primers for the People*, no. 2, *Chemistry* (London, 1883).

Odling translated Auguste Laurent, *Chemical Method, Notation, Classification and Nomenclature* (London, 1855; some copies released in 1854). Odling's final book was the extraordinary *The Technic of Versification: Notes and Illustrations* (Oxford–London, 1916), which Marsh (below) aptly described as "a kind of type theory of verse with a symbolic notation almost chemical."

The principal archival sources are, in London: Chemical Society (B Club and Roscoe papers, photographs), Imperial College Archives, Royal Institute of Chemistry (several MSS, including drafts of pt. II of the *Manual*), Royal Institution, Royal Society (referee reports); at Harpenden: Rothamsted Experimental Station (J. H. Gilbert papers); at Oxford: Museum of History of Science (Rev. F. J. J. Smith papers).

II. SECONDARY LITERATURE. There are two good obituaries: J. E. Marsh, in *Journal of the Chemical Society*, **119** (1921), 553–564, with portrait; and H. B. D.[ixon], in *Proceedings of the Royal Society*, **100A** (1922), i–vii, with portrait. An Oxford student's caricature of Odling lecturing is reproduced in R. T. Gunther, *Early Science at Oxford*, XI (Oxford, 1937), 293. To Freeman, and Thornton and Wiles (above), add K. R. Webb, "William Odling, Third President 1883–88," in *Journal of the Royal Institute of Chemistry*, **81** (1957), 728–733; and J. R. Brown and J. L. Thornton, "William Odling as Medical Officer of Health at Lambeth," in *Medical Officer*, **102** (1959), 77–78.

No detailed study of Odling's influence on theoretical chemistry in the 1850's and 1860's has yet been made. For some indications see, on the problem of Odling's influence on Kekulé, R. Anschütz, *August Kekulé*, I (Berlin, 1929), *passim*; on Odling's contribution to valence, C. A. Russell, *History of Valency* (Leicester, 1970), *passim*; on Odling's attitude toward Brodie and atomism, W. H. Brock, *The Atomic Debates* (Leicester, 1967), *passim*, which includes four letters; on Odling and the periodic law, J. W. van Spronsen, "William Odling wegbereider en ontdekker van het periodiek systeem der elementen 1864–1964," in *Chemisch Weekblad*, **60** (1964), 683–686; and his *Periodic System of Chemical Elements* (Amsterdam–London–New York, 1969), 87–90, 112–116, 349–350; and, for general orientation, J. R. Partington, *A History of Chemistry*, IV (London, 1964), *passim*. Finally, for a glimpse of Odling the administrator, see R. B. Pilcher, *The Institute of Chemistry of Great Britain and Ireland. History of the Institute, 1877–1914* (London, 1914), *passim*.

W. H. BROCK

OENOPIDES OF CHIOS (*b.* Chios; *fl.* fifth century B.C.), *astronomy, mathematics.*

The notice of Pythagoras in Proclus' summary of the history of geometry is followed by the sentence,[1] "After him Anaxagoras of Clazomenae touched many questions concerning geometry, as also did Oenopides of Chios, being a little younger than Anaxagoras, both of whom Plato mentioned in the *Erastae*[2] as having acquired a reputation for mathematics." This fixes the birthplace of Oenopides as the island of Chios and puts his active life in the second third of the fifth

century B.C.[3] Anaxagoras was born about 500 B.C. and died about 428 B.C. There is confirmation from Oenopides' researches into the "great year" (see below), which suggest that he could not have differed greatly in date from Meton, who proposed his own Great Year in 432. Like Anaxagoras, Oenopides almost certainly conducted his researches in Athens.

In the opening words of the *Erastae*, to which Proclus refers, Socrates is represented as going into the school of Dionysius the grammarian, Plato's own teacher,[4] and seeing two youths earnestly discussing some astronomical subject. He could not quite catch what they were saying, but they appeared to be disputing about Anaxagoras or Oenopides, and to be drawing circles and imitating some inclinations with their hands. In the light of other passages in Greek authors, this is a clear reference to the obliquity of the ecliptic in relation to the celestial equator. Eudemus in his history of astronomy, according to Dercyllides as transmitted by Theon of Smyrna, related that Oenopides was the first to discover the obliquity of the zodiac,[5] and there appears to have been a widespread Greek belief to that effect. Macrobius,[6] for example, drawing on Apollodorus, notes that Apollo was given the epithet $\Lambda o\xi i\alpha s$ because the sun moves in an oblique circle from west to east, "as Oenopides says." Aëtius[7] says that Pythagoras was the first to discover the obliquity of the ecliptic, and that Oenopides claimed the discovery as his own, while Diodorus[8] says that it was from the Egyptian priests and astronomers that he learned the path of the sun to be oblique and opposite to the motion of the stars (that is, fixed stars). He is not recorded as having given any value to the obliquity, but it was probably he who settled on the value of 24°, which was accepted in Greece until refined by Eratosthenes.[9] Indeed, if Oenopides did not fix on this or some other figure, it is difficult to know in what his achievement consisted, for the Babylonians no less than the Pythagoreans and Egyptians must have realized from early days that the apparent path of the sun was inclined to the celestial equator.

In the same passage as that already mentioned, Theon of Smyrna[10] attributes to Oenopides the discovery of the period of the Great Year. This came to mean a period in which all the heavenly bodies returned to their original relative positions, but in early days only the motions of the sun and moon were taken into account and the Great Year was the least number of solar years which coincided with an exact number of lunations. Before Oenopides it was calculated that the sun and the moon returned to the same relative positions after a period of eight years, the *octaëteris*, in which three years of thirteen months or

384 days were distributed among five years of twelve months or 354 days, giving the solar year an average of $365\frac{1}{4}$ days and making the lunar month a shade over $29\frac{1}{2}$ days. Oenopides appears to have been the first to give a more exact rendering, possibly in an attempt to take account also of the planetary motions. Aelian records that he set up at Olympia a bronze inscription stating that the Great Year consisted of fifty-nine years, and Aëtius confirms the period,[11] while Censorinus[12] states that he made the year to be $365\frac{22}{59}$ days, which implies a Great Year of 21,557 days. Oenopides no doubt fixed upon a period of fifty-nine years, as P. Tannery[13] first showed, by taking the figures of $29\frac{1}{2}$ days for a lunar month and 365 days for a solar year, and deducing that in fifty-nine years there would on this basis be exactly 730 lunations. Observation would have established, Tannery argued, that in 730 lunar months there were 21,557 days, from which it follows that the year consists of $365\frac{22}{59}$ or 365.37288 days and the month of 29.53013 days. The cycle of nineteen years that Meton and Euctemon proposed in 432 B.C., on which the present ecclesiastical calendar is ultimately based, gives a year of $365\frac{5}{19}$ or 365.26315 days and a month of 29.53191 days. The modern value for the sidereal year is 365.25637 days and for the mean synodic month is 29.53059 days.

Oenopides' figure for the lunar month is, therefore, if Tannery is right, more exact than that of Meton (indeed, very exact, for the error does not exceed a third of a day in the whole fifty-nine years), but his figure for the year is considerably less exact, amounting to seven days for the whole period.

But could Oenopides have calculated at that date so exact a figure for the mean synodic month (which requires a long period of observation) when he had so inaccurate a figure for the solar year (to establish which as about $365\frac{1}{4}$ days would require only a few consecutive observations of the times of the solstices)? In a private communication G. J. Toomer is skeptical. He believes that Oenopides did not assign any specific number of days to the Great Year, and the year-length of $365\frac{22}{59}$ days attributed to him by Censorinus is a later reconstruction. Someone at this later date asked himself what is the length of the year according to Oenopides. He answered the question by taking the standard length of the mean synodic month of his own time, namely (expressed sexagesimally) 29; 31, 50, 8, 20 days. This is found in Geminus as well as the *Almagest* and was a fundamental Babylonian parameter adopted by Hipparchus. The hypothetical investigator multiplied this by the 730 months of Oenopides' period and obtained 21,557 days and a fraction of a day. Dividing 21,557 by the

59 years of the cycle, he declared that Oenopides' year consisted of $365\frac{22}{59}$ days—that is to say, the figure is a later deduction using a completely anachronistic value for the month. This is credible. The critical question is whether Oenopides could have had at his disposal records extending over more than his own adult life showing that in 730 lunations there were 21,557 days; if he did, it would be strange for him not to have known a more exact figure for the year.

Tannery[14] holds that Oenopides' Great Year was intended to cover the revolutions of the planets and of the sun and moon, but he is forced to conclude that Oenopides could not have taken them all into account. The ancient cosmographers gave the time for Saturn to traverse its orbit as thirty years, for Jupiter twelve years, and for Mars two years, which would allow two revolutions for Saturn in the Great Year, five for Jupiter, and thirty or thirty-one for Mars. If the latter figure is taken as the more correct, and the figure of 21,557 days in the Great Year is divided by these numbers, we get values for the revolutions of the three planets which do not differ by more than one percent from the correct values. Tannery considers that the degree of inaccuracy ought rather to be judged by the error in the mean position of the heavenly body at the end of the period; this would be only 2° in the case of Saturn and 9° for the sun, but 107° for Mars. If Oenopides had indicated in which sign of the zodiac the planet would be found at the end of the period, the error would have been obvious when the time came.

According to Achilles Tatius,[15] Oenopides was among those who believed that the path of the sun was formerly the Milky Way; the sun turned away in horror from the banquet of Thyestes and has ever since moved in the path defined by the zodiac.

Two propositions in geometry were discovered by Oenopides according to Eudemus as preserved by Proclus. Commenting on Euclid I.12 ("to a given infinite straight line from a given point which is not upon it to draw a perpendicular straight line") Proclus[16] says: "Oenopides was the first to investigate this problem, thinking it useful for astronomy. But, in the ancient manner, he calls the perpendicular 'a line drawn gnomon-wise,' because the gnomon is at right angles to the horizon." When he comes to Euclid I.23 ("on a given straight line and at a given point on it, to construct a rectilineal angle equal to a given rectilineal angle") Proclus[17] comments: "This problem is rather the discovery of Oenopides, as Eudemus relates." Heath[18] justly observes that the geometrical reputation of Oenopides can hardly have rested on such simple propositions as these, nor could he have been the first to draw a perpendicular in practice. Possibly he was the first to draw a perpendicular to a straight line by means of a ruler and compass (instead of a set-square), and it may have been he who introduced into Greek geometry the limitation of the use of instruments in all plane constructions—that is, in all problems equivalent to the solution of algebraic equations of the second degree—to the ruler and compasses. He also may have been the first to give a theoretical construction to Euclid I.23.

This question bears on an interesting problem to which Kurt von Fritz[19] has devoted much attention. According to Proclus,[20] "Zenodotus, who stood in the succession of Oenopides but was one of the pupils of Andron, distinguished the theorem from the problem by the fact that the theorem seeks what is the property predicated of its subject-matter, but the problem seeks to find what is the cause of what effect" (as translated by Heath,[21] but Glenn R. Morrow[22] translates τίνος ὄντος τί ἐστιν as "under what conditions something exists"). The meaning was probably no clearer to Proclus than it is to us, but it may be that Oenopides was one of those who helped to create the distinction between theorems and problems. Taken in conjunction with what was said in the previous paragraph, it would appear that he made a special study of the methodology of mathematics.

Oenopides had an original theory to account for the Nile floods. He held that the water beneath the earth is cold in the summer and warm in the winter, a phenomenon proved by the temperature of deep wells. In winter, when there are no rains in Egypt, the heat that is shut up in the earth carries off most of the moisture, but in summer the moisture is not so carried off and overflows the Nile. Diodorus Siculus, who recorded the theory, reasonably objected that other rivers of Libya, similar in position and direction to the Nile, are not so affected.[23]

It is related that Oenopides, seeing an uneducated youth who had amassed many books, observed, "Not in your coffer but in your breast."[24] Sextus Empiricus[25] says that Oenopides laid special emphasis on fire and air as first principles. Aëtius[26] says that Diogenes (of Apollonia), Cleanthes, and Oenopides made the soul of the world to be divine. Cleanthes left a hymn to Zeus in which the universe is considered a living being with God as its soul, and if Aëtius is correct then Oenopides must have anticipated these views by more than a century. Diogenes is known to have revived the doctrine of Anaximenes that the primary substance is air, and presumably Oenopides in part shared this view but gave equal primacy to fire as a first principle.

NOTES

1. Proclus: *Procli Diadochi in primum Euclidis, Elementorum librum commentarii*, G. Friedlein, ed. (Leipzig, 1873, repr. 1967), pp. 65.21–66.4.
2. Plato, *Erastae (Amatores)*, 132 A.B, in J. Burnet, ed., *Platonis opera*, II (Oxford, 1901, repr. 1946). The Platonic authorship of the *Erastae* has been denied, but this does not affect its evidence for Oenopides.
3. The "Vita Ptolemaei e schedis Savilianis descripta" found in a Naples MS (Erwin Rohde, *Kleine Schriften*, I [Tübingen–Leipzig, 1901], p. 123, n. 4) is therefore in error in saying that Oenopides lived "towards the end of the Peloponnesian war" but more accurate in adding "at the same time as Gorgias the orator and Zeno of Elea and, as some say, Herodotus, the historian, of Halicarnassus." Diogenes Laërtius IX.41 (H.S. Long, ed., II [Oxford, 1964], 450. 23–25) says that Democritus "would be a contemporary of Archelaus, the pupil of Anaxagoras, and of the circle of Oenopides"; and he adds that Democritus makes mention of Oenopides—presumably in a work that has not survived.
4. Diogenes Laërtius III. 4 (H. S. Long, ed., I [Oxford, 1964], 122.13).
5. Theon of Smyrna, *Expositio rerum mathematicarum ad legendum Platonem utilium*, E. Hiller, ed. (Leipzig, 1878), 198.14–16. H. Diels's conjecture λόξωσιν ("obliquity") for διάζωσιν ("girdle") is almost certainly correct.
6. Macrobius, *Saturnalia* I.17.31, F. Eyssenhardt, ed., 2nd ed. (Leipzig, 1893), 93.28–94.2.
7. Aëtius, II.12, 2, Ps.-Plutarch, *De placitis philosophorum*, B. N. Bernardakis, ed. (*Plutarchi Chaeronensis Moralia*, Teubner, V [Leipzig, 1893]), 284.8–9.
8. Diodorus Siculus, *Bibliotheca historica*, I.98.3, C. II. Oldfather, ed., I (London–New York, 1933), pp. 334.29, 337.4.
9. Proclus, *In primum Euclidis*, Friedlein, ed., p. 269.11–21, states that Euclid IV.16 (which shows how to construct a regular polygon of fifteen sides in a circle, each side therefore subtending an angle of 24° at the center) was inserted "in view of its use in astronomy." Erastosthenes found the distance between the tropical circles to be 11/83 of the whole meridian, giving a value for the obliquity of 23°51′20″ as Ptolemy records in *Syntaxis*, J. L. Heiberg, ed., I.12 (Leipzig, 1898), p. 68.3–6.
10. Theon of Smyrna, *op. cit.*, p. 198.15.
11. Aelian, *Varia historia*, X.7, C. G. Kuehn ed., II (Leipzig, 1780), 65–67; Aëtius, II.32.2, *op. cit.*, 316.1–7.
12. Censorinus, *De die natali* 19.2, F. Hultsch, ed. (Leipzig, 1867), 40.19–20.
13. Paul Tannery, *Mémoires scientifiques*, II (Toulouse–Paris, 1912), 359.
14. *Ibid.*, 358, 362–363.
15. Achilles Tatius, *Introductio in Aratum* 24, E. Maass ed., *Commentariorum in Aratum reliquiae* (Berlin, 1898), p. 55.18–21. Aristotle, *Meteorologica* I.8, 345A, 13–25, Fobes, ed. (Cambridge, Mass. 1919, repr. Hildesheim, 1967), notes that certain of the so-called Pythagoreans held the same view and pointedly asks why the zodiac circle was not scorched in the same way.
16. Proclus, *In primum Euclidis*, Friedlein, ed., 283.7–10.
17. *Ibid.*, 333.5–6.
18. Thomas Heath, *A History of Greek Mathematics*, I (Oxford, 1921), 175.
19. Kurt von Fritz, "Oinopides" in Pauly-Wissowa, **17** (Stuttgart, 1937), cols. 2267–2271.
20. Proclus, *In primum Euclidis*, Friedlein, ed., p. 80.15–20.
21. Thomas L. Heath, *The Thirteen Books of Euclid's Elements*, 2nd ed., I (Cambridge, 1926; New York, 1956), 126.
22. Glenn R. Morrow, *Proclus: A Commentary on the First Book of Euclid's Elements* (Princeton, 1970), p. 66.
23. Diodorus Siculus I. 41.1–3, *op. cit.*, vol. 1, pp. 144.23–147.17.

24. *Gnomologium Vaticanum* 743, L. Sternbach, ed. (Berlin, 1963), n. 420.
25. Sextus Empiricus, *Pyrrhoniae hypotyposes*, iii. 30.
26. Aëtius, I.7, 17, *op. cit.*, 284.8–9.

BIBLIOGRAPHY

No works by Oenopides have survived, nor are the titles of any known. The ancient references to him are collected in Diels-Kranz, *Die Fragmente der Vorsokratiker*, 6th ed. (Dublin–Zurich, 1969), 41(29), 393–395. The most useful modern studies are Paul Tannery, "La grande année d'Aristarque de Samos," in *Mémoires de la Société des sciences physiques et naturelles de Bordeaux*, 3rd ser., **4** (1888), 79–96, reprinted in *Mémoires scientifiques*, J. L. Heiberg and H. G. Zeuthen, ed., **2** (Paris–Toulouse, 1912), 345–366; Thomas Heath, *Aristarchus of Samos. The Ancient Copernicus* (Oxford, 1913), 130–133; Kurt von Fritz, "Oinopides," in Pauly-Wissowa-Kroll, *Real-Encyclopädie der classischen Altertumswissenschaft*, **17** (Stuttgart, 1937), cols. 2258–2272; D. R. Dicks, *Early Greek Astronomy to Aristotle* (London, 1970), 88–89, 157, 172; Jürgen Mau, "Oinopides," in *Der Kleine Pauly*, IV (Stuttgart, 1972), cols. 263–264.

IVOR BULMER-THOMAS

OERSTED, HANS CHRISTIAN (*b*. Rudkøbing, Langeland, Denmark, 14 August 1777; *d*. Copenhagen, Denmark, 9 March 1851), *physics*.

Oersted was the elder son of an apothecary, Søren Christian Oersted, and his wife, the former Karen Hermansen. The demands of his father's business and his mother's superintendence of a large family forced his parents to place Hans Christian and his younger brother, Anders Sandøe, with a German wigmaker and his wife while they were still young boys. It was there that Oersted learned German by translating a German Bible and speaking with the couple. The brothers' intellectual abilities were soon apparent, and neighbors did what they could to stimulate and educate them. In this way they picked up the rudiments of Latin, French, and mathematics. When Oersted was eleven, he began to serve as his father's assistant in the pharmacy, thereby gaining a practical knowledge of the fundamentals of chemistry.

This was not much formal education; but when the two brothers arrived in Copenhagen in 1794, they were able to pass the entrance examination for the university with honors. At this point they parted intellectual company; Anders went on to become a jurist and Hans Christian pursued a career in natural philosophy. The most important of Oersted's courses for his intellectual development was that offered on Kant and the critical philosophy. Oersted became a passionate Kantian and defender of Kant's philosophical views, which were to be of fundamental importance to his scientific development. They were even to be the agent that led him to his most important discovery, electromagnetism.

At the University of Copenhagen, Oersted studied astronomy, physics, mathematics, chemistry, and pharmacy. In 1797 he received his pharmaceutical degree with high honors. The following year he became a member of the editorial staff of a new periodical, *Philosophisk repertorium for faedrelandets nyeste litteratur*, which was devoted to the propagation and defense of Kantian philosophy. Although short-lived, the journal provided Oersted with an opportunity to mature his philosophical thinking. An unpublished article that he wrote for it served as the starting point for his doctoral dissertation. In 1799 he received his doctorate with a thesis entitled "Dissertatio de forma metaphysices elementaris naturae externae," which states Oersted's appreciation of the importance of Kantian philosophy for natural philosophy and, in addition, provides a clue to the two areas in which he was to apply his scientific training: electromagnetism and research on the compressibility of gases and liquids.

After a brief stint as the manager of a pharmacy, Oersted set out in the summer of 1801 on a journey that was to complete his scientific education. The scientific world was in ferment over the recently announced discovery of the voltaic pile (1800), and Oersted eagerly pursued information relating to galvanism and its relation to chemistry. A small voltaic battery of his own invention gained him entry to others' laboratories, and he gathered knowledge and ideas as he visited Berlin, Göttingen, and Weimar. Again the influences at work on him were twofold. At Göttingen he was given an introduction to Johann Ritter, who was then publishing on the chemical effects of current electricity. Ritter focused Oersted's attention on the forces of chemical affinity and their relationship to electricity. Ritter's highly unorthodox ideas on matter and force also stimulated Oersted to develop his own concepts. At Berlin he attended lectures on *Naturphilosophie* and met such *Naturphilosophen* as Henrik Steffens and Franz von Baader. He read Schelling and heard Friedrich Schlegel. As a result he developed his philosophical insights by comparing his own metaphysics with those of the *Naturphilosophen*. Since both Oersted and the *Naturphilosophen* drew their inspiration and basic ideas from Kant, it is no coincidence that Oersted's later philosophy closely resembled *Naturphilosophie.*

Oersted was saved from the extravagances of a Schelling by his basic respect for empirical fact. Nevertheless, during this trip it was his philosophical penchant that dominated, for although he was suspicious of Schelling's system-building, he swallowed as fact what were only wild guesses by Ritter and the Hungarian chemist J. J. Winterl. Indeed, it was as a defender of Winterl and Ritter that Oersted made his scientific debut in Paris.

The result was disastrous. Winterl's "system" rested on two archetypal substances—Andronia and Thelycke—the essences of acidity and basicity. From these Winterl developed a chemistry of conflicting opposites which, because of its philosophical beauty, completely seduced Oersted. The French chemists, however, were scornful; and Oersted was blasted in the *Annales de chimie et de physique.* It was a valuable lesson. Henceforth, Oersted tended increasingly to hold his philosophical enthusiasms in check at least until he had some evidence for their plausibility. The lesson was driven home by his championing of Ritter's work. To his dismay, he discovered that many of the experimental results his friend reported in the journals were, like Winterl's Andronia, mere figments of his imagination. The pain of having made a scientific fool of himself taught Oersted the critical attitude necessary for the successful pursuit of scientific knowledge.

Oersted returned to Denmark in 1804, preceded by his reputation as an uncritical enthusiast. He had hoped for a professorship in physics but was disappointed by the failure of the warden of the University of Copenhagen to nominate him. He turned, instead, to public lectures, which became so popular that he finally gained an extraordinary professorship in 1806. He then began his own scientific work in earnest. A series of sober publications, among which was an excellent paper on acoustical figures (1810), gradually erased his earlier reputation. He began a steady advance in the academic hierarchy and in reputation. In 1824 he founded the Society for the Promotion of Natural Science and in 1829 became the director of the Polytechnic Institute in Copenhagen, a position that he held until his death. Oersted was a superb teacher and, almost single-handed, raised the level of Danish science to that of the major countries of Europe. He was also an ardent popularizer of science, writing articles and reviews for popular journals. Some of these writings, collected and published as *The Soul in Nature,* reveal his deepest philosophical and scientific beliefs.

There is a unity in Oersted's scientific work that is rarely found in the results of someone whose researches ranged from the forces of chemical affinity, electromagnetism, and the compressibility of fluids and gases to the new phenomenon of diamagnetism. This unity was drawn from Oersted's philosophy, inspired by his reading of Kant. Most Kantian scholars today would insist that Oersted totally misread Kant and came to conclusions to which Kant would have objected. That charge is probably correct; but what is important is that Oersted, and a number of other philosophers and scientists of the time, misread Kant in the same way. Basically, what Oersted thought Kant was saying was that science was not merely the *dis*-covery of Nature; that is, the scientist did not just record empirical facts and sum them up in mathematical formulas. Rather, the human mind imposed patterns upon perceptions; and the patterns were scientific laws. That those patterns were not arbitrary was guaranteed by the existence of Reason. Human reason corresponded to the Divine Reason, for man was made in the image of God. And, inasmuch as God had created Nature, it too shared in the Divine Reason. Thus human reason, unaided, could construct the laws of nature by virtue of its congruence with the Divine Reason. "Was der Geist versprecht, leistet die Natur" is a misquotation from Schiller's *Columbus*—"Mit dem Genius steht die Natur in ewigem Bunde, Was der Eine Verspricht, leistet die andre gewiss"—that Oersted used more than once in *The Soul in Nature.* It represents the basic position of *Naturphilosophie.*

Oersted's reading of Kant led him to more than an attitude toward nature. It also gave him what he felt was a firm metaphysical foundation for his beliefs. In a now neglected treatise, *Metaphysische Anfangsgründe der Naturwissenschaft* (1786), Kant had abandoned some of his agnosticism expressed in the antinomies in the *Critique of Pure Reason.* More particularly, whereas in the *Critique* he had argued that it was impossible for reason to decide between an atomistic or a plenist concept of matter, in the *Metaphysische Anfangsgründe* he came down on the side of the antiatomists. He argued that we experience only force; that force manifests itself in matter as the force of attraction that defines the limits of a body and the force of repulsion that gives a body the property of impenetrability. These two forces Kant called *Grundkräfte* (basic forces). Other forces, such as electricity, magnetism, heat, and light, he hinted, were merely modifications of the *Grundkräfte* under different conditions.

Oersted read both the *Critique of Pure Reason* and the *Metaphysische Anfangsgründe* while still at the university. His doctoral dissertation is a defense of the *Metaphysische Anfangsgründe* and an attempt to have it accepted in Denmark as a basic philosophical treatise. As early as 1800 it is possible to discern the two elements that were fundamental in Oersted's later scientific work: the clear enunciation of the doctrine of forces and the disbelief in atoms. The first was to lead him, through the convertibility of forces, to the discovery of electromagnetism; the second seems to have been the stimulus behind his work on compressibility, for if solid, incompressible atoms existed, there ought to come a point when further compression of a gas or fluid was impossible.

In 1800, however, Oersted's ideas were only half-formed. He was far more *au courant* in philosophy than he was in science. This is why his journey to Germany and France was so crucial. It acquainted him with men who were at the frontiers of science and forced him to bring his philosophical speculations down to earth.

The reentry was a difficult one. The "new" chemistry of Lavoisier and the other French chemists left him unmoved because it turned its back on the very questions, such as elective affinity and the true nature of acids and bases, that fascinated Oersted. Winterl's system, on the other hand, was just what he was looking for. Instead of some thirty-odd elements, defined only empirically as the last products of a laboratory analysis, Winterl offered two fundamental and opposed substances. Andronia and Thelycke could be viewed as materializations of the *Grundkräfte* and chemistry could then, it was hoped, be seen as a Kantian science. Similarly, Ritter's work in electro-chemistry appeared to Oersted as a development of Kantian thought and all of a piece with his own philosophy of forces. It was only when his philosophical theories and the empirical facts refused to fit together in repeatable experiments that Oersted's critical faculties were awakened. It is significant that, at this point, he did not reject his philosophical faith. Instead, he rejected the physical systems of Winterl and Ritter. His first real scientific achievement was to create his own system, based upon his own experiments. The results appeared in German in 1812 and in a French translation in 1813. The title of the latter, *Recherches sur l'identité des forces chimiques et électriques*, indicates its purpose. From the *Grundkräfte*, Oersted hoped to deduce a system of chemistry that would be in accordance with the results of experiment.

The *Recherches* is an undeservedly neglected work of theoretical chemistry. The standard histories of chemistry barely mention it, yet it tried to come to grips with some of the major problems of the day. Specifically, it sought to make some sense of the various chemical reactions involved in combustion and the neutralization of acids and bases. By 1813 Lavoisier's theory of acids and of combustion could be severely criticized. Humphry Davy's work on chlorine showed that oxygen was not the only supporter of combustion. The fact that hydrochloric acid contained no oxygen also proved that oxygen was not, as Lavoisier had claimed, the principle of acidity. Oersted now tried to show how one could create a new chemistry based on forces, not elements.

According to Oersted, the Kantian *Grundkräfte* of attraction and repulsion manifest themselves in chemistry as combustibles and combusters. These forces are in conflict and when allowed, in combustion, to come to grips with one another, so to speak, produce the light and heat that are so preeminently the effects of combustion. But these two forces do not annihilate one another chemically; instead, they produce a higher synthesis—the acids and bases. Acidity and basicity, in turn, are opposites which unite to form the neutral salts. The supposedly Hegelian triad of thesis-antithesis-synthesis is here clear and is a standard aspect of *Naturphilosophie*. Although this analysis of fundamental chemical processes did provide a conceptual unity where before there was chaos, it left little impression upon Oersted's colleagues. Nor did his final chapters, in which he examined the convertibility of other forces. By 1813 everyone admitted the chemical role of electricity, but Oersted's treatment of it seemed to be of little help. What is of interest, at least to historians of science, is his discussion of the possibility of the conversion of electricity into magnetism.

It is important to stress that electromagnetism was not an effect to be expected according to the orthodox, corpuscular theories of the day. Coulomb seemingly had proved in the 1780's that electricity and magnetism were two entirely different species of matter whose laws of action were mathematically similar but whose natures were fundamentally different. The conversion of one into the other was, literally, unthinkable. Hence, those who accepted Coulomb's findings simply did not look for a magnetic effect.

For Oersted the situation was quite different. The Kantian doctrine of *Grundkräfte* led directly to the idea of conversion of forces. All that was necessary was to discover the conditions under which such conversions took place. The particular conditions for the conversion of electricity into magnetism were deduced by Oersted from the nature of electricity. Electricity to him was a conflict of the positive and negative aspects of magnetism, which conflict spread out in wave fashion in space. When the electric conflict was confined in a rather narrow-gauge wire, the result was heat. When the conflict was restricted still further by decreasing the diameter of the wire, light was produced. So, Oersted suggested in his treatise on the identity of chemical and electrical forces, the magnetic force should be produced when the electrical conflict is still further confined in a very narrow-gauge wire. In 1813, therefore, he had already predicted the existence of the electromagnetic effect. He was wrong, of course, on the conditions; and this error, together with his increasing teaching duties in the years that followed, prevented him from bringing his prediction to reality. The actual discovery was made in the early spring of 1820 and may best be given in Oersted's own words.

Electromagnetism itself was discovered in the year 1820, by Professor Hans Christian Oersted, of the University of Copenhagen. Throughout his literary career, he adhered to the opinion, that the magnetical effects are produced by the same powers as the electrical. He was not so much led to this, by the reasons commonly alleged for this opinion, as by the philosophical principle, that all phenomena are produced by the same original power. . . . His researches upon this subject, were still fruitless, until the year 1820. In the winter of 1819-20, he delivered a course of lectures upon electricity, galvanism, and magnetism, before an audience that had been previously acquainted with the principles of natural philosophy. In composing the lecture, in which he was to treat of the analogy between electricity and magnetism, he conjectured, that if it were possible to produce any magnetical effect by electricity, this could not be in the direction of the current, since this had been so often tried in vain, but that it must be produced by a lateral action. This was strictly connected with his other ideas; for he did not consider the transmission of electricity through a conductor as an uniform stream, but as a succession of interruptions and reestablishments of equilibrium, in such a manner that the electrical powers in the current were not in quiet equilibrium, but in a state of continual conflict. . . . The plan of the first experiment was, to make the current of a little galvanic trough apparatus, commonly used in his lectures, pass through a very thin platina wire, which was placed over a compass covered with glass. The preparations for the experiments were made, but some accident having hindered him from trying it before the lecture, he intended to defer it to another opportunity; yet during the lecture, the probability of its success appeared stronger, so that he made the first experiment in the presence of the audience. The magnetical needle, though included in a box, was disturbed; but as the effect was very feeble, and must, before its law was discovered, seem very irregular, the experiment made no strong impression on the audience ["Thermo-electricity," in *Edinburgh Encyclopaedia* (1830), XVIII, 573–589; repr. in Oersted's *Scientific Papers*, II, 356].

Oersted could not be sure that the effect was the one he had anticipated, and therefore he deferred working on it for some three months. In July he resumed his researches and made certain that a current-carrying wire is surrounded by a circular magnetic field. The results appeared in a short paper, written in Latin, sent to the major scientific journals in Europe. The "Experimenta circa effectum conflictus electrici in acum magneticam," dated 21 July 1820, opened a new epoch in the history of physics. From it followed the creation of electrodynamics by Ampère and Faraday's *Experimental Researches in Electricity*.

Oersted's second major area of research involved the compressibility of gases and fluids. It may be, as his biographer Kirstine Meyer implies, that he became interested in this problem by noting inconsistencies in the experiments of previous investigators. There may also, however, be a matter of theoretical importance involved. In all his experiments on compressibility, especially the compressibility of fluids, Oersted was intent upon proving that the reduction in volume was proportional to the pressure. If this were so, then the law of compressibility would provide a smooth pv curve. The existence of incompressible atoms, occupying space, would force a discontinuity in this curve if and when the point could be reached when the atoms were packed tightly together. Oersted's system of forces permitted continual compression, and it seems plausible that his experiments on compressibility were intended to test the atomic hypothesis. The results were inconclusive, but his apparatus and critical acumen in detecting sources of error were of basic importance for later investigations of compressibility.

Oersted's last scientific researches were on the phenomena of diamagnetism. He tried to account for diamagnetic substances by assuming reverse polarity and reverse inductive effects in substances that were repelled from, rather than attracted to, a magnetic pole. This work, in the late 1840's, was made obsolete by Faraday's investigations, which showed that the concept of polarity could not be applied to diamagnetics.

In his last years Oersted returned to his first love, philosophy. In a series of articles, published together in *The Soul in Nature*, he considered the relation between beauty and science. He still saw the hand of God in both. Beauty in art and music was the Divine Reason manifested in the harmonies of sight and sound. "Spirit and nature are one, viewed under two different aspects. Thus we cease to wonder at their harmony." Oersted's last work, *The Soul in Nature*, was left unfinished when he died on 9 March 1851. It was intended to express, in final form, the faith that had guided his entire scientific career.

BIBLIOGRAPHY

I. ORIGINAL WORKS. There is an autobiography, in Danish, in *Kofod's Konversationslexikon*, XXVIII (Copenhagen, 1828), but it deals only with Oersted's earlier years. The published primary sources are *H. C. Ørsted, Scientific Papers. Collected Edition With Two Essays on His Work* by Kirstine Meyer, 3 vols. (Copenhagen, 1920); and *Correspondance de H. C. Orsted avec divers savants*, H. C. Harding, ed., 2 vols. (Copenhagen, 1920). There is also a considerable amount of unpublished MS material at the Royal Academy of Sciences in Copenhagen. Oersted's views on philosophy, nature, and aesthetics are found in *The Soul in Nature* (London, 1852; repr. 1966).

II. SECONDARY LITERATURE. The only biography to deal with Oersted's entire scientific life is that by Kirstine Meyer, which introduces the *Scientific Papers*.

There are a number of specialized studies on Oersted. Bern Dibner, *Oersted and the Discovery of Electromagnetism* (Norwalk, Conn., 1961), is a study of Oersted's most important work. Robert C. Stauffer's "Speculation and Experiment in the Background of Oersted's Discovery of Electromagnetism," in *Isis*, **48** (1957), 33 ff.; and "Persistent Errors Regarding Oersted's Discovery of Electromagnetism," *ibid.*, **44** (1953), 307 ff., first drew scholarly attention to the importance of *Naturphilosophie* for an understanding of Oersted's scientific career.

L. PEARCE WILLIAMS

OHM, GEORG SIMON (*b.* Erlangen, Bavaria, 16 March 1789; *d.* Munich, Bavaria, 6 July 1854), *physics.*

Ohm was the oldest son of Johann Wolfgang Ohm, master locksmith, and Maria Elisabeth Beck, daughter of a master tailor. Of the Protestant couple's seven children, only two others survived childhood: Martin the mathematician and Elisabeth Barbara. The father, a self-sacrificing autodidact, gave his sons a solid education in mathematics, physics, chemistry, and the philosophies of Kant and Fichte; their considerable mathematical ability was recognized in 1804 by the Erlangen professor Karl Christian von Langsdorf, who enthusiastically likened them to the Bernoullis. Of considerably less importance than his father's tutoring was Ohm's attendance (1800–1805) at the Erlangen Gymnasium, where the predominantly classical instruction stressed recitation, translation, and interpretation of texts. On 3 May 1805 he matriculated at the University of Erlangen, where he studied for three semesters until his father's displeasure at his supposed overindulgence in dancing, billiards, and ice skating forced him to withdraw in virtual exile to rural Switzerland. In September 1806 Ohm began a two-and-a-half-year stint teaching mathematics at one

Pfarrer Zehender's *Erziehungsinstitut* in Gottstadt bei Nydau, Bern canton; in March 1809, he went to Neuchâtel for two years as a private tutor. Just before this move he had expressed to Langsdorf the desire to follow him to Heidelberg; but he was dissuaded with the advice that he would be better off studying Euler, Laplace, and Lacroix on his own.

By Easter of 1811 Ohm was back at the University of Erlangen, where on 25 October, after having passed the required examinations, he received the Ph.D. He subsequently taught mathematics for three semesters as a *Privatdozent*, his only university affiliation until near the end of his life. Lack of money and the poor prospects for advancement at Erlangen forced Ohm to seek other employment from the Bavarian government; but the best he could obtain was a post as a teacher of mathematics and physics at the low-prestige, poorly attended *Realschule* in Bamberg, where he worked with great dissatisfaction from January 1813 until the school's dissolution on 17 February 1816. From 11 March 1816 until his release from Bavarian employ on 9 November 1817, he was assigned, in the capacity of an auxiliary instructor, to teach a section of mathematics at the overcrowded Bamberg *Oberprimärschule*.

On 11 September 1817 Ohm had been offered the position of *Oberlehrer* of mathematics and physics at the recently reformed Jesuit Gymnasium at Cologne, and he began work there (evidently) sometime before the end of the year. The ideals of *wissenschaftliche Bildung* had infused the school with enthusiasm for learning and teaching; and this atmosphere—which appears later to have waned—coupled with the requirement that he teach physics and the existence of a well-equipped laboratory, stimulated Ohm to concern himself for the first time avidly with physics. He studied the French classics—at first Lagrange, Legendre, Laplace, Biot, and Poisson, later Fourier and Fresnel—and, especially after Oersted's discovery of electromagnetism in 1820, did experimental work in electricity and magnetism. It was not until early in 1825, however, that he undertook research with an eye toward eventual publication. On 10 August 1826 Ohm was granted a year's leave of absence, at half pay, to go to Berlin to continue this work. When his leave ended in September 1827, he had not yet attained his fervently sought goal of a university appointment.

Not wishing to return to Cologne, Ohm formally severed his connections there in March 1828 and accepted a temporary job to teach three recitation classes of mathematics a week at the Allgemeine Kriegsschule in Berlin. Sometime during 1832 he also took on a class at the Vereinigte Artillerie- und Ingenieurschule there. Continuing to find all higher academic doors closed to him in Prussia, Ohm hoped to have better luck in Bavaria; but although his ample qualifications were duly recognized, he could elicit no better offer (18 October 1833) than the professorship of physics at the Polytechnische Schule in Nuremberg, a job that brought him no improvement over his previous circumstances except the desirable title of professor.

Finally Ohm began to receive belated official recognition of the importance of his earlier work: he became a corresponding member of the Berlin (1839) and Turin (1841) academies, and on 30 November 1841 he received the Royal Society's Copley Medal. He became a full member of the Bavarian Academy in 1845 and was called to Munich on 23 November 1849 to be curator of the Academy's physical cabinet, with the obligation to lecture at the University of Munich as a full professor. He did not receive the chair of physics until 1 October 1852, less than two years before his death.

Ohm's first work was an elementary geometry text, *Grundlinien zu einer zweckmässigen Behandlung der Geometrie als höheren Bildungsmittels an vorbereitenden Lehranstalten* (Erlangen, 1817), which embodied his ideas on the role of mathematics in education. The student, he believed, should learn mathematics as if it were the free product of his own mind, not as a finished product imposed from without. Ideally, by fostering the conviction that the highest life is that devoted to pure knowledge, education should create a self-reliance and self-respect capable of withstanding all vicissitudes in one's external circumstances. One detects in these sentiments the reflection not only of his own early education but also of the years of isolation in Switzerland and of personal and intellectual deprivation at Bamberg. The resulting inwardness of Ohm's character and the highly intellectualized nature of his ideals of personal worth were an essential aspect of the man who would bring the abstractness of mathematics into the hitherto physical and chemical domain of galvanic electricity.

Ohm's decision in 1825 to undertake, and publish, the original research that was to immortalize his name was made only after he had become convinced that his life had run into a dead end, that he must extricate himself from what had become a stultifying situation at Cologne. Overburdened with students, finding little appreciation for his conscientious efforts, and realizing that he would never marry, he turned to science both to prove himself to the world and to have something solid on which to base his petition for a position in a more stimulating environment. (Similarly, the occasion for the publication of his geometry book had been the desire to leave Bamberg.)

Ohm's first scientific paper was "Vorläufige Anzeige des Gesetzes, nach welchem Metalle die Contaktelektricität leiten" (May 1825).[1] In it he sought a functional relationship between the decrease in the electromagnetic force exerted by a current-carrying wire and the length of the wire. A brief discussion of his procedure is necessary to understand his results and their implications for his further work. From the zinc and copper poles of a voltaic pile he ran two wires, A and B, the free ends of which terminated in small mercury-filled cups, M and N; between M and another cup, O, he ran a third wire, C. Together A, B, and C formed what he called the "invariable conductor," to distinguish it from one of the seven wires of different lengths that, when placed in the circuit between O and N, constituted the "variable conductor." Among the latter was one "very thick" wire, four inches long, and six thinner ones, 0.3 line (.025″) in diameter, ranging in length from one foot to seventy-five feet. Finally, over wire C hung the magnetic needle of a Coulomb torsion balance, which served to measure the electromagnetic force exerted when one of the variable conductors completed the circuit.

Ohm referred all his force readings to the so-called normal force produced by the short, thick wire and chose as his variable the loss in force (*Kraftverlust*) brought about by one of the six longer and thinner test wires. This loss in force was equal to the difference between the normal force and the lesser force occasioned by one of the other wires, divided by the normal force. Tabulating these values against the lengths of the wires, he found that his data were well represented by the formula $v = 0.41 \log (1 + x)$, where v is the loss in force and x is the length of the wire in feet. (This seems to have been a purely empirical fit to his data.) Differentiating this equation—whereby he apparently forgot he was using common logarithms—to get $dv = m \left[dx/(1 + x) \right]$, Ohm then speculated that its general form might be $dv = m \left[dx/(a + x) \right]$; a would represent the equivalent length of the invariable conductor (which in the previous case by chance had been equal to 1). Hence the general equation, ignoring an additive constant, is $v = m \log (1 + x/a)$, which he found quite well confirmed by subsequent experiments and took as the sought-for law. Ohm believed that the coefficient m was a function of the normal force, the thickness of the wire, the value of a, and the "electric tension of the force." He seems actually to have believed that the loss in force would be total (that is, $v = 1$) for a sufficiently long conductor, as required by his formula. One of the striking features of this and Ohm's other early papers was their direct foundation on experiment. Indeed, several could be taken as models of inductive derivation of mathematical laws from empirical data. In his mature work of 1827, however, Ohm, under the influence of Fourier, adopted a highly abstract theoretical mode of presentation that obscured the theory's close relationship with experiment.

It is not obvious why Ohm chose to measure the loss in force and not the force itself. It should be noted, however, that he nowhere spoke of measuring the current; rather, he wanted to find out by what amount the electromagnetic force exerted by a given conductor was weakened when another, longer conductor was placed in the same circuit. From the beginning he sought a law that would elucidate the complex relationship between battery and conductor, and it is possible that he regarded the progressive attenuation of the battery's force by ever longer conductors as the central phenomenon to be explained. In this regard it is significant that three of Ohm's cryptic references to his formula's applicability were to the behavior of different forms of the pile; the other reference was to a series of experiments in which Poggendorff had shown that the magnifying effect of a multiplier eventually reached a limit as the number of turns—and thereby also the length of the conductor—was increased.[2]

In the same month that Ohm's first paper was published (May 1825) there appeared an extract in Férussac's *Bulletin des sciences mathématiques* of A.-C. Becquerel's and Barlow's work on the electric conductibility of metals.[3] Becquerel, like Davy before him, was primarily interested in comparing the "conducting powers" of different wires.[4] Their findings were similar: Becquerel said that to obtain the same conductibility with wires of the same metal, their lengths should be in the same ratio as their cross sections; Davy had said that the conducting powers of wires of the same metal varied directly with their mass (per unit length) and inversely with their length. Each also determined the relative conductibility of different metals, although their results differed markedly. Whereas neither Becquerel nor Davy actually measured anything like the current or the electromagnetic effect—both preferring an equilibrium or null-effect type of experiment —Barlow sought a direct relationship between current intensity, as measured by the deflection of a magnetic needle, and the length and diameter of the conductor. He found that this intensity varied roughly with the inverse square root of the length of the wire and that, for wires all of the same length, it increased with their diameters only up to a certain point, after which any further increase in the diameter of the wire had no effect on the intensity.

Additional experiments by both Barlow and Becquerel had corroborated that the electromagnetic effect did not vary sensibly at different points along the same wire, thereby proving that something having to do with the current remained constant throughout the circuit. Barlow had expected to find a steady diminution of effect either from the positive pole to the negative or from both poles toward the center, and thereby to be able to decide in favor of either the one-fluid or the two-fluid theory of electricity; hence the apparent inconclusiveness of this experiment puzzled him. Becquerel, however, used the same observation, in conjunction with his finding that conductibility decreased with length, in his explanation of the nature of the electric current. He conceived of it as a double stream, going in opposite directions, of positive and negative electricity, such that the intensity or quantity of each—Becquerel was not precise in his distinctions —decreased arithmetically from its pole of origin, resulting in a constant net current at all points. This conjecture, along with Becquerel's original observation that the electromagnetic effect did not vary over the length of the conductor, may have influenced Ohm's subsequent work. In it Ohm clarified with mathematical precision exactly what remained constant (the current) and what gradually decreased (the tension, or electroscopic force) along a conducting wire. At the least Ohm now took it upon himself to eliminate the discrepancies among these related findings. His suspicion, subsequently disproved, that conductibility varied with the strength of the current, made it all the more natural for him to incorporate the force into the relationship for conductibilities.

In February and April 1826, Ohm published two important papers that dealt separately with the two major aspects of his ultimately unified theory of galvanic electricity. The first, "Bestimmung des Gesetzes, nach welchem Metalle die Contaktelektricität leiten, nebst einem Entwurfe zu einer Theorie des Voltaischen Apparates und des Schweiggerschen Multiplicators," announced a comprehensive law for electric current that brought order into the hitherto confused collection of phenomena pertaining to the closed circuit, including the solution to the problem of conductibility as he and others had conceived of it.[5] The second paper, "Versuch einer Theorie der durch galvanische Kräfte hervorgebrachten elektroskopischen Erscheinungen," broke new ground in associating an electric tension with both open and closed galvanic circuits.[6]

Ohm's experimental procedure in the first of these papers was analogous to that which he had used earlier but was modified in several significant ways. First, at Poggendorff's suggestion he now used a thermoelectric pile in order to eliminate the fluctuations in current strength accompanying the voltaic pile, fluctuations that Ohm attributed to changes produced by the current in the distribution (*Vertheilung*) of the components of the liquid conductor. Second, he sought a direct relationship between the electromagnetic force of the current and the entire length of the connecting wire. Although there is some evidence that Ohm may have been in possession of his new, correct law before he undertook this later series of experiments, he presented it as if it were a straightforward induction from his data and later consistently referred to it as having been derived from his experiments.

Be that as it may, in the paper in question Ohm simply observed that the data from each of his several series of experiments were very closely represented by the formula $X = a/(b + x)$, where X is the strength of the electromagnetic effect—which he took as a measure of the electric current—of a conductor of length x on the magnetic needle of a Coulomb torsion balance, and where a and b are constants the exact nature of which he proposed to determine from additional series of carefully controlled experiments. The observation that b remained constant for all series of experiments, whereas a varied with temperature, led Ohm to conclude that a depended solely on the electromotive force (*erregende Kraft*) of the pile and b solely on the resistance (*Leitungswiderstand* or, more commonly, *Widerstandslänge*) of the remaining portion of the circuit, in particular that of the pile itself. He also observed that the electromotive force of the thermoelectric pile appeared to be exactly proportional to the temperature difference at its end points. This process of reasoning back and forth between the experimental data and their mathematical representation, through which he was able to discover the physical significance of the terms, is a characteristic of Ohm's methodology.

After reconfirming the validity of his law by further series of experiments, Ohm exhibited its explanatory powers on some of the chief unsolved problems which had occupied scientists working on the pile; and he showed how it also cast light on a number of other previously reported but poorly understood experimental findings. For example, he was able to explain the apparent differences in behavior between voltaic and thermoelectric pile by pointing out that although both the electromotive force a and the resistance b are normally much greater in the voltaic pile than in the thermoelectric pile, the current in a circuit composed solely of a thermoelectric element bent back upon itself—for which $x = 0$ in the expression $a/(b + x)$ —could exert just as great an electromagnetic effect as the voltaic pile. According to Ohm's formula, however, the introduction of another conductor into each circuit would result in a relatively much greater diminution in the electromagnetic effect of the thermoelectric circuit than of the hydroelectric circuit, which was known to be the case. It had previously seemed anomalous that of two piles capable of registering the same electromagnetic action, one, the thermoelectric, should be incapable of producing either chemical actions or the ignition of fine wires. Such differences had either been attributed to a qualitative difference between electricities stemming from different sources or had been explained by saying that the electricity produced by the thermoelectric pile was greater in quantity but lower in intensity relative to that of the hydroelectric, or voltaic, pile. In addition, Ohm developed a simple mathematical theory of the multiplier that enabled him to say under exactly what conditions it would either amplify or diminish the electromagnetic effect, why this amplification eventually reached a maximum, and why the multiplier usually seemed to weaken the electromagnetic effect of a thermoelectric circuit, whereas it markedly strengthened that of a hydroelectric circuit. The fruitful application of Ohm's simple law to existing problems was an explanatory tour de force.

Ohm's second major paper of 1826 announced the beginnings of a comprehensive theory of galvanic electricity based, he said, on the fact that the contact of heterogeneous bodies produced and maintained a constant electric tension (*Spannung*). He deferred the systematic exposition of this theory to a later work, however, and limited himself to stating without derivation the two equations that constituted its heart: $X = kw(a/l)$ and $u - c = \pm(x/l)a$, where X is the strength of the electric current in a conductor of length l, cross section w, and conductibility (*Leitungsvermögen*) k produced by a difference in electric tension a at its end points; where u is the electroscopic force at a variable point x of the conductor; and where c is a constant independent of x. By means of the first equation one can, with respect to overall conducting power (or resistance), reduce the actual length of a wire of whatever cross section and conductibility to the equivalent length of one wire chosen arbitrarily as a standard. Letting l now be this equivalent length—called the reduced length (*reducirte Länge*) of the conductor—Ohm wrote his first law in the simpler form $X = a/l$, the expression which has become known as Ohm's law.

After pointing out briefly how this law, which corresponded to the one he had developed in his previous paper, embraced his and others' findings on the conductibility of different wires, Ohm devoted the rest of the paper to developing the implications of the second, electroscopic law and to comparing these implications with previously known facts. In this work he showed that his formula successfully explained those experiments which measured the electroscopic force at different points (especially the poles) of open and closed, and grounded and ungrounded, circuits. Here again the explanatory power of his law was impressive.

The fully developed presentation of his theory of electricity appeared in Ohm's great work, *Die galvanische Kette, mathematisch bearbeitet* (Berlin, 1827). Hoping to make the book more accessible to the mathematically unsophisticated, he devoted the first third of it to an introduction in which he attempted an essentially geometric presentation of his theory. The introduction, which contained a discussion of the theory's success in explaining the property of conductibility, the phenomena of the pile, and the behavior of the electromagnetic multiplier, was virtually the only part of the book in which he referred explicitly to the theory's very close connections with experiment. But in neither the introduction nor in the body of the work, which contained the more rigorous development of the theory, did Ohm bring decisively home either the underlying unity of the whole or the connections between fundamental assumptions and major deductions. For example, although his theory was conceived as a strict deductive system based on three fundamental laws (*Grundgesetze*), he nowhere indicated precisely which of their several mathematical and verbal expressions he wished to be taken as the canonical form. The following exposition, although simplified by the omission of steps in the derivation and of the theory's more specialized developments, follows the letter of Ohm's work as it attempts to provide a clearer synopsis than is sometimes afforded by the book.

As a preliminary to the formulation of his fundamental laws, Ohm defined the electroscopic force operationally as that force the presence of which was detected by means of an electroscope, and the quantity of electricity of a body as the product of the magnitude of its electroscopic force times its volume. These definitions, in the context of the larger theory, gave the previously vague but universally used notions of intensity and quantity of electricity a precise interpretation.

Ohm's first *Grundgesetz* pertained to the communication of electricity from one body to another, and it involved the explicit assumption that the quantity of electricity communicated was proportional to the difference in the bodies' electroscopic force, an assumption the validity of which would be proved by the subsequent correspondence between theory and experiment. This hypothesis, coupled with the definition of conductibility as the quantity of electricity

transferred per unit time across a unit distance, led directly to the expression

$$(1) \qquad \frac{\kappa(u' - u)\, dt}{s}$$

for the quantity of electricity communicated in time dt between two bodies of electroscopic force u' and u, separated by a distance s, where κ is the conductibility relative to these bodies. This may be taken as the mathematical expression of his first fundamental law.

Ohm's second *Grundgesetz*—which he based on the results of experiments Coulomb had done on the loss into the surrounding air of the electricity of a charged body—declared that, for an infinitesimal slice of thickness dx of a current-carrying conductor of circumference c, this loss across the surface in the time interval dt was proportional to that time, to the electroscopic force of the slice, and to its surface area, or to

$$(2) \qquad bcu\,dx\,dt,$$

where b is a constant dependent only on the condition of the air. As Ohm himself observed, this law has little or no applicability to galvanic phenomena; it was included for the sake of completeness and to maintain the desired parallelism between the fundamental equations of electricity and heat.

Ohm's third *Grundgesetz* embodied the fundamental tenet of the contact theory of electricity by asserting that heterogeneous bodies in contact maintain a constant difference in electroscopic force (tension) across their common surface. Mathematically,

$$(3) \qquad (u) - (u') = a,$$

where the parentheses simply indicate that the quantities they enclose are to be evaluated at the common surface between the two conductors, and where a is the magnitude of the constant difference. This fact he considered to be the basis (*Grundlage*) of all galvanic phenomena.

Ohm derived several important results directly from the first fundamental law. Applying it to three infinitesimal slices M', M, and $M_{,}$ of a homogeneous prismatic current-carrying conductor, the quantities of electricity transferred from M' to M, and from $M_{,}$ to M, are

$$(4) \qquad \frac{\kappa(u' - u)\, dt}{dx} \qquad \text{and} \qquad \frac{\kappa(u_{,} - u)\, dt}{dx},$$

respectively, where u', u, and $u_{,}$ are the electroscopic force and $x + dx$, x, and $x - dx$ are the abscissas of M', M, and $M_{,}$. Hence the total increase in the quantity of electricity of slice M is $[\kappa(u' + u_{,} - 2u)dt]/dx$, which, by means of the Taylor series expansions for u' and $u,$, can be written as

$$(5) \qquad \kappa\omega \frac{d^2u}{dx^2}\, dxdt,$$

where the conductibility κ has now been referred to unit cross section, ω being the cross section of the conductor. Furthermore, observing that each of the expressions in (4) is individually equal to $\kappa\omega(du/dx)dt$, Ohm defined the electric current S as the quantity of electricity passing through a given cross section of the conductor in unit time, and wrote

$$(6) \qquad S = \kappa\omega \frac{du}{dx},$$

which related the current directly to the (change in) electroscopic force. He then used this equation as the basis of the important condition for the continuity of current between two conductors,

$$(7) \qquad \kappa\omega \left(\frac{du}{dx}\right) = \kappa'\omega' \left(\frac{du'}{dx}\right),$$

where the parentheses have the same meaning as in (3).

The total change in the quantity of electricity of an infinitesimal slice of conductor is found by adding expressions (2) and (5). But, from the definition of quantity of electricity, this change is just equal to $\omega(du/dt)dxdt$—which quantity must, however, be multiplied by a factor γ, analogous to the coefficient for heat capacity, if equal changes in electroscopic force are not always accompanied by equal changes in the quantity of electricity. From these considerations Ohm derived the important general equation

$$(8) \qquad \gamma\frac{du}{dt} = \kappa\frac{d^2u}{dx^2} - \frac{bc}{\omega}u.$$

Although Ohm solved this equation in its full generality, as well as for the steady-state case when $b \neq 0$ (that is, when the influence of the air may not be ignored), the only really useful solution was for the steady-state case when $b = 0$. Under these conditions the equation reduces to $0 = d^2u/dx^2$, the general solution of which is

$$(9) \qquad u = fx + c.$$

For the idealized case of a simple circuit composed of a conductor of length l, bent back upon itself so that the cross sections at $x = 0$ and $x = l$ are in contact, and of a single source of tension (*Erregungsstelle*) located at this common point, equation (3), taken in conjunction with (9), implies that

$$(u)_{x=l} - (u)_{x=0} = f \cdot l - f \cdot 0 = a.$$

Hence $f = a/l$; and for this simple circuit

$$(10) \qquad u = (a/l)x + c,$$

where the constant c is determined whenever the electroscopic force at any one point is known—as, for example, by the circuit's being grounded.

In a derivation too lengthy to recapitulate here, Ohm showed that equation (10) can be generalized to circuits composed of any number of different conductors and sources of electromotive force, for which

$$(11) \qquad u = (A/L)y - O + c,$$

where A is the sum of the tensions of all sources of electromotive force; L is the total reduced length of the entire circuit; y is the so-called reduced abscissa, equal to the reduced length of that portion of the circuit between the origin and the point in question; and O is the sum of the tensions of all sources lying between the origin and that point.

Now from equations (6) and (11) one has

$$S = \kappa\omega \frac{du}{dy} \cdot \frac{dy}{dx} = \kappa\omega \frac{A}{L} \cdot \frac{dy}{dx}.$$

As Ohm showed from the (here omitted) derivation of equation (11), dy/dx, which simply relates the change in reduced length to the change in real length of the conductor, is just equal to $1/\kappa\omega$. Hence

$$(12) \qquad S = A/L.$$

This equation—which is, again, Ohm's law as we know it—states that the current in a galvanic circuit is constant across all cross sections and is equal to the sum of all the tensions divided by the total reduced length of the circuit.

Equations (11) and (12) epitomize the theory as it pertains to the electroscopic and current manifestations of the galvanic circuit, respectively. Ohm's major conceptual originality lay in explicating the intrinsic relationship between tension and current, and in associating a varying electric tension, or electroscopic force, with each point of a current-carrying wire. The relationship between these two classes of phenomena had at best been obscure when, as was often the case, they were not regarded as mutually exclusive. This belief was, however, not without foundation, since in general one had been able to measure the electric tension of a pile only when no current flowed. Earlier experiments of Erman, Ritter, and C. C. F. Jäger, to which Ohm referred, had demonstrated not only the presence of an electroscopic force at the poles of a pile closed by means of a poor conductor (such as water) but also the progressive decrease in this force from the poles toward the center of the connecting conductor.[7] To the extent to which these experiments had not simply been forgotten, however, they were thought inapplicable to the case of metallic conduction because of the traditional classification of substances into perfect, imperfect, and nonconductors, each with its own peculiar characteristics. To Ohm, who had the mathematical physicist's tendency to regard properties less as an "either-or" of some quality than as a "more-or-less" of some quantity, such distinctions could have no intrinsic validity; and he did not hesitate to apply to metals findings originally restricted to imperfect conductors.

It was not a matter of casual importance that Ohm regarded the force arising at the contact surface of heterogeneous substances as the cardinal fact and starting point of his theory, for his acceptance of the contact theory of electricity was probably crucial to the genesis of his own theory. It was the contact theory that asserted the existence of an impulsive electromotive force, and it was this electromotive force (of the closed pile) which Ohm identified conceptually with the electroscopic force (of the open pile). Measurement of the electric tension of the open pile (while no current flowed and no chemical activity took place) by means of an electroscope was one of the foundation stones of the contact theory, as was the fact that this tension increased as the number of metallic couples was increased. Indeed, the very existence of such an additive electromotive force was an acute embarrassment to the defenders of the chemical theory of the pile, who consequently tended to play down the very phenomena from which Ohm borrowed one of his central concepts.

Ohm structured his theory in conscious imitation of Fourier's *Théorie analytique de la chaleur* (1822), a fact that may have induced him to deemphasize its experimental side in favor of an abstract deductive rigor, in striking contrast with the inductivist tone of his earliest papers. In particular his basic expressions for the conduction of electricity through a solid (1) and for the loss of electricity from the surface into the air (2), as well as his resulting general equation (8), are exactly analogous to Fourier's equations for the motion of heat. Although he did not spell out just how, Ohm wished the analogy between electricity and heat to be taken seriously, not as something merely coincidental but as revealing some underlying relationship. It is possible that Seebeck's thermoelectric pile had powerfully suggested the intimate relationship between the two phenomena that Ohm endeavored to exploit in his own theory.

Although Ohm's work was not immediately and universally appreciated even within Germany—largely because the majority of German physicists in 1827 represented a soon-to-be-superseded nonmathematical approach to physics—already by the early 1830's it was beginning to be used by all the younger physicists working in electricity: Gustav Theodor Fechner gave Ohm's theory a prominent place in his *Lehrbuch des Galvanismus und der Elektrochemie* (Leipzig, 1829) and subjected it to rigorous experimental testing (and confirmation) in his *Massbestimmungen über die galvanische Kette* (Leipzig, 1831); Heinrich Friedrich Emil Lenz used it in his first paper on electromagnetic induction, "Über die Gesetze nach welchen der Magnet auf eine Spirale einwirkt wenn er ihr plötzlich genähert oder von ihr entfernt wird und über die vortheilhafteste Construction der Spiralen zu magneto-electrischem Behufe," read on 7 November 1832;[8] Wilhelm Eduard Weber and Karl Friedrich Gauss used it from 1832–1833 in connection with their investigations on terrestrial magnetism and their construction of precision instruments; and Moritz Hermann Jacobi became familiar with it sometime after 1833 and used it in his first appreciable publication, *Mémoire sur l'application de l'Électro-Magnétisme au Mouvement des Machines* (Potsdam, 1835). On the other hand, the question of how fast Ohm's work became known and appreciated by the majority of scientists who were not particularly concerned with that branch of physics has still to be answered. One would like to know, for instance, how soon it entered the textbooks; suggesting its rather quick adoption was its inclusion in the *Supplementband* (Vienna, 1830–1831) to Andreas Baumgartner's *Naturlehre* (a popular text that went through eight editions between 1824 and 1845), although it remains to be seen whether this example was typical. English and French physicists seem not to have become aware of Ohm's work and its profound implications for electrical science until the late 1830's and early 1840's.[9]

It has been repeatedly asserted ever since the middle of the last century that Ohm's work had to await the recognition of foreign scientists around 1840 before it became well known in Germany. Insofar as his fame among the larger scientific and nonscientific community is concerned, there may be some truth to that assertion. However, by then his work had already been used by those working in electricity who should have appreciated it, at least among the scientists born after 1800. Nor does that traditional explanation gain plausibility from the observation that in the nineteenth century the notion had become a commonplace in Germany that Germans only esteemed what came from abroad, hence the uncritical commentator had a familiar and convenient dictum ready at hand to explain a complex situation.[10] The issue of the acceptance of Ohm's work by contemporary scientists has been further confounded with his lack of success in securing an academic appointment. In connection with the latter, to make matters worse, the fact that his chief adversaries in Berlin—Johannes Schulze, a powerful figure in the ministry of education, and Georg Friedrich Pohl, professor of physics at the Friedrich-Wilhelms-Gymnasium—were followers of Hegel and of *Naturphilosophie* has wrongly been taken as characteristic of the general situation in German physics. And even this confrontation was not simply a matter of ideologies: Martin Ohm, several years before, had incurred Schulze's dislike and had gained the reputation in Berlin of being a dangerous revolutionary because of his criticisms of the educational system; among his suggestions for reform had been the use of his brother's geometry text, which did not find favor in Berlin.

NOTES

1. In Schweigger's *Journal für Chemie und Physik*, **44** (1825), 110–118. Also in Poggendorff's *Annalen der Physik und Chemie*, **4** (1825), 79–88.
2. J. C. Poggendorff, "Physisch-chemische Untersuchungen zur nähern Kenntniss des Magnetismus der voltaischen Säule," in *Isis von Oken* (1821), **2** (9 in the series), no. 8, cols. 687–710.
3. A.-C. Becquerel, "Du pouvoir conducteur de l'électricité dans les métaux, et de l'intensité de la force électro-dynamique en un point quelconque d'un fil métallique qui joint les deux extrémités d'une pile lu à l'Académie royale des sciences le 31 Janvier 1825," in *Annales de chimie et de physique*, **32** (Aug. 1826), 420–430; and Peter Barlow, "On the Laws of Electro-Magnetic Action, as Depending on the Length and Dimensions of the Conducting Wire, and on the Question, Whether Electrical Phenomena Are Due to the Transmission of a Single or of a Compound Fluid?" in *Edinburgh Philosophical Journal*, **12**, no. 23 (Jan. 1825), 105–114. Extracts of these, which Ohm saw, appeared in *Bulletin des sciences mathématiques, astronomiques, physiques et chimiques*, **3**, no. 5 (May 1825), 293–296 and 296–298, respectively.
4. Humphry Davy, "Farther Researches on the Magnetic Phaenomena Produced by Electricity; With Some New Experiments on the Properties of Electrified Bodies in Their Relations to Conducting Powers and Temperature," in *Philosophical Transactions of the Royal Society*, **111** (1821), 425–439. Ohm knew the German trans. in Gilbert's *Annalen der Physik*, **71** (1822), 241–261.
5. In Schweigger's *Journal für Chemie und Physik*, **46** (1826), 137–166.
6. In Poggendorff's *Annalen der Physik und Chemie*, **6** (1826), 459–469; *ibid.*, **7** (1826), 45–54, 117–118.
7. Paul Erman, "Ueber die electroskopischen Phänomene der Voltaischen Säule," in Gilbert's *Annalen der Physik*, **8** (1801), 197–209; and "Ueber die electroskopischen Phänomene des Gasapparats an der Voltaischen Säule," *ibid.*, **10** (1802), 1–23; J. W. Ritter, "Versuche und Bemerkungen über den Galvanismus der Voltaischen Batterie. . . . Dritter Brief," *ibid.*, **8** (1801), 385–473; C. C. F. Jäger, "Ueber die electroskopischen Aeusserungen der Voltaischen Ketten und Säulen," *ibid.*, **13** (1803), 399–433. Even the

recent experiment of Ampère and Becquerel had left open the question of whether tension was associated with complete conduction by metals, since they too detected a tension only at the poles of a pile closed by means of a so-called incomplete conductor; see "Note sur une Expérience relative à la nature du courant électrique, faite par MM. Ampère et Becquerel," in *Annales de chimie et de physique*, **27** (Sept. 1824), 29–31.

8. *Mémoires de l'Académie impériale des sciences de St.-Pétersbourg*, 6th ser. Sciences mathématiques, physiques et naturelles, **2** (1833), 427–457; repr. in Poggendorff's *Annalen der Physik und Chemie*, **34** (1835), 385–418; and trans. in Taylor's *Scientific Memoirs*, **1** (1837), 608–630.
9. The first exposition of Ohm's work in French that I know of was Élie Wartmann, "Des travaux et des opinions des Allemands sur la pile voltaïque," in *Archives de l'électricité*, **1** (1841), 31–66, followed by Auguste de la Rive, "Observations sur l'article de M. Wartmann . . .," *ibid.*, 67–73.
10. See, for example, Schweigger's *Journal für Chemie und Physik*, **10** (1814), 355; **23** (1818), 372; **33** (1821), 20; and Poggendorff's *Annalen der Physik und Chemie*, **3** (1825), 191. Leibniz' comment on his countrymen, "nil nisi aliena mirantur," was often cited to support the generality of this supposed nationality trait.

BIBLIOGRAPHY

I. ORIGINAL WORKS. A nearly complete list of Ohm's scientific papers is found in the Royal Society *Catalogue of Scientific Papers*, IV, 665–666. Also useful is Poggendorff, II, cols. 316–318, which lists books as well as papers. All but two of Ohm's papers, plus the book *Die galvanische Kette*, are collected in *Gesammelte Abhandlungen von G. S. Ohm*, edited with an intro. by E. Lommel (Leipzig, 1892). Ohm also wrote a textbook, *Grundzüge der Physik als Compendium zu seinen Vorlesungen*, 2 vols. (Nuremberg, 1853–1854). Two of his earlier papers—"Vorläufige Anzeige . . ." and "Bestimmung des Gesetzes . . ."—are reprinted in *Das Grundgesetz des elektrischen Stromes. Drei Abhandlungen von Georg Simon Ohm (1825 und 1826) und Gustav Theodor Fechner (1829)*, C. Piel, ed. (Leipzig, 1938), which is Ostwald's Klassiker der exakten Wissenschaften, no. 244. An English trans. of the second of these papers has been published by Niels H. de Vaudrey Heathcote as "A Translation of the Paper in Which Ohm First Announced His Law of the Galvanic Circuit, Prefaced by Some Account of the Work of His Predecessors," in *Science Progress*, **26**, no. 101 (July 1931), 51–75.

The 1st ed. of *Die galvanische Kette* has been reprinted in facs. (Brussels, 1969). It was translated into English by William Francis as "The Galvanic Circuit Investigated Mathematically," in R. Taylor, J. Tyndall, and W. Francis, eds., *Scientific Memoirs*, *Selected From the Transactions of Foreign Academies and Learned Societies and From Foreign Journals*, II (London, 1841), 401–506, and later reprinted (New York, 1891), no. 102 in the Van Nostrand Science Series. There is a French ed., *Théorie mathématique des courants électriques*, translated with preface and notes by Jean-Mothée Gaugain (Paris, 1860); and an Italian one (not seen), "Teoria matematica del circuito galvanico," in *Cimento* (Pisa), **3** (1845), 311–348; **4** (1846), 85–96, 169–183, 246–266. A very useful and informative source is *Aus Georg Simon Ohms handschrift-lichem Nachlass. Briefe, Urkunden und Dokumente*, Ludwig Hartmann, ed. (Munich, 1927), which contains much of the MS material on Ohm in the Deutsches Museum in Munich.

II. SECONDARY LITERATURE. The fullest biography is Heinrich von Füchtbauer, *Georg Simon Ohm. Ein Forscher wächst aus seiner Väter Art* (Berlin, 1939), which contains extracts of letters not available elsewhere. Also very informative is the article by Carl Maximilian von Bauernfeind in *Allgemeine deutsche Biographie*, XXIV (Leipzig, 1887), 187–203. Useful for some aspects of his background and life is Ernst G. Deuerlein, *Georg Simon Ohm 1789–1854. Leben und Wirken des grossen Physikers* (Erlangen, 1939; 2nd ed., enl., 1954). Two contemporary eulogies are valuable: Friedrich von Thiersch, "Rede zur Feier des hohen Geburtsfestes Sr. Majestät des Königs Maximilian II. von Bayern," in *Gelehrte Anzeigen der k. bayerischen Akademie der Wissenschaften*, **40** (Jan.–June 1855), Bulletins der drei Classen, nos. 3–4 (Jan. 5–8), cols. 26–32, 33–35 (indicated here are only those portions of the speech dealing with Ohm; the bulk of the published article is a long footnote on Ohm by Philipp Ludwig Seidel, cols. 29–35); and Johann von Lamont, *Denkrede auf die Akademiker Dr. Thaddäus Siber und Dr. Georg Simon Ohm . . .* (Munich, 1855).

The best account of Ohm's electrical work is Morton L. Schagrin, "Resistance to Ohm's Law," in *American Journal of Physics*, **31**, no. 7 (July 1963), 536–547. Not to be trusted, especially in its translations, is Henry James Jacques Winter, "The Reception of Ohm's Electrical Researches by His Contemporaries," in *London, Edinburgh and Dublin Philosophical Magazine and Journal of Science*, 7th ser., **35**, no. 245 (June 1944), 371–386. Worth consulting are two articles by John L. McKnight: "The Intellectual Development of Georg Simon Ohm," in *Actes du XIᵉ Congrès international d'histoire des sciences, Varsovie-Toruń-Kielce-Cracovie, 24–31 août 1965*, III (Wrocław-Warsaw–Cracow, 1968), 318–322; and "Laboratory Note-books of G. S. Ohm: A Case Study in Experimental Method," in *American Journal of Physics*, **35**, no. 2 (Feb. 1967), 110–114, although his account is rather too Baconian. See also Eugen Lommel, *Georg Simon Ohm's wissenschaftliche Leistungen. . . .* (Munich, 1889), English trans. by William Hallock, "The Scientific Work of George Simon Ohm," in *Annual Report of the Board of Regents of the Smithsonian Institution, . . . 1891* (Washington, 1893), 247–256.

There were several contemporary reviews of *Die galvanische Kette*: Georg Friedrich Pohl, in *Jahrbücher für wissenschaftliche Kritik* (Berlin) (1828), **1**, nos. 11/12–13/14, Jan., cols. 85–96, 97–103; Ludwig Friedrich Kämtz, in *Allgemeine Literatur-Zeitung* (Halle–Leipzig) (1828), **1**, nos. 13–14, Jan., cols. 97–104, 105–109; and *Leipziger Literatur-Zeitung* (18 Dec. 1828), cols. 2562–2565, anonymous, although possibly written by Heinrich Wilhelm Brandes, professor of physics at Leipzig and an editor of the journal. Problematical is the review that appeared anonymously in the obscure journal edited by K. W. G.

Kastner, *Proteus. Zeitschrift für Geschichte der gesammten Naturlehre*, **1**, no. 2 (1828), 349–377. Ohm referred to it as if it had been written by Johann Wilhelm Andreas Pfaff, but Füchtbauer says Ohm himself was really the author, as evidenced by a letter from Martin Ohm to his brother; in fact it seems as if Kastner, Pfaff, and Ohm all had a hand in it. It is less a review than a complete recapitulation and reformulation of the full mathematical theory, an undertaking which probably only Ohm would have ventured. As such it should perhaps be numbered among Ohm's works.

KENNETH L. CANEVA

OKEN (or **Okenfuss**), **LORENZ** (*b.* Bohlsbach bei Offenburg, Baden, Germany, 1 August 1779; *d.* Zurich, Switzerland, 11 August 1851), *natural science, philosophy, scientific congresses.*

The son of poor farmers in the Black Forest, Oken studied at the universities of Freiburg, Würzburg, and Göttingen. In 1803, at the age of twenty-four, he published a system of *Naturphilosophie*, thereby marking his adherence to the school of thought founded by Schelling a few years earlier. Throughout his life he remained faithful to this way of thinking, which he outlined in 1805 in a small book of methodological importance, *Die Zeugung*. Oken was a prolific writer whose works record his growing erudition and developing conceptions about nature. After graduating from the University of Freiburg in 1804, he held various teaching posts at Göttingen, Jena, Munich, and Erlangen. The frequent changes in his place of employment were occasioned by the boldness of the ideas he taught; the violence of the scientific polemics in which he engaged; and his political activities in revolutionary youth movements, which the German principalities severely repressed. Finally, in 1832 he secured a post at the recently founded University of Zurich, where he was a respected teacher until his death in 1851.

Oken took an active interest in all branches of natural history and of human knowledge in general, including optics, mineralogy, and even military science. His contributions to anatomy deal with the osteology of the skull and the vertebrae, the organogenesis of the intestinal tract and the umbilical cord, and, more generally, with the subject of comparative anatomy. Oken's importance lies far more in the formulation of a number of fundamental concepts, which constitute the guiding threads of his many publications. A good example of his treatment of one of the major themes of his corpus is offered by *Die Zeugung*, in which he discusses the elementary units of living organisms, "the infusoria." In this work Oken contended that all flesh can be broken down into infusoria and that all higher animals consist of constituent animalcules. "For this reason," he wrote, "we shall call them primal animals (*Urthiere*)." From the semantic point of view, this word is crucial; it was long used to designate the protozoans, and the prefix *Ur-* is one of the key elements of *Naturphilosophie* and of Romantic thought in general.

According to Oken, these primal animals constitute the original material not only of the animals as we know them but also of the plants; they may thus be called the primal material of all organized beings. The primal animals are subordinated to a higher organism in which they facilitate a unique common function, or in which they carry out this function by realizing their own potentialities. When the entities are combined they form another entity, the organism, which is a fusion of primal beings, each element having lost its individuality in favor of a higher unity.

In his treatise on the philosophy of nature Oken postulated the existence of a primal slime. It results from a combination of various processes that—when they reach equilibrium—must produce a sphere; for the organism is the image of the planet and therefore possesses an analogous spherical form. This primal plasm supposedly formed along the boundary of the seas and the earth. Oken held that a primal mucous follicle emerged from this plasm or infusorian, and that the genesis of the organism is merely the accumulation of an infinite number of mucous particles. According to Oken, organisms are not preformed; no organism is created that is larger than an infusorial particle; no organism is created or has ever been created that is not microscopic. Everything that is larger has not been created but has developed. Man was not created; he developed. These aphoristic pronouncements were repeatedly reprinted in the re-editions of the book until 1843, that is, until five years after the appearance of Schwann's work on the cell theory. These formulations of Oken's prefigure some of the fundamental concepts of nineteenth-century natural science.

In the preceding paragraphs we have summarized one aspect of Oken's thought; his own prose has become virtually impenetrable to the modern reader unfamiliar with the enthusiastic outpourings of Romantic philosophy. Throughout his scientific career Oken devoted his greatest efforts to fostering the study of natural science, a subject then at the height of its development. In communicating his enthusiasm for it, he was, of course, also attempting to promote his own views. He was one of the first to stress the pedagogical value of natural history at all levels of instruction, and he wrote many books for both students and adults.

Sometimes these were modest works, but often they were major treatises in several volumes. Further, Oken founded his own journal, *Isis oder enzyklopädische Zeitung von Oken*, which for three decades (1817–1847) published popular scientific articles of a very high caliber. Oken himself wrote the majority of the articles; and in them he set forth his basic views, particularly the theory that the skull is composed of several vertebrae. In claiming priority for this theory he became involved in a long and bitter polemic with Goethe, a complicated affair that has been the subject of many historical studies. Several times Oken discussed the traditional explanations of the origin of the first man. Oken often gave free vent to his anger regarding the contemporary political situation and thus ran afoul of the official censors. By the variety of its contents, *Isis* offers a remarkable picture of the development of the field of natural history in the first half of the nineteenth century.

Oken made a lasting contribution to science through his role in the creation of scientific congresses organized outside the framework of the universities. Accordingly, at the Congrès Scientifique de France, held at Strasbourg in 1842, Oken, despite his absence, was acclaimed the father of scientific meetings. He was the founder of the Gesellschaft Deutscher Naturforscher und Aerzte, which first met at Leipzig in 1822, and the 107th meeting of which was held in Munich in October 1972. The proceedings of this organization constitute a precious record of the fruitful union of biology and medicine in the first half of the nineteenth century. After a very agitated university and scientific career, Oken found a peaceful life and a definite appointment at the University of Zurich, and as the rector of this newly created university he had to receive the young Georg Büchner, who now figures prominently in the history of European thought by virtue of the recent vogue for his literary works. By profession Büchner was a naturalist who had received his doctorate at Strasbourg under Georges Louis Duvernoy and was appointed to the University of Zurich after giving an inaugural lecture that recently has been republished. Unfortunately, Büchner died before he was able to take up his post.

Contemporary judgments of Oken's work and personality varied considerably, but there was general agreement on the importance of his contributions to comparative anatomy, which were well known even outside the German-speaking countries. One of his shorter books was published in French in 1821, when Oken was already known among scientists in Paris. For example, Cuvier's lecture notes contain analyses of Oken's writings. In 1830 Oken's name was mentioned again during the famous controversy at the

Académie des Sciences, in which Goethe played an important, although indirect role.

Oken has never been completely forgotten, but during his lifetime sharply differing assessments were made of his role. Claude Bernard, in his *Introduction à l'étude de la médecine expérimentale*, mentioned Oken along with Goethe, Carus, Geoffroy Saint-Hilaire, and Darwin. On the hundredth anniversary of his birth (1879) he was the subject of an article in *Die Gartenlaube*, one of the most widely read popular German newspapers. A. Ecker (1880) wrote a fervent biography of Oken, which was translated into English. Then, with the rise of experimental natural science— the founders of which were hostile to *Naturphilosophie* —Oken's reputation was temporarily eclipsed. Interest in him revived around 1930 when historians of science began to study the Romantic period more closely. Indeed, their opinions of Oken tend to reflect their overall assessment of Romantic biology and its repercussions in modern biology.

Oken has also been exploited for ideological purposes. In 1939 J. Schuster interpreted certain passages in Oken's writings as favorable to German nationalism. The philosopher Ernst Bloch has treated Oken from the opposite point of view in his treatise on the problem of materialism.

The centennial of Oken's death was commemorated by a colloquium held in 1951 in his native region, at Freiburg im Breisgau. The few quotations given above show that despite his obscurity and combativeness, Oken remains a subject of considerable interest for the historian of modern biology.

BIBLIOGRAPHY

I. ORIGINAL WORKS. A complete list of Oken's publications can be found in the works of Ecker (1880) and Pfannenstihl (1953), both of which are cited below. The following works are referred to in the text: *Die Zeugung* (Bamberg, 1805); *Beiträge zur vergleichenden Zoologie, Anatomie und Physiologie*, 2 pts. (Bamberg–Würzburg, 1806–1807), written with D. G. Kieser; *Über Bedeutung der Schädelknochen* (Bamberg, 1807); *Erste Ideen zur Theorie des Lichts, der Finsternis, der Farben und der Wärme* (Jena, 1808); *Grundzeichnung des natürlischen Systems der Erze* (Jena, 1809); *Über den Wert der Naturgeschichte besonders für die Bildung der Deutschen* (Jena, 1809); *Lehrbuch der Naturphilosophie* (Jena, 1809, 1831; 3rd ed., Zurich, 1843); "Über die Bedeutung der Schädelknochen . . .," in *Isis*, **1** (1817), 1204–1208; and "Oken, wie er zur Bedeutung der Schädelknochen gekommen," in *Isis*, **2** (1818), 511–512.

See also "Entstehung des ersten Menschen," in *Isis*, **5** (1819), 1117–1123; *Esquisse du système d'anatomie, de physiologie et d'histoire naturelle* (Paris, 1821), *Natur-*

geschichte für Schüler (Bamberg, 1821); "Vergleichung alter Sagen und Überlieferungen mit Okens Ansicht der Entstehung des Menschen aus dem Meere," in *Isis*, **9** (1821), 1113–1115; *Allgemeine Naturgeschichte für alle Stände*, 13 vols. (Stuttgart, 1839–1842); *Elements of Physiophilosophy*, trans. from the German by A. Tulk (London, 1847); and "Über die Schädelwirbel gegen Hegel und Göthe," in *Isis* (1847), 557–560.

II. SECONDARY LITERATURE. See E. Bloch, *Das Materialismusproblem. Seine Geschichte und Substanz* (Frankfurt am Main, 1972), esp. 258–260; H. Bräuning-Oktavio, *Oken und Goethe im Lichte neuer Quellen. Beiträge zur deutschen Klassik* (Weimar, 1959); G. Büchner, "Mémoire sur le système nerveux du barbeau," in *Mémoires de la Société du Muséum d'histoire naturelle de Strasbourg*, **2** (1835), 1–57; *Über Schädelnerven. Probevorlesung* (Zurich, 1836), in Büchner, *Sämmtliche Werke und Briefe*, W. R. Lehmann, ed. (Hamburg, 1971); *Congrès scientifique de France*, I (1843), esp. 87, 581; A. Ecker, *Lorenz Oken* (Stuttgart, 1880), trans. into English by A. Tulk (London, 1883); E. Gagliardi, H. Nabholz, J. Strohl, *Die Universität Zürich 1833–1933 und ihre Vorläufer* (Zurich, 1938), esp. 262–276; M. Klein, *Histoire des origines de la théorie cellulaire* (Paris, 1936), esp. 18–22; "Sur les résonances de la philosophie de la nature en biologie moderne et contemporaine," in *Revue philosophique*, **144** (1954), 514–543; and "Goethe et les naturalistes français," in *Goethe et l'esprit français* (Paris, 1958), 169–191, esp. 177; D. Kuhn, *Empirische und ideelle Wirklichkeit. Studien über Goethes Kritik des französischen Akademiestreites* (Graz, 1967); A. Lang, "Oken, Lorenz (eigentlich Okenfuss)," in *Allgemeine deutsche Biographie*, XXIV (Leipzig, 1881), 216–226; E. T. Nauk, "Lorenz Oken und die medizinische Fakultät Freiburg im Breisgau," in *Oken Heft* (1951), 21–74; E. Nordenskiöld, *Die Geschichte der Biologie* (Jena, 1926), esp. 290–294; and "Oken-Heft," in *Berichte der Naturforschenden Gesellschaft zu Freiburg im Breisgau*, **41**, no. 1 (1951).

See also J. L. Pagel, "Oken," in *Biographisches Lexikon der hervorragenden Aerzte aller Zeiten und Völker*, **4** (Vienna–Leipzig, 1886), 416; M. Pfannenstiehl, "Lorenz Oken," in *Oken-Heft* (1951), 7–20; "Schriften und Varia über Lorenz Oken von 1806 bis 1951," *ibid.*, 101–118; and "Lorenz Oken. Sein Leben und Werken," in *Freiburger Universitätsreden*, n.s. **14** (1953); J. Schuster, "Oken, Welt und Wesen, Werk und Wirkung," in *Archiv für Geschichte der Mathematik, der Naturwissenschaften und der Technik*, n.s. **3** (1929), 54–70; J. Schuster, ed., *Laurentius Oken gesammelte Schriften, Programme zur Naturphilosophie* (Berlin, 1939), esp. 320–328, Oken Geistesgeschichtliche Stellung; C. Sterne [Ernst Krause], "Ludwig Lorenz Oken. Zum hundertjährigen Geburtstag eines Vielgeschmähten," in *Gartenlaube* (1879), 518–520; J. Strohl, *Oken und Büchner. Zwei Gestalten aus der Uebergangszeit von Naturphilosophie zu Naturwissenschaft* (Zurich, 1936); and G. von Wyss, *Die Hochschule Zürich in den Jahren 1833–1883* (Zurich, 1883).

MARC KLEIN

OLAUS MAGNUS (*b*. Linköping, Sweden, October 1490; *d*. Rome, Italy, 1557), *geography*, *ethnology*.

Olaus Magnus was born to a middle-class family. He attended school in Linköping and in 1510 traveled abroad to prepare himself for a career in the Swedish church. With the support of a canonry he studied for almost seven years on the Continent, among other places at the University of Rostock, where, probably in 1513, he received his baccalaureate. Upon his return to Sweden, Olaus became in 1518 a deputy to Arcimboldi, the papal seller of indulgences; and in that capacity he traversed the wilderness of Norrland and the high mountains of Norway. He may have reached Lofoten and southern Finnmark before returning to Sweden and proceeding south via Torneå (Tornio, Finland). Later he was a vicar in Stockholm and cathedral dean in Strängnäs. In 1523 the Church ordered him to Rome and he never returned to Sweden. The Lutheran Reformation erupted in Sweden, but Olaus, together with his brother, Archbishop Johannes Magnus, remained loyal to the Catholic faith. Both brothers spent several years as refugees in Danzig, but in 1537 they traveled to Italy, where with gusto they took part in the game of church politics. In 1544, after his brother's death, Olaus was appointed archbishop of Sweden and in that capacity attended some of the meetings of the Council of Trent. He continued to live in Rome for the rest of his life.

During his long exile Olaus Magnus published two scientific works which give him a pioneering position in the geographic research of Scandinavia. The first was the monumental map of the Scandinavian countries, *Carta marina* (Venice, 1539), of which only two copies are extant. It is executed in woodcut and also shows the Atlantic Ocean with its islands from Scotland to Iceland and Greenland. It was the first fairly reliable map of northern Europe and was based on older maps (Claudius Clavus, Ziegler) and Olaus' own notes—and perhaps also on some no longer extant nautical charts. Olaus used a few astronomical latitude determinations. His vivid illustrations of wild animals, skiing Lapps, and tumbling sea monsters gave the *Carta marina* life and movement.

In 1555, at Rome, Olaus published his great description of the Scandinavian peoples, *Historia de gentibus septentrionalibus*. Originally this work was planned as a detailed description of the more noteworthy features of the map. Olaus dealt with nature and the life of the people in Scandinavia—especially Sweden—the Lapps and Finns, the climate and physical geography, agriculture and mining, the wild animals, and the Swedish people in their daily occupations. The work has to be used with care, since large parts were simply copied from older European literature. But he also builds upon his own memories and experiences in this description of an entire country at the beginning of a new period. The basic thread is primitivistic, and Olaus Magnus, a warm patriot, praises the freezing winter cold and the harsh Scandinavian virtues.

Both of Olaus' works were of great influence. The *Carta marina* was indispensable for later cartographers; and the historical work, which was published in many editions, for generations informed the educated European about Scandinavia.

BIBLIOGRAPHY

I. ORIGINAL WORKS. The *Carta marina* has been published in many facs. eds., including Lychnosbibliotek, XI, 1 (Malmö, 1949). A copperplate engraving on a reduced scale was produced by Antonio Lafreri (Rome, 1572). The *Historia* is available in Latin, French, Italian, Dutch, and German; facs. ed. (Copenhagen, 1972). A modern Swedish trans., *Historia om de nordiska folken*, 4 vols. (Uppsala, 1909–1925), has a vol. of commentary by John Granlund (Uppsala, 1951).

II. SECONDARY LITERATURE. The most recent biography is Hjalmar Grape, *Olaus Magnus* (Stockholm, 1970), in Swedish. A basic work is Herman Richter, *Olaus Magnus Carta marina 1539*, Lychnosbibliotek, XI, 2 (Lund, 1967). See also Karl Ahlenius, *Olaus Magnus och hans framställning af Nordens geografi* (Uppsala, 1895).

STEN LINDROTH

OLBERS, HEINRICH WILHELM MATTHIAS (*b*. Arbergen, near Bremen, Germany, 11 October 1758; *d*. Bremen, 2 March 1840), *medicine*, *astronomy*.

Olbers was the eighth of the sixteen children of Johann Jürgen Olbers, a Protestant minister. He became interested in astronomy when he was about fourteen, but the Gymnasium in Bremen which he attended was a typical humanistic institution of that time where almost no mathematics or science was taught. In order to understand astronomy Olbers taught himself mathematics and tried to compute the solar eclipse of 1774. In 1777 he began the study of medicine in Göttingen under Blumenbach and Ernst Baldinger, and also attended lectures in physics and mathematics by G. C. Lichtenberg and, especially, A. G. Kästner, who was in charge of the small observatory at Göttingen. But mainly he studied astronomy on his own. His lifelong concern with comets dates from January 1779, when he used his observations of Bode's comet to calculate its orbit according to Euclid's method. In 1780 he independently discovered a comet that was simultaneously observed by Montaigne. Meanwhile, Olbers continued his medical studies, concentrating on a problem that involved the application of mathematics to physiology. His dissertation, *De oculi mutationibus* (Göttingen, 1780), explains how the eye adapts to a change in focus by changing the shape of the eyeball; only much later was it discovered that only the lens changes shape. Later, as a practicing physician he specialized in ophthalmology, a field hardly recognized at that time.

In 1781, after receiving his medical degree at Göttingen, Olbers went on a study trip to Vienna, where he visited hospitals during the day, enjoyed the aristocratic social life of the city in the evenings and spent the nights at the Vienna observatory. Throughout his life he profited from needing only four hours of sleep, so that after a long and busy day of practicing medicine he could "relax" by observing the sky. In Vienna he was thus able to follow the course of the recently discovered planet Uranus.

At the end of 1781 Olbers settled in Bremen and soon acquired an extensive medical practice. It was mainly through his efforts that inoculation was introduced in the city, and he was highly praised for his work during several cholera epidemics. When the "magnetic cures" of Mesmer started a great controversy, Olbers published an article admitting the reality of some of them but also expressed the opinion that future understanding of physiology would explain them without the assumption of a special power.

In 1785 Olbers married Dorothea Köhne, who died a year later at the birth of their daughter. In 1789 he married Anna Adelheid Lurssen, by whom he had one son. After the death of his daughter in 1818 and of his second wife in 1820, he retired from active medical practice to devote the rest of his life to astronomy.

Olbers installed an observatory on the second floor of his house, using its two large bay windows for his telescopes. At various times he possessed two achromatic Dollond refractors, a Schröter reflector, a heliometer and refractor from Fraunhofer's workshop, and three comet seekers, made by Hofmann, Weickhardt, and Fraunhofer. He had no transit instrument or fixed instrument of any kind. His library became one of the best private astronomical collections in Europe. For over fifty years he carefully gathered astronomical literature and assembled a collection in the field of cometography that was practically complete. After Olbers' death, F. G. W. Struve bought this library for the new Pulkovo observatory, near St. Petersburg. Struve's new catalog of the collection listed 4,361 items, consisting of 39 sky charts, 1,607 monographs, and 2,715 articles.

Busy with his new medical practice when he first moved to Bremen, Olbers had less time for astronomy; but in 1786 he met J. H. Schröter, whose private observatory in nearby Lilienthal was one of the best-equipped on the Continent, and they worked closely together for many years. In 1796 Olbers discovered a comet and calculated its parabolic orbit with a new method, simpler than that used by Laplace. In a letter to F. X. von Zach, director of the newly founded observatory on the Seeberg, near Gotha, Olbers asked whether his treatise on this method should be printed, and if so, how this could best be done. After reading the treatise and using it with excellent results to compute the orbit of the comet of 1779, which had presented great difficulties to many astronomers, von Zach decided to see it through the press himself. It appeared at Weimar in 1797 under the title *Über die leichteste und bequemste Methode, die Bahn eines Kometen aus einigen Beobachtungen zu berechnen*. This work immediately established Olbers among the foremost astronomers of his time, and his method was used throughout the nineteenth century.

Despite the work of Newton and Lambert, the computation of cometary orbits had until then been a very laborious process. Laplace had given formulas for the computation of a parabola through successive approximations, but the procedure was cumbersome and unsatisfactory. It had been assumed that when three observations of a comet had been obtained within a short period of time, the radius vector of the middle observation would divide the chord of the orbit of the comet from the first to the last observation in relation to the traversed time. The finding that this assumption could be applied with equal advantage to the three positions of the earth in its orbit was Olbers' contribution. This basic idea led to a rapidly converging process of calculation, and Olbers worked out simple and easily calculated formulas.

The space between the planets Mars and Jupiter, shown mathematically by Bode's law, had long intrigued astronomers. The first asteroid was discovered by G. Piazzi at the Palermo observatory on 1 January 1801. He noticed a starlike object that moved during the succeeding days. He communicated this news to other astronomers; and although it was soon realized that this must be a new planet, named Ceres by Piazzi, it disappeared before more observations could be made. At that time it was still impossible to compute an orbit from such a small arc without assuming the eccentricity. Then the twenty-three-year-old Gauss was able to determine the orbit by a new method; and it was Olbers who, on 1 January 1802, found the new planet very near where Gauss had calculated it would be. This episode was the beginning of their lifelong friendship; and when Gauss visited Olbers in 1803, each had his portrait painted to give to the other. The two portraits now hang in the Göttingen observatory. While following Ceres, Olbers discovered a second asteroid, Pallas, on 28 March 1802; a third, Juno, was discovered by Harding at Lilienthal in 1804. The orbits of these small planets suggested to Olbers that they had a common point of origin and might have originated from one large planet. Accordingly, for years he searched the sky where the orbits of Ceres, Pallas, and Juno approached each other; the result was the discovery of Vesta on 29 March 1807.

The search for comets remained Olbers' main interest, and his industry was rewarded with the discovery of four. Of particular interest is the comet that he discovered on 6 March 1815, which has an orbit of seventy-two years, similar to Halley's. Olbers also calculated the orbits of eighteen other comets. Noticing that comets consist of a starlike nucleus and a parabolic cloud of matter, he supposed that this matter was expelled by the nucleus and repelled by the sun. In "Über die Durchsichtigkeit des Weltraums," published in 1823 in *Berliner astronomisches Jahrbuch für das Jahr 1826,* Olbers discussed the paradox that now bears his name: If we accept an infinite, uniform universe, the whole sky would be covered by stars shining as brightly as our sun. Olbers explained the paradox of the dark night sky by assuming that space is not absolutely transparent and that some interspace matter absorbs a very minute percentage of starlight. This effect is sufficient to dim the light of the stars, so that they are seen as points against the dark sky. The idea was not absolutely new; Halley had written about it and a young Swiss astronomer, Jean Philippe Loys de Chéseaux, had published an essay in 1744 using a very similar argument.

Olbers was also interested in the influence of the moon on weather, the origin of meteorite showers, and the history of astronomy. He was a member of Museum, the scientific society in Bremen, and through the years gave over eighty lectures there (of which only one was on a medical subject).

Although Olbers usually declined official posts, he felt it his duty to participate in the government during the time that Bremen was part of the French empire (1811–1813). This commitment forced him to spend time in Paris, where he met some of the French astronomers.

Olbers was held in great esteem by his contemporaries. He conducted an extensive correspondence with Gauss, Bessel, Encke, Schröter, and other astronomers. He also encouraged many young astronomers with good advice and made great efforts to obtain positions for them at various observatories. One of them, Friedrich Wilhelm Bessel, a twenty-year-old apprentice in a merchant's office, had approached Olbers in 1804 with his calculation of the orbit of Halley's comet. Olbers was so impressed with his work that, after suggesting some additions, he recommended it for publication and sought to obtain the directorship of the new observatory at Königsberg for Bessel.

A very modest man, Olbers later claimed that his greatest contribution to astronomy had been to lead Bessel to become a professional astronomer. Bessel's eulogy, written in 1845, ended: "He was to me the most noble friend. With wise and fatherly counsel he guided my youth; 171 letters which I possess from him are written proof of my right to extend my devotion beyond the limits of science."

BIBLIOGRAPHY

I. ORIGINAL WORKS. Olbers' article on Mesmer's cures is "Erklärung über die in Bremen durch den sogenannten Magnetismus vorgenommenen Kuren," in *Deutsches Museum* (Oct. 1787), 296–312. A complete listing of his almost 200 articles is in vol. I of C. Schilling, *Wilhelm Olbers, sein Leben und seine Werke,* 2 vols. in 3 pts. and supp. (Berlin, 1894–1909); this work also contains the complete correspondence with Gauss. Olbers' correspondence with Bessel was published by A. Erman, *Briefwechsel zwischen W. Olbers und F. W. Bessel,* 2 vols. (Leipzig, 1852). The Staatsbibliothek in Bremen has a collection of Olbers' papers.

II. SECONDARY LITERATURE. *Von Bremer Astronomen und Sternfreunden,* W. Stein, ed. (Bremen, 1958), contains six papers on various aspects of Olbers' career and a partial listing of his works. Bessel's obituary is in *Astronomische Nachrichten,* **22** (1845), cols. 265–270. Another, unsigned obituary is in *Proceedings of the Royal Society,* **4** (1837–1843), 267–269. Struve reported on the purchase of Olbers' library for the observatory at Pulkovo in *Astronomische Nachrichten,* **19** (1842), 307–312. The paradox of the dark night sky is extensively treated by Stanley L. Jaki in *The Paradox of Olbers' Paradox* (New York, 1969). See also Otto Struve, "Some Thoughts on Olbers' Paradox," in *Sky and Telescope,* **25** (1963), 140–142; and Stanley L. Jaki, "New Light on Olbers' Dependence on Chéseaux," in *Journal for the History of Astronomy,* **1** (1970), 53–55. F. X. von Zach describes Olbers' observatory and instruments in "Auszug aus einem astronomischen Tagebuche, geführt auf einer Reise nach Celle, Bremen und Lilienthal in Sept. 1800," in *Monatliche Correspondenz* . . ., **3** (1801), 113–145. There is a biographical notice in *Allgemeine deutsche Biographie,* XXIV, 236–238.

LETTIE S. MULTHAUF

OLDENBURG, HENRY (*b.* Bremen, Germany, *ca.* 1618; *d.* London, England, 5 September 1677), *scientific administration.*

There were three eminent secretaries of seventeenth-century scientific societies: Lorenzo Magalotti, Henry Oldenburg, and J. B. du Hamel. Although both the Italian and the Frenchman left behind substantial memorials of the societies with which they were associated, Oldenburg alone made a profession of scientific administration. In his fifteen years of service to the Royal Society he founded a complete system of records (still extant), created an international correspondence among scientists, and furnished a monthly account of scientific developments.

The Oldenburg family, which had moved to Bremen from Münster in the sixteenth century, was long associated with education. Henry's father, for whom he was named, taught from about 1610 to 1630 at the Paedagogium in Bremen; his last years were spent in the new university that Gustavus II founded at Dorpat (now Tartu), Estonia, where he died in 1634. The year of his son's birth can only be deduced from the facts that the boy entered the Gymnasium Illustre of Bremen in May 1633 and, after proceeding to the degree of Master of Theology in November 1639, went on to the University of Utrecht in 1641. Moreover, it seems likely that at his second marriage in 1668 Oldenburg described himself as "about fifty" years old. There are no details concerning his early life, and the only known means for his support during his minority was a lease of some ecclesiastical property, acquired by his grandfather, which he retained all his life—although apparently not as a useful source of income. His studies at the Gymnasium were largely theological, with Hebrew, Latin, Greek, rhetoric, logic, and mathematics as other subjects. Again, there is no evidence to show how he acquired his mastery of modern languages.

After a brief appearance at the University of Utrecht, where he possibly became acquainted with the philosophy of Descartes, Oldenburg vanishes for twelve years. It is likely that he followed the plan indicated in his letter to G. J. Vossius (August 1641) of acting as a private tutor, for in these years he acquired, apparently, a wide knowledge of France, Italy, Switzerland, Germany, and possibly England, and command of their respective languages. It also seems likely that when Oldenburg reappears he had already been tutor to a number of young Englishmen (among them Edward Lawrence, Robert Honywood, and William Cavendish, later first duke of Devonshire); he had now (as Milton testified) a perfect knowledge of English. Hence it is likely that he had spent some period in England, a deduction

confirmed by the next certain event in his life—his selection by the city government of Bremen, at a moment when he had returned to his birthplace, to go on a diplomatic mission to Oliver Cromwell, with the object of protecting the maritime interests of Bremen. Oldenburg arrived in England at the end of July 1653 and presented a memorial to Cromwell in December without achieving much result (partly owing to the state of confusion in the English government) before the conclusion of peace between England and Holland brought an end to the seizures at sea. Oldenburg remained in England, where he made new acquaintances or revived old ones, until a second call arrived from Bremen in August 1654 asking him to enlist Cromwell's friendship in aid of Bremen's resistance against a Swedish onslaught. This time Oldenburg (despite his laments of lack of money) achieved a partial diplomatic success. When this business was done—and possibly even before—Oldenburg returned to his tutorial employment, although there is no positive evidence of it before March 1656, when he was negotiating with the two Boyle families of Cork and Ranelagh.

By this time Oldenburg was certainly acquainted with John Dury, Samuel Hartlib, John Milton, Thomas Hobbes, the learned and pious Lady Ranelagh and her more famous brother, Robert Boyle, and no doubt many others who moved in the circles of persons who as yet were more inclined toward religion than toward philosophy or science and, insofar as they hoped for material progress in this life, saw it as dependent on the mysteries of technical invention. Like Boyle, Oldenburg did not figure in the Gresham College group; but his tutorship of Boyle's nephew Richard Jones (later third viscount and first earl of Ranelagh, 1641–1712) took him to Oxford in 1656, and so to acquaintance with John Wilkins and, no doubt, others residing at the university and constituting its Philosophical Club. In the summer of 1657 Oldenburg took young Jones for a long stay in France, with excursions into Germany. In several cities, but in Paris above all, Oldenburg and his pupil participated in learned societies, while, under the simultaneous promptings of Boyle and Hartlib, his interests and his acquaintanceships moved steadily toward science and medicine, especially chemistry. On these travels Oldenburg began to learn his trade as a scientific intelligencer and to become the friend of scientists. His return to London with Jones slightly preceded that of Charles II, and he soon began to develop his correspondence with the Continent. On 29 November 1660, at the famous meeting of the Gresham College group, he was listed as a candidate member of a formal scientific society—later to be the

Royal Society of London for Improving Natural Knowledge—which he joined in January 1661.

Thereafter Oldenburg's whole life was devoted to the Royal Society. He made one more trip abroad, to Bremen in the summer of 1661; returning through Holland, he met both Huygens and Spinoza. He was twice married. On 22 October 1663 he married Dorothy West, a woman not much younger than he, who possessed an estate of £400 with which (in part) his house in Pall Mall, near Lady Ranelagh's, was bought; she died early in 1665. In August 1668 Oldenburg married (with her father's consent) Dora Katherina Dury, aged about sixteen, who had been his ward for some years. She brought him a small property in Kent, near Charlton, which was their summer home. There were two children of this marriage, Rupert, born ca. 1673, and a younger daughter, Sophia.

In the first royal charter granted to the Royal Society (15 July 1662), as in the second (1663), Oldenburg was named one of its two secretaries, although he had not hitherto played a great part in its affairs. Probably, like Hooke, he owed his position to Robert Boyle, his constant friend and occasional employer over many years. His obvious chief qualifications for this honorary office were his industry, knowledge of languages, and literary gifts. Few Englishmen at this time possessed close contacts with the learned men of the Continent or knew much about work being done abroad. Certainly neither John Wilkins nor any of his successors in the titular first secretaryship hesitated to leave all conduct of the Society's affairs in Oldenburg's hands.

Oldenburg thus defined (British Museum MS Add 4441, fol. 27) the secretary's business as it had matured by the spring of 1668:

> He attends constantly the Meetings both of ye Society and Councill; noteth the Observables, said and done there; digesteth ym in private; takes care to have ym entred in the Journal- and Register-books; reads over and corrects all entrys; sollicites the performances of tasks recommended and undertaken; writes all Letters abroad and answers the returns made to ym, entertaining a correspondence wth at least 30. persons; employes a great deal of time, and takes much pain in inquiring after and satisfying forrain demands about philosophicall matters, dispenseth farr and near store of directions and inquiries for the society's purpose, and sees them well recommended etc.
>
> Query. Whether such a person ought to be left unassisted?

Besides the journal book, which held notes of meetings, and the register book, in which copies of important contributions were entered, Oldenburg kept the Council minutes and a letter book in which all the more important incoming and outgoing letters were extracted, as well as the files of original letters and papers, records of membership, and a cipher record of discoveries. Since he could pursue no regular career—although he did have earnings as an editor and translator, especially from the *Philosophical Transactions*—Oldenburg suffered increasing impoverishment until the Society allowed him an annual salary of £40 beginning in April 1668; also about this time he gained the assistance of an amanuensis.

Between them the Royal Society's two permanent officers, Robert Hooke and Henry Oldenburg, provided a great part of the matter discussed at the weekly meetings, Oldenburg drawing upon his correspondence and the books presented to the Society through himself. Apart from the week-by-week business of the Society this correspondence was Oldenburg's greatest burden, involving as it did receiving and answering an average of probably six or seven letters a week during the working period of the year, some of them long and difficult documents. The postal service to many points abroad was nonexistent or unreliable and, in any case, expensive; but in the last ten years of his service Oldenburg was able to exploit diplomatic channels by enlisting young men in embassies as his correspondents and agents. From 1666 he instructed correspondents to write by post to "Grubendol, London." This was a code address; it seems that Grubendol letters were delivered to the office of the secretary of state (and there paid for); in return Oldenburg reported any news of events abroad his letters might contain. Despite the Royal Society's privileges, maintaining correspondence with foreigners could be perilous, especially in time of war—as Oldenburg discovered when he was thrown in the Tower for some weeks during the summer of 1667. The probability is that in a letter to some foreigner that was seized he had expressed a patriotic but injudicious resentment that the English government had fallen down in its measures to protect England from the Dutch fleet. Thereafter he was very scrupulous in sticking to scientific matters.

From 6 March 1665 selected portions of the letters submitted to him were published in the *Philosophical Transactions: Giving Some Accompt of the Present Undertakings, Studies and Labours of the Ingenious in Many Considerable Parts of the World*, which were interrupted only twice in Oldenburg's lifetime: once by the plague, when a few issues were printed at Oxford although Oldenburg remained in London, attentive to the Society's concerns, and again when Oldenburg was imprisoned. The *Philosophical*

Transactions formed the first purely scientific journal containing both formal contributions and short notes about work in progress, as well as book reviews that were often long and of critical value. They became the principal vehicle of interchange between English and Continental science, supplementing Oldenburg's correspondence; and for some investigators—of whom Leeuwenhoek is the most obvious example—they were their sole vehicle of publication. Oldenburg also encouraged the Royal Society to undertake, and personally managed, the publication of separate works: those of Malpighi are best known in this category. He both translated and published Steno's *Prodromus*; and generally through his letters and the open pages of the *Transactions* he gave encouragement to all the younger English scientists of the decade 1667–1677, including Isaac Newton, as well as many on the Continent.

As a scientific journalist and administrator of the Royal Society, Oldenburg has been accused of over-enthusiasm. At a time when the line between a private letter and a paper for publication was dubious, he committed some errors of discretion; but he was never guilty of a breach of confidence. He tended to regard everything disclosed at an ordinary meeting of the Royal Society as public, unless a special request was made—and, indeed, the Society was opposed to secrecy about discoveries. He can hardly be censured for communicating accounts of meetings to absent fellows, whether native or, like Huygens and Hevelius, foreign. Oldenburg perhaps had an excessive faith in the power of the process of critique-and-rebuttal to elicit truth, but this was often for the sake of enhancing English prestige in a manner that his contemporaries expected of him. There is no evidence that Oldenburg (who was careful not to claim English nationality, which he sought only in the last months of his life) favored foreigners; the accusations on this score leveled against him by Hooke were without foundation, and he was fully vindicated by the Royal Society's Council. Hooke was Oldenburg's sole enemy, and then only after the Huygens' spring-balance watch patent application of 1675.

Oldenburg's conception of the Royal Society's function was consistently and simply Baconian; it was the task of the learned and the well-endowed of his age to compile an authentic natural history from which posterity would elucidate a sound natural philosophy. "Natural history" included, besides passive investigation of flora and fauna, minerals, the heavens, and even wonders and prodigies, active experimentation, such as blood transfusion and medical injection, with which he was much concerned. All this Oldenburg regarded as an international enterprise, in which the efforts of established societies should be strengthened by individual zeal in every nation. He regretted the poverty of the Royal Society, contrasting it with the lavish resources enjoyed by the Académie Royale des Sciences. Like Boyle and Newton he distrusted a priorist systems of nature and sometimes, like Bacon, spoke of the amelioration of human life as a major object of the scientific movement. But in practice he gave a warm welcome to any piece of solid work, whether in scientific description, pure mathematics, experimental physics, or astronomical calculation. As an editor he had a sound instinct, although (like his age) distorted by an excessive preoccupation with medical curiosities and teratology. If Oldenburg's approach to the advancement of science was not greatly ahead of that general in his time, it did not lag behind.

Oldenburg remained steadily active until the last months of his life. He died on 5 September 1677 after a brief illness and was buried at Bexley, Kent; his wife died on 17 September. Since Oldenburg was intestate, letters of administration were taken out to make provision for the children; Boyle probably had a hand in the arrangements. Rupert Oldenburg, then serving as a lieutenant, committed suicide in 1724; of the fate of Sophia no trace remains. Oldenburg's considerable library was bought by the earl of Anglesey, whose vast collection was in turn dispersed in 1686. Some of Oldenburg's books are now in the British Museum, and others appear on the antiquarian market.

BIBLIOGRAPHY

I. ORIGINAL WORKS. Besides the *Philosophical Transactions* and the literary activities already mentioned, Oldenburg translated several of Boyle's books into Latin and probably acted as a literary assistant to John Evelyn. He also published an English translation of François Bernier's *History of the Late Revolution of the Empire of the Great Mogul* and was possibly the translator of some other works published over the initials "H.O." For his correspondence see A. Rupert Hall and Marie Boas Hall, eds., *The Correspondence of Henry Oldenburg*, I–IX (Madison–Milwaukee–London, 1965–1973), a work that is still continuing.

II. SECONDARY LITERATURE. Friedrich Althaus in the Munich *Beilage zur Allgemeinen Zeitung*, no. 212 (2 August 1889), pp. 1–3, gave an account of Oldenburg's family and early life in Bremen. For the rest, see A. Rupert Hall and Marie Boas Hall, "Why Blame Oldenburg?" in *Isis*, **53** (1962), 482–491; "Some Hitherto Unknown Facts About the Private Career of Henry Oldenburg," in *Notes and Records of the Royal Society of London*, **18** (1963), 94–103; "Further Notes on Henry Oldenburg," *ibid.*, **23** (1968), 33–42; M.

B. Hall, "Henry Oldenburg and the Art of Scientific Communication," in *British Journal for the History of Science*, **2** (1964–1965), 277–290; and A. R. Hall, "Henry Oldenburg et les relations scientifiques au XVIIe siècle," in *Revue d'histoire des sciences*, **23** (1970), 285–304. See also T. Sprat, *History of the Royal Society* (London, 1667); T. Birch, *History of the Royal Society* (London, 1756–1757; repr. 1968), and Robert Hooke, *Diary, 1672–80*, H. W. Robinson and W. Adams, eds. (London, 1935).

A. RUPERT HALL

OLDHAM, RICHARD DIXON (*b*. Dublin, Ireland, 31 July 1858; *d*. Llandrindod Wells, Wales, 15 July 1936), *geology, seismology*.

Oldham was the third son of Thomas Oldham, a distinguished geologist who was professor of geology at Trinity College, Dublin, and then a director of the geological surveys of Ireland and India. He was educated in England, first at Rugby and then at the Royal School of Mines. He followed in his father's footsteps by joining the staff of the Geological Survey of India in 1879. He devoted much energy to completing the unfinished work of his father, who died in 1878, notably an extensive investigation of a great earthquake in Cachar in 1869.

Oldham became superintendent of the Geological Survey of India and wrote some forty of its publications, chiefly on earthquakes in India, the hot springs of India, the geology of the Son Valley, and the structure of the Himalayas and the Ganges plain, taking account of geodetic observations. He developed a great interest in the then emerging science of seismology and is now noted more for his contribuions to seismology than to geology. He left India in 1903, partly because of ill health, and returned to England, spending some time working with the seismologist John Milne on the Isle of Wight. Later, for health reasons, he lived in the Rhone Valley and then in Wales; but he remained an active contributor to science until about eight years before his death. He was awarded the Lyell Medal of the Geological Society of London in 1908 and was elected to the Royal Society in 1911.

Oldham became famous for his report on the great Assam earthquake of 12 June 1897, one of the most violent of modern times, which caused complete devastation over 9,000 square miles and was felt over 1.75 million square miles. It far surpassed in quality all reports on previous earthquakes, describing the remarkable Chedrang fault, with a thirty-five-foot uplift at one point; gave evidence of the occurrence of fractures without apparent rock displacement; showed that in some places accelerations of the ground

motion had exceeded the vertical acceleration of gravity; and reported the results of the first resurvey ever carried out after a large earthquake. From the point of view of seismology, the most far-reaching result was the first clear identification on seismograms of the onsets of the primary (P), secondary (S), and tertiary (surface) waves, previously predicted in longstanding mathematical theory. This identification showed that the earth could be treated as perfectly elastic to good approximation in studying seismic waves, a result of supreme importance to the further development of seismology.

Oldham also supplied the first clear evidence that the earth has a central core (1906). Others had suspected its existence but had not succeeded in obtaining direct evidence. In the course of analyzing some of Milne's records of large earthquakes, Oldham invariably found delays in the arrival of P waves at points on the earth diametrically opposite to earthquake sources; and he showed that the delays could be interpreted only in terms of the presence of a sizable core inside which the average P velocity is substantially less than in the surrounding shell.

Oldham was an original and independent thinker whose writings, whatever the subject, were always interesting and suggestive. One account describes him as "a little too independent sometimes for those in authority." There is a suggestion that he was impatient with the red tape of administrators less brilliant than himself. Above all, he is noted as a pioneer in the application of seismology to the study of the interior of the earth.

BIBLIOGRAPHY

I. ORIGINAL WORKS. Oldham's "Report on the Great Earthquake of 12th June 1897" was published in *Memoirs of the Geological Survey of India*, **29** (1899), i–xxx, 1–379, along with a supplementary report in **30** (1900), 1–102. "On the Propagation of Earthquake Motion to Great Distances," in *Philosophical Transactions of the Royal Society*, **194A** (1900), 135–174, includes his work on P, S, and surface waves. Most of his other papers were published in *Memoirs of the Geological Survey of India*.

II. SECONDARY LITERATURE. See the accounts of Oldham's life by C. Davison, in *Obituary Notices of Fellows of the Royal Society of London*, **2** (1936–1938), 111–113; and by P. L., in *Nature*, **138** (Aug. 1936), 316–317.

K. E. BULLEN

OLDHAM, THOMAS (*b*. Dublin, Ireland, 4 May 1816; *d*. Rugby, England, 17 July 1878), *geology*.

Oldham was educated privately in Dublin and

received his B.A. from Trinity College, Dublin, in 1836. Next, at Edinburgh he studied engineering; also geology and mineralogy under Robert Jameson, professor of natural history. On his return to Ireland in 1839, Oldham became chief geological assistant to J. E. Portlock, who was in charge of the Ordnance Survey in Ireland. Oldham supplied the mineral identifications for Portlock's *Report on the Geology of Londonderry* . . . (London, 1843). In 1844 he was appointed assistant professor of engineering at Trinity College, and a year later he became professor of geology there. In 1846 he also became local director of the Irish branch of the Geological Surveys of the United Kingdom, but continued to occupy the chair of geology.

During the next four years Oldham carried out much geological work. His noteworthy discovery in 1849 of hitherto unnoticed radiating fanlike impressions in the Cambrian rocks of Bray Head, County Wicklow, aroused intense interest; and the paleontologist Edward Forbes gave the name *Oldhamia* to the presumed fossil. The nature of this fossil has been disputed, but it is now thought to be a trace fossil—that is, a sedimentary structure caused by a living creature.

In November 1850 Oldham was appointed, on a five-year agreement, as geological surveyor to the East India Company. Although he succeeded another surveyor, D. H. Williams, he took no narrow view of his new post, immediately describing himself as the "Superintendent of the Geological Survey of India," and began to recruit other geologists to his staff. His office was renewed every five years until his retirement in 1876.

Oldham is justifiably regarded as the architect of the Geological Survey of India; under his guidance a remarkable amount of work was carried out, and large areas of India were surveyed geologically. Particular attention was given to a survey of the Indian coalfields, and in 1864 Oldham issued an elaborate report, *On the Coal Resources of India.* At the same time, under his supervision several serial publications were begun: *Annual Reports, Records, Memoirs,* and the important *Palaeontologia Indica.* Oldham initiated the scientific study of earthquakes in India and published a catalog of earthquakes. He also brought to the attention of European geologists much new information on the Cretaceous rocks. A vast collection of Indian rocks and fossils was accumulated, and shortly before Oldham's retirement it was transferred to the Indian Museum in Calcutta.

Oldham was elected a fellow of the Royal Society in 1848, and in 1875 the Society awarded him a Royal Medal.

BIBLIOGRAPHY

Oldham's scientific papers are listed in the Royal Society *Catalogue of Scientific Papers,* IV, 672; VIII, 528. His geological work in India was published by the Geological Survey of India.

There is no biography of Oldham, but details of his career are given by T. G. Bonney, in *Dictionary of National Biography,* XLII (1895), 111, which is based partly on an obituary notice in *Quarterly Journal of the Geological Society of London,* **35** (1879), "Proceedings," 16. The circumstances relating to his appointment in India are given by Sir Cyril S. Fox, "The Geological Survey of India, 1846 to 1947," in *Nature,* **160** (1947), 889. For a brief appraisal of his work there, see Sir Lewis Fermor, "Geological Survey of India, Centenary Celebrations," *ibid.,* **167** (1951), 10.

JOAN M. EYLES

OLIVER, GEORGE (*b.* Middleton-in-Teesdale, Durham, England, 13 April 1841; *d.* Farnham, Surrey, England, 27 December 1915), *physiology.*

Oliver was the second son of W. Oliver, a surgeon. He prepared at Gainford School, Yorkshire, for medical studies at University College, London, qualifying for membership in the Royal College of Surgeons in 1863 and receiving the M.B. in 1865. After brief periods of practice at Stockton-on-Tees and Redcar, he won the gold medal in obtaining his M.D. (London) in 1873. Oliver settled in Harrogate, where he practiced medicine from 1876 to 1908, then retired to Farnham. His first wife, Alice Hunt, died in 1898. Two years later he married Mary Ledyard, who survived him. Winter residence in London, afforded him by the seasonal nature of his Harrogate practice, allowed Oliver to be active in a number of medical and scientific societies. He was a member of the Physiological Society and of the Medical Society of London and a fellow of the Royal College of Physicians of London, the Royal Society of Medicine, and the Royal Microscopical Society.

Oliver was one of the many medical students influenced by William Sharpey, professor of anatomy and physiology at University College, to devote himself to the development of more scientific methods of diagnosis and therapy. With extensive clinical experience, knowledge of physiology and chemistry, and considerable technical ingenuity, he devised accurate and convenient techniques for, among other things, the analysis of blood and of urine, the measurement of circulatory phenomena, and the assessment of the therapeutic effects of medicinal waters. Notable examples of his contributions in this area are his introduction of urinary testing papers and of his hemacytometer, hemoglobinometer, arteriometer, and sphygmomanometer.

Oliver's interest in the circulation and his facility with instruments led to his most important scientific contribution, a collaboration with Edward A. Schäfer (later Sir Edward Sharpey-Schafer) in 1893–1895, in which the two elucidated the cardiovascular effects of the administration of extracts of the adrenal medulla and of the pituitary. Oliver administered glycerin extracts of a number of different organs to his son, noting their various effects with particular reference to the caliber of the peripheral arteries, as measured by his arteriometer. In Schäfer's words:

> Dr. George Oliver had been making a large number of clinical observations upon the effect of various organ extracts upon the circulation, but had been unable to arrive at any very definite conclusions regarding them. Amongst these was extract of suprarenal capsule, extract of thyroid gland, extract of brain and so on. He consulted me as to what steps might be taken to arrive at a clearer understanding in regard to their action, and I invited him to investigate their physiological action along with me upon animals in the laboratory. This we proceeded to do; and the result of the investigation was that the majority of the extracts from which he supposed that he had obtained definite results in man gave no indications of physiological activity; whereas on the other hand, the extract of suprarenal capsule gave such manifest indications of activity that it was quite clear that a very important principle was contained within this organ. The properties of this principle we then proceeded to work out . . . [from Schäfer's testimony before the second Royal Commission on Vivisection, in *British Parliamentary Papers*, **57** (1908), 430].

Addison in 1849 had associated a diseased state of the adrenal glands with the set of clinical symptoms characteristic of the disease that now bears his name. Brown-Séquard (1856) showed that excision of the entire adrenal glands of animals was inevitably fatal. Oliver and Schäfer's experiments demonstrated conclusively that intravenous injection of small quantities of aqueous extract of adrenal gland into various animals produced striking effects: a sharp increase in blood pressure owing to contraction of the arterioles, cardiac inhibition, shallower respiration, and prolongation of muscular contractions. They showed that the extract took effect through direct action on the peripheral arterioles; that the activity of the extract was preserved through digestion; that the active principle was produced by the medulla and not by the cortex of the gland; and that the active principle was absent in extracts of glands from patients with advanced Addison's disease. Oliver and Schäfer identified the active principle which they had dem-

onstrated in the adrenals with a substance described by Vulpian (1856) in his distinction between the cortex and the medulla of the gland. They contrasted their results with those of Paolo Pellacani (1874) and Pio Foà and Pellacani (1884), who had found that injection of adrenal extract into animals was generally fatal. In related work they demonstrated that extract of pituitary in relatively large quantities caused a somewhat smaller rise in blood pressure due to contraction of arterioles and augmentation of heart action.

Oliver and Schäfer's accomplishment was the first detailed study of the effect of the active principle of a ductless gland. By explicitly rejecting the autointoxication theory, which held that fatalities following excision of the adrenals were due to the accumulation in the blood of toxins that it was the normal function of the adrenals to destroy, they helped to shape the endocrine doctrine. They pointed out that the production of a specific active principle, diffused through the blood, appeared to be the essential function of certain ductless glands, notably the thyroid and the adrenals. Their work was the basis for subsequent research in which J. J. Abel (1899) isolated and named the active principle of the adrenal medulla, epinephrine, and Thomas Bell Aldrich (1901) and Jokichi Takamine (1901) prepared it in crystalline form.

BIBLIOGRAPHY

I. ORIGINAL WORKS. Oliver's many medical writings are listed in *Index medicus*. His endocrinological researches are dealt with in four papers written with E. A. Schäfer: "On the Physiological Action of Extract of the Suprarenal Capsules," in *Journal of Physiology*, **16** (1894), i–iv, and **17** (1894–1895), ix–xiv; "The Physiological Effects of Extracts of the Suprarenal Capsules," *ibid.*, **18** (1895), 230–276; and "On the Physiological Action of Extracts of Pituitary Body and Certain Other Glandular Organs," *ibid.*, 277–279. See also "The Croonian Lectures: A Contribution to the Study of the Blood and the Circulation. Lecture II," in *British Medical Journal* (1896), **1**, 1433–1437; and "The Action of Animal Extracts on the Peripheral Vessels," in *Journal of Physiology*, **21** (1897), xxii–xxiii; and the book *Pulse-Gauging. A Clinical Study of Radial Measurement and Pulse-Pressure* (London, 1895). A few letters by Oliver are in the Wellcome Institute of the History of Medicine, London, and in the library of the Royal College of Physicians, London. His MS notes of William Jenner's lectures in medicine for the session of 1862–1863 are in the library of University College Hospital, London.

II. SECONDARY LITERATURE. Sources for Oliver's life and work are the notices in *Lancet* (1916), **1**, 105; and

British Medical Journal (1916), **1**, 73; *Munk's Roll* (London, 1955), IV, 324; *Presidential Address to the Royal College of Physicians of London* (London, 1916), 27–29; and T. R. Elliot, "Sir William Jenner and Dr. George Oliver," in *University College Hospital Magazine*, **19** (1934), 159–163. On Oliver's work in the context of early endocrinology, see E. A. Schäfer, "Internal Secretions," in *Lancet* (1895), **2**, 321–324, an important theoretical discussion, and "On the Present Condition of Our Knowledge Regarding the Functions of the Suprarenal Capsules," in *British Medical Journal* (1908), **1**, 1277–1281, 1346–1351. See also the following books: L. F. Barker, ed., *Endocrinology and Metabolism* (London, 1922); A. Biedl, *The Internal Secretory Organs: Their Physiology and Pathology*, L. Forster, trans. (London, 1913); C. McC. Brooks, J. L. Gilbert, H. A. Levey, and D. R. Curtis, *Humors, Hormones and Neurosecretions* (New York, 1962); J. F. Fulton and L. G. Wilson, eds., *Selected Readings in the History of Physiology*, 2nd ed. (Springfield, Ill., 1966); E. Gley, *The Internal Secretions. Their Physiology and Application to Pathology*, M. Fishberg, trans. (New York, 1917), H. D. Rolleston, *The Endocrine Organs in Health and Disease, With an Historical Review* (London, 1936); E. A. Schäfer, ed., *Text-Book of Physiology*, I (Edinburgh–London, 1898); and *The Endocrine Organs. An Introduction to the Study of Internal Secretion* (London, 1916); and S. Vincent, *Internal Secretion and the Ductless Glands* (London, 1912).

RICHARD D. FRENCH

OLSZEWSKI, KAROL STANISŁAW (*b.* Broniszow, Poland, 29 January 1846; *d.* Cracow, Poland, 24 March 1915), *chemistry*, *physics*.

Olszewski was a pioneer in the field of low-temperature phenomena who became famous, along with Z. von Wroblewski, for achieving the liquefaction of air. His father, a Polish landowner, was killed during a peasants' uprising a few months after the birth of his son; and Olszewski was brought up by relatives. From 1866 to 1872 he studied natural science at Cracow and at Heidelberg, from which he received the doctorate in 1872. He then became assistant to Emil Czyrnianski, professor of chemistry at the Jagiellonian University in Cracow; in 1891 he was appointed professor of chemistry there, a post he held until his death. Olszewski was a member of the Cracow Academy of Sciences.

In 1883 Olszewski and Wroblewski liquefied air, oxygen, nitrogen, and carbon monoxide. Their successes owed much to Olszewski's previous work on the liquefaction of carbon dioxide. After Wroblewski's death Olszewski was the only expert in Poland on the liquefaction of gases. He determined the inversion temperatures of oxygen and nitrogen and, in 1902,

that of hydrogen. He also liquefied argon and fluorine. Olszewski and Wroblewski were able to liquefy hydrogen only in its dynamic state; it appeared as a cloud of fog in the midst of escaping hydrogen gas. Olszewski attempted to liquefy hydrogen in its static state, but the first to do so was James Dewar (1898), who used the new procedure of air liquefaction developed by Linde and Hampson: the cooling of gases by means of their internal efficiency, using the counterflow principle. Olszewski, however, improved Dewar's methods and adapted them to practical laboratory work.

Olszewski worked on the liquefaction of helium as early as 1895, but without success; the existing methods were not applicable because of the low critical temperature of helium, and Linde's process was unavailable to him because of its high cost. (The liquefaction of helium was achieved in 1908 by H. Kamerlingh Onnes.) Olszewski was a thorough researcher with great manual dexterity and experimental intuition. His devices for air and hydrogen liquefaction were very highly regarded and were manufactured under license by the Cracow mechanic L. Grodzicki.

BIBLIOGRAPHY

I. ORIGINAL WORKS. Olszewski's numerous scientific papers include "Ueber die Verflüssigung des Sauerstoffs, Stickstoffs und Kohlenoxyds," in *Annalen der Physik und Chemie*, n.s. **20** (1883), 243–257, written with Z. von Wroblewski; "Ueber die Dichte des flüssigen Methans, sowie des verflüssigten Sauerstoffs und Stickstoffs," *ibid.*, **31** (1887), 58–74; "Ueber das Absorptionsspectrum des flüssigen Sauerstoffs und der verflüssigten Luft," *ibid.*, **33** (1888), 570–575; "Bestimmung des Siedepunkts des Ozons und der Erstarrungstemperatur des Aethylens," *ibid.*, **37** (1889), 337–340; "Bestimmung der kritischen- und der Siedetemperatur des Wasserstoffs," *ibid.*, **56** (1895), 133–143; "Liquefaction of Gases," in *Philosophical Magazine*, 5th ser., **39** (1895), 188–213; "Ein Versuch, das Helium zu verflüssigen," in *Annalen der Physik und Chemie*, n.s. **59** (1896), 184–192; "Experimentelle Bestimmung der Inversionstemperatur der Kelvinschen Erscheinung," in *Annalen der Physik*, 4th ser., **7** (1902), 818–823; "Apparate zur Verflüssigung von Luft und Wasserstoff," *ibid.*, **10** (1903), 768–782; "Ein neuer Apparat zur Verflüssigung des Wasserstoffs," *ibid.*, **12** (1903), 196–201; "Ein Beitrag zur Bestimmung des kritischen Punktes des Wasserstoffs," *ibid.*, **17** (1905), 986–993; "Weitere Versuche, das Helium zu verflüssigen," *ibid.*, 994–998; and "On the Temperature of Inversion of the Joule-Kelvin Effect for Air and Nitrogen," in *Philosophical Magazine*, 6th ser., **13** (1907), 722–724.

Bibliographies of Olszewski's writings are in Academy of Sciences, Cracow, *Katalog der Akademischen Publika-*

tionen seit 1873 bis 1909 (Cracow, 1910); and Poggendorff, IV, 1095; and V, 922–923.

II. Secondary Literature. M. von Smoluchowski, "Karl Olszewski—ein Gelehrtenleben," in *Naturwissenschaften*, **5** (1917), 738–740, includes a biographical note on Wroblewski; see also H. Kamerlingh Onnes, "Karol Olszewski," in *Chemikerzeitung*, **39** (1915), 517–519.

A chronological list of publications in Polish—courtesy of Dr. I. Stroński, Cracow—includes the following: *Kronika Uniwersytetu Jagiellońskiego 1864–1887* (Cracow, 1887), 83–86, 184; E. Kurzyniec, "O pierszeństwie skroplenia wodoru w stanie dynamicznym" ("On the Priority of the Liquefaction of Hydrogen in the Dynamic State"), in *Prace Komisji historii medycyny*, **3** (1953), 303–315; K. Adwentowski, A. Pasternak, and Z. Wojtaszek, "Dewar czy Olszewski?" ("Dewar or Olszewski?"), in *Kwartalnik historii nauki . . .*, **1** (1956), 539–561, including letters from M. Pattison Muir and Sir William Ramsay to Olszewski; A. Pasternak, "Karol Olszewski (1846–1915) i Zygmunt Wroblewski (1845–1888)," in *Polscy badacze przyrody* ("Polish Investigators of Nature"; Warsaw, 1959), 174–203; K. Adwentowski, A. Pasternak, and Z. Wojtaszek, "Karol Olszewski jako uczony i nauczyciel" ("Karol Olszewski as Teacher and Scientist"), in *Studia i materiały z dziejów nauki polskiej*, ser. C, **3** (1959), 193–229, including a report on Olszewski's laboratory by his former co-worker K. Adwentowski; and Z. Wojtaszck, "O działalności naukowej Karola Olszewskiego poza dziedzina kriogeniki" ("On Olszewski's Scientific Work Outside Cryogenics"), *ibid.*, **9** (1964), 135–173 (which includes Olszewski's researches on the chemistry of water and a bibliography of these papers); and "Zarys historii katedr chemicznych Uniwersytetu Jagiellońskiego" ("Compendium of the History of the Chairs of Chemistry in the Jagiellonian University of Cracow"), in *Studia ad universitatis Iagellonicae Cracoviensis facultatis mathematicae, physicae, chemiae cathedrarum historiam pertinentia* (Cracow, 1964), 133–219.

Hans-Günther Körber

OLUFSEN, CHRISTIAN FRIIS ROTTBØLL (*b.* Copenhagen, Denmark, 15 April 1802; *d.* Copenhagen, 29 May 1855), *astronomy.*

Olufsen was the son of the Danish political economist Christian Olufsen. During his studies at the University of Copenhagen he was awarded a gold medal for a mathematical treatment of eclipses, and he later spent two years with Bessel at Königsberg. In 1829 he became senior astronomer at the University of Copenhagen observatory and, three years later, was promoted to professor of astronomy and director of the observatory. In 1840 he received his doctorate with a dissertation on the derivation of the lunar parallax.

In 1829 Schumacher had suggested that the Royal Danish Academy of Sciences and Letters produce new tables for the sun, some preparatory work having already been done by Bessel; but more than twenty years elapsed before the tables were completed through cooperation between Hansen, in Gotha, and Olufsen. The former derived the perturbations in the movement of the earth, and the latter made comparisons with a long series of observations and the final determination of the mean motion of the earth. Olufsen's investigation in 1831 of the systematic errors in the observations made with the Greenwich mural quadrant when Maskelyne was astronomer royal was a prerequisite for the use of the Greenwich observations of the sun for his work with Hansen.

For the series of star maps covering the declinations $-15°$ to $+15°$, which were initiated and published by the Berlin Academy (*Akademische Sternkarten*), Olufsen took over the right ascension 1^h; and he gave a detailed report on the course of the total solar eclipse of 28 July 1851, as observed from Kalmar, Sweden.

Olufsen worked in several fields, but he was often hampered by illness. His main contribution was made in connection with the work of his contemporaries, particularly that of Bessel, toward reforming and improving the foundation of astronomy.

BIBLIOGRAPHY

Olufsen's memoirs include "Untersuchungen über den Greenwicher Mauerquadranten während Maskelynes Direction der dortigen Sternwarte," in *Astronomische Nachrichten*, **9** (1831), 85–106; "Untersuchungen über den Werth der Mondsparallaxe, die aus den in der Mitte des vorigen Jahrhunderts angestellten correspondirenden Beobachtungen abgeleiten werden kann," *ibid.*, **14** (1837), 209–226; "Ueber die Sonnenfinsterniss am 7ten Juli 1842," *ibid.*, **22** (1844), 217–230, 232–242; and "Beobachtung der totalen Sonnenfinsterniss am 28sten Juli 1851 in Calmar," *ibid.*, **33** (1851), 219–222. Among his books are *Disquisitio de parallaxi lunae* (Copenhagen, 1840), his dissertation; *Tentamen de longitudine speculae Havniensis. Praemittuntur considerationes de conaminibus, quae initio seculi octavi decimi ad astronomiam practicam reformandam instituit inclytissimus Roemerus* (Copenhagen, 1840); *Begyndelsesgrunde af astronomien med anvendelse paa den mathematiske Geographie* (Copenhagen, 1848); and *Tables du soleil, exécutées d'après les ordres de la Société royale des sciences de Copenhague* (Copenhagen, 1853; supp., 1857), written with P. A. Hansen.

There is an obituary by P. Pedersen in *Oversigt over det K. Danske Videnskabernes Selskabs Forhandlinger* (1856), 96–103.

Axel V. Nielsen

OLYMPIODORUS (*b.* Thebes, Egypt, *ca.* 360–385; *d.* after 425), *history, alchemy.*

The earliest known event in the life of Olympiodorus is a mission in 412 for Emperor Honorius to Donatus, leader of the Huns. About 415 he was in Athens; and about 423 he went to Egypt, where he visited Nubia, Thebes, Talmis, Syene (now Aswan), the oasis of Siwa, and the priests of Isis at Philae. He probably lived at times in Byzantium, Ravenna, and Rome; and he knew the latter city well. He was not a Christian. At Athens, Olympiodorus associated with the Sophists and was a friend of the grammarian Philtatius. He was personally acquainted with Valerius, the prefect of Thrace. He called himself a poet (ποιητής), a word that is sometimes interpreted as "alchemist."

Olympiodorus is known primarily for his Greek history, *Materials for History*, a continuation of the work of Eunapius (*d.* after 414). The original work, covering the period from 407–425, is preserved only in fragments in the *Bibliotheca* of Photius, the ninth-century patriarch of Constantinople. Olympiodorus' history is dedicated to the Emperor Theodosius II and describes in twenty-two books the history of the Western Empire from the seventh consulship of Honorius to the accession of Valentinian III. The work is an impartial and interesting commentary by an educated observer who had firsthand knowledge of the troubled decades of the early fifth century.

Certain authorities, such as Berthelot and Lippmann, credit Olympiodorus of Thebes with being the author of a Greek work on alchemy entitled variously "The Philosopher Olympiodorus to Pelasius, King of Armenia, on the Divine and Sacred Art" and "The Alexandrian Philosopher Olympiodorus on the Book of Deeds by Zosimus and on the Sayings of Hermes and the Philosophers." The work is quite extensive, with a wealth of disconnected quotations; some of those from Zosimus of Panopolis (late third century) are new. The author presents a very confused and poor explanation of alchemy and displays little practical understanding of his subject, although there is considerable alchemical imagery with Gnostic and Egyptian influence and language. He attempts to draw parallels between the views of the great alchemists and the views of such philosophers as Thales, Anaximander, Anaximenes, Parmenides, and Xenophanes on the origin of matter. He cites the many books of the ancients that were to be found in the Ptolemaic library at Alexandria, written in allegory, with the words having a mystical, double sense which only the initiate can understand. There is little mention of alchemical apparatus. Among his alchem-ical predecessors he mentions Agathodaemon, Chimes, Maria the Jewess, and Synesius.

Other authorities, especially Hammer-Jensen, consider the author of this alchemical work to have been a Neoplatonic philosopher of the sixth century known as Olympiodorus of Alexandria. The author of commentaries on the works of Plato and Aristotle, this Olympiodorus is much esteemed as an interpreter of Plato.

BIBLIOGRAPHY

I. ORIGINAL WORKS. The work on alchemy is found in Marcellin P. E. Berthelot, *Collection des anciens alchimistes grecs,* 3 vols. (Paris, 1887–1888; Osnabrück, 1967), II, 69–106, III, 75–115. The excerpts from Olympiodorus' historical work, as preserved by Photius, are published in Ludwig A. Dindorf, *Historici graeci minores,* I (Leipzig, 1870), 450–472.

II. SECONDARY LITERATURE. See M. P. E. Berthelot, *Les origines de l'alchimie* (Paris, 1885), 191–199 and *passim*; and *Introduction à l'étude de la chimie des anciens et du moyen âge* (Paris, 1889; Brussels, 1966), *passim*; Walter Haedicke, "Olympiodoros" no. 11, in Pauly-Wissowa, *Real-Encyclopädie der classischen Altertumswissenschaft,* 1st ser.; XVIII, pt. 1 (Stuttgart, 1939), cols. 201–207; Ingeborg Hammer-Jensen, *Die älteste Alchemie, Meddelelser fra den K. Danske Videnskabernes Selskab, Hist.-fil. Meddel.,* IV, no. 2 (Copenhagen, 1921); Arthur J. Hopkins, *Alchemy, Child of Greek Philosophy* (New York, 1967), 77; Edmund O. von Lippmann, *Entstehung und Ausbreitung der Alchemie,* I (Berlin, 1919), 96–102; Riess, "Alchemie," in Pauly-Wissowa, 1st ser., I (Stuttgart, 1894), col. 1349; and George Sarton, *Introduction to the History of Science,* I (Baltimore, 1927), 389.

KARL H. DANNENFELDT

OMALIUS D'HALLOY, JEAN BAPTISTE JULIEN D' (*b.* Liège, Belgium, 16 February 1783; *d.* Brussels, Belgium, 15 January 1875), *geology.*

D'Omalius d'Halloy, who played a major role in the transition from the stratigraphic systems of Werner or Guettard to those of de la Beche and Murchison, was the only son of Jean Bernard d'Omalius d'Halloy, the son of an old and wealthy family, and Sophie de Thier de Skeuvre. Following his parents' wishes, he was educated in the family tradition of law and public service. In 1801 he was sent to Paris, where they expected him to become acquainted with literature, art, and theater. But Paris was also the scientific center of Europe, and d'Omalius was attracted to the natural sciences. In 1803, over parental protests, he began serious scientific study, attending the lectures of Lacépède, the zoologist; Antoine de Fourcroy, the chemist; and Cuvier.

D'Omalius made his first geological tour in the Ardennes and Lorraine in 1804. In 1805–1806 he traveled throughout France, including the Belgian provinces, making the observations for his first important paper, "Essai sur la géologie du nord de la France" (1808), which established his scientific reputation. In this publication d'Omalius began, on the Continent, stratigraphic subdivision of the major Wernerian classes by superposition and paleontological criteria. This type of subdivision was later associated in England with the work of Bakewell and Smith and in America with that of Maclure and Eaton. The success of the essay led Coquebert de Montbret, head of the Bureau of Statistics of France, to engage d'Omalius to prepare a geological map of the Empire. This work was begun in 1809 and completed in 1813, but new administrative duties prevented d'Omalius from preparing the map for publication until 1823. In 1813 he presented to the Institut de France a "Mémoire sur l'étendue géographique du terrain des environs de Paris," extending and significantly modifying the work on the Paris basin begun by Cuvier and Brongniart.

Political events ended the first period of d'Omalius' scientific career. From 1813 to 1830, with his father's urging, d'Omalius served in a succession of public offices: mayor of Brabant (1813); superintendent of Dinant (1814), then secretary general of Liège; and governor of the province of Namur, Netherlands (1815–1830). A notable achievement of his administration was the *Code administratif de la province de Namur* (1827), on which he worked for several years. The establishment of Belgian independence in 1830 ended his governorship of Namur and allowed him to resume his scientific career. He never again entirely gave up science for public service, although in 1848 he was elected to the Belgian senate from Dinant, holding office until his death. From 1851 to 1870 he was vice-president of the senate.

In the first period of his scientific career, from 1804 to 1813, d'Omalius worked in stratigraphy and mineralogy. His *Essai* of 1808 opposed Wernerian geology by arguing that the inclination of strata is not due to deposition and that, in the same basin, inclined strata are older than horizontal strata. He also distinguished ten terrains among the strata of northern France. In his *Observations sur un essai de carte géologique de la France, des Pays-Bas et des contrées voisines* (1823), d'Omalius brought the local descriptions of the geology of France into a uniform and sophisticated stratigraphic column, one that, in conjunction with the parallel efforts of Alexandre Brongniart, enjoyed wide acceptance and formed the basis for the development of Continental stratigraphy in the first half of the nineteenth century.

After returning to geology in 1830, d'Omalius was more speculative than in the earlier period. He also wrote about ethnology and defended the theory of evolution. His controversial views grew out of his conservative refusal to accept complete uniformitarianism in geology. In papers and in his textbook, *Éléments de géologie* (1831), d'Omalius argued that contemporary geological processes are not capable of having produced all formations. Reasoning from the traditional hypothesis that the earth was originally a hot mass cooling slowly, he insisted that the deepest structures—Werner's primitive terrain, which he renamed plutonic terrain—had been formed by heat agencies no longer intensely active. Even in later epochs, when upper strata were formed by deposition in water, heat remained a secondary cause. Thus d'Omalius believed that many deposits of sand in Belgium had been ejected from the hot interior. These views, which he strongly defended in the 1840's and 1850's, when uniformitarianism was being accepted by the scientific community, were d'Omalius' resolution of the contest between Werner's and Hutton's theories, which influenced his early career. In 1833, with the aim of completing an introduction to the science that he called "inorganic natural history," he published a 900-page tome on astronomy, meteorology, and mineralogy, the *Introduction à la géologie*.

While d'Omalius nominally eschewed hypotheses, he early adopted the catastrophic idea of craters of elevation, and he was one of the first to accept glacial concepts. D'Omalius was, in 1831, an early defender of the theory of organic evolution, rejecting Cuvier's theory of successive creations as a "purely gratuitous hypothesis" (*Éléments de géologie*, pp. 526–527). He believed that species are not absolutely fixed, but change in response to changes in environment. Domestication, in which man alters species by controlling nutrition, for instance, is strong analogical evidence for similar processes in nature. While he rejected the notion that man had developed from a polyp, he did believe that the human species had evolved to some extent, suggesting that if man had existed at the beginning of the coal age, then at that time he must have possessed lungs permitting him to live in an atmosphere with more carbon dioxide than his lungs now allow. Contemporary man's racial differentiation similarly resulted from changes in environment.

In his later years d'Omalius was reluctant to accept Charles Darwin's theory of the origin of species. He agreed that natural selection occurs and alters species to a small degree, but he did not think natural selection is powerful enough to explain the major developments in paleontological series. He continued to believe that only environmental changes were sufficient to make major alterations in species.

D'Omalius' evolutionary views were undoubtedly inspired by Lamarck and Geoffroy St.-Hilaire, whose famous debate with Cuvier over evolution had occurred in 1830, but they also derived from a fundamental belief in vital forces. D'Omalius thought that the hypothesis of physical-chemical forces was unable to explain living phenomena; rather, he believed that "each form of living being is determined by a special force" ("Quatrième note sur les forces naturelles," in *Bulletin de l'Académie royale des sciences . . . de Belgique*, **32** [1871], 48–49). He conceived of the vital forces as analogous to the director of an industrial plant who oversees the assembly of a product according to his design. The vital forces thus directed organic responses to environmental change, thereby making evolution possible. This concept of vital force was compatible with the concept of an immortal soul—a matter of importance to d'Omalius, who was a practicing Catholic.

D'Omalius d'Halloy was a member of the Royal Academy of Sciences, Letters, and Fine Arts of Belgium and a foreign member of the Academy of Sciences (Paris).

BIBLIOGRAPHY

I. ORIGINAL WORKS. Most of d'Omalius' articles were published in the *Journal des mines* and the *Annales des mines*, its successor; and the *Bulletin* and *Mémoires* of the Royal Academy of Sciences, Letters, and Fine Arts of Belgium. Scattered pieces of correspondence are listed in the *Catalogue générale des manuscrits des bibliothèques publiques en France*, **48, 55**; and "Paris: Tome II," *passim*.

His most important works are "Essai sur la géologie du nord de la France," in *Journal des mines*, **24** (1808), 123–158, 271–318, 345–392, 439–466; "Observations sur un essai de carte géologique de la France, des Pays-Bas, et des contrées voisines," in *Annales des mines*, **7** (1823), 353–376; *Éléments de géologie* (Paris, 1831); *Introduction à la géologie ou première partie des éléments d'histoire naturelle inorganique, comprenant des notions d'astronomie, de météorologie et de minéralogie* (Paris, 1833); and *Coup d'oeil sur la géologie de la Belgique* (Brussels, 1842).

II. SECONDARY LITERATURE. The best biographical memoir is J. Guequier, "Omalius d'Halloy," in *Biographie nationale . . . de Belgique*, **16** (1901), 157–166, with partial bibliography. There is a detailed biography by Jules Gosselet, in *Bulletin de la Société géologique de France*, **6** (1878), 453–467, which succeeds the major study by

E. Dupont, "Notice sur la vie et les travaux de J. B. J. d'Omalius d'Halloy," in *Annuaire de l'Académie royale de Belgique*, **42** (1876), 181–296, with a complete bibliography.

RONALD C. TOBEY

OMAR KHAYYAM. See **al-Khayyāmī.**

OMORI, FUSAKICHI (*b.* Fukui, Japan, 30 October 1868; *d.* Tokyo, Japan, 8 November 1923), *seismology*.

Omori entered the College of Science of the Imperial University, Tokyo, in 1886. After graduating in physics in 1890, he turned his attention to the then rapidly emerging science of seismology. He became a lecturer at the university in 1893; and after some further study in Italy and Germany he became professor of seismology in 1897, a post which he held until his death. During this period he was secretary of the Japanese Committee for the Prevention of Earthquake Disasters, becoming noted as Japan's foremost seismologist of the time and one of the world's great early seismologists.

Omori's work was inspired by Seikei Sekiya and by John Milne, who in Tokyo had become one of the great pioneers of modern seismology. Under Milne's encouragement Omori made the first precise studies of earthquake aftershocks and published an important memoir on this subject in 1894. His studies, principally of a great earthquake in the Japanese provinces of Mino and Owari in 1891, led him to evolve a formula, still quoted, for the rate of falloff of aftershocks following major earthquakes.

Omori is probably most noted today for his work in designing seismological instruments. One of these, a horizontal-pendulum-type seismograph, was used in many countries and, with certain modifications, is still in use in some observatories. Omori was the first to experiment with the tiltmeter, an instrument designed to measure small tilting of geological blocks before, during, and after large earthquakes. An important innovation, this instrument led to the gathering of much information useful in predicting earthquakes.

Omori carried out pioneering work on earthquake zoning—the division of a region into areas of greater and less earthquake risk. He showed, incidentally, that destructive Japanese earthquakes were centered predominantly under the steeply sloping ocean floors on the Pacific side of Japan, a result of some importance to modern theories of earthquake occurrence.

Omori's contributions touched on practically all aspects of seismology, and his published papers are numerous. Further topics treated by him include the characteristics of earthquake motions as recorded on seismograms; detailed measurements of periods, displacements, and accelerations of the motions; the location of earthquake sources from seismograph records; the evolution of earthquake intensity scales based on acceleration measurements; experiments on the overturning of brick columns on shaking tables designed to simulate earthquakes; measurements of vibrations of buildings, bridges, chimneys, and towers during earthquakes; and the compilation of earthquake catalogs. He was also interested in the mechanism of volcanoes and used seismic methods in studying them. Omori also applied his ideas in investigations of large earthquakes in India, California, Sicily, and Formosa.

Omori's approach was that of the practical physicist. It has been stated that his achievements, important as they are, could have been greatly enhanced had he been more mathematically minded. But that judgment does not detract from his central importance in maintaining unbroken the distinguished reputation of Japanese seismological research since Milne's time.

On 1 September 1923 Omori, who had gone to Australia to attend a Pan-Pacific Science Congress, visited the Riverview Observatory in Sydney. While he was there, the seismographs started to trace out records of a large distant earthquake. This event proved to be a great earthquake in the province of Kanto, Japan, which caused the loss of 140,000 lives and left Tokyo in ruins. During Omori's return by sea to Japan, his health declined sharply. He died shortly after his return in the university hospital close by the wrecked buildings where he had carried out his lifework.

BIBLIOGRAPHY

Omori's many seismological papers, some of which were written in English, appeared mainly in Japanese journals, especially *Publications of the Imperial Earthquake Investigation Committee, Transactions of the Seismological Society of Japan*, and *Journal of the College of Science, Imperial University of Tokyo*. Other papers were published in *Bollettino della Società sismologica italiana*. Omori's major papers include "On the Aftershocks of Earthquakes," in *Journal of the College of Science, Imperial University of Tokyo*, **7** (1895), 111–200; and "Materials for the Earthquake History of Japan From the Earliest Times Down to 1866," which is *Publications of the Imperial Earthquake Investigation Committee*, **46**, nos. 1 and 2 (1904), written in Japanese with S. Sekiya.

On Omori's life and work, see Charles Davison, *The Founders of Seismology* (Cambridge, 1927), ch. 11;

publication details (without titles) of about 100 of Omori's papers are given.

See also *Who's Who in Japan* (Tokyo, 1912), 691.

K. E. BULLEN

ONNES, HEIKE KAMERLINGH. See **Kamerlingh Onnes, Heike.**

OPPEL, ALBERT (*b.* Hohenheim, Württemberg, Germany, 19 December 1831; *d.* Munich, Germany, 22 December 1865), *paleontology, biostratigraphy.*

Oppel was the son of a professor at the agricultural college in Hohenheim, near Stuttgart. He spent most of his school years in Stuttgart, where he was introduced to geology and mineralogy by J. G. von Kurr. In 1851 he entered the University of Tübingen, where he became one of Quenstedt's most talented students. Oppel was a passionate and gifted collector, and even as a student he amassed a first-rate collection of fossils of the Württemberg Jurassic.

Oppel received his doctorate in 1853 with the dissertation "Über den Mittleren Lias in Schwaben." In the following years he visited the Jurassic exposures in Germany, France, England, and Switzerland and met the most important investigators of the Jurassic in these countries. He formed a particularly close friendship with d'Orbigny in Paris. In 1858 he became an assistant to Andreas Wagner at the Bavarian State Paleontological Collection in Munich. Oppel became an assistant professor there in 1860 and, following Wagner's death in 1861, was appointed full professor of paleontology and curator of the paleontological collections at the University of Munich—posts he held until his death. In 1861 he married Anna Herbort, a friend of his sister; they had two children. Their younger child died at the beginning of December 1865. Soon afterward Oppel fell ill and died of typhoid fever at the age of thirty-four.

With his dissertation Oppel laid the foundation for his scientific lifework, the investigation of the Jurassic system. His fundamental work was *Die Juraformation Englands, Frankreichs und des südwestlichen Deutschlands* (1856–1858). Previously the Jurassic deposits of these countries had been subdivided according to local, and frequently lithological, features. Oppel showed, however, that a subdivision may be based solely on paleontological content—that is, on certain faunal species or assemblages—even when the lithological character of the sediments involved is quite varied. By means of fossils he divided the Jurassic formation into thirty-three sections, which he called zones. Each zone was characterized by a number of typical animal species, mostly ammonites. Thus the Jurassic deposits of western Europe were correlated independently of their lithology.

Like d'Orbigny, whose methodology he followed, Oppel based his stratigraphic division on the acceptance of sharply delineated faunal assemblages or faunal species that suddenly appear and disappear. This approach presupposed Linnaeus' concept of the immutability of species and Cuvier's catastrophism. When Darwin's work on the origin of species appeared in 1859, Oppel experienced a great inner conflict. He accepted the theory of evolution only hesitatingly, in the last years of his life. Nevertheless, his concept of the zone is an indispensable resource of modern biostratigraphy, despite the altered theoretical foundations.

Following the appearance of his comparative studies on the Jurassic, Oppel began publishing *Paläontologische Mittheilungen* at Munich. The first five essays, which he himself wrote, dealt chiefly with the invertebrates of the Jurassic and demonstrated his taxonomic acuity. The nearness of the Alps directed his attention to problems of Alpine Jurassic stratigraphy, and in his last work (1865) he distinguished the Tithonian stage. In this designation he included the boundary layers between the Jurassic and Cretaceous in the Alpine and transalpine regions and characterized them through the ammonites they contained. Oppel devoted much time and energy to his collections, and he enriched them to an extraordinary degree; further expanded by his successor Zittel, they became world famous.

BIBLIOGRAPHY

I. ORIGINAL WORKS. Oppel's writings include *Die Juraformation Englands, Frankreichs und des südwestlichen Deutschlands* (Stuttgart, 1856–1858); *Paläontologische Mittheilungen* . . ., 5 pts. (Stuttgart, 1862–1865); and "Die tithonische Etage," in *Zeitschrift der Deutschen geologischen Gesellschaft*, **17** (1865), 535–558.

II. SECONDARY LITERATURE. See F. von Hochstetter, "Zur Erinnerung an Dr. Albert Oppel," in *Jahrbuch der Geologischen Reichsanstalt*, **16** (1866), 59–67; J. G. von Kurr, "Nekrolog des Professor Dr. Albert Oppel," in *Jahreshefte des Vereins für vaterländische Naturkunde in Württemberg*, **23** (1867), 26–30; K. Lambrecht and W. and A. Quenstedt, "Palaeontologi. Catalogus biobibliographicus," in *Fossilium catalogus*, **2**, pt. 72 (1938), 320; and the obituaries by K. F. P. von Martius, in *Sitzungsberichte der Bayerischen Akademie der Wissenschaften zu München*, **1** (1866), 380–386, with bibliography; W. W. Smyth, in *Quarterly Journal of the Geological Society of London*, **23** (1867), "Proceedings," 48–49; and H. Woodward, in *Geological Magazine*, **3** (1866), 95–96, with bibliography.

HEINZ TOBIEN

OPPENHEIM, SAMUEL (*b.* Braunsberg, Moravia [now Brušperk, Czechoslovakia], 19 November 1857; *d.* Vienna, Austria, 15 August 1928), *astronomy*.

After leaving the Gymnasium at Teschen, Austrian Silesia, Oppenheim began his studies of mathematics, physics, and astronomy in 1875 at the University of Vienna. His teachers included Boltzmann, Petzval, Stefan, and Weiss. In 1878 he had to undergo a year of military service. He obtained his teaching diploma in mathematics and physics in 1880 and was employed as a teacher at the Akademisches Gymnasium in Vienna. From 1883 onward, he also worked at the university observatory. After receiving the Ph.D., he became assistant astronomer and in 1889 lecturer in astronomy. From 1888 he worked for some time as associate astronomer at Kuffner's private observatory at Ottakring, then a suburb of Vienna. In order to have a safe economic basis, Oppenheim again accepted employment as a teacher in secondary schools: in Vienna (1891), Arnau, Bohemia (1896), and Karolinenthal, near Prague (1899). He also gave lectures in astronomy at Charles University, where in 1902 he became associate professor. In 1911 he was finally called to Vienna and appointed full professor at the university. Oppenheim became a member of the Astronomische Gesellschaft in 1889 and of the Austrian Academy of Sciences in 1920.

The major part of Oppenheim's work was devoted to theoretical astronomy. He studied the influence of rotation on the shape of heavenly bodies, and he published valuable contributions to the three-body and *n*-body problem and to the theory of gravitation. A considerable part of his work dealt with the motions of the stars and with stellar statistics. Oppenheim also performed many numerical calculations of the orbits of comets and minor planets, and he also promoted astrophysics by a great number of visual and photographic observations. After 1917 he was editor of the astronomy volumes of the *Encyklopädie der Mathematischen Wissenschaften*.

BIBLIOGRAPHY

I. ORIGINAL WORKS. Oppenheim's works include "Eine neue Integration der Differential-Gleichungen der Planetenbewegung," in *Sitzungsberichte der Akademie der Wissenschaften in Wien*, **87** (1883); "Rotation und Präcession eines flüssigen Sphäroids," *ibid.*, **92** (1885); "Eine

Gleichung, deren Wurzeln die mittleren Bewegungen im n-Körperproblem sind," in *Publikationen der von Kuffnerschen Sternwarte*, **1** (1889); "Bahnbestimmung des Kometen 1846," in *Sitzungsberichte der Akademie der Wissenschaften in Wien*, **99** (1890); "Bahnbestimmung des Planeten (290) Bruna," *ibid.*, **100** (1891); and "Ausmessung des Sternhaufens G.C. Nr. 1166," in *Publikationen der von Kuffnerschen Sternwarte*, **3** (1894).

See also "Bestimmung der Kräfte, durch welche die Bewegung dreier Körper in gegebenen Curven erzeugt werden," *ibid.*, **3** (1894); *Zur Lehre von den Bewegungen der Doppelsterne* (Vienna, 1894); *Fortpflanzungsgeschwindigkeit der Gravitation* (Vienna, 1895); "Specielle periodische Lösungen im Problem der drei Körper," in *Publikationen der von Kuffnerschen Sternwarte*, **4** (1896); *Kritik des Newton'schen Gravitationsgesetzes* (Prague, 1903); "Bestimmung der Periode einer periodischen Erscheinung nebst Anwendung auf die Theorie des Erdmagnetismus," in *Sitzungsberichte der Akademie der Wissenschaften in Wien*, **118** (1909); "Die Eigenbewegungen der Fixsterne," in *Denkschriften der Akademie der Wissenschaften*, **87** (1912); **92** (1916); **93** (1917); **97** (1921); "Zur Frage nach der Fortpflanzungsgeschwindigkeit der Gravitation," in *Annalen der Physik*, **53** (1917); "Theorie der Gleichgewichtsfiguren der Himmelskörper," in *Encyklopädie der Mathematischen Wissenschaften* (Leipzig, 1919); and *Das astronomische Weltbild im Wandel der Zeit* (Leipzig, 1920).

Other works include "Die scheinbare Verteilung der Sterne," in *Sitzungsberichte der Akademie der Wissenschaften in Wien*, **130** (1921); "Statistische Untersuchungen über die Bewegung der kleinen Planeten," in *Denkschriften der Akademie der Wissenschaften*, **97** (1921); *Weltuntergang in Sage und Wissenschaft* (1921), written with K. Ziegler; *Kometen* (Vienna, 1922); "Perioden der Sonnenflecken," in *Sitzungsberichte der Akademie der Wissenschaften in Wien*, **137** (1928). Besides, there are about thirty papers that are mainly concerned with the determination of orbits of planets, comets, stellar statistics and proper motions, and with theoretical mechanics; these papers are published in the *Astronomische Nachrichten*, **113** (1886), to **232** (1928), and in other periodicals.

II. Secondary Literature. See W. E. Bernheimer, in *Beiträge zur Geophysik*, **20** (1928), in *Forschungen und Fortschritte*, **4** (1928), and in *Nature*, **122** (London, 1928), 657; K. Graff, in *Almanach. Österreichische Akademie der Wissenschaften*, **79** (1929), 183–186; J. Rheden, in *Astronomische Nachrichten*, **233** (1928), 295; C. Wirtz, in *Vierteljahrsschrift der Astronomischen Gesellschaft*, **64** (1929), 20–30, with a portrait of Oppenheim; and Poggendorff, vols. III, 988; IV, 1096–1097; V, 923; VI, 1913.

Konradin Ferrari d'Occhieppo

OPPENHEIMER, J. ROBERT (*b.* New York, N.Y., 22 April 1904; *d.* Princeton, New Jersey, 18 February 1967), *theoretical physics.*

Robert Oppenheimer achieved great distinction in four very different ways: through his personal research, as a teacher, as director of Los Alamos, and as the elder statesman of postwar physics. These different activities belong to different periods, except that his role as teacher overlaps in time with several of these periods. We may therefore review these different contributions separately, while following a chronological order.

J. Robert Oppenheimer was the son of Julius Oppenheimer, who had immigrated as a young man from Germany.[1] The father was a successful businessman, and the family was well-to-do. His mother, the former Ella Freedman, was a painter of near professional standard, and both parents had taste for art and music.

As a boy Oppenheimer showed a wide curiosity and the ability to learn quickly. He went to the Ethical Culture School in New York, a school with high academic standards and liberal ideas. He went as a student to Harvard in 1922, and in spite of following a very broad curriculum, which included classical languages as well as chemistry and physics, he completed the four-year undergraduate course in three years and graduated *summa cum laude* in 1925.

With all the breadth of his interests, Oppenheimer was quite clear that his own subject was physics. During his undergraduate course he profited much from the contact with Percy Bridgman, an eminent physicist who himself had wide-ranging interests and whose publications dealt with topics far beyond the field of his own experiments; they included philosophical questions.

After graduating, Oppenheimer went to Europe; and during his four years of travel he established himself as a theoretical physicist.

Research in Quantum Mechanics. The year 1925 marked the beginning of an exhilarating period in theoretical physics. During that year Heisenberg's first paper on the new quantum mechanics appeared, and Dirac started to develop his own version of Heisenberg's theory in a paper which appeared in the same year. Schrödinger's first paper on his wave equation was published early in 1926. Up to that time the principles of the quantum theory had been grafted onto the classical equations of mechanics, with which they were not consistent. The resulting rules sometimes gave unique predictions which agreed with observation; sometimes the answers were ambiguous; and sometimes the rules could not be applied at all. The new ideas showed the way of obtaining a logically consistent and mathematically clear description, and it looked as if all the old paradoxes of atomic theory would resolve themselves.

This started a period of intense activity, during which all atomic phenomena had to be reexamined in the light of the new ideas. Oppenheimer's quickness in grasping new ideas helped him to play a part in this process. His first paper was submitted for publication in May 1926, less than four years from his entering Harvard and less than a year after Heisenberg's first paper on quantum mechanics.[2] It shows him in full command of the new methods, with which he showed that the frequencies and intensities of molecular band spectra could be obtained unambiguously from the new mechanics. A second paper, submitted in July, is concerned with the hydrogen atom;[3] by this time he was making use of the full apparatus of matrix mechanics developed by Born, Heisenberg, and E. P. Jordan, of the alternative techniques of Dirac, and of Schrödinger's wave mechanics. These two papers were written in Cambridge, and he acknowledged help from Ralph H. Fowler and Paul Dirac.

In the second paper Oppenheimer raises the question of the continuous spectrum and discusses the question of how to formulate the normalization of the wave functions for that case. This was the beginning of his interest in a range of problems which were to occupy him for some time.

In 1926 Max Born invited Oppenheimer to come to Göttingen, where he continued his work on transitions in the continuous spectrum, leading to his first calculations of the emission of X rays. He also developed, jointly with Born, the method for handling the electronic, vibrational, and rotational degrees of freedom of molecules, now one of the classical parts of quantum theory, referred to as the "Born-Oppenheimer method."[4] He obtained his Ph.D. degree in the spring of 1927.

Oppenheimer remained in Europe until 1929, spending some time with Paul Ehrenfest in Leiden and with Wolfgang Pauli in Zurich; the influence of both these men helped further to deepen his understanding of the subject. He continued with the work on radiative effects in the continuous spectrum, which he recognized as one of the important and difficult problems of the time, and found ways of improving the approximations used, which still serve as a pattern for work in this field. Among his minor papers, one deals with electron pickup by ions, a problem which requires the use of nonorthogonal wave functions.[5]

In 1929 Oppenheimer accepted academic positions both at the University of California, Berkeley, and at the California Institute of Technology; and between 1929 and 1942 he divided his time between these two institutions. The list of his papers during this period might almost serve as a guide to what was important in physics at that time. He was now at the top of his form in research work, and he knew what was important, so that he did not waste his time on pedantic detail. In some of these papers Oppenheimer struggled with key problems which were not yet ripe for solution, such as the difficulties of the electromagnetic self-energy, or the paradox of the "wrong" statistics of the nitrogen nucleus (wrong because, before the discovery of the neutron, nuclei were believed to consist of protons and electrons).[6] But on others he was able to take important steps forward. He saw the importance of Dirac's idea to avoid the difficulty of negative energy states for electrons by assuming them all filled except for a few holes, which were then positively charged particles. He showed, however, that Dirac could not be right in identifying these as protons, since they would have to have the same mass as electrons.[7] Thus he practically predicted the positron three years before its discovery by Carl Anderson.

When cosmic-ray experiments showed serious contradiction with theory, Oppenheimer studied the possibility that this might indicate a breakdown of the accepted quantum theory of radiation.[8] When the discovery of the meson resolved the paradox, he took great interest in the properties of the new particle. He also developed, in a paper with J. F. Carlson, an elegant method for investigating electron-photon showers in cosmic rays.[9] In the 1930's the cyclotron and other accelerators opened up the atomic nucleus to serious study, and Oppenheimer participated in asking important questions and in answering some of them. His paper with G. Volkoff shows a very early interest in stars with massive neutron cores.[10]

During the California period Oppenheimer proved to be an outstanding teacher of theoretical physics. He attracted many pupils, both graduate students and more senior collaborators, many of whom, under his inspiration, became first-rate scholars. His important qualities as a teacher were those which characterized his research: his flair for the key question, his quick understanding, and his readiness to admit ignorance and to invite others to share his struggle for the answer. His influence on his pupils was enhanced by his perceptive interest in people and by his habit of informal and charming hospitality. After his marriage in 1940 his wife, the former Katherine Harrison, helped maintain this easy and warm hospitality.

Oppenheimer still maintained a great breadth of interests, adding even Sanskrit to the languages he could, and did, read. At first his interests were exclusively academic; and he showed little interest in political questions, or in the national and world events of the day. But in the mid-1930's he became acutely aware of the disturbing state of the world—unemployment at home, Hitler, Mussolini, and the Spanish Civil War in Europe. He became interested in politics and, like many liberal intellectuals of the day, became for a time involved with the ideas of left-wing groups.

The list of publications by Oppenheimer and his group shows a break in 1941, and this marks almost the end of his personal research (the exception being three papers published after the war) but by no means of his influence on the development of physics.

Atomic Energy: Los Alamos. The change was the result of Oppenheimer's involvement with atomic energy. After the discovery of fission he, like many others, had started thinking about the possibility of the practical release of nuclear energy. With his quick perception he was aware of the importance of fast neutrons for any possible bomb. In 1940 and 1941 the idea of releasing nuclear energy was beginning to be taken seriously. A number of groups in different universities were working on the feasibility of a nuclear reactor, and others on methods for separating uranium isotopes. The latter would ultimately lead to the production of the light isotope (U^{235}) in nearly pure form, and this is capable of sustaining a chain reaction with fast neutrons. The reactor work led to the production of plutonium, which can be used for the same purpose. While these efforts were well under way by the beginning of 1942, there was no coordinated work on the design of an atomic weapon, its critical size, methods of detonating it, and so on. Oppenheimer had attended some meetings at which such matters were discussed, and early in 1942 he was asked to take charge of the work on fast neutrons and on the problem of the atomic bomb.

On the theoretical side Oppenheimer assembled at Berkeley a conference of first-rate theoreticians, including Edward Teller, who on that occasion first suggested the possibility of a thermonuclear explosion. The work continued in a theoretical group led by Oppenheimer at Berkeley. The experimental determination of the relevant nuclear data was divided between a large number of small nuclear physics laboratories; this hampered progress, since it was difficult for these groups to maintain adequate contact, particularly in view of the secrecy with which the whole project had to be treated.

When, therefore, the United States government brought the atomic energy work under the auspices of the army and put Colonel (later General) Leslie Groves in charge of the project under the code name "Manhattan District," Oppenheimer suggested to Groves that the weapon development be concentrated in a single laboratory. This should include the theory and the nuclear physics work as well as the chemical, metallurgical, and ordnance aspects of the project. In this way the different groups could work together effectively.

Groves accepted the proposal, and on Oppenheimer's advice chose the site of a boys' boarding school at Los Alamos, New Mexico, a region Oppenheimer knew and loved—he had a ranch there. The remoteness of the site made access and transport problems difficult but seemed to have an advantage in reducing contacts with the outside—and therefore the risk of leakage of information.

Groves not only followed Oppenheimer's advice in the creation and location of the laboratory, but he selected Oppenheimer as its director. This was a bold decision, since Oppenheimer was a theoretician with no experience of administration or of organizing experimental work. Events proved Groves right, and the work of the laboratory was extremely effective. In the view of most of the wartime members of Los Alamos, its success owed much to Oppenheimer's leadership.

He attracted a strong team of first-rate scientists, who came because of their respect for Oppenheimer as a scientist and because of his evident sense of purpose. Inside the laboratory he was able to maintain completely free exchange of information between its scientific members; in other words, in exchange for the isolation of the laboratory and the restrictions on travel which its members had to accept, there was none of the "compartmentalization" favored in other atomic energy laboratories for the sake of security. Oppenheimer was able to delegate responsibility and to make people feel they were being trusted. At the same time his quick perception enabled him to remain in touch with all phases of the work. When there were major problems or major decisions to be taken, he guided the discussions of the people concerned in the same spirit of a joint search for the answer in which he had guided the discussions with his students. In the work he did not spare himself, and in response he obtained a sustained effort from all his staff.

It seems that the laboratory was set up just in time, because when the design of the plutonium bomb was ready, enough plutonium was available for the first bomb. The plutonium bomb required a greater design and development effort than the uranium bomb, since the more intense neutron background required a much more rapid assembly from subcritical conditions to the final, highly critical configuration. Failing this, a stray neutron is likely to set off the chain reaction when the assembly is only just critical, giving an explosion of very poor efficiency.

When the test of the first bomb at Alamogordo demonstrated the power of the new weapon, all spectators felt a terrified awe of the new power, mixed with pride and satisfaction at the success of their endeavors. Initially some were more conscious of the one emotion, some of the other. Oppenheimer, whose attitude to his own faults was as unmerciful as to those of others, if not more so, admitted later that he could not resist feeling satisfaction with the key part he had played in the work. Many accounts have quoted the verses from his Sanskrit studies of the *Bhagavad-Gita* which went through his mind at the time of the test, the first referring to the "radiance of a thousand suns" and the other saying, "I am become Death, the destroyer of worlds." Besides the awareness of the technical achievement, Oppenheimer clearly did not lose sight of the seriousness of the implications.

None of this was public knowledge until 6 August 1945, when the first uranium bomb was dropped on Hiroshima. The implications of the decision to use the bomb to destroy a city will continue to occupy historians for a long time. Oppenheimer played some part in this decision: he was one of a panel of four scientists (the others being A. H. Compton, E. Fermi, and E. O. Lawrence) who were asked in May 1945 to discuss the case for the military use of the bomb on Japan. They were told that it would be impossible to cancel or delay the planned invasion of Japan, which was sure to be very costly in lives, unless Japan surrendered beforehand. Their opinion, which Oppenheimer supported, was that a demonstration on an uninhabited island would not be effective, and that the only way in which the atom bomb could be used to end the war was by actual use on a "military" target in a populated area. Today, in retrospect, many people, including many scientists, deplore this advice and the use of the bomb. Oppenheimer commented in 1962: "I believe there was very little deliberation. . . . The actual military plans at that time . . . were clearly much more terrible in every way and for everyone concerned than the use of the bomb. Nevertheless, my own feeling is that if the bombs were to be used there could have been more effective warning and much less wanton killing. . . ."[11] He remained for the rest of his life acutely conscious of the responsibility he bore for his part in developing the weapon and in the decision to use it.

The Aftermath of the Bomb: Princeton. At the end of 1945 Oppenheimer returned to California. This did not mean, however, returning to an ivory tower. He was by now a national figure, and his advice much in demand; he was also very seriously concerned with the issues raised by the invention of atomic weapons.

He took part in the drafting of the "Acheson-Lilienthal Report," which proposed the international control of atomic energy. Most of the language of this report is undoubtedly Oppenheimer's and so, probably, are many of its ideas. The authors of this report wrote it in a generous spirit: international control of the new weapons would be used to ensure peace and to prevent any nation's threatening another with the formidable new weapons. It probably never had much chance of becoming a political reality. A proposal embodying the outline of the report, but hardly its spirit, was presented to the United Nations by Bernard Baruch as the "Baruch Plan," but nothing came of it.

In 1946 the Atomic Energy Commission was set up under the McMahon Act, which provided for civilian control of atomic energy. The first proposal, the May-Johnson Bill, which would have led to military control, was defeated very largely because of the opposition from scientists, although Oppenheimer was prepared to accept it. The commission appointed a General Advisory Committee, with Oppenheimer as chairman; and he served in that capacity until 1952. The committee did more than give technical advice; it had great influence on the policy of the commission. Oppenheimer's role as chairman was not to dominate opinion but to clarify the issues and to formulate people's thoughts. In addition to the General Advisory Committee, he served on numerous other committees concerned with policy questions relating to atomic weapons and defense.

In October 1947, Oppenheimer moved to Princeton, New Jersey, to become director of the Institute for Advanced Study. Until then the Institute had been a kind of retreat for great scientists and scholars who wanted to get on with their studies in peace. Under Oppenheimer's regime the population of the Institute grew in number, and it included many young scientists, mostly as short-term members for a year or two. They included many visitors from other countries. Oppenheimer was an active member of the physics department and usually presided at seminar meetings.

Under Oppenheimer's influence the physics group became one of the centers at which the current problems of modern physics were most clearly understood. Many colleagues came to discuss their ideas with Oppenheimer, and to do so meant exposing one's thoughts to penetrating scrutiny and sometimes to withering criticism. Oppenheimer now had less time for physics than in the prewar days, and he had to form his judgments more rapidly. He was fallible, and there were occasions when he violently and effectively attacked some unfortunate speaker whose ideas were perhaps not proved but were worth debating; there were other instances when he hailed as very promising ideas which later proved barren.

The early Princeton years were a time when there was again a buoyant optimism in physics. The theory of electrons and their electromagnetic field had been stagnant for many years because of the infinities predicted by quantum theory for the field energy of a point charge. The discovery of the "Lamb shift" in the hydrogen spectrum showed that there were some questions to which theoretical answers were needed, and the attempts to find the answers showed how one could bypass the troublesome infinities. S. Tomonaga, J. Schwinger, R. P. Feynman, and F. J. Dyson developed consistent formulations for the new form of the theory, and it was hoped that they could be extended to the proton and neutron and their interactions with the newly discovered meson field. It was a time of intense debate and discussion, and much of this took place at small ad hoc meetings of theoreticians, at which Oppenheimer was at his best in guiding discussion and in helping people to understand each other (and sometimes themselves). The phrase he used in an interview to describe the work at the Institute, "What we do not know we try to explain to each other," is very appropriate for these sessions. He had always had a remarkable gift for finding the right phrase, and he had now become an absolute master of the epigram.

While he did not resume personal research on any substantial scale (he was coauthor of three papers on physics after the war, one of them being a criticism of somebody else's theory), Oppenheimer's participation in meetings at the Institute and elsewhere was still a major factor in the development of ideas in physics.

As director of the Institute, Oppenheimer was responsible also for the policy in other fields, including pure mathematics and history. Here the breadth of his knowledge was a unique qualification. He did not, of course, take part in the work of the other groups as he did in physics, but he could understand what was being done and could comment in a manner respected by the experts.

Throughout the postwar period Oppenheimer wrote and lectured much. At first the subject was predominantly atomic energy and its implications, and the scheme for its international control. Later he became more concerned with the relations between the scientist and society and, from this, with the problem of conveying an adequate understanding of science to the layman. In his Reith lectures on the B.B.C., "Science and the Common Understanding," he attempted to set out what science is about.[12] The language of such lectures was probably not easily followed in detail by the nonscientist, but it had a poetic quality which to many listeners brought the subject closer.

The "Oppenheimer Case." In December 1953, Oppenheimer was informed that his security clearance—that is, his access to secret information—was being withdrawn, because of accusations that his loyalty was in doubt. He exerted his right to ask for hearings, and he was exposed to the grueling experience of over three weeks' quasi-judicial hearings, in which all his past was exposed to detailed scrutiny. The charges were in part his opposition in 1949 to a crash program for developing the hydrogen bomb, and in part his contacts or associations in the late 1930's and early 1940's with Communists and fellow travelers, contacts which had been known to the A.E.C. many years before and had then not been considered sufficiently derogatory to impede his clearance.

It is impossible to understand how these charges could be raised without remembering the atmosphere of hysterical fear of Communism of the Joseph McCarthy era and also without noting that Oppenheimer had made many enemies, who were delighted at this opportunity of curbing his influence. Some of these enemies were people he had bested in public debate, whom his devastating logic had not only shown to be wrong but also made to appear ridiculous. Others were people interested in military policy who feared his influence, which could act contrary to their interests.

The hearings before the three-man Personnel Security Board were originally intended to be confidential, but eventually the transcript was published.[13] It remains an interesting historical document. The board found that Oppenheimer was "a loyal citizen" but, by a two-to-one majority, that he was to blame for opposing the hydrogen-bomb program and later was lacking in enthusiasm for it.

The report of the board went to the Atomic Energy Commission. The commissioners did not uphold the board's (majority) decision censuring Oppenheimer for his views on the hydrogen bomb—this would have caused a powerful reaction in the scientific community—but confirmed the withdrawal of his clearance, in a majority verdict, mainly on grounds of "defects of character." This was opposed by one of the commissioners, the physicist Henry Smyth, who wrote a minority report in favor of Oppenheimer and criticizing the arguments of his colleagues.[14]

Oppenheimer continued as director of the Institute and with his writing and lecturing. On many occasions audiences at his lectures gave him ovations clearly intended to express their sympathy for him and their indignation at the treatment he had received.

In 1963, when the McCarthy era was an embarrassing memory, when many of the people who had conducted the Oppenheimer investigation and made decisions had been succeeded by others, and when tempers had cooled, it was decided to make a gesture of reconciliation. Oppenheimer was given the Enrico Fermi Award for 1963, a prize of high prestige awarded by the Atomic Energy Commission. The award is usually conferred by the president, and John F. Kennedy had the intention of doing so when he was assassinated. It was then conferred by Lyndon Johnson, and Oppenheimer acknowledged it with the words he had intended to say to President Kennedy: "I think it is just possible . . . that it has taken some charity and some courage for you to make this award today."

Oppenheimer knew for almost a year that he had throat cancer, and he could contemplate this fact and talk about it as lucidly as about a conclusion in physics.

NOTES

1. There has been controversy whether in "J. Robert" the "J" stood for "Julius." P. M. Stern (footnote at the beginning of ch. 2 of the book cited in the bibliography) quotes evidence that this was the case. We use the style Oppenheimer used, with the explanation that the letter J "stood for nothing."
2. Oppenheimer, "On the Quantum Theory of Vibration-Rotation Bands," in *Proceedings of the Cambridge Philosophical Society*, **23** (1926), 327–335.
3. Oppenheimer, "On the Quantum Theory of the Problem of the Two Bodies," *ibid.*, 422–431.
4. Max Born and Oppenheimer, "Zur Quantentheorie der Molekeln," in *Annalen der Physik*, 4th ser., **84** (1927), 457–484.
5. Oppenheimer, "On the Quantum Theory of the Capture of Electrons," in *Physical Review*, **31** (1928), 349–356.
6. Oppenheimer, "Note on the Theory of the Interaction of Field and Matter," *ibid.*, **35** (1930), 461–477; P. Ehrenfest and Oppenheimer, "Note on the Statistics of Nuclei," *ibid.*, **37** (1931), 333–338.
7. Oppenheimer, "On the Theory of Electrons and Protons," *ibid.*, **35** (1930), 562–563.
8. Oppenheimer, "Are the Formulas for the Absorption of High Energy Radiation Valid?" *ibid.*, **47** (1935), 44–52.
9. Oppenheimer and J. F. Carlson, "On Multiplicative Showers," *ibid.*, **51** (1937), 220–231.
10. Oppenheimer and G. Volkoff, "On Massive Neutron Cores," *ibid.*, **55** (1937), 374–381.
11. Oppenheimer, *The Flying Trapeze*, the Whidden lectures for 1962 (London, 1964), pp. 59–60.
12. Oppenheimer, *Science and the Common Understanding*, Reith lectures, British Broadcasting Corporation, Nov. 1953 (New York, 1953; London, 1954).
13. United States Atomic Energy Commission, *In the Matter of J. Robert Oppenheimer. Transcript of Hearings Before the Personnel Security Board* (Washington, D.C., 1954).
14. United States Atomic Energy Commission, *In the Matter of J. Robert Oppenheimer. Text of Principal Documents* (Washington, D.C., 1954).

BIBLIOGRAPHY

I. ORIGINAL WORKS. A full list of Oppenheimer's writings can be found in the article by H. A. Bethe, in *Biographical Memoirs of Fellows of the Royal Society*, **14** (1968), 391–416.

II. SECONDARY LITERATURE. There is as yet no book-length biography of Oppenheimer. Among his obituary notices the most important are the one by Bethe, cited above, and the record of speeches at a memorial meeting by R. Serber, V. F. Weisskopf, A. Pais, and G. T. Seaborg, in *Physics Today*, **20**, no. 10 (Oct. 1967), 34–53. The dual biography by Nuel Pharr Davis, *Lawrence and Oppenheimer* (New York, 1968), has been strongly criticized by many reviewers—for instance, F. Oppenheimer, in *Physics Today*, **22**, no. 2 (Feb. 1969), 77–80.

Numerous books are primarily concerned with the "Oppenheimer case" but bring in much biographical material. The most scholarly of these is P. M. Stern, *The Oppenheimer Case; Security on Trial* (New York, 1969). In addition there are C. P. Curtis, *The Oppenheimer Case. The Trial of a Security System* (New York, 1955); and J. Major, *The Oppenheimer Hearing* (London, 1971). H. Chevalier, *Oppenheimer, The Story of a Friendship* (New York, 1965), criticizes Oppenheimer for his conduct when questioned on security; it also contains many interesting facets of Oppenheimer's life at Berkeley.

There is also a considerable literature on the history of the Manhattan Project, including Oppenheimer's part in it. The official record is *A History of the United States Atomic Energy Commission*, I, R. G. Hewlett and D. E. Anderson, Jr., *The New World* (University Park, Pa., 1962), II, R. G. Hewlett and F. Duncan, *Atomic Shield* (University Park, Pa., 1969). Other examples are Leslie R. Groves, *Now It Can Be Told* (New York, 1962); Lewis L. Strauss, *Men and Decisions* (New York, 1962); D. E. Lilienthal, *Journals*, II, *The Atomic Energy Years 1945–1950* (New York, 1964), and III, *The Venturesome Years 1950–1955* (New York, 1966); and L. Giovanetti and F. Freed, *The Decision to Drop the Bomb* (New York, 1965).

RUDOLF PEIERLS

OPPOLZER, THEODOR RITTER VON (*b.* Prague, Bohemia [now Czechoslovakia], 26 October 1841; *d.* Vienna, Austria, 26 December 1886), *astronomy, geodesy.*

His father, Johann von Oppolzer, was a leader of the Vienna school of medicine and professor at the universities of Prague, Leipzig, and Vienna. Oppolzer's first teacher, Franz Jahne, discovered and encouraged his outstanding mathematical abilities. After attending the Piaristen-Gymnasium in Vienna from 1851 to 1859 he studied medicine—in accordance with his father's wishes—and received the M.D. in 1865. Having also studied astronomy, he built a private observatory in the Josephstadt, a recently incorporated suburb of

Vienna. His main instrument, a seven-inch refracting telescope, was then probably the largest in the Austrian empire. By 1866 he had published more than seventy papers on astronomy, comprising observations, computations of the orbits of comets and asteroids, and analytical investigations of related problems. In March 1866 he became lecturer on astronomy at the University of Vienna. In 1868 he participated in the Austrian expedition to Aden to observe a solar eclipse, and in 1874 he observed the transit of Venus at Iaşi, Rumania.

Elected to the Imperial Academy of Sciences of Vienna in 1869, Oppolzer subsequently became a member of nearly every European and American learned society. In 1870 he was appointed associate professor and, in 1875, full professor of astronomy and geodesy at the University of Vienna. In 1873 he became director of the Gradmessungs-Bureau, the Austrian geodetic survey, which was very active under his direction. At the eighth conference of the Internationale Erdmessung, held at Berlin in 1886, he was elected vice-president of the International Geodetic Association. He died a few months later, after having revised the major part of the proofs of his last work, "Canon der Finsternisse."

On 1 June 1865 Oppolzer married Coelestine Mautner von Markhof, daughter of a prominent Austrian industrialist; they had six children. Three planetoids are named for two of their three daughters, Hilda and Agatha, and for his wife. A son, Egon Ritter von Oppolzer, founded the astronomical observatory at Innsbruck.

The great majority of Oppolzer's more than 300 papers deal with the determination and improvement of the orbits of comets and asteroids—sometimes based on Oppolzer's own observations—and with the computation of ephemerides derived from the orbital elements. Dissatisfied with merely routine work, Oppolzer improved existing methods: as early as 1864, for example, he developed new formulas for calculating the differential correction of planetary or cometary orbital elements directly from the deviations from the computed positions. His two-volume *Lehrbuch zur Bahnbestimmung der Cometen und Planeten* (1870–1880) comprises all the materials then necessary for understanding and determining both preliminary and definitive orbits: the basic concepts, mathematical tools, practically arranged formulas, extensive auxiliary tables, and examples drawn from the author's own experience.

About 1868 Oppolzer began to study the computation of ancient and modern eclipses, intending to compile a catalog of the relevant data of all eclipses from the beginning of reliable history, whether observations of the eclipses were actually known by him.

These data were to be computed on the basis of modern knowledge of the exact laws of solar and lunar motion. After several years of discouraging setbacks, Oppolzer realized the impossibility of completing the work within a reasonable time by using Hansen's tables, then the best available. Instead of abandoning the work, however, he devised new methods and tables that, despite their greater accuracy, were much easier to use. They were published in 1881 as "Syzygien-Tafeln für den Mond nebst ausführlicher Anweisung. . . . "

Oppolzer then organized—partly at his own expense —the immense project that resulted in the "Canon der Finsternisse." The "Canon" contains, with minor exceptions, the relevant data of every lunar and solar eclipse, with charts of the central paths of the latter, from 1207 B.C. to A.D. 2163. Oppolzer also planned a fundamental improvement of the lunar theory. Left unfinished at his death, the expansions of the derivatives necessary for this purpose were completed under the supervision of his collaborator R. Schram, who followed Oppolzer's ideas.

In his work in geodesy Oppolzer revealed uncommon administrative ability. He introduced technical improvements in the registration of time signals and in the use of the reversible pendulum for gravimetry. Many differences of longitude between primary stations of the European triangulation frame were determined by Oppolzer or under his supervision. He represented Austria with distinction at international conferences and soon won esteem for his profound knowledge. Apart from his admirable scientific qualities, he showed great social responsibility. Beloved for his generous liberality, he devoted his last public speech to the association for the welfare of sick students founded by his father.

BIBLIOGRAPHY

I. ORIGINAL WORKS. Oppolzer's works include "Entwickelung von Differentialformeln zur Verbesserung einer Planeten- oder Cometenbahn," in *Sitzungsberichte der Akademie der Wissenschaften in Wien*, **49** (1864), 271–288; "Definitive Bahnbestimmung des Planeten (58) Concordia," *ibid.*, **57** (1868), 343–383; *Lehrbuch zur Bahnbestimmung der Cometen und Planeten*, 2 vols. (Leipzig, 1870–1880; 2nd ed., rev. and enl., 1882), French trans. by Ernest Pasquier, *Traité de la détermination des orbites des comètes et des planètes* (Paris, 1886); "Über den Venusdurchgang des Jahres 1874," in *Sitzungsberichte der Akademie der Wissenschaften in Wien*, **61** (1870), 515–599; "Das Schaltbrett der österreichischen Gradmessung," *ibid.*, **69** (1874), 379–398; "Entwickelung der Differentialquotienten der wahren Anomalie und des

Radiusvectors nach der Excentricität in nahezu parabolischen Bahnen," in *Monatsberichte der Deutschen Akademie der Wissenschaften zu Berlin* (1878), 852–859; and "Syzygien-Tafeln für den Mond nebst ausführlicher Anweisung . . .," in *Publikationen der Astronomischen Gesellschaft*, **16** (1881).

See also "Ermittlung der Störungswerthe in den Coordinaten durch die Variation entsprechend gewählter Constanten," in *Denkschriften der Akademie der Wissenschaften*, **46** (1882), 45–75; "Tafeln für den Planeten (58) Concordia," *ibid.*, **47** (1883), 149–159; "Tafeln zur Berechnung der Mondesfinsternisse," *ibid.*, 243–275; "Bestimmung der Schwere mit Hilfe verschiedener Apparate," in *Zeitschrift für Instrumentenkunde*, **4** (1884), 303–316, 379–387; "Entwurf einer Mondtheorie," in *Denkschriften der Akademie der Wissenschaften*, **51** (1885), 69–105; "Canon der Finsternisse," *ibid.*, **52** (1887), 1–376, repr. as *Canon of Eclipses* (New York, 1962), with trans. of text and pref. by Owen Gingerich and Donald H. Menzel; and "Astronomische Refraction," *ibid.*, **53** (1887), 1–52.

II. Secondary Literature. Robert Schram, "Nekrolog Theodor von Oppolzer," in *Vierteljahrsschrift der Astronomischen Gesellschaft*, **22** (1887), 177–208, contains a bibliography of Oppolzer's work. See also Eduard Suess, "Bericht," in *Almanach der Akademie der Wissenschaften in Wien*, **37** (1887), 183–189, with partial bibliography.

Konradin Ferrari d'Occhieppo

ORBELI, LEON ABGAROVICH (*b.* Tsakhkadzor, Russia, 7 July 1882; *d.* Leningrad, U.S.S.R., 9 December 1958), physiology.

Orbeli was the son of Abgar Iosifovich Orbeli, a well-known jurist in Transcaucasia. After graduating from the Gymnasium in Tbilisi in 1899, he entered the Military Medical Academy in St. Petersburg. Orbeli's general biological views were formed under the influence of the lectures of the zoologist N. A. Kholodkovsky and the histologist M. A. Lavdovsky. While still a student in the second course, Orbeli studied physiology and began to work in the laboratory of I. P. Pavlov. Here he carried out his first experimental research—the activity of pepsin iron before and after the severing of the vagus nerves (1903). For the next thirty-five years, Orbeli's life and scientific career were closely connected with the work of Pavlov.

Following his graduation from the Military Medical Academy (1904), Orbeli became an intern at the Nikolai Hospital in Kronshtadt. His move to the Naval Hospital in St. Petersburg gave him the opportunity to continue his experimental research in Pavlov's laboratory. Orbeli joined Pavlov at the very height of Pavlov's research on conditioned reflexes.

In Orbeli's dissertation, "Conditioned Reflexes of the Eye in Dogs" (1908), he showed that a change in the intensity of light could serve as a conditioned stimulus for a dog, even though the dog could not distinguish the color. On Pavlov's recommendation Orbeli worked for two years with Hering in Germany, Langley and Barcroft in England, and at the Marine Biological Station in Naples.

Orbeli's scientific career was spent in the leading Russian physiological centers. He worked in the physiology departments of the Institute of Experimental Medicine; the Military Medical Academy, where he was chairman of the department from 1925 to 1950; and the First Leningrad Medical Institute, where he was also chairman from 1920 to 1930. He also worked in the physiology laboratory of P. F. Lesgaft at the Petrograd Scientific Institute in the Biological Station in Koltushakh.

After Pavlov's death Orbeli was the most prominent physiological scientist in the U.S.S.R.; he directed the I. P. Pavlov Institute of Physiology of the Academy of Sciences of the U.S.S.R., the Institute of Evolutionary Physiology and Pathology of Higher Nervous Activity in Koltushakh (now Pavlovo). In 1956 Orbeli organized the I. M. Sechenov Institute of Evolutionary Physiology (now the Institute of Evolutionary Physiology and Biochemistry of the Academy of Sciences of the U.S.S.R.).

Orbeli wrote more than 200 works on experimental and theoretical science. They embrace a varied range of problems in physiology and theoretical medicine. Most of them are grouped around the following subjects: physiology of the higher nervous activity and the sense organs; of the regularities of cerebrospinal coordination; physiology of the autonomic nervous system, the rapid development of which led to his creation of the theory of the adaptive-trophic role of the sympathetic nervous system in the organism (the classic Orbeli–Ginedinsky phenomenon, 1923); the theory of the physiological role of the cerebellum as regulator of the autonomic functions; the physiology of kidney activity and the problem of pain; and environmental physiology particularly in deep-sea diving.

Orbeli was responsible for the development of evolutionary physiology, and he proposed special experimental methods of research to study regularities of the evolution of functions. Orbeli's basic ideas in this direction are generalized in his program report "Basic Problems and Methods of Evolutionary Physiology" (1956). He created a large physiological school, and among his students were Y. M. Kreps, A. G. Ginetsinsky, A. V. Lebedinsky, and A. V. Tonkikh.

Orbeli's scientific and organizational talent was highly appreciated by the Soviet government. In 1935 he was elected an active member of the Academy of Sciences of the U.S.S.R., and in 1945 he was awarded the title of Hero of Socialist Labor. He was also a member of various foreign academies.

BIBLIOGRAPHY

Orbeli's major writings are included in *Izbrannye trudy* ("Selected Works") 5 vols. (Moscow–Leningrad, 1961–1968).

On Orbeli and his work see L. G. Leybson, in L. A. Orbeli, *Izbrannye trudy*, **1**, 13–55; and *Leon Abgarovich Orbeli* (Leningrad, 1973).

N. A. GRIGORIAN

ORBIGNY, ALCIDE CHARLES VICTOR DES-SALINES D' (*b.* Couëron, Loire-Atlantique, France, 6 September 1802; *d.* Pierrefitte-sur-Seine, near Saint-Denis, France, 30 June 1857), *paleontology.*

D'Orbigny's father, Charles-Marie Dessalines d'Orbigny, came from Santo Domingo. After serving as a naval doctor, he practiced medicine in Couëron and finally in La Rochelle on the Atlantic coast. He was an enthusiastic scientist and often took his sons Alcide and Charles collecting with him on excursions along the coast near their house. As a result of this experience, Alcide decided on a career in science. In 1819 he began systematic zoological research, studying in Paris under Cordier. In June 1826 he left for South America on a commission for the Muséum d'Histoire Naturelle and did not return until March 1834. During these eight years he traveled through the entire continent, making extensive scientific studies under difficult and often dangerous conditions. At the time, much of the continent had been explored only slightly or not at all.

Following his return d'Orbigny spent the rest of his life in Paris, except for brief periods of travel. He was but little concerned about his career. Because of his novel, unorthodox ideas and hypotheses, he had many opponents among his French colleagues. The zoologists dismissed his taxonomic and systematic works and his views concerning the geographic distribution of animals. Many geologists opposed his stratigraphic conceptions. His division of the history of the earth into stages evoked repeated criticism. Lastly, zoologists and geologists were united against him; they thought that paleontology was not an independent science, but that it was only the zoology and botany of fossil organisms.

Consequently, d'Orbigny's initial attempt to obtain a professorship in Paris was unsuccessful. In 1853 a government decree finally created—especially for him —a chair of paleontology at the Muséum d'Histoire Naturelle; the position still exists. Although with his appointment to this chair he had attained his life's goal, he had become embittered by the years of hostility and criticism from his colleagues. He thought that he could forget this adversity by working harder, but the increased activity helped undermine his health and he died of a heart ailment, which had caused him much pain during the last year of his life. D'Orbigny was survived by a wife and children. He was a member of many scientific societies and academies in France and abroad, and on two occasions he won the Wollaston Medal of the Geological Society of London.

D'Orbigny's first scientific publications were brief studies of recent and Jurassic gastropods and of the masticatory apparatus of the nautiluses. From 1819 much of his early research was devoted to recent and fossil Foraminifera. After seven years of work in this field, he published *Tableau méthodique de la classe des Céphalopodes* (1826). In Lamarck's classification the protozoans were still grouped under the cephalopods. D'Orbigny accepted this view, but he separated— under the name Foraminifera—the microscopic forms from the other cephalopods. His classification encompassed five classes, fifty-three genera, and 600 species. He based his classification on the number and arrangement of the chambers of the shell. Among the forms that he described were living taxa from South America, the Canary Islands, Cuba, and the Antilles. He also described Cretaceous fossils from the Paris Basin and Tertiary fossils from the Vienna Basin. Although d'Orbigny knew the entire group of Foraminifera better than anyone else at the time, he did not grasp their true systematic position. This was first perceived in 1835 by Dujardin, who discovered their protozoan nature and grouped them with the infusorians.

Between 1834 and 1847 d'Orbigny published in ten volumes the results of his eight-year expedition to South America. The material—which extended to zoology, geography, geology, paleontology, ethnography, and anthropology—constituted the most detailed description of a continent ever made. While supervising this publication, d'Orbigny was occupied with many other projects. With Férussac he published *Histoire naturelle des Céphalopodes vivants et fossiles* (1839–1848). He wrote the sections on mollusks, echinoderms, sponges, and Foraminifera for Webb and Berthelot's *Histoire naturelle des îles Canaries* (1839–1840) and the sections on ornithology, Foraminifera, and mollusks for Ramon de la Sagra's *Histoire naturelle de Cuba et des Antilles* (1839–1843). His *Histoire naturelle des Crinoides* appeared in 1840 and his *Galérie ornithologique des Oiseaux d'Europe* in 1836–1838 in fifty-two installments. He was the author of a series of paleontological monographs, including one on the Foraminifera of the Upper Cretaceous of the Paris Basin (1840) and one on the Mesozoic and Tertiary fossils of European Russia and of the Ural Mountains (in the great work by Murchison, P. E. de Verneuil, and Keyserling [1845]). Finally, he published a series of brief studies on Cretaceous and Jurassic ammonites, belemnites, and gastropods, on Cretaceous Rudista, and on Tertiary Sepioideans.

From 1840 until his death, d'Orbigny was involved with the publication of his principal work, *Paléontologie française*. In this work he set forth the paleontology and the stratigraphic distribution of all the known forms of mollusks, echinoderms, brachiopods, and bryozoans found in the French Jurassic and Cretaceous deposits. For many years this critical catalog was of great assistance to French geologists and stratigraphers. A notable feature of the work was its treatment of the bryozoans. With the exception of isolated works by other authors, there had previously existed no comprehensive survey of the bryozoans. D'Orbigny provided a critical synthesis of all the living and fossil forms of this phylum, which embraced 1,929 species, of which 879 species came from the Cretaceous period alone. D'Orbigny did not complete *Paléontologie française*. After his death the work was continued, with the aid of the French Geological Society, by Cotteau, Deslongchamps, Piette, De Loriol, and Fromentel, but it was never finished.

D'Orbigny published a still more comprehensive paleontological work, *Prodrome de paléontologie stratigraphique universelle* (1850–1852). It consisted of critical lists of all the fossil mollusks and of other invertebrate groups, which were arranged according to their stratigraphic distribution. D'Orbigny made consistent use of this novel approach and divided the sediments and their fossil contents into twenty-seven stages (*étages*). The stages were named for localities or regions and all were spelled with the same -*ian* ending (-*ien* in French)—Silurian, Callovian, Aptian, Cenomanian, and so forth. Furthermore, the stages were designated by characteristic fossils, and the 18,000 species under consideration were divided into twenty-seven stages.

In this manner d'Orbigny obtained twenty-seven successive extinct faunas. He examined the faunas and ascertained that most species in any given stage no longer appeared in the next younger one; rather, they were replaced by new species. He therefore arrived at a conception of successive destructions and creations of animals in the course of the earth's history. This conception corresponded to the views that Cuvier had set forth in his theory of catastrophism. The theory of

evolution has put an end to all such ideas about new creations, including d'Orbigny's. Nevertheless, the term and important elements of the concept of the stage are still valid, and many of the names that d'Orbigny created for the stages remain in use. D'Orbigny may thus be considered one of the founders of modern biostratigraphy. In *Prodrome* d'Orbigny presented a great number of new species, but did not illustrate them. Between 1906 and 1937 the *Annales de paléontologie* (volumes 1–26) published the expanded diagnoses and illustrations of a large portion of the types first described by d'Orbigny.

With the publication of *Prodrome* and of another basic work with similar aims, *Cours élémentaire de paléontologie et de géologie stratigraphiques* (1849–1852), d'Orbigny established the close and enduring connection between invertebrate paleontology and stratigraphic geology that has proved so fruitful for both disciplines.

BIBLIOGRAPHY

I. ORIGINAL WORKS. D'Orbigny's works include *Tableau méthodique de la classe des Céphalopodes* (Paris, 1826); *Voyage dans l'Amérique méridionale*, 10 vols. (Paris, 1834–1847); *Galérie ornithologique des Oiseaux d'Europe* (Paris, 1836–1838); *Histoire naturelle générale et particulière des Céphalopodes acétabulifères vivants et fossiles* (Paris, 1839–1848), with Férussac; *Histoire naturelle générale et particulière des Crinoides vivants et fossiles, comprenant la description zoologique et géologique de ces animaux* (Paris, 1840); *Paléontologie française. Description zoologique et géologique de tous les animaux mollusques et rayonnés fossiles de France*, 8 vols. (Paris, 1840–1856); *Cours élémentaire de paléontologie et de géologie stratigraphiques*, 3 vols. (Paris, 1849–1852); *Prodrome de paléontologie stratigraphique universelle des animaux mollusques et rayonnés*, 3 vols. (Paris, 1850–1852).

II. SECONDARY LITERATURE. On d'Orbigny and his work, see *Notice analytique sur les travaux de Géologie, de Paléontologie et de Zoologie de M. Alcide d'Orbigny, 1823–1856* (Paris, 1856); P. Fischer, "Notice sur la vie et sur les travaux d'Alcide d'Orbigny," in *Bulletin de la Société géologique de France*, ser. 3, **6** (Paris, 1878), 434–453, which contains a bibliography; A. Gaudry, "Alcide d'Orbigny, ses voyages et ses travaux," in *Revue des Deux Mondes* (Paris, 15 February 1859); C. L. V. Monty, "D'Orbigny's Concepts of Stage and Zone," in *Journal of Paleontology*, **42**, no. 3 (1968), 689–701; J. E. Portlock, "Obituary," in *Quarterly Journal of the Geological Society of London*, **14** (London, 1858), lxxiii–lxxix; and K. A. Zittel, *Geschichte der Geologie und Paläontologie bis Ende des 19. Jahrhunderts* (Munich–Leipzig, 1899), pp. 297, 441, 669–670, 692, 696, 705–706, 777, 796, 800, 811.

HEINZ TOBIEN

ORESME, NICOLE (*b*. France, *ca*. 1320; *d*. Lisieux, France, 1382), *mathematics, natural philosophy*.

Oresme was of Norman origin and perhaps born near Caen. Little is known of his early life and family. In a document originally drawn in 1348, "Henry Oresme" is named along with Nicole in a list of masters of arts of the Norman nation at Paris. Presumably this is a brother of Nicole, for a contemporary manuscript[1] mentions a nephew of Nicole named Henricus *iunior*. A "Guillaume Oresme" also appears in the records of the College of Navarre at Paris as the holder of a scholarship in grammar in 1352 and in theology in 1353; he is later mentioned as a bachelor of theology and canon of Bayeux in 1376.

Nothing is known of Nicole Oresme's early academic career. Apparently he took his arts training at the University of Paris in the 1340's and studied with the celebrated master Jean Buridan, whose influence on Oresme's writing is evident. This is plausible in that Oresme's name appears on a list of scholarship holders in theology at the College of Navarre at Paris in 1348. Moreover, in the same year he is listed among certain masters of the Norman nation, as was noted above. After teaching arts and pursuing his theological training, he took his theological mastership in 1355 or 1356; he became grand master of the College of Navarre in 1356.

His friendship with the dauphin of France (the future King Charles V) seems to have begun about this time. In 1359 he signed a document as "secretary of the king," whereas King John II had been in England since 1356 with the dauphin acting as regent. In 1360 Oresme was sent to Rouen to negotiate a loan for the dauphin.

Oresme was appointed archdeacon of Bayeux in 1361. He attempted to hold this new position together with his grand-mastership, but his petition to do so was denied and he decided to remain in Navarre. Presumably he left Navarre after being appointed canon at Rouen on 23 November 1362. A few months later (10 February 1363) he was appointed canon at Sainte-Chapelle, Paris, obtaining a semiprebend. A year later (18 March 1364) he was appointed dean of the cathedral of Rouen. He held this dignity until his appointment as bishop of Lisieux in 1377, but he does not appear to have taken up residency at Lisieux until 1380. From the occasional mention of him in university documents it is presumed that from 1364 to 1380 Oresme divided his time between Paris and Rouen, probably residing regularly in Rouen until 1369 and in Paris thereafter. From about 1369 he was busy translating certain Aristotelian Latin texts into French and writing commentaries on them. This was done at the behest of King Charles V, and his appointment as bishop was in part a reward for this service. Little is known of his last years at Lisieux.

Scientific Thought. The writings of Oresme show him at once as a subtle Schoolman disputing the fashionable problems of the day, a vigorous opponent of astrology, a dynamic preacher and theologian, an adviser of princes, a scientific popularizer, and a skillful translator of Latin into French.

One of the novelties of thought associated with Oresme is his use of the metaphor of the heavens as a mechanical clock. It has been suggested that this metaphor—which appears to mechanize the heavenly regions in a modern manner—arises from Oresme's acceptance of the medieval impetus theory, a theory that explained the continuance of projectile motion on the basis of impressed force or impetus. Buridan, Oresme's apparent master, had suggested the possibility that God could have impressed impetuses in the heavenly bodies, and that these, acting without resistance or contrary inclination, could continue their motion indefinitely, thus dispensing with the Aristotelian intelligences as the continuing movers. A reading of several different works of Oresme, ranging from the 1340's to 1377, all of which discuss celestial movers, however, shows that Oresme never abandoned the concept of the intelligences as movers, while he specifically rejected impetuses as heavenly movers in his *Questiones de celo*.[2] In these discussions he stressed the essential differences between the mechanics governing terrestrial motion and that involved in celestial motions. In two passages of his last work, *Livre du ciel et du monde d'Aristote*,[3] he suggests (1) the possibility that God implanted in the heavens at the time of their creation special forces and resistances by which the heavens move continually like a mechanical clock, but without violence, the forces and resistances differing from those on earth; and (2) that "it is not impossible that the heavens are moved by a power or corporeal quality in it, without violence and without work, because the resistance in the heavens does not incline them to any other movement nor to rest but only [effects] that they are not moved more quickly." The latter statement sounds inertial, yet it stresses the difference between celestial resistance and resistance on the earth, even while introducing analogues to natural force and resistance. In other treatments of celestial motions Oresme stated that "voluntary" forces rather than "natural" forces are involved, but that the "voluntary" forces differ from "natural" ones in not being quantifiable in terms of the numerical proportionality theorems applicable to natural forces and resistances.[4] In addition to his retention of intelligences as movers, a further factor prevents the identification of any of Oresme's treatments of celestial movers with the proposal of Buridan. For Buridan, *impetus* was a thing of permanent nature (*res natura permanens*) which was corruptible by resistance and contrary inclination. But Oresme seems to hold in his *Questiones de celo*[5] that impetus is not permanent, but is self-expending by the very fact that it produces motion. If this is truly what Oresme meant, it would be obviously of no advantage to use such impetuses in the explanation of celestial motions, for unless such impetuses were of infinite power (and he would reject this hypothesis for all such powers) they would have to be renewed continually by God. One might just as well keep the intelligences as movers. An even more crucial argument against the idea that Oresme used the impetus theory to explain heavenly motion is that he seems to have associated impetus with accelerated motion, and yet insisted on the uniform motion of the heavens. Returning to the clock metaphor, it should be noted that in the two places in which the metaphor is employed, Oresme did not apply it to the whole universe but only to celestial motions.

One of these passages in which the clock metaphor is cited leads into one of Oresme's most intriguing ideas—the probable irrationality of the movements of the celestial motions. The idea itself was not original with Oresme, but the mathematical argument by which he attempted to develop it was certainly novel. This argument occurs in his treatise *Proportiones proportionum* ("*The Ratios of Ratios*"). His point of departure in this tract is Thomas Bradwardine's fundamental exponential relationship, suggested in 1328 to represent the relationships between forces, resistances, and velocities in motions:

$$\frac{F_2}{R_2} = \left(\frac{F_1}{R_1}\right)^{\frac{V_2}{V_1}}.$$

Oresme went on to give an extraordinary elaboration of the whole problem of relating ratios exponentially. It is essentially a treatment of fractional exponents conceived as "ratios of ratios."

In this treatment Oresme made a new and apparently original distinction between irrational ratios of which the fractional exponents are rational, for example, $(\frac{2}{1})^{\frac{1}{2}}$, and those of which the exponents are themselves irrational, apparently of the form $(\frac{2}{1})^{\sqrt{1/2}}$. In making this distinction Oresme introduced new significations for the terms *pars*, *partes*, *commensurabilis*, and *incommensurabilis*. Thus *pars* was used to stand for the exponential part that one ratio is of another. For example, starting with the ratio $(\frac{2}{1})^{\frac{1}{2}}$, Oresme would say, in terms of his exponential calculus, that this irrational ratio is "one half part" of the ratio $\frac{2}{1}$—

meaning, of course, that if one took the original ratio twice and composed a ratio therefrom, $\frac{2}{1}$ would result. Or one would say that the ratio $\frac{2}{1}$ can be divided into two "parts" exponentially, each part being $(\frac{2}{1})^{\frac{1}{2}}$, or more succinctly in modern representation:

$$\frac{2}{1} = \left[\left(\frac{2}{1}\right)^{\frac{1}{2}}\right]^2.$$

Furthermore, Oresme would say that such a ratio as $(\frac{3}{1})^{\frac{2}{3}}$ is "two third parts" of $\frac{3}{1}$, meaning that if we exponentially divided $\frac{3}{1}$ into

$$\left(\frac{3}{1}\right)^{\frac{1}{3}} \cdot \left(\frac{3}{1}\right)^{\frac{1}{3}} \cdot \left(\frac{3}{1}\right)^{\frac{1}{3}},$$

then $(\frac{3}{1})^{\frac{2}{3}}$ is two of the three "parts" by which we compose the ratio $\frac{3}{1}$, again representable in modern symbols as

$$\left(\frac{3}{1}\right) = \left(\frac{3}{1}\right)^{\frac{2}{3}} \cdot \left(\frac{3}{1}\right)^{\frac{1}{3}}.$$

This new signification of *pars* and *partes* also led to a new exponential treatment of commensurability. After this detailed mathematical treatment, Oresme claimed (without any real proof) that as we take a larger and larger number of the possible whole number ratios greater than one and attempt to relate them exponentially two at a time, the number of irrational ratios of ratios (that is, of irrational fractional exponents relating the pairs of whole number ratios) rises in relation to the number of rational ratios of ratios. From such an unproved mathematical conclusion, Oresme then jumps to his central theme, the implications of which reappear in a number of his works: it is probable that the ratio of any two unknown ratios, each of which represents a celestial motion, time, or distance, will be an irrational ratio. This then renders astrology—the predictions of which, he seems to believe, are based on the precise determinations of successively repeating conjunctions, oppositions, and other aspects—fallacious at the very beginning of its operations. A kind of basic numerical indeterminateness exists, which even the best astronomical data cannot overcome. It should also be noted that Oresme composed an independent tract, the *Algorism of Ratios*, in which he elucidated in an original way the rules for manipulating ratios.

Oresme's consideration of a very old cosmological problem, the possible existence of a plurality of worlds, was also novel. Like the great majority of his contemporaries, he ultimately rejected such a plurality in favor of a single Aristotelian cosmos, but before doing so he stressed in a cogent paragraph the possibility that God by His omnipotence could so create such a plurality.[6]

All heavy things of this world tend to be conjoined in one mass [*masse*] such that the center of gravity [*centre de pesanteur*] of this mass is in the center of this world, and the whole constitutes a single body in number. And consequently they all have one [natural] place according to number. And if a part of the [element] earth of another world was in this world, it would tend towards the center of this world and be conjoined to its mass. . . . But it does not accordingly follow that the parts of the [element] earth or heavy things of the other world (if it exists) tend to the center of this world, for in their world they would make a mass which would be a single body according to number, and which would have a single place according to number, and which would be ordered according to high and low [in respect to its own center] just as is the mass of heavy things in this world. . . . I conclude then that God can and would be able by His omnipotence [*par toute sa puissance*] to make another world other than this one, or several of them whether similar or dissimilar, and Aristotle offers no sufficient proof to the contrary. But as it was said before, in fact [*de fait*] there never was, nor will there be, any but a single corporeal world. . . .

This passage is also of interest in that it reveals Oresme's willingness to consider the possible treatment of all parts of the universe by ideas of center of gravity developed in connection with terrestrial physics.

The passage also illustrates the technique of expression used by Oresme and his Parisian contemporaries, which permitted them to suggest the most unorthodox and radical philosophical ideas while disclaiming any commitment to them.

The picture of Oresme's view of celestial physics and its relationship to terrestrial phenomena would not be complete without further mention of his well-developed opposition to astrology. In his *Questio contra divinatores* with *Quodlibeta annexa* we are told again and again that the diverse and apparently marvelous phenomena of this lower world arise from natural and immediate causes rather than from celestial, incorporeal influences. Ignorance, he claims, causes men to attribute these phenomena to the heavens, to God, or to demons, and recourse to such explanations is the "destruction of philosophy." He excepted, of course, the obvious influences of the light of the sun on living things or of the motions of celestial bodies on the tides and like phenomena in which the connections appear evident to observers. In the same work he presented a lucid discussion of the existence of demons. "Moreover, if the Faith did not pose their existence," he wrote, "I would say that from no natural effect can they be proved to exist, for all things [supposedly arising from them] can be saved naturally."[7]

In examining his views on terrestrial physics, we should note first that Oresme, along with many fourteenth-century Schoolmen, accepted the conclusion that the earth could move in a small motion of translation.[8] Such a motion would be brought about by the fact that the center of gravity of the earth is constantly being altered by climatic and geologic changes. He held that the center of gravity of the earth strives always for the center of the world; whence arises the translatory motion of the earth. The whole discussion is of interest mainly because of its application of the doctrine of center of gravity to large bodies. Still another question of the motion of the earth fascinated Oresme, that is, its possible rotation, which he discussed in some detail in at least three different works. His treatment in the *Du ciel*[9] is well known, but many of its essential arguments for the possibility of the diurnal rotation of the earth already appear in his *Questiones de celo*[10] and his *Questiones de spera*.[11] These include, for example, the argument on the complete relativity of the detection of motion, the argument that the phenomena of astronomy as given in astronomical tables would be just as well saved by the diurnal rotation of the earth as by the rotation of the heavens, and so on. At the conclusion of the argument, Oresme says in the *Questiones de spera* (as he did in the later work): "The truth is, that the earth is not so moved but rather the heavens." He goes on to add, "However I say that the conclusion [concerning the rotation of the heavens] cannot be demonstrated but only argued by persuasion." This gives a rather probabilistic tone to his acceptance of the common opinion, a tone we often find in Oresme's treatment of physical theory. The more one examines the works of Oresme, the more certain one becomes that a strongly skeptical temper was coupled with his rationalism and naturalism (of course restrained by rather orthodox religious views) and that Oresme was influenced deeply by the probabilistic and skeptical currents that swept through various phases of philosophy in the fourteenth century. He twice tells us in the *Quodlibeta* that, except for the true knowledge of faith, "I indeed know nothing except that I know that I know nothing."[12]

In discussing the motion of individual objects on the surface of the earth, Oresme seems to suggest (against the prevailing opinion) that the speed of the fall of bodies is directly proportional to the time of fall, rather than to the distance of fall, implying as he does that the acceleration of falling bodies is of the type in which equal increments of velocity are acquired in equal periods of time.[13] He did not, however, apply the Merton rule of the measure of uniform acceleration of velocity by its mean speed, discovered at Oxford in the

1330's, to the problem of free fall, as did Galileo almost three hundred years later. Oresme knew the Merton theorem, to be sure, and in fact gave the first geometric proof of it in another work, but as applied to uniform acceleration in the abstract rather than directly to the natural acceleration of falling bodies. In his treatment of falling bodies, despite his different interpretation of *impetus*, he did follow Buridan in explaining the acceleration of falling bodies by continually accumulating impetus. Furthermore, he presented (as Plutarch had done in a more primitive form) an *imaginatio*—the device of a hypothetical, but often impossible, case to illustrate a theory—of a body that falls through a channel in the earth until it reaches the center. Its impetus then carries it beyond the center until the acquired impetus is destroyed, whence it falls once more to the center, thus oscillating about the center.[14]

The mention of Oresme's geometrical proof of the Merton mean speed theorem brings us to a work of unusual scope and inventiveness, the *Tractatus de configurationibus qualitatum et motuum*, composed in the 1350's while Oresme was at the College of Navarre. This work applies two-dimensional figures to hypothetical uniform and nonuniform distributions of the intensity of qualities in a subject and to equally hypothetical uniform and nonuniform velocities in time.

There are two keys to our proper understanding of the *De configurationibus*. To begin with, Oresme used the term *configuratio* in two distinguishable but related meanings, that is, a primitive meaning and a derived meaning. In its initial, primitive meaning it refers to the fictional and imaginative use of geometrical figures to represent or graph intensities in qualities and velocities in motions. Thus the base line of such figures is the subject when discussing linear qualities or the time when discussing velocities, and the perpendiculars raised on the base line represent the intensities of the quality from point to point in the subject, or they represent the velocity from instant to instant in the motion (Figs. 1–4). The whole figure, consisting of all the perpendiculars, represents the whole distribution of intensities in the quality, that is, the quantity of the quality, or in case of motion the so-called total velocity, dimensionally equivalent to the total space traversed in the given time. A quality of uniform intensity (Fig. 1) is thus represented by a rectangle, which is its *configuratio*; a quality of uniformly nonuniform intensity starting from zero intensity is represented as to its configuration by a right triangle (Fig. 3), that is, a figure where the slope is constant ($GK/EH = CK/GH$). Similarly, motions of uniform velocity and uniform acceleration are represented,

respectively, by a rectangle and a right triangle. There is a considerable discussion of other possible configurations.

Differences in configuration—taken in its primitive meaning—reflect for Oresme in a useful and suitable fashion internal differences in the subject. Thus we can say by shorthand that the external configuration represents some kind of internal arrangement of intensities, which we can call its essential internal *configuratio*. So we arrive at the second usage of the term configuration, in which the purely spatial or geometrical meaning is abandoned, since one of the variables involved (namely intensity) is not essentially spatial, although, as Oresme tells us, variations in intensity can be represented by variations in the length of straight lines. He suggests at great length how differences in internal configuration may explain many physical and even psychological phenomena, which are not simply explicable on the basis of the primary elements that make up a body. Thus two bodies might have the same amounts of primary elements in them and even in the same intensity, but the configuration of their intensities may well differ, and so produce different effects in natural actions.

The second key to the understanding of the configuration doctrine of Oresme is what we may call the suitability doctrine. It pertains to the nature of configurations in their primitive meaning of external figures and, briefly, holds that any figure or configuration is suitable or fitting for description of a quality, when its altitudes (ordinates, we would say in modern parlance) on any two points of its base or subject line are in the same ratio as the intensities of the quality at those points in the subject. The phrase used by Oresme to describe the key relationship of intensities and altitudes occurs at the beginning of Chapter 7 of the first part, where he tells us that:

> Any linear quality can be designated by every plane figure which is imagined as standing perpendicularly on the linear extension of the quality and which is proportional in altitude to the quality in intensity. Moreover a figure erected on a line informed with a quality is said to be "proportional in altitude to the quality in intensity" when any two lines perpendicularly erected on the quality line as a base and rising to the summit of the surface or figure have the same ratio to each other as do the intensities at the points on which they stand.

Thus, if you have a uniform linear quality, it can be suitably represented by *every* rectangle erected on the given base line designating the extension of the subject (for example, either *ADCB* or *AFEB*, or any other rectangle on *AB* in Fig. 1), because any rectangle on that base line will be "proportional in altitude to the

$$\frac{MK}{IG} = \frac{LK}{HG} = 1$$

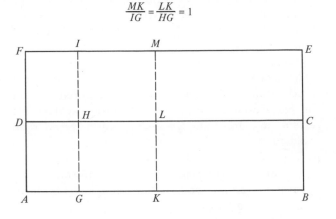

FIGURE 1

intense as the first one, we would have a rectangle whose altitude is everywhere twice as high as that of the rectangle specifying the first uniform quality.

The essential nature of this suitability doctrine was not present in the *Questiones super geometriam Euclidis*, and in fact it is specifically stated there that some specific quality must be represented by a specific

$$\frac{GK}{EH} = \frac{CK}{GH}$$

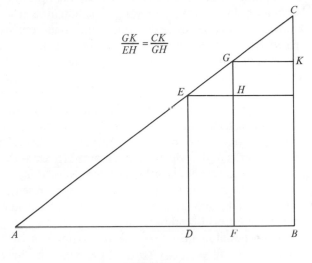

FIGURE 3

quality in intensity," the ratio of any two intensities always being equal to one (that is, $MK/IG = LK/HG = 1$). Similarly, a uniformly difform quality will be represented by *every* right triangle on the given base line, since two altitudes on any one right triangle will have the same ratio to each other as the corresponding two altitudes over the same points of the base line of any other triangle (that is, in Fig. 2, $DB/FE - CB/GE$).

figure rather than a specific kind of figure; that is, a quality represented by a semicircle (Fig. 4) is representable only by that single semicircle on the given base line. But in the *De configurationibus* (pt. 1, ch. 14) Oresme decided in accordance with his fully developed suitability doctrine that such a quality that is representable by a semicircle can be represented by any curved

$$\frac{DB}{FE} = \frac{CB}{GE}$$

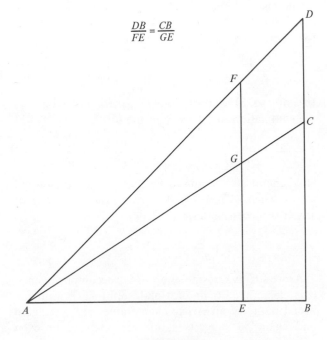

FIGURE 2

The only proviso is, of course, that when we compare figures—say, one uniform quality with another—we must retain some specific figure (say rectangle) as the point of departure for the comparison. Thus, in representing some uniform quality that is twice as

$$\frac{CD}{EF} = \frac{HD}{FG} = \frac{JD}{IF}$$

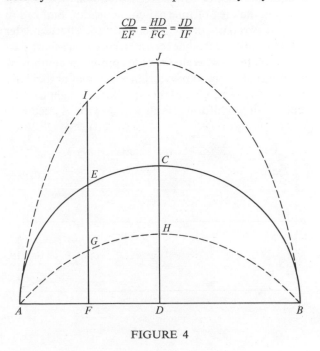

FIGURE 4

figure on the same base whose altitudes (ordinates) would have any greater or lesser constant ratio with the corresponding altitudes (ordinates) of the semicircle (for example, in Fig. 4, $CD/EF = HD/FG = JD/IF$). He was puzzled as to what these higher or lower figures would be. For the figures of higher altitudes, he definitely rejected their identification with segments of circles, and he said he would not treat the figures of lower altitudes. Unfortunately, Oresme had little or no knowledge of conic sections. In fact the conditions he specified for these curves comprise one of the basic ways of defining ellipses: if the ordinates of a circle $x^2 + y^2 = a^2$ are all shrunk (or stretched) in the same ratio b/a, the resulting curve is an ellipse whose equation is $x^2/a^2 + y^2/b^2 = 1$. Oresme, without realizing it, has given conditions that show that the circle is merely one form of a class of curves that are elliptical. It is quite evident that Oresme arrived at the conclusion of this chapter by systematically applying the basic and sole criterion of suitability of representation, which he has already applied to uniform and uniformly difform qualities; namely, "that the figure be proportional in altitude to the quality in intensity," which is to say that any two altitudes on the base line have the same ratios as the intensities at the corresponding points in the subject. He had not adequately framed this doctrine in the *Questiones super geometriam Euclidis*, and in fact he denied it there, at least in the case of a quality represented by a semicircle or of a uniform or uniformly difform quality formed from such a difform quality. In this denial he confused the question of sufficiently representing a quality and that of comparing one quality to another.

While the idea of internal configuration outlined in the first two parts of the book had little effect on later writers and is scarcely ever referred to, the third part of the treatise—wherein Oresme compared motions by the external figures representing them, and particularly where he showed (Fig. 5) the equality of a right triangle representing uniform acceleration with a rectangle

representing a uniform motion at the velocity of the middle instant of acceleration—was of profound historical importance. The use of this equation of figures can be traced successively to the time of its use by Galileo in the third day of his famous *Discorsi* (Theorem I). And indeed the other two forms of the acceleration law in Galileo's work (Theorem II and its first corollary) are anticipated to a remarkable extent in Oresme's *Questiones super geometriam Euclidis*.[15]

The third part of the *De configurationibus* is also noteworthy for Oresme's geometric illustrations of certain converging series, as for example his proof in chap. 8 of the series

$$1 + \frac{1}{2} \cdot 2 + \frac{1}{4} \cdot 3 \cdots + \frac{1}{2^{n-1}} \cdot n \cdots = 4.$$

He had showed similar interest in such a series in his *Questions on the Physics* and particularly in his *Questiones super geometriam Euclidis*. In the latter work he clearly distinguished some convergent from divergent series. He stated that when the infinite series is of the nature that to a given magnitude there are added "proportional parts to infinity" and the ratio a/b determining the proportional parts is less than one, the series has a finite sum. But when $a > b$, "the total would be infinite," that is, the series would be divergent. In the same work he gave the procedure for finding the following summation:

$$1 + \frac{1}{3} + \frac{1}{9} + \frac{1}{27} + \cdots + \frac{1}{3^n} + \frac{1}{3^{n+1}} + \cdots = \frac{3}{2}.$$

In doing so, he seems to imply a general procedure for the summation of all series of the form:

$$1 + \frac{1}{m} + \frac{1}{m^2} + \frac{1}{m^3} + \cdots + \frac{1}{m^n} + \frac{1}{m^{n+1}} + \cdots.$$

His general rule seems to be that the series is equal to y/x when, $(1/m^i - 1/m^{i+1})$ being the difference of any two successive terms,

$$m^i \left(\frac{1}{m^i} - \frac{1}{m^{i+1}} \right) = \frac{x}{y}.$$

As we survey Oresme's impressive accomplishments, it is clear that his natural philosophy lay within the broad limits of an Aristotelian framework, yet again and again he suggests subtle emendations or even radical speculations.

NOTES

1. MS Paris, BN lat. 7380, 83v: cf. MS Avranches, Bibl. Munic. 223, 348v.
2. Bk. II, quest. 2.

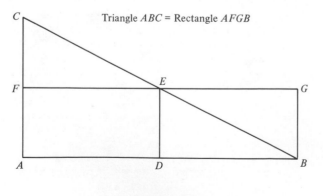

Triangle ABC = Rectangle $AFGB$

FIGURE 5

3. Menut text, 70d–71a; 73d.

4. *Questiones de spera*, quest. 9; *Questiones de celo*, bk. II, quest. 2.

5. Bk. II, quest. 13.

6. *Du ciel*, 38b, 39b–c.

7. MS Paris, BN lat. 15126, 127v.

8. *Questiones de spera*, quest. 3.

9. 138b–144c; see also Clagett, *Science of Mechanics*, 600–608.

10. Bk. II, quest. 13.

11. Quest. 6[8]; see also Clagett, *Science of Mechanics*, 608, n. 23.

12. BN lat. 15126, 98v, 118v.

13. *Questiones de celo*, bk. II, quest. 7.

14. *Questiones de celo*, ibid.; *Du ciel*, 30a–b; Clagett, *Science of Mechanics*, 570.

15. Clagett, *Nicole Oresme and the Medieval Geometry of Qualities*, etc., ch. 2, pt. A.

BIBLIOGRAPHY

I. ORIGINAL WORKS. Oresme's scholarly writings reflect a wide range of interests and considerable originality. He was the author of more than thirty different writings, the majority of which are unpublished and remain in manuscript. They can be conveniently grouped into five categories:

1. Collections of, or individual, *questiones*. These include questions on various works of Aristotle: *Meteorologica* (perhaps in two versions, with MS St. Gall 839, 1–175v being the most complete MS of the vest version); *De sensu et sensato* (MS Erfurt, Amplon. Q. 299, 128–157v); *De anima* (MSS Bruges 514, 71–111v; Munich, Staatsbibl. Clm 761, 1–40v; a different version with an *expositio* in Bruges 477, 238v–264r, may also be by Oresme); *De generatione et corruptione* (MS Florence, Bibl. Naz. Centr., Conv. Soppr. H. ix. 1628, 1–77v; a different version in MS Vatican lat. 3097, 103–146; and Vat. lat. 2185, 40v–61v, may be by him); *Physica* (MS Seville, Bibl. Colomb. 7–6–30, 2–79v); and *De celo* (MSS Erfurt, Amplon. Q. 299, 1–50; Q. 325, 57–90). These also include questions on the *Elementa* of Euclid (edit. of H. L. L. Busard [Leiden, 1961]; additional MS Seville, Bibl. Colomb. 7–7–13, 102v–112) and on the *Sphere* of Sacrobosco (MSS Florence, Bibl. Riccard. 117, 125r–135r; Vat. lat. 2185, 71–77v; Venice Bibl. Naz. Marc. Lat. VIII, 74, 1–8; Seville, Bibl. Colomb. 7–7–13; a different version is attributed to him in Erfurt, Amplon. Q. 299, 113–126). There are other individual questions that are perhaps by him: *Utrum omnes impressiones* (MS Vat. lat. 4082, 82v–85v; edit. of R. Mathieu, 1959), *Utrum aliqua res videatur* (MS Erfurt, Amplon. Q. 231, 146–150), *Utrum dyameter alicuius quadrati sit commensurabilis coste eiusdem* (MS Bern A. 50, 172–176; H. Suter, ed., 1887; see *Isis*, **50** [1959], 130–133), and *Questiones de perfectione specierum* (MS Vat. lat. 986, 125–133v). This whole group of writings seems to date from the late 1340's and early 1350's, that is, from the period when Oresme was teaching arts.

2. A group of mathematico-physical works. This includes a tract beginning *Ad pauca respicientes* (E. Grant, ed., 1966), which is sometimes assigned the title *De motibus sperarum* (MS Brit. Mus. 2542, 59r); a *De proportionibus proportionum* (E. Grant, ed. [Madison, Wisc., 1966]); *De commensurabilitate sive incommensurabilitate motuum celi* (E. Grant, ed. [Madison, Wisc., 1971]); *Algorimus proportionum* (M. Curtze, ed. [Thorn, 1868], and a partial ed. by E. Grant, thesis [Wisconsin, 1957]); and *De configurationibus qualitatum et motuum* (M. Clagett, ed. [Madison, Wisc., 1968]). These works also probably date from the period of teaching arts, although some may date as late as 1360.

3. A small group of works vehemently opposing astrology and the magical arts. Here we find a *Tractatus contra iudiciarios astronomos* (H. Pruckner, ed., 1933; G. W. Coopland, ed., 1952); a somewhat similar but longer exposition in French, *Le livre de divinacions* (G. W. Coopland, ed., 1952); and a complex collection commonly known as *Questio contra divinatores* with *Quodlibeta annexa* (MS Paris, BN lat. 15126, 1–158; Florence, Bibl. Laurent. Ashb. 210, 3–70v; the *Quodlibeta* has been edited by B. Hansen in a Princeton University diss. of 1973). The first two works almost certainly date before 1364; the last is dated 1370 in the manuscripts but in all likelihood is earlier.

4. A collection of theological and nonscientific works. This includes an economic tract *De mutationibus monetarum* (many early editions; cf. C. Johnson, ed. [London, 1956]; this work was soon translated into French, cf. E. Bridrey's study), a *Commentary on the Sentences of Peter Lombard* (now lost but referred to by Oresme); a short theological tract *De communicatione ydiomatum* (E. Borchert, ed., 1940); *Ars sermonicinandi*, i.e., on the preaching art (MSS Paris, BN lat. 7371, 279–282; Munich, Clm 18225); a short legal tract, *Expositio cuiusdam legis* (Paris, BN lat. 14580, 220–222v); a *Determinatio facta in resumpta in domo Navarre* (MS Paris, BN lat. 16535, 111–114v); a tract predicting bad times for the Church, *De malis venturis super Ecclesiam* (Paris, BN 14533, 77–83v); a popular and oft-published *Sermo coram Urbano V* (delivered in 1363; Flaccus Illyricus, ed. [Basel, 1556; Lyons, 1597]), a *Decisio an in omni casu* (possibly identical with a *determinatio* in MS Brussels, Bibl. Royale 18977–81, 51v–54v); a *Contra mendicacionem* (MSS Munich, Clm 14265; Kiel, Univ. Bibl. 127; Vienna, Nat.-bibl. 11799); and finally some 115 short sermons for Sundays and Feast Days, *Sacre conciones* (Paris, BN lat. 16893, 1–128v). The dating of this group is no doubt varied, but presumably all of them except the *Commentary on the Sentences* postdate his assumption of the grand-mastership at Navarre.

5. A group of French texts and translations. This embraces a popular tract on cosmology, *Traité de l'espere* (L. M. McCarthy, ed., thesis [Toronto, 1943]), which dates from about 1365; a translation and commentary, *Le livre de ethiques d'Aristote* (A. D. Menut, ed., [New York, 1940]), completed in 1372; a similar translation and commentary of the *Politics—Le livre de politique d'Aristote* (Vérard, ed. [Paris, 1489; cf. Menut's ed., in *Transactions of the American Philosophical Society*, n.s. **60**, pt. 6 (1970)]), completed by 1374; the *Livre de ycono-*

mique d'Aristote (Vérard, ed. [Paris, 1489]; A. D. Menut, ed. [Philadelphia, 1957]), completed about the same time; and finally, *Livre du ciel et du monde d'Aristote* (A. D. Menut and A. J. Denomy, eds. [Toronto, 1943], new ed., Madison, Wisc., 1968), completed in 1377. To these perhaps can be added a translation of *Le Quadripartit de Ptholomee* (J. F. Gossner, ed., thesis [Syracuse, 1951]), although it is attributed to G. Oresme.

6. Modern editions. These comprise "De configurationibus qualitatum et motuum," in M. Clagett, ed., *Nicole Oresme and the Medieval Geometry of Qualities* (Madison, Wisc., 1968); E. Grant, ed., *"De proportionibus proportionum"* and *"Ad pauca respicientes"* (Madison, Wisc., 1966); *Nicole Oresme and the Kinematics of Circular Motion* (Madison, Wisc., 1971); A. D. Menut, ed., *Le livre de ethiques d'Aristote* (New York, 1940); A. D. Menut and M. J. Denomy, eds., *Le livre de ciel et du monde d'Aristote*, in *Mediaeval Studies*, 3–5 (1941–1943), rev. with English trans. by Menut (Madison, Wisc., 1968).

II. SECONDARY LITERATURE. Only a brief bibliography is given here because the extensive literature on Oresme appears in full in the editions of Grant, Clagett, and Menut listed above. These editions include full bibliographical references to the other editions mentioned in the list of Oresme's works.

Works on Oresme include E. Borchert, "Die Lehre von der Bewegung bei Nicolaus Oresme," in *Beiträge zur Geschichte der Philosophie und Theologie des Mittelalters*, **31**, no. 3 (1934); M. Clagett, *The Science of Mechanics in the Middle Ages* (Madison, Wisc., 1959, 1961); M. Curtze, *Die mathematischen Schriften des Nicole Oresme (ca. 1320–1382)* (Berlin, 1870); P. Duhem, *Études sur Léonard de Vinci*, 3 vols., (Paris, 1906–1913); *Le système du monde*, VI–X (Paris, 1954–1959). See also the following works by A. Maier, *An der Grenze von Scholastik und Naturwissenschaft*, 2nd ed. (Rome, 1952); *Die Vorläufer Galileis im 14. Jahrhundert* (Rome, 1949); *Zwei Grundproblem der scholastischen Naturphilosophie*, 2nd ed. (Rome, 1952); and O. Pederson, *Nicole Oresme, og hans Naturfilosofiske System. En undersøgelse af hans skrift* "Le livre du ciel et du monde" (Copenhagen, 1956).

MARSHALL CLAGETT

ORIBASIUS (*fl.* Pergamum, fourth century), *medicine.*

The life of Oribasius (or Oreibasius, the correct form of his name is not certain) is described by Eunapius in his *Lives of the Philosophers and Sophists.* This article follows Schröder's presentation, which is based on Eunapius and other sources. Since Oribasius is mentioned among the Sophists, he was an "iatrosophist"—a concept which appeared before the fourth century and which referred to a physician of a particular rhetorical and philosophical orientation.[1] He came from a prominent family in Pergamum, where he was born at the beginning of the fourth century. He may have studied medicine there, but most of his medical education was obtained at Alexandria. In the late Hellenistic period the study of medicine at Alexandria had become "scholastic," as Galen termed it—it was divorced from practice and was purely theoretical.[2] Oribasius, however, dissociated himself from physicians who were overly concerned with rhetoric and philosophy.

In Pergamum, Oribasius belonged to the circles representing the intellectual elite of the age; there he met the future Emperor Julian the Apostate, who later made Oribasius his physician in ordinary and head of his library. The relationship between the two plainly was very close, and Oribasius' political influence was correspondingly great. He also was a political official, quaestor of Constantinople. In addition he was closely associated with the emperor's cultural program, including the restoration of pagan religion. Oribasius' notes (a *hypomnema*) on the emperor's life have not survived, but they served as an essential source for Eunapius' biography of Julian and, evidently, as a source for some parts of the historical writings of Ammianus Marcellinus. Banished after Julian's death along with other of his supporters, Oribasius was later rehabilitated. He was married and had four children; a son named Eustathius was also a physician.

The initial stimulus for Oribasius' work as a medical writer was a suggestion by Julian that he prepare abstracts *(epitomai)* of Galen's works; this composition has not survived. His most extensive surviving work (although it was not transmitted intact) is *Iatrikai synagogai* (or *Collectiones medicae*), which contains excerpts from the writings of the more important Greek physicians. These extracts are primarily, but not entirely, verbatim.[3] From this large work he produced *Synopsis for Eustathius* (also extant), a kind of abridged edition or vade mecum for his son. There still exists *For Eunapius*, a collection of easily procured medicines compiled for the layman. The known lost works, in addition to the historical account already mentioned, are *To the Perplexed Physicians, On Diseases, Anatomy of the Intestines*, and, outside the field of medicine, *On Royal Rule* (only the title of the last work is known). Two spurious writings are extant: *Introductions to Anatomy* and a commentary on the *Aphorisms* of Hippocrates. (The authorship of the commentary, which is preserved only in Latin translation, should be carefully examined since it contains material of interest for the history of medicine.)[4]

Oribasius' encyclopedic medical writings became the model for such authors as Aëtius of Amida. They also found a large audience in the Latin West, as the early (fifth century [?]) Latin translations of them testify. The Arabs also drew freely on Oribasius' works. For the historian of medicine Oribasius is especially important for his role in preserving earlier, more important medical authors, whom we know about, in part, only through his excerpts.

NOTES

1. See F. Kudlien, "The Third Century A. D.—a Blank Spot in the History of Medicine?" in L. G. Stevenson and R. P. Multhauf, eds., *Medicine, Science and Culture. Historical Essays in Honor of Owsei Temkin* (Baltimore, 1968), 32 ff.
2. See F. Kudlien, "Medical Education in Classical Antiquity," in C. D. O'Malley, ed., *The History of Medical Education* (Berkeley–Los Angeles–London, 1970), 23 ff.
3. For the rather complicated situation, see F. Kudlien, *Die handschriftliche Überlieferung des Galenkommentars zu Hippokrates De articulis* (Berlin, 1960), 49–54.
4. See F. Kudlien, "Pelops no. 5," in Pauly-Wissowa, *Real-Encyclopädie*, supp. X (Stuttgart, 1965), col. 531.

BIBLIOGRAPHY

The best ed. of the genuine writings is by H. Raeder in *Corpus medicorum Graecorum*, VI, 1–3 (Amsterdam, 1964). The best survey is H. O. Schröder, "Oreibasios," in Pauly-Wissowa, supp. VII (Stuttgart, 1940), cols. 797–812.

FRIDOLF KUDLIEN

ORLOV, ALEKSANDR YAKOVLEVICH (*b.* Smolensk, Russia, 6 April 1880; *d.* Kiev, Ukrainian S.S.R., 28 January 1954), *astronomy, gravimetry, seismology.*

The thirteenth child of a priest, Orlov graduated from the Voronezh Gymnasium in 1898. He revealed a strong interest in astronomy while attending the mathematical section of St. Petersburg University; a student work published in 1901 on the total solar eclipse of 1907 was awarded a prize by the Society of Natural Scientists. He graduated with distinction in 1902 and the following year broadened his scientific background by studying at the Sorbonne, at Lund with C. L. W. Charlier, and at Göttingen with Johann Wiechert.

In 1905–1906 Orlov was an assistant at the Yurev [now Tartu, Estonian S.S.R.] observatory and inspected seismic stations in Transcaucasia for the Permanent Central Seismic Commission. At Pulkovo observatory (1906–1908) he made observations on the zenith telescope, analyzed observations, and improved existing methods. In 1908 he returned to Yurev to undertake seismic research, and in 1909 he became director of the seismic station of the Yurev observatory. He was an active member of the Perma-nent Central Seismic Commission in his capacity as representative of Yurev University, where he also lectured on seismology, the theory of seismic instruments, celestial mechanics, and geodesy. His remarkable series of observations on tidal lunar-solar deformations of the earth, made with the horizontal pendulum, provided the subject of his thesis, defended in 1910 at St. Petersburg, for the degree of master of astronomy and geodesy. In July 1911 Orlov was one of three Russian delegates to the congress of the International Seismological Association at Manchester, at which he was elected a member of the international commission for the study of tidal deformations of the earth. In 1911, on the recommendation of the congress, he organized a new seismic station in Tomsk. He also visited Yerkes Observatory in connection with his research on the motion of matter in comet tails. In the summer of 1912 Orlov took part in a major gravimetric expedition to western Siberia. In December of that year he was named extraordinary professor at Novorossysk University in Odessa and director of the Odessa observatory. After defending his doctoral dissertation in 1915, he became professor at Odessa University, where he taught spherical and theoretical astronomy, celestial mechanics, and advanced geodesy.

After the 1917 Revolution, Orlov took part in renewing the destroyed triangulation network of southern Russia from the Dnieper to the Dniester rivers. In 1921 he organized computation and publication of the marine astronomical yearbook, issued until 1924. Remaining as director of the Odessa observatory, Orlov was elected rector of Kiev University in 1919 and from 1920 to 1923 was academician of the Academy of Sciences of the Ukrainian S.S.R. In 1924 a gravimetric observatory was organized, at Orlov's suggestion, in Poltava, to produce gravimetric maps of the Ukrainian S.S.R. and to study tidal deformations of the earth and polar perturbation. In 1926 this observatory began to conduct regular work at Poltava and gravimetric expeditions.

In 1927 Orlov was elected corresponding member of the Soviet Academy of Sciences; from 1934 to 1938 he was professor of astronomy at the P. K. Sternberg Astronomical Institute in Moscow. From 1938 to 1951 he again headed the Poltava observatory, and in 1939 he became a member of the Academy of Sciences of the Ukrainian S.S.R. While he was director of the Main Astronomical Observatory of the Academy (1944–1950) construction was begun on a new observatory in Goloseevo, near Kiev. At Orlov's initiative the first All-Union Conference on Latitude was held in October 1939; on its recommendation a commission on latitude of the Astronomical Council of the Soviet Academy of Sciences was created. Orlov was its president until 1952.

Orlov's scientific work touched on several areas: (1) the motion of the poles and variations in latitude; (2) tidal deformations of the earth; (3) seismology; and (4) geodesy and geophysics. He also studied comets, the rotation of the sun, precalculations of the circumstances of solar eclipses, problems of theoretical astronomy, analysis of curves of brightness of variable stars, and curves of radial velocities of spectroscopic binary stars.

Work in the first area inaugurated a yearlong series (1906–1907) of extremely precise observations on the zenith telescope at Pulkovo. Orlov developed a graphic method of selecting pairs of stars for determining latitudes (so-called latitude pairs) from observations by the method of equal zenith angles. A group of works beginning in 1916 was completed with the publication of articles that were of great importance in interpreting the results of observations of the International Latitude Service. Orlov introduced a new definition of the concept of "mean latitude" and, using harmonic analysis of the variations of altitude of the pole, confirmed Chandler's indication that there were variations of latitude besides the fourteen-month period in the motion of the pole.

At the Poltava gravimetric observatory, extensive observations were begun on the two bright stars α Persei and α Ursae Majoris, which could be observed there at their highest culmination near the zenith both day and night. Orlov proposed the establishment of stations at the same latitude, at Blagoveshchensk (on the Amur River) and Winnipeg, Canada.

Orlov discovered slow nonpolar variations of latitude and devised a method for excluding them and for correcting the polar coordinates for the period during which the International Latitude Service existed (1892–1952). His numerous investigations led him to develop a new method of determining the polar coordinates from latitude observations at an isolated station.

Orlov's last works deal with an explanation of semimonthly changes in latitude and with the determination of the coefficients of the principal member of nutation based on declination. A posthumously published work on secular polar motion contains a vast amount of observational and theoretical material (259,000 observations of latitude) on the basis of which Orlov discovered the annual secular motion of the pole to be 0.004″ per year, proceeding along a meridian of 69° W.

Orlov's son Boris (1906–1963) was an astrometrist at Pulkovo. His son Aleksandr (b. 1915) became a specialist in celestial mechanics at the P. K. Sternberg Astronomical Institute.

BIBLIOGRAPHY

I. ORIGINAL WORKS. Orlov's selected works were published as *Izbrannye trudy*, 3 vols. (Kiev, 1961). His writings include "O polnom zatmenii Solntsa 1907 goda" ("On the Total Solar Eclipse of 1907"), in *Izvestiya Russkago astronomicheskago obshchestva*, no. 9 (1901), 48–52, with map; and *ibid.*, no. 10 (1903), 131–145; "Nablyudenia potoka Perseid v 1901 g., sdelannye v Pulkove" ("Observations at Pulkovo on the Stream of Perseids in 1901"), in *Izvestiya Imperatorskoi akademii nauk*, 36 (1902), 45–52; "Sur la théorie des appareils seismiques," in *Bulletin astronomique*, 23 (1906), 286–291; "Über die Untersuchungen der Schwankungen der Erdrinde," in *Protokoly Obshchestva estestvoispytatelei pri Imperatorskom yurevskom universitete*, 15 no. 3 (1906), 147–162; "Über die von Fürst Golitzin angestellte Versuch mit einem nahezu aperiodischen Seismographen," *ibid.*, 167–173; "Beobachtungen am grossen Zenitellescop von 7 Februar 1907 bis zum 28 Februar 1908," in *Publications de l'Observatoire central (Nicolas) à Poulkova*, 2nd ser., 18 (1908), 1–66; "Ob opredeleny postoyannykh k i n uravnenia $d^2\theta/dt^2 + 2k(d\theta/dt) + n^2\theta = 0$" ("On the Determination of the Constants k and n of the Equation . . ."), in *Protokoly Obshchestva estestvoispytatelei pri Imperatorskom yurevskom universitete*, 10, pt. 4 (1908), 243–258; "Graphische Methode zur Auswahl der Sternpaare für die Breitenbestimmung nach der Methode gleicher Zenitdistanzen," in *Trudy Astronomicheskoi observatorii, Yurevskogo universitet*, 21, pt. 2 (1909), 3–12; "Beobachtungen über die Deformation des Erdkörpers unter dem Attractionseinfluss des Mondes an Zöllner'schen Horizontalpendeln," in *Astronomische Nachrichten*, 186 (1910), 81–88; and "Novy sposob opredelenia velichiny ottalkivatelnoy sily Solntsa" ("A New Method for Determining the Value of the Repulsive Force of the Sun"), in *Izvestiya Imperatorskoi akademii nauk*, no. 7 (1910), 517–522.

Subsequent works include "Pervy ryad nablyudeny s gorizontalnymi mayatnikami v Yurieve nad deformatsiami Zemli pod vlianiem lunnogo prityazhenia" ("First Series of Observations with the Horizontal Pendulums at Yurev on the Deformation of the Earth Under the Influence of Lunar Gravity"), in *Trudy Astronomicheskoi observatorii, Yurevskogo universiteta*, 23, pt. 1 (1911), his master's diss.; "Sur la théorie des queues des comètes," in *Astronomische Nachrichten*, 196 (1914), 231; "Über der ursprüngliche Bredichinsche Teorie des Kometenschweife," *ibid.*, 198 (1914), 161; "Opredelenie sily tyazhesti v Zapadnoy Sibiri" ("Determination of the Force of Gravity in Western Siberia"), in *Trudy Astronomicheskoi observatorii* (Odessa), no. 1 (1914), 1–22; "Rezultaty yurievskikh, tomskikh i potsdamskikh nablyudeny nad lunnosolnechnymi deformatsiami Zemli" ("Results of Yurev, Tomsk, and Potsdam Observations on the Lunar-Solar Deformation of the Earth"), *ibid.*, no. 2 (1915), 1–281, his doctoral diss.; "Rezultaty 18-letnego ryada nablyudeny solnechnykh pyaten, proizvedennogo v Odesse s konstantinovskim geliografom" ("Results of an Eighteen-Year Series of Observations of Sunspots Made at Odessa With a Constantinov Heliograph"), in *Izvestiya Imperatorskoi akademii nauk*, no. 2 (1915), 135–144; *Teoreticheskaya astronomia s prilozheniem tablits* ("Theoretical Astronomy With Appended Tables"; Odessa, 1920); Odessa Astronomical Observatory, "Harmonic Analysis of the Latitude Observations. I. Kazan, Carlo-forte, Greenwich" (Odessa, 1925), 7–30; "Harmonic Tables for Spectroscopic Binaries," *ibid.*, (1930), 1–8; "Über die Dreiachsigkeit des Trägheitsellipsoids der Erde aus Breitenbeobachtungen," in *Verhandlungen der siebenten Tagung der Baltischen geodetischen Kommission* (1934), 319–339; und "Opredelenie lunnykh geomagnitnykh variatsy pri pomoshchi schetnykh mashin" ("Determination of the Lunar Geomagnetic Variations With the Aid of Computing Machines"), in *Izvestiya akademii nauk SSSR*, Ser. Geograf. i geofiz., no. 2 (1937), 195-206.

His later works include "O deformatsiakh Zemli po nablyudeniam v Tomske i Poltave s gorizontalnymi mayatnikami" ("On the Deformations of the Earth According to Observations in Tomsk and Poltava With Horizontal Pendulums"), *ibid.*, no. 1 (1939), 3–29; *Kurs teoreticheskoy astronomii* ("Course of Theoretical Astronomy"; Moscow, 1940), written with his son, Boris; "Dvizhenie zemnogo polyusa po nablyudeniam shiroty v Pulkovo . . ." ("The Motion of the Earth's Pole According to Latitude Observations at Pulkovo . . ."), in *Byulleten Gosudarstvennogo astronomicheskogo instituta imeni Shternberga*, no. 7 (1941), 5–26; "Dvizhenie mgnovennogo polyusa Zemli otnositelno srednego polyusa za 46 let" ("Motion of the Instantaneous Pole of the Earth Relative to the Mean Pole for Forty-Six Years"), *ibid.*, no. 8 (1941), 5–34; "On Variations of Greenwich Mean Latitude," in *Doklady Akademii nauk SSSR*, **42**, no. 9 (1944), 377–381; "On the 'Ellipcity' of the Earth's Equator," *ibid.*, **43**, no. 8 (1944), 327–328; "The Mean Annual Motion of the Earth's Principal Axes of Inertia," *ibid.*, **51**, no. 7 (1946), 509; "O vekovom dvizheny polyusov" ("On the Secular Motion of the Poles"), in *O zadachakh i programme nablyudeny Mezhdunarodnoy Sluzhby Shiroty* ("On the Problems and Program of Observations of the International Latitude Service"; Moscow, 1954), 13–18; "Analiz pulkovskikh nablyudeny na zenit-teleskope s 1915 po 1928" ("An Analysis of Observations at Pulkovo on the Zenith Telescope from 1915 to 1928"), in Orlov's *Izbrannye trudy*, I (Kiev, 1961), 234–261; and "Sluzhba shiroty" ("Latitude Service"), *ibid.*, 270–334.

II. Secondary Literature. On Orlov and his work, see Z. N. Aksentieva, "Ocherk zhizni i tvorchestva Orlova" ("Sketch of the Life and Work of Orlov"), in *Izbrannye trudy*, I, 3–37; and the obituary by Z. N. Aksentieva and V. P. Fedorov, in *Trudy Glavnoi astronomicheskoi observatorii v Pulkove*, no. 146 (1954).

P. G. Kulikovsky

ORLOV, SERGEY VLADIMIROVICH (*b.* Moscow, Russia, 18 August 1880; *d.* Moscow, 12 January 1958), *astronomy, astrophysics.*

Orlov was the son of a physician. After graduating in 1899 from the First Gymnasium in Moscow, he entered the department of physics and mathematics of Moscow University. Orlov began his scientific career while a student, when, influenced by the lectures of Vitold Ceraski, he became a non-staff assistant at the university's observatory and conducted observations with the transit instrument. Following graduation in 1904, Orlov continued to work in the observatory, began teaching, and served as an artillery officer in the Russo-Japanese War. Since his former position in the Moscow University observatory was filled, from 1906 to 1918 Orlov taught at the First Gymnasium and began his study of comets. During 1914–1917 Orlov again was on active duty in the army. After recovering from a compound fracture of the leg, he was demobilized in 1917 and returned to the Gymnasium, where he taught mathematics and physics and served as vice-director until 1920, meanwhile continuing his study of comets. In 1917 he had received the right to teach at the university level; and in 1920–1922 he was professor at Perm University, where he headed the department of astronomy and physics.

In 1922 Orlov was again in Moscow, where he became a staff member of the State Astrophysical Institute (acting director 1923–1931) and at the Moscow University Astronomical-Geodesical Scientific Research Institute, which in 1931, after merging with the university observatory, became the P. K. Sternberg Astronomical Institute. From 1931 to 1935 Orlov was its vice-director and from 1943 to 1952 its director.

In 1926 Orlov became professor at Moscow University, where he gave courses in astrophysics and comet astronomy; in 1935 he received the doctorate in physical and mathematical sciences, and from 1938 he was head of the department of comet astronomy. From 1935 to 1957 he was president of the Commission on Comets and Meteors of the Astronomical Council of the USSR Academy of Sciences. In 1943 Orlov was elected associate member of the Academy of Sciences and was awarded the state prize for scientific work on comet and meteor astronomy. His other honors include two Orders of Lenin, two Orders of the Red Banner of Labor, and several state medals. As early as 1908 he had photographed and studied photographs of Morehouse's comet, and in 1910 he had observed Halley's comet. This work formed the beginning of investigations that led to more than seventy publications on the astronomy of comets.

Bredikhin's research in the mechanical theory of

comet forms was further developed by Orlov and his school. Orlov faced the problem of creating a theory that would embrace the mechanistic properties of motion, as well as the physical peculiarities of comets and their changes through time. At first he examined the mechanistic theory and put its formulas into a form more convenient for calculation. He then gave an improved method of determining the values of the repulsive accelerations of the action of the sun on the particles of comets' tails; these accelerations were multiples of 22.3 ($I + M = 22.3 \cdot n$, where n can take a value from 1 to 9). This method was based on careful study of the displacements of separate details of the tails as functions of time.

Enlarging on Bredikhin's ideas, Orlov examined and returned to the improvement of Bredikhin's classification of comet forms and developed his own classification of the forms of comet heads. In connection with the latter he produced a theory of the head of the comet, based on the proposition that both the sun and the nucleus of the comet are centers of repulsion forces acting on molecules that separate from the body of the comet's nucleus as the comet approaches the sun and are pushed out into the tail. According to this theory, cross sections of the nuclei of comets were on the order of several kilometers, a dimension confirmed by further research. This theory was also proved by analysis of the structure of the envelopes of comet heads and calculation of the masses of comets.

While continuing Bredikhin's work Orlov also pioneered in the astrophysical study of comets, taking into consideration the mechanism of luminescence of a comet and variations in its spectra. He repeatedly returned to the study of cometary luminescence and the laws of its variation in a periodic comet from one appearance to another. Orlov provided a method of determining the parameters of comet's light and for many comets established the integral, or absolute stellar, magnitudes (the stellar magnitudes reduced to so-called standard conditions, for which one takes the distance of the comet from the sun and its distance from the earth as equal to astronomical unity). As Orlov showed, the law of variation of the parameters of a comet's light is of great importance for the study of the origin and evolution of comets. In particular he noted that a comet's brightness, related to standard conditions, depends on the phase of solar activity.

Orlov's cosmogonic hypothesis suggested that the formation of comets was a result of accidental collisions between two asteroids, which led to explosions that destroyed these small bodies. Fragments acquired varied orbits, usually elliptical. As they approached the sun and came under the influence of its radiation, the fragments released gases that later formed the envelopes of the heads and of the tails of comets. Research on spectra enabled Orlov to determine the gas composition of the straight-tail (type I) comets; less was known at that time about tails of types II and III—he took them to be dust. He was the first to identify lines of nickel in the spectrum of comets.

Orlov's construction of new astronomical instruments was related to the organization of observations of comets and meteors in the Soviet Union. He created a special camera for photographing comets and developed a method for their photogrammetry. Orlov was widely known as an excellent lecturer.

BIBLIOGRAPHY

I. ORIGINAL WORKS. Orlov's writings include "Issledovanie ochertany golovy komety" ("Research on Outlining the Head of a Comet"), in *Zhurnal fizikomatematicheskogo obshchestva pri Permskom Gosudarstvennom Universitete* (1919), no. 2, 139–144; "Opredelenie ottalkivatelnykh sil Solntsa v khvoste komety po dvum nablyudeniam polozhenia oblachnogo obrazovania" ("Determination of the Repulsive Force of the Sun on the Tail of a Comet From Two Observations of the Position of the Cloud Formation"), in *Trudy Glavnoi rossiiskoi astrofizicheskoi observatorii*, **1** (1922), 231–236; "O svyazi mezhdu yarkostyu komet i deyatelnostyu na poverkhnosti Solntsa" ("On the Relations Between the Brightness of Comets and Activity on the Solar Surface"), *ibid.*, **2** (1923), 150; "Opredelenie ottalkivatelnykh sil Solntsa–kometa Galleya (1910 II)" ("Determination of the Repulsive Forces of the Sun and Halley's Comet . . ."), in *Russkii astronomicheskii zhurnal*, **2**, no. 3 (1925), 4–21; "The Series of Carbon Monoxide in the Spectrum of Comets. 1908 III (Morehouse)," in *Astronomische Nachrichten*, **225** (1925), 397–400; "The Spectrum of the Comet 1882 II," in *Russkii astronomicheskii zhurnal*, **4**, no. 1 (1927), 1–9; and "Oblachnye obrazovania v khvoste komety 1908 III (Morehouse), 14–17 oktyabrya" ("Cloud Formations in the Tail of Comet 1908 III [Morehouse] 14–17 October"), in *Astronomicheskii zhurnal*, **5**, no. 4 (1928), 193–202.

Other works are "Mekhanicheskaya teoria kometnykh form" ("Mechanical Theory of Comet Forms"), in *Trudy Gosudarstvennogo astrofizicheskogo instituta*, **3**, no. 4 (1928), 3–79, also in *Astronomischeskii zhurnal*, **6**, no. 2 (1929), 180–186; "Priroda ottalkivatelnykh sil Solntsa v khvostakh komet" ("The Nature of the Repulsive Forces of the Sun in the Tails of Comets"), in *Astronomicheskii zhurnal*, **8**, no. 3–4 (1931), 199–205; "Stereoskopichesky metod fotografirovania komet" ("The Stereoscopic Method of Photographing Comets"), *ibid.*, **9**, nos. 1–2 (1932), 71–81; "O dvizhenii oblachnykh obrazovany v khvoste komety 1908 III (Morehouse)" ("On the Motion of the Cloud Formation in the Tail of Comet 1908 III . . ."), *ibid.*, nos. 3–4 (1932), 163–165; *Komety*

("Comets"; Moscow, 1935); "Spectroskopia komet" ("Spectroscopy of Comets"), in *Uspekhi astronomicheskikh nauk*, **4** (1935), 46–60; "Stroenie golovy komety" ("Structure of the Head of a Comet"), in *Astronomicheskii zhurnal*, **12**, no. 1 (1935), 1–20; and "Origin of Sporadic Meteors," in *Observatory*, **59**, no. 743 (1936), 132–135.

Subsequent writings are "Vidimye radianty kosmicheskikh meteornykh potokov" ("Visible Radiants of Meteor Showers in Space"), in *Astronomicheskii zhurnal*, **13** (1936), 388–396; "Mnogoyarusnye obolochki komet s khvostami I tipa" ("Many-Layered Envelopes of Comets With Tails of Type I"), *ibid.*, **14**, no. 2 (1937), 130–134; "Evolyutsia i proiskhozhdenie komet" ("Evolution and Origin of Comets"), *ibid.*, **16**, no. 1 (1939), 3–27; "Istoria Gosudarstvennogo astrofizicheskogo instituta, 1922–1931" ("History of the State Astrophysical Institute . . ."), in *Uchenye zapiski Moskovskogo gosudarstvennogo universiteta*, **58** (1940), 121–136; "Proiskhozhdenie komet" ("Origin of Comets"), in *Uspekhi astronomicheskikh nauk* (1941), no. 2, 101–121; "Isklyuchitelnye komety. Bolshaya sentyabrskaya kometa 1882 II" ("Exceptional Comets. The Great September Comet 1882 II"), in *Astronomicheskii zhurnal*, **21**, no. 5 (1944), 201–202; *Priroda komet* ("The Nature of Comets"; Moscow, 1944); *Golova komety i novaya klassifikatsia kometnykh form* ("Head of a Comet and a New Classification of Comet Forms"; Moscow, 1945); "Moshchnost i svetosila astrografa i spektrografa" ("Power and Optical Efficiency of the Astrograph and Spectrograph"), in *Astronomicheskii zhurnal*, **22**, no. 1 (1945), 1–10; and "Sinkhrony v khvostakh komet" ("Synchrones in the Tails of Comets"), *ibid.*, no. 4, 202–214.

Later works are "Rol' F. A. Bredikhina v razvitii mirovoy nauki" ("The Role of F. A. Bredikhin in the Development of World Science"), in *Uchenye zapiski Moskovskogo gosudarstvennogo universiteta*, no. 91 (1947), 157–185; *Fedor Aleksandrovich Bredikhin, 1871–1904* (Moscow, 1948); "Komety," in *Astronomia v SSSR za tridtsat let. 1917–1947* ("Astronomy in the USSR for Thirty Years . . ."; Moscow, 1948), 83–88; "Asteroidy i meteority" ("Asteroids and Meteorites"), in *Meteoritika*, no. 5 (1949), 3–13; "Meteornye potoki i komety" ("Meteor Showers and Comets"), in *Astronomicheskii zhurnal*, **17**, no. 1 (1940), 4–7; "Reflektory Maksutova i Shmidta" ("The Reflectors of Maksutov and Schmidt"), *ibid.*, **30**, no. 5 (1953), 546–551; "Rol bazisa pri opredelenii meteornykh orbit" ("The Role of the Basis for the Determination of Meteor Orbits"), in *Byulleten Komissii po kometam i meteoram Astrosoveta, Akademiya nauk SSSR*, no. 1 (1954), 24–28; and "Komety," in *Astronomia v SSSR za 40 let* ("Astronomy in the USSR for Forty Years"; Moscow, 1960), written with S. M. Poloskov.

II. SECONDARY LITERATURE. See "Chestvovanie chlenakorrespondenta AN SSSR S. V. Orlova" ("Celebration in Honor of Associate Member . . . Academy of Sciences . . ."), in *Vestnik Akademii nauk SSSR* (1951), no. 6, 81–83; "Orlov, Sergey Vladimirovich," in *Bolshaya Sovetskaya entsiklopedia* ("Great Soviet Encyclopaedia"), 2nd ed., XXXI (1955), 203; S. M. Poloskov, "Vydayu-

shchiysya issledovatel' komet S. V. Orlov (k 70-letiyu so dnya rozhdenia)" ("Outstanding Investigator of Comets S. V. Orlov [on His Seventieth Birthday]"), in *Priroda* (1951), no. 11, 73–75; "S. V. Orlov (k 75-letiyu so dnya rozhdenia" (". . . on His Seventy-Fifth Birthday"), in *Byulleten Stalinabadskoi astronomicheskoi observatorii*, no. 14 (1955), 3–4; "S. V. Orlov (Nekrolog)," in *Astronomicheskii tsirkulyar Akademii nauk SSSR*, no. 190 (1958), 1–3; "Semidesyatiletie S. V. Orlova" ("Seventieth Birthday of S. V. Orlov"), in *Byulleten Vsesoyuznogo astronomo-geodezicheskogo obshchestva*, no. 10 (1951), 3–4; "Sergey Vladimirovich Orlov (k 40-letiyu nauchnoy i pedagogicheskoy deyatelnosti)" (". . . on the Fortieth Anniversary of His Scientific and Teaching Career"), in *Tsirkulyar Stalinabadskoi astronomicheskoi observatorii*, nos. 64–65 (1948), 1; and "Sergey Vladimirovich Orlov (nekrolog)," in *Astronomicheskii zhurnal*, **35**, no. 3 (1958), 321–322.

P. G. KULIKOVSKY

ORNSTEIN, LEONARD SALOMON (*b*. Nijmegen, Netherlands, 12 November 1880; *d*. Utrecht, Netherlands, 20 May 1941), *physics*.

At the suggestion of his teacher, H. A. Lorentz, Ornstein took as the subject of his doctoral dissertation (Leiden, 1908) the application of J. W. Gibbs's general methods in statistical mechanics (published in 1902) to various concrete problems in molecular theory, including the determination of the equation of state of a nonideal gas.

Ornstein generalized Boltzmann's definition of the probability of a macroscopically definable state of a gas to include systems in which the interactions between the molecules could no longer be neglected. He then calculated the probability that in a homogeneous system a given spatial distribution of density arises. This was the basis of virtually all of Ornstein's subsequent work as a theoretical physicist, and, in particular, of his collaboration with F. Zernike from 1914 to 1917 on the formation of molecular "swarms." They were thus able to add an important correction to the Einstein-Smoluchowski theory of opalescence of a fluid at its critical point, taking account of the correlation of the density fluctuations in volume elements separated by distances comparable to the wavelength of the scattered light.

From 1909 to 1914 Ornstein was lecturer in theoretical physics at the University of Groningen, where Hermanus Haga tried unsuccessfully to interest him in the experimental work of the physical institute. Late in 1914 Ornstein succeeded Peter Debye in the chair of theoretical physics at the University of Utrecht, where W. H. Julius provided him with a room in the physical institute. There, largely through contact with and in collaboration with W. J. H. Moll,

Ornstein began to experiment on liquid crystals, regarded as an exemplification of his theory of molecular swarms.

It was, however, only in 1920, when Ornstein became acting director of the Utrecht physical institute (substituting for the ailing Julius, whom he succeeded officially in 1925), that his work shifted decisively into experiment, and his organizational talent began to unfold. In the preceding dozen years he had published about fifty papers; in the following twenty years over two hundred bore his own name, and almost five hundred additional papers were published from his institute, which underwent three substantial enlargements in this period. Among these publications were eighty-eight doctoral dissertations: about one per year in the early 1920's, increasing to three per year in the middle and late 1920's, and reaching a peak of about seven per year in the mid-1930's.

With great acumen Ornstein had recognized around 1918 that the advance of atomic physics would require that the exceedingly precise measurements of spectral frequencies be supplemented by quantitative measurements of intensities. Immediately upon taking charge of the Utrecht institute, which had had under Julius a strong tradition in spectroscopy and radiation intensity measurements in the service of solar physics, Ornstein charted an ambitious, coordinated program for the systematic investigation of techniques of intensity measurement—especially the blackening of photographic plates—for exploitation in the service of atomic physics. Although generally regarded by his colleagues as a difficult man, within his own institute "the boss" maintained a harmonious collaboration of all the staff upon his tightly integrated program.

In the period 1923–1925 the publications from his institute on the simple integral relations ("sum rules") between the intensities of spectral lines originating in transitions out of or into a complex spectral term, and also between the intensities of the several components into which a spectral line is split in a magnetic field, were an important stimulus and a unique source of data for theoretical atomic physicists seeking a quantum mechanics via Bohr's correspondence principle.

In the late 1920's and early 1930's, after the development of a quantum mechanics whose arbitrary character he found unsatisfying, Ornstein and his co-workers turned these same techniques—for which his institute was then world-famous—to a wide variety of problems: the investigation of electric arcs; the Raman effect; liquid crystals; the determination of isotopic ratios; and purely technical problems of illumination engineering and lightbulb lifetimes.

From the mid-1920's Ornstein, although an active Zionist, cultivated the closest relations with Dutch industry, providing space in his institute and his personal supervision for technical chores in electrical and heat, as well as light, engineering. "The physicist *in* society" was one of his watchwords.

In the late 1930's, on the proposal and with the support of the Rockefeller Foundation, Ornstein moved into biophysics, concentrating upon bacterial luminescence and photosynthesis. Far more would have emerged from this effort had not the war and German occupation intervened. In November 1940 Ornstein was forbidden entrance to his laboratory; he died six months later.

BIBLIOGRAPHY

A complete annotated bibliography of Ornstein's publications and the publications from his institute to 1933 is given in *L. S. Ornstein; A Survey of His Work From 1908 to 1933 Dedicated to Him by His Fellow-Workers and Pupils* (Utrecht, 1933), reviewed by W. Gerlach in *Naturwissenschaften*, **22** (1934), 111–112. The text of this publication, pp. 1–86, gives semipopular expositions of the various areas of research conducted by Ornstein and his institute. The publications of the "Biophysical Group Utrecht–Delft," 1936–1940, are listed in A. F. Kamp *et al.*, eds., *Albert Jan Kluyver. His Life and Work* (Amsterdam, 1959), 548–553. Ornstein's style in the direction of research is also described, pp. 30–31.

Valuable obituary notices are H. A. Kramers, "Levensbericht van L. S. Ornstein," in *Jaarboek van het Koninkl. Akademie van Wetenschappen, Amsterdam* (1940–1941), 225–231; F. Zernike, "Ornsteins Levenswerk," in *Nederlandsch Tijdschrift voor Naturkunde*, **8** (1941), 253–265; and R. C. Mason, "Leonard Salomon Ornstein," in *Science*, **102** (1945), 638–639.

Additional biographical data is given in *Wie is dat*, 4th ed. (The Hague, 1938), pp. 314–315. Some twenty-five letters by Ornstein are listed in T. S. Kuhn *et al.*, *Sources for History of Quantum Physics* (Philadelphia, 1967), 71–72.

PAUL FORMAN

ORTA, GARCIA D' (or **da Orta**) (*b*. Castelo de Vide, Portugal, *ca*. 1500; *d*. Goa, India, *ca*. 1568), *botany, pharmacology, tropical medicine, anthropology*.

Among the Portuguese voyagers and travelers in Asia, d'Orta was the first to use his position to add to the knowledge in Europe of South Asian flora. He thus showed how inadequate were the inherited Greek and Arabic sources on Indian botany and pharmacology. His work provided Western scholars with their introduction to tropical medicine and with their basic data on almost all of the major cultivated plants of the region.

His parents, Fernão and Leonor d'Orta, were Spanish Jews who had taken refuge at Castelo de Vide, in the Portuguese province of Alentejo, when the Jews were banished from Spain in 1492. Faced again in 1497 with the choice between conversion or exile, they became Christians. Probably their eldest son, Garcia, was born soon afterward. The family presumably retained cultural links with Spain, for d'Orta was sent to study at the universities of Salamanca and Alcalá de Henares; he returned to his native town in 1523. He was officially examined and became qualified to practice medicine in 1526 and then moved to Lisbon. In 1530, after two unsuccessful applications, he was appointed to lecture on natural philosophy at the University of Lisbon, where he was elected to the council in 1533. Despite this apparently rapid progress in his career, he sailed for Goa on 12 March 1534, as personal physician to M. A. de Sousa, who had been appointed "captain general by sea" of the Portuguese in India and was later viceroy. From 1534 to 1538 d'Orta traveled extensively along the western coast of India and Ceylon attending de Sousa on his campaigns. He thus met and treated some of the leading Indian princes of the Deccan, notably Burhān Nizām Shah, the sultan of Ahmadnagar, who became a personal friend.

In 1538 he settled permanently in Goa and acquired a country estate on the island of Bombay. Once established, he began to bring over his sisters, who had already been in the hands of the Inquisition and might have hoped that they would be safe from persecution in Goa. In 1541 he married a distant relative, Brianda de Solis; the couple had several daughters. After de Sousa's return to Portugal, d'Orta remained in India as vice-regal physician. It has been assumed that, as the most eminent doctor of Goa, he must also have been a physician at the Goa hospital and prison, but documentary evidence is lacking.

D'Orta participated in a public disputation on philosophy and medicine in 1559, when he was described as very old—indeed "already decrepit"—and learned. Feeling that old age was pressing in on him, he decided to make known the information he had collected during his thirty years in India. This work, *Coloquios dos simples e drogas he cousas medicinais da India* (Goa, 1563), is in the form of dialogues between d'Orta and a colleague, newly arrived in Goa and anxious to know about the materia medica of India. Most of the simples discussed were of vegetable origin, but amber, ivory, and pearls were also among his topics. For each specimen he provided the names in the local languages as well as the names in Greek and Arabic. He then described the size and form of the plant, its leaves, flowers, and fruit; what parts were used; the methods of cultivation and preparation; and the exact location where each plant was grown.

Although d'Orta's central concern was medicinal substances, he often digressed to include other edible plants unknown in Europe. Besides verbal inquiry he used his mercantile contacts to procure specimens, which he attempted to cultivate in his garden (for example, *Eugenia malaccensis* from Malaya). Although he made his own mistakes, he corrected many more, and first reported on several important local food plants, notably mangoes, mangosteens, durians, and jakfruit, which shares a chapter with three other fruit trees then new to European botany. He also described accurately other plants formerly known only as processed commodities or from garbled texts. He was a pioneer in the study of Indian diseases then new to European medicine. His description of the symptoms of Asian cholera became a standard reference, and he carefully observed the effects of chronic dysentery, cobra bite, and datura poisoning.

Besides the plants, drugs, and diseases he found in India, d'Orta was greatly interested in Indian sociology. He described the caste system, the Parsee religion, and the social role of such practices as betel chewing and the consumption of *bangue* (cannabis). D'Orta established friendships with both Muslims and Hindus, and he learned much from their medicine. Although he wrote of Portuguese achievements patriotically, he could appreciate other cultures. He had after all assumed Portuguese Catholicism as a mask. He also reported his discussions with Arab and Jewish merchants from the Middle East. One of these last, who styled himself Isaac of Cairo, and so a Turkish subject, was really a kinsman from Castelo de Vide.

D'Orta was one of the first European scholars to express admiration for the civilization of China, and believed that Western medicine would benefit from closer contact. He realized, too, that the medieval Arabic authors on materia medica knew more about India than the Greeks, and he did not hesitate to challenge the authority of classical texts. This cultural relativism and skepticism toward Western tradition may be attributed in part to his origins.

These origins at last caught up with him. Investigations by the Holy Office brought up his name, and perhaps only his influential position protected his family, for soon after his death his sister Catarina was arrested. From her interrogations it appears that d'Orta had secretly encouraged his family to honor the sabbath and the fasts of Judaism as faithfully as possible. Catarina was martyred in 1569, and the rest of the family was deported to Portugal. In 1580 d'Orta's remains were exhumed and burned.

D'Orta's book may then have been suppressed in Goa. The Flemish botanist L'Écluse came across a copy in Lisbon. He extracted the essential information on the characteristics and properties of the economic and medicinal plants of India, and published an epitome in Latin as *Aromatum et simplicium . . . historia* (Antwerp, 1567); Italian and French translations were also published. Much of d'Orta's material later reappeared in a Spanish work. Although his entertaining dialogue and thoughtful comments were lost, his contributions to botany and tropical medicine were thus saved and absorbed into the mainstream of European natural history.

BIBLIOGRAPHY

D'Orta's work was entitled *Coloquios dos simples e drogas he cousas medicinais da India e assi dalgũas frutas achadas . . .* (Goa, 1563). Two nineteenth-century eds. appeared; the standard one was edited and annotated by de Ficalho, 2 vols. (Lisbon, 1891–1895). This ed. was translated into English by C. Markham as *Colloquies on the Simples and Drugs of India* (London, 1913), but without the introductory material or notes.

L'Écluse's epitome appeared as *Aromatum et simplicium aliquot medicamentorum apud Indos nascentium historia ante biennium quidem Lusitanica lingua . . . conscripta, D. Garcia ab Horto auctore* (Antwerp, 1567); five eds. appeared between 1567 and 1605, and a facs. ed. was produced in 1963. An Italian trans. was made in 1576 (later eds. appeared between 1582 and 1616), and a French trans. was made in 1602 (2nd ed., 1619). C. Acosta, *Tractado de las drogas y medicinas de las Indias orientales* (Burgos, 1588), corrects, epitomizes, and illustrates d'Orta's work.

There are two biographies of d'Orta: A. de Silva Carvalho, "Garcia d'Orta," in *Revista da Universidade de Coimbra*, **12** (1934), 61–246; and Count de Ficalho, *Garcia da Orta e o seu tempo* (Lisbon, 1886).

The journal *Garcia de Orta. Revista da Junta das missões geográficas e de investigacões do ultramar* has been named in his honor; **10**, no. 4 (1963), is a special issue commemorating the publication of *Coloquios dos simples*; an extensive bibliography by J. Walter is included.

A. G. KELLER

ORTEGA, JUAN DE (*b.* Palencia, Spain, *ca.* 1480; *d. ca.* 1568), *mathematics.*

Ortega was a member of the Order of Preachers and was assigned to the province of Aragon. He taught arithmetic and geometry in Spain and Italy. Ortega followed the classical tradition and drew inspiration, like his Spanish contemporaries, from the arithmetic of Boethius. His work reveals the influence of the more important mathematicians of the thirteenth and fourteenth centuries, but he was apparently unfamiliar with fifteenth-century works.

Ortega wrote *Cursus quattuor mathematicarum artium liberalium* (Paris, 1516) and *Tractado subtilisimo d'aritmética y de geometria* (Barcelona, 1512). The first part of the latter was devoted to commercial arithmetic and contains many examples, practical rules, and conversion tables for the various currencies then in use in the different regions of Spain. The second part gives instruction in practical rules of geometry "whereby anybody can measure any figure."

This work is of historical interest mainly for the numerical values that he obtained in extracting square roots, which appear in some of the geometric applications in the second part of the book. Almost identical editions were published in Seville in 1534, 1537, and 1542 (each published by Ortega himself), in which he modified the roots extracted in the first edition. He replaced them with values satisfying the Pell equation $(x^2 - Ay^2 = 1)$; these values thereby gave the best approximation of square roots. Mathematicians have wondered how Ortega managed to evolve a method enabling him to find such closely approximate values, when a general solution of the Pell equation was presumably not achieved before Fermat (1601–1665).

Ortega's *Aritmética* became famous throughout Europe; the work was published in Lyons (1515), Rome (1515), Messina (1522), and Cambray (1612). It was also published in Seville (1552), probably posthumously, as it contained inadmissible changes. (This publication was later corrected.) The Lyons edition was the first book on commercial arithmetic to be published in French.

BIBLIOGRAPHY

Works that discuss Ortega and his work are Cantor, *Vorlesungen über die Geschichte der Mathematik*, II (Leipzig, 1908), 388; J. E. Hofmann, *Geschichte der Mathematik*, trans. into Spanish as *Historia de la Matemática* (Mexico City, 1960), I, 109–110; J. Rey Pastor, "Los matemáticos españoles del siglo XVI," in *Biblioteca scientia*, no. 2 (1926), 67, and "Las aproximaciones de Fr. Juan de Ortega," in *Revista matemática hispanoamericana*, **7** (1925), 158.

MARÍA ASUNCIÓN CATALÁ

ORTELIUS (or **Oertel**), **ABRAHAM** (*b.* Antwerp, Brabant [now Belgium], 14 April 1527; *d.* Antwerp, 4 July 1598), *cartography, geography.*

With the exception of his friend Mercator, Ortelius was the principal cartographer of the sixteenth century. He was born to a Catholic family whose origins were in Augsburg. At the age of twenty he was admitted as an illuminator of maps into the guild of St. Luke in his native town. Soon he was able to earn his living by buying, coloring, and selling maps produced by map makers in various countries. Ortelius traveled widely in his profession; he went regularly to the Frankfurt Fair and visited Italy several times before 1558. In the period 1559–1560 he traveled through Lorraine and Poitou in the company of Mercator, who encouraged him to become a cartographer and to draw his own maps. The first product of this new activity was an eight-sheet map of the world published in 1564. In 1565 he published a map of Egypt (two sheets), in 1567 a map of Asia (two sheets), and in 1570 a map of Spain (six sheets).

The growing demand for maps of distant countries, caused by the rapidly expanding colonization and the development of commerce, had already led to the production of large collections of maps of various size and provenance, for instance, Lafreri's atlas published *ca.* 1553. At the suggestion of the Dutch merchant and map collector Hooftman, and of his friend Radermacher, Ortelius undertook the publication of a comprehensive atlas of the world. It appeared in May 1570 in the form of a single volume, in folio, entitled *Theatrum orbis terrarum*, published by Egidius Coppens Diesth and printed by Plantin in Antwerp. It contained fifty-three sheets with a total of seventy copperplate maps, most of them engraved by Frans Hoogenberg, and thirty-five leaves of text.

The atlas clearly reveals that Ortelius was more an editor of maps than an original mathematical cartographer. Unlike Mercator, Ortelius never devised new projections; but acquiring the rights to utilize maps produced by others, he reduced them to a uniform size and brought their geographic contents up-to-date. To cite a single example, his map of Denmark, entitled *Daniae regni typus*, had as its immediate prototype a map with the same title made in 1552 by Marcus Jordan. But Ortelius' map also included a number of features taken from *Caerte van oostland*, drawn *ca.* 1543 by Cornelis Anthoniszoon, and from Niccolò Zeno's map published in 1558. The map was, however, an unmistakable improvement on previous maps of the region, which was also true for most of his other maps, although Ortelius still relied to a certain extent on material later shown to be legendary, for example the travels of Prester John.

A unique feature of the *Theatrum* was the *Catalogus cartographorum*, in which Ortelius listed eighty-seven map makers as authorities for his own work. Much of what we know of the minor cartographers of the fifteenth and sixteenth centuries derives from this catalog.

The *Theatrum* was an immediate success and the Plantin press published a long series of editions and epitomes in Latin between 1570 and 1624. In 1625 the copyright was acquired by Willem Blaeu, who in 1631 published an appendix to the work and then edited his own *Theatrum orbis terrarum sive atlas novus* in 1634. Ortelius' atlas was translated into Dutch (*Toonneel des aertbodems*) in 1571 and 1598; German (*Schawplatz des erdbodems*) in 1572, 1573, 1580, 1602; French (*Théâtre de l'univers*) in 1572, 1574, 1578, 1581, 1587, 1598; Spanish (*Theatro de la tierra universal*) in 1588, 1600, 1602, 1612; Italian (*Theatro del mondo*) in 1608 and 1612; and English (*Abraham Ortelius his Epitome of the Theatre of the Worlde*) in 1603 and 1606. Ortelius continually revised the new editions, adding new maps and reediting the old. In 1573 he published the first *Additamentum theatri orbis terrarum*. This work was later incorporated into the *Theatrum* (1601), which contained no fewer than 161 maps and 183 authorities.

The *Theatrum* won for Ortelius the title of geographer to King Philip II of Spain. (Arias Montanus vouched for Ortelius' orthodox faith, which had been under suspicion.) It also secured for him a substantial income, enabling him to continue his travels to collect new material. In 1577 he visited England and Ireland, making the personal acquaintance of John Dee, Camden, Hakluyt, and other British geographers. The report of a similar journey in 1575 appeared as *Itinerarium per nonnullas Galliae Belgicae partes*, written in collaboration with J. Vivianus and published in 1584 by Plantin.

During the later part of his life, Ortelius spent much time on classical studies. His large collection of ancient coins and other antiquities was described in the *Deorum dearumque capita ex vetustis numismatibus . . . effigiata et edita ex museo A. Ortelii*, published by P. Gallaeus in 1573 (later editions are 1582, 1602, 1680, 1683, 1699). An edition of *C. J. Caesaris omnia quae extant* (1593) appeared in Leiden and *Aurei saeculi imago, sive Germanorum veterum vita, mores, ritus et religio iconibus delineata* (1596) was published in Antwerp. Of particular interest are Ortelius' works on ancient geography, which began with his *Synonymia geographica*, published by Plantin in 1578 and later revised as *Thesaurus geographicus* (1587, 1596). In 1584 he published *Nomenclator Ptolemaicus*, which dealt with place names in Ptolemy's geography, and *Parergon*, a collection of maps illustrating ancient history, printed by Plantin. The *Nomenclator* and the

Parergon were incorporated into several of the later editions of the *Theatrum;* thus the 1601 edition contained forty maps from the *Parergon.* Ortelius also collaborated with Marcus Welser on his edition of the *Tabula Peutingeriana* (Venice, 1591), a fourth-century Roman military itinerary map.

BIBLIOGRAPHY

On Ortelius and his work, see L. Bagrow, *Abrahami Ortelii Catalogus Cartographorum* (Gotha, 1928–1930); J. Denucé, *Oud–Nederlandsche Kaartmakers in betrekking met Plantin,* II (Antwerp 1913), 1–252, which contains a good biography of Ortelius and a complete bibliography of the *Theatrum;* J. H. Hessels, "Abrahami Ortelii . . . et virorum eruditorum . . . epistolae," in J. H. Hessels, *Ecclesiae Londino-Batavae archivum,* I (Cambridge, 1887); and H. E. Wauermans, *Histoire de l'école cartographique belge et anversoise du XVIe siècle* (Brussels, 1895).

OLAF PEDERSEN

ORTON, JAMES (*b.* Seneca Falls, N.Y., 21 April 1830; *d.* Lake Titicaca, Bolivia, 24 September 1877), *natural history, exploration.*

James Orton was the fifth of eight sons of Azariah Giles Orton, preacher, poet, and classicist, and Minerva Squire Orton. He wrote *The Miner's Guide and Metallurgist's Directory* at nineteen, in the year of the gold rush; but he did not go to California. After graduating from Williams College (B.A. 1855), he attended Andover Theological Seminary and held three pastorates, but Mark Hopkins, president of Williams College, turned Orton permanently toward natural history.

Under the auspices of Williams College and with a loan of instruments from the Smithsonian Institution, Orton directed an Andean expedition in 1867 to determine whether deposits in the upper Amazon Valley were of marine or, as Louis Agassiz insisted, glacial origin. He crossed the Ecuadorian Andes and by canoe descended the Rio Napo, "a steaming vapor-bath." He found marine shells at Pebas, Peru. Only the botanist William Jameson and the zoologist Gaetano Osculati had preceded Orton's party across the Guamani Pass on a scientific expedition. Orton's *Andes and Amazon* (1870) was dedicated to Charles Darwin.

In 1869 Orton, a staunch supporter of coeducation, introduced natural history instruction at Vassar College and recounted his experiences in *Liberal Education of Women* (1873). His *Comparative Zoology, Structural and Systematic* (1876), expounding Agassiz's functional approach, was an influential text. In 1873

Orton directed a second Andean expedition, from Pará to Yurimaguas, across the Andes and down to Lima, collecting for specialists in a wide number of fields and telling of these experiences in the third edition of *Andes and Amazon* (1876).

In 1876 Orton set out on a third expedition, traveling to the trans-Andean rain forests. Although the expedition seemed well planned, the hired porters and much of the escort provided by the Bolivian government mutinied, leaving the small party to make its way through most difficult terrain to Lake Titicaca. Orton had never enjoyed good health, and he succumbed from exhaustion while crossing the lake. He was buried on Estaves Island. Unfortunately, Orton's collections and notes from this last expedition were lost during shipment to New York.

BIBLIOGRAPHY

I. ORIGINAL WORKS. Orton's principal writings include *The Miner's Guide and Metallurgist's Directory* (New York–Cincinnati, 1849); *The Proverbialist and the Poet: Proverbs Illustrated by Parallel or Relative Passages From the Poets, to which are Added Latin, French, Spanish, and Italian Proverbs* (Philadelphia, 1852); *Andes and the Amazon; or, Across the Continent of South America* (New York, 1870; repr., 1871; 2nd ed., 1876); *Underground Treasures, How and Where to Find Them* (Hartford, 1872); and *Comparative Zoology, Structural and Systematic, for Use in Schools and Colleges* (New York, 1876).

Orton published a number of short papers in the *American Journal of Science, Geological Magazine, Proceedings of the American Association for the Advancement of Science, Annals and Magazine of Natural History,* and *American Naturalist,* including one in the latter, "The Great Auk, *Alca impennis,*" concerning the former model for Audubon's drawing in the Vassar College collection, **3** (1869), 539–542.

He edited *The Liberal Education of Women, the Demand and the Method, Current Thoughts in America and England* (New York, 1873), to which he contributed 8 chapters. Four of Orton's letters, written between 1867 and 1868, are preserved in the S. F. Baird correspondence, Smithsonian Institution. Manuscript "Notes for New Edition" of *Andes and Amazon,* including 251 queries and references, is preserved in De Golyer Library, University of Oklahoma.

II. SECONDARY LITERATURE. There is no published bibliography of his writings. The essential sketch is Susan R. Orton, "A Sketch of James Orton," in *Vassar Quarterly,* **1** (1916), 1–8, in which the date of death accepted here appears. See also E. D. Cope, "An Examination of the Reptilia and Batrachia Obtained by the Orton Expedition to Ecuador and the Upper Amazon, With Notes on Other Species," in *Proceedings of the Academy of Natural Sciences of Philadelphia,* **20** (1868), 96–140, and "On Some Batrachia and Nematognathi Brought From the Upper Amazon by Professor Orton," *ibid.,* **26** (1874), 120–137;

Philip Reese Uhler, "Notices of the Hemiptera Obtained by the Expedition of Prof. James Orton in Ecuador and Brazil," in *Proceedings of the Boston Society of Natural History*, **12** (1869), 321–327; George Dale Smith, "List of Coleoptera Collected by Professor James Orton in Ecuador and Brazil," *ibid.*, 327–330; and Samuel Hubbard Scudder, "Notes on Orthoptera Collected by Professor James Orton on Either Side of the Andes of Equatorial South America," *ibid.* 330–345. Ruth D. Turner, "James H. Orton. His Contributions to the Field of Fossil and Recent Mollusks," in *Revista del Museo argentino de ciencias naturales "Bernardino Rivadavia." Ciencias zoológicas*, **8** (1962), 89–99—the title included an erroneous middle initial.

Henry Morris Myers and Philip Van Ness Myers, *Life and Nature Under the Tropics* (New York, 1871), 194–323, relates to a contingent of the first Andean expedition.

JOSEPH EWAN

OSBORN, HENRY FAIRFIELD (*b*. Fairfield, Connecticut, 8 August 1857; *d*. Garrison, New York, 6 November 1935), *vertebrate paleontology*.

Osborn was the eldest son of William Henry Osborn, president of the Illinois Central Railroad, and of Virginia Reed Sturges. He spent his early life in the vicinity of New York City. He attended the College of New Jersey (now Princeton University), where he was much influenced by President James McCosh and Arnold Guyot, director of the museum. At Princeton he began a lifelong friendship with William Berryman Scott. In their junior year, Scott and Osborn became intensely interested in the fossil remains of extinct reptiles and mammals. The young men accordingly organized their first paleontological expedition. They spent the summer of 1877 in Colorado and Wyoming, still a wild land inhabited by less than friendly Indians and by some of the "old mountain men." In 1878 there was a second expedition, and it was at this time that they met and became disciples of Edward Drinker Cope of Philadelphia, the rival of O. C. Marsh of Yale.

After completing their undergraduate work at Princeton, Scott and Osborn went abroad for postgraduate studies. Osborn studied under T. H. Huxley and Francis Maitland Balfour in London. He also met Charles Darwin, an encounter that he never forgot.

He returned to join the faculty at Princeton, and in 1881 married Lucretia Perry; they had five children. In 1891 he was called to Columbia University to found a department of biology and to the American Museum of Natural History to found a department of mammalian paleontology (soon to become the department of vertebrate paleontology). He spent the remainder of his life in New York City, where he was actively associated with Columbia until 1910 and with the American Museum of Natural History until his death.

In addition to his career as first head of the biology department at Columbia, Osborn was first dean of the graduate faculty, and for many years was Da Costa professor of zoology, in which capacity he trained numerous students, many of whom became distinguished zoologists and paleontologists. At the same time he served as head of the department of vertebrate paleontology, where he was instrumental in building a collection of worldwide importance. For twenty-five years he was also president of the American Museum of Natural History and was largely responsible for making it probably the largest natural history museum in the world.

In spite of his involvement with these several concurrent careers, Osborn was primarily a research scientist. He continually studied fossil vertebrates, and with the aid of assistants and colleagues, who did much of the detailed work for him, he published some 600 papers, books, and monographs.

Although Osborn was concerned with the details of vertebrate evolution—particularly that of reptiles and mammals—he was especially interested in the larger problems of life. He was a theorist and proposed various explanations for many aspects of evolution. His important contributions to the knowledge of evolution within many groups of mammals and reptiles were, nonetheless, based upon the fossil evidence. He had a grand concept of the adaptive radiation of life; yet in spite of his penetrating mind, he never seemed to appreciate fully the significance of genetic studies to the modern concept of evolution. Osborn was also a master of synthesis, a capacity illustrated by his enormous monographs on the titanotheres and the proboscideans.

BIBLIOGRAPHY

A full bibliography of Osborn's works (exclusive of newspaper articles, abstracts, and some popular articles) will be found in William K. Gregory, "Biographical Memoir of Henry Fairfield Osborn 1857–1935," in *Biographical Memoirs. National Academy of Sciences*, **19** (1938), 53–119. See also George Gaylord Simpson, "Henry Fairfield Osborn," in *Dictionary of American Biography*, **11**, supp. 1 (New York, 1944), 584–587, which includes a bibliography.

EDWIN H. COLBERT

OSBORNE, THOMAS BURR (*b*. New Haven, Connecticut, 5 August 1859; *d*. New Haven, 29 January 1929), *protein chemistry*.

Osborne was the son of Arthur Dimon Osborne, who was educated in law but subsequently became the president of a local bank, and Frances Louisa Blake. His ancestors on both sides can be traced in the history of New Haven to its earliest years. Osborne prepared for college at the Hopkins Grammar School in New Haven and was graduated from Yale in 1881. A year was spent in the study of medicine before he entered the Yale graduate school, where he studied chemistry under W. G. Mixter. His doctoral dissertation (1885) described the analytical determination of niobium in columbite, the mineral occurring in Connecticut in which niobium (originally named columbium) had been discovered in 1801 by Charles Hatchett. In 1886, at the invitation of Samuel W. Johnson, director of the recently established Connecticut Agricultural Experiment Station and professor of agricultural chemistry of the Sheffield Scientific School of Yale University, Osborne joined the staff of the experiment station as an analytical chemist. In the same year he married Elizabeth Anna Johnson, his director's daughter.

While a graduate student at Yale, and during a year spent as an instructor, Osborne published several papers on analytical methods. At the experiment station he developed what became known as the Osborne beaker method for the mechanical analysis of soils, a method still in use. In 1889, owing to the passage of the Hatch Act of 1887, which provided for additional funds, Osborne began the investigations of the proteins of plant seeds, which became his lifelong work. The initial suggestion to begin this research was made by Johnson, impressed with the related work of Heinrich Ritthausen in Germany.

Johnson's former teacher at Yale, J. P. Norton, had studied the proteins of the oat kernel some forty years earlier, and Johnson, noting that Ritthausen had not investigated this seed, suggested that further work was desirable, Although in later years Osborne stated that no seed that he subsequently worked with ever presented such difficulties as had the oat kernel, he succeeded in preparing what appeared to be a homogeneous alcohol-soluble protein and also a globulin that was obtained in crystalline form.

This success led to broadly planned research into the proteins of seeds used as human or animal food. Within two years he had obtained crystalline globulins from six different seeds, and from 1889 to 1901 he examined no less than thirty-two species, including a number of legumes, many common nuts, and the most important cereal grains. His skillful use of saline solvents, his control of acidity by the intelligent use of indicators long before the theory of pH had been developed, the use of temperature gradients, dialysis, and in certain instances of alcohol to precipitate the components of the extracts, demonstrate an instinctive appreciation of the physicochemical properties of proteins, which was many years in advance of theoretical explanation of these matters. He established what since have become the classical methods for the isolation of proteins from plant seeds.

Osborne was somewhat restricted during this early period of research by two considerations. Liebig's dictum of fifty years earlier that there are only four kinds of protein in nature (albumin, casein, fibrin, and gelatin), although shown to be greatly oversimplified by Ritthausen and others, was still a dominating principle. Second, the motive for many studies was to show that identical proteins could be prepared from analogous tissues of different species. Inasmuch as the main criterion for the differentiation of preparations from different species was the comparison of the content of carbon, hydrogen, nitrogen, and sulfur, it can be understood how Osborne was at first frequently misled into believing that he had obtained the same protein from two or more different seeds. Thus, in 1894, he stated that, since their ultimate composition was essentially the same, the globulins of hempseed, castor bean, squashseed, flax, wheat, maize, and cottonseed are identical. For this widely distributed protein he suggested the name edestin (from the Greek for "edible"), a name later applied only to the globulin of hempseed.

Several other instances of apparent identity between pairs or small groups of proteins of different origin were later encountered. Nevertheless, as his experience broadened, Osborne became increasingly suspicious of the validity of such conclusions, and, at the turn of the century, he began to subject his extensive collection of proteins to detailed chemical study. He examined such properties as the solubility in saline solution, coagulation temperature, specific rotation, heat of combustion, color tests, the behavior of sulfur when the protein was heated with alkali in the presence of lead, and the quantitative behavior of protein toward acid and alkali, in which he sought for differences between proteins that seemed to be identical. Osborne's closest attention, however, was given to the determination of the different forms of nitrogen in the products of complete acid hydrolysis of the proteins and to the determination of the basic amino acids by the recently published method of Kossel and Kutcher. Glutamic and aspartic acids were also determined by direct isolation.

Osborne soon came to the conclusion that the detection of differences was the fundamental problem. To obtain more complete characterizations, for about five years beginning in 1906, he devoted the full resources of his laboratory to the determination of the amino acid composition of many of the most important proteins. He used the ester distillation method of Emil Fischer for these determinations. The outcome of this labor was that, with only a few exceptions, proteins that closely resembled each other in ultimate composition could be distinguished from each other in terms of amino acid composition. When the highly sensitive biologic test dependent upon the anaphylaxis reaction became available, Osborne, from 1911 to 1916, collaborated with H. Gideon Wells of the University of Chicago in a comprehensive study of the seed proteins. Their studies showed that only two or three doubtful instances remained where proteins of different origin could not be distinguished from each other. This demonstration of the specificity of vegetable proteins with respect to source remains one of Osborne's fundamental contributions to protein chemistry.

In 1909, Osborne invited Lafayette B. Mendel of Yale to join him in a study of the nutritive properties of the seed proteins. It was widely believed that, with a few exceptions, all proteins are alike in nutritive effect. The striking differences in the amino acid composition that had been found for a number of common food proteins raised the question of the validity of this view. The collaboration with Mendel continued from 1909 until Osborne's retirement in 1928. They developed a technique for feeding rats that enabled them to measure the food intake, and within a few years obtained convincing proof that the amino acids tryptophan and lysine are essential in the diet. Although it was clear that the rat can synthesize some of the amino acids, this capacity is strictly limited. The study of the effect of lysine was especially rewarding since it showed that the growth of a young rat could be quantitatively controlled by the supply of lysine, either as such or combined in the protein of the diet. Animals stunted by low levels of lysine intake could be induced to grow at any age by increasing the supply.

The outstanding accomplishment of the first few years of this collaboration was the discovery of what became known as vitamin A. This discovery resulted from the comparison of the growth of rats on diets consisting of purified components, of which one contained dried whole milk and the other only the lactose and inorganic salts of milk. The substitution of butter for some of the lard in the second diet prevented the loss of weight and eventual death of the animals. This observation was made early in 1913. The conclusion was obvious that butter contains a trace amount of some fat-soluble organic substance

that is essential in nutrition. Unfortunately the submission to a journal of a similar observation by E. V. McCollum of the University of Wisconsin preceded by three weeks the receipt of the Osborne and Mendel paper, and McCollum is accordingly regarded as the discoverer of the first vitamin to be recognized. Although Osborne and Mendel devoted considerable study to the natural distribution of the fat-soluble vitamin (notably finding that cod liver oil is a rich source) and the later-discovered water-soluble vitamin, their main interest during the extremely active period from 1911 to 1924 was in the phenomena of growth and in the nutritive properties of various proteins. They studied the effects of high-protein diets, low-carbohydrate and low-fat diets, and variations in the supply of inorganic salts. They obtained rational explanations for many empirical practices in animal feeding that had been found advantageous, and they cleared up the relation between nutritional ophthalmia and vitamin A. They also contributed to the demonstration of the nutritional origin of rickets; the common use of cod liver oil and orange juice in the diets of children stems largely from their work.

Although the main interest of the laboratory continued to be in nutrition, Osborne, with the aid of his assistants, also devoted much effort to the many purely chemical problems that arose. In 1919 he and Alfred J. Wakeman prepared the first vitamin-rich concentrate from an extract of brewer's yeast. The concentrate was used for many years in the laboratory and was marketed successfully by a former assistant, Isaac F. Harris, who had become a manufacturing chemist. The observation that the alfalfa plant is rich in vitamins led to attempts to prepare the proteins from green leaves. Only moderate success attended these efforts, but A. C. Chibnall of the Imperial College, London, who joined Osborne's group in 1923 and 1924, was later successful. In his last years Osborne also stimulated the investigations by his assistants of the simpler nitrogenous substances present in plants, a field of study that had been neglected since the early work of Ernst Schulze in Switzerland in the last decades of the nineteenth century.

Unlike his collaborator Mendel, Osborne did not have a large group of loyal and devoted students to keep his memory alive. To those who worked with him he was a rare stimulus, a formidable opponent in argument, and an ever genial but just critic. His major, in fact almost his only, interest was in the work of the laboratory. He served for many years as a director of the local bank of which his father had been president, but this and the group of close friends at his club, together with his interest in the birds of Connecticut, upon which he was an authority, provided the major relief from his daily work at the laboratory bench.

BIBLIOGRAPHY

I. ORIGINAL WORKS. Osborne's bibliography published in Vickery's memoir (see below) lists titles of 252 papers that appeared in various chemical journals between 1884 and 1929. A nearly complete bound collection of his work is in the Osborne Library at the Connecticut Agricultural Experiment Station in New Haven. The papers on the preparation of proteins appeared in the *American Chemical Journal* or *Journal of the American Chemical Society* until 1904; nearly all were reprinted in the annual *Report of the Connecticut Agricultural Experiment Station*.

Most of the papers from 1891 to 1897 were translated into German by V. Griessmayer in *Die Proteide der Getreidarten, Hülsenfrüchte und Ölsamen sowie einiger Steinfruchte* (Heidelberg, 1897). Griessmayer continued to translate and publich most of Osborne's papers, which appeared up to 1908, in *Zeitschrift für das landwirtschaftliche Versuchswesen in Österreich* or, after 1904, in *Zeitschrift für analytische Chemie*.

From 1904 to 1910 Osborne's papers were published in the *American Journal of Physiology*; subsequent papers appeared in the *Journal of Biological Chemistry*, to which Osborne and Mendel contributed most of their collaborative papers on nutrition between 1912 and 1927. Including annual reports to the Carnegie Institution of Washington there were 111 of these. The six papers on the anaphylaxis reactions of the seed proteins, written with H. Gideon Wells, appeared in the *Journal of Infectious Diseases* between 1911 and 1916.

Osborne's works also include *The Proteins of the Wheat Kernel*, Carnegie Institution of Washington Publication no. 84 (Washington, D.C., 1907); *The Vegetable Proteins*, in R. H. Plimmer and F. G. Hopkins, eds., Monographs on Biochemistry (London, 1909; 2nd ed., rev., 1924); and *Feeding Experiments with Isolated Food-Substances, Parts I and II*, Carnegie Institution of Washington Publication no. 156 (Washington, D.C., 1911), written with Mendel.

II. SECONDARY LITERATURE. Hubert Bradford Vickery has written three articles on Osborne: "Thomas Burr Osborne, 1859–1929," in *Biographical Memoirs. National Academy of Sciences*, **14** (1931), 261–304; "Thomas B. Osborne, a Memorial," in *Bulletin. Connecticut Agricultural Experiment Station*, **312** (1930); and "Thomas Burr Osborne," in *Journal of Nutrition*, **59** (1956), 1–26.

The bulletin published by the experiment station contains several obituary notices, the records of the presentation of an honorary degree by Yale University in 1910, the presentation of the John Scott Medal by the board of directors of City Trusts of Philadelphia in 1922, and the presentation of the Thomas Burr Osborne Medal by the American Association of Cereal Chemists in 1928. It also contains reprints of Osborne's addresses on protein

chemistry to several organizations, a previously unpublished paper on bird migration, and a complete bibliography of his papers.

HUBERT BRADFORD VICKERY

OSGOOD, WILLIAM FOGG (*b*. Boston, Massachusetts, 10 March 1864; *d*. Belmont, Massachusetts, 22 July 1943), *mathematics*.

Osgood was the son of William Osgood and Mary Rogers Gannett. After preparing for college at the Boston Latin School, he entered Harvard College in 1882 and was graduated second in his class in 1886. He remained at Harvard for a year of graduate work in mathematics and was awarded the A.M. in 1887. Osgood spent much of his first two years at Harvard studying the classics but was largely influenced by the mathematical physicist Benjamin Osgood Peirce, one of his favorite teachers, and by Frank Nelson Cole. Cole had attended Felix Klein's lectures on function theory and lectured on the subject, following Klein's ideas, at Harvard during 1885–1887. Osgood went to the great German center of mathematics at Göttingen in 1887, largely because of Klein's presence there.

In 1887 there was great mathematical activity in Europe, brought about especially by the introduction of rigor into current research. Under the influence of Klein, Osgood embraced this tendency, which remained a commitment throughout his life. Osgood went to Erlangen in 1889 to continue his graduate work. His dissertation, a study of Abelian integrals of the first, second, and third kinds, was based on previous work by Klein and Max Noether. The topic was part of the theory of functions, to which Osgood devoted much of his later life. After receiving his Ph.D. at Erlangen in 1890, Osgood married Anna Terese Ruprecht of Göttingen and returned to the United States. He then joined the Harvard department of mathematics, where he remained for forty-three years. He brought with him the spirit of research, then new in the United States, as well as that of rigor. A year later Maxime Bôcher returned to Harvard, and the two were influential in fostering the new attitude there.

Osgood's main research papers concerned convergence of sequences of continuous functions, solutions of differential equations, Riemann's theorem on the mapping of a simply connected region, the calculus of variations, and space-filling curves. These topics are classical, and Osgood's results are important and deep. Klein invited Osgood to write an article for the *Encyklopädie* on the theory of functions; the writing of it (1901) gave Osgood an unparalleled knowledge of the field and its history. His *Lehrbuch der Funktionentheorie* (1907) subsequently became the standard treatise. Osgood was one of the world's outstanding mathematics teachers through that work and through others on analytic geometry, calculus, and advanced calculus. Over the years he instilled ideals and habits of careful and accurate thought in hundreds of elementary as well as advanced students. After his retirement from Harvard in 1933, he lectured for two years at the National University of Peking.

Osgood's favorite recreations were travel by car, smoking cigars, and occasional games of tennis and golf. He was kindly although somewhat reserved, but warm to those who knew him. He and his first wife had two sons and a daughter. He married Celeste Phelps Morse in 1932.

BIBLIOGRAPHY

Personal recollections; Harvard Class of 1886 *Reports* for 1886, 1889, 1894, 1898, 1901, 1906, 1911, 1926, 1936; and clippings in Harvard University Archives. See also *Dictionary of American Biography*, supp. 3, 574–575.

J. L. WALSH

OSIANDER, ANDREAS (*b.* Gunzenhausen, Bavaria, Germany, 19 December 1498; *d.* Königsberg, Germany [now Kaliningrad, U.S.S.R.], 17 October 1552), *theology, astronomical and mathematical publishing.*

On 9 July 1515 Osiander was admitted to the University of Ingolstadt as a "cleric of the Eichstätt" diocese.[1] Without obtaining a degree he moved to Nuremberg, where he taught Hebrew and was ordained a priest in 1520. He enthusiastically embraced the new Lutheran movement and soon became one of its most militant spokesmen. When Nuremberg accepted the pro-Catholic Augsburg Interim, Osiander left and joined the Protestant Duke Albert of Prussia. On 27 January 1549 he arrived in Königsberg, where the recently founded university appointed him professor of theology.[2] His doctrinal views were bitterly opposed by the more orthodox followers of Martin Luther in the "Osiander Controversy," which continued after Osiander's death.

In 1538 Rheticus obtained a leave of absence from Wittenberg University in order to visit German astronomers. In Nuremberg he met Osiander, whose hobby was the mathematical sciences. Hence, when Rheticus' *Narratio prima*, the first printed discussion of the Copernican astronomy, was published in 1540, a copy was sent to Osiander, who was shocked by the claim of the new system to be true; he regarded divine revelation as the sole source of truth. In similar letters to Rheticus and Copernicus on 20 April 1541, when Rheticus was waiting in Frombork (Frauenburg) for Copernicus to put the final touches on the manuscript of *De revolutionibus orbium coelestium*, Osiander urged the inclusion in the introduction of the statement that even if the Copernican system provided a basis for correct astronomical computations, it might still be false. Copernicus firmly rejected Osiander's recommendation.

Nevertheless, subsequent events enabled Osiander to impose his fictionalist philosophy of science on *De revolutionibus*, while its author lay helpless and dying in far-off Frombork. Copernicus had entrusted the printing of *De revolutionibus* to Rheticus, who supervised the early stages of the process in the shop of Johannes Petreius (Hans Peter) in Nuremberg. When Rheticus had to go to the University of Leipzig, which had just appointed him professor of mathematics, he was replaced as editor of *De revolutionibus* by Osiander, who surreptitiously slipped into the authentic front matter an unsigned preface composed by himself and expounding his anti-Copernican fictionalism.[3]

When copies of *De revolutionibus* reached Rheticus in Leipzig, he became enraged and sent to the City Council of Nuremberg a sharp protest that was written by Tiedemann Giese, the closest friend of Copernicus, who had died in the meantime. Petreius replied that he had received the false preface in a form undifferentiated from the rest of the material. Whereas Osiander never publicly acknowledged his authorship of the interpolated preface, he did so privately,[4] and thus finally in 1609 Kepler's *Astronomia nova* was able to identify Osiander as the culprit.

Osiander was more sympathetic to the mathematician Cardano. Both of them were astrologers, and they exchanged letters about horoscopes for some five years before Cardano on 9 January 1545 dedicated *Artis magnae sive de regulis algebraicis liber unus*—which initiated the theory of algebraic equations—to Osiander, who edited the work for Petreius.[5]

NOTES

1. Götz F. v. Pölnitz, ed., *Die Matrikel der Ludwig-Maximilians-Universität Ingolstadt-Landshut-München*, I (Munich, 1937), 381.
2. His son Lucas was admitted to the university in the summer semester of 1549 (Georg Erler, ed., *Die Matrikel der Universität Königsberg in Preussen*, I [Leipzig, 1908–1910], 10).
3. Osiander's preface was translated into English by Edward Rosen, *Three Copernican Treatises*, 3rd ed. (New York, 1971), pp. 24–25.

4. Ernst Zinner, *Entstehung und Ausbreitung der copperni-canischen Lehre* (Erlangen, 1943), p. 453.

5. Cardano's dedication was translated into English by T. Richard Witmer, *The Great Art or the Rules of Algebra by Girolamo Cardano* (Cambridge, Mass., 1968), p. 2.

BIBLIOGRAPHY

I. ORIGINAL WORKS. Osiander's works are chronologically enumerated (1522–1552) in Gottfried Seebass, *Das reformatorische Werk des Andreas Osiander* (Nuremberg, 1967), pp. 6–58, with nine portraits of Osiander as frontispiece and supplement.

II. SECONDARY LITERATURE. On Osiander and his work, see Wilhelm Möller, *Andreas Osiander* (Elberfeld, 1870; repr. Nieuwkoop, 1965), and his article, "Osiander," in *Allgemeine deutsche Biographie*, XXIV (1887; 1970), 473–483; and G. Seebass, *op. cit.*, pp. xi–xviii.

EDWARD ROSEN

OSMOND, FLORIS (*b.* Paris, France, 10 March 1849; *d.* St. Leu, Seine-et-Oise, France, 18 June 1912), *metallography.*

Osmond studied metallurgy under Samson Jordan at the École Centrale des Arts et Manufactures. After a short period with the Fives-Lille machine shop he joined Denain et Anzin, where he worked with Bessemer and open-hearth installations. From 1880 to 1884 Osmond was chief of the chemical laboratory of Schneider, Creusot, where he began his microscopic study of iron and steel in collaboration with a colleague in the physical testing laboratories. After 1884 Osmond, who was of a retiring disposition, left active business and returned to Paris, where he continued his research, corresponding with professional friends and publishing some eighty papers before his death.

Osmond's earliest interests concerned the effects of tempering and hardening cast steel and, particularly, the phenomena that occur during the heating and cooling of steel. The Le Chatelier pyrometer became available in 1886; and with the help of it Osmond took up the studies suggested by Tschernoff in 1868, by W. F. Barrett in 1873, and by Le Chatelier and others. Osmond proceeded to determine the so-called critical points at which the abnormal retardation or acceleration in the temperature drop occurs during the cooling of an iron sample—effects which indicate a liberation or an absorption of heat. From these investigations he concluded that allotropic β iron is the principal cause of the new properties communicated to steel by hardening. Osmond's experiments with tungsten steel showed that variations in the hardness of steel could be obtained by altering the initial temperature of heating and the rate of cooling; he did not publish this finding, which, in a sense, anticipated the Taylor-White process (1898).

By 1890 Osmond recognized three modifications of iron: α, β, and γ. His research led to the allotropic theory, the subject of much argument in the 1890's. It was opposed by the "carbonists," including John Oliver Arnold, who maintained that all the phenomena observed in the hardening of steel are explained by changes in the condition of the carbon and are in no way due to allotropic modifications of the iron. The Iron and Steel Institute (London) recognized the merits of both arguments by awarding the Bessemer Medal to Arnold in 1905 and to Osmond in 1906.

Osmond made substantial contributions to microscopical investigations of the structure of iron and steel. Although his interest may have been derived from the work of Hermann Vogelsang of Delft, he started with H. C. Sorby's methods, which he developed, especially in the preparation of samples. In the final polishing Osmond developed a method of "polish attack," in which the sample was rubbed on a sheet of parchment covered with calcium sulfate moistened with an infusion of licorice by which some of the constituents of the steel were colored.

Osmond's observations led him to identify and name sorbite, austenite, and troostite, commemorating Sorby, Sir W. C. Roberts-Austen, and Troost, an early associate of Osmond's who presented the latter's early papers to the Académie des Sciences in 1886–1887. Osmond rechristened H. M. Howe's hardenite "martensite" in honor of Adolf Martens, another pioneer in metallography. His own name was commemorated in osmondite, a term now obsolete in the nomenclature.

Osmond was awarded prizes by the Société d'Encouragement pour l'Industrie Nationale in 1888 and 1895, and the Lavoisier Medal in 1897.

BIBLIOGRAPHY

I. ORIGINAL WORKS. Among Osmond's more than 80 papers are: "Théorie cellulaire des propriétés de l'acier," in *Annales des mines* (Mémoires), 8th ser., **8** (1885), 5–84, written with Jean Werth; "Sur les phénomènes qui se produisent pendant le chauffage et le refroidissement de l'acier fondu," in *Comptes rendus . . . de l'Académie des sciences*, **103** (1886), 743–746, 1135–1137; "Rôle chimique du manganèse," *ibid.*, **104** (1887), 985–987; "Sur les residues que l'on extrait des aciers," *ibid.*, 1800–1812, written with J. Werth; "Die Metallographie als Untersuchungsmethode," in *Stahl und Eisen*, **17** (1897), 904–913; "Metallography as a Testing Method," in *Metallographist*, **1** (1898), 5–27; "What is the Inferior Limit of the Critical Point A$_2$?" *ibid.*, **2** (1899), 169–186; "On the Crystallography of Iron," *ibid.*, **3** (1900), 181–219; 275–290; *The Microscopic Analysis of Metal*, J. E. Stead, ed. (London, 1904); "Les expériences du Prof. Heyn sur la trempe et le revenu des aciers," in *Revue de métallurgie* (Mémoires), **3** (1906), 621–632; and "Crystallization of Iron," in *Journal of the Iron and Steel Institute*, **71**, no. 3 (1906), 444–492, written with G. Cartaud.

II. SECONDARY LITERATURE. See John O. Arnold and A. McWilliams, "The Diffusion of Elements in Iron," in *Engineering*, **68** (1899), 249; Henry M. Howe, *The Metallurgy of Steel* (New York, 1890), 163 ff.; and "The Heat Treatment of Steel: Note on Osmond's Theory," in *Transactions of the American Institute of Mining Engineers*, **23** (1893), 520; and the unsigned obituary in *Engineering*, **94** (1912), 56–58.

P. W. BISHOP

OSTROGRADSKY, MIKHAIL VASILIEVICH (*b.* Pashennaya [now in Poltava oblast], Russia, 24 September 1801; *d.* Poltava [now Ukrainian S.S.R.], 1 January 1862), *mathematics, mechanics.*

Ostrogradsky was born on the estate of his father, Vasily Ivanovich Ostrogradsky, a landowner of modest means; his mother was Irina Andreevna Sakhno-Ustimovich. After he had spent several years at the Poltava Gymnasium, the question of his future arose. Ostrogradsky hoped to become a soldier; but the life of an officer was expensive, the salary alone would not support him, and the family had little money to spare. It was decided to prepare him for the civil service and to give him a university education, without which his career would be limited. In 1816 Ostrogradsky enrolled in the physics and mathematics department of Kharkov University, where he received a good mathematical education under A. F. Pavlovsky and T. F. Osipovsky. He was especially influenced by the latter, an outstanding teacher and author of the three-volume *Kurs matematiki* (1801–1823), which was well known in its time, and also of philosophical papers in which he criticized Kant's apriorism from the materialistic point of view. In 1820 Ostrogradsky passed the examinations for the candidate's degree, and the university council voted to award it to him. But the minister of religious affairs and national education refused to confirm the council's decision and proposed that Ostrogradsky take the examinations again if he wished to receive his degree. Ostrogradsky rejected this proposal, and therefore did not obtain a university diploma.

The true reason for the arbitrary reversal of the council's decision was the government's struggle with the nonconformist and revolutionary attitudes prevalent among the Russian intelligentsia. The national educational system was headed by conservative bureaucrats who encouraged a combination of piety and mysticism at the universities. In the autumn of 1820 Osipovsky was suspended after having been rector of Kharkov University for a number of years. The animosity felt toward him was extended to Ostrogradsky, his best and favorite pupil, who, according to his own account later, was at that time a complete materialist and atheist. The ground for the refusal to grant him a diploma was that, under the influence of Osipovsky, he and the other students of mathematics did not attend lectures on philosophy and theology.

Ostrogradsky continued his mathematical studies in Paris, where Laplace and Fourier, Legendre and Poisson, Binet and Cauchy worked, and where outstanding courses were offered at the École Polytechnique and other educational institutions. Ostrogradsky's rapid progress gained him the friendship and respect of the senior French mathematicians and of his contemporaries, including Sturm. The Paris period of his life (1822–1827) was for Ostrogradsky not only "years of traveling and apprenticeship" but also a period of intense creative work. Between 1824 and 1827 he presented to the Paris Academy several papers containing important new discoveries in mathematical physics and integral calculus. Most of these discoveries were incorporated in his later papers; a memoir on hydrodynamics was published by the Paris Academy in 1832, and individual results in residue theory appeared, with his approval, in the works of Cauchy.

In the spring of 1828 Ostrogradsky arrived in St. Petersburg. There, over a period of several months, he presented three papers to the Academy of Sciences. In the first, on potential theory, he gave a new, more exact derivation of Poisson's equation for the case of a point lying within or on the surface of an attracting mass. The second was on heat theory, and the third on the theory of double integrals. All three appeared in *Mémoires de l'Académie impériale des sciences de St.-Pétersbourg*, 6th ser., **1** (1831). On 29 December 1828 Ostrogradsky was elected a junior academician in the section of applied mathematics. In 1830 he was elected an associate and in 1832 a full academician. His work at the Academy of Sciences restored to it the brilliance in mathematics that it had won in the eighteenth century but had lost in the first quarter of the nineteenth.

Ostrogradsky's activity at the Academy was manifold. He contributed some eighty-odd reports in mathematics and mechanics, delivered public lectures, wrote detailed reviews of papers submitted to the Academy, and participated in the work of commissions on the introduction of the Gregorian calendar and the decimal system of measurement. At the behest of the government he also investigated exterior ballistics problems. Ostrogradsky also devoted a great deal of time to teaching and did much to improve mathematical instruction in Russia. From 1828 he lectured at the Naval Corps (later the Naval Academy); from 1830, at the Institute of Means of Communication; and from 1832, at the General Pedagogical Institute. Later he also lectured at the General Engineering College and at the General Artillery College.

From 1847 Ostrogradsky accomplished a great deal as chief inspector for the teaching of the mathematical sciences in military schools. His textbooks on elementary and higher mathematics include a very interesting course on algebra and an exposition of the theory of numbers. Ostrogradsky's educational views were ahead of their time in many respects, particularly his program for the education of children between the ages of seven and twelve, which is expounded in *Considérations sur l'enseignement* (St. Petersburg–Paris, 1860), written with I. A. Blum.

It was mainly Ostrogradsky who established the conditions for the rise of the St. Petersburg mathematical school organized by Chebyshev, and who was the founder of the Russian school of theoretical mechanics. His direct disciples included I. A. Vyshnegradsky, the creator of the theory of automatic regulation, and N. P. Petrov, the author of the hydrodynamic theory of lubricants. Ostrogradsky's services were greatly appreciated by his contemporaries. He was elected a member of the American Academy of Arts and Sciences in 1834, the Turin Academy of Sciences in 1841, and the Rome Academy of Sciences in 1853; in 1856 he was elected a corresponding member of the Paris Academy of Sciences.

Ostrogradsky's scientific work closely bordered upon the developments originating in the École Polytechnique in applied mathematics and in directly related areas of analysis. In mathematical physics he sought a grandiose synthesis that would embrace hydromechanics, the theory of elasticity, the theory of heat, and the theory of electricity by means of a unique homogeneous method. The realization of this plan was beyond the capacity of one man and beyond the resources of the nineteenth century; it remains uncompleted to date.

Ostrogradsky contributed significantly to the development of the method of separating variables that was so successfully applied by Fourier in his work on the conduction of heat (1822). In "Note sur la théorie de la chaleur," presented in 1828 and published in 1831 (see his *Polnoe sobranie trudov*, I,

62–69), Ostrogradsky was the first to formulate a general schema of the method of solving boundary-value problems, which Fourier and Poisson had applied to the solution of individual problems.

For linear partial differential equations with constant coefficients Ostrogradsky established the orthogonality of the corresponding system of proper functions (eigenfunctions). Auxiliary means of calculation in this determination were Ostrogradsky's theorem for the reduction of certain volume integrals to surface integrals and the general formula for arbitrary conjugate linear differential operators with constant coefficients for a three-dimensional space, generally called Green's theorem. In terms of modern vector analysis Ostrogradsky's theorem states that the volume integral of the divergence of a vector field A taken over any volume v is equal to the surface integral of A taken over the closed surface s surrounding the volume v:

$$\iiint (\nabla \cdot A)\, dv = \iint A\, d\bar{s}.$$

(Ostrogradsky himself expressed this proposition in terms of ordinary integral calculus.) This theorem is also called Gauss's theorem, Green's theorem, or Riemann's theorem.

Ostrogradsky next applied his general results to the theory of heat, deriving formulas for the coefficients a_k in the expansion of an arbitrary function $f(x, y, z)$ into a series $\sum_{k=0}^{\infty} a_k u_k$ of eigenfunctions $u_k(x, y, z, \theta_k)$ of the corresponding boundary-value problem—a generalized Fourier series. He noted the difficulty connected with investigating the convergence of this type of series expansion and only touched on the problem of the existence of eigenvalues of θ_k; satisfactory solutions to these questions were not found until the turn of the twentieth century, by Poincaré and V. A. Steklov, among others.

A large part of these discoveries was contained in two memoirs presented by Ostrogradsky to the Paris Academy of Sciences in 1826–1827. In the second of these he solved the problem of the conduction of heat in a right prism with an isosceles right triangle as a base; Fourier and Poisson had previously examined the cases of a sphere, a cylinder, and a right rectangular parallelepiped. Lamé mentioned this solution, which was not published during Ostrogradsky's lifetime, in an 1833 paper. General results in the theory of heat analogous to Ostrogradsky's (but without his integral theorem) were also obtained by Lamé and Duhamel, who presented their papers to the Paris Academy of Sciences in 1829 (published in 1833).

At first Ostrogradsky investigated heat conduction in a solid body surrounded by a medium having a constant temperature. In "Deuxième note sur la théorie de la chaleur," presented in 1829 and published in 1831 (see *Polnoe sobranie trudov*, I, 70–72), he reduced this problem to the case when the temperature of the surrounding medium is a given function of the coordinates of space and time. Finally, in "Sur l'équation relative à la propagation de la chaleur dans l'intérieur des liquides," presented in 1836 and published in 1838 (*ibid.*, pp. 75–79), he derived the corresponding differential equation for an uncompressed moving liquid free of internal friction, thereby confirming Fourier's results by more thorough analysis.

At the same time Ostrogradsky studied the theory of elasticity; in this field his work meshed with Poisson's parallel investigations. Starting from the work of Poisson, who was the first to establish precisely the necessary condition of the extremum of a double integral with variable limits (1833), Ostrogradsky obtained important results in the calculus of variations. In "Mémoire sur le calcul des variations des intégrales multiples," presented in 1834 and published in 1838 (*ibid.*, III, 45–64), he derived equations containing the necessary conditions of the extremum of an integral of any multiplicity. To accomplish this he had to develop substantially the theory of multiple integrals. He generalized the integral theorem which he had found earlier, that is, reduced an n-tuple integral from an expression of the divergent type taken over any hypervolume to an $(n-1)$-tuple integral taken over the corresponding boundary hypersurface; derived a formula for the substitution of new variables in an n-tuple integral (independently of Jacobi, who published it in 1834); and described in detail the general method for computing an n-tuple integral by means of n consecutive integrations with respect to each variable.

In "Sur la transformation des variables dans les intégrales multiples," presented in 1836 and published in 1838 (*ibid.*, pp. 109–114), Ostrogradsky was the first to derive in a very modern manner (with a geometrical interpretation) the rule of the substitution of new variables in a double integral; he later extended this method to triple integrals. His work in the calculus of variations was directly related to his work in mechanics.

Ostrogradsky made two important discoveries in the theory of ordinary differential equations. In "Note sur la méthode des approximations successives," presented in 1835 and published in 1838 (*ibid.*, pp. 71–75), he proposed a method of solving nonlinear equations by expanding the unknown quantity into a power series in α, where α is a small parameter, in order to avoid "secular terms" containing the independent variable outside the sign of trigonometric functions. This important idea received further development in the investigations of H. Gylden (1881), Anders Lindstedt (1883), Poincaré, and Lyapunov. In "Note sur les équations différentielles linéaires," presented in 1838 and published in 1839 (*ibid.*, pp. 124–126), Ostrogradsky derived, simultaneously with Liouville, a well-known expression for Wronski's determinant, one of the basic formulas in the theory of differential linear equations.

Ostrogradsky also wrote several papers on the theory of algebraic functions and their integrals (*ibid.*, pp. 13 44, 175 179). The foundation of this theory was laid in 1826 by Abel, whom Ostrogradsky may have met in Paris. From Ostrogradsky's general results there follows the transcendency of a logarithmic function and of the arc tangent. His investigations were parallel to Liouville's work in the same area; they were continued in Russia by Chebyshev and his pupils. In "De l'intégration des fractions rationnelles," presented in 1844 and published in 1845 (*ibid.*, pp. 180–214), Ostrogradsky proposed a method for finding the algebraic part of an integral of a rational function without preliminary expansion of the integrand into the sum of partial fractions. This algebraic (and rational) part is calculated with the aid of rational operations and differentiations. Hermite rediscovered this method in 1872 and included it in his textbook on analysis (1873). It is sometimes called Hermite's method.

In "Mémoire sur les quadratures définies," written in 1839 and published in 1841 (*ibid.*, pp. 127–153), which grew out of his work in ballistics, Ostrogradsky gave a new derivation of the Euler-Maclaurin summation formula with a remainder term in the form in which it is now often presented (Jacobi published an equivalent result in 1834) and applied the general formulas to the approximation calculus of definite integrals. Several articles are devoted to probability theory—for example, one on the sample control of production, presented in 1846 and published in 1848 (*ibid.*, pp. 215–237), and to algebra. In general, however, as a mathematician Ostrogradsky was always an analyst.

Ostrogradsky's memoirs in mechanics can be divided into three areas: the principle of virtual displacements; dynamic differential equations; and the solution of specific problems.

Ostrogradsky's most important investigations in mechanics deal with generalizations of its basic principles and methods. He made a substantial contribution to the development of variational

OSTROGRADSKY

principles. The fundamental "Mémoire sur les équations différentielles relatives au problème des isopérimètres," presented in 1848 and published in 1850 (*ibid.*, II, 139–233), belongs in equal measure to mechanics and the calculus of variations. Because of his mathematical approach Ostrogradsky's investigations significantly deepened the understanding of variational principles.

In the paper just cited Ostrogradsky examined the variational problem in which the integrand depends on an arbitrary number of unknown functions of one independent variable and their derivatives of an arbitrary order and proved that the problem can be reduced to the integration of canonical Hamiltonian equations, which can be viewed as the form into which any equations arising in a variational problem can be transformed. This transformation requires no operation other than differentiation and algebraic operations. The credit for this interpretation of the dynamics problem belongs to Ostrogradsky. He also eased the restrictions on constraints, which had always been considered stationary, and thus significantly generalized the problem. Therefore the variational principle formulated by Hamilton in 1834–1835 might more accurately be called the Hamilton-Ostrogradsky principle. Jacobi also worked in the same direction, but his results were published later (1866).

At the same time Ostrogradsky prepared the important paper "Sur les intégrales des équations générales de la dynamique," also presented in 1848 and published in 1850 (*ibid.*, III, 129–138). In it he showed that even in the more general case, when the constraints and the force function depend on time (this case was not considered by Hamilton and Jacobi), the equations of motion can be transformed into Hamiltonian form. Generally, the development of the classical theory of the integration of canonical equations was carried out by Hamilton, Jacobi, and Ostrogradsky.

Ostrogradsky's results related to the development of the principle of virtual displacements are stated in "Considérations générales sur les moments des forces," presented in 1834 and published in 1838 (*ibid.*, II, 13–28). This paper significantly broadened the sphere of application of the principle of virtual displacements, extending it to the relieving constraints.

In "Mémoire sur les déplacements instantanés des systèmes assujettis à des conditions variables," presented and published in 1838 (*ibid.*, pp. 32–59), and "Sur le principe des vitesses virtuelles et sur la force d'inertie," presented in 1841 and published in 1842 (*ibid.*, pp. 104–109), Ostrogradsky gave a rigorous proof of the formula expressing the principle of virtual displacements for the case of nonstationary constraints.

"Mémoire sur la théorie générale de la percussion," presented in 1854 and published in 1857 (*ibid.*, pp. 234–266), presents Ostrogradsky's investigations of the impact of systems, in which he assumed that the constraints arising at the moment of impact are preserved after the impact. The principle of virtual displacements is extended here to the phenomenon of inelastic impact, and `the basic formula of the analytical theory of impact is derived.

Ostrogradsky also wrote papers containing solutions to particular problems of mechanics that had arisen in the technology of his time. A series of his papers on ballistics deserves special mention: "Note sur le mouvement des projectiles sphériques dans un milieu résistant" and "Mémoire sur le mouvement des projectiles sphériques dans l'air," both presented in 1840 and published in 1841; and "Tables pour faciliter le calcul de la trajectoire que décrit un mobile dans un milieu résistant," presented in 1839 and published in 1841 (*ibid.*, pp. 70–94). In the first two papers Ostrogradsky investigated the motion of the center of gravity and the rotation of a spherical projectile the geometrical center of which does not coincide with the center of gravity; both topics were important for artillery at that time. The third paper contains tables, computed by Ostrogradsky, of the function $\Phi(\theta) = 2 \int d\theta / \sin^3 \theta$, used in ballistics. These papers stimulated the creation of the Russian school of ballistics in the second half of the nineteenth century.

BIBLIOGRAPHY

I. Original Works. Most of Ostrogradsky's papers appeared in French in publications of the St. Petersburg Academy of Sciences. The most complete bibliography of his works and of writings concerning him is by M. G. Novlyanskaya in Ostrogradsky's *Izbrannye trudy* ("Selected Works"), V. I. Smirnov, ed. (Moscow, 1958), 540–581. Other collections of Ostrogradsky's writings are *Polnoe sobranie sochineny* ("Complete Collected Works"), I, pt. 2, *Lektsii po analiticheskoy mekhanike, 1834* ("Lectures on Analytic Mechanics"), and II, *Lektsii algebraicheskogo i transtsendentnogo analiza, 1837* ("Lectures on Algebraic and Transcendental Analysis"; Moscow-Leningrad, 1940–1946), never completed; and *Polnoe sobranie trudov* ("Complete Collected Works"), I. Z. Shtokalo, ed., 3 vols. (Kiev, 1959–1961), which contains commentaries and articles by I. Z. Shtokalo, I. B. Pogrebyssky, E. Y. Remez, Y. D. Sokolov, S. M. Targ, and others but does not include the 1834 and 1837 works above or the two articles that follow; and "Dokazatelstvo odnoy teoremy integralnogo ischisleniia" ("Proof of One Theorem in the Integral Calculus") and "Memuar o rasprostranenii tepla vnutri tverdykh tel" ("Memoir on the Conduction of Heat Within Solid Bodies"), in *Istoriko-matematicheskie issledovaniya*, **16** (1965), 49–96, Russian translations of two previously unpublished articles presented to the Paris Academy in 1826–1827, with an introduction by A. P. Youschkevitch.

II. SECONDARY LITERATURE. See Y. L. Geronimus, *Ocherki o rabotakh korifeev russkoy mekhaniki* ("Essays on the Work of the Leading Figures in Russian Mechanics"; Moscow, 1952), 13–57; B. V. Gnedenko and I. B. Pogrebyssky, *Mikhail Vasilievich Ostrogradsky (1801–1862). Zhizn i rabota. Nauchnoe i pedagogicheskoe nasledie* (". . . Life and Work. Scientific and Pedagogical Heritage"; Moscow, 1963), the most complete work on his life and accomplishments; A. T. Grigorian, *Mikhail Vasilievich Ostrogradsky (1801–1862)* (Moscow, 1961); and *Ocherki istorii mekhaniki v Rossii* ("Essays on the History of Mechanics in Russia"; Moscow, 1961), see index; *Istoria otechestvennoy matematiki* ("History of Russian Mathematics"), I. Z. Shtokalo, ed.-in-chief, II (Kiev, 1967), see index; A. I. Kropotov and I. A. Maron, *M. V. Ostrogradsky i ego pedagogicheskoe nasledie* ("Ostrogradsky and His Pedagogical Heritage"; Moscow, 1961); *Mikhail Vasilievich Ostrogradsky. 1862–1962. Pedagogicheskoe nasledie. Dokumenty o zhizni i deyatelnosti* (". . . Pedagogical Heritage. Documents on His Life and Activity"), I. B. Pogrebyssky and A. P. Youschkevitch, eds. (Moscow, 1961), a supp. to *Polnoe sobranie trudov* containing a Russian trans. of Ostrogradsky and Blum's *Considérations sur l'enseignement* (St. Petersburg–Paris, 1860), and Ostrogradsky's "Zapiski integralnogo ischislenia" ("Lectures on Integral Calculus"); E. Y. Remez, "O matematicheskikh rukopisyakh akademika M. V. Ostrogradskogo" ("On the Mathematical Manuscripts of Academician M. V. Ostrogradsky"), in *Istoriko-matematicheskie issledovaniya*, **4** (1951), 9–98; S. P. Timoshenko, *History of Strength of Materials* (New York–Toronto–London, 1953); I. Todhunter, *A History of the Progress of the Calculus of Variations During the Nineteenth Century* (Cambridge, 1861); P. I. Tripolsky, ed., *Mikhail Vasilievich Ostrogradsky. Prazdnovanie stoletia dnya ego rozhdenia* (". . . Celebration of the Centenary of His Birth"; Poltava, 1902), which contains short sketches on his life and scientific and educational activities—of special interest are an article by Lyapunov on his work in mechanics (pp. 115–118) and one by Steklov on Ostrogradsky's paper in mathematical physics (pp. 118–131); A. Youschkevitch, *Michel Ostrogradski et le progrès de la science au XIXᵉ siècle* (Paris, 1967); and *Istoria matematiki v Rossii do 1917 goda* ("History of Mathematics in Russia to 1917"; Moscow, 1968), see index; and N. E. Zhukovsky, "Uchenye trudy M. V. Ostrogradskogo po mekhanike" ("Ostrogradsky's Scientific Works in Mechanics"), in Zhukovsky's *Polnoe sobranie sochineny* ("Complete Collected Works"), VII (Moscow–Leningrad, 1950), 229–246.

A. P. YOUSCHKEVITCH

OSTWALD, CARL WILHELM WOLFGANG (*b.* Riga, Latvia, Russia, 27 May 1883; *d.* Dresden, Germany, 22 November 1943), *colloid chemistry, zoology.*

Ostwald, the second child of Wilhelm Ostwald, was a founder of colloid chemistry. He attended the Realgymnasium in Leipzig and at the age of fifteen composed a scientific work on the cases of the larvae of the caddis fly. After completing his secondary education he studied zoology at Leipzig under Carl Chun. From 1904 to 1906 he was a research assistant to Jacques Loeb at Berkeley, California. There he became friendly with the physiologist and physician M. H. Fischer, with whom he worked on the theory of fertilization. He qualified as a lecturer in biology at Leipzig in 1907 and he became professor of colloid chemistry in 1915. In 1907 he became editor of *Zeitschrift für Chemie und Industrie der Kolloide* and, beginning in 1909, he also edited *Kolloidchemische Beihefte*. Through these journals and through the Kolloid Gesellschaft, founded in 1922 at his suggestion—he was its first president and held that post for two decades—Ostwald organized and encouraged research in colloid chemistry. In 1923 he was appointed director of the colloid chemistry division of the physical-chemical institute at the University of Leipzig. He became a full professor there in 1935 and had a large circle of students.

In his zoological studies Ostwald explained the suspension of plankton and described the process of fertilization as a colloidal phenomenon. He established that there are no sharp differences between mechanical decompositions and colloidal and molecular solutions. He also defined colloids as disperse systems that are generally polyphasic and that possess particles 1–100 millimicrons in size. Ostwald worked on colloid chemistry problems involving, for example, bread and rubber. In addition he discovered the rule of color dispersion in the optics of colloidal systems and explained the irregular flow behavior of colloids, their textural viscosity, and their textural turbulence. He also worked on the law governing precipitation in saturated colloidal solutions, electrolytic coagulation, and other colloidal properties. In addition he developed a method of foam analysis. Through the lectures he gave outside Leipzig, especially in the United States, and through his books Ostwald made an essential contribution to obtaining international recognition of colloid chemistry as an independent field.

BIBLIOGRAPHY

I. ORIGINAL WORKS. Ostwald's approximately 200 scientific papers include "Kolloidwissenschaft, Elektrotechnik und heterogene Katalyse," in *Kolloidchemische Beihefte*, **32** (1930), 1–48; "Über mesomorphe und kolloide Systeme," in *Zeitschrift für Kristallographie . . .*, **79** (1932), 222–254; "Über Osmose und Solvation disperser Systeme," in *Zeitschrift für physikalische Chemie*, **159A** (1932), 375–392; "Elektrolytkoagulation und Elektrolytaktivitätskoeffizient," in *Kolloidzeitschrift*, **73** (1935)–**87** (1939), and **94** (1941), 169–184 (12 papers on this topic); "Metastrukturen der Materie," in *Kolloidchemische Beihefte*, **42** (1935), 109–124; "Über die andere geschichtliche Wurzel der Kolloidwissenschaft," in *Kolloid-Zeitschrift*, **84** (1938), 258–265; and "Physikalisch-chemische Metastasen," *ibid.*, **100** (1942), 2–57.

Ostwald's books include *Neue theoretische Betrachtungsweise in der Planktologie* (Stuttgart, 1903); *Grundriss der Kolloidchemie* (Leipzig, 1909); *Die Welt der vernachlässigten Dimensionen* (Leipzig, 1914), which consists of lectures given in the United States; *Praktikum der Kolloidchemie* (Leipzig, 1920); and *Licht und Farbe in Kolloiden* (Dresden–Leipzig, 1924).

Bibliographies of his works are in: Poggendorff, IV, 1103; V, 930–931; VI, 1929–1931; and VIIa, pt. 3, 484–486; and in the biographical article by Lottermoser.

II. SECONDARY LITERATURE. See the following, listed chronologically: A. Lottermoser, "Wolfgang Ostwald 60 Jahre alt," in *Kolloidzeitschrift*, **103**, no. 2 (1943), 89–94 (bibliography 91–94); G. F. Hüttig, "Wolfgang Ostwald," in *Forschungen und Fortschritte*, **20** (1944), 118–119; and other obituaries by R. E. Oesper, in *Journal of Chemical Education*, **22** (1945), 263; by H. Ebring, in *Kolloidzeitschrift*, **115** (1949), 3–5; by E. A. Hauser, in *Journal of Chemical Education*, **32** (1955), 2–9; and by M. H. Fischer, "Wolfgang Ostwalds Weg zur Kolloidchemie," in *Kolloidzeitschrift*, **145** (1956), 1–2.

HANS-GÜNTHER KÖRBER

OSTWALD, FRIEDRICH WILHELM (*b.* Riga, Latvia, Russia [now Latvian S.S.R.], 2 September 1853; *d.* Leipzig, Germany, 4 April 1932), *chemistry, color science.*

For a detailed study of his life and work, see Supplement.

OTT, ISAAC (*b.* Northampton County, Pennsylvania, 30 November 1847; *d.* Easton, Pennsylvania, 1 January 1916), *physiology.*

Discoverer of the heat-regulating center of the brain in 1887, Ott received the B.A. and M.A. from Lafayette College and the M.D. from the University of Pennsylvania in 1869, with a dissertation on typhoid fever. Following an internship at St. Mary's Hospital in Philadelphia, he did postgraduate study at Leipzig, Würzburg, and Berlin. In 1873 he was appointed demonstrator of experimental physiology at the University of Pennsylvania, where he organized a physiological laboratory and lectured on physiology until 1878. He became a fellow in biology at the Johns Hopkins University in 1879, lecturing the same year in physiology at the Medico-Chirurgical College of Philadelphia while it was still a society. In 1894 Ott was appointed professor of physiology at the Medico-Chirurgical College, filling the chair until the college merged with the University of Pennsylvania about the time of his death in 1916. He served as dean in 1895, and each year he selected five of his most promising students as members of the American Physiological Society.

In 1876 Ott settled at Easton. He wrote more than fifty scientific papers, the last one in 1910 on internal secretions, and wrote the book *The Action of Medicines* (1878).

Ott performed experiments demonstrating that there are areas in the brain which exert considerable control over the body temperature and pinpointed the center for temperature regulation in the region of the corpora striata. From his pioneering work in neurophysiological technique have come a multitude of studies. He also devoted considerable study to the physiological action of drugs and discovered the path and decussation of the sudorific, sphincter-inhibitory and thermo-inhibitory fibers in the spinal cord and the innervation of the sphincters.

He served as president of the American Neurological Association. In his opening address as president of the Section on Physiology at the first Pan American Medical Congress in 1895, he reviewed work in physiology in the United States and noted that research required special commitment because it was exhausting financially as well as physically.

BIBLIOGRAPHY

I. ORIGINAL WORKS. Ott's article "The Relation of the Nervous System to the Temperature of the Body," in *Journal of Nervous and Mental Diseases*, **11** (1884), 141–152, is item 1416 in F. H. Garrison and L. T. Morton, *A Medical Bibliography* (London, 1943), with a statement that Ott wrote important papers on the nervous regulation of body temperature. His papers on the heat center in the brain and on the thermo-inhibitory apparatus were published in the same journal, **14** (1887), 150–162, 428–438; and **15** (1888), 85–104. His book *Fever: Its Thermotaxis and Metabolism* (New York, 1914) is listed in Garrison and Morton as item 2115. He also published *Cocaine, Veratria and Gelsemium: Toxicological Studies* (Philadelphia, 1874). His works on lobelia, thebaine, lycotomia, poisonous mushrooms, ethyl bromide, Jamaica dogwood, loco weed, lily of the valley, rattlesnake venom, copperhead snake venom, absinthism epilepsy, antipyretics, heroin, and adrenalin are listed in the *Surgeon General's Catalogue.* Further writings are *Textbook of Physiology* (Philadelphia, 1904; 2nd ed., 1907; 3rd ed., 1909; 4th ed., 1913); *The Parathyroid Glandules From a Physiological and Pathological Standpoint* (Philadelphia, 1910); *Internal Secretions From a Physiological and Therapeutical Standpoint* (Easton, Pa., 1910); and *Contributions From the Physiological Laboratory of the Medico-Chirurgical College of Philadelphia* (Philladelphia, 1914), written with John C. Scott.

II. SECONDARY LITERATURE. A good biographical sketch is presented in Howard A. Kelly and Walter L. Burrage, eds., *American Medical Biographies* (Baltimore, 1920), 869. There is a contemporary sketch by W. B. Atkinson in *Physicians and Surgeons of the United States* (Philadelphia, 1878), 172–173. Ott's photograph is reproduced on plate 69, facing p. 343, accompanied by a sketch and an excerpt from his classic article "The Heat-Center in the Brain" (in *Journal of Nervous and Mental Diseases,* **14** [1887], 150–162), in John F. Fulton and Leonard G. Wilson, *Selected Readings in the History of Physiology,* 2nd ed. (Springfield, Ill., 1966), 337. There is a biographical sketch in *Appleton's Cyclopaedia of American Biography,* IV (1888), 608; and obituaries in *Journal of the American Medical Association,* **26** (1916), 206; by Joseph McFarland, in *Journal of Nervous and Mental Diseases,* **43** (1916), 201; in *Medical Record,* **89** (1916), 72; and in *New York Medical Journal,* **103** (1916), 80. G. Clark, Magoun, and Ranson refer to his work in "Hypothalamic Regulation of Body Temperature," in *Journal of Neurophysiology,* **2** (1939), 61–80.

SAMUEL X. RADBILL

OUDEMANS, CORNEILLE ANTOINE JEAN ABRAM (*b.* Amsterdam, Netherlands, 7 December 1825; *d.* Arnhem, Netherlands, 29 August 1906), *medicine, botany, mycology.*

Oudemans was the son of Anthonie Cornelis Oudemans, an educator, and Jacoba Adriana Hammecker. Two of their other children became prominent scientists: Jean Abraham Crétien Oudemans, an astronomer, and Antoine Corneille Oudemans, a chemist. Oudemans received his elementary education in Weltevreden, Java, where his father was the principal of a grammar school; at the age of fourteen he was sent back to the Netherlands to study Latin and Greek in preparation for admission to a university. Two years later he became a medical student at Leiden, where he was granted the M.D. on 5 November 1847. A subsequent study trip to Paris and Vienna was cut short by the March Revolution of 1848. Soon after his return on 9 August 1848, Oudemans was appointed lecturer in botany, materia medica, and natural history at the clinical school of Rotterdam, where he also set up a practice. While in Rotterdam he was very active in the field of public

health and also published the results of his pharmacological investigations.

In 1859 Oudemans was offered the chair of medicine and botany at the Athenaeum of Amsterdam, vacant after Miquel moved to the University of Utrecht. He gave his inaugural lecture on 21 November. When the Athenaeum obtained university status in 1877, Oudemans became its first *rector magnificus.* In the same year his teaching duty was reduced to systematic botany and pharmacognosy; Hugo de Vries was appointed lecturer in plant physiology and anatomy. After his retirement in 1896 he settled in Arnhem.

While at Amsterdam, Oudemans became increasingly interested in the fungi of the Netherlands, a subject on which he became the national expert. His *Révision des champignons* (1892–1897) and *Catalogue raisonné* (1904) are still standard works on Dutch mycology, as is his posthumously published *Enumeratio systematica fungorum,* on which he worked for twenty-five years. In this book he described all the known European parasitic fungi. The work was published under the supervision of J. W. Moll, professor of botany at Groningen, to which university Oudemans left his collection of parasitic fungi.

BIBLIOGRAPHY

I. ORIGINAL WORKS. The library of the University of Amsterdam has the following MS notes by Oudemans: "Hebra's Klinik über Hautkrankheiten. Angefangen 20 März (1848). Aufgeschrieben in einem Privatkurs von C. A. J. A. Oudemans."

His earliest published works are *De fluxu menstruo* (Leiden, 1847), his dissertation; *Algemeen verslag der subcommissie voor den Aziatischen braakloop, geheerscht hebbende te Rotterdam* (Rotterdam, 1849); *Systematisch overzicht der geneeskundige gewassen* (Rotterdam, 1851); *Aanteekeningen op het systematisch- en pharmacognostisch botanische gedeelte der Pharmacopoea Neerlandica,* 2 vols. (Rotterdam, 1854–1856); *Bijdrage tot de kennis van de morphologische en anatomische structuur van de vrucht en het zaad des kamferbooms (Dryobalanops camphora, Colebr.) van Sumatra* (Rotterdam, 1855); *Brief van de openbare gezondheidscommissie te Rotterdam omtrent het planten van boomen aldaar* (n.p., 1855); *Flora van Nederland,* 3 vols. and atlas (Haarlem, 1859–1862; 2nd ed., Amsterdam, 1872–1874); and *Over de plantkunde, beschouwd in hare trapsgewijze ontwikkeling van de vroegste tijden* (Amsterdam, 1859), his inaugural lecture.

Writings from the 1860's and 1870's are *Brief over de hervorming en uitbreiding van het natuur- en geneeskundig onderwijs aan het Athenaeum Illustre te Amsterdam . . .* (Amsterdam, 1860), written with C. E. V. Schneevoogt; *Ueber den Sitz der Oberhaut bei den Luftwurzeln der Orchideen* (Amsterdam, 1861); *Annotationes criticae in Cupuliferas nonnulas Javanicas* (Amsterdam, 1865); *Hand-*

leiding tot de pharmacognosie van het planten- en dierenrijk (Haarlem, 1865); *Leerboek der plantenkunde,* 2 vols. (Utrecht–Amsterdam, 1866–1870); *Eerste beginselen der plantenkunde* (Amsterdam–Rotterdam–Utrecht, 1868); and *Rede ter herdenking van den sterfdag van Carolus Linnaeus, eene eeuw na diens verscheiden* (Amsterdam, 1878).

His latest works were *Leerboek der plantenkunde, ten gebruike bij het hooger onderwijs,* I, *Vormleer en rang-schikking der planten* (Zaltbommel, 1883; 2nd ed., Nijmegen, 1896)—vols. II and III written by Hugo de Vries; *Revisio pyrenomycetum in regno Batavorum, hujusque detectorum* (Amsterdam, 1884); *Révision des champignons, tout supérieurs qu'inférieurs, trouvés jusqu'à ce jour dans les Pays-Bas,* 2 vols. (Amsterdam, 1892–1897); *Beteekenis der geslachtsnamen van de phanerogamen en de vaat kryptogamen* (Bussum, 1899); *Catalogue raisonné des champignons des Pays-Bas* (Amsterdam, 1904); and *Enumeratio systematica fungorum,* J. W. Moll, R. de Boer, and L. Vuyck, eds., 5 vols. (The Hague, 1919–1924).

In addition Oudemans wrote a large number of papers, a list of more than eighty is in the obituary by J. W. Moll and in the Royal Society *Catalogue of Scientific Papers,* IV, 715; VIII, 543–544; X, 970–971; XII, 552; and XVII, 657.

II. Secondary Literature. See P. J. Lotsy, "Corneille Antoine Jean Abram Oudemans," in *Nieuw nederlandsch biografisch woordenboek,* I (Leiden, 1911), 1396–1397; J. W. Moll, "C. A. J. A. Oudemans," in *Jaarboek van de K. Akademie van wetenschappen . . . Amsterdam,* **62** (1909), 57–105, with bibliography; W. F. R. Suringar, "C. A. J. A. Oudemans," in *Eigen Haard,* **21** (1895), 773–775; and J. S. Theissen, "Corneille Antoine Jean Abram Oudemans," in *Gedenkboek van het Athenaeum en de Universiteit van Amsterdam, 1632–1932,* I (Amsterdam, 1932), 649–650.

Peter W. van der Pas

OUGHTRED, WILLIAM (*b.* Eton, Buckinghamshire, England, 5 March 1575; *d.* Albury, near Guildford, Surrey, England, 30 June 1660), *mathematics.*

Oughtred's father was a scrivener who taught writing at Eton and instructed his young son in arithmetic. Oughtred was educated as a king's scholar at Eton, from which he proceeded to King's College, Cambridge, at the age of fifteen. He became a fellow of his college in 1595, graduated B.A. in 1596, and was awarded the M.A. in 1600.

Ordained a priest in 1603, Oughtred at once began his ecclesiastical duties, being presented with the living of Shalford, Surrey. Five years later he became rector of Albury and retained this post until his death. Despite his parochial duties he continued to devote considerable time to mathematics, and in 1628 he was called upon to instruct Lord William Howard, the young son of the earl of Arundel. In carrying out this task he prepared a treatise on arithmetic and algebra.

This slight volume, of barely 100 pages, contained almost all that was then known of these two branches of mathematics; it was published in 1631 as *Clavis mathematicae.*

Oughtred's best-remembered work, the *Clavis* exerted considerable influence in England and on the Continent and immediately established him as a capable mathematician. Both Boyle and Newton held a very high opinion of the work. In a letter to Nathaniel Hawes, treasurer of Christ's Hospital, dated 25 May 1694 and entitled "A New Scheme of Learning for the Mathematical Boys at Christ's Hospital," Newton referred to Oughtred as "a man whose judgment (if any man's) may be relyed on." In Lord King's *Life of Locke* we read: "The best Algebra yet extant is Oughtred's" (I, 227). John Aubrey, in *Brief Lives,* maintained that Oughtred was more famous abroad for his learning than at home and that several great men came to England for the purpose of meeting him (II, 471).

John Wallis dedicated his *Arithmetica infinitorum* (1655) to Oughtred. A pupil of Oughtred, Wallis never wearied of sounding his praises. In his *Algebra* (1695) he wrote: "The *Clavis* doth in as little room deliver as much of the fundamental and useful parts of geometry (as well as of arithmetic and algebra) as any book I know," and in its preface he classed Oughtred with the English mathematician Thomas Harriot.

The *Clavis* is not easy reading. The style is very obscure, and rules are so involved as to make them difficult to follow. Oughtred carried symbolism to excess, using signs to denote quantities, their powers, and the fundamental operations in arithmetic and algebra. Chief among these were X for multiplication, $\sqsupset$ for "greater than"; $\sqsubset$ for "less than"; and $\sim$ for "difference between." Ratio was denoted by a dot; proportion, by ::. Thus the proportion $A : B = \alpha : \beta$ was written $A \cdot B :: \alpha \cdot \beta$. Continued proportion was written $\div$. Of the maze of symbols employed by Oughtred, only those for multiplication and proportion are still used. Yet, surprisingly, there is a complete absence of indices or exponents from his work. Even in later editions of the *Clavis,* Oughtred used *Aq, Ac, Aqq, Aqc, Acc, Aqqc, Aqcc, Accc, Aqqcc,* to denote successive powers of *A* up to the tenth. In his *Géométrie* (1637) Descartes had introduced the notation x^n but restricted its use to cases in which *n* was a positive whole number. Newton extended this notation to include fractional and negative indices. These first appeared in a letter to Oldenburg for transmission to Leibniz—the famous *Epistola prior* of June 1676—in which Newton illustrated the newly discovered binomial theorem.

In *La disme*, a short tract published in 1585, Simon Stevin had outlined the principles of decimal fractions. Although a warm admirer of Stevin's work, Oughtred avoided his clumsy notation and substituted his own, which, although an improvement, was far from satisfactory. He did not use the dot to separate the decimal from the whole number, undoubtedly because he already used it to denote ratio; instead, he wrote a decimal such as 0.56 as 0/56.

Oughtred is generally regarded as the inventor of the circular and rectilinear slide rules. Although the former is described in his *Circles of Proportion and the Horizontal Instrument* (1632), a description of the instrument had been published two years earlier by one of his pupils, Richard Delamain, in *Grammelogie, or the Mathematical Ring*. A bitter quarrel ensued between the two, each claiming priority in the invention. There seems to be no very good reason why each should not be credited as an independent inventor. Oughtred's claim to priority in the invention of the rectilinear slide rule, however, is beyond dispute, since it is known that he had designed the instrument as early as 1621.

In 1657 Oughtred published *Trigonometria*, a work of thirty-six pages dealing with both plane and spherical triangles. Oughtred made free use of the abbreviations *s* for sine, *t* for tangent, *se* for secant, *sco* for sine of the complement (or cosine), *tco* for cotangent, and *seco* for cosecant. The work also contains tables of sines, tangents, and secants to seven decimal places as well as tables of logarithms, also to seven places.

It is said that Oughtred, a staunch royalist, died in a transport of joy on hearing the news of the restoration of Charles II.

BIBLIOGRAPHY

I. Original Works. Oughtred's chief writing is *Arithmeticae in numeris et speciebus institutio . . . quasi clavis mathematicae est* (London, 1631); 2nd ed., *Clavis mathematicae* (London, 1648). English translations were made by Robert Wood (1647) and Edmond Halley (1694). Subsequent Latin eds. appeared at Oxford in 1652, 1667, and 1693.

His other works are *The Circles of Proportion and the Horizontal Instrument*, W. Forster, trans. (London, 1632), a treatise on navigation; *The Description and Use of the Double Horizontal Dial* (London, 1636); *A Most Easy Way for the Delineation of Plain Sundials, Only by Geometry* (1647); *The Solution of All Spherical Triangles* (Oxford, 1651); *Description and Use of the General Horological Ring and the Double Horizontal Dial* (London, 1653); *Trigonometria* (London, 1657), trans. by R. Stokes

as *Trigonometrie* (London, 1657); and *Canones sinuum, tangentium, secantium et logarithmorum* (London, 1657).

A collection of Oughtred's papers, mainly on mathematical subjects, was published posthumously under the direction of Charles Scarborough as *Opuscula mathematica hactenus inedita* (Oxford, 1677).

II. Secondary Literature. On Oughtred or his work, see John Aubrey, *Brief Lives*, Andrew Clark, ed. (Oxford, 1898), II, 106, 113–114, 471. W. W. R. Ball, *A History of the Study of Mathematics at Cambridge* (Cambridge, 1889); Florian Cajori, *William Oughtred, a Great Seventeenth-Century Teacher of Mathematics* (Chicago–London, 1916); Moritz Cantor, *Vorlesungen über Geschichte der Mathematik*, 2nd ed., II (Leipzig, 1913), 720–721; Charles Hutton, *Philosophical and Mathematical Dictionary*, new ed. (London, 1815), II, 141–142; and S. J. Rigaud, ed., *Correspondence of Scientific Men of the Seventeenth Century*, I (Oxford, 1841), 11, 16, 66.

J. F. Scott

OUTHIER, RÉGINALD (*b*. La Marre-Jousserans, near Poligny, France, 16 August 1694; *d*. Bayeux, France, 12 April 1774), *astronomy, cartography.*

Outhier, for many years canon of the cathedral of Bayeux, was one of the many provincial amateur scientists who supplied the academicians in Paris with somewhat raw observations, which they, in turn, used in order to support their more general theories and treatises. His scientific observations covered astronomy, meteorology, and cartography, both terrestrial and celestial.

Outhier's scientific communications began in 1727, when he presented a celestial globe of his own invention to the Académie Royale des Sciences. In addition to the positions of the stars, this globe, moved by clockwork, indicated the apparent path of the sun along the ecliptic and various motions of the moon. On 1 December 1731 Outhier was named correspondent of Jacques Cassini and, twenty-five years later, correspondent of Cassini de Thury.

In preparation for an exact map of France, Cassini in 1733 drew a line perpendicular to the meridian of Paris westward from Paris to the sea. Outhier, then secretary to Paul d'Albert de Luynes, the very scientific bishop of Bayeux, joined the surveying party from Caen to St.-Malo. After the triangulation was accomplished, the party went to Bayeux to make some celestial observations. Cassini was impressed by the large sundial with lines at five-minute intervals that Outhier had traced on the cathedral library. Around this time Outhier drew a map of the diocese of Bayeux, published in 1736, and others of the bishopric of Meaux and of the archbishopric of Sens.

In 1736–1737 the Academy sponsored an expedition to Lapland to measure the length of a degree of latitude near the North Pole, in order to determine the actual figure of the earth; and Outhier, "dont la capacité dans l'ouvrage que nous allions faire, etoit connuë . . ." (Maupertuis, *La figure de la terre*, p. xv), was invited to participate. He assisted in the astronomical observations, drew eighteen maps of the lands through which they passed, and studied the religious and social customs of the Lapps. His detailed journal of the voyage was published in 1744.

In 1752 Outhier drew, and presented to the Academy, a map of the Pleiades that was by far the most accurate map of the region. It included ninety-nine stars of the third through the tenth magnitudes, thirty-five of which had been measured by Le Monnier; coordinates were given for every ten minutes of celestial latitude and longitude and every twenty minutes of right ascension and declination. Other reports to the Academy concerned the weather at Bayeux, the transit of Venus of 1761, six lunar eclipses, and two solar eclipses.

BIBLIOGRAPHY

I. ORIGINAL WORKS. Outhier's account of his journey to Lapland is *Journal d'un voyage au nord, en 1736 et 1737* (Paris, 1744; repub. Amsterdam, 1746), English trans. in John Pinkerton, ed., *A General Collection of the Best and Most Interesting Voyages and Travels*, I (London, 1808), 259–336. Two of his maps appeared as *Carte topographique du diocèse de Bayeux, divisé en ses quatre archidiaconés et ses dix sept doyenés . . . par l'Abbé Outhier*, 2 sheets (1736); and *Cartes de l'évêché de Meaux et de l'archévêché de Sens*.

His earlier articles include "Globe mouvant inventé par M. l'Abbé Outhier, prestre," in *Machines et inventions approuvées par l'Académie royale des sciences*, V (Paris, 1735), 15–17; "Le mesme globe perfectionné et presenté en MDCCXXXI," *ibid.*, pp. 19–20; "Addition au globe mouvant, par M. l'Abbé Outhier," *ibid.*, 21–22; "Observations de l'éclipse de Jupiter & de ses satellites par la lune, faites à Sommervieux près de Bayeux par M. l'Évêque de Bayeux le 17 juin 1744, par M. Cassini," in *Mémoires de l'Académie royale des sciences . . .* (1744), 415–416; "Extrait des observations de l'éclipse de lune, faites à Bayeux le 2 novembre 1743 au matin, & communiquées à l'Académie, par M. le Monnier fils," *ibid.* (1745), 511; "Observation de l'éclipse du soleil, du 25 juillet 1748, faite à Bayeux par M. l'Abbé Outhier," in *Mémoires . . . présentés par divers sçavans*, 2 (1755), 307–308; "Observation de l'éclipse de lune, du 8 août 1748, faite à Bayeux, dans l'évêché par M. l'Abbé Outhier," *ibid.*, pp. 309–310; "Observation de l'éclipse de lune, du 23 décembre 1749, faite à Bayeux, par M. l'Abbé Outhier, correspondent de l'Académie," *ibid.*, pp. 311–312; "Observation de l'éclipse du soleil du 8 janvier 1750, faite à Bayeux, par M. l'Abbé

Outhier," *ibid.*, pp. 313–314; "Sur une nouvelle quadrature par approximation, par M. l'Abbé Outhier . . .," *ibid.*, p. 333; and "Cartes des Pléyades . . .," *ibid.*, pp. 607–608 and pl. XXV; "Observations météorologiques faites à Bayeux en 1756," *ibid.*, **4** (1763), 612–613; "Autre observation du passage de Vénus, faite à Bayeux le 6 juin 1761, avec une lunette de 34 pouces garnis d'un micromètre dont chaque tour de vis est divisé en 42 parties," *ibid.*, **6** (1764), 133–134; "Observation de l'éclipse de lune, faite à Bayeux le 18 mai 1761," *ibid.*, p. 134; and "Observation de l'éclipse de lune du 8 mai 1762, au matin, faite à Bayeux," *ibid.*, p. 176.

II. SECONDARY LITERATURE. See C. F. Cassini de Thury, "De la carte de la France et de la perpendiculaire à la méridienne de Paris," in *Mémoires de l'Académie royale des sciences . . .* (1733), 389–405; H. F., "Outhier (Réginald ou Regnauld)," in *Nouvelle biographie générale*, XXXVIII (Paris, 1864), cols. 982–983; and P. Maupertuis, *La figure de la terre* (Paris, 1738).

DEBORAH JEAN WARNER

OVERTON, CHARLES ERNEST (*b.* Stretton, Cheshire, England, 25 February 1865; *d.* Lund, Sweden, 27 January 1933), *cell physiology, pharmacology.*

Overton was the son of the Reverend Samuel Charlesworth Overton and Harriet Jane Fox, daughter of the Reverend W. Darwin Fox, a second cousin of Charles Darwin. He was educated at Newport Grammar School until 1882, when his mother, for health reasons, moved with her children to Switzerland. He studied biology, especially botany, at the University of Zurich, where in 1889 he obtained the Ph.D. and, in 1890, was appointed *Dozent* in biology. From Zurich, Overton moved to the University of Würzburg in 1901 as assistant to Max von Frey in the physiology department. In 1907 he accepted the chair of pharmacology at the University of Lund, where he remained until his retirement in 1930. In 1912 he married Dr. Louise Petrén. Overton published his most important papers between about 1893 and 1902. His productivity subsequently decreased considerably, owing to impaired health.

As early as 1890–1893, before finding his final field of research, Overton had done pioneering work in plant cytology, in which he showed that the haploid chromosome number is characteristic not only of the sex cells themselves but also of the whole gametophyte.

At about this time Overton became interested in the fundamental problem of how living cells, isolated from their surroundings so that the solutes in the sap are prevented from diffusing out, are nevertheless able to take up nutrients from without and to throw off the waste products of their metabolism. In the 1890's living cells were commonly thought to be virtually impermeable to the great majority of solutes but readily permeable to water. Overton, however, observed that there is a whole series of intermediate cases between substances totally unable to penetrate living protoplasts and those that do so as rapidly as water. Moreover, he found that all the widely different kinds of plant and animal cells are surprisingly similar in their permeability properties. In 1899 Overton pointed out a striking parallel between the permeating powers of different substances and their relative fat solubility—that is, their partition coefficient in a system composed of fat and water. The smaller this coefficient, the more difficult the passage of the substance through the protoplast. This was at first sight a very surprising result, but Overton explained it by assuming that the invisible plasma membranes, already theoretically postulated by Pfeffer, are "impregnated" with fatlike substances, such as cholesterol or phosphatides.

This hypothesis, now universally known as Overton's lipoid (or lipide) theory of plasma permeability, was first published in a preliminary form, his intention being to present the detailed basis for it in a later extensive publication. The larger work containing definite proof of the theory was, however, never finished. Thus, it is understandable that, although the theory aroused a great deal of interest, it also met with doubt and even violent opposition, especially since Overton never replied to the attacks on his views. Apart from minor modifications, however, later experiments have confirmed his results.

In 1896 Overton pointed out that both plant and animal cells can transport solutes against the concentration gradient. Such an active transport carried out at the expense of energy set free by metabolic processes is a phenomenon quite different from the simple diffusion of substances through the protoplasts. Active transport, as Overton anticipated, has proved to be of fundamental importance to living cells.

In carrying out permeability experiments with muscle cells, Overton found that their irritability is reversibly lost when the sodium ions that are normally present between them diffuse out from the muscles. To explain this and other related observations, he tentatively proposed the hypothesis that for an extremely short interval the surface of the contracting muscle fibers becomes permeable to sodium and potassium ions. This fundamental idea in the theory of propagation of impulses in nerves and muscles was worked out almost fifty years later by A. L. Hodgkin and A. F. Huxley, for which they were awarded the Nobel Prize in physiology or medicine in 1963.

In studying the permeability properties of plant and animal cells, Overton observed that those substances which, owing to their great lipide solubility, penetrate the protoplasts most rapidly also have the ability to produce narcosis. It was only natural that he assumed their narcotizing effect to be in some way dependent on their lipide solubility. Almost simultaneously with Overton but independently of him, the pharmacologist Hans Horst Meyer reached much the same conclusion. Although the Meyer-Overton theory does not offer a complete explanation of the mechanism of narcosis, it remains an important starting point for newer, more elaborate theories of this phenomenon.

A gentle and placid man, Overton had a striking intuitive ability to recognize the great, fundamental problems and to envision a means of solving them without recourse to complicated apparatus. He never founded a school in the proper sense of the word, and his publications, almost all of which were written in German, do not seem to have been widely read in the original, especially in English-speaking countries. Nevertheless, his influence on the development of cell physiology and pharmacology has been strong and long-lasting. He was one of those scientists whose stature is more obvious after their death than it was during their lifetime.

BIBLIOGRAPHY

Overton's most important publications are "On the Reduction of the Chromosomes in the Nuclei of Plants," in *Annals of Botany*, **7** (1893), 139–143; "Über die allgemeinen osmotischen Eigenschaften der Zelle, ihre vermutlichen Ursachen und ihre Bedeutung für die Physiologie," in *Vierteljahrsschrift der Naturforschenden Gesellschaft in Zürich*, **44** (1899), 88–135; *Studien über die Narkose* (Jena, 1901); "Beiträge zur allgemeinen Muskel- und Nervenphysiologie," in *Pflügers Archiv für die gesamte Physiologie*, **92** (1902), 346–386; and "Über den Mechanismus der Resorption und Sekretion," in W. Nagel, ed., *Handbuch der Physiologie des Menschen*, II (Brunswick, 1907), 744–898.

For a more complete biography and bibliography, see P. R. Collander, "Ernest Overton (1865–1933), a Pioneer to Remember," in *Leopoldina*, 3rd ser., **8–9** (1962–1963), 242–254.

RUNAR COLLANDER

OWEN, DAVID DALE (*b*. New Lanark, Scotland, 24 June 1807; *d*. New Harmony, Indiana, 13 November 1860), *geology*.

Owen was the son of Robert Owen, the utopian philanthropist and progressive mill owner, and Anne

Caroline Dale Owen. He was educated at home in the classics, mechanics, and architectural drawing and, from the age of seventeen to twenty, at P. E. von Fellenberg's "progressive school" in Hofwyl, near Bern, Switzerland, at which he studied the classics, music, drawing, chemistry, and natural history. He then spent a year in Glasgow, studying principally chemistry under Andrew Ure at the Andersonian Institution. In 1825 Owen's father and William Maclure purchased the village, factories, and lands of New Harmony, Indiana, from George Rapp. In 1828, Owen came to New Harmony, which remained his home for the rest of his life. With Henry D. Rogers he went back to London in 1831 to study chemistry, then returned to New Harmony in 1833 and studied medicine in Cincinnati at various times from 1835 to 1837. He graduated in 1837 and used the title of doctor, although he never practiced. His medical training was to gain more scientific background, especially for his developing interest in geology. He spent part of the summer of 1836 as assistant to Gerard Troost, state geologist of Tennessee. He married Caroline Neef in 1837.

When the Indiana Geological Survey was established in 1837, Owen was immediately appointed state geologist. Always mindful of the practical application of science, he made a regional survey to determine the major rock divisions, the limits of the coal-bearing rocks, the iron ore deposits, and building stones. He was the first American to use the term "Carboniferous" in the present restricted sense. He also recognized the Cincinnati arch just east of Indiana, a structural axis that controlled the westward-dipping strata in Indiana. Owen's Indiana reports led to his appointment in 1839 to explore the United States mineral lands of the Dubuque lead district in southwestern Wisconsin, southeastern Iowa, and northeastern Illinois, then the most important lead mining area in the country. Aided by John Locke and a corps of 139 assistants, in two months Owen covered 11,000 square miles; he presented maps in February 1840 and a report in June 1840. The expertly colored geologic maps and sections, the sketches of topographic features, and the lithographic fossil plates, all by Owen, added greatly to the value of the report.

In 1847 Owen was appointed to survey the mineral lands of the Chippewa land district, an area extending from northeastern Iowa and southern Wisconsin to Lake Superior. In his report, presented the following year, he correctly analyzed the stratigraphy and structure and paid particular attention to the economic geology. Owen and his assistants continued explorations into Minnesota and to Lake Winnipeg,

then into Iowa and the South Dakota Badlands. The resulting report (1852) included an atlas of maps and plates engraved from sketches by Owen and his brother Richard. The most sumptuous American geological publication to that time, it is still of great significance.

Appointed state geologist of Kentucky in 1854, Owen not only made detailed geologic, chemical, economic, and soil studies but also constructed base maps. His medical training enabled him to relate certain diseases to soil and mineral types. After Owen's part in the Kentucky fieldwork was completed and the third volume of the surveys was published, he accepted an appointment as state geologist of Arkansas in 1857, at very little salary, for the opportunity to examine unknown territory.

In 1859 the Indiana Geological Survey was reactivated and Owen was appointed state geologist, with the understanding that his brother Richard, who had long been associated with him, could begin the fieldwork while Owen was completing the second volume of the Arkansas survey. But Owen, who had long suffered from recurrent malaria, was seized by other ailments, including acute rheumatism, and soon became practically immobilized. Nevertheless, he dictated the last of the Arkansas report to two secretaries and completed the work three days before he died.

A superb field geologist, Owen attracted and retained capable assistants who could lead his field parties and could also contribute important parts of the final reports. In a day when verbosity was not uncommon he wrote in a lucid, well-outlined, compact manner and completed the writing and editing of his reports in remarkably short time. He was a talented artist; and his works contain hundreds of maps, sections, and diagrams and scores of lithographic plates, some of which are today sought by collectors.

Owen's reports contain meticulous and accurate descriptions, reasonable analysis of origin, and wide correlation with American and foreign strata; they also introduced to America some of the terminology for Paleozoic systems used today. A skilled chemist with a knowledge of mechanics and a naturalist-physician, he produced geological writings ranging through paleontology, stratigraphy, mineralogy, and structure. Above all he related economic resources to geology in a way that endeared him to "practical" men and to legislators.

Many of his assistants and associates, some of whom received their first geological experience under him, become important geologists: Robert Peter, F. B. Meek, Richard Owen, John Evans, J. G. Norwood, E. T. Cox, C. C. Parry, Benjamin F. Shumard,

G. C. Swallow, Peter Lesley, Charles Whittlesey, and John Locke.

BIBLIOGRAPHY

I. ORIGINAL WORKS. Owen's major works are *Report of a Geological Reconnaissance of the State of Indiana*, 2 pts. (Indianapolis, 1838–1839); *Report of a Geological Exploration of Part of Iowa, Wisconsin and Illinois . . .* (Washington, 1840–1844); *Report of a Geological Reconnaissance of the Chippewa Land District* (Washington, 1848); *Report of a Geological Survey of Wisconsin, Iowa and Minnesota*, 2 vols. (Philadelphia, 1852); *Report of the Geological Survey in Kentucky*, 4 vols. (Frankfort, Ky., 1856–1861); and *Report of a Geological Reconnaissance . . . of Arkansas*, 2 vols. (Little Rock, 1858; Philadelphia, 1860). One of the most significant of his many short papers is that read before the Geological Society of London in 1842, "On the Geology of the Western States of North America," in *Quarterly Journal of the Geological Society of London*, **2** (1846), 433–447, with an important map and correlation of English and American Paleozoic rocks. Scores of papers, reviews, and short reports that form additional records of his travels and activities are listed most completely in Hendrickson (see below). Each larger report contains a long introduction describing the establishment, organization, associates, progress of the fieldwork, and publications. The body of most reports gives an account of day-to-day activities, which together form a detailed "scientific biography."

In addition to the bibliography of Owen's publications in Hendrickson see those in J. M. Nickles, "Geologic Literature of North America 1785–1918," in *Bulletin of the United States Geological Survey*, no. 746 (1923), 804–805; and detailed and annotated lists in Max Meisel, *A Bibliography of American Natural History* (New York, 1929), see III, 633, for the many entries. J. B. Marcou, "Writings of D. D. Owen," in *Bulletin. United States National Museum*, **30** (1885), 247–251, presents a partially annotated list of fossil genera and species described by Owen and his associates.

II. SECONDARY LITERATURE. An excellent biography, with a portrait of Owen and extensive bibliographies of his publications, of source materials, and of related documents and publications is W. B. Hendrickson, *David Dale Owen, Pioneer Geologist of the Middle West* (Indianapolis, 1943). Caroline Dale Snedecker, a granddaughter of Owen's, relates much personal history and includes interesting illustrations in *The Town of the Fearless* (Garden City, N.Y., 1931). Various obituary notices, most of them listed by Hendrickson, were published at intervals after Owen's death. William E. Wilson, in *The Angel and the Serpent, the Story of New Harmony* (Bloomington, Ind., 1964), gives the best account, with many illustrations and portraits, of Robert Owen and William Maclure at New Harmony and the later activities of Robert Owen's family. The "Obituary Notice," in *Fourth Report of the Geological Survey in Kentucky* (1861),
323–330, is of especial interest and value because it formed the basis for later obituaries. The unsigned obituary by one of the editors (Benjamin Silliman, Jr.?) in *American Journal of Science*, **31** (1861), 153–155, has information on scientific associates and an evaluation of Owen's work by an editor who published many of his papers. A very brief sketch by N. H. Winchell(?) with a portrait is in *American Geologist*, **4** (1889), 65–72. The account by W. J. Youmans in *Pioneers of Science in America* (New York, 1896), 500–508, is mostly derived from Winchell. That in H. A. Kelly and W. L. Burrage, *Dictionary of American Medical Biography* (New York–London, 1928), 927–928, adds little new material.

G. P. Merrill, in *First One Hundred Years of American Geology* (New Haven, 1924; New York, 1962), 194–200, 217–218, 271–275, 321–323, 365–367, has summarized Owen's geological contributions and reproduced important illustrations. Merrill's article in *Dictionary of American Biography*, XIV, 116–117, is a summary of these longer notes. See also *National Cyclopaedia of American Biography*, VIII, 113. A number of biographies of geologists contain considerable information on Owen's association with them (see list in Hendrickson, pp. 160–164). Charles Keyes, "The Transplantation of English Terranal Classification to America by David Dale Owen," in *Pan-American Geologist*, **34** (1923), 81–94, is a fulsome description with some minor inaccuracies of Owen's introduction of English names for Paleozoic periods in which the strata of the Mississippi Valley were deposited. Sir Charles Lyell, *A Second Visit to the United States of North America*, II (London, 1849), 269–274, recounts his visit to Owen at New Harmony and his excursions to see Wabash Valley geology.

GEORGE W. WHITE

OWEN, GEORGE (*b.* Henllys, Pembrokeshire, Wales, 1552; *d.* 1613), *geology.*

A member of an old and distinguished South Wales family, Owen became vice admiral of the maritime counties of Pembroke and Cardigan and was twice sheriff of Cardigan. He was eminent as a local historian and topographer. In geology he is important not so much for the few paragraphs he wrote that happen to come within that subject as for the historical context in which he wrote them.

The description of the geology of Britain can hardly be said to have been begun at any definite time. There are, first of all, the casual remarks of the medieval writers and those made by John Leland in his *Itinerary* (*ca.* 1538) and by William Camden in his *Britannia* (1586). But in 1603 Owen included in his manuscript "Description of Pembrokeshire" an account of the occurrence of the (Carboniferous) limestone and coal measures of South Wales. He did so for the practical guidance of those wishing to exploit these materials; but in detailing the course of the limestone, he established the geological fact of bands of outcrop traceable across country. His account is thus the first attempt to "map" a British geological formation, if only verbally. He prepared a topographical map to accompany his description of Pembrokeshire; had he delineated his information on it, he would have provided a true geological map some two centuries before any other was made. Owen described the course of the limestone as being in two separate "veins"; these are really both the same limestone, outcropping on the north and south sides of the syncline of the South Wales coalfield. Owen clearly had no idea of geological structure, and his remarks cannot be said to form part of a continuous evolution of geological knowledge. It was not until the second half of the seventeenth century that the scientific spirit really came alive and produced a band of naturalists who, among their wide-ranging scholarly researches, collected, described, and discussed truly geological matters.

BIBLIOGRAPHY

Owen's most important work is *The Description of Pembrokeshire*, written in 1603; the authoritative ed. is that by his descendant, Henry Owen, published as no. 1 in Cymmrodorion Record Series (London, 1892), with geological commentary in the footnotes.

Owen's biography is given by Henry Owen in the intro. to his ed. of . . . *Pembrokeshire* (see above). See also D. Lleufer Thomas, in *Dictionary of National Biography*, XLII (1895), 408–410. Detailed commentaries on Owen's geological observations are made by A. Ramsay, in *Passages in the History of Geology*, pt. 2 (London, 1849), 8–11; by F. J. North, "From Giraldus Cambrensis to the Geological Map," in *Transactions of the Cardiff Naturalists' Society*, **64** (1931), 20–97, see 24–29; and by J. Challinor, "The Early Progress of British Geology—I," in *Annals of Science*, **9** (1953), 124–153, see 127–129.

JOHN CHALLINOR

OWEN, RICHARD (*b*. Lancaster, England, 20 July 1804; *d*. Richmond Park, London, England, 18 December 1892), *comparative anatomy, vertebrate paleontology, geology.*

Owen, the younger son of Richard and Catherine Parrin Owen, lost his father in 1809. When six years old Owen was enrolled at the Lancaster Grammar School, where he was a younger schoolmate of William Whewell. In 1820 Owen was apprenticed to the first of three Lancaster surgeons under whom he studied. As an apprentice he had access to postmortems and

dissections at the local jail, which sparked an early interest in anatomy and started him collecting anatomical specimens. Before completing his apprenticeship, Owen matriculated in October 1824 at the University of Edinburgh, where he attended the anatomical lectures of Alexander Munro Tertius. More importantly, Owen was able to attend the extramural lectures on anatomy given by John Barclay, from whom Owen gained considerable knowledge of comparative anatomy. In April 1825 Barclay recommended that Owen go to London to study at St. Bartholomew's Hospital with John Abernethy, to whom Barclay addressed a letter of introduction on Owen's behalf. Abernethy immediately appointed Owen to be his prosector. After qualifying as a member of the Royal College of Surgeons in August 1826, Owen set up practice in Lincoln's Inn Fields.

Abernethy had recognized Owen's dissecting ability and knowledge of comparative anatomy. As president of the Royal College of Surgeons, Abernethy had Owen appointed assistant to the conservator, William Clift, of the Hunterian Collection. Owen soon became engaged to Clift's only daughter, Caroline, whom he married in 1835. His primary task was to assist Clift in the preparation of the long-needed catalogue of John Hunter's wide-ranging collection, which had been purchased for the College of Surgeons and served as the nucleus of the College's Museum. Since most of Hunter's notes concerning the specimens had been lost, Owen was obliged to perform many fresh dissections in order to identify the specimens. His general assistance to Clift included serving as Georges Cuvier's guide around the Museum in 1830. This encounter led to an invitation to visit Cuvier in Paris, which Owen did the following year. He later considered the experiences of that trip and the contact with Cuvier a major influence on his work. In 1836 Owen was appointed Hunterian professor at the Royal College of Surgeons, an appointment that necessitated his presenting annually a course of twenty-four lectures based on some aspect of the Hunterian Collection.

Owen succeeded Clift as conservator of the Museum and continued in that position until his appointment in 1856 as superintendent of the natural history departments of the British Museum. At that time these departments were still housed with all the other departments of the British Museum in Bloomsbury. In 1859 Owen sent a forceful report to the trustees of the Museum detailing his views and plans for a new building in a separate location to house the natural history departments. There was much talk and little action, until Gladstone took an interest in Owen's scheme and introduced a bill into Parliament. Finally, in 1871 work was begun on the new Natural History Museum in South Kensington, with the galleries laid out after the design Owen had submitted in 1859. Owen continued as superintendent of the Natural History Museum until after it was fully installed in the new building. He retired in 1884 and was then made K.C.B. After leaving the Royal College of Surgeons, Owen was free to accept the Fullerian lectureship in physiology at the Royal Institution. He also lectured at the Royal School of Mines and on many natural history topics in London and throughout Great Britain. During his career he received most major awards in his fields, including both the Royal and Copley medals from the Royal Society; he was also a member of many British and foreign scientific societies. He served on several royal commissions that dealt with aspects of public health and was president of the British Association for the Advancement of Science in 1858. After a lengthy decline in his health, he died on 18 December 1892 at Sheen Lodge (in Richmond Park), the use of which Queen Victoria had granted him in 1851.

Unfortunately Owen is principally remembered as T. H. Huxley's antagonist at the 1860 meeting of the British Association and in the ensuing debates over Darwin's *On the Origin of Species*. This view neglects his authorship of massive quantities of detailed monographs and papers, which made known many new organisms (both recent and fossil), helped to delineate several natural groups, and laid the bases for much later work by many investigators. The attention of the scientific community was first focused on Owen in 1832 when he published *Memoir on the Pearly Nautilus* (*Nautilus Pompilius, Linn.*), which was based on a single specimen of this delicate organism that had previously been known only by its shell. In this superb piece of descriptive anatomy he also modified Cuvier's Cephalopoda and proposed two orders that were considered valid until 1894. He reviewed the Cephalopoda in an 1836 article for Robert Todd's *Cyclopaedia of Anatomy and Physiology*. Among many other works on invertebrates, Owen in 1835 described the parasite that causes trichinosis.

In 1828 Owen began dissecting the animals that died in the gardens of the Zoological Society of London and soon after helped to organize the evening scientific meetings, the publication of which became *Proceedings of the Zoological Society of London*. Of all the exotic forms to which he thus had access probably none interested him more than the monotremes and marsupials. Before his work the means of generation and of feeding the young of these groups was very much a matter for discussion. Through specimens from the Zoological Society and the many specimens

collected for him in Australia and New Zealand, Owen was able to establish in a series of papers both the mammalian nature and the egg-laying mode of reproduction of the monotremes. Similarly he was able to present details of the reproductive processes of the marsupials. This work was brought together in the articles "Monotremes" and "Marsupials" in Todd's *Cyclopaedia*. Later in his career he was sent and described numerous fossil monotremes and marsupials, which further supported his argument that these forms compose two distinct groups within the Mammalia and that they have long been geographically isolated.

Primates in general and anthropoid apes in particular were of early and lasting interest to Owen, especially in their relation to man. He published many accounts of the anatomy of various primates from the aye-aye to the gorilla. In 1839 Owen began a series, "Contributions to the Natural History of the Anthropoid Apes," which at first was concerned with the osteology of the orangutans but was broadened to include the other apes as specimens became available, often being sent to him by African explorers. Owen separated man from the anthropoid apes into a separate subclass of Mammalia, the Archencephala, primarily on the basis of several supposed differences in the gross structure of their brains.

Lyell introduced Owen to Charles Darwin in October 1836, and thus began a long friendship. The following year Darwin turned over to Owen, for description, his South American fossils. Up to this time Owen had not published on any fossils but did have a broad knowledge of the anatomy, especially the osteology, of recent vertebrates. He described Darwin's *Toxodon platensis* (1837), and his description of Darwin's fossils from South America was published as the first volume of *The Zoology of the Voyage of H.M.S. "Beagle"* (1840). The teeth of some of these fossils intrigued Owen and led him into a major study of the structure of teeth. He addressed a report to the British Association in 1838, which served as the nucleus of his *Odontography* (1840–1845) and his article, "Odontology," in *Encyclopaedia Britannica* (1858). This work on teeth contained a great deal of new information and presented a uniform nomenclature for the teeth and their parts that was of considerable service to zoologists.

In addition to the monographs on comparative anatomy, Owen published several general works. Certain of his Hunterian lectures were published as separate volumes: on invertebrates (1843), on fishes (1844, 1846), and again on invertebrates (1855). Between 1866 and 1868 Owen published the massive *On the Anatomy and Physiology of Vertebrates*, the conclusion of which contains some of Owen's views on Darwin's hypothesis. All of these works were based on the prodigious amount of dissection and observation performed by Owen in preparing the five-volume *Descriptive and Illustrative Catalogue of the Physiological Series of Comparative Anatomy* of the Royal College of Surgeons' Museum, of his nearly twenty courses of Hunterian lectures, and of his many research papers.

Owen's paleontological work began in 1837 with Darwin's South American fossils and especially with the monograph on the *Toxodon* that Owen recognized as an intermediate type, with anatomical characteristics normally identified with rodents, cetaceans, and pachyderms. His works on Darwin's other fossils, for example, *Glyptodon* and *Macrauchenia*, are no less important. Owen also published on the marsupial characteristics of a group of fossils from the Stonesfield Slate (1838) and the first part of his major *Report on British Fossil Reptiles* to the British Association (1839, part two in 1841). This two-part *Report* was the framework on which Owen developed his exhaustive four-volume *History of British Fossil Reptiles* (1849–1884), which is a separate publication of his collected papers issued principally by the Palaeontographical Society. Also in 1839 Owen received a fragment of a femur from New Zealand, which he identified as belonging to a previously unknown giant terrestrial bird. This first paper on the New Zealand moa developed into a major series of publications on *Dinornis* and similar flightless birds. In addition, Owen paid particular attention to fossils from South Africa and Australia, the latter in relation to his interest in marsupials, and published many new species and new descriptions of these faunae. Also of interest are his 1842 studies of English Triassic labyrinthodonts and his description of the Jurassic bird *Archaeopteryx* (1863).

Despite the quantity of Owen's paleontological work before 1856, his career can be divided in two segments, not only by his place of employment but also by the different emphases of his work. While at the College of Surgeons the principal thrust of his work, and also of that museum's collections, was comparative-anatomical. After his transfer to the British Museum with its rich collections of fossils, which Owen further enriched, he naturally changed the emphasis of his work to paleontology. One aspect of this changed emphasis was his series of lecture courses on paleontology at the Royal School of Mines beginning in 1857; they were well-received and later compiled in his popular text *Paleontology* (1860).

Owen made a number of contributions to taxonomy, often modifying and clarifying one or another taxon in the course of his anatomical investigations and in describing many previously unknown species and genera. An excellent example of this work is his recognition of the marsupials as a natural, geographically defined group. Owen did undertake a classification of the Mammalia, in his Rede lecture in May 1859, in which he gave primal import to certain characteristics of the cerebral hemispheres. By these criteria he divided the Mammalia into four subclasses of equivalent value: Lyencephala, Lissencephala, Gyrencephala, and Archencephala (in order of increasing complexity). A strength of Owen's classification was the close association of the monotremes and marsupials in his Lyencephala. The other three subclasses graded imperceptibly into one another. The Archencephala, moreover, contained just one species, man. Owen believed that his cerebral criteria—anterior and posterior extension of the cerebral hemispheres, the posterior horn of the lateral ventricle, and the presence of a *hippocampus minor*—separated man further from the anthropoid apes than the latter were separated from the most primitive primates.

Owen's views on the transmutation of species are not entirely clear, partly on account of his writing style. In 1848 he claimed to have no idea of what the secondary causes may have been by which the Creator introduced new species, and he refrained from publishing on the subject. He did think that there were six possible ways in which the Creator might have acted but would not enumerate them. This, of course, was soon after the publication of Chambers' *Vestiges of the Natural History of Creation*, a much talked-about book. He had no objection to the notion that the Creator may have worked through secondary causes and recognized that, among animals, there had been an ascent and progression. Owen responded very vigorously to Darwin's *Origin* in a long, anonymous attack in the *Edinburgh Review* for April 1860. He was totally unable to accept the possibility that selective action of external circumstances might cause new species to arise. He observed that no effects of any of the hypothetical transmuting influences had been recorded. His objections were not to evolution's having occurred but rather that Darwin's mechanism, natural selection, had not been demonstrated as adequate. He thought "an innate tendency to deviate from parental type" the most probable way that secondary causes have produced one species from another (*On the Anatomy and Physiology of the Vertebrates*, III, p. 807).

The basic ideas Owen put forth in his Rede lecture had been presented previously in London meetings, one of which T. H. Huxley attended. Huxley doubted the validity of Owen's subclass Archencephala, investigated the matter to his own satisfaction, and incorporated his opposing findings in his teaching without publishing them. When Owen repeated his views in a discussion following another's paper at the 1860 meeting of the British Association in Oxford, Huxley was prepared to contradict Owen directly and publicly, stating that he would give evidence to support his contradiction in a more appropriate place. This Huxley did, with the assistance of others, particularly Flower, in a series of publications from 1860 to 1863. Owen simply failed to see certain anatomical structures and relationships. He appears to have operated on the assumption that man possessed unique mental capabilities and that any such unique capabilities must be based in some unique anatomical structure or structures; therefore man could be distinguished from the anthropoid apes by just such structures. Not to be ignored is the fact that many considered Owen to be the preeminent anatomist of his time, and he had held two prominent positions in the British scientific community. In contrast, Darwin had not held any similar position and had already retired, seemingly, to the country; and Huxley, who had backed the argumentative Owen into a corner, was a relative youngster in 1860. These personal factors must have played a role in this whole controversy.

Owen's comparative-anatomical and paleontological work is in the best Cuvierian tradition and perhaps comparable only to that of Cuvier. At the same time Owen was guided by a strong affinity to that school of thought which strongly repelled Cuvier—German *Naturphilosophie*. This affinity is amply evidenced by Owen's further development of the idea of a vertebral archetype, promulgated by Goethe and Carus, in his *On the Archetype and Homologies of the Vertebrate Skeleton* (1848), his *Anatomy of Fishes* (1846), and *On the Nature of Limbs* (1849). It was hardly coincidence that Owen was instrumental in having Oken's *Lehrbuch der Naturphilosophie* translated and published in London in 1847. Also, Owen wrote the article "Oken" for the eighth edition of *Encyclopaedia Britannica*. Through his elaboration of his theory of archetypes, Owen provided a major assist to the much-needed standardization of anatomical nomenclature and greatly clarified the distinction between the anatomical concepts of homology and analogy. In addition, from the *Naturphilosophen* Owen acquired the notion of a specific character resulting from the interaction of two opposing forces working within the developing embryo. His view that one species might develop from another by "an innate tendency to deviate from the parental type" meshes well with the developmental forces he saw operative in each individual.

BIBLIOGRAPHY

I. ORIGINAL WORKS. There are more than 600 titles in Owen's bibliography. The greatest bulk of his papers are in the collections of the British Museum (Natural History). These include correspondence, notebooks, drafts of papers, and interleaved copies of most of his own books. The Royal College of Surgeons has a smaller but important collection of Owen's papers, mostly dating from the period when he was there. In addition, letters by Owen are to be found in the papers of his many correspondents.

The most important of Owen's separate publications include *Memoir on the Pearly Nautilus* (*Nautilus Pompilius, Linn.*) (London, 1832); *Descriptive and Illustrative Catalogue of the Physiological Series of Comparative Anatomy*, 5 vols. (London, 1833–1840); *Fossil Mammalia, pt. 1 of The Zoology of the Voyage of H.M.S "Beagle"* (London, 1840); *Odontography; or a Treatise on the Comparative Anatomy of the Teeth; Their Physiological Relations, Mode of Development, and Microscopic Structure in the Vertebrate Animals* (London, 1840–1845); *On the Archetype and Homologies of the Vertebrate Skeleton* (London, 1848); *On the Classification and Geographical Distribution of the Mammalia, Being the Lecture on Sir Robert Rede's Foundation* (London, 1859); *Palaeontology, or a Systematic Summary of Extinct Animals and Their Geological Relations* (Edinburgh, 1860; 2nd ed., Edinburgh, 1861); and *On the Anatomy and Physiology of Vertebrates*, 3 vols. (London, 1866–1868). *The Life of Sir Richard Owen*, cited below, contains an exhaustive chronological bibliography of about 650 items; this is the most complete listing of his works.

II. SECONDARY LITERATURE. The most important source for Owen's life and work is by his grandson, Rev. Richard Owen, *The Life of Sir Richard Owen* (London, 1894), which contains an essay by Thomas Henry Huxley, "Owen's Position in the History of Anatomical Science," II, 273–332, and the bibliography cited above, II, 333–382. See also William Henry Flower, "Richard Owen," in *Dictionary of National Biography*, XIV (1894–1895), 1329–1338.

WESLEY C. WILLIAMS

OZANAM, JACQUES (*b.* Bouligneux, Bresse, France, 1640; *d.* Paris, France, 3 April 1717 [?]), *mathematics*.

Ozanam came from a Jewish family that had converted to Catholicism. As the younger of two sons he was educated for the clergy, but chemistry and mechanics interested him more than theology. He was said to be generous, witty, and gallant; and probably he was too tolerant to have made a good churchman of his day. Except for a tutor who may have helped him slightly, Ozanam taught himself mathematics.

Four years after Ozanam had begun studying for the church, his father died; he then devoted himself to mastering mathematics, with considerable success.

He taught mathematics at Lyons without charge until the state of his finances led him to charge a fee. A lucky circumstance took him to Paris, where his teaching brought him a substantial income. Being young and handsome, his gallantry as well as his penchant for gambling drained his resources; Ozanam sought a way out by marrying a modest, virtuous young woman without means. Although his financial problems remained unsolved, the marriage was happy and fruitful; there were twelve children, most of whom died young. After his marriage Ozanam's conduct was exemplary; always of a mild and cheerful disposition, he became sincerely pious and shunned disputes about theology. He was wont to say that it was the business of the Sorbonne doctors to discuss, of the pope to decide, and of a mathematician to go straight to heaven in a perpendicular line.

Following the death of his wife in 1701, misfortune quickly befell Ozanam. In the same year the War of the Spanish Succession broke out; and many of his students, being foreign, had to leave Paris. From then on, the income from his professional activities became small and uncertain. The last years of his life were melancholy, relieved only by the dubious satisfaction of being admitted as an *élève* of the Academy of Sciences. Ozanam never regained his customary health and spirits, and died of apoplexy, probably on 3 April 1717, although there is some reason to believe that it may have been between 1 April and 6 April 1718.

By almost any criterion Ozanam cannot be regarded as a first-rate mathematician, even of his own time. But he had a flair for writing and during his career wrote a number of books, some of which were very popular, passing through many editions. According to Montucla:

> He promoted mathematics by his treatise on lines of the second order; and had he pursued the same branch of research, he would have acquired a more solid reputation than by the publication of his *Course, Récréations,* or *Dictionnaire mathématique*; but having to look to the support of himself and family, he wisely consulted the taste of his purchasers rather than his own [*Histoire des mathématiques*, II, 168].

In short, his contributions consisted of popular treatises and reference works on "useful and practical mathematics," and an extremely popular work on mathematical recreations; the latter had by far the more lasting impact. Ozanam's *Récréations* may be regarded as the forerunner of modern books on mathematical recreations. He drew heavily on the works of Bachet de Méziriac, Mydorge, Leurechon, and Daniel Schwenter; his own contributions were somewhat less significant, for he was not a particularly creative mathematician. The work was later augmented and revised by Montucla and, still later, was translated into English by Hutton (1803).

Ozanam is not to be confounded with a contemporary geometer, Sébastien Leclerc (1637–1714), who upon occasion used the pseudonym Ozanam.

BIBLIOGRAPHY

I. ORIGINAL WORKS. Ozanam's writings include *Méthode pour tracer les cadrans* (Paris, 1673, 1685, 1730); *La géométrie pratique du sr Boulenger* (Paris, 1684, 1689, 1691, 1736, 1764); *Tables de sinus, tangentes et sécantes; et des logarithmes . . .* (Paris, 1685, 1697, 1720, 1741); *Traité de la construction des équations pour la solution des problèmes indéterminez* (Paris, 1687); *Traité des lieux géométriques, expliquez par une méthode courte et facile* (Paris, 1687); *Traité des lignes du premier genre, expliquées par une méthode nouvelle et facile* (Paris, 1687); *Usage du compas de proportion . . . augmenté d'un traité de la division des champs* (Paris, 1688, 1691, 1700, 1736, 1748, 1794); *Usage de l'instrument universel. . . .* (Paris, 1688, 1700, 1748); and *Méthode de lever les plans et les cartes de terre et de mer, avec toutes sortes d'instrumens, et sans instrumens. . . .* (Paris, 1693, 1700, 1750, 1781).

His major works are *Dictionnaire mathématique, ou, idée générale des mathématiques. . . .* (Amsterdam–Paris, 1691), translated and abridged by Joseph Raphson (London, 1702); *Cours de mathématique, qui comprend toutes les parties les plus utiles et les plus nécessaires à un homme de guerre, & à tous ceux qui se veulent perfectionner dans les mathématiques,* 5 vols. (Paris, 1693), also 3 vols. in 1 (Amsterdam, 1697), translated as *Cursus mathematicus: Or a Compleat Course of the Mathematicks. . . ,* 5 vols. (London, 1712); and *Récréations mathématiques et physiques . . . ,* 4 vols. (Paris, 1694, 1696, 1698, 1720, 1725, 1735, 1778, 1790; Amsterdam, 1698), translated as *Recreations Mathematical and Physical . . .* (London, 1708); as *Recreations in Mathematics and Natural Philosophy . . . First Composed by M. Ozanam . . . Lately Recomposed by M. Montucla, and Now Translated into English . . . by Charles Hutton* (London, 1803, 1814), rev. by Edward Riddle (London, 1840, 1844); and as *Recreations for Gentlemen and Ladies, or, Ingenious Amusements . . .* (Dublin, 1756).

Among his other works are *Traité des fortifications . . .* (Paris, 1694), translated by J. T. Desaguliers as *Treatise of Fortification . . .* (Oxford, 1711, 1727); *Nouveaux élémens d'algèbre . . . ,* 2 vols. (Amsterdam, 1702); *Géographie et cosmographie* (Paris, 1711); *La perspective, théorique et pratique* (Paris, 1711, 1720); *La méchanique . . . tirée du cours de mathématique de M. Ozanam* (Paris, 1720); *La gnomonique . . . tirée du cours de mathématique de M. Ozanam* (Paris, 1746); and *Traité de l'arpentage et du toisé, nouvelle édition, mise dans un nouvel ordre par M. Audierne*

(Paris, 1779). Ozanam also published several articles in the *Journal des sçavans*, including a proof of the theorem that neither the sum nor the difference of two fourth powers can be a fourth power.

His translations or editions of works by others include a revised and enlarged ed. of Adriaan Vlacq, *La trigonométrie rectiligne et sphérique . . . avec tables* (Paris, 1720, 1741, 1765); and *Les élémens d'Euclide du R. P. Dechalles . . . et de M. Ozanam . . . démontrés d'une manière . . . par M. Audierne* (Paris, 1753).

II. SECONDARY LITERATURE. See Heinrich Zeitlinger, ed., *Bibliotheca chemico-mathematica* (London, 1921), I, 171, and II, 643; Moritz Cantor, *Vorlesungen über die Geschichte der Mathematik*, 2nd ed. (Leipzig, 1913), II, 770, and III, 102–103, 270, 364; Fontenelle, "Éloge . . .," in *Oeuvres diverses*, III (The Hague, 1729), 260–265; Charles Hutton, *Philosophical and Mathematical Dictionary*, II (London, 1815), 144; J. E. Montucla, *Histoire des mathématiques*, II (Paris, 1799), 168; *The Penny Cyclopaedia of the Society for the Diffusion of Useful Knowledge*, XVII (London, 1840), 111–112; and Edward Riddle, *Dr. Hutton's Philosophical Recreations* (London, 1840), v–vii.

WILLIAM L. SCHAAF

OZERSKY, ALEKSANDR DMITRIEVICH (*b.* Chernigov guberniya, Russia, 21 September 1813; *d.* St. Petersburg, Russia, 1 October 1880), *mining engineering, geology.*

Ozersky's father, Dmitry Nikitich Ozersky, owned a small estate and had the rank of state councillor. His mother, Varvara Aleksandrovna, came from a noble family. In 1831 Ozersky, who had graduated from the Mining Cadet Corps (now the Leningrad G. V. Plekhanov Mining Institute), returned to the corps as a tutor in chemistry; lectured on mining statistics and mineralogy from 1833 to 1857; and from 1848 to 1851 was school inspector. From 1857 to 1864 he was the head of the Altay mines and for several years during the period was civilian governor of Tomsk. Upon his return to St. Petersburg, Ozersky worked in the Mining Department and until almost the end of his life was a member of the Committee on Mining Science. In 1857 he was given the rank of major general and in 1866 that of lieutenant general. He married Sofia Semenovna Gurieva and had two daughters, Olga and Sofia.

Ozersky's extremely varied scientific interests at the beginning of his career included the chemical analysis of minerals, rocks, and alloys. Through these precise investigations he established the composition of a number of Russian minerals, pointing out a number of cases in which new names had been suggested for already known minerals. Commissioned by the Free Economic Society to systematize its collection of natural stones according to use, he distinguished thirteen groups of minerals, rocks, and ores.

In his study of ore deposits—following the ideas on the origin of ores then current—Ozersky accepted the sublimation theory: that metalliferous veins are formed by a cooling of "metallic sublimates" that penetrate into cavities, fissures, and pores of a rock. During his expeditions he tried not only to study outcrops of ore and mineral deposits but also to deduce their genesis, in order to assist further prospecting.

While working in Transbaikalia, Ozersky established that ore deposits do not depend upon the enclosing strata but are directly associated with intrusive igneous rocks. He determined a pattern according to which all the deposits of Transbaikalia could be grouped into several isolated stretches. This regularity was later confirmed and was of great practical importance in prospecting.

Ozersky was also interested in the origin of sulfur, saltpeter, and other nonmetallic minerals. He believed in the organic origin of oil, assuming that it could have an animal beginning, particularly a molluscan one. In his regional investigations he attached great importance to the problems of stratigraphic subdivision and solved a number of complicated problems of geological age.

While working in the Baltic provinces in 1843, Ozersky was the first to compile a detailed sequence of Silurian strata of this area, which is now regarded as a classic example of the Lower Paleozoic of northern Europe. Minor subdivisions that he distinguished according to paleontological and lithological data are still valid. Although at that time there were no adequate tables for making paleontological determinations, the stratigraphic scheme worked out by Ozersky proved so accurate that all subsequent studies have confirmed it without introducing any vital changes. Later, in Transbaikalia, he discovered Jurassic deposits which had long been overlooked, an omission resulting in the compilation of erroneous tectonic and paleogeographical schemes of that vast territory. Not until the middle of the twentieth century were his conclusions fully confirmed.

In tectonics Ozersky was a plutonist, believing that all uplifts are determined by injections of a liquid magma into a sedimentary shell. At the same time he admitted the possibility of alternating ascending and descending movements, suggesting that they be called oscillation movements, a term later accepted in geological literature. He indicated that vertical crustal movements could be divided into "local," involving only small portions of the crust, and "general," resulting in an uplift or subsidence of an entire continent.

Ozersky's Russian translation (1845) of Murchison's *The Geology of Russia in Europe and the Ural Mountains* included much new data obtained through extensive research conducted during the four years following the appearance of Murchison's book. He also supplied many footnotes with references to the studies of Russian geologists that had served as a basis for Murchison's work.

Ozersky was a materialist, stating that only experience and its practical application can be depended upon to determine the laws of nature. In public lectures he discussed the interrelations between material objects and natural phenomena, the cycle of matter (the circulation of substances through chemical change), the process of development as reflected in everything that surrounds us, and the fact that light can be emitted only by existing bodies.

Advocating the development of industry and the national economy, Ozersky urged the expansion of railway transport in Russia, the construction of canals to connect the major rivers, the use of hard coal instead of charcoal by industrial enterprises, and the introduction of modern methods in metallurgy.

BIBLIOGRAPHY

Ozersky's major writings are "Geognostichesky ocherk severo-zapadnoy Estlyandii" ("Geognostic Outline of Northwestern Estonia"), in *Gornyi zhurnal*, **2** (1844), 157–208, 285–338; "Vstupitelnye lektsii i kurs prikladnoy mineralogii" ("Introductory Lectures of the Course in Applied Mineralogy"), in *Zhurnal Ministerstva narodnogo prosveschenia*, **46**, sec. 2 (1845), 1–38, 87–111, 161–224; and "Ocherk geologii, mineralnykh bogatstv i gornogo promysla Zabaykalya" ("Outline of the Geology, Mineral Reserves, and Mining Industry of Transbaikalia"), in *Izdaniya SPb. Mineral. Obshchestva*, **8** (1867), 89c.

On Ozersky and his work, see V. V. Tikhomirov and T. A. Sofiano, "Zabyty russky geolog A. D. Ozersky" ("A. D. Ozersky, Forgotten Russian Geologist"), in *Byulleten Moskovskogo obshchestva ispytatelei prirody*, geological ser., **29**, no. 1 (1954).

V. V. TIKHOMIROV

PACCHIONI, ANTONIO (*b.* Reggio nell' Emilia, Italy, 13 June 1665; *d.* Rome, Italy, 5 November 1726), *medicine.*

Pacchioni studied in his native town and obtained his degree in medicine on 25 April 1688. In 1689 he moved to Rome, where at first he attended the Santo Spirito hospital. He was assistant physician at the Ospedale della Consolazione from 26 May 1690 to 3 June 1693, and then remained for six years in Tivoli as the town doctor. In 1699 Pacchioni returned to Rome and established a successful medical practice; he later became head doctor at the Hospital of San Giovanni in Laterano and then at the Ospedale della Consolazione. Interested in anatomy, he was guided by Malpighi (who lived in Rome from 1691 to 1694) and collaborated with Lancisi.

Among Pacchioni's dissertations, from 1701 on, dealing with the structure and functions of the dura mater, the *Dissertatio epistolaris de glandulis conglobatis durae meningis humanae* (1705) is particularly well known and contains his description of the arachnoidal, or so-called Pacchioni, granulations. Pacchioni attributed to these bodies the faculty of secreting lymph for lubricating the sliding movement between the meninges and the brain. He believed that the contraction of the dura mater, then considered to be muscular in nature, served to compress the glands, which, according to Malpighi's doctrine, constituted the cerebral cortex. Pacchioni also collaborated with Lancisi on the explanatory text to Eustachi's *Tabulae anatomicae* (1714).

BIBLIOGRAPHY

I. ORIGINAL WORKS. Pacchioni's principal work is *Dissertatio epistolaris de glandulis conglobatis durae meningis humanae, indeque ortis lymphaticis ad piam meningem productis* (Rome, 1705), reprinted in his *Opera* (Rome, 1741).

II. SECONDARY LITERATURE. On Pacchioni and his work, see Enrico Benassi, "Carteggi inediti fra il Lancisi, il Pacchioni ed il Morgagni," in *Rivista di storia delle scienze mediche e naturali*, **23** (1932), 145–169; Maria Bertolani del Rio, "Antonio Pacchioni 1665–1726," in Luigi Barchi, ed., *Medici e naturalisti Reggiani* (Reggio nell' Emilia, 1935), 659–667; Pietro Capparoni, "Lo stato di servizio di Antonio Pacchioni all'Ospedale della Consolazione in Roma ed un suo medaglione onorario," in *Rivista di storia critica delle scienze mediche e naturali*, **2** (1914), 241–245; Jacopo Chiappelli, "Notizie intorno alla vita di Antonio Pacchioni da Reggio," in *Raccolta d'opuscoli scientifici e filologici*, **3** (1730), 79–102; and Girolamo Tiraboschi, *Biblioteca Modenese*, III (Modena, 1783), 415–419.

LUIGI BELLONI

PACINI, FILIPPO (*b.* Pistoia, Italy, 25 May 1812; *d.* Florence, Italy, 9 July 1883), *anatomy, histology.*

Pacini was the son of Francesco Pacini, a cobbler, and Umiltà Dolfi. He was educated, with public assistance, at the Pistoia episcopal seminary and later at the classical academy. In 1830 he entered the medical school attached to the Ospedale del Ceppo; he completed his studies at the University of Pisa, where he graduated in surgery in 1839 and in medicine in 1840. In the latter year Pacini was also appointed assistant at the Institute of Comparative Anatomy in Pisa; he assumed a similar post at the Institute of Human Anatomy in 1843, and became a substitute teacher there the following year.

In 1847 Pacini began to teach descriptive anatomy at the Lyceum in Florence; he subsequently (1849) became director of the anatomical museum and professor of topographical anatomy at the medical school there, and from 1859 also teacher of microscopical anatomy. (Throughout Pacini's career at the Florence medical school, the professor of descriptive anatomy was Luigi Paganucci.) As a teacher Pacini, convinced of the fundamental importance of the biological sciences to medical education, initiated a number of new programs; he was, however, occasionally frustrated and embittered by the antagonism of Bufalini, director of the department of internal medicine.

Pacini was primarily interested in microscopical research; as early as 1833 he had access to a primitive instrument, and in 1843 was given a good one by the Pistoian philanthropist Niccolò Puccini. The following year Pacini designed his own microscope, which he constructed the next year with the help of Amici; this was the best to which he ever had access. In 1868 he constructed another compound (which he called "inverted") instrument for photographic and chemical use; this, together with the 1845 microscope, is preserved in the Museo di Storia della Scienza in Florence.

Pacini saw the corpuscles that are now named for him early in his career; indeed, he discovered them in a hand that he was dissecting as a student in the Pistoia hospital in 1831, when he was nineteen. He first saw the corpuscles around the digital branches of the median nerve, and suggested that they were "nervous ganglia of touch"; but he soon found them also in the abdominal cavity. Although he studied these corpuscles microscopically from 1833 on, Pacini published his research only in 1840, when his *Nuovi organi scoperti nel corpo umano* appeared. The name "Pacini's corpuscles" was proposed in 1844 by Koelliker, who had confirmed their existence; in 1862, however, the Viennese anatomist Carl Langer claimed priority for Abraham Vater—although Vater's work, published in 1741, had been forgotten and was certainly unknown to Pacini. At all events, Pacini was the first to describe the distribution of the corpuscles in the body, their microscopic structure, and their nerve connections; he also interpreted the function of the corpuscles as being concerned with the sensation of touch and deep pressure.

Pacini made another important observation in 1854, when, in the midst of an epidemic in Florence, he discovered the cholera vibrio. He microscopically examined the blood and feces of those afflicted with the disease and the intestines of those dead from it. He published his findings in a report, *Osservazioni microscopiche e deduzioni patologiche sul cholera asiatico*, in which he stated that cholera is a contagious disease, characterized by destruction of the intestinal epithelium, followed by extreme loss of water from the blood (for which condition he later recommended, in 1879, the therapeutic intravenous injection of saline solution). Pacini went on to declare that the intestinal injuries common to the disease were caused by living microorganisms (which he called "vibrions"); he further provided drawings of the vibrions that he had observed microscopically in abundance in the intestines of cholera victims.

Despite the significance of his researches, Pacini was overlooked when, following the epidemic of 1866, the Italian government distributed medals for meritorious work against cholera. In 1884 Koch rediscovered the cholera vibrio, which he isolated in pure culture, and named it "Komma Bacillus"; by applying his rigorous postulates, he was further able to prove that the bacillus was the sole cause of the disease. Koch presented his findings to the Cholera Commission of the Imperial Health Office in Berlin; the commission also recognized Pacini's priority in discovering the microorganism.

In addition to conducting his own histological research, Pacini enthusiastically advocated the teaching of microscopic anatomy. He himself gave a course in practical microscopy as early as 1843, while he was still at Pisa; in 1847 he published a plea for the teaching of histology, and in 1861 he presented a collection of selected microscopical preparations to the first Italian Exposition, held at Florence. He published further notes on histological technique as late as 1880. His specific contributions include a description of the *membrana limitans interna* of the human retina (1845) and reports on the electric organ of the Nile *Silurus* (1846 and 1852) and on the structure of bone (1851). He also published work in practical anatomy, including a study of the muscular mechanics of respiration in man (1847); he later (1870) developed a method of artificial respiration based upon a rhythmic movement of the shoulders of the unconscious subject.

Pacini was a pious and charitable man. He never married, and his work was generally unrecognized; he died in a poorhouse, and was buried in the cemetery of the Misericordia in Florence. In 1835 his remains were transferred, with the remains of two other anatomists, Atto Tigri and Filippo Civinini (Castaldi), to the church of Santa Maria delle Grazie in Pistoia.

BIBLIOGRAPHY

I. ORIGINAL WORKS. For a complete bibliography of Pacini's fifty-five works, see Castaldi, below. Works of particular interest are "Sopra un particulare genere di piccoli corpi globulari scoperti nel corpo umano da Filippo Pacini," in *Archivio delle scienze medico-fisiche*, **8** (1835), and in *Nuovo giornale dei letterati*, parte scientifica, **32** (1836), 109–114; *Nuovi organi scoperti nel corpo umano* (Pistoia, 1840); "Nuove ricerche microscopiche sulla tessitura intima della retina," in *Nuovi annali delle scienze naturali* (July-Aug. 1845), and separately repr. (Bologna, 1845); "Sopra l'organo elettrico del Siluro del Nilo," *ibid.* (July 1846); "Sulla questione della meccanica dei muscoli intercostali," in *Gazzetta toscana delle scienze medico-fisiche*, **5** (1847), 153–156; "Cosa è ed a che è buona l'anatomia microscopica del corpo umano," *ibid.*, 193–199; "Nuovo ricerche microscopiche sulla tessitura intima delle ossa," in *Gazzetta medica italiana federativa* (Nov. 1851); "Osservazioni microscopiche e deduzioni patologiche sul colera asiatico," *ibid.* (Dec. 1854), and repr. in *Sperimentale*, **78** (1924), 277–282; "Della natura del colera asiatico," in *Cronaca medica di Firenze* (10 Aug. and 10 Nov. 1866); and "Il mio metodo di respirazione artificiale per la cura dell'asfissia," in *Imparziale*, **10** (1870), 481–486.

See also "Dei fenomeni e delle funzioni di trasudamento nell'organismo animale," in *Sperimentale*, **28** (1874), 436–438, 537–563, 681–722; "Del processo morboso del colera asiatico del suo stadio di morte apparente e della legge matematica da cui è regolato," *ibid.*, **33** (1879), 355–369, 466–499, 573–597; "Di alcuni metodi di preparazione e di conservazione degli elementi microscopici dei tessuti animali o vegetali," in *Giornale internazionale delle scienze mediche*, **2** (1880), 337–350; and *Nuove osservazioni microscopiche sul colera* (Milan, 1885).

II. SECONDARY LITERATURE. On Pacini and his work see A. Bianchi, *Relazione e catalogo dei manoscritti di Filippo Pacini esistenti nella R. Biblioteca Nazionale di Firenze* (Florence, 1889); L. Castaldi, "Filippo Pacini nel quarantesimo anniversario della sua morte," in *Rivista di storia delle scienze mediche e naturali*, **14** (1923), 182–212, with complete bibliography; "Filippo Pacini," in *Sperimentale*, **78** (1924), 275–283; "Un manoscritto inedito di Filippo Pacini sull'ordinamento degli studi anatomici," in *Rivista di storia delle scienze mediche e naturali*, **16** (1925), 13–17; "Discorso per la translazione delle salme di Filippo Civinini, Filippo Pacini ed Atto Tigri nella Chiesa di S. Maria delle Grazie presso l'Ospedale del Ceppo. Letto in 29 Settembre 1935 nel Palazzo Comunale di Pistoia," *ibid.*, **26** (1935), 289–310; G. Chiarugi, "Corpuscoli lamellosi del Pacini," in *Istituzioni di anatomia dell'uomo*, IV (Milan, 1921), 789–793; A. Filippi, "Filippo Pacini," in *Sperimentale*, **37** (1883), 109–111; P. Franceschini, "Filippo Pacini e il colera," in *Physis*, **13** (1971), 324–332; J. Herrick, *Introduction to Neurology* (Philadelphia, 1928), 89; A. Koelliker, *Ueber die Pacinischen Körperchen des Menschen und der Säugethiere* (Zurich, 1844); C. Langer, "Zur Anatomie und Physiologie der Haut," in *Sitzungsberichte der Akademie der Wissenschaften in Wien*, Math.-naturwiss. Klasse, **44** (1861), 19–46, and **45** (1862), 133–188; and G. Sanarelli, *Il Colera* (Milan, 1931), 73, 74, 80.

PIETRO FRANCESCHINI

PACINOTTI, ANTONIO (*b.* Pisa, Italy, 17 June 1841; *d.* Pisa, 24 March 1912), *electrophysics*.

Although Pacinotti spent most of his life as a physics professor at various Italian universities, his subsequent reputation was due largely to his invention of a new form of armature used in electric motors and generators. The armature design that Pacinotti first described in a paper published in *Nuovo cimento* (June 1864) became a key element in the evolution from the magnetoelectric generator to the commercial self-excited dynamo during the next decade. The Pacinotti armature consisted of an iron ring with projecting teeth interspersed with coils which formed a closed series circuit with connections to a commutator. In his paper Pacinotti pointed out that his new machine could be used as either a direct-current motor or a generator. A similar ring armature design was developed, apparently independently, by Gramme by 1869.

Pacinotti developed his armature while a student at the University of Pisa. His electrical investigations were encouraged by his father, Luigi Pacinotti, a professor of mathematics and physics at Pisa who had himself engaged in electrical studies during the 1840's. A laboratory notebook kept by the younger Pacinotti indicates that he began his armature experiments in 1858. His work was interrupted by a year of service in the corps of engineers during the war for Italian independence. Pacinotti later claimed to have conceived the idea for radial teeth on his armature after having seen radially stacked muskets during the war. He returned to Pisa and resumed his electrical experiments, which culminated in a small test machine described in his 1864 paper. Following his graduation from Pisa in 1861, Pacinotti taught at Florence until 1864. He then taught physics at the Royal Institute of Technology in Bologna and at the University of Cagliari before returning to the University of Pisa, where he spent the rest of his life.

In the wake of the widespread publicity given the Gramme dynamo, Pacinotti called attention to his own earlier work in a note published in *Comptes rendus . . . de l'Académie des sciences* in 1871. Belated recognition followed at the Vienna Exposition of 1873 and the Paris Electrical Exhibition of 1881. From the perspective of the historian of science, Pacinotti provides an interesting example of a scientist whose contribution was not especially impressive but whose reputation ultimately derived from his recognition by the new electrical engineering profession for his invention of a device that was largely ignored until its apparently independent invention some years later.

BIBLIOGRAPHY

I. ORIGINAL WORKS. See the Royal Society *Catalogue of Scientific Papers*, IV, 733; VIII, 549; X, 977–978; XII, 553; XVII, 668; for lists of Pacinotti's published papers, most of which appeared in *Nuovo cimento*. His paper on armature design, "Correnti elettriche generate dall'azione del calorico e della luce," in *Nuovo cimento*, **19** (1864), 378–384, was reprinted as *Descrizione di una macchina elettro-magnetica* (Bergamo, 1912), with accompanying French, English, German, and Latin translations.

II. SECONDARY LITERATURE. There is a three-part biographical essay based on original sources by Franklin L. Pope, in *Electrical Engineer* (New York), **14** (1892), 259–262, 283–284, 339–341. See S. P. Thompson, *Dynamo-Electric Machinery*, 3rd ed. (London, 1888), for a detailed discussion of Pacinotti's design and the results of Thompson's experiments comparing the electrical performance of the Pacinotti and Gramme armatures. An obituary appeared in *Electrical World*, **59** (1912), 732–733. See also G. Polvani, *Antonio Pacinotti: la vita, l'opera* (Milan, 1932).

JAMES E. BRITTAIN

PACIOLI, LUCA (*b.* Sansepolcro, Italy, *ca.* 1445; *d.* Sansepolcro, 1517), *mathematics, bookkeeping.*

Luca Pacioli (Lucas de Burgo), son of Bartolomeo Pacioli, belonged to a modest family of Sansepolcro, a small commercial town in the Tiber valley about forty miles north of Perugia. All we know of his early life is that he was brought up by the Befolci family of Sansepolcro. It has been suggested that he may have received part of his early education in the atelier of his older compatriot Piero della Francesca (1410–1492). As a young man he entered the service of Antonio Rompiansi, a Venetian merchant who lived in the fashionable Giudecca district. Pacioli lived in Rompiansi's house and helped to educate his three sons. While doing so he studied mathematics under Domenico Bragadino, who held classes in Venice, probably at the school that the republic had established near the Church of San Giovanni di Rialto for those who did not want to go to Padua. The experience Pacioli gained in Rompiansi's business and the knowledge he gathered at Bragadino's school prompted him to write his works on arithmetic, the first of which he dedicated to the Rompiansi brothers in 1470. Their father was dead by then and Pacioli's employment probably had ended. He then stayed for several months in Rome as the guest of the architect Leone Battista Alberti.

Sometime between 1470 and 1477 Pacioli was ordained as a friar in the Franciscan order in fulfillment of a vow. After completing his theological studies he began a life of peregrination, teaching mathematics in various cities of Italy. From 1477 to 1480 he gave lessons in arithmetic at the University of Perugia and wrote a treatise on arithmetic for the benefit of his students (1478). In 1481 he was in Zara (now Zadar, Yugoslavia), then under Venetian rule, where he wrote another work on arithmetic. After teaching mathematics successively at the universities of Perugia, Naples, and Rome in 1487–1489, Pacioli returned to Sansepolcro. In 1494 his major work, *Summa de arithmetica, geometria, proportioni et proportionalita,* was ready for the publisher and he went to Venice to supervise the printing. He dedicated the book to the young duke of Urbino, Guidobaldo da Montefeltro (1472–1508), who, it is believed, was his pupil. The dedicatory letter suggests that Pacioli had been closely associated with the court of Urbino. This is confirmed by the altarpiece painted by Piero della Francesca for the Church of San Bernardino in Urbino (now in Milan), in which the figure of St. Peter the Martyr is portrayed by Pacioli. The painting shows Duke Federigo (Guidobaldo's father) praying before the Virgin and Child surrounded by angels and saints. A painting by Jacopo de' Barbari in the Naples Museum shows Pacioli demonstrating a lesson in geometry to Guidobaldo.

In 1497 Pacioli was invited to the court of Ludovico Sforza, duke of Milan, to teach mathematics. Here he met Leonardo da Vinci, who was already in Sforza's employment. That Leonardo consulted Pacioli on matters relating to mathematics is evident from entries in Leonardo's notebooks. The first part of Pacioli's *Divina proportione* was composed at Milan during 1496–1497, and it was Leonardo who drew the figures of the solid bodies for it. Their stay in Milan ended in 1499 with the entry of the French army and the consequent capture of Sforza. Journeying through Mantua and Venice, they arrived in Florence, where they shared quarters. Leonardo's stay in Florence, which lasted until the middle of 1506, was interrupted by a short period in the service of Cesare Borgia.

In 1500 Pacioli was appointed to teach Euclid's *Elements* at the University of Pisa, which had been transferred to Florence because of the revolt of Pisa in 1494. The appointment was renewed annually until 1506. In 1504 he made a set of geometrical figures for the Signoria of Florence, for which he was paid 52.9 lire. He was elected superior of his order for the province of Romagna and shortly afterward (1505) was accepted as a member of the monastery of Santa Croce in Florence. During his stay in Florence, Pacioli also held an appointment at the University of Bologna as *lector ad mathematicam* (1501–1502). At this time the University of Bologna had several *lectores ad arithmeticam*, one of whom was Scipione dal Ferro, who was to become famous for solving the cubic equation. It has been suggested that Pacioli's presence in Bologna may have encouraged Scipione to seek a solution of the cubic equation, but there is no evidence to support this apart from Pacioli's statement in the *Summa* that the cubic equation could not be solved algebraically.

Since his arrival in Florence, Pacioli had been preparing a Latin edition of Euclid's *Elements* and an Italian translation. He had also written a book on chess and had prepared a collection of recreational problems. On 11 August 1508 Pacioli was in Venice, where he read to a large gathering in the Church of San Bartolomeo in the Rialto an introduction to book V of Euclid's *Elements*. A few months later, on a supplication made by him to the doge of Venice, he was granted the privilege that no one but he could publish his works within the republic for fifteen years. The works listed were the fifteen books of Euclid, *Divina proportione*, "De viribus quantitatis," "De ludo scachorum," and *Summa de arithmetica*. The Latin edition of Euclid and the *Divina proportione* were published in 1509. Pacioli was called once more to lecture in Perugia in 1510 and in Rome in 1514.

On several occasions Pacioli came into conflict with the brethren of his order in Sansepolcro. In 1491, on a complaint made to the general of the order, he was prohibited from teaching the young men of the town; but this did not prevent his being called to preach the Lenten sermons there in 1493. It is likely that certain minor privileges granted to him by the Pope had aroused enmity or jealousy. Although a petition had been sent to the general of the order in 1509, he was shortly afterward elected commissioner of his convent in Sansepolcro. A few years later Pacioli renounced these privileges and in 1517, shortly before his death, his fellow townsmen petitioned that he be appointed minister of the order for the province of Assisi.

The commercial activity of Italy in the late Middle Ages had led to the composition of a large number of treatises on practical arithmetic to meet the needs of merchant apprentices. Evidence of this is found in the extant works of the *maestri d'abbaco* of central and northern Italy. Some of them even contained chapters devoted to the rules of algebra and their application, no doubt influenced by the *Liber abbaci* of Leonardo Fibonacci. The first printed commercial arithmetic was an anonymous work that appeared at Treviso in 1478. By the end of the sixteenth century about 200 such works had been published in Italy. Pacioli wrote three such treatises: one at Venice (1470), one at Perugia (1478), and one at Zara (1481). None of them was published and only the second has been preserved.

Pacioli's *Summa de arithmetica* . . . (1494) was more comprehensive. Unlike the practical arithmetics, it was not addressed to a particular section of the community. An encyclopedic work (600 pages of close print, in folio) written in Italian, it contains a general treatise on theoretical and practical arithmetic; the elements of algebra; a table of moneys, weights, and measures used in the various Italian states; a treatise on double-entry bookkeeping; and a summary of Euclid's geometry. He admitted to having borrowed freely from Euclid, Boethius, Sacrobosco, Leonardo Fibonacci, Prosdocimo de' Beldamandi, and others.

Although it lacked originality, the *Summa* was widely circulated and studied by the mathematicians of the sixteenth century. Cardano, while devoting a chapter of his *Practica arithmetice* (1539) to correcting the errors in the *Summa*, acknowledged his debt to Pacioli. Tartaglia's *General trattato de' numeri et misure* (1556–1560) was styled on Pacioli's *Summa*. In the introduction to his *Algebra*, Bombelli says that Pacioli was the first mathematician after Leonardo Fibonacci to have thrown light on the science of algebra—"primo fu che luce diede a quella scientia."[1] This statement, however, does not mean that algebra had been neglected in Italy for 300 years. Another edition of Pacioli's *Summa* was published in 1523.

Pacioli's treatise on bookkeeping, "De computis et scripturis," contained in the *Summa*, was the first printed work setting out the "method of Venice," that is, double-entry bookkeeping. Brown has said, "The history of bookkeeping during the next century consists of little else than registering the progress of the *De computis* through the various countries of Europe."[2]

The *Divina proportione*, written in Italian and published in 1509, was dedicated to Piero Soderini, perpetual gonfalonier of Florence. It comprised three books: "Compendio de divina proportione," "Tractato de l'architectura," and "Libellus in tres partiales tractatus divisus quinque corporum regularium." The first book, completed at Milan in 1497, is dedicated to Ludovico Sforza. Its subject is the golden section or divine proportion, as Pacioli called it, the ratio obtained by dividing a line in extreme and mean ratio. It contains a summary of Euclid's propositions (including those in Campanus' version) relating to the golden section, a study of the properties of regular polyhedrons, and a description of semi-regular polyhedrons obtained by truncation or stellation of regular polyhedrons. Book 2 is a treatise on architecture, based on Vitruvius, dedicated to Pacioli's pupils at Sansepolcro. To this he added a treatise on the right proportions of roman lettering. The third book is an Italian translation, dedicated to Soderini, of Piero della Francesca's *De corporibus regularibus*.

Also in 1509 Pacioli published his Latin translation of Euclid's *Elements*. The first printed edition of Euclid (a Latin translation made in the thirteenth century by Campanus of Novara from an Arabic text) had appeared at Venice in 1482. It was severely criticized by Bartolomeo Zamberti in 1505 when he was publishing a Latin translation from the Greek. Pacioli's edition is based on Campanus but contains his own emendations and annotations. It was published in order to vindicate Campanus, apparently at the expense of Ratdolt, the publisher of Campanus' translation.

Among the works that Pacioli had intended to publish is "De viribus quantitatis," a copy of which, in the hand of an amanuensis, is in the University Library of Bologna.[3] The name of the person to whom the work was dedicated has been left blank. It is an extensive work (309 folios) divided into three parts: the first is a collection of eighty-one mathematical recreational problems, a collection larger than those published a century later by Bachet de Méziriac and others; the second is a collection of geometrical problems and games; the third is a collection of proverbs and verses. No originality attaches to this work, for the problems are found scattered among earlier arithmetics and, in fact, a collection is attributed to Alcuin of York. Pacioli himself called the work a compendium. Some of the problems are found in the notebooks of Leonardo da Vinci, and the work itself contains frequent allusions to him.

Pacioli's Italian translation of Euclid's *Elements* and his work on chess, "De ludo scachorum," dedicated to the marquis of Mantua, Francesco Gonzaga, and his wife, Isabella d'Este, were not published and there is no trace of the manuscripts.

Vasari, in writing the biography of Piero della Francesca, accused Pacioli of having plagiarized the work of his compatriot on perspective, arithmetic, and geometry.[4] The accusations relate to three works by Piero—*De prospectiva pingendi*, "Libellus de quinque corporibus regularibus," and *Trattato d'abaco*, all of which have been published only since the turn of the twentieth century.[5] In 1908 Pittarelli came to the defense of Pacioli, pointing out that any accusation of plagiarism in regard to *De prospectiva* was unjust, since Pacioli had acknowledged Piero's work in both the *Summa* and the *Divina proportione*.[6] As for the *Libellus*, it has been established by Mancini that Pacioli's work is a translation of it that lacks the clarity of the original.[7] In the case of the *Trattato*, although Piero can claim no originality for it, it has been possible to find in it at least 105 problems of the *Summa*.[8]

The writings of Pacioli have provided historians of the Renaissance with important source material for the study of Leonardo da Vinci. The numerous editions and translations of the *De computis et scripturis* are evidence of the worldwide esteem in which Pacioli is held by the accounting profession. Pacioli made no original contribution to mathematics; but his *Summa*, written in the vulgar tongue, provided his countrymen, especially those not schooled in Latin, with an encyclopedia of the existing knowledge of the subject and enabled them to contribute to the advancement of algebra in the sixteenth century.

NOTES

1. Rafael Bombelli, *Algebra* (Bologna, 1572), d 2v.
2. Brown, *History of Accounting*, p. 119.
3. An ed. of the MS by Paul Lawrence Rose of New York University is in press.
4. Vasari, *Vite*, pp. 360, 361, 365.
5. Codex Palat. Parma, published by C. Winterberg (1899); Codex Vat. Urb. lat. 632, published in 1915 by Mancini; Codex Ash. 280, published in 1971 by Arrighi.
6. Pittarelli, "Luca Pacioli . . . ."
7. Mancini, "L'opera 'De corporibus regularibus' . . . ."
8. Jayawardene, "The *Trattato d'abaco* of Piero della Francesca."

BIBLIOGRAPHY

I. ORIGINAL WORKS. Pacioli's writings include *Summa de arithmetica, geometria, proportioni et proportionalita* (Venice, 1494; 2nd ed. Toscolano, 1523)—there are several eds. of the treatise on bookkeeping, "De computis et scripturis," contained in the *Summa*, fols. 197v–210v, in the original Italian and in trans.; *Divina proportione* (Venice, 1509)—there are two extant MSS containing the "Compendio de divina proportione," one in the University of Geneva Library (Codex 250) and the other in the Biblioteca Ambrosiana, Milan (Codex 170, parte superiore), the second published as no. XXXI of Fontes Ambrosiani, Giuseppina Masotti Biggiogero, ed. (Verona, 1956); *Euclid megarensis opera . . . a Campano . . . tralata. Lucas Paciolus emendavit* (Venice, 1509); "De viribus quantitatis" (University of Bologna Library, Codex 250), described by Amedeo Agostini in "Il 'De viribus quantitatis' di Luca Pacioli," in *Periodico di matematiche*, **4** (1924), 165–192, and by Carlo Pedretti in "Nuovi documenti riguardanti Leonardo da Vinci," in *Sapere* (15 Apr. 1952), 65–70.

An unpublished arithmetic, written in Perugia (1478), is in the Vatican Library (Codex Vat. lat. 3129).

II. SECONDARY LITERATURE. Studies of Pacioli's life and work are listed by G. Masotti Biggiogero in "Luca Pacioli e la sua 'Divina proportione,'" in *Rendiconti dell'Istituto lombardo di scienze e lettere*, ser. A, **94** (1960), 3–30.

The earliest biographical sketch, written by Bernardino Baldi in 1589, was not published. Baldassare Boncompagni made a critical study of it with the help of archival documents: "Intorno alle vite inedite di tre matematici . . . scritte da Bernadino Baldi," in *Bullettino di bibliografia e di storia delle scienze mathematiche e fisiche*, **12** (1879), 352–438, 863–872. Other archival documents were published by D. Ivano Ricci in *Luca Pacioli, l'uomo e lo scienziato* (Sansepolcro, 1940). R. E. Taylor, *No Royal Road: Luca Pacioli and His Times* (Chapel Hill, N. C., 1942), is a lively narrative but unreliable as a biography. Pacioli's work is discussed by L. Olschki in *Geschichte der neusprachlichen wissenschaftlichen Literatur*, I (Leipzig, 1919), 151–239.

Stanley Morison, *Fra Luca Pacioli of Borgo San Sepolcro* (New York, 1933), contains a study of that part of the *Divina proportione* dealing with roman lettering. The history of bookkeeping is discussed by Richard Brown in *A History of Accounting and Accountants* (London, 1905), 108–131.

On the accusations of plagiarism see Giorgio Vasari's life of Piero della Francesca in *Le vite de' più eccellenti architetti, pittori e scultori italiani* (Florence, 1550); G. Pittarelli, "Luca Pacioli usurpò per se stesso qualche libro di Piero de' Franceschi," in *Atti, IV Congresso internazionale dei matematici, Roma, 6–11 aprile 1908*, III (Rome, 1909), 436–440; G. Mancini, "L'opera 'De corporibus regularibus' di Pietro Franceschi detto Della Francesca usurpata da fra Luca Pacioli," in *Memorie della R. Accademia dei Lincei*, classe di scienze morali, storiche e filologiche, ser. 5, **14** (1915), 446–477, 488–580; and Gino Arrighi's ed. of Piero della Francesca's *Trattato d'abaco* (Pisa, 1971), 24–34. See also S. A. Jayawardene, "The *Trattato d'abaco*" of Piero della Francesca," in *Studies in the Italian Renaissance: A Collection in Honour of P. O. Kristeller* (in press).

S. A. JAYAWARDENE

PACKARD, ALPHEUS SPRING, JR. (*b.* Brunswick, Maine, 19 February 1839; *d.* Providence, Rhode Island, 14 February 1905), *entomology*.

Packard was the son of Alpheus Spring Packard, professor of Greek and Latin at Bowdoin College, and Frances Elizabeth Appleton, daughter of Jesse Appleton, president of Bowdoin College. His boyhood was spent exploring nature, a pastime in which he was encouraged by his father. By the time he had matriculated at Bowdoin College in 1857, he had investigated most branches of natural history. Packard's attention early turned to entomology, and in 1860 he was invited to join an expedition to Labrador arranged by Chadbourne. After graduating in 1861, he spent the summer with the Maine Geological Survey and published his first two scientific papers, on entomology and on geology.

In the fall of 1861 Packard went to the Lawrence Scientific School to study under Louis Agassiz. Packard was simultaneously able to pursue his medical studies, mainly human anatomy and medicine, and was awarded the M.D. from the Maine Medical School at Bowdoin College in 1864. By now he appeared so well established in his assistantship that there was every reason to believe he would be appointed one of the permanent curators of the new Museum of Comparative Zoology. Unfortunately a smoldering quarrel between the junior assistants and Agassiz relating to their duties and obligations to the museum led to a complete break; Packard, A. Hyatt, E. S. Morse, F. W. Putnam, S. H. Scudder, and A. E. Verrill left Cambridge in 1864.

Immediately after leaving Cambridge, Packard was again invited to join an expedition to Labrador, this time under the direction of the artist William Bradford. On his return to the United States in the fall of 1864 he received a commission as assistant surgeon of the First Maine Veteran Volunteers. But Packard's Civil War experience was of short duration, and it appears that his medical practice was equally brief, being confined entirely to these few months.

For the next thirteen years Packard led an almost itinerant existence of writing and editing, interrupted by short appointments at various institutions and agencies. He was acting librarian and custodian of the Boston Society of Natural History for a year. In 1867 he was one of the curators of the Peabody Academy of Science, Salem, Massachusetts, and, in 1877–1878, was its director. He lectured on economic entomology at the Maine State College of Agriculture and the Mechanical Arts (now the University of Maine) for a year and for several years at the Massachusetts Agricultural College (now University of Massachusetts). At Bowdoin he lectured first on entomology and later on comparative anatomy. During the winter of 1869–1870 he studied marine life at Key West and in the Dry Tortugas, then did similar work in Charleston, South Carolina. In March 1867 he joined forces with E. S. Morse, A. Hyatt, and F. W. Putnam to found *American Naturalist*, a popular scientific monthly.

Packard was its editor for some twenty years, writing many of the articles.

In 1874 he was associated with the Kentucky Geological Survey, investigating the fauna of Mammoth Cave; and in 1875–1876 he was with the U.S. Geological Survey of the Territories under F. V. Hayden. In 1877 Packard was appointed secretary to the U.S. Entomological Commission, headed by C. V. Riley.

With his appointment as professor of zoology and geology at Brown University, a greater maturity may be seen in his approach to scientific matters. During these years he produced some of his finest writings: *The Cave Fauna of North America* (1888), *The Labrador Coast* (1891), *Textbook of Entomology* (1898), and the three-volume *Monograph of the Bombycine Moths of North America* (1895–1914). He was a foreign member of the Royal Entomological and the Linnean societies of London and held an honorary Ph.D. and an honorary LL.D. from Bowdoin.

By inclination Packard was a naturalist in the early nineteenth-century tradition at a time when specialization was the fashion. His bibliography therefore appears miscellaneous, and the quality of his writings is varied. In his own time he was considered a general zoologist and geologist; today he is generally thought of as an entomologist, since with only a few exceptions it is his entomological publications that have real currency. As an educator, he provided a sound basis for training a new generation of professional entomologists with his *Half Hours With Insects* (1873), *Our Common Insects* (1873), *Guide to the Study of Insects* (1869), and *Textbook of Entomology* (1898).

Much of Packard's reputation now rests in the more enduring area of taxonomy, and it has been estimated that he described as new over 50 genera and about 580 species of invertebrates. About a quarter of these have now been placed in synonymy. Packard's descriptive methods varied greatly in quality. He turned out a good many inadequately analyzed and artificial descriptions, which accounts in part for a high share of the synonyms noted; yet, as with the bombycid moths, he delineated careful morphological features. Packard's reputation therefore rests with *A Monograph of the Geometrid Moths or Phalaenidae of the United States* (1876) and *Monograph of the Bombycine Moths of North America* (1895–1914). The latter work in particular more nearly corresponds to present-day expectations.

Attention is frequently drawn to Packard's place in the history of economic entomology; but although he contributed an impressive list of shorter papers, bulletins, and books on injurious insects, he was not an original or really professional applied entomologist.

The value of these writings consisted in providing sound life history studies and calling attention to potential problems. *Insects Injurious to Forest and Shade Trees* (1881, 1890), a compilation with some original observations, represents his best and most useful effort in this field.

Packard's work in marine invertebrate zoology was divided among taxonomic treatments, both living and fossil, one of his best being *A Monograph of the Phyllopod Crustacea of North America* (1883); and embryological and anatomical investigations, typical of which is *On the Embryology of Limulus polyphemus* (1871).

Packard's embryological studies, perhaps reflecting the influence of Agassiz, were fairly inclusive of the invertebrates, embracing both primitive and higher insects, crustaceans, and some anomalous forms, such as *Peripatus*. The first serious American student of insect embryology, he was one of the first in the United States to introduce the concept of comparative embryology. His preliminary *Life Histories of Animals, Including Man; or, Outlines of Comparative Embryology* (1876) was followed by *Outlines of Comparative Embryology* (1878); these pioneer efforts, however, were soon superseded by Francis Maitland Balfour's masterly two-volume *A Treatise on Comparative Embryology* (1880–1881).

An undoubted pioneer masterpiece of Packard's was *The Cave Fauna of North America, With Remarks on the Anatomy of the Brain and Origin of the Blind Species* (1888), combining the disciplines of taxonomy, anatomy, and evolution.

Packard's sustained interest in evolution was more Lamarckian than Darwinian, more teleologic than mechanistic. His interest in Lamarck's zoological philosophy led to *Lamarck, the Founder of Evolution; His Life and Work, With Translations of His Writings on Organic Evolution* (1901) and, with E. D. Cope and A. Hyatt, virtually to found the neo-Lamarckian movement, which influenced the writings of later nineteenth- and early twentieth-century American taxonomists.

BIBLIOGRAPHY

A rather complete listing of the many biographical notices of Packard is in Mathilde M. Carpenter, "Bibliography of Biographies of Entomologists," in *American Midland Naturalist*, **33** (1945), 76–77. Of those listed, J. S. Kingsley, "Sketch of Alpheus Spring Packard," in *Popular Science Monthly*, **33** (1888), 260–267, and A. D. Mead, "Alpheus Spring Packard," *ibid.*, **67** (1905), 43–48, are especially good; but the definitive reference is T. D. A. Cockerell, "Biographical Memoir of Alpheus Spring

Packard," in *Biographical Memoirs. National Academy of Sciences*, **9** (1920), 181–236, which quotes extensively from Packard's unpublished diaries and includes a complete bibliography of his writings. No modern evaluation of Packard's impact on American science has been published.

CALVERT E. NORLAND

PADOA, ALESSANDRO (*b.* Venice, Italy, 14 October 1868; *d.* Genoa, Italy, 25 November 1937), *mathematical logic, mathematics.*

Padoa attended a secondary school in Venice, the engineering school in Padua, and the University in Turin, from which he received a degree in mathematics in 1895. He taught in secondary schools at Pinerolo, Rome, and Cagliari, and (from 1909) at the Technical Institute in Genoa.

Padoa was the first to devise a method for proving that a primitive term of a theory cannot be defined within the system by the remaining primitive terms. This method was presented in his lectures at Rome early in 1900 and was made public at the International Congress of Philosophy held at Paris later that year. He defined a system of undefined symbols as irreducible with respect to the system of unproved propositions when no symbolic definition of any undefined symbol can be deduced from the system of unproved propositions. He also said:

> To prove that the system of undefined symbols is irreducible with respect to the system of unproved propositions, it is necessary and sufficient to find, for each undefined symbol, an interpretation of the system of undefined symbols that verifies the system of unproved propositions and that continues to do so if we suitably change the meaning of only the symbol considered ["Essai . . .," p. 322].

Although it took the development of model theory to bring out the importance of this method in the theory of definition, Padoa was already convinced of its significance. (A proof of Padoa's method was given by Alfred Tarski in 1926 and, independently, by J. C. C. McKinsey in 1935.)

In lectures at the universities of Brussels, Pavia, Bern, Padua, Cagliari, and Geneva, Padoa was an effective popularizer of the mathematical logic developed by Giuseppe Peano's "school," of which Padoa was a prominent member. He was also active in the organization of secondary school teachers of mathematics and participated in many congresses of philosophy and mathematics. In 1934 he was awarded the ministerial prize in mathematics by the Accademia dei Lincei.

BIBLIOGRAPHY

I. ORIGINAL WORKS. A list of 34 of Padoa's publications in logic and related areas of mathematics (about half of all his scientific publications) is in Antonio Giannattasio, "Due inediti di Alessandro Padoa," in *Physis* (Florence), **10** (1968), 309–336. To this may be added three papers presented to the Congrès International de Philosophie Scientifique at Paris in 1935 and published in *Actualités scientifiques et industrielles* (1936): "Classes et pseudo-classes," no. 390, 26–28; "Les extensions successives de l'ensemble des nombres au point de vue déductif," no. 394, 52–59; and "Ce que la logique doit à Peano," no. 395, 31–37.

Padoa's method was stated in "Essai d'une théorie algébrique des nombres entiers, précédé d'une introduction logique à une théorie déductive quelconque," in *Bibliothèque du Congrès international de philosophie, Paris, 1900*, III (Paris, 1901), 309–365. An English trans. (with references to Padoa's method) is in Jean van Heijenoort, ed., *From Frege to Gödel: A Source Book in Mathematical Logic 1879–1931* (Cambridge, Mass., 1967), 118–123. Padoa's major work is "La logique déductive dans sa dernière phase de développement," in *Revue de métaphysique et de morale*, **19** (1911), 828–832; **20** (1912), 48–67, 207–231, also published separately, with a preface by G. Peano (Paris, 1912).

II. SECONDARY LITERATURE. There is no biography of Padoa. Some information on his life and work may be found in the obituaries in *Bollettino dell'Unione matematica italiana*, **16** (1937), 248; and *Revue de métaphysique et de morale*, **45** (1938), Apr. supp., 32; and in F. G. Tricomi, "Matematici italiani del primo secolo dello stato unitario," in *Memorie della Accademia delle scienze di Torino*, 4th ser., no. 1 (1962), 81.

HUBERT C. KENNEDY

PAGANO, GIUSEPPE (*b.* Palermo, Sicily, 21 September 1872; *d.* Palermo, 9 August 1959), *physiology.*

For a detailed study of his life and work, see Supplement.

PAINLEVÉ, PAUL (*b.* Paris, France, 5 December 1863; *d.* Paris, France, 29 October 1933), *mathematics.*

Painlevé's father, Léon Painlevé, and grandfather, Jean-Baptiste Painlevé, were lithographers. Through his grandmother, Euphrosine Marchand, he was a descendant of Napoleon I's valet. As gifted in literature as in the sciences, Painlevé received excellent marks in secondary school.

After hesitating between a career as a politician, engineer, and researcher Painlevé chose the last, which had been offered him by the École Normale Supérieure. Admitted in 1883, he received his *agrégation* in mathematics in 1886. He worked for a time at Göttingen, where Schwarz and Klein were teaching, and at the same time completed his doctoral dissertation (1887). Painlevé became professor at Lille in 1887. In 1892 he moved to Paris, where he taught at the Faculty of Sciences and the École Polytechnique, the Collège de France (1896), and the École Normale Supérieure (1897).

Painlevé received the Grand Prix des Sciences Mathématiques (1890), the Prix Bordin (1894), and the Prix Poncelet (1896); and was elected a member of the geometry section of the Académie des Sciences in 1900. In 1901 he married Marguerite Petit de Villeneuve, niece of the painter Georges Clairin; she died at the birth of their son Jean (1902), who became one of the creators of scientific cinematography.

Painlevé was interested in the infant field of aviation, and as the passenger with Wilbur Wright and Henri Farman he even shared for a time the record for duration of biplane flights (1908). He was a professor at the École Supérieure d'Aéronautique (1909) and president of several commissions on aerial navigation.

In 1910 Painlevé turned to politics. Elected a deputy from the fifth arrondissement of Paris, the "Quartier Latin," he headed naval and aeronautical commissions established to prepare for the country's defense. In 1914 he created the Service des Inventions pour les Besoins de la Défense Nationale, which became a ministry in 1915. Minister of war in 1917, Painlevé played an important role in the conduct of military operations: he supported the efforts of the Army of the Near East in the hope of detaching Austria-Hungary from the German alliance. He conducted the negotiations with Woodrow Wilson over the sending of American combat troops to France. He also had Foch appointed as head of the allied chiefs of staff.

In 1920 Painlevé was commissioned by the Chinese government to reorganize the country's railroads. From 1925 to 1933 he was several times minister of war and of aviation, president of the Council of Ministers, and an active participant in the League of Nations and in its International Institute of Intellectual Cooperation.

As a mathematician Painlevé always considered questions in their greatest generality. After his first works concerning rational transformations of algebraic curves and surfaces, in which he introduced biuniform transformations, he was remarkably successful in the study of singular points of algebraic differential equations. His goal was to obtain general propositions on the nature of the integral considered as a function of the variable and of the constants, par-

ticularly through distinguishing the "perfect integrals," definable throughout their domain of existence by a unique development.

In old problems in which the difficulties seemed insurmountable, Painlevé defined new transcendentals for singular points of differential equations of a higher order than the first. In particular he determined every equation of the second order and first degree whose critical points are fixed. This work was presented in notes published in the *Comptes rendus . . . de l'Académie des sciences* beginning in 1887.

The results of these studies are applicable to the equations of analytical mechanics which admit rational or algebraic first integrals with respect to the velocities. Proving, in the words of Hadamard's *éloge*, that "continuing [the work of] Henri Poincaré was not beyond human capacity," Painlevé extended the known results concerning the *n*-body problem. He also corrected certain accepted results in problems of friction and of the conditions of certain equilibriums when the force function does not pass through a maximum.

BIBLIOGRAPHY

I. ORIGINAL WORKS. Painlevé's mathematical writings are "Sur les lignes singulières des fonctions analytiques," in *Annales de la Faculté des sciences de Toulouse* (1888), his doctoral dissertation; "Sur la transformation des fonctions harmoniques et les systèmes triples de surfaces orthogonales," in *Travaux et mémoires de la Faculté des sciences de Lille*, **1** (Aug. 1889), 1–29; "Sur les équations différentielles du premier ordre," in *Annales scientifiques de l'École normale supérieure*, 3rd ser., **8** (Jan.–Mar. 1891), 9–58, 103–140; (Aug.–Sept. 1891), 201–226, 267–284; **9** (Jan. 1892), 9–30; (Apr.–June 1892), 101–144, 283–308; "Mémoire sur la transformation des équations de la dynamique," in *Journal de mathématiques pures et appliquées*, 4th ser., **10** (Jan. 1894), 5–92; "Sur les mouvements et les trajectoires réels des systèmes," in *Bulletin de la Société mathématique de France*, **22** (Oct. 1894), 136–184; *Leçons sur l'intégration des équations de la dynamique et applications* (Paris, 1894); *Leçons sur le frottement* (Paris, 1895); *Leçons sur l'intégration des équations différentielles de la mécanique et applications* (Paris, 1895); *Leçons sur la théorie analytique des équations différentielles professées à Stockholm . . .* (Paris, 1897); "Sur les équations différentielles dont l'intégrale générale est uniforme," in *Bulletin de la Société mathématique de France*, **28** (June 1900), 201–261; "Sur les équations différentielles du second ordre et d'ordre supérieur dont l'intégrale générale est uniforme," in *Acta mathematica*, **25** (Sept. 1900), 1–80; and contributions to Émile Borel, *Sur les fonctions de variables réelles et les développements en série de polynomes* (Paris, 1905), 101–147; and Pierre Boutroux, *Leçons sur les fonctions* *définies par les équations différentielles du premier ordre* (Paris, 1908), 141–187.

Painlevé's other works include *L'aviation* (Paris, 1910; 2nd ed., 1911), written with Émile Borel; *Cours de mécanique de l'École polytechnique*, 2 vols. (Paris, 1920–1921); *Les axiomes de la mécanique. Examen critique et note sur la propagation de la lumière* (Paris, 1922); *Cours de mécanique* (Paris, 1929), written with Charles Platrier; *Leçons sur la résistance des fluides non visqueux*, 2 vols. (Paris, 1930–1931); and *Paroles et écrits* (Paris, 1936).

II. SECONDARY LITERATURE. See the collection made by the Société des Amis de Paul Painlevé, *Paroles et écrits de Paul Painlevé* (Paris, 1936), with prefaces by Paul Langevin and Jean Perrin; and Jean Painlevé, *Textes inédites et analyse des travaux scientifiques jusqu'en 1900.*

LUCIENNE FÉLIX

PAINTER, THEOPHILUS SHICKEL (*b.* Salem, Virginia, 22 August 1889; *d.* Fort Stockton, Texas, 5 October 1969), *genetics, cytogenetics.*

Painter is best known for introducing the use of the giant salivary gland chromosomes of the fruit fly, *Drosophila melanogaster*, into cytogenetic studies. With this material he was able to demonstrate in 1933 what until then had been only an assumption: that Mendelian genes could be identified with specific bands on physical structures in cell nuclei, the chromosomes.

The son of the Reverend Franklin Verzelius Newton Painter, professor of modern languages at Roanoke College, Virginia, and Laura Shickel, Painter received his early education from tutors. He entered Roanoke College in 1904 and received the B.A. in 1908. He then went to Yale on a fellowship in chemistry but soon found biology more to his liking. Working under A. Petrunkevitch and R. G. Harrison, Painter received the Ph.D. in 1913, then studied during 1913–1914 under Theodor Boveri at Würzburg. Returning to Yale in 1914, he served as an instructor in zoology for two years (1914–1916); during the summers of 1914 and 1915 he was an instructor in the invertebrate zoology course at the Marine Biological Laboratory, Woods Hole, Massachusetts. In 1916 he accepted a post as adjunct professor of zoology at the University of Texas, beginning a long and distinguished association with that university. In 1922 he was promoted to full professor and in 1939 became a distinguished professor in the graduate school. From 1944 to 1946 he was acting president of the university and from 1946 until 1952 was president. In 1952 he resigned the presidency to return to full-time teaching and research. In 1966 he retired but continued his research and participated regularly in graduate seminars until his death.

By the 1930's most geneticists were convinced that Mendel's genes had an actual physical existence and were arranged in a linear fashion on the cell's chromosomes (the common analogy was to beads on a string). At that time, however, there was no direct proof for the validity of this assumption. The linkage maps for *Drosophila* prepared by T. H. Morgan, C. B. Bridges, and their associates between 1915 and 1925 were only formalisms derived almost wholly from analysis of crossover frequencies (that is, breeding data). Positions on these maps represented only relative distances between the various genes. Several studies in the 1920's had suggested that a point-by-point correspondence between linkage maps and the structure of actual chromosomes could be determined. In 1929, however, Painter and H. J. Muller (both at the University of Texas) cast doubt on this idea by showing that while the linear sequence determined by crude cytological methods and that determined by crossover data were the same, the spatial correspondences were not. That is, there appeared to be long areas of the chromosome in which no crossovers occurred, and other, shorter areas where a great deal seemed to occur.

The major problem in determining the correspondence between linkage maps and the structure of chromosomes was the small size of the latter. Workers before the 1930's studied various types of somatic (body) or oögonial cells, in which the chromosomes were so small that detailed observation, particularly of the banding pattern, was impossible. Larger chromosomes had been observed in the 1880's and, in the 1920's, in salivary gland cells of young larval dipterans; but these cells had been found difficult to work with and observational studies with them had not been carried very far. In 1930 Painter found that if older larvae (almost ready to pupate) were used, large and easily observable chromosomes could be obtained. They offered ideal material for the study of small chromosomal segments and thus for the detection of modifications of chromosomal structure that could be correlated with variations in linkage maps. Painter's paper of December 1933 established a method that made possible the detailed analysis of *Drosophila* and other insect chromosomes and provided the long-awaited confirmation of the chromosomal theory of heredity—the idea that genes are located on chromosomes.

In addition to studying the chromosomes of insects, Painter pioneered in the structural analysis of human chromosomes. He provided new techniques for studying human karyotypes (the full complement of chromosomes from a species, observed in squash or other preparations) and suggested ways of relating chromosomal aberrations to disease. He was also interested in the relationship of heterochromatin and chromosome puffing to ribonucleic acid (RNA) synthesis, and at the time of his death he was studying the nucleic acids found in the royal jelly of the honeybee. It was Painter's original count of the human karyotype, in 1929 and subsequently, that established the erroneous total of 48 chromosomes (rather than 46), believed for many years to be the actual number for the human species.

Painter was a member of the U.S. National Academy of Sciences (1938), the American Philosophical Society (1939), the American Society of Zoologists, the American Genetics Society, the American Society of Naturalists, and Sigma Xi. He received the David Girard Elliott Medal of the National Academy of Sciences (1934) in recognition of his work on the giant chromosomes of *Drosophila*, and the M. D. Anderson Award from the University of Texas, for his "scientific creativity and teaching" (1969). He was also awarded an honorary D.Sc. from Yale (1936) and an LL.D. from Roanoke College (1942).

In 1917 Painter married Anna Mary Thomas, whom he had met at Woods Hole in 1914. They had four children.

BIBLIOGRAPHY

Painter's last scientific publication, "The Origin of the Nucleic Acid Bases Found in the Royal Jelly of the Honeybee," appeared posthumously in *Proceedings of the National Academy of Sciences . . .*, **64** (Sept. 1969), 64–66. His major work on the giant salivary gland chromosomes in *Drosophila* is "A New Method for the Study of Chromosome Rearrangements and Plotting of Chromosome Maps," in *Science*, **78** (1933), 585–586.

No full-scale biographical study exists, although presumably one will be issued by the National Academy of Sciences. My major sources of information have been a brochure from the University of Texas, announcing the M. D. Anderson Award in 1969 (supplied by Mrs. T. S. Painter), and several personal communications from Mrs. Painter in 1970.

GARLAND E. ALLEN

PALEY, WILLIAM (*b.* Peterborough, England, July 1743; *d.* Lincoln, England, 25 May 1805), *natural theology*.

Paley was the eldest son of Elizabeth and William Paley. His father, a graduate of Christ's College, Cambridge, was a vicar and minor canon of the Church of England, and was headmaster of the grammar school at Giggleswick. Paley was educated at his father's school and entered Christ's College, Cambridge, in 1759, receiving his B.A. in January 1763. Following graduation he began to teach at an academy in Greenwich, but in June 1766 he was elected a fellow of his college and returned to Cambridge. Paley's last formal connection with Christ's College was as tutor from 1771 to 1774.

While an undergraduate, Paley had shown promise in mathematics; he continued his interest in that field during his tenure as tutor, when he corrected the proofs of *Miscellanea analytica*, written by Edward Waring, the Lucasian professor of mathematics. Paley had been ordained a deacon in the Church of England by 1766. While a fellow of Christ's College, he gave a lecture entitled "Metaphysics, Morals and the Greek Testament" and discussed the *Being and Attributes of God*, written by the Reverend Samuel Clarke. It was at this time that Paley became friendly with a number of other fellows interested in natural theology, including John Jebb, and joined the Hyson Club. His interest in metaphysics and in Clarke's work led him to support an attempt of other latitudinarians to relax the stringency of the church's organization and government.

In 1775 Paley was presented with the rectorship of Musgrave in Cumberland, the first of several ecclesiastical posts he was to hold. By 1782 he had become archdeacon of Carlisle, and his financial position was assured. Written at this time, his *Principles of Moral and Political Philosophy* was taken from his lectures and enjoyed wide success. His rise in the church continued, and by the end of 1785 he had become chancellor of the diocese of Carlisle. Having become interested in the abolition of the slave trade, he lectured against slavery and became, on the local level, very much of a public figure.

Paley's abandonment of a purely academic career may be seen in his refusal of the mastership of Jesus College, Cambridge, in 1792, for financial reasons. Instead of returning to the university he continued to accumulate increasingly lucrative ecclesiastical holdings and continued to publish. By 1794 his writings advanced his religious career, for his *Evidences of Christianity* was warmly regarded by the church and he was rewarded with new benefices. In 1795 Paley received the Doctorate of Divinity at Cambridge and the rectorship of Bishop-Wearmouth, a post worth £1,200 a year. He remained in residence at Carlisle and was appointed a justice of the peace for the region.

Although much in demand as a public speaker, illness in 1800 forced Paley to give up this aspect of his career. In 1802 he published his most significant book, *Natural Theology; or, Evidences of the Existence and*

Attributes of the Deity. He died three years later. Paley was married twice: to Jane Hewitt, who died in 1791; and in 1795 to a Miss Dobinson. His son by his first marriage, Edmund, wrote a life of his father.

Paley's fame is as a writer of textbooks. His works were used at Cambridge for nearly half a century after his death. His own religious views inclined toward liberalism; and while he never embraced the Unitarian point of view, as did so many of his friends, he was not hostile toward Arianism or Unitarianism. *Natural Theology* is perhaps most significant for Paley's efforts to reconcile liberal orthodox Christianity with divine providence. As an undergraduate at Cambridge, Charles Darwin read much of Paley's writings:

> In order to pass the B.A. examination, it was also necessary to get up Paley's *Evidences of Christianity*, and his *Moral Philosophy*. This was done in a thorough manner, and I am convinced that I could have written out the whole of the *Evidences* with perfect correctness, but not of course in the clear language of Paley. The logic of this book, and, as I may add, of his *Natural Theology*, gave me as much delight as did Euclid. The careful study of these works, without attempting to learn any part by rote, was the only part of the academical course which, as I then felt and as I still believe, was of the least use to me in the education of my mind. I did not at that time trouble myself about Paley's premises; and taking these on trust, I was charmed and convinced by the long line of argumentation [*Charles Darwin's Autobiography*, Sir Francis Darwin, ed. (New York, 1961), 34–35].

Paley's underlying belief, expressed in *Natural Theology*, was that the world is essentially a happy place. Nature was God and God was good; the proof of the goodness of God and Nature could be found in day-to-day experiences. In the most often quoted passage of his work Paley says:

> It is a happy world after all. The air, the earth, the water teem with delighted existence. In a spring noon, or a summer evening, on whichever side I turn my eyes, myriads of happy beings crowd upon my view. "The insect youth are on the wing." Swarms of new-born flies are trying their pinions in the air. Their sportive motions, their wanton mazes, their gratuitous activity, testify their joy and the exultation which they feel in their lately discovered faculties. . . . The whole winged insect tribe, it is probable, are equally intent upon their proper employments, and under every variety of constitution, gratified, and perhaps equally gratified, by the offices which the author of their nature has assigned to them [*Natural Theology*, p. 236].

The work itself, written as a treatise against atheism and teleological in the extreme, shows how the workings of the body, the functions of animals and plants, and the arrangement of the human frame all manifest the workings of the deity. Throughout, Paley dwells on how things could not possibly have been organized otherwise, using mechanical examples to illustrate further the existence of the deity. In his description of the muscles Paley attempted to work out a dynamic approach to muscular action (*Natural Theology*, in *The Works of William Paley*, I [Cambridge, 1830], 71; hereafter cited by page only). In his treatment of organisms Paley cited symmetry as a further proof of divinity (pp. 101, 166). He also used the relations of "parts one to another" to show the works of God; his classic example was that the sexes are "manifestly made for each other" (p. 143).

Believing that the various parts of animals complement each other, Paley used the term "compensation" —which, to him, was "a relation, when the defects of one part, or one organ, are supplied by the structure of another part, or of another organ" (p. 146). He showed how the "short, unbending neck of the elephant" is compensated by the trunk, and in the course of this description he took issue with the ideas of Erasmus Darwin.

> If it be suggested, that this proboscis may have been produced in a long course of generations, by the constant endeavour of the elephant to thrust out his nose, (which is the general hypothesis by which it has been lately attempted to account for the forms of animated nature), I would ask, how was the animal to subsist in the mean time; during the process; *until* this prolongation of snout were completed? What was to become of the individual, whilst the species was perfecting? (pp. 146–147)

Paley took no stand on evolution as such, believing that "our business is simply to point out the relation which an organ bears to the peculiar figure of the animal to which it belongs" (p. 147).

After dealing with animate matter Paley turned to a very brief treatment of the elements—a highly simplistic and almost Aristotelian one. His comments on astronomy sum up his idea of the purpose of scientific studies: "My opinion of [it] has always been, that it is *not* the best medium through which to prove the agency of an intelligent Creator; but that, this being proved, it shows, beyond all other sciences, the magnificence of his operation" (p. 197). Paley's conclusion seems quite clear. "In the observable portion of nature organisms are formed one beneath another . . . the Deity can mould and fashion the parts in material nature so as to fulfill any purpose whatsoever which he is pleased to appoint" (p. 280).

Paley's significance in the history of science is twofold. His writings on natural theology clearly reveal the changed framework of the late eighteenth and early nineteenth centuries as opposed to the late seventeenth century. The purely physical universe no longer could suffice to furnish proof for God's existence, but emphasis had turned to biological evidence to show the beneficence of the deity's workings. On the whole Paley's universe was a benevolent one. This very benevolence, coupled with Paley's popularity as a textbook writer, helped to create the atmosphere so hostile to Charles Darwin in the 1850's and 1860's.

BIBLIOGRAPHY

I. ORIGINAL WORKS. Paley's published works were collected as *The Works of William Paley, D.D.*, 6 vols. (Cambridge, 1825; 2nd ed., 1830). Included are *Natural Theology; or, Evidences of the Existence and Attributes of the Deity, Sermons on Various Subjects, Horae Paulinae, Clergyman's Companion, The Young Christian Instructed, Principles of Moral and Political Philosophy*, and *A View of the Evidences of Christianity*. In 1820 *Natural Theology* was reprinted for the twentieth time, and in 1835–1839, it formed the core of a work entitled *Natural Theology* by Lord Brougham. Paley's work was translated into Spanish, French, and Italian.

II. SECONDARY LITERATURE. G. W. Meadley, "Memoirs of William Paley, D.D.," in *The Works of William Paley, D.D.*, I, is the best treatment of the subject. Meadley had been a close friend of Paley, and his work is more detailed than Edmund Paley's "Life of William Paley," which is prefixed to the 1825 ed. of Paley's *Works*. Other treatments are derivative and depend on Meadley's. Passing reference is paid to Paley by L. E. Elliott-Binns, *Religion in the Victorian Era* (London–Redhill, 1946). Although the most extensive treatment is to be found in Leslie Stephen's article in *Dictionary of National Biography*, XV (1967–1968), 101–107, Stephen is concerned less with Paley's influence on science than in the recounting of personal anecdotes.

JOEL M. RODNEY

PALISA, JOHANN (*b.* Troppau, Austrian Silesia [now Czechoslovakia], 6 December 1848; *d.* Vienna, Austria, 2 May 1925), *astronomy.*

While a student Palisa became known for his skill in mathematics, and in 1866 he entered the University of Vienna to study that subject. He soon became attracted to astronomy, the science to which he devoted the rest of his life. In 1870 he was appointed assistant astronomer at the Vienna observatory. There he performed routine observations: at night, of positions of stars with the meridian circle; during the day, of the spots on the sun's disk. In 1871 Palisa became associate astronomer at the Geneva observatory. A

few months later, at the age of twenty-three, he was appointed director of the Austro-Hungarian naval observatory at Pola, with the rank of commander. His main task was precise timekeeping by astronomical observations. For this purpose a new meridian circle was acquired; and he himself invented the "Chronodeik," a small instrument for determining time by measuring equal heights of stars east and west of the meridian. Palisa was also eager to promote scientific research. Inspired by Oppolzer, he began to observe asteroids systematically with the small telescope at Pola; he obtained a great many positions of asteroids already known and discovered twenty-eight new ones between 1874 and 1880.

Meanwhile, a splendid new observatory had been built at Vienna with a refracting telescope of twenty-seven inches aperture, the largest at that time. Palisa agreed to join the observatory as associate astronomer after being assured that the large telescope would always be at his disposal. From 1883 to the fall of 1924 he used it to the utmost, an undertaking made arduous because there was no automation: the telescope, the observer's stage, and the dome were moved manually. The discovery of 120 asteroids is Palisa's best-known work but not his greatest. About 1893 Max Wolf at Heidelberg had begun to discover asteroids photographically; and the two scientists, after a short period of rivalry, achieved an effective collaboration: Wolf continued to discover asteroids near their opposition, while Palisa followed them to great distances with his powerful telescope so that their orbits could be determined with greater precision. Valuable products of Palisa's work are two catalogs containing the positions of 4,696 stars and, from his collaboration with Wolf, the 210 sheets of the Palisa-Wolf photographic charts of the sky. Undoubtedly, Palisa was the most effective observer of the Austrian astronomers.

BIBLIOGRAPHY

I. ORIGINAL WORKS. Palisa's writings are listed in Poggendorff, III, 1000–1001; IV, 1113; V, 937–938; and VI, 1941. They include "Das Meridian-Instrument zu Pola," in *Repertorium für Experimental-Physik physikalische Technik* . . ., **13** (1877); "Beobachtungen während der Sonnenfinsternis 6. Mai 1883," in *Sitzungsberichte der Akademie der Wissenschaften in Wien*, Abt. IIa, **88** (1884), 1018–1031; "Katalog von 1238 Sternen," in *Denkschriften der Akademie der Wissenschaften* (Vienna), **67** (1899), written with F. Bidschof; "Sternlexikon von −1° bis +19° Deklination," in *Annalen der Universitätssternwarte in Wien*, 4th ser., **17** (1902); "Über einen Plan zur Herstellung von Ekliptikal-Sternkarten," in *Vierteljahrsschrift der Astronomischen Gesellschaft* (Leipzig), **39** (1904) and **41** (1906); and "Katalog von 3458 Sternen," in *Annalen der Universitätssternwarte in Wien*, 4th ser., **19** (1908). There are also many observational notes in *Astronomische Nachrichten*, **76–222** (1870–1924).

II. SECONDARY LITERATURE. See J. Hepperger, "J. Palisa," in *Astronomische Nachrichten*, **225** (1925); S. Oppenheim, "J. Palisa," in *Vierteljahrsschrift der Astronomischen Gesellschaft* (Leipzig), **60** (1925); and J. Rheden, *Johann Palisa* (Vienna, 1925), a pamphlet.

KONRADIN FERRARI D'OCCHIEPPO

PALISSY, BERNARD (*b*. La Capelle Biron, France, *ca*. 1510; *d*. Paris, France, *ca*. 1590), *natural history, hydrology.*

Palissy was first trained in the manufacture and decoration of stained glass windows. As his profession became less in demand, however, he took up land surveying in order to support his wife and children (of whom there were at least six). Some time around 1539 he became interested in enameled pottery and, after sixteen years of tireless experimentation (during which, by his own account, he burned his furniture and floorboards to fuel his kiln), perfected a technique for making a "rustic" enameled earthenware that brought him fame and a modest fortune. Some of his works are preserved in the Louvre and the Cluny Museum in Paris and in the Victoria and Albert Museum and the British Museum in London. These extant pieces are molded and decorated with modeling or applied ornaments, often in patterns derived from contemporary engravings; Palissy probably never used the potter's wheel, and no identifying mark of his is known. The governor of Saintes, where Palissy settled, was the constable Anne, Duc de Montmorency, who had a keen interest in the fine arts and became Palissy's patron.

Palissy converted to Protestantism in about 1546. He was one of the first Huguenots in Saintes, and was much persecuted for his religion. He was imprisoned in Bordeaux around 1559 and, had it not been for Anne de Montmorency, who took his case directly to the queen mother, Catherine de Médicis, he would almost certainly have been executed. The queen mother appointed him *inventeur des rustiques figulines du roy*, and commissioned him to decorate the new Tuileries palace. Palissy thus became established in Paris, where in 1575 he began to give public lectures on natural history. Despite his lack of formal education Palissy's lectures, according to Désiré Leroux, attracted the most learned men in the capital.

Palissy wrote two major books, *Recepte véritable*, published in 1563, and *Discours admirables*, published in 1580. (A small pamphlet describing the building of a grotto for Anne de Montmorency was also published in 1563.) The form of the two works is similar; each is a dialogue, between "Demande" and "Réponse" in the *Recepte*, and between "Théorique" and "Pratique" in the *Discours*. "Réponse" and "Pratique" give voice to Palissy's own ideas and concepts.

In *Recepte véritable*, Palissy discussed a wide variety of topics, including agriculture (for which he proposed better methods for farming and for the use of fertilizers), geology (in which he touched upon the origin of salts, springs, precious stones, and rock formations), mines, and forestry. He also suggested plans for an ideal garden, to be decorated with his earthenware and with biblical quotations, and discussed the founding and persecution of the Protestant church at Saintes. As part of this ecclesiastic history he included plans for a spiral fortress, which he claimed would be invincible and which would presumably offer a refuge for Protestants in time of war.

The second book, *Discours admirables*, probably incorporates Palissy's Paris lectures. It, like the earlier work, deals with an impressive array of subjects: agriculture, alchemy, botany, ceramics, embalming, engineering, geology, hydrology, medicine, metallurgy, meteorology, mineralogy, paleontology, philosophy, physics, toxicology, and zoology. The book is divided into several chapters, the first and longest of which is concerned with water. The others take up metals and their nature and generation; drugs; ice; different types of salts and their nature, effects, and methods of generation; characteristics of common and precious stones; clay and marl; and the potter's art.

Palissy's views on hydrology and paleontology, as expressed in the *Discours*, are of particular interest. He was one of the few men of his century to have a correct notion of the origins of rivers and streams, and he stated it forcefully, denying categorically that rivers can have any source other than rainfall. An early advocate of the infiltration theory, he refuted, with great skill and logic, the old theories that streams came from seawater or from air that had condensed into water. He also wrote on the principles of artesian wells, the recharging of wells from nearby rivers, and forestation for the prevention of soil erosion, and presented plans for constructing "fountains" for domestic water supply.

Palissy discussed fossils extensively. Like Xenophanes of Colophon, he believed them to be remnants of animals and plants. He firmly rejected the idea that they were detritus of the biblical flood, suggesting that inland fossils are found on site as the result of the congelation of a lake. He recognized the relation between these fossils and living species and, in some cases, extinct ones. He was one of the first to hold a reasonably correct view of the process of petrification.

(Duhem in *Études sur Léonard de Vinci* has pointed out that all these ideas may well be derived from Cardano's *De subtilitate*, with which Palissy was familiar, and hence from the thought of Leonardo da Vinci.)

Palissy held other advanced views. From experimentation he concluded that all minerals with geometric crystal forms must have crystallized in water; his classification of salts was nearly correct; and he suggested the concept of superposition for the development of sedimentary rocks. In his writings on medicine he demonstrated that potable gold was neither potable nor beneficial, and he showed that mithridate, a remedy composed of some 300 ingredients, was useless and probably harmful. He presented observations in support of his scientific ideas, and scathingly denounced established authorities if their findings did not agree with his own data. While there is some question concerning his originality—La Rocque discussed his dependence on thirty-one other writers on earth sciences whose works were available in the sixteenth century, and Thorndike charged him with plagiarizing Jacques Besson's *L'art et la science de trouver les eaux* of 1567—there is little doubt that Palissy was probably one of the first men in France to teach natural sciences from facts, specimens, and demonstrations rather than hypotheses.

Although he was well known as a potter, Palissy's scientific work was not widely recognized in his lifetime. In 1588, soon after religious warfare once more broke out in France, Palissy was again imprisoned. He was taken to the Conciergerie, then transferred to the Bastille, where he died.

BIBLIOGRAPHY

I. ORIGINAL WORKS. Palissy's works are *Recepte véritable par laquelle tous les hommes de la France pourront apprendre à multiplier et augmenter leurs trésors* (La Rochelle, 1563); *Architecture et ordonnance de la grotte rustique de Monseigneur le duc de Montmorency* (La Rochelle, 1563; repr. Paris, 1919); and *Discours admirables de la nature des eaux et fontaines* (Paris, 1581), translated by Aurèle La Rocque as *The Admirable Discourses of Bernard Palissy* (Urbana, Ill., 1957).

Collected eds. of Palissy's works include those of B. Faujas de Saint-Fond and N. Gobet (Paris, 1777), which contains incorrectly attributed works and a dedication to Benjamin Franklin; and of Anatole France (Paris, 1880).

II. SECONDARY LITERATURE. See C. L. Brightwell, *Palissy the Potter; or the Huguenot, Artist and Martyr* (New York, 1835); H. Morley, *Palissy the Potter*, 2 vols. (London, 1852); E. Dupuy, *Bernard Palissy, l'homme, l'artiste, le savant, l'écrivain* (Paris, 1894); Désiré Leroux, *La vie de Bernard Palissy* (Paris, 1927); Lynn Thorndike,

A History of Magic and Experimental Science, V (New York, 1941), 441, 465, 596–599; H. R. Thompson, "The Geographical and Geological Observations of Bernard Palissy, the Potter," in *Annals of Science*, **10**, no. 2 (1954), 149–165; and A. K. Biswas, *History of Hydrology* (Amsterdam, 1970), 149–155.

MARGARET R. BISWAS
ASIT K. BISWAS

PALLADIN, VLADIMIR IVANOVICH (*b.* Moscow, Russia, 23 July 1859; *d.* Petrograd [now Leningrad], U.S.S.R., 3 February 1922), *biochemistry, plant physiology.*

Palladin attended the Gymnasium in Moscow and in 1883 graduated from Moscow University, where he remained to prepare for a career in teaching. In 1886 he defended his thesis, "The Meaning of Oxygen for Plants," for the M.A. From 1886 Palladin was an instructor and then a professor of botany at the Institute of Agriculture and Forestry in Novaya Aleksandriya, and from 1889 he was professor of botany at Kharkov University. In 1889 he defended his doctoral dissertation, "The Influence of Oxygen on the Decomposition of Proteins in Plants," at the University of Warsaw, to which he had transferred in 1897. In 1901 Palladin was appointed to the chair of physiology at St. Petersburg University and in the Higher Courses for Women. Here Palladin began his lengthy teaching career; among his students were the physiologists S. P. Kostychev, N. A. Maksimov, and D. A. Sabinin.

Palladin was the author of two well-known textbooks: *Fisiologia rasteny* ("Plant Physiology"), which for more than thirty years was used as the basic text in all Russian higher educational institutions, and *Anatomia rasteny* ("Plant Anatomy"). In 1906 he was elected corresponding member of the Academy of Sciences, and in 1914 academician. He then retired from St. Petersburg University and conducted his scientific work at the academy.

In his two graduate dissertations Palladin showed the existence of a close bond between the two most important biological processes: respiration and protein metabolism. He established that the carbons formed in plants are the products of the incomplete oxidation of proteins, for which the assimilation of oxygen from the air is necessary. Palladin also studied the process of evaporation of water, the content of proteins and mineral substances, the process of respiration in green and etiolated plants, and the conditions under which etiolated plants become green. He then advanced to questions concerning the chemical physiology of plants, first studying the transformation of nitrogenous substances and the energy processes in plants, and then studying the process of plant respiration, to which he devoted the last year of his life.

Three basic stages can be noted in Palladin's research into plant respiration. First, basing his work on the discovery of oxidizing enzymes at the end of the nineteenth century, he concluded that the oxidation-reduction processes, which represent a chain of strictly coordinated enzyme reactions, are the basis of respiration in plants. His monograph "The Respiration of Plants as the Sum of the Enzyme Processes" (1907) attracted much attention from Russian and foreign scientists; it clarified the details of the anaerobic and aerobic phases of respiration from the point of view of the activity of specific enzymes, which transform in succession the intermediate products of respiration. A careful study of the action of the oxidase and peroxidase enzymes showed that their oxidizing energy is limited and cannot have an oxidizing effect on the respiratory substrate: carbohydrates or the products of carbohydrate decomposition. In the second stage of his research into respiration, Palladin sought to discover the intermediaries between oxidases and carbohydrates. They proved to be aromatic compounds of the polyphenol type, which he called respiratory chromogens. Palladin formulated the role of the respiratory chromogens in "The Significance of Respiratory Pigments in the Oxidizing Processes of Plants and Animals" (1912). A new point in this work was the discovery of intermediate agents: carriers of oxygen. But the process of respiration was still understood in accordance with Lavoisier's hypothesis of a process analogous to burning. In the last stage of his research Palladin showed that this hypothesis was false. He stated that respiratory chromogens do not activate the oxygen in the air; instead, they activate the hydrogen in carbohydrates with the aid of the enzyme reductase (dehydrogenase). Respiratory chromogens were thus carriers of hydrogen, not oxygen. He discovered that simultaneously with the decomposition of water, the oxygen of which goes into the oxidation of the respiratory substrate and forms carbonic acid, the hydrogen is temporarily bonded to the respiratory pigment. This work predated that of H. O. Wieland, with whom the phenomenon is usually associated.

This first phase of respiration is the most basic. It occurs under anaerobic conditions and the carbonic acid separated out is formed by the respiratory substrate (carbohydrates), not by atmospheric oxygen. The oxygen in the air takes part only in the second phase of respiration, interacting with hydrogen in the pigments and restoring their activity. Palladin's

theory of respiration brought him an international reputation. His concept of the active role of hydrogen was new, as well as his theory of the active participation of water in the oxidation-reduction process of respiration.

BIBLIOGRAPHY

I. ORIGINAL WORKS. Palladin's major works include "Bedeutung des Sauerstoffes für die Pflanzen," in *Byulletin' Moskovskogo obschestva ispytalelii prirody*, **62**, no. 3 (1882), 44–126; *Vliyanie kisloroda na raspadenie belkovykh veshchestv v rasteniyakh* ("The Influence of Oxygen on the Decomposition of Albuminous Substances in Plants"; Warsaw, 1889), which also appeared in *Bericht der Deutschen botanischen Gesellschaft*, **5** (1887), 326–328, **6** (1888), 205–212, and **7** (1889), 126–130; *Fiziologia rasteny* ("Plant Physiology," Kharkov, 1891; 9th ed., Petrograd, 1922); "Fiziologicheskie issledovania nad etiolirovannymi listyami" ("Physiological Research on Etiolated Leaves"), in *Trudy Obschestva ispytatelei prirody pri Imperatorskom khar'kovskom universite*, **26** (1892), 67–68; this article also appeared in *Bericht der Deutschen botanischen Gesellschaft*, **9** (1891), 194–198, 229–232; "Recherche sur la respiration des feuilles vertes et étiolées," in *Revue générale de botanique*, **5** (1893), 449–473; and *Anatomia rasteny* ("Plant Anatomy," Kharkov, 1895; 7th ed. Petrograd, 1924).

Palladin's subsequent writings include "Dykhanie rasteny kak summa fermentativnykh protsessov" ("Breathing of Plants as the Sum of Enzyme Processes"), in *Zapiski Imperatorskoi akademii nauk. Fiziko–Matematicheskomu*, ser. 8, **20** (1907), no. 5, 5–64; "Die Atmungspigmente der Pflanzen," in *Hoppe–Seyler's Zeitschrift fur physiologische Chemie*, **55** (1908), 207–222; "Znachenie vody v protsesse spirtovogo brozhenia i dykhania" ("The Importance of Water in the Process of Alcohol Fermentation and Breathing"), in F. N. Krasheninnikov, ed., *Sbornik statey; posvyashchenny K. A. Timiryazevy ego uchenikami v oznamenovanie Semidesyatogo dlya ego rozhdenia* ("A collection of articles offered to K. A. Timiryazev by his pupils in honor of his seventieth birthday," Moscow, 1916), pp. 1–34; and *Izbrannye trudy* ("Selected Works"; Moscow, 1960), which gives a bibliography of Palladin's works.

II. SECONDARY LITERATURE. For works on Palladin and his work, see S. Kostychev, "V. I. Palladin. Nekrolog" ("V. I. Palladin, Obituary"), in *Zhurnal Russkago botanicheskogo obshchestva*, **7** (1922), 173–186; C. N., "W. Palladin," in *Biochemische Zeitschrift*, **130** (1922) 321–322; S. D. Lvov, "V. I. Palladin kak osnovopolozhnik sovremennogo uchemia o dykhanii" ("V. I. Palladin as the Founder of the Contemporary Theory of Breathing"), in *Vestnik Leningradskogo gosudarstvennogo universiteta*, nos. 4, 5, 50–71; "Zesedanie i doklady, posvyashchennye pamyati V. I. Palladin" ("Session and Reports Devoted to the Memory of V. I. Palladin"), in *Biokhimiya*, **17**, no. 2 (1952), 246–254; B. A. Rubin, "Idei V. I. Palladina i sovremennoe sostoyanie uchenia o dykhanii rasteny" ("V. I. Palladin's Ideas and the Present State of the Theory of Breathing"), in *Vestnik sel'skokhozyaistvennoi nauki*, no. 9 (1960), 39–49; and E. M. Senchenkova, "Vydayush-chysya russky biokhimik i fiziolog rasteny. K stoletiyu so dyna rozhdenia V. I. Palladin" ("Distinguished Russian Biochemist and Plant Physiologist. For the Hundredth Anniversary of the Birthday of V. I. Palladin"), in *Voprosy istorii estestvoznaniya i tekhniki*, no. 9 (1960), 134–138.

E. M. SENCHENKOVA

PALLAS, PYOTR SIMON (*b*. Berlin, Germany, 3 October 1741; *d*. Berlin, 20 September 1811), *natural science, geography*.

Pallas was the son of a professor at the Berlin Medical-Surgical Academy. He received his early education at home and from 1754 to 1759 studied at the Medical-Surgical Academy and the universities of Halle, Göttingen, and Leiden. In his dissertation for the doctorate in medicine, which he defended at Leiden, Pallas refuted the Linnaean classification of worms. From 1761 to 1766 he studied collections of marine animals in England and Holland. In *Elenchus zoophytorum* (1766) he gave a detailed classification of corals and sponges, which had just been transferred by zoologists from the plant kingdom to the animal. In 1763 Pallas was elected a member of the Royal Society of London and the Academia Caesarea Leopoldina.

In 1767 Pallas was invited to work at the St. Petersburg Academy of Sciences. He was elected ordinary academician and had the rank of acting state councillor. For more than forty years Pallas was associated exclusively with the development of Russian science. During his first years there he studied nature and the peoples of the Russian empire, participating in the "Academic expeditions" of 1768–1774. His research as leader of the first Orenburg detachment of the expeditions covered both European Russia and Asia. Pallas and his companions journeyed from St. Petersburg to Moscow; crossed the Volga at Simbirsk (now Ulyanovsk); and explored the Zhiguli Mountains and the southern Urals, the steppes of western Siberia and the Altay, Lake Baikal, and the mountains of Transbaikalia. The easternmost regions visited were the basins of the Shilka and Argun rivers. On his way back to St. Petersburg, Pallas studied the Caspian depression and the lower reaches of the Volga. His results were published in *Reise durch verschiedenen Provinzen des russischen Reichs* . . . (1771–1776), which later appeared in Russian (1773–1778) and in French, English, and Italian. Pallas' writings and the other materials of the "Academic expeditions" enriched

natural history by providing massive amounts of empirical data which made it possible to generalize on the geographical distribution of plants and animals and to gain knowledge about the orography, climate, population, and economy of varied and little-studied regions of Russia.

In St. Petersburg Pallas published a series of works, including a monograph on rodents (1778) and on the genus *Astragalus* (1780); assembled a collection of botanical, zoological, and mineralogical specimens; and was the Admiralty historiographer and teacher of the future Emperor Alexander I and his brother Constantine. At the Academy of Sciences he proposed bold projects for new expeditions to northern and eastern Siberia. Pallas' discussions of the formation of mountains (1777) and the variability of animals (1780) are of great importance. Pallas offered a paleogeographic interpretation of fossil animal remains found in the frozen strata of Siberia, although he was influenced by ideas that explained these phenomena in terms of the sudden catastrophic incursion of oceanic water from the south. In an illustrated collection, *Flora Rossia*, he described 283 species of ancient trees and began work on the description of the fauna of Russia.

In 1793–1794 Pallas studied the southern provinces of Russia—the steppes near the Caspian Sea, the northern Caucasus, and the Crimea. The natural beauty of the Crimea and its healthy climate made him decide to live there permanently. Catherine II granted him two estates on the shore and a house in Simferpol, as well as a subsidy to establish a school of horticulture and enology. In 1795 Pallas moved to the Crimea, where he studied nature and developed gardens and vineyards in the Sudak and Koz valleys. He published *Fizicheskoe i topograficheskoe opisanie Tavricheskoy gubernii* ("Physical and Topographical Description of Taurida Province"; 1795) and wrote articles on the agricultural technology of the warm areas of the Crimea. His main efforts were devoted to preparing materials of the 1793–1794 trip for publication and to compiling a complete description of the fauna of Russia. In 1799–1801 he published an account of the trip that included an important description of the Crimea.

The writing of a zoological geography of the Russian empire, which was the main goal of Pallas' life, took much work and money; and its preparation for publication went slowly. Because of his declining health, and his wish to hasten the appearance of his work in print, Pallas moved in 1810 to Berlin, where he died a year later. The St. Petersburg Academy of Sciences, without waiting to prepare the drawings for publication, began in 1811 to publish Pallas'

Zoographia Rosso-Asiatica . . ., the last volume of which appeared in 1831.

A versatile scientist, Pallas was in many ways reminiscent of the scientific encyclopedists of antiquity. Among his contemporaries he was a peer of Linnaeus and Buffon; in zoology, he was a predecessor of Cuvier. As a geographer he may be considered a predecessor of Humboldt. Pallas sought to advance from merely describing nature to finding the causal interrelationships and hidden regularities of natural phenomena. Using the comparative method, he laid the bases of a new natural history that excluded the metaphysical approach. Pallas' achievements in zoology and botany were especially important. He was one of the first to use anatomical characteristics in classifying animals. His research in comparative anatomy provided the foundations for animal taxonomy. He described hundreds of species of animals and plants; expressed interesting ideas on their relationships to the environment; and noted the boundaries and areas of their distribution, which led to the development of the science of biogeography.

Pallas' views on the evolution of animals and plants reflected the contradictions in the science of his age and underwent changes during his lifetime. In the 1760's and 1770's he assumed the unity of origin and historical development of the organic world. In 1766 he proposed the first known scheme to express the sequential development of animal organisms in terms of a family tree. Later he spoke as a metaphysician and catastrophist, recognizing the constancy and nonvariability of species. In 1780 Pallas showed that all known species arose at one general time. He denied Buffon's idea that food, climate, and way of life influence the variation of species and Linnaeus' idea that species vary through the process of hybridization.

Pallas' contribution to geology and geography was great. From his descriptions of the natural features of Russia later generations of scientists drew much that was new and useful. He formulated the first general hypothesis of the formation of mountains. In his opinion, granite constituted the skeleton of the earth and its nucleus. Emerging after some time in the form of marine islands, the granite appeared framed with slate, the product of the disintegration of the granite. Limestones containing organic remains and constituting a Secondary formation are even younger. The friable rocks of adjacent foothills were separated out into a Tertiary formation. The raising of the mountains and the receding of the seas occurred, in Pallas' opinion, as a result of volcanic processes. These processes caused the inclined position of layers, especially of the steep position of the most ancient

rocks. Pallas' ideas on the structure and origin of mountains played an important role in the further development of theoretical geology, as Cuvier pointed out.

The progressive significance of Pallas' views consisted in the recognition of a prolonged geological history of the earth and of the important role of both volcanic (inner) and external forces and their mutual influence in the development of the earth. In many ways, however, he shared the opinions of seventeenth- and eighteenth-century diluvialists. His work was influential in the development of evolutionary ideas of nature, as was acknowledged by Charles Darwin in England and K. F. Rulye in Russia.

Pallas left a deep impression in paleogeography, medicine, ethnography, the history of geography, and philology. His impressive capacity for work resulted in 170 published writings, including dozens of major reports on research. He was an active member of many Russian and foreign scientific societies, institutes, and academies. Plants and animals—including the plant genus *Pallasia* (the name given by Linnaeus) and the Crimean pine *Pinus Pallasiana*—were named in honor of Pallas. Stony meteorites are called pallasite; and a volcano (Pallasa) in the Kuril Islands and a reef in New Guinea bear his name.

BIBLIOGRAPHY

I. ORIGINAL WORKS. Pallas' writings include *Reise durch verschiedenen Provinzen des russischen Reichs in den Jahren 1768–1773,* 2 vols. (St. Petersburg, 1771–1776); "Observations sur la formation des montagnes et sur les changements arrivés au globe," in *Acta academiae scientiarum imperialis Petropolitanae,* pt. 1 (1777), 21–64; *Novae species quadrupedum et glirium ordine* (Erlangen, 1778); *Species astragalorum* (Leipzig, 1780); "Mémoire sur la variation des animaux," in *Acta academiae scientiarum imperialis Petropolitanae,* **4,** pt. 2 (1780), 69–102; "O Rossyskikh otkrytiakh na moryakh mezhdu Aziey i Amerikoy" ("On Russian Discoveries in the Seas Between Asia and America"), in *Mesyatseslov istorichesky i geografichesky* (1781), 1–150, also in German (1782) and Danish (1784); *Flora Rossia . . .* (St. Petersburg, 1784–1788), also in Russian (St. Petersburg, 1786); *Bemerkungen auf einer Reise in die südlichen Statthalterschaften des russischen Reichs in den Jahren 1793 und 1794,* 2 vols. (Leipzig, 1799–1801); and *Zoographia Rosso-Asiatica,* 3 vols. (St. Petersburg, 1811–1831).

II. SECONDARY LITERATURE. See V. V. Belousov, "Pallas–puteshestvennik i geolog" ("Pallas—Traveler and Geologist"), in *Priroda* (1941), no. 3, 111–116; G. P. Dementev, "Pyotr Simon Pallas (1741–1811)," in *Lyudi russkoy nauki. Biologia . . .* ("People of Russian Science. Biology . . ."; Moscow, 1963), 34–44, with bibliography;

Y. K. Efremov, "Pyotr Simon Pallas," in N. N. Baransky *et al.*, eds., *Otechestvennye fiziki-geografy i puteshestvenniki* ("Native Physical Geographers and Travelers"; Moscow, 1950), 132–144, with bibliography; V. Marakuev, *Pyotr Simon Pallas, ego zhizn, uchenye trudy i puteshestvia* (". . . His Life, Scientific Works and Travels"; Moscow, 1877); "Peter Simon Pallas (1741–1811)," in *Lomonosov. Schlözer. Pallas. Deutsch-Russische Wissenschaftsbeziehungen im 18. Jahrhundert* (Berlin, 1962), 245–317; and B. E. Raykov, "Russkie biologi-evolyutsionisty do Darvina" ("Russian Evolutionist Biologists Before Darwin"), in *Materialy k istorii evolyutsionnoy idei v Rossii* ("Material for a History of the Idea of Evolution in Russia"), I (Moscow–Leningrad, 1952), 42–105, with bibliography.

VASILIY A. ESAKOV

PALMER, EDWARD (*b.* Hockwold cum Wilton, England, 12 January 1831; *d.* Washington, D.C., 10 April 1911), *natural history*.

Although Palmer had little formal education and was never robust in health, he was a gifted collector and made significant contributions to knowledge, especially from about 1860 to 1880. During this period he worked primarily in the western United States and mostly in areas that were still sparsely or not at all occupied by Europeans. His notes and observations on the manners and customs of the western Indians, and his collections of ancient and modern Indian artifacts, are among the more important sources of information on the ethnology and archaeology of the tribes in question. Throughout his career he collected botanical and zoological specimens, and also those of anthropological interest, but in his later years he increasingly restricted himself to the collection of herbarium specimens. His most-quoted paper is "Food Products of the North American Indians," in *Report of the Commissioner of Agriculture* (1871), and most of his other publications are short papers on the same or similar subjects.

Palmer came to the United States in 1849. He was introduced to natural history and to the practice of medicine by serving as hospital steward on a naval expedition to Paraguay (1853–1855). He attended lectures at the Homeopathic College in Cleveland, Ohio (1856–1857) and, having thus qualified himself, earned much of his living for the next eleven years as a physician and surgeon, while at the same time collecting and distributing biological specimens. He served as a contract surgeon at various army posts in Colorado, Kansas, and Arizona (1862–1867), and as medical officer at an Indian agency in what is now Oklahoma (1868). After this he gave up medicine and devoted himself exclusively to collecting in Mexico and the western United States, with intermittent support from government agencies, including the U.S. Department of Agriculture, the Smithsonian Institution, the Bureau of Ethnology, and the Commission of Fish and Fisheries. Private sponsors included the Peabody Museum of Archaeology and Ethnology, and other biologically oriented museums at Harvard University. In 1878 and thereafter, Palmer helped to finance several of his own trips to Mexico by selling subscriptions to his sets of exsiccatae. Asa Gray and his successors at Harvard supplied determinations for the botanical specimens that Palmer collected and helped with the sale and distribution of his duplicates. In Palmer's later years J. N. Rose of the U.S. National Herbarium performed a similar service for him.

Palmer's zoological collections include representatives of most of the major groups of macroscopic animals, but he seems never to have collected extensively in any group except the insects. His botanical collections, which were widely distributed, included an estimated 100,000 specimens, or about 20,000 different gatherings, of which about 2,000 represented species new to science. Although lacking the unique quality of his early ethnological collections, his botanical specimens were often from areas seldom or never before visited by experienced collectors. They provided a basis for modern taxonomic and phytogeographic studies, especially of northern and western Mexico, and they stimulated further exploration in western North America.

BIBLIOGRAPHY

I. ORIGINAL WORKS. Palmer's own publications comprise 25 papers published in scientific periodicals and government documents. Most of the papers deal with the uses of plants or other articles by the American Indians; all are cited in full in McVaugh's book on Palmer, which is mentioned below.

About 650 of Palmer's letters (1852–1911), and many handwritten documents pertaining to specimens, are extant. The richest sources of these are the governmental archives in Washington, D.C. (especially those of the Smithsonian Institution), and the archives and libraries of Harvard University.

Palmer's personal collection of MSS and correspondence was sold at auction in 1914, and much of it has never been located since that time (McVaugh, *Edward Palmer*, p. 407, item 45 of "References and Sources").

II. SECONDARY LITERATURE. Rogers McVaugh, *Edward Palmer: Plant Explorer of the American West* (Norman,

1956), includes a detailed listing of Palmer's itineraries by date and locality, copies of some early field notes, and a bibliography of all known books and papers written by or about Palmer to 1955.

ROGERS McVAUGH

PAMBOUR, FRANÇOIS MARIE GUYONNEAU DE (*b.* Noyon, France, 1795), *civil engineering.*

Pambour attended the École Polytechnique (1813–1815) and upon being commissioned he entered the artillery; later he transferred to the general staff. His principal contributions were to the theory and practice of steam engines and steam locomotives.

His *Théorie de la machine à vapeur,* which went through several editions and translations, had a fundamental and mathematical approach such as might be expected from an applied physicist rather than a practical engineer. As late as 1876 the work was authoritatively referred to as "the most celebrated treatise of Pambour . . . published in 1844, then far superior to other works and still in many respects one of the best standards on the subject." In his definitive treatise, R. H. Thurston frequently refers to Pambour's work in the highest terms. He points out that much of his original work has been "demonstrated anew by a certain number of modern writers who appear to ignore the works of Pambour." Pambour was certainly not a mere empiricist. His original researches were reported in papers communicated to *Comptes rendus* of the Academy of Sciences. In addition to his treatise on the steam engine, he wrote an equally successful practical work, *Traité théorique et pratique des machines locomotives* (1835).

Despite his productivity, Pambour was never a member of the Academy. A candidate for the Section de Mécanique in 1837, 1840, and 1843, he failed to be elected, quite possibly as a result of scientific differences with Poncelet, probably intensified by a personal clash. There was a polemic between Pambour and Poncelet's protégé, Morin, over the choice of "frictional coefficients" for calculating the work of piston expansion. This quantity relates the volumes occupied by a unit weight of steam in the boiler and in the cylinder. According to the older theory of Poncelet and Morin, the ratio can be determined by a constant coefficient. In the new theory of Pambour, the coefficient is no longer constant, but varies with operating conditions. Pambour's denunciation of Poncelet's earlier work elicited a sharp response. Not only was Pambour rejected by the Academy, but his name does not appear in the *École Polytechnique, Livre du centenaire,* which includes biographical sketches of considerably less distinguished graduates.

Pambour's most important contribution to the theory of the steam engine dealt with the calculation of the work obtained under a given set of operating conditions. An earlier treatment, developed by Poncelet and Morin, calculated the work of expansion by the use of Boyle's law but did not take into account the drop in steam temperature upon expansion. Pambour, on the other hand, assumed that the steam remained saturated throughout the engine; and since the temperature of saturated steam varies with pressure, Boyle's law is quite incapable of representing this situation. Instead, Pambour used an empirical formula that involved two experimentally determined constants. He assumed various pressure situations between the boiler and the cylinder and with his formula calculated the work for these cases. The assumption that steam is saturated during expansion is not used today; the Rankine cycle—where the expansion is from superheated steam into wet steam—has replaced Pambour's scheme. The improvement over the assumption of Boyle's law was tremendous and represented a major advance. Clapeyron used Pambour's formula in his 1851 lectures but recognized the shortcomings inherent in the assumption that the steam was "dry."

BIBLIOGRAPHY

There are forty-four papers by Pambour on the steam engine in *Comptes rendus hebdomadaires des séances de l'Académie des sciences,* **4–21** (1837–1845). His subsequent interest in hydraulic turbines was reflected in seventeen papers in vols. **32–75** (1851–1872). *Théorie de la machine à vapeur* appeared in French (Brussels, 1837; Paris, 1839, 1844; Liège, 1847, 1848), in English (London, 1839; Philadelphia, 1840), and in German, with intro. by A. L. Crelle (Berlin, 1849).

On Pambour's candidature at the Academy, see *Comptes rendus,* **4** (1837), 556; **10** (1840), 504; and **17** (1843), 1310.

On Pambour and his work, see James Renwick, *Treatise on the Steam Engine,* 3rd ed. (New York, 1848), pref.; R. S. McCullock, *Treatise on the Mechanical Theory of Heat and Its Application to the Steam Engine* (New York, 1876), pp. 24, 261–263; R. H. Thurston, *Traité de la machine à vapeur,* I (Paris, 1893), 260; and F. Zernikow, *Die Theorie der Dampfmaschinen* (Brunswick, 1857), 14–23.

MILTON KERKER

PANDER, CHRISTIAN HEINRICH (*b.* Riga, Latvia, Russia, 24 July 1794; *d.* St. Petersburg, Russia, 22 September 1865), *embryology, anatomy, paleontology.*

Pander was the son of a wealthy banker of German descent. After studying in the local schools of Riga, he entered the University of Dorpat in 1812. Dorpat had been refounded in 1798, and its faculty was German trained. Prior to this the Baltic gentry had traditionally sent their sons to German universities. Although his father had wanted him to study medicine, Pander was more interested in natural history, but he attempted to combine the two. At Dorpat he came under the influence of the anatomist Karl Friedrich Burdach, who had also taught Karl Ernst von Baer; Baer later continued Pander's embryologic researches.

In 1814 Pander left Dorpat for Berlin and from there he went on to Göttingen. In March 1816, at a congress of Baltic students resident in Germany, he renewed his acquaintance with Baer, who persuaded him to come to the University of Würzburg and study under Ignaz Döllinger. In his autobiography Baer states that he, Pander, and Döllinger had discussed Döllinger's hope that someone would study anew the development of the chick embryo. Pander took on the task and he received his M.D. at Würzburg in 1817. His dissertation, "Historia metamorphoseos quam ovum incubatum prioribus quinque diebus subit," was amplified and then published in German (1817) with illustrations by the elder E. J. d'Alton.

Pander discovered the trilaminar structure of the chick blastoderm, a term he also coined. He stated that he used the term blastoderm, from the Greek *blastos*, germ, and *derma*, skin, because the embryo chose it as "its seat and its domicile, contributing much to its configuration out of its own substance, therefore in the future we shall call it blastoderm." He described the three layers as the serous or outer, the vascular or middle, and the mucous or inner. In the twelfth hour of embryonic development he reported that the blastoderm consisted of two entirely separate layers: an inner layer, thick and opaque; and an outer layer, thin, smooth, and transparent. Between these two a third layer developed, in which blood vessels formed and from which "events of the greatest importance subsequently occur." When Baer received a copy of Pander's work in 1818 at Königsberg University, where he was serving as prosector to his old Dorpat professor, Burdach, he began his own investigations, which ultimately revolutionized embryology. Baer's first treatise on the subject includes an introduction styled as a personal letter to Pander, explaining his differences with his old friend.

Pander, for reasons that are not entirely clear, never pursued his early research, although he regarded his studies as incomplete and had expressed himself only briefly on the subsequent transformations that took place in the embryo. After receiving his degree, Pander traveled in a leisurely manner through Germany, France, Spain, Holland, and England with d'Alton as a companion, visiting anatomical museums and making various paleontological, geological, and biological observations. In 1821 he began publishing a series of papers on comparative osteology with illustrations by d'Alton. In these osteological studies Pander developed an evolutionary theory of the development of animal forms which had strong Lamarckian overtones. Goethe endorsed his transformist ideas, and Darwin was aware of them through secondary sources.

In 1821 he became a member of the Academy of Sciences in St. Petersburg. He also traveled extensively in Russia at this time and wrote an account of the natural history of Bukhara in central Asia. In 1826 he became a fellow of the Zoological Academy in St. Petersburg, but in 1827 he returned to his estate near Riga, where he remained until 1842. In that year he returned to St. Petersburg as a member of the Mining Institute. He then resumed his travels in Russia, observing geological characteristics and gathering paleontological materials. Although he wrote almost exclusively on geological matters, he began a zoological collection and surveyed geological formations around St. Petersburg. Little of his later work has received the attention paid his earlier studies.

BIBLIOGRAPHY

I. ORIGINAL WORKS. Pander's major works include *Dissertatio inauguralis, sistens historiam metamorphoseos, quam ovum incubatum prioribus quinque diebus subit* (Würzburg, 1817); *Beiträge zur Entwickelungsgeschichte des Hühnchens im Eie* (Würzburg, 1817); *Der vergleichende Osteologie*, 12 vols. (Bonn, 1821–1831), written with E. d'Alton, and divided into individually titled sections *Riesenfaulthier* (1821), *Pachydermata* (1821), *Raubthiere* (1822), *Widerkauer* (1823), *Nagathiere*, 2 vols. (1823–1824), *Vierhänder* (1825), *Zahnlose Thiere* (1826), *Robben und Lamantine* (1826), *Cetaceen* (1827), *Beutelthiere* (1828), and *Chiropteren und Insectivoren* (1831); "Naturgeschichte der Bukharei," in George Meyendorf, *Reise von Orenburg nach Buchara* (Jena, 1826), trans. into French as *Voyage d'Orenbourg à Boukhara* (Paris, 1826); *Beiträge zur Geognosie des russischen Reichs* (St. Petersburg, 1830); *Monographie der Fossilen Fische des silurischen Systems der Russisch–Baltischen Gouvernements* (St. Petersburg, 1856); *Über die Placodermen des devonischen Systems* (St. Petersburg, 1857); *Über die Ctenodipterinen des devonischen Systems* (St. Petersburg, 1858); and *Über die Saurodipterinen, Dendrodonten, Glyptolepiden und Cheirolepiden des devonischen Systems* (St. Petersburg, 1860).

II. SECONDARY LITERATURE. For Pander's contributions to embryology, see Erik Nordenskiöld, *The History of Biology* (New York, 1928), 368–369; Jane M. Oppenheimer,

"The Non-Specificity of the Germ Layers," in her *Essays in the History of Embryology and Biology* (Cambridge, Mass., 1967), 256–294, which is reprinted with additional bibliography from the *Quarterly Review of Biology*, **15** (1940), 1–27; and Alexander Vucinich, *Science in Russian Culture: A History to 1860* (Stanford, 1963), 206, 362.

Personal information about Pander is found in the autobiography of Karl Ernst von Baer, *Nachrichten über Leben und Schriften des Geheimrathes Dr. Karl Ernst von Baer, mitgetheilt von ihm selbst. Veröffentlicht bei Gelegenheit seines fünfzigjährigen Doctor-Jubiläums, am 29. August 1864, von der Ritterschaft Ehstlands* (St. Petersburg, 1866); and in L. Steidt's article in *Allgemeine Deutsche Biographie*, XXV (Leipzig, 1875–1901), 117–119.

VERN L. BULLOUGH

PANETH, FRIEDRICH ADOLF (*b.* Vienna, Austria, 31 August 1887; *d.* Mainz, Germany, 17 September 1958), *radiochemistry, inorganic chemistry.*

Paneth was the second of three sons of Joseph and Sophie Schwab Paneth. His father was a noted physiologist who discovered the histological cells that bear his name. Paneth completed his education at the universities of Munich and Glasgow, and received the Ph.D. from the University of Vienna in 1910. On 6 December 1913 he married Else Hartmann; the couple had two children, Eva and Heinrich Rudolph. From 1912 to 1918 Paneth served as an assistant to Stefan Meyer at the Vienna Institute for Radium Research. In 1913 he spent a short period of time with Soddy at the University of Glasgow and visited Rutherford's laboratory in Manchester. After a brief stay at the Prague Institute of Technology, he spent three years at Hamburg University (1919–1922). He then worked at the University of Berlin, where he remained until 1929. He was invited to give the George Fisher Baker lectures at Cornell University in 1926–1927.

From 1929 to 1933 Paneth was professor and director of the chemistry laboratories at the University of Königsberg. The growth of the Nazi movement, however, was a factor in his decision to leave Königsberg for good and become a guest lecturer at the Imperial College of Science and Technology in London, a position he held for five years. After serving one year as a reader in atomic chemistry at the University of London, he accepted a professorship at the University of Durham, where he remained from 1939 until 1953, when he returned to Germany as director of the Max Planck Institute for Chemistry in Mainz. From 1943 to 1945 he was head of the chemistry division of the Joint British-Canadian Atomic Energy Team in Montreal. He served as president of the Joint Commission on Radioactivity, an organization of the International Council of Scientific Unions, from 1949 to 1955. He received the Lavoisier, Stas, Liebig, and Auer von Welsbach medals from the chemical societies of France, Belgium, Germany, and Austria.

Paneth's intellectual career manifested a progressively broader and deeper range of interests as his professional competence increased. He contributed significantly to the development of radioactive tracer techniques, synthesized and characterized new metal hydrides, and experimentally verified the existence of free radicals in the thermal decomposition of organic compounds. In subsequent research he developed methods for determining the age of rocks and meteorites by measuring the helium content, and he applied exceedingly sensitive methods of helium measurement to determine the composition of the stratosphere as a function of altitude up to 45 miles. In addition to his purely experimental research, Paneth was keenly interested in the philosophical, cosmological, and historical aspects of science. His involvement in radiochemical studies soon led him to an active interest in the history of alchemy, while his experimental work in the quantitative determination of trace amounts of helium led him to a consuming, lifelong interest in the study of meteorites, from a historical as well as a cosmological perspective. After his death a trust fund was established to administer his meteorite collection housed at the Max Planck Institute, to further and encourage research concerned with meteorites, and to augment the collection.

One of Paneth's first papers in chemistry dealt with the acid-catalyzed rearrangement of quinidine and cinchonidine. But his work at the Radium Institute soon involved him in the study of radioactive substances. All of Paneth's future experimental work progressed from this early research. Several unsuccessful efforts to separate radium D and thorium B from lead and its compounds gradually led him to the realization that radium D and thorium B must be "isotopes" of lead. These studies, carried out in collaboration with the Hungarian radiochemist Georg von Hevesy, developed into the exploration of radium D and thorium B as indicators to determine the solubility of the slightly soluble compounds lead sulfide and lead chromate. A similar attempt to separate the radioactive products of thorium led to the preparation and isolation of BiH_3 and the realization that thorium C and radium E were isotopes of bismuth. The yield of bismuth hydride was exceedingly low when produced by the ordinary methods of preparation; it was thus undetected for a long time, and only the use of radioactive isotopes permitted the detection of the minute quantities formed.

While studying the metal hydrides of bismuth, lead, tin, and polonium, Paneth employed the mirror deposition technique to decompose the hydride and concentrate the corresponding metal. Although it seems a short step from a study of the unstable metal hydrides to a study of the metal alkyls, this step took twelve years. During his stay at the University of Berlin, Paneth's classic paper, written with Wilhelm Hofeditz, appeared (1929), announcing the preparation and identification of the free methyl radical from lead tetramethyl.

During the intervening period of time (1917–1929), Paneth worked at developing the sensitive methods for determining trace amounts of helium for which he is justly famous. Using spectroscopic techniques first, and mass spectrometry later, he successfully applied these techniques (1) to the determination of the content of natural gas from various sources, (2) to the quantitative determination of the rate of diffusion through glass, (3) to several unsuccessful efforts to measure helium produced by the attempted transmutation of various lighter elements into helium, and (4) to the quantitative determination of helium in rocks, artificial glasses, and meteorites. From 1929 to the end of his life the study of meteorites increasingly dominated his interests. He refined ever more accurately his techniques for determining the age of rocks by their helium content and the helium : radium ratio. These determinations were further refined when it was discovered that part of the ^{4}He is converted into ^{3}He by cosmic-ray bombardment in space. From these measurements he estimated the ages of iron meteorites to be in the range of 10^8 to 10^9 years and speculated that they were formed within the solar system. Until 1935 Paneth also continued his studies of organic free radicals. (This field was later developed by the physical and organic chemists.) About this same time he succeeded in his efforts to induce artificial transmutation by obtaining measurable amounts of helium from the neutron bombardment of boron.

In 1935 Paneth began to investigate trace components of the stratosphere. In an interesting series of papers he determined the He, O_3, and NO_2 content of the atmosphere and investigated the extent of gravitational separation of the components of the atmosphere. His basic finding was that there is no appreciable gravitational separation below 40 miles, while there appears to be a measurable change in relative concentration above 40 miles. Paneth subsequently returned to the field of free radical chemistry and explored the use of radioactive isotopes for the study of free radicals with the mirror removal technique. His last paper, on meteorites, appeared posthumously in *Geochimica et cosmochimica acta* as an introduction to a series of studies on the Breitscheid meteorite, which fell in Breitscheid, Dillkreis, West Germany, on 11 August 1956.

BIBLIOGRAPHY

I. ORIGINAL WORKS. Paneth's principal works are *Lehrbuch der Radioaktivität* (Leipzig, 1923; 2nd ed., 1931), written with G. von Hevesy, trans. into English, by R. W. Lawson, as *A Manual of Radioactivity* (London, 1926; 2nd ed., 1938), and also into Russian and Hungarian (1924–1925); *Radioelements as Indicators and Other Selected Topics in Inorganic Chemistry* (New York, 1928), the George Fisher Baker lectures; "Über die Darstellung von freiem Methyl," in *Berichte der Deutschen chemischen Gesellschaft*, **62B** (1929), 1335–1347, written with W. Hofeditz; *The Origin of Meteorites* (Oxford, 1940), the Halley lectures, and "Der Meteorit von Breitscheid," in *Geochimica et cosmochimica acta*, **17** (1959), 315–320. *Chemistry and Beyond*, H. Dingle and G. R. Martin, eds. (New York, 1964), is a selection of Paneth's writings, and also contains an extensive bibliography.

II. SECONDARY LITERATURE. See Otto Hahn, "Friedrich A. Paneth," in *Zeitschrift für Electrochemie*, **61** (1957), 1121, written on the occasion of Paneth's seventieth birthday; and K. Peters' bibliographical appendix to one of Paneth's last articles, "Hat Chladni das Pallas-Eisen in Petersburg gesehen," in *Österreichische Chemikerzeitung*, **59** (1958), 289–291.

ERNEST G. SPITTLER, S.J.

PANNEKOEK, ANTONIE (*b.* Vaassen, Netherlands, 2 January 1873; *d.* Wageningen, Netherlands, 28 April 1960), *astronomy*.

Pannekoek was the son of Johannes Pannekoek and Wilhelmina Dorothea Beins. In 1903 he married Johanna Maria Nassau Noordewier, a teacher of Dutch literature. His family belonged to the rural middle class, and through his wife Pannekoek entered literary and musical circles. He was a member of the Royal Netherlands Academy of Sciences and an honorary member of the American Astronomical Society. In addition he received an honorary doctorate from Harvard University and the gold medal of the Royal Astronomical Society.

An amateur astronomer since his youth, Pannekoek studied astronomy at Leiden University. He began his career in 1895 as a geodesist and became observer at the Leiden observatory in 1898, but he grew disenchanted with the old-fashioned meridian work, which he considered of little scientific use. A teacher of Marxist theory at the Socialist party school in

Berlin from 1905, and later in Bremen, he came to oppose the increasing opportunism in the German Socialist party.

At the outbreak of World War I, Pannekoek returned to the Netherlands, where he became a high-school teacher. Since leaving the observatory he had followed the progress of astronomy and had written several scientific papers. He now finished his book *De wonderbouw der wereld* (1920), an excellent and original historical introduction to astronomy. Long interested in Babylonian astronomy, he published several papers on this subject, while continuing his lectures on Marxism at Leiden. His nomination as a vice-director of the Leiden observatory was rejected by the minister of education; but the city of Amsterdam, not dependent on the state, appointed him lecturer in mathematics and astronomy at its municipal university, where he founded a modest but very active astronomical institute. Named professor in 1925, he was dismissed by the German occupation government in 1941.

A chance readings of Saha's paper on ionization in stellar atmospheres prompted Pannekoek to begin work in astrophysics, and he became the founder of modern astrophysics in the Netherlands. His investigations of the structure of the galaxy that includes our solar system extended over sixty years. He made careful and detailed drawings, with isophotes, of the northern and southern Milky Way, and later repeated this work on extrafocal photographs. Improving on the work of Kapteyn, he studied our galaxy as a function of galactic longitude as well as latitude. Dissatisfied by smoothed mean values, he gave full attention to star clouds and dark nebulae. He discovered the typical groups of early stars that were later called associations.

In the area of ionization theory and the composition of stellar atmospheres, Pannekoek was the first to modify Henry Norris Russell's work and to assume a huge preponderance of hydrogen, a view subsequently confirmed. He was also the first to apply "detailed analysis" to stellar atmospheres, taking into account the change in physical properties of the successive layers. With M. Minnaert he published the first quantitative analysis of the flash spectrum during a solar eclipse. Calling attention to the surprisingly low value of gravitation that may be deduced from the spectra of giant stars, he interpreted the brightness maxima of Cepheids as the ejection of gaseous shells.

Pannekoek's work on the history of astronomy, culminating in his *History of Astronomy*, emphasized the broad lines of the evolution of the disciplines and the relation between astronomy and society. Of still wider scope is his *Anthropogenesis*, in which he traced the origin of man and the development into *Homo sapiens*.

BIBLIOGRAPHY

I. ORIGINAL WORKS. Among Pannekoek's earlier writings are *Untersuchungen über den Lichtwechsel Algols* (Leiden, 1902), his diss.; *De astrologie en hare betekenis voor de ontwikkeling der sterrekunde* (Leiden, 1916), his inaugural lecture; "Die nördliche Milchstrasse," in *Annalen van de Sterrewacht te Leiden*, **11**, no. 3 (1920); *De wonderbouw der wereld* (Amsterdam, 1920); *Researches on the Structure of the Universe*, Publications of the Astronomical Institute of the University of Amsterdam, nos. 1–2 (1924–1929); "The Ionization Formula for Atmospheres Not in Thermodynamic Equilibrium," in *Bulletin of the Astronomical Institutes of the Netherlands*, **3** (1926), 207–209; *Results of Observations of the Solar Eclipse of June 29, 1927. Photometry of the Flash Spectrum* (Amsterdam, 1928), written with M. Minnaert; "Die südliche Milchstrasse," in *Annalen van der Bosscha-Sterrewacht* (Lembang), **2**, no. 1 (1929), 1–73; "Die Ionisation in den Atmosphären der Himmelskörper," in *Handbuch der Astrophysik*, III, pt. 1 (Berlin, 1930), 256–350; "The Theoretical Contours of Absorption Lines," in *Monthly Notices of the Royal Astronomical Society*, **91** (1930), 139–169, 519–531; *Photographische Photometrie der nördlichen Milchstrasse*, Publications of the Astronomical Institute of the University of Amsterdam, no. 3 (1933); "Theoretical Colour Temperatures," in *Monthly Notices of the Royal Astronomical Society*, **95** (1935), 529–535; *The Theoretical Intensities of Absorption Lines in Stellar Spectra*, Publications of the Astronomical Institute of the University of Amsterdam, no. 4 (1935); and "Ionization and Excitation in the Upper Layers of an Atmosphere," in *Monthly Notices of the Royal Astromical Society*, **96** (1936), 785–793.

Later works include "The Hydrogen Lines Near the Balmer Limit," *ibid.*, **98** (1938), 694–709; *A Photometric Study of Some Stellar Spectra*, Publications of the Astronomical Institute of the University of Amsterdam, no. 6, 2 pts. (1939–1946), written with G. B. van Albada; *Investigations on Dark Nebulae, ibid.*, no. 7 (1942); "Anthropogenese, een studie over het ontstaan van den mens," in *Verhandelingen der K. akademie van wetenschappen*, **42**, no. 1 (1945), translated as *Anthropogenesis, a Study of the Origin of Man* (Amsterdam, 1953); "The Line Spectra of Delta Cephei," in *Physica*, **12** (1946), 761–767; "Planetary Theories," in *Popular Astronomy*, **55** (1947), 422–438, and **56** (1948), 2–13 (Copernicus), 63–75 (Kepler), 177–192 (Newton), 300–312 (Laplace); *Photographic Photometry of the Southern Milky Way*, Publications of the Astronomical Institute of the University of Amsterdam, no. 9 (1949), written with D. Koelbloed; "Line Intensities in Spectra of Advanced Types," in *Publications of the Dominion Astrophysical Observatory*,

Victoria, B.C., **8** (1950), 141–223; *De groei van ons wereld-beeld* (Amsterdam–Antwerp, 1951), translated as *A History of Astronomy* (London, 1961); and "The Origin of Astronomy," in *Monthly Notices of the Royal Astronomical Society*, **111** (1951), 347–356.

II. SECONDARY LITERATURE. Two short biographies are G. B. van Albada, "Ter nagedachtenis van Prof. Panne-koek," in *Hemel en dampkring*, **58** (1960), 105; and B. J. Bok, "Two Famous Dutch Astronomers," in *Sky and Telescope*, **20** (1960), 74–76.

M. MINNAERT

PAPANICOLAOU, GEORGE NICHOLAS (*b.* Kími, Greece, 13 May 1883; *d.* Miami, Florida, 19 February 1962), *anatomy*.

The son of a physician, George Nicholas undertook the study of medicine and received the M.D. from the University of Athens in 1904. After postgraduate work in biology at the universities of Jena, Freiburg, and Munich, from which he received his doctorate in 1910, he returned to Greece and married Mary Mavroyeni, the daughter of a high-ranking military officer.

Papanicolaou decided to forgo the practice of medicine in favor of an academic career, in which his wife served as his lifelong associate. En route to Paris, Papanicolaou stopped for a visit at the Oceanographic Institute of Monaco and accepted an unexpected offer to join its staff. He worked for one year as a physiologist and then returned to Greece upon the death of his mother. After serving for two years as second lieutenant in the medical corps of the Greek army during the Balkan War, he immigrated to the United States.

In 1913 Papanicolaou was appointed assistant in the pathology department of New York Hospital, and in 1914 he became assistant in anatomy at Cornell Medical College. Until 1961 he conducted all of his scientific research, devoted almost exclusively to the physiology of reproduction and exfoliative cytology, at these two affiliated institutions, each of which named a laboratory in his honor. He was designated professor emeritus of clinical anatomy at Cornell in 1951. In November 1961 Papanicolaou moved to Florida and became director of the Miami Cancer Institute, but died three months later of acute myocardial infarction. The institute was renamed the Papanicolaou Cancer Research Institute in November 1962. An indefatigable worker, Papanicolaou is said never to have taken a vacation.

Papanicolaou is best known for his development of the technique, eponymically termed the Papanicolaou smear, or "Pap test," for the cytologic diagnosis of cancer, especially cancer of the uterus—second only to the breast as the site of origin of fatal cancers in American women.

The history of cancer cytology dates from 1867, when Beale observed tumor cells in the smears of sputum from a patient with carcinoma of the pharynx. He suggested the microscopic examination of desquamated cells for the detection of cancer of other organs, including the uterus and urinary tract.[1] Friedlaender noted, in his subsequent microscopic examination of fluid exuding from ulcerating cancers of the uterus, distinctive cellular elements that helped establish the diagnosis.[2] In 1908 Königer called attention to the striking differences in the size and shape of cancer cells obtained from serous cavities, the abundance of vacuoles and fatty droplets in the cytoplasm, the enlargement of the nucleus, and the presence of multiple nucleoli within it.[3]

Papanicolaou was invited by Charles R. Stockard, chairman of the Cornell Medical School department of anatomy, to join him in his work in experimental genetics. In 1917 he began a study of the vaginal discharge of the guinea pig, with the hope of finding an indicator of the time of ovulation; he would thus be able to obtain ova at specific stages of development. He sought traces of blood, as seen during estrus in certain other species, such as the cow and bitch, and in the menstrual discharge of primates and women. In the course of his daily examination of the guinea pig vaginal fluid, obtained through a small nasal speculum, Papanicolaou saw no blood. He noted instead a diversity in the forms of the epithelial cells in a sequence of cytologic patterns recurring in a fifteen- to sixteen-day cycle, which he was able to correlate with the cyclic morphologic changes in the uterus and ovary. Papanicolaou thus established the technique that became the standard for studying the sexual (estrous) cycle in other laboratory animals, especially the mouse and rat, and for measuring the effect of the sex hormones.

In 1923 Papanicolaou extended his studies to human beings in an effort to learn whether comparable vaginal changes occur in woman in association with the menstrual cycle. His first observation of distinctive cells in the vaginal fluid of a woman with cervical cancer gave Papanicolaou what he later described as "one of the most thrilling experiences of my scientific career" and soon led to a redirection of his work.

His early reports on cancer detection, however, which appeared from 1928, failed to arouse the interest of clinicians. Cytologic examination of the vaginal fluid seemed an unnecessary addition to the proven procedures for uterine cancer diagnosis—cervical biopsy and endometrial curettage. In 1939, while collaborating with the gynecologist Herbert Traut, Papanicolaou began to concentrate his studies on human beings. Their research culminated in the publication of *Diagnosis of Uterine Cancer by the Vaginal Smear.* This monograph encompassed a variety of physiologic and pathologic states, including the menstrual cycle, puerperium, abortion, ectopic pregnancy, prepuberty, menopause, amenorrhea, endometrial hyperplasia, vaginal and cervical infections, and 179 cases of uterine cancer (127 cervical and 52 corporeal). The work was instrumental in gaining clinical acceptance of the smear as a means of cancer diagnosis, for superficial lesions could thus be detected in their incipient, preinvasive phase, before the appearance of any symptoms.

The Papanicolaou smear soon achieved wide application as a routine screening technique. The death rate from cancer of the uterus among women aged thirty-five to forty-four who were insured under industrial policies by the Metropolitan Life Insurance Company was almost halved in the decade from 1951 to 1961, decreasing from 16.0 to 8.2 per 100,000; while the corresponding reduction in the death rate from cancer of all sites was from 74.0 to 66.0.

Although the *Atlas of Exfoliative Cytology* lists the criteria for malignancy in the shed cells, Papanicolaou used to state that he could not explain how he recognized a smear as positive for malignancy any more than he could explain how to recognize an acquaintance by describing his facial expression. Yet he taught thousands of students how to detect cancer cells under the microscope, and they carried his teachings to all parts of the world. Papanicolaou's technique was rapidly extended to the diagnosis of cancer of other organs from which scrapings, washings, or exudates could be obtained. The principal value of the Papanicolaou smear lies in cancer screening, but it is also applied to the prediction of cancer radiosensitivity, the evaluation of the effectiveness of radiotherapy, and the detection of recurrence after treatment.

It has been suggested that Papanicolaou's work ranks with the discoveries of Roentgen and Marie Curie in reducing the burden of cancer. Cancer of the uterine cervix is nearly 100 percent curable when recognized in its incipiency.

NOTES

1. Beale, L. S., *The Microscope in Its Application to Practical Medicine*, 3rd ed. (Philadelphia, 1867), p. 197.
2. Friedlaender, C., *The Use of the Microscope in Clinical and Pathological Examinations*, 2nd ed., trans. by H. C. Coe (New York, 1885), pp. 168–169.
3. Königer, H., *Die Zytologische Untersuchungsmethode, ihre Entwicklung und ihre Klinische Verwerthung an den Ergüssen Seröser Höhlen* (Jena, 1908), pp. 99–100.

BIBLIOGRAPHY

I. ORIGINAL WORKS. Papanicolaou's works include "The Existence of a Typical Oestrous Cycle in the Guinea Pig—With a Study of its Histological and Physiological Changes," in *American Journal of Anatomy*, **22** (1917), 225–283, written with C. Stockard; "New Cancer Diagnosis," in *Proceedings. Third Race Betterment Conference, January 2–6, 1928* (1928), 528–534; *Diagnosis of Uterine Cancer by the Vaginal Smear* (New York, 1943), written with H. Traut; and *Atlas of Exfoliative Cytology* (Cambridge, Mass., 1954).

II. SECONDARY LITERATURE. On Papanicolaou and his work, see "Dedication of the Papanicolaou Cancer Research Institute," in *Journal of the American Medical Association*, **182** (1962), 556–559; H. Speert, *Obstetric and Gynecologic Milestones* (New York, 1958), 286; and D. E. Carmichael, *The Pap Smear: Life of George N. Papanicolaou* (Springfield, Ill., 1973).

HAROLD SPEERT

PAPIN, DENIS (*b.* Blois, France, 22 August 1647; *d.* London [?], England, *ca.* 1712), *technology.*

Papin was the son of Denys Papin and Magdaleine Pineau. He studied medicine at the University of Angers, from which he received the M.D. in 1669. He was apparently early intent upon a scientific career, since shortly after graduation he went to Paris, where he began working as an assistant to Christiaan Huygens. Papin was a skillful mechanic; he constructed an air pump, with which he performed a number of experiments under Huygens' direction. These were eventually published (1674), and included some attempts at preserving food in a vacuum that testify to Papin's utilitarian bent of mind.

In 1675 Papin went to London. He took with him letters of introduction to Henry Oldenburg, but it was with Robert Boyle that he soon established himself. In *A Continuation of New Experiments*, published by Boyle in 1680, Papin described both the investigations that he had made with Boyle (chiefly on the air pump) and those that he had conducted himself. In Boyle's scientific household Papin also invented his "steam digester," a pressure cooker for which he invented a safety valve that was to be technologically important in the development of steam power. He demonstrated the digester to the Royal Society, under the auspices of Robert Hooke, in May 1679. In the latter part of the same year, he was employed by Hooke to write letters for the society, at two shillings each. He was not elected a fellow until late in 1680.

Papin was again in Paris with Huygens at some time in 1680; in 1681 he went to Venice, where he was director of experiments at Ambrose Sarotti's academy.

He remained there for three years; among his duties was the performance of diverse experiments for the entertainment of the members, who periodically gathered in Sarotti's library. Papin returned to London in 1684 to serve as temporary curator of experiments to the Royal Society, at a salary of £30 a year. He sought the more lucrative post of secretary, but Halley was elected in his stead. His own work at this time consisted primarily of experiments in hydraulics and pneumatics, a number of which were published in the Royal Society's *Philosophical Transactions*.

In 1687 Papin went to Germany and joined a number of his fellow Huguenots at the University of Marburg, where he had been appointed professor of mathematics. He married and acquired a large family, which further strained his always inadequate finances. At this time Papin's interests in air pumps and steam pressure merged to provide an innovative solution to the widespread need for raising water. He considered first a piston ballistic pump using gunpowder, the idea for which he had earlier discussed with Huygens but claimed as his own (in a letter of 6 March 1704 to Leibniz). Papin met the problem of a 20 percent residue of elastic air remaining in the chamber after combustion by substituting steam for the gunpowder. In 1690 he published an account of a single cylinder engine in which water was both boiled and condensed in a tube beneath a piston. Atmospheric pressure forced the piston down again. While not immediately practical in actual operation, the piston arrangement had the advantage, Papin noted, of requiring steam at pressure low enough to be accommodated by vessels artisans of the time could make. Thomas Newcomen independently achieved great success following this line.

Papin remained in correspondence with Huygens during these years, and at one point, having tired of his heavy teaching load and low salary, appealed to him for help in finding a new position. Huygens could offer him nothing in The Hague, however, and Papin in 1695 was given a place in the court of the landgrave of Hesse, in Kassel. Here he devised a number of pumps and other practical inventions that intermittently interested his patron. He was made counsellor to the landgrave, and received recognition for his work in raising water from the Fulde. In 1705 Leibniz sent him a diagram of T. Savery's high-pressure steam pump. Papin designed a modification to this engine, published in *Ars nova ad aquam ignis adminiculo efficacissime elevandam* (1707), which though workable was not to prove as fruitful as the original piston model.

In 1707 Papin returned to England, but his old friends were gone, and he received no permanent appointment from the Royal Society. He drifted into obscurity and died, probably about 1712, but certainly at some date before 1714.

BIBLIOGRAPHY

Papin's more important writings include: *Nouvelles expériences du vuide* (Paris, 1674), repr. in Huygens, *Oeuvres complètes*, XIX (The Hague, 1937), 231; *A New Digester or Engine for Softening Bones . . .* (London, 1681;) *A Continuation of the New Digester of Bones, Together With Some Improvements and New Uses of the Air Pump* (London, 1687); "Nova methodus ad vires motrices validissimas levi pretio comparandas," in *Acta Eruditorum* (1690), and *Ars nova ad aquam ignis adminiculo efficacissime elevandam* (Kassel, 1707). A complete bibliography of Papin's writings, together with a biography, was published by Ernst Gerland, *Leibnizens und Huygens' Briefwechsel mit Papin, nebst der Biographie Papins* (Berlin, 1881), which contains the letter from Papin to Leibniz of 6 March 1704. See also Bannister, *Denis Papin, sa vie et ses écrits* (Blois, 1847); and Louis de Saussaye, *La vie et les ouvrages de Denis Papin* (Lyons, 1869).

For evaluation of Papin's place in the development of steam power see R. Thurston, *A History of the Growth of the Steam Engine* (New York, 1878); R. L. Galloway, *The Steam Engine and Its Inventors* (London, 1881); and H. W. Dickenson, *A Short History of Steam Power* (Cambridge, 1938).

PATRICIA P. MacLACHLAN

PAPPUS OF ALEXANDRIA (*b.* Alexandria, *fl.* A.D. 300–350), *mathematics, astronomy, geography.*

In the silver age of Greek mathematics Pappus stands out as an accomplished and versatile geometer. His treatise known as the *Synagoge* or *Collection* is a chief, and sometimes the only, source for our knowledge of his predecessors' achievements.

The *Collection* is in eight books, perhaps originally in twelve, of which the first and part of the second are missing. That Pappus was an Alexandrian is affirmed by the titles of his surviving books and also by an entry in the *Suda Lexicon*.[1] The dedication of the seventh and eighth books to his son Hermodorus[2] provides the sole detail known of his family life. Only one of Pappus' other works has survived in Greek, and that in fragmentary form—his commentary on Ptolemy's *Syntaxis* (the *Almagest*). A commentary on book X of Euclid's *Elements*, which exists in Arabic, is generally thought to be a translation of the commentary that Pappus is known to have written, but some doubts may be allowed. A geographical work, *Description of the World*, has survived in an early Armenian translation.

The dates of Pappus are approximately fixed by his

reference in the commentary on Ptolemy to an eclipse of the sun that took place on the seventeenth day of the Egyptian month Tybi in the year 1068 of the era of Nabonasar. This is 18 October 320 in the Christian era, and Pappus writes as though it were an eclipse that he had recently seen.[3] The *Suda Lexicon*, which is followed by Eudocia, would make Pappus a contemporary of Theon of Alexandria and place both in the reign of Theodosius I (A.D. 379–395), but the compiler was clearly not well informed. The entry runs: "Pappus, of Alexandria, philosopher, lived about the time of the Emperor Theodosius the Elder, when Theon the Philosopher, who wrote on the *Canon* of Ptolemy, also flourished. His books are: *Description of the World, Commentary on the Four Books of Ptolemy's Great Syntaxis, Rivers of Libya, Interpretation of Dreams.*" The omission of Pappus' chief work and the apparent confusion of the *Syntaxis* with the *Tetrabiblos* of Ptolemy[4] does not inspire confidence. The argument that two scholars could not have written in the same city, on the same subject, at the same time, without referring to each other may not be convincing, for that is precisely what scholars are liable, deliberately or inadvertently, to do. But detailed examination shows that when Theon wrote his commentary on the *Syntaxis* he must have had Pappus' commentary before him.[5] A scholium to a Leiden manuscript of chronological tables, written by Theon, would place Pappus at the turn of the third century, for opposite the name Diocletian (A.D. 284–305) it notes: "In his time Pappus wrote."[6] This statement cannot be reconciled with the eclipse of A.D. 320, but it is more than likely that Pappus' early life was spent under Diocletian, for he would certainly have been older than fifteen when he wrote his commentary on the *Syntaxis*.

The several books of the *Collection* may well have been written as separate treatises at different dates and later brought together, as the name suggests. It is certain that the *Collection*, as it has come down to us, is posterior to the *Commentary on the Syntaxis*, for in book VIII Pappus notes that the rectangle contained by the perimeter of a circle and its radius is double the area of the circle, "as Archimedes showed, and as is proved by us in the commentary on the first book of the *Mathematics* [*sc.*, the *Syntaxis mathematica* of Ptolemy] by a theorem of our own."[7] A. Rome concludes that the *Collection* was put together about A.D. 340, but K. Ziegler states that a long interval is not necessary, and that the *Collection* may have been compiled soon after A.D. 320.[8] It has come down to us from a single twelfth-century manuscript, Codex Vaticanus Graecus 218, from which all the other manuscripts are derived.[9]

T. L. Heath judiciously observes that the *Collection*, while covering practically the whole field of Greek geometry, is a handbook rather than an encyclopedia; and that it was intended to be read with the original works, where extant, rather than take their place. But where the history of a particular topic is given, Pappus reproduces the various solutions, probably because of the difficulty of studying them in many different sources. Even when a text is readily available, he often gives alternative proofs and makes improvements or extensions.[10] The portion of book II that survives, beginning with proposition 14, expounds Apollonius' system of large numbers expressed as powers of 10,000. It is probable that book I was also arithmetical.

Book III is in four parts. The first part deals with the problem of finding two mean proportionals between two given straight lines, the second develops the theory of means, the third sets out some "paradoxes" of an otherwise unknown Erycinus, and the fourth treats of the inscription of the five regular solids in a sphere, but in a manner quite different from that of Euclid in his *Elements*, XIII.13–17.

Book IV is in five sections. The first section is a series of unrelated propositions, of which the opening one is a generalization of Pythagoras' theorem even wider than that found in Euclid VI.31. In the triangle

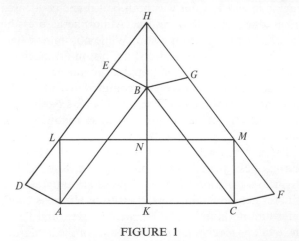

FIGURE 1

ABC let any parallelograms *ABED, BCFG* be drawn on *AB, AC* and let *DE, FG* meet in *H*. Join *HB* and produce it to meet *AC* in *K*. The sum of the parallelograms *ABED, BCFG* can then be shown to be equal to the parallelogram contained by *AC, HB* in an angle equal to the sum of the angles *BAC, DHB*. (It is, in fact, equal to the sum of *ALNK, CMNK*; that is, to the figure *ALMC*, which is easily shown to be a parallelogram having the angle *LAC* equal to the sum of the angles *BAC, DHB*.)

The second section deals with circles inscribed in the figure known as the ἄρβηλος or "shoemaker's knife." It is formed when the diameter *AC* of a semi-

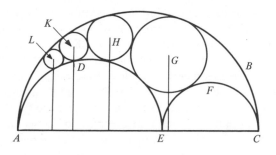

FIGURE 2

circle *ABC* is divided in any way at *E* and semicircles *ADE*, *EFC* are erected. The space between these two semicircles and the semicircle *ABC* is the ἄρβηλος. In a series of elegant theorems Pappus shows that if a circle with center *G* is drawn so as to touch all three semicircles, and then a circle with center *H* to touch this circle and the semicircles *ABC*, *ADE*, and so on *ad infinitum*, then the perpendicular from *G* to *AC* is equal to the diameter of the circle with center *G*, the perpendicular from *H* to *AC* is double the diameter of the circle with center *H*, the perpendicular from *K* to *AC* is triple the diameter of the circle with center *K*, and so on indefinitely. Pappus records this as "an ancient proposition" and proceeds to give variants. This section covers as particular cases propositions in the *Book of Lemmas* that Arabian tradition attributes to Archimedes.

In the third section Pappus turns to the squaring of the circle. He professes to give the solutions of Archimedes (by means of a spiral) and of Nicomedes (by means of the conchoid), and the solution by means of the quadratrix, but his proof is different from that of Archimedes. To the traditional method of generating the quadratrix (see the articles on Dinostratus and Hippias of Elis), Pappus adds two further methods "by means of surface loci," that is, curves drawn on surfaces. As a digression he examines the properties of a spiral described on a sphere.

The fourth section is devoted to another famous problem in Greek mathematics, the trisection of an angle. Pappus' first solution is by means of a νεῦσις or verging—the construction of a line that has to pass through a certain point—which involves the use of a hyperbola. He next proceeds to solve the problem directly, by means of a hyperbola, in two ways; on one occasion he uses the diameter-and-ordinate property (as in Apollonius), and on another he uses the focus-directrix property. This property is proved in book VII. Pappus then reproduces the solutions by means of the quadratrix and the spiral of Archimedes; he also gives the solution of a νεῦσις, which he believes

Archimedes to have unnecessarily assumed in *On Spirals*, proposition 8.

In the preface to book V, which deals with isoperimetry, Pappus praises the sagacity of bees who make the cells of the honeycomb hexagonal because of all the figures which can be fitted together the hexagon contains the greatest area. The literary quality of this preface has been warmly praised. Within the limits of his subject, Pappus looks back to the great Attic writers from a world in which Greek had degenerated into Hellenistic. In the first part of the book Pappus appears to be reproducing Zenodorus fairly closely; in the second part he compares the volumes of solids that have equal surfaces. He gives an account of thirteen semiregular solids, discovered and discussed by Archimedes (but not in any surviving works of that mathematician) that are contained by polygons all equilateral and equiangular but not all similar. He then shows, following Zenodorus, that the sphere is greater in volume than any of the regular solids that have surfaces equal to that of the sphere. He also proves, independently, that, of the regular solids with equal surfaces, that solid is greater which has the more faces.

Book VI is astronomical and deals with the books in the so-called *Little Astronomy*—the smaller treatises regarded as an introduction to Ptolemy's *Syntaxis*. In magistral manner he reviews the works of Theodosius, Autolycus, Aristarchus, and Euclid, and he corrects common misrepresentations. In the section on Euclid's *Optics*, Pappus examines the apparent form of a circle when seen from a point outside the plane in which it lies.

Book VII is the most fascinating in the whole *Collection*, not merely by its intrinsic interest and by what it preserves of earlier writers, but by its influence on modern mathematics. It gives an account of the following books in the so-called *Treasury of Analysis* (those marked by an asterisk are lost works): Euclid's *Data* and *Porisms*,* Apollonius' *Cutting Off of a Ratio*, *Cutting Off of an Area*,* *Determinate Section*,* *Tangencies*,* *Inclinations*,* *Plane Loci*,* and *Conics*. In his account of Apollonius' *Conics*, Pappus makes a reference to the "locus with respect to three or four lines" (a conic section); this statement is quoted in the article on Euclid (IV, 427 *ad fin.*). He also adds a remarkable comment of his own. If, he says, there are more than four straight lines given in position, and from a point straight lines are drawn to meet them at given angles, the point will lie on a curve that cannot yet be identified. If there are five lines, and the parallelepiped formed by the product of three of the lines drawn from the point at fixed angles bears a constant ratio to the parallelepiped formed by the product of the other two lines drawn from the point and a given length, the point will be on a certain curve given in position. If there are six lines, and the solid figure contained by three of the lines bears a constant ratio to the solid figure formed by the other three, then the point will again lie on a curve given in position. If there are more than six lines it is not possible to conceive of solids formed by the product of more than three lines, but Pappus surmounts the difficulty by means of compounded ratios. If from any point straight lines are drawn so as to meet at a given angle any number of straight lines given in position, and the ratio of one of those lines to another is compounded with the ratio of a third to a fourth, and so on (or the ratio of the last to a given length if the number of lines is odd) and the compounded ratio is a constant, then the locus of the point will be one of the higher curves. Pappus had, of course, no symbolism at his disposition, nor did he even use a figure, but his meaning can be made clearer by saying that if $p_1, p_2, \ldots, p_n$ are the lengths of the lines drawn at fixed angles to the lines given in position, and if (a having a given length and k being a constant)

$$\frac{p_1}{p_2} \cdot \frac{p_3}{p_4} \ldots \frac{p_{n-1}}{p_n} = k \text{ when } n \text{ is even, or}$$

$$\frac{p_1}{p_2} \cdot \frac{p_3}{p_4} \ldots \frac{p_n}{a} = k \text{ when } n \text{ is odd,}$$

then the locus of the point is a certain curve.

In 1631 Jacob Golius drew the attention of Descartes to this passage in Pappus, and in 1637 "Pappus' problem," as Descartes called it, formed a major part of his *Géométrie*.[11] Descartes begins his work by showing how the problems of conceiving the product of more than three straight lines as geometrical entities, which so troubled Pappus, can be avoided by the use of his new algebraic symbols. He shows how the locus with respect to three or four lines may be represented as an equation of degree not higher than the second, that is, a conic section which may degenerate into a circle or straight line. Where there are five, six, seven, or eight lines, the required points lie on the next highest curve of degree after the conic sections, that is, a cubic; if there are nine, ten, eleven, or twelve lines on a curve, one degree still higher, that is, a quartic, and so on to infinity. Pappus' problem thus inspired the new method of analytical geometry that has proved such a powerful tool in subsequent centuries. (See the article on Descartes, IV, 57.)

In his *Principia* (1687) Newton also found inspiration in Pappus; he proved in a purely geometrical manner that the locus with respect to four lines is a conic section, which may degenerate into a circle. It is impossible to avoid seeing in Newton's conclusion to lemma XIX, cor. ii, a criticism of Descartes: "Atque ita Problematis veterum de quatuor lineis ab *Euclide* incaepti et ab *Apollonio* continuati non calculus, sed compositio Geometrica, qualem Veteres quaerebant, in hoc Corollario exhibetur."[12] But in this instance it was Descartes, and not Newton, who had the forward vision. Pappus observes that the study of these curves had not attracted men comparable to the geometers of previous ages. But there were still great discoveries to be made, and in order that he might not appear to have left the subject untouched, Pappus would himself make a contribution. It turns out to be nothing less than an anticipation of what is commonly called "Guldin's theorem."[13] Only the enunciations, however, were given, which state

Figures generated by complete revolutions of a plane figure about an axis are in a ratio compounded (*a*) of the ratio [of the areas] of the figures, and (*b*) of the ratio of the straight lines similarly drawn to [*sc.* drawn to meet at the same angles] the axes of rotation from the respective centers of gravity. Figures generated by incomplete revolutions are in a ratio compounded (*a*) of the ratio [of the areas] of the figures and (*b*) of the ratio of the arcs described by the respective centers of gravity; it is clear that the ratio of the arcs is itself compounded (1) of the ratio of the straight lines similarly drawn [from the respective centers of gravity to the axis of rotation] and (2) of the ratio of the angles contained about the axes of rotation by the extremities of these straight lines.

Pappus concludes this section by noting that these propositions, which are virtually one, cover many theorems of all kinds about curves, surfaces, and solids, "in particular, those proved in the twelfth book of these elements." This implies that the *Collection* originally ran to at least twelve books.

Pappus proceeds to give a series of lemmas to each of the books he has described, except Euclid's *Data*, presumably with a view to helping students to understand them. (He was half a millennium from Apollonius and elucidation was probably necessary.) It is mainly from these lemmas that we can form any knowledge of the contents of the missing works, and they have enabled mathematicians to attempt reconstructions of Euclid's *Porisms* and Apollonius' *Cutting Off of an Area, Plane Loci, Determinate Section, Tangencies,* and *Inclinations*. It is from Pappus' lemmas that we can form some idea of the eighth book of Apollonius' *Conics*.

The lemmas to the *Cutting Off of a Ratio* and the *Cutting Off of an Area* are elementary, but those to the *Determinate Section* show that this work amounted to a theory of involution. The most interesting lemmas concern the values of the ratio $AP \cdot PD : BP \cdot PC$, where (A, D), (B, C) are point-pairs on a straight line and P is another point on the straight line. Pappus investigates the "singular and least" values of the ratio and shows what it is for three different positions of P.

The lemmas to the *Inclinations* do not call for comment. The lemmas to the second book of the *Tangencies* are all concerned with the problem of drawing a circle so as to touch three given circles, a problem that Viète and Newton did not consider it beneath their dignity to solve.[14] The most interesting of Pappus' lemmas states: Given a circle and three points in a straight line external to it, inscribe in the circle a triangle, the sides of which shall pass through the three points.

The lemmas to the *Plane Loci* are chiefly propositions in algebraic geometry, one of which is equivalent to the theorem discovered by R. Simson, but generally known as Stewart's theorem:[15] If A, B, C, D are any four points on a straight line, then

$$AD^2 \cdot BC + BD^2 \cdot CA + CD^2 \cdot AB + BC \cdot CA \cdot AB = 0.$$

The remarkable proposition that Pappus gives in his description of Euclid's *Porisms* about any system of straight lines cutting each other two by two has already been set out in modern notation in the article on Euclid (IV, 426–427). The thirty-eight lemmas that he himself provides to facilitate an understanding of the *Porisms* strike an equally modern note. Lemma 3, proposition 129 shows that Pappus had a clear understanding of what Chasles called the anharmonic ratio and is now generally called the cross-ratio of four points. It proves the equality of the cross-ratios that

are made by any two transversals on a pencil of four lines issuing from the same point. The transversals are, in fact, drawn from the same point on one of the straight lines—in Figure 3 they are *HBCD* and *HEFG*, cutting the lines *AH*, *AL*, *AF*, and *AG*—but it is a simple matter to extend the proof, and Pappus proves that

$$\frac{HE \cdot GF}{HG \cdot FE} = \frac{HB \cdot DC}{HD \cdot BC},$$

that is to say, the cross-ratio is thus invariant under projection.

Lemma 4, proposition 130 shows, even more convincingly than the lemmas to the *Determinate Section*, that Pappus had an equally clear grasp of involution. In Figure 4, *GHKL* is a quadrilateral and *ABCDEF* is

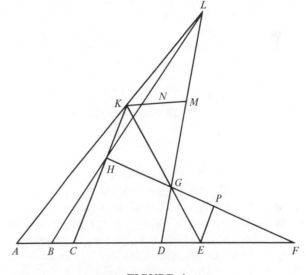

FIGURE 4

any transversal cutting pairs of opposite sides and the diagonals in (A,F), (C,D), (B,E). Pappus shows that

$$\frac{AF \cdot BC}{AB \cdot CF} = \frac{AF \cdot DE}{AD \cdot EF}.$$

(Strictly, what Pappus does is to show that if, in the figure, which he does not set out in detail, this relationship holds, then F, G, H lie on a straight line, but this is equivalent to what has been said above.) This equation is one of the ways of expressing the relationship between three pairs of conjugate points in involution. That Pappus gives these propositions as lemmas to Euclid's *Porisms* implies that they must have been assumed by Euclid. The geometers living just before Euclid must therefore have had an understanding of cross-ratios and involution, although these properties were not named for 2,250 years.

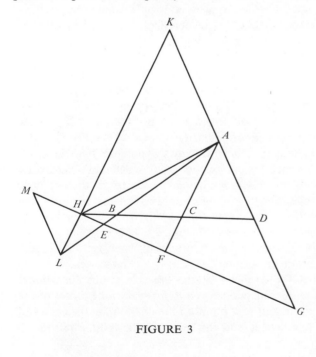

FIGURE 3

Lemma 13, proposition 139 has won its way into text books of modern geometry as "The Theorem of Pappus."[16] It establishes that if, from a point C, two transversals CE, CD cut the straight lines AN, AF, AD (see Figure 5) so that A, E, B and C, F, D are two sets of collinear points, then the points G, M, K are collinear. GMK is called the "Pappus line" of the two sets of collinear points.

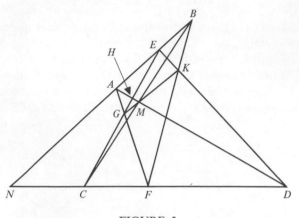

FIGURE 5

In the second of the two lemmas that Pappus gives to the *Surface Loci*, he enunciates and proves the focus-directrix property of a conic, which, as we have seen, he had already once employed. There is only one other place in any surviving Greek text in which this property is used—the fragment of Anthemius' *On Remarkable Mechanical Devices*. G. L. Toomer, however, has recently discovered this property in an Arabic translation of Diocles' treatise *On Burning Mirrors* in Mashhad (Shrine Library, MS 392/5593) and Dublin (Chester Beatty Library, Arabic MS 5255). But Pappus' passage remains the only place in ancient writing in which the property is proved.

Book VIII is devoted mainly to mechanics, but it incidentally gives some propositions of geometrical interest. In a historical preface Pappus justifies the claim that mechanics is a truly mathematical subject as opposed to one of merely utilitarian value. He begins by defining "center of gravity"—the only place in Greek mathematics where it is so defined—gives the theory of the inclined plane; shows how to construct a conic through five given points; solves the problem of constructing six equal hexagons around the circumference of a circle so as to touch each other and a seventh equal hexagon at the center; discourses on toothed wheels; and in a final section (which may be wholly interpolated) gives extracts from Heron's description of the five mechanical powers: the wheel and axle, the lever, the pulley, the wedge, and the screw.

Commentary on the Almagest. A commentary by Pappus on book V (with lacunae) and book VI of Ptolemy's *Syntaxis* exists in the Florentine manuscript designated L (ninth century) and in various other manuscripts. But this commentary is only part of a larger original. In the *Collection* Pappus refers to his commentary (*scholion*) on the first book of the *Almagest*, and in the surviving sixth book he makes the same reference, repeating a proof of his own for Archimedes' theorem about the area of a circle which, he says, he had given in the first book. In the compilation of uncertain authorship known as the *Introduction to the Almagest* there is a reference to a method of division "according to the geometer Pappus," which would seem to hark back to the third book.[17] In the fifth book of the commentary Pappus refers to a theorem in connection with parallax proved in his fourth book.[18] Although there is no direct reference to the second book, there is sufficient evidence that he commented on the first six books, and he may have written on all thirteen. The date of the commentary, as we have seen, must be soon after 320.

At the outset of his fifth book Pappus gives a summary of Ptolemy's fourth book, and at the beginning of his sixth book he summarizes Ptolemy's fifth book, which suggests that his commentary was a course of lectures. This theory is borne out by the painstaking and methodical way in which he explains, apparently for an audience of beginners, the details of Ptolemy's theory.

Ptolemy's fourth book introduces his lunar theory, and he explains the "first or simple anomaly" (irregularity of the movements of the moon) by postulating that the moon moves uniformly round the circumference of a circle (the epicycle), the center of which is carried uniformly round a circle concentric with the ecliptic. Pappus, following Ptolemy closely, explains in his fifth book that this needs correction for a second anomaly, which disappears at the new and full moons but is again noticeable when the moon is at the quadratures—provided that it is not then near its apogee or perigee, an irregularity later called evection. He also explains in detail Ptolemy's hypothesis that the circle on which the epicycle moves (the deferent) is eccentric with the ecliptic, and that the center of the eccentric circle itself moves uniformly round the center of the earth. To account for certain irregularities not explained by these anomalies, Ptolemy postulates a further correction which he calls prosneusis (that is, inclination or verging). In this context prosneusis means that the diameter of the epicycle which determines apogee and perigee is not directed to the center of the ecliptic but to a point on the line joining the center of the eccentric and the center of the ecliptic produced, and as far distant from the latter as the latter is from the former. After a gap in the manuscript, Pappus begins his comment again in the middle of this subject and proceeds to deal with a further complication. He states that the true position of the moon may not be where it is seen in the heavens on account of parallax, which may be neglected for the sun but not for the moon. He gives details for the construction of a "parallactic instrument" (an alidade) used for finding the zenithal distances of heavenly bodies when crossing the meridian. He had previously given details of "an astrolabe" (really an armillary sphere) described by Ptolemy.[19] He also follows Ptolemy closely in his deduction of the sizes and distances of the sun and moon, the diameter of the shadow of the earth in eclipses, and the size of the earth.

In the sixth book, again following Ptolemy closely, Pappus explains the conditions under which conjunctions and oppositions of the sun and moon occur. This explanation leads to a study of the conditions for eclipses of the sun and moon and to rules for predicting when eclipses will occur. The book closes with a study of the points of first and last contact during eclipses.

Pappus, like Theon after him, not only follows Ptolemy's division into chapters but enumerates theorems as Ptolemy does not. It is clear that Theon had Pappus' commentary before him when he wrote over a century later, and in some cases Theon lifted passages directly from Pappus.

Commentary on Euclid's Elements. Eutocius[20] refers to a commentary by Pappus on the *Elements* of Euclid and it probably extended to all thirteen books. In Proclus' commentary on book I there are three references to Pappus,[21] and it is reasonable to believe that they relate to Pappus' own commentary on the *Elements* as they do not relate to anything in the *Collection*. Pappus is said to have pointed out that while all right angles are equal to one another, it is not true that an angle equal to a right angle is always

a right angle—it may be an angle formed by arcs of circles and thus cannot be called a right angle. He is also alleged to have added a superfluous axiom: If unequals are added to equals, the excess of one sum over the other is equal to the excess of one of the added quantities over the other. He also added a complementary axiom about equals added to unequals, as well as certain axioms that can be deduced from the definitions. He gave a neat alternative proof of Euclid I.5 (the angles at the base of an isosceles triangle are equal) by comparing the triangle *ABC* with the triangle *ACB*, that is, the same triangle with the sides taken in reverse order (Figure 6).

Eutocius states that Pappus, in his commentary on the *Elements*, explains how to inscribe in a circle a polygon similar to a polygon inscribed in another circle. This would doubtless be in his commentary on book XII, and Pappus probably solved the problem in the same manner as a scholiast to XII.1, that is, by making the angles at the center of the second circle equal to the angles at the center of the first.[22]

If Pappus wrote on books I and XII it is likely that he also commented on the intermediate books, and the fact that he commented on book X is attested by a scholiast to Euclid's *Data*[23] and by the *Fihrist*, in which it is stated that the commentary was in two parts.[24]

A two-part commentary on the tenth book of Euclid's *Elements* does actually exist in Arabic,[25] and it is usually identified with that of Pappus. It was discovered in a Paris manuscript by F. Woepcke in 1850, but the manuscript lacks diacritical marks and Woepcke himself read the consonantal skeleton of the author's name as Bls, which he interpreted as meaning Valens, probably Vettius Valens, an astronomer of the age of Ptolemy.[26] Heiberg showed this interpretation to be impossible, and was the first scholar to identify the commentary with that which Pappus was known to have written.[27] H. Suter pointed out that the Arabic for Bls could easily be confused with Bbs, and as there is no P in Arabic, Pappus would be the author indicated.[28] This was accepted by T. L. Heath,[29] and indeed generally, but when Suter's translation of Woepcke's text was published in 1922[30] he raised the question whether the prolixity and Neoplatonic character of the treatise did not indicate Proclus as the author. In the latest study of the subject (1930) William Thomson denied the charges of prolixity and mysticism and accepted the authorship of Pappus.[31] It must be admitted that the commentary is in a wholly different style from the severely mathematical nature of the *Collection*, or even of the more elementary commentary on the *Almagest*, and the question of authorship cannot be regarded as entirely free from doubt.

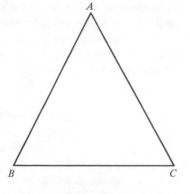

A

B   C

FIGURE 6

The superscription to the first part of the commentary and the subscription to the second part state that the Arabic translation is the work of Abū 'Uthman al-Dimishqī (*fl. ca.* 908–932), who also translated the tenth book of Euclid's *Elements*. The postscript to the second part adds that the copy of the commentary was written in 969 by Aḥmad ibn Muḥammad ibn 'Abd al-Jalīl, that is, the Persian geometer generally known as al-Sizjī (*ca.* 951–1029).

Some two dozen passages in the commentary have parallels in the scholia to Euclid's book X, sometimes remarkably close parallels. The simplest explanation is that the scholiast made his marginal notes with Pappus' commentary in front of him.

Euclid's book X is a work of immense subtlety, but there is little in the commentary that calls for comment. The opening section has an interest for the historian of mathematics as it distinguishes the parts played by the Pythagoreans, Theaetetus, Euclid, and Apollonius in the study of irrationals. It also credits Theaetetus with a classification of irrationals according to the different means.[32] He is said to have assigned the medial line to geometry ($\sqrt{xy}$ is the geometric mean between x, y), the binomial to arithmetic ($\frac{1}{2}[x + y]$ is the arithmetic mean between x, y), and the apotome to harmony (the harmonic mean $[2xy]/[x + y]$ between x, y is $[(2xy)/(x^2 - y^2)] \cdot [x - y]$, which is the product of a binomial and an apotome.)

Other Mathematical Works. Marinus, in the final sentence of his commentary on Euclid's *Data*,[33] reveals that Pappus also commented on the *Data*. Pappus apparently showed that Euclid's teaching followed the method of analysis rather than synthesis. Pappus also mentions a commentary that he wrote on the *Analemma* of Diodorus, in which he used the conchoid of Nicomedes to trisect an angle.[34]

The *Fihrist* includes among Pappus' works "A commentary on the book of Ptolemy on the *Planisphaerium*, translated by Thābit into Arabic." The entry leaves it uncertain whether Thābit ibn Qurra (*d.* 901) translated Ptolemy's work or Pappus' commentary, but Ḥājjī Khalīfa states that Ptolemy was the author of a treatise on the *Planisphaerium* translated by Thābit. He also adds that Ptolemy's work was commented on by "Battus al Roûmi [that is, late Greek], an Alexandrian geometer." "Battus" is clearly "Babbus," that is Pappus.[35]

Geography. The *Description of the World* mentioned in the *Suda Lexicon* has not survived in Greek, but the *Geography* bearing the name of the Armenian Moses of Khoren (although some scholars see in it the work of Anania Shirakatsi) appears to be a translation, or so closely based on Pappus' work as to be virtually a translation. The *Geography*, if correctly ascribed to Moses, was written about the beginning of the fifth century. The archetype has not survived, and the manuscripts contain both a long and a short recension. The character of Pappus' work may be deduced from two passages of Moses, or the pseudo-Moses, which may be thus rendered:[36] "We shall begin therefore after the *Geography* of Pappus of Alexandria, who has followed the circle or the special map of Claudius Ptolemy" and "Having spoken of geography in general, we shall now begin to explain each of the countries according to Pappus of Alexandria." From these and other passages J. Fischer[37] deduced that Pappus' work was based on the world map and on the special maps of Ptolemy rather than on the text itself, and as Pappus flourished only a century and a half after Ptolemy it is a fair inference that the world map and the special maps date back to Ptolemy himself. Pappus appears to have written with Ptolemy's maps as his basis, but about the world as he knew it in the fourth century.

Nothing is known of the second geographical work, *Rivers of Libya*, mentioned in the *Suda Lexicon*, or of the *Interpretation of Dreams*. The interpretation of dreams is akin to astrology, and there would be nothing surprising in a work on the subject by an ancient mathematician.

Music. It is possible that the commentary on Ptolemy's *Harmonica*, which was first edited by Wallis as the work of Porphyry, is, from the fifth chapter of the first book on, the work of Pappus. Several manuscripts contain the first four chapters only, and Lucas Holstein found in the Vatican a manuscript containing a definite statement that Porphyry's commentary was confined to the first four chapters of the first book and that Pappus was responsible for the remainder. Montfaucon also noted the same manuscript under the title "Pappi De Musica." Wallis did not accept the attribution because the title of the whole work and the titles of the chapters imply that it is wholly the work of Porphyry and because he could detect no stylistic difference between the parts. But the titles prove nothing, as Porphyry no doubt did comment, or intended to comment, on the whole work, and only missing parts would have been taken from another commentary, and arguments based on differences of style, especially in a technical work, are notoriously difficult. Hultsch and Jan were satisfied that Pappus was the author, but Düring was emphatically of the opinion that the whole is the work of Porphyry, and Ver Eecke agreed.[38] It must be left an open question.

Hydrostatics. An Arabic manuscript discovered in Iran by N. Khanikoff and published in 1860 under the title *Book of the Balance of Wisdom, an Arabic Work on the Water Balance, Written by al-Khazini in the Twelfth Century*[39] attributes to Pappus an instrument for measuring liquids and describes it in detail. The instrument is said by Khanikoff to be nearly identical with the volumeter of Gay-Lussac. If the attribution is correct—and there seems no reason to doubt it—the instrument may have been described in the missing part of the eighth book of the *Collection* or it may have had a place in a separate work on hydrostatics, of which no other trace has survived.

An Alchemical Oath. An oath attributed to "Pappus, philosopher" in a collection of alchemical writings may be genuine—if not *vero*, it is at least *ben trovato*—and if so it may tell us something of Pappus' syncretistic religious views in an age when paganism was retreating before Christianity. It is an oath that could have been taken equally by a pagan or a Christian, and it would fit in with the dates of Pappus. It could be gnostic, it has a Pythagorean element in it, there may be a veiled reference to the Trinity, and there is a Byzantine ring to its closing words. It reads: "I therefore swear to thee, whoever thou art, the great oath, I declare God to be one in form but not in number, the maker of heaven and earth, as well as the tetrad of the elements and things formed from them, who has furthermore harmonized our rational and intellectual souls with our bodies, who is borne upon the chariots of the cherubim and hymned by angelic throngs."[40]

A Vatican manuscript containing Ptolemy's *Handy Tables* has on one folio a short text about the entry of the sun into the signs of the zodiac, which F. Boll has shown must refer to the second half of the third century and which E. Honigmann attributes to Pappus. But this is no more than an unsubstantiated guess, which Boll himself refrained from making.[41]

A Florentine manuscript catalogued by Bandini notices Ἡμεροδρόμιον Πάππου τῶν διεπόντων καὶ πολευόντων, that is, daily tables of governing and presiding stars compiled by Pappus.[42]

NOTES

1. *Suda Lexicon*, Adler, ed., Vol. I, Pars IV (Leipzig, 1935), P 265, p. 26.
2. Pappus, *Collectio*, III.1, F. Hultsch, ed., I, 30.4; VII.1, Hultsch, ed., II, 634.1. Nothing more is known of Hermodorus or of Pandrosion and Megethion, to whom the third and fifth books are dedicated; or of his philosopher-friend Hierius, who pressed him to give a solution to the problem of finding two mean proportionals (Hultsch, ed., III, 3–8). A phrase in Proclus, *In primum Euclidis*, Friedlein, ed. (Leipzig, 1873; repr. Hildesheim, 1967), p. 429.13, οἱ . . . περὶ Πάππον, implies that he had a school.

3. A. Rome, *Commentaires de Pappus et de Théon d'Alexandrie sur l'Almageste*, I (Rome, 1931), 180.8–181.23, *Studi e Testi*, no. 54 (1931). The eclipse is no. 402 in F. K. Ginzel, *Spezialler Kanon der Sonnen und Mond Finsternisse* (Berlin, 1899), p. 87, and no. 3642 in T. von Oppolzer, *Canon der Finsternisse* (Vienna, 1887), repr. translated by Owen Gingerich (New York, 1962), p. 146. Rome, who first perceived the bearing of this eclipse on the date of Pappus, argues that if the total, or nearly total, eclipse of A.D. 346 had taken place, Pappus would certainly have chosen it for his example, and that the better eclipse of A.D. 291 was already too distant to be used (A. Rome, *op. cit.*, pp. x–xiii).
4. So A. Rome, *op. cit.*, I, xvii, note 1, suggests. This is more convincing than the conjecture of F. Hultsch, *op. cit.*, III, viii, note 3, that Δ is a copyist's error for ΙΓ.
5. A. Rome, *op. cit.*, II, lxxxiii, *Studi e Testi*, no. 72 (1936).
6. Leiden MS, no. 78, of Theon's ed. of the *Handy Tables*, fol. 55. This was first noted by J. van der Hagen, *Observationes in Theonis Fastos Graecos priores* (Amsterdam, 1735), p. 320, and his view was followed by H. Usener, "Vergessenes III," in *Rheinisches Museum*, n.s. **28** (1873), 403–404, and F. Hultsch, *op. cit.*, III, vi–vii, but none of these scholars realized the significance of Pappus' reference to the eclipse of A.D. 320.
7. Pappus, *Collectio* VIII.46, *op. cit.*, III, 1106.13–15. Rome, *op. cit.*, I, 254, note 1, gives reasons for thinking that the third theorem of book V of the *Collectio* is a fragment, all that now survives, of book I of the *Commentary on the Syntaxis*, and that it is an interpolation by an ed.
8. A. Rome, see previous note; K. Ziegler, in Pauly-Wissowa, XVIII (Waldsee, 1949), col. 1094.
9. F. Hultsch, *op. cit.*, I, p. vii–xiv.
10. Thomas Heath, *A History of Greek Mathematics*, II (Oxford, 1921), 357–358. A full and excellent conspectus of the *Collection* is given by Heath, *loc. cit.*, pp. 361–439; Gino Loria, *Le scienze esatte nell'antica Grecia*, 2nd ed. (Milan, 1914), pp. 658–700; and Paul Ver Eecke, *Pappus d'Alexandrie: La Collection mathématique*, I (Paris–Bruges, 1933), xiii–cxiv.
11. René Descartes, *Des matières de la géométrie* (Leiden, 1637), book I, 304–314, book II, 323–350; David Eugene Smith and Marcia C. Latham, *The Geometry of René Descartes With a Facsimile of the First Edition* (New York, 1925; repr. 1954), book I, 17–37, book II, 59–111.
12. Isaac Newton, *Philosophiae naturalis principia mathematica* (London, 1687; repr. London, 1953), "De motu corporum," lib. 1, sect. 5, lemma XIX, pp. 74–75.
13. Pappus, VII.42, *op. cit.*, II, 682.7–15. The whole passage in which this occurs is attributed by Hultsch to an interpolator, but without reasons given, and by Ver Eecke (*op. cit.*, I, xcvi) for unconvincing stylistic reasons and lack of connection with the context. But Heath pertinently observes (*A History of Greek Mathematics*, II, 403) that no Greek after Pappus would have been capable of framing such an advanced proposition. Ver Eecke (*op. cit.*, I, xcv, cxxiii) observes that Paul Guldin (1577–1643) could not have been inspired by the passage in Pappus as Commandino did not include it in his first ed. (Pesaro, 1588) and he could not have seen the second ed. (Bologna, 1660), augmented with this passage by Manolessius. But this conclusion is an error; the passage is in the first no less than the second ed. See also the article on Guldin.
14. F. Vieta, *Apollonius Gallus* (Paris, 1600), problem x, pp. 7–8; Isaac Newton, *Arithmetica universalis* (Cambridge, 1707), problem xli *ad finem*, pp. 181–182, 2nd ed. (London, 1722), problem xlvii *ad finem*, p. 195; *Principia* (London, 1687; repr. London, 1953), lemma XVI, pp. 67–68.
15. Robert Simson, *Apollonii Pergaei locorum planorum libri II restituti* (Glasgow, 1749), pp. 156–221; Matthew Stewart, *Some General Theorems of Considerable Use in the Higher Parts of Mathematics* (Edinburgh, 1746), pp. 1–2. See also

Moritz Cantor, *Vorlesungen über Geschichte der Mathematik*, III (Leipzig, 1898), 523–528.

16. For example, E. A. Maxwell, *Geometry For Advanced Pupils* (Oxford, 1949), p. 97. The term "Pappus' Theorem" is thus used by Renaissance and modern geometers in two different ways.

17. C. Henry, *Opusculum de multiplicatione et divisione sexagesimalibus, Diophanto vel Pappo tribuendum* (Halle, 1879), p. viii; A. Rome, *op. cit.*, **1**, xvi.

18. A. Rome, *op. cit.*, I, 76.19–77.1.

19. For a reconstruction of the astrolabe and parallactic instrument as described by Pappus, with illustrations, see A. Rome, *Annales de la Société scientifique de Bruxelles*, **47** (1927), 77–102, 129–140, and *op. cit.*, **1**, 3–5, 69–77.

20. Eutocius, *Commentarii in libros Archimedis De Sphaera et cylindro*, p. 1.13, *ad init.*, *Archimedis opera omnia*, J. L. Heiberg, ed., 2nd ed., III (Leipzig, 1915), corr. repr. Evangelos S. Stamatis (Stuttgart, 1972), p. 28.19–22: ὅπως μὲν οὖν ἔστιν εἰς τὸν δοθέντα κύκλον πολύγωνον ἐγγράψαι ὅμοιον τῷ ἐν ἑτέρῳ ἐγγεγραμμένῳ, δῆλον, εἴρηται δὲ καὶ Πάππῳ εἰς τὸ ὑπόμνημα τῶν Στοιχείων.

21. Proclus, *In primum Euclidis*, Friedlein, ed., pp. 189.12–191.4, 197.6–198.15, 249.20–250.19.

22. *Euclidis opera omnia*, J. L. Heiberg and H. Menge, eds., V (Leipzig, 1888), scholium 2, 616.6–617.21.

23. *Ibid.*, VI (Leipzig, 1896), scholium 4 *ad definitiones*, 262.4–6 : δύναται δὲ καὶ ῥητὸν καὶ ἄλογον δεδομένον εἶναι, ὡς λέγει Πάππος ἐν ἀρχῇ τοῦ εἰς τὸ ι′ Εὐκλείδου.

24. H. Suter, "Das Mathematiker Verzeichniss im Fihrist des Ibn abî Ja'kûb an-Nadîm," in *Zeitschrift für Mathematik und Physik*, **37** (1892), suppl. (or *Abhandlungen zur Geschichte der Mathematik*, **6**), p. 22. The whole entry runs, in English: "Pappus the Greek. His writings are: A Commentary on the book of Ptolemy concerning the representation of the sphere in a plane, translated by Thābit into Arabic. A commentary on the tenth book of Euclid, in two parts."

25. Bibliothèque Nationale (Paris), MS no. 2457 (Supplément arabe de la Bibliothèque impériale no. 952.2). The manuscript contains about fifty treatises, of which nos. 5 and 6 constitute the two books of the commentary.

26. Woepcke described the manuscript and translated four passages into French in his "Essai d'une restitution de travaux perdus d'Apollonius sur les quantités irrationelles," in *Mémoires présentés par divers savants à l'Académie des sciences*, **14** (1856), 658–720. He developed his theory about the authorship in *The Commentary on the Tenth Book of Euclid's Elements by Bls*, which he published anonymously and without date or place of publication. Woepcke read the name of the author in the title of the first book of the commentary as B.los (the dot representing a vowel) and in other manuscripts as B.lis, B.n.s, or B.l.s.

27. J. L. Heiberg, *Litterärgeschichtliche Studien über Euklid* (Leipzig, 1882), pp. 169–170. Heiberg points out that one of the manuscripts cited by Woepcke states that "B.n.s le Roumi" (that is, late Greek) was later than Claudius Ptolemy, while the *Fihrist* says that "B.l.s le Roumi" wrote a commentary on Ptolemy's *Planisphaerium*. As Vettius Valens lived under Hadrian, he was therefore older than Ptolemy—an elder contemporary. Moreover the *Fihrist* gives separate entries to B.l.s and Valens. See also Suter, *op. cit.*, p. 54, note 92.

28. H. Suter, "Das Mathematiker Verzeichniss im Fihrist," pp. 22, 54, note 92.

29. T. L. Heath, *The Thirteen Books of Euclid's Elements*, 2nd ed., III (Cambridge, 1905, 1925; repr. New York, 1956), 3; Heath, *A History of Greek Mathematics*, I (Oxford, 1921), 154–155, 209, II, 356.

30. H. Suter, "Der Kommentar des Pappus zum X Buche des Eukleides," in *Abhandlungen zur Geschichte der Naturwissenschaften und der Medizin*, **4** (1922), 9–78; see p. 78 for the question of authorship.

31. William Thomson and Gustav Junge, *The Commentary of Pappus on Book X of Euclid's Elements* (Cambridge, Mass., 1930; repr. New York, 1968), pp. 38–42.

32. There is nothing in the opening section about the rational and irrational being "given," as Pappus is stated by a scholiast (see note 23) to have maintained at the beginning of his commentary. This may be evidence against the ascription of the Arabic treatise to Pappus.

33. *Euclidis opera omnia*, J. L. Heiberg and H. Menge, eds., VI, 256.22–25.

34. F. Hultsch, *op. cit.*, I, 246.1–3. Ἀνάλημμα, as in Ptolemy's work with that title, means the projection of the circles of a celestial sphere on the plane. Neither the work of Diodorus nor the commentary of Pappus has survived. In Ptolemy's work certain segments of a semicircle are required to be divided into six equal parts, and it is easy to see how Pappus would need to trisect an arc or angle.

35. H. Suter, "Das Mathematiker Verzeichniss im Fihrist," p. 22 (see note 24, supra); Hājjī Khalīfa, *Lexikon bibliographicum et encyclopaedicum*, G. Fluegel, ed., V (London, 1850), 61–62, no. 9970, *s.v.* Kitab testih el koret. The *Planisphaerium* is a system of stereographic projection by which points on the heavenly sphere are represented on the plane of the equator by projection from a pole.

36. Translated from the French of P. Arsène Soukry, *Géographie de Moïse de Corène d'après Ptolémée* (Venice, 1881), p. 7.

37. J. Fischer, "Pappus und die Ptolemaeus Karten," in *Zeitschrift der Gesellschaft für Erdkunde zu Berlin*, **54** (1919), 336–358.

38. John Wallis, *Claudii Ptolemaei Harmonicorum libri III* (Oxford, 1682), reprinted in *Opera mathematica*, III (Oxford, 1699); the commentary is on pp. 183–355 of the latter work, and the authorship is discussed on p. 187. It has been edited in modern times by Ingemar Düring as *Porphyrios' Kommentar zur Harmonienlehre des Ptolemaios* (Göteborg, 1932). His discussion of the authorship is on pp. xxxvii–xxxix. Lucas Holstenius, *Dissertatio De vita et scriptis Porphyrii* (Rome, 1630), c. vi, p. 55: Neque tamen in universum ἁρμονικῶν opus scripsit Porphyrius, sed in quatuor duntaxat prima capita: cetera dein Pappus pertexuit. Ita enim in alio manuscripto Vaticano titulus indicat: Πορφυρίου ἐξήγησις εἰς δ′ πρῶτα κεφάλαια τοῦ πρώτου τῶν ἁρμονικῶν Πτολεμαίου. Sequitur deinde, Πάππου ὑπόμνημα εἰς τὰ ἀπὸ τοῦ ε′ κεφαλαίου καὶ ἐφεξῆς. Bernard de Montfaucon, *Bibliotheca bibliothecarum manuscriptorum nova*, I (Paris, 1739), 11B. Paul Ver Eecke, *Pappus d'Alexandrie: La Collection mathématique*, I (Paris–Bruges, 1933), cxv–cxvi. F. Hultsch, *op. cit.*, III, xii. C. Jan, *Musici scriptores graeci* (Leipzig, 1895; repr. Hildesheim, 1962), p. 116 and note 1.

39. See *Journal of the American Oriental Society*, **6** (1860), 40–53; and the article on al-Khāzinī, IV, 338–341; and bibliography, 349–351.

40. C. G. Grumer, *Isidis, Christiani et Pappi philosophi Iusjurandum chemicum nunc primum graece et latine editum* (Jena, 1807); M. Berthelot and C. E. Ruelle, *Collection des anciens alchimistes grecs* (Paris, 1888), pp. 27–28, traduction, pp. 29–30; Paul Tannery, "Sur la réligion des derniers mathématiciens de l'antiquité," in *Annales de philosophie chrétienne*, **34** (1896), 26–36, repr. in *Mémoires scientifiques*, **2** (1912), 527–539, esp. pp. 533–535. Tannery seems inclined to think that the oath may be correctly attributed to Pappus the mathematician, and he speculates that he may have been a gnostic.

41. Vaticanus Graecus 1291, fol. 9r. F. Boll, "Eine illustrierte Prakthandschrift der astronomischen Tafeln des Ptolemaios," in *Sitzungsberichte der Königliche Bayerische Akademie der Wissenschaften, philosophisch-philologischen und historischen Classe*, **29** (1899), 110–138. E. Honigmann, *Die sieben Klimata und die πόλεις ἐπίσημοι* (Heidelberg, 1929), p. 73.

42. Codex Laurentianus XXXIV plut. XXVIII; A. M. Bandini, *Catalogus Bibliothecae Laurentianae*, II (Florence, 1767), 61.

BIBLIOGRAPHY

I. ORIGINAL WORKS. *Collection.* The only complete ed. of the extant Greek text is F. Hultsch, *Pappi Alexandrini Collectionis quae supersunt e libris manu scriptis edidit latina interpretatione et commentariis instruxit Fridericus Hultsch*, 3 vols. (Berlin, 1876–1878). The Greek text is accompanied by a Latin translation on the opposite page and there are invaluable introductions, notes, and appendixes. Apart from a tendency to invoke interpolators too readily, the work is a model of scholarship.

The only translation of the whole extant text into a modern language is that of Paul Ver Eecke, *Pappus d'Alexandrie, La Collection Mathématique: oeuvre traduite pour la première fois du grec en français avec une introduction et des notes*, 2 vols. (Paris–Bruges, 1933). A German translation of books III and VIII is given by C. J. Gerhardt, *Die Sammlung des Pappus von Alexandrien, griechisch und deutsch herausgegeben*, 2 vols. (Halle, 1871).

The *Collection* first became known to the learned world when Commandino included Latin translations of various extracts in his editions of Apollonius (Bologna, 1566) and Aristarchus (Pesaro, 1572). After Commandino's death, his complete Latin trans. of the extant Greek text, except the unknown fragment of book II, appeared as *Pappi Alexandrini Mathematicae Collectiones a Federico Commandino Urbinate in Latinum conversae et commentariis illustratae* (Pesaro, 1588). Reprints appeared in 1589 (Venice) and 1602 (Pesaro) and a second ed. was published by C. Manolessius in 1660 (Bologna); despite the editor's claims it was inferior to the first ed.

Extracts from the Greek text were published in works by Marc Meiboom (1655), John Wallis (1688; first publication of the missing fragment of book II, which he found in a MS in the Savilian Library at Oxford), David Gregory (1703), Edmond Halley (1706, 1710), Robert Simson (1749), Joseph Torelli (1769), Samuel Horsley (1770), J. G. Camerer (1795), G. G. Bredow (1812), Hermann J. Eisenmann (1824), C. J. Gerhardt (1871).

Commentary on Ptolemy's Syntaxes (Almagest). The only complete ed. of the extant Greek text (part of book V and book VI) is Adolphe Rome, *Commentaires de Pappus et de Théon d'Alexandrie sur l'Almageste, texte établi et annoté par A. Rome*; vol. I is *Pappus d'Alexandrie: Commentaire sur les livres 5 et 6 de l'Almageste* (Rome, 1931), *Studi e Testi* no. 54. The work lacks only the indexes that would have been published at the end of the commentaries if Rome's design had not been interrupted by the destruction of his papers in the war.

The extant Greek text of book V was printed, with numerous errors and together with Theon's commentary, at the end of the *editio princeps* of the *Almagest*. This ed. was published by Grynaeus and Camerarius (Basel, 1538), but contained no mention of Pappus on the title page. F. Hultsch began, but was not able to complete, an ed. of the commentary by Pappus and Theon; see his "Hipparchos über die Grosse und Entfernung der Sonne," in *Berichte über die Verhandlungen der königlich sachsischen Gesellschaft der Wissenschaften*, Philologisch-Historische

Klasse, **52** (1900), 169–200. This work is vitiated by a fundamental error—what he thought was a working over of Pappus' text by Theon was really the same text—an error he would undoubtedly have recognized had he been able to continue his research.

Commentary on Euclid's Elements. The text of Abū ʿUthman al-Dimishqī's Arabic translation of a Greek commentary on the tenth book of Euclid's *Elements*, generally believed to be part of Pappus' commentary on the *Elements*, is published—with an English trans. and notes—in William Thomson and Gustav Junge, *The Commentary of Pappus on Book X of Euclid's Elements*, VIII in Harvard Semitic Series (Cambridge, Mass., 1930; repr. New York, 1968), 189–260. This supersedes the first printed version of the text by F. Woepcke, *The Commentary on the Tenth Book of Euclid's Elements by Bls* (Paris, 1855)—published without indication of author, place, or date. The Arabic text and trans. are the work of William Thomson. There is a German translation in H. Suter, "Der Kommentar des Pappus zum X Buche des Eukleides," in *Abhandlungen zur Geschichte der Naturwissenschaften und der Medizin* (1922), 9–78.

Commentary on Ptolemy's Harmonics. John Wallis, *Claudii Ptolemaei Harmonicorum libri III (graece et latine), Joh. Wallis recensuit, edidit, versione et notis illustravit, et auctarium adjecit* (Oxford, 1682). The commentary, which follows Ptolemy's text, is the work of Porphyry for the first four chapters, but possibly of Pappus from the fifth chapter on. The work was reprinted in *Johannis Wallis S.T.D. Operum mathematicorum Vol. III* (Oxford, 1699), 183–355, as *Porphyrii in Harmonica Ptolemaei commentarius nunc primum ex Codd. MSS. (Graece et latine) editus*, with (?) Pappus' share of the commentary on pp. 266–355. There is a modern text, with copious notes, by Ingemar Düring, "Porphyrios' Kommentar zur Harmonielehre des Ptolemaios," in *Göteborgs högskolas årsskrift*, **38** (1932), i–xliv, 1–217; see also Bengt Alexanderson, *Textual Remarks on Ptolemy's Harmonica and Porphyry's Commentary*, which is *Studia Graeca et latina Gothoburgensia*, XXVII (Göteborg, 1969).

Geography. What is believed to be essentially an early Armenian trans. of Pappus' *Geography* is given, with a French rendering, in P. Arsène Soukry, *Géographie de Moïse de Corène d'après Ptolémée, texte arménien, traduit en français* (Venice, 1881).

II. SECONDARY LITERATURE. *General.* Konrat Ziegler, "Pappos 2," in Pauly-Wissowa, XVIII (1949), cols. 1084–1106; the prefatory matter, notes, and appendices to the works by Hultsch, Rome, and Ver Eecke are cited above; Moritz Cantor, *Vorlesungen über Geschichte der Mathematik*, I, 3rd ed. (Leipzig, 1907), 441–455; Gino Loria, *Le scienze esatte nell'antica Grecia*, 2nd ed. (Milan, 1914), pp. 656–703; T. L. Heath, *A History of Greek Mathematics*, II (Oxford, 1921), 355–439.

Collection. The works cited in the previous paragraph are helpful. See also Robert Simson, *Apollonii Pergaei locorum planorum libri II restituti* (Glasgow, 1749); "De porismatibus tractatus," in *Opera quaedam reliqua*

(Glasgow, 1776), pp. 315–594; Michel Chasles, *Les trois livres de porismes d'Euclide, rétablis pour la première fois, d'après la notice et les lemmes de Pappus* (Paris, 1860); Paul Tannery, "L'arithmetique des Grecs dans Pappus" in *Mémoires de la Société des sciences physiques et naturelles de Bordeaux*, **3** (1880), 351–371, repr. in *Mémoires scientifiques*, **1** (1912), pp. 80–105; "Note sur le problème de Pappus" ("Pappus' problem" in the sense used by Descartes), in *Oeuvres de Descartes*, C. Adam and P. Tannery, eds., VI (Paris, 1902), 721–725, repr. in *Mémoires scientifiques*, **3** (1915), 42–50; J. S. MacKay, "Pappus on the Progressions" (a translation of Pappus on means), in *Proceedings of the Edinburgh Mathematical Society*, **6** (1888), 48–58; J. H. Weaver, "Pappus," in *Bulletin of the American Mathematical Society*, **23** (1916–1917), 127–135; "On Foci of Conics," *ibid.*, 361–365; N. Khanikoff, "Analysis and Extracts of *Book of the Balance of Wisdom*, an Arabic Work on the Water Balance, Written" by al-Khāzinī in the Twelfth Century, in *Journal of the American Oriental Society*, **6** (1860), lecture 1, ch. 7, 40–53; and al-Khāzinī, *Kitāb mīzān al-ḥikma* (Hyderabad, Deccan, A.H. 1359 [A.D. 1940–1941]). For further references see Bibliography to article on al-Khāzinī, in *Dictionary of Scientific Biography*, IV, 349–351. An article by Malcolm Brown, "Pappus, Plato and the Harmonic Mean," is promised for *Phronesis*.

Commentary on Ptolemy's Syntaxis (*Almagest*). F. Hultsch, *Hipparchos über die Grosse und Entfernung der Sonne* as above; S. Gunther, "Über eine merkwürdige Beziehung zwischen Pappus und Kepler," in *Bibliotheca mathematica*, n.s. **2** (1888), 81–87; A. Rome, "L'astrolabe et le météoroscope, d'après le commentaire de Pappus sur le 5e livre de l'Almageste," in *Annales de la Société scientifique de Bruxelles*, **47** (1927), 77–102; "L'instrument parallactique d'après le commentaire de Pappus sur le 5e livre de l'Almageste," *ibid.*, 129–140; *Pappus d'Alexandrie: Commentaire sur les livres 5 et 6 de l'Almageste* as above.

Commentary on Euclid's Elements. F. Woepcke, "Essai d'une restitution de travaux perdus d'Apollonius sur les quantités irrationelles," in *Mémoires présentés par divers savants à l'Académie des sciences de l'Institut de France*, **14** (1856), 658–720; J. L. Heiberg, *Litterärgeschichtliche Studien uber Euklid* (Leipzig, 1882), pp. 169–170; H. Suter, *Der Kommentar des Pappus zum X Buche des Eukleides* as above; William Thomson and Gustav Junge, *The Commentary of Pappus on Book X of Euclid's Elements* as above.

Geography. J. Fischer, "Pappus und die Ptolemaeus Karten," in *Zeitschrift der Gesellschaft für Erdkunde zu Berlin*, **54** (1919), 336–358; *Claudii Ptolemaei Geographiae Codex Urbinas Graecus 82, Tomus prodromus* (Leiden–Leipzig, 1922), 419–436; E. Honigmann, *Die sieben Klimata und die* πόλεις ἐπίσημοι (Heidelberg, 1929), c.x., "Pappus und Theon," pp. 72–81.

Commentary on Ptolemy's Harmonics. Ingemar Düring, "Die Harmonielehre des Klaudios Ptolemaios," in *Göteborgs högskolas årsskrift*, **36** (1930); and "Ptolemaios und Porphyrios uber die Musik," *ibid.*, **40** (1934), 1–293.

IVOR BULMER-THOMAS

PARACELSUS, THEOPHRASTUS PHILIPPUS AUREOLUS BOMBASTUS VON HOHENHEIM

(*b.* Einsiedeln, Switzerland, *ca.* 1493 [or 1 May 1494(?)]; *d.* Salzburg, Austria, 24 September 1541), *chemistry, medicine, natural philosophy, cosmology, theology, occultism, iatrochemistry.*

"Paracelsus," a nickname dating from about 1529, may denote "surpassing Celsus"; it might also represent a latinization of "Hohenheim," or even refer to his authorship of "para [doxical]" works that overturned tradition. Paracelsus was the son of William of Hohenheim, a member of the Bombast (Banbast) family of Swabia, who practiced medicine from 1502 to 1534 at Villach, in Carinthia; his mother was a bondswoman of the Benedictine abbey at Einsiedeln. Paracelsus received his early education–particularly in mining, mineralogy, botany, and natural philosophy—from his father. He was later taught by several bishops and apparently by Johannes Trithemius, abbot of Sponheim and a famous exponent of the occult, who was also in contact with Heinrich Cornelius Agrippa von Nettesheim. Paracelsus did practical work in the Fugger mines of Hutenberg, near Villach, and in those of Siegfried Fueger at Swaz.

In addition, Paracelsus probably studied at various Italian universities, perhaps including that of Ferrara. It is not certain that he received the doctorate; the only documentation would seem to be a personal deposition made before a magistrate in Basel. (This deposition was accepted in lieu of an oath by a witness in a lawsuit between two Strasbourg burghers, one of whom had been a patient of Paracelsus.) At any rate, in his laudatory preface to Paracelsus' *Grosse Wundartzney* (Augsburg, 1536), Wolfgang Thalhauser, municipal physician at Augsburg, called Paracelsus "Doctor of both medicines." It is possible that Paracelsus took a lower medical degree at Ferrara, as may be borne out by his subsequent service as a military surgeon, first in the service of Venice, then elsewhere on his early travels (including those to Scandinavia and probably to the Middle East and Rhodes). His work as a surgeon reflected his nonconformity; in reply to the traditional separation of medicine and surgery he coined the phrase "*In judicando*, a physician; *in curando*, a surgeon."

In 1525 Paracelsus was in Salzburg for a short time. While there he barely escaped prosecution for exhibiting sympathy for the Peasants' War. Following some abortive attempts to establish himself in southern Germany and Switzerland, he set up a successful practice in Strasbourg. Called in consultation to Basel, he saved the life of the influential humanist and publisher Johannes Froben. His conservative and cautious treatment of Froben and the medical advice that he gave Erasmus, who was then staying in Froben's house, won Paracelsus the post of municipal physician and professor of medicine at Basel in March 1527. His appointment was sponsored by Strasbourg and Basel church reformers, especially Johannes Oecolampadius, and was not approved by the academic authorities. The latter refused to admit into their company a man who not only failed to submit qualifying documents and declined to take the required oath, but also issued instead an iconoclastic document, the *Intimatio*. In this work (which, published as a broadside, is extant in the 1575 edition of Michael Toxites' *Libri paragraphorum*, although it has been lost in its original form since 1616) he professed disagreement with Galenic medicine and promised to introduce a new syllabus based upon his own firsthand experience as a naturalist and in treating patients at the sickbed.

Paracelsus next offended by burning a copy of Ibn Sīnā's *Canon* at a student rag on St. John's Day (24 June). He further lectured in German, contrary to academic tradition, and admitted barber-surgeons to his courses. When his patron Froben died suddenly in October 1527 his opponents (who had at first been subdued by the enthusiastic response to Paracelsus' teaching by the students, humanists, and reformed churchmen) gained ground. Chief among his enemies were the professors and, especially, the apothecaries, who objected to his control of the pharmacies and his criticism of the profits that they made. The public mood began to turn against Paracelsus, and his protests to the town council—directed against the apothecaries and against the lampoons that the fickle students had begun to publish about him—were ignored.

The final clash came in February 1528, when Paracelsus publicly denounced a magistrate who had found against him in a lawsuit against a church dignitary who had had Paracelsus called in for consultation in an acute abdominal emergency. He promised Paracelsus the enormous fee that he demanded; having been cured by a few of Paracelsus' laudanum pellets, the patient refused to pay, and Paracelsus charged him with default. Having made his denunciation, Paracelsus had to leave Basel, thereby relinquishing all his property. He never obtained academic preferment or contractual employment again.

Paracelsus then paid a short visit to Lorenz Fries at Colmar, stopped for a brief time at Esslingen, and reached Nuremberg in 1529. He remained there until 1530, leaving after a series of altercations, the chief of which developed from his stated disapproval of the treatment of syphilis by guaiacum and poisonous

doses of mercury; his criticism of Lutheran orthodoxy; and his assertion of his right to publish (which was followed by censure elicited from the Leipzig Medical Faculty). He proceeded to Beratzhausen, where he worked on his *Buch paragranum*, then spent an uneasy period of about two years at St. Gall. There Paracelsus completed his main medical work, the *Opus paramirum*, which he dedicated to Joachim de Watt (Vadianus), humanist, Zwinglian churchman, geographer, and acting mayor. He left despite influential friends and patients and good chemical laboratory facilities.

Paracelsus then embarked upon a career as a wandering lay preacher, appearing in "beggar's garb" in Appenzell, Innsbruck, and Sterzing (Vipiteno). He failed to secure the medical work he hoped for, but was able to study miners' diseases— silicosis and tuberculosis—at Solbad Hall in Tirol and at Schwaz, to which he returned in 1533. He found better luck in Merano, St. Moritz, and especially Pfäfers-Bad Ragaz, where in August 1535 he was consulted by the abbot John Jacob Russinger. The following summer he was at Augsburg and Ulm, where he supervised the printing of his *Grosse Wundartzney*. He traveled on through Bavaria (where he wrote a work on tartar) to Kromau in Bohemia, where he wrote a work on the occult-metaphysical *philosophia sagax* and continued chemical laboratory work. In Austria he had audiences with Ferdinand of Bohemia, brother of Charles V, and thus temporarily recovered much of his former status.

In 1538 Paracelsus reached Villach, where his father had died four years before. Here he completed his *Carinthian Trilogy*, which included a *Chronica* of the land, his last work *On Tartar*, the *Labyrinth of Doctors Perplexed*, and the *Seven Defenses* against his critics. Although the Carinthian authorities promised him publication, the work was not published until 1564, and then in Cologne. Paracelsus again practiced medicine, although his own health was failing. Finally he was called to Salzburg by Ernest of Wittelsbach, suffragan of that city; he died there and was buried in the almshouse of St. Sebastian. The site of his grave was a place of pilgrimage for the sick for a long time after.

Paracelsus' difficult personality may have been formed from his resentment of his father's illegitimate birth and of his mother's status as a bondswoman. He was an angry man, and his career followed a pattern of initial triumphs followed by losing battles, in the course of which he alienated even his best friends and patrons. His wholesale condemnation of traditional science and medicine found its parallel in his rough behavior and in his unwillingness to make concessions to custom and authority. He sought to learn new cures and remedies from the common people, and spent many hours drinking with them in low taverns; his expertise concerning wines and vintages is apparent in some of his medical writings. Paracelsus was prepared to treat the poor without any reward, but required high fees of the rich and reviled them if they defaulted (or, indeed, if he even thought that they had). Some of his cures were probably not as brilliant as they appeared to be at the time, and some may even have done more harm than good in the long run (although some of these criticisms must be discounted as the canards of more traditional practitioners).

A portrait of Paracelsus painted when he was in his thirties shows him as beardless, but with a shock of hair, and almost pathologically obese. Pictures made a decade later show him still beardless and mostly bald, while in his older years he is depicted as looking haggard and ill. The best eyewitness account of him is that of his amanuensis, Johannes Oporinus, which was published in Daniel Sennert's *De chymicorum cum Aristotelicis et Galenicis consensu et dissensu* (Wittenberg, 1619). Oporinus was one of the few men for whom Paracelsus himself had words of praise, and he in his turn admired Paracelsus and his medicine although, as a young and timid scholar, he was often overawed by his master's unconventional behavior.

Oporinus found fault with Paracelsus' rejection of organized religion and classical scholarship, as well as his addiction to drink, noting that he had been averse to wine until his twenty-fifth year, but later challenged peasants to drinking contests from which he emerged victorious. He gave a vivid report of Paracelsus' astonishing resilience, describing him dictating, late at night after a drinking bout, with perfect coherence and sense, in a manner that could not have been bettered by a sober person. Then Paracelsus threw himself on his bed with his long sword (which he said he had got from a hangman) still girded about him, and, suddenly leaping up, brandished his sword like a madman, frightening his famulus to distraction. Oporinus further states that Paracelsus was busy all day in his laboratory, but lived luxuriously, never short of money. As part of his treatment for ulcers, in which he ignored the usual restrictive diets, he dined lavishly with his patients, curing them "with a full stomach." He was not interested in women, and never had sexual intercourse. He liked to buy expensive new clothes, and tried to give his old ones away, although no one would accept them because they were extremely dirty. (This last comment is at variance with Paracelsus' announced scorn of academic robes

and with the modest and practical dress shown in his portraits.)

In his own writings Paracelsus dealt in paradoxes, interlarded with undisguised obscenities and endless outbursts against traditional doctrines and their professors. His works might have at times appeared to be the ravings of a megalomaniac, enjoining the whole learned world to follow him in new paths, away from deceitfully wrong and "excrementitious" humoral lore. Nonetheless, he created a new style and a refreshing and witty language, perfectly suited to the ideas that he wished to convey. These ideas—those of a naturalist physician, spiritualist and symbolist thinker, and passionately religious and charitable fighter against perceived evil—are reflected in the contradictory interpretations that posterity has placed upon Paracelsus' work. He was, for example, extolled in the early years of the nineteenth century, the era of Romanticism and *Naturphilosophie*, and reviled before and after, at the beginning of the age of scientific medicine.

Only a few of Paracelsus' works were published during his lifetime. Among these were some astrological-mantic forecasts, including the *Practica gemacht auf Europen in dem nechstkunfftigen Dreyssigtsen Jahr* (Nuremberg, 1529); *Usslegung des Commeten erschynen zu mitlem Augsten anno 1531*; *Practica teutsch auf das MDXXXV Jar*; and *Prognostication auff XXIIII jar*. More important were his critical appraisal of the treatment of syphilis by guaiacum (*Vom Holtz Guaiaco gründlicher heylung* [Nuremberg, 1529]); a related treatise on the "impostures" committed therein (*Von der Französischen kranckheit Drey Bücher* [Nuremberg, 1530]); a booklet on Bad Pfäfers (*Von dem Bad Pfeffers Tugenden, Krefften und würckung, ursprung und herkommen, Regiment und ordinantz* [1535]); and the *Grosse Wundartzney* (Augsburg, 1536). Most of his writings came to light in the decades following his death, and their publication reached a peak in about 1570 with the *Archidoxis*, a handbook of Paracelsian chemistry that went through many editions after the first one, issued at Cracow in 1569. The *Archidoxis* was edited or translated by Adam Schröter, Adam of Bodenstein, Michael Toxites, Gerard Dorn, Balthassar Flöter, and G. Forberger, among others. The work of all of them predated that of John Huser, who edited the first definitive collected editions—ten quarto volumes in 1589–1591, folio editions of 1603 and 1605, and the surgical folio of 1605.

Among Paracelsus' practical achievements was his management of wounds and chronic ulcers. These conditions were overtreated at the time, and Paracelsus' success lay in his conservative, noninterventionist approach, which was based upon his belief in natural healing power and *mumia*, an active principle in tissues. He thus continued the tradition of Theodoric Borgognoni of Lucca and his pupil Henry of Mondeville, both of whom had advocated, in the thirteenth and fourteenth centuries, aseptic and pus-preventing treatment, the method of *rara vulnerum medicatio* (as Cesare Magati named it in 1616). Chemical therapy had been used chiefly externally by the ancients, but Paracelsus recognized the superiority of chemicals taken internally over the traditional, mostly herbal, internal medicines. He imposed strict controls upon their use, however, holding that chemicals must be given only in moderate doses (in contrast to the toxic doses of mercury then used in treating syphilis) and only in detoxified form, achieved by washing the chemical substance with water and alcohol, "to cleanse the sharpness," or by oxidation and the induction of solubility (as, for example, in heating white crystalline arsenic with saltpeter or in converting harmful iron sulfides into therapeutic sulfates).

Paracelsus also knew of the diuretic action of mercury in the treatment of dropsy and of the narcotic and sedative properties of ether-like preparations that he obtained from the interaction of alcohol and sulfur. He demonstrated the latter in an early pharmacological experiment on chickens, which he probably selected because of the well-known narcotic effect of *Hyoscyamus* (henbane) upon them (an effect also called *mort aux poules*).

Paracelsus' description of miners' diseases was the first to identify silicosis and tuberculosis as occupational hazards. He was also the first to recognize the congenital form of syphilis, and to distinguish it from postpartum infection. He studied visceral—notably osseous and nervous—syphilis in its protean manifestations, and differentiated it from hydrargyrosis, the morbid syndrome caused by toxic doses of mercury. (He did, however, regard syphilis as a specific modification of other diseases, rather than as a separate entity.) Paracelsus also gave the first purely medical account of dancing mania and chorea, proposing a natural explanation in place of previous supernatural theories (including possession by demons). He described the symptoms of hysteria, hysterical blindness among them.

Paracelsus further drew the connection between cretinism and goiter, which he identifed as being endemic and related to the mineral content of drinking water. He recognized the significance of acid in mineral waters as a powerful aid to gastric digestion and wrote of the "hungry acid" *(acetosum esurinum)* in the stomach of some animals as permitting them to digest metals and stone. He was not, however, aware of the essential role of acid in the gastric digestion of all animals—this was recognized and studied thoroughly only by J. B. van Helmont, between 1624 and 1644, and to a lesser degree by slightly earlier workers, including Quercetanus (Duchesne), Petrus Castelli, Fabius Violet (perhaps Quercetanus writing under another name), and Johannes Walaeus. Paracelsus also observed the precipitation of albumin in urine after acid (rennet or vinegar) is added.

Chief among Paracelsus' contributions to medical theory was his new concept of disease. He demolished the ancients' notion of disease as an upset of humoral balance—either an excess *(hyperballonta)* or an insufficiency *(elleiponta)*—or as a displacement or putrefaction of humors. Each of these conditions depended on the constitution (or *physis*, or "temperament") of the individual, as determined by the humoral variations appropriate to him. There were therefore as many diseases as there were individuals, and no disease was considered to be a classifiably separate entity, having a specific agent and specific anatomical effects.

Paracelsus completely reversed this concept, emphasizing the external cause of a disease, its selection of a particular locus, and its consequent seat. He sought and found the causes of diseases chiefly in the mineral world (notably in salts) and in the atmosphere, carrier of star-born "poisons." He considered each of these agents to be a real *ens*, a substance in its own right (as opposed to humors, or temperaments, which he regarded as fictitious). He thus interpreted disease itself as an *ens*, determined by a specific agent foreign to the body, which takes possession of one of its parts, imposing its own rules on form and function and thereby threatening life. This is the parasitistic or ontological concept of disease—and essentially the modern one. It was substantially elaborated by Helmont. The significance of specific disease-semina, its connection with imagination, ideas, and passions, and the bodily manifestation of spiritual impulses, as inculcated by Helmont, is clearly anticipated in Paracelsus' concept of disease.

Paracelsus' new idea of disease led him to new modes of therapy. He directed his treatment specifically against the agent of the disease, rather than resorting to the general anti-humoral measures (such as sweating, purging, bloodletting, and inducing vomiting) that had been paramount in ancient therapy for "removal of excess and addition of the deficient." For Galenic remedies derived from plants, he substituted specifics, often applied on homeopathic principles. Here his notion of "signatures" came into play, in the selection of herbs that in color and shape resembled the affected organ (as, for example, a yellow plant for the liver or an orchid for the testicle). Paracelsus' search for such specific medicines led him to attempt to isolate the efficient kernel (the *quinta essentia*) of each substance. His method was thus one of separating drugs into their component parts, rather than compounding them as the ancients had done.

In nontherapeutic chemistry Paracelsus described new products arising from the combination of metals and devised a method of concentrating alcohol by freezing out its watery component. He also developed a new way to prepare aquafortis, and demonstrated its transformation into an oil at the bottom of its container when laminated metals were dissolved in it. In the *Archidoxis* he grouped chemicals according to their susceptibility to similar chemical processes, although it has been stated (and disputed) that many of the chemicals that Paracelsus believed to be discrete entities were in fact identical distillates containing nitric or hydrochloric acid. It is difficult to reproduce some of the processes that Paracelsus described, partly because he made deliberate omissions in the interest of secrecy (as, for example, in his instructions for producing the *arbor Dianae*). It is no easier to decide what in his work is truly original or to what degree it had been anticipated by the Lullists and by Johannes de Rupiscissa, the latter in the middle of the fourteenth century, particularly in regard to the preparation of potable metals and *quintae essentiae*. Certainly Paracelsus was the first to devise such advanced laboratory techniques as the use of detoxification and freezing to concentrate alcohol and invented new preparations (including those of the ether group and probably tartar emetic); he was, moreover, the first to attempt to construct a chemical system.

Much has been written about Paracelsus as an alchemist, but he was not really interested in the classical alchemists' problems of transmutation, the philosopher's stone, or making gold. Rather, "alchemy" meant to him the invention of new and nontoxic metals for medicinal uses. He was, however, perceptibly influenced by the medieval alchemists and by a number of contemporary herbalist-distillers, including Hieronymus Brunschwig and Ulstadt.

While the observations and achievements in medicine and chemistry cited may be regarded as stepping-stones to modern science, it must be realized that they are selected from the larger body of Paracelsus' writings, which, in their totality, evoke a world of *magia naturalis* far removed from the modern spirit of independent inquiry. Paracelsus, on the whole, was as much (and on occasion more) of a seer, a cosmosophic, and religious metaphysician, than he was a naturalist and scientist. Having turned against book learning, formal logic, and complacent human reasoning, he espoused the study of nature, which must be "read" by traveling from land to land—"one land, one page." He thus sought to find the invisible, spiritual forces that make visible bodies act.

Paracelsus believed that these invisible forces achieved their purpose through what he called "knowledge," which is not of the observer but rather of the object observed—the vital principle that, for instance, insures that the seed of a pear tree will grow into a pear tree, and not any other kind. Knowledge therefore lies in the object itself and in its specific function; man can acquire this knowledge only through union with the object—a meeting of the spirit of the inquirer with the spirit of the object. It is through this traffic between astral bodies (which Paracelsus defined as ethereal spirits of finest corporality, the star-born carriers of vital principles—"souls"—on their descent from heaven) that knowledge is obtained in the "light of nature," which represents the total of the specific forces embedded in the visible objects of nature and their grasping by the mind through union with them. These forces, the divine arcana, are specific for every object and are visualized as volatile. Knowledge through union with the object is possible to man because all the substances and objects of the ambient world are somewhere and somehow represented in him. This follows from the close parallelism between the macrocosm and the microcosm, and from the attraction of like to like (universal sympathy).

Paracelsus believed that the microcosmic state of man permitted the study of the universe, so that science and knowledge are possible. He called the study of nature and medicine "astronomy," and urged that every physician be an astronomer—that is, that he study the *astra*. Paracelsus' term *astra* denoted not so much the stars themselves and their influences on sublunary objects (so important in traditional astrology) as the essential virtues and functions of individual objects and their correspondences within all realms of nature, including the stars.

Indeed, each object (or part thereof) has its vital principles—*astra*—as well as its celestial star, with which it shares specific properties. In the realm of plants, for example, a certain herb represents a certain star, as well as a corresponding mineral, organ, part of the body, disease, and remedy. A certain fungus is thus a "fruit" of the earth; its equivalent is vitriol, a "fruit" of water. Arsenic, a mineral product of water, emerges as a terrestrial "fruit" in the form of another kind of fungus. *Vitriolum terrae album* is equivalent to *Pfifferling*, a kind of chanterelle; *vitriolum aquae* is the copper of water.

In explaining the curative power of mercury in the treatment of dropsy, Paracelsus was able to reach a rational and protoscientific statement: the cure results from the expulsion of a "wrong" salt, which tends to be dissolved, and its replacement by one that remains in a fixed, coagulated state. Less scientifically, however, this "life of salts" depends upon celestial impression—a "shot" fired by the star that represents the salt in its own world "divides" the bodily salt in the same way that the sun melts snow. The salt is then restored by the celestial virtue of the mercury. Paracelsus thus retained much of traditional astrology, although giving it an original, astrosophical interpretation and denying the exclusive power of the stars over human life. Moreover he corrected or dismissed a great deal of traditional lore, and argued generally against complacent human reasoning, which is "from the stars" and comes to us with the astral body.

Paracelsus' notion of knowledge led him to advocate humanitarian treatment of imbeciles; he posited that since man's reason and pseudo-knowledge are "astral," the simpleton, unaffected by the astral snares of human reasoning, retains a closeness to God (which incidentally allows him to make accurate predictions). Paracelsus also—although not unequivocally—recommended humane treatment of the insane, stating that their illness is perfectly natural and not simply the work of demons. There are nevertheless certain retrogressive features in his system of therapy—among them many popular superstitions, including *Dreck-Apotheke*—that are the result of his adherence to *magia naturalis* and the idea of cosmic sympathy.

Paracelsus' general natural philosophy is spiritualist. The important forces in nature are the invisible "spirits," such as the *quintae essentiae*; these are the life substances of objects, and the *magus* may know how to extract them, particularly from herbs and chemicals. These "spirits" may not be defined in terms of the merely passive ("female") elements, qualities, humors, and elemental mixtures of the ancients; they are rather the specific, active ("male") *arcana* and primordial seeds (*semina*) that emanate immediately from God and direct and inform nature. Each contains its own *archeus* (*vulcanus*), which determines individual form and function. The *archeus* is also called the "internal alchemist," the digestive principle that, acting in the "kitchen" ("stomach") of each organ (most notably the stomach proper), separates nourishment from poison, the pure from the impure, and the assimilable from waste. Its failure leads to the deposit of sediment which constitutes pathological change, the Paracelsian tartar. The *semina* are preformed in an invisible, nonmaterial

foreworld, the *iliastrum*, or prime matter. This has nothing to do with matter in any modern sense of the word; rather, it denotes in themselves uncreated (divine) impulses (*logoi*), the word *Fiat* that directs an original watery "matter" to form individual objects. This matter is an archetype of water, an invisible "creative" water, that is linked to ordinary water (that is, the material, elementary world) through bearing the *semina* of all things; it is thus the mother element, the mother of all things. Earth, air, and fire also occur in the Paracelsian world, not in the ancient sense of elements, but rather in the Platonic and cabalistic (*sepher jezirah*) sense of mothers. They are the wombs that give birth to groups of objects, each specific to its source; thus, minerals and metals are the "fruit" of water, and plants and animals—including man—the "fruit" of earth. Each of these "fruits" has its corresponding "fruit" in each of the mothers.

The three Paracelsian principles—salt, sulfur, and mercury—likewise do not replace the elements of the ancients, nor are they matter of any kind. They are rather principles within matter that condition the state in which matter can occur. There is thus in every object a principle (salt) responsible for its solid state; a principle (sulfur) responsible for its inflammable, or "fatty," state; and a third (mercury) responsible for its smoky (vaporous) or fluid state. Of these, salt is of particular importance in medicine. It represents a state of fixation, or coagulation and sedimentation, and appears in the pathological form of tartar. According to Paracelsus, tartar is any pathological change that can be interpreted as a deposit, and the remains of unassimilable nourishment for an organ; it is coagulated under the influence of acid and affects the function and vitality of all parts of the body. It is the opposite pole of spirit, that is, of what is active and alive; it reflects the pain of hell and its curse in the life of man. It is for this reason named "tartar" (*cagastrum*), which also denotes the useless and troublesome deposits in wine vats, comparable with the stones and calcifications in the channels of the kidneys, bladder, bronchi, and other organs. (In the lungs such deposits cause pulmonary tuberculosis through bronchial obstruction.) A universal solvent, the *liquor alcahest*, was therefore a medical necessity, and one was eagerly sought.

Of the Paracelsian principles, mercury denotes the highest spiritual state and sulfur an intermediate one. Sulfur is also called the soul, and forms the link between the spirit (*geist*, mercury) and the solid body (salt). It is, of course, the spirit that animates an object—that is, that accounts for its specific form and function—and each object is an "essential thing" by virtue of its specific spirit. This spirit gives life, a "spiritual, invisible, incomprehensible thing"; it makes dead things "male" (*männisch*)—that is, alive and responsive.

Paracelsus was conversant with traditional academic medicine and naturalism, both ancient and medieval. Although he was in principle intent on destroying tradition, he retained much of it in his system, often merely changing its emphasis or giving it an original interpretation. For example, during the Middle Ages salt as a third principle was known as *faex*, or earth; its admixture to sulfur and mercury had been thought to influence proportionally the nature of a metal (by Michael Scott) or any other substance (as in the *Seven Hermetic Tracts*, Archelaus [Arisleus], and the Lullists). Paracelsus assigned salt a much wider, cosmological significance. For him it stood for not only a bodily admixture to a mineral or metal, determining its baseness or nobility, but also for anything that makes an object appear in solid form—that is, for whatever causes a deposit in a nonsolid medium or promotes any change in normal appearance, as in an organ. In the latter sense, salt can denote any morbid anatomical change, although it can at the same time mean any particular salt, such as sodium chloride, that has caused this change. (Paracelsus referred to an ulcer as a salt mine.)

Obviously, then, Paracelsus was not the first to introduce the concept of the third principle, but he did give it an original meaning. Similarly, he adapted the *quintae essentiae* and their use in medicine, merely studying them further and applying them in greater depth and compass. He did the same thing with the notion of the astral body, a Neoplatonic concept that he probably owed to Marsilio Ficino, whose influence is apparent in the work of Paracelsus as a whole, as well as in detail in his medical system (most notably in his ideas on the cause of the plague, the role of the stars, and *magia naturalis*). Natural magic meant, to Paracelsus, capturing and demonstrating heavenly "gifts," rather than cultivating demons, in which parallels between his work and that of Agrippa von Nettesheim may be seen.

Among the medieval antecedents of Paracelsus' work, Konrad of Megenberg's *Buch der Natur*, of about 1350, would seem to be of importance. Paracelsus used the phrase "Buch der Natur," recommending that it be studied instead of the printed books of scholars and professors. Doctrines that are common to Paracelsus and Konrad of Megenberg may also be traced to earlier sources. Some of these ideas bear the clear stamp of gnosticism, as transmitted in the esoteric and largely suppressed medieval literature of the "prohibited arts" of alchemy and astrology. These ideas include the notion of the lower, "incompetent," astral "administrators" responsible for the creation of our evil world, which emerges in Paracelsian (and notably pseudo-Paracelsian) treatises as the concept of the *vulcani* or *archei*. Likewise gnostic are the ideas of prime and uncreated matter (and its offspring, the original "water"); of the elemental and material world as the workshop of the devil; of missiles from the stars as the agents of insanity, aggression, delinquency, and physical màlformations; of the splitting off of a female principle in the person of God; and of the ultimate return of the immortal soul to God and of the fine pneumatic shell of the soul (the astral body) to the stars.

Paracelsus made a distinct contribution to medicine and chemistry in his nomenclature for substances that were already known—for example, he substituted the word "alcohol" (which had previously meant any subtle substance in dispersion) for "spirit of wine" and "synovia" for the "gluten" contained within the joints. His more general reforms were, however, less scientific in character (although protoscientific elements are prominent in them). Chief among his posthumous accomplishments was the introduction of Paracelsian chemicals into the *London Pharmacopoeia* of 1618—some of these, calomel among them, owed their inclusion to Croll, Turquet de Mayerne, and other Paracelsists. But however his specific contributions may be qualified, there is no doubt of Paracelsus' essential influence, both direct and indirect, on medical reform, as there can be no doubt of his truly naturalist empiricism and skepticism toward the prevalent Galenic tradition.

Medicine was the chief focus of Paracelsus' labors, the center of his anthropocentric world. Nonetheless, it was by no means his only concern—he was further committed to the reformation of religion and society. At heart neither Protestant nor Catholic, he opposed any closed church (*Mauerkirche*) and fought against what he considered to be the fraudulent rationalism of dogma and formal juridical logic, the man-made snares "sold" by jurists as divine laws and institutions. He belonged to the group of spiritualist and individualist reformers that included Sebastian Franck, whom he had probably met at Nuremberg and Augsburg. Like Franck, he wrote in paradoxical language to advocate a return to the ideals of early Christianity, including poverty, the redistribution of wealth, and regeneration ("glorification of the flesh") through the sacraments.

In sum, Paracelsus was a great doctor and an able chemist. That he achieved little in his lifetime (apart from his success in his practice and in the laboratory) may be attributed in part to his uncompromisingly destructive attitude toward tradition. His views encompassed both astrological superstitions and quite conspicuously modern descriptions of diseases, together with shrewd appraisals of their nature and causes. He remained ignorant of a number of important surgical methods that were practiced widely by his contemporaries and, although repudiating astrological beliefs in many instances, he nonetheless incorporated them into his own work and added multifarious mantic lore of his own. It must be noted, however, that his credulousness was part of his unprejudiced and empirical attitude; he was intent on testing all reported observations, no matter how unlikely they might be. All these factors are reflected in the varied quality of his writings—a mixture of pansophic and religious parables with naturalism and medicine, the mixture of the "medieval" and the modern. Nevertheless, Paracelsus is basically consistent in theory and practice. A number of apparent contradictions in his work disappear when they are considered in their proper context, while others are clearly the result of developmental changes in his life and general outlook.

What is in the end most remarkable in Paracelsus' work is that he achieved real advances in chemistry and medicine through the revival and original development of lore that had been kept alive only at a very low level (or had, indeed, been suppressed as heresy). This lore—alchemy, astrology, and the "prohibited arts"—can be traced to Hellenistic and Oriental Neoplatonism, gnosticism, and syncretism; in Paracelsus' hands it became, if not scientific, at least protoscientific. It is difficult to overrate the effect of Paracelsus' achievement on the development of medicine and chemistry. Some thirty years after his death a powerful Paracelsian movement began to agitate naturalists and physicians all over Europe. It was set in motion by the need to find new and immediately effective medicines, and even orthodox traditionalists joined in in some form (usually in attempting to devise a conciliatory and eclectic synopsis of Paracelsian and Galenic practice). Despite opposition and vilification, the influence of Paracelsus and the Paracelsians is apparent in the work of Van Helmont, Boyle, Willis, Sylvius, Stahl, Boerhaave, and others, well into the eighteenth century.

BIBLIOGRAPHY

I. ORIGINAL WORKS. The few works appearing during Paracelsus' lifetime and the first definitive collected ed. by Huser are mentioned in the text. The complete modern and critical ed. of the medical, chemical, metaphysical, and mantic works is Karl Sudhoff, *Theophrast von Hohenheim, genannt Paracelsus, sämtliche Werke*, 14 vols. (Munich, 1922–1933). An index to the Sudhoff ed. is found in Martin Müller, *Registerband zu Sudhoffs Paracelsus Gesamtausgabe* (Einsiedeln, 1960), which is *Nova acta paracelsica*, supp. (1960). Of the planned *Die theologischen und religionswissenschaftlichen Schriften*, only 1 vol. appeared, Wilhelm Matthiessen, ed. (Munich, 1923). It was resumed in a new critical ed. by Kurt Goldammer, of which 6 vols. (of 14 planned) have appeared (Wiesbaden, 1955–1973). An annotated version of the Huser quarto ed. in modern German appeared under the name of B. Aschner, 4 vols. (Jena, 1926–1932); a "study ed." of the most important works in slightly modernized form by Will-E. Peuckert, 5 vols. (Basel–Stuttgart, 1965–1968); and an annotated digest by J. Strebel, 8 vols. (St. Gall, 1944–1949).

Modern individual eds. and translations of single or several treatises include A. E. Waite, *The Hermetic and Alchemical Writings of Paracelsus the Great*, 2 vols. (London, 1894; repr. 1966); Franz Strunz, *Das Buch Paragranum* (Jena, 1903), and *Volumen und Opus Paramirum* (Jena, 1904); H. E. Sigerist et al., *Four Treatises of Theophrastus of Hohenheim* (Baltimore, 1941); K. Leidecker, *Volumen Medicinae Paramirum*, which is *Bulletin of the History of Medicine*, supp. 3 (Baltimore, 1949); Kurt Goldammer, *Paracelsus. Sozial-ethische und sozialpolitische Schriften* (Tübingen, 1952); K. Goldammer et al., *Die Kärntner Schriften* (Klagenfurt, 1955); Robert Blaser, *Theophrastus von Hohenheim, Liber de nymphis, sylphis, pygmaeis et salamandris et caeteris spiritibus* (Bern, 1960), Altdeutsche Übungstexte, XVI; K. Goldammer and K.-H. Weimann, *Paracelsus vom Licht der Natur und des Geistes* (Leipzig, 1960), *Labyrinthus medicorum* and selected theological treatises with bibliography and critical notes; Paul F. Cranefield and W. Federn, "Paracelsus on Goitre and Cretinism," in *Bulletin of the History of Medicine*, **37** (1963), 463–471; K. Goldammer, *Das Buch der Erkanntnus des Theophrast von Hohenheim. Aus der Handschrift mit einer Einleitung* (Berlin, 1964), Texte des Späten Mittelalters, XVIII; Paul F. Cranefield and W. Federn, "The Begetting of Fools. An Annotated Translation of Paracelsus, De generatione Stultorum," in *Bulletin of the History of Medicine*, **41** (1967), 56–74, 161–174.

II. SECONDARY LITERATURE. Biographical material may be found in W. Artelt et al., *Theophrastus Paracelsus*, F. Jaeger, ed. (Salzburg, 1941); K. Bittel, *Paracelsus-Museum, Stuttgart. Paracelsus-Dokumentation. Referatenblätter* (Stuttgart, 1943); R. H. Blaser, "Neue Erkenntnisse zur Basler Zeit des Paracelsus," in *Nova acta Paracelsica*, supp. VI (Einsiedeln, 1953); R. J. Hartmann, *Theophrast von Hohenheim* (Stuttgart–Berlin, 1905); E. Schubert and K. Sudhoff, *Paracelsus-Forschungen*, 2 vols. (Frankfurt, 1887–1889); K. Sudhoff, *Paracelsus. Ein deutsches Lebensbild aus den Tagen der Renaissance* (Leipzig, 1936); and E. Wickersheimer, "Paracelse à Strasbourg," in *Centaurus*, **1** (1951), 356–365, which includes documentation concerning Paracelsus' doctorate (?) at Ferrara.

Literary criticism and a bibliography of the corpus of Paracelsian writings, together with a discussion of questions of authenticity, can be found in K. Sudhoff, *Versuch einer Kritik der Echtheit der Paracelsischen Schriften*, 2 vols. (Berlin, 1894–1899). Vol. I, *Bibliographia Paracelsica* (repr. Graz, 1958), contains a complete annotated catalog and collation of all works issued under Paracelsus' name from 1527 to 1893. Vol. II, *Paracelsus Handschriften*, contains an analysis and collation of letters, documents, and MSS of treatises on medical, chemical, alchemical, theological, and magical subjects (there are no autographs other than of letters, recipes, and documents).

A bibliography of secondary Paracelsian literature is given in K. Sudhoff, *Nachweise zur Paracelsus Literatur* (Munich, 1932), continued in K.-H. Weimann, *Paracelsus-Bibliographie 1932–1960. Mit einem Verzeichnis neuentdecker Paracelsus Handschriften* (Wiesbaden, 1963), which is vol. II of K. Goldammer, ed., *Kosmosophie*.

Paracelsus' doctrines and sources are discussed in K. Goldammer, "Der Beitrag des Paracelsus zur neuen wissenschaftlichen Methodologie und zur Erkenntnislehre," in *Medizin-historisches Journal*, 1 (1966), 75–95; "Die Paracelsische Kosmologie und Materietheorie in ihrer wissenschaftsgeschichtlichen Stellung und Eigenart," *ibid.*, 6 (1971), 5–35; and "Bemerkungen zur Struktur des Kosmos und der Materie bei Paracelsus," in *Medizingeschichte in unserer Zeit. Festgabe für Edith Heischkel und Walter Artelt* (Stuttgart, 1971), 121–144; C. G. Jung, *Paracelsica* (Zurich-Leipzig, 1942); Walter Pagel, "Religious Motives in the Medical Biology of the XVIIth Century," in *Bulletin of the Institute of History of Medicine, Johns Hopkins University*, 3 (1935), 97–312; *Paracelsus—Introduction to Philosophical Medicine in the Era of the Renaissance* (Basel–New York, 1958), trans. into French by M. Deutsch (Paris, 1963); "Paracelsus and Techellus the Jew," in *Bulletin of the History of Medicine*, 34 (1960), 274–277; "Paracelsus and the Neoplatonic and Gnostic Tradition," in *Ambix*, 8 (1960), 125–166; "The Prime Matter of Paracelsus," *ibid.*, 9 (1961), 117–135; *Das medizinische Weltbild des Paracelsus. Seine Zusammenhänge mit Neuplatonismus und Gnosis* (Wiesbaden, 1962), which is vol. I of K. Goldammer, ed., *Kosmosophie*; "The Wild Spirit (Gas) of J. B. Van Helmont (1579–1644) and Paracelsus," in *Ambix*, 10 (1962), 1–13; "Paracelsus' aether-ähnliche Substanzen und ihre pharmakologische Auswertung an Hühnern. Sprachgebrauch (*henbane*) und Konrad von Megenbergs *Buch der Natur* als mögliche Quellen," in *Gesnerus*, 21 (1964), 113–125: "Paracelsus: Traditionalism and Mediaeval Sources," in *Medicine, Science and Culture. Historical Essays in Honor of Owsei Temkin* (Baltimore, 1968), 51–75; and "Van Helmont's Concept of Disease—to be or not to be? The Influence of Paracelsus," in *Bulletin of the History of Medicine*, 46 (1972), 419–454.

See also Walter Pagel and P. Rattansi, "Vesalius and Paracelsus," in *Medical History*, 8 (1964), 309–328; Walter Pagel and Marianne Winder, "Gnostisches bei Paracelsus und Konrad von Megenberg," in *Fachliteratur des Mittelalters. Festschrift für Gerhard Eis* (Stuttgart,

1968), 359–371; "The Eightness of Adam and Related 'Gnostic' Ideas in the Paracelsian Corpus," in *Ambix*, 16 (1969), 119–139; and "The Higher Elements and Prime Matter in Renaissance Naturalism and the Paracelsian Corpus," in *Ambix*, 21 (in press); and O. Temkin, "The Elusiveness of Paracelsus," in *Bulletin of the History of Medicine*, 26 (1952), 201–217.

The moral philosophy, sociology, and theology of Paracelsus are discussed in K. Goldammer, "Paracelsische Eschatologie," in *Nova acta Paracelsica*, 5 (1948), 45–85, and 6 (1954), 3–37; *Paracelsus. Natur und Offenbarung* (Hannover, 1953); *Paracelsus-Studien* (Klagenfurt, 1954); "Das theologische Werk des Paracelsus," in *Nova acta Paracelsica*, 7 (1954), 78–102; and "Friedensidee und Toleranzgedanke bei Paracelsus und den Spiritualisten," in *Archiv für Reformationsgeschichte*, 47 (1956), 20–46, 180–212. See also Bodo Sartorius von Waltershausen, *Paracelsus am Eingang der Deutschen Bildungsgeschichte* (Leipzig, 1936).

Critical assessments of Paracelsus' achievements in medicine and chemistry are in E. Darmstaedter, *Arznei und Alchemie. Paracelsus-Studien* (Leipzig, 1931), which is vol. XX in the series Studien zur Geschichte der Medizin; and "Paracelsus 'De natura rerum,'" in *Janus*, 37 (1933), 1–18, 48–62, 109–115, 323–324; F. Dobler, "Chemische Arzneibereitung bei Paracelsus am Beispiel seiner Antimonpräparate," in *Pharmaceutica acta helvetiae*, 37 (1957), 181–193, 226–252; W. Ganzenmüller, "Paracelsus und die Alchemie des Mittelalters," in *Angewandte Chemie*, 54 (1941), 417–431, repr. in his *Beiträge zur Geschichte der Technologie und Alchemie* (Weinheim, 1956), 300–314; R. Hooykaas, "Die Elementenlehre des Paracelsus," in *Janus*, 39 (1935), 175–187; "Die Elementenlehre der Iatrochemiker," *ibid.*, 41 (1937), 1–28; and "Chemical Trichotomy Before Paracelsus?," in *Archives internationales d'histoire des sciences*, 28 (1949), 1063–1074; R. Multhauf, "Medical Chemistry and the Paracelsians," in *Bulletin of the History of Medicine*, 28 (1954), 101–126; "J. B. Van Helmont's Reformation of the Galenic Doctrine of Digestion," *ibid.*, 29 (1955), 154–163; and "The Significance of Distillation in Renaissance Medical Chemistry," *ibid.*, 30 (1956), 329–346; W. Pagel, "J. B. Van Helmont's Reformation of the Galenic Doctrine of Digestion—and Paracelsus," *ibid.*, 29 (1955), 563–568; and "Van Helmont's Ideas on Gastric Digestion and the Gastric Acid," *ibid.*, 30 (1956), 524–536; J. R. Partington, *A History of Chemistry*, II (London, 1961), 115–151; J. K. Proksch, *Paracelsus über die venerischen Krankheiten und die Hydrargyrose* (Vienna, 1882); *Paracelsus als medizinischer Schriftsteller* (Vienna–Leipzig, 1911); and *Zur Paracelsus-Forschung* (Vienna–Leipzig, 1912); W. Schneider, "Der Wandel des Arzneischatzes im 17. Jahrhundert und Paracelsus," in *Sudhoffs Archiv für Geschichte der Medizin und der Naturwissenschaften*, 45 (1961), 201–215; "Grundlagen für Paracelsus' Arzneitherapie," *ibid.*, 49 (1965), 28–36; and "Paracelsus und die Entwickelung der pharmazeutischen Chemie," in *Archiv der Pharmazie*, 299 (1967), 737–746; and *Geschichte der pharmazeutische Chemie* (Weinheim, 1973); T. P. Sherlock, "The Chemical

Work of Paracelsus," in *Ambix*, **3** (1948), 33–63; G. Urdang, "How Chemicals Entered the Official Pharmacopoeias," in *Archives internationales d'histoire des sciences*, **7** (1954), 303–314; and P. Walden, "Paracelsus als Chemiker," in *Angewandte Chemie*, **54** (1941), 421–427.

Paracelsus' influence is discussed in Allen G. Debus, "The Paracelsian Compromise in Elizabethan England," in *Ambix*, **8** (1960), 71–97; "Solution Analyses Prior to Robert Boyle," in *Chymia*, **8** (1962), 41–61; "The Paracelsian Aerial Niter," in *Isis*, **55** (1964), 43–61; "An Elizabethan History of Medical Chemistry," in *Annals of Science*, **18** (1962), 1–29; and *The English Paracelsians* (London, 1965); P. M. Rattansi, "Paracelsus and the Puritan Revolution," in *Ambix*, **11** (1963), 24–32; Dietlinde Goltz, *Studien zur Geschichte der Mineralnamen in Pharmazie, Chemie und Medizin von den Anfängen bis auf Paracelsus* (Wiesbaden, 1972), which was supp. in *Sudhoffs Archiv für Geschichte der Medizin und der Naturwissenschaften*, **14**; and Audrey B. Davis, *Circulation Physiology and Medical Chemistry in England 1650–1680* (Lawrence, Kansas, 1973).

WALTER PAGEL

PARAMEŚVARA (*b*. Ālattūr, Kerala, India, *ca*. 1380; *d*. *ca*. 1460), *astronomy*.

Parameśvara was born into a learned Nampūtiri Brāhmaṇa family of Kerala, which belonged to the Bhṛgugotra and followed the Āśvalāyanasūtra of the *Ṛgveda*. His father remains obscure, but his grandfather studied under the astrologer Govindabhaṭṭa of Ālattūr (1236–1314). The family resided in an *illam* ("house") called Vaṭaśśeri (Vaṭaśreṇi) in the village of Ālattūr (Aśvatthagrāma) on the north bank of the river Nīlā at its mouth in Kerala. Parameśvara states that this place lies eighteen *yojanas* west of the meridian of Ujjain, and that the sine of its latitude is 647 (with R = 3,438); its latitude, then, is 10°51′N.

Parameśvara names Rudra as his teacher. Nīlakaṇṭha (*b*. 1444), the pupil of his son Dāmodara, states that Parameśvara studied under Nārāyaṇa and Mādhava; the latter was a well-known astronomer of Saṅgamagrāma in Kerala who lived between *ca*. 1340 and *ca*. 1425. Parameśvara's dates are fixed not only by the epochs of his several astronomical works, but also by his eclipse observations which extended from 1393 to 1432 (see D. Pingree, in *Journal of the American Oriental Society*, **87** [1967], 337–339). His latest recorded observation was made in 1445, although he states in a verse cited by Nīlakaṇṭha that he made observations for fifty-five years—that is, until 1448 if the observations commenced in 1393. Since Nīlakaṇṭha, who was born in 1444, knew him personally, Parameśvara could not have died much before 1460.

Parameśvara's greatest achievements were the revisions of the accepted parameters of planetary motions, the *parahita* that were based on the *Āryabhaṭīya* of Āryabhaṭa I (*b*. 476), and the accepted procedure of eclipse-computations on the basis of his observations. He called this new system the *dṛggaṇita* (see essay in Supplement). He was also active in the composition of commentaries on the standard astronomical texts that were in use in Kerala.

BIBLIOGRAPHY

I. ORIGINAL WORKS. Parameśvara's works include the following. *Parameśvara* (*ca*. 1408), B. D. Āpaṭe, ed. (Poona, 1946), is a commentary on the *Laghubhāskarīya* of Bhāskara I (*fl*. 629); *Grahaṇamaṇḍana*, K. V. Sarma, ed. (Hoshiarpur, 1965), is a treatise on eclipses, of which an earlier version contained 87 verses, and a later 100; the epoch is 15 July 1411. The *Dṛggaṇita* (1431), K. V. Sarma, ed. (Hoshiarpur, 1963), gives his new parameters, which modify those of the *parahita* system. The work contains new parameters of mean motions of the planets, of their mean longitudes at the beginning of the Kaliyuga, and of their two equations, and a table of their equations at intervals of 6° of argument. It also mentions the *Grahaṇamaṇḍana*. Nīlakaṇṭha in the *Āryabhaṭīyabhāṣya* written after 1501 understood the fifty-five years of Parameśvara's observations to antedate the *Dṛggaṇita*, but this would make him nearly a century old in Nīlakaṇṭha's own youth.

The *Siddhāntadīpikā*, published by T. S. Kuppanna Sastri (Madras, 1957), is a commentary on the *Bhāṣya*, written by Govindasvāmin (*fl*. *ca*. 800–850) on the *Mahābhāskarīya* of Bhāskara I (*fl*. 629). In this work Parameśvara cites the series of eclipse observations (including one at Nāvākṣetra in 1422 and two at Gokarṇa in 1425 and 1430), which extended from 1393 to 1432. The *Grahaṇanyāyadīpikā*, K. V. Sarma, ed. (Hoshiarpur, 1966), discusses eclipse theory in eighty-five verses and cites both the *Grahaṇamaṇḍana* and the *Siddhāntadīpikā*. The first *Goladīpikā* (1443) contains four chapters that deal respectively with the armillary sphere, the motions of the planets, geography, and gnomon-problems. It was edited with Parameśvara's own commentary, *Vivṛti*, by K. V. Sarma (Madras, 1957). *Grahaṇāṣṭaka*, a short treatise in ten verses, gives the fundamental information required for the computation of eclipses. It was edited by K. V. Sarma, in *Journal of Oriental Research, Madras*, **28** (1958–1959), 47–60.

Other works include *Vākyakaraṇa*, an unpublished treatise on the *vākya* system of astronomy (see essay in Supplement); *Bhaṭadīpikā*, H. Kern, ed. (Leiden, 1874), a commentary on the *Āryabhaṭīya* of Āryabhaṭa I (*b*. 476); *Vivaraṇa*, an unpublished commentary on the *Līlāvatī* of Bhāskara II (*b*. 1115); and *Karmadīpikā*, B. Āpaṭe, ed. (Poona, 1945), is a commentary on the *Mahābhāskarīya* of Bhāskara I (*fl*. 629), in which Parameśvara mentions his *Siddhāntadīpikā*, his *Vākyadīpikā* (= *Vākyakaraṇa*), his (*Grahaṇa*)*nyāyadīpikā*, his *Goladīpikā*, and his *Bhaṭadīpikā*, and also two lost works: a *Muhūrtāṣṭakadīpikā* on astrology and a *Bhādīpikā*.

Vivaraṇa is a commentary on the *Sūryasiddhānta*, K. S. Shukla, ed. (Lucknow, 1957), in which the amount of precession is reckoned for 1432. This *Vivaraṇa* refers to his *Pārameśvara* on the *Laghubhāskarīya*, his *Siddhāntadīpikā*, his *Līlāvatīvivaraṇa*, and his *Karmadīpikā*. The *Pārameśvara*, B. D. Āpaṭe, ed. (Poona, 1952), is a commentary on the *Laghumānasa* of Muñjāla (*fl.* 932). A second *Goladīpikā*, T. G. Śāstrī, ed. (Trivandrum, 1916), consists of 302 verses and discusses a number of problems that relate to the celestial spheres. In this work Parameśvara refers to his *Siddhāntadīpikā*, to his first *Goladīpikā*, and to his *Karmadīpikā*. A *Jātakapaddhati*, K. S. Menon, ed. (Trivandrum, n.d.), is on horoscopes; and an unpublished commentary, *Vṛtti*, is on the *Vyatīpātāṣṭaka*, which is a work on the *pātas* of the sun and moon. A number of astrological works by Parameśvara exist in MSS in South India: *Ācārasaṅgraha*, a commentary on the *Muhūrtaratna* of Govindabhaṭṭa (1236–1314), the teacher of Parameśvara's grandfather; a commentary on the *Jātakapaddhati* of Śrīpati (*fl.* 1040); and a commentary on the *Ṣaṭpañcāśikā* of Pṛthuyaśas (*fl. ca.* 575).

II. SECONDARY LITERATURE. The best source of information on Parameśvara is in the introductions to K. V. Sarma's works. Unfortunately, there is as yet no study of how Parameśvara's observations affected his astronomy. A brief summary of what was then known about him is given by K. K. Raja, "Astronomy and Mathematics in Kerala," in *Brahmavidyā*, **27** (1963), 118–167, esp. 136–143.

DAVID PINGREE

PARDIES, IGNACE GASTON (*b.* Pau, France, 5 September 1636; *d.* Paris, France, 21 April 1673), *physics*.

A Jesuit, Pardies deserves a place in the history of physics for having intervened in the debate on the ideas of Newton and of Huygens at certain decisive moments. His work, which is not extensive, is characteristic of a transitional period. The establishment of the Jesuits at Pau in 1622 determined the course of Pardies's life. His Christian name resulted from the friendship of his father, a royal counselor at the Parlement of Navarre, for the Jesuits. It was at their *collège* that he began his studies.

After finishing his secondary education in 1652, Pardies decided to become a Jesuit. He entered into the novitiate and with it the remarkably well-organized network of Jesuit studies and schools. From 1654 to 1656 at Toulouse he completed the philosophical phase of the curriculum by the study of logic and physics. From 1656 to 1660 he taught humanities at Bordeaux. After studying theology, he was ordained a priest in 1663 and was admitted to the order in 1665.

During the remaining eight years of his life Pardies taught at La Rochelle (1666–1668), Bordeaux (1668–1670), and the Collège Clermont in Paris (1670–1673). During this period he demonstrated his ability to conduct scientific research while teaching—without neglecting his clerical duties. Indeed, it was while carrying out his ministry at the hospital of Bicêtre during the Easter season of 1673 that he contracted a fatal illness.

"As good a cleric as a scientist," according to the Jesuit chronicler of the *Mémoires de Trévoux* (1726), Pardies nevertheless presented a problem to his order. From the time of his appointment at La Rochelle his superiors distrusted him because he was known "to pursue strange opinions avidly," and until his death he was continually obliged to compromise his true views on philosophy and science, to the point that they cannot be established with certainty.

Pardies's first work, *Horologium thaumanticum duplex*, dates from 1652; it is not known whether it was ever published. He discussed the subject more completely in a treatise published in 1673. His correspondence from 1661 to 1665 with Kircher offers insight into the source of his initial inspiration, the influence of Maignan on him, and reveals the originality of his "two marvelous clocks." This originality consists not only in the optical device—a cone receiving light on its base that transformed a stopped-down pencil of solar rays into a luminous plane perpendicular to this pencil; its originality is also reflected in the use of this plane, which rotated with the sun, with either a sundial or a translucent terrestrial sphere. Thus, while still a student of theology, Pardies was engaged in scientific research at a level indicating that he possessed a good education, keen intelligence, and skill in handling instruments.

These qualities also marked his subsequent work. In *Discours du mouvement local* (1670), *Élémens de géométrie* (1671), and *La statique ou la science des forces mouvantes* (1673) he presented his material tersely and suggestively. Despite certain inadequacies (notably his account of the laws of impact) it is easy to see in these writings a striving for the most economical axioms obtained through rational reflection on empirical data. During this period Pardies also wrote works of a more philosophical character; the titles indicate criticism of Descartes and reveal how greatly their author felt the need to clarify his position. *Discours du mouvement local* was published with additional remarks designed to counter the charge of Cartesianism. Yet although Pardies clearly derived a great deal from the Cartesian heritage and felt obliged to defend himself in this regard, Cartesianism was not his principal source. Through the *Philosophical Transactions of the Royal Society* he was directly informed of the advances of English science (quadrature of the hyperbola and the competition concerning the laws of impact); and in Paris he closely followed the work of the newly established Académie Royale des Sciences and especially that of Huygens, with whom he was in personal contact.

Pardies's last book offers more of his ideas, which were based on knowledge derived from widely different sources. It contains, for example, his critical study of Descartes's letter to Beeckman on the speed of light (1634) and his demonstration of the tautochronism of the cycloidal pendulum.

Hindered by the philosophical climate, Pardies made his most important scientific contribution not in his writings, but in his correspondence. It is there that we find the objections that Pardies expressed to Newton concerning his theory of colors and the *experimentum crucis*—objections that enabled Newton to clarify certain difficult points. Pardies's unpublished manuscripts contain a theory of waves and vibrations that—judging from the fragments presented by Pierre Ango in 1682—might well have played an important role in the development of physics.

Although Pardies did not have the time to devote the full measure of his abilities to science, he was undoubtedly one of those vigorous intellects that science always needs, along with great discoverers, especially in an age of transition. That he was just such an intellect is evident from his pedagogical writings and his contacts with the pioneers of physics. Leibniz' impression of him confirms this view. A member of the great line of Jesuit scientists that persisted throughout the seventeenth century, he was, to a greater degree than his predecessors, embroiled in philosophical disputes. Beneath the Aristotelian language that he sometimes sought to preserve, new meanings emerge. His notions, as bold as they were naïve, purported to demonstrate the spirituality of the soul by virtue of its capacity to understand the infinite through the "clear and distinct ideas" of certain geometric arguments.

BIBLIOGRAPHY

I. ORIGINAL WORKS. Pardies's writings include *Horologium thaumanticum duplex* (? Paris, 1662); *Dissertatio de motu et natura cometarum* (Bordeaux, 1665); *Theses mathematicae ex mechanica* (Bordeaux, 1669); *Discours du mouvement local* (Paris, 1670), also translated into English (London, 1670); *Élémens de géométrie* (Paris, 1671), also translated into Dutch (Amsterdam, 1690),

Latin (Jena, 1693), and English (London, 1746); *Discours de la connaissance des bestes* (Paris, 1672); *Lettre d'un philosophe à un cartésien de ses amis* (Paris, 1672); *La créance des miracles* (Paris, 1673); *Deux machines propres à faire les quadrans avec une très grande facilité* (Paris, 1673); *La statique ou la science des forces mouvantes* (Paris, 1673); *Atlas céleste* (Paris, 1674); and *Oeuvres de mathématiques* (Paris, 1691, 1694, 1701, 1721).

Letters written by Pardies or concerning him can be found in *The Correspondence of Isaac Newton*, H. W. Turnbull, ed., I (Cambridge, 1959); *Oeuvres complètes de Huygens*, VI-VIII, *passim*; and *The Correspondence of Henry Oldenburg*, R. Hall and M. Hall, eds., VIII. Portions of his correspondence remain unpublished.

II. SECONDARY LITERATURE. See Pierre Ango, S.J., *L'optique* (Paris, 1682), which draws on Pardies's MSS; and the unsigned article in *Mémoires pour servir à l'histoire des sciences et des beaux-arts (Mémoires de Trévoux)* (Apr. 1726), 667–668. August Ziggelaar, S.J., *Le physicien Ignace Gaston Pardies S.J. (1636–1673)*, vol. XXVI of Bibliotheca Universitatis Havniensis (Odense, 1971), contains the most complete documentation available and eliminates the need to present a more detailed listing of secondary works here.

PIERRE COSTABEL

PARÉ, AMBROISE (*b.* Laval, Mayenne, France, 1510 [?]; *d.* Paris, France, 22 December 1590), *surgery*.

Paré was the son of an artisan. He served an apprenticeship to a barber-surgeon in the provinces (probably at Angers or Vitré), then went to Paris, where he became house surgical student at the Hôtel-Dieu, a post that provided him a valuable opportunity to study anatomy by dissection. About 1536 Paré became a master barber-surgeon and entered military service under Maréchal Montejan; he accompanied the army on an expedition to Italy, where he spent two years. He returned to Paris in 1539, but intermittently participated in military campaigns throughout most of the next three decades. In 1552 Henry II appointed him one of his *chirurgiens ordinaires*; he became *premier chirurgien* to Charles IX in 1562 and served Henry III in the same capacity. He had a flourishing practice at court and in Paris, and, as a military surgeon, treated the wounded of both sides during the Wars of Religion. (Although often reported to have been a Huguenot, Paré remained a Roman Catholic throughout his life.)

Military practice afforded Paré experience in treating a wide variety of injuries. In particular, he revolutionized the treatment of gunshot wounds, which had been considered to be poisonous and were routinely cauterized with boiling oil. At the siege of Turin in 1536, Paré (according to his own account, published almost half a century later) ran out of hot oil and instead used a "digestive" dressing composed of egg yolk, oil of roses, and turpentine. The following day, he noted that the soldiers who had had their wounds dressed in this improvised manner were recovering better than the soldiers treated by the conventional method; they were free from pain, and their wounds were neither inflamed nor swollen. Paré then experimented with a number of different dressings (including some containing *aqua vitae*, which would, together with turpentine, have acted as a topical antiseptic) and concluded that gunshot wounds were not in themselves poisonous, and did not require cautery. He reported his discovery in his first treatise, *La méthode de traicter les playes faites par les arquebuses et aultres bastons à feu*, published in 1545. This treatise, written in the vernacular because Paré knew no Latin, brought him immediate fame.

Paré also rejected cautery as a method of achieving hemostasis and advocated the ligature of blood vessels to control hemorrhage during amputations. He devised a new instrument for this purpose—the "crow's beak," a sort of hemostat that he used to grasp the vessels to be ligated. His obstetrical surgery was also innovative, and he revived the ancient technique of podalic version for difficult deliveries. (Paré's method was widely used after his own time; one of his chief disciples, Jacques Guillemeau, was primarily an obstetrician, and his influence on French surgeon-obstetricians extended throughout the seventeenth century.)

Paré's motto was "Je le pensai, Dieu le guarist"—"I dressed him, God cured him." Many of the details of his surgery are no longer of scientific interest; despite his innovations, he labored under the humoral theories and superstitions common to sixteenth-century surgery and was ignorant of such considerations as circulation of the blood and asepsis. Nonetheless, he saved many patients who would be the despair of a modern surgeon, and he came to represent the ideal practitioner, both for his technical competence and for his humanitarian concern for his patients. He had a vague, reasoned anticipation of some form of transmissible infection and a crude appreciation of public health measures. Although his knowledge of pathology was at best rudimentary, he advocated and practiced (and left records of) autopsy investigations of fatal illnesses.

Paré's theories and writings were often in opposition to those of the university authorities. He desired to spread anatomical knowledge among his fellow barber-surgeons, and to this end performed dissections and wrote a number of works on anatomy. His use of the vernacular and the advent of the printing press assured his books a wide distribution, although they were published, for the most part, only after legal conflicts with the members of the Paris Faculty of Medicine, who wished to suppress them. Paré was, however, widely supported by his noble clientele, and their support brought him the acceptance of professional associations that were usually closed to all except university graduates. (He was, for example, invited to join the guild of academic surgeons of Paris in the Collège de Saint-Côme, despite his lack of Latin—although the physicians and the Faculty of Medicine always scorned and snubbed him.)

Paré's personal life was marked by honesty, piety, and concern for the poor and defenseless. His last recorded act is his having, at the age of eighty, stopped a religious procession in the streets of Paris so that he might plead with its leader, the archbishop of Lyons, to come to terms with Henry of Navarre (later Henry IV), who was then besieging the city. Paré hoped thus to alleviate the lot of the starving Parisians, and whether or not his unprecedented act exerted any influence, the siege was lifted about a week later. He died shortly thereafter, in the house in which he had lived throughout most of his active career. He was buried in his parish church, St. André-des-Artes (destroyed in 1807, in which year Paré's bones were transferred to the catacombs). Twice married, Paré had nine children, of whom three daughters survived him.

Paré left a powerfully reactivated surgical tradition at his death. His many publications, which were translated into both Latin and modern languages, circulated throughout Europe, and had considerable influence during his life and well into the following century. But in France itself surgeons were again under the Hippocratic yoke within two generations, and the art of surgery had reverted to about the level at which Paré had found it. Part of the blame for this must be attached to the reactionary character of French academic medicine, and to the prevailing moral and religious antipathy toward the scientific principle; the reforms for which Paré struggled did not come until both the Collège de Saint-Côme and the once powerful and privileged Faculty of Medicine were abolished in the French Revolution.

BIBLIOGRAPHY

Paré's writings have been collated and described in Janet Doe, *A Bibliography of the Works of Ambroise Paré; Premier Chirurgien et Conseiller du Roy* (Chicago, 1937). His best books are in J. F. Malgaigne, *Oeuvres complètes d'Ambroise Paré*, 3 vols. (Paris, 1840). Accounts of Paré's life and works are available in W. B. Hamby, *The Case Reports and Autopsy Records of Ambroise Paré* (Springfield, Ill., 1960), *Surgery and Ambroise Paré* (Norman, Okla., 1965), trans. and ed. from J. F. Malgaigne, *op cit.*, and

Ambroise Paré; Surgeon of the Renaissance (St. Louis, Mo., 1967). See also G. Keynes, ed., *The Apologie and Treatise of Ambroise Paré, Containing the Voyages Made Into Divers Places With Many of His Writings Upon Surgery* (Chicago, 1952); F. P. Packard, ed., *The Life and Times of Ambroise Paré* (New York, 1926); and Stephen Paget, *Ambroise Paré and His Times: 1510–1590* (New York–London, 1897).

WALLACE B. HAMBY

PARENAGO, PAVEL PETROVICH (*b*. Ekaterinodar [now Krasnodar], Russia, 20 March 1906; *d*. Moscow, U.S.S.R., 5 January 1960), *astronomy*.

The son of a physician and surgeon, Parenago lived in Moscow from 1912. He graduated from secondary school in 1922 and, seven years later, from the Faculty of Physics and Mathematics of the University of Moscow. The sudden appearance in 1920 of a nova in the constellation Cygnus aroused Parenago's interest in the observation of variable stars. He began his scientific work as a serious observer of variable stars in 1921–1922. In 1925, while still a student, Parenago became a computer at the Astrophysical Institute, which in 1931 became part of the P. K. Sternberg State Astronomical Institute at the University of Moscow. From 1932 he was a senior scientific worker.

Parenago began teaching in 1930 as an assistant at the Steel Institute, then was a lecturer in the department of mathematics. In 1935 he was awarded a doctorate in the physical and mathematical sciences without defense of a dissertation. In 1937 Parenago became a lecturer, and in 1938 professor, in the department of astronomy of the Faculty of Mechanics and Mathematics of the University of Moscow. From 1940 he was the head of the department of stellar astronomy there, which had been organized on his initiative. He gave courses in stellar astronomy, spherical astronomy, probability theory and mathematical analysis of observations, and stellar dynamics. In 1953 he was elected corresponding member of the Soviet Academy of Sciences.

Parenago began his scientific career with photometric research on variable stars—first visually and then from photographs in the collection at the Moscow and Simeiz observatories—in all he investigated more than 600 variable stars. He subsequently advanced to a study of all the properties of variable stars, including their motion. He discovered statistical relationships of their physical and kinematic properties to their spatial distribution in the galaxy, and investigated the use of variable stars in studying its structure. For these purposes he collected and systematized a vast amount of observational material that reflected all aspects of contemporary knowledge of the stars. The foremost Soviet stellar astronomer, Parenago was head of a school of specialists in this field and the organizer of the first department of stellar astronomy in the Soviet Union. His textbook *Kurs zvezdnoy astronomii* ("Course of Stellar Astronomy") went through three editions (1938, 1946, and 1954) and was translated into some foreign languages.

The numerous investigations of variable stars by Parenago and other Moscow astronomers and their rich collection of references to the existing world literature led the Executive Committee of the International Astronomical Union in 1946 to commission them to name new variable stars and to compile and edit *Obshchy katalog peremennykh zvezd* ("General Catalog of Variable Stars"). Parenago was coauthor of its two editions (1948, 1958) and of the first edition of *Katalog zvezd, zapodozrennykh v peremennosti* ("Catalog of Stars Suspected of Being Variable"; 1951). His long monograph, *Fizicheskie peremennye zvezdy* ("Physical Variable Stars"; 1937), written with B. V. Kukarkin, and the popular *Peremennye zvezdy i sposoby ikh nablyudenia* ("Variable Stars and Methods of Observing Them"; 1938; 2nd ed., 1947), were of great value for amateur astronomers.

His interest in the structure of the galaxy and in using variable stars as indicators of distance led Parenago to develop a method of taking into account the absorption of light in galactic space by particles of interstellar dust. This method substantially increased the precision of determining galactic distances. A number of important works by Parenago concern the Hertzsprung-Russell diagram (the "spectrum-luminosity" relation and the "mass-radius-luminosity" relation). Parenago also studied the kinematics of stars and stellar dynamics. With Kukarkin he developed and published a new, evolutionary meaning for the concept of subsystems of various objects in the galaxy; and, using extensive statistical material, he obtained fundamental quantitative properties of these subsystems and provided a method for evaluating the total number of objects in each of them. Parenago studied the law of rotation of the galaxy and its spiral structure. He also developed a new theory of galactic potential (that is, of the law of the variation of the force of galactic attraction with the distance from the center of the galaxy) and the theory of the galactic orbit of stars and the sun. He published 225 works, more than 40 reviews, and more than 150 popular articles and books.

From 1947 to 1951 Parenago was president of the Moscow Astronomical and Geodetic Society. In 1949 he received the Bredikhin Prize of the Soviet

Academy of Sciences for a series of works on the structure of the galaxy. He was awarded the Order of Lenin in 1951. Parenago was a member of the International Astronomical Union and participated in a number of international and Soviet congresses and scientific conferences.

BIBLIOGRAPHY

I. ORIGINAL WORKS. Parenago's writings of the 1930's are "O periode i krivoy izmenenia yarkosti SW Cygni" ("On the Period and Curve of the Variation of Brightness of SW Cygni"), in *Astronomicheskii zhurnal*, 8, nos. 3–4 (1931), 229–239; "Shkaly zvezdnykh velichin" ("Stellar Magnitude Scales"), in *Uspekhi astronomicheskikh nauk*, 2 (1933), 104–122; "The Catalogue of Parallaxes of Variable Stars," in *Astronomicheskii zhurnal*, 11, no. 1 (1934), 29–39; "Untersuchungen über veränderliche Sterne mit unbekannten Lichtwechsel," in *Peremennye zvezdy*, 4, no. 9 (1934), 301–317; "O vrashchenii Urana vokrug osi" ("On the Rotation of Uranus Around Its Axis"), in *Astronomicheskii zhurnal*, 11, no. 5 (1934), 487–496; "The Shapes of Light Curves of Long-Period Cepheids," in *Zeitschrift für Astrophysik*, 11, no. 5 (1936), 337–355, written with B. V. Kukarkin; "The Mass-Luminosity Relation," in *Astronomicheskii zhurnal*, 14, no. 1 (1937), 33–48; "Standard Light Curves of Cepheids," *ibid.*, 14, no. 3 (1937), 181–193, written with B. V. Kukarkin; "Issledovania izmeneny bleska 208 peremennykh zvezd (1920–1937)" ("Research on the Variations in Brightness of 208 Variable Stars"), in *Trudy Gosudarstvennogo astronomicheskogo instituta im. P. K. Shternberga*, 12, iss. 1 (1938), 1–132; "Obobshchennaya zavisimost massa-svetimost" ("Generalized Mass-Luminosity Relation"), in *Astronomicheskii zhurnal*, 16, no. 6 (1939), 7–14; and "Opredelenie galakticheskoy orbity Solntsa" ("Determination of the Galactic Orbit of the Sun"), *ibid.*, 16, no. 4 (1939), 18–24.

During the 1940's Parenago published "Issledovania, osnovannye na svodnom kataloge zvezdnykh parallaksov" ("Researchs Based on the Summary Catalog of Stellar Parallaxes"), in *Trudy Gosudarstvennogo astronomicheskogo instituta im. P. K. Shternberga*, 13, pt. 1 (1940), 59–117; "O temnykh tumannostyakh i pogloshchenii sveta v galaktike" ("On Dark Nebulae and the Absorption of Light in the Galaxy"), in *Astronomicheskii zhurnal*, 17, no. 4 (1940), 1–22, also in *Byulleten Gosudarstvennogo astronomicheskogo instituta im. P. K. Shternberga*, 4 (1940), 3–24; "O diagramme Rassela-Khertsshprunga" ("On the Hertzsprung-Russell Diagram"), in *Astronomicheskii zhurnal*, 21, no. 5 (1944), 223–229; "O mezhzvezdnom pogloshchenii sveta" ("On the Interstellar Absorption of Light"), *ibid.*, 22, no. 3 (1945), 129–150; "Some Works on the Structure of the Galaxy," in *Popular Astronomy*, 53 (1945), 441–446; "Fizicheskie kharakteristiki subkarlikov" ("Physical Characteristics of Subdwarfs"), in *Astronomicheskii zhurnal*, 23, no. 1 (1946), 31–39; "O dvizheniakh sharovykh skopleny" ("On the Motions of Globular Clusters"), *ibid.*, 24, no. 3 (1947), 167–176; "Prostranst-

vennoe dvizhenie peremennykh zvezd tipa RR Lyrae" ("Spatial Motion of Variable Stars of Type RR Lyrae"), in *Peremennye zvezdy*, 6, no. 2 (1948), 79–88; "Shkaly i katalogi zvezdnykh velichin" ("Scales and Catalogs of Stellar Magnitudes"), in *Uspekhi astronomicheskikh nauk*, 2nd ser., 4 (1948), 257–287; and "Stroenie Galaktiki" ("Structure of the Galaxy"), *ibid.*, pp. 69–171, translated into German in *Abhandlungen aus der Sowjetischen Astronomie*, 3 (1953), 7–113.

Writings by Parenago that appeared in the 1950's were "O gravitatsionnom potentsiale Galaktiki" ("On the Gravitational Potential of the Galaxy"), 2 pts., in *Astronomicheskii zhurnal*, 27, no. 6 (1950), 329–340, and 29, no. 3 (1952), 245–287; "Issledovanie prostranstvennykh skorosteyzvezd" ("Research on the Spatial Velocities of Stars"), *ibid.*, no. 3 (1950), 150–168, also in *Trudy Gosudarstvennogo astronomicheskogo instituta im. P. K. Shternberga*, 20 (1951), 26–80; "Issledovanie zavisimosti massa-radius-svetimost. I. Opredelenie empiricheskoy zavisimosti massa-radius-svetimost. II. Teoreticheskaya interpretatsia empiricheskikh zavisimostey" ("Research on the Mass-Radius-Luminosity Relation. I. Determination of the Empirical Mass-Radius-Luminosity Relation. II. Theoretical Interpretation of Empirical Relations"), in *Trudy Gosudarstvennogo astronomicheskogo instituta im. P. K. Shternberga*, 20 (1951), 81–146, written with A. G. Masevich, also in *Astronomicheskii zhurnal*, 27, no. 3 (1950), 137–149, and no. 4 (1950), 202–210; "O gravitatsionnom potentsiale galaktiki. II" ("On the Gravitational Potential of the Galaxy. II"), in *Astronomicheskii zhurnal*, 29, no. 3 (1952), 245–287; "Issledovanie zvezd v oblasti tumannosti Oriona" ("Research on Stars in Areas of Nebulae of Orion"), *ibid.*, 30, no. 3 (1953), 249–264, also in *Byulleten "Peremennye zvezdy,"* 9, no. 2 (1953), 89–93, and in *Trudy Gosudarstvennogo astronomicheskogo instituta im. P. K. Shternberga*, 25 (1954), 1–547; "O spiralnoy strukture galaktiki po radionablyudeniam na volne 21 sm." ("On the Spiral Structure of the Galaxy According to Radio Observations on a Wave of 21 cm."), in *Astronomicheskii zhurnal*, 32, no. 3 (1955), 226–238; "Plan kompleksnogo izuchenia izbrannykh oblastey Mlechnogo Puti" ("Plan of Complex Study of Selected Areas of the Milky Way"), *ibid.*, 33, no. 5 (1956), 749–755; "O kinematike razlichnykh posledovatelnostey na diagramme spektr-svetimost" ("On the Kinematics of Various Sequences in the Spectrum-Luminosity Diagram"), *ibid.*, 35, no. 3 (1958), 488–490; and "The Hertzsprung-Russell Diagram From Photoelectric Observations of Nearby Stars," in J. Greenstein, ed., *The Hertzsprung-Russell Diagram* (Paris, 1959), 11–18.

In 1960 he published "Zvezdnaya astronomia" ("Stellar Astronomy"), in *Astronomia v SSSR za 40 let. 1917–1957* ("Astronomy in the U.S.S.R. for Forty Years . . ."; Moscow, 1960), 227–259.

II. SECONDARY LITERATURE. See *Astronomichesky tsirkulyar SSSR*, no. 169 (1956), 23, on Parenago's 50th birthday; *Astronomicheskii zhurnal*, 37, no. 1 (1960), 191–192, an obituary; *Bolshaya sovetskaya entsiklopedia*, 2nd ed., XXXII (1955), 88; B. V. Kukarkin, "P. P. Parenago

(1906–1960)," in *Peremennye zvezdy*, **13**, no. 1 (1960), 3–5; D. Y. Martynov, *Astronomichesky kalendar na 1951 g.* ("Astronomical Calendar for 1951"; Gorky, 1951), 144–145, on Parenago's receiving the Bredikhin Prize; "P. P. Parenago (1906–1960)," in *Istoriko-astronomicheskie issledovania*, no. 7 (1961), 335–394, which consists of articles by B. A. Vorontsov-Velyaminov, B. V. Kukarkin, A. S. Sharov, and F. A. Tsitsin, and a bibliography of Parenago's works; A. S. Sharov, "On the Photometric Catalogue of Stars in the Region of Orion Nebulae, Compiled by P. P. Parenago," in *Astronomical Journal*, **66**, no. 2 (1961), 103; and W. Zonn, "Pavel Petrowich Parenago," in *Postępy astronomii*, **8**, no. 3 (1960), 175.

P. G. KULIKOVSKY

PARENT, ANTOINE (*b.* Paris, France, 16 September 1666; *d.* Paris, 26 September 1716), *physics*.

Parent was the son of an *avocat au conseil*. His mother's uncle, Antoine Mallet, took charge of the boy's education when he was only three; Fontenelle, our source for this information, does not indicate why the father relinquished the duty. An elderly and pious man, Mallet pointed Parent toward a career in law. After dutifully completing that study, Parent turned to mathematics, for which he had independently acquired a taste. He attended the lectures of La Hire and Sauveur—the latter considered Parent a rare genius. For a short time Parent accompanied the Marquis d'Alègre on military campaigns, studying fortifications, and then devoted his time exclusively to science.

In 1699, when Gilles Filleau des Billettes was elected to the Académie des Sciences, he selected Parent as his *élève*. Parent carried the title until his death. His failure to advance was due to a lack of clarity in his writing, his antipathy to Cartesian science, and his aggressive, tactless, critical, and uncompromising candor in dealing with colleagues. Fontenelle declared that he had "goodness without showing it," scarcely a generous remark in an official eulogy. Parent, who never married, lived alone according to an austere, disciplined regimen. In 1716 he contracted a fatal case of smallpox.

Parent's interests were very wide-ranging, although such broad scope was not uncommon in his day, before the branches of science were carefully delineated. He wrote on astronomy, cartography, chemistry, biology, sensationalist psychology and epistemology, music, practical and abstract mathematics, and various mechanical phenomena, particularly those of the strength of materials and the effects of friction on motion. He often reviewed and commented on the works of others. He read many papers to the Académie des Sciences but few were published in the *Mémoires*. His most frequent avenues of publication were the *Journal des sçavans* and the *Journal de Trévoux*. In 1705 he launched his own periodical, *Essais et recherches de mathématiques et de physique*, which, although short-lived, provided a means of publishing much of his completed work. A three-volume sequel (1713) remains his best-known and most comprehensive collection.

Some of Parent's work was clearly original. The work of 1705 contained a memoir, originally delivered to the Academy in 1700, on the description of a sphere according to the techniques of analytic geometry. Although the treatment is awkward by modern standards, the clear understanding and use of space coordinates was not to become routine for many years. Typically, Parent aimed at extending the power both of geometry and of the new calculus, although he was far from moving to pure analysis. Some of his earliest work was in cartography, and it seems to have left a permanent mark on his style. The ever-present correspondence between the descriptive device of geometry and the physical space being described is characteristic of mapping. Parent never went the full journey to pure abstraction. He anticipated neither Lagrange nor Laplace but, rather, Coulomb, the engineer who absorbed enough science to emerge as an early physicist. The similarity is confirmed in Parent's work. The early study of fortifications has been mentioned. The publication of 1713 included an article describing the conditions of stress on a loaded beam, in which Parent first recognized the existence of a shear stress. Certain aspects of the analysis were not extended or even repeated for over half a century, by Coulomb.

Parent's contributions to science are not best characterized by the listing of "firsts." The power of the new mathematics was such that originality became common during the first decade of the eighteenth century. Parent learned from La Hire and Sauveur, and he shared the stage during his prime with Varignon, Hermann, Jakob I Bernoulli, and others. If Parent had a particular characteristic, it is perhaps his sense of the practical. The utilitarian aspect, seldom absent in his work, is noticeable from his first paper, on the calculation of frictional forces in machines, to his last, on the theoretical and practical applications of arithmetic.

Also remarkable is the degree to which Parent's criticisms of scientific work extended into the thematic or paradigmatic foundations of science. This tendency is evident even in the first volume of the 1713 publication; the bulk of that book is devoted to an attack on Descartes's *Principia philosophiae*, a work then nearly seventy years old. Parent went through it almost paragraph by paragraph; the reviewer in the *Journal des sçavans* needed three pages just to list the points upon which Parent and Descartes disagreed. For Parent, who was an atomist, motion could not produce hardness in objects, nor could it account for their specific shapes; Cartesian laws of motion were entirely incorrect. Parent refuted Cartesian notions on the formation of the elements, on comets, weight, the nature and effects of fire, on air, winds, hail and lightning, subterranean heat, light and color, the nature of ideas and the principles of music. Parent did not, as might be suspected, consider Newton to be Descartes's principal adversary, although Parent and Newton clearly shared many concepts. But Parent seems to have viewed Descartes as having been refuted by the whole range of seventeenth-century mechanical philosophers who embraced atomism. His attack on Descartes seems also to have been aimed at the Academy, most of whose members still clung to Cartesian science.

Parent emerges from the skimpy historical record as rather stiff, pious, solitary, independent, hardworking, and intelligent. He foreshadowed the Enlightenment in his unflagging critical spirit, his attempt to develop the scientific view of nature, and his conviction that the seemingly esoteric nature of mathematics had a very real utility.

BIBLIOGRAPHY

I. ORIGINAL WORKS. Parent's most comprehensive single work is *Essais et recherches de mathématiques et de physique*, 3 vols. (Paris, 1713). Also valuable are his reviews and articles in the *Journal des sçavans* and the *Journal de Trévoux*.

II. SECONDARY LITERATURE. Parent has not received much attention. His official *éloge* by Fontenelle appeared in the *Histoire de l'Académie Royale des Sciences* for 1716 and constitutes the bulk of the available biographical information. An account of his mathematics can be found in C. B. Boyer, *History of Analytic Geometry* (New York, 1956), 156 ff. The most extensive treatment of his physics is in Clifford Truesdell, *The Rational Mechanics of Flexible or Elastic Bodies*, in Euler's *Opera omnia*, 2nd ser., XI, pt. 2 (Lausanne, 1950), 109–114. Truesdell repeats some of his comments in "The Creation and Unfolding of the Concept of Stress," in *Essays in the History of Mechanics* (New York, 1968), 184–238. See also C. S. Gillmor, *Coulomb and the Evolution of Physics and Engineering in Eighteenth-Century France* (Princeton, 1971), *passim*; Isaac Todhunter, *A History of the Theory of Elasticity and of the Strength of Materials* (New York, 1960), *passim*; and Hunter Rouse and Simon Ince, *History of Hydraulics* (New York, 1963), *passim*.

J. MORTON BRIGGS JR.

PARKHURST, JOHN ADELBERT (*b.* Dixon, Illinois, 24 September 1861; *d.* Williams Bay, Wisconsin, 1 March 1925), *astronomy*.

Parkhurst was the son of Sanford and Clarissa J. Hubbard Parkhurst. Upon the death of his mother, when he was five years old, he was adopted by his aunt and uncle Dr. and Mrs. Abner Hagar, who lived in Marengo, Illinois. After completing public schools there, he attended Wheaton College, Wheaton, Illinois, from 1878 to 1881. Parkhurst graduated from the Rose Polytechnic Institute, Terre Haute, Indiana, in 1886 with a B.S. in mechanical engineering and remained there as instructor of mathematics for the next two years; in 1897 he received an M.S. from Rose.

He married Anna Greenleaf of Terre Haute, Indiana, in 1888; their only child died in infancy. From childhood, when he walked with crutches, until his death, caused by a cerebral hemorrhage, Parkhurst suffered from poor health but nevertheless worked diligently. He was a member of the American Astronomical Society, the British Astronomical Association, and the Astronomische Gesellschaft of Hamburg, and was a fellow of the Royal Astronomical Society. For many years he was active in the Congregational Church in Williams Bay and was elected the first town supervisor.

Parkhurst's interest in astronomy was stimulated by reading the works of Thomas Dick. Although his time in Marengo was devoted principally to business, he spent his leisure hours making astronomical observations, mainly of variable stars. Within a decade that part-time research had led to approximately fifty published papers.

After occasionally serving as a nonresident computer for the Washburn Observatory, Parkhurst made an important change in his professional life with the opening in 1897 of the University of Chicago's Yerkes Observatory. In 1898 he became a volunteer research assistant at Yerkes; and in 1900, with his appointment as assistant, he began working full time on astronomy. He remained at Yerkes until his death twenty-five years later, having progressed to the rank of associate professor in 1919.

Parkhurst's first published paper at Yerkes, "The Spectra of Stars of Secchi's Fourth Type," was written with George E. Hale and Ferdinand Ellerman. His specialty was stellar photometry, both visual and photographic. In 1906 the Carnegie Institution of Washington published his longest work, *Researches in Stellar Photometry During the Years 1894 to 1906, Made Chiefly at the Yerkes Observatory*. Perhaps his most important paper, however, was "Yerkes Actinometry," published in 1912. It contained his determinations of the visual and photographic magnitudes, color indexes, and spectral classes of all stars brighter than apparent magnitude 7.5 between $+73°$ north declination and the celestial north pole.

As Yerkes' representative, Parkhurst began collaborating in 1900 with Harvard, Lick, and McCormick observatories in a comparison, published in 1923, of the brightnesses of faint stars with those of known bright stars. He also helped prepare no. XII of the appendix to J. G. Hagen's *Atlas stellarum variabilium*; and he determined the photographic magnitudes and color indexes of 1,500 stars in twenty-four Kapteyn Fields, the report of which was published posthumously.

Parkhurst participated in three solar eclipse expeditions to measure coronal brightness but encountered clear skies for only one—that of 24 January 1925, shortly before his death.

BIBLIOGRAPHY

I. Original Works. Parkhurst published nearly 100 papers, principally in *Astronomical Journal, Astrophysical Journal, Astronomische Nachrichten*, and *Popular Astronomy*. His key works include *Researches in Stellar Photometry During the Years 1894 to 1906, Made Chiefly at the Yerkes Observatory* (Washington, D.C., 1906); "Yerkes Actinometry," in *Astrophysical Journal*, **36** (1912), 169–227; "Photometric Magnitudes of Faint Standard Stars Measured Visually at Harvard, Yerkes, Lick and McCormick Observatories," in *Memoirs of the American Academy of Arts and Sciences*, **14**, no. 4 (1923), 209–307, written with S. A. Mitchell *et al.*; "Methods Used in Stellar Photographic Photometry at the Yerkes Observatory Between 1914 to 1924," in *Astrophysical Journal*, **62** (1925), 179–190, written with Alice Hall Farnsworth; and "Zone $+45°$ of Kapteyn's Selected Area: Photographic Photometry for 1,550 Stars," in *Publications of the Yerkes Observatory*, **4**, pt. 6 (1927), 230–289.

II. Secondary Literature. Biographical information is given in J. McKeen and Dean R. Brimell, eds., *American Men of Science* (Lancaster, Pa., 1921), 526; and in Poggendorff, VI, 1951. A biographical sketch by Raymond S. Dugan is in *Dictionary of American Biography*, XIV, 246–247. Obituaries are by R. G. Aitken and E. B. Frost, in *Publications of the Astronomical Society of the Pacific*, **37** (1925), 85–88; by Storrs B. Barrett, in *Popular Astronomy*, **33** (1925), 280–284, which includes a portrait from 1923; and by E. B. Frost in *Astrophysical Journal*, **61** (1925), 454. There are unsigned obituaries in *Astronomische Nachrichten*, **224** (1925), 147–148; in *Observatory*, **48** (1925), 120; and in *Monthly Notices of the Royal Astronomical Society*, **86** (1926), 185–186.

Richard Berendzen

PARKINSON, JAMES (*b*. Hoxton Square, London, England, 11 April 1755; *d*. London, 21 December 1824), *medicine, paleontology.*

Parkinson's father, John Parkinson, was a surgeon. Where James studied is not known, but in 1784 his name appeared on a list of surgeons approved by the Corporation of London, and in 1785 he attended a series of lectures by John Hunter. On 21 May 1783 he married Mary Dale of Hoxton Square; they had six children.

Parkinson's early career was overshadowed by his involvement in a variety of social and revolutionary causes. This involvement was mainly through pamphlets that he wrote anonymously or under the pseudonym "Old Hubert." He advocated reform and representation of the people in the House of Commons, the institution of annual parliaments, and universal suffrage. Parkinson joined the London Corresponding Society for Reform of Parliamentary Representation in 1792, and it was between then and 1795 that he was most often heard from with regard to social and political change.

In 1780 Parkinson published, anonymously, *Observations on Dr. Hugh Smith's Philosophy of Physic*, a critical appraisal of Smith's theories. With the exception of a brief account of the effects of lightning (1789), Parkinson published nothing more in the sciences until his political and social activities lessened near the end of the century. His medical practice continued to flourish, however, and during this period he became interested in geology and paleontology. In 1799 his *Chemical Pocket-Book*, a guide for the student and layman, was published; it reflected his interests in medicine, geology, and fossils. In 1799 a work called *Medical Admonitions* was also published. It was the first in a series of popular medical works by Parkinson aimed toward the improvement of the general health and well-being of the population. It is likely that these works represented a continuation of the same zeal for the welfare of the people that was expressed by his political activism. His humanitarianism appeared again in 1811, when he crusaded for better safeguards in regulating madhouses and for legal protection for the mental patients, their keepers, doctors, and families.

Parkinson was the author of several medical treatises of particular interest to the profession. These included a work on gout (1805) and a report on a perforated and gangrenous appendix with peritonitis (1812). The latter is probably the earliest description of that condition in the English medical literature. Parkinson's most important medical work was *An Essay on the Shaking Palsy* (1817). In this short essay Parkinson established the disease as a clinical entity. Sorting through a variety of palsied conditions, which he had observed throughout his career, Parkinson gave the classic, albeit in modern terms limited, clinical description of the illness: "Involuntary tremulous motion, with lessened muscular power, in parts not in action and even when supported; with a propensity to bend the trunk forwards, and to pass from a walking to a running pace: the senses and intellect being uninjured." Symptoms that had been assumed to be characteristic of distinct illnesses, such as tremulous agitans and the violent propensity to run, were shown to be part of a single ailment. A study of several cases and a sorting-out of the symptoms comprises most of the work. Parkinson made no decision concerning the cause but suggested that it arose from "a disordered state of that part of the medulla which is contained in the cervical vertebrae." The illness described by Parkinson, now called Parkinson's disease, is understood today as one form of several clinical events.

Sometime in the late eighteenth century, Parkinson began to collect and study fossils. This was a pleasant avocation for him, and he enjoyed making short trips with his children and his friends to collect or observe fossil plants and animals. In the second edition of the *Chemical Pocket-Book* (1801) he made a public appeal for information on fossils. As he attempted to learn more about their identification and interpretation he discovered that there was little help available in English works. He decided, therefore, to write an introduction to the study of fossils. The first of three volumes of *Organic Remains of a Former World* was published in 1804, the second in 1808, and the third in 1811. Parkinson wanted these volumes to be useful to the beginning student as well as to the advanced collector. Volume I discusses the plant kingdom. The work is somewhat more theoretical than either of the other volumes and is also the least interesting; indeed, this volume met with only moderate success and was soundly criticized for its dullness and poor grammar. At a time when new discoveries in geology were causing concern among the theologians, the volume was also criticized for its failure to offer any mode of reconciliation between geology and theology. Much of the book is devoted to the question of whether coal, peat, and other bituminous products are vegetable in origin; a small portion is devoted to fossil woods, ferns, and other plants. There was considerable disagreement on this issue among Parkinson's contemporaries. Parkinson believed these products originated from plants, and he developed a theory of "bituminous fermentation" to explain the transformation. This fermentation, one of several kinds he recognized as normal to the vegetable kingdom, operated in the absence of external air and under conditions that prohibited the escape of volatile principles in the vegetation. A fluid was thus created. A modification of this fluid occurred through the "oxygenization" of carbon by the mixture of earthy and metallic salts.

Volume II (on the fossil zoophytes) and volume III (on the fossil starfish, echini, shells, insects, amphibia, and mammals) are more descriptive and met with a better reception. In volume III Parkinson introduced the discoveries of Lamarck, Cuvier, and William Smith. From Smith he adopted the use of fossils as stratigraphic markers, from Lamarck information on shells, and from Cuvier knowledge of the amphibia and land mammals. These volumes, though descriptive, give insight into Parkinson's basic position with regard to geological theory.

He was opposed to the Huttonian theory of the earth. Although probably not a strict adherent of Werner's neptunism, he favored it. In studying the relation of fossils to their strata he was convinced that the creation of life had taken a long time and had proceeded in an orderly fashion, in keeping with scriptural history. After the creation of primary rocks, vegetables were created, then animals of the water and air, followed by land animals and man. He emphasized the Biblical Flood in some cases, but creation and extinction were continuing processes guided by the hand of God. To reconcile his concept of geological time with theology, he adopted from some of his contemporaries the notion that each day of creation represented a long period of time. Parkinson was adamantly opposed to any theory of gradual, natural evolution. The "creative power," he argued, worked continually through new creations.

The volumes of *Organic Remains* were well illustrated with many plates (some in color) done by Parkinson. The plates were later republished in Gideon Mantell's *Pictorial Atlas of Fossil Remains* (1850). The work was a major contribution to the development of British paleontology, particularly as a thorough and usable compilation of information on British fossils.

On 13 November 1807 Parkinson met with several of his friends, including Sir Humphry Davy and George Greenough, at the Freemason's Tavern. Together they formed the Geological Society of London. Parkinson was a contributor to the first volume (1811) of the society's *Transactions* with a detailed study of the London basin entitled "Observations on Some of the Strata in the Neighbourhood of London, and on the Fossil Remains Contained in Them."

In 1822 Parkinson published *Outlines of Oryctology*,

which he considered a supplement to Conybeare and Phillips' *Outlines of the Geology of England and Wales, With an Introductory Compendium of the General Principles of That Science, and Comparative Views of the Structure of Foreign Countries.* It is similar to *Organic Remains,* with some additions and changes based on newer developments in geology. He adopted catastrophism and viewed the creation of life in a sequence and manner like that outlined by Cuvier.

BIBLIOGRAPHY

I. ORIGINAL WORKS. Parkinson's major works are *The Chemical Pocket-Book, or Memoranda Chemica: Arranged in a Compendium of Chemistry: With Tables of Attractions, etc. Calculated as Well for the Occasional Reference of the Professional Student, As to Supply Others With a General Knowledge of Chemistry* (London, 1799); *Organic Remains of a Former World. An Examination of the Mineralized Remains of the Vegetables and Animals of the Antediluvian World Generally Termed Extraneous Fossils* (London, 1804–1811); *An Essay on the Shaking Palsy* (London, 1817); and *Outlines of Oryctology: An Introduction to the Study of Fossil Organic Remains; Especially of Those Found in the British Strata: Intended to Aid the Student in His Inquiries Respecting the Nature of Fossils and Their Connection With the Formation of the Earth* (London, 1822).

Parkinson's notes on J. Hunter's lectures were transcribed by his son and published as *Hunterian Reminiscences* (London, 1833).

II. SECONDARY LITERATURE. On Parkinson and his work see W. R. Bett, "James Parkinson: Practitioner, Pamphleteer, Politician and Pioneer in Neurology," in *Medical Press,* **234** (1955), 148; G. S. Boulger, "James Parkinson," in *Dictionary of National Biography*; J. Challinor, "Beginnings of Scientific Paleontology in Britain," in *Annals of Science,* **6** (1948), 46–53; M. Critchley, ed., *James Parkinson (1755–1824). A Bicentenary Volume of Papers Dealing with Parkinson's Disease Incorporating the Original Essay on the Shaking Palsy* (London, 1955), contains a biography of Parkinson by W. H. McMenemey and a bibliography; J. M. Eyles, "James Parkinson (1755–1824)," in *Nature,* **176** (1955), 580–581; and L. G. Rowntree, "James Parkinson," in *Johns Hopkins Hospital Bulletin,* **23** (1912), 33–45.

PATSY A. GERSTNER

PARKINSON, SYDNEY (*b.* Edinburgh, Scotland, *ca.* 1745; *d.* at sea 26 January 1771), *natural history drawing.*

Parkinson, a young Scottish artist, who died on the return voyage of the *Endeavour* after the disastrous stay for refitting at Batavia (where nearly everyone on board contracted malaria or dysentery, or both),

was an extremely gifted and versatile draftsman and colorist. His beautiful and accurate drawings of the plants and animals collected on Cook's first voyage round the world, his studies of exotic landscapes, their peoples, and artifacts, together with Joseph Banks's collections and manuscripts, combined to make that voyage one of the most memorable in the annals of scientific discovery.

Sydney was the younger son of Joel Parkinson, an Edinburgh brewer, and his wife Elizabeth. Nothing is known of his education—not a very formal one since he signed himself both Sydney and Sidney—but in his teens he was apprenticed to a woolen draper. He seems to have had innate aptitude for drawing. His brother Stanfield wrote in the introduction to his posthumously published journal that from an early age "taking a delight in drawing flowers, fruits and other objects of natural history, he soon became as proficient in that stile of painting as to attract the notice of the most celebrated botanists and connoisseurs in that study."

When Parkinson was about twenty his widowed mother moved to London, where he exhibited with the Free Society in 1765 and 1766. About that time he was engaged by another Scot, James Lee of the Vineyard Nursery, Hammersmith, to teach his favorite daughter Ann, some thirteen years old. It was to her that Parkinson bequeathed his "utensils" and some botanical paintings that remained in the possession of the Lee family until 1970. The paints and brushes have been lost, but the paintings are now in the National Library, Canberra; Ann's paintings, considered by the great Danish entomologist J. C. Fabricius to be the best British natural history drawings of the day, are in the library of the Royal Botanic Gardens, Kew. Early in 1767 Lee introduced Parkinson to Banks, and from then on the young artist worked extensively on Banks's collections, first on the plates (now in the British Museum [Natural History]) of the Loten collection from Ceylon, then on the invertebrates, fishes, and birds collected by Banks in Newfoundland and Labrador in 1766. These drawings of Newfoundland animals, and of other exotic species in Banks's possession, many of which are still unidentified, are in the Print Room, British Museum.

Banks himself wrote in warm terms of Parkinson's industry in the *Endeavour.* During the voyage the young Scot made nearly 1,000 drawings of plants, about 300 of animals ranging from pellucid coelenterates to tropical birds, all of which may be seen in the British Museum (Natural History); he also executed some 200 topographical and ethnographical drawings, now in the Manuscript Room, British Museum.

Parkinson also recorded Polynesian and other vocabularies whenever the opportunity arose. In some cases his lists exceeded those compiled by Banks, who, more cautiously, recorded only ninety-one Tahitian words against Parkinson's 300. Parkinson also listed eighty-one Tahitian plants, with their economic uses as fish poisons, dyes, medicines, textiles, and as building material. These lists appeared in the illegally published edition (1773) of his completed journal (which was lost) when his brother Stanfield attempted to forestall the official account of the voyage. A second edition appeared in 1784. A self-portrait is owned by the British Museum (Natural History); an engraving of him at an earlier age forms the frontispiece to his journal.

BIBLIOGRAPHY

The illegally published edition of Parkinson's journal is Sydney Parkinson, *A Journal of a Voyage to the South Seas in His Majesty's Ship the Endeavour* (London, 1773, 2nd ed. 1784). See also F. C. Sawyer, "Some Natural History Drawings Made During Captain Cook's First Voyage Round the World," in *Journal of the Society for the Bibliography of Natural History*, **2** (1950), 190–193; J. C. Beaglehole, ed., *The Journals of Captain James Cook*, I, *The Voyage of the Endeavour* (Cambridge, 1955); and *The Endeavour Journal of Joseph Banks*, 2 vols. (Sydney, 1962); A. M. Lysaght, *Joseph Banks in Newfoundland and Labrador, 1766* (London, 1971); A. M. Lysaght and D. L. Serventy, "Some Erroneous Distribution Records in Parkinson's Journal of a Voyage to the South Seas," in *Emu*, **56** (1956), 129–130; W. F. Miller, "Sydney Parkinson and His Drawings," in *Journal of the Friends' Historical Society*, **8** (1911), 123–127; and E. J. Willson, *James Lee and the Vineyard Nursery* (London, 1961).

AVERIL M. LYSAGHT

PARMENIDES OF ELEA (*b. ca.* 515 B.C.; *d.* after 450 B.C.), *natural philosophy.*

Parmenides' dates are inferred from the dramatic situation in Plato's *Parmenides*. A different chronology, which ultimately comes from Apollodorus of Athens, should be rejected, since it is based on an attempt to place Parmenides' birth in 540/539 B.C., the year of the founding of Elea. (See Tarán, *Parmenides*, pp. 3–4.)

Parmenides puts forward his philosophy in a poem in dactylic hexameter. Mainly through Simplicius, who cites it in his commentaries on Aristotle's *Physics* and *De Caelo*, we have approximately 155 lines of it; there are, in addition, six lines extant only in a Latin translation. More information on his thought may be obtained from Plato, Aristotle, Theophrastus, and the doxographers who depend mainly upon Aristotle and Theophrastus. Because one must depend on others for his thought and because of Aristotle's notorious tendency to interpret his predecessors in the light of his own philosophy, the indirect information about Parmenides cannot be taken at face value but must be analyzed critically. (This has been done by Cherniss in *Aristotle's Criticism of Presocratic Philosophy*. On the secondary sources of information about Parmenides, see Tarán, *Parmenides*, pp. 269–295.)

To emphasize the objectivity of his method, Parmenides presents his doctrine through a nameless goddess whom the poet reaches after traveling in a chariot driven by the daughters of the sun. According to this goddess, only two ways of inquiry can be conceived of: that which asserts the existence of being and that which accepts as necessary the existence of not-being. Since it is impossible to think that which in no way is, only the first way can be pursued. Nevertheless the goddess, with a probable allusion to Heraclitus' doctrine of the unity of contraries, attacks as the extreme of folly those mortals who believe that being and not-being are the same and yet not the same. She asks her hearer to judge her argument by reason and not to let himself be led astray by the senses; for there is but one way, that which maintains that only being exists. By assuming that there is no *tertium quid* between being and absolute not-being, the goddess construes a tight and cogent reasoning which shows that that which is (being) must be ungenerated, imperishable, homogeneous, changeless, immovable, complete, and unique. These characteristics are meant to emphasize from the negative side the unique and unalterable existence of being, for it is implied that if being did not have any one of these characteristics, one would have to admit the existence of something different from being; and such an admission, given the original assumption, would be tantamount to accepting the existence of not-being. Consequently mortals' opinions about the phenomenal world are meaningless, since they refer to something that has no existence whatever. Yet the pupil must learn the opinions of men, for it is essential to know the source of error so that no one should outstrip him. The minimal error is the belief, conscious or not, that difference is real. Since the minimal difference implies the existence of two things, the goddess shows how from it a whole world of difference and change can be derived. In accordance with this purpose of offering a cosmogony or cosmology as a model of reference, the goddess describes doctrines that were more or less current at Parmenides' time.

Parmenides' basic mistake is his misapplication of the law of the excluded middle to the disjunction being:: not-being. Otherwise his reasoning is flawless, and none of the philosophers who came immediately after him was able to refute him. The refutation was reserved for Plato, especially in his *Sophist*; but Plato recognized the importance of Parmenides' attempt to apply the exigencies of logical proofs to thought and its object.

BIBLIOGRAPHY

The fragments of Parmenides' poem and most of the evidence from secondary sources are in H. Diels and W. Kranz, eds., *Die Fragmente der Vorsokratiker*, 6th ed., I (Berlin, 1952), 217–246.

Modern works dealing with Parmenides are P. Albertelli, *Gli Eleati. Testimonianze e frammenti* (Bari, 1939); K. Bormann, *Parmenides. Untersuchungen zu den Fragmenten* (Hamburg, 1971); J. Burnet, *Early Greek Philosophy*, 4th ed. (London, 1930), 169–196; G. Calogero, *Studi sull'eleatismo* (Rome, 1932); H. Cherniss, *Aristotle's Criticism of Presocratic Philosophy* (Baltimore, 1935); H. Diels, *Parmenides Lehrgedicht. Griechisch und Deutsch* (Berlin, 1897); H. Fränkel, *Wege und Formen frühgriechischen Denkens*, 2nd ed. (Munich, 1960); W. K. C. Guthrie, *A History of Greek Philosophy*, II (Cambridge, 1965), 1–80; U. Hölscher, *Parmenides. Vom Wesen des Seiendes* (Frankfurt, 1969); J. B. McDiarmid, "Theophrastus on the Presocratic Causes," in *Harvard Studies in Classical Philology*, **61** (1953), 85–156; J. Mansfeld, *Die Offenbarung des Parmenides und die menschliche Welt* (Assen, 1964); A. Mourelatos, *The Route of Parmenides* (New Haven, 1970); G. Reale, in his ed. of E. Zeller's *Die Philosophie der Griechen, La filosofia dei greci nel suo sviluppo storico*, I, pt. 3 (Florence, 1967); K. Reinhardt, *Parmenides und die Geschichte griechischen Philosophie* (Bonn, 1916); L. Tarán, *Parmenides. A Text With Translation, Commentary, and Critical Essays* (Princeton, 1965); M. Untersteiner, *Parmenide. Testimonianze e frammenti* (Florence, 1958); W. J. Verdenius, *Parmenides. Some Comments on His Poem* (Groningen, 1942); and E. Zeller, *Die Philosophie der Griechen*, 7th ed., W. Nestle, ed., I (Leipzig, 1923), 679–741.

LEONARDO TARÁN

PARMENTIER, ANTOINE-AUGUSTIN (*b*. Montdidier, France, 12 or 17 August 1737; *d*. Paris, France, 17 December 1813), *chemistry, nutrition, agriculture, public health, pharmacy.*

Born into a bourgeois family of modest means, Parmentier was apprenticed at an early age to an apothecary in Montdidier. In 1755 he left for Paris to continue his apprenticeship; but two years later, during the Seven Years War, he joined the French army in Germany as *apothicaire sous-aide*. Wounded in action and captured five times by the Prussians, he nevertheless returned safely to Paris in 1763. To support himself he worked in an apothecary shop and in his spare time attended lectures given by Nollet, Bernard de Jussieu, and G.-F. Rouelle. In 1766 he competed successfully for the post of *apothicaire gagnant-maîtrise* at the Hôtel Royal des Invalides and in 1772 was commissioned *apothicaire-major* of that institution. Two years later the Sisters of Charity, the nursing order in charge of the pharmacy service at the Invalides since 1676, caused Parmentier's commission to be revoked. Despite this temporary setback, he carved out a brilliant career in military pharmacy, eventually achieving the rank of inspector general in the army health service.

Parmentier's earliest investigation, dating from about 1771, concerned the chemical and nutritive constituents of the potato. This research was soon broadened to include a large number of indigenous plants which he recommended as food in times of scarcity and famine, ascribing their nutritive value to their starch content. These early efforts resulted in a published memoir (1773), which was awarded a prize by the Besançon Academy of Sciences, Belles-Lettres, and Arts and later formed the basis of a greatly expanded work, *Recherches sur les végétaux nourissants qui, dans les temps de disette, peuvent remplacer les alimens ordinaires* (1781).

Of all these plants it was the potato that most interested Parmentier, and it is unfortunate that his long and successful campaign to popularize the cultivation and use of the potato in France as a cheap and abundant source of food has tended to obscure his other accomplishments in food chemistry and nutrition. Typical and worthy of note are his chemical analyses of wheat and flour (1776), chestnuts (1780), milk (1790 and 1799, in collaboration with Nicolas Deyeux), and chocolate (1786 and 1803). Parmentier devoted considerable time to formulating cheap and nutritious soups for the poor and to the technology of bread-making. In 1780 he was instrumental in founding, with his colleague Cadet de Vaux, the first government-sponsored school of baking in France. During France's economic warfare with England (1806–1812), Parmentier achieved some success in fostering the production of grape syrup as a substitute for cane sugar, which had become scarce and expensive.

A member of the prestigious Royal Society of Agriculture in Paris and an *agronome* of repute,

Parmentier conducted far-ranging investigations that included preservation of grain and flour; improvements in milling; cultivation of corn; and preservation of vinegar, wine, and meat, as well as methods for detecting their adulteration. He contributed articles to the twelve-volume *Cours complet d'agriculture*, launched by Abbé François Rozier in 1781; he collaborated in the writing of the twenty-four-volume *Nouveau dictionnaire d'histoire naturelle* (Paris, 1803–1804); and he was the author of *Économie rurale et domestique*, of which six volumes of the projected eight appeared (Paris, 1788–1793).

Parmentier also evinced a strong interest in public health, reflected in his publications on the quality of water from the Seine (1775 and 1787), chemical studies with Deyeux of pathological changes in the blood (1791 and 1794), and his collaboration with Laborie and Cadet de Vaux on cesspools (1778) and with them and Hecquet on exhumations (1783). Parmentier was active in the movement to provide free smallpox vaccinations to the poor, and in 1802 he was appointed to the newly created Council of Health for the Department of the Seine.

Frankly utilitarian in his scientific orientation, Parmentier in his life and work personified the best sentiments and aspirations of the Enlightenment. In addition to his close association with Cadet de Vaux and Deyeux, Parmentier numbered among his collaborators Bertrand Pelletier, Chaptal, Huzard, Rozier, Thouin and d'Ussieux. A member of many learned societies, he was admitted to the Academy of Sciences in 1795 and in 1801 was one of the founding members of the Société d'Encouragement pour l'Industrie Nationale.

BIBLIOGRAPHY

I. Original Works. An annotated bibliography of Parmentier's publications is given in A. Balland, *La chimie alimentaire dans l'oeuvre de Parmentier* (Paris, 1902), 377–426. See also J.-M. Quérard, *La France littéraire ou dictionnaire bibliographique* (Paris, 1827–1839), VI, 603–606; and the Royal Society *Catalogue of Scientific Papers* (*1800–1863*), IV, 762–763.

II. Secondary Literature. For older material covering the period 1781–1897, see Balland (above), pp. 427–434, which lists 34 references. Recent sources include Arthur Birembaut, "L'école gratuite de boulangerie," in René Taton, ed., *Enseignement et diffusion des sciences en France au XVIIIᵉ siècle* (Paris, 1964), 493–509; A. J. Bourde, *Agronomie et agronomes en France au XVIIIᵉ siècle*, 3 vols. (Paris, 1967), II, 637–643, 913; and III, 1291, 1331, 1533–1534; Maurice Bouvet, "Hommage à Parmentier," in *Revue d'histoire de la pharmacie*, **12**, no. 151 (Dec. 1956), 478–480; Maurice Javillier, "Antoine Parmentier," in *Figures pharmaceutiques françaises* (Paris, 1953), 29–34; and R. Massy, "À l'apothicairerie de l'Hôtel royal des Invalides: Le conflit de 1772 entre l'administration de l'hôtel et les Filles de la Charité," in *Revue d'histoire de la pharmacie*, **11**, no. 142 (Sept. 1954), 315–324.

Alex Berman

PARNAS, JAKUB KAROL (*b.* Tarnopol, Poland [now Ukrainian S.S.R.], 16 January 1884; *d.* Moscow, U.S.S.R., 29 January 1949), *biochemistry*.

Parnas studied chemistry in the universities of Berlin, Strasbourg, Zurich, and Munich, where he received the Ph.D. in 1907. He was associate professor of chemistry at Strasbourg in 1913 and professor of physiological chemistry at Warsaw (1916–1919) and Lvov (1920–1941). From 1943 he was head of the Biological and Medical Chemistry Institute of the Soviet Academy of Medical Sciences in Moscow, where he also established a Laboratory of Physiological Chemistry as part of the Soviet Academy of Sciences.

In the course of his career Parnas educated a large number of biochemists and exerted an important influence on the development of biochemistry, both in Poland and throughout the world. As a researcher, his chief fields of investigation were the biochemistry of muscles, especially the interdependence of the metabolism of carbohydrates and that of phosphorus; ammonia production in its relationship to the function of muscles; and the connection between nitrogen metabolism and the metabolism of adenosine monophosphate, including its deamination and dephosphorylation. He discovered the phosphorolysis of glycogen, and, by establishing reaction sequences linking the metabolism of carbohydrates with that of phosphorus, initiated the method of studying life processes now characteristic of molecular biology. In 1937, in collaboration with the Niels Bohr Institute in Copenhagen, Parnas became one of the first to apply P^{32} to biochemical investigations, particularly to that of the metabolism of muscles in vitro. He thus attained a detailed picture of the functional metabolism of muscles; the enzymatic pathway that he thereby established is sometimes known as the Embden, Meyerhof, and Parnas (EMP) scheme.

Parnas was a member of the Polish Academy of Sciences, the Soviet Academy of Sciences, the Soviet Academy of Medical Sciences, the Academy of Medicine in Paris, and the Leopoldina. He received honorary degrees from the universities of Athens and Paris.

BIBLIOGRAPHY

I. ORIGINAL WORKS. Parnas published about 120 scientific papers and a number of reviews, of which a list of twenty may be found in Dorothy M. Needham, *Machina carnis* (Cambridge, 1971), p. 706. A complete list of Parnas' works has been compiled by Irena Mochnacka in *Acta Biochimica Polonica*, **3** (1956), 3–39. His textbooks include *Chemja Fizjologiczna* ("Physiological Chemistry"; Warsaw–Lvov, 1922).

II. SECONDARY LITERATURE. An article on Parnas and his work appears in *Wielka Encyklopedia Powszechna* (Warsaw, 1966), and J. Heller and W. Mozołowski have described his teaching activity in *Postępy Biochemii*, **4** (1958), 5–16, where there is also a bibliography.

T. W. KORZYBSKI

PARSEVAL DES CHÊNES, MARC-ANTOINE

(*b*. Rosières-aux-Salines, France, 27 April 1755; *d*. Paris, France, 16 August 1836), *mathematics*.

Little is known of Parseval's life or work. He was a member of a distinguished French family and described himself as a squire; his marriage in 1795 to Ursule Guerillot soon ended in divorce. An ardent royalist, he was imprisoned in 1792 and later fled the country when Napoleon ordered his arrest for publishing poetry against the regime. He was nominated for election to the Paris Academy of Sciences in 1796, 1799, 1802, 1813, and 1828; but the closest he came to being elected was to place third to Lacroix in 1799.

Parseval's only publications seem to have been five memoirs presented to the Academy of Sciences. The second of these (dated 5 April 1799) contains the famous Parseval theorem, given here in his own notation:

If there are two series

$$A + Bf + Cf^2 + Ff^3 + \cdots = T$$

$$a + b\frac{1}{f} + c\frac{1}{f^2} + f\frac{1}{f^3} + \cdots = T'$$

as well as the respective sums T, T', then we obtain the sum of the series

$$Aa + Bb + Cc + Ff + \cdots = V$$

by multiplying T by T' and, in the new function $T \times T'$, substituting

$$\cos u + \sqrt{-1} \sin u$$

for the variable f, which will yield the function V'. Then for f substitute

$$\cos u - \sqrt{-1} \sin u$$

which will yield the new function V''. We then obtain

$$V = \frac{1}{u} \int \frac{V' + V''}{2} \, du,$$

u being made equal to 180° after integrating.

According to Parseval, the theorem was suggested by a method of summing special cases of series of products, presented by Euler in his *Institutiones calculi differentialis* of 1755. He believed the theorem to be self-evident, suggesting that the reader multiply the two series and recall that $(\cos u + i \sin u)^m = \cos mu + i \sin mu$, and gave a simple example that would "confirm its validity." He noted that it could be used only if the imaginaries in V' and V'' cancel one another, and he hoped to overcome this inconvenience. This hope was realized in a note appended to his next memoir (dated 5 July 1801), in which he gave a simplified version of the theorem. In modern notation the theorem states:

If, in the series $M = A + Bs + Cs^2 + \cdots$ and $m = a + bs + cs^2 + \cdots$, s is replaced by $\cos u + i \sin u$, and the real and imaginary parts are separated so that

$$M = P + Qi$$

and

$$m = p + qi,$$

then

$$\frac{2}{\pi} \int_0^\pi Pp \, du = 2Aa + Bb + Cc + \cdots.$$

(There is an error in Parseval's statement: the 2 in the right-hand side of the last equation is missing.)

In his memoirs, which were not published until 1806, Parseval applied his theorem to the solution of certain differential equations suggested by Lagrange and d'Alembert. The theorem first appeared in print in 1800, in Lacroix's *Traité des différences et des séries* (p. 377). By 1810 Delambre, in his *Rapport historique sur les progrès des sciences mathématiques depuis 1789, et sur leur état actuel*, could report that Prony had given, and published, lectures at the École Polytechnique taking Parseval's procedure into account and that Poisson had used a method dependent on an equation of this type. Since then dozens of equations have been called Parseval equations, although some only remotely resemble the original. Although Parseval's method involves trigonometric series, he never tried to find a general expression for the series coefficients; and hence he did not contribute directly to the theory of Fourier series. It should be noted that although Parseval viewed his theorem as a formula for summing infinite series, it was taken up at the end of the century as defining properties in more abstract treatments of analysis.

BIBLIOGRAPHY

I. Original Works. Parseval's five memoirs appeared in *Mémoires présentés à l'Institut des Sciences, Lettres et Arts, par divers savans, et lus dans ses assemblées. Sciences mathématiques et physiques.* (*Savans étrangers.*), **1** (1806): "Mémoire sur la résolution des équations aux différences partielles linéaires du second ordre" (5 May 1798), 478–492; "Mémoire sur les séries et sur l'intégration complète d'une équation aux différences partielles linéaires du second ordre, à coefficiens constans" (5 Apr. 1799), 638–648; "Intégration générale et complète des équations de la propagation du son, l'air étant considéré avec ses trois dimensions" (5 July 1801), 379–398; "Intégration générale et complète de deux équations importantes dans la mécanique des fluides" (16 Aug. 1803), 524–545; and "Méthode générale pour sommer, par le moyen des intégrales définies, la suite donnée par le théorème de M. Lagrange, au moyen de laquelle il trouve une valeur qui satisfait à une équation algébrique ou transcendente" (7 May 1804), 567–586.

II. Secondary Literature. A brief biography is in *Généalogies et souvenirs de famille; les Parseval et leurs alliances pendant trois siècles, 1594–1900*, I (Bergerac, 1901), 281–282. The memoirs are described in Niels Nielsen, *Géomètres français sous la Révolution* (Copenhagen, 1929), 192–194. The relation of Parseval's theorem to the work of Fourier is discussed in Ivor Grattan-Guinness, *Joseph Fourier, 1768–1830* (Cambridge, Mass., 1972), 238–241, written with J. R. Ravetz.

HUBERT C. KENNEDY

PARSONS, WILLIAM, Third Earl of Rosse (*b.* York, England, 17 June 1800; *d.* Monkstown, Ireland, 31 October 1867), *astronomy.*

William Parsons was the eldest son of Lawrence Parsons, second Earl of Rosse, and a descendant of the Sir William Parsons who had gone to Ireland in the sixteenth century. Prior to the death of his father, in 1841, he held the title Lord Oxmantown, under which style some of his scientific papers were published. (His own eldest son, Lawrence Parsons, held the same succession of titles; since he too was an astronomer, this has given rise to some confusion.) He received his early education privately at Birr Castle, the family seat, then in 1818 went for a year to Trinity College, Dublin. He next attended Magdalen College, Oxford, matriculating in 1821 and graduating with first-class honors in mathematics in 1822.

Since the nobility of his time took their responsibilities seriously, it was expected that Oxmantown would follow his father's example and take his place in the Irish government. As an undergraduate, in 1821, he was returned as a member of parliament for King's County, a seat that he held until 1834. He proved to be an able political economist and an effective committee member. He was appointed to further civil duties; in 1831 he was named lord lieutenant of County Offaly, in which Birr is situated, and in 1834 he became colonel of the local militia. In 1845, as the earl of Rosse, he was elected Irish representative peer and sat in the English House of Lords.

Rosse's scientific achievements were all the more remarkable in light of his activities as an administrator and public servant. His chief contributions were to astronomical instrumentation, particularly the design and construction of large telescopes. He early realized the need for instruments of greater aperture and light-grasp than were provided by William Herschel's forty-eight-inch aperture telescope of 1789; his own experiments, which he began in about 1826, were first concentrated on instruments incorporating the new optically excellent small-aperture Fraunhofer refractors. Having without success investigated the possibility of devising large fluid lenses, he was soon convinced that large apertures could be achieved only with reflectors. He therefore took up the search for an appropriate material for casting large mirrors and, after a number of experiments, decided to use an alloy of four parts of copper and one of tin. This alloy was both harder and more brittle than steel, it crystallized easily, and thus casting it was difficult. Rosse first tried making sectional mirrors composed of annular rings surrounding a central disk, all soldered to a brass disk having the same coefficient of expansion, but these proved ineffective in instruments of greater than eighteen-inch aperture.

Rosse was thus forced to develop a technique for casting solid disks. Having designed a mold ventilated so as to permit the mirror to cool evenly all over in an annealing oven, he finally achieved his aim. He completed a sectional thirty-six-inch speculum in 1839 and a superior solid mirror of the same size in 1840. In 1842 he cast the first seventy-two-inch disk, which, mounted in the meridian between two brick walls nearly sixty feet high, became known as the "Leviathan of Parsonstown" (Parsonstown being an old name of Birr). The telescope was completed in 1845; it had a focal length of fifty-four feet (with a nominal maximum magnification of 6,000), and a tube about seven feet in diameter. The mirror itself weighed nearly four tons, and its flexure under gravitation was controlled by twenty-seven felt-covered cast iron platforms. While it was not completely maneuverable, it was mounted so that a considerable portion of the sky was visible, and Rosse and his collaborator, the Reverend Thomas Romney Robinson, were able to utilize it to carry out, especially between 1848 and 1878, a number of important observations of nebulae.

With the new telescope Rosse and his co-workers were able to see hitherto unsuspected detail in many hundreds of nebulae, and to resolve many of these nebulae into stars. They abolished some of the existing distinctions (annular/planetary, for example) and added some new classes. Rosse himself was the first to detect the spiral nature of some nebulae, of which he published a number of fine drawings that clearly demonstrated the value of a large reflector of high optical quality.

In addition to overcoming the problems inherent in casting large solid mirrors (he eventually cast one of eighty-four inches), Rosse devised improvements in grinding and polishing techniques. Although he had initially believed that only hand finishing would be delicate enough to give a good conformation, he found this to be incorrect. He then designed an apparatus in which the mirror was rotated horizontally in a water bath (for constant temperature) beneath a grinding and polishing tool that could be moved in either a straight line or an ellipse of any eccentricity. The mirror could be tested *in situ* by observing its image in a watch dial fixed some fifty feet above it. The machine was driven by steam and was widely copied. Rosse also designed and executed a simple but effective clockwork drive for a large (eighteen-inch) equatorial. His interests extended further to the building of iron-armored ships, on which some correspondence is printed in his *Scientific Papers*. He took some of the earliest lunar photographs.

Rosse was married in 1836 to a Yorkshirewoman, Mary Field; they had four sons. He was president of the British Association at its 1843 meeting in Cork and president of the Royal Society from 1848 to 1854. In 1852 he served as chancellor of Trinity College, Dublin, and he was a member of the board of visitors of both Greenwich Observatory and Maynooth College. Following the potato famine of 1846 Rosse devoted the major part of the rents from his Irish properties to alleviating the poverty of the local inhabitants; he was held in great affection by his tenants, some 4,000 of whom attended his funeral.

BIBLIOGRAPHY

I. ORIGINAL WORKS. All of Rosse's scientific papers have been reprinted in Charles Parsons, ed., *The Scientific Papers of William Parsons, Third Earl of Rosse 1800–1867* (London, 1926). Rosse's chief publications are "An Account of Experiments on the Reflecting Telescope," in *Philosophical Transactions of the Royal Society*, **130** (1840), 503–528; "Observations of Some of the Nebulae," *ibid.*, **134** (1844), 321–323; "Observations of the Nebulae," *ibid.*, **140** (1850), 499–514; and "On the Construction of Specula of Six-Feet Aperture; and a Selection From the Observations of Nebulae Made With Them," *ibid.*, **151** (1861), 681–745.

II. SECONDARY LITERATURE. Two useful notes on Rosse are in *Proceedings of the Royal Society*, **16** (1868), xxxvi–xlii; and *Monthly Notices of the Royal Astronomical Society*, **29** (1869), 123–130. See also J. D. North, *The Measure of the Universe* (Oxford, 1965), esp. ch. 1.

J. D. NORTH
COLIN A. RONAN

PARTINGTON, JAMES RIDDICK (*b.* Bolton, Lancashire, England, 20 June 1886; *d.* Weaverham, Cheshire, England, 9 October 1965), *chemistry, dissemination of knowledge.*

Partington studied chemistry at the University of Manchester and, after a short period of research in organic chemistry under Arthur Lapworth, received an 1851 Exhibition scholarship. He worked under Nernst in Berlin on the specific heats of gases, continuing his research after his appointment as lecturer in chemistry at Manchester in 1913. During World War I he carried out investigations with E. K. Rideal for the Ministry of Munitions on the purification of water and the oxidation of nitrogen; he was subsequently knighted for this work. From 1919 to 1951 he was professor of chemistry at Queen Mary College, London University, where he continued his research on the specific heats of gases.

Remembered primarily as a historian of chemistry, Partington was gifted with an encyclopedic mind and a great facility for writing. His chief work, *A History of Chemistry*, is an outstanding accomplishment that surpasses any work on the subject since Hermann Kopp's *Geschichte der Chemie* (1843–1847). Its four volumes deal with the history of chemistry from antiquity to the present. Although at his best in describing the personalities and contributions of the great pioneers, Partington also included accounts of their less important contemporaries. His method consisted of summarizing the successive accomplishments of contributors to chemistry, rather than of organizing the history of the subject around a given sequence of themes or topics. The vein is biographical, not narrative, but the comprehensive accounts permit the reader to constitute his own narrative.

In 1965 Partington was awarded the Sarton Medal of the American History of Science Society during the Eleventh International Congress of the History of Science held in Warsaw and Cracow.

BIBLIOGRAPHY

I. ORIGINAL WORKS. Partington published several historical papers in *Annals of Science*. They include "Joan Baptista van Helmont," **1** (1936), 359–384; "Historical Studies on the Phlogiston Theory," **2** (1937), 361–404; **3** (1938), 1–58, 337–371; **4** (1939), 113–149, written with D. McKie; "The Origins of the Atomic Theory," **4** (1939), 245–282; and "Jeremias Benjamin Richter and the Law of Reciprocal Proportions," **7** (1951), 173–198; **9** (1953), 289–314.

His early books are *Higher Mathematics for Chemical Students* (London, 1911; 4th ed., 1931); *A Textbook of Thermodynamics* (London, 1913); *The Alkali Industry* (London, 1918); *A Textbook of Inorganic Chemistry for University Students* (London, 1921; 6th ed., 1950); *The Nitrogen Industry* (London, 1922), written with L. H. Parker; *Chemical Thermodynamics* (London, 1924; 4th ed., rev. and enl., 1950); *The Specific Heats of Gases* (London, 1924), written with W. G. Shilling; *Calculations in Physical Chemistry* (London–Glasgow, 1928), written with S. K. Tweedy; *The Composition of Water* (London, 1928); and *Everyday Chemistry* (London, 1929; 3rd ed., 1952).

Subsequent works are *A School Course of Chemistry* (London, 1930); *Origins and Development of Applied Chemistry* (London, 1935); *A Short History of Chemistry* (London, 1937; 3rd ed., rev. and enl., 1965); *A College Course of Inorganic Chemistry* (London, 1939); and *Intermediate Chemical Calculations* (London, 1939), written with K. Stratton.

His later writings are *General and Inorganic Chemistry for University Students* (London, 1946; 4th ed., 1966); *An Advanced Treatise on Physical Chemistry*, 4 vols. (London, 1949–1953); *A History of Greek Fire and Gunpowder* (Cambridge, 1960); *The Life and Work of William Higgins, Chemist (1763–1825)* (New York, 1960), written with T. S. Wheeler; and *A History of Chemistry*, 4 vols. (London–New York, 1961–1970).

II. SECONDARY LITERATURE. See the obituary notice in *The Times* (11 Oct. 1965), p. 12.

HAROLD HARTLEY

PASCAL, BLAISE (*b.* Clermont-Ferrand, Puy-de-Dôme, France, 19 June 1623; *d.* Paris, France, 19 August 1662), *mathematics, mechanical computation, physics, epistemology.*

Varied, original, and important, although often the subject of controversy, Pascal's scientific work was intimately linked with other aspects of his writings, with his personal life, and with the development of several areas of science. Consequently a proper understanding of his contribution requires a biographical framework offering as precise a chronology as possible.

Pascal's mother, Antoinette Begon, died when he was three; and the boy was brought up by his father, Étienne, who took complete charge of his education.

In 1631 the elder Pascal left Clermont and moved to Paris with his son and two daughters, Gilberte (1620–1687), who married Florin Périer in 1641, and Jacqueline (1625–1661), who entered the convent of Port-Royal in 1652.

The young Pascal began his scientific studies about 1635 with the reading of Euclid's *Elements*. His exceptional abilities, immediately and strikingly apparent, aroused general admiration. His sister Gilberte Périer left an account, more doting than objective, of her brother's life and, in particular, of his first contacts with mathematics. According to her, Pascal accompanied his father to the meetings of the "Académie Parisienne" soon after its founding by Mersenne in 1635 and played an important role in it from the first. This assertion, however, is not documented; and it appears more likely that it was at the beginning of 1639 that Pascal, not yet sixteen, began to participate in the activities of Mersenne's academy. In that year Girard Desargues had just published his *Brouillon project d'une atteinte aux événemens des rencontres du cone avec un plan*; but his originality, his highly personal style and vocabulary, and his refusal to use Cartesian algebraic symbols baffled most contemporary mathematicians. As the only one to appreciate the richness of this work, which laid the foundations of projective geometry and of a unified theory of conic sections, Pascal became Desargues's principal disciple in geometry.

Projective Geometry. Grasping the significance of Desargues's new conception of conics, Pascal adopted the basic ideas of the *Brouillon project:* the introduction of elements at infinity; the definition of a conic as any plane section of a cone with a circular base; the study of conics as perspectives of circles; and the involution determined on any straight line by a conic and the opposite sides of an inscribed quadrilateral. As early as June 1639 Pascal made his first great discovery, that of a property equivalent to the theorem now known as Pascal's "mystic hexagram"; according to it, the three points of intersection of the pairs of opposite sides of a hexagon inscribed in a conic are collinear.[1] He also soon saw the possibility of basing a comprehensive projective study of conics on this property. (The property amounts to an elegant formulation, in geometric language, of the condition under which six points of one plane belong to a single conic.) Next he wrote *Essay pour les coniques* (February 1640), a pamphlet, of which only a few copies were published [1].[2] A plan for further research, illustrated with statements of several typical propositions that he had already discovered, the *Essay* constituted the outline of a great treatise on conics that he had just conceived and begun to prepare.

Pascal seems to have made considerable progress by December 1640, having deduced from his theorem most of the propositions contained in the *Conics* of Apollonius.[3] Subsequently, however, he worked only intermittently on completing the treatise. Although Desargues and Mersenne alluded to the work in November 1642 and 1644, respectively, it was apparently not until March 1648 that Pascal obtained a purely geometric definitive general solution to the celebrated problem of Pappus, which had furnished Descartes with the principal example for illustrating the power of his new analytic geometry (1637).[4] Pascal's success marked an important step in the elaboration of his treatise on conics, for it demonstrated that in this domain projective geometry might prove as effective as the Cartesian analytic methods. Pascal therefore reserved the sixth, and final, section of his treatise, "Des lieux solides" (geometric loci composed of conics), for this problem.

In 1654 Pascal indicated that he had nearly completed the treatise [12], conceived "on the basis of a single proposition"—a work for which he had "had the idea before reaching the age of sixteen" and which he then "constructed and put in order." He also mentioned some special geometric problems to which his projective method could usefully be applied: circles or spheres defined by three or four conditions; conics determined by five elements (points or tangents); geometric loci composed of straight lines, circles, or conics; and a general method of perspective.

Pascal made no further mention of this treatise, which was never published. It seems that only Leibniz saw it in manuscript, and the most precise details known about the work were provided by him. In a letter [23] of 30 August 1676 to E. Périer, one of Pascal's heirs, Leibniz stated that the work merited publication and mentioned a number of points concerning its contents, which he divided into six parts: (1) the projective generation of conics; (2) the definition and properties of the "mystic hexagram"—Pascal's theorem and its applications; (3) the projective theory of poles and polars and of centers and diameters; (4) various properties related to the classic definitions of conics on the basis of their axes and foci; (5) *contacts coniques*, the construction of conics defined by five elements (points or tangents); and (6) solid loci (the problem of Pappus). Besides reading notes on a number of passages of Pascal's treatise [15], Leibniz's papers preserve the text of the first part, "Generatio conisectionum" [14].

The content and inspiration of this introductory chapter are readily apparent from the full title: "The Generation of Conics, Tangents, and Secants; or the Projection of the Circumference, Tangents, and Secants of the Circle for Every Position of the Eye and of the Plane of the Figure." The text presents in an exceptionally elegant form the basic ideas of projective geometry already set forth, in a much less explicit fashion, in Desargues's *Brouillon project*.[5] Although these few elements of Pascal's treatise preserved by Leibniz do not provide a complete picture of its contents, they are sufficient to show the richness and clarity of Pascal's conceptions once he had become fully aware of the power of projective methods. It is reasonable to assume that publication of this work would have hastened the development of projective geometry, impeded until then by the obscurity of Desargues's writings and by their limited availability. Despite the efforts of Philippe de la Hire,[6] the ultimate disappearance of the treatise on conics and the temporary eclipse of both *Essay pour les coniques* (which was not republished until 1779) and Desargues's *Brouillon project* (rediscovered in 1864) hindered the progress of projective geometry. It was not truly developed until the nineteenth century, in the work of Poncelet and his successors. Poncelet, in fact, was one of the first to draw attention to the importance of Pascal's contribution in this area.

Pascal was soon obliged to suspend the contact with the "Académie Parisienne" that had encouraged the precocious flowering of his mathematical abilities. In 1640 he and his sisters joined their father, who since the beginning of that year had been living in Rouen as a royal tax official. From the end of 1640 until 1647 Pascal made only brief and occasional visits to Paris, and no information has survived concerning his scientific activity at the beginning of this long provincial interlude. Moreover, in 1641 he began to suffer from problems of health that several times forced him to give up all activity. From 1642 he pursued his geometric research in a more or less regular fashion; but he began to take an interest in a new problem, to the solution of which he made a major contribution.

Mechanical Computation. Anxious to assist his father, whose duties entailed a great deal of accounting, Pascal sought to mechanize the two elementary operations of arithmetic, addition and subtraction. Toward the end of 1642 he began a project of designing a machine that would reduce these operations to the simple movements of gears. Having solved the theoretical problem of mechanizing computation, it remained for him to produce such a machine that would be convenient, rapid, dependable, and easy to operate. The actual construction, however, required relatively complicated wheel arrangements and proved to be extremely difficult with the rudimentary and inaccurate techniques available. In this venture Pascal displayed remarkable practical sense, great concern for efficiency, and undeniable stubbornness. Supervising a team of workers, he constructed the first model within a few months but, judging it unsatisfactory, he decided to modify and improve it. The considerable problems he encountered soon discouraged him and caused him to interrupt his project. At the beginning of 1644 encouragement from several people, including the chancellor of France, Pierre Séguier, induced Pascal to resume the development of his "arithmetic machine." After having constructed, in his words, "more than fifty models, all different," he finally produced the definitive model in 1645. He himself organized the manufacture and sale of the machine.

This activity is the context of Pascal's second publication, an eighteen-page pamphlet [2] consisting of a "Lettre dédicatoire" to Séguier and a report on the calculating machine—its purpose, operating principles, capabilities, and the circumstances of its construction ("Avis nécessaire à ceux qui auront curiosité de voir ladite machine et de s'en servir"). The text concludes with the announcement that the machine can be seen in operation and purchased at the residence of Roberval. Pascal's first work of this scope, the pamphlet is both a valuable source of information on the guiding ideas of his project and an important document on his personality and style.

It is difficult to estimate the success achieved by Pascal's computing machine, the first of its kind to be offered for sale—an earlier one designed by W. Schickard (1623) seems to have reached only the prototype stage. Although its mechanism was quite complicated, Pascal's machine functioned in a relatively simple fashion—at least for the two operations to which it was actually applied.[7] Its high price, however, limited its sale and rendered it more a curiosity than a useful device. It is not known how many machines were built and sold; seven still exist in public and private collections.[8] For a few years Pascal was actively involved in their manufacture and distribution, for which he had obtained a monopoly by royal decree (22 May 1649) [22]. In 1652 he demonstrated his machine during a lecture before fashionable audience and presented one to Queen Christina of Sweden. For some time, however, he had been directing his attention to problems of a very different kind.

Raised in a Christian milieu, Pascal had been a practicing Catholic throughout his youth but had never given any special consideration to problems of faith. Early in 1646, however, he became converted to the austere and demanding doctrine of Saint-Cyran (Jean Duvergier de Hauranne), whose views were close to those of the Jansenists. This event profoundly marked the rest of Pascal's life. The intransigence of his new convictions was underscored at Rouen between February and April 1647, when Pascal and two friends denounced certain bold theological positions defended by Jacques Forton de Saint-Ange. This change in attitude did not, however, prevent Pascal from embarking on a new phase of scientific activity.

Fluid Statics and the Problem of the Vacuum. To understand and evaluate Pascal's work in the statics of gases and liquids, it is necessary to trace the origins of the subject and to establish a precise chronology. In his *Discorsi* (1638) Galileo had noted that a suction pump cannot raise water to more than a certain height, approximately ten meters. This observation, which seemed to contradict the Aristotelian theory that nature abhors a vacuum, was experimentally verified about 1641 by R. Maggiotti and G. Berti. V. Viviani and E. Torricelli modified the experiment by substituting mercury for water, thereby reducing the height of the column to about seventy-six centimeters. Torricelli announced the successful execution of this experiment in two letters to M. Ricci of 11 and 28 June 1644. Describing the experiment in detail, he gave a correct interpretation of it based on the weight of the external column of air and the reality of the existence of the vacuum.[9] Mersenne, informed of the work of the Italian scientists, attempted unsuccessfully to repeat the experiment, which for some time fell into neglect.

In October 1646 Mersenne's friend P. Petit, who was passing through Rouen, repeated the experiment with the assistance of Étienne and Blaise Pascal. At the end of November 1646 Petit described the event in a letter to Pierre Chanut. Meanwhile, Pascal, seeking to arrive at firm conclusions, had repeated the experiment in various forms, asserting that the results contradicted the doctrine of the *horror vacui*. Profiting from the existence at Rouen of an excellent glassworks, Pascal conducted a series of further experiments in January and February 1647. He repeated Torricelli's experiment with water and wine, using tubes of different shapes, some as long as twelve meters, affixed to the masts of ships. These experiments became known in Paris in the spring of 1647. Gassendi wrote the first commentary on them, and Mersenne and Roberval undertook their own experiments. The first printed account of the entire group of Pascal's experiments was *Discours sur le vide* by P. Guiffart, of Rouen, written in April 1647 and published in August of that year. Just as it was published, word reached Paris that a barometric experiment had been conducted at Warsaw in July 1647 by V. Magni, who implicitly claimed priority. Roberval responded on 22 September with a Latin *Narratio* (published at Warsaw in December), in which he established the priority of Torricelli's and Pascal's experiments and revealed new details concerning the latter.

Pascal soon intervened directly in the debate. During the summer of 1647 his health had deteriorated; and he left Rouen with his sister Jacqueline to move to Paris, where their father joined them a year later. Henceforth, Pascal maintained contacts both with the Jansenists of Port-Royal and with the secular intellectuals of Paris, who were greatly interested in the interpretation of the experiments with the vacuum. He had two discussions on this topic with Descartes (23 and 24 September), who may have suggested that he compare barometric observations made at different altitudes.[10] This idea was also proposed by Mersenne in his *Reflexiones physico-mathematicae* (beginning of October 1647).[11] At this time Pascal wrote a report of his experiments at Rouen, a thirty-two-page pamphlet published in October 1647 as *Expériences nouvelles touchant le vide* [3]. In this "abridgment" of a larger work that he planned to write, Pascal admitted that his initial inspiration derived from the Italian barometric experiment and stated that his primary goal was to combat the idea of the impossibility of the vacuum. From his experiments he had deduced the existence of an apparent vacuum, but he asserted that the existence of an absolute vacuum was still an unconfirmed hypothesis. Consequently his pamphlet makes no reference to the explanation of the barometric experiment by means of the weight of the air, proposed by Torricelli in 1644.[12] According to his sister Jacqueline, however, Pascal had been a firm proponent of this view from 1647.[13] In any case his concern was to convince his readers; he therefore proceeded cautiously, affirming only what had been irrefutably demonstrated by experiment.

Despite his moderate position, Pascal's rejection of the theory of the impossibility of the vacuum involved him in vigorous debate. With the publication of the *Expériences nouvelles*, a friend of Descartes's, the Jesuit Estienne Noël, declared in a letter to Pascal that the upper portion of Torricelli's tube was filled with a purified air that had entered through the pores of the glass.[14] In a dazzling reply (29 October 1647) [4] Pascal clearly set forth the rules of his scientific method and vigorously upheld his position. Several days later Noël reaffirmed the essence of his views but expressed a desire to end the dispute.[15] It was indirectly resumed, however, after Noël published a new and violent critique of the *Expériences nouvelles*.[16] In a letter to his friend F. Le Pailleur [5], Pascal refuted Noël's second letter and criticized his recent publication. In April 1648 Étienne Pascal entered the debate against Noël.[17] The dispute soon ended, however, when Noël published a much more moderate Latin version of his short treatise.[18]

During this controversy scientists in Paris had become interested in the problem of the vacuum, devoting many experiments to it and proposing a number of hypotheses to explain it. Having participated in discussions on the topic, Pascal conceived one of the variants of the famous experiment of the vacuum within the vacuum, designed to verify the hypothesis of the column of air.[19] He seems, however, to have expected a still better confirmation of the hypothesis from a program of simultaneous barometric observations at different altitudes (at Clermont-Ferrand and at the summit of Puy de Dôme), the execution of which he entrusted to his brother-in-law, Périer. One of these observations, now known as the "Puy de Dôme experiment," was carried out on 19 September 1648. Pascal immediately published a detailed, twenty-page account of it, *Récit de la grande expérience de l'équilibre des liqueurs . . .* [6], consisting principally of Périer's letter and report. In a short introduction he presented the experiment as the direct consequence of his *Expériences nouvelles*, and the text of a letter of 15 November 1647 to Périer, in which he explained the goal of the experiment and the principle on which it was based. He concluded by pointing out his analogous experiment at the Tour St. Jacques in Paris and by announcing his conversion to the principles of the existence of the absolute vacuum and of the weight of air.

The *Récit*, which marks an important phase of Pascal's research on the vacuum, gave rise to two heated controversies.[20] The first arose at the end of the seventeenth century, when several authors denied Pascal's priority with regard to the basic principle of the Puy de Dôme experiment. This question, however, is of only secondary importance. While it appears that the principle was formulated simultaneously—on the basis of different presuppositions—by Pascal, Descartes, and Mersenne, only Pascal tested it and integrated it into an exceptionally cogent chain of reasoning.

The second controversy was launched in 1906–1907 by F. Mathieu, who challenged both Pascal's scientific originality and his honesty. He accused Pascal of having fabricated the letter to Périer of 15 November 1647 after completion of the event, in order to take credit for the experiments of the vacuum within the vacuum and of Puy de Dôme. Although the heated debate that ensued did not produce any unanimously accepted conclusions, it did stimulate research that brought to light many unpublished documents. In an assessment of the question J. Mesnard, after examining the arguments and clarifying many points, suggests that Pascal probably did send the contested letter to Périer on 15 November 1647 but may have altered the text slightly for publication. This compromise judgment is probably close to the truth.

At the beginning of 1649 Périer, following Pascal's instructions, began an uninterrupted series of barometric observations designed to ascertain the possible relationship between the height of a column of mercury at a given location and the state of the atmosphere. The *expérience continuelle*, which was a forerunner of the use of the barometer as an instrument in weather forecasting, lasted until March 1651 and was supplemented by parallel observations made at Paris and Stockholm.[21] Pascal continued working on a major treatise on the vacuum; but only a few fragments, dating from 1651, have survived: a draft of a preface [7] on the relationships between reason and authority and between science and religion, and two short passages published by Périer in 1663.[22] In June 1651 a Jesuit accused Pascal of claiming credit for Torricelli's experiment. In two letters [9, 10], of which only the first was printed, Pascal recounted—with several serious errors—the history of that experiment and laid claim to the idea of the Puy de Dôme experiment.

Pascal soon put aside his great treatise on the vacuum in order to write a shorter but more synthetic work. Divided into two closely related parts, this work is devoted to the laws of hydrostatics and to the demonstration and description of the various effects of the weight of air. It was completed about the beginning of 1654 and marked the end of Pascal's active research in physics. It was published posthumously by Périer, along with several appendices, in 1663 as *Traités de l'équilibre des liqueurs et de la pesanteur de la masse de l'air* . . . [13]. The fruit of several years of observations, experiments, and reflection, it is a remarkable synthesis of new knowledge and theories elaborated since the work of Stevin and Galileo. The highly persuasive *Traités*, assembling and coordinating earlier results and recent discoveries, are characterized above all by their rigorous experimental method and by the categorical rejection of Scholasticism. In hydrostatics Pascal continued the investigations of Stevin, Galileo, Torricelli, and Mersenne. He clearly set forth the basic principles of the science, although he did not fully succeed in demonstrating them satisfactorily. In particular he provided a lucid account of the fundamental concept of pressure.

The untoward delay in the publication of the *Traités* obviously reduced its timeliness; for in the meanwhile the study of the weight of air and the existence of the vacuum had been profoundly affected by the work of Otto von Guericke and Robert Boyle.[23] In this area, in fact, the *Traités* essentially systematized, refined, and

developed experiments, concepts, and theories that, for the most part, had already been discussed in the *Expériences nouvelles* and the *Récit*. Pascal's influence, therefore, must be measured as much by the effect of these preliminary publications and the contemporary writings of Mersenne and Pecquet, which reflect his thinking, as by the posthumous *Traités*.[24] This influence was certainly considerable, for it partially conditioned all subsequent research on the subject; but it cannot easily be separated from that of, for instance, Roberval and Auzout, who participated in the rapid progress of research on the vacuum at Paris in 1647 and 1648. Nevertheless, for their synthetic treatment of the subject, clarity, and rigor, the *Traités* are indisputably a classic of seventeenth-century science.

Although from October 1646 Pascal had been deeply interested in problems of the vacuum, he was often impeded in his research by poor health and by religious concerns. The death of his father in September 1651 and the entry of his sister Jacqueline into the convent of Port-Royal in January 1652 marked a turning point in his life. In better health and less preoccupied with religious problems, he pursued his scientific work while leading a more worldly existence. Beginning in the summer of 1653 he frequently visited the duke of Roannez. Through the duke he met the Chevalier de Méré, who introduced him to the problems of games of chance. At the beginning of 1654, in an address [12] to the Académie Parisienne de Mathématique, which was directed by F. Le Pailleur, Pascal listed the works on geometry, arithmetic, and physics that he had already completed or begun writing and mentioned, in particular, his recent research on the division of stakes.[25]

Calculus of Probabilities. The Arithmetical Triangle. The year 1654 was exceptionally fruitful for Pascal. He not only did the last refining of his treatises on geometry and physics but also conducted his principal studies on arithmetic, combinatorial analysis, and the calculus of probability. This work can be seen in his correspondence with Fermat [16] and his *Traité du triangle arithmétique* [17].

Pascal's correspondence with Fermat between July and October 1654 marks the beginning of the calculus of probability. Their discussion focused on two main problems. The first concerned the probability that a player will obtain a certain face of the die in a given number of throws. The second, more complex, consisted in determining, for any game involving several players, the portion of the stakes to be returned to each player if the game is interrupted. Fermat succeeded in solving these problems by using only combinatorial analysis. Pascal, on the other hand, seems gradually to have discovered the advantages of the systematic application of reasoning by recursion. This recourse to mathematical induction, however, is not clearly evident until the final section of the *Traité du triangle arithmétique*, of which Fermat received a copy before 29 August 1654.

The *Traité* was printed in 1654 but was not distributed until 1665. Composed partly in French and partly in Latin, it has a complex structure; but the discovery of a preliminary Latin version of the first part makes it easier to trace its genesis.[26] Although the principle of the arithmetical triangle was already known,[27] Pascal was the first to make a comprehensive study of it. He derived from it the greatest number of applications, the most important and original of which are related to combinatorial analysis and especially to the study of the problems of stakes. Yet it is impossible to appreciate Pascal's contribution if it is considered solely from the perspective of combinatorial analysis and the calculus of probability. Several modern authors have shown that Pascal's letters to Fermat and the *Traité du triangle arithmétique* can be fully understood only when they are seen as preliminary steps toward a theory of decision.[28]

As E. Coumet has pointed out, Pascal's concern, beyond the purely mathematical aspect of the problems, was to link decisions and uncertain events. His aim was not to define the mathematical status of the concept of probability—a term that he did not employ—but to solve the problem of dividing stakes. This innovative effort must therefore be viewed in the context of the discussions conducted by jurists, theologians, and moralists in the sixteenth and seventeenth centuries on the implications of chance in the most varied circumstances of individual and community life. Unrecognized until recently, this aspect of Pascal's creative work is revealed in its full significance in the light of recent ideas on game theory and decision theory.

On the other hand, Pascal's research on combinatorial analysis now appears much less original. Considered in the context of the vigorous current of ideas on the subject in the sixteenth and seventeenth centuries, it is noteworthy less for the originality of its results than for the clarity, generality, and rigor with which they are presented.[29] Pascal's contribution to the calculus of probability is much more direct and indisputable: indeed, with Fermat he laid the earliest foundations of this discipline.[30] The *Traité du triangle arithmétique* contains only scattered remarks on the subject; in addition, only a part of the correspondence with Fermat [16] has been preserved, and its late publication (1679 and 1779) certainly reduced its direct influence. Fortunately, through Huygens the original contribution of Pascal and Fermat in this area became quickly known. During a stay in Paris in 1655 Huygens was informed in detail of their work, and he recast their ideas in the light of his own conceptions in his *Tractatus de ratiociniis in aleae ludo*. With its publication in 1657 the essential elements of the new science were revealed.[31] Nevertheless, the calculus of probability did not experience further development until the beginning of the eighteenth century, with Jakob I Bernoulli, P. R. de Montmort, and A. de Moivre.

Unsatisfied by his worldly life and intense scientific activity, Pascal was again drawn to religious concerns. Following a second conversion, during the famous "nuit de feu" of 23 November 1654, he abandoned his scientific work in order to devote himself to meditation and religious activity and to assist the Jansenists in their battle against many enemies, particularly the Jesuits. Working anonymously, between 13 January 1656 and 24 March 1657 Pascal composed the eighteen *Lettres provinciales* with the assistance of his friends from Port-Royal, Antoine Arnauld and Pierre Nicole. A masterpiece of polemic, this eminent contribution to the debate then agitating Christian doctrine was first published as a collection in 1657 under the pseudonym Louis de Montalte. Although Pascal produced other polemical writings, he worked primarily on preparing a defense of Christianity directed to nonbelievers. This unfinished project was the source of several posthumously published writings, the most important being the *Pensées*, published in 1670. The object of numerous commentaries and penetrating critical studies, this basic work fully displays Pascal's outstanding philosophical and literary talents.

Although concerned above all with meditation and religious activities during this period, Pascal was not totally estranged from scientific life thanks to his friends, particularly Carcavi. Around 1657, at the request of Arnauld, Pascal prepared a work entitled *Éléments de géométrie*, of which there remain only a few passages concerning methodology: the brief "Introduction à la géométrie," preserved among Leibniz's papers [18]; and two fragments, "De l'esprit géométrique" and "De l'art de persuader" [19]. Finally, in 1658 Pascal undertook a brilliant, if short-lived, series of scientific studies.

The Calculus of Indivisibles and the Study of Infinitesimal Problems. During 1658 and the first months of 1659 Pascal devoted most of his time to perfecting the "theory of indivisibles," a forerunner of the methods of integral calculus. This new theory enabled him to study problems involving infinitesimals: calculations of areas and volumes, determinations of centers of gravity, and rectifications of curves.

From the end of the sixteenth century many authors, including Stevin (1586), L. Valerio (1604), and Kepler

(1609 and 1615), had tried to solve these fundamental problems by using simpler and more intuitive methods than that of Archimedes, which was considered a model of virtually unattainable rigor.[32] The publication in 1635 of Cavalieri's *Geometria* marked the debut of the method of indivisibles;[33] its principles, presentation, and applications were discussed and elaborated in the later writings of Cavalieri (1647 and 1653) and in those of Galileo (1638), Torricelli (1644), Guldin (1635–1641), Gregory of Saint-Vincent (1647), and A. Tacquet (1651). (The research of Fermat and Roberval on this topic remained unpublished.)[34] The method, which assumed various forms, constituted the initial phase of development of the basic procedures of integral calculus, with the exception of the algorithm.

Pascal first referred to the method of indivisibles in a work on arithmetic of 1654, "Potestatum numericarum summa."[35] He observed that the results concerning the summation of numerical powers made possible the solution of certain quadrature problems. As an example he stated a known result concerning the integral of x^n for whole n, $\int_0^a x^n \, dx = a^{n+1}/(n+1)$, in modern notation.[36] This arithmetical interpretation of the theory of indivisibles permitted Pascal to give a sufficiently precise idea of the order of infinitude[37] and to establish the natural relationship between "la mesure d'une grandeur continue" and "la sommation des puissances numériques." In the fragment "De l'esprit géométrique" [19], composed in 1657, he returned to the notion of the indivisible in order to specify its relationship to the notions of the infinitely small and of the infinitely large and to refute the most widespread errors concerning it.

At the beginning of 1658 Pascal believed that he had perfected the calculus of indivisibles by refining his method and broadening its field of application. Persuaded that in this manner he had discovered the solution to several infinitesimal problems relating to the cycloid or *roulette*, he decided to challenge other mathematicians to solve these problems.[38] Although rather complicated, the history of this contest is worth a brief recounting because of its important repercussions during a crucial phase in the birth of infinitesimal calculus. In an unsigned circular distributed in June 1658, Pascal stated the conditions of the contest and set its closing date at 1 October [20a]. In further unsigned circulars and pamphlets [20], issued between July 1658 and January 1659, he modified or specified certain of the conditions and announced the results. He also responded to the criticism of some participants and sought to demonstrate the importance and the originality of his own solutions.

Most of the leading mathematicians of the time followed the contest with interest, either as participants (A. de Lalouvère and J. Wallis) or as spectators working on one or several of the questions proposed by Pascal or on related problems—as did R. F. de Sluse, M. Ricci, Huygens, and Wren.[39] Their solutions having been judged incomplete and marred by errors, Lalouvère and Wallis were eliminated. Their heated reactions to this decision were partially justified by the bias it displayed and the commentaries that accompanied it.[40] This bias, which also appears in certain passages of Pascal's *Histoire de la roulette* [20b, 20d], was the source of intense polemics concerning, in particular, the importance of Torricelli's original contribution.[41] At the end of the contest Pascal published his own solutions to some of the original problems and to certain problems that had been added in the meantime. In December 1658 and January 1659 he brought out, under the pseudonym A. Dettonville, four letters setting forth the principles of his method and its applications to various problems concerning the cycloid, as well as to such questions as the quadrature of surfaces, cubature of volumes, determination of centers of gravity, and rectification of curved lines. In February 1659 these four pamphlets were collected in *Lettres de A. Dettonville contenant quelques-unes de ses inventions de géométrie . . .* [21].

This publication of some 120 pages has a very complex structure. The first of the *Lettres* consists of five sections with independent paginations, and the three others appear in inverse order of their composition.[42] Thus only by returning to the original order is it possible to understand the logical sequence of the whole, follow the development of Pascal's method, and appreciate the influence on it of the new information he received and of his progress in mastering infinitesimal problems.[43]

When he began the contest, Pascal knew of the methods and the chief results of Stevin, Cavalieri, Torricelli, Gregory of Saint-Vincent, and Tacquet; but he was not familiar with the bulk of the unpublished research of Roberval and Fermat. Apart from this information, and in addition to the arithmetical procedures that he applied, starting in 1654, to the solution of problems of the calculus of indivisibles, Pascal possessed a new method inspired by Archimedes. It was elaborated on a geometric foundation, its point of departure being the principle of the balance and the concepts of static moment and center of gravity. Pascal learned of the importance of the results obtained by Fermat and Roberval—notably in the study of the cycloid—at the time he issued his first circular. This information led him to modify the subject of the contest and to develop his own method further. Similarly, in August 1658, when he was informed of the result of the rectification of the cycloid, Pascal extended rectification to other arcs of curves and then undertook to determine the center of gravity of these arcs, as well as the area and center of gravity of the surfaces of revolution generated by their revolution about an axis. Consequently the *Lettres* present a method that is in continual development, appearing increasingly complex as it becomes more precise and more firmly based. The most notable characteristics of this work, which remained unfinished, are the importance accorded to the determination of centers of gravity, the crucial role of triangular sums and statical considerations, its stylistic rigor and elegance, and the use of a clear and precise geometric language that partially compensates for the absence of algebraic symbolism.[44] Among outstanding contributions of the work are the discovery of the equality of curvature of the generalized cycloid and the ellipse; the deepening of the concept of the indivisible; a first step toward the concept of the definite integral and the determination of its fundamental properties; and the indirect recourse to certain methods of calculation, such as integration by parts.

Assimilated and exploited by Pascal's successors, these innovations contributed to the elaboration of infinitesimal methods. His most productive contribution, however, appears to have been his implicit use of the characteristic triangle.[45] Indeed, Leibniz stated that Pascal's writings on the characteristic triangle were an especially fruitful stimulus for him.[46] This testimony from one of the creators of infinitesimal calculus indicates that Pascal's work marked an important stage in the transition from the calculus of indivisibles to integral calculus. Pascal was unable, however, to transcend the overly specific nature of his conceptions. Neither could he utilize to full effect the power and generality of the underlying methods nor develop the results he obtained. This partial failure can be attributed to two causes. First, his systematic refusal to adopt Cartesian algebraic symbolism prevented him from realizing the necessity of the formalization that permitted Leibniz to create the integral calculus. Second, his preoccupation with mystic concerns led him to interrupt his research only a short time after he had begun it.

Early in 1659 Pascal again fell gravely ill and abandoned almost all his intellectual undertakings in order to devote himself to prayer and to charitable works.[47] In 1661 his desire for solitude increased after the death of his sister Jacqueline and a dispute with his friends from Port-Royal. Paradoxically, it was at this time that Pascal participated in a project to establish a public transportation system in Paris, in the form of carriages charging five *sols* per ride—a

scheme that went into effect in 1662.[48] Some writers have asserted that Pascal's doctrinal intransigence had diminished in this period to such a point that at the moment of his death he renounced his Jansenist convictions, but most of the evidence does not support this interpretation.

Pascal was a complex person whose pride constantly contended with a profound desire to submit to a rigorous, Augustinian insistence on self-denial. An exceptionally gifted polemicist, moralist, and writer, he was also a scientist anxious to help solve the major problems of his day. He did not, it is true, produce a body of work distinguished by profound creativity, on the model of such contemporaries as Descartes, Fermat, and Torricelli. Still, he was able to elucidate and systematize several rapidly developing fields of science (projective geometry, the calculus of probability, infinitesimal calculus, fluid statics, and scientific methodology) and to make major original contributions to them. In light of this manifold achievement Pascal, a leading opponent of Descartes, was undoubtedly one of the outstanding scientists of the mid-seventeenth century.

NOTES

1. The first known formulation of this theorem was as lemma 1 of *Essay pour les coniques*. It clearly differs from the modern statement by not referring explicitly to the inscribed hexagon and by apparently being limited to the case of the circle (even though the corresponding figure illustrates the case of the ellipse). According to remarks made by Leibniz, it seems that this theorem, in its hexagonal formulation and under the name "hexagramme mystique," held a central place in Pascal's treatise on conics, now lost. The fact that the *Essay pour les coniques* contains only statements without demonstrations makes it impossible to ascertain the precise role Pascal assigned to this theorem in 1640.
2. The numbers in square brackets refer to the corresponding works listed in sec. 1 of the bibliography. For a more detailed study of the *Essay*, see R. Taton, in *Revue d'histoire des sciences*, **8** (1955), 1–18, and in *L'oeuvre scientifique de Pascal* (Paris, 1964), 21–29; and J. Mesnard, ed., *Blaise Pascal. Oeuvres complètes*, II (1971), 220–225 (cited below as Mesnard).
3. See Mersenne's letter to Theodore Haak of 18 Nov. 1640, in Mesnard, II, 239.
4. On the references by Desargues and Mersenne, see *ibid.*, 279–280, 299. On the problem of Pappus, see Mersenne's letter to Constantijn Huygens of 17 Mar. 1648 in C. Huygens, *Oeuvres complètes de Christiaan Huygens, publiées par la Société Hollandaise des Sciences*, II (1888), 33, and in Mesnard, II, 577–578. On Descartes, see Taton, in *L'oeuvre scientifique de Pascal*, 45–50; and M. S. Mahoney, "Descartes: Mathematics and Physics," in *DSB*, IV, 56.
5. See Taton, in *L'oeuvre scientifique . . .*, 55–59 (for "Generatio conisectionum") and 53–72 (for the treatise as a whole). See also his "Desargues," in *DSB*, IV, 46–51.
6. See Taton, "La Hire, Philippe de," in *DSB*, VII, 576–578.
7. See D. Diderot, "Arithmétique (Machine)," in *Encyclopédie*, I (1751), 680–684.

8. See J. Payen, in *L'oeuvre scientifique de Pascal*, 229–247.

9. See, in particular, C. De Waard, *L'expérience barométrique, ses antécédents et ses explications* (Thouars, 1936), 110–123; M. Gliozzi, "Origine e sviluppi dell'esperienza torricelliana," in *Opere de Evangelista Torricelli*, G. Loria and G. Vassura, eds., IV (Faenza, 1944), 231–294; and W. E. K. Middleton, *The History of the Barometer* (London, 1964).

10. Jacqueline Pascal gave some details of these meetings in a letter to her sister Gilberte of 25 Sept. 1647. (See Mesnard, II, 478–482.) In a letter to Mersenne of 13 Dec. 1647 and in two letters to Carcavi of 11 June and 17 Aug. 1649 (see *ibid.*, 548–550, 655–658, 716–719) Descartes stated that he had suggested this idea, which was the origin of the celebrated Puy de Dôme experiment of 19 Sept. 1648, to Pascal.

11. See *ibid.*, 483–489.

12. Torricelli held that the space above the column of mercury was empty. Considering the horizontal plane determined by the exterior level of the mercury, he asserted that the weight of the column of mercury equaled the weight of a column of air of the same base, which implied simultaneously the existence of the vacuum, the weight of the air, and the finiteness of the terrestrial atmosphere. In 1651 Pascal admitted that he was aware of Torricelli's explanation as early as 1647 (see *ibid.*, 812), but he insisted that at that time the explanation was only a conjecture; it had yet to be verified by experiment, and for this reason he undertook the experiment of Puy de Dôme.

13. Letter to Gilberte Pascal of 25 Sept. 1647 (see *ibid.*, 482).

14. See *ibid.*, 513–518.

15. See *ibid.*, 528–540.

16. It was a brief work with the picturesque title *Le plein du vide* (Paris, 1648); see Mesnard, II, 556–558. This work was reprinted by Bossut in *Oeuvres de Blaise Pascal*, C. Bossut, ed., IV (The Hague, 1779), 108–146.

17. See Mesnard, II, 584–602.

18. E. Noël, *Plenum experimentis novis confirmatum* (Paris, 1648); see Mesnard, II, 585.

19. This experiment is mentioned without details in Pascal's *Récit . . .* (see Mesnard, II, 678). The reality of the experiment is confirmed by the quite precise description of it that Noël gave in his *Gravitas comparata* (Paris, 1648); on this point see Mesnard, II, 635–636, which presents the Latin text, a French translation, and an explanatory diagram derived from an earlier study by P. Thirion. The principle of this experiment consists of conducting Torricelli's experiment in an environment where the pressure can be varied from atmospheric pressure to zero. Other variants were devised at almost the same time by Roberval (Mesnard, II, 637–639) and by Auzout (*ibid.*, 767–771). A fourth variant, easier to carry out in practice, is described in Pascal's *Traités de l'équilibre des liqueurs et de la pesanteur de la masse de l'air . . .* (*ibid.*, 1086–1088).

20. See *ibid.*, 653–676.

21. F. Périer published an account of them in 1663 as an appendix to Pascal's *Traités de l'équilibre . . .* (pp. 195–209); see Mesnard, II, 738–745. The fact that the first observations made at Stockholm were carried out by Descartes appears to indicate that he had become reconciled with Pascal.

22. The preface was not published until 1779, when it appeared under the title "De l'autorité en matière de philosophie" (Bossut, II, 1–12). The passages published by Périer appear at the end of Pascal's *Traités de l'équilibre . . .* (pp. 141–163).

23. See F. Krafft, "Guericke," in *DSB*, V, 574–576; and C. Webster, "The Discovery of Boyle's Law and the Concept of the Elasticity of Air in the Seventeenth Century," in *Archive for History of the Exact Sciences*, 2 (1965), 441–502, esp. 447–458.

24. M. Mersenne, *Reflectiones physico-mathematicae* (Paris, 1647); and J. Pecquet, *Experimenta nova anatomica* (Paris, 1651). To these works should be added publications by Noël, already cited, as well as those of Roberval and of V. Magni (see Webster, *op. cit.*), and, above all, the correspondence of scientists from Italy, France, England, Poland, and other European countries.

25. The word used in French to designate this problem, *parti*, is the past participle (considered as the noun form) of the verb *partir*, understood in the sense of "to share." The problem consists in finding, for a game interrupted before the end, the way of dividing the stakes among the players in proportion to their chances of winning at the time of interruption.

26. See Mesnard, II, which provides an introduction to the texts (pp. 1166–1175) and the texts themselves, both of the first printing, in Latin with French translation (pp. 1176–1286), and of the second, with translation of the Latin passages (pp. 1288–1332).

27. This figure, in more or less elaborated forms that were equivalent to lists of coefficients of the binomial theorem, appeared as early as the Middle Ages in the works of Naṣīr al-Dīn al Ṭūsī (1265) and Chu Shih-chieh (1303). The arithmetical triangle reappeared in the sixteenth and seventeenth centuries in the writings of Apian (1527), Stifel, Scheubel, Tartaglia, Bombelli, Peletier, Trenchant, and Oughtred. But Pascal was the first to devote to it a systematic study linked to many questions of arithmetic and combinatorial analysis.

28. See, for example, E. Coumet, "La théorie du hasard est-elle née par hasard?" in *Annales. Économies, sociétés, civilisations* (1970), 574–598, as well as the studies of G.-T. Guilbaud (1952) and the other works on operational research, cybernetics, game theory, and other fields cited in Coumet's article (p. 575, notes 1 and 2).

29. See E. Coumet, "Mersenne, Frénicle et l'élaboration de l'analyse combinatoire dans la première moitié du XVIIe siècle" (a typescript thesis, Paris, 1968), and "Mersenne: Dénombrements, répertoires, numérotations de permutations," in *Mathématiques et sciences humaines*, 10 (1972), 5–37.

30. See I. Todhunter, *A History of the Mathematical Theory of Probability From the Time of Pascal to That of Laplace* (Cambridge–London, 1865; repr. New York, 1949), 7–21.

31. See F. Van Schooten, *Exercitationum mathematicarum libri quinque* (Leiden, 1657), 519–534, and H. J. M. Bos's article on Huygens in *DSB*, VI, 600.

32. On Archimedes see the article by M. Clagett in *DSB*, I, 213–231, esp. 215–222, for his infinitesimal methods and 229 for the diffusion of his writings in the sixteenth and seventeenth centuries. It should be noted that at this period mathematicians were aware only of his rigorous method of presentation, which Gregory of Saint-Vincent termed the "method of exhaustion." Archimedes' much more intuitive method of discovery did not become known until the rediscovery of his *Method* in 1906. On the infinitesimal work of Stevin, Valerio, and Kepler, see C. B. Boyer, *The Concept of Calculus* (New York, 1949), 98–111.

33. B. Cavalieri, *Geometria indivisibilibus continuorum nova quadam ratione promota* (Bologna, 1635). On this subject see Boyer, *op. cit.*, pp. 111–123; A. Koyré, in *Études d'histoire de la pensée scientifique* (Paris, 1966), 297–324; and the article on Cavalieri by E. Carruccio in *DSB*, III, 149–153.

34. See Boyer, *op. cit.*, pp. 123–147, 154–165.

35. Reprinted in Mesnard, II, 1259–1272; see esp. 1270–1272. This work is the next to last—but also one of the earliest written—of the brief treatises making up the *Traité du triangle arithmétique* [17].

36. "The sum of all the lines of any degree whatever is to the larger line and to the higher degree as unity is to the exponent of the higher degree" (Mesnard, II, 1271). On Pascal's infinitesimal work see H. Bosmans, in *Archivio di storia della scienza*, 4 (1923), 369–379; Boyer, *op. cit.*, pp. 147–153; F. Russo, in *L'oeuvre scientifique de Pascal* (Paris, 1964), 136–153; and P. Costabel, *ibid.*, 169–206.

37. "In the case of a continuous magnitude (*grandeur continue*), magnitudes of any type (*genre*), when added in any number desired to a magnitude of higher type, do not increase it at all. Thus, points add nothing to lines, [nor] lines to surfaces, [nor] surfaces to solids, or, to use the language of numbers in a treatise devoted to numbers, roots do not count with respect to squares, [nor] squares with respect to cubes . . . . Therefore, lower degrees should be neglected as possessing no value" (Mesnard, II, 1271–1272).

38. The cycloid is the curve generated by a point M of the circumference of a circle (C) that rolls without sliding on a straight line D. AB, the base of the cycloid, is equal to $2\pi r$ (where r is the radius of the circle C). Derived curves are obtained by the displacement of a point M' situated on the interior (curtate cycloid) or M'' on the exterior (prolate cycloid) of the moving circle. Defined by Roberval in 1637,

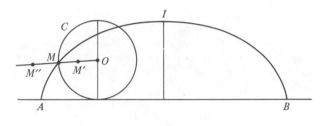

FIGURE 1

these curves had served since that year—under the name of *roulettes*, trochoids, or cycloids—as key examples for the solution of various problems pertaining to the infinitesimal calculus. These problems included the construction of tangents to plane curves by the use of the method of indivisibles, the determination of plane areas, the calculation of volumes, and the determination of centers of gravity. The cycloid thus played an important role in the patient efforts that resulted in the transition from the method of indivisibles to the infinitesimal calculus. Between 1637 and 1647 Roberval, then Fermat and Descartes, and finally Torricelli were particularly interested in the solution of infinitesimal problems associated with the cycloid; and bitter priority disputes broke out between Roberval and Descartes and then between Roberval and Torricelli. But in June 1658, when Pascal distributed his first circular, it appears that he had only a very imperfect knowledge of prior work on this subject.

The practice of setting up a contest was very common at the time. A similar contest, initiated by Fermat in January 1657 on questions of number theory, continued to set Fermat against some of the participants, notably Wallis. See O. Becker and J. E. Hofmann, *Geschichte der Mathematik* (Bonn, 1951), 192–194.

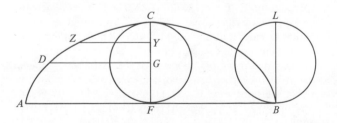

FIGURE 2

The contest problem was the following: Given an arch of the cycloid of base AB and of axis CF, one considers the semicurvilinear surface CZY defined by the curve, the axis, and a semichord ZY parallel to the base. The problem is to find (1) the area of CZY and its center of gravity; (2) the volumes of the solids V_1 and V_2 generated by the revolution of CZY about CY and about ZY, as well as their centers of gravity; and (3) the centers of gravity of the semisolids obtained by cutting V_1 and V_2 by midplanes.

39. In his *Histoire de la roulette* [20b], Pascal mentions the results sent to him by these four authors and notes, in particular, the rectification of the arch of the cycloid communicated to him by Wren. He points out that he has extended this operation to an arbitrary arc AZ originating at the summit of the cycloid and that he has determined the center of gravity of this arc AZ, as well as the areas and centers of gravity of the surfaces of revolution generated by the rotation of AZ about the base or about the axis of the cycloid. Carcavi, the president of the jury, also mentioned the results sent by Fermat, particularly those on the areas of the surfaces of revolution.

40. See A. Lalouvère, *Veterum geometria promota in septem de cycloide libris* (Toulouse, 1660); and J. Wallis, *Tractatus duo, prior de cycloide, posterior de cissoide* (Oxford, 1659). On the latter publication see K. Hara, "Pascal et Wallis au sujet de la cycloïde," in two parts: the first in *Annals of the Japanese Association for the Philosophy of Science*, **3**, no. 4 (1969), 36–57, and the second in *Gallia* (Osaka), nos. 10–11 (1971), 231–249.

41. See, in particular, C. Dati, *Lettera della vera storia della cicloide* (Florence, 1663).

42. This question is raised by K. Hara, in "Quelques additions à l'examen des textes mathématiques de Pascal," in *Gallia* (Osaka), no. 7 (1962); by P. Costabel, in *L'oeuvre scientifique de Pascal*, 169–198; and by J. Mesnard, in Mesnard, I, 31–33.

43. The original order is reproduced in vol. III of Mesnard's ed. of Pascal's works (in preparation).

44. See Bosmans, *op. cit.*; Boyer, *op. cit.*, pp. 147–153; Russo, *op. cit.*, pp. 136–153; and Costabel, *ibid.*, pp. 169–206.

45. See Russo, *op. cit.*, pp. 149–151. It should be noted that the expression "characteristic triangle" was introduced not by Pascal but by Leibniz. See also Boyer, *op. cit.*, pp. 152–153; Boyer points out that this figure had previously been used by Torricelli and Roberval and even by Snell (1624). In modern notation, the characteristic triangle at a point $M(x_0, y_0)$ of a plane curve (C) of equation $y = f(x)$ is a right triangle, the first two sides of which, parallel to the axes Ox and Oy, are of length dx and dy; its diagonal, of length ds, is parallel to the tangent to the curve (C) at M.

46. See a letter from Leibniz to Jakob I Bernoulli of Apr. 1703, in Leibniz, *Mathematische Schriften*, C. I. Gerhardt, ed., III (Halle, 1856), 72–73. This letter is reproduced by J. Itard in *Histoire générale des sciences*, 2nd ed., II (Paris, 1969), 245–246. For other statements by Leibniz concerning his knowledge of Pascal's writtings, see P. Costabel, in *L'oeuvre scientifique de Pascal*, 201–205.

47. Pascal wrote again to Fermat (10 Aug. 1660), met Huygens (5 and 13 Dec. 1660), and conversed with the duke of Roannez on the force of rarefied air and on flying. These are the few indications that we have regarding Pascal's scientific activity during the last three years of his life.

48. See M. Duclou, *Les carrosses à cinq sols* (Paris, 1950).

BIBLIOGRAPHY

I. ORIGINAL WORKS. There have been many complete eds. of Pascal's works. The most important from the point of view of scholarship are the following:

a. *Oeuvres de Blaise Pascal*, C. Bossut, ed., 5 vols. (The Hague, 1779), abbrev. as Bossut.

b. *Oeuvres de Blaise Pascal publiées selon l'ordre chronologique*, L. Brunschvicg, P. Boutroux, and F. Gazier, eds., 14 vols. (Paris, 1904–1914), part of the Collection des Grands Écrivains de la France, abbrev. as G.E.

c. *Oeuvres complètes de Blaise Pascal*, J. Chevalier, ed. (Paris, 1954), in Bibliothèque de la Pléiade," abbrev. as PL.

d. *Blaise Pascal. Oeuvres complètes*, J. Mesnard, ed., 2 vols. to date (Paris, 1964–1971); abbrev. as Mesnard. This last ed., which surpasses all previous ones, so far comprises only vol. I (*Introduction générale* and *Documents généraux*) and vol. II (*Oeuvres diverses, 1623–1654*). It has been used in preparing this article.

Each reference to a passage in one of these eds. will consist of the abbreviation, the volume number, year of publication of the volume, and page number. The list below includes most of Pascal's surviving scientific writings, cited in the order in which they were written. For each writing there is the title, its presumed date of composition, and its various eds.: the first (indicated as "orig." if published during Pascal's lifetime and as "1st ed." if posthumous) and the chief subsequent eds. (in separate vols. and in the sets of complete works cited above, as well as any other ed. containing important original material).

1. *Essay pour les coniques* (1639–1640). Orig. (Paris, Feb. 1640); Bossut, IV (1779), 1–7; G.E., I (1908), 243–260 and XI (1914), 347; PL (1954), 57–63, 1380–1382; R. Taton, "L' 'Essay pour les coniques' de Pascal," in *Revue d'histoire des sciences*, **8** (1955), 1–18; Mesnard, II (1971), 220–235.

2. *Lettre dédicatoire à Monseigneur le Chancelier sur le sujet de la machine nouvellement inventée par le sieur B. P. pour faire toutes sortes d'opérations d'arithmétique par un mouvement réglé sans plume ni jetons avec un avis nécessaire à ceux qui auront curiosité de voir ladite machine et de s'en servir* (1645). Orig. (Paris, 1645); Bossut, IV (1779), 7–24; G.E., I (1908), 291–314; PL (1954), 347–358; Mesnard, II (1971), 329–341.

3. *Expériences nouvelles touchant le vide. . . . Avec un discours sur le même sujet . . . dédié à Monsieur Pascal, conseiller du roi . . . par le sieur B. P. son fils. Le tout réduit en abrégé et donné par avance d'un plus grand traité sur le même sujet* (Sept.–early Oct. 1647). Orig. (Paris, Oct. 1647); Bossut, IV (1779), 51–68; G.E., II (1908), 53–76; PL (1954), 359–370; Mesnard, II (1971), 493–508.

4. Pascal's correspondence with Noël (late Oct.–early Nov. 1647). 1st ed., Bossut, IV (1779), 69–108; G.E., II (1908), pp. 77–125; PL (1954), 370–377, 1438–1452; Mesnard, II (1971), 509–540.

5. Pascal's letter to Le Pailleur (Feb. 1648). 1st ed., Bossut, IV (1779), 147–177; G.E., II (1908), 177–211; PL (1954), 377–391; Mesnard, II (1971), 555–576.

6. *Récit de la grande expérience de l'équilibre des liqueurs projetée par le sieur B. P. pour l'accomplissement du traité qu'il a promis dans son abrégé touchant le vide et faite par le sieur F. P. en une des plus hautes montagnes*

d'Auvergne (autumn 1648). Orig. (Paris, 1648), repr. in facs. with intro. by G. Hellmann (Berlin, 1893) and in *Traités de l'équilibre des liqueurs et de la pesanteur de la masse de l'air . . .* (Paris, 1663; repr. 1664, 1698); Bossut, IV (1779), 345–369; G.E., II (1908), 147–162, 349–358, and 363–373; PL (1954), 392–401; Mesnard, II (1971), 653–690.

7. Preface to the treatise on the vacuum ("De l'autorité en matière de philosophie") (1651). 1st ed., Bossut, II (1779), 1–12; G.E., II (1908), 127–145, and XI (1914), 348–349; PL (1954), 529–535; Mesnard, II (1971), 772–785.

8. Fragments of "Traité du vide" (1651). 1st ed., in *Traités de l'équilibre des liqueurs et de la pesanteur de la masse de l'air . . .* (Paris, 1663), 141–163; Bossut, IV (1779), 326–344; G.E., II (1908), 513–529; PL (1954), 462–471; Mesnard, II (1971), 786–798.

9. *Lettre de M. Pascal le fils adressante à M. le Premier Président de la Cour des aides de Clermont-Ferrand . . .* (July 1651). Orig. (Clermont-Ferrand, 1651); Bossut, IV (1779), 198–214; G.E., II (1908), 475–495; PL (1954), 402–409; Mesnard, II (1971), 799–813.

10. Continuation of the correspondence with M. de Ribeyre (July–Aug. 1651). 1st ed., Bossut, IV (1779), 214–221; G.E., II (1908), 496–502; PL (1954), 409–411; Mesnard, II (1971), 814–818.

11. Letter from Pascal to Queen Christina of Sweden (June 1652). 1st ed., in F. Granet and P. N. Desmolets, eds., *Recueil de pièces d'histoire et de littérature*, III (Paris, 1738), 117–123; Bossut, IV (1779), 25–29; G.E., III (1908), 23–34; PL (1954), 502–504; Mesnard, II (1971), 920–926.

12. "Celeberrimae matheseos academiae Parisiensis" (Paris, 1654). 1st. ed., Bossut, IV (1779), 408–411; G.E., III (1908), 293–308; PL (1954), 71–74, 1400–1404 (French trans.); Mesnard, II (1971), 1121–1135 (with French trans.).

13. *Traités de l'équilibre des liqueurs et de la pesanteur de la masse de l'air. Contenant l'explication des causes de divers effets de la nature qui n'avaient point été bien connus jusques ici, et particulièrement de ceux que l'on avait attribués à l'horreur du vide* (completed at the latest in 1654). 1st ed. (Paris, Nov. 1663). The text of the *Traités* corresponds to pp. 1–140; pp. 141–163 reproduce the only two fragments known of the great treatise on the vacuum prepared by Pascal in 1651; the rest of the volume contains (pp. 164–194) a repr. of the *Récit de la grande expérience . . .* and (pp. 195–232) texts by F. Périer and others. Important subsequent eds. are those of 1664 and 1698; Bossut, IV (1779), 222–325; G.E., III (1908), 143–292, and IX (1914), 352; PL (1954), 412–471; Mesnard, I (1964), 679–689 (preface by F. Périer), and II (1971), 739–745 (account of Périer's observations), 787–798 (two "Fragments d'un traité du vide"), and 1036–1101 (the actual *Traités*).

14. "Generatio conisectionum" (completed about 1654). 1st ed. in *Sitzungsberichte der K. Preussischen Akademie der Wissenschaften zu Berlin*, **1** (1892), 197–202 (edited by C. I. Gerhardt); G.E., II (1908), 234–243; PL (1954), 66–70, 1382–1387 (French trans.); Mesnard, II (1971), 1108–1119.

15. Leibniz's notes on Pascal's treatise on conics (the notes date from 1676, but the treatise was finished about

1654). 1st ed. (partial) in *Sitzungsberichte der K. Preussischen Akademie der Wissenschaften zu Berlin*, **1** (1892), 195–197, edited by C. I. Gerhardt; G.E., II (1908), 227–233; P. Costabel, in *L'oeuvre scientifique de Pascal* (1964), 85–101 (with French trans.); Mesnard, II (1971), 1120–1131 (with French trans.).

16. Correspondence with Fermat (July–Oct. 1654). 1st ed., P. Fermat, *Varia opera mathematica* . . . (Toulouse, 1679), 179–188 (for the three letters by Pascal; for the other four see Bossut); Bossut, IV (1779), 412–445; Fermat, *Oeuvres*, P. Tannery and C. Henry, eds., II (1894), 288–314, and III (1896), 310–311; PL (1954), 74–90; Mesnard, II (1971), 1132–1158.

17. *Traité du triangle arithmétique, avec quelques petits traités sur la même matière* (1654). 1st ed. (Paris, 1665). Without the first four pages (title page, foreword, and table of contents) and the plate, this work was printed during Pascal's lifetime (1654) but was not distributed. It consists of four parts: the "Traité du triangle arithmétique" itself; two papers devoted to various applications of the triangle; and a fourth paper on numerical orders, powers, combinations, and multiple numbers that is formed of seven sections, the first in French and the rest in Latin. J. Mesnard has identified a preliminary Latin version of the part of this treatise that was published in French.

Subsequent eds.: Bossut, V (1779), 1–134; *Oeuvres complètes de Pascal*, C. Lahure, ed., II (1858), 415–494 (with French trans. of the Latin passages); G.E., III (1908), 311–339, 341–367, 433–598, and XI (1914), 353, 364–390; PL (1954), 91–171, 1404–1432 (translations); Mesnard, II (1971), 1166–1332—repr. with French trans. of the entire preliminary Latin ed., *Triangulus arithmeticus*, followed by the new sections of the *Traité*.

18. "Introduction à la géométrie" (written about the end of 1657). 1st ed. in *Sitzungsberichte der K. Preussischen Akademie der Wissenschaften zu Berlin*, **1** (1892), 202–204 (C. I. Gerhardt, ed.); G. E., IX (1914), 291–294; PL (1954), 602–604, 1476; J. Itard, in *L'oeuvre scientifique de Pascal* (1964), 102–119.

19. "De l'esprit géométrique" and "De l'art de persuader" (written about 1657–1658). 1st ed. (partial), P. N. Desmolets in *Continuation des mémoires de littérature et d'histoire*, V, pt. 2 (Paris, 1728), 271–296; Bossut, II (1779), 12–38, 39–57; G.E., IX (1914), 240–290; PL (1954), 574–602.

20. Various items pertaining to the cycloid competition (June 1658–Jan. 1659).

a. Three circulars addressed to the contestants: the first in Latin (June 1658); the second in Latin (July 1658); the third in French and Latin (dated 7 Oct. in the French text and 9 Oct. in the Latin version).

b. *Histoire de la roulette* . . . (10 Oct. 1658), also in Latin, *Historia trochoidis* (same date).

c. *Récit de l'examen et du jugement des écrits envoyés pour les prix proposés publiquement sur le sujet de la roulette* . . . (25 Nov. 1658).

d. *Suite de l'histoire de la roulette* . . . (12 Dec. 1658, with an addition on 20 Jan. 1659); the Latin version exists only in MS.

A more detailed description of this group of writings is provided by L. Scheler, in *L'oeuvre scientifique de Pascal* (1964), 30–31, and in Mesnard, I (1964), 163–167. Subsequent eds. are Bossut, V (1779), 135–213; G.E., VII (1914), 337–347, and VIII (1914), 15–19, 155–223, 231–246, 289–319; PL (1954), 180–223, 1433–1435 (French trans. of the circulars of June and July 1658).

21. *Lettres de A. Dettonville contenant quelques-unes de ses inventions de géométrie* . . . (Paris, Feb. 1659). This vol. contains a title page (written after the rest of contents), four sheets of plates, and four letters published between Dec. 1658 and Jan. 1659 (in the order 1, 4, 3, 2).

Letter no. 1: *Lettre de A. Dettonville à Monsieur de Carcavy, en lui envoyant: Une méthode générale pour trouver les centres de gravité de toutes sortes de grandeurs. Un traité des trilignes et de leurs onglets. Un traité des sinus du quart de cercle. Un traité des solides circulaires. Et enfin un traité général de la roulette, contenant la solution de tous les problèmes touchant la roulette qu'il avait proposés publiquement au mois de juin 1658.* Orig. (Paris, 1658).

Letter no. 2: *Lettre de A. Dettonville à Monsieur A. D. D. S. en lui envoyant: La démonstration à la manière des anciens de l'égalité des lignes spirale et parabolique.* Orig. (Paris, 1658).

Letter no. 3: *Lettre de A. Dettonville à Monsieur de Sluze, chanoine de la cathédrale de Liège, en lui envoyant: La dimension et le centre de gravité de l'escalier. La dimension et le centre de gravité des triangles cylindriques. La dimension d'un solide formé par le moyen d'une spirale autour d'un cône.* Orig. (Paris, 1658).

Letter no. 4: *Lettre de A. Dettonville à Monsieur Huggyens [sic] de Zulichem, en lui envoyant: La dimension des lignes de toutes sortes de roulettes, lesquelles il montre être égales à des lignes elliptiques.* Orig. (Paris, 1659).

Later eds.: Bossut, V (1779), 229–452; G.E., VIII (1914), 247–288, 325–384, and IX (1914), 1–149, 187–204; PL (1954), 224–340, 1436–1437; a facs. of the original ed. has recently appeared (London, 1966).

Two other important documents relating to Pascal's scientific work are the following:

22. The license for his calculating machine (22 May 1649). 1st ed. in *Recueil de diverses pièces pour servir à l'histoire de Port-Royal* (Utrecht, 1740), 244–248; Bossut, IV (1779), 30–33; G.E., II (1908), 399–404; Mesnard, II (1971), 711–715.

23. Letter from Leibniz to Étienne Périer of 30 Aug. 1676 concerning Pascal's treatise on conics. 1st ed., Bossut, V (1779), 459–462; G.E., II (1908), 193–194; PL (1954), 63–65; J. Mesnard and R. Taton, in *L'oeuvre scientifique de Pascal* (1964), 73–84.

II. SECONDARY LITERATURE. A very complete bibliography of studies on Pascal's scientific work published before 1925 can be found in A. Maire, *Bibliographie générale des oeuvres de Pascal*, 2nd ed., I, *Pascal savant* (Paris, 1925). Most of the more recent works on the subject (except for those dealing with the cycloid) are cited in the bibliographies in Mesnard, II (1971)—geometry, 227–228, 1108; combinatorial theory and the calculus of probability, 1135, 1175; the calculating machine, 327–

328; physics, 349, 459, 513, 675–676, 777, 804, 1040; miscellaneous, 1031.

Two general studies in particular should be mentioned: P. Humbert, *L'oeuvre scientifique de Pascal* (Paris, 1947), a survey written for a broad audience; and *L'oeuvre scientifique de Pascal* (Paris, 1964), a joint effort that restates the main aspects of Pascal's career and scientific work (with the exception of the theory of combinations and the calculus of probability). Other recent studies worth consulting are A. Koyré, "Pascal savant," in *Blaise Pascal, l'homme et l'oeuvre* (Paris, 1956), pp. 259–285; K. Hara, "Examen des textes mathématiques dans les oeuvres complètes de Pascal d'après les Grands Écrivains de la France," in *Gallia* (Osaka), no. 6 (1961); "Quelques additions à l'examen des textes mathématiques de Pascal," *ibid.*, no. 7 (1962); and "Pascal et Wallis au sujet de la cycloïde, I," in *Annals of the Japan Association for Philosophy of Science*, 3, no. 4 (1969), 166–187; "Pascal et Wallis . . . , II," in *Gallia*, nos. 10–11 (1971), 231–249; and "Pascal et Wallis . . . , III," in *Japanese Studies in the History of Science*, no. 10 (1971), 95–112; N. Bourbaki, *Éléments d'histoire des mathématiques*, 2nd ed. (Paris, 1969), see index; M. E. Baron, *The Origins of the Infinitesimal Calculus* (London, 1969), esp. 196–205; and E. Coumet, "La théorie du hasard est-elle née par hasard?" in *Annales. Économies, sociétés, civilisations*, **5** (May–June 1970), 574–598.

RENÉ TATON

PASCAL, ÉTIENNE (*b.* Clermont-Ferrand, France, 2 May 1588; *d.* Paris, France, 24 September 1651), *mathematics*.

The son of Martin Pascal, treasurer of France, and Marguerite Pascal de Mons, Pascal married Antoinette Begon in 1616. They had three children: Gilberte (1620–1687), who in 1641 married Florin Périer; Blaise (1623–1662), the philosopher and scientist; and Jacqueline (1625–1661), who in 1652 entered the convent of Port-Royal.

Elected counselor for Bas-Auvergne in 1610, Pascal became president of the Cour des Aides in 1625. His wife died in 1626, and in 1631 he left Clermont to settle in Paris with his children. He devoted himself to his son's education while gaining a reputation as a talented mathematician and musician. In 1634 Pascal was one of five commissioners named to examine J. B. Morin's "invention" for the determination of longitudes. As early as 1635 he frequented "Mersenne's academy" and was in contact with Roberval, Desargues, and Mydorge.

In November 1635 Mersenne dedicated to Pascal the "Traité des orgues" of his *Harmonie universelle* (1636). Roberval communicated to Pascal his first discoveries concerning the cycloid and intervened on his side in the debate concerning the nature of gravity (interpreting it in terms of attraction—letter to Fermat of 16 August 1636; Fermat's response of 23 August). At the beginning of 1637 Fermat wrote his "Solution d'un problème proposé par M. Pascal." At about the same time Pascal introduced a special curve, the conchoid of a circle with respect to one of its points, to be applied to the problem of trisecting an angle. Roberval called it the "limaçon de M. Pascal" and determined its tangent by his kinematic method. In February 1638 Roberval joined Pascal in defending Fermat's *De maximis et minimis*, which had been attacked by Descartes.

Having been obliged to return to Auvergne from March 1638 to April 1639, Pascal then moved to Rouen, where he was appointed intendant of the province, a post he held until 1648. He had given his son Blaise a solid foundation in mathematics, and he now fostered the development of his work, mainly through his contacts with many scientists. In October 1646 Pascal participated with his son and P. Petit in the first repetition in France of Torricelli's experiment. In April 1648 he joined in the debate between Blaise and the Père E. Noël concerning the problem of the vacuum. He returned to Paris in August 1648, was in Auvergne from May 1649 to November 1650, then spent his last months in Paris.

BIBLIOGRAPHY

I. ORIGINAL WORKS. The rare documents concerning Pascal's scientific work are reproduced in the major eds. of his son's complete works: *Oeuvres de Blaise Pascal publiées selon l'ordre chronologique*, L. Brunschvicg, P. Boutroux, and F. Gazier, eds., 14 vols. (Paris, 1908–1914), in the collection Grands Écrivains de la France (hereafter cited as G.E.); and *Blaise Pascal. Oeuvres complètes*, J. Mesnard, ed., I, II (Paris, 1964, 1971) (hereafter cited as Mesnard).

They include "Jugement porté par les commissaires Étienne Pascal, Mydorge, Beaugrand, Boulanger, Hérigone sur l'invention du sieur J. B. Morin," in G.E., I, 194–195, and Mesnard, II, 82–99; "Lettre d'Étienne Pascal et Roberval à Fermat, samedi 16 août 1636," in *Oeuvres de Fermat*, P. Tannery, C. Henry, and C. de Waard, eds., 5 vols. (Paris, 1891–1922), II, 35–50 (hereafter cited as Fermat), also in G.E., I, 177–193, and Mesnard, II, 123–140; "Lettre de Fermat à Étienne Pascal et Roberval, 23 août 1636," in Fermat, II, 50–56, and in Mesnard, II, 140–146; "Solutio problematis a Domino de Pascal propositi" (Jan. or Feb. 1637), in Fermat, I, 70–74, also in G.E., I, 196–201, and Mesnard, II, 148–156, also translated into French as "Solution d'un problème proposé par M. de Pascal," in Fermat, III, 67–71, and Mesnard, II, 149–156; "Réponse de Descartes à un écrit des amis de M. de Fermat" (1 Mar. 1638), in *Oeuvres de Descartes*, C. Adam and P. Tannery, eds., II (Paris, 1898), 1–15, also in *Descartes. Correspondance*, C. Adam and G. Milhaud, eds., II (Paris, 1939), 143–153, *Correspondance du P. Marin Mersenne*, C. De Waard and B. Rochot, eds., VII (Paris, 1962), 64–73, and Mesnard, II, 164–174; and "Lettre de M. Pascal le Père au R. P. Noël" (Apr. 1648), in G.E., II, 255–282, and in Mesnard, II, 584–602.

II. SECONDARY LITERATURE. Documents, notices, and details concerning the life and work of Pascal can be found in G.E., I, 5–28, 170–176, and II, 533–562; Mesnard, I, 459–464, 510–515, 571–576, 721–722, 727–729, 754–771, 1077–1079, 1091–1100, and II, 119–123, 157–163, 174–188, 217, 253–254, 841–863; the ed. of Descartes's *Oeuvres* cited above, index, V, 607; the ed. of Descartes's correspondence cited above, II, 379–381 and index; and Mersenne's correspondence cited above, vols. IV–VII, see index.

The catalog of a commemorative exhibition held at the Bibliothèque Nationale in 1962, *Blaise Pascal, 1623–1662* (Paris, 1962), furnishes references to many documents concerning Étienne Pascal: nos. 1, 9, 10, 14, 17, 18, 22–27, 31, 32, 34, 36, 38, 41, 60, 67, 69–72, 76, 77, 168. Other references are in A. Maire, *Pascal savant* (Paris, 1925), 270–275 and index.

Additional details are in M. Cantor, *Vorlesungen über Geschichte der Mathematik*, 2nd ed., II (Leipzig, 1900), 675, 679, 681, 875, 881, 882; J. Mesnard, *Pascal et les Roannez*, 2 vols. (Paris, 1965), see index; and P. Tannery, *Mémoires scientifiques*, X (Paris, 1930), 372, 382–383, and XIII (Paris, 1934), 337–338.

RENÉ TATON

PASCH, MORITZ (*b.* Breslau, Germany [now Wrocław, Poland], 8 November 1843; *d.* Bad Homburg, Germany, 20 September 1930), *mathematics*.

Pasch studied chemistry at Breslau but changed to mathematics at the suggestion of Heinrich Schröter, to whom, along with Kambly, his teacher at the Elisabeth Gymnasium, he dedicated his dissertation (1865). Later, at Berlin, he was influenced by Weierstrass and Kronecker. He maintained his mathematical activity with scarcely a break for sixty-five years, for the first seventeen years in algebraic geometry and later in foundations, the work on which his fame rests. His first two papers were written in collaboration with his lifelong friend J. Rosanes. Except for rapid promotion, Pasch's career at the University of Giessen was not unusual: in 1870, *Dozent*; in 1873, extraordinary professor; in 1875, after an offer of an extraordinary professorship from the University of Breslau, ordinary professor. In 1888 he obtained the chair left vacant by the death of Heinrich Baltzer. He was also active in administration, becoming dean in 1883 and rector in 1893–1894. In order to dedicate himself more fully to his scientific work, he retired in 1911. In celebration of his eightieth birthday Pasch received honorary Ph.D.'s from the

universities of Frankfurt and Freiburg. He was a member of the Deutsche Mathematiker-Vereinigung. His name is perpetuated in Pasch's axiom, which states that in a plane, if a line meets one side of a triangle, then it meets another. His outward life was simple, although saddened by the early death of his wife and one of two daughters. He died while on a vacation trip away from Giessen.

The axiomatic method as it is understood today was initiated by Pasch in his *Vorlesungen über neuere Geometrie* (Leipzig, 1882; 2nd ed., Berlin, 1926). It consists in isolating from a given study certain notions that are left undefined and are expressly declared to be such (the *Kernbegriffe*, in Pasch's terminology of 1916), and certain theorems that are accepted without proof (the *Kernsätze*, or axioms). From this initial fund of notions and theorems, the other notions are to be defined and the theorems proved using only logical arguments, without appeal to experience or intuition. The resulting theory takes the form of purely logical relations between undefined concepts.

To be sure, there are preliminary explanations, and a definite philosophy is disclosed for choosing the axioms. According to Pasch the initial notions and theorems should be founded on observations. Thus the notion of point is allowed but not that of line, since no one has ever observed a complete (straight) line; rather, the notion of segment is taken as primitive. Similarly, a planar surface, but not a plane, is primitive.

Pasch's analysis relating to the order of points on a line and in the plane is both striking and pertinent to its understanding. Every student can draw diagrams and see that if a point *B* is between point *A* and point *C*, then *C* is not between *A* and *B*, or that every line divides a plane into two parts. But no one before Pasch had laid a basis for dealing logically with such observations. These matters may have been considered too obvious; but the result of such neglect is the need to refer constantly to intuition, so that the logical status of what is being done cannot become clear. According to Pasch, the appeal to intuition formally ceases once the *Kernbegriffe* and *Kernsätze* are stated.

The higher geometry of Pasch's day was projective geometry that used real numbers as coordinates. Pasch therefore considered that the foundation would be laid once the coordinates had been introduced. In doing this he presented notions of congruence, which were nonprojective. This is somewhat disappointing in view of Staudt's 1847 program for founding projective geometry solely on projective terms (though we may emphasize that the congruence axioms are original with Pasch). But F. Klein had uncovered some nonrigorous thinking in Staudt's proof that a one-to-one mapping between two lines that sends harmonic quadruples into harmonic quadruples is uniquely determined by the images of three points—without, however, obtaining notable success in clarifying this matter. Pasch proved this fundamental theorem on the basis of the Archimedean character of the ordering on the line, and not on its completeness, as Klein proposed to do. The congruence notions were introduced, at least in part, in order to state Archimedes' axiom. Once the fundamental theorem was proved, the introduction of coordinates could be easily accomplished—as M. Dehn remarks in a historical appendix to Pasch's *Vorlesungen*—on the basis of the Eudoxian theory of book V of Euclid's *Elements*. But for Pasch this procedure was complicated by his empiricist point of view.

It would be easy to overlook the significance of Pasch's foundational achievements for several reasons. First, it is now a commonplace to present theories in an axiomatic way, so that even logic itself is presented axiomatically. Thus Pasch's innovation achieves the status of being a trifle.

There are also widespread misconceptions as to what is in book I of the *Elements*: it is thought that Euclid had an axiomatic way of presenting geometry. This view is further confounded by a lack of clarity as to what the axiomatic method is and what geometry is. Anyone who looks at book I of the *Elements* with modern hindsight sees that something is wrong, but it would take delicate historical considerations to place the source of the faults in a correct light.

The Greeks of Euclid's time had the axiomatic method; Aristotle's description of it can be considered a close approximation to the modern one. Or, better yet, one may consider Eudoxus' theory of magnitude as presented in book V of the *Elements*. Except for style (which, however, may indicate a difference in point of view), the procedure presented there coincides with Pasch's. It is known, however, that the *Elements* is a compilation of uneven quality, so that even with the definitions, postulates, and common notions of book I, it is unwarranted to assume that book I is written from the same point of view as book V.

In some versions of book I, as it has come down to us, there are five "common notions" and five postulates. T. L. Heath considers it probable that common notions 4 and 5 were interpolations; and P. Tannery maintains that they were none of them authentic. The first three postulates are the "postulates of construction," the fourth states that all right angles are equal, and the fifth is the parallel postulate. It has been argued that the first three postulates were meant to help meet the injunction to limit the means of construction to "straightedge and compass"; that there was no intention to say anything about space. One could eliminate these three, as well as the fourth, without changing the rigor of the book or the points of view disclosed relative to geometry or to the axiomatic method. The fifth does not appear until proposition 29, so that the first twenty-eight propositions (minus the constructions) are, from a modern axiomatic point of view, based on nothing.

Although deduction is a prominent feature of book I of the *Elements*, the contents of the book and the history of the parallel postulate show that geometry was conceived as the study of a definite object, "external space." With the invention of non-Euclidean geometry around 1800, it began to dawn on mathematicians that their concern is with deduction, and not with a supposed external reality. Applications, if any, may be left to the physicist. With G. Fano's miniature projective plane of just seven points and seven lines (1892), the revolution may be considered to have been completed. Hilbert, through his work in geometry and logic, consolidated it.

Pasch initiated the axiomatic method, although the foundational developments of his time were against this point of view. Thus Cantor's striking discoveries were based, from an axiomatic point of view, on nothing. Dedekind rightly contrasted his own treatment of magnitude with Eudoxus'; Dedekind's was constructive, whereas Eudoxus' was axiomatic. As late as 1903 Frege poked fun at the axiomatic method as presented in Hilbert's *Grundlagen der Geometrie*.

The Italian geometers, particularly Peano, continued Pasch's work. In 1889 Peano published both his exposition of geometry, following Pasch, and his treatment of number. It is tempting to see in the former work a source of the latter, although there were many other sources.

Pasch played a crucial role in the innovation of the axiomatic method. This method, with contributions from logic and algebra, is a central feature of twentieth-century mathematics.

BIBLIOGRAPHY

See M. Dehn and F. Engel, "Moritz Pasch," in *Jahresbericht der deutschen Mathematiker-Vereinigung*, **44** (1934), 120–142; P. Tannery, "Sur l'authenticité des axiomes d'Euclide," in *Bulletin des sciences mathématiques et astronomiques* (1884), 162; G. Fano, "Sui postulati fondamentali della geometria proiettiva," in *Giornale di matematiche* (Naples), **30** (1892), 106–132; G. Frege, "Über die Grundlagen der Geometrie," in *Jahresbericht der deutschen Mathematiker-Vereinigung*, **12** (1903), 319–324,

368–375; H. Freudenthal, "Zur Geschichte der Grundlagen der Geometrie," in *Nieuwe Archieff voor Wiskunde*, **5** (1957), 105–142; T. L. Heath, *The Thirteen Books of Euclid's Elements*, 2nd ed. (New York, 1956), esp. 221, 225, 232; and A. Seidenberg, "The Ritual Origin of Geometry," in *Archive for History of Exact Sciences*, **1** (1962), 488–527, esp. 497 f.

A. SEIDENBERG

PASCHEN, LOUIS CARL HEINRICH FRIEDRICH

(*b.* Schwerin, Mecklenburg, 22 January 1865; *d.* Potsdam, Germany, 25 February 1947), *experimental physics.*

Friedrich Paschen, "probably the greatest experimental spectroscopist of his time,"[1] was born into a Lutheran family of scientifically inclined Mecklenburg officers, military and civil. His paternal grandfather, H. C. Friedrich Paschen (1804–1873), was director of the Mecklenburg geodetic survey and a noted astronomer. An uncle, Carl Paschen (1835–1911), who rose to the rank of admiral in the German navy, was a well-known hydrographer. Paschen himself, although he incorporated some official virtues—and although, as was customary, he became a lieutenant in the reserve[2]—seems nonetheless to have reacted against the authoritarian structure and the social-political attitudes of the German officer class. Apparently against the wishes of his family, and with no independent income, he resolved to accept the greater hazards of an academic career.[3]

After completing his secondary education in Schwerin, Paschen began his university studies in 1884 at Strasbourg, where he joined the group of disciples around August Kundt, the most charismatic and influential professor of physics in Germany, who happened also to be a native of Mecklenburg and a graduate of the Schwerin Gymnasium. After two years at Strasbourg, Paschen studied for one year at the University of Berlin, then returned to Kundt for supervision of his doctoral research. The degree was conferred in September 1888.[4] Paschen's doctoral research, suggested to him by Kundt, established "Paschen's law": that the sparking voltage depends only on the product of the gas pressure and the distance between the electrodes—one of the first and most important of the numerous scaling laws in this field.[5]

From October 1888 to April 1891 Paschen was Wilhelm Hittorf's last assistant in the Physical Institute of the Catholic Academy (subsequently University) of Münster. In keeping with Hittorf's interests and the experimental facilities available in consequence of them, Paschen turned to electrolytic solutions and, giving the first proofs of his enormous energy, in two years published seven papers on a variety of investigations of electrolytic potentials. It was here, under Hittorf, that Paschen learned the value and technique of precision measurements.[6] Hittorf retired in 1890, and at Easter 1891 Paschen became Heinrich Kayser's teaching assistant in the Physical Institute of the Technische Hochschule at Hannover. Paschen continued in this position until Easter 1901, serving under Conrad Dieterici after Kayser's departure for Bonn in the summer of 1894.

Paschen had qualified as lecturer (*habilitiert*) at Hannover in the spring of 1893; and in March 1895, in return for his refusal of a position at Aachen, the Prussian government created a permanent lectureship (*etatsmässige Dozentur*) in physics and photography for him. This post gave him a relatively comfortable income of 3,300 marks in 1895, rising to about 4,000 marks by 1900, and a relatively large amount of time for research.[7]

In the late 1880's Kirchhoff's function (the universal but unknown temperature and wavelength dependence of the ratio of the radiant energy emitted to that absorbed by a body in thermal equilibrium—and, consequently also the dependence of the radiant energy in a cavity in thermal equilibrium upon those two variables) was beginning to draw considerable attention from theorists following the bolometric measurements of S. P. Langley and others.[8] Kayser proposed that Paschen improve upon Langley's results by more extensive measurements using the reflection gratings with which the institute had been well supplied for Kayser's and Carl Runge's spectroscopic work.[9] Gratings should have the advantage that their spectra, in contrast to prismatic spectra, may be chosen "normal" —that is, to disperse equal wavelength intervals into equal angular intervals—so that intensity measurements will give the desired distribution function directly. Only after a year spent building up the necessary apparatus—including the most sensitive galvanometer (of the Thomson astatic type) constructed until then or for years afterward—did Paschen discover late in 1892 that the gratings were unusable because the metal on which they were ruled showed irregular selective reflection in the infrared.[10]

But now committed to this problem, which would absorb most of his research efforts for the ten years at Hannover, Paschen turned to prismatic spectra and made a very accurate investigation of the dispersion of fluorite (correcting Rubens' measurements). At the same time he determined the infrared absorption by carbon dioxide and water vapor (obtaining results which, although presumed to have been superseded by Rubens, remained in 1913 the strongest evidence in favor of Bjerrum's quantum theory of molecular absorption).[11] Paschen also investigated the much mooted question of whether heat alone could bring gases to radiate, demonstrating—in contrast with the results of Ernst Pringsheim—the existence of infrared spectral lines produced by merely heating the gas.[12]

Paschen spent much of 1894 observing the deflections of his galvanometer attached to a very delicate bolometer irradiated by heated platinum with various surfacings; but the reduction of this data to emissive power as a function of λ and T, especially the transformation from a prismatic to a normal spectrum, required extremely laborious computations. By the summer of 1894 he had strong indications that $\lambda_{max} \cdot T = $ constant, "or: the frequency of the main thermal vibrations of the molecular parts of an absolutely black body is proportional to the absolute temperature."[13] Paschen, who was never willing to take time from the laboratory to find out in the library what others had done—nor, indeed, ever to write a review article in any of the fields in which he was to become an authority—seems to have been ignorant of W. Wien's publication of thermodynamic deductions of this "displacement law" in 1893 and 1894. Paschen was, however, aware of the general growth of interest and activity in this field, especially in Berlin (Rubens, Pringsheim, Lummer, among others); and in the summer of 1895, in view of the growing competition, Paschen published his result.[14]

But to complete the computation of all those "hundreds of curves" from which Paschen hoped to induce Kirchhoff's function would take many months more. It was thus not difficult for Carl Runge, excited by Ramsay's announcement in March 1895 of the discovery of terrestrial helium and bereft of his experimental collaborator Kayser, to persuade Paschen that the investigation of the spectrum of this new element was far more important to science. Compared with Paschen's infrared researches, this optical spectroscopy proved to be child's play: in one day he obtained for Runge the yellow D_3 helium line, and within three months they brought out two papers giving an astonishingly accurate inventory of the helium lines and an astonishingly successful arrangement of them into series.[15] Overnight Paschen acquired an international reputation; and accompanying Runge to England in September 1895, he was received most warmly by British physicists.[16]

In the fall of 1895 Paschen returned to the calculation of his emissive power curves, and by the spring of 1896 he had found $I = c_1 \lambda^{-\alpha} \exp(-c_2/\lambda T)$ with $\alpha = 5.5$, for an iron oxide surface.[17] The formulas for this curve previously proposed by V. A. Michelson and H. F. Weber, involving exponential dependence, had undoubtedly been suggestive; and Runge's

suggestion that the energy curves be plotted on logarithmic scales was also helpful.[18] Wien, who had evidently gotten into contact with Paschen after the publication of Paschen's preliminary announcement in the summer of 1895, was informed in advance of these results by mail. Wien replied that he had deduced exactly this formula, but with $\alpha = 5$, some time earlier. The derivation of what soon became known as Wien's law—doubtless previously withheld from publication because of its highly arbitrary character—now appeared immediately following Paschen's paper in the *Annalen*.[19]

In the laboratory, however, Paschen had been obliged by lack of space and funds to forgo entirely his bolometric work from mid-1895 to the end of 1896. Instead he joined Runge in the quest for spectral series, first unsuccessfully with argon and then successfully with the homologous oxygen-sulfur-scandium-tellurium spectra. Through this collaboration Paschen became fully familiar with the field that would occupy him almost exclusively after the question of the blackbody radiation formula had finally been settled. That question certainly could not be settled by measurements on heated surfaces; to assert definitely that his (and Wien's) formula was the true one, and to fix the value of α, would require a far more perfect realization of ideal blackbody radiation.

For this purpose Paschen's competitors, enjoying the ample resources of the Physikalisch-Technische Reichsanstalt at Berlin, had in 1895 begun the construction of elaborate "thermostatic cavities." In the spring of 1897 Paschen, with a grant from the Berlin Academy and with the enlargement of the Hannover Institute, began to construct similar equipment.[20] By the summer of 1898 he had found $\alpha = 5$ and was "convinced that there can remain no further doubt about the correctness of the formula itself and of its constants."[21] Indeed, he was so convinced that when deviations between theory and experiment began to appear in 1899, he took them as indicative of undetected sources of experimental error. Only in 1900, when the Berlin experimentalists, working with much larger values of $\lambda \cdot T$, found clear deviations from Wien's law, did Paschen (like Planck) reconceptualize his experiments as a search for the limits of the law's range of validity. Paschen construed the results positively as strong evidence for the validity of Planck's formula in the intermediate region between Wien's and Rayleigh's formulas.[22] In striking and curious contrast with the Berlin experimentalists, who were literally enraged at him, throughout his work on the blackbody radiation problem Paschen the pure experimentalist showed himself to be more than ready to enlist experiment in the service of theory.

This continued to be characteristic of the man, of his work, and of some of his greatest successes.

In these years, despite the volume and importance of his work, it looked very much as if Paschen, like Runge, would remain stuck at Hannover.[23] Finally, however, in February 1901, the University of Tübingen, after failing successively to secure Paul Drude, Philipp Lenard, and Hermann Ebert, appointed Paschen professor of physics at a salary of 3,500 marks, including living quarters in a moderately good institute.[24] Here Paschen brought a wife in September 1901; here he raised a daughter and married her to his student Hermann Schüler in August 1920;[25] here he kept a guest room "always standing ready for the physicists." In 1908 the institute was substantially enlarged to accommodate the growing number of advanced students, including eventually many from abroad.[26] In July 1915 Paschen refused a call to Göttingen as Eduard Riecke's successor, gaining in return 9,000 marks for his institute and 3,000 marks per annum salary supplement.[27] In 1919 he was offered and actually accepted the Bonn chair of physics in succession to Kayser; but he reneged early in 1920 because he was persuaded that, in consequence of the political and above all the economic situation, the move would be to the disadvantage of his research work.[28]

Paschen had lost a year or two of research in transferring to Tübingen, and the diverse resources of the institute there led to forays into other fields—radioactivity and the nature of X rays, canal rays, and the mechanism of light emission. By 1908, however, he was focusing again on the problem of spectral series. Important forces bringing his attention back to this problem, to which he would devote himself exclusively for the remainder of his career, were, on the one hand, the presence of Walther Ritz at Tübingen during the winter of 1907–1908 and, on the other hand, Arno Bergmann's discovery in 1907 of new series in the infrared spectra of the alkalies (the so-called f series). Paschen now had, as he had not had at Hannover in the early 1890's, the facilities necessary for a systematic bolometric search for infrared spectral lines, above all the large-capacity high-voltage storage batteries to maintain intense, steady discharges. Returning to helium, in the spectrum of which he had previously detected bolometrically (June 1895) a few lines predicted by Runge's series formulas, he found in the spring of 1908 additional lines that did not fit in that series system. Paschen was looking everywhere for the impurity responsible for these lines when a letter arrived from Ritz announcing his newly invented combination principle and suggesting that helium

lines might exist at precisely those wavelengths Paschen had observed. Following this striking confirmation, Ritz suggested that Paschen look for hydrogen lines at frequencies $\nu = N \ (1/3^2 - 1/m^2)$, $m = 4,5 \ldots$, and this "Paschen series" was soon found.[29]

In 1899 Thomas Preston had presented evidence that the magnetic splitting of spectral lines (Zeeman effect) was characteristic for the series to which they belonged, and in 1900 Runge and Paschen had begun a very careful investigation of Preston's rule. Paschen had been able to do no more than make the requisite photographs before he left for Tübingen; the striking quantitative results published under their names were entirely Runge's.[30] By 1905, however, Paschen had begun to equip himself to continue this work; and from 1907 he and his students employed the Zeeman effect extensively and with great success as an aid in identifying series lines.

At the same time, however, they found a large number of apparent exceptions to Preston's rule. In the simplest case those were very narrow doublet or triplet line groups showing the "normal" splitting pattern characteristic of a single line rather than the anticipated superposition of the "anomalous" splittings of the individual components of the group. Paschen, investigating this general circumstance with his student Ernst Back, and basing himself upon Ritz's conception of a spectral line as the combination of two independently subsisting terms, showed in 1912 that in sufficiently strong magnetic fields—i.e., fields strong enough for the magnetic splitting to be large compared with the separation of the components of the line group—all the splitting patterns transform themselves into the "normal" pattern. This "Paschen-Back effect" was immediately seized upon as potentially one of the most revealing clues to atomic structure and the mechanism of emission of spectral lines.[31]

In the last days of July 1914 the intense activity at Paschen's institute ceased abruptly. The German students and the institute staff rushed to the colors, and the foreign students fled over the Swiss border; Paschen himself seems not to have had the least inclination to participate in the war effort.[32] In the summer of 1915, with the aid of a single technician recalled from the army, Paschen again took up the most interesting problem upon which he had been working in 1914—"Bohr's helium lines," the lines previously construed as the sharp series of hydrogen but now ascribed by Bohr to ionized helium. In the course of this work, which was initially intended to check Bohr's prediction of a small difference between the Rydberg constant, N, for hydrogen and helium, and which was hampered by the diffuseness of the lines, Paschen discovered that a particular layer in the negative glow inside the common cylindrical-cathode Geissler tube gave especially sharp and complete spectra. Following up this observation, he developed the Paschen hollow-cathode discharge tube, in which, under the right conditions, the glow discharge retreats entirely into the largely field-free interior of a boxlike cathode. This device, which was the basis of much of the subsequent work on series and multiplet structure by Paschen and his students, showed the fine structure of Bohr's helium lines with extraordinary clarity and completeness.[33] (Here the series structure is the fine structure.)

Paschen had already reached this point when, late in 1915, Arnold Sommerfeld wrote inquiring about data with which to compare the relativistic fine structure demanded by the extension of Bohr's theory that he was then developing. Paschen was impressed; enlisting himself in the service of Sommerfeld's theory, he spent all his free time in the following six months confirming its predictions in detail, so far as possible.[34] The single paper presenting his results was immediately recognized as the tremendous advance in knowledge that it was.[35]

After the war spectroscopic activity in Paschen's institute increased rapidly. During the six years before his departure in 1924 Tübingen was unquestionably the most important center of atomic spectroscopy in Germany, at a time when this technique was far and away the most important for the advance of theoretical atomic physics. Paschen's own outstanding successes were the ordering of the neon spectrum—almost 1,000 lines—into spectral series; the evocation of the missing combinations between complex spectral terms by magnetic fields of appropriate strength (violation of the selection rule for the total angular momentum quantum number); and the first analysis of the spectra of an atom in its doubly ionized, as well as its neutral, and singly ionized states.[36] At the same time his associates Ernst Back and Alfred Landé were in the forefront of research on multiplet structure and Zeeman effects.

Paschen accepted, as few other experimentalists did, the priorities and guidance of atomic theorists. In 1922, persuaded that Landé could do more for him in this respect than any other available young theorist, he fought recklessly, tenaciously, and ultimately successfully against the social-political prejudices of his university for Landé's appointment to Tübingen's professorship (Extraordinariat) for theoretical physics.[37]

In July 1924 Paschen was looking forward to spending that fall and winter in the United States as the second German physicist (after Sommerfeld) to receive the compliment of a visiting professorship there since the war. But September found Paschen in Berlin, not Ann Arbor, for the month before he had been offered the presidency of the Physikalisch-Technische Reichsanstalt, as successor to Nernst.[38] Paschen accepted the post at the urging of the leading Berlin physicists, and with the intent of restoring basic research as a principal function of the institution. In this endeavor he had only very limited success because of budgetary constraints, bureaucratic resistance, and Paschen's own limitations as administrator and politician. After scarcely a year in the post he was letting it be known that he would be glad to return to a university chair.[39] He stayed on, however, gradually building up a spectroscopic laboratory to continue his previous line of research. As honorary professor, Paschen lectured at the University of Berlin on some topic in spectroscopy or physical optics for two hours a week every term. As a member of the Berlin Academy (from July 1925) and of various committees and commissions, and as president of the Deutsche Physikalische Gesellschaft (1925–1927), he played a prominent role—although not a key role—in the lively scientific life in Berlin during the later Weimar period.

Paschen's post, the highest to which a German experimental physicist could aspire, was *ipso facto* coveted by Johannes Stark; immediately following the Nazi seizure of power, Stark had himself appointed to it, effective 1 May 1933.[40] Forced out of his office and into retirement, Paschen was still able to continue working for a few years in his laboratory—at the cost of considerable difficulty and personal humiliation. Finally he withdrew to his home in Charlottenburg, where he confined himself to the evaluation of his spectrographs.[41] In November 1943 his home and all his possessions went up in flames in a bombing raid. Paschen then moved to Potsdam, where, weakened by postwar deprivations, he died of pneumonia early in 1947.

NOTES

1. S. Tolansky, "Friedrich Paschen," p. 1040.
2. Paschen, "Vita," Dissertation (1888); University of Tübingen Archives, 128/Paschen.
3. W. Gerlach, "Friedrich Paschen," p. 277; Paschen to Kayser, 14 Nov. 1895.
4. Paschen, "Vita," Dissertation (1888); "Antrittsrede," in *Sitzungsberichte der Deutschen Akademie der Wissenschaften zu Berlin* (1925), cii.
5. Paschen, "Ueber die zum Funkenübergang . . . erforderliche Potentialdifferenz," in *Annalen der Physik und Chemie*, n.s. **37** (1889), 69–96; J. J. Thomson, *The Conduction of Electricity Through Gases*, 2nd ed. (Cambridge, 1906), pp. 451 ff.

6. Paschen, "Antrittsrede" (1925), p. cii.

7. Paschen to Kayser, 17 Mar. 1895; 18 July 1895; 14 Nov. 1895; 8 Feb. 1898.

8. H. Kangro, *Vorgeschichte des Planckschen Strahlungsgesetzes.*

9. H. Kayser, "Erinnerungen aus meinem Leben" (1936), pp. 162–163 (typescript). Copy in the Library of the American Philosophical Society, Philadelphia.

10. Kangro, *Vorgeschichte . . .*, pp. 60–73.

11. Kangro, "Ultrarotstrahlung . . .," p. 181.

12. Kangro, *Vorgeschichte . . .*, loc. cit.

13. Paschen, "Über Gesetzmässigkeiten in den Spectren fester Körper und über eine neue Bestimmung der Sonnentemperatur," in *Nachrichten der Gesellschaft der Wissenschaften zu Göttingen*, Math.-phys. Kl. (1895), 294–304, dated June 1895.

14. *Ibid.*

15. "Spielerei": Paschen to Kayser, 18 July 1895; Iris Runge, *Carl Runge*, pp. 73–74. Henry Crew, visiting Hannover at this time, found Paschen reminded him of J. E. Keeler, while his "laboratory like Nernst's in apparent dissorder—using concave grating without any mounting, simply sets up the three parts in a room." Crew, "Diary," 12 July 1895 (American Institute of Physics, New York).

16. Paschen to Kayser, 14 Nov. 1895; Runge, *op. cit.*, p. 76.

17. Paschen, "Ueber Gesetzmässigkeiten in den Spectren fester Körper. Erste Mittheilung," in *Annalen der Physik*, 3rd ser., **58** (1896), 455–492, dated May 1896; Kangro, *Vorgeschichte . . .*, pp. 74–89.

18. Paschen, "Ueber Gesetzmässigkeiten in den Spectren fester Körper. Zweite Mittheilung," in *Annalen der Physik*, **60** (1897), 663–723, dated Jan. 1897, see 723.

19. Paschen to Kayser, 4 June [1896]; H. Kangro, "Das Paschen-Wiensche Strahlungsgesetz."

20. Paschen to Kayser, 2 Aug. 1896; *Sitzungsberichte der Preussischen Akademie der Wissenschaften* (8 Apr. 1897), 453; and (18 May 1899), 438.

21. Paschen to Kayser, 17 July 1898. This result was not published, however, until almost one year later in *Sitzungsberichte der Akademie der Wissenschaften zu Berlin* (1899), 405–420.

22. Kangro, *Vorgeschichte . . .*, pp. 165–179, 223.

23. Paschen to Kayser, 19 Jan. 1901.

24. University of Tübingen Archives, 128/Paschen; Paschen to L. Graetz, 22 July 1901 (Deutsches Museum, Munich); Paschen to Kayser, 18 Feb. 1901. "Der Neubau des physikalischen Instituts für die kgl. württemb. Landes-Universität Tübingen," in *Deutsche Bauzeitung*, **24** (1890), 213, 217.

25. Paschen to Sommerfeld, 25.8.20 (SHQP mf33); Paschen to E. Wiedemann, 10.6.13 (Darmst.).

26. Württemberg, Landtag, Kammer der Abgeordneten, "Begründung einer Exigenz von 125000 Mk. zur Erweiterung des physikalischen Instituts der Universität Tübingen," in *Verhandlungen*, 37. Landtag (1907), Beilagenband 1, Heft 15, pp. 16–18. H. M. Randall, who spent the year 1910-1911 at Tübingen, recalled that "Paschen offered to show me how each element of his entire infrared setup was constructed . . . . By 1914 a complete infrared installation of the Paschen type had been set up at Michigan. . . ." "Infrared Spectroscopy at the University of Michigan," in *Journal of the Optical Society of America*, **44** (1954), 97–103. Many examples could be given of the imitation of Paschen's installations by former students.

27. University of Tübingen Archives, 128/Paschen and 117/904; Akten der Naturwissenchaftlichen Fakultät, Tübingen.

28. Paschen to Kayser, 18 June 1919; Paschen to Sommerfeld, 25 Jan. 1919 [sic; actually 1920], Mar. 1920 (SHQP mf 33).

29. Paschen, "Zur Kenntnis ultraroter Linienspektra. I. (Normalwellenlängen bis 27000 Å.-E)," in *Annalen der Physik*, **27** (1908), 537–570, received 12 Aug. 1908; W. Ritz, *Gesammelte Werke*, Pierre Weiss, ed. (Paris, 1911), 521–525.

30. Runge, *op. cit.*, p. 108.

31. Paschen and E. Back, "Normale und anomale Zeemaneffekte," in *Annalen der Physik*, **39** (1912), 897–932; Paul Forman, "Back," in DSB, I, 370–371; J. B. Spencer, *Zeeman Effect*, 1896–1913.

32. Paschen to Kayser, 4 Feb. 1916.

33. H. Schüler, "Erinnerungen eines Spektrokopikers . . .," in H. Leussink *et al.*, *Studium Berolinense* (Berlin, 1960), 816–826.

34. Paschen to Sommerfeld, 32 letters Nov. 1915–Aug. 1916 (Archive for History of Quantum Physics).

35. Paschen, "Bohr's Heliumlinien," in *Annalen der Physik*, 4th ser., **50** (1916), 901–940, received 1 July 1916.

36. Paschen, "Das Spektrum des Neon," *ibid.*, **60** (1919), 405–453, and "Nachtrag," *ibid.*, **63** (1920), 201–220; Paschen and E. Back, "Liniengruppen magnetisch vervollständigt," in *Physica* (Eindhoven), **1** (1921), 261–273; and Paschen, "Die Funkenspektren des Aluminiums," in *Annalen der Physik*, 4th ser., **71** (1923), 142–161, 537–571.

37. Paul Forman, *Environment and Practice of Atomic Physics in Weimar Germany*, Ph.D. diss., Univ. of California, Berkeley, 1967 (Ann Arbor, Mich., 1968), 455–489.

38. University of Tübingen Archives, 128/Paschen; Paschen to Bohr, 11 Jan. 1924; 10 July 1924 (Archive for History of Quantum Physics).

39. Paschen to Sommerfeld, 14 Dec. 1924 (Archive for History of Quantum Physics); W. Wien to Ministerialrat [?], 14 Jan. 1926 (University of Munich Archives, Personalakten W. Wien, EII-698); H. Schüler, in *Physikalische Blätter*, **3** (1947), 232–233.

40. Armin Hermann, "Albert Einstein und Johannes Stark," in *Sudhoffs Archiv . . .*, **50** (1966), 267–286, see 283, which includes material on Paschen's role in the consideration of Stark for membership in the Berlin Academy, Dec. 1933–Jan. 1934.

41. Gerlach, *op. cit.*, p. 279.

BIBLIOGRAPHY

I. ORIGINAL WORKS. The only lists of Paschen's publications are the Royal Society *Catalogue of Scientific Papers*, XVII, 721–722; and Poggendorff, IV, 1121, 1286–1287 (under Runge); V, 618 (under Kayser), 946, 1078–1079 (under Runge), 1349 (under Weinland); VI, 1956–1957, 2291 (under R. A. Sawyer); VIIa, pt.3, 506–507. The following additional items have come to my attention: *Ueber die zum Funkenübergang in Luft, Wasserstoff und Kohlensäure bei verschiedenen Drucken erforderliche Potentialdifferenz*, his doctoral dissertation at Strasbourg (Leipzig, 1889), differs significantly from the version in *Annalen der Physik*, **37** (1889), 69–96; "Terrestrial Helium," in *Nature*, **52** (6 June 1895), 128, *Chemical News . . .*, **71** (14 June 1895), 286; and *Chemiker-zeitung*, **19** (1895), 977, written with C. Runge; "Ueber das Strahlungsgesetz des schwarzen Körpers," in *Annalen der Physik*, 4th ser., **4** (1901), 277–298; "Eine neue Bestimmung der Dispersion des Flusspates im Ultrarot," *ibid.*, 299–303; "Bestimmung des selectiven Reflexionsvermögens einer Planspiegel," *ibid.*, 304–306; "Erweiterung des Seriengesetzes der Linienspectra auf Grund genauer Wellenlängenmessungen im Ultraroth," in *Comptes rendus du Congrès international de radiologie et électricité, Brussels 1910*, I (Brussels, 1911), 588–600, also in *Jahrbuch der Radioaktivität und Elektronik*, **8** (1911), 174–186;

and "Antrittsrede," in *Sitzungsberichte der Preussischen Akademie der Wissenschaften* (2 July 1925), cii–civ.

Paschen's MSS apparently were destroyed with his home in 1943. Some 4 letters from Paschen to N. Bohr, 4 to W. Gerlach, 1 to S. A. Goudsmit, 1 to L. Graetz, 37 to H. Kayser, 1 to J. Königsberger, 14 to A. Landé, 1 to A. G. Shenstone, 87 to A. Sommerfeld, 2 to J. R. Swinne, and 1 to E. Wiedemann are listed or cited in T. S. Kuhn *et al.*, *Sources for History of Quantum Physics* (Philadelphia, 1967), 72–73. The items in the Darmstädter Collection, F1c(4) 1893, cited there, particularly the important collection of 37 letters to Kayser—17 Mar. 1895; 24 Mar. (1895); 18 July (1895), 1 Aug. 1895; 14 Nov. 1895; 25 Nov. 1895; 30 Dec. 1895; 7 Jan. 1896; 13 Feb. 1896; 6 May 1896; 4 June (1896); 19 July 1896; 25 July 1896; 2 Aug. 1896; 8 Feb. 1898; 23 Feb. 1898; 17 July 1898; 30 Dec. 1900; 3 Jan. 1901; 9 Jan. 1900 [*sic*; actually 1901]; 19 Jan. 1901; 22 Jan. 1901; 18 Feb. 1901; 7 June 1902; 5 July 1903; 7 July 1903; 9 June 1905; 16 June 1905; 19 Nov. 1910; 3 Oct. 1912; 14 Oct. 1913; 4 Feb. 1916; 2 July 1915 [*sic*; actually 1916]; 29 Mar. 1919; 18 June 1919; 11 Oct. 1921; 14 Sept. 1923—are now in the Staatsbibliothek Preussischer Kulturbesitz, Berlin-Dahlem. The Nachlass Stark in the same depository includes 25 letters from Paschen to Stark: 11 Jan. 1905; 28 Jan. 1905; 6 Mar. 1905; 19 May (1906); 10 July 1906; 2 Aug. 1906; 29 Sept. 1906; 3 Oct. 1906; 10 Nov. (1906); 12 Feb. 1907; 3 June 1907; 19 June (1907); 21 June (1907); 27 June (1907); 29 Feb. 1908; 18 Mar. 1911; 15 Oct. 1911; 18 Oct. 1911; 20 Oct. 1911; 22 Oct. 1911; 3 Oct. 1918; 20 Oct. 1918; 4 May 1927; 6 July 1927; 2 Oct. 1927. There are 3 additional letters to N. Bohr—11 Jan. 1924; 30 Mar. 1924; 10 July 1924—in the Bohr Collection, Niels Bohr Institutet, Copenhagen; and at least 3 letters to W. F. Meggers —6 Sept. 1921; 14 June 1924; 15 Oct. 1925—in the Meggers Papers, American Institute of Physics, New York.

II. Secondary Literature. Paschen's work on Kirchhoff's emission function is discussed in detail by Hans Kangro, *Vorgeschichte des Planckschen Strahlungsgesetzes. Messungen und Theorien der spektralen Energieverteilung . . .* (Wiesbaden, 1970), summarized in Kangro's "Das Paschen-Wiensche Strahlungsgesetz und seine Abänderung durch Max Planck," in *Physikalische Blätter*, **25** (1969), 216–220, and touched upon in his "Ultrarotstrahlung bis zur Grenze elektrisch erzeugter Wellen: Das Lebenswerk von Heinrich Rubens," in *Annals of Science*, **26** (1970), 235–259, and **27** (1971), 165–200. Paschen's collaboration and personal relations with Carl Runge are described in Iris Runge, *Carl Runge und sein wissenschaftliches Werk* (Göttingen, 1949). The magneto-optical work of Paschen and his school up through the discovery of the Paschen-Back effect is discussed in detail in James Brooks Spencer, *An Historical Investigation of the Zeeman Effect, 1896–1913*, Ph.D. diss., U. of Wisconsin, 1964 (Ann Arbor, 1964). Some of their later work is discussed by P. Forman, "Alfred Landé and the Anomalous Zeeman Effect, 1919–1921," in *Historical Studies in the Physical Sciences*, **2** (1970), 153–262.

There are no biographical studies of Paschen apart from the very few and spare obituary notices. The best of these is Walther Gerlach, "Friedrich Paschen," in *Jahrbuch der Bayerischen Akademie der Wissenschaften* (1944–1948), 277–280—Paschen had been elected a corresponding member in 1922. Others are S. Tolansky, "Friedrich Paschen," in *Proceedings of the Physical Society of London*, **59** (1947), 1040–1041; H. Schüler, "Friedrich Paschen," in *Physikalische Blätter*, **3** (1947), 232–233; R. Seeliger, "Nachruf auf Friedrich Paschen," in *Jahrbuch der Deutschen Akademie der Wissenschaften zu Berlin* (1946–1949), 199–201; W. Heisenberg et al., "Friedrich Paschen," in *Annalen der Physik*, 6th ser., **1** (1947), 137–138. A notice by Carl Runge in honor of Paschen's sixtieth birthday, "Friedrich Paschen," in *Naturwissenschaften*, **13** (1925), 133–134, gives reminiscences of the origin of their collaboration in 1895; Niels Bohr, "Friedrich Paschen zum siebzigsten Geburtstag," *ibid.*, **23** (1935), 73, testifies to Paschen's "happy intuition, by which he always has pursued experimentally those problems the investigation of which proved to be of decisive significance for the extension of general theoretical conceptions."

PAUL FORMAN

PASTEUR, LOUIS (*b*. Dole, Jura, France, 27 December 1822; *d*. Chateau Villeneuve-l'Étang, near Paris, France, 28 September 1895), *crystallography, chemistry, microbiology, immunology*.

Outline of Pasteur's Career

1829–1831	Student at École Primaire, Arbois
1831–1839	Student at Collège d'Arbois
1839–1842	Student at Collège Royal de Besançon
1842–1843	Student at Barbet's School and Lycée St.-Louis, Paris
1843–1846	Student at École Normale Supérieure (Paris)
1846–1848	Préparateur in chemistry, École Normale
1849–1854	Professor of chemistry, Faculty of Sciences, Strasbourg suppléant, 1849–1852 titulaire, 1852–1854
1854–1857	Professor of chemistry and dean of the Faculty of Sciences, Lille
1857–1867	Administrator and director of scientific studies, École Normale
1867–1874	Professor of chemistry, Sorbonne
1867–1888	Director of the laboratory of physiological chemistry, École Normale
1888–1895	Director of the Institut Pasteur (Paris)

In addition:

Sept.–Dec. 1848   Professor of physics, Lycée de Dijon
1863–1868   Professor of geology, physics, and chemistry in their application to the fine arts, École des Beaux-Arts (Paris)

List of Pasteur's Major Prizes and Honors

1853   Chevalier of the Imperial Order of the Legion of Honor
1853   Prize on racemic acid, Société de Pharmacie de Paris
1856   Rumford Medal, Royal Society (for work in crystallography)
1859   Montyon Prize for Experimental Physiology, Académie des Sciences
1861   Zecker Prize, Académie des Sciences (chemistry section)
1862   Alhumbert Prize, Académie des Sciences
1862   Elected member of the Académie des Sciences (mineralogy section)
1866   Gold Medal, Comité Central Agricole de Sologne (for work on diseases of wine)
1867   Grand Prize Medal of the Exposition Universelle (Paris), for method of preserving wine by heating
1868   Honorary M.D., University of Bonn (returned during Franco-Prussian War, 1870–1871)
1868   Promoted to commander of the Legion of Honor
1869   Elected fellow of the Royal Society
1871   Prize for silkworm remedies, Austrian government
1873   Commander of the Imperial Order of the Rose, Brazil
1873   Elected member of the Académie de Médecine
1874   Copley Medal, Royal Society (for work on fermentation and silkworm diseases)
1874   Voted national recompense of 12,000 francs
1878   Promoted to grand officer of the Legion of Honor
1881   Awarded Grand Cross of the Legion of Honor
1882   Grand Cordon of the Order of Isabella the Catholic
1882   National recompense augmented to 25,000 francs
1882   Elected to Académie Française
1886   Jean Reynaud Prize, Académie des Sciences
1887   Elected perpetual secretary, Académie des Sciences (resigned because of illness in January 1888)
1892   Jubilee celebration at the Sorbonne

Chronological Outline of Pasteur's Major Research Interests

1847–1857   Crystallography: optical activity and crystalline asymmetry
1857–1865   Fermentation and spontaneous generation; studies on vinegar and wine
1865–1870   Silkworm diseases: *pébrine* and *flacherie*
1871–1876   Studies on beer; further debates over fermentation and spontaneous generation
1877–1895   Etiology and prophylaxis of infectious diseases: anthrax, fowl cholera, swine erysipelas, rabies

Pasteur and His Place in History. If Pasteur was a genius, it was not through ethereal subtlety of mind. Although often bold and imaginative, his work was characterized mainly by clearheadedness, extraordinary experimental skill, and tenacity—almost obstinacy—of purpose. His contributions to basic science were extensive and very significant, but less revolutionary than his reputation suggests. The most profound and original contributions are also the least famous. Beginning about 1847 Pasteur carried out an impressive series of investigations into the relation between optical activity, crystalline structure, and chemical composition in organic compounds, particularly tartaric and paratartaric acids. This work focused attention on the relationship between optical activity and life and provided much inspiration and several of the most important techniques for an entirely new approach to the study of chemical structure and composition. In essence, Pasteur opened the way to a consideration of the disposition of atoms in space, and his early memoirs constitute founding documents of stereochemistry.

From crystallography and structural chemistry Pasteur moved to the controversial and interrelated topics of fermentation and spontaneous generation. If he did more than anyone to promote the biological theory of fermentation and to discredit the theory of spontaneous generation, his effect was due less to profound conceptual originality than to experimental ingenuity and polemical virtuosity. He did broach and contribute fundamentally to important questions in microbial physiology—including the relationship between microorganisms and their environment—but he was readily distracted from such basic issues by more practical concerns—the manufacture of wine, vinegar, and beer, the diseases of silkworms, and the etiology and prophylaxis of diseases in general.

To an extent, Pasteur's interest in practical problems evolved naturally from his basic research, especially that on fermentation, for the biological theory of fermentation contained obvious implications for industry. By insisting that each fermentative process could be traced to a specific living microorganism, Pasteur not only drew attention to the purity of the causative organism and the amount of oxygen employed, but also suggested that the primary industrial product could be preserved by appropriate sterilizing procedures, called "pasteurization" almost from the outset. Furthermore, the old and widely accepted analogy between fermentation and disease made any theory of the former immediately relevant to the latter. Pasteur's biological theory of fermentation virtually implied a biological or "germ" theory of disease. This implication was more rapidly developed by others, particularly Joseph Lister; but Pasteur also perceived it from the first and devoted his last twenty years almost exclusively to the germ theory of disease.

No one insisted more strongly than Pasteur himself on the degree to which his pragmatic concerns grew out of his prior basic research. He saw the progression from crystallography through fermentation to disease as not only natural but virtually inevitable; he had been "enchained," he wrote, by the "almost inflexible logic of my studies."[1] This view, however enduring and widely accepted, has not gone entirely unchallenged. René Dubos has emphasized how Pasteur's work could have taken many other directions with equal fidelity to the internal logic of his research.[2] To some extent Pasteur chose, or at least allowed himself to pursue, the practical consequences of his work at the expense of his potential contributions to basic science. Without disputing the immense value and fertility of the basic research he did accomplish, it is fascinating to speculate on what might have been. Late in life, Pasteur indulged in similar speculation and expressed regret that he had abandoned his youthful researches before fully resolving the relationship between asymmetry and life. Had he contributed as much as he had once hoped toward this problem, he would surely have fulfilled his ambition of becoming the Newton or Galileo of biology.

By taking another direction, however, Pasteur revealed the enormous medical and economic potential of experimental biology. He himself developed only one treatment directly applicable to a human disease—his treatment for rabies—but his widely publicized and highly successful efforts on behalf of the germ theory were immediately credited with saving much money and many lives. It is for this reason above all that he was recognized and honored during his lifetime and that his name remains a household word.

As his letters make clear, Pasteur chose his path under the impulse of complex and mixed motives.

Apart from the internal logic of his research, these motives included ambition for fame and imperial favor, his wish to serve his country and humanity, and his concern for financial security (more for the sake of his work and his family than for himself). In the highly competitive academic life of mid-nineteenth-century France, he was unabashedly ambitious and opportunistic. Not yet thirty, he consoled his rather neglected wife by telling her that he would "lead her to posterity."[3] Pasteur's correspondence is filled with references to academic politics and with appeals for support from his influential friends—notably Biot and Dumas at the outset of his career, and later a number of important ministers and government officials, including Emperor Louis Napoleon and Empress Eugénie.

Pasteur sometimes complained bitterly of the neglect of science by the French state; but once his concern with practical problems became manifest, he had remarkable success in getting what he sought—a new laboratory, additional personnel, a larger research budget, a national pension for himself, even railroad passes for himself and his assistants. His support, although not spectacular in comparison with that provided to some scientists in German universities, was unusually generous by French governmental standards.

To supplement it, Pasteur competed actively for awards from private societies and foreign governments. Here too he enjoyed considerable success. For his work on racemic acid, for example, he received a prize of 1,500 francs from the Société de Pharmacie de Paris in 1853; and for his efforts to aid the silkworm industry, he was awarded 5,000 florins by the Austrian government. By far the most spectacular award for which Pasteur competed—in this case unsuccessfully —was a prize of 625,000 francs offered in 1887 by the government of New South Wales for practical measures to reduce the rabbit population. As unpublished correspondence makes clear,[4] Pasteur sought this fortune partly for the sake of his family and partly to support the projected Institut Pasteur, toward the creation of which a widely publicized and highly successful drive had been launched. The fame of Pasteur's treatment for rabies attracted donors throughout the world, and the value of their contributions surpassed 2 million francs by November 1888,[5] when the Institut Pasteur was officially inaugurated. The French National Assembly had already voted him two national recompenses—one in 1874 with an annual value of 12,000 francs and another in 1883 that increased his life annuity to 25,000 francs and made it transferable upon his death to his wife and then to his children.[6]

Pasteur secured yet other revenues from patents or

licenses for products and processes that resulted from his research. In 1861 he patented his method of making vinegar; and he later received patents or licenses for his methods of preserving wine and manufacturing beer, for a bacterial filter (the Chamberland-Pasteur filter), and for his vaccines against fowl cholera, anthrax, and swine erysipelas. No adequate account exists of the fate of these patents and licenses, but some were allowed to enter the public domain or were otherwise unexploited, while those for the filter and vaccines apparently yielded large revenues, most of which seem to have gone to the state or to the Institut Pasteur. Apparently at the urging of his wife and family, Pasteur accepted some unknown amount of the income from his patents. His will reveals only that he left his wife "all that the law allows."[7] Apparently Pasteur amassed no large personal fortune. Although exaggerated, his insistence that he worked solely for the love of science and country and the standard portrayal of him as a "savant désintéressé" carry more conviction than attempts to depict him as a scientific prostitute. Compared, for example, with Liebig, he was a model of commercial restraint.[8]

Pasteur displayed no comparable restraint in controversy. Combative and enormously self-assured, he could be devastating to the point of cruelty. He so offended one opponent, an eighty-year-old surgeon, that the latter challenged him to a duel.[9] Although often counseled to spend his energy more productively, Pasteur was constitutionally incapable of suffering criticism in silence. A few debates, notably on spontaneous generation, did stimulate valuable work and produce important clarifications, but most were barren. Sharing with many contemporary scientists a zealous concern for his intellectual property, he spent considerable time and effort to establish the priority of concepts and discoveries, particularly his process for preserving wines. Pasteur generally gave credit to others only grudgingly and mistrusted those who claimed to have reached similar views independently. He also shared a rather simpleminded and absolutist notion of scientific truth, rarely conceding the possibility of its being multifaceted and relative. By appeal to public demonstrations—notably in the sensational vaccination experiments at Pouilly-le-Fort—and by frequent recourse to "judiciary" commissions of the Académie des Sciences, Pasteur almost invariably won public and quasi-official sanction for his views.[10]

Although in some ways unfortunate, Pasteur's polemical inclinations and talents were a major factor in his success. Intuitively at least, he perceived that the essential measure of a scientist's achievement is the degree to which he can persuade the scientific community of his views. By this measure, Pasteur was enormously successful, thanks in part to his tendency toward self-advertisement. The most obvious factor contributing to his success was his tremendous capacity for work; equally important was his ability to concentrate intensely on one problem for remarkably long periods. Other factors, especially obvious in his early work in crystallography, were his powerful visual imagination and highly developed aesthetic sense. Perhaps the most surprising factor invoked to explain Pasteur's success was his myopia, which reportedly enhanced his close vision so that, in an object under the microscope or between his hands, he saw things hidden to those around him.[11]

His father's constant concern for his health suggests that Pasteur had never been robust, and excessive physical and mental exertion further undermined his constitution. On 19 October 1868, in the midst of silkworm studies, Pasteur suffered a cerebral hemorrhage that completely paralyzed his left side. Treated with leeches and later by electricity and mineral waters, he improved somewhat but retained a lifelong hemiplegia that impaired his speech and prevented his performing most experiments. He continued to design and direct experiments with his usual care and ingenuity, but their execution was often left to collaborators. For nearly twenty years Pasteur's health remained fairly stable; but in the autumn of 1886 he began to experience cardiac deficiency and in October 1887 he suffered another stroke that further impaired his speech and mobility. His strength fading steadily, Pasteur was visibly feeble when he moved into the Institut Pasteur in 1889. In 1892 he expressed a brief enthusiasm for Charles Brown-Séquard's controversial testicular injections, but in 1894 he suffered what was probably a third stroke.[12] At his death he was almost completely paralyzed.

Virtually obsessed with science and its applications, Pasteur devoted little thought to political, philosophical, or religious matters. His beliefs in these areas were basically visceral or instinctive. His close association with the Second Empire reflects his political instincts. Despite a youthful flirtation with republicanism during the Revolution of 1848, Pasteur was essentially conservative, not to say reactionary. He considered strong leadership, firm law enforcement, and the maintenance of domestic order more important than civil liberty or even democracy, which he distrusted lest it lead to national mediocrity or vulgar tyranny. Yearning for the past glory of France, which he traced to Napoleon, he believed that Louis Napoleon might somehow restore it.[13]

From the coup d'état of 2 December 1851, by which Louis Napoleon dissolved the Constituent Assembly, Pasteur declared himself a "partisan" of the new leader.[14] Partly through Dumas, whom Napoleon III named a senator, Pasteur developed personal relations with the imperial household, to which he sent copies of his works on fermentation and spontaneous generation. Especially after 1863, when Dumas presented him to Louis Napoleon, Pasteur openly sought to attract imperial interest to his research. He dedicated his book on wines (1866) to the emperor and his book on silkworm diseases (1870) to the empress, who had encouraged him during the difficult early stages of this work.[15]

Louis Napoleon's deposition in 1870 nullified an imperial decree of 27 July 1870 by which Pasteur would have been awarded a national pension and made a senator. In 1868 the emperor had promoted Pasteur to commander of the Legion of Honor, and in 1865 had invited him to Compiègne, the most elegant imperial residence. During a week there Pasteur, in giddy letters to his wife, betrayed his awe of, and fascination with, imperial power, pomp, and wealth.[16] No mere political opportunist, however, he continued to acknowledge his association with and indebtedness to the empress after the abdication—in the face of advice that it could be politically imprudent to do so.[17]

However firm Pasteur's loyalty to the Second Empire, his general patriotism was even stronger. In 1871, despite tempting offers from Milan and Pisa, Pasteur remained in France, partly because of his wife's unwillingness to expatriate but especially because he felt it would be an act of desertion to leave his country in the wake of its crushing defeat by Prussia.[18] That defeat and the excesses of the Prussian army so aroused Pasteur that he vowed to inscribe all of his remaining works with the words, "Hatred toward Prussia. Revenge! Revenge!"[19] Also in 1871 he returned in protest an honorary M.D. awarded in 1868 by the University of Bonn. In an exchange of letters with the dean of the faculty of medicine there, which he published as a brochure, Pasteur cried out in rage at the "barbarity" being visited upon his country by Prussia and its king. In another brochure of 1871, "Some Reflections on Science in France," Pasteur emphasized the disparity between the state support of science in France and in Germany, and traced the defeat of France in the war to its excessive tolerance toward the "Prussian canker [chancre]" and to its neglect of science during the preceding half-century.

During the war and, later, the Commune, Pasteur withdrew to the provinces and launched his studies on beer—his explicit object being to bring France into competition with the superior German breweries. In 1873, when he patented the process that resulted from these studies, Pasteur stipulated that beer made by his method should bear in France the name "Bières de la revanche nationale" and abroad the name "Bières françaises."[20] Chauvinism undoubtedly played some part in his refusal to grant permission to translate his Études sur la bière into German and in his bitter and protracted controversy with Robert Koch in the 1880's. Even on the eve of his death, Pasteur's memories of the war remained so strong that he declined the Prussian Ordre Pour le Mérite.[21]

In 1875 Pasteur was asked by friends in Arbois to run for the Senate. Saying that he had no right to a political opinion because he had never studied politics, he nonetheless consented to run as a conservative. Presenting himself as the candidate of science and patriotism, he rehearsed his published explanations for the fall of France in the Franco-Prussian War and made his central political pledge "never [to] enter into any combinations the goal of which is to upset the established order of things."[22] Although Pasteur's strong commitment to scientific professionalism probably struck some as elitist, the main issues against him were his conservatism, his links with the Second Empire, and his suspected Bonapartist loyalties. In response, Pasteur reported that the emperor had died owing him 4,000 francs and disclaimed any link with organized Bonapartist groups. He was soundly defeated, receiving only 62 votes, nearly 400 less than each of the two successful candidates (both republicans). Although asked at least twice during the 1880's to run again for the Senate, Pasteur declined while his strength for scientific work remained. By then he referred to politics as ephemeral and sterile compared with science, a view that can only have been reinforced by his hostile reception on a visit to Arbois in 1888.[23] In 1892, no longer strong enough for research, Pasteur began soliciting support for a place in the Senate but eventually withdrew.[24]

At the center of Pasteur's public views on religion and philosophy lay his insistence on an absolute separation between matters of science and matters of faith or sentiment.[25] Although he was reared and died a Catholic, religious ritual and sectarian doctrine held little attraction for him. He cared as little for formal philosophy. By 1865 he had read only a few "absurd passages" in Comte, and he described his own philosophy as one "entirely of the heart."[26] Throughout his life he disdained materialists, atheists, freethinkers, and positivists. In 1882, in his inaugural address to the Académie Française, Pasteur found wanting the positivistic philosophy of Émile Littré, whom he was replacing. For Pasteur, the failures of positivism included its lack of real intellectual novelty, its confusion of the true experimental method with the "restricted method" of observation, and above all its disregard for "the most important of positive notions, that of the Infinite,'' one form of which is the idea of God. Pasteur never doubted the existence of the spiritual realm or of the immortal soul. In that sense, and in his opposition to philosophical materialism, he was a spiritualist. Indeed, in his inaugural address he spoke of the service his research had rendered to the "spiritualistic doctrine, much neglected elsewhere, but certain at least to find a glorious refuge in your ranks."[27]

Pasteur's chief contribution to the "spiritualist doctrine" was his campaign against spontaneous generation, the religiophilosophical consequences of which he emphasized in an address at the Sorbonne in 1864 while fervently denying that these broader issues had influenced his actual research. To the extent that any question was truly scientific, he argued, neither spiritualism nor any other philosophical school had a place in it. The "experimental method" alone could arbitrate scientific disputes. And while limited hypotheses played an essential role in the experimental method, speculation on the ultimate origin and end of things was beyond the realm of science. Despite this public posture, Pasteur sometimes speculated on the origin of life and attempted to create it experimentally, as he finally confessed in 1883.[28] And while the results of his work on fermentation, spontaneous generation, and disease may point toward a vitalistic rather than a mechanistic position, it would be misleading if not erroneous to label Pasteur a vitalist.

Pasteur was frank, stubborn, prodigiously self-confident, intensely serious—almost somber—and rather aloof toward those outside his select circle. Obsessed with his work, he brooked no interference with it. Sincerely kind to children, he could be insensitive and exploitative to others. His passion for tidiness and cleanliness approached the eccentric, and fear of infection allegedly made him wary of shaking hands or of eating without first wiping the dinnerware and scrutinizing his food.[29] Pasteur tended to be highly secretive about the general direction of his current work, even with his most trusted assistants; and his insistence on absolute control of his laboratory reportedly extended even to the recording of experimental notes and the labeling of animal cages.[30]

An innovative administrator and fastidious organizer, Pasteur showed a legendary devotion to detail. As director of scientific studies at the École Normale Supérieure, he proposed procedural and structural reforms, notably with regard to the *agrégés-préparateurs* (laboratory assistants who were graduates of the school); founded a journal, *Annales scientifiques de l'École normale supérieure*; and raised the standards and reputation of the scientific section so that it began to challenge the École Polytechnique. On the other hand, Pasteur's handling of student discipline betrayed

an inflexible and rather authoritarian spirit. His relations with students were described as "hardly frequent" but "often disagreeable."[31] He dealt summarily, unsympathetically, and sometimes arbitrarily with student complaints about food and rules; and by 1863 he was openly appalled by what he considered student insubordination. In 1867 Pasteur was removed from his post as administrator and director of scientific studies precisely because of his rigid and unpopular stand against a student protest involving free speech and anti-imperial sentiment.[32]

Pasteur was considered an excellent teacher, and his lectures were beautifully organized if not spellbinding. During the last two decades of his life, however, he taught only by precept and example in the laboratory and only those few who could simultaneously contribute to his own work and meet his exacting standards. He therefore trained very few students directly, but several of them—notably Émile Duclaux and Émile Roux—transmitted the spirit of his work to others who established and staffed the more than 100 medical institutes and scientific centers that now bear Pasteur's name. Despite his tendency to be as demanding of others as he was of himself, Pasteur inspired tremendous loyalty. If any assistant-collaborator felt that his contributions were being unduly appropriated to Pasteur's name, none ever expressed that feeling publicly.

In realizing most if not all of his ambitions, Pasteur became a national hero and "benefactor of humanity" to many while arousing the envy and hostility of others. A portion of the medical profession and of what he denigrated as the "so-called scientific press" vilified him as an intolerant representative of "official" science, an egomaniacal and greedy opportunist, and a would-be suppressor of dissident views. Some fervently denied that his work had brought the immense industrial, agricultural, or medical benefits claimed for it. In addition to debates over the safety and efficacy of Pasteur's treatment for rabies, there were questions about the degree of success of his other vaccines, preservative processes, and remedies.[33] These questions deserve more detailed examination; but the contemporary attacks on Pasteur were generally so exaggerated and badly argued that they fail now, as then, to persuade others of the residue of truth they contain.

Early Life and Education. Until the late seventeenth century the Pasteurs were simple laborers or tenant farmers in the Franche-Comté, on the eastern border of France. Then, for two generations, Pasteur's ancestors were millers at Lemuy, in service to the count of Udressier. About the middle of the eighteenth century his great-grandfather migrated to Salins-les-Bains, where he became a tanner and, by payment to and "special grace" of the count of Udressier, achieved independence for himself and his posterity. Pasteur's grandfather, Jean-Henri Pasteur (1769–1796), moved to Besançon, where he too worked as a tanner. His only son, Jean-Joseph Pasteur, was Louis Pasteur's father.

Born in 1791, Jean-Joseph Pasteur was drafted into the French army in 1811. As a member of the celebrated Third Regiment of Napoleon's army, he served with distinction in the Peninsular War during 1812–1813. By 1814, when he was discharged, he had attained the rank of sergeant major and had been awarded the cross of the Legion of Honor. Upon his return to civilian life, Jean-Joseph also became a tanner, initally at Besançon. In 1816 he married Jeanne-Étiennette Roqui, daughter of a gardener from a family of the Franche-Comté. They moved to Dole, where the first four of their five children were born. Louis, their third child, was preceded by a son who died in infancy and by a daughter born in 1818; two daughters were born later. About 1826 the family moved to Marnoz, the native village of the Roqui family, and in 1827 to the neighboring town of Arbois, on the Cuisance River, where a tannery had become available for lease. It was in Arbois, a town of about 8,000 inhabitants, that Louis grew up and to which he returned periodically.

From his parents Louis absorbed the traditional *petit bourgeois* values: familial loyalty, moral earnestness, respect for hard work, and concern for financial security. Jean-Joseph, who had received little education, wished only that his son should join the faculty of a local *lycée*. Louis, who at one time apparently shared this goal, gradually directed his vision toward the scientific elite in Paris. Jean-Joseph's modest ambitions for his son seem entirely in keeping with Louis's early performance at school. In 1831, after two years in the associated École Primaire, Louis entered the Collège d'Arbois as a day pupil; he was for several years considered only a slightly better-than-average student. Until quite near the end of his secondary schooling, nothing in his record presaged his later success and fame. Only his genuine, if immature, artistic talent seemed to promise anything exceptional. Several early portraits of friends, teachers, and acquaintances have been preserved; two sensitive character sketches of his parents reveal a talent quite beyond the ordinary.

If Louis ever seriously considered an artistic career, he was dissuaded by his pragmatic father and by Bousson de Mairet, a family friend and headmaster of the Collège d'Arbois until 1837. Under Bousson and his successor, Romanet, Louis's scholarly enthusiasm was at last aroused; and he swept the school prizes during the academic year 1837–1838. Bousson and Romanet also awakened his ambition to prepare for the École Normale Supérieure. Apparently with this end in view, it was arranged that he enter the preparatory school in Paris headed by M. Barbet, himself a Franc-Comtois. Louis arrived in Paris in October 1838; less than a month later, overwhelmed by homesickness, he returned to Arbois. His superb performance that year at the Collège d'Arbois inspired him to prepare again for the École Normale.

Because the Collège d'Arbois had no class in philosophy leading to the baccalaureate in letters, Louis was compelled to continue his studies elsewhere. On 29 August 1840 he received his bachelor's degree in letters from the Collège Royal de Besançon. He received a mark of "good" in all subjects except elementary science, in which he received a "very good." Consumed with the ambition of entering the science section of the École Normale, he had first to obtain a bachelor's degree in science. His family's financial burdens were eased by his appointment as "preparation master" or tutor at the Collège Royal de Besançon. After two years in the class of special mathematics there, Pasteur received his baccalaureate in science on 13 August 1842, although in physics he was considered merely "passable," and in chemistry "mediocre." Two weeks later he was declared admissible to the École Normale, but he was dissatisfied with his rank of fifteenth among twenty-two candidates and declined admittance. Having also considered a career as a civil engineer, Pasteur took the entrance examination for the École Polytechnique in September but failed.[34] He decided to spend another year preparing for the École Normale. In letters to his parents he emphasized the importance of study in Paris; and in October 1842 he returned to Barbet's boarding school.

Like all students at the Barbet school, Pasteur attended the classes of the Lycée St.-Louis; but he also went to hear Jean-Baptiste Dumas, professor of chemistry at the Sorbonne, whose fervent admirer he quickly became. At the end of the academic year 1842–1843, he took first prize in physics at the Lycée St.-Louis, sixth "accessit" in physics in the annual general competition, and was admitted fourth on the list of candidates to the science section of the École Normale, which he entered in the autumn of 1843.

Until November 1848 Pasteur studied and worked at the École Normale. Before he could join even a secondary school faculty, he had to pass the license examination and to compete in the annual *agrégation*. In the license examination, which he took in 1845, Louis placed seventh. In September 1846 he placed third in the annual *agrégation* in the physical sciences. His appointment in October as *préparateur* in chemistry to Antoine Jérome Balard at the École Normale enabled Pasteur to continue toward his doctorate, which he received in August 1847 with dissertations in both physics and chemistry. While awaiting an appropriate post, he continued to work as *préparateur* at the École Normale and launched those studies on optical activity which were to make his early reputation.

Optical Activity, Asymmetry, Crystal Structure. By the time he completed his dissertation in physics, Pasteur's interest in optical activity had emerged. Already attracted to crystallography by the lectures of Gabriel Delafosse, professor of mineralogy at the École Normale, he found his interest intensified by his association with Auguste Laurent, who worked in the same laboratory from late in 1846 until April 1847. In his dissertation Pasteur also expressed indebtedness to Biot, whose own polarimeter Pasteur had used and whose pioneering papers on the optical activity of organic liquids had served as a guide. Essentially a preliminary methodological study, Pasteur's dissertation focused in part on the relation between isomorphism and optical activity. The results, based on two pairs of isomorphic substances, supported Laurent's view that substances of the same crystalline form possess the same optical activity in solution. One of these isomorphic pairs belonged to the tartrates, and Pasteur's other references to the tartrates and paratartrates suggest that he had already begun a systematic study of them.

Ordinary tartaric acid had been known since the eighteenth century. Prepared from salts of the tartar deposited as a by-product in wine vats, it had become especially important in medicine and in dyeing. Racemic or paratartaric acid had come to the attention of chemists only in the 1820's, when Gay-Lussac established that it possessed the same chemical composition as ordinary tartaric acid. Because of their importance for the emerging concept of isomerism, the two acids had thereafter attracted considerable notice. The studies of Biot and Eilhard Mitscherlich had established that aqueous solutions of tartaric acid and its derivatives rotated the plane of polarized light to the right, while aqueous solutions of racemic acid and its derivatives exerted no effect on it. Indeed, in a brief note of 1844 Mitscherlich had claimed that in one case—the sodium-ammonium double salts—the tartrates and paratartrates were identical in every respect, including crystalline form and atomic arrangement, except for this difference in optical activity.

Pasteur later emphasized the seminal role of Mitscherlich's note in his work. He had been deeply disturbed, he said, by the notion that "two substances could be as similar as claimed by Mitscherlich without being completely identical."[35] Pasteur's approach to the problem reflects his tutelage under Delafosse, who had made a special study of hemihedrism and naturally emphasized it in his lectures.[36] Through him Pasteur learned of the earlier work of Haüy, Biot, and John Herschel on crystallized quartz. Haüy had shown that some quartz crystals are hemihedral to the left, while others are hemihedral to the right. Biot had shown that some quartz crystals rotate the plane of polarized light to the left, while others of the same thickness rotate it an equal amount to the right. Herschel in 1820 had established a causal connection between the asymmetrical crystalline forms and the direction of optical activity. Because quartz displays optical activity only in the crystallized state and loses it when dissolved, it had been recognized that only the quartz crystal as a whole, and not its constituent molecules, is asymmetrical. But Biot had also found a number of natural organic substances—oil of turpentine, camphor, sugar, tartaric acid—that were optically active in aqueous solutions or in the fluid state. As he emphasized, optical activity in such cases—unlike that of quartz—must depend on an asymmetry in the form of the constituent molecules.

Obviously prepared in part by the ideas of Delafosse and Laurent, Pasteur became convinced that the molecular asymmetry of optically active liquids ought to find expression in an asymmetry or hemihedrism in their crystalline form. In May 1848—having published several related papers on isomorphism and dimorphism in various compounds—Pasteur announced the discovery of small hemihedral facets on the crystals of all nineteen tartrate compounds he had studied. In all of them the hemihedral facets inclined in the same direction, and the direction of optical activity was the same. In the optically inactive paratartrates Pasteur expected to find perfectly symmetrical crystals. This expectation was confirmed with the notable exception of the sodium-ammonium paratartrate on which Mitscherlich's claims specifically rested. At first disappointed when he found hemihedrism in these crystals, Pasteur soon noticed that certain crystals inclined to the right, others to the left. Pasteur meticulously separated them by hand, dissolved them, and found that solutions of the right-handed crystals rotated the plane of polarized light in one direction while solutions of the left-handed crystals rotated it in the opposite direction to approximately the same degree. When equal weights of the two kinds of crystals were dissolved separately and then combined, the result was an optically inactive sodium-ammonium paratartrate.

Similar results were obtained with the acids from which the sodium-ammonium salts had been derived.

Right-handed salts gave a right-handed acid identical to ordinary tartaric acid. Left-handed salts gave a hitherto unknown acid identical to tartaric acid except for the left-handed direction of both its hemihedrism and optical activity. Combinations of equal weights of the left-handed and right-handed acids yielded an acid identical to racemic or paratartaric acid. Pasteur now concluded that the optical inactivity of paratartaric acid (and hence of its derivatives) resulted from its being a combination of two optically active acids that were mirror images of each other, the separate optical activities of which, in opposite directions, compensated for or canceled each other.

These results, quickly confirmed by Biot and further developed by Pasteur in a series of papers between 1848 and 1850, bear striking testimony to the fertility of an admittedly a priori conception. Indeed, so powerful was Pasteur's conviction that tartrates and other optically active substances must possess hemihedral facets that he was able not only to see subtle distinctions that had eluded earlier observers, but in a sense even to produce them by appropriate adjustments in the conditions of crystallization. The hemihedral forms of sodium-ammonium paratartrate appear only under quite special and delicate conditions, especially with regard to temperature, a circumstance that leads some to assign luck a rather large role in Pasteur's first great discovery.[37] His decision to begin with the tartrates and paratartrates seems at least as fortunate, for in no other optically active compounds is the relationship between molecular asymmetry and crystalline structure so clear or straightforward; and Pasteur soon had to contend with several "exceptions" to his "law of hemihedral correlation."

Meanwhile, his credentials having been established, Pasteur was appointed professeur suppléant in chemistry at the Faculty of Sciences in Strasbourg on 29 December 1848. On 29 May 1849 he married Marie Laurent, daughter of the rector of the Strasbourg Academy. Devoted to her husband and his career, tolerating his intense absorption in his work,[38] and often serving as his stenographer or secretary, she bore him three daughters who died before reaching maturity, a son, Jean-Baptiste (b. 1851), who became a diplomat, and a fourth daughter, Marie-Louise (b. 1858), who in 1879 married René Vallery-Radot, later Pasteur's biographer.

At Strasbourg, Pasteur continued and greatly extended his work on optical activity and molecular asymmetry despite expanding teaching duties. During 1850 and 1851 he turned to asparagine and its derivatives (aspartic acid, malic acid, the aspartates and malates), which were among the very few optically active compounds from which crystals could be ob-

tained in sizes and amounts adequate for his investigations. Most of these compounds, too, display hemihedral facets as well as optical activity and, at least in this respect, fulfilled Pasteur's expectations. Indeed, malic acid shares so many analogies with tartaric acid (with which it occurs naturally in the grape) that Pasteur was led to postulate a common atomic grouping for the two and to predict the existence of a hitherto unknown left-handed malic acid and of an optically inactive malic acid analogous to, and appearing naturally with, racemic acid. Several of the asparates and malates do not, however, conform to Pasteur's conclusions concerning the tartrates and paratartrates. Certain compounds, for example, rotate the plane of polarized light in a direction contrary to the direction of their hemihedrism. A few display hemihedrism in the absence of optical activity, while others display optical activity in the absence of hemihedral crystals. Even in cases where the relationship between optical activity and crystalline form does seem to conform to Pasteur's "law," the evidence is more ambiguous. Similar difficulties emerged when other groups of optically active compounds were investigated.

Some of these difficulties escaped Pasteur, who naturally sought confirmation and not refutation of his earlier conclusions. His response to those "exceptions" which he did recognize was sometimes brilliant, sometimes evasive, but always ingenious. For cases of hemihedrism in the absence of optical activity, he had a ready explanation derived from the case of quartz. Like quartz, he argued, such substances must possess not true molecular asymmetry but merely a fortuitous asymmetry in the form of their crystal as a whole. More generally and more importantly, he suggested that minor aspects of the conditions of crystallization could mask the existence of a clear and consistent correlation between molecular and crystalline asymmetry; and he even managed in several cases to adjust the crystallizing medium and conditions so as to produce the "hidden" hemihedral facets he sought.[39] This bold achievement perhaps accounts for the confidence with which Pasteur announced as late as 1856 that the only legitimate exception to his law was one which he himself had discovered: amyl alcohol, which shared with a few other compounds the property of being optically active in the absence of crystalline asymmetry but which also displayed in its mode of crystallization unique features that convinced Pasteur that any "hidden" asymmetry could never be revealed.[40]

By 1860, as the number of apparent "exceptions" multiplied, Pasteur had subtly shifted the emphasis of his position so that optical activity became the primary index of molecular asymmetry, while crystalline form was relegated to a secondary although still important position.[41] Never, it seems, did he fully and openly abandon his basic conviction that optical activity (and hence molecular asymmetry) must somehow find expression in crystalline form.[42]

In speculating on the kind of atomic arrangements that could produce molecular asymmetry, Pasteur suggested tentatively in 1860 that the atoms of a right-handed compound, for example, might be "arranged in the form of a right-handed spiral, or . . . situated at the corners of an irregular tetrahedron."[43] But he never developed these suggestions, and it was left to others—notably Le Bel and van't Hoff in 1874—to link his work with Kekulé's theory of the tetrahedral carbon atom. From this linkage emerged the concept of the asymmetrical carbon atom, which underlies all subsequent developments in stereochemistry. Besides adding precision and clarity to Pasteur's earlier investigations of molecular asymmetry, these developments in stereochemistry raised further doubts about the validity of some of his principles.

Asymmetry and Life. In the meantime, Pasteur's preconceptions had opened a fertile new territory to him. But scarcely had he entered it when he committed himself firmly and permanently to another guiding idea—that optical activity was somehow intimately associated with life and could not be produced artificially by ordinary chemical procedures. The precise origin and basis of this idea are the subject of some controversy;[44] but Pasteur's commitment to it seems undeniable by 1852, and he may have held it implicitly from the outset of his career. Even then, evidence existed (especially from the work of Biot and Laurent) that optical activity was generally present in organic products and uniformly absent from inorganic substances. In any case, Pasteur's conviction of an association between life and optical activity ultimately became far more fundamental to him than his belief in a correlation between molecular and crystalline asymmetry.

Quite probably because of this conviction, Pasteur reacted dramatically to the work of Victor Dessaignes, who announced in 1850 that he had prepared aspartic acid by heating optically inactive starting materials (maleic and fumaric acids). Since the only known aspartic acid was optically active, Dessaignes's discovery seemed to constitute the artificial creation of optical activity. Upon hearing of this work, Pasteur went immediately to Dessaignes's laboratory in Vendôme to obtain samples of the new acid. As he expected, it proved to be a hitherto unknown inactive aspartic acid, as did the malic acid prepared from it. The possibility remained, however, that these newly discovered inactive acids were "racemic"—that is, that they owed their optical inactivity to a compensation between left-handed and right-handed forms. Initially, in a memoir of 1852, Pasteur rejected this possibility on the ground that such "racemic" acids could be synthesized only from "racemic" starting materials, while the available evidence suggested that neither the maleic nor the fumaric acid with which Dessaignes had begun could possess such a constitution.

Having rejected this explanation for the inactivity of Dessaignes's aspartic and malic acids, Pasteur boldly suggested that they belonged to an entirely new class of compounds—those the original asymmetry of which had been "untwisted" so that they had become inactive by total absence of any asymmetry, "inactive by nature" rather than "inactive by compensation." The existence of such compounds (subsequently designated by the prefix "meso") was quickly confirmed by Pasteur's preparation of "mesotartaric" acid, a compound he predicted on the basis of his belief that all forms of malic acid should have counterpart forms of tartaric acid. His hypothetical "mesomalic" acid has never been found, however, and it now seems certain that Dessaignes's synthetic malic acid was in fact "racemic" or "inactive by compensation." That Pasteur did not recognize it as such has led to the assumption that he operated under the sway of preconceived ideas—an assumption that gains immense force from Pasteur's remark of 1860 that if Dessaignes's malic acid were inactive by compensation between left-handed and right-handed forms, he would have performed the remarkable feat of producing not just one but two optically active substances from inactive starting materials.[45]

A similar interpretation can be given to Pasteur's trip of October 1852 through the tartaric acid factories of Germany and Austria. His explicit aim was to find the origin of and new sources for paratartaric or racemic acid, which had become scarce and which resisted attempts to produce it in the laboratory. For these reasons the Société de Pharmacie in 1851 had established a prize of 1,500 francs for the resolution of two questions: Does racemic acid preexist in certain tartrates? How can racemic acid be produced from tartaric acid?

Another chemist might have sought the answers solely within the laboratory, but Pasteur's conviction that asymmetry could not be produced chemically suggested another approach. Since racemic acid is a combination of right- and left-handed tartaric acids, its production from ordinary (right-handed) tartaric acid implied the transformation of a portion of right-handed tartaric acid into its left-handed form. By 1852 Pasteur had become convinced that such a transformation was chemically impossible and that racemic acid might best be sought by tracing it to its natural origin. He therefore visited the tartaric acid factories where racemic acid had once appeared or was now believed to appear, in order to compare the sources and natures of the tartars they used as well as their modes of manufacture. A survey of factories in Saxony, Vienna, and Prague revealed a correlation between the appearance of racemic acid and the use of crude tartars, especially from Italy. Pasteur concluded that racemic acid preexisted naturally to varying degrees in crude tartars and resulted not from some accidentally discovered industrial procedure. Since most manufacturers used semirefined rather than crude tartars, Pasteur asked one of them to switch back to crude Italian tartars, with the expected result that racemic acid soon reappeared in the factory. In addition he persuaded two manufacturers to seek racemic acid by treating the mother liquids left from the initial purification of their semirefined tartars, and this effort too had rapid success.

During this journey Pasteur met a German industrial chemist who claimed to have achieved what Pasteur then considered impossible—the chemical transformation of tartaric into racemic acid. Although he soon confirmed his belief that this particular claim was inaccurate, Pasteur unexpectedly achieved the transformation in May 1853 by heating cinchonine tartrate at 170° C. for five to six hours. This procedure also yielded a small amount of inactive "mesotartaric" acid, the existence of which Pasteur had predicted the year before and in search of which he had apparently undertaken the experiment. In the memoir (1 August 1853) in which he announced these two discoveries, Pasteur disclosed a new method for separating racemic acid into its left- and right-handed components. His original method, involving the manual separation of the crystals, was laborious and extremely limited in applicability. The central feature of the new method was the chemical combination of racemic acid with optically active bases. Under appropriate conditions they affected the solubility of the resulting paratartrates in such a way as to favor the crystallization of only one of the two forms that together compose the paratartrate. Although introduced by Pasteur only for the case of racemic acid, this new method clearly had wider applicability and was soon used to separate the left- and right-handed components in other "racemic" substances (substances inactive by compensation).

In November 1852, immediately after his foreign tour, Pasteur was promoted to *professeur titulaire* at Strasbourg. For his work on racemic acid and crystallography he received the prize of 1,500 francs from the Société de Pharmacie (1853), membership in the Legion of Honor, and the Rumford Medal of the Royal Society (1856). In December 1857, having moved to Lille and become deeply involved in the study of fermentation, Pasteur announced in preliminary fashion the discovery of a third method for separating racemic acid. If the first method is considered as manual and the second as chemical, then the new method was biological or physiological. In essence, it depended on the capacity of certain microorganisms to "discriminate" between left- and right-handed forms and selectively to metabolize one or the other.

The particular example that Pasteur described grew out of his study of the fermentation of ammonium paratartrate. Following this fermentation with a polarimeter, he found that the fermenting fluid displayed increasing optical activity to the left. Eventually, the fluid yielded only left-handed ammonium tartrate. The right-handed form originally present in the paratartrate had been selectively attacked during the fermentation, while the left-handed form had been left alone. Pasteur linked this discriminatory action with the nutritional needs of a living microorganism presumed to be responsible for the fermentation. Initially vague about its nature, he showed in 1860 that a specific mold, *Penicillium glaucum*, selectively metabolized the right-handed form in a solution of ammonium paratartrate containing a little phosphate. Later qualified, modified, and generalized by others, Pasteur's new method became applicable to the separation of left- and right-handed forms in a number of compounds. Another method of wide applicability was discovered in 1868 by Désiré Gernez, one of Pasteur's assistants. He showed that a single crystal of either the left- or the right-handed form, when sown into a supersaturated solution of a paratartrate, induced the selective crystallization of the form sown.

Pasteur retained a lifelong conviction that asymmetry and life are intimately associated. To do so, however, he had to refine, qualify, and even deny some aspects of his original position, especially in the face of accumulating evidence that racemic acid and other racemic substances could be produced from optically inactive compounds by ordinary chemical procedures. Ultimately Pasteur merely insisted that the artificial production of racemic substances should in no way be compared with the production of a single active substance unaccompanied by its inverse form. Ascribing the latter faculty to nature alone, he perceived in it the last barrier between organic and inorganic phenomena.[46]

If this mode of thought seems to stamp Pasteur as a vitalist, a slightly different perspective can make him seem a mechanist, for he spoke not of "vital forces" but of "asymmetrical forces." While emphasizing that these asymmetrical forces were not deployed in ordinary chemical procedures, he nonetheless connected them with, and sought them among, physical forces at work in the cosmos. In particular, he suggested that the earth is asymmetrical, in the sense that when it turns on its axis, its mirror image rotates in a different direction. And if an ether moving with the rotating earth presides over electrical and magnetic phenomena, the latter must be considered asymmetrical in the same sense. Solar light, too, presents an asymmetrical aspect, for it strikes the earth (and its organisms) at an angle which would be inverted in a mirror. Somehow, Pasteur believed, these or other asymmetrical forces must generate asymmetry (and thus life) in matter.

Not content merely to harbor such boldly speculative ideas, Pasteur sought experimental evidence for them. As early as 1853, while still at Strasbourg, he tried to bring asymmetrical forces to bear upon crystallization by means of powerful magnets built to his specifications. At Lille he tried to modify the normal character of optically active substances by using a large clockwork mechanism to rotate a plant continuously in alternate directions and by using a reflector-and-heliostat arrangement to reverse the natural movement of solar rays directed on a plant from its moment of germination. Biot and others discouraged such experiments as a waste of physical and mental resources, and Pasteur admitted that he must have been a "little mad" to undertake them.[47] Nonetheless, despite his lack of success, Pasteur never abandoned hope that life might someday be created, or at least profoundly modified, in the laboratory under the influence of such asymmetric forces. It seems a remarkable paradox that he could retain this hope while attacking all attempts by others to achieve spontaneous generation.[48] In any case, all subsequent research has supported Pasteur's convictions that optical activity and life are somehow intimately associated and that the production of a single active substance unaccompanied by its mirror image is indeed nature's prerogative except under highly exceptional and basically "asymmetrical" conditions.

Fermentation: The Background. In December 1854 Pasteur was named professor of chemistry and dean of the newly established Faculty of Sciences at Lille. Located at the center of the most flourishing industrial region in France, it was designed in part to bring science to the service of local industry. While resisting any emphasis on applied subjects at the expense of basic science, Pasteur strongly supported this goal and sought to link industry and the Faculty of Sciences in his own courses and activities. For instance, he taught the principles and techniques of bleaching, of extracting and refining sugar, and especially of fermentation and the manufacture of beetroot alcohol, an important local industry. During 1856, he went regularly to the beetroot alcohol factory of M. Bigo, seeking the cause of and remedies for recent disappointments in the quality of that product. For this reason especially, Pasteur's interest in fermentation has often been traced to the brewing industry in Lille.

Pasteur, however, traced his interest to 1849, when Biot informed him that amyl alcohol displayed optical activity.[49] For a brief period during that year, he apparently tried to study the compound, but the problem of securing pure amyl alcohol in adequate quantities led him to abandon the topic. His transfer to Lille may well have reactivated his intention to continue these studies, for amyl alcohol was readily available as a by-product of several industrial fermentations. By August 1855 Pasteur had published a paper showing that the crude amyl alcohol found in industrial fermentations was composed of two isomeric forms, one optically active and the other optically inactive. A careful study of the two forms and their derivatives convinced him by June 1856 that he had found the first legitimate exception to his "law of hemihedral correlation." His determination to investigate this exception thoroughly probably helped to direct his attention to fermentations.

Once attracted to the study of fermentation, Pasteur naturally pondered the source of asymmetry in its optically active products, notably amyl alcohol. The prevailing view traced the optical activity of amyl alcohol to the sugar (also optically active) that served as the starting material in fermentations. Pasteur, however, believed that the molecular structure of amyl alcohol differed too greatly from that of sugar for its optical activity to originate there. His tendency to associate asymmetry and optical activity with life may then have brought him to the view that fermentation depends on the activity of living microorganisms. In taking this view Pasteur defied the dominant chemical theory of fermentation, but his basic position was by no means novel or obscure. Since 1837 several observers—notably Charles Cagniard de Latour and Theodor Schwann—had insisted that alcoholic fermentation depended on the vital activity of brewer's yeast. This view had been ridiculed and eventually overwhelmed by Liebig and Berzelius, who insisted that the process was chemical rather than vital or biological. Their position drew impressive support from indisputably chemical processes considered analogous to fermentation—most notably the action of the soluble digestive "ferments" (enzymes) diastase and pepsin. But the alternative biological theory had also been founded and developed on the basis of persuasive evidence that must have given Pasteur enormous comfort when he launched his campaign against the chemical theory.

Lactic Fermentation. The opening salvo in that campaign was a short memoir on lactic fermentation, presented in August 1857 to the Society of the Sciences, Agriculture, and the Arts in Lille. Émile Duclaux has suggested that two factors induced Pasteur to focus first on the relatively unimportant lactic fermentation (most familiar as the process producing sour milk) rather than alcoholic fermentation: (1) a large quantity of amyl alcohol is produced during lactic fermentation and (2) alcoholic fermentation had already been thoroughly investigated without seriously threatening the dominant chemical theory. In a sense, unless and until living organisms were implicated in other fermentations, advocates of the chemical theory could continue to doubt the essential role of living yeast in alcoholic fermentation.[50]

Pasteur's memoir expressed the basic approach and point of view which informed all of his subsequent work on fermentation. After a historical introduction he began by claiming that "just as an alcoholic ferment exists—namely, brewer's yeast—which is found wherever sugar breaks down into alcohol and carbonic acid—so too there is a special ferment—a lactic yeast—always present when sugar becomes lactic acid." In an ordinary lactic fermentation, this "lactic yeast" appeared as a gray deposit the central role of which could be demonstrated by isolating and purifying it. To do this Pasteur took the soluble extract from brewer's yeast, added to it some sugar and some chalk, and then sprinkled in a trace of the gray deposit from an ordinary lactic fermentation. In this way he invariably produced a lively and indisputably lactic fermentation, with the gray deposit increasing in amount as the fermentation progressed. Viewed macroscopically, this deposit resembled ordinary pressed or drained brewer's yeast. Under the microscope it seemed to be composed of "little globules or very short segmented filaments, isolated or in clusters, which form irregular flakes resembling those of certain amorphous precipitates." An extremely small amount of the deposit sufficed to decompose a large amount of sugar. Although smaller and harder to see than brewer's yeast, the lactic ferment seemed to Pasteur so analogous to it that he supposed the two "yeasts" might belong to closely related species or families.

Throughout the memoir Pasteur more nearly assumed than proved that lactic yeast "is a living organism, . . . that its chemical action on sugar corresponds to its development and organization," and that the nitrogenous substances in the fermenting medium served merely as its food. Nonetheless, his

convictions were firm and his conception of fermentation was already remarkably complete. Nothing demonstrates this more forcefully than his discussion of the conditions essential for good fermentations, which include not only a pure and homogeneous ferment but also an appropriate nutrient medium, well adapted to the "individual nature" of the ferment. "In this respect," he wrote, "it is important to realize that the circumstances of neutrality, alkalinity, acidity, or chemical composition of the liquids play a great part in the predominant growth of . . . a ferment, for the life of each does not adapt itself to the same degree to different states of the environment." Acidity, for example, favors the development of the alcoholic over the lactic fermentation, while in neutral or slightly alkaline media the situation is reversed. Furthermore, the purity of the fermentation is greatly enhanced by protecting it from air and by the method of sowing pure ferments, for both prevent the invasion of "foreign vegetation or infusoria." An unsown fermentable medium, like an unseeded plot of land, "soon becomes crowded with various plants and insects that are mutually harmful." Pasteur even referred to the capacity of "the essential oil of onion" to inhibit the development of both brewer's yeast and infusoria without affecting the growth of the lactic ferment—a remark to which some have traced the concept of antibiotics.

With two striking exceptions this memoir contains the central theoretical and methodological features of all of Pasteur's work on fermentation—the biological conception of fermentation as the result of the activity of living microorganisms; the view that the substances in the fermenting medium serve as food for the causative microorganism and must therefore be appropriate to its nutritional requirements; the notion of specificity, according to which each fermentation can be traced to a specific microorganism; the recognition that particular chemical features of the medium can promote or impede the development of any one microorganism in it; the notion of competition among different microorganisms for the aliments contained in the media; the assumption that air might be the source of the microorganisms that appear in fermentations; and the technique of directly and actively sowing the microorganism presumed responsible for a given fermentation in order to isolate and purify it. The two missing features, which soon completed Pasteur's basic conception, were the technique of cultivating microorganisms (and thereby producing fermentations) in a medium free of organic nitrogen and his notion of fermentation as "life without air."

In October 1857, two months after presenting his memoir on the lactic fermentation, Pasteur left Lille for the École Normale in Paris, where he had been named director of scientific studies and administrator, his duties including "the surveillance of the economic and hygienic management, the care of general discipline, intercourse with the families of the pupils and the literary or scientific establishments frequented by them."[51] Because these positions included neither laboratory nor allowance for research expenses, Pasteur was obliged to make frequent appeals to governmental agencies for financial support. Although he considered such appeals "antipathetic to the character of a scientist worthy of the name,"[52] he made them with sufficient success to secure his own research laboratory, which consisted at first of two rooms in an attic of the École Normale. By December 1859 he had gained possession of a small pavilion, which was expanded considerably in 1862. In these surroundings Pasteur pursued his study of fermentation and quickly extended his basic conclusions on lactic fermentation to various others, notably the tartaric, butyric, and acetic as well as alcoholic.

Alcoholic Fermentation. In December 1857 Pasteur published the first in a series of abstracts, notes, and letters on alcoholic fermentation that culminated in a long and classic memoir of 1860. Divided into two major sections, dealing respectively with the fate of sugar and of yeast in alcoholic fermentation, it inflicted on the chemical theory what Duclaux called "a series of blows straight from the shoulder, delivered with agility and assurance."[53] Pasteur established that alcoholic fermentation invariably produces not only carbonic acid and ethyl alcohol—as was well known—but also appreciable quantities of glycerin and succinic acid as well as trace amounts of cellulose, "fatty matters," and "indeterminate products." On the basis of these results, Pasteur emphasized the complexity of alcoholic fermentation and attacked the tendency of chemists since Lavoisier to depict it as the simple conversion of sugar into carbonic acid and alcohol. If the alleged simplicity of the process had formerly been seen as evidence of its chemical nature, he argued, then its actual complexity ought now to be seen as evidence of its dependence on the activity of a living organism. In truth, the complexity of alcoholic fermentation was such as to prevent the writing of a complete equation for it, a fact which was only to be expected, since chemistry was "too little advanced to hope to put into a rigorous equation a chemical act correlative with a vital phenomenon."

However impressive this line of attack against the chemical theory, an even more decisive mode of argument derived from Pasteur's ability to produce yeast and alcoholic fermentation in a medium free of organic nitrogen. To a pure solution of cane sugar he added only an ammonium salt and the minerals obtained by incineration of yeast, then sprinkled in a trace of pure brewer's yeast. Although the experiment was difficult and not always successful, this method could produce an alcoholic fermentation accompanied by growth and reproduction in the yeast and the evolution of all the usual products. If any one constituent of this medium were eliminated, no alcoholic fermentation took place. Obviously, argued Pasteur, the yeast must grow and develop in this mineral medium by assimilating its nitrogen from the ammonium salt, its mineral constituents from the yeast ash, and its carbon from the sugar. In fact, it is precisely the capacity of yeast to assimilate combined carbon from sugar that explains why it can decompose sugar into carbonic acid and alcohol. Above all, there is in this medium none of the "unstable organic matter" required by Liebig's theory.

When this memoir on alcoholic fermentation appeared, Pasteur had already begun to exploit more widely his new method of cultivating microorganisms in a medium free of organic nitrogen. Described initially in a note of December 1858, this method had been applied to the lactic ferment by February 1859. Indeed, "Pasteur's fluid"—a solution of sugar, yeast ash, and ammonium salt—proved far more conducive to the growth of the lactic ferment than to that of brewer's yeast. Sometimes, the lactic fermentation appeared "spontaneously" in this medium, even when only brewer's yeast had been sown. From similar events in ordinary crude alcoholic fermentations, some chemists had concluded that lactic acid was a normal by-product of alcoholic fermentation. Pasteur showed, however, that the appearance of lactic acid in such cases could be associated with an accidental contamination of the fermenting medium by the lactic ferment. To ensure the uncontaminated growth of the lactic ferment itself, it was necessary only to add calcium carbonate to the solution of sugar, yeast ash, and ammonium salt.

Fermentation and Putrefaction as "Life Without Air." In November 1860 Pasteur described the successful cultivation of *Penicillium* "or any mucedinous fungus" in a medium of pure water, cane sugar, phosphates, and an acid ammonium salt. By February 1861 he had isolated a specific butyric ferment and had produced butyric fermentation in a similar medium. In two respects this new butyric ferment greatly suprised him: (1) unlike brewer's yeast and the lactic ferment, it was motile and thus, presumably, a member of the animal kingdom; and (2) while examining microscopically the liquid from a butyric fermentation, he noticed that the rodlike "infusoria" lost their motility and vitality at the margins of the slide glass but remained active in the center. Assuming that this phenomenon depended on the presence of atmospheric air at the margins of the slide glass, Pasteur passed a current of ordinary air through a butyric fermentation. Within an hour or two the butyric fermentation had ceased and all the motile rods had been killed. Carbonic acid gas, on the other hand, exerted no appreciable effect on their life and reproduction. Pasteur concluded that the butyric ferment is an infusorium and that this infusorium lives without free oxygen gas. This was, he believed, the first known example of an animal ferment and of an animal capable of living without free oxygen.

From the beginning naturalists challenged Pasteur's belief that the butyric ferment was an animal, because for many of them motility had ceased to be an automatic index of animality. More specifically, the genus *Vibrionia*, to which Pasteur assigned his new ferment, had been identified as vegetable in 1854 by Ferdinand Cohn, who had linked it with the algae and bacteria. Not surprisingly, then, an English translator immediately suggested that Pasteur's supposed butyric "infusorium" probably belonged instead among the algae.[54] Cohn later placed it among the bacteria (*Bacillus subtilis*).[55] Although Pasteur quickly qualified his assertion of the animality of the new ferment, he demonstrated little concern about the taxonomic issue and little serious interest in the literature of the naturalists, whom he seemed sometimes to despise. This attitude and Pasteur's inadequacies as a naturalist led to some confusion about and hostility toward his work—and by no means solely in the case of the butyric ferment. In later years Pasteur became somewhat more sensitive to taxonomic issues and emphasized the importance of physiological characters as a taxonomic criterion; but his generally casual attitude toward microbial morphology and nomenclature helped to exacerbate some of the debates over spontaneous generation, the transformation of microbial species, and the germ theory of disease. Cohn and Koch, among others, chastised Pasteur severely for his lack of rigor in these areas.

Pasteur's discovery of the butyric ferment and of its death in air gave a new direction to his studies on fermentation. He quickly investigated the effect of free oxygen on other ferments and moved gradually toward a new definition of fermentation as "life without air." In June 1861 he reported that the activity of brewer's yeast depended fundamentally on the degree of free oxygen available to it. Like ordinary fungi or infusoria, it grew and reproduced with great vigor in the presence of air. As a ferment, however, it was virtually powerless under such circumstances; only in the absence of free oxygen did it display a significant capacity to ferment sugar. For Pasteur the explanation was obvious: when deprived of free oxygen, the yeast of necessity attacked the sugar in order to extract its combined oxygen.

In March 1863 Pasteur announced that calcium tartrate fermented in a medium free of organic nitrogen by the action of a motile infusorium analogous to the butyric ferment. Like the butyric, the new ferment lived only in the absence of air and belonged to the genus *Vibrionia*, although its external form differed greatly from the butyric ferment. In a medium exposed to the air, the new ferment developed only when protected by organisms that consumed free oxygen at the surface of the medium, while the ferment lived and developed at lower, oxygen-free levels. Fermentation, Pasteur now suggested, is merely "nutrition without the consumption of free oxygen gas." In this conception, he believed, lay the key to "the secret and mysterious character of all true fermentations and, possibly, that of many normal and abnormal actions in the organization of living things."

Among these "normal and abnormal actions" was putrefaction, generally defined as the decomposition of vegetable or animal matter with the evolution of fetid gases. In April and June 1863, on the basis of rather sketchy evidence, Pasteur extended to the phenomena of putrefaction the central conclusions of his work on fermentation. Like fermentation, he insisted, putrefaction can be traced to the vital activity of living ferments. Indeed, except for the action of microorganisms, the constituents of dead plants and animals could be considered "relatively indestructible." To express the matter in more poetic terms, "life takes part in the work of death in all its phases," for the decomposition associated with death depends on the development and multiplication of microorganisms. Moreover, death is as essential to the cycle of life as life is to the phenomena of death. For it is only as a consequence of death and putrefaction that carbon, nitrogen, and oxygen become available as nutrients to support the life of other organisms. Thus, in an eternal cycle, life stems from death and death from life.

Within this cosmic perspective, reformulated and reemphasized on other occasions, Pasteur developed a more prosaic analysis of the nature and action of the microorganisms involved in the decomposition of dead substances. These organisms are of two kinds: (1) the oxidative microorganisms—the mycodermas and their relatives—which in the course of their vital activity transfer atmospheric oxygen to the dead organic substances and thereby enormously increase the rate of combustion and (2) the putrefactive ferments per se, which (like the butyric ferment) belong to the genus *Vibrionia* and live only in the absence of air. Putrefaction and fermentation are, therefore, analogous processes, for both involve the decomposition of substances by organisms living in the absence of air. In fact, putrefaction is merely the fermentation of substances containing a relatively high proportion of sulfur, and the release of this sulfur in gaseous form produces the fetid odors commonly associated with putrefaction.

In other words, Pasteur emphasized, a putrescible liquid exposed to atmospheric air experiences two distinct sorts of chemical decomposition correlative with the life and development of two distinct sorts of microscopic organisms. On the one hand the anaerobes—putrefactive ferments living below the surface, in the absence of air—determine "acts of fermentation": they transform nitrogenous materials into simpler but still complex substances. On the other hand the aerobes—oxidative microorganisms living at the surface, in the presence of air—can assimilate these intermediate products and transform them into the "simplest binary combinations"—water, ammonia, and carbonic acid. Bulloch has traced the concept of anaerobism or "life without air" to Leeuwenhoek and Spallanzani.[56] Their work in this regard having been completely forgotten, however, Pasteur has always been recognized as the architect of the idea.

Studies on Acetic Fermentation and Vinegar. By the time he published his papers on putrefaction, Pasteur was deeply involved in the study of acetic fermentation and the manufacture of vinegar. Beginning in July 1861, he produced a series of papers on acetic fermentation that linked theory with industrial practice and culminated in a long memoir (1864) and in *Études sur le vinaigre* (1868). When he began this work, acetic fermentation was widely viewed as a chemical, catalytic process, comparable with the well-known oxidation of alcohol to aldehyde and acetic acid in the presence of finely divided platinum. This conception seemed in accord with the German method of manufacturing vinegar, in which the fermenting medium consisted of a dilute alcohol solution, a trace of acetic acid, and some "unstable organic matter" such as sharp wine or acid beer. When this liquid trickled through a hollow column of wine casks containing loosely piled beechwood shavings, the alcohol was oxidized to acetic acid with the release of heat and the production of an upward current of air that constantly renewed the supply of oxygen. As Liebig interpreted this method, the "unstable organic matter" initiated fermentation and the beechwood shavings facilitated the oxidation process while remaining unaltered (that is, they acted as a catalyst). In all of this there was no hint of biological action.

Pasteur approached acetic fermentation fully confident that he would find in this case, too, that a microorganism was essential to the process. The rela-

tive ease with which he· succeeded can be partly ascribed to the character of the French method of vinegar production, for which the leading center was Orléans. This method differed markedly from the German method. In Orléans vinegar was produced by the slow oxidation of wine in covered casks stacked on end, about one-third empty and exposed to the air by an opening or "window" above the surface of the fermenting liquid. On the surface of the liquid, which consisted of a mixture of finished vinegar and new wine, there appeared a delicate pellicle—long known as "mother of vinegar"—the presence of which was recognized as essential to the process. From his earlier studies of fermentation, Pasteur knew that such pellicles could be formed by microorganisms. Moreover, several observers had already suggested that the "mother of vinegar" consisted of living organisms. In 1822 Persoon had named it "mycoderma" precisely to suggest that it was a fungal skin. And in 1837 Friedrich Kützing had drawn a connection between the life of this skin and the production of vinegar—as indeed, in the same year he had also connected the life of yeast with the production of alcohol in ordinary alcoholic fermentation. As in alcoholic fermentation, Pasteur could draw inspiration from a tradition that viewed fermentation as a vital process. His task was to present this case so persuasively as to override the dominant authority and arguments of Liebig.

To do so, Pasteur resorted again to media free of organic nitrogen. By July 1862 he had succeeded in cultivating *Mycoderma aceti* in a medium of dilute alcohol, ammonia, and mineral salts. When sown into such a medium, *Mycoderma aceti* consistently produced acetic acid; and Pasteur again emphasized the ability of a microorganism to yield fermentation in the absence of the "unstable organic matter" required by Liebig's theory. Moreover, he was able to detect a thin film of *Mycoderma aceti* on the beechwood shavings so important in the German method of vinegar production. Protected from or deprived of the *Mycoderma*, the shavings lost their capacity to produce acetic acid. Their only role, Pasteur insisted, was to provide a site for the growth and development of *Mycoderma aceti*. In his view *Mycoderma aceti* acted by transmitting the "combustive action" of atmospheric oxygen to alcohol and thus oxidizing it to acetic acid. If no alcohol remained in the fermenting medium, the *Mycoderma* could attack the acetic acid it had produced and complete the oxidation to water and carbonic acid. *Mycoderma aceti* also ceased to produce acetic acid if submerged; only at the surface of the fermenting medium, in the presence of abundant oxygen, did it support acetic fermentation. Although this latter fact posed an obvious difficulty for his concept of fermentation as "life without air," Pasteur made no attempt to resolve the issue at the time.

From the beginning of his research on acetic fermentation, Pasteur recognized its industrial significance; and in July 1861 he took out a patent "for the manufacture of vinegar or acetic acid by means of molds, in particular *Mycoderma vini* and *Mycoderma aceti*."[57] To a considerable extent Pasteur's interpretation of acetic fermentation merely provided a rationale for industrial practices that had already been introduced empirically, although it did allow somewhat greater confidence in and control over them. Perhaps the most important advantage that Pasteur ascribed to his method of manufacturing vinegar was that it permitted the process to be directed at will. No longer was it necessary to await the "spontaneous" appearance of the mycodermic pellicle, which sometimes took several weeks. Manufacturers could now produce acetification quickly and reliably by direct sowing of *Mycoderma aceti*. Moreover, he claimed, his method produced acetic acid three to five times as rapidly as the Orléans method and greatly reduced the losses by evaporation experienced in the German method. By 1868, when he published his *Études sur le vinaigre*, Pasteur could appeal by analogy to his recent studies on the "diseases" of wine in order to discuss the diseases of vinegar, all of which (like the diseases of wine) could be prevented by heating finished vinegar to about 55° C.

Studies on Wine. In December 1863 Pasteur published the first of the papers that culminated in his *Études sur le vin* (1866; 2nd ed. 1873). In that first paper, dealing with the role of atmospheric oxygen in vinification, he sought to establish that the aging of wine resulted from the slow penetration of atmospheric oxygen through the porous wood casks into which new wine was decanted. By virtue of this slow oxidation, he claimed, new wine grows less harsh and acid to the taste as it becomes clearer and lighter from the precipitation of dark coloring matters. In his second paper (January 1864) Pasteur examined the "alterations" or "diseases" of wine, especially wine from the Jura, his native department. Reviewing the familiar diseases of "turned," "acid," "ropy," or "oily" wine, he associated each with a microscopic organism. He summarized the results of his first two papers by noting that "wine, which is produced by a cellular vegetation acting as a ferment [namely, yeast], is altered only by the influence of other vegetations of the same order; and once removed from the effects of their parasitism, it is made or matured principally by the action of atmospheric oxygen penetrating slowly through the staves of the casks."

Since the diseases of wine are due to the development of foreign organisms, which are present before the wine becomes sensibly "sick" and the germs of which are bottled with the wine, the crucial task was to find a way of killing these germs without damaging the taste or other qualities of wine. On 1 May 1865 Pasteur told the Académie des Sciences that his attempts to cure diseased wines with chemical antiseptics had been less than satisfying, but that he had found a perfectly reliable and practical procedure for preserving healthy wine: by heating it in closed vessels for an hour or two at a temperature between 60° and 100° C. As a result of small-scale preliminary trials, Pasteur progressively lowered the temperature to between 50° and 60° C. Within this range, he claimed, wine could be perfectly protected from disease at minimum risk to its taste, bouquet, and color.

As soon as Pasteur publicly disclosed this method, which he patented in April 1865, alternative claims began to appear. In a series of letters and notes published between 1865 and 1872, nearly all of which were reproduced or incorporated into the two editions of his *Études sur le vin*, Pasteur repeatedly defended his priority rights, even as he became increasingly informed of the long history of "empirical" attempts to preserve wine. Eventually he admitted that he had been anticipated by Nicolas Appert, who had specifically proposed the application to wine of his method of preserving foodstuffs by heating them in closed vessels. Nonetheless, he insisted that he had rescued from oblivion and established on the basis of rigorous scientific experiments what had been only a poorly tested and entirely empirical technique.

In support of the practicability of his method, Pasteur cited a series of commissions the members of which generally preferred the taste of heated to untreated wine. One commission was appointed by the French navy in 1868 to test the feasibility of applying Pasteur's process to wines destined for the fleet and the French colonies. The results were impressive enough for the navy to adopt Pasteur's process. Further evidence of the value of his method was reflected in the grand prize awarded Pasteur by the jury of the Exposition Universelle (1867); the use abroad of the word "pasteurization" to denote the heating of wine; and the prizes from agricultural societies and from the Société d'Encouragement pour l'Industrie Nationale for the best apparatus for heating wine (fifteen examples of which Pasteur described and illustrated in the second edition of *Études sur le vin*).

Spontaneous Generation: The Background. Almost from the beginning of his work on fermentation and despite attempts by Biot and Dumas to dissuade him, Pasteur became embroiled in the controversial issue of spontaneous generation. Although advanced in several more or less sophisticated versions, the doctrine of spontaneous generation rests at bottom on the notion that living organisms can arise independently of any immediate living parent, whether from inorganic substances (abiogenesis) or from organic debris (heterogenesis). In his classic paper of 1861, "Mémoire sur les corpuscules organisés qui existent dans l'atmosphère . . .," Pasteur included a fairly substantial historical introduction, which seems greatly to have influenced subsequent histories of the debate. To account for the modern rise of the doctrine—following its apparent destruction in the seventeenth century by Francesco Redi's experiments on the generation of insects—Pasteur emphasized the influence of the microscope. By revealing a teeming world of hitherto unseen living organisms of dubious or unknown parentage, the microscope gave the doctrine a new lease on life and led to a celebrated eighteenth-century dispute between Spallanzani and Needham. Spallanzani seemed largely to carry the day by showing that infusions boiled for forty-five minutes in closed vessels (to destroy any organisms they might already contain) thereafter remained free of alteration and microbial life. But his technique was open to the objection that the air in his sealed flasks might have been altered in such a way as to render spontaneous generation impossible. In the early nineteenth century this objection took special force from Gay-Lussac's study of the role of oxygen in fermentation and putrefaction. Having found that oxygen was absent from substances preserved by Appert's canning process, and that grapes crushed under mercury in a bell jar fermented only upon the introduction of air, Gay-Lussac concluded that oxygen was essential to the onset of fermentation and putrefaction (and hence to the appearance of any microorganisms associated with these alterations).

As Pasteur emphasized, Gay-Lussac's experiments made it imperative to remove any doubts about the possible alteration of air in Spallanzani's flasks. Toward this end Theodor Schwann made "a great step forward" in 1837 by showing that boiled meat infusions could be preserved from alteration in flasks in which the air was continually renewed, provided only that the added air had been heated or "calcined" before entering the flasks. Schwann's experiment extended that of Franz Schulze, who in 1836 had achieved similar results by drawing the added air through potassium hydroxide and sulfuric acid; it also helped to set the stage for the work of Heinrich Schröder and Theodor von Dusch, who in the 1850's exposed alterable substances to ordinary air filtered through cotton. By these means Schwann, Schulze, Schröder, and Dusch prevented putrefaction, fermen-

tation, and microbial life in many alterable substances—including meat infusions, beer, must, starch paste, and the constituents of milk taken separately—and tended to suppose that they had done so by eliminating airborne germs. But in the case of other substances—notably milk, egg yolk, and dry meat—their experiments often failed and helped to sustain the view that something like spontaneous generation could occur.

Moreover, Pasteur insisted, even those experiments which seemed to contradict spontaneous generation did so only in the sense of showing that an unknown something in atmospheric air was essential to life in organic infusions. This unknown principle seemed often to be eliminated by heat, cotton, or certain chemical reagents; but insofar as Schwann and others tended to suppose that atmospheric germs had thus been killed or eliminated, they "had no more proofs for their opinion," wrote Pasteur, "than those who believed that [the unknown principle] might be a gas, fluid, noxious effluvia, etc., and who consequently were inclined to believe in spontaneous generation." There, according to Pasteur, the issue lay when Félix Pouchet launched his attempt to establish the doctrine of spontaneous generation on the basis of irrefutable experiments. Pouchet, a respected naturalist from Rouen and a corresponding member of the Académie des Sciences, published in 1859 his long and controversial *Hétérogénie ou traité de la génération spontanée*, which created a sensation in France and probably stimulated the Académie des Sciences to institute the Alhumbert Prize in 1860 for the best "attempt, by well conducted experiments, to throw new light on the question of so-called spontaneous generation."

Pasteur won this competition with his "Mémoire sur les corpuscules. . . ." By ignoring a wide range of other factors that helped to discredit spontaneous generation (notably studies of cell division and the debate, by then resolved, over the origin of parasitic worms),[58] it magnified the importance of his own contributions; and nearly all subsequent accounts have followed suit. At the end of his historical introduction, Pasteur traced his interest in spontaneous generation to his work on fermentation, and particularly to his recognition that the ferments were living organisms:

> Then, I said to myself, one of two things must be true. The true ferments being living organisms, if they are produced by the contact of albuminous materials with oxygen alone, considered merely as oxygen, then they are spontaneously generated. But if these living ferments are not of spontaneous origin, then it is not just the oxygen as such that intervenes in their production—the gas acts as a stimulant to a germ carried

with it or already existing in the nitrogenous or fermentable materials. At this point, to which my study of fermentation brought me, I was thus obliged to form an opinion on the question of spontaneous generation. I thought I might find here a powerful support for my ideas on those fermentations which are properly called fermentations.

As this passage suggests, it is perhaps artificial to separate Pasteur's study of spontaneous generation from his work on fermentation, especially since some of his adversaries contended that microorganisms could appear as a result of fermentation rather than as its cause. The question of the origin of the ferments was therefore crucial, and Pasteur's concern with it is apparent from his earliest paper on fermentation.

In 1858, in his initial paper on fermentation, Pasteur wrote that the lactic ferment "originates spontaneously, with as much facility as brewer's yeast, whenever conditions are favorable," but immediately emphasized in a footnote that he used the word "spontaneously" merely to "describe the fact, leaving entirely aside any judgment on the question of spontaneous generation." In February 1859 he addressed the issue

somewhat more directly, asserting that in his experiments the lactic ferment always came "uniquely by way of the atmospheric air." If he boiled his medium and then removed it from all contact with air or exposed it only to previously calcined air, no microbial life or fermentation of any kind appeared. "On this point," he wrote, "the question of spontaneous generation has made an advance."

Spontaneous Generation, 1860–1861. Beginning in February 1860, Pasteur presented to the Académie des Sciences a series of notes focusing specifically on spontaneous generation. In the first and most important of these papers, he began by examining the solid particles of the air, which he collected by aspirating atmospheric air through a tube plugged with guncotton. When this guncotton was dissolved in a sedimentation tube containing an alcohol-ether mixture, the solid particles trapped by it settled at the bottom. Although this method killed any germs or microorganisms in the trapped particles, microscopic examination always revealed a variable number of corpuscles, the form and structure of which closely resembled those of living organisms. But were these

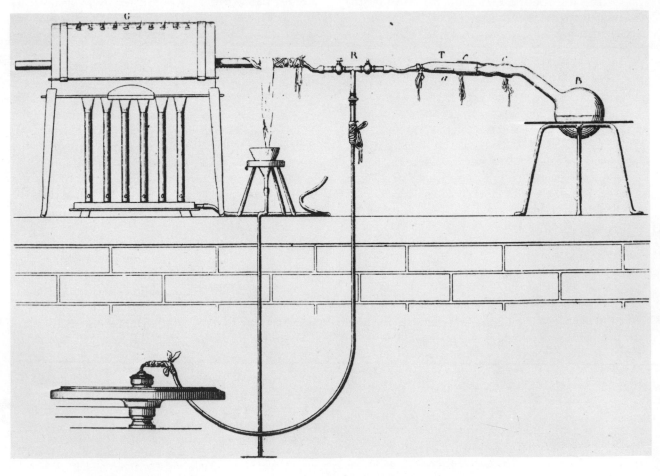

FIGURE 1

"organized corpuscles" in fact the "fecund germs" of the microorganisms which appeared in alterable media exposed to the air? In search of an answer, Pasteur employed three distinct methods. With the first, involving the use of a pneumatic trough filled with mercury, he obtained somewhat dubious or inconsistent results and abandoned it in favor of a second method, which he characterized as "unassailable and decisive." In a flask of about 300 cubic centimeters, he placed 100 to 150 cubic centimeters of sugared yeast water, which he boiled for a few minutes. After the flask had cooled, he filled it with calcined air (by means of a neck connected to a red-hot platinum tube) and then sealed it in a flame. The liquid in such a flask, deposited in a stove at 28–32° C., could remain there indefinitely without alteration.

Having thus far only repeated the experiments of Schwann and others, Pasteur now introduced an important modification. After a month to six weeks he removed the flask from the stove and connected it to an elaborate apparatus so arranged that a small wad of guncotton previously charged with atmospheric dust could be made to slide into the hitherto sterile liquid in the flask (see Figure 1). In twenty-four to thirty-six hours, the liquid swarmed with familiar microorganisms. Thus, Pasteur concluded, the dust of the air, sown in an otherwise sterile medium, produces organisms of the same sort and in the same period of time as would appear if the liquid were freely exposed to ordinary air. Finally, to counter the objection that these microorganisms arose not from germs in the atmospheric dust but "spontaneously" from the organic matter in the guncotton, Pasteur replaced the guncotton with dust-charged asbestos, a mineral substance, and obtained the same results. With dust-free or precalcined asbestos, on the other hand, no growths appeared in the flask.

To confirm and extend these conclusions on the role of atmospheric dust, Pasteur employed a third method, perhaps the most influential by virtue of its elegant simplicity: the famous "swan-necked" flask. After preparing a series of flasks in the same manner as in the second method, he drew their necks out into very narrow extensions, curved in various ways and exposed to the air by an opening one to two millimeters in diameter (see Figure 2). Without sealing these flasks, he boiled the liquid in most of them for several minutes, leaving three or four unboiled to serve as controls. If all the flasks were then placed in calm air, the unboiled liquids became covered with various molds in twenty-four to forty-eight hours, while the boiled flasks remained unaltered indefinitely despite their exposure. Moreover, if one of the curved necks were detached from a hitherto sterile flask and placed up-

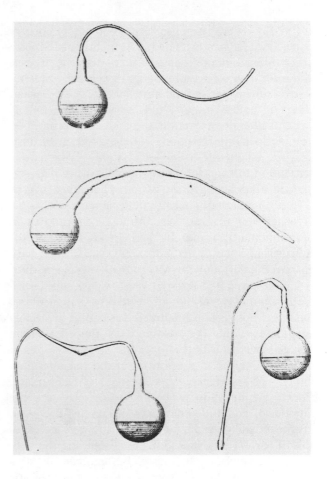

FIGURE 2

right in it, vegetative growths appeared in a day or two. Pasteur concluded that the "sinuosities and inclinations" of his swan-necked flasks protected the liquids from growths by capturing the dusts that entered with the air. In fact, Pasteur insisted, nothing in the air—whether gases, fluids, electricity, magnetism, ozone, or some unknown or occult agent—constitutes a condition of microbial life except the germs carried by atmospheric dusts.

According to Duclaux, the swan-necked flask method was suggested to Pasteur by Balard; and Pasteur admitted that Chevreul had already done "similar experiments" in his chemistry lectures.[59] But if in this case, as in his experiments with calcined air, Pasteur borrowed importantly from the techniques of his predecessors, he also developed and exploited them with greater effect and influence. By the force of its conclusions and the variety and ingenuity of its experimental techniques, his paper of 6 February 1860 propelled Pasteur to preeminence among the opponents of spontaneous generation. All of his subsequent work in this field can be seen as an extension, elaboration, and defense of the principles and methods set forth here.

By May 1860, as promised at the end of his February paper, Pasteur had extended his conclusions to media other than albuminous sugar water—namely, to urine and milk, two substances highly susceptible to alteration in air. Deprived of atmospheric dust, Pasteur claimed, boiled urine could be stored indefinitely without alteration, even at the temperature most favorable to its putrefaction. But the addition of dust-charged asbestos to a previously sterile flask of urine resulted in the appearance of various microorganisms and an abundant deposit of phosphates and urates. One of the microorganisms could be identified as the "true ferment of urine," responsible for the production of ammoniacal urine. Its germ, like those of the infusoria and molds that appeared with it, could have entered the flask only by way of the atmospheric dust.

Unlike urine and sugared yeast water, milk boiled for two minutes and then protected from atmospheric dusts did not remain unaltered. Instead, it invariably coagulated within three to ten days, this coagulation being associated with the appearance and development of vibrios. By no means, however, did this alteration imply that spontaneous generation had taken place. For if the duration of boiling were increased, the number of flasks in which milk coagulated decreased proportionately. And if the temperature were increased to 110° or 112° C., no vibrios appeared and the milk did not coagulate. Obviously, Pasteur concluded, a temperature of 100° C. does not entirely destroy the fecundity of the vibrio germs, while a temperature of 110° to 112° C. does.

In September and November 1860, Pasteur described another famous set of experiments in which he exposed alterable liquids to the natural atmosphere of different locations and altitudes, hoping thereby to discredit the belief that any quantity of ordinary air, however minute, is sufficient for the production of organized growths in any kind of infusion. In his view this belief enjoyed currency chiefly because of Gay-Lussac's analysis of Appert's preserves and his experiment with grapes crushed under mercury, for these studies led him to associate fermentation or putrefaction with the presence of oxygen, even in minute quantities. On this basis the partisans of spontaneous generation had elaborated a seemingly impressive argument against the notion of airborne germs. For if the most minute quantity of air can produce the microorganisms appropriate to any infusion, and if these organisms are supposed to derive from pre-existent germs, then the air must be so loaded with a multitude of different germs as to be foggy at least, if not as dense as iron.

Pasteur's approach to this problem was deceptively simple. After boiling sugared yeast water in sealed flasks, he broke the necks to admit the surrounding air, immediately resealed the flasks in a flame, and stored them in a stove at a temperature favorable to the development of microorganisms. Under these conditions the liquids in the flasks sometimes remained entirely unaffected, a "simple and unobjectionable proof" that a limited quantity of ordinary air does not invariably produce infusorial growths. On the other hand, the result accorded well with the notion of the variable dissemination of germs in the air. The latter notion received further support from the fact that it was easy to alter the proportion of flasks in which microbial life appeared merely by exposing them to the air in various locations or altitudes. In the vaults of the Paris observatory, for example, the proportion of exposed flasks that later showed infusorial growths was much lower than in Pasteur's laboratory at the École Normale. This proportion also decreased with increased altitude. Thus, of twenty flasks opened at the foot of the Jura plateau, eight later showed vegetative growths; of twenty exposed on one of the Jura mountains, 850 meters above sea level, five produced growths; and of twenty opened on a glacier at Montanvert, 2,000 meters above sea level, only one flask underwent subsequent alteration. For Pasteur such results authorized the conclusion that germs are variably disseminated in the air, their relative abundance depending on locality, altitude, and other environmental circumstances.

In January 1861, in his fifth paper on spontaneous generation, Pasteur described the influence of temperature on the fecundity of fungal spores. Spallanzani had found that fungal spores could survive boiling in water at 100° C. and—without assigning a precise upper limit—had claimed that they could even resist the heat of a furnace when dry. Pasteur denied that this upper limit was as high as Spallanzani had supposed and criticized his experimental technique for its failure to ensure that any observed fungi derived solely from the spores he had sown and not from additional spores in the air or on the experimental apparatus. His own method, which seemed to Pasteur "beyond reproach," was a modification of the technique he had used to sow dust-charged asbestos into sterile media in an atmosphere of calcined air. In this case the asbestos was charged with fungal spores and then heated to a determined temperature before sowing. Pasteur found that in a vacuum or in dry air, such spores could remain fecund even after being heated at 120–125° C. for as long as an hour. On the other hand, their fecundity was completely destroyed by heating them at a temperature of 127–130° C. for twenty to thirty minutes. These results also offered a means of proving that fungal spores exist in the atmospheric dust, for the sowing of such dust at 120–125° C. produced fungi, while none appeared when the dust was sown at 125–130° C.

The Memoir of 1861. In May 1861, at a meeting of the Société Chimique de Paris, Pasteur presented the major results of his work on spontaneous generation in a lecture later expanded into his prize-winning memoir. Although this memoir is essentially a restatement of his earlier papers on the topic, it is richer in detail and contains some new material, including the historical introduction. The appearance under the microscope of atmospheric dust and of the organisms found in infusions received considerable attention, as did the role of contaminated mercury as a source of error in the experiments of Pouchet and others. Pasteur had barely hinted at the latter possibility in his initial paper of 6 February 1860 and had made it explicit in a note of September 1860. Pouchet's experimental case for spontaneous generation rested chiefly on his ability to produce microbial life by adding germ-free air to boiled hay infusions under mercury. Pasteur admitted that Pouchet's precautions seemed to eliminate every source of possible contamination by living germs with one exception—the mercury. But this exception was crucial, Pasteur argued, since ordinary laboratory mercury often contains germs. As proof he cited the following comparative experiments. If a globule of ordinary mercury is dropped into an alterable liquid in an atmosphere of calcined (and hence germ-free) air, microbial life appears within two days. But if the mercury is previously calcined, not a single living organism will appear. Indeed, so thoroughly did Pasteur mistrust experiments with the mercury trough that he insisted that this mode of experimentation be banished from the field.

The most important new material in the 1861 memoir concerned the effect of the alkalinity of a medium on the heat-resistance of germs in it. Pasteur identified the alkalinity of milk as the chief reason why boiling at 100° C. failed to protect it from subsequent alteration. As evidence he noted that sugared yeast water—ordinarily protected by boiling at 100° C.—must be heated at 105–110° if its alkalinity is increased by the addition of chalk.

This memoir seriously damaged the doctrine of spontaneous generation, but the blow was far from fatal and many unresolved issues remained. In Pasteur's mind the most obvious weakness of his work on spontaneous generation was its exclusive reliance on experiments involving heated substances—"organic matters which are not only dead but which have also been carried to the temperature of boiling." To all such experiments, partisans of spontaneous generation could object that so high a temperature profoundly modified organic substances and perhaps destroyed a "vegetative force" or some other condition essential for spontaneous generation. For this reason Pasteur long sought to extend his conclusions to "natural organic substances, not previously heated"—in short, to "natural substances such as life elaborates them." In April 1863 he announced that he had found a way to take fresh blood and urine directly from healthy, living organisms and to preserve both substances from putrefaction without preliminary boiling. He immediately asserted that these results "carry a final blow to the doctrine of spontaneous generation," and he attached enormous importance to them in all subsequent debates over spontaneous generation and the germ theory of disease.

The Pasteur-Pouchet Debate. Pasteur's work on spontaneous generation created as great a sensation in France as had Pouchet's *Hétérogénie* (1859), and in neither case was the sensation confined to scientific circles. The wide public interest in the debate stemmed from its presumed religiophilosophical and even political implications, for the issue of spontaneous generation formed part of the general debate raging in France between materialism and spiritualism. Pouchet's results were invoked in support of materialism, evolutionism, and radical politics, while Pasteur's opposing results were used to support spiritualism, the Biblical account of creation, and conservative politics. In April 1864, in a lecture at the Sorbonne, Pasteur emphasized that the doctrine of spontaneous generation (like materialism in general) threatened the very concept of God the Creator. And although he insisted that he had approached the issue without preconceived ideas, and would willingly have announced in favor of spontaneous generation had "experiment imposed the view on me," there is reason to believe that he wanted a priori to deny the existence of spontaneous generation at least as fervently as Pouchet wanted to affirm it.[60] For Pasteur's position in the debate was in keeping both with his conservative religious and political convictions and with certain aspects of his concept of fermentation—notably the idea of specificity, which implied the transmission of hereditary characters and led to a belief in an ordinary kind of generation among microorganisms. That Pasteur was influenced by such a priori convictions seems clear from his tendency automatically to suspect error in any experiment—including his own—which might be used in support of spontaneous generation and from the eagerness with which he accused Pouchet and other heterogeneticists of technical errors without having repeated their experiments carefully.

Perhaps partly for this reason, as well as the public notoriety of Pasteur's experiments on the glacier at

Montanvert, Pouchet decided to expose his usual hay infusions to the atmosphere at high altitude, following Pasteur's procedure and without using mercury. In November 1863 Pouchet and two collaborators, Nicolas Joly and Charles Musset, announced that the results of their experiments, conducted in the Spanish Pyrenees, contradicted Pasteur's results at Montanvert. For when they exposed their flasks to the air, all subsequently showed microbial growths, as one would expect if the organic material in infusions required only oxygen to organize itself spontaneously into living organisms. In his contemptuous reply to this announcement, Pasteur criticized Pouchet and his collaborators for using a short file instead of long pincers to break the necks of their flasks and for limiting their flasks to so small a number as eight.

In January 1864 the Académie des Sciences named a commission to adjudicate the dispute. When the commission proposed that the participants in the debate repeat their principal experiments before it in March, Pouchet and his collaborators asked that the meeting be delayed until the summer, on the ground that warm weather was conducive to the success of their experiments. In June the commission met with Pasteur and his adversaries, but the latter objected to the program as arranged by the commission and withdrew without repeating their experiments. The commission then observed a series of Pasteur's experiments and verified their exactitude in a report that scarcely veiled its contempt for the opposite side.[61]

As Duclaux has emphasized, this episode might have had a different outcome had Pouchet and his collaborators maintained their nerve in the face of Pasteur's self-assurance and the contempt of the commission.[62] For although no one seemed to realize it immediately, there was a crucial difference between the experiments of Pasteur and those of Pouchet—namely, that Pasteur used yeast water as his alterable medium, while Pouchet used hay infusions. And while boiling easily kills the microorganisms common to yeast water, decoctions of desiccated hay often contain heat-resistant bacilli endospores which can survive high heat and subsequently develop in the presence of oxygen. For this reason Pouchet's flasks could have given microbial life and could have been used in support of spontaneous generation. Only after 1876, especially as a result of the work of Ferdinand Cohn and John Tyndall, did the heat-resistant hay bacillus endospore become fully recognized. Ironically, Pasteur had briefly considered a possibility of this sort in his Sorbonne lecture of 1864, but his attention seems to have been diverted by his zeal to ascribe technical errors to Pouchet. Thus, even though Pasteur had examined the heat resistance of fungal spores and had recognized the role of heat resistance in other cases, the full complexity and importance of the issue became clear to him only during his debate with Henry Charlton Bastian in the 1870's and in the wake of work by Cohn, Tyndall, Koch, and others.

The Silkworm Problem: The Background. On 8 December 1862, three weeks before he won the Alhumbert Prize, Pasteur had been elected to membership in the mineralogy section of the Académie des Sciences, succeeding in his third formal campaign for the honor. His often active participation in the weekly meetings of the Academy regularly took him away from his laboratory and administrative tasks. So did his lectures at the École des Beaux-Arts, where from November 1863 to October 1867 he was the first professor of geology, physics, and chemistry in their application to the fine arts, and where he introduced laboratory procedures oriented toward the problems of art and its materials. Pasteur also found time to write historical articles on Lavoisier in 1865 and on his friend Claude Bernard in 1866. But the most exhausting demand on his time from 1865 through 1870 was the silkworm problem, which took him away from Paris for several months each year.

By 1865 French sericulturists had become almost frantic about a blight which had afflicted their silkworms for the past fifteen to twenty years—a disease so disastrous as to reduce silk production over this period by a factor of six. In Alais [now Alès] alone, the center of French sericulture, the revenue loss was estimated at 120 million francs for the fifteen years before 1865.[63] The gravity of the situation aroused the concern of the ministry of agriculture and of Dumas, Pasteur's mentor and patron, who was from Alais. In May 1865 Dumas asked Pasteur to study the silkworm blight. Confessing utter ignorance of the problem and noting that he had never even touched a silkworm,[64] Pasteur nonetheless acceded to Dumas's request and immersed himself in the relevant literature, notably Quatrefages's 1859 work.

According to most authorities, the blight resulted from a disease called *pébrine* (pepper) by Quatrefages because of the small black spots frequently seen on sick worms. Its symptoms included stunted or interrupted growth, sluggishness, loss of appetite, and premature death. A general association had also been established between *pébrine* and the existence of microscopic "corpuscles" within the internal organs of diseased worms. Although considerable controversy surrounded the precise role and nature of these corpuscles, several authorities considered them to be the cause of the disease. Those who did tended to suppose that the corpuscles were living parasites, a position that drew support from Agostino Bassi's pioneering studies in the 1830's of another major silkworm disease, muscardine, which he had traced to a fungal parasite. Unfortunately the microscopic corpuscles of *pébrine* could sometimes be found in apparently healthy broods, while their absence failed to guarantee either healthy worms or good silk cocoons. Nonetheless, in 1859, after detecting the corpuscles even in silkworm eggs, where they increased in size and number as hatching time approached, Marco Osimo had tried to establish a preventive measure based on the rejection of corpuscular eggs and pupae. Preliminary trials of Osimo's method were unimpressive, however, and the problem remained obscure.

Pasteur's Early Silkworm Studies. Pasteur's initial firsthand experience with *pébrine* disposed him to doubt both its contagiousness and the causative role of the corpuscles. On his first trip to Alais, in June 1865, he observed two neighboring cultures or broods the opposite fates of which seemed to refute the supposed connection between *pébrine* and the internal corpuscles. The first brood, a successful one, had already spun its cocoons and had therefore entered the pupa stage of its life cycle; the second brood, which had proceeded sluggishly and poorly, as if diseased, had not yet made its passage from silkworms to pupae. Surprisingly, the pupae and moths of the successful brood contained corpuscles in abundance, while the worms of the poor brood contained almost none. Similar cases appeared in other silkworm nurseries around Alais. Some of the surprise abated as the second brood continued to pass through its life cycle. The previously rare corpuscles became increasingly frequent in the pupae, and eventually every moth contained them in profusion. Nonetheless, from the rarity of corpuscles in the sick worms of the second brood, Pasteur concluded that *pébrine* must be a constitutional, hereditary disease, existing prior to and independently of the corpuscles. These corpuscles he supposed to be products of the disease, perhaps resulting from tissue disintegration. Since both broods displayed corpuscles, both must have been diseased; but presumably the first brood had been attacked only late in its life cycle (and thus without serious damage to its silk crop), while the second brood had suffered more severely since an earlier stage.

This conception led Pasteur to essentially the same preventive remedy proposed by Osimo—the selection of eggs from noncorpuscular moths and the rejection of those from corpuscular moths. That Pasteur could advocate this method of egg selection while denying the causative role of the corpuscles becomes less paradoxical if the corpuscles are regarded as an index of the severity of the disease. In Pasteur's view corpuscular moths were obviously in an advanced state of

the disease; and although noncorpuscular moths might also be sick, they must be less seriously so and thus less likely to produce diseased offspring. This method of egg selection, which Pasteur announced only two weeks after his arrival in Alais, remained at the core of his remedial proposals even as his conception of the silkworm plague underwent a dramatic change.

For various reasons this change took place with almost agonizing slowness. In the first place, the tentative conclusions drawn from one year's silk culture could be overturned by the results of the next year, and no way existed to circumvent fully this prolonged natural delay. Moreover, if the material selected happened to fail for reasons unconnected with the prevailing blight, it became useless as a guide to the disease. Personal tragedies and burdens further frustrated Pasteur's efforts. During his first brief trip to Alais, toward the end of the silkworm season of 1865, his father died. The studies of the following year were briefly interrupted by the death of his two-year-old daughter. Immediately after the 1867 season he became the focus of the student protest which ended with his dismissal from the administration of the École Normale. His activities during the 1869 and 1870 seasons were restricted by his debilitating stroke of October 1868.

But the most fundamental obstacle lay in the inherent complexity of the task. Only gradually did it become clear that the silkworm plague involved at least two independent diseases, which differed in ways precisely calculated to confuse students of the problem. Under the weight of these burdens, Pasteur leaned heavily on the moral support of Dumas and Empress Eugénie, and—beginning in 1866—on the companionship and assistance of his loyal collaborators Désiré Gernez, Maillot, Jules Raulin, and Émile Duclaux. For about five months of every year through 1870, one or more of these collaborators joined Pasteur and his wife at Pont-Gisquet, near Alais, where in an abandoned orangery they arranged a makeshift laboratory and carried out the experiments which the master had designed.

From the outset Pasteur's basic experimental strategy was to compare carefully the results of cultures from relatively corpuscular moths with those from relatively noncorpuscular moths. These painstaking studies established the following general conclusions: (1) the more corpuscular the parent moths, the less successful the resulting crop of silk cocoons; (2) while the offspring from partially corpuscular moths sometimes gave a good first crop, they never gave a good second crop; (3) in any brood, however corpuscular the eggs from which it derived, some noncorpuscular moths could always be found. If this third result offered hope that healthy moths (and hence cultures) could always appear even in the midst of disease, the first two tended to emphasize the connection between the corpuscles and the disease and to reinforce the value of selecting eggs from noncorpuscular moths. Indeed, this method had so won Pasteur's confidence by the end of the 1866 season that he began to rely on it to make bold public prophecies. In a letter to the mayor of St.-Hippolyte-du-Fort he predicted the fate during the 1867 season of fourteen batches of eggs he had examined there the year before. In twelve of the fourteen cases, the results conformed closely to his predictions.[65]

None of these results, however, really demonstrated either that the corpuscles caused the disease or that they were living parasites. Nor did a clear answer emerge from preliminary feeding experiments conducted by Pasteur in 1866. For when he fed healthy worms mulberry leaves smeared with corpuscles—to see if *pébrine* could be transmitted in this way—many of the young worms died without becoming corpuscular. On the other hand, similar feeding experiments by Gernez seemed strongly to support the parasitic theory of *pébrine*. Besides establishing a general association between a corpuscular diet and *pébrine*, Gernez showed more precisely that the time at which the corpuscles of *pébrine* appeared in a brood depended directly on the time at which the corpuscular diet had been introduced. Pasteur, however, was not yet convinced. When he reported the results of Gernez's experiments in November 1866, he focused chiefly on those which showed that broods from noncorpuscular moths gave good silk crops—in other words, he reemphasized the practical value of his method of egg selection.

By now, it seems, Pasteur's collaborators were thoroughly convinced both that the corpuscles caused *pébrine* and that they were living parasites. His reluctance to accept this view greatly surprised them, and Duclaux went so far as to accuse him of obstinacy.[66] Pasteur's hesitation is indeed remarkable, not only in view of Gernez's persuasive results but more emphatically in view of his abiding faith in the pathological implications of the germ theory of fermentation—a faith which ought presumably to have disposed him toward a parasitic etiology for *pébrine*. Nonetheless, his initial observations in 1865, and the evidence which he knew best from his own research, conflicted in some respects with the parasitic theory. As late as January 1867, he listed four major objections to a parasitic etiology for *pébrine*: "(1) the disease is certainly constitutional in a number of circumstances and precedes the appearance of corpuscles; (2) the feeding of corpuscular matter often kills young worms without corpus-

cles appearing in their bodies; (3) I have been unable thus far to discover a mode of reproduction for the corpuscles; (4) their mode of appearance resembles a transformation of tissues."[67]

These objections depended in part on Pasteur's inadequate knowledge of protozoan reproduction and on his then defective technique for detecting corpuscles. But they derived in larger measure from a general confusion between *pébrine* and another disease, *morts-flats* or *flacherie*, the complex etiology of which was even more obscure than that of *pébrine*. Perhaps partly because he shared this confusion with so many other authorities on *pébrine*, Pasteur resisted a rapid and careless extension of the germ theory to the diseases of silkworms. Indeed, no other work by Pasteur displays greater sensitivity to the complex relationships between heredity, environment, and parasitism; and Duclaux—while accusing Pasteur of obstinacy—wrote that he did not know a "more beautiful example of scientific investigation" than Pasteur's study of the silkworm problem.[68]

The Silkworm Season of 1867. The silkworm season of 1867 marked a watershed in Pasteur's investigations. Before it ended, he had become a convert to the parasitic theory of *pébrine* and had come to recognize that *morts-flats* or *flacherie*—which most authorities linked with *pébrine*—was an independent disease, with its own character and etiology.[69] His conversion to the parasitic theory of *pébrine* depended chiefly on mounting evidence of its contagiousness. To establish this characteristic, it was necessary to discredit the notion that the disease arose in consequence of a mysterious epidemic environment. Pasteur rejected this notion on the ground that broods derived from noncorpuscular moths—of which he had secured a large supply—usually remained sound and noncorpuscular even in the midst of the allegedly epidemic environment. This result helped to clear the way for further feeding experiments, for it undermined the objection that worms which became sick on a corpuscular diet might owe their disease to an epidemic environment having no connection with their diet.

Against this background Pasteur and his collaborators repeated on a large scale Gernez's feeding experiments and supplemented them with experiments in which healthy silkworms were directly inoculated with corpuscles through surface punctures. In both ways, although especially by corpuscular diets, otherwise healthy worms contracted *pébrine* and became highly corpuscular. Having reached this point, Pasteur seems to have encountered little difficulty in discovering a mode of reproduction for the corpuscles, a mode strikingly different from the budding and binary fission of the microorganisms which he knew best but a mode familiar to protozoologists.

While these studies seemed, therefore, to establish the contagiousness of *pébrine*, with parasitic corpuscles as its cause, they raised another question: If *pébrine* is contagious, of what use is the method of egg selection as a remedy? In the first place, Pasteur replied, the corpuscles of diseased parent moths can be transmitted directly to their eggs; and in this sense *pébrine* is simultaneously hereditary and contagious. Moreover, if the offspring of noncorpuscular moths later contract *pébrine*—whether by eating corpuscular leaves or by inoculation—the incubation period is long enough to ensure that all, or virtually all, the worms will spin cocoons and yield a silk crop. And since the corpuscles lose their fecundity and pathogenicity from one silkworm season to the next, the only effective source of contagion in each season must be the corpuscles contained in the eggs produced by corpuscular moths. If, therefore, all the eggs from corpuscular moths are rejected, *pébrine* ought to disappear quickly. In this way Pasteur developed a new and more impressive rationale for his method of egg selection, but his hope that it could lead to total elimination of *pébrine* was doomed by the fact that the corpuscle enjoys hosts other than the silkworm.[70]

Studies on Flacherie, 1867–1870. Pasteur's recognition of *flacherie* as an independent disease can be traced at least in part to his confidence in the method of egg selection, undoubtedly reinforced by his new conviction of the parasitic nature of *pébrine*. For what especially alerted him to the independence of *flacherie* was the failure during the 1867 season of entire broods descended from noncorpuscular moths. Most of these unsuccessful broods, which appeared in Pasteur's cultures as well as those of several breeders to whom he had sent the eggs, displayed neither the corpuscles nor the black external spots of *pébrine*. Instead, nearly all the worms died with the familiar symptoms of *flacherie* —symptoms different enough from those of *pébrine* to have received a separate name, although most authorities (including Pasteur) had hitherto supposed that these symptoms merely represented a special stage or effect of *pébrine*. That *flacherie* represented a well-defined and independent hereditary disease now seemed clear not only from the absence of corpuscles in these diseased broods but also from the way it attacked all of the offspring of certain batches of eggs, even though these eggs had been cultivated in widely different environments.

Although these events aroused great practical concern, they also helped to clarify much of the apparently contradictory evidence. In the case of Pasteur's work, it now seemed clear that his initial observations at Alais, as well as his preliminary experiments with corpuscular diets, had miscarried through the intervention of *flacherie*. Because, in both cases, he had observed death and disease in the absence of corpuscles, he had supposed that *pébrine* must be a constitutional disease. The events of the 1867 season strongly suggested that such a constitutional disease did exist, but that this disease was *flacherie* rather than *pébrine*. Compared with *pébrine*, *flacherie* had contributed rather little to the ruinous silkworm blight; but its character and etiology demanded great attention because it threatened the method of egg selection on which Pasteur had based his hopes for the rejuvenation of French sericulture. At first Pasteur merely advised the rejection of eggs from broods which displayed high mortality, languor, or any other symptom of *flacherie*. Then, during the silkworm seasons of 1868 to 1870, he sought to unravel the etiology of *flacherie* from that of *pébrine* and to find a prophylactic method for it as reliable as the method of egg selection he had devised for *pébrine*.

At the outset of these studies on *flacherie*, two striking phenomena arrested Pasteur's attention: (1) the strongly hereditary aspect of the disease, as revealed by the almost constant and devastating appearance of *flacherie* in descendants of broods which had shown some symptoms of the disease before spinning their cocoons and laying their eggs; and (2) the abundant presence of microorganisms in the intestinal canals of worms attacked by *flacherie*. Notable among these microorganisms, which were virtually absent from healthy worms, were vibrions (bacilli) and a "petit ferment en chapelets de grains" (a micrococcus), which resembled an organism he had already associated with certain fermentations.[71] As with the corpuscles of *pébrine*, Pasteur at first supposed that these microorganisms were a consequence of the disease rather than its cause, their chief significance being diagnostic rather than etiological.[72] More specifically, he conceived of *flacherie* as a sort of hereditary susceptibility to indigestion, in consequence of which ingested mulberry leaves underwent fermentation in the intestinal canal. On this view the microorganisms associated with intestinal fermentation, and especially the small ferment in chains, served as a physical index of a late stage in the disease. But even while thus denying the intestinal microorganisms a direct causative role in *flacherie*, Pasteur put them at the center of his efforts to develop a prophylactic measure against it. In brief, he counseled the rejection of pupae the stomachs of which contained the small ferment in chains, since they were certain to transmit the hereditary predisposition to their offspring.

During the silkworm season of 1869, Pasteur considerably modified his conception of *flacherie*.[73] As in the case of *pébrine*, feeding experiments seem to have been chiefly responsible for this shift. On a diet of leaves smeared with excrement from worms with *flacherie*, previously healthy worms fell sick with the disease. Thus *flacherie*, like *pébrine*, was contagious as well as hereditary. Unlike *pébrine*, however, *flacherie* owed its hereditary character not to the direct transmission of a microorganism from the parent moths to the eggs but to a constitutional weakness of which there was no immediately visible sign. While thus retaining part of his original conception of the disease, Pasteur now perceived—however dimly—that this hereditary weakness involved a susceptibility not so much to indigestion per se as to the germs of the microorganisms later seen in the intestinal canal. Henceforth he identified the intestinal microorganisms as the proximate cause of *flacherie*. Unlike the corpuscles of *pébrine*, these microorganisms are common and universally distributed. They must therefore become pathogenic in silkworms only under special circumstances. Hereditary susceptibility to them in certain silkworms clearly forms one of these special circumstances; but other such conditions must exist, for *flacherie* sometimes appears "accidentally" or "spontaneously" in a brood without any hereditary predisposition. In such cases, Pasteur suggested, unusual conditions of temperature, humidity, or ventilation in the nursery must either promote the multiplication of the causative microorganisms on the leaves or lower the resistance of the silkworms to the ingested germs. To prevent or reduce all forms of *flacherie*, therefore, it was necessary not only to reject infected pupae but also to monitor and to control as far as possible the environmental conditions in the nursery.

According to René Dubos, the etiology of *flacherie* is even more complex than Pasteur realized.[74] Among other things, the susceptibility of silkworms to the bacteria of *flacherie* seems to depend on the intervention of a filterable virus. However that may be, Pasteur had attained a remarkably keen insight into the essential features of *pébrine* and *flacherie*. He recognized the subtlety and importance of the questions this work raised about the interaction of parasite, host, and environment in the production of disease; and he later advised young physicians to study his *Études sur la maladie des vers à soie* (1870) as an introduction to such issues.[75] But Pasteur had grown increasingly tired of this work, especially as he became confident that he had provided the basis for a practical solution to the problems of French sericulture. In fact, between 1868 and 1870 study of the etiology of *flacherie* occupied him less fully and directly than his efforts to establish and proselytize his practical measures against the silk-

worm blight. Toward this end he engaged in an enormous correspondence with sericulturists and their trade journals, distributed vast quantities of eggs for industrial trials, and became a practical sericulturist. These efforts brought Pasteur recognition and testimonials from commissions and sericulturists, many of whom adopted his methods. If his success was less than total, it was certainly considerable and he did not lose confidence even during a serious depression in French sericulture from 1879 to 1881, which he ascribed not to a failure of his methods but to bad weather and to the comparatively low prices of Oriental silk.[76]

Debates Over Fermentation, 1871–1876. From 1865 to 1870, while Pasteur was preoccupied with the silkworm problem, his theory of fermentation enjoyed increasing favor, especially abroad. What criticism did appear during that period failed to distract him from his central task. In 1871, however, the *Annales de chimie et de physique* published a French translation of a wide-ranging critique by Liebig, who had broken a long silence on the issue in two lectures (1868, 1869). In a reply of almost arrogant brevity, Pasteur discussed only two aspects of Liebig's critique, both of which involved direct challenges to experimental claims made a decade before by Pasteur: (1) that pure yeast and a simple alcoholic fermentation could be produced in a medium free of organic nitrogen and (2) that acetic fermentation required the intervention of *Mycoderma aceti*. Pasteur responded by challenging Liebig to submit the dispute to a commission of the Académie des Sciences. Before this commission, Pasteur boldly predicted, he would prepare, in a medium free of organic nitrogen, as much beer yeast as Liebig might reasonably demand and would demonstrate the existence of *Mycoderma aceti* on the surface of the beechwood shavings used in the German method of acetification.[77]

Although Liebig died in 1873 without accepting Pasteur's challenge, some aspects of his critique were adopted in France by Edmond Frémy and Auguste Trécul, among others. These critics earned the scorn and ridicule of Pasteur who went so far as to impugn the patriotism of those who dared to defend a "German theory" against a "French theory" after the Franco-Prussian War.[78] Despite their often personal and repetitive character, the ensuing debates nonetheless contributed to Pasteur's understanding and articulation of the issues surrounding fermentation and spontaneous generation. Insofar as the debates concerned fermentation as such, their chief value was to induce Pasteur to clarify his views on the role of oxygen in the process, to extend to all living cells his theory of fermentation without air, and to begin at last to face directly and explicitly the ambiguities of his definition of fermentation.

In his papers of the 1860's Pasteur had implied that oxygen played no role in fermentation, unless to impede it. In fact, some brewers supposed that he advocated the total elimination of air during brewing, a natural enough conclusion from his theory of fermentation as "life without air."[79] Only gradually, under prodding from such critics as Frémy, Oscar Brefeld, and Moritz Traube, did Pasteur begin to emphasize that oxygen played an essential, if strictly limited, role. In the face of Frémy's repeated insistence that some contact with oxygen was essential to the fermentation of grape juice, Pasteur finally acknowledged in 1872 that this view contained a kernel of truth, in that yeast—the true agent of fermentation—did require some oxygen in order to germinate.[80] In 1875 he responded in essentially similar fashion to the objections of Brefeld and Traube, whose careful experiments suggested that yeast deprived of free oxygen either could not live at all or else provoked at most a very feeble and incomplete fermentation. In his reply Pasteur suggested that they had been misled by using contaminated yeast or yeast too old and "exhausted" to germinate in an oxygen-free environment.[81] In his *Études sur la bière* (1876), in which he also described a new and perfected method of preparing pure yeast, Pasteur emphasized that yeast occasionally required small quantities of oxygen in order to retain its "youth" and its capacity to germinate in oxygen-free environments. Having now achieved a new appreciation for the importance of oxygen in brewing, and especially the advantages of aerated wort, he insisted only that air should be carefully limited and freed of foreign germs rather than entirely eliminated.

In the meantime Pasteur had extended his theory of fermentation to all living cells, a development that Dumas believed might well mark "an epoch in the history of general physiology."[82] Beginning in October 1872, Pasteur set forth and elaborated the view that because fermentation is a manifestation of life in the absence of free oxygen, and because every living cell can survive at least temporarily under such conditions, "all living things are ferments in certain conditions of their life." As evidence he cited experiments showing that *Mycoderma vini* and *Penicillium glaucum*, ordinarily aerobic organisms that consume free oxygen, can live for a time in the absence of free oxygen—when forcibly submerged in a sugared liquid medium, for example. Under these anaerobic conditions the *Mycoderma* and *Penicillium* become ferments: they decompose the sugar in order to extract its combined oxygen and carbon, producing alcohol in the process. Similarly, intact grapes, prunes, plums, and other fruits

give off a small quantity of alcohol in an oxygen-free environment. In the latter case the cells of the fruit decompose the sugar in the fruit to obtain carbon and oxygen and thus the heat (or energy) required for physiological processes. As early as 1861 Pasteur had described in preliminary fashion a converse phenomenon—the capacity of yeast, ordinarily an anaerobic organism, to become adapted to a more or less aerobic existence, in which case its power as a ferment decreased or disappeared. In August 1875 he specified the conditions under which yeast could become a fully aerobic plant, living exactly like common molds. The essential task was to germinate the yeast on a liquid of large surface area in the presence of abundant oxygen. Under these circumstances it consumed free oxygen and did not produce fermentation.[83]

In several respects these ideas confused Pasteur's contemporaries, and some of his opponents thought he had unwittingly exposed fundamental flaws in his germ theory of fermentation. By revealing the protean character of yeast and other lower organisms—which might live as either anaerobes or aerobes, as ferments or not—he seemed to undermine his insistence on the specificity and peculiarity of fermentative microorganisms. More directly, his suggestion that fruit cells could produce alcohol—without the intervention of living microorganisms—struck some as an outright contradiction of his earlier views and the entire germ theory of fermentation. While responding to such confusion and criticism, Pasteur finally emphasized and clarified several points hitherto largely implicit or otherwise submerged in his work. Above all, he revealed how much his theory of fermentation depended on his carefully circumscribed definition of the process.

The Circularity of Pasteur's Theory of Fermentation. From the beginning of his work on fermentation, Pasteur had restricted the germ theory to "fermentations proprement dites" ("fermentations properly so-called"). When, in February 1872, Frémy demanded to know what he meant by this expression, "so vague and so elastic," Pasteur said that he applied it to "the fermentations that I have studied and which include all the best characterized fermentations, those which are as old as the world, those which give bread, wine, beer, sour milk, ammoniacal urine, etc., etc., those in which the ferments are, according to my researches, living beings which arise and multiply during the act of fermentation."[84] On the other hand, processes such as the so-called diastatic fermentation, by which starch was converted into sugar, did not merit inclusion among the fermentations "properly so-called," because they involve a soluble chemical ferment (an enzyme) rather than a living microorganism. In other words, Pasteur excluded from his definition of fermentation those processes of decomposition which he admitted to be chemical rather than biological.

But Pasteur also excluded from the list of true fermentations certain processes of decomposition that he had identified as biological. He probably acted intentionally, for example, when he omitted acetic fermentation from the list of the "best characterized fermentations" that he had studied. This obvious omission can be explained by supposing that Pasteur defined as "fermentations properly so-called" only those processes associated with anaerobic microorganisms. Because acetification depended on *Mycoderma aceti*, an aerobic organism, it must be excluded from the true fermentations, even though it met two other fundamental criteria—it was microbial and it involved the decomposition of a weight of substance vastly greater than the weight of the responsible microorganism. Along somewhat similar lines, Pasteur differentiated between alcoholic fermentation "properly so-called" and the nonmicrobial production of alcohol by fruit cells in the absence of free oxygen. By itself, he insisted, the production of alcohol is no index of true alcoholic fermentation, for the latter process also yields glycerin, succinic acid, and other substances. This process is called "alcoholic fermentation" only by abbreviation; to be precise, one ought to designate it by its complete equation, the complexity of which reflects its dependence on living yeast.

As these examples make clear, Pasteur's theory of fermentation reduced to a virtual tautology, for any process which failed to conform to that theory in every respect automatically failed to qualify as a fermentation "properly so-called." In similar fashion Liebig might have maintained an unassailable chemical theory of fermentation had he been willing to exclude from his definition of fermentation those processes which Pasteur associated with microorganisms. In so doing, however, Liebig would have excluded many of the decomposition processes traditionally regarded as fermentations—most notably ordinary alcoholic fermentation, which had always been considered the archetypal fermentative process. The fertility and power of Pasteur's theory derived precisely from its applicability to these familiar processes, and he seemed remarkably unconcerned that it did not also apply to those processes associated with such soluble chemical ferments as diastase, emulsin, or pepsin. By admitting, or at least implying, that his theory also failed to apply to certain biological processes—including acetification and the nonmicrobial production of alcohol by fruit cells—Pasteur invited confusion and threatened his own attempt to generalize the theory to all living cells. That his study of fermentation nonetheless produced

valuable insights, both theoretical and practical, illustrates forcefully that not all circles are vicious.

The Issue of a Soluble Alcoholic Ferment. In retrospect, the most intriguing feature of the debate between Pasteur and Liebig is the extent to which they seemed ultimately to approach a mutually acceptable conception of fermentation. By 1869, at least, Liebig was prepared to admit the possibility that alcoholic fermentation depended in part on the life of yeast. Adopting a hypothesis by no means original with him, he suggested that living yeast cells might secrete a soluble chemical ferment, analogous to diastase or pepsin, which then induced the decomposition of sugar into alcohol and carbonic acid. This hypothesis drew particular support from the knowledge that yeast did produce at least one other soluble ferment, *ferment glycosique* or invertase, responsible for inverting cane sugar.

Pasteur made no immediate objection to Liebig's suggestion; indeed, in his memoir of 1860 on alcoholic fermentation, he had mentioned the possibility that yeast might act by secreting a soluble ferment. In 1875, two years after Liebig's death, Pasteur suggested that the processes resulting from soluble ferments might someday be reunited with the true fermentations "in some way as yet unknown."[85] In July 1876 he conceded that the ammoniacal fermentation of urine, which he had ascribed since 1860 to a living microorganism, could be traced more immediately to a soluble chemical ferment produced by the living ferment. When his opponents tried to exploit this concession, Pasteur emphasized that for twenty years he had devoted himself chiefly to demonstrating that the agents of fermentations were microorganisms. The precise mechanism by which these agents acted was a problem of a different order and required further investigation.[86]

From this perspective the debate between Pasteur and Liebig seems to have ended as an essentially semantic dispute, a disagreement born of their approach to the phenomena of fermentation at different levels, with Liebig seeking its proximate cause and Pasteur content to establish more remote correlations. As Duclaux emphasized, however, the two positions implied strikingly different experimental strategies.[87] Because this difference was reinforced by long-standing disagreements over experimental results, and by personal and national antagonisms, Pasteur and Liebig found it difficult to make concessions; and their potential rapprochement remained largely submerged in mutual hostility.

Even in the absence of these difficulties, Pasteur and Liebig might never have achieved a fully compatible conception of fermentation, for some of the issues which divided them reemerged in Pasteur's debate with Marcelin Berthelot, the leading French advocate of the modified chemical theory of fermentation. Like Liebig, Berthelot had initially opposed Pasteur's attempt to implicate living organisms in fermentation and had then moved to the view that living yeast might act by secreting a soluble alcoholic ferment. His views on fermentation derived particular authority from his having isolated from yeast the soluble ferment responsible for the inversion of cane sugar. In 1878 Berthelot arranged for the posthumous publication of manuscript notes in which Claude Bernard criticized Pasteur's theory of fermentation and claimed to have isolated a soluble ferment capable of producing alcoholic fermentation independently of living yeast.

The publication of this manuscript placed Pasteur in an awkward position, for Bernard had long contributed his immense authority and support to Pasteur's cause. To some extent Pasteur adopted the strategy of impugning Berthelot's motives rather than the work of the revered Bernard, who had neither authorized the publication of his manuscript notes nor described their contents to Pasteur. Nonetheless, in a full-length critique of Bernard's manuscript (1879), Pasteur attacked in devastating fashion the experiments by which Bernard believed he had destroyed Pasteur's theory of fermentation as life without air. By carefully repeating these experiments and comparing them with his own, Pasteur went a long way toward justifying his claim that Bernard's results were mistaken, dubious, or badly interpreted. In this task Pasteur benefited from the patently crude and preliminary character of Bernard's experiments (at least as they were represented in the manuscript notes) and from their author's inability to reply or defend himself. While expressing reluctance about taking advantage of these circumstances, Pasteur justified his action on methodological grounds. In his view Bernard's manuscript offered a dramatic example of the danger of "systems" and "preconceived ideas," a danger which Bernard himself had done so much to expose in his *Introduction à l'étude de la médecine expérimentale* (1865).

Saying that Bernard had somehow forgotten his own wise precepts, Pasteur suggested that he had been led astray by an a priori conviction of a fundamental opposition between organic syntheses, which he supposed to be peculiarly vital phenomena, and organic decompositions (including fermentation, combustion, and putrefaction), which he supposed to be physicochemical rather than vital processes. Because his theory of fermentation linked life and organic syntheses with a process of organic decomposition, Pasteur continued, it conflicted with Bernard's general conception of life and thereby earned his rejection. From this perspective it was easy to understand why Bernard not only embraced the view that the immediate cause of fermentation was a soluble alcoholic ferment but also claimed that this soluble ferment existed—independently of yeast cells—in the juice of grapes at a certain stage of their maturity. By this claim Bernard sought to deny living yeast any role in fermentation, while even Liebig and Berthelot were willing to concede that it might be essential for the production of the hypothetical soluble ferment. Unfortunately for Bernard, said Pasteur, his claim was refuted by the fact that grapes of any degree of maturity never fermented when carefully protected from yeast germs.

If this version of Bernard's "preconceived ideas" was less than fair or accurate—as Duclaux suggests[88] —Pasteur may have been driven to it by the extravagance of Bernard's views. But it is clear from his critique of Bernard, and from the associated debate with Berthelot, that he was also suspicious of the more moderate attempts by Berthelot and Liebig to incorporate his "physiological" theory of fermentation into the modified chemical theory that yeast acted by secreting a soluble alcoholic ferment. Even as he insisted that he would be neither surprised nor disturbed by the discovery of such a chemical ferment—indeed, he reportedly sought it himself by grinding and plasmolyzing yeast cells[89]—Pasteur asserted that the role of soluble ferments would one day be eclipsed by that of life without air.[90]

Until his death Pasteur could retain this hope as he surveyed a long tradition of unsuccessful attempts to isolate a soluble alcoholic ferment. In 1897, however, while engaged in apparently unrelated immunological research, Eduard Buchner achieved this goal and thereby cast Pasteur's physiological theory of fermentation into the shade. Even then, however, the phenomenon known as the "Pasteur effect"—the inhibition of fermentation in the presence of free oxygen —remained as real as it was inexplicable. More recently, the physiological and chemical theories of fermentation have come to be seen as complementary rather than opposed. If, at some level, Pasteur perceived this possibility, he never explained precisely how the notion of a soluble alcoholic ferment could be reconciled with the doctrine of fermentation as life without air. He sought instead to defend the conclusions he had already reached and challenged the wisdom or necessity of invoking the concept of a soluble alcoholic ferment. For him this concept remained a gratuitous and unproved assumption. For his opponents, and particularly for Berthelot, the concept of life without air was an equally gratuitous, unproved and unnecessary hypothesis. In short, if our present conception of fermentation suggests that the debate was largely semantic and capable of easy resolution, its participants were unable to see it that way.

Studies on Beer. During the late 1860's the "pasteurization" of wine and vinegar became increasingly common. The process found a new application in Austria and Germany, where the practice of heating bottled beer to 55° C. became widespread following the publication of Pasteur's *Études sur le vin* (1866). Beginning in May 1871, largely under the stimulus of the Franco-Prussian War, Pasteur launched a study of beer in hopes of serving "a branch of industry in which Germany is superior to us."[91] This effort, begun in Émile Duclaux's laboratory at Clermont-Ferrand, led to a series of patents and to Pasteur's *Études sur la bière* (1876). Meanwhile, Pasteur had become embroiled in a series of debates over fermentation and spontaneous generation; and the book on beer consists for the most part of a sometimes oddly organized and largely tedious rehearsal of those debates.

Only two chapters in the book were directed specifically toward the practical problems of brewing. In the first chapter Pasteur sought to demonstrate that the alterations or "diseases" of beer depend on the appearance and development of foreign microorganisms, "not at this time a new idea," according to Duclaux.[92] In the last chapter Pasteur described his process for manufacturing beer, which emphasized the use of pure yeast and carefully limited quantities of pure air. As in his books on vinegar and wine, he gave considerable space to descriptions and drawings of the industrial apparatus his new method would require. Perhaps because of its wide adoption in the German brewing industry, the method of preserving beer by heat received only passing and skeptical attention.[93]

Among the advantages that Pasteur claimed for his new method of manufacturing beer, the most important were the elimination or reduction of costly cooling techniques (introduced empirically, but now explicable as a means of impeding the development of pathogenic organisms) and the protection of finished beer from disease. Nonetheless, Pasteur admitted that his process had "not yet been practically adopted,"[94] a result he ascribed chiefly to the costly retooling it would require. If attempts were ever made to exploit Pasteur's patents on beer, their fate has yet to be described. Nonetheless, his more general contributions to the study of brewing attracted the attention and admiration of some industrial brewers, notably J. C. Jacobsen, founder of the Carlsberg brewery in Denmark. In the late 1870's Jacobsen gave 1.5 million francs for the creation of a magnificent laboratory at his Carlsberg brewery. For this laboratory, which soon became a leading center of biochemical research, he commissioned a bust of Pasteur, who responded by dedicating his 1879 critique of Bernard to Jacobsen.[95]

Pasteur and Spontaneous Generation, 1871–1879. If Pasteur believed that his triumph over Pouchet would silence the partisans of spontaneous generation, he was soon disappointed. The issue remained a subject of lively debate, especially in England and Germany, where Pasteur's critics had rather less to fear from the judiciary proceedings of the Académie des Sciences and from the presumed association of spontaneous generation with Darwinian evolution and radical politics. When Pasteur rejoined the controversy in 1871 his chief French opponents were those who simultaneously challenged his theory of fermentation—notably Frémy and Trécul. In France the debate on spontaneous generation now focused on the origin of the alcoholic yeasts, although attention was also paid to the origin of the microorganisms found in putrefying eggs and in human abscesses. Bound up with these specific concerns were the broader issues of the transmutation of microbial species, the nature and distribution of germs, and the distinction between aerobic and anaerobic life. From July 1876 to July 1877 Pasteur also engaged in a celebrated controversy with the English naturalist H. Charlton Bastian, who claimed he could produce microorganisms spontaneously in neutral or alkaline urine. From this debate—the most productive in the series—Pasteur emerged with a firmer grasp of the relative distribution of germs in air, in water, and on solid objects, and—most important—with a greater appreciation for the heat resistance of certain microorganisms.

Pasteur rejoined the spontaneous generation controversy by attacking Frémy's claim that the yeasts of vinification arose internally and spontaneously from grape juice upon contact with the air. In 1872, in an attempt to make his point decisively, Pasteur showed that a drop of unheated natural grape juice, aspirated from the interior of a ripe grape, would neither ferment nor give yeasts in germ-free air.[96] He took great delight in this delicate experiment, which he often linked with his earlier demonstrations that natural urine and blood could be preserved in germ-free air even without preliminary heating. Although Frémy and Trécul managed to find objections against even this experiment, Pasteur disposed of them quite readily and continued to cite the experiment as definitive proof against the internal, spontaneous origin of yeasts.

When Frémy then sought support for spontaneous generation in Pasteur's demonstration that fruits could remain intact (hence closed to external germs) and yet produce alcohol in an oxygen-free environment, Pasteur was obliged to emphasize that no microorganisms participated in this process; it was a case of the fruit cells themselves acting as "ferments" under anaerobic conditions.

But Pasteur went much further. Denying that the yeasts of wine originated spontaneously within the grape, he sought to establish their precise external origin and to clarify their more general properties. By 1876, when he reported his results in his *Études sur la bière*, he felt confident that he had established the following generalizations about the alcoholic yeasts: (1) a great many yeasts exist, differing in form, physiological properties, and in the taste and other qualities that they impart to the fermenting liquid; (2) the yeasts of wine derive from germs that are particularly abundant on the wood of the grape cluster, somewhat less abundant on the surfaces of the grapes themselves, and rare in ordinary atmospheric air; (3) these germs gradually decrease in number and fecundity during the winter and are entirely absent from the surfaces of immature grapes; (4) these germs increase in number and fecundity as the grapes mature and as the time of the vintage approaches (so that when the ripe grapes are crushed, no yeasts need be sown, as they must in brewing beer); (5) these germs require oxygen to retain their vitality and thus their capacity to produce fermentation; and (6) the species of yeast are distinct, are not transformed one into the other, and do not represent special developmental forms of another plant.[97]

In 1878, after Bernard's manuscript on fermentation had revived the notion of an internal origin for the yeast of wine, Pasteur confirmed under natural conditions the central conclusions of his *Études sur la bière*. In July of that year, immediately after reading Bernard's manuscript, he ordered the construction of several glass hothouses, with which he intended to cover some of the still immature vines in his own vineyard near Arbois. This plan had been executed by early August, before any yeast germs had appeared on the grape clusters. As a further precaution he wrapped some of the clusters within the hothouses in sterile cotton. By 10 October all the grapes had ripened and the time of vintage had arrived. As Pasteur expected, the exposed grapes easily and rapidly fermented when crushed, while those protected from yeast germs by the hothouses did not, except in one case. The grapes wrapped in cotton within the hothouses never fermented when proper precautions were taken. On the other hand, if these grapes were subsequently exposed in the open air, they soon fermented when crushed with the yeast germs that they had in the meantime received.[98]

By these experiments Pasteur went a long way toward a definitive demonstration of the external origin of the yeast of wine. He had by then reached an equally firm position on the issue of the transmutation of microbial species. From the 1840's to the early 1870's, an increasing number of botanists claimed that they had observed the transformation of one microbial species into another; and their claims had been enlisted in support of Darwinian evolution and spontaneous generation. In 1861 Pasteur specifically challenged several presumed cases of microbial transmutation—notably of *Penicillium glaucum* into beer yeast—and his more general opposition to the doctrine seems implicit in his work on fermentation and spontaneous generation, with its dependence on the specificity and hereditary continuity of microorganisms. Nonetheless, Pasteur gave little explicit attention to the issue before the 1870's, and his general position had been obscured by his claim of 1862 that he had observed the transformation of *Mycoderma vini* into the alcoholic yeast of wine under anaerobic conditions, more specifically when submerged in a fermentable liquid. For the next decade, as he continued to hold this view, Pasteur used it in support of his theory of fermentation as life without air. Then quite suddenly, in October and November 1872, he reconsidered and abandoned his earlier claim.[99]

By Pasteur's own account, this change of view had its origin in two sorts of observational evidence. First, even when he had sown only *Mycoderma vini* into the fermentable liquid, he sometimes found cells of *Mucor mucedo* or *racemosus* as well as yeast cells among the submerged mycodermic pellicle. Assuming that this *Mucor* could have entered the medium only from the surrounding air, he began to wonder if the air could not also be the source of the yeast cells he had hitherto supposed to be the transformed cells of *Mycoderma vini*. Second, yeast cells sometimes failed to appear in the submerged pellicle, even when the experimental conditions seemed identical. Why should the presumed transmutation fail to take place in these cases? To resolve his doubts Pasteur modified his swan-necked flasks in such a way as to permit the comparative study of the same microorganism under anaerobic conditions (when submerged) and under aerobic conditions (on the surface of a shallow liquid) without exposing the liquid medium to the ambient air or to any other external source of germs. Under these conditions Pasteur never again observed the supposed transformation of *Mycoderma vini* into yeast, and he never again wavered in his opposition to the notion of direct microbial transmutation.

If Pasteur felt any embarrassment about rejecting his original belief in the transmutability of *Mycoderma vini*, he probably found more than adequate consolation in the circumstance that his theory of fermentation not only remained intact but also acquired a new extension and generality. For his rejection of the transmutability of *Mycoderma vini* coincided with, and perhaps depended upon, the extension to all living cells of his theory of fermentation as life without air. In the light of this generalized version of his theory, he could and did ascribe fermentative power directly to the cells of *Mycoderma vini* under anaerobic conditions, without needing to suppose that they acquired this power by virtue of a transformation into yeast cells. Pasteur may also have been encouraged to take this position and to reassert his general opposition to microbial transformism by the influential work of the German botanists Anton de Bary and Ferdinand Cohn. Certainly he was not alone in his opposition to immediate microbial transformism; and de Bary, Cohn, and others contributed more than he to the general rejection of the doctrine.

With regard, finally, to Pasteur's general position on the transmutation of species, it should be emphasized that he did not directly and explicitly repudiate Darwinian evolutionary theory per se. Although clearly skeptical of the theory and suspicious of its popularity—which he ascribed to its failure to require "rigorous experimentation" or "profound observations"[100]—Pasteur insisted only that no one had demonstrated the immediate transformation of one microbial species into another.

The Pasteur-Bastian Debate. By July 1876, when Pasteur locked horns with H. Charlton Bastian, that influential English advocate of spontaneous generation had already established his reputation through his long and controversial *The Beginnings of Life* (1872) and had engaged the attention and opposition of the English physicist John Tyndall. Although Bastian's advocacy of spontaneous generation depended on a wide range of experimental evidence and theoretical considerations, his dispute with Pasteur focused very narrowly on one issue: whether microorganisms can originate spontaneously in neutral or alkaline urine. Pasteur seems publicly to have ignored Bastian's work until the latter sent a note to the Académie des Sciences in which he claimed that microorganisms appeared under carefully specified conditions in urine that had been boiled and subsequently protected from atmospheric germs. According to Bastian, the requisite physicochemical conditions were the intervention of potash and oxygen and a storage temperature of 50° C. On the assumption that the boiling killed any organism in the urine, Bastian claimed to have produced spontaneous generation.

Within a week Pasteur had repeated Bastian's experiment and had confirmed in most cases his central result—boiled urine rendered alkaline by aqueous potash did indeed yield microbial life in germ-free air.

With Bastian's interpretation of this result, however, Pasteur profoundly disagreed. In his view Bastian's result merely proved "that certain inferior germs resist 100° C. in neutral or slightly alkaline media, no doubt because their envelopes are not penetrated by water under these conditions as they are . . . [in] slightly acid media."[101] He referred Bastian to his memoir of 1861 on organized corpuscles in the atmosphere, in which he had discussed the heat resistance of microorganisms in alkaline media, and challenged him to repeat his experiments using potash—whether solid or in aqueous solution—that had been previously heated to 110° C. Under these conditions, Pasteur asserted, the urine would remain sterile and Bastian's "spontaneous generation" would cease to exist.

The terms of Pasteur's challenge imply his belief that Bastian had unwittingly introduced the germs of microbial life into his urine flasks by using germ-charged potash or germ-charged water. Over the next several months Bastian refused to abandon his claim, insisting on the absurdity of the notion that germs could resist so caustic a substance as potash, demanding a direct demonstration of the heat resistance of germs, and complaining that his experimental procedures (including the exact neutralization of urine by potash) had not been faithfully reproduced by Pasteur and his collaborators, Jules Joubert and Charles Chamberland. As they fended off these objections, Pasteur and his collaborators sought to establish more precisely the external origin and degree of heat resistance of the germs supposedly introduced into Bastian's flasks. Pasteur and Joubert launched a study of the distribution of germs in water, reinforcing and extending the earlier results of the English physiologist Burdon-Sanderson concerning the enormous quantity of bacteria in ordinary streams and the presence of germs even in distilled water unless it was stored in vessels rendered germ-free by flaming. They also noted the absence of germs in water from deep sources, where surface germs could not penetrate, and insisted on the extreme minuteness of the bacterial germs, which passed through all ordinary filters and required the invention of a new method for their collection (presumably a prototype of Chamberland's porcelain bacterial filter).

In July 1877, having accepted Pasteur's challenge to submit their dispute to a commission of the Académie des Sciences, Bastian went to Paris to repeat his experiment in the presence of this commission. Like Pouchet, however, Bastian eventually withdrew after a long and confusing dispute with the commissioners.[102] Once again facing a commission on spontaneous generation without an opponent, Pasteur reaffirmed his claim that neutral urine could be kept sterile if all proper precautions were observed. By this time he had clearly identified three possible sources of germ contamination in Bastian's experiments: to the potash solution originally suspected he added the experimental apparatus (even when carefully washed, since all water contains germs) and the urine, which can from the outset harbor germs capable of surviving boiling at 100° C. He did not yet fully appreciate the latter possibility, however, believing that the acidity of the normal urine with which Bastian began would prevent the appearance of these heat-resistant germs, and he chose instead to indict contaminated apparatus as the source of germs in Bastian's experiments.

Only after Cohn, Koch, Tyndall, and others had established the existence of highly resistant bacterial endospores; only when it became clear that certain microorganisms could survive a temperature of 100° C. even in acid media; and only as microbial life continued to appear in certain liquids (notably urine and infusions of hay or cheese) despite every precaution to eliminate germs from the experimental apparatus— only then did Pasteur begin fully to perceive the possibility that the liquids used by Pouchet, Bastian, and other advocates of spontaneous generation may sometimes have harbored microbial life from the beginning rather than having subsequently acquired it through careless experimental technique.

By this time other aspects of Pasteur's doctrine had come under open and serious challenge, especially in England.[103] Some challenged his evidence that the "organized corpuscles" in the air were living organisms, for that evidence was largely indirect and failed to establish a direct link between any particular living microorganism and its presumed antecedent germ or corpuscle. Others asked how germs living in the air— and thus presumably aerobic—could be responsible for processes that Pasteur ascribed to the activity of anaerobic microorganisms. To meet this argument, Pasteur suggested that germs possessed only latent life while in the air and therefore should not be called aerobic organisms in the ordinary sense of the word.[104]

More or less convergent with these challenges were two doubts shared even by those who fully accepted his claim that the air contained living ferments. One doubt concerned whether the atmosphere in fact carried as much microbial life as Pasteur supposed. Pasteur himself had contributed toward this question by showing that microbial life was variably disseminated in the atmosphere and was certainly not so widespread as to exist in every sample of air. He had also drawn attention to the relatively high concentration of microbial life on grape clusters and in water as compared with the atmosphere, but some of his contemporaries advocated an even greater shift of emphasis to liquids and solid surfaces. The second doubt concerned the precise meaning of Pasteur's often casual use of "germ." In 1877 Burdon-Sanderson argued that Pasteur's "organized corpuscles" were in fact finished, adult microorganisms and not their "germs" or precursors.[105]

In both cases subsequent research has tended to confirm the doubts. Indeed, Pasteur himself emphasized in 1878 that surgeons had far more to fear from germs on their instruments or hands than from germs in the air,[106] and he seems not to have disputed the growing belief that many of his "germs" were adult microorganisms. Insofar as the word "germs" is used for adult microorganisms today, it is merely a perpetuation of Pasteur's vague designation.

On the other hand, none of these doubts and criticisms really undermined Pasteur's central positions on spontaneous generation and on "the infinite role of infinitely small" organisms. If some of his earlier views now required modification, and if Cohn, Tyndall, and others ultimately contributed as much as he to the still dominant sentiment against the doctrine of spontaneous generation, he had nonetheless laid the groundwork. Nor did Pasteur fail to derive practical benefit from the new attention to bacterial spores and to liquids and solids as the main vehicles of germ contamination. In Pasteur's laboratory, and almost certainly under his watchful eye, Chamberland pursued some of the issues arising from the dispute with Bastian. In his doctoral dissertation (1879) Chamberland established the basic rules of modern bacteriological technique by showing that temperatures of at least 115° C. were required to ensure the destruction of heat-resistant microorganisms in liquids, while temperatures of at least 180° C. were required to achieve the same result on dry surfaces. Especially in the wake of Chamberland's work, the autoclave and the flaming of glassware became standard in microbiological equipment and technique.[107]

Pasteur and Medicine: The Background. Almost from the beginning of his work on fermentation and spontaneous generation, Pasteur made frequent reference to its potential medical implications. Sharing the common belief that fermentation and disease were analogous processes, he naturally supposed that the germ theory could apply to disease as well as to fermentation—as Theodor Schwann, among others, had supposed before him. In fact, in the late 1850's, when Pasteur began his study of fermentation and spontaneous generation, the status of the germ theory of disease paralleled almost precisely the status of the germ theory of fermentation. In both cases the germ theory held less favor than alternative theories, but serious claims had been made for it on the basis of solid and highly suggestive evidence. Advocates of the germ theory of fermentation appealed chiefly to evidence that yeast was a living organism; the germ theory of disease drew its most impressive support from accumulating evidence of the important role played by living parasites in a number of plant and animal diseases, including such human maladies as trichinosis, scabies, and the fungal skin diseases, notably scalp favus.

At the same time, however, critics of the germ theory could cite apparently contradictory evidence, could insist that any microorganisms associated with disease or fermentation were merely epiphenomenal products of these processes rather than their cause, and could argue that the alleged examples of microbial processes were atypical or unimportant. With regard to disease, even those who accepted the pathogenic role of microscopic parasites in certain diseases often doubted or denied their role in the major killer diseases of man or other vertebrates. The notion that tiny living agents could kill vastly larger organisms struck many as absurd. Moreover, the complexity of disease, and the peculiarity of its expression in each patient, impressed most physicians with the seeming irregularity, spontaneity, and mystery of the process. From this perspective the germ theory of disease seemed too simplistic, inflexible, and remote, particularly because it emphasized the role of agents possessing a life and origin independent of the organisms in which disease became manifest.

In contrast with the emphasis of the germ theory on the "exteriority" of disease, the dominant concepts of the process stressed the internal state and quality of the affected organism. When external agents found a place in these schemes—and the existence of epidemics virtually required their inclusion—they were generally denied a life of their own and accorded a distinctly secondary role. In traditional medical doctrine these external agents—whether meteorological conditions, "cosmic-telluric" forces, subtle fluids, noxious effluvia, chemical poisons, or inanimate particles—acted chiefly as contributors to, or as transmitters of, pathological states the proximate genesis of which was internal and spontaneous. In Pasteur's view the future of medicine depended on a literally life-and-death struggle against this traditional doctrine of the interiority and spontaneity of disease, a doctrine which found capsule expression in the slogan "Disease is in us, of us, by us."[108]

Through his efforts on behalf of the germ theory of fermentation and against spontaneous generation, Pasteur became a highly influential, if largely indirect, participant in this struggle during the two decades after 1857. His studies on the silkworm diseases may seem to represent his most direct and important contribution to the germ theory of disease, but persuasive evidence of microbial participation in certain insect diseases had long existed without transforming medical theory. Vastly more influential in this regard were two medical contributions immediately inspired and encouraged by Pasteur's work on fermentation. The more familiar and dramatic of these was antiseptic surgery, introduced in the 1860's by Lister, who openly saluted Pasteur for having provided in the germ theory of fermentation "the sole principle" upon which the antiseptic system had been built.[109] Although only gradually and rather reluctantly accepted, especially in England, Lister's method eventually created a revolution in surgery and enormously advanced the cause of the germ theory of disease.

Almost simultaneously the French pathologist Casimir Joseph Davaine sought to establish a microbial etiology for anthrax or splenic fever, taking as his point of departure a paper by Pasteur on the fermentation of butyric acid. Struck by the similarity between Pasteur's butyric ferment and some rods he had observed more than a decade before in anthrax blood, Davaine in 1863 launched his attempt to demonstrate experimentally that anthrax was caused by these rod-like organisms or "bacteridia." Ultimately the path from Pasteur's work on fermentation to Davaine's on anthrax carried traffic both ways, for anthrax became the subject of Pasteur's first excursion into medical research per se. Twice in 1865 Pasteur took part in discussions on anthrax at the Académie des Sciences. On both occasions he gave qualified support to Davaine's basic position, but the tone of his remarks betrayed his belief that anthrax remained obscure in many respects.[110] As early as 1867 he specifically identified anthrax as the disease he hoped soon to study.[111] Not until 1877, however, did he publish the first of his papers on anthrax.

For a man of his bold readiness to tackle the major problems of the day, and for a man whose research had so long approached the medical domain, Pasteur seems to have hesitated a surprisingly long time before entering the struggle against traditional medical doctrine. His hesitation is all the more surprising because it persisted despite his expressed desire to undertake specifically medical research and his possessing ample opportunity, adequate resources, and—in a sense—an imperial mandate to do so. This mandate—along with the resources and facilities to carry it out—followed a remarkable appeal that Pasteur addressed simultaneously (on 5 September 1867) to Louis Napoleon and to the minister of public instruction.

Having just removed Pasteur from his administrative posts at the École Normale, the Ministry of Public

Instruction had offered him a professorship in chemistry at the Sorbonne and a position as *maître de conférences* in organic chemistry at the École Normale, with the right to retain his old apartment and laboratory there. Pasteur submitted a counter proposal. He agreed fully with his appointment at the Sorbonne but objected to the proposed position at the École Normale on several grounds, including his concern that two teaching posts might impede his research. Instead, he proposed the construction at the École Normale of a new, spacious, and well-endowed laboratory of physiological chemistry in which he would not teach but would continue his research. He supported his proposal by referring to "the necessity of maintaining the scientific superiority of France against the efforts of rival nations" and by projecting studies of immense practical importance on infectious diseases in general and on anthrax in particular.[112]

The emperor immediately expressed his support for Pasteur's project in a letter to the minister of public instruction. Construction began in August 1868, the cost of 60,000 francs being shared equally by the Ministry of Public Instruction and the Ministry of the House of the Emperor. The new laboratory, thirty meters long, was to be linked by a gallery with the pavilion Pasteur had occupied since 1859. Largely because of the Franco-Prussian War, however, the laboratory remained incomplete as late as 1871. In September of that year, following the departure from Paris of the Prussian troops and the Communards, Pasteur returned from the provinces and immediately asked to be relieved of his remaining teaching duties at the Sorbonne because of his health. Claiming thirty years in university service (including his days as a tutor at Besançon), he requested a retirement pension as well as a separate national recompense in recognition of his contributions.[113]

By 1874, when Pasteur achieved the last of these goals, he had still taken no direct steps toward the study of anthrax projected in 1867. For the first four of the intervening years, his attention had been diverted by his desire to complete the silkworm studies under way since 1865 and by the Franco-Prussian War. By late 1871, however, he had solved the silkworm problem to his satisfaction and had at his disposal the new and presumably disease-oriented laboratory, as well as an annual research allowance of 6,000 francs. And yet, instead of turning to the direct study of disease, he continued through 1876 to devote his energies and the resources of his laboratory to his studies on beer and to the persistent controversies over spontaneous generation and his germ theory of fermentation.

To a degree Pasteur considered the solution of these problems—and especially the destruction of the doctrine of spontaneous generation—a prerequisite to the direct and effective study of disease.[114] But in the paper of 1877 that marked his full-fledged entry into the medical arena, Pasteur offered another explanation for his prior absence. Although long "tormented" with the desire of tackling the great medical problems of the day, he wrote, he had hesitated until now for two reasons: (1) he had needed a "courageous and devoted collaborator," a requirement at last fulfilled in Jules Joubert, and (2) being "a stranger to medical and veterinary knowledge," he had needed to overcome his fear of his own "insufficiency."[115]

That Pasteur required assistance to undertake the experimental study of disease can scarcely be denied—not only because of his partial paralysis but also because of his attitude toward vivisection. As one who found vivisection personally repugnant,[116] and yet considered it essential to his task, he needed collaborators who were willing and able to undertake the animal experiments he designed. But in view of the seeming ease with which he attracted such assistants—not only Joubert but also Duclaux, Chamberland, Émile Roux, Louis Thuillier, and Adrien Loir—one wonders whether he could not have found them long before 1877 had he really tried. On the other hand, Pasteur's fear of "insufficiency"—while scarcely in keeping with his usual self-assurance and his bold excursions into other fields in which he could claim no professional competence—does find some echo in his general ambivalence toward holders of the M.D. degree. Although he tended to disdain doctors for their traditionalism, their pretensions to scientific knowledge, and their preference for ritual and oratory over experiment, he envied their social status, their clinical experience, and their immediate, dramatic utility.

Much of this ambivalence emerged during meetings of the Académie de Médecine, where Pasteur became a frequent and controversial participant after his election to membership in 1873. Besides repeatedly defending his views on fermentation, putrefaction, and spontaneous generation, he occasionally ventured into discussions of more strictly medical topics even before 1877—most notably on urinary disorders and the use of cotton wool dressings in surgery. As might be expected, he linked ammoniacal urine with the "true ferment of urine" which he had discovered in the early 1860's and which had since been studied in great detail by van Tieghem. For the treatment of such disorders he proposed the injection into the bladder of antiseptics, particularly dilute boric acid, the destructive action of which on the ammoniacal ferment he examined and the therapeutic efficacy of which he later affirmed on the basis of clinical reports from those willing to adopt his suggestion.[117]

With regard to cotton wool dressings, Pasteur argued that their efficacy depended not on the exclusion of air, as many surgeons supposed, but on the capacity of cotton wool to trap germs without impeding the circulation over the wound of presumably beneficial pure oxygen.[118] If physicians and surgeons were annoyed by these unsolicited incursions into their domain by a "mere chemist," they were incensed by his implicit charge that they often produced disease by carrying pathogenic microorganisms into their patients on contaminated hands or instruments. As early as 1874, in a passage reflecting his deep commitment to the germ theory of disease before he had entered strictly medical research, Pasteur wrote: "If I had the honor of being a surgeon, I would never introduce any instrument into the human body without having passed it through boiling water, or better yet through a flame, immediately before the operation."[119]

The Etiology of Anthrax: The Background. By the time Pasteur finally did undertake his study of anthrax, its etiology had been largely resolved. Perhaps because it was a well-defined, economically important, and often fatal epidemic disease of large animals—particularly of cattle and sheep, although it could occur in humans in the form of "the malignant pustule"—anthrax had long been the subject of intense study and controversy. Davaine's work of the 1860's therefore aroused great interest, and anthrax quickly became a major focus for the debate between advocates and opponents of the germ theory of disease. Advocates of the germ theory emphasized Davaine's claim that bacteridia always appeared in the blood of animals afflicted with anthrax but never in that of animals free of its symptoms, while opponents of the theory denied this invariable association and insisted that Davaine had failed in any case to prove the causative role of the bacteridia. If he had shown that anthrax blood could transmit the disease from one animal to another, he had not fully demonstrated that the bacteridia were the agents of this transmission. Moreover, Davaine's conception of anthrax scarcely helped to explain its behavior under natural conditions—its appearance or frequency in any given season or why it should selectively attack certain herds or fields while sparing others. His attempt to implicate flies as vectors of the infection failed to account persuasively for these and other features of the disease.[120]

Into this breach stepped Robert Koch, whose classic study of 1876 unraveled the complete life cycle of Davaine's bacteridia (Koch's *Bacillus anthracis*) and established the existence of an endospore phase. These anthrax spores, which preserved the virulence of the rods, could form in the blood and tissues of an animal after death and, once formed, resisted subsequent putrefaction or drying. Koch immediately recognized that these resistant spores held the key to understanding the natural behavior of anthrax, for they could retain their pathogenicity from one season to the next and could produce a recurrence of the disease in specific localities under appropriate conditions of temperature and moisture. Suggesting that natural infection probably took place through the food, he proposed preventive measures against the disease. In addition he developed new techniques for cultivating the anthrax bacillus and showed that successive cultures remained virulent despite repeated dilution.

Pasteur on the Etiology of Anthrax and Septicemia. Despite these achievements, which attracted widespread attention and acclaim, Pasteur believed that some doubts remained. As evidence he cited Paul Bert's claim of January 1877 that anthrax blood could produce death even after its bacteridia had been killed by compressed oxygen. Since death occurred "without any trace" of bacteridia, Bert concluded that the latter were "neither the cause nor the necessary effect of anthrax." Instead, he ascribed the disease to a "virus," by which he meant a soluble chemical poison or some other inanimate agent. In his first memoir on anthrax (April 1877), Pasteur challenged Bert's hypothesis by extending Koch's successive dilution experiments. By greatly increasing the number of cultures (Koch had stopped at eight) and by using a much larger volume of cultural liquid each time, Pasteur diluted an initial drop of anthrax blood to the point of virtual disappearance. Nonetheless, each successive culture retained the original virulence. In his view this result persuasively established the dependence of anthrax on a living microorganism, for no other agent could have retained its power through so drastic a dilution. Only an agent which reproduced itself in each successive culture—almost certainly a living organism—could be responsible for the continued virulence of the original drop of blood. If Bert's hypothetical chemical poison did exist, it must be capable of self-reproduction or must be continuously secreted by the multiplying bacteridia. But these possibilities, remote in any case, became even more so in view of the fact that the filtered liquid from each culture (which ought to contain any soluble poison) produced no effect when injected.

In his next paper on anthrax (July 1877), Pasteur offered his own interpretation of Bert's experiment and applied it as well to the most damaging earlier evidence against Davaine's work. In essence, he argued that the architects of this earlier evidence (notably Leplat and Jaillard), and probably Bert as well, had confused anthrax with a form of septicemia. As early as 1865, when Davaine made a similar charge, Pasteur had lent credence to it by reporting that Leplat and Jaillard's supposed anthrax blood contained putrefactive microorganisms foreign to anthrax.[121] What he sought now to do was to develop this argument and, more generally, to clarify the relationship between anthrax and septicemia. In this relationship, he insisted, the crucial factor is the time that elapses between death and the extraction of blood. At first, for perhaps eighteen hours, the blood of an animal dead of anthrax contains only the anthrax bacteridia. Eventually, however, this blood undergoes putrefaction and the bacteridia progressively disappear. Despite this disappearance, or despite the destruction of the bacteridia by compressed oxygen, the blood can remain virulent and can produce death in another animal.

One reason for the continued virulence, Pasteur suggested, was that such blood might continue to harbor anthrax bacteridia in the endospore phase, for the anthrax spores not only resist putrefaction (as Koch had already shown) but also survive the action of compressed oxygen. In such cases, however, the spores ought to germinate when injected into another animal, reproducing ordinary anthrax with its familiar rods. But Leplat and Jaillard, and apparently Bert as well, had insisted that their injections of anthrax blood had produced death in the absence of any microorganisms whatever. In these cases, Pasteur argued, the blood must have ceased to carry anthrax and must have become putrid or septic instead. More important, he claimed that the most familiar effects of putrid or septic injections also depended upon a microorganism —the hitherto unknown *vibrion septique*—and not an inanimate septic "virus," as was commonly believed. To explain how the *vibrion septique* had previously escaped detection, Pasteur focused on the preoccupation of earlier observers with the blood, a concern that had distracted them from a systematic search for pathogenic microorganisms in other parts of the body. In an animal dying of septicemia, microorganisms could be found in abundance in the muscles and in the abdominal serosities near the intestinal canal, but not in the blood until just before death. And when these organisms finally did enter the bloodstream, they became peculiarly long and translucent and easily escaped detection.

But even if such organisms did exist, and even if they had invaded the blood used by Bert, how could they have retained their virulence after being subjected to compressed oxygen? Pasteur's answer hinged on the assertion that the new septic vibrio, like the anthrax bacteridium, had a resistant spore phase. In fact, he insisted, this spore phase appears within hours of the application of compressed oxygen to septic blood. Preserved in this immobile, resistant phase from further attack by oxygen, the septic vibrio can return to its motile, filamentary phase upon injection into another animal, producing death with the usual symptoms of septicemia. With only slightly less confidence, Pasteur suggested that the septic vibrio was one of the putrefactive vibrios found in the intestinal canal. If so, septicemia might properly be called "putrefaction on the living." And since various putrefactive vibrios exist, one could expect a corresponding range of septic infections from the inoculation of putrid materials.

On the way to this new interpretation of Bert's experiment—which Bert soon adopted—Pasteur offered some novel views on the physiological properties and modus operandi of the anthrax bacteridia. Having observed that filtered anthrax serum produced agglutination of the blood, he suggested that this familiar symptom of the disease might be due to a soluble ferment produced by the bacteridia. But this suggestion produced no shift in his basic conviction that the bacteridia themselves, and not any soluble ferment, were responsible for death from anthrax. In search of a mechanism by which the bacteridia might kill, he began by insisting on their aerobic character. Once in the blood, he supposed, these aerobic bacteridia would compete with the red blood cells, "those aerobic beings *par excellence*," for oxygen. If the bacteridia won this struggle for existence, the animal would die of asphyxia, as suggested by the black color of the blood and viscera. In support of this notion, Pasteur reported that other aerobic microorganisms could impede the development of the bacteridia in cultural liquids or in animal bodies. Most remarkably, even animals highly susceptible to anthrax could survive an injection of bacteridia so long as the latter were accompanied by competing aerobic microorganisms. By his suggestion that these facts "authorize the greatest hopes from the therapeutic point of view," Pasteur has won credit as a prophet of bacteriotherapy, in the development of which he played no direct or substantial role.[122]

In March 1878 Pasteur described a remarkable new experiment on which he placed great importance for both the etiology and the treatment of anthrax. He showed that it was possible to transmit anthrax to hens, which are ordinarily refractory, merely by lowering their body temperature a few degrees. Aware that anthrax bacteridia could not develop in otherwise appropriate media at a temperature above 44° C., Pasteur had wondered whether the natural immunity of hens to anthrax might be due to the naturally elevated temperature of their blood. By plunging the legs of a chicken in an ice bath, he lowered its blood temperature several degrees; previously injected bacteridia were then able to develop and to induce death from anthrax. Conversely, he was able to prevent anthrax in rabbits, which are ordinarily susceptible, by raising their blood temperature several degrees. On this basis he hoped that it might prove possible to cure humans of "malignant pustule" by placing them in a bath warm enough to maintain a blood temperature of 41–42° C. By July 1878 he had cured a chilled hen of advanced anthrax by warming it. When some members of the Académie de Médecine raised objections against these experiments, Pasteur effectively demolished them in dramatic confrontations before the full Academy and by demanding a judiciary commission, which verified the exactitude of his results. In the light of subsequent research, Pasteur's interpretation of these results, as well as the therapeutic hopes he based on them, seem somewhat naïve, for such drastic changes in body temperature produce effects far more general and profound than those bearing directly on the anthrax bacteridia. Nonetheless, his results offered striking experimental evidence that receptivity to disease depends on factors beyond the mere presence of pathogenic agents.

Pasteur on the Etiology of Natural Anthrax. Beginning with reports to the minister of agriculture in September and October 1879, and more fully in a memoir of July 1880, Pasteur extended and refined Koch's views on the etiology of natural anthrax. Through feeding experiments on large domestic animals (which Koch had not used), he confirmed Koch's suggestion that the natural mode of transmission was the food. More specifically, he showed that sheep could contract anthrax by ingesting bacteridia spores, especially when the spores were mixed with a prickly diet of thistle leaves or short barbs of oats and barley. The resulting lesions strongly suggested that the disease began in the mouth and back of the throat. To explain how sheep and cattle came upon anthrax spores under natural conditions, Pasteur recalled that these spores withstood putrefaction and could therefore persist for months or even years in soil where diseased animals had been buried. Indeed, these spores could be found on the soil above such graves—where grazing animals might ingest them—while no spores could be found on the soil just a few meters away. In this way the existence of "infected fields" could be readily understood; they were fields in which animals dead of anthrax had been buried.

Pasteur's most original contribution to the problem concerned the mechanism by which the immotile anthrax spores were brought from animal graves to the surface of the earth. The agent of this transfer, he insisted, was the common earthworm. After several days in soil containing anthrax spores, earthworms carried the spores in their intestinal canals. When they rose to the surface, they ejected these spores along with their earth castings. Once on the surface, the anthrax spores could attach to the plants on which sheep and cattle grazed or—as Pasteur recognized in January 1881[123]—could be inhaled. These conclusions authorized a fairly obvious and simple prophylactic measure: animals dead of anthrax must never be buried in fields intended for grazing or the growing of fodder, at least not unless the soil in such fields was inimical to earthworms. If this measure were followed, Pasteur rather extravagantly predicted, anthrax could be a thing of the past, for the disease is never spontaneous and can be found only where its germs have been disseminated "by the innocent complicity of earthworms."[124]

The Extension of the Germ Theory to Other Diseases. Although Pasteur's work on the etiology of anthrax and septicemia was largely a confirmation and extension of Koch's work, it helped to raise anthrax to its special status as the first major killer disease of large animals widely admitted to be parasitic. Besides lending credence and interest to a series of earlier but inconclusive attempts to implicate microorganisms in major vertebrate and human diseases, this achievement ushered in what came to be known as the golden age of bacteriology. In less than two decades the microbial theory of disease was extended to tuberculosis, cholera, diphtheria, typhoid, gonorrhea, pneumonia, tetanus, and plague. Surprisingly, Pasteur and the French school contributed only minimally. The vast majority of these pathogenic microorganisms were isolated and studied by Koch and the German school, thanks in part to Koch's mastery of microscopic morphology, classification, and technique and more particularly to his method of pure solid cultures, which Pasteur praised without adopting. For the most part Pasteur and the French school focused instead on the problems of immunity from and prophylaxis against microbial diseases—in a word, on vaccination.[125] But only after 1880 did these differences become dramatically clear, to be quickly reinforced by national and personal rivalries. Between 1878 and 1880 Pasteur and Koch seemed to be aiming toward similar goals: the elucidation of septicemia in its various forms and the extension of the germ theory to diseases other than anthrax.

Pasteur's contributions toward these goals include a lecture of April 1878, "La théorie des germes et ses applications à la médecine et la chirurgie," and a memoir of May 1880 on the extension of the germ theory to the etiology of certain common diseases. In the 1878 lecture, delivered before the Académie de Médecine, Pasteur described the results of studies undertaken on the *vibrion septique* since discovering it the year before. To a large degree these results merely gave more explicit, elaborate, and confident form to his original conception of the septic vibrio. After several unsuccessful attempts to cultivate this organism by ordinary means, Pasteur and his collaborators had decided that it might be an obligate anaerobe, incapable of living in the presence of the oxygen dissolved in ordinary cultural liquids. They therefore switched to cultures in a vacuum or an atmosphere of carbon dioxide, with immediate success. But this obligate anaerobism applied only to the motile, filamentary phase of the vibrio. In its spore phase, the *vibrion septique* could obviously live in oxygen; it even survived the compressed oxygen used by Bert. The persistent virulence of the septic blood in Bert's experiment—as well as the existence of natural septicemia in any form—depended absolutely on this spore phase. Only in the form of resistant spores could the otherwise anaerobic vibrio exist in ordinary air, ready to germinate and to produce septicemia if the spores penetrated a portion of an animal where oxygen was absent or nearly so. Until they reached such a site, the spores could not germinate and thus remained harmless.

In other words, Pasteur argued, the *vibrion septique* may be harmless or pathogenic according to environmental circumstances, just as its form, reproductive capacity, and virulence vary in different artificial media. Similarly, one of the most common bacteria resembles the anthrax bacillus in its physiological properties—including obligate aerobism—and yet is harmless because it cannot live at the temperature of the animal body. Yet another vibrio—the hitherto unrecognized "microbe of pus"—resembles yeast in its capacity to live either aerobically or anaerobically. And, like any solid body, the microbe of pus produces an abscess, or pocket of pus, upon injection into a guinea pig or rabbit. But the inordinate size of the resulting abscess clearly depends on the vital activity of the new microbe; if killed by heat before injection, it produces a much smaller abscess. Although far less dangerous than the anthrax bacillus or the *vibrion septique*, the microbe of pus can sometimes produce metastatic abscesses, purulent infection, and death. It can also modify the action and virulence of those more dangerous microorganisms when associated with them. More generally, the nature and relative proportions of specific microbes determine a richly varied set of pathological states.

If this is the central thrust of Pasteur's lecture of April 1878, the message must be extracted from a diffuse and atypically obscure presentation of his views. In the same lecture, and more or less haphazardly, he also described methods for separating aerobic

from anaerobic microorganisms; mentioned the difficulties his results posed for microbial classification; offered hygienic advice to surgeons; insisted that the acquired knowledge of anthrax and septicemia upset the doctrine of spontaneity; and argued that the *vibrion septique* was the true cause (rather than a product) of septicemia, probably without the intervention of any soluble ferment. In his advice to surgeons, probably the most famous section of the lecture, Pasteur repeated and embellished the counsel he had given in 1874, before his entry into the medical arena. After the same opening phrase ("if I had the honor to be a surgeon"), he stated: "Impressed as I am with the dangers to which the patient is exposed by the germs of microbes scattered over the surface of all objects, particularly in hospitals, not only would I use none but perfectly clean instruments, but after having cleansed my hands with the greatest care and subjected them to a rapid flaming . . . I would use only lint, bandages and sponges previously exposed to air of a temperature of 130 to 150° C.; I would never use any water which had not been subjected to a temperature of 110 to 120° C." Finally, Pasteur quoted with pride from a lecture given at the Académie des Sciences several weeks earlier by the distinguished surgeon Sédillot, who introduced the word "microbe" for microorganism and enthusiastically supported the germ theory and the new "Listerian" surgery arising from it.

In his paper of May 1880, "De l'extension de la théorie des germes à l'étiologie de quelques maladies communes," Pasteur implicated microbes in furuncles (boils), osteomyelitis, and puerperal fever. He reached his views on boils and on osteomyelitis after studying a single case of each. The case of boils belonged to one of Pasteur's own assistants (Duclaux). When pricked and submitted to culture, these boils gave a unique aerobic microbe of the form later called staphylococcus, to which Pasteur ascribed the local inflammation and consequent pus. When he found this same microbe in pus taken from the infected bone of a girl, he boldly asserted that "osteomyelitis is the boil of the bone marrow." In his discussion of puerperal fever, Pasteur described seven cases of the disease, in each of which he found highly presumptive evidence of microbial participation, and then developed the views he had already expressed during a debate on puerperal fever at the Académie de Médecine in March 1879.[126] During that debate Pasteur asserted that a microbe shaped like strings of beads caused most childbed infections, and he joined Semmelweiss in charging doctors themselves with the transmission of these infections. With his usual tone of disdain toward those who tried to classify microbes, he noted that some German authors had given the Latin name "micrococcus" to organisms having the form of the new puerperal microbe—including the ferment of ammoniacal urine and the microbe of *flacherie*—and had even tried to implicate micrococci in puerperal fever. Despite these attempts the etiology of puerperal fever remained obscure, chiefly because various microbes associated with pus could intervene to modify the symptoms and course of the disease. Finally, for the treatment of puerperal infections, Pasteur advocated the use of sterile water and bandages and, more specifically, the application to the infected genital tissues of a 4 percent solution of boric acid, which combined the advantages of known destructiveness toward at least one micrococcus (the ferment of ammoniacal urine) and inoffensiveness to mucous membranes.

Immunity, Virus Diseases, and the Discovery of Vaccines: The Background. From the outset of his work on anthrax, and even as his study of septic infections converged with the German effort to identify new pathogenic microbes, Pasteur pondered what were then known in France as the "virus diseases." Typified by smallpox and presumed to be nonmicrobial, their most striking feature was that they did not recur (or recurred in milder form) in the same individual. The strength of the "virus" (or poison) considered responsible for each of these diseases was usually assumed to be fixed and uniform for any given species but variable from one species to another. In particular the cowpox virus, which maintained a constant virulence through hundreds of transfers from man to man, clearly declined in strength when passed from cow to man. Thus "humanized," the cowpox virus became the "vaccine" introduced by Edward Jenner at the end of the eighteenth century to protect man from attacks of smallpox. Most authorities adopted Jenner's belief that his vaccine was simply a milder form of the smallpox virus, modified by passage through the cow. But others claimed that smallpox and cowpox were independent diseases, due to distinct viruses of inherently different strengths. Variations in severity between different smallpox epidemics and in the course of the same epidemic, as well as variations in the duration of the immunity produced, further obscured the nature of the virus diseases. Moreover, attempts to find "vaccines" or modified viruses against other diseases had produced nothing, and Jenner's vaccine remained unique.

As early as June 1877, Pasteur announced that he had begun to study the virus diseases, and particularly the cowpox virus that served as Jenner's vaccine.[127] He clearly hoped to isolate a cowpox microbe (a vain hope), and he may already have perceived some con-

nection between the virus diseases and the microbial diseases of anthrax and septicemia. In fact, Davaine and others had already shown that anthrax and septicemia shared one property of the virus diseases: their virulence could be modified by passage through living animals. But the meaning of this isolated fact was obscure, and the possibility that such variations might be related to variations in the microbes of anthrax and septicemia ran afoul of the doctrine of microbial specificity. Although Pasteur had done much to establish this doctrine, and continued to deny the transmutability of microbial species, his position was somewhat more flexible than that of Cohn or Koch. During his study of septicemia, he noticed that different cultures of the *vibrion septique* varied in virulence when injected into animals. At first, in keeping with the doctrine of microbial specificity, he supposed that these variable virulences depended on different species or varieties of septic vibrio. In April 1878, however, in his lecture on the germ theory to the Académie de Médecine, he suggested that these variations should be ascribed to the effects of different cultural media on the properties of a single *vibrion septique*. To suspect a connection between microbial diseases and the virus diseases, and to recognize that the virulence of the *vibrion septique* could be artificially modified, were to take some preliminary steps toward the concept of attenuated viruses and the technique of vaccination. But these early, almost instinctive steps gained real force and direction only through Pasteur's study of fowl cholera.

Fowl Cholera and the Discovery of Vaccines. In December 1878 Toussaint, a professor at the Alfort Veterinary School, sent Pasteur some blood from a cock dead of fowl cholera.[128] The symptoms of this disease, which has no relation to human cholera, include weakness, loss of coordination, droopy wings, erect feathers, and somnolence usually ending in death. Its progress through an infected poultry yard can be extremely swift, with most of the hens dead or dying in a few days. Like a few others before him, Toussaint linked the disease with a microbe, which he found in the blood of all hens having the disease. Beginning with the blood sent him by Toussaint, Pasteur immediately sought to isolate the microbe in a state of perfect purity[129] and to demonstrate by the method of successive cultures that it was the true and sole cause of fowl cholera. He soon found that this nonmotile microbe—in the form of a figure eight but so tiny as to resemble isolated dots—developed much more readily in neutral chicken broth than in the neutral urine used by Toussaint. By March 1879 he had found that a culture almost uniformly fatal for chickens was relatively benign for guinea pigs, and he drew an analogy between the guinea pig and yeast extract, both being cultural media ill-suited to the development of the fowl cholera microbe.[130]

In February 1880 Pasteur announced that although the fowl cholera microbe retained its virulence through successive cultures in chicken broth, he had found a way of decreasing its virulence "by certain changes in the mode of culture." In this milder form the microbe usually produced disease, but not death, in chickens. More important, the chickens that recovered from this less virulent form of the microbe became relatively immune to the highly virulent form. Unlike ordinary chickens they did not die from an injection of the microbe in its usual form. In other words, Pasteur concluded, "The disease is its own preventive. It has the character of the virus diseases, which do not recur." What gave this result special importance and novelty was the demonstrably microbial nature of fowl cholera. Preventive inoculations were not new, but they had never been used against a disease known to be caused by a microorganism that might be cultivated outside of living organisms. Never had it been known that the property of nonrecurrence, associated with the so-called virus diseases, could belong to a microbial disease. Fowl cholera thus formed the first clear link between microbial diseases and diseases "in the virus of which life has never been recognized." Although many difficulties remained before the attenuated microbe of fowl cholera could be properly compared with Jenner's vaccine—in particular, its constancy through a series of inoculations had yet to be assured —it offered hope that every "virus" might be artificially cultivated and that "vaccines" might be obtained against the infectious diseases "which afflict humanity, and which are the greatest scourge of agriculture in the rearing of domestic animals."

In announcing these dramatic results, Pasteur declined to reveal the method by which he had obtained the attenuated form of the fowl cholera microbe, saying that he wished to assure independence in his studies. Despite complaints from members of the Académie de Médecine in particular, he persisted in this course for nine months, during which period he reported the results of his subsequent studies. In April 1880 he admitted that inoculation with the attenuated form of the fowl cholera microbe produced very different results in different hens, but he insisted that the procedure always conferred some benefit. Even when two or more inoculations were required for complete protection against the disease, each acted in some measure to impede its course. He emphasized that "vaccinated" chickens, as well as species naturally resistant to the disease, must represent cultural media somehow ill-suited for the development of the microbe and suggested that this immunity probably resulted from the absence of some substance essential to the life of the microbe.

This suggestion drew support from the fact that cultivations of whatever sort (whether ordinary plants, parasites, or microbes) modify a given medium (or "soil") in such a way as to make subsequent cultivations of the same species difficult or impossible. Thus, after four days as a medium for the fowl cholera microbe, chicken broth will not support a new inoculation of the microbe. After the second day it will do so, but less readily than at first, which suggests that some essential substance is progressively withdrawn from the medium by the microbe. The same effects might be explained by supposing that the developing microbe produces some substance which is toxic to itself, but Pasteur rejected this hypothesis on the ground that cultural extracts developed easily in new chicken broth, although such extracts should contain any self-toxic substance secreted by the fowl cholera microbe.

In May 1880 Pasteur suggested that the fowl cholera microbe produces a soluble narcotic responsible for the characteristic somnolence of the disease. This suggestion echoes his earlier proposal that the anthrax bacillus produces a soluble substance responsible for the agglutination of the blood in that disease. Now, as then, he made the soluble substance responsible for only one symptom of the disease and ascribed death chiefly to asphyxia, citing the violet-tinged combs of diseased chickens and the aerobic character of the fowl cholera microbe, which implied a struggle for oxygen with the red blood cells. As evidence that somnolence and death had independent causes, he reported that vaccination prevented death but not extract-induced somnolence.

From late May to early October 1880, Pasteur participated in heated debates at the Académie de Médecine over the significance of his work on fowl cholera vis-à-vis smallpox and Jenner's vaccine. Having shown that the fowl cholera "vaccine" was only modified fowl cholera "virus" (or microbe), he felt confident that Jenner's vaccine was only modified smallpox virus. His opponents denied the relevance to this question of experiments on fowl cholera, claimed that physicians had long held the view that Pasteur was now needlessly repeating, and criticized him for keeping secret his method of attenuating the fowl cholera microbe. In return Pasteur insisted on the importance of experimental evidence, accused his opponents of failing to grasp the real issue in dispute (the relation between smallpox and vaccine, not between cowpox and vaccine), defended his "reserve" on the method of attenuation, and ridiculed one opponent's surgical procedures so viciously that the latter had to be restrained from physically assaulting Pasteur, whom he soon challenged to a duel.[131]

Finally, in October 1880, Pasteur described his method of attenuating the fowl cholera microbe. The first step was to procure the microbe in its most virulent form by taking it from a chicken dead of the chronic form of the disease. In successive cultures made at brief intervals, this virulence remained constant; but attenuation set in when the intervals reached two or three months. In general, the longer the intervals, the weaker the virulence became, although the results defied mathematical regularity. Throughout these changes in virulence, the microbe remained essentially constant in form. Furthermore, a virus (or microbe) of any given virulence retained this degree of virulence so long as successive cultures were made at brief intervals. To explain attenuation, Pasteur invoked the effect on the microbe of prolonged exposure to atmospheric oxygen. As proof he reported that no attenuation occurred in closed tubes, however long the intervals between cultures might be. He suggested that oxygen might have a similar effect on other viruses or microbes and might even be responsible for the natural limits characteristic of great epidemics. Neither here nor anywhere else did Pasteur specify why oxygen should weaken microbes, especially those aerobic microbes (including the anthrax bacillus and the fowl cholera microbe) which ordinarily depended on it for life.

At one point in this memoir, Pasteur alluded again to his prior silence on the method of attenuation. The "true reason" for that silence, he said, ought now to be clear: "Time was an element in my researches." What he did not reveal even now was the remarkable manner in which the crucial role of time had become known. In this case, as in his discovery of hemihedrism in the paratartrates, Pasteur seemed to enjoy extremely good luck.[132] During his early experiments on fowl cholera, he followed his usual practice of making fresh cultures of the microbe every day or so. From late July to October 1879, however, the cultures were allowed to lie idle while he vacationed at Arbois.[133] During this period nearly all the cultures had become sterile and resisted attempts to restore their fecundity by inoculation into chickens. The seemingly useless cultures were about to be discarded when Pasteur proposed that the chickens in which they had produced no apparent effect be subjected to a fresh inoculation from a fecund, virulent culture. The chickens survived. "With [this] one blow," wrote Duclaux, "fowl cholera passed to the list of virus diseases and vaccination was discovered!"[134] Against those who might call this discovery mere luck, Duclaux insisted that some "secret instinct," some "spirit of divination" had led

his master to it, while Pasteur himself might have repeated his famous phrase, "Chance favors only the prepared mind."[135]

In any case Pasteur immediately recognized that he had found a technique capable of extension to other diseases, and he moved toward this goal even as he kept secret his method of attenuating the fowl cholera microbe. Anthrax, the disease he knew best, served naturally as his first choice in the effort to find other vaccines. One may wonder how far this effort would have gone or how successful it would have been without a major expansion in Pasteur's facilities and resources. In May 1880, shortly after the discovery of the fowl cholera vaccine, the city of Paris gave him access to some unoccupied land near his laboratory. On this site, which belonged to the old Collège Rollin, he made extensive provisions for the care and shelter of the many animals used in his experiments. Simultaneously the annual budget for his laboratory—fixed at 6,000 francs since 1871—was supplemented by an annual credit of 50,000 francs from the Ministry of Agriculture.[136] As he surveyed his new domain and as his team of assistants grew larger, Pasteur found new scope for those qualities that led Duclaux to compare him to "a chief of industry who watches everything, lets no detail escape him, wishes to know everything, to have a hand in everything, and who, at the same time, puts himself in personal relation with all his clientele. . . ."[137]

Pasteur and the Discovery of Anthrax Vaccine. In his attempt to place anthrax among the virus or non-recurring diseases and to find a vaccine against it, Pasteur faced competitors, notably Auguste Chaveau and Toussaint. As early as September 1879, Chaveau undertook to explain the relative immunity of Algerian sheep from anthrax and to reinforce that immunity by preventive inoculations. In July 1880 Toussaint announced that he had obtained an effective vaccine against anthrax. In opposition to Pasteur, Chaveau and Toussaint shared an essentially chemical theory of immunity, ascribing it to a soluble substance released by and noxious to the developing anthrax bacilli. Toussaint's proposed vaccine reflects this view: he used filtered and defibrinated anthrax blood heated for ten minutes at 55° C. He supposed that these procedures freed a soluble vaccine from its microbial companions and claimed that sheep injected with this serum survived inoculations of virulent anthrax.

Toussaint's announcement clearly shook Pasteur, whose biological theory of immunity and vaccination it directly threatened. Immediately upon hearing of the announcement, while on vacation at Arbois, he wrote Chamberland and Roux, his collaborators throughout his studies on anthrax, and asked them to join him for experiments designed to examine Toussaint's claims.[138] They soon found that Toussaint's proposed vaccine did indeed provide protection in most cases; but they rejected his interpretation of how this process took place, criticized his experimental technique on several grounds, and disputed the general safety and practicability of his method of vaccination. While doing so, they defended Pasteur's alternative conception of immunity and developed a different anthrax vaccine, based on fundamentally the same principles and techniques employed in the discovery of the fowl cholera vaccine.

As a matter of fact, Pasteur briefly considered the possibility that the fowl cholera vaccine might also serve as an anthrax vaccine. In August 1880, on the basis of preliminary experiments, he claimed that chickens inoculated with the fowl cholera vaccine became simultaneously immune from anthrax. Unlike ordinary chickens, they did not contract anthrax when injected with its bacilli and subsequently chilled. Pasteur noted that this result, if established, would constitute the creation of immunity from anthrax by means of an entirely different parasitic disease. If applicable to other virulent diseases, it gave hope of immense therapeutic consequences, even in human diseases. Since he made no further mention of this result, one can only surmise that subsequent experiments failed to corroborate these preliminary claims.

Slightly earlier, in July 1880, Pasteur had made brief and passing reference to another possible mode of vaccination against anthrax: the gradual and moderate feeding of anthrax spores. He claimed that this idea had first occurred to him in the late summer of 1878, during his experiments on the etiology of natural anthrax. Having noticed that some sheep fell sick but did not die from the ingestion of anthrax spores, he injected eight of them with virulent anthrax blood. Of these eight sheep all but one survived the virulent injection, leading Pasteur to conclude that their recovery from diet-induced anthrax had rendered them immune to subsequent attacks of the disease. In reporting these results, nearly two years after they had been achieved, Pasteur recalled that Toussaint, who had just announced the discovery of a new anthrax vaccine, had witnessed these experiments, initially with skepticism but ultimately with conviction as to their accuracy.[139]

Pasteur drew additional attention to these experiments and extended their basic result to cows in a letter of 27 September 1880. The occasion was a report to the minister of agriculture on a proposed empirical treatment for anthrax in cows. He reported that no valid judgment could be made of the proposed treatment because cows inoculated with anthrax sometimes succumbed despite the treatment, while others recovered in the absence of any treatment whatever. A far more interesting and significant conclusion—based on experiments conducted in August 1879 and in mid-September 1880—was that recovery from an initial attack of anthrax preserved cows subsequently injected with virulent anthrax blood. Thus in cows, as in sheep, anthrax does not recur and inoculations that do not kill act as preventives. In the same report Pasteur defended his biological theory of immunity against Chaveau's chemical theory. Contrary to Chaveau, he insisted that no toxic substance need be invoked to explain the relative immunity from anthrax of Algerian sheep and the reinforcement of the immunity by preventive inoculations. Instead, Algerian sheep ought to be compared with chickens, which are naturally and inherently resistant to anthrax without the intervention of any substance toxic to the anthrax bacillus. The proof of this contention lay in the fact that the mere act of chilling (which could hardly destroy any such substance) permitted the development of the anthrax bacillus in otherwise refractory hens. Moreover, the reinforcement of immunity by preventive inoculations could be likened to the progressive sterility of successive cultures of the bacilli in a given medium.

Pasteur undoubtedly realized that defending his theory of immunity or claiming priority for the discovery of nonrecurrence in anthrax was quite different from producing a safe and effective vaccine. After his "accidental" discovery of the fowl cholera vaccine, the path to such a vaccine must have seemed fairly direct: by increasing the interval between successive cultures of the anthrax microbe, and thus prolonging its exposure to atmospheric oxygen, he could hope to attenuate it. However, the extension of this method to the anthrax microbe was neither so obvious as he might have feared nor so rapid and straightforward as he might have hoped. Not until February 1881 did Pasteur announce the production of the new anthrax vaccine; the resistant spore phase of the anthrax bacillus (a phase which the fowl cholera microbe does not possess) had formed the chief obstacle because it undergoes no alteration upon exposure to atmospheric oxygen.

To attenuate the anthrax microbe, therefore, it was necessary to prevent the production of spores without simultaneously killing the microbe. This feat could be accomplished only by a quite delicate application of heat during cultivation. More specifically, in a medium of neutral chicken broth, the bacillus could live and grow without forming spores at a temperature between 42° and 44° C., while a temperature of 45° C. killed it. Once obtained, however, this asporogenous culture underwent rapid attenuation. After only eight days at 42–44° C., the culture proved harmless to guinea pigs, rabbits, and sheep, three species otherwise highly susceptible to anthrax. Most important, the microbe could be cultivated and conserved in this harmless state, as well as in each degree of attenuation achieved during the previous eight days; and each of these attenuated strains acted as a preventive or vaccine for the less attenuated strain that immediately preceded it. Pasteur claimed that he had already had great success in protecting sheep from anthrax with these vaccines and announced that the method would be given a large-scale trial when the sheep-penning season arrived in the Beauce district.

Also in the memoir of February 1881, Pasteur described the results of experiments in which animals of various ages and species had been injected with variously attenuated strains of the anthrax microbe. Despite the almost random character these experiments must sometimes have presented, they led to a general conclusion of great theoretical and practical importance—that attenuated viruses (or microbes) could return to their original virulence after successive cultures in appropriate animals. Thus a one-day-old guinea pig might succumb to an anthrax microbe that had been attenuated to the point of harmlessness for an adult of the species. If passed from this one-day-old guinea pig to progressively older ones, the microbe gained steadily in virulence until it reached its original capacity to kill adult guinea pigs and even sheep. Unless subjected anew to the attenuation procedure, the microbe would retain this original virulence. In similar fashion a fowl cholera microbe attenuated to harmlessness for chickens might remain virulent for canaries or other small birds and might regain its original virulence by passage through them. This progressive return to original virulence not only offered a means of preparing vaccines of all intermediate degrees but also suggested a possible explanation for new eruptions of old epidemic diseases and for the occasional appearance of entirely new epidemic diseases. By progressive passage through other species, a microorganism might regain a virulence once lost through natural attenuation or might become virulent to a species for which it had hitherto been harmless. With remarkable prescience Pasteur thus broached the question of the evolutionary relationship between parasites and their hosts. In essence, he had perceived that different animal species, including man, can serve as reservoirs of infection for each other; and he recognized that there was virtually no hope of a complete and final victory over epidemic diseases by preventive measures of any sort, including his own.

When this memoir appeared, Toussaint had not yet published the results obtained with his proposed anthrax vaccine. But Pasteur already felt confident that Toussaint's "uncertain" method would compare poorly with his own, which rested on the existence of vaccines producible at will and without resort to anthrax blood. A month later, in March 1881, he subjected Toussaint's proposed vaccine to a probing critique. In the first place, he argued, whatever success Toussaint had achieved resulted not from the death of the anthrax microbe (and consequent isolation of a presumed soluble vaccine) but from its unintentional attenuation by heat. Unfortunately, this protective modification of the anthrax bacillus was only one of three possible effects of Toussaint's unreliable method of heating anthrax blood to 55° C. In certain cases the microbe might survive without modification and thus retain its original virulence upon injection. In still other cases it might indeed be killed, as Toussaint supposed; but its injection would then fail to protect the animal from a subsequent attack of anthrax. Nor did the use of filtration improve the reliability of the method. Filtered anthrax blood might retain all its original virulence; more commonly, it would fail to act at all and would thus confer no protection against a subsequent attack. In short, no anthrax vaccine could be produced by successive filtrations or dilutions of an original quantity of anthrax blood. Moreover, even when Toussaint's method did attenuate the anthrax microbe, and even if it could be made to do so consistently and reliably, it still presented serious practical difficulties. Unlike Pasteur's fowl cholera vaccine or his new anthrax vaccine, Toussaint's heat-modified anthrax microbe could not be reproduced in culture so as to preserve its modified virulence. His method therefore required a large and continually renewed supply of anthrax blood.

In a separate paper of the same day (21 March 1881), Pasteur reported that he and his collaborators had produced an anthrax vaccine so attenuated that it failed to kill even newborn guinea pigs. This vaccine, the product of forty-three days of attenuation at 42–43° C., could therefore regain its original virulence only through some new species even more susceptible to anthrax. Nonetheless, the new vaccine displayed no appreciable morphological differences from the most virulent form of the bacillus and grew with equal facility in artificial media. Most important, this fully attenuated microbe (and all others of intermediate virulence) shared with the original, fully virulent culture the capacity to form spores that preserved the virulence of the anthrax rods. This meant that anthrax vaccines of whatever degree of virulence could be fixed in that state by passage into the spore phase and could then be stored or transported over long distances without fear of alteration.

The Experiments at Pouilly-le-Fort. Unlike fowl cholera—which was quite rare and local in its effects—anthrax posed a severe economic threat to French agriculture and animal husbandry. According to Pasteur, estimates of the annual loss from anthrax ranged from 20 to 30 million francs.[140] His announcement of an effective anthrax vaccine therefore excited great interest, and the Agricultural Society of Melun quickly proposed a public field test of the new method. Much of the initiative came from H. Rossignol, a veterinarian who had earlier satirized the growing deification of the germ theory and of Pasteur as its "pontiff" and "prophet," and who now produced a list of about 100 subscribers willing to underwrite the costs of a field trial of Pasteur's anthrax vaccine.[141] At the end of April 1881, Pasteur and the Agricultural Society of Melun agreed upon a course of experiments, to be arranged and supervised by Rossignol, who gave the program wide publicity by sending copies throughout the world. The program captured international attention as much by its uncompromising and boldly prophetic character as by its inherent importance—so much so that the *Times* of London sent its Paris correspondent to Rossignol's farm at Pouilly-le-Fort to provide a serial eyewitness account.[142]

As initially agreed upon, the program called for the injection of virulent anthrax culture into fifty sheep of any age, variety, or sex, of which half were to be unvaccinated while the other half were to be previously vaccinated by separate inoculations of two unequally attenuated anthrax cultures. Pasteur predicted that all twenty-five unvaccinated sheep would die from the virulent injection, while all twenty-five vaccinated sheep would recover completely and would be indistinguishable from ten additional sheep kept apart as an index of normalcy. At the request of the Agricultural Society of Melun, Pasteur later agreed to substitute two goats for two of the fifty sheep and to extend the trial to ten cows, of which six were to be vaccinated and four unvaccinated. Although somewhat less confident of the results on cows, he predicted that the six vaccinated cows would remain healthy when injected with the virulent culture, while the four unvaccinated cows would die or at least become very ill.

The experiments began on 5 May 1881 with the injection of an attenuated anthrax culture into twenty-four sheep, one goat, and six cows. On 17 May each of these animals was inoculated with a second attenuated culture, somewhat more virulent than the first. On 31 May Pasteur and his assistants—Chamberland, Roux, and Thuillier—injected a fully virulent anthrax culture into each of these thirty-one vaccinated animals and into twenty-nine unvaccinated animals —twenty-four sheep, one goat, and four cows. They inoculated the vaccinated and unvaccinated animals alternately, "to render the experiments more comparative," and set 2 June as the date on which the crowd should reassemble to observe the results. In the meantime some of the vaccinated animals became feverish and Pasteur's faith wavered briefly; indeed, it has been asserted that he temporarily feared the possibility of public ridicule and, in an overwrought state, accused Roux of carelessness and thought of sending him to face the crowd alone.[143] But a telegram from Rossignol informed him on the morning of 2 June that he would find a "stunning success" when he arrived at Pouilly-le-Fort that afternoon.[144] When he and his collaborators made their triumphant arrival at two o'clock, all of the vaccinated sheep were alive and apparently healthy; all but three of the unvaccinated sheep were dead, and they were failing rapidly. Two dropped before the spectators' eyes, and the third died at the end of the day. The six vaccinated cows were also perfectly healthy, while the four unvaccinated ones were swollen and feverish. Upon seeing Pasteur, the crowd burst into applause and congratulations. It was perhaps the single most dramatic moment in a singularly dramatic scientific career.

In his published account of these experiments (13 June 1881), Pasteur reported that one of the vaccinated sheep (a ewe) had died on 3 June. But an autopsy revealed that this ewe had been pregnant and that her fetus had been dead for two weeks. Rossignol and a fellow veterinarian, who had jointly conducted the autopsy, therefore linked the ewe's death with that of her fetus, a diagnosis that aroused acrimonious but inconclusive debate. In the same report Pasteur insisted that the vaccine should be prepared and controlled in his laboratory, at least for the time being, lest a poor application of the method compromise its future. Finally, he emphasized that the new vaccine, as an artificial product of the laboratory, marked a great advance over Jenner's smallpox vaccine, which was a unique and mysterious natural product. On 22 June 1881 he developed this distinction further, noting that the smallpox microbe remained unknown, if indeed it existed at all, and that the preservative powers of the Jennerian vaccine gradually deteriorated, presumably because it could not be conserved in the form of spores.[145]

Anthrax Vaccination After 1881. Controversy and Triumph. In the wake of the dramatic success at Pouilly-le-Fort, Pasteur and his laboratory received a flood of requests for supplies of the new anthrax vaccine. On Christmas Day 1881, in a private note to the president of the Council of Ministers, Pasteur proposed the creation of a state factory for the manufacture of anthrax vaccine, of which he should be the director, assisted by Chamberland and Roux. By its support for this project, the French state would gain prestige and gratitude as the disease disappeared. In return Pasteur asked only that he and his family "be freed of material preoccupations."[146] Ultimately the government rejected Pasteur's proposal, and his laboratory remained the center for the manufacture of anthrax vaccine; one annex of the laboratory, under Chamberland's supervision, was given over entirely to the production of this and other vaccines discovered subsequently.

As efforts were made to meet the growing demand for the anthrax vaccine, Pasteur noted that his achievement raised at least one important new problem—the duration of immunity conferred by the vaccine. By June 1881 his experiments suggested that protection against injections of highly virulent anthrax culture lasted at least six months, leading him to suppose that it would last at least a year under normal conditions of field exposure. If it proved necessary, annual revaccination should pose no serious obstacles, for the procedure took little time and the vaccine cost very little to produce.[147] In late January 1882 Pasteur injected a new virulent anthrax culture into the sheep vaccinated nearly eight months before at Pouilly-le-Fort. All survived. In his view this result solved the question from a practical point of view, since the normal anthrax season ran only from April to October. Animals vaccinated in April of each year would therefore acquire complete protection from the disease.[148] By March 1883 Pasteur realized that the duration of immunity followed no general law, varying from animal to animal, so that annual revaccination was indeed indicated.[149]

In the meantime Pasteur basked in the fame and general success of his method of anthrax vaccination, while seeking to explain and to minimize those failures or "accidents" which occurred as the procedure became increasingly common and increasingly distant from his direct control. In August 1881 he went in triumph to London, where he addressed the International Congress of Medicine on vaccination. While summarizing his earlier achievements, Pasteur reported that a commission of doctors and veterinarians had asked him to repeat the Pouilly-le-Fort experiments using infected anthrax blood in place of a virulent anthrax culture as a test of the preservative powers of the attenuated vaccine. These experiments, conducted at Chartres, produced equally decisive and favorable results. Pasteur characterized vaccination as a great advance in "microbiology" (the word he preferred to the more restrictive and "Germanic" word "bacteriology")[150] and emphasized that his extension of the word "vaccination" to include preventive inoculations of any sort of attenuated culture was meant as homage to Jenner. What he had seen and heard during the Congress (including Koch's technique of solid culture) struck him as evidence not merely of the advance but of the triumph of the germ theory of disease.[151]

Late in January 1882, during his return to Pouilly-le-Fort for experiments on the duration of immunity, Pasteur received three medals commemorating his original experiments there. At the festive meeting of the Agricultural Society of Melun, where this honor was bestowed, Pasteur reported that more than 32,000 sheep had already been vaccinated, with a mortality rate about one-tenth that of unvaccinated sheep under ordinary conditions of field exposure. In fact, about 400 sheep had been saved, and the number would have been even greater had the vaccinations been made earlier in the season. As for those deaths which did occur immediately after vaccination, only a portion should be ascribed to accidents in the procedure itself; the others should be charged to the disease having already invaded the animal before its vaccination.

By June 1882, however, as reports of accidents increased, Pasteur admitted that the vaccines supplied by his laboratory from November 1881 to March 1882 had been less than adequate, despite their being direct cultural descendants of earlier, completely successful vaccines. Experience revealed that the vaccines gradually deteriorated (like Jenner's vaccine), leading to two sorts of unfortunate accidents: (1) the first of the two preventive inoculations might be made with a culture too weak compared with the second, so that the latter produced death upon injection; and (2) both vaccines might be too weak to act as a preventive against the natural disease. When these problems and their causes became clear, effective new vaccines were developed and sent free of charge to all who requested them. Pasteur also insisted again that accidents could occur through no fault of the vaccine itself: not even Jenner's vaccine could prevent smallpox once the disease had become established. Moreover, because of interspecific or interracial differences in susceptibility to anthrax, a vaccine perfectly appropriate for, say, one race of sheep might be entirely unsuited to another. Therefore vaccination should be extended to a new race of sheep or cattle only after preliminary tests had determined the appropriate degree of attenuation. In any case, occasional accidents should not be allowed to obscure the demonstrable overall value of anthrax vaccination. To encourage its general adoption, Pasteur proposed that farmers be reimbursed for any losses suffered from accidents in the procedure, with the revenues for this guarantee to be raised by a surcharge of ten centimes on each vaccination.[152]

At the end of this paper of June 1882, in response to a remark from the floor, Pasteur charged the veterinary school at Turin with a careless experimental error that had undermined confidence in his method of vaccination. A commission from that school had found that his vaccines failed to prevent death from the injection of virulent anthrax blood. In a bold assertion from afar, Pasteur ascribed their failure to the inadvertent use of anthrax blood contaminated with septicemia. For nearly a year thereafter, Pasteur and the Turin school exchanged charges and invective in open forum. When the Turin school denied his assertion and accused him of arrogance for his diagnosis-at-a-distance, Pasteur offered to come to Turin to demonstrate that anthrax blood becomes partially septic within a day. The Turin school replied that no such simple and restricted demonstration could decide the real issues in dispute and compared Pasteur to a "duelist who challenges all those who dare to contradict him . . . but who has the habit of choosing the weapons and of obliging his adversaries to fight with their hands tied."[153]

In his rejoinder Pasteur continued to limit the debate to the narrow confines within which he had placed it. He reported that Roux had confirmed the point he wished to demonstrate before the Turin school by showing that the blood of an anthrax victim dead for twenty-six hours contained both the anthrax bacillus and the *vibrion septique*, which could be separated by appropriate methods of culture (the bacillus grew in air; the vibrio *in vacuo*). Besides implying that his adversaries feared a direct confrontation with him, Pasteur impugned their motives by citing a passage in which they had distorted his views by quoting him out of context. According to Pasteur Vallery-Radot, the Turin school never admitted defeat; nevertheless anthrax vaccination soon became as widespread in Italy as elsewhere.[154]

More disturbing criticism of Pasteur's work came from Germany, where Koch and his school contributed their impressive authority to the cause. Scarcely concealed beneath the scientific and methodological issues dividing Pasteur and Koch were powerful personal and national antagonisms. As one whose basic training lay in chemistry, and whose attitude toward naturalists and physicians sometimes approached the contemptuous, Pasteur belonged to a tradition different from that of Koch, whose training had been in medicine and whose career owed so much to the botanist Ferdinand Cohn. A more immediate source of their later confrontation lay in Pasteur's tendency to minimize the originality and decisiveness of Koch's work on anthrax. Indeed, from 1877 he repeatedly claimed priority for the discovery of

resistant bacilli endospores, citing passages in which he had described the formation of resistant "corpuscules brilliants" or "corpuscules-germs" in *flacherie*.[155] To him Koch's discovery of a resistant endospore phase for the anthrax microbe amounted to merely a confirmation and extension of this earlier discovery. With a convenient disregard for the difference between his rather brief, ambiguous description of "corpuscules brilliants" in *flacherie* and Koch's precise and full-fledged account of the anthrax endospore, Pasteur implied that the special character and full significance of these "corpuscules" had always been clear to him and ought therefore to have been clear to Koch and other naturalists. In fact, as Koch well knew, the existence and significance of bacilli endospores had received little attention before 1875, when Ferdinand Cohn recognized their crucial place in the life cycle of *Bacillus subtilis*.

However deep and long-standing these tensions between Koch and Pasteur may have been, they remained largely suppressed until 1881, when the German Sanitary Office published the first volume of its journal, *Mittheilungen aus dem Kaiserlichen Gesundheitsamt*. In this volume Koch and his students attacked Pasteur's work on disease on several grounds, of which perhaps the most damning was their charge that his liquid media (as opposed to Koch's solid media) failed to guarantee pure cultures. In fact, the German school alleged that Pasteur's supposedly "attenuated" anthrax cultures or "vaccines" were merely contaminated cultures.[156] They also accused him of confusing several other diseases with septicemia and of unacknowledged dependence on Koch and others for the most accurate and valuable portions of his work. Koch disputed Pasteur's claims that earthworms play a central role in the spread of anthrax and that domestic animals ordinarily contract it through lesions of the mouth and throat caused by prickly diets.

Pasteur was apparently unaware of these charges when he met Koch at the International Congress of Medicine in August 1881 and described the latter's solid media as a "great progress." But in September 1882, during the International Congress of Hygiene and Demography at Geneva, he mounted a vigorous defense of his work against Koch and his pupils, blaming their "inexperience" for the "multitude of errors" they had committed.[157] Fortified by the results of his experiments at Pouilly-le-Fort, he virtually demanded a response from Koch, who sat among the audience. Considering the Congress an inappropriate forum for such a discussion, Koch had little to say, although he promised to respond in print to Pasteur's address. Three months later he kept his promise with

Ueber die Milzbrandimpfung. Eine Entgegnung auf den von Pasteur in Genf gehaltenen Vortrag. In an abrupt shift of position, Koch hailed the discovery of attenuation as a major achievement but gave Toussaint, rather than Pasteur, priority for it and justified his own earlier skepticism on the ground that his French rival had failed at first to provide a complete and explicit account of his method of attenuating the anthrax microbe. Moreover, he continued to condemn Pasteur's method of vaccination from a practical point of view, citing the experiments of the veterinary school of Turin as well as other "accidents" and unresolved issues, including the duration of immunity. He continued also to cast aspersions on the purity of Pasteur's cultures, on his secrecy, and on his more general knowledge of medicine and pathological bacteriology. Pasteur's rejoinder took the form of a long open letter to Koch dated Christmas Day 1882. Combining heavy sarcasm with considerable persuasion, he refuted Koch's critique point by point until it seemed to contain nothing of value but belated and grudging concessions to Pasteur's point of view.

For several years thereafter, the Pasteur-Koch dispute remained mostly in the shadows, as Pasteur's method of anthrax vaccination spread throughout Europe with striking success. In April 1883 Pasteur could insist that the new anthrax vaccines—introduced in November 1882—were so safe that not a single animal had fallen victim to a vaccination accident in the meantime, while their efficacy was so great that he could not have been consoled had attenuation been other than a "French discovery."[158] One month later Pasteur reported that a field trial of his anthrax vaccine had been conducted in two regions of Germany, under the auspices of the Prussian minister of agriculture, and that the results of the first year, released that month in Berlin, had been so favorable that the farmers of those regions had decided to adopt the procedure.[159] In August 1887, after Pasteur announced that the "Berlin school" had been converted, Koch denied that he had modified his views on the practical value of vaccination and insisted that no guarantee existed as to the accuracy of Pasteur's glowing statistics on the procedure. To Pasteur this position represented blind obstinacy in the face of the testimony of veterinarians, whose reports he promised to submit to the forthcoming International Congress of Hygiene and Demography in Vienna. These reports, like all that followed, can only have embarrassed Koch. By 1894 Chamberland could report that 3,400,000 sheep and 438,000 cattle had been vaccinated against anthrax, with respective mortality rates of 1 and 0.3 percent. Comparing these rates with earlier mortalities among unvaccinated animals, he estimated a saving through vaccination of five million francs for sheep and two million francs for cattle.[160]

The Attenuation of the "Saliva Microbe" and of a Microbe Found in "Horse Typhoid." Pasteur's work on anthrax vaccines reinforced his belief in the general applicability of the method of attenuation discovered for the fowl cholera microbe. As early as June 1881, soon after the Pouilly-le-Fort experiment, he reported the extension of this method to a third microbe: the "saliva microbe" (later recognized to be a pneumococcus), first obtained in December 1880 from the saliva of a child dead of rabies. This saliva produced rapid death upon injection into dogs or rabbits, the blood of which became infested by the new microbe, similar morphologically (a figure eight) but not physiologically to the fowl cholera microbe. The origin of the saliva raised the possibility that the new microbe might play some role in rabies; and Pasteur spent several weeks investigating this possibility, while carefully refraining from publishing any definite conclusions. In March 1881, having found the new microbe in the saliva of young victims of other diseases and in healthy adults, he denied any connection between it and rabies. Indeed, by the time he announced his success in attenuating this new microbe, again by prolonged exposure to atmospheric oxygen, he suggested that it might be entirely harmless to man, however lethal its effects when injected into rabbits or dogs.[161]

In September 1882, at the International Congress of Hygiene and Demography in Geneva, Pasteur gave a much fuller account of his work on the saliva microbe and disclosed the discovery of a fourth example of attenuation by atmospheric oxygen—that of a microbe obtained from the nasal discharges of a horse dead of "horse typhoid." Rabbits injected with these discharges died in less than twenty-four hours of a "veritable typhoid fever," accompanied by the appearance in their blood of a new microbe—once again in the form of a figure eight. Like the microbes of fowl cholera, anthrax, and saliva, the aerobic character of which it shared, this new microbe underwent no change in virulence in closed tubes but became progressively less virulent (or more attenuated) upon exposure to the air. As in his early work on the saliva microbe, Pasteur carefully avoided any conclusion as to the possible role of this microbe in horse typhoid.[162] Despite such caution, his adversaries accused him of trying to forge an etiological link between these microbes and the diseases of the subjects from which they had been taken, especially in the case of the microbe taken from the rabid youth. Koch referred sarcastically to Pasteur's fondness for microbes in the form of a figure eight and suggested that the animals allegedly killed by these suspicious new microbes had merely died of different forms of septicemia.

In part Koch's objections reflect a more general difference of emphasis between him and Pasteur (or between the German and French schools). For while they basically agreed on the specificity of microbes, they differed as to the range of variability within a given species and as to the relative importance of morphological and physiological properties in microbial identification. Probably because of his mastery of technique in the naturalist tradition, Koch gave pride of place to morphology—to careful, detailed descriptions and pictorial representations of microbial form. The relative reliability and constancy of form in microbes grown in his solid cultural media tended naturally to reinforce this morphological bias. Pasteur's lack of training in and relative disdain for the naturalist tradition led him to focus instead on the physiological properties of microbes, and this functional bias drew additional force from observations of morphological variability in the richly varied liquid media he used.

This is not to say that Koch ignored physiological considerations, or that Pasteur ignored morphology,[163] but merely to assert a difference in emphasis. From this perspective some of their specific disagreements can be more readily understood. Pasteur's claim that microbes of similar form (notably the figure eight) had radically different functions—produced different diseases—was bound to arouse Koch's skepticism. But Pasteur's physiological bias made him rather more sensitive to the variable behavior of a given microbe in different environments, and he early recognized that different animal species constitute different cultural media or "terrains" for the microbe to which they are host. Not surprisingly, therefore, he tended to identify microbes by virtue of their biological action when injected into a given animal species. Thus, his claim that the "saliva microbe" differed from the *vibrion septique* rested above all on the fact that guinea pigs, which were strikingly susceptible to septicemia, proved entirely refractory to injections of the new microbe.[164]

For somewhat similar reasons Pasteur was more disposed than Koch to suppose that a given microbe could undergo intrinsic changes in its properties by successive passages through the same or different animal species. That the virulence of a microbe could be increased by successive passages within a species was known before Pasteur began his work. Indeed, Koch had drawn attention to this fact in the cases of anthrax and traumatic infectious diseases. But Koch emphasized the effect of such passages on microbial purity—he described the technique in 1878 as "the best and surest method of pure cultivation"—and did not suppose that the intrinsic properties of the microbe had thereby been changed.[165] This helps to explain his assumption that Pasteur's "attenuated" anthrax cultures must have been impure. Pasteur, by contrast, insisted that his attenuated anthrax cultures were pure and that they resulted from real changes in the properties of the microbe itself. These changes could be reversed and the microbe returned to its original virulence by passage through animals of different ages and species.[166]

In his address at the Geneva Congress in 1882, Pasteur extended these conclusions to the saliva microbe and to the microbe found in "horse typhoid." He reported that the virulence of the former microbe in guinea pigs could be increased by successive passages through that species, while the virulence of the latter in rabbits could be increased by successive passages through that species. More important, he now recognized that successive passages through one species could reduce the virulence of a microbe toward another species. Thus the saliva microbe became increasingly less virulent to rabbits by successive passages through guinea pigs, and the microbe found in "horse typhoid" became progressively less virulent to guinea pigs by successive passages through rabbits. In effect this amounted to the discovery of a new method of attenuation, which Pasteur was soon to exploit against swine erysipelas and rabies.

Discovery of the Vaccine Against Swine Erysipelas. Although Pasteur's attention had been drawn to swine erysipelas (*rouget du porc* or hog cholera) as early as 1877 by Achille Maucuer, a veterinarian in the township of Bollène, in Vaucluse,[167] he was then too preoccupied with other work to give it any serious attention. In the summer of 1881, he sent Chamberland to Bollène to study the disease, but nothing seems to have come of that effort. Six months later Louis Thuillier, another of Pasteur's assistants, went to Peux, in Vienne, where in March 1882 he isolated a new microbe (now called *Erysipelothrix insidiosa*), which he implicated in swine erysipelas. Almost immediately Thuillier returned with cultures of this new microbe to Pasteur's laboratory at the École Normale, where they began searching for a means of attenuating it. Early in April, however, Thuillier was sent to Germany to supervise a field trial of anthrax vaccination on the model of the Pouilly-le-Fort experiments, as he had done in Hungary the year before. For the next two months Thuillier remained in Germany as Pasteur pursued the search for a vaccine against swine erysipelas. By mid-October, Pasteur apparently had made considerable progress; and in November he, Thuillier, and Adrien Loir went to Bollène to conduct preliminary small-scale trials. From there, on

3 December 1882, Pasteur sent J.-B. Dumas a letter, to be read at the Académie des Sciences, in which he outlined the basic results to date of their hitherto unpublished studies. He included Thuillier's new microbe among those having the form of a figure eight and reported that it killed rabbits and sheep as well as hogs but had no effect on chickens. More important, he announced that they had proved the nonrecurrence of swine erysipelas and had prepared an attenuated form of the microbe, inoculation with which made hogs refractory to the disease. While noting that additional confirmatory experiments needed to be done, Pasteur expressed confidence that the new vaccine would be ready by the next spring to save hogs from this seasonal blight, which in 1882 had claimed an estimated 20,000 animals in the departments of the Rhône Valley alone and in 1879 an estimated 900,000 hogs in the United States.[168]

In November 1883, after further successful testing of the new vaccine, Pasteur gave the Académie des Sciences a more extended account of the studies on swine erysipelas. He began with a warm tribute to Thuillier, who had died of cholera in September, at the age of twenty-seven. His death affected Pasteur deeply, in part because it came while Thuillier served on the ill-fated French Cholera Commission, sent to Egypt at Pasteur's urging and under his guidance to study the very disease that killed him. As if to intensify the tragedy, the German Cholera Commission, in Egypt at the same time under Koch's leadership, made considerable progress and eventually isolated a comma-shaped bacillus to which Koch definitely and triumphantly ascribed cholera in the early months of 1884.

Pasteur took consolation in the heroic quality of Thuillier's death and in the outcome of their joint study of swine erysipelas, the results of which he presented in both their names. He reported that the immunity conferred by the new vaccine lasted at least a year, but that its general diffusion faced practical difficulties owing to wide variations in the susceptibility of different breeds of hogs to the disease. Studies were already under way, however, to prepare vaccines of a strength appropriate to each breed; and while absolutely definitive results could not yet be claimed, he decided to disclose the method by which the microbe had been attenuated. By way of introduction, Pasteur recalled his earlier discovery that the saliva microbe became attenuated for rabbits by successive passages through guinea pigs.

Having learned that pigeons and rabbits, as well as hogs, suffered severely from infectious disease in the department of Vaucluse, Pasteur and his team wondered whether these species might share with hogs a susceptibility to the microbe of swine erysipelas—and if so, what effects its successive passage through them might have. They quickly established that pigeons and rabbits did indeed die from injections of the microbe; and while successive passages through pigeons increased the virulence of the microbe for hogs, successive passages through rabbits had the opposite effect. In fact, several passages through rabbits so attenuated its virulence in hogs that it became harmless to them. At this point inoculation of the cultures protected hogs from the effects of somewhat less attenuated cultures. By injecting hogs with a series of progressively more virulent cultures, they could be rendered immune to the natural disease. According to Bulloch, this method of vaccination was used on more than 100,000 hogs in France between 1886 and 1892, and on more than 1 million hogs in Hungary from 1889 to 1894.[169]

In revealing this new method of attenuation, Pasteur emphasized the variability of viruses or microbes in different media and made an arresting comparison between their variability and that of higher organisms. In fact, he suggested, microbes are no more variable than higher organisms; they seem to be only because they reproduce so rapidly, with an immense number of generations succeeding each other in short order. By contrast, higher organisms require thousands or millions of years to achieve the same number of generations. Thus, even though higher organisms, no less than microbes, display "plasticity" under the influence of the environmental conditions in which successive generations live, they seem static to us. As usual, Pasteur said nothing about the possible implications of such ideas for the transmutability of species or for Darwinian evolutionary theory.

The Search for a Rabies Vaccine, 1881–1884. Because rabies is so rare in man (in France its victims probably never reached more than 100 in any year) and can be quite readily controlled by muzzling and quarantine of dogs, many observers of Pasteur's career have been somewhat puzzled by his interest in it. Some have traced his concern to a traumatic childhood experience. In October 1831 a rabid wolf bit several Arboisiens and terrorized the entire region. The standard treatment, then as since antiquity, was to cauterize the wounds immediately with a red-hot iron; and the youthful Pasteur reportedly saw a man submit to this excruciating procedure at a blacksmith's shop near his home. Despite all efforts some of the wolf's victims died, including at least one whose name and circumstances Pasteur recalled more than half a century later.[170]

As a result of this episode, Pasteur may long have shared the popular horror of the disease. Indeed, in several ways rabies was precisely suited to inspire terror and a sense of mystery. Its rarity made it seem that its victims had been perversely singled out, especially since they were often children. Its usual victim and agent was man's favorite pet. Its long incubation period, ordinarily a month, at least, produced suspense and dread in any victim of an animal bite, especially because medical care was utterly powerless and death absolutely certain once the symptoms became manifest. Above all, the symptoms were believed to embody the ultimate in agony and degradation, stripping the victims of their sanity and reducing them to quivering, convulsive, animal-like shadows of their former selves. Although this conception of rabies depended more on observations of "mad" dogs than on clinical evidence, it so gripped the public imagination that the short, dry cough of human victims was compared to the bark of a dog. Few realized that the disease had a quite peaceful "paralytic" form as well as a "mad" form, or that the supposed fear of water—which gave the disease its other popular name, hydrophobia—stemmed from difficulty in swallowing and not from a fear of water per se.

Thus, however unimportant rabies may have been in terms of vital statistics, Pasteur must have realized that its conqueror would be hailed as a popular savior. And indeed he was. For if the anthrax experiments at Pouilly-le-Fort had created public confidence in the germ theory of disease, his treatment for rabies set off an international chorus of cheers the tangible echo of which was the Institut Pasteur. Not even Pasteur could have hoped for such a result from the outset, however; and before he had fully achieved it, he offered an additional explanation for his interest in rabies—an explanation at once more prosaic and plausible than the others. Speaking at Copenhagen in 1884, he emphasized that the extension of vaccination to human diseases presented special difficulties, notably because "experimentation, [if] allowable on animals, is criminal on man." For this reason vaccination could be extended to man only on the basis of a deep knowledge of animal diseases, "in particular those which affect animals in common with man." As the oldest, most familiar, and most striking example of such a disease, rabies was a natural choice to satisfy Pasteur's "desire to penetrate further" into the problem.[171]

Initially, from December 1880 through March 1881, Pasteur's work on rabies was bound up with that on the "saliva microbe." Once convinced that this microbe had no connection with rabies, and finding himself unable to implicate any other microbe in the disease, Pasteur approached rabies rather differently from the way in which he had so successfully attacked fowl cholera and anthrax. The central feature of his

work on these diseases, as he often insisted, was the cultivation and attenuation of the implicated microbe in sterile cultural media, outside the animal economy. With a flexibility born partly of necessity, Pasteur now made the living organism the sole cultural medium for the rabies virus. In this, as in so much of his work, a thread of continuity runs through the seemingly dramatic shift in approach. For he had long conceived of living organisms as cultural media, and he already knew that the microbes of fowl cholera and anthrax could vary in virulence in different living media. Moreover, believing that Jenner's still mysterious vaccine was merely attenuated smallpox virus, he had additional reason to hope that any "virus," including that of rabies, might be altered in virulence by passage through appropriate animals, even though it resisted attempts to cultivate it in vitro. In fact, as we now know, Pasteur could have accomplished what he did toward the conquest of rabies only by this rather indirect approach. Of the "virus" diseases that he studied, only rabies is a virus disease in the modern sense; its agent is a filterable virus, invisible under the ordinary microscope, the in vitro cultivation of which has not yet been achieved. In this connection it is interesting that Robert Koch studied rabid brains during the 1880's.[172] That this work was apparently fruitless may well have been partly due to Koch's tendency to emphasize the visible and tangible aspects of disease agents over their physiological behavior in different media.

Although fortunate and essential, Pasteur's decision to proceed in the absence of an in vitro rabies culture did not lead far by itself. The lengthy incubation period, as well as the uncertainty of the standard modes of transmission, made new techniques imperative. Neither the injection of rabid saliva nor the bite of a rabid animal produced rabies consistently, and neither method reduced the incubation period. Similar objections applied to the subcutaneous inoculation of rabid nerve tissue, a method that seemed well chosen in view of the patently neuropathic symptoms of the disease. In May 1881, in his first memoir on rabies per se, Pasteur described a new experimental method for transmitting the disease with certainty and with a greatly reduced incubation period. The new method, perhaps suggested by Roux,[173] involved the extraction of cerebral matter from a rabid dog under sterile procedures and its subsequent inoculation directly onto the surface of the brain of a healthy animal, under the dura mater, after trephining. Under these conditions the inoculated animal invariably contracted rabies after an incubation period of about two weeks.

In December 1882, Pasteur reported that rabies could also be transmitted (usually in paralytic form) by the intravenous injection of its virus, the character of which remained obscure. Whether transmitted by this intravenous method or by the intracranial method announced earlier, the incubation period had now been reduced to six to ten days, although Pasteur declined to reveal how, "leaving aside for the moment all details." Among the other results of his 200 experiments, perhaps the most important was the discovery that a few dogs were "accidentally" or inherently resistant to injections of the virulent virus. After recovering from the effects of one such injection, these dogs became immune to subsequent injections. This result established that rabies shared the distinguishing feature of the other "virus" diseases—it did not recur in an animal that had survived an attack. That rabies shared this feature had been far from certain, since death so consistently claimed its victims. Only with the removal of this doubt did it become entirely reasonable to hope that the search for a vaccine might eventually succeed.

Fortified by this assurance and armed with their new techniques of transmission, Pasteur and his collaborators pressed toward a rabies vaccine. In February 1884 Pasteur announced that they had reached their goal. By now they had returned to the method of intracranial inoculation, described as easy to learn and almost always successful. Although the virus continued to resist all attempts at artificial cultivation, Pasteur held to his assumption that a microbe of rabies did exist. At the very least, he maintained, a rabid brain could easily be distinguished from a normal one, for the medulla of the former contained numerous fine granules, resembling simple dots and suggesting a microbe of extreme tenuity. Whether or not further research established that these granules were "actually the germ of rabies," Pasteur and his team had made what seemed to him a vastly more important discovery: the rabies virus (like the microbes of fowl cholera, anthrax, saliva, and "rabbit typhoid") could be prepared in varying degrees of virulence by successive passages through different animal species. In any given species a series of passages led eventually to a fixed degree of virulence, measured by the number of days of incubation for a given quantity of inoculated virus. This maximum or "fixed" virulence varied in different animals and had already been reached naturally in the dog by virtue of countless transfers by bites through past ages.

As this suggestion implies, Pasteur emphatically rejected the notion that rabies could arise "spontaneously" in the absence of the virus. But the really important consequence of the varying states of virulence was that they allowed "a method of rendering dogs refractory to rabies in numbers as large as

desired." Like his earlier methods of vaccination, this method involved the serial inoculation of progressively virulent cultures, beginning with one attenuated to the point of harmlessness. By this method Pasteur and his team had already produced twenty-three dogs capable of sustaining the most virulent rabies virus. Indirectly the problem of prophylaxis in man had also thus been essentially solved, for he ordinarily contracted rabies only from dogs. Moreover, the lengthy incubation period of the disease offered hope that a victim might be rendered refractory before the symptoms became manifest.

In his fourth memoir on rabies (May 1884), Pasteur elaborated very briefly on the methods by which the rabies virus had been prepared in varying degrees of virulence. To weaken or attenuate the virus, it was passed from dog to monkey and then successively from monkey to monkey. After just a few such passages it had become so attenuated that its hypodermic injection into dogs never resulted in rabies; indeed, even intracranial inoculation usually produced no effect. On the other hand, the virulence of ordinary canine rabies could be increased by successive passages through guinea pigs or rabbits; in the latter it achieved its maximum fixed virulence only after a considerable number of passages. By these means, Pasteur noted, one can prepare and keep on hand a series of viruses of various strengths, the most attenuated of which are nonlethal from the outset but protect the inoculated animal from the effects of somewhat more virulent viruses, which in their turn act as a vaccine against still more virulent strains, until eventually the animal is always rendered refractory to even the most virulent and ordinarily fatal virus. If all dogs were vaccinated in this way, rabies could eventually be eliminated; but until that "distant period" it seemed important to search for a means of preventing the disease during the long incubation that followed the bite of a rabid animal. Indeed, Pasteur believed that the method was already at hand to render bitten patients refractory before the disease became manifest. "But," he emphasized, "proofs must be collected from different animal species, and almost *ad infinitum*, before human therapeutics can make bold to try this mode of prophylaxis on man himself."

Toward this end Pasteur requested the convening of a commission, to be appointed by the minister of public instruction, to which he could submit his present results and future experiments. Two sorts of experiments seemed to him best calculated to carry conviction. First, twenty of his vaccinated dogs should be placed with twenty unvaccinated dogs, and all forty should then be subjected to the bites of rabid dogs. Second, the same experiment should be made, except that the forty dogs should sustain the intracranial inoculation of ordinary canine rabies instead of the bites of rabid dogs. "If the facts announced by me are real," Pasteur predicted, "not one of my twenty [vaccinated] dogs will contract rabies, while the twenty control animals will." The proposed commission was duly appointed that very month and issued its initial report early in August 1884. After two months of experiments conducted under its scrutiny, none of Pasteur's twenty-three vaccinated dogs had contracted rabies—whether from the bites of rabid dogs or from inoculation of the rabies virus. By contrast, two-thirds of the unvaccinated control dogs had already become rabid.

Later in August, in a major address to the International Congress of Medicine at Copenhagen, Pasteur proudly repeated these results and finally described in considerable detail the method of intracranial inoculation and his process of preparing the rabies virus in varying degrees of virulence. He reported that the search for an organism which would act as an attenuating medium for the virus had been long and frustrating. Through a great number of experiments, the animals selected as candidates for this role proved to increase rather than to attenuate the virulence of the virus. Not until December 1883 did they happen upon the proper "attenuating" organism—the monkey. Toward the end of this address, Pasteur again raised the issue of the rabies microbe: "You must be feeling, gentlemen, that there is a great blank in my communication; I do not speak of the microorganism of rabies. We have not got it. . . . Long still will the art of preventing diseases have to grapple with virulent diseases, the microorganic germs of which escape our investigation."

Despite the encouraging initial results, it gradually became clear that Pasteur's proposed method was not infallible—no more than fifteen or sixteen dogs in twenty could be rendered refractory to rabies with absolute certainty. Furthermore, the results of the method could be ascertained only after three or four months, a circumstance that would have severely limited its scope in human practice, particularly in emergency cases. For these reasons Pasteur undertook to discover a new method of prophylaxis that would be both more rapid and more certain.

In doing so, Pasteur could look forward to yet another major government-financed expansion of his facilities. Very early in its deliberations, the rabies commission recommended the establishment of a large kennel yard for the housing and observation of Pasteur's experimental dogs. The site initially chosen, in the Bois de Meudon, was quickly abandoned in the face of vigorous protests from inhabitants of the neighborhood. Similar local protests erupted upon the selection of a second site—in the park of Villeneuve l'Étang, near St.-Cloud, a state domain that had once belonged to Louis Napoleon. Although these protests helped to delay an appropriation of 100,000 francs promised to Pasteur, they ultimately proved ineffectual. By May 1885 the old stables of the château of St.-Cloud had been converted into a large paved kennel with accommodations for sixty dogs. A laboratory was also established, and living quarters nearby were renovated for Pasteur's private use.[174]

Rabies Vaccination, 1884–1886: Its Extension to Man. Awaiting the completion of this new complex—which eventually became a branch of the Institut Pasteur and was the site of his death—Pasteur pursued his quest for a perfected method of preventing rabies. In December 1884 he reluctantly declined to treat a bitten child by the means at his disposal, noting that he had not yet established that his method would work on dogs after they had been bitten and confessing that even if he proved successful at that, his hand would "tremble" before applying the treatment to humans, "for what is possible on the dog may not be so on man."[175] By March 1885, however, he had begun to test his method on dogs already bitten;[176] and on 6 July 1885 he decided to treat nine-year-old Joseph Meister, from Alsace, "not without feelings of utmost anxiety," even though he had been assured by two sympathetic physicians that the boy was otherwise "doomed to inevitable death" and even though his new method of prophylaxis had never failed in dogs.

In a memoir of 26 October 1885, Pasteur described this new method and the circumstances under which he had made his fateful decision. In essence the new method involved *in vitro* attenuation rather than the earlier method of passage through monkeys. It depended first on the preparation of a virus both pure and perfectly consistent in its virulence. This had been accomplished by using a virus passed successively through rabbits over a period of three years. Now in its ninetieth passage, this virus invariably produced an incubation period of seven days and had done so for nearly forty consecutive passages. In two earlier memoirs Pasteur had reported that a given rabies virus retained its virulence for weeks in the encephalon and spinal cord of the infected animal, as long as these tissues were preserved from putrefaction by storage at 0–12° C. He now revealed that this technique could be modified in such a way as to attenuate the virus. Adopting a technique introduced by Roux, who prevented putrefaction of rabbit spinal cords by suspending them in a dry atmosphere instead of by cooling,[177] Pasteur excised strips of spinal cord from rabbits dead of the seven-day "fixed" virus and suspended them in flasks in which the atmosphere was kept dry by addition of caustic potash. He found that the virulence of the virus in these strips gradually diminished and eventually disappeared. The time required for this process depended somewhat on the thickness of the strips but more importantly on atmospheric temperature. Up to a point, the higher the temperature, the more quickly attenuation was achieved. Ordinarily the virus became attenuated to the point of harmlessness in about two weeks.

Using a spinal strip that had been drying for some two weeks, the first step in the actual treatment was to mash a portion of it in a sterile broth and then to inject the resulting paste into the animal to be protected. On successive days the injections came from progressively fresher marrows and eventually from a highly virulent strip that had been drying for only a day or two. By this method, Pasteur reported, he had rendered fifty dogs of all ages and types refractory to rabies when young Meister appeared unexpectedly at his laboratory, accompanied by his mother and the owner of the dog responsible for the attack. Two days before, on 4 July, Meister had been bitten in fourteen places on his hands, lower legs, and thighs. These wounds, some so deep that he could scarcely walk, had been cauterized with carbolic acid by a local physician twelve hours after the attack. The dog had been killed by its owner, whom Pasteur sent home after having been assured that his skin had not been broken by the dog's fangs. That the dog was indeed rabid seemed certain from its behavior and from the presence in its stomach of hay, straw, and wood chips.

Pasteur immediately consulted Alfred Vulpian, a member of the rabies commission, and Jacques Joseph Grancher, who worked in his laboratory. Both considered young Meister doomed; and after Pasteur told them of his new results, both urged him to use the new method on the boy. The treatment, begun that evening, lasted ten days, during which Meister received thirteen abdominal injections derived from progressively more virulent rabbit marrows. By the end of the treatment, Meister was being inoculated with the most virulent rabies virus known—that of a mad dog augmented by a long series of passages through rabbits. Nonetheless, he had remained healthy during the nearly four months since he had been bitten, and his recovery therefore seemed assured. According to Dubos, Meister eventually became a concierge at the Institut Pasteur and lived until 1940, when he chose to commit suicide rather than open Pasteur's burial crypt to the advancing German army.[178]

At the end of his memoir of 26 October 1885, Pasteur announced that a week earlier he had begun to treat a second boy, a fifteen-year-old shepherd named Jean-Baptiste Jupille, who had been viciously bitten while killing a rabid dog that threatened the lives of six younger comrades. He had not arrived at Pasteur's laboratory for treatment until six days after having been bitten (as compared with two days for Meister), prompting Pasteur to emphasize that the length of time that could safely be allowed to pass between bites and treatment presented the "most anxious question for now." During the brief and uniformly laudatory discussion that followed Pasteur's memoir, Vulpian proposed the founding of a special service for the treatment of rabies by Pasteur's method (a proposal ultimately realized in the Institut Pasteur) and the president of the Académie des Sciences predicted that the date of this meeting would "remain forever memorable in the history of medicine and forever glorious for French science." When, a day later, Pasteur read the same memoir to the Académie de Médecine, its president expressed the nearly identical sentiment that the date of the meeting would "remain one of the most memorable, if not the most memorable, in the history of the conquests of science and in the annals of the Academy."[179]

In March 1886, Pasteur reported that young Jupille remained well (like Meister, Jupille ultimately joined the staff of the Institut Pasteur, where he served until his death in 1923)[180] and that 350 patients had now submitted to his rabies treatment. One had died despite the treatment, but Pasteur defended his method by emphasizing that ten-year-old Louise Pelletier had not arrived for treatment until thirty-seven days after being attacked and by showing that the fatal virus had an incubation period characteristic of dog-bite virus and not of the virus used in his prophylactic treatment.

In the same memoir Pasteur referred briefly to the problem of reliable statistics, which remained at the center of all subsequent debate over his antirabies treatment. Admitting his surprise at the large number of people who came for treatment, he suggested that the frequency of rabid bites had previously been underestimated out of reluctance to inform victims that they might have contracted a fatal disease. Moreover, he emphasized that he had drawn up a very rigorous catalog of the cases, insisting where possible that the victims bring certificates from veterinarians or doctors testifying to the rabid state of the attacking animal. Although it nonetheless proved necessary to treat cases in which dogs were merely suspected of being rabid, Pasteur declined to treat anyone whose clothes had not been visibly penetrated. Supporting himself particularly on statistics giving an average of one death per six bitten victims in the department of the Seine from 1878 to 1883, he insisted that his treatment was "henceforth an established fact" and deserved a special new institution. In the discussion which followed, he argued that one such center in Paris would suffice for all of Europe if those who would eventually apply the treatment abroad came there for training.[181]

Pasteur and the Rabies Treatment After 1886. Even a few of Pasteur's disciples and collaborators opposed his quickness in applying the prophylactic treatment to human cases. Indeed, Roux broke with Pasteur over the issue, refusing to sign the first report on the treatment and leaving the laboratory for several months.[182] Naturally opposition was far more severe outside Pasteur's circle, particularly among traditional medical men, antivivisectionists, and antivaccinationists, and especially as others died after receiving the treatment. Some critics charged that these deaths occurred not despite the treatment but because of it, in effect accusing Pasteur of involuntary manslaughter, and the father of one dead child actually filed suit against him.[183] Despite overwhelming statistical evidence as to the safety of his treatment, Pasteur was not allowed to forget the occasional failures. By May 1886 he complained, with some justice, that his efforts had made him the target of a "hostile press" and of "malevolent persons" in the Académie de Médecine.[184] Nonetheless, it was impossible to claim absolute safety and efficacy for his treatment, and Pasteur's attempts to perfect it may have done more to exacerbate doubts than to dispel them.

In Meister's case the last injection in the series had been prepared from spinal marrow only one day old, but soon afterward Pasteur decided that five-day-old marrow should suffice for the final injection. For certain severe cases, however, he developed a more intensive version of the treatment, which he had begun to apply by September 1886. In these cases he returned to one-day-old marrow for the last injection in each series and increased the number of injections per day so that the patient went through three series of injections in the same period of time (ten days) that Meister and other victims had gone through one series.[185] Besides raising some doubt as to Pasteur's full confidence in his treatment, these modifications failed to eliminate occasional failures. In a very few cases death occurred under circumstances suggesting that the "intensive" method of treatment may have been responsible,[186] and Pasteur abandoned it within a year of its introduction. To some this indecision served as evidence that Pasteur's method was empirical rather than truly "scientific," as did the rather casual leap from animal experiments to human therapeutics and Pasteur's practice of keeping certain details of the method secret.[187] Against the latter criticism, however, Pasteur could appeal to the need for quality control

and could produce a list of those to whom every detail of the method had been taught in his laboratory.[188]

Ultimately the chief and most persuasive criticism of Pasteur's treatment concerned the statistical evidence of its efficacy. In its report of 1887, probably the most judicious contemporary evaluation of the treatment, the English Rabies Commission emphasized the unreliability of statistics on rabies. Besides the frequent difficulty or impossibility of establishing that the attacking animal had in fact been rabid, immense uncertainty surrounded the exact influence of the character and location of bites, of interracial and interspecific differences among attacking animals, and of cauterization and other treatments applied before Pasteur's vaccine. The uncertainty of these and other factors helped to explain why previous estimates of the mortality from the bites of rabid dogs varied from 5 percent to 60 percent. Despite its testimony as to the exactitude of Pasteur's experiments and its conviction that his treatment had saved a considerable number of lives, the English Rabies Commission recommended the less dramatic course of enacting and enforcing more stringent police regulations on dogs. By this approach, already operating with striking success in Australia and Germany, rabies was virtually eliminated from England by the turn of the century.[189]

Meanwhile, however, English citizens were among those making the pilgrimage to Paris in hope of being saved from rabies. If Pasteur's treatment evoked strong opposition from certain quarters, it won lavish praise and gratitude from nearly all who submitted to it; and centers for the treatment quickly spread to other nations. Despite the cavils of unbitten and unthreatened adversaries, a steady stream of fearful victims came to Paris and offered Pasteur living testimony of the value of his achievement. By November 1886, about a year after the first treatment, nearly 2,500 persons had been treated in Paris alone. Of 1,726 French citizens treated, only 12 had died; and Pasteur refused to acknowledge failure in two of these cases, including that of Louise Pelletier. On Pasteur's reckoning, therefore, the mortality rate after his treatment amounted to about 0.6 percent, as compared with the most optimistic estimate of 5 percent in the absence of his treatment.[190]

At Pasteur's death about 20,000 persons had undergone his rabies treatment at centers throughout the world, with a mortality rate of less than 0.5 percent.[191] By 1905 this number had reached 100,000; and by 1935, 51,057 persons had been treated at the Institut Pasteur alone, with only 151 deaths—a mortality rate of 0.29 percent.[192] Despite these statistics, controversy continued to surround the safety and efficacy of Pasteur's original method of vaccination and of the modified versions introduced subsequently. By the mid-twentieth century it had become clear that the repeated injection of rabid nerve tissue could sometimes produce paralysis and that such accidents could be strikingly reduced by resort to dead vaccines in place of Pasteur's living, attenuated vaccine. Even better results were achieved with live vaccine cultivated in duck eggs rather than in nerve tissue.[193] By 1973, another rabies vaccine had been developed in the hope that a single preventive injection could replace the long and painful series of abdominal injections.[194] If most epidemiologists now doubt that Pasteur's treatment has saved as many lives as once believed, if others deny its value under present social circumstances, and if all agree that muzzling and quarantine of dogs is a preferable approach to the rabies problem, Pasteur's achievement nonetheless had an impact and importance not fully represented in statistical terms—not only for those whose lives or peace of mind were saved by it but also for the promise and foundation it gave to the immensely successful campaign to extend immunization to other human diseases.[195]

Pasteur on Pest Control. On the basis of a few isolated passages in his work, Pasteur has been called a prophet not only of bacteriotherapy but also of chemotherapy. If this was indeed true, he was scarcely a toiler in the vineyard of either discipline. A rather similar judgment attaches to his few scattered remarks on biological methods of pest control, the prophetic character of which may seem more compelling in an era when ecology is in the ascendant and insecticides under suspicion. One pest of particular concern to him was phylloxera, a plant louse which, by its ruinous effects on vineyards in France and elsewhere, interfered for several years with the adoption and spread of his process for preserving wine. "In a time of famine," wrote Duclaux, "no one need consider how to keep grapes, and the heating of wines was little practiced except for those which must be shipped under bad conditions as to keeping, for example, in the commissariat of the Navy."[196] In 1882 Pasteur suggested that if phylloxera were subject to some contagious disease, and if the causative microbe of this disease could be isolated and cultivated, then the pest might be controlled by introducing the microbe into infested vineyards. This suggestion seems not to have been seriously pursued, however, and the phylloxera plague eventually declined as mysteriously as it had arisen.[197]

Under the stimulus of a 625,000-franc prize offered by the afflicted countries, Pasteur sought far more seriously a practical means of reducing the destructively large rabbit population in Australia and New Zealand. Having observed the remarkable susceptibility of rabbits to fowl cholera, he proposed that their food be contaminated with the fowl cholera bacillus, in hopes of establishing an epizootic outbreak of the disease among them. In 1888, following a highly successful preliminary trial of this method on an estate in Rheims, he sent a team of his collaborators to Sydney, Australia, where they were to organize and launch the antirabbit campaign. Ultimately, however, the Australian government refused to authorize a full-scale field trial and Pasteur failed to win the prize. He ascribed this outcome chiefly to the irrational fear aroused in Australia by the word "cholera," even though fowl cholera has nothing in common with human cholera.[198] Subsequent attempts along similar lines, however, have made it clear that Pasteur underestimated the difficulty of establishing a progressive epizootic disease in any animal population. Whether they arise naturally or are produced artificially, epizootics and epidemics are limited in their spread by factors which Pasteur did not fully appreciate and which remain to some degree obscure.[199]

Pasteur and Chemical Theories of Immunity. Like some of Pasteur's contemporary critics, Dubos has characterized his work on vaccination as largely "empirical" rather than "scientific."[200] Compared with the time and energy he invested in the search for effective vaccines, his efforts to establish a theoretical basis for attenuation and immunity were rather casual and undeveloped. Nonetheless, his concepts of immunity are interesting, the more so because they underwent a dramatic shift as a result of his work on rabies. Throughout his work on fowl cholera, anthrax, and swine erysipelas, Pasteur linked immunity with the biological, and particularly the nutritional, requirements of the pathogenic organism. In the case of animals inherently immune to a given disease, he supposed either that their natural body temperature was inimical to the development of the appropriate microbe or that they lacked some substance(s) essential to its life and nutrition. In animals rendered immune by recovery from a prior attack or by preventive inoculations, he supposed that each invasion by a given microbe (even in the attenuated state) removed a portion or all of some essential nutritional element(s), thereby rendering subsequent cultivation difficult or impossible. In January 1880, during a discussion of his work on fowl cholera, Pasteur illustrated his conception by applying it to cases of long-lasting immunity. Such cases could be explained by supposing that elements as rare as cesium or rubidium were essential to the life of the appropriate microbe and present only in trace amounts in the tissues of the invaded animal. Under these circumstances the initial invasion of the microbe could exhaust the supply of the essential element(s), rendering the animal refractory for as long as it took it to recoup a sufficient supply of the rare substance(s).[201]

At some point during his work on rabies, however, Pasteur began to doubt the validity of this biological "exhaustion" theory in the case of immunity against rabies. By his own account, he converted to a chemical "toxin" theory for rabies early in 1884;[202] but he gave no public indication of his conversion until his memoir of 26 October 1885, where it paled into insignificance beside the drama of young Meister and Jupille. Moreover, his conversion remained tentative and undeveloped, with the details of the supporting experiments reserved for a later paper. For the time being, Pasteur merely asserted that the vaccinal properties of the desiccated rabbit marrows seemed to result not from a decrease in the intrinsic virulence of the rabies virus but from a progressive quantitative decrease in the amount of living virus contained in the marrows. Then, citing other evidence that microbes could produce substances toxic to themselves (evidence that he had minimized while holding the "exhaustion" theory), Pasteur suggested that the virus might be composed of two distinct substances, "the one living and capable of multiplying in the nervous system, the other not living but nonetheless capable in suitable proportion of arresting the development of the former."

In January 1887, in the first issue of the *Annales de l'Institut Pasteur*, Pasteur gave a somewhat fuller account of the considerations that had led him to adopt a chemical theory of immunity for rabies. He noted that in rabbits the same rabies virus could give either a prolonged incubation period or a minimum incubation of seven days, depending on the manner and hence the quantity in which it was injected. This finding upset Pasteur's earlier assumption that length of incubation depended only on the intrinsic virulence and not on the quantity of the virus. Even more remarkable, large quantities of a given vaccine generally seemed to produce immunity more readily than smaller quantities. If immunity depended only on the action of an attenuated, living virus capable of self-reproduction, then small quantities ought to work just as effectively as large ones. Finally, Pasteur cited cases in which vaccination rendered animals immediately refractory to rabies without their showing any prior symptoms of an attenuated form of the disease.

To Pasteur these results seemed explicable only on the assumption that the rabies virus (or microbe) produced a nonliving vaccinal substance inimical to its own development. If this were so, the result of any given injection would depend on the relative proportions of living virus and vaccinal substance at the time of injection. The situation was complicated by the fact that the quantity of vaccinal substance depended to some extent on the amount of living virus from which it was derived. If the quantity of living virus introduced was small, as in intracranial inoculation or animal bites, the quantity of associated vaccinal substance would also necessarily be small. In such cases the supply of vaccinal substance might be inadequate to prevent the multiplication of the virus, and rabies would appear. Such a conception helped to explain why intracranial inoculation invariably produced rabies and why the bites of rabid dogs never conferred immunity. On the other hand, if the preexisting supply of vaccinal substance were large compared with the amount of living virus, then it might prevent the virus from developing at all—as seemed to be the case in animals rendered refractory to rabies without showing any prior symptoms of an attenuated form of the disease. The progressive loss of virulence in desiccated rabbit marrows could be explained by supposing that the drying process destroyed the living virus more rapidly than it destroyed the nonliving vaccinal substance. On such grounds, Pasteur reported, he had sought marrows in which the rabies virus had been entirely destroyed but in which some vaccinal substance remained. Although his search for such nonliving vaccines had been inconclusive, he continued to hope they would be found, for their discovery would constitute "both a first-rate scientific fact and a priceless improvement on the present method of prophylaxis against rabies." On 20 August 1888 he announced encouraging results with injections of rabid spinal cord heated at 35° C. for forty-eight hours to kill the virus—results that led him to predict that a chemical vaccine against rabies would soon be found and utilized.[203]

In January 1888, Pasteur had thrown his unqualified support behind Roux and Chamberland's claim that they had found a soluble chemical vaccine against septicemia in guinea pigs. At the same time he described his own preliminary attempts to find a chemical vaccine against anthrax.[204] Toward this end he used anthrax blood heated at 45° C. for several days to kill the anthrax microbe—a technique strikingly similar to that which Toussaint had proposed in 1880 and which Pasteur had criticized severely. Thus, at the very end of his scientific life Pasteur proved willing to modify profoundly the biological point of view that underlay his most celebrated achievements in the study of fermentation, putrefaction, and disease. He did, however, retain the notion that a living virus or microbe was essential to the production of the chemical vaccine. And he did reveal a continuing sympathy for biological theories of immunity—most notably by drawing early and favorable attention to Élie Metchnikoff's "phagocytic" theory.[205] But in doing so he no longer insisted on the inviolability of his earlier views.

In short, the aging Pasteur demonstrated a remarkable flexibility of mind. Moreover, as Dubos suggests, he seemed to end by groping "towards the new continent where the chemical controls of disease and immunity were hidden."[206] How far he might have progressed toward chemical theories of disease and chemotherapy must remain unknown. But without fully acknowledging it—perhaps without fully recognizing it—he seemed to draw ever closer not only to his erstwhile opponents Liebig, Bernard, and Chaveau but also to his own roots in chemistry. Given just a little more time, he might have closed the circle.

Honored Life, Honored Death. The final decade of Pasteur's life brought him additional honors, of which the most tangible were the second national recompense of 1883 and the establishment of the Institut Pasteur in 1888. Perhaps the most cherished were his election on 8 December 1881 to the Académie Française; an official celebration in July 1883 at Dole, where a commemmorative plaque was placed on the house in which he was born; and, above all, the moving jubilee celebration in the grand amphitheater of the Sorbonne on 27 December 1892, depicted in the painting by Rixens.

So frail that he had to be led in on the arm of Sadi Carnot, president of the Third Republic, Pasteur found the huge amphitheater filled to overflowing with students from the French *lycées* and universities, with his former pupils and assistants, with delegations from all the major French scientific schools and societies, and with government officials, foreign ambassadors and dignitaries. Of the many speakers who honored his life and work, the surgeon Sir Joseph Lister was perhaps the most notable and certainly the best qualified to testify to the direct influence of Pasteur's work. Unable to deliver his own brief speech of appreciation, Pasteur delegated this task to his son. In it he counseled the young students to "live in the serene peace of laboratories and libraries" and spoke to the foreign delegates of his "invincible belief that Science and Peace will triumph over Ignorance and War, that nations will unite, not to destroy, but to build, and that the future will belong to those who have done most for suffering humanity."[207]

It was Pasteur's last public appearance but far from his last honor. By the time of his death, his name had been given to the *collège* in Arbois, to a village in Algeria, to a district in Canada, and to streets and schools throughout France and the world, not to mention the proliferating Pasteur institutes. On 5 October 1895 France honored Pasteur's passing with a state funeral at Nôtre Dame, complete with full military honors. Temporarily placed in one of the chapels at Nôtre Dame, his body was moved in January 1896 to the resplendent funeral crypt in the Institut Pasteur where it now reposes, and where his wife was interred in 1910.

NOTES

Pasteur's scientific papers have been cited only when it seemed that the information provided in the text (notably the dates of memoirs), combined with that given by the editor of Pasteur's *Oeuvres*, might be insufficient to guide the reader to the pertinent paper. Similarly, for more strictly biographical material, references have been provided only when that material seemed sufficiently unfamiliar or controversial to warrant documentation.

1. Pasteur, *Oeuvres*, I, 376.
2. See Dubos, *Louis Pasteur*, 359–362, 377–384.
3. Pasteur, *Correspondance*, I, 228.
4. Pasteur to John Tyndall, 8 Mar. 1888, Archives of the Royal Institution of Great Britain.
5. *Ibid*. Cf. Pasteur, *Correspondance*, IV, 229–231 and *passim*.
6. René Vallery-Radot, *The Life of Pasteur*, 245–246, 374–376. Cf. Pasteur, *Correspondance*, II, 552, 565–570, 573–574, 580–583; III, 350, 364, 373, 384.
7. See Pasteur, *Correspondance*, IV, 365.
8. See Cuny, *Louis Pasteur*, 15–18; and Dubos, *op. cit.*, 80–82. For a contemporary attempt to portray Pasteur as greedy and unscrupulous, see Auguste J. Lutaud, *M. Pasteur et la rage* (Paris, 1887), esp. 405–431. Fanatically opposed to Pasteur, Lutaud often distorted and misused the documents he adduced in support of his claims, but those documents are suggestive enough to deserve a more dispassionate reexamination.
9. See Pasteur, *Oeuvres*, VI, 489; and Pasteur, *Correspondance*, III, 173 ff.
10. For a valuable but rather uncritical survey of Pasteur's involvement in controversy, see Pasteur Vallery-Radot, *Pasteur inconnu*, 62–131.
11. See Roux, "The Medical Work of Pasteur," 384; Dubos, *op. cit.*, 80, 370; and Louis Chauvois, D. Wrotnowska, and E. Perrin, "L'optique de Pasteur," in *Revue d'optique théorique et instrumentale*, **45** (1966), 197–213, esp. 197 f.
12. See Pasteur, *Correspondance*, IV, 336, 341, and 357, n. 1.
13. On Pasteur's general political views, see Cuny, *Louis Pasteur*, 19–25; Pasteur Vallery-Radot, *op. cit.*, 175–220; and Pasteur, *Correspondance*, II, 355, 459, 461–463, 489, 523, 534, 593, 600, 611–630; III, 424, 436–437; IV, 268–270, 300.
14. See Pasteur, *Correspondance*, I, 228, 230.
15. On the origins of Pasteur's study of wine, see especially *ibid.*, II, 128–129; and Pasteur, *Oeuvres*, III, 481–482. On his relationship with the imperial house, see *Correspondance*, II, 62, 215–235, 245–246, 268, 286–287, 297, 345–346, 355, 385, 387–388, 407–408, 451, 459, 461–463, 471, 484–485, 489, 586, 627; and his correspondence with Col. Fave, Louis Napoleon's aide-de-camp, *ibid.*, 98–100, 110–111, 120–121, 125–126, 146–148, 160–161, 236–238. In an unpub. letter of 7 Aug. 1863, announced for sale in *The Month at Goodspeed's* (May 1965), 249–250, Pasteur refers to a request from the emperor that he "take care of the aged and their illnesses," an invitation that Pasteur thought "might be useful to me with public officials whose help I might have to ask."
16. Pasteur, *Correspondance*, II, 216–236.
17. See Pasteur Vallery-Radot, ed., *Pages illustres de Pasteur*, 8.

18. See Pasteur, *Correspondance*, II, 502–503, 511–514, 517–519.
19. *Ibid.*, 491–492.
20. See "Fabrication de la bière," in *Journal de pharmacie*, **17** (1873), 330–331.
21. See Pasteur, *Correspondance*, III, 115–116, 313–314, 335–346, 430–431; IV, 209, 213–214, 358–359. More generally on Pasteur as "patriote," see Pasteur Vallery-Radot, *Pasteur inconnu*, 175–192.
22. Pasteur, *Correspondance*, II, 612. More generally on his campaign and the election, see *ibid.*, 611–630; and Pasteur Vallery-Radot, *Pasteur inconnu*, 203–215.
23. See Ledoux, *Pasteur et la Franche-Comté*, 55 ff.
24. Pasteur, *Correspondance*, IV, 340.
25. On Pasteur's general philosophical and religious positions, see René Vallery-Radot, *op. cit.*, 242–245, 342–343; Dubos, *op. cit.*, 385–400; Pasteur Vallery-Radot, *Pasteur inconnu*, 221–238; André George, *Pasteur* (Paris, 1958); and Pasteur, *Oeuvres*, II, 328–346; VI, 55–58; VII, 326–339.
26. Pasteur, *Correspondance*, II, 213–214.
27. Pasteur, *Oeuvres*, VII, 326–339, quote on 326. For an English trans. of Pasteur's inaugural address, see Eli Moschcowitz, "Louis Pasteur's Credo of Science: His Address When He Was Inducted Into the French Academy," in *Bulletin of the History of Medicine*, **22** (1948), 451–466.
28. Pasteur, *Oeuvres*, I, 376. For the Sorbonne address of 1864, see *ibid.*, II, 328–346. More generally, see Farley and Geison, "Science, Politics and Spontaneous Generation . . ." (in press).
29. See Adrien Loir, "L'ombre de Pasteur," **15** (1938), 508; and Dubos, *op. cit.*, 79–80, 370.
30. See Duclaux, *Pasteur*, 147–148, 174–175; Roux, "The Medical Work of Pasteur," 384–387; Loir, *op. cit.*, esp. **14** (1937), 144–146, 659–664; and Dubos, *op. cit.*, 370.
31. See Victor Glachant, "Pasteur disciplinaire: Un incident à l'École normale supérieure (novembre 1864)," in *Revue universitaire*, **47** (1938), 97–104, quote on p. 97.
32. *Ibid.*; Pasteur Vallery-Radot, *Pasteur inconnu*, 36–58; and Pasteur, *Correspondance*, II, 136–142, 332–339.
33. See esp. Lutaud, *op. cit.*, 418–430.
34. Ledoux, *op. cit.*, 33.
35. Pasteur, *Oeuvres*, I, 370. Cf. *ibid.*, 323 ff.
36. Pasteur later wrote that he might never have discovered hemihedrism in the tartrates had not Delafosse given such "particular development and special attention" to hemihedrism in his lectures. See Pasteur, *Correspondance*, IV, 386. For other expressions of his indebtedness to Delafosse, see Pasteur, *Oeuvres*, I, 66, 322, 398.
37. See J. R. Partington, *A History of Chemistry*, IV (London, 1964), 751–752; and Aaron Ihde, *The Development of Modern Chemistry* (New York, 1964), 322–323.
38. In 1884 Marie wrote to her daughter: "Your father, always very busy, says little to me, sleeps little, gets up at dawn— in a word continues the life that I began with him 35 years ago today." Pasteur, *Correspondance*, III, 418.
39. See esp. Pasteur, *Oeuvres*, I, 203–241.
40. *Ibid.*, 275–279, 284–288.
41. *Ibid.*, 314–344, esp. 331.
42. *Ibid.*, 369–380, 391–394.
43. *Ibid.*, 327.
44. See esp. Dorian Huber, "Louis Pasteur and Molecular Dissymmetry: 1844–1857" (M.A. thesis, Johns Hopkins University, 1969).
45. Pasteur, *Oeuvres*, I, 334–336. But see Huber, *op. cit.*, esp. 40–58.
46. See Pasteur, *Oeuvres*, I, 345–350, 360–365, 369–386.
47. Pasteur, *Correspondance*, I, 325–326. Cf. Pasteur Vallery-Radot, ed., *Pages illustres de Pasteur*, 10–13.
48. This paradox is explored in Farley and Geison, *op. cit.*
49. See Pasteur, *Oeuvres*, I, 275; II, 3.
50. Duclaux, *Pasteur*, 69. Cf. Pasteur, *Oeuvres*, II, 85–86.
51. René Vallery-Radot, *op. cit.*, 84. Cf. Pasteur, *Oeuvres*, VII, 186.
52. Pasteur, *Correspondance*, II, 183.
53. Duclaux, *op. cit.*, 73.
54. See *Annals and Magazine of Natural History*, 3rd ser., **7** (1861), 343, n.
55. See Ferdinand Cohn, "Untersuchungen über Bacterien, II.," in *Beiträge zur Biologie der Pflanzen*, **1**, no. 3 (1875), 141–207, esp. 194–196. More generally on Cohn, see Gerald L. Geison, "Ferdinand Cohn," in *Dictionary of Scientific Biography*, III, 336–341.
56. Bulloch, *History of Bacteriology*, 232.
57. Pasteur, *Oeuvres*, II, 13–14, n. 3.
58. See John Farley, "The Spontaneous Generation Controversy (1700–1860): The Origin of Parasitic Worms," in *Journal of the History of Biology*, **5** (1972), 95–125.
59. See Duclaux, *op. cit.*, 107; and Pasteur, *Oeuvres*, II, 190.
60. See Farley and Geison, *op. cit.*
61. This report is reproduced in Pasteur, *Oeuvres*, II, 637–647.
62. Duclaux, *op. cit.*, 109–111.
63. Pasteur, *Correspondance*, II, 198.
64. *Ibid.*, 193–195.
65. Pasteur, *Oeuvres*, IV, 86.
66. Duclaux, *op. cit.*, 163.
67. Pasteur, *Oeuvres*, IV, 465.
68. See Duclaux, *op. cit.*, 147, 158–159, 165, quote on 147.
69. See esp. Pasteur, *Oeuvres*, IV, 100–134, 188–199, 500–510.
70. See Duclaux, *op. cit.*, 172–173.
71. See Pasteur, *Oeuvres*, IV, 544.
72. *Ibid.*, 564–571.
73. *Ibid.*, 590–595.
74. Dubos, *op. cit.*, 225.
75. Pasteur, *Oeuvres*, VI, 132.
76. *Ibid.*, IV, 729–732.
77. *Ibid.*, II, 361–366.
78. *Ibid.*, 379, 396.
79. *Ibid.*, V, 265, n. 1.
80. *Ibid.*, II, 403–404, n. 3. Cf. *ibid.*, 427–429.
81. *Ibid.*, 430–435, 443–444.
82. *Ibid.*, 387.
83. *Ibid.*, 440–442.
84. *Ibid.*, 374–380, quote on 375.
85. *Ibid.*, VI, 33.
86. *Ibid.*, 80–86.
87. Duclaux, *op. cit.*, 128–131.
88. *Ibid.*, 206–209.
89. See Robert Kohler, "The Background to Eduard Buchner's Discovery of Cell-Free Fermentation," in *Journal of the History of Biology*, **4** (1971), 35–61, on 39–40.
90. See Pasteur, *Oeuvres*, II, 353, 538, 588–593, esp. 535.
91. *Ibid.*, V, 5.
92. Duclaux, *op. cit.*, 188.
93. See Pasteur, *Oeuvres*, V, 18, n. 1.
94. *Ibid.*, 307.
95. See Pasteur, *Correspondance*, III, 71, 78–79. For facsimiles of these letters, as well as several others exchanged between Pasteur and Jacobsen (including two previously unpublished letters from Pasteur), see *Lettres échangées entre J. C. Jacobsen et Louis Pasteur au cours des années 1878–1882* (Copenhagen, 1964).
96. Pasteur, *Oeuvres*, II, 385–386.
97. *Ibid.*, 453–455; V, *passim*; and Duclaux, *op. cit.*, 214–218.
98. Pasteur, *Oeuvres*, II, 541–545, 559–567.
99. *Ibid.*, 150–158, 373, 383, 389 n. 1, 407–408, esp. n. 2; V, 98–101; and Duclaux, *op. cit.*, 192–197.
100. Pasteur, *Oeuvres*, V, 101; II, 411. Pasteur only once used Darwin's name in print—while pointing out that the belief in microbial transformism was losing ground by 1876, "in spite of the growing favor of Darwin's system." *Ibid.*, V, 79.
101. *Ibid.*, II, 461.

102. For Bastian's account of his disagreements with the commission, see Henry Charlton Bastian, "The Commission of the French Academy and the Pasteur-Bastian Experiments," in *Nature*, **16** (1877), 277–279. Cf. Pasteur, *Oeuvres*, II, 459–473. More generally, see Glenn Vandervliet, *Microbiology and the Spontaneous Generation Debate During the 1870's* (Lawrence, Kan., 1971), 55–64; and J. K. Crellin, "The Problem of Heat Resistance of Microorganisms in the British Spontaneous Generation Controversy of 1860–1880," in *Medical History*, **10** (1966), 50–59.

103. See Vandervliet, *op. cit.*, *passim*; and J. K. Crellin, "Airborne Particles and the Germ Theory; 1860–1880," in *Annals of Science*, **22** (1966), 49–60.

104. Pasteur, *Oeuvres*, II, 478–481.

105. J. Burdon-Sanderson, "Bacteria," in *Nature*, **17** (1877), 84–87, on 84. More generally, see Crellin, "Airborne Particles and the Germ Theory."

106. Pasteur, *Oeuvres*, VI, 124.

107. See Duclaux, *op. cit.*, 119; Bulloch, *op. cit.*, 109; and Vandervliet, *op. cit.*, 63–64.

108. See Pasteur, *Oeuvres*, VI, 167, 188, 590.

109. See Pasteur, *Correspondance*, II, 577.

110. Pasteur, *Oeuvres*, VI, 161–163. Cf. *ibid.*, 469.

111. Pasteur, *Correspondance*, II, 350.

112. *Ibid.*, 346–351.

113. *Ibid.*, 551–552, 564–568, 570, 573–574, 580–584.

114. See Pasteur, *Oeuvres*, VI, 166–167, 188; II, 465.

115. *Ibid.*, VI, 167.

116. See Roux, *op. cit.*, 382. Pasteur's work made him the target of antivivisectionists and antivaccinationists, especially in England. For his contemptuous attitude toward these movements, see Pasteur, *Correspondance*, IV, 86, 109, 143, 193, 232, 294, 296–297.

117. Pasteur, *Oeuvres*, VI, 71–84, 138, 140, 157, 543.

118. *Ibid.*, 89–103.

119. *Ibid.*, 71.

120. See Duclaux, *op. cit.*, 237–241; and Bulloch, *op. cit.*, 179–182, 207, and *passim*.

121. Pasteur, *Oeuvres*, VI, 162–163.

122. *Ibid.*, 178; and Dubos, *op. cit.*, 309–310, 380–381.

123. Pasteur, *Oeuvres*, VI, 271–272.

124. *Ibid.*, 262.

125. Bulloch, *op. cit.*, 213, 236–238; and Dubos, *op. cit.*, 261.

126. Pasteur, *Oeuvres*, VI, 131–138.

127. *Ibid.*, 470.

128. *Ibid.*, 495.

129. Claiming, in private, that Toussaint had failed to do so. See *ibid.*, VII, 49.

130. *Ibid.*, VI, 132–133.

131. *Ibid.*, 471–489, esp. 489. Cf. Pasteur, *Correspondance*, III, 173–179.

132. But, more generally on luck and chance in Pasteur's work, see Dubos, *op. cit.*, 100–101, 219, 327, 340, 342.

133. Throughout that period all of Pasteur's correspondence is addressed from Arbois. See Pasteur, *Correspondance*, III, 98–115.

134. Duclaux, *op. cit.*, 281.

135. First used by Pasteur in his 1854 inaugural address at Lille. See Pasteur, *Oeuvres*, VII, 131. He used it again in 1871, in an address at Lyons, and in 1881, while discussing his famous Pouilly-le-Fort experiments on anthrax vaccination. See *ibid.*, 215; VI, 348.

136. See Pasteur, *Correspondance*, III, 121, 138–140.

137. Duclaux, *op. cit.*, 178.

138. Pasteur, *Correspondance*, III, 158–171, esp. 159, 166.

139. Pasteur, *Oeuvres*, VI, 256, n. 2.

140. *Ibid.*, 371.

141. See René Vallery-Radot, *op. cit.*, 313–315.

142. See Pasteur, *Oeuvres*, VI, 350, 710–711.

143. Charles Nicolle, *Biologie de l'invention* (Paris, 1932), 62–65. Cf. Roux, *op. cit.*, 379.

144. See Pasteur, *Correspondance*, III, 196–199.

145. Pasteur, *Oeuvres*, VI, 358, 360, 363–364.

146. See Pasteur, *Correspondance*, III, 271, n. 2.

147. Pasteur, *Oeuvres*, VI, 365–366.

148. *Ibid.*, 385.

149. *Ibid.*, 441.

150. See Pasteur, *Correspondance*, IV, 262–263, 286–287.

151. Pasteur, *Oeuvres*, VI, 370.

152. *Ibid.*, 386–390.

153. *Ibid.*, 454.

154. *Ibid.*, 458, n. 1.

155. See *ibid.*, 115, 165, 174, 424.

156. Perhaps with some justice, since Chamberland reportedly added cultures of *Bacillus subtilis* to some tubes of anthrax vaccine. See Dubos, *op. cit.*, 341.

157. Pasteur, *Oeuvres*, VI, 403–411.

158. See *ibid.*, 446–447, 450.

159. *Ibid.*, 459.

160. See Duclaux, *op. cit.*, 293.

161. Pasteur, *Oeuvres*, VI, 367–368. Cf. 398–399, 570–571.

162. *Ibid.*, esp. 402, n. 1.

163. Cf. Dubos, *op. cit.*, 193–194.

164. Pasteur, *Oeuvres*, VI, 555.

165. See Bulloch, *op. cit.*, 226.

166. Pasteur, *Oeuvres*, VI, 332–338, esp. 335–336.

167. *Ibid.*, 525. More generally on Pasteur's work on this disease, see Frank and Wrotnowska, *Correspondence of Pasteur and Thuillier*, 53 ff.

168. See Pasteur, *Oeuvres*, VI, 523, 525.

169. See Bulloch, *op. cit.*, 246–247.

170. Ledoux, *op. cit.*, 16–17. Cf. Dubos, *op. cit.*, 332.

171. See Pasteur, *Oeuvres*, VI, 591.

172. See Frank and Wrotnowska, *op. cit.*, 137.

173. See Dubos, *op. cit.*, 264.

174. See Pasteur, *Correspondance*, III, 421, 425–428, 441–445; and René Vallery-Radot, *op. cit.*, 398, 406, 410–411.

175. Pasteur, *Correspondance*, III, 445–446.

176. *Ibid.*, IV, 14–15.

177. See Dubos, *op. cit.*, 333–334.

178. *Ibid.*, 336. But if Dubos's romantic version of Meister's suicide is true, it seems remarkable that his death should have been reported so briefly and casually in *Isis*, **37** (1947), 183, where no mention is made of suicide or the German army and where the year of his death is given as 1941 rather than 1940.

179. See Pasteur, *Oeuvres*, VI, 611–612.

180. See *Journal of the American Medical Association*, **81** (1923), 1445.

181. Pasteur, *Oeuvres*, VI, 621.

182. See Dubos, *op. cit.*, 335, 347.

183. *Ibid.*, 347.

184. Pasteur, *Oeuvres*, VI, 626–627.

185. *Ibid.*, 633–634.

186. See *ibid.*, 875–876.

187. See *ibid.*, 836–844, esp. 841–842.

188. Pasteur, *Correspondance*, IV, 75–76.

189. See Pasteur, *Oeuvres*, VI, 870–877; and *Black's Medical Dictionary*, 27th ed. (London, 1967), 743. Rabies did return to England, however, between 1918 and 1940, presumably because of violations of the quarantine regulations. See H. J. Parish, *A History of Immunization* (Edinburgh, 1965), 56–57.

190. Pasteur, *Oeuvres*, VI, 628–629.

191. Duclaux, *op. cit.*, 299.

192. Bulloch, *op. cit.*, 251.

193. See Parish, *op. cit.*, 58.

194. See *New York Times*, 21 Aug. 1973, 1:4.

195. Cf. Dubos, *op. cit.*, 350–353.

196. Duclaux, *op. cit.*, 143.

197. See Dubos, *op. cit.*, 310; and Pasteur, *Oeuvres*, VII, 32–35.

198. See Pasteur, *Oeuvres*, VII, 86–93; and Pasteur, *Correspondance*, IV, 227–229, 231–232, 237, 240–251, 257–260, 270–273, 278–280, 287–290.

199. Dubos, *op. cit.*, 312. Cf. Bulloch, *op. cit.*, 243.
200. Dubos, *op. cit.*, 379–382 and *passim*.
201. Pasteur, *Oeuvres*, VI, 290–291.
202. *Ibid.*, 463.
203. *Ibid.*, 550.
204. *Ibid.*, 464–466.
205. *Ibid.*, 645, n. 2.
206. Dubos, *op. cit.*, 357–358.
207. See René Vallery-Radot, *op. cit.*, 447–451. For the text of Pasteur's address, see Pasteur, *Oeuvres*, VII, 426–428.

BIBLIOGRAPHY

I. Original Works. Virtually every word that Pasteur published during his lifetime, including all of his books, monographs, and scientific papers, has been reproduced in the monumental and magnificent *Oeuvres de Pasteur*, Pasteur Vallery-Radot, ed., 7 vols. (Paris, 1922–1939). This work also contains a number of letters, notes, and MSS that were not published during Pasteur's lifetime and a number of documents by others relating to his work, including several reports by commissions of the Académie des Sciences. Each volume has a brief introduction by Pasteur Vallery-Radot, who adds helpful editorial notes and comments throughout. The volumes are organized topically as follows: I, molecular asymmetry; II, fermentations and spontaneous generation; III, studies on vinegar and wine; IV, studies on the silkworm disease; V, studies on beer; VI, infectious diseases, virus vaccines, and rabies prophylaxis; VII, scientific and literary miscellania. Vol. VII also contains a complete index of names cited in all of the volumes, a complete chronological bibliography of Pasteur's publications, and a masterful "analytic and synthetic" subject index. In every way *Oeuvres de Pasteur* is a triumph of careful and diligent scholarship.

Of the approximately 500 communications published by Pasteur during his lifetime, many cover essentially similar ground, and the great majority are very brief notes or letters. Many others are nonscientific in content. The Royal Society *Catalogue of Scientific Papers* lists nearly 200 papers. Only the most important and influential of his published works can be listed here. His published books and monographs were *Études sur le vin. Ses maladies, causes qui les provoquent. Procédés nouveaux pour le conserver et pour le vieillir* (Paris, 1866; 2nd ed., rev. and enl., 1873); *Études sur le vinaigre, sa fabrication, ses maladies, moyens de les prévenir; nouvelles observations sur la conservation des vins par la chaleur* (Paris, 1868); *Études sur la maladie des vers à soie. Moyen pratique assuré de la combattre et d'en prévenir le retour*, 2 vols. (Paris, 1870); *Études sur la bière. Ses maladies, causes qui les provoquent, procédé pour la rendre inaltérable, avec une théorie nouvelle de la fermentation* (Paris, 1876), trans. by Frank Faulkner and D. Constable Robb as *Studies on Fermentation; the Diseases of Beer, Their Causes and the Means of Preventing Them* (London, 1879); and *Examen critique d'un écrit posthume de Claude Bernard sur la fermentation* (Paris, 1879).

Of Pasteur's papers on molecular asymmetry, the most important are "Recherches sur le dimorphism," in *Annales de chimie et de physique*, 3rd ser., **23** (1848), 267–294; "Recherches sur les relations qui peuvent exister entre la forme cristalline, la composition chimique et le sens de la polarisation rotatoire," *ibid.*, **24** (1848), 442–459; "Recherches sur les propriétés spécifiques des deux acides qui composent l'acide racémique," *ibid.*, **28** (1850), 56–99; "Nouvelles recherches sur les relations qui peuvent exister entre la forme cristalline, la composition chimique et le phénomène de la polarisation rotatoire," *ibid.*, **31** (1851), 67–102; "Mémoire sur les acides aspartique et malique," *ibid.*, **34** (1852), 30–64; "Nouvelles recherches sur les relations qui peuvent exister entre la forme cristalline, la composition chimique et le phénomène rotatoire moléculaire," *ibid.*, **38** (1853), 437–483; "Notice sur l'origine de l'acide racémique," in *Comptes rendus hebdomadaires . . . de l'Académie des sciences* (hereafter *Comptes rendus*), **36** (1853), 19–26; "Transformation des acides tartriques en acide racémique. Découverte de l'acide tartrique inactif. Nouvelle méthode de séparation de l'acide racémique en acides tartriques droit et gauche," *ibid.*, **37** (1853), 162–166; "Sur le dimorphisme dans les substances actives. Tetartoédrie," *ibid.*, **39** (1854), 20–26; "Mémoire sur l'alcool amylique," *ibid.*, **41** (1855), 296–300; "Isomorphisme entre les corps isomères, les uns actifs les autres inactifs sur la lumière polarisée," *ibid.*, **42** (1856), 1259–1264; "Études sur les modes d'accroissement des cristaux et sur les causes des variations de leurs formes secondaires," in *Annales de chimie et de physique*, 3rd ser., **49** (1857), 5–31; and "Note relative au *Penicillium glaucum* et à la dissymétrie moléculaire des produits organiques naturels," in *Comptes rendus*, **51** (1860), 298–299.

Pasteur's views on molecular asymmetry and optical activity, as they stood at the end of his active research on the problem, are admirably summarized in "Recherches sur la dissymétrie moléculaire des produits organiques naturels," in *Leçons de chimie professées en 1860* (Paris, 1861), 1–48, trans. by George Mann Richardson as "On the Asymmetry of Naturally Occurring Organic Compounds," in *The Foundations of Stereochemistry; Memoirs by Pasteur, van't Hoff, Lebel, and Wislicenus* (New York, 1901), 3–33. Pasteur's continuing interest in the relationship between asymmetry and life can be seen in ["Observations sur les forces dissymétriques"], in *Comptes rendus*, **78** (1874), 1515–1518; "Sur une distinction entre les produits organiques naturels et les produits organiques artificiels," *ibid.*, **81** (1875), 128–130; "La dissymétrie moléculaire," in *Revue scientifique*, 3rd ser., **7** (1884), 2–6; and "Réponses aux remarques de MM. Wyrouboff et Jungfleisch sur 'La dissymétrie moléculaire,'" in *Bulletin de la Société chimique de Paris*, n.s. (1884), 215–220. For a projected volume that would gather his earlier works on molecular asymmetry Pasteur wrote a preface, an introduction, and a historical note (1878); published posthumously by Pasteur Vallery-Radot in *Oeuvres de Pasteur*, I, 389–412, they serve as an excellent introduction to Pasteur's mature views on the subject.

Excluding his works on vinegar, wine, and beer (discussed below), the longest and most important of Pasteur's papers on fermentation and spontaneous generations is

"Mémoire sur les corpuscules organisés qui existent dans l'atmosphère, examen de la doctrine des générations spontanées," in *Annales des sciences naturelles.* Zoologie, 4th ser., **16** (1861), 5–98, significant portions of which are trans. into English in Conant, *Harvard Case Histories* (see below), 494–504, 509–516. Also important are "Mémoire sur la fermentation appelée lactique," in *Mémoires de la Société des sciences, de l'agriculture et des arts de Lille*, 2nd ser., **5** (1858), 13–26, trans. into English with the omission of three paragraphs in Conant, *Harvard Case Histories*, 453–460; "Mémoire sur la fermentation alcoolique," in *Annales de chimie et de physique*, 3rd ser., **58** (1860), 323–426; "De l'origine des ferments. Nouvelles expériences relatives aux générations dites spontanées," in *Comptes rendus*, **50** (1860), 849–854, of which an English trans. appeared in *Quarterly Journal of Microscopical Science*, **8** (1860), 255–259; "Recherches sur le mode de nutrition des Mucédinées," in *Comptes rendus*, **51** (1860), 709–712, of which an English trans. appeared in *Quarterly Journal of Microscopical Science*, 2nd ser., **1** (1861), 213–215; "Animalcules infusoires vivant sans gaz oxygène libre et déterminant des fermentations," in *Comptes rendus*, **52** (1861), 344–347, of which an English version appeared in *Annals and Magazine of Natural History*, 3rd ser., **7** (1861), 343–344; "Expériences et vues nouvelles sur la nature des fermentations," in *Comptes rendus*, **52** (1861), 1260–1264; and "Quelques faits nouveaux au sujet des levûres alcooliques," in *Bulletin de la Société chimique de Paris* (1862), 66–74.

Also see "Nouvel exemple de fermentation déterminée par des animalcules infusoires pouvant vivre sans gaz oxygène libre, et en dehors de tout contact avec l'air de l'atmosphère," in *Comptes rendus*, **56** (1863), 416–421, of which an English version appeared in *Annals and Magazine of Natural History*, 3rd ser., **11** (1863), 313–317; "Examen du rôle attribué au gaz oxygène atmosphérique dans la destruction des matières animales et végétales après la mort," in *Comptes rendus*, **56** (1863), 734–740, of which an English version appeared in *Chemical News and Journal of Physical (Industrial) Science*, **7** (1863), 280–282; "Recherches sur la putréfaction," in *Comptes rendus*, **56** (1863), 1189–1194; "Des générations spontanées," in *Revue des cours scientifiques*, **1** (1864), 257–265; "Note sur un mémoire de M. Liebig, relatif aux fermentations," in *Comptes rendus*, **73** (1871), 1419–1424; "Sur la nature et l'origine des ferments," *ibid.*, **74** (1872), 209–212; "Réponse à M. Frémy," *ibid.*, 403–404; "Faits nouveaux pour servir à la connaissance de la théorie des fermentations proprement dites," *ibid.*, **75** (1872), 784–790, of which an English trans. appeared in *Quarterly Journal of Microscopical Science*, 2nd ser., **13** (1873), 351–356; "Nouvelles expériences pour démontrer que le germe de la levure qui fait le vin provient de l'extérieur des grains de raisin," in *Comptes rendus*, **75** (1872), 781–782; "Note sur la fermentation des fruits et sur la diffusion des germes des levures alcooliques," *ibid.*, **83** (1876), 173–176; "Note sur l'altération de l'urine, à propos d'une communication du Dr Bastian, de Londres," *ibid.*, 176–180; "Sur l'altération de l'urine. Réponse à M. le

Dr Bastian," *ibid.*, 377–378; "Note sur l'altération de l'urine, à propos des communications récentes du Dr Bastian," *ibid.*, **84** (1877), 64–66, written with Jules François Joubert; "Réponse à M. le Dr Bastian," *ibid.*, 206; "Sur les germes des bactéries en suspension dans l'atmosphère et dans les eaux," *ibid.*, 206–209, written with J. F. Joubert; and "Note au sujet de l'expérience du Dr Bastian, relative à l'urine neutralisée par la potasse," *ibid.*, **85** (1887), 178–180. Also of interest are Pasteur's papers on Claude Bernard's posthumous MS on fermentation. These papers, published in 1878 and 1879, are reproduced in the appendix to Pasteur's *Examen critique d'un écrit posthume de Claude Bernard* (cited above).

The most important of Pasteur's papers on vinegar and acetic acid fermentation are "Sur la fermentation acétique," in *Bulletin de la Société chimique de Paris* (1861), 94–96, repr. in *Oeuvres*, III, 3–5; "Études sur les mycoderms. Rôle de ces plantes dans la fermentation acétique," in *Comptes rendus*, **54** (1862), 265–270; "Suite à une précédente communication sur les mycodermes. Nouveau procédé industriel de fabrication du vinaigre," *ibid.*, **55** (1862), 28–32; and "Mémoire sur la fermentation acétique," in *Annales scientifiques de l'École normale supérieure*, **1** (1864), 115–158. The last paper was combined with an otherwise unpublished lecture (delivered at Orléans in Nov. 1867) to yield Pasteur's *Études sur le vinaigre* (cited above).

Of Pasteur's papers on wine, the most important are "Études sur les vins. Première partie: De l'influence de l'oxygène de l'air dans la vinification," in *Comptes rendus*, **57** (1863), 936–942; "Études sur les vins. Deuxième partie: Des altérations spontanées ou maladies des vins, particulièrement dans le Jura," *ibid.*, **58** (1864), 142–150; "Procédé pratique de conservation et d'amélioration des vins," *ibid.*, **60** (1865), 899–901; "Note sur les dépôts qui se forment dans les vins," *ibid.*, 1109–1113; and "Nouvelles observations au sujet de la conservation des vins," *ibid.*, **61** (1865), 274–278. These papers form the basis of and were developed into Pasteur's *Études sur le vin* (cited above). Apart from his book *Études sur la bière* (cited above), Pasteur's only important publication on beer is "Études sur la bière; nouveau procédé de fabrication pour la rendre inaltérable," in *Comptes rendus*, **77** (1873), 1140–1148.

In *Études sur la maladie des vers à soie* (cited above), Pasteur reproduced all his important papers on silkworm disease written between 1865 and 1869 with the exception of "Sur la nature des corpuscules des vers à soie. Lettre à M. Dumas," in *Comptes rendus*, **64** (1867), 835–836. Of the post-1869 papers on silkworm disease, the most important are "Rapport adressé à l'Académie sur les résultats des éducations pratiques de vers à soie, effectuées au moyen de graines préparées par les procédés de sélection," *ibid.*, **71** (1870), 182–185; "Note sur l'application de la méthode de M. Pasteur pour vaincre la pébrine," in *Annales scientifiques de l'École normale supérieure*, 2nd ser., **1** (1872), 1–9, written with Jules Raulin; and "Note sur la flacherie," *ibid.*, 11–21, written with Jules Raulin.

The most important of Pasteur's communications on anthrax and septicemia are "Charbon et septicémie," in *Comptes rendus*, **85** (1877), 101–115, written with J. F. Joubert; ["Discussion sur l'étiologie du charbon"], in *Bulletin de l'Académie de médecine*, 2nd ser., **6** (1877), 921–926; ["Discussion sur l'étiologie du charbon. Poules rendues charbonneuses"], *ibid.*, **7** (1878), 253–255, 259–261; "Sur le charbon des poules," in *Comptes rendus*, **87** (1878), 47–48, written with J. F. Joubert and C. E. Chamberland; "Recherches sur l'étiologie et la prophylaxie de la maladie charbonneuse dans le département d'Eure-et-Loir," in *Recueil de médecine vétérinaire*, **56** (1879), 193–198; "Sur l'étiologie de l'affection charbonneuse," in *Bulletin de l'Académie de médecine*, 2nd ser., **8** (1879), 1063–1065, written with C. E. Chamberland and Émile Roux; "Étiologie du charbon [discussion]," *ibid.*, 1152–1157, 1159, 1183–1186, 1222–1234; and "Sur l'étiologie du charbon," in *Comptes rendus*, **91** (1880), 86–94, written with C. E. Chamberland and E. Roux, of which an English version appeared in *Chemical News*, **42** (1880), 225–227.

See also "Sur l'étiologie des affections charbonneuses," in *Comptes rendus*, **91** (1880), 455–457; "Sur la non-récidive de l'affection charbonneuse," *ibid.*, 531–538, written with C. E. Chamberland; "Sur la longue durée de la vie des germes charbonneux et sur leur conservation dans les terres cultivées," *ibid.*, **92** (1881), 209–211, written with C. E. Chamberland and E. Roux; "Note sur la constatation des germes du charbon dans les terres de la surface des fosses où on a enfoui des animaux charbonneux," in *Bulletin de l'Académie de médecine*, 2nd ser., **10** (1881), 308–311, written with C. E. Chamberland and E. Roux; "De la possibilité de rendre les moutons réfractaires au charbon par la méthode des inoculations préventives," in *Comptes rendus*, **92** (1881), 662–665, written with C. E. Chamberland and E. Roux; "Le vaccin du charbon," *ibid.*, 666–668, written with C. E. Chamberland and E. Roux; "Compte rendu sommaire des expériences faites à Pouilly-le-Fort, près Melun, sur la vaccination charbonneuse," *ibid.*, 1378–1383, written with C. E. Chamberland and E. Roux; "La vaccination charbonneuse. Réponse à un mémoire de M. Koch," in *Revue scientifique*, 3rd ser., **5** (1883), 74–84; "Sur la vaccination charbonneuse," in *Comptes rendus*, **96** (1883), 967–982; "Les doctrines dites microbiennes et la vaccination charbonneuse," in *Bulletin de l'Académie de médecine*, 2nd ser., **12** (1883), 509–514; and "La commission de l'École vétérinaire de Turin," in *Comptes rendus*, **96** (1883), 1457–1462.

Of Pasteur's communications on fowl cholera, the most important are "Sur les maladies virulentes, et en particulier sur la maladie appelée vulgairement choléra des poules," in *Comptes rendus*, **90** (1880), 239–248, of which an English version appeared in *Chemical News*, **42** (1880), 4–7; "Sur le choléra des poules; études des conditions de la non-récidive de la maladie et de quelques autres de ses caractères," in *Comptes rendus*, **90** (1880), 952–958, of which an English version appeared in *Chemical News*, **42** (1880), 321–322, and **43** (1881), 5–6; "Expériences tendant à démontrer que les poules vaccinées pour le

choléra sont réfractaires au charbon," in *Comptes rendus*, **91** (1880), 315; and "De l'atténuation de virus du choléra des poules," *ibid.*, 673–680, of which an English version appeared in *Chemical News*, **43** (1881), 179–180.

Of Pasteur's papers on rabies, the most important are "Sur une maladie nouvelle provoquée par la saliva d'un enfant mort de la rage," in *Comptes rendus*, **92** (1881), 159–165, written with C. E. Chamberland and E. Roux; "Sur la rage," *ibid.*, 1259–1260, written with C. E. Chamberland, E. Roux, and Louis Ferdinand Thuillier; "Nouveaux faits pour servir à la connaissance de la rage," *ibid.*, **95** (1882), 1187–1192, written with C. E. Chamberland, E. Roux, and L. F. Thuillier; "Nouvelle communication sur la rage," *ibid.*, **98** (1884), 457–463, written with C. E. Chamberland and E. Roux; "Sur la rage," *ibid.*, 1229–1231, written with C. E. Chamberland and E. Roux; "Méthode pour prévenir la rage après morsure," *ibid.*, **101** (1885), 765–773, 774; "Nouvelle communication sur la rage," *ibid.*, **103** (1886), 777–784; and "Lettre sur la rage," in *Annales de l'Institut Pasteur*, **1** (1887), 1–18. These communications, as well as two others, are trans. into English in Jean R. Suzor, *Hydrophobia: An Account of M. Pasteur's System* (London, 1887). The two additional communications trans. by Suzor are "Résultats de l'application de la méthode pour prévenir la rage après morsure," in *Comptes rendus*, **102** (1886), 459–466, 468–469; and "Note complémentaire sur les résultats de l'application de la méthode de prophylaxie de la rage après morsure," *ibid.*, 835–838.

Pasteur also published a number of papers on infectious diseases other than anthrax, fowl cholera, and rabies. The most important of these are ["Discussion sur la peste en Orient"] in *Bulletin de l'Académie de médecine*, 2nd ser., **8** (1879), 176–182; "Septicémie puerpérale," *ibid.*, 256–260, 271–274, 488–493; "Commission dite de la peste," *ibid.*, **9** (1880), 386–390; "De l'extension de la théorie des germes à l'étiologie de quelques maladies communes [I. Sur les furoncles. II. Sur l'ostéomyélite. III. Sur la fièvre puerpérale]," in *Comptes rendus*, **90** (1880), 1033–1044; "Note sur la péripneumonie contagieuse des bêtes à cornes," in *Recueil de médecine vétérinaire*, **59** (1882), 1215–1223; and "La vaccination du rouget des porcs à l'aide du virus mortel atténué de cette maladie," in *Comptes rendus*, **97** (1883), 1163–1169, written with L. F. Thuillier.

For Pasteur's more general views on infectious diseases and vaccines, see especially "Observations verbales, à l'occasion du rapport de M. Gosselin," in *Comptes rendus*, **80** (1875), 87–95; "Discussion sur la fermentation," in *Bulletin de l'Académie de médecine*, 2nd ser., **4** (1875), 247–257, 265–282, 283, 284–290; "La théorie des germes et ses applications à la médecine et la chirurgie," in *Comptes rendus*, **86** (1878), 1037–1043, written with J. F. Joubert and C. E. Chamberland; "De l'atténuation des virus et de leur retour à la virulence," *ibid.*, **92** (1881), 429–435, written with C. E. Chamberland and E. Roux; "Vaccination in Relation to Chicken-Cholera and Splenic Fever," in *Transactions of the International Medical Congress, Seventh Session Held in London . . . 1881*,

4 vols. (London, 1881), I, 85–90; "Des virus-vaccins," in *Revue scientifique*, 3rd ser., **3** (1881), 225–228; "De l'atténuation des virus," *ibid.*, **4** (1882), 353–361, written with C. E. Chamberland, É. Roux, and L. F. Thuillier; and "Microbes pathogènes et vaccins," in *Semaine médicale*, **4** (1884), 318–320.

Of Pasteur's nonscientific writings the most interesting are "Lavoisier," in *Moniteur universel*, 4 Sept. 1865, 1198; "Claude Bernard. Idée de l'importance de ses travaux, de son enseignement et de sa méthode," *ibid.*, 7 Nov. 1866, 1284–1285; *Quelques réflexions sur la science en France* (Paris, 1871); *Discours de réception à l'Académie française* (Paris, 1882); *Réponse au discours de M. J. Bertrand à l'Académie française* (Paris, 1885); "Discours prononcé à l'inauguration de l'Institut Pasteur, le 14 novembre 1888," in *Inauguration de l'Institut Pasteur* (Paris, 1888), 26–30; and "Discours prononcé par Pasteur, le 27 décembre 1892, à l'occasion de son jubilé," in *Jubilé de M. Pasteur* (Paris, 1893), 24–26.

A major portion of Pasteur's vast correspondence was assembled and published in his *Correspondance*, Pasteur Vallery-Radot, ed., 4 vols. (Paris, 1940–1951). Arranged chronologically over the period 1840–1895, these letters provide a detailed account of Pasteur's activities and vividly illuminate every aspect of his life and career. Pasteur's own letters dominate the collection, but many letters to him and many by members of his family are included. For published versions of nearly 100 additional letters to or by Pasteur, as well as several other previously unpublished documents, see *Pages illustres de Pasteur*, Pasteur Vallery-Radot, ed. (Paris, 1968), 7–55; and *Correspondence of Pasteur and Thuillier Concerning Anthrax and Swine Fever Vaccination*, translated and edited by Robert M. Frank and Denise Wrotnowska with a preface by Pasteur Vallery-Radot (University, Ala., 1968).

Pasteur's grandson, Pasteur Vallery-Radot, spent his life seeking and collecting his grandfather's letters, MSS, and papers. In 1964 he gave most of his collection to the Bibliothèque Nationale. It comprises 7 file boxes of correspondence to Pasteur, 6 file boxes of correspondence by Pasteur, 1 file box of letters about him, and 22 packets containing MSS of his works and his laboratory and course notebooks. Although this material became generally accessible upon Pasteur Vallery-Radot's death in 1971, the collection is not yet classified for use. Apart from this material, some letters or MSS by and relating to Pasteur are deposited in the Reynolds collection at the University of Alabama at Birmingham, the Institut Pasteur in Paris, the Maucuer family in Paris, the Carlsberg Foundation in Copenhagen, the Bayerische Staatsbibliothek in Munich, the Laboratoire Arago in Banyuls-sur-Mer, the Royal Institution and the Wellcome Institute of the History of Medecine in London, the National Library of Medicine in Bethesda, Maryland, and the Burndy Library in Norwalk, Connecticut. Still other letters or MSS may be deposited in other libraries or may be privately owned. A number of official and administrative documents by and about Pasteur are deposited in French national and provincial archives. Many such documents have been extracted or otherwise put to use in the articles by Denise Wrotnowska (see below).

In addition to its small collection of Pasteur's personal letters and the resplendent funeral chapel where Pasteur and his wife are interred, the Institut Pasteur houses the Musée Pasteur, which includes the following: Pasteur's personal apartment, preserved as it was when he lived there; Pasteur's personal library, including annotated volumes of his communications to the Académie des Sciences; about 1,000 pieces of Pasteur's laboratory instruments and equipment, including chemical products with his labels, microscopes, wood models of crystals, flasks, and bottles; Pasteur's medals, diplomas, and other personal souvenirs; several of the portraits and pastel drawings he did as a youth (including the superb portraits of his parents); an iconography of about 5,000 photographs, drawings, and portraits of Pasteur, his disciples, and the Institut Pasteur; as yet uncataloged MS material on Émile Roux, Alexandre Yersin, Élie Metchnikoff, and Albert Calmette; documents concerning the Institut Pasteur; and a historical library. Pasteur museums also exist in Arbois, Dole, and Strasbourg.

II. SECONDARY LITERATURE. Perhaps no life in science has been so minutely described as Pasteur's, and rarely does a biographer or historian have access to such a wealth of carefully preserved primary material. Nonetheless, no fully adequate scientific biography of Pasteur exists, and the vast majority of the literature on him is derivative and essentially useless. Only the most important and valuable of the literature can be listed here.

There are three basic sources for Pasteur's life and work. The standard biography is René Vallery-Radot, *La vie de Pasteur* (Paris, 1900), trans. by Mrs. R. L. Devonshire as *The Life of Pasteur*, 2 vols. (London, 1901; 2nd, abr. ed., 1906)—references in the notes are to the 2nd ed. This biography, from which most of the literature on Pasteur derives, is distinguished for its extensive use of Pasteur's correspondence (including some still not published) and for its extraordinary detail. But it is without scholarly apparatus, occasionally obscure about dates, weak on historical background, and too exclusively concerned with Pasteur as an isolated genius at the expense of the more general context of his scientific work. Moreover, Vallery-Radot, who was Pasteur's son-in-law, is often openly hostile toward Pasteur's opponents and is so devoid of critical judgment as to approach hagiography. A second basic source is Émile Duclaux, *Pasteur: Histoire d'un esprit* (Paris, 1896), trans. by Erwin F. Smith and Florence Hedges as *Pasteur: The History of a Mind* (Philadelphia, 1920). Although also virtually devoid of scholarly apparatus, this book provides a lucidly brilliant and critical analysis of Pasteur's work by one of his most celebrated students. Illuminated by a prescient historiography, it remains one of the most impressive and perceptive books ever written on the development of a scientist's thought. The third basic source is René Dubos, *Louis Pasteur: Free Lance of Science* (Boston, 1950), trans. by Elisabeth Dussauze as *Louis Pasteur: Franc-tireur de la science*, with a preface by Robert Debré (Paris, 1955). Although sometimes almost embarrassingly dependent on Duclaux, and although virtually undocumented, this book is more sensitive to the larger context of Pasteur's work and surpasses Duclaux's by interweaving the evolution of Pasteur's scientific thought with his other activities and attitudes. Distinguished by a lucid and graceful style, it offers insights and perspectives unavailable to Duclaux so soon after Pasteur's death.

Of the remaining full-scale general accounts of Pasteur's life and work, the most valuable are Hilaire Cuny, *Louis Pasteur: L'homme et ses théories* (Paris, 1963), trans. by Patrick Evans as *Louis Pasteur: The Man and His Theories* (London, 1965); Jacques Nicolle, *Un maître de l'enquête scientifique, Louis Pasteur* (Paris, 1953), trans. as *Louis Pasteur; a Master of Scientific Enquiry* (London, 1961); and *Pasteur: sa vie, sa méthode, ses découvertes* (Paris, 1969); and Percy F. and Grace C. Frankland, *Pasteur* (New York, 1898). René Dubos, *Pasteur and Modern Science* (New York, 1960), is essentially an elegantly spare reworking of Dubos's earlier full-bodied biography. René Vallery-Radot foreshadowed his later full-scale biography in the anonymously published *Pasteur, histoire d'un savant par un ignorant* (Paris, 1883), which appeared twelve years before Pasteur's death. Also of interest is René Vallery-Radot, *Madame Pasteur* (Paris, 1941), a brief panegyric written in 1913 and eventually released for publication by Pasteur Vallery-Radot, whose own *Louis Pasteur: A Great Life in Brief*, trans. by Alfred Joseph (New York, 1958), is perhaps the best short biography of Pasteur.

Of the remaining books on Pasteur, several deserve mention on rather more specialized grounds. François Dagognet, *Méthodes et doctrines dans l'oeuvre de Pasteur* (Paris, 1967), is a highly suggestive, sometimes brilliant, but essentially ahistorical account of Pasteur's scientific work. Particularly valuable for their insights into the modern consequences of Pasteur's program are Henri Simonnet, *L'oeuvre de Louis Pasteur* (Paris, 1947); and Albert Delaunay, *Pasteur et la microbiologie* (Paris, 1967). For a valuable account of some of the less familiar and essentially nonscientific aspects of Pasteur's career, see Pasteur Vallery-Radot, *Pasteur inconnu* (Paris, 1954). Pasteur's early life receives detailed scrutiny in E. Ledoux, *Pasteur et la Franche-Comté; Dole, Arbois, Besançon* (Besançon, 1941), an appealing attempt to elucidate the influences on him of the land, climate, and demography of his native region. Louis Blaringhem, *Pasteur et le transformisme* (Paris, 1923), approaches Pasteur's work from an interesting perspective and seeks to trace to his work on fermentation, the genetic technique of "pure lines" and other intervening developments in biology. *The Pasteur Fermentation Centennial, 1857–1957* (New York, 1958) contains the contributions of Pasteur Vallery-Radot and René Dubos to a symposium held on the centennial of the publication of Pasteur's first memoir on lactic fermentation. Among the books that reprint extracts or selections from Pasteur's works are *Les plus belles pages de Pasteur*, Pasteur Vallery-Radot, ed. (Paris, 1943); *Pasteur: Pages choisies*, Ernest Kahane, ed. (Paris, 1957);

Louis Pasteur: Choix de textes, bibliographie, portraits, fac-similés, Hilaire Cuny, ed. (Paris, 1963); *Louis Pasteur; recueil de travaux*, Pasteur Vallery-Radot, ed. (Paris, 1966); and *Louis Pasteur: Extraits de ses oeuvres*, R. Dujarric de la Rivière, ed. (Paris, 1967).

Of the multitude of articles on Pasteur, the most generally valuable are those written by his students. Particularly informative with regard to Pasteur's personality and interaction with his assistants are Émile Roux, "L'oeuvre médicale de Pasteur," in *Agenda du chimiste* (Paris, 1896), trans. by Erwin F. Smith as "The Medical Work of Pasteur," in *Scientific Monthly*, **21** (1925), 365–389, to which version the notes refer; and Adrien Loir, "L'ombre de Pasteur," in *Mouvement sanitaire*, **14** (1937), 43–47, 84–93, 135–146, 188–192, 269–282, 328–348, 387–399, 138–145, 187–197, 572–573, 619–621, 659–661; **15** (1938), 179–181, 370–376, 503–508.

See also Émile Duclaux, "Le laboratoire de M. Pasteur à l'École normale," in *Revue scientifique*, 4th ser., **15** (Apr. 1895), 449–454; and "Le laboratoire de M. Pasteur," in *Le centenaire de l'École normale, 1795–1895* (Paris, 1895), 458 ff., and repro. in the centenary volume sponsored by the Institut Pasteur, *Pasteur, 1822–1922* (Paris, 1922), 39–54. Also repro. in the centenary volume are Roux's paper of 1896, "L'oeuvre médicale de Pasteur" (55–87); his "L'oeuvre agricole de Pasteur" (89–101), originally delivered to the Société Nationale d'Agriculture on 22 Mar. 1911; and his "Madame Pasteur" (102–104), a speech originally delivered on 28 Sept. 1910, when she was interred in the Pasteur crypt at the Institut Pasteur. See also Élie Metchnikoff, "Recollections of Pasteur," in *Ciba–Symposium*, **13** (1965), 108–111; and *The Founders of Modern Medicine: Pasteur, Koch, Lister* (New York, 1939). For a lengthy list of obituary notices on Pasteur, see the Royal Society *Catalogue of Scientific Papers*, XVII, 726–727.

Of the more narrowly focused literature on Pasteur (including that cited in full in the notes above), several works deserve special mention. Pasteur's religious position is explored in great detail in George (n. 25). On his handling of student discipline, see Glachant (n. 31). Various aspects of his career are explored in the articles of Denise Wrotnowska, among which the most significant are "Pasteur, professeur à Strasbourg (1849–1854)," in *92nd Congrès national des sociétés savantes*, I (Strasbourg–Colmar, 1967), 135–144; "Candidatures de Pasteur à l'Académie des sciences," in *Histoire de la médicine*, spec. no. (1958), 1–23; "Pasteur et Lacaze–Duthiers, professeur d'histoire naturelle à la Faculté des sciences de Lille," in *Histoire des sciences médicales* (1967), no. 1, 1–13; "Pasteur, précurseur des laboratoires auprès des musées," in *Bulletin du Laboratoire du Musée du Louvre* (1959), no. 4, 46–61; and "Recherches de Pasteur sur le rouget du porc," in *90th Congrès nationale des sociétés savantes*, III (Nice, 1965), 147–159. Pasteur's work on crystallography and molecular asymmetry is explored in admirable detail in Huber (n. 44). Seymour Mauskopf, *Crystals and Compounds* (forthcoming), examines the French crystallographic tradition from which Pasteur emerged, and offers a novel interpretation of his discovery of optical isomerism, emphasizing Laurent's influence and the issue of isomorphism. See also J. D. Bernal, "Molecular Asymmetry," in *Science and Industry in the Nineteenth Century* (London, 1953), 181–219; and Nils Roll-Hansen, "Louis Pasteur—a Case Against Reductionist Historiography," in *British Journal for the Philosophy of Science*, **23** (1972), 347–361.

For an English trans. of nearly all of Pasteur's first memoir on fermentation, together with a brief account of its genesis and impact, see James Bryant Conant, "Pasteur's Study of Fermentation," in *Harvard Case Histories in Experimental Science*, II (Cambridge, Mass., 1957), 437–485. On the relationship of Pasteur's work on fermentation to Buchner's discovery of zymase, see Kohler (n. 89). For an English trans. of significant portions of Pasteur's prize-winning memoir of 1861 on organized particles in the atmosphere, together with a more general discussion of the controversy over spontaneous generation, see Conant, "Pasteur's and Tyndall's Study of Spontaneous Generation," *op cit.*, 487–539. For an attempt to show that Pasteur's work on and public posture toward spontaneous generation were motivated in part by political factors, see John Farley and Gerald L. Geison, "Science, Politics and Spontaneous Generation in Nineteenth-Century France: The Pasteur-Pouchet Debate," in *Bulletin of the History of Medicine*, **48** (1974). The same debate is treated at length by Pouchet's disciple Georges Pennetier, *Un débat scientifique: Pouchet et Pasteur, 1858–1868* (Rouen, 1907). More generally on spontaneous generation, see Crellin (n. 102 and n. 103) and Vandervliet (n. 102). On the larger historical context of Pasteur's biological work, see William Bulloch, *The History of Bacteriology* (London, 1938); and William D. Foster, *A History of Medical Bacteriology and Immunology* (London, 1970).

GERALD L. GEISON

PASTOR, JULIO REY. See **Rey Pastor, Julio.**

PATRIZI, FRANCESCO (also **Patrizzi** or **Patricio;** Latin form, **Franciscus Patricius**) (*b.* Cherso, Istria, Italy, 25 April 1529; *d.* Rome, Italy, 7 February 1597), *mathematics, natural philosophy.*

Patrizi studied at Ingolstadt, at the University of Padua (1547–1554), and at Venice. While in the service of various noblemen in Rome and Venice he made several trips to the East, where he perfected his knowledge of Greek, and to Spain. He lived for a time at Modena and at Ferrara, before being appointed to a personal chair of Platonic philosophy at the University of Ferrara by Duke Alfonso II d'Este in 1578. He remained there until 1592, when Pope Clement VIII summoned him to a similar professorship in Rome, a post he held until his death.

Patrizi had interests in many different intellectual fields; he published works on poetry, history, rhetoric, literary criticism, metaphysics, ethics, natural philosophy, and mathematics, besides translating a number of Greek works into Latin. His thought is a characteristic blend of Platonism (in the widest sense in which the word is used when referring to the Renaissance) and natural philosophy, with a very strong anti-Aristotelian bent. The latter critical tendency is developed in his *Discussiones peripateticae* (Venice, 1571; much enlarged edition, Basel, 1581).

Patrizi's importance in the history of science rests primarily on his highly original views concerning the nature of space, which have striking similarities to those later developed by Henry More and Isaac Newton. His position was first set out in *De rerum natura libri II priores, alter de spacio physico, alter de spacio mathematico* (Ferrara, 1587) and was later revised and incorporated into his *Nova de universis philosophia* (Ferrara, 1591; reprinted Venice, 1593), which is his major systematic work. Rejecting the Aristotelian doctrines of *horror vacui* and of determinate "place," Patrizi argued that the physical existence of a void is possible and that space is a necessary precondition of all that exists in it. Space, for Patrizi, was "merely the simple capacity (*aptitudo*) for receiving bodies, and nothing else." It was no longer a category, as it was for Aristotle, but an indeterminate receptacle of infinite extent. His distinction between "mathematical" and "physical" space points the way toward later philosophical and scientific theories.

The primacy of space (*spazio*) in Patrizi's system is also seen in his *Della nuova geometria* (Ferrara, 1587), the essence of which was later incorporated into the *Nova de universis philosophia*. In it Patrizi attempted to found a system of geometry in which space was a fundamental, undefined concept that entered into the basic definitions (point, line, angle) of the system.

The full impact of Patrizi's works on later thought has yet to be evaluated.

BIBLIOGRAPHY

Lega Nazionale di Trieste, *Onoranze a Francesco Patrizi da Cherso: Catalogo della mostra bibliografica* (Trieste, 1957), presents the most complete listing of primary and secondary works to 1957. Other general works are B. Brickman, *An Introduction to Francesco Patrizi's Nova de universis philosophia* (New York, 1941); P. O. Kristeller, *Eight Philosophers of the Italian Renaissance* (Stanford, 1964), ch. 7; and G. Saitta, *Il pensiero italiano nell'umanesimo e nel Rinascimento*, 2nd ed. (Florence, 1961), II, ch. 9.

Works on Patrizi's concept of space are B. Brickman, "Francesco Patrizi on Physical Space," in *Journal of the History of Ideas*, **4** (1943), 224–245; E. Cassirer, *Das Erkenntnisproblem*, 3rd ed. (Berlin, 1922), I, 260–267; W. Gent, *Die Philosophie des Raumes und der Zeit*, 2nd ed. (Hildesheim, 1962), 81–83; and M. Jammer, *Concepts of Space* (Cambridge, Mass., 1954), 84–85.

CHARLES B. SCHMITT

PAUL OF AEGINA (*b*. Aegina; *fl*. Alexandria, A.D. 640), *medicine*.

The details of Paul of Aegina's life are meager. He was born on the island of Aegina in the Saronic Gulf and studied and practiced medicine at Alexandria, where he remained after the Arabic invasion of 640.

Paul's most important and only extant work is his seven-book medical encyclopedia, *Epitome medicae libri septem*. According to Islamic sources, he also wrote two other works, a volume on gynecology and one on toxicology. Muslim physicians considered him one of the most eminent of Greek medical authorities, and he is frequently quoted in their works. In the preface to his work, Paul indicated that he prepared his review of earlier Greek medical practices in order that physicians, regardless of where they found themselves, could have a brief synopsis of pertinent medical procedures. He did not claim to be original; and, indeed, he noted that he had added only a few practices of his own. His study was based primarily on Oribasius' seventy-volume medical encyclopedia. Through Oribasius, Paul acquired and transmitted many of the Galenic medical concepts. Although he used other sources, unlike Oribasius, he did not cite them.

Paul divided the *Epitome* into the following sections:

Book I.   Hygiene and regimen
Book II.   Fevers
Book III. Bodily afflictions arranged topically
Book IV. Cutaneous complaints and intestinal worms
Book V.   Toxicology
Book VI. Surgery
Book VII. Properties of medicines.

In the first book Paul examined in some detail the general principles of hygiene. Beginning with an analysis of the problems of pregnant women, he proceeded to a review of the problems of hygiene in the successive ages of man. He was interested in the establishment of the proper regimen for every stage of human development. In the Galenic tradition he subscribed to the earlier Greek humoral pathology of the four elements with their respective qualities. Paul contended that through various forms of dietary, medical, and physical manipulations, a proper balance could be achieved in the body and man would thus enjoy good health. He provided instructions for the care of the eyes and teeth, the retention of hearing, and the problems of impotence. His attitudes toward the role of the temperaments is clearly based on Oribasius' interpretation of Galen's thoughts on this subject. Paul maintained that man is in his best temperament when he exists in a middle position between all extremes—leanness and obesity, softness and hardness, hot and cold, and wet and dry. Individuals have particular attributes as their bodies vary from the mean. Bodies with hot and dry temperaments differ substantially from those with cold and moist temperaments. Depending upon their constituency of humors, internal organs also have different temperaments. The numerous permutations of possible temperaments and humors both explain the diverse medical conditions of men and necessitate the numerous varieties of medicines and treatments. Since food is vital to sound health and to the balance of the humors, he presented a sustained discussion of dietary therapeutics with a description of numerous foods and their medicinal virtues.

In Book II, Paul analyzed the nature and manifestations of fevers as characteristics of particular diseases. He utilized the duration and degree of fever as one of the prognoses for the course of a disease. High fevers indicate an acute illness; low fevers, a chronic sickness. The pulse is another important prognostic tool, and he classified sixty-two varieties of pulse. He defined pulse

> . . . as a movement of the heart and arteries, taking place by a diastole and systole. Its object is two fold; for, by the diastole, which is, as it were, an unfolding and expansion of the artery, the cold air enters, ventilating and resuscitating the animal vigour, and hence the formation of vital spirits; and by the systole, which is, as it were, a falling down and contraction of the circumference of the artery towards the centre, the evacuation of the fuliginous superfluities is effected [Adams, *Seven Books*, I, 202].

Paul also utilized alvine discharges, urine, and sputa as indications of the body's conditions.

In Book III Paul surveyed ailments that affect the body. Beginning with afflictions of the hair, he proceeded through diseases of the head (eye, ear, nose, and throat) to mental problems and then to internal ailments (heart, stomach, kidney, liver, and uterus). He concluded with comments on corns, calluses, and nails. Paul's topical approach enabled him to critique the general medical complications of the body's organs and their respective treatments. He recommended bleeding for cephalalgia, hemicrania, phrenitis, erysipelas of the brain, and lethargy, and he encouraged diverse medicines and select bleedings for the control of epilepsy, melancholy, apoplexy, and nervous diseases. His review of the kidneys, liver, and spleen embodies the best traditions of classical medical thought. Kidney stones are formed by thick earthy humors that are heated by the body. Baths and compound medicines are methods of expelling these stones. Diseases and afflictions of the uterus, and complicated labors are examined thoroughly in the final passages of this book. Paul maintained that when the fetus is in a preternatural position it should be restored to its natural position.

> . . . sometimes drawing it down, sometimes pressing it back, sometimes rectifying the whole. If a hand or foot protrude we must seize upon the limb and drag it down, for thereby it will be more wedged in, or may be dislocated or fractured; but fixing the fingers about the shoulders or the hip joint of the foetus, the part that had protruded is to be restored to its proper position. If there be a wrong position of the whole foetus, attended with impaction, we must first push it upwards from the mouth of the womb, then lay hold of it, and direct it properly to the mouth of the uterus [Adams, *Seven Books*, I, 648].

Paul did not describe podalic version, and Islamic surgeons followed his example and consequently failed to include this in their medical procedures. His comments on complicated labors were closely studied by Muslim medical thinkers.

Cutaneous afflictions and their treatments are outlined in Book IV. Some diseases, such as elephantiasis, leprosy, and cancer, could not be healed because it was impossible to find medicines that were stronger than the ailments; but it was possible in certain cases to control the progress of the disease. Paul's description of cancer is abridged from Galen. According to Galenic theory, cancers are formed by the overheating of black bile. Because of the thickness of the humor that precipitated cancer, it was incurable. His description of the three types of intestinal worms (round, broad, and ascarids) is rather curious. The round worms were generated in the small intestinal membrane from bilious humors; the broad worm was converted from the intestinal membrane into a living animal; and ascarids, formed by bad diet, arose in the region near the rectum. All of these worms were to be treated with bitter astringents.

Toxicology was of interest to classical medical authorities; and in Book V Paul summarized the principal comments of ancient authors upon this theme. Information is provided for the treatment of bites or stings of vipers, mad dogs, spiders, scorpions, and crocodiles. This section terminates with a series of antidotes for henbane, fleawort, hemlock, wolfsbane, smilax, gypsum, arsenic, and lead.

Paul's most important and original contributions are in Book VI, on surgery. He divided this book into a section that examines manual operations on the flesh and into passages that review treatment of fractures and dislocations. The work contains one of the most detailed descriptions of ophthalmic surgery in antiquity and describes procedures for the removal of cataracts, and operations for trichiasis, ectropion, cysts, symblepharon, and staphyloma. Surgical techniques for tracheotomies, tonsilectomies, nasal polyps, abdominal paracentesis, catheterization, hemorrhoidectomies, and lithotomies are outlined. Since bleeding was an important aspect of his medical procedures, he spared few details in his descriptions of venesection, cupping, cauterization, and ligation for bleeding vessels. In Book III Paul had sought to alleviate the problems of difficult labor with drugs and repositioning of the fetus, but in Book VI he offered surgical techniques for cases in which the fetus must be removed to save the mother's life. This book concludes with a survey of useful methods for the treatment of fractures and dislocations.

His concluding book is a summary of simple and compound medicines used in the practice of the healing art. The majority of this information was derived from the Dioscoridian tradition, for Paul utilized ninety minerals, 600 plants, and 168 animals from Dioscorides' *De materia medica*.

Paul's *Epitome* provided Islamic physicians with their most substantial account of Greek surgical procedures. Al-Zahrāwī and al-Razi used it extensively in their works, and Fabrici based much of his surgery on the techniques detailed in Paul's sixth book. The *Epitome* also transmitted the whole range of classical Greek medical thought to the Islamic world.

BIBLIOGRAPHY

I. ORIGINAL WORKS. The *editio princeps* of Paul's medical encyclopedia was the Aldine ed. (Venice, 1528). Francis Adams' very satisfactory English trans. of Paul's work, prepared for the Sydenham Society, *The Seven Books of Paulus Aegineta*, 3 vols. (London, 1844–1847), contains an excellent commentary on Paul's relationship with Greek and Arabic medical traditions. René Briau prepared a Greek ed. and French trans. of Paul's Book VI, on surgery, *La chirurgie de Paul d'Égine* (Paris, 1855); there is a German trans. by J. Berendes (Leiden, 1914).

II. SECONDARY LITERATURE. For discussions of Paul's contributions and thought see E. Gurlt, "Paulus von Aegina," in *Geschichte der Chirurgie*, I (Berlin, 1898), 558–590; Signorelli Remo, "Ostetricia e ginecologia nel bizantino Paolo d'Egina e nell' arabo Albucasi," in *Minerva medica*, **58** (24 Nov. 1967), 4118–4131; and Konrad Straubel, "Zahn- und Mundleiden und deren Behandlung bei Paulos von Aigina" (diss., University of Leipzig, 1922).

PHILLIP DRENNON THOMAS

PAUL OF ALEXANDRIA (*fl.* Alexandria, *ca.* A.D. 378), *astrology.*

Paul composed an elementary textbook, Εἰσαγωγικά, which was designed to instruct students in the fundamental concepts of astrology. The second edition of this brief text, addressed to his son Cronamon, is extant; in chapter twenty Paul gives as an example for the determination of the weekday the computation for "today, 20 Mecheir 94 Diocletian," or 14 February A.D. 378. No further biographical details are known.

Paul names as his sources Ptolemy, Apollinarius, Apollonius of Laodicea, the *Panaretus* (of Hermes Trismegistus), the wise men of the Egyptians, and Hermes Trismegistus himself. In addition, relations of his text to a number of other astrological texts—for example, those of Firmicus Maternus and Rhetorius—can be discerned. Astronomically, Paul was not incompetent but never became profound. He discussed the planets' heliacal risings and settings (ch. 14) and their stationary points (ch. 15; he referred the reader desiring accurate computations to Ptolemy's *Handy Tables*); and he treated the moon's phases (ch. 16), the sun's longitude for any day (ch. 28), and the establishment of the ascendant (ch. 29) and the midheaven (ch. 30).

Paul's work became reasonably popular. It was used as the basis for a course of lectures delivered at Alexandria between May and July A.D. 564—probably by Olympiodorus (*Heliodori, ut dicitur, in Paulum Alexandrinum Commentarium*, E. Boer, ed. [Leipzig, 1962]; compare L. G. Westerink, "Ein astrologisches Kolleg aus dem Jahre 564," in *Byzantinische Zeitschrift*, **64** [1971], 6–21). Chapters 1 and 2 (p. 1, line 1–p. 10, line 8 in E. Boer's edition) were translated into Armenian by Ananias of Shirak in the seventh century (A. G. Abrahamyan, ed., item 21 of Ananias' collected works [Yerevan, 1944], pp. 327–330. I owe this reference to Prof. R. C. Thompson of Harvard). A summary of Paul's work was included in an important Byzantine treatise on astrological authorities (pp. xxi–xxiv in E. Boer's ed.), and the text was illuminated by numerous scholia (pp. 102–134, in E. Boer's ed.), at least some of which are of the twelfth century (O. Neugebauer, in E. Boer's ed., pp. 136–137).

Modern interest in Paul has largely centered on two problems. Al-Bīrūnī alleged that the Indian astronomer Pauliśa (or Puliśa) was a Greek, Paulus of Alexandria. Although al-Bīrūnī later corrected his error, many more recent scholars have continued to repeat it. The reasons for the rejection of the identification will be found in O. Neugebauer and D. Pingree, *The Pañcasiddhāntikā of Varāhamihira*, I (Copenhagen, 1970), 12–13 (Pauliśa's peculiar Greco-Babylonian astronomy is summarized by Varāhamihira in his *Pañcasiddhāntikā*, I, 11–13; III; VI–VII; and XVII, 65–80 [?]); and in D. Pingree, "The Later Pauliśasiddhānta," in *Centaurus*, **14** (1969), 172–241, where it is shown that al-Bīrūnī's *Pauliśasiddhānta* was written at Sthāneśvara in the eighth century, and that it follows the *ardharatrikapakṣa* that was founded by Āryabhaṭa.

Several scholars have contended that there is a relation of direct dependence between a geographical list in Acts of the Apostles and the astrological geography in Paul's Εἰσαγωγικά. This relation has been disproved by B. M. Metzger, "Ancient Astrological Geography and Acts 2: 9–11," in W. W. Gasque and R. P. Martin, eds., *Apostolic History and the Gospel* (Exeter, 1970), 123–133.

BIBLIOGRAPHY

The standard ed. of Paul is E. Boer, *Pauli Alexandrini Elementa apotelesmatica* (Leipzig, 1958). The articles on Paul by W. Gundel, in Pauly-Wissowa, *Real-Encyclopädie der classischen Altertumswissenschaft*, XVIII, pt. 2, cols. 2376–2386; and W. Gundel and H. G. Gundel, *Astrologumena* (Wiesbaden, 1966), 236–239, are no longer of much value.

DAVID PINGREE

PAUL OF VENICE (*b.* Udine, Italy, *ca.* 1370; *d.* Padua, Italy, 15 June 1429), *natural philosophy, logic.*

Christened Paolo Nicoletti da Udine, Paul of Venice was a highly respected scholar and leader of the Hermits of St. Augustine. He was the son of Nicoletto di Venezia, a noble citizen of Udine, and his wife Elena. Paul received his early religious and literary training at the monastery of St. Stephen in Venice. In 1390 the Augustinian order sent him for university training to Oxford, where he studied both natural philosophy and terminist logic and seems to have been influenced by Ockhamism. But his sympathies seem to have lain primarily with the Averroists, although he also adopted some doctrines of earlier Augustinians, especially Gregory of Rimini. After a fairly brief period at Oxford, Paul apparently studied at Paris, where he likely knew and studied with Pierre d'Ailly, a leading nominalist of the period.

Paul returned to Italy about 1395, and although little is known of his activities for nearly twelve years after that date, he must have been occupied with preaching and lecturing, since by 1408 he had already acquired a considerable reputation. In that year he was listed among the masters at Padua.

In 1413 Paul served briefly as Venetian ambassador to the king of Poland, and during the next two years, he lectured at Siena, Bologna, and Paris. In 1415 he was summoned before the Venetian Council of Ten, apparently on a charge of having interrupted his lectures at Padua in order to lecture elsewhere. He was ordered not to travel outside Venice for a year. In 1416 he was allowed to leave Venice, on the condition that he not attend the Council of Constance. He returned to Padua, where he remained for three years.

Most of Paul's work was written between 1409 and 1417; and because of his growing reputation as a philosopher, in 1417 the friars of his convent received the rare honor of being entitled to wear the black beret reserved for patricians of Venice. In 1420, when he was elected prior provincial of Siena and of the province of Marche Tarvisine, he was at the height of his fame. He was accorded such honorific titles as *monarcha sapientiae, summus Italiae philosophus*, and *Aristotelis genius*.

Paul's fame apparently carried with it a certain immunity. In 1420 a dispute with a Friar Francesco Porcerio led to a trial for heresy, and in that same year he was again summoned before the Council of Ten and exiled to Ravenna, where he was ordered to remain for at least five years. Neither of these difficulties seems to have affected his fortunes, and he simply ignored the sentence of the Council. In 1421 he was reelected prior provincial of Marche Tarvisine, and in 1422 he became regent at the Siena convent. He was deputed to lecture at Bologna in May 1424, moved to Perugia in November of that year, and was granted a faculty to visit Rome in 1426. In 1427 he was a professor at Siena, and he was rector of the university during 1428.

On 16 June 1428 Paul's petition to return to Padua was granted, and a year later he died and was buried there. The cause of his death is unknown.

Although Paul was widely known as a prominent rationalist with Averroist tendencies, and although his work in natural philosophy was widely read, his real importance seems to have been primarily in the field of logic. In the late fifteenth and early sixteenth centuries, his *Logica* was inscribed in the list of required texts at Venice, Padua, and Ferrara. And his logic remained widely read in many parts of Italy even until near the end of the seventeenth century, when it was still used as a text in Jesuit schools.

Paul's four logical works—although not markedly original—probably constitute the most thorough and encyclopedic exposition of the so-called terminist logic written during the Middle Ages. He seems to have read and thoroughly digested the most important logical work since Peter of Spain, and one finds in his writings, presented with admirable clarity, order, and understanding, almost all of the important concepts, problems, and proposed solutions of problems of terminist logic. His *Logica* is undoubtedly his most important and enduring contribution.

Paul's work in natural philosophy, on the other hand, is much less impressive in every respect. Although he wrote extensively in both natural philosophy and geology, his work seems to be wholly derivative and eclectic in a not very discriminating fashion.

In approaching Paul's work in natural philosophy, Duhem has shown the importance of distinguishing clearly between the early *Expositio super octo phisicorum* (completed in 1409) and the later *Summa naturalium*.[1] In the *Expositio*, Paul revealed himself as an orthodox Averroist not only on the question of the unicity of the agent intellect, but also on other issues. By the time of the *Summa*, he had moved away from Averroës in important respects and located his primary influences among the Parisian natural philosophers of the fourteenth century. In part this move away from Averroës can probably be explained as an attempt to maintain the orthodox position on God's omnipotence, as expressed in the 1277 condemnations. Thus when in the *Summa* Paul admitted the logical possibility of an actually infinite magnitude, while still maintaining that such a magnitude cannot occur in nature, he did not merely abandon Averroës to follow Albert of Saxony, but he also affirmed an accepted condition of divine omnipotence.[2] The same must be said of his admission that God could move the entire universe.[3] Paul often attempted unsuccessfully to reconcile Averroistic positions with the assertion of divine omnipotence. For example, he continued to uphold a notion of absolute place (he calls it *locus situalis*) as a relation of objects to the center of the universe, even though he had abandoned the notion of an immobile earth as the center of the universe and treated the center merely as a geometrical point.[4]

At least some of the shifts in Paul's positions should be treated as genuine changes of opinion, not merely as efforts at orthodoxy. A good example is the change in his view of projectile motion. In the *Expositio*, he takes the view that a projectile, after losing contact with the projecting instrument, is carried by successive waves of air.[5] For this view Paul found support not only in Aristotle and Averroës, but also in Walter Burley, a realist and terminist who remained with the standard Peripatetic position. In the *Summa* he had come to accept an account of projectile motion in terms of an "impetus" imparted to the object by the projecting instrument, a theory most importantly linked with Jean Buridan.[6] While this does seem to reflect a genuine change of opinion, it is also a good example of Paul's eclecticism. Although he supported his new view in language reminiscent of Buridan and Albert of Saxony, and although he followed Buridan's and Albert's arguments in extending the theory of the impetus to account for the acceleration of freely falling bodies,[7] the version of the theory that he accepted is not Buridan's, but a version usually associated with the Scotist Francis of Marchia. For Buridan the impetus transferred to the projectile would keep it moving indefinitely, were it not for the resistance of the air. Paul followed Francis of Marchia in explaining the tendency of the projectile to lose velocity by the view that the impetus, since it is not natural to the projectile but is impressed on it by violence, is gradually lost as the motion continues.

As Duhem has shown, Paul's work is repeatedly marred by elementary confusions. Thus in the *Expositio*, after attributing projectile motion to the push of air, he wrote about how much further a projectile would move in a void.[8] In attempting to defend Aristotle against Ockham's view that motion is identical with the thing moved, he used an argument based on the possibility of God's removing all form from prime matter and then moving the prime matter, hardly a defense that Aristotle would have appreciated.[9]

When we turn to Paul's geological theories in his *De compositione mundi*, the judgment must be much the same. Despite the fact that the intervening century and a half had witnessed both important theoretical advances and a number of significant discoveries and empirical observations, Paul's work is heavily dependent on the *Composizione del mondo* of Ristoro (written in 1282). Duhem goes so far as to characterize Paul as no more than a plagiarist of Ristoro.[10] Thus he not merely copied Ristoro's accounts of the origin of mountains and rivers and of the Mediterranean Sea, failing to take account of the discoveries of Marco Polo and others, but he even failed to include some of Ristoro's most interesting observations, such as the presence of fossils high on mountains.[11] Furthermore, Paul continued to rely heavily on astrological arguments and failed to take account of the strong antiastrological arguments of earlier philosophers such as Oresme.

Although Paul undoubtedly aided in the dissemination of Parisian natural philosophy in Italy, he should probably not be accounted an important figure in medieval science.

NOTES

1. Duhem, *Études sur Léonard de Vinci*, vol. III, p. 104.
2. Paul of Venice, *Summa naturalium Aristotelis*, pt. II (*De caelo et mundo*), 7.
3. *Ibid.*, pt. VI (*Metaphysica*), sec. 37.
4. Paul of Venice, *Expositio super octo phisicorum libros Aristotelis*, book IV, tract I, ch. 3, pt. 2, note 6.
5. *Ibid.*, pt. 1.
6. Paul of Venice, *Summa naturalium Aristotelis*, pt. II (*De caelo et mundo*), sec. 22.
7. *Ibid.*, pt. I (*Physica*), sec. 32.
8. Paul of Venice, *Expositio super octo phisicorum libros Aristotelis*, book VII, tract II, ch. 2, pt. 1.
9. *Ibid.*, book III, tract I, ch. 3, *dubium secundum*.
10. P. Duhem, *Le système du monde*, vol. IV, pp. 199–210, esp. pp. 209–210, where Duhem compares a number of passages from Paul and Ristoro. See also L. Thorndike, *Science and Thought in the Fifteenth Century*, pp. 195–232.
11. Paul of Venice, *De compositione mundi*, esp. chs. 18–27.

BIBLIOGRAPHY

I. ORIGINAL WORKS. Paul's most important works on logic and natural philosophy are *Logica* (Bologna, [?], 1472; Venice, 1475, 1478, 1480, 1485, 1488, 1492, 1493, 1498, 1565; Milan, 1474, 1478, 1484); *Expositio super libros de generatione et corruptione* (Perugia, 1475 [?]; Venice, 1498); *Summa naturalium Aristotelis* (Venice, 1476, 1503; Milan, 1476; Paris, 1514, 1521); *Expositio in libros Posteriorum Aristotelis* (Venice, 1477, 1481, 1486, 1491, 1494, 1518); *Quadratura* (Pavia, 1483; Venice, 1493; Paris, 1513); *Sophismata* (Pavia, 1483; Venice, 1493; Paris, 1514); *Universalia predicamenta sexque principia* (Venice, 1494); *De compositione mundi* (Venice, 1498); *Expositio super octo phisicorum libros Aristotelis* (Venice, 1499); *Logica magna* (Venice, 1499); and *In libros de anima* (Venice, 1504).

II. SECONDARY LITERATURE. On Paul and his work, see I. M. Bochenski, *History of Formal Logic* (Notre Dame, Indiana, 1961); P. Duhem, *Études sur Léonard de Vinci*, II (Paris, 1955), 319–327, and index in vol. III; P. Duhem, *Le système du monde*, IV (Paris, 1954), 199–210, and vol. X (Paris, 1959), 377–439; A. B. Emden, *A Biographical Register of Oxford University*, III (Oxford, 1959), 1944–1945, which contains a bibliography; A. Maier, *An der Grenze von Scholastik und Naturwissenschaft* (Essen, 1943), p. 207; A. Maier, *Zwei Grundprobleme der scholastischen Naturphilosophie*, 2nd ed. (Rome, 1951), 273–274; F. Momigliano, *Paolo Veneto e le correnti de pensiero religioso e filosofico nel tempo suo* (Udine, 1907); D. A. Perini, *Bibliographia Augustiniana*, III (Florence, 1929–1938), 29–46, contains biographical note and bibliography; and L. Thorndike, *Science and Thought in the Fifteenth Century* (New York, 1929), 195–232.

T. K. SCOTT, JR.

PAULI, SIMON. See **Paulli, Simon.**

PAULI, WOLFGANG (*b*. Vienna, Austria, 25 April 1900; *d*. Zurich, Switzerland, 14 December 1958), *physics.*

Wolfgang Pauli's father, a distinguished and original scholar, was professor of colloid chemistry at the University of Vienna and was also named Wolfgang. Thus his son, in his early work, called himself Wolfgang Pauli, Jr. The child was baptized a Catholic, his godfather being Ernst Mach, the physicist and critical philosopher. Pauli went to school in Vienna. Toward the end of his high school studies he became acquainted with Einstein's general theory of relativity, which at that time was completely new. He read it secretly during dull classroom hours. He was truly proficient in higher mathematics, for he had previously studied Jordan's *Cours d'analyse* in the same manner. Einstein's papers had made a deep impression on him. It was, he said, as if scales had fallen from his eyes; one day, so it appeared to him, he suddenly understood the general theory of relativity.

After finishing high school Pauli decided to study theoretical physics. He went to Arnold Sommerfeld in Munich, who was then the most imposing teacher of theoretical physics, in Germany or elsewhere. Many outstanding theoreticians were his pupils, including Heisenberg and Bethe. Here Pauli further perfected his analytical skills, which he later again and again masterfully put to use. Felix Klein was then publishing the *Encyklopädie der mathematischen Wissenschaften*, a monumental compilation that was to examine the current state of science from all sides. Leading scholars—mathematicians and physicists—were contributors. Klein had requested Sommerfeld to write an article on relativity theory for the *Encyklopädie*. Sommerfeld ventured to entrust the task to Pauli, who although scarcely twenty years old had published several papers on the subject. (Sommerfeld revealed admirable courage and insight in letting a student in his fourth semester write this important article.)

Pauli soon completed a monograph of about 250 pages, which critically presented the mathematical foundations of the theory as well as its physical significance. He took thorough account of the already very considerable literature on the subject but at the same time clearly put forth his own interpretation. Despite the necessary brevity of discussion, the monograph is a superior introduction to the special and general theories of relativity; it is in addition a first-rate historical document of science, since, together with H. Weyl's *Raum, Zeit, Materie* ("Space, Time, and Matter"), it is the first comprehensive presentation of the mathematical and physical ideas of Einstein, who himself never wrote a large work about his theory.

Sommerfeld was elated by this performance and wrote to Einstein that Pauli's article was "simply masterful"—and so it has remained to the present day. Pauli showed here for the first time his art of presenting science, which marks everything he wrote.

In Sommerfeld's institute Pauli also became acquainted with the quantum theory of the atom. He wrote in his Nobel lecture:

> While, in school in Vienna, I had already obtained some knowledge of classical physics and the then new Einstein relativity theory, it was at the University of Munich that I was introduced by Sommerfeld to the structure of the atom, somewhat strange from the point of view of classical physics. I was not spared the shock which every physicist, accustomed to the classical way of thinking, experienced when he came to know of Bohr's "basic postulate of quantum theory" for the first time.

It is a modest expression when Pauli speaks of "some knowledge of classical physics and the . . . Einstein relativity theory." This must be taken into account to understand what it means for a "physicist, accustomed to the classical way of thinking," to experience a shock from Bohr's postulate. There were, to be sure, few students scarcely twenty years of age who had penetrated the classical way of thinking as deeply as Pauli had. At this age the shock must have been great.

In 1922 Pauli obtained the doctorate with the thesis "Über das Modell der Wasserstoffmolekülions." Soon thereafter he began to work on the anomalous Zeeman effect. As he reports in his Nobel lecture, these studies finally culminated in the discovery of the exclusion principle, announced in "Ueber den Zusammenhang des Abschlusses der Elektronen-gruppen im Atom mit der Komplexstruktur der Spektren" (*Zeitschrift für Physik*, **31** [1925], 765). The markedly complicated title shows that here Pauli had solved an intricate problem. Landé, Sommerfeld, and Bohr among others believed, particularly in the case of the alkali metals, that the atomic core around which the valence electron moved possessed an angular momentum and that this was the cause of the magnetic anomaly. Why the atomic core should possess a half-integral angular momentum and a magnetic moment was, to be sure, unclear. Even more incomprehensible was the situation regarding the alkaline earths which possess both a singlet and a triplet system; these two systems should also be explained from the properties of the core. Indeed, the core should always possess the same electron configuration; but in the two cases it would interact differently with the valence electrons. No one could say how this would happen; and Bohr spoke of a *Zwang*, or constraint, which had no mechanical analogue. Now because the core, the closed noble gas configuration, should possess such peculiar properties, it was further believed that the core could not be characterized by the quantum numbers of the individual electrons: the "permanence of the quantum numbers" would have to be given up.

Pauli now proposed that the magnetic anomaly be understood as a result of the properties of the valence electron: in it appears, as he wrote, "a classically nondescribable two-valuedness in the quantum-theoretic properties of the electron." The atomic core, on the other hand, possesses no angular momentum and no magnetic moment. This assumption meant that the "permanence of the quantum numbers," Bohr's *Aufbauprinzip*, could be retained: each electron, even in a closed shell, could in principle be described by quantum numbers. In addition to the already known n, l, and m, one now needed a fourth, which is denoted today by the spin quantum number s. After such a strong foundation was laid, Pauli went on to study the structure of the core, which had previously been considered by E. C. Stoner (*Philosophical Magazine*, **48** [1924], 709). Pauli was able to explain Stoner's rule by means of his famous exclusion principle:

> There can never be two or more equivalent electrons in an atom, for which in a strong field the values of all the quantum numbers n, k_1, k_2 and m are the same. If an electron is present, for which these quantum numbers (in an external field) have definite values, then this state is "occupied."

In this formulation the atom is first considered in a strong external field (Paschen-Back effect), since only then can the quantum numbers for single electrons be defined. However, on thermodynamic grounds (the invariance of the statistical weights during an adiabatic transformation of the system) the number of possible states in strong and weak fields must, as Pauli observed, be the same. Thus the number of possible configurations of the various unclosed electron shells could now be ascertained.

The discovery of the exclusion principle builds the crowning conclusion to the old quantum theory based on the correspondence principle, which Pauli described in *Handbuch der Physik*, XXIII (1926). When the article was published, new developments had already occurred; in rapid succession the fundamental work of Heisenberg, Dirac, and Schrödinger appeared, leading to a proper, mathematically consistent quantum mechanics.

Following Dirac's precedent, Jordan, Heisenberg, and Pauli developed the relativistic quantum electrodynamics. This theory occupied physicists for a good twenty years before it became clear that, in spite of all the doubts and disappointments, one of the most precise physical theories had been discovered. Disappointment and doubt had arisen primarily from the following circumstances: It was known for a long time that in the quantum theory of light and the electron, the Sommerfeld fine structure constant $e^2/hc = \alpha$ plays an exceptional role: α is a dimensionless quantity and has the value 1/137. In it three areas of theoretical physics are symbolically united: electromagnetism, which is represented by e; relativity, represented by c; and quantum theory, represented by h. It was therefore believed that if a relativistic quantum electrodynamics was successfully developed, it would at the same time yield a theory of α. Thereby, so it was further hoped, a natural solution would be found for the problem of the infinite self-energy of the electron, an insurmountable problem in the classical electron theory. These hopes have not been fulfilled.

In order to accommodate the new developments, Pauli wrote an article on wave mechanics for the second edition of the *Handbuch der Physik* (XXIV, pt.1 [1933]), "Die allgemeinen Prinzipien der Wellenmechanik." A student at the time, the author well remembers meeting Hermann Weyl on the street and his saying, "What Pauli has written on wave mechanics is again completely outstanding!" This judgment of a connoisseur is still valid today: the same article, twenty-five years later, was used unchanged in the new handbook (1958). Pauli's presentation was thoroughly modern and well thought out, considering that such articles frequently become outdated after only a few years.

While the work on the Pauli principle and the first *Handbuch* article—"the Old Testament"—was done in Hamburg, the second article—"the New Testament"— was written in Zurich. After finishing his thesis under Sommerfeld's guidance, Pauli had gone to Göttingen as an assistant to Max Born. Here he met Niels Bohr, who invited him to Copenhagen. From there he soon went to Hamburg, where he held an assistantship under Wilhelm Lenz and gave his inaugural lecture as *Privatdozent*. In 1928 the Swiss Board of Education appointed him Debye's successor as professor at the Eidgenössische Technische Hochschule, where he remained until his death in 1958. At the same time Schrödinger had left the University of Zurich, where wave mechanics was developed, and he was succeeded by Gregor Wentzel. Both professors were very young and brought a rich and active scientific life to Zurich. For many years Pauli and Wentzel organized a seminar together, in which the more important new work from practically all areas of theoretical physics was critically discussed.

By today's standards facilities at both schools were at that time rather limited. At the Technical University, Pauli was the only lecturer for theoretical physics, and students specializing in this field were practically nonexistent. But Pauli—in contrast to Wentzel at the university—did have an assistantship at his disposal. This was a research position, and he always filled it with someone who had already attained the doctorate. These assistants became his true pupils: R. Kronig, Rudolf Peierls, H. B. G. Casimir, and V. F. Weisskopf were his assistants during his first ten years in Zurich, and all were scholars who later became well-known in the field.

Pauli was never what one would call a good lecturer. He mumbled to himself, and his writing on the blackboard was small and disorganized. Above all, though, he had the tendency during the lecture to think over the subject at hand—which, as Wilhelm Ostwald remarked in *Great Men*, hinders teaching. And so his lectures were difficult to understand—but nevertheless his students were fascinated and greatly stimulated. On the whole he radiated a very strong personal force. One was immediately impressed by his sharp and critical judgment. In discussions he was in no way willing, and perhaps completely unable, to accept unclear formulations. He seemed hard to convince, or he reacted in a sharply negative manner. Thereby he forced his partner in discussion to self-criticism and to a more logical organization of his thoughts. If, however, one succeeded in convincing Pauli of an idea, then at the same time one's own thoughts were brought to a greater clarity. In this sense he was a truly Socratic teacher who helped in the birth of the ideas of others.

The great influence that Pauli exerted on students and colleagues cannot be ascribed to his imposing critical understanding alone. Nor did the respect that one had for him originate solely from his often caustic way of jumping at his discussion partner, which put many into disarray. Such attacks, although occasionally malicious, were not intended to be mean and had a humorous, ironic side. It was the daemon of the man that one sensed. Theoretical physics surely appears quite rational, but it rises from irrational depths. And so it rests on a daemonic background that can lead to serious conflicts. Pauli had experienced and endured this deep within himself. He had, as few others, earnestly endeavored to master this conflict rationally. Since mathematics and theoretical physics are creations of the human soul, and since they come out of the structure of the soul, he took up the ideas of C. G. Jung in order to better understand

the meaning of scientific activity. The results of these efforts are numerous essays and lectures, and particularly his study "Der Einfluss archetypischer Vorstellungen auf die Bildung naturwissenschaftlicher Theorien bei Kepler." It appeared—and Pauli attached importance to this—in the book *Naturerklärung und Psyche* (1952), which he published with C. G. Jung.

It appears that Pauli's colleagues did not always understand how earnestly he wrestled with the philosophical foundations of science and how strongly he experienced their irrational origin. But in some obscure manner they felt it and realized it in outward experiences. These experiences took form in the strange phenomena known as the "Pauli effect": Pauli's mere presence in a laboratory would cause all sorts of misfortunes. So believed critical scholars, such as Otto Stern, who was friendly with Pauli, and so Pauli himself believed. The great impression that his personality made on all who came in contact with him can be correctly assessed only when this mysterious side of his complex being is taken into account.

One of Pauli's most significant accomplishments in physics while in Zurich is the neutrino hypothesis. With it he correctly explained the continuous β spectrum, at that time very puzzling. In a lecture before the Naturforschende Gesellschaft in Zurich in 1957 he presented the history of this discovery. Niels Bohr was of the opinion that in the case of β decay the conservation of energy should be only statistically valid. If this were conceded, then the conservation of angular momentum and the statistical laws for particles of spin 1/2 would be violated. In the early days of the development of atomic theory, Bohr was ready to sacrifice the *Aufbauprinzip* and the permanence of the quantum numbers and to introduce a mechanically unexplainable *Zwang*; and he was now also prepared to give up the classical conservation laws. He was always "ready and willing" to discover the unexpected in the realm of atomic dimensions. Pauli, on the other hand, resolved only with great difficulty to let fall natural laws that had previously been confirmed everywhere. Just as he held on to the permanence of the quantum numbers in his theory of the closing of shells in atoms, which led him to the exclusion principle, so it appeared to him right to retain the conservation laws. Thus he proposed in a letter of 4 December 1930 to Lise Meitner and associates "the continuous β-spectrum would be understandable under the assumption that during β-decay a neutron is emitted along with the electron. . . ."

Since the letter was written before Chadwick had discovered the neutron in the nucleus, the discussion here involved another particle, which Fermi then christened "neutrino." At the Solvay Congress in 1933, Pauli again extensively justified his proposal, which was published in the Congress report. Shortly thereafter, in 1934, Fermi worked out his theory of β decay, which, in spite of unsolved basic difficulties, has been confirmed amazingly well.

During the war Pauli was active at the Institute for Advanced Study in Princeton; but later, after careful consideration, he returned to Zurich. He lived happily with his wife in Zollikon, near great forests that invited meditative strolls. Consistent as he was, he now earned Swiss citizenship.

This article has intentionally avoided giving even an approximately complete review of Pauli's scientific work, for there is practically no area of theoretical physics in which he did not decisively take part. The aim has been to make clear, in connection with his most important contributions, the manner in which he worked. A last example to be mentioned is his important work on discrete symmetries in field theory. He dedicated it to Niels Bohr on his seventieth birthday under the title "Exclusion Principle, Lorentz Group and Reflection of Space-time and Charge." Starting from investigations by Schwinger and Lüders, Pauli showed that every Lorentz invariant Lagrangian field theory is invariant under the operation CTP, whereas C, T, and P separately do not have to be symmetries of the theory. This study had greatly occupied him, as he occasionally told me, and I guessed that he had hidden thoughts about the matter which he did not express. So I asked him if in this work there was not in fact another problem between the lines and if he might not say something about it. But he denied my conjecture: he was interested in these symmetries in their own right.

Not much later it was discovered that in weak interactions—for example, in β decay—the parity (P) is not conserved (Lee and Yang, 1956). Pauli was greatly stirred by this discovery. It seemed to him at first extraordinarily repugnant that in nature right and left should not enjoy equal status. But then he realized that the symbolic, to some extent natural-philosophic, concept which he saw in this symmetry did indeed remain: for as he had made clear one year earlier, CTP must be a valid symmetry if only the natural laws are Lorentz invariant. Thus, guided by his own genius, he had meaningfully prepared for the coming developments.

Just as Pauli received a shock when, as a student, he first became acquainted with the strange laws of quantum theory, so did he receive a shock from the nonconservation of parity. For it was always his hope

that physics would indicate the mysterious harmony of God and Nature. This hope was not illusory. Precisely in his most important work he had shown how apparently paradoxical phenomena could be explained through a harmonious extension of the previously confirmed theory. And so theoretical physics since Kepler, Galileo, and Newton appeared to him as a great house the foundations of which, despite many changes, would never be shaken. It was because he felt this way, and because he considered himself a representative of a great tradition, that he reacted so sharply against obscure arguments and superficial speculation. He expressed himself thus concerning his position to a colleague: "In my youth I believed myself to be a revolutionary; now I see that I was a classicist."

In December 1958, Pauli became violently and seriously ill, and on December 14 he died. At the funeral Viktor Weisskopf said he was "the conscience of theoretical physics." This is truly the shortest statement that can render the impression which this rare man made on all who knew him.

BIBLIOGRAPHY

A complete list of Pauli's books, articles, and studies is in *Theoretical Physics in the Twentieth Century, a Memorial Volume to Wolfgang Pauli* (New York, 1960). Collections include his scientific papers (New York, 1964) and *Aufsätze und Vorträge über Physik und Erkenntnistheorie* (Brunswick, 1961).

                                            M. FIERZ

PAULIŚA (*fl.* India, fourth or fifth century), *astronomy.*

Pauliśa was the author of a textbook *(siddhānta)* on astronomy in Sanskrit. The work was largely based on the Greek adaptations of Mesopotamian astronomy that began to be introduced into India in the third century by Sphujidhvaja (*fl.* 269/270) and perhaps earlier, in the second century, by Yavaneśvara (*fl.* 149/150) (see essay in Supplement). Since the *Pauliśasiddhānta* was revised by Lāṭadeva (*fl.* 505), the original must have been written between *ca.* 300 and *ca.* 450; it is probably, then, to be associated with the patronage of the Guptas, of whom the one most noted for his interest in literary efforts is Candragupta II (*fl. ca.* 375–415). Of Pauliśa himself we can say nothing save that his name may be a transliteration of the Greek Παῦλος. His identification with Paul of Alexandria (*fl.* 378)—at which al-Bīrūnī first hinted—is certainly false, as it is based on a misreading of the place-name Tanaysar (Sthānesvara or Sthānvīsvara) in a later *Paulisasiddhānta* that was written in the eighth century and that followed the *ārdharātrikapakṣa* of Āryabhaṭa I (*b.* 476) (see D. Pingree, "The Later Paulisasiddhānta," in *Centaurus*, **14** [1969], 172–241).

The original *Paulisasiddhānta*, as revised by Lāṭadeva, is known to us only through the *Pañcasiddhāntikā* of Varāhamihira (*fl. ca.* 550). From that work we learn of Pauliśa's method of computing the days lapsed since epoch (I, 11–13); his solar and lunar equations, the former computed from a Greek model, the latter going back to Babylonian techniques (III; 1–3, 5–8); his method of computing oblique ascensions, longitudinal differences, and the daily motion of the sun (III, 10–17); his rules relating to the Indian time-units called *karaṇas* (sixtieths of a synodic month), *tithis* (thirtieths of a synodic month), and *ṛtus* (seasons of two synodic months), and to the *pātas* of the sun and moon, the *ṣaḍasītimukhas* (ecliptic arcs of 86° beginning from Libra 0°), and the *saṅkrāntis* (entries of the sun into the several zodiacal signs) (III, 18–27); his computation of lunar latitude (III, 28–29); his theory of lunar and solar eclipses (VI, VII); and his planetary theory, based on a Greek adaptation of Babylonian astronomy in which the synodic arcs of the planets and their elongations from the sun at the occurrence of the "Greek-letter" phenomena are utilized (XVII, 64–80).

BIBLIOGRAPHY

All of the material relevant to Pauliśa will be found in O. Neugebauer and D. Pingree, *The Pañcasiddhāntikā of Varāhamihira*, 2 vols. (Copenhagen, 1970–1971).

DAVID PINGREE

PAULLI, SIMON (*b.* Rostock, Mecklenburg, 6 December 1603; *d.* Copenhagen, Denmark, 23 April 1680), *botany, anatomy.*

Paulli was the son of Heinrich Paulli, a professor at Rostock and physician in ordinary at the Danish court. He studied anatomy at Rostock and Leiden, and later at Paris under Jean Riolan. After a trip to England he received his medical degree at Wittenberg in 1630. He practiced medicine at Rostock and Lübeck from 1634 to 1639 and from 1639 to 1648 was professor of medicine at Rostock. In 1648 Paulli was appointed professor of anatomy, surgery, and botany at Copenhagen. Simultaneously he became physician in ordinary to the Danish king, who granted him the revenue from the bishopric of Aarhus. In 1655 he gave a series of botany lectures in Rostock.

Paulli made notable contributions to the technical literature of anatomy and botany. His botanical writings were discussed in detail by Albrecht von Haller, who praised him not only for compiling existing botanical knowledge but also for comparing it with information derived from his own experiments. More a practitioner than a theoretician, he recommended the use of simple medications. His biography is included in the posthumous Frankfurt edition of *Quadripartitum botanicum* (1708).

BIBLIOGRAPHY

I. ORIGINAL WORKS. Paulli's major work is *Quadripartitum botanicum de simplicium medicamentorum facultatibus* . . . (Rostock, 1640; Strasbourg, 1667–1668; Frankfurt, 1708), in which he arranges plants according to the seasons, in the form of a floral almanac; within each season the plants are listed in alphabetical order. Along with the uses and effects of the vegetal medicines, he provides bibliographical information. The star-thistle (*Centaurea calcitrapa*) is discussed here, apparently for the first time. An appendix reprints his Rostock inaugural lecture, "De officio medicorum, pharmacopoeorum et chirurgorum," which contains the first mention of the use of a cow's bladder in giving enemas. The lecture was printed separately at Rostock in 1639.

He also wrote *Flora Danica, det er Dansk Urtebog* . . . (Copenhagen, 1648), which is also arranged according to the seasons and, besides descriptions of plants, includes information on their synonyms and medicinal properties and 393 illustrations, some original and some taken from Matthias de Lobel and Joannes Moretus (Moerentorf); *Viridaria varia regia et academica publica* . . . (Copenhagen, 1653), which consists of catalogs of the botanical gardens of Copenhagen, Paris, Warsaw, Oxford, Leiden, and Groningen, as well as catalogs of exotic and native plants, listed according to location; *Parekbasis seu digressio de . . . causa febrium . . . Appendix, seu Historica relatio de . . . anatomico et chirurgico casu ad . . . Johannem Riolanum . . . anno 1652* (Frankfurt, 1660), which includes a description of scurvy and venereal diseases; *Miscella antiquae lectionis cujus quatuor monumenta in praefatione enumerata in publicam lucem reduxit* . . . (Strasbourg, 1664), a historical work; *Commentarius de abusu tabaci Americanorum veteri et herbae Theé Asiaticorum in Europa novo* . . . (Strasbourg, 1665, 1681), also in English trans. by Robert James (London, 1746)—according to Haller, Paulli also published *Libellum de usu et abusu tabaci et herbae Theae* in 1635; *Orbis terraqueus in tabulis geographicis et hydrographicis descriptus* . . . (Strasbourg, 1670), a geographical work; and *Historia litteraria, sive Dispositio librorum omnium facultatum* . . . (Strasbourg, 1671), an encyclopedic work.

Miscella . . ., *Orbis* . . ., and *Historia* . . . are cited in *Catalogue général de la Bibliothèque Nationale*, CXXXI (Paris, 1935), cols. 671 ff. Haller mentions a letter entitled

"De gramine ossifrago epistola ad Th. Bartholinum a Beughemio citatur."

II. Secondary Literature. See A. Blanck, *Die mecklenburgischen Aerzte* (Schwerin, 1874), 30; A. von Haller. *Bibliotheca botanica*, 2 vols. (Zurich, 1771–1772; repr, Hildesheim–New York, 1969): I, 459, and II, 333; C. Krause, in *Allgemeine deutsche Biographie*, XXV (1885), 274; J. Krey, *Andenken an die Rostocker Gelehrten*, VI, 8 f.; Linnaeus, *Bibliotheca botanica* (Amsterdam, 1736), 36, 48, 69–71, 74, 78–79, 86, 92, 97, 143; and H. Schelenz, *Geschichte der Pharmazie* (Berlin, 1904), 495, 526.

Karin Figala

PAULY, AUGUST (*b.* Munich, Germany, 13 March 1850; *d.* Munich, 9 February 1914), *zoology, entomology.*

Pauly's development as a scientist was completely self-motivated and self-directed. His father, Cölestin Pauly, was from the south of France; formerly a farrier, and during Pauly's childhood a wine merchant and innkeeper in Munich, he was known for his hot temper. Pauly's mother, Johanna Riehle, a Bavarian, was more sympathetic toward the boy, but neither parent understood his deep longing for a good education. They intended him for a career in commerce, but in the depths of the wine cellar Pauly secretly read to provide himself with the equivalent of the Gymnasium studies. Adolf Bayersdorfer, a lifelong friend of Pauly and later his brother-in-law, helped him in his plans to pass the examinations and enter the University of Munich. Whenever Pauly could, he attended lectures on a wide variety of subjects at the Konservator an der alten Pinakothek in Munich. He had a sensitive disposition, was interested in art, and thought that he might become a painter.

Pauly took his examinations in 1873, and in 1877 received the doctorate with a dissertation in zoology. His interest in biology had most probably been influenced by his teacher Carl Theodor Ernst von Siebold, professor of zoology and comparative anatomy, whose assistant Pauly became. From 1877 to 1885 Pauly edited an ornithological journal; since he had access to a large store of histological material, he became an expert in avian pathological anatomy. He gave lectures on both the theoretical and practical aspects of forest entomology, and donated considerable material for the study of insects, insect damage, and forest zoology to the Royal Institute for Experimental Forestry in Munich. He was appointed extraordinary professor of applied zoology at the University of Munich in 1896. His wife, Mathilde von Portheim, gave him invaluable help in

his work as he suffered progressive difficulties with his vision, including retinal detachment.

Since Pauly set zoology within the framework of a philosophically oriented outlook that combined the love of nature with a broad interest in art, pressing biological questions were frequently discussed within the group of his friends, which included artists and a poet, and later, the scientists Boveri and Spemann when he came to Munich.

Pauly's zoological lectures reflected his dissatisfaction with Darwin's explanation of the evolutionary process, for Pauly thought it highly unlikely that chance variations could accumulate and coincide to account for the adaptation and correlation of organs. Pauly looked back, rather, to Lamarck, discounting the emphasis that had been placed on Lamarck's view of the role of use and disuse and stressing the psychic factor that entered into the Lamarckian doctrine. *Darwinismus und Lamarckismus. Entwurf einer psychophysischen Teleologie*, published in 1905, represented the sum of Pauly's thirty years' work in evolutionary theory.

Pauly conceived of evolution as being the result of an "inner teleology," a capacity for change in response to a consciously apprehended need within the organism itself. Adaptation was a "discovery," a change in response to this necessity. Adaptive changes were inherited but could be maintained only through use; the changed organ or organism tended to revert to its former condition should the function cease. Pauly referred the underlying psychic circumstances not only to the brain but also to each organ and cell; variation on this psychological basis was, of course, present in the plant as well as the animal world. He maintained this neo-Lamarckian evolutionary theory—a vitalistic viewpoint that he believed was derived from Lamarck, but which was actually uniquely his own—throughout his lifetime.

BIBLIOGRAPHY

I. Original Works. Pauly's most important work was *Darwinismus und Lamarckismus. Entwurf einer psychophysischen Teleologie* (Munich, 1905). He also published his aphorisms in that year and wrote short essays on his evolutionary beliefs.

II. Secondary Literature. On Pauly and his work, see Fritz Baltzer, *Theodor Boveri, Life and Work of a Great Biologist 1862–1915*, trans. by Dorothea Rudnick (Berkeley–Los Angeles, 1967), 8–10, 36, 48, 130–131, 141–142, which describes their friendship and correspondence and the milieu in Munich. See also Friedrich Wilhelm Spemann, ed., *Hans Spemann, Forschung und Leben* (Stuttgart, 1948), 145–150, 157–164, which presents a valuable reminiscence of Pauly and his background, as well as an excellent account of his theory.

Obituaries are M. Merk-Buchberg, "Zum Gedächtnis August Paulys," in *Zoologischer Beobachter* (1914), 87–88; K. Escherich, "August Pauly," in *Zeitschrift für angewandte Entomologie*, **1** (1914), 370–373; Max Friedemann, "Psychobiologie. Zum andenken an August Pauly," in *Berliner klinische Wochenschrift*, **51**, pt. 2 (1914), 1441–1443; Adolf Leiber, "August Pauly," in *Süddeutsche Monatshefte*, **11**, no. 2 (1914), 161–166; and the *Deutsche biographisches Jahrbuch, 1914–1916* (Berlin, 1925), 303, which has further biographical references.

GLORIA ROBINSON

PAVLOV, ALEKSEI PETROVICH (*b.* Moscow, Russia, 13 November 1854; *d.* Bad Tölz, Germany, 9 September 1929), *geology*.

Pavlov was the son of a retired military man. He entered the Moscow Gymnasium in 1866, then in 1874 enrolled in the Faculty of Physics and Mathematics of Moscow University. He was talented in both art and music, and his eventual choice of a scientific career may have been influenced by his Gymnasium teachers. At the university he attended the lectures of the distinguished geologists G. E. Shchurovsky and M. A. Tolstopiatov; his diploma topic, ammonites, was suggested to him by Shchurovsky, and his work won him a gold medal. After graduating from the university, Pavlov taught natural history in the secondary schools of Tver (now Kalinin) from 1878 to 1880; in the latter year he went to Moscow, at Shchurovsky's invitation, to become curator of the geological and mineralogical collections of the university. At the same time he began to study for the master's degree, make practical studies in mineralogy, and teach in the Higher Courses for Women.

In 1883 Pavlov, at the request of the St. Petersburg Mineralogical Society, conducted field research in the lower and middle Volga regions; this research formed the basis for his master's thesis, *Nizhnevolzhskaya yura* ("The Jurassic Period of the Lower Volga"), which he defended the following year. He then traveled abroad, first to Paris and the Auvergne, then to Vienna, where he attended the lectures of Suess. While in Paris he met M. V. Illich-Shishatskaya, a young widow who was auditing lectures on geology and paleontology there; they were married in 1886. Pavlov returned to the Volga to do further fieldwork in the summer of 1885; he studied Cretaceous deposits and made important observations regarding the stratigraphy of Cretaceous and Tertiary deposits. In January 1886 he became a professor at the Uni-

versity of Moscow—a post that he held for the rest of his life—and in May of that year he defended a doctoral dissertation on the *Aspidcervas acanthicum* of eastern Russia.

Pavlov's teaching was inseparable from his scientific work. His course on introductory geology, which he gave for about ten years, was extremely popular, as were the field excursions that he conducted for his students. His courses at the Moscow Archaeological Institute and at the Moscow Mining Academy, together with those at the university, brought him a large number of pupils who formed the nucleus of the Moscow school of geologists that he trained. His concern for the reform of secondary education in Russia culminated in a book, published in 1905, in which he stressed the need for the teaching of science at that level. He later devoted a number of articles to the subject.

Pavlov's purely scientific works comprised a wide range of topics, including stratigraphy, paleontology, tectonics, Quaternary geology, and practical geology. A single, early work is devoted to vertebrate paleontology; in an article on *Archaeopteryx*, published in 1884, Pavlov suggested that this genus, having achieved its greatest development in the Jurassic period, was an evolutionary side branch, destined to extinction through poor adaptation to life.

Pavlov spent a number of years studying the Mesozoic deposits of the Russian platform and the Boreal phases of the Mesozoic era throughout northern Europe. In his master's thesis of 1884 he had traced the upper and lower boundaries of the Volga Jurassic deposits and had studied their fauna; he later established a discontinuity in the Jurassic deposits of the same region, associated with the perturbations of the Jurassic sea, and showed the sharp line of contact between the Jurassic and Cretaceous deposits. In 1888, while attending the Fourth International Geological Congress in London, Pavlov studied the local Jurassic and Cretaceous profiles and examined the collections of Jurassic and Cretaceous fossils in English museums. He utilized this new material in a comparative stratigraphic analysis of the Jurassic deposits of England and of the central part of European Russia. His conclusion was that these deposits were possibly equivalent.

Pavlov drew upon later studies of the profile of the province of Boulogne to make still wider generalizations and to compare deposits. He thus discovered a great similarity between the Jurassic fauna of the Volga region and that of Europe. By 1896 he had synthesized an enormous amount of material into a comprehensive classification of the Upper Jurassic and Lower Cretaceous deposits of Europe and Russia and had completed a paleogeographic survey of these areas. He presented the results of these researches to the International Geological Congresses of 1897 and 1900.

In his study of the stratigraphy of the Lower Cretaceous Pavlov used materials drawn from his investigations of the Russian plains and the Pechersky caves, as well as from collections gathered in northern Siberia. He established that there had been two Boreal periods in the Lower Cretaceous and that the sea which had flooded the lower Volga in the Albian stage had been connected to the sea of Western Europe. He proposed a series of paleogeographic maps and described the character of these Lower Cretaceous deposits; he also studied the Upper Cretaceous deposits of the same area and incorporated them into a stratigraphical scheme in which he noted a number of new paleontologically distinct horizons. He further established the distribution of the Lower Tertiary deposits of the Volga and differentiated them paleographically.

Pavlov's work in Quaternary geology also began early; indeed, his interest in the period dated from Shchurovsky's lectures at the university. He studied Quaternary deposits in his first expedition to the Volga, then, during the Third International Geological Congress, held in 1885 in Berlin, investigated the glacial deposits of Germany. After several years of investigating and comparing Quaternary deposits Pavlov was able to reach a number of conclusions concerning the genetic types of continental deposits, the number of glaciations that had caused them, and the genesis of modern topography. He summed these up in a paper of 1888, "Geneticheskie tipy materikovykh obrazovany lednikovoy i poslelednikovoy epokhi" ("Genetic Types of Continental Formations of Glacial and Post-glacial Epochs").

Pavlov defined two types of glacial deposits. The first, the talus, consists of deposits formed by the weathering and decomposition of bedrock which have formed a slope at the bottom of a steeper declivity. This process played a large part in the formation of the topography of the Russian platform; Pavlov included a number of different types of rocks within this concept and assigned an aqueous origin to all of them, even loess. He studied the loess of the Volga region, Turkestan, and Western Europe to conclude that the process by which the Turkestan loess had been formed was very similar to that of the talus, save only that the loess had been formed by torrential mountain deluges running through the valleys, rather than by rain. He proposed to call these deposits, his second type, "proluvium." Pavlov emphasized the importance of talus and proluvial deposits in his studies of ancient continental deposits, suggesting that these were the result of weathering processes that had taken place in the earliest geological age. He integrated his findings into his investigations of contemporary topology.

In his researches on the history of the glacial epoch Pavlov compared Russian and Western European Neogene and Quaternary deposits to establish threefold glaciation. He noted two waves of cold in the Pliocene period, then a first glaciation, covering a large part of Europe, in the Quaternary. Following the moderate and moist Chellian and Achellian periods, a second glacier covered the whole of northern Europe, developing a glacial cover almost equal to the first. The characteristic morainic landscape of Europe was formed during the second interglacial epoch; the third glaciation was less widespread than the first two, and was followed by the present warm and moist period.

Pavlov conducted paleontological research as an adjunct to his stratigraphic work. He was particularly interested in Mesozoic ammonites and belemnites and devoted several works to the description of belemnites from the Spiton deposits, in which he showed the similarity of their forms and established their genetic series and natural classification. In a report given to the Eighth International Geological Congress, which met in Paris in 1900, Pavlov proposed a new genetic classification for fossil organisms, arguing that the morphological classification then accepted did not correspond to evolutionary theory. His own system was based upon phylogenetic properties; he suggested that the terms "genetic series," "genetic line," "phyletic branch," "generation," and "species and variety" be used for more detailed subdivision. A convinced Darwinian, he drew upon the example of the ammonites to analyze questions of phylogeny and ontogeny and thereby discovered the phenomenon of phylogenetic acceleration. He applied his own classification to aucella, comparing examples from Russian and Western European deposits, and described Pliocene paludinas as part of his analysis of Quaternary material. Pavlov's wife assisted him actively in his paleontological work, and several of his students continued it.

In the course of his work on the Volga Pavlov also became concerned with tectonic phenomena. In 1887 he suggested the existence of faulting in the northern border region of Zhigulaya. An adherent of the contractionist theory, he ascribed this faulting to that cause and noted further that petroleum deposits might be associated with this dislocation, a prediction that was later confirmed. Pavlov also discovered a fault on the right bank of the Volga and thus accounted for the general tectonic features of that area. He further found a new element in the structure of the Russian platform, the great gentle down-warpings that he called "synclines." He interpreted these as local uplifts and depressions in the crust of the earth.

In the field of theoretical tectonics Pavlov, as early as the end of the 1890's, began to study the topography of the moon and its genesis. He later made a comparative analysis of the topography of the moon and that of the earth, which he reported in a paper of 1908, "Lik zemli i lik luni" ("The Face of the Earth and the Face of the Moon"), and in another read to the Astronomical Society in 1922. He emphasized the importance of the study of lunar topography for understanding terrestrial processes. In his investigation of the basic morphology of the earth he concluded that its structure was determined at an early stage of its development, but that its fundamental topography was then obscured by its massive sedimentary cover and the action of the hydrosphere. The moon, which because of its weak gravity lacks an air and water cover, may therefore, in its continents and in its depressions, serve as a model of the first stages of the development of the surface of the earth. Beginning with the contraction hypothesis, Pavlov suggested that lunar forms were shaped by the solidification of the molten moon and by volcanic action; such forms, he added, had previously existed on earth, but had been transformed by the forces of contraction and the processes of weathering.

Although he was primarily interested in theoretical geology, Pavlov did not neglect its practical aspects. He investigated the landslides on the shores of the Volga and concluded that they resulted from the geological structure of the slope of the river bank, its steepness, the activity of underground water, and the leaching-out effect of the river itself. He divided landslides into two types—gravity slides, embracing the lower part of the slope; and pushing slides, whose movement begins at the top of the slope and embraces it almost in its entirety. (Some landslides may partake of both types.) Pavlov also treated the distribution of forces acting in massive landslides and suggested preventive measures. He provided a classification of rocks for engineering purposes and was frequently consulted about the construction of railroads and bridges, work related to the then new field of engineering geology.

Pavlov was, in addition, often consulted on hydrogeological problems, including the irrigation of arid areas and the reasons for the hardness of water. He was interested in soil and emphasized the relationship between soil and bedrock and topology and stressed the geological processes of soil formation. He thus contributed a good deal of the basic geological research upon which the Russian discipline of soil science was founded.

In addition to his geological works, Pavlov published a number of books in the history of science and a number of popular scientific works. He gave well-attended popular lectures, too, and several of his books went through multiple editions. He was an active member of several scientific societies and received many honors. He died at the spa of Bad Tölz, where he went with his wife to recover from a serious illness. He was active until the last days of his life, investigating the mineral springs of the resort.

BIBLIOGRAPHY

I. ORIGINAL WORKS. Pavlov's writings include *Nizhnevolzhskaya yura. Klassifikatsia otlozheny i spiski iskopaemykh* ("The Jurassic of the Lower Volga. Classification of Deposits and Notes on Fossils"; Moscow, 1884); "Notes sur l'histoire géologique des oiseaux," in *Bulletin de la Société impériale des naturalistes de Moscou*, **60** (1884), 100–123; "Samarskaya luka i Zheguli" ("The Samara Bend and the Zhiguli Hills"), in *Trudy Geologicheskago komiteta*, **2**, no. 5 (1885–1887), 1–63; "Geneticheskie tipy materikovykh obrazovany lednikovoy i poslelednikovoy epokhi" ("Genetic Types of Continental Formations of Glacial and Post-glacial Epochs"), in *Izvestiya Geologicheskago komiteta*, **7** (1889), 243–261; "Études sur les couches jurassiques et crétacées de la Russie," in *Bulletin de la Société impériale des naturalistes de Moscou*, n.s. **3** (1890), 61–127, 176–179; "Argiles de Speeton et leurs équivalents," *ibid.*, **5** (1892), 214–276, 455–570; "On the Classification of the Strata Between the Kimheridgian and Aptian," in *Quarterly Journal of the Geological Society of London*, **52** (1896), 542–554; *Polveka v istorii nauki ob iskopaemykh · organizmakh* ("Half a Century in the History of Science of Fossil Organisms"; Moscow, 1897); "O reliefe ravnin i ego izmeneniakh pod vlinaniem raboty podzemnykh i poverkhnostnykh vod" ("On the Topography of Plains and Its Changes Under the Influence of Underground and Surface Waters"), in *Zemlevedenie*, **5** (1898), 91–147; and *Vulkany na Zemle i vulkanicheskie yavlenia vo vselennoy* ("Volcanoes on the Earth and Volcanic Phenomena in the Universe"; St. Petersburg, 1899).

Works published in the twentieth century include *Kratky ocherk istorii geologii* ("A Brief Sketch of the History of Geology"; Moscow, 1901); "Ob izmeneniakh v geografii Rossii v yurskoe i melovoe vremya" ("On the Changes in the Geography of Russia in the Jurassic and Cretaceous Eras"), in *Nauchnoe slovo*, **1** (1903), 143–145; *Opolzni Simbirskogo i Saratovskogo povolzhya* ("Landslips in the Simbirsk and Saratov Volga Region"; Moscow,

1903); *Geologichesky ocherk okrestnostey Moskvy* ("Geological Sketch of the Surroundings of Moscow"), 5th ed. (Moscow, 1907). "Enchaînement des aucelles et aucellines du crétacé russe," in *Nouveaux mémoires de la Société des naturalistes de Moscou,* **17,** no. 1 (1907), 1–92; *Geologia nastoyashchego vremeni* ("Geology of the Present Time"; Moscow, 1914); "Yurskie i nizhnemelovye Cephalopods severnoy Sibiri" ("The Jurassic and Lower Crétaceous Cephalopoda of Northern Siberia"), in *Zapiski Imperatorskoi akademii nauk,* 8th ser., **21,** no. 4 (1914), 1–68; *Ocherki istorii geologicheskikh znany* ("Sketches of the History of Geological Knowledge"; Moscow, 1921); and *Neogenovye i posletretichnye otlozhenia Yuzhnoy i Vostochnoy Evropy* ("Neocene and Post-Tertiary Deposits of Southern and Eastern Europe"; Moscow, 1925).

II. Secondary Literature. On Pavlov and his work, see A. P. Mazarovich, *Aleksey Petrovich Pavlov* (Moscow, 1948); N. S. Shatsky, "O sineklizakh A. P. Pavlova" ("On Pavlov's Syneclises"), in *Byulleten Moskovskogo obshchestva ispytatelei prirody,* Otdel. geolog., **18,** nos. 3–4 (1940), 39–45; and V. A. Varsanofieva, *Aleksey Petrovich Pavlov i ego rol v razvitii geologii* ("Aleksey Petrovich Pavlov and His Role in the Development of Geology"; Moscow, 1947).

Irina V. Batyushkova

PAVLOV, IVAN PETROVICH (*b.* Ryazan, Russia, 27 September 1849; *d.* Leningrad, U.S.S.R., 27 February 1936), *physiology, psychology.*

Pavlov was the son of a priest, Pyotr Dmitrievich Pavlov, and his wife, Varvara Ivanova. He was sent at the age of eleven to the religious school in Ryazan and, after graduating, entered the seminary of that town, where he studied the current literature on natural science, including I. M. Sechenov's *Refleksy golovnogo mozga* ("Reflexes of the Brain") and the popular works of D. I. Pisarev. He did not complete his studies there, but in 1870 entered the natural sciences section of the Faculty of Physics and Mathematics at St. Petersburg University. While he was a third-year student the lectures and experimental work of E. F. Cyon decisively stimulated his interest in physiology and he carried out experimental research on the influence of the nerves on the circulation of the blood. Pavlov was awarded a gold medal for a student work on the nerves that govern the pancreas (1875), written with M. I. Afanasiev.

To broaden his knowledge of physiology Pavlov entered the third-year course at the Military Medical Academy after graduating from the university in 1875. His studies were directed primarily toward theoretical medicine. In the physiology laboratory of the veterinary section of the academy, directed by K. N.

Ustimovich, Pavlov conducted the research on the physiology of the circulation of the blood that brought him into contact with S. P. Botkin. He subsequently organized and headed the physiology laboratory of Botkin's clinic (1878–1890) and conducted investigations on the physiology of circulation and of digestion. On 19 December 1879 he received the degree of doctor of medicine; in 1881 he married Serafima Vasilievna Karchevskaya.

In Botkin's laboratory Pavlov was exposed to an atmosphere of "nervism," which "extended the influence of the nervous system to the greatest possible amount of an organism's activity."[1] During this period Pavlov wrote his doctoral dissertation, on the efferent nerves of the heart, which he defended on 21 May 1883. In 1884–1886 he worked in the laboratories of Karl Ludwig in Leipzig and Rudolf Heidenhain in Breslau and, at the latter, carried out his only research in the physiology of invertebrates, published in 1885.

In 1883 Pavlov became *Privatdozent* in physiology at the Military Medical Academy and in 1890 was appointed professor in the department of pharmacology. At the same time he became director of the physiology section of the Institute of Experimental Medicine and conducted research on the physiology of digestion that was summarized in a work published in 1897. In 1895, after the retirement of I. R. Tarkhanov, Pavlov moved to the department of physiology, which he headed until 1925. For the rest of his life his activity was concentrated at three institutes: the Institute of Physiology of the Soviet Academy of Sciences that now bears his name, the Institute of Experimental Medicine, and the biological station at Koltushy (now Pavlovo), near Leningrad.

Pavlov's scientific work received worldwide recognition. In 1904 he was awarded the Nobel Prize in physiology or medicine for his research on digestion. In 1907 he was elected an academician of the Russian Academy of Sciences. In August 1935 he presided over the Fifteenth International Physiological Congress, held at Leningrad and Moscow.

Pavlov enriched physiology and the natural sciences with a new method and a new methodology. The latter derived from his general biological thought, which was directed toward the study of the whole organism under the conditions of its normal activity. For Pavlov the living organism was a complex system, the study of which—like that of any system—demanded the use of both the analytic and synthetic methods of scientific research. He considered the main problem of experimental research in physiology to be the study of reciprocal influence and reciprocal action within the organism, and the relation of the organism to its environment. In his first study of circulation he emphasized that such work was possible only by a method that allowed the systematic investigation of "those mutual relationships in which the separate constituent parts of the complex hemodynamic machine are found during its life activity."[2] Research must be conducted under normal conditions on unprepared animal specimens.

Toward the end of the nineteenth century the essential problem of physiology was becoming the replacement of the traditional, vivisectional method with a long-term, environmental one. Such replacement was called for by the logic of the development of physiology; a vast amount of data had been accumulated by means of the vivisectional method, but it was becoming increasingly apparent that the entire organism must be studied in its natural conditions. On the limitations of vivisection Pavlov said:

> Strict experiment . . . can serve the aims of physiological analysis—that is, the general clarification of the functions of a given part of an organism and its conditions—more successfully. But when, how, and to what degree the activity of the separate parts is connected . . . constitutes the content of physiological synthesis, and . . . is frequently difficult or simply impossible to deduce from the data of strict experiment, for the setting of the experiment (narcosis, curarization, operations) is inevitably linked to a certain amount of destruction of the normal processes of the organism.[3]

Pavlov conceived the method of long-term experiment, which he introduced into the laboratory, not only as a technique of experimental research but also as a way of thinking. The continuous method inaugurated a new era in the physiology of digestion and led to new work and concepts, especially in experimental surgery and in the physiology of the brain. In his first lecture on the physiology of digestion, Pavlov said, "Science moves in spurts, depending on progress made in its methods. With each step forward in methods we rise, so to speak, to a higher step, from which a wider horizon opens to us, with subjects previously unseen."[4] He therefore developed a synthetic physiology designed to "determine precisely the actual course of particular physiological phenomena in a whole and normal organism."[5]

The object of Pavlov's research was both the organism as a system and any of its separate organs that fulfilled a definite function. He was not concerned with the basic principles and foundations of life, believing them to be the proper subjects of not physiological but rather physicochemical research. Characterizing his approach, he wrote:

> I would prefer to remain a pure physiologist, that is, an investigator who studies the functions of separate

organs, the conditions of their activity, and the synthesis of their function in the total mechanism of a part or in the whole of the organism; and I am little interested in the ultimate, deep basis for the function of an organ or of its tissues, for which primarily chemical or physical analysis is required.[6]

His devotion to the synthetic approach did not, however, hinder Pavlov from analytical study of the organism, "going into the depths of cellular and molecular physiology."[7] Emphasizing the problems and goals of physiological analysis, he pointed out its role in elucidating the functional mechanisms of the organs. He distinguished four levels, or degrees, of experimental physiological research—organismic, organic, cellular, and molecular—all of which must, in the final analysis, reflect the properties of a living substance. Pavlov was well aware of the necessity of a definite, regular relationship between the holistic and analytical (or organicist and reductionist) approaches of scientific research. As a founder of organicism he clearly foresaw the advent of the cellular and molecular physiology that would greatly alter the course of organic physiology.

Pavlov stated his notion of the levels of physiological research in a speech dedicated to the memory of Heidenhain (1897), in which he said that "organic physiology . . . began its study with the middle of life; its principle, the basis of life, is in the cell."[8] He considered Heidenhain "a cellular physiologist, a representative of that physiology which must replace . . . contemporary organic physiology and which must be considered the forerunner of the last step in the science of life—the physiology of the living molecule."[9]

The greatest part of Pavlov's research is devoted to three major areas: the physiology of the circulation of the blood (1874–1888), the physiology of digestion (1879–1897), and the physiology of the brain and of higher nervous activity (1902–1936). His earliest research in the physiology of circulation was devoted to the mechanisms that regulate blood pressure. He described the role of the nerve mechanism in the adaptive activity of the blood vessels, specifying the role of the vagus nerve as a regulator of blood pressure. In his doctoral dissertation he showed that cardiac function is governed by four nerves which respectively inhibit, accelerate, weaken, and intensify it. (Prior to his work and that of Gaskell it was believed that the influence of the nerves on the heart was limited to changing its rhythm.) Pavlov's research in this area culminated with the publication in 1888 of his work on the intensifying nerve, in which he proposed that its influence be understood as trophic. In the 1920's he returned to trophic innervation, the idea upon which

L. A. Orbeli had based his theory of the adaptive-trophic role of the sympathetic nervous system.

Pavlov's research on the physiology of digestion (1897, 1906, 1911) required him to devise new techniques and thereby marked a turning point in his work. His method for studying the action of the digestive organs involved surgical intervention on the entire digestive tract, performed under conditions of strict asepsis and antisepsis, which allowed him to observe the normal activity of a particular digestive gland in a healthy animal. (A mastery of surgery was, for Pavlov, as necessary to the physiologist as a knowledge of physical and chemical methods of research.) His surgical procedures included the formation of various types of fistulas from the salivary glands, the stomach, and the pancreas to the body surface, known as esophagotomy; "imaginary feeding," carried out with E. O. Shumova-Simanovskaya (1889); the operation on the small ventricle of the stomach, formed with P. P. Khizhin (1894); and the severing of two branches of the vagus nerve and the application of the fistula of Eck (1892). He was thus enabled to investigate, more or less directly, the mechanisms governing the salivary glands, stomach, pancreas, kidneys, and intestines.

Pavlov's experiments proceeded from contemporary ideas about the neural and humoral regulation of the digestive process and of its consequences in various parts of the digestive tract. He showed that there is a close connection between the properties of salivary secretion and the kind of food consumed (the Pavlovian curves of salivary secretion). He elucidated the role of enzymes in digestion and, with N. P. Shepovalnikov, discovered enterokinase—which he called "the enzyme of enzymes"—in the intestinal secretion (1894). His theoretical conclusions were of broad biological significance. His theory of specific irritability was of particular importance—in showing that the concept of general irritability is scientifically untenable, he demonstrated specific irritability in various parts of the digestive tract. The Pavlovian theory of digestion was of great value in the clinical pathology of the stomach and intestines.

Following his work on the physiology of digestion, Pavlov turned to the physiology of behavior. By the beginning of the twentieth century many physiologists, zoologists, and psychologists had already undertaken experiments to study the function of the brain, but had assembled only fragmentary data. Pavlov drew upon Darwin's theory of evolution—which stressed psychological as well as physiological continuity—and Sechenov's reflexology to create his own theory of behavior. Pavlov thus described the genesis of his behaviorism: "The time is ripe for the transition to experimental analysis of the subject from the objective, external side, as in all the other natural sciences. This transition has made possible the recently born [study of] comparative physiology, which itself arose as one of the results of the influence of evolutionary theory."[10]

Pavlov investigated the activity of the cortex and the cerebral hemispheres, basing his work on fundamental facts, concepts, and terminology of the physiology of the nervous system. He chose to approach these areas through studying the salivary glands, which had attracted his attention because of their modest role in the organism and because their activity could be subjected to strict quantitative measurement. He had, moreover, already encountered the phenomenon of "psychic" salivation in the course of his investigations on the physiology of digestion, and wished to study it further. Subjective psychology held that saliva flowed because the dog wished to receive a choice bit of meat, but Pavlov, "an experimenter from head to foot," rejected this method as fallacious and chose to pursue the investigation objectively.

Pavlov could not help but see the "psychic" stimulation of the salivary glands as a phenomenon analogous to the normal digestive reflex. Both digestion and salivation were reflexive; only the external agents that evoked the reflexes were different. The digestive reflex was triggered by the essential mechanical and chemical properties of the food; the salivary by nonphysiological "signals," including the form and odor of the food. Using the concept of the reflex as an elementary response of the organism to external stimulus, Pavlov termed the normal digestive reaction an unconditioned reflex, and the activity of the salivary glands, stimulated by various environmental agents, a conditioned reflex.

Pavlov described the formation of the conditioned reflex, showing it to be based, like the unconditioned reflex, on the innate activity of the organism. He demonstrated that any environmental factor can enter into a temporary relation with the natural activity of the organism through combination with the unconditioned reflex. He noted that the chief characteristics of conditioned reflexes are that they are developed throughout the life of an organism (and are therefore extraordinarily subject to change, depending on the environment) and that they are provoked by stimuli that act as signals. Taken together, these qualities ensure the organism a completely individual adaptive activity. Pavlov saw in the conditioned reflex a mechanism through which the ameliorative potentialities of the organism are increased.

Pavlov made his first public statement on the conditioned reflex in 1903, in a paper presented to the

Fourteenth International Medical Congress in Madrid. He expanded upon the subject three years later, when he wrote that

> . . . with the general biological point of view before us we find in this conditioned reflex an improved adaptive mechanism or, in other words, a more precise mechanism for counterbalance with the environment. The organism reacts with natural phenomena that are vital to it in the most sensible and most precautionary way, since all other, even the smallest phenomena . . ., although accompanying the first only temporarily, present themselves as signals of the first—signals of the stimulus. The subtlety of the procedure makes itself known in the formation of the conditioned reflex as well as in its suppression, when it ceases to be a correct signal. Here, we must think, lies one of the main mechanisms of progress in the more finely differentiated nervous system. . . . The concept of the conditioned stimulus must be seen as the fruit of the previous work of biologists. . . .[11]

Pavlov found in the conditioned reflex a mechanism of individual adaptation which, he held, exists throughout the entire animal world. "A temporary nervous connection is a universal physiological phenomenon in the animal world and exists in us ourselves."[12]

Pavlov localized conditioned-reflex activity in the cerebral hemispheres of the brain, demonstrating that the center for such activity is to be found in the cortex, among the cortical agents of innate reflexes. Pavlov considered the possibility that subcortical formations may be responsible for the placement of the conditioned-reflex centers, but did not offer any direct evidence for this. He showed that with the formation of conditioned reflexes in the functional state of nerve centers displacements occur in the form of increases in irritability. The cells of the higher sections of the central nervous system, and their branches, he suggested, must therefore undergo definite subtle structural and physicochemical changes. "The locking-in, the formation of new connections," he wrote, "we relate to the function of the separating membrane, if it exists, or simply to the fine branching between neurons [that is], between the separate nerve cells."[13] Pavlov's hypothesis has been verified by more recent neurophysiological data, which have demonstrated the plastic character of the changes in the synactial apparatus as a result of excitation. Through work on the conditioned reflex investigators were able to establish that the activity of the cerebral hemispheres is based on the processes of excitation and inhibition. Further experiments, designed to elucidate the dynamics and mutual relationships of these processes, revealed a definite regularity in their development.

An important concomitant of Pavlov's experimental work was his creation of experimental neuroses, which arose when contradictory stimuli were offered the subject. Such neuroses may serve as a rough model for functional disease of the human nervous system; Pavlov and his co-workers attributed them to the disturbance of balance between the cortical processes of excitation and inhibition. In 1924, in Pavlov's laboratory, I. P. Razenkov, investigating the induced conflict of basic nerve processes in the activity of the cerebral cortex, observed the same phase states as N. E. Vvedensky had observed in the nerve fiber. It was shown that disturbance of cortical activity passed through four stages: inhibiting, characterized by the absence of all reflexes; paradoxical, in which strong stimuli produce little or no effect, while weak stimuli induce greater effects; equalizing, in which all conditioned stimuli, regardless of their intensity, produce the same effect; and intermediate to the norm, in which stimuli of average intensity produce the greatest effect, and strong or weak conditioned stimuli induce little or no effect. Pavlov applied Razenkov's work, which provided the first description of phase states of the central nervous system, toward understanding the nature of human psychic illness. From 1918 on, he regularly visited a psychiatric clinic in Udelnaya, near Leningrad, to study the patients.

A. G. Ivanov-Smolensky, V. V. Rikman, I. S. Rosenthal, I. O. Narbutovich, and L. N. Fedorov were active in the creation of the theory of experimental neuroses. Pavlov's student M. K. Petrova was able to induce deliberately various specific neuroses in animals and subsequently to suppress them. This study of experimental neuroses was closely related to the development of the theory of types of behavior. In 1909 Pavlov reported his pioneering work on behavior to the Society of Russian Physicians in St. Petersburg; his paper *Dalneyshie shagi obektivnogo analiza slozhnonervnykh yavleny* ("Further Steps in the Objective Analysis of Complex Nerve Phenomena") discussed carefully conditioned, "weak-nerved" dogs, in which it was difficult to induce inhibition.

In addition to studying animal behavior and the accumulating experimental material, Pavlov and his co-workers made the first attempt to provide a scientific basis for the ancient Hippocratic classification of temperaments. They established the existence of four basic types of behavior, which they classified according to the strength, mobility, and constancy of the basic nerve processes.

During the 1920's two ramifications emerged from Pavlov's basic theory: the study of comparative physiology of behavior and the theory of human behavior. Pavlov had experimented on dogs, mice, and monkeys; his students expanded the range of animal subjects, E. M. Kreps working with Ascidia, Y. P. Frolov with fish, N. A. Popov and B. I. Bayandurov with doves, N. M. Nikiforovsky and E. A. Asratyan with amphibians and reptiles, and G. A. Vasiliev and A. N. Promptov with birds. In the next decade Pavlov himself took up the idea of the genetic study of behavior; a biological station was established for this purpose at Koltushy, near Leningrad. On the basis of comparative physiological data an attempt was made, chiefly by Pavlov's student L. A. Orbeli, to create an evolutionary physiology of behavior.

Pavlov attributed decisive importance to the signals that characterize conditioned-reflex activity. He assumed the existence of two signal systems, of which one, the primary system, is found in both animals and man, whereas the secondary system is peculiar to man, and it is this system that makes possible the distinctively human activities of abstract thought and speech. In recent years he has come to be regarded as a mechanist who saw complex behavior as the sum of individual conditioned reflexes. This is a profound error, since in Pavlov's view the brain, through its capacity for subtle analysis and complex synthesis, integrates a vast range of conditioned reflexes into coherent behavior corresponding to the specific circumstances and needs of the organism. If in the early stages of his work Pavlov and his students were chiefly concerned with the study of elementary conditioned reflexes, they later turned to purposeful study of the more complex forms.

A distinguished scientific administrator, Pavlov created a large research school that, at various times, employed about 300 physiologists and physicians. He also organized a number of major research centers, including the physiological section of the Institute of Experimental Medicine, the Institute of Physiology of the Soviet Academy of Sciences, and the biological station at Koltushy. With Pavlov's active cooperation the Russian Physiological Society (now the I. P. Pavlov All-Union Physiological Society) was organized in 1917. He was an active member of the Society of Russian Physicians in St. Petersburg, and his services were highly valued by the Soviet government.

NOTES

1. I. P. Pavlov, *Polnoe sobranie sochineny* ("Complete Collected Works"), 2nd ed. (Moscow–Leningrad, 1951–1952), I, 197.
2. *Ibid.*, I, 82.
3. *Ibid.*, VI, 321.
4. *Ibid.*, II, bk. 2, p. 22.
5. *Ibid.*, 36.
6. A. F. Samoylov, *Izbrannye trudy* ("Selected Works"), V. V. Parin, ed. (Moscow, 1967), 301.

7. I. P. Pavlov, *Polnoe sobranie sochineny*, I, 574.
8. *Ibid.*, VI, 104.
9. *Ibid.*, 107.
10. *Ibid.*, IV, 19.
11. *Ibid.*, II, bk. 1, p. 71.
12. *Ibid.*, II, bk. 2, p. 182.
13. *Ibid.*, II, bk. 2, p. 61.

BIBLIOGRAPHY

I. ORIGINAL WORKS. Pavlov's writings were collected as *Polnoe sobranie trudov* ("Complete Collected Works"), 5 vols. (Moscow, 1940–1949). The 2nd ed. is *Polnoe sobranie sochineny* ("Complete Collected Works"), 6 vols. (Moscow–Leningrad, 1951–1952). There is a German trans. of this ed., *Sämtliche Werke*, L. Pickenhain, ed., 6 vols. (Berlin, 1953–1956).

Works referred to in the text are *O nervakh, zavedyvayushchikh rabotoy v podzheludochnoy zheleze* ("On the Nerves That Govern the Pancreas"; 1875), written with M. I. Afanasiev; *O tsentrobezhnykh nervakh serdtsa* ("On the Efferent Nerves of the Heart"; St. Petersburg, 1883), his doctoral diss.; "Kak bezzubka raskryvaet svoi stvorki" ("How the Anodonta Opens Its Valves"; *Polnoe sobranie sochineny*, 1, 466–493, also in *Pflügers Archiv*, 37 [1885], 6–31); *Lektsii o rabote glavnykh pishchevaritelnykh zhelez* ("Lectures on the Function of the Main Food-Digesting Glands"; 1897); *Eksperimentalnaya psikhologia i psikhopatologia na zhivotnykh* ("Experimental Psychology and Psychopathology in Animals"; 1903), his first public statement on the conditioned reflex; "Vneshnyaya rabota pishchevaritelnykh zhelez i ee mekhanizm" ("The External Function of the Digestive Glands and Its Mechanism"), in W. Nagel, ed., *Handbuch der Physiologie des Menschen*, II (Brunswick, 1907), 666–743; "Operativnaya metodika izuchenia pishchevaritelnykh zhelez" ("An Operative Method of Studying the Digestive Glands"; in Tigerstedt's *Handbuch der physiologischen Methodik*, Band II, IH, Leipzig, 1911); *Dvadtsatiletny opyt obektivnogo izuchenia vysshey nervnoy deyatelnosti (povedenia) zhivotnykh* ("Twenty Years of Experiments in the Objective Study of Higher Nervous Activity [Behavior] of Animals"; Moscow–Petrograd, 1923); and *Lektsii o rabote bolshikh polushary golovnogo mozga* ("Lectures on the Function of the Cerebral Hemispheres"; Moscow, 1927), Pavlov edited vols. 1–6 (1924–1936) of *Trudy fiziologicheskikh laboratorii imeni I. P. Pavlova*.

Important English translations of his works include *The Work of the Digestive Glands*, W. H. Thompson, trans. (London, 1902; 2nd ed., 1910); *Conditioned Reflexes*, G. V. Anrep, trans. and ed. (London, 1927; repr. New York, 1960), a trans. of the 1923 work cited above; and *Lectures on Conditioned Reflexes*, W. H. Gantt, trans. (New York, 1928).

II. SECONDARY LITERATURE. On Pavlov's life and work, see P. K. Anokhin, *Ivan Petrovich Pavlov Zhizn, deyatelnost i nauchnaya shkola* (". . . Life, Work, and Scientific School"; Moscow–Leningrad, 1949); E. A. Asratyan, *Ivan Petrovitch Pavlov, Work* (Moscow, 1974), in English;

B. P. Babkin, *Pavlov* (Chicago, 1949); Y. P. Frolov, *Pavlov and His School* (London, 1937), written by a student of Pavlov; and E. M. Kreps, ed., *I. P. Pavlov v vospominaniakh sovremennikov* ("Pavlov Recalled by His Contemporaries"; Leningrad, 1967).

N. A. GRIGORIAN

PAYEN, ANSELME (*b*. Paris, France, 17 January 1795; *d*. Paris, 13 May 1871), *industrial chemistry, agricultural chemistry*.

Payen's father owned a factory in Grenelle, a suburb of Paris, in which sal ammoniac was made from animal waste. He would not permit his son to go to school and himself took charge of his education; the boy grew up well-informed on scientific matters but rather unsociable—traits that persisted throughout his life. The turmoil of the Hundred Days and its aftermath prevented him from entering the École Polytechnique, but he studied chemistry privately with Vauquelin and Chevreul. Payen's first industrial venture was the manufacture of borax, which until then had been imported; but more significant was his advocacy of animal charcoal (the carbonaceous residues from the Grenelle works) as superior to wood charcoal for decolorizing purposes in the recently established beet-sugar industry. He also had his own beet-sugar factory at Vaugirard.

In 1829 Payen began to teach industrial chemistry at the École Centrale des Arts et Manufactures; ten years later he was also appointed to a similar chair at the Conservatoire des Arts et Métiers, although he did not abandon his industrial interests. He wrote a large number of papers, mostly on technological matters of local and temporary concern. The subjects included manures (some in collaboration with Boussingault), sugar refining, rubber and gutta-percha, water supply, potato blight, and phylloxera. Such extensive publication would imply some dilution of quality, and Berzelius had an uncharitably low opinion of Payen's rank as a chemist. "I know the man so well," Berzelius wrote to Wöhler on 12 January 1847, "that I never rely on him where accuracy is concerned. But when it is a matter of writing pamphlet-fodder for the general public, then he is in his element."

Payen is remembered mainly for his work on carbohydrates, some of it done with Persoz. In 1833 they found that starch was hydrolyzed to sugar by a substance contained in malt, which they called diastase, now known to be a mixture of extracellular enzymes. (Their priority in this matter was disputed.) Payen later showed that starch has the same chemical composition, regardless of the species of plant from which it is prepared. In 1838 he distinguished two components in woody tissue, an isomer of starch for which he coined the name cellulose and the "true woody material," later called lignin; the two could be separated chemically.

Payen spent all his life in the same poor quarter of Paris, much respected by his working-class neighbors. Of his five children only one daughter survived him. He is reputed never to have missed a lecture until, toward the end of 1869, he collapsed in front of his class. Even so, during the siege of Paris he devoted himself to attempts to make various unusual materials edible. He died during the Commune and was given an unpublicized and perfunctory funeral to the distant rattle of musketry.

BIBLIOGRAPHY

I. ORIGINAL WORKS. Approximately 200 papers written by Payen or in collaboration with others are listed in the Royal Society *Catalogue of Scientific Papers*, IV, 783–789; VIII, 574–575; XII, 563. His books, in their various eds., are listed in Bibliothèque Nationale *Catalogue général des livres imprimés*, CXXXI, cols. 947–964. His most important work is the printed version of his lecture course, *Manuel du cours de chimie organique appliquée aux arts industriels et agricoles*, J. J. Garnier, ed., 2 vols. (Paris, 1842–1843).

II. SECONDARY LITERATURE. The most informative obituary of Payen is by J.-A. Barral, in *Mémoires publiés par la Société centrale d'agriculture de France* (1873), 67–87. A. Girard, in *Annales du Conservatoire des arts et métiers*, **9** (1870) [*sic*], 317–331, admits to knowing little of Payen's private life and confines himself to an account of his work. An anonymous notice in *Revue scientifique*, **8** (1871), 94–96, is no more than a list of some of Payen's papers with brief comments.

W. V. FARRAR

PAYKULL, GUSTAF (*b*. Stockholm, Sweden, 21 August 1757; *d*. Vallox-Säby, Sweden, 28 January 1826), *entomology*.

Paykull, a civil servant, became a chamberlain at the royal court in 1796 and was appointed master of the royal household in 1815. He received the title of baron in 1818.

In his twenties Paykull had a moderately successful career in literature, and wrote dramas and satirical plays. Later, however, his interest turned to natural history, where the possibilities for original contributions were decidedly greater than in belles lettres. On his estate, Vallox-Säby, in Uppland, he amassed the largest private zoological collection ever assembled in Scandinavia. The bird collections reportedly occupied

1,362 drawers, and the insects were said to have included 8,600 species. The shellfish and fish collections were comparatively large, but the collection of animals preserved in alcohol was unimportant. The extensive group of the larger tropical mammals—lion, leopard, camel, zebra—was noteworthy. Some of Paykull's animals were purchased during foreign travels—in Holland and France, for instance. The entire collection was donated in 1819 to the state and became the nucleus of the present National Museum of Natural History in Stockholm.

Although Paykull was a general zoologist, his primary interest was in entomology, and it was there that he made his lasting contributions. His first publications (1785–1786) concerned moths; he later concentrated on beetles, although he did produce a short article on the Lepidoptera in 1793. His main work, *Fauna Suecica*, appeared in three parts (1798–1800). Intending from the outset to publish a complete Swedish fauna, Paykull began with the insects—"to finish them off." His aim was not realized, however, and the three published volumes concern only beetles. An extraordinarily fine and well executed work, it clearly shows Paykull's taxonomical competence. In his *Fauna*, as well as in smaller monographs on various beetle families, Paykull accurately described a great number of new species.

BIBLIOGRAPHY

Paykull's major writings are *Monographia staphylinorum Sueciae* (Uppsala, 1789); *Monographia caraborum Sueciae* (Uppsala, 1790); *Monographia curculionum Sueciae* (Uppsala, 1792); *Fauna Suecica. Insecta*, 3 vols. (Uppsala, 1789–1800); and *Monographia histeroidum* (Uppsala, 1811). For the best account of Paykull and his work see Sten Lindroth, *Kungl. Svenska Vetenskapsakademiens Historia 1759–1818*, II (Stockholm, 1967), *passim*.

BENGT-OLOF LANDIN

PEACOCK, GEORGE (*b*. Denton, near Darlington, Durham, England, 9 April 1791; *d*. Ely, England, 8 November 1858), *mathematics*.

Peacock is known for his role in the reform of the teaching of mathematics at Cambridge and his writings on algebra. His father, Thomas, was perpetual curate at Denton; and Peacock was educated at home. He entered Trinity College, Cambridge, in 1809 and received the B.A. in 1813, as second wrangler; the M.A. in 1816; and the D.D. in 1839. In 1815 he was named lecturer at Trinity and was a tutor from 1823 to 1839. He was a moderator of the tripos examination in 1817,

1819, and 1821. Peacock was a member of the Analytical Society, founded by Charles Babbage for the purpose of revitalizing mathematical studies at Cambridge. Toward this end Peacock, Babbage, and John Herschel published a translation of an elementary calculus text by Lacroix (1816). In 1820 Peacock published a collection of examples in differential and integral calculus. These works, and his influence as moderator, tutor, and lecturer, were major factors in replacing the fluxional notation and the geometric methods, which had been entrenched at Cambridge since the time of Newton, with the more fruitful analysis and Leibnizian notation.

In 1837 Peacock became Lowndean professor of geometry and astronomy at Cambridge, but in 1839 he was appointed dean of Ely. (He had been ordained in 1822.) Although he moved to Ely and no longer lectured, he remained active in the affairs of Cambridge. In 1841 he published a book on the statutes of the university in which he urged reform, and he served on two government commissions dealing with the question. Peacock was a member of the Cambridge Philosophical Society, the Royal Astronomical Society, the Geological Society of London, and the British Association for the Advancement of Science. He was elected a fellow of the Royal Society in 1818. He married Frances Elizabeth Selwyn in 1847. They had no children.

Peacock's mathematical work, although not extensive, is significant in the evolution of a concept of abstract algebra. In the textbook *A Treatise on Algebra* (1830), revised in 1842–1845, he attempted to put the theory of negative and complex numbers on a firm logical basis by dividing the field of algebra into arithmetical algebra and symbolic algebra. In the former the symbols represented positive integers; in the latter the domain of the symbols was extended by his principle of the permanence of equivalent forms. This principle asserts that rules in arithmetical algebra, which hold only when the values of the variables are restricted, remain valid when the restriction is removed. Although it was a step toward abstraction, Peacock's view was limited because he insisted that if the variables were properly chosen, any formula in symbolic algebra would yield a true formula in arithmetical algebra. Thus a noncommutative algebra would not be possible.

Peacock's other works include a survey on the state of analysis in 1833, prepared for the British Association for the Advancement of Science. It is an invaluable source for a contemporary view of the important problems at that time. Peacock also wrote a biography of Thomas Young and was one of the editors of his miscellaneous works.

BIBLIOGRAPHY

Early works are Sylvestre Lacroix, *An Elementary Treatise on the Differential and Integral Calculus*, translated by Charles Babbage, George Peacock, and John Herschel, with notes by Peacock and Herschel (Cambridge, 1816); and *A Collection of Examples of the Differential and Integral Calculus* (Cambridge, 1820). *A Treatise on Algebra* (Cambridge, 1830) is rare, but there is a rev. ed., 2 vols. (Cambridge, 1842–1845; repr. New York, 1940). Other writings include "Report on the Recent Progress and Present State of Certain Branches of Analysis," in *Report of the British Association for the Advancement of Science* (1834), 185–352; "Arithmetic," in *Encyclopaedia Metropolitana*, I (London, 1845); 369–523; *The Life of Thomas Young* (London, 1855); *Miscellaneous Works of the Late Thomas Young*, vols. I and II, George Peacock, ed., vol. III, John Leitch, ed. (London, 1855); and *Observations on the Statutes of the University of Cambridge* (London, 1841).

A complete bibliography of his writings can be found in Daniel Clock, "A New British Concept of Algebra: 1825–1850" (Ph.D. diss., U. of Wisconsin, 1964), 10–12; this work also contains an extensive discussion of Peacock's life and work.

ELAINE KOPPELMAN

PEALE, CHARLES WILLSON (*b*. Queen Anne's County, Maryland, 15 April 1741; *d*. Philadelphia, Pennsylvania, 22 February 1827), *museum direction*.

Eldest of the five children of Charles Peale, sometime clerk in the General Post Office, London, and Margaret Triggs of Annapolis, Maryland, Peale grew up in Chestertown, Maryland, where his father was master of the Kent County school. Deciding at the age of twenty-one that painting might be more profitable than saddlemaking, for which he had been trained, he sought instruction from John Hesselius in Maryland and from John Singleton Copley in Boston. Thereafter he displayed such skill in his portraits of the Maryland gentry that in 1767 several joined to send him abroad for two years to study under Benjamin West, who was later historical painter to George III. In 1776 Peale settled in Philadelphia, the largest and wealthiest city in the British colonies. During the American Revolution, Peale, a zealous patriot, served as a militia officer in the campaign of Trenton and Princeton (1776–1777) and the defense of Philadelphia (1777–1778); and as a "furious Whig" he took a prominent role in political controversies of the period. All the while he continued to paint—Washington, his officers, and the men of the Revolution are known today largely through Peale's eyes. With the return of peace Peale's artistic genius, mechanical skill, and patriotic vision of America's future found expression in designs for grand public displays, such as Philadelphia's Federal Procession of 4 July 1788.

A commission to make drawings of bones of a prehistoric creature from the banks of the Ohio River gave Peale the idea of establishing a natural history museum. It was the first in the United States, for the American Museum of Pierre Eugène du Simitière, although containing natural history specimens, was primarily historical. The museum was opened in Peale's house at Third and Lombard Streets in 1786; thereafter, without entirely giving up painting, he devoted his principal energies to it. It was moved in 1794 to the hall of the American Philosophical Society, the members of which took a warm interest in it and seemed thereby to endorse Peale's plans; and in 1802 it was established in the State House (now Independence Hall). Most of the exhibits were gifts or deposits (for instance, specimens collected by Lewis and Clark presented by President Jefferson); others were secured by Peale himself, most notably the nearly complete skeletons of two mastodons from Orange County, New York, in 1801. When the museum collections were sold in 1848 and 1854 the catalog listed 1,824 birds, 250 quadrupeds, 650 fish, 135 reptiles, lizards, and tortoises, 269 portraits, and thirty-three cases of shells.

Peale's museum demonstrated sound principles of scientific exposition. The exhibits were arranged according to the modified Linnaean system, from fossils and insects to "animal man" (although Peale never obtained a preserved specimen of *Homo sapiens*); and as far as possible they were shown in their natural forms, attitudes, and backgrounds, which Peale as painter readily provided. Special attention was directed to likenesses between species and to distinctive features: a rattlesnake, for example, was mounted with its jaws open and a glass was placed so that all might see the fangs and venom sacs.

Peale viewed the museum as an element in a reformed system of education suitable for virtuous republicans and hoped it would become a national institution, comparable with the Muséum National d'Histoire Naturelle in Paris, with salaried staff, lecturers, laboratories, and publications. This would have required greater support than the federal government was prepared to give. Peale had, therefore, to depend on admission charges, which, although they produced a satisfactory income, constantly exposed the museum—especially when Peale was not personally in charge—to pressures to compromise with scientific integrity. The museum was a school for such young naturalists as Alexander Wilson, John D. Godman, and Richard Harlan, who drew upon its collections for their earliest researches. Similar institutions were established in Baltimore and New York by Peale's sons Rubens and Rembrandt; and catchpenny imitations which did not scorn, as Peale's museum did, to "catch the eye of the gaping multitude," sprang up throughout the country after 1820. These cabinets of jumbled curiosities gave a few young men an introduction to science, but they misled many as to science's nature and scope and fell far short of Peale's goal.

Peale was married three times: to Rachel Brewer of Annapolis in 1762; to Elizabeth DePeyster of New York, in 1791; and to Hannah Moore of Philadelphia, in 1805. From the two first marriages he had seventeen children, of whom eleven reached maturity. Most of them displayed artistic talents of high order; two—Titian Ramsay and Franklin—achieved distinction in natural history and mechanics, respectively.

BIBLIOGRAPHY

Peale's paintings have been listed and illustrated in Charles Coleman Sellers, "Portraits and Miniatures by Charles Willson Peale" and "Charles Willson Peale With Patron and Populace," in *Transactions of the American Philosophical Society*, n.s. **42**, pt. 1 (1952), and **59**, pt. 3 (1969), respectively. The contents of the museum are described in Peale and A. F. M. J. Palisot de Beauvois, *A Scientific and Descriptive Catalogue of Peale's Museum* (Philadelphia, 1796); and Peale's *Guide to the Philadelphia Museum* (Philadelphia, 1804). Peale explained his purpose and philosophy in *Introduction to a Course of Lectures on Natural History* (Philadelphia, 1800). His letter books, diary, autobiography, and other MSS are in the American Philosophical Society library.

Charles Coleman Sellers, *Charles Willson Peale* (New York, 1969), based upon a lifetime of study, is a sufficient introduction to, as well as the last authority on, the subject and its sources.

WHITFIELD J. BELL, JR.

PEALE, REMBRANDT (*b.* near Richboro, Pennsylvania, 22 February 1778; *d.* Philadelphia, Pennsylvania, 3 October 1860), *biology.*

For a detailed study of his life and work, see Supplement.

PEALE, TITIAN RAMSAY (*b.* Philadelphia, Pennsylvania, 2 November 1799; *d.* Philadelphia, 13 March 1885), *natural history.*

Titian Peale, youngest son of Charles Willson Peale and his second wife, Elizabeth DePeyster Peale, knew Philadelphia's scientific men from childhood.

His formal education ended at age thirteen. At sixteen he was sketching for volume I of Thomas Say's *American Entomology* (1824). At eighteen he was elected to the Academy of Natural Sciences of Philadelphia.

Peale's first natural history collecting expedition was in 1817–1818, to Florida and the Sea Islands of Georgia, with Thomas Say, George Ord, and William Maclure. In 1819–1820 he was assistant naturalist with Stephen Long's expedition to the Rocky Mountains, making 122 sketches and drawings.

During 1822–1838 Peale was employed chiefly at the Philadelphia Museum. In the winter of 1824–1825 he collected in Florida for Charles Lucien Bonaparte and then drew all but one of the plates for volume I of Bonaparte's *American Ornithology* (1825); many of the specimens from which the plates were drawn were of Peale's collecting. He visited Maine in 1829 and returned from a trip to Colombia (1830–1832) with 500 bird skins, as well as drawings and butterflies, for exhibition in the Philadelphia Museum. In 1833 he issued a prospectus for what he hoped would be his most important publication, *Lepidoptera Americana*, temporarily abandoned because it was too expensive. He was elected to the American Philosophical Society in 1833.

Peale's great opportunity came when he was appointed as a naturalist on the United States South Seas Surveying and Exploring Expedition (the Wilkes expedition) of 1838–1842. On the homeward journey, in June 1841, one of the expedition's ships, the *Peacock*, was wrecked. A large proportion, and the best, of Peale's bird and animal specimens, all of his butterflies, and an extensive collection of native artifacts were lost—the results of three years' collecting. Still other specimens, which had been shipped back, were improperly handled. Bureaucratic restrictions, lack of library facilities, and Peale's sometimes difficult temper and financial problems combined with quarrels over the quality of engravings to present difficulties during the preparation of his book, which Charles Wilkes titled *Mammalia and Ornithology* (1848).

Wilkes objected to Peale's preface, in which he said that although the government specified that only new species should be described, he felt it would have been more appropriate also to record times and places of observations of known species. There was some criticism of Peale's nomenclature, and therefore Wilkes suppressed the volume shortly after its publication. In 1852 John Cassin, a brilliant taxonomist, was appointed to rewrite it. In his *Mammalogy and Ornithology* (1858) the classifications and names of the species are often different, but Peale's field observations are quoted extensively. According to Harley Harris Bartlett, "Cassin went too far afield to find species to which Peale's might be reduced, and the more modern conception of geographic species might justify the reinstatement of [a number of] Peale's species" ("Reports of the Wilkes Expedition," p. 689). It was a crushing professional defeat for Peale.

Peale was later an examiner in the U.S. Patent Office (1849–1872), did amateur photography, wrote occasional articles, painted, and worked on his manuscript on butterflies. He was a passionate and careful field observer and collector, rather than a "closet naturalist" or skilled taxonomist, at a time when questions of synonymy and nomenclature were deemed of increasing importance. Consequently, he often observed and collected species that others subsequently recorded and described.

BIBLIOGRAPHY

I. ORIGINAL WORKS. Peale's papers are in the collections of the American Philosophical Society, the Historical Society of Pennsylvania, the Academy of Natural Sciences of Philadelphia, and the Library of Congress. The American Museum of Natural History, New York, possesses Peale's unpublished MS "The Butterflies of North America, Diurnal Lepidoptera, Whence They Come; Where They Go; and What They Do," with 3 vols. of accompanying drawings and paintings. His *Lepidoptera Americana. Prospectus* (Philadelphia, 1833) and *Mammalia and Ornithology*, vol. VIII of the Scientific Reports of the U.S. Exploring Expedition of 1838–1842 (Philadelphia, 1848), are extremely rare.

II. SECONDARY LITERATURE. Jessie Poesch, *Titian Ramsay Peale, 1799–1885, and His Journals of the Wilkes Expedition*, which is *Memoirs of the American Philosophical Society*, **52** (1961), an extensive bibliography. See also Harley Harris Bartlett, "The Reports of the Wilkes Expedition, and the Work of the Specialists in Science," in *Proceedings of the American Philosophical Society*, **82** (1940), 601–705; Mary E. Cooley, "The Exploring Expedition in the Pacific," *ibid.*, 707–719; Clifford Merrill Drury, *Diary of Titian Ramsay Peale* (Los Angeles, 1957); Daniel C. Haskell, *The United States Exploring Expedition, 1838–1842, and Its Publications 1844–1874—a Bibliography* (New York, 1942); and Asa Orrin Weese, ed., "The Journal of Titian Ramsay Peale, Pioneer Naturalist," in *Missouri Historical Review*, **41** (1947), 147–163, 266–284.

JESSIE POESCH

PÉAN DE SAINT-GILLES, LÉON (*b.* Paris, France, 4 January 1832; *d.* Cannes, France, 22 March 1862), *analytical chemistry*.

Péan de Saint-Gilles was born into an old and very rich family. His father, like his ancestors, was a notary.

Sickly and weak, he never attended public schools but received private tutoring instead. At the age of seventeen he earned his bachelor of letters degree. Departing from family tradition, he chose scientific research as a profession, but his poor health made it impossible for him to pursue university studies on a regular basis. Thus, he gained his knowledge of chemistry by himself and acquired practical laboratory experience under the guidance of Pelouze, a student and successor of Gay-Lussac at the École Polytechnique. Independently wealthy, Péan de Saint-Gilles later had a laboratory built for himself in which he carried out chemical investigations. He had already achieved some success when death ended his very promising career. The symptoms of consumption appeared at the beginning of 1861; he moved to Cannes to aid his cure, but it was no longer of any help. He was survived by his widow and two children.

Péan de Saint-Gilles's most important work was in the field of titrimetry. In 1846 Frédéric Marguerite introduced the standard solution of potassium permanganate (then called chameleon solution) into the volumetric analysis employed in the determination of iron. Pelouze applied this method to other determinations. Péan de Saint-Gilles extended the use of potassium permanganate as a titrimetric solution for the quantitative determination of nitrite and iodide, as well as of oxalic acid and other organic substances. All of these procedures are still used. He also worked on the identification of the oxidation products of organic substances. His investigations in the area of inorganic chemistry are of no particular importance.

In physical chemistry he examined, in collaboration with Berthelot, the esterification of alcohols with acids. They found that the reaction was never complete but reached a state of equilibrium. This state was independent of the quality of the alcohol and acid. Finding that "the amount of ester formed in each moment is proportional to the product of the reacting substances," they attempted to give a mathematical formulation of the phenomenon. It was the crucial reaction to which Guldberg and Waage referred in their enunciation of the law of mass action in 1864.

BIBLIOGRAPHY

There is a bibliography of Péan de Saint-Gilles's works in Poggendorff, III, 1010–1011. See also the Royal Society *Catalogue of Scientific Papers*, which lists eighteen works, seven of them written with Berthelot. The latter include the important "Recherches sur les affinités," in *Annales de chimie et de physique*, 3rd ser., **65** (1862), 385–422; **66** (1862), 5–110; **68** (1863), 225–359.

On his life and work, see M. Berthelot, "Nécrologie," in *Bulletin. Société chimique de France*, **A5** (1863), 226–227; J. R. Partington, *A History of Chemistry*, IV (London, 1964), 584–585; and F. Szabadváry, *History of Analytical Chemistry* (Oxford, 1966), 251.

F. SZABADVÁRY

PEANO, GIUSEPPE (*b*. Spinetta, near Cuneo, Italy, 27 August 1858; *d*. Turin, Italy, 20 April 1932), *mathematics, logic.*

Giuseppe Peano was the second of the five children of Bartolomeo Peano and Rosa Cavallo. His brother Michele was seven years older. There were two younger brothers, Francesco and Bartolomeo, and a sister, Rosa. Peano's first home was the farm Tetto Galant, near the village of Spinetta, three miles from Cuneo, the capital of Cuneo province, in Piedmont. When Peano entered school, both he and his brother walked the distance to Cuneo each day. The family later moved to Cuneo so that the children would not have so far to walk. The older brother became a successful surveyor and remained in Cuneo. In 1974 Tetto Galant was still in the possession of the Peano family.

Peano's maternal uncle, Michele Cavallo, a priest and lawyer, lived in Turin. On this uncle's invitation Peano moved to Turin when he was twelve or thirteen. There he received private lessons (some from his uncle) and studied on his own, so that in 1873 he was able to pass the lower secondary examination of the Cavour School. He then attended the school as a regular pupil and in 1876 completed the upper secondary program. His performance won him a room-and-board scholarship at the Collegio delle Provincie, which was established to assist students from the provinces to attend the University of Turin.

Peano's professors of mathematics at the University of Turin included Enrico D'Ovidio, Angelo Genocchi, Francesco Siacci, Giuseppe Basso, Francesco Faà di Bruno, and Giuseppe Erba. On 16 July 1880 he completed his final examination "with high honors." For the academic year 1880–1881 he was assistant to D'Ovidio. From the fall of 1881 he was assistant and later substitute for Genocchi until the latter's death in 1889. On 21 July 1887 Peano married Carola Crosio, whose father, Luigi Crosio (1835–1915), was a genre painter.

On 1 December 1890, after regular competition, Peano was named extraordinary professor of infinitesimal calculus at the University of Turin. He was promoted to ordinary professor in 1895. In 1886 he had been named professor at the military academy, which was close to the university. In 1901 he gave up his position at the military academy but retained his professorship at the university until his death in 1932, having transferred in 1931 to the chair of complementary mathematics. He was elected to a number of scientific societies, among them the Academy of Sciences of Turin, in which he played a very active role. He was also a knight of the Order of the Crown of Italy and of the Order of Saint Maurizio and Saint Lazzaro. Although he was not active politically, his views tended toward socialism; and he once invited a group of striking textile workers to a party at his home. During World War I he advocated a closer federation of the allied countries, to better prosecute the war and, after the peace, to form the nucleus of a world federation. Peano was a nonpracticing Roman Catholic.

Peano's father died in 1888; his mother, in 1910. Although he was rather frail as a child, Peano's health was generally good. His most serious illness was an attack of smallpox in August 1889. After having taught his regular class the previous afternoon, Peano died of a heart attack the morning of 20 April 1932. At his request the funeral was very simple, and he was buried in the Turin General Cemetery. Peano was survived by his wife (who died in Turin on 9 April 1940), his sister, and a brother. He had no children. In 1963 his remains were transferred to the family tomb in Spinetta.

Peano is perhaps most widely known as a pioneer of symbolic logic and a promoter of the axiomatic method, but he considered his work in analysis most important. In 1915 he printed a list of his publications, adding: "My works refer especially to infinitesimal calculus, and they have not been entirely useless, seeing that, in the judgment of competent persons, they contributed to the constitution of this science as we have it today." This "judgment of competent persons" refers in part to the *Encyklopädie der mathematischen Wissenschaften*, in which Alfred Pringsheim lists two of Peano's books among nineteen important calculus texts since the time of Euler and Cauchy. The first of these books was Peano's first major publication and is something of an oddity in the history of mathematics, since the title page gives the author as Angelo Genocchi, not Peano: *Angelo Genocchi, Calcolo differenziale e principii di calcolo integrale, publicato con aggiunte dal D.ʳ Giuseppe Peano*. The origin of the book is that Bocca Brothers wished to publish a calculus text based on Genocchi's lectures. Genocchi did not wish to write such a text but gave Peano permission to do so. After its publication Genocchi, thinking Peano lacked regard for him, publicly disclaimed all credit for the book, for which Peano then assumed full responsibility.

Of the many notable things in this book, the *Encyklopädie der mathematischen Wissenschaften* cites theorems and remarks on limits of indeterminate expressions, pointing out errors in the better texts then in use; a generalization of the mean-value theorem for derivatives; a theorem on uniform continuity of functions of several variables; theorems on the existence and differentiability of implicit functions; an example of a function the partial derivatives of which do not commute; conditions for expressing a function of several variables with Taylor's formula; a counterexample to the current theory of minima; and rules for integrating rational functions when roots of the denominator are not known. The other text of Peano cited in the *Encyklopädie* was the two-volume *Lezioni di analisi infinitesimale* of 1893. This work contains fewer new results but is notable for its rigor and clarity of exposition.

Peano began publication in 1881 with articles on the theory of connectivity and of algebraic forms. They were along the lines of work done by D'Ovidio and Faà di Bruno. Peano's work in analysis began in 1883 with an article on the integrability of functions. The article of 1890 contains original notions of integrals and areas. Peano was the first to show that the first-order differential equation $y' = f(x, y)$ is solvable on the sole assumption that f is continuous. His first proof dates from 1886, but its rigor leaves something to be desired. In 1890 this result was generalized to systems of differential equations using a different method of proof. This work is also notable for containing the first explicit statement of the axiom of choice. Peano rejected the axiom of choice as being outside the ordinary logic used in mathematical proofs. In the *Calcolo geometrico* of 1884 Peano had already given many counterexamples to commonly accepted notions in mathematics, but his most famous example was the space-filling curve that was published in 1890. This curve is given by continuous parametric functions and goes through every point in a square as the parameter ranges over some interval. Some of Peano's work in analysis was quite original, and he has not always been given credit for his priority; but much of his publication was designed to clarify and to make rigorous the current definitions and theories. In this regard we may mention his clarification of the notion of area of a surface (1882, independently discovered by H. A. Schwarz); his work with Wronskians, Jacobians, and other special determinants, and with Taylor's formula; and his generalizations of quadrature formulas.

Peano's work in logic and in the foundations of mathematics may be considered together, although he never subscribed to Bertrand Russell's reduction of mathematics to logic. Peano's first publication in logic

was a twenty-page preliminary section on the operations of deductive logic in *Calcolo geometrico secondo l'Ausdehnungslehre di H. Grassmann* (1888). This section, which has almost no connection with the rest of the text, is a synthesis of, and improvement on, some of the work of Boole, Schröder, Peirce, and McColl. The following year, with the publication of *Arithmetices principia, nova methodo exposita*, Peano not only improved his logical symbolism but also used his new method to achieve important new results in mathematics; this short booklet contains Peano's first statement of his famous postulates for the natural numbers, perhaps the best known of all his creations. His research was done independently of the work of Dedekind, who the previous year had published an analysis of the natural numbers, which was essentially that of Peano but without the clarity of Peano. (This was the only work Peano wrote in Latin.) *Arithmetices principia* made important innovations in logical notation, such as $\in$ for set membership and a new notation for universal quantification. Indeed, much of Peano's notation found its way, either directly or in a somewhat modified form, into mid-twentieth-century logic.

In the 1890's he continued his development of logic, and he presented an exposition of his system to the First International Congress of Mathematicians (Zurich, 1897). At the Paris Philosophical Congress of 1900, Peano and his collaborators—Burali-Forti, Padoa, and Pieri—dominated the discussion. Bertrand Russell later wrote, "The Congress was a turning point in my intellectual life, because I there met Peano."

In 1891 Peano founded the journal *Rivista di matematica*, which continued publication until 1906. In the journal were published the results of his research and that of his followers, in logic and the foundations of mathematics. In 1892 he announced in the *Rivista* the *Formulario* project, which was to take much of his mathematical and editorial energies for the next sixteen years. He hoped that the result of this project would be the publication of a collection of all known theorems in the various branches of mathematics. The notations of his mathematical logic were to be used, and proofs of the theorems were to be given. There were five editions of the *Formulario*. The first appeared in 1895; the last was completed in 1908, and contained some 4,200 theorems. But Peano was less interested in logic as a science per se than in logic as used in mathematics. (For this reason he called his system "mathematical logic.") Thus the last two editions of the *Formulario* introduce sections on logic only as it is needed in the proofs of mathematical theorems. The editions through 1901 do contain separate, well-organized sections on logic.

The postulates for the natural numbers received minor modifications after 1889 and assumed their definitive form in 1898. Peano was aware that the postulates do not characterize the natural numbers and, therefore, do not furnish a definition of "number." Nor did he use his mathematical logic for the reduction of mathematical concepts to logical concepts. Indeed, he denied the validity of such a reduction. In a letter to Felix Klein (19 September 1894) he wrote: "The purpose of mathematical logic is to analyze the ideas and reasoning that especially figure in the mathematical sciences." Peano was neither a logicist nor a formalist. He believed rather that mathematical ideas are ultimately derived from our experience of the material world.

In addition to his research in logic and arithmetic, Peano also applied the axiomatic method to other fields, notably geometry, for which he gave several axiom systems. His first axiomatic treatment of elementary geometry appeared in 1889 and was extended in 1894. His work was based on that of Pasch but reduced the number of undefined terms from four to three: point and segment, for the geometry of position (1889), and motion, also necessary for metric geometry (1894). (This number was reduced to two by Pieri in 1899.)

The treatise *Applicazioni geometriche del calcolo infinitesimale* (1887) was based on a course Peano began teaching at the University of Turin in 1885 and contains the beginnings of his "geometrical calculus" (here still influenced by Bellavitis' method of equipollences), new forms of remainders in quadrature formulas, new definitions of length of an arc of a curve and of area of a surface, the notion of a figure tangent to a curve, a determination of the error term in Simpson's formula, and the notion of the limit of a variable figure. There is also a discussion of the measure of a point set, of additive functions of sets, and of integration applied to sets. Peano here generalized the notion of measure that he had introduced in 1883. Peano's popularization of the vectorial methods of H. Grassmann—beginning with the publication in 1888 of the *Calcolo geometrico secondo l'Ausdehnungslehre di H. Grassmann*—was of more importance in geometry. Grassmann's own publications have been criticized for their abstruseness. Nothing could be clearer than Peano's presentation, and he gave great impetus to the Italian school of vector analysis.

Peano's interest in numerical calculation led him to give formulas for the error terms in many commonly used quadrature formulas and to develop a theory of "gradual operations," which gave a new method for the resolution of numerical equations. From 1901 until 1906 he also contributed to actuarial mathematics, when as a member of a state commission he was asked to review a pension fund.

Peano also wrote articles on rational mechanics (1895–1896). Several of these articles dealt with the motion of the earth's axis and had their origin in the famous "falling cat" experiment of the Paris Academy of Sciences in the session of 29 October 1894. This experiment raised the question: "Can the earth change its own orientation in space, using only internal actions as animals do?" Peano took the occasion to apply his geometrical calculus in order to show that, for example, the Gulf Stream alone was able to alter the orientation of the earth's axis. This topic was the occasion of a brief polemic with Volterra over both priority and substance.

By 1900 Peano was already interested in an international auxiliary language, especially for science. On 26 December 1908 he was elected president of the Akademi Internasional de Lingu Universal, a continuation of the Kadem Volapüka, which had been organized in 1887 by the Reverend Johann Martin Schleyer in order to promote Volapük, the artificial language first published by Schleyer in 1879. Under Peano's guidance the Academy was transformed into a free discussion association, symbolized by the change of its name to Academia pro Interlingua in 1910. (The term "interlingua" was understood to represent the emerging language of the future.) Peano remained president of the Academia until his death. During these years Peano's role as interlinguist eclipsed his role as professor of mathematics.

Peano's mathematical logic and his ideography for mathematics were his response to Leibniz' dream of a "universal characteristic," whereas Interlingua was to be the modern substitute for medieval Latin, that is, an international language for scholars, especially scientists. Peano's proposal for an "interlingua" was *latino sine flexione* ("Latin without grammar"), which he published in 1903. He believed that there already existed an international scientific vocabulary, principally of Latin origin; and he tried to select the form of each word which would be most readily recognized by those whose native language was either English or a Romance language. He thought that the best grammar was no grammar, and he demonstrated how easily grammatical structure may be eliminated. His research led him to two areas: one was the algebra of grammar, and the other was philology. The latter preoccupation resulted most notably in *Vocabulario commune ad latino-italiano-français-english-deutsch* (1915), a greatly expanded version of an earlier publication (1909). This second edition contains some 14,000 entries and gives for each the form to be adopted in Interlingua, the classic Latin form, and its version in Italian, French, English, and German (and sometimes in other languages), with indications of synonyms, derivatives, and other items of information.

In his early years Peano was an inspiring teacher; but with the publication of the various editions of the *Formulario*, he adopted it as his text, and his lectures suffered from an excess of formalism. Because of objections to this method of teaching, he resigned from the military academy in 1901 and a few years later stopped lecturing at the Polytechnic. His interest in pedagogy was strong, and his influence was positive. He was active in the Mathesis Society of school teachers of mathematics (founded in 1895); and in 1914 he organized a series of conferences for secondary teachers of mathematics in Turin, which continued through 1919. Peano constantly sought to promote clarity, rigor, and simplicity in the teaching of mathematics. "Mathematical rigor," he wrote, "is very simple. It consists in affirming true statements and in not affirming what we know is not true. It does not consist in affirming every truth possible."

As historian of mathematics Peano contributed many precise indications of origins of mathematical terms and identified the first appearance of certain symbols and theorems. In his teaching of mathematics he recommended the study of original sources, and he always tried to see in his own work a continuation of the ideas of Leibniz, Newton, and others.

The influence of Peano on his contemporaries was great, most notably in the instance of Bertrand Russell. There was also a school of Peano: the collaborators on the *Formulario* project and others who were proud to call themselves his disciples. Pieri, for example, had great success with the axiomatic method, Burali-Forti applied Peano's mathematical logic, and Burali-Forti and Marcolongo developed Peano's geometrical calculus into a form of vector analysis. A largely different group was attracted to Peano after his shift of interest to the promotion of an international auxiliary language. This group was even more devoted; and those such as Ugo Cassina, who shared both the mathematical and philological interests of Peano, felt the closest of all.

It has been said that the apostle in Peano impeded the work of the mathematician. This is no doubt true, especially of his later years; but there can be no question of his very real influence on the development of mathematics. He contributed in great measure to the popularity of the axiomatic method, and his discovery of the space-filling curve must be considered remarkable. While many of his notions, such as area and integral, were "in the air," his originality is undeniable. He was not an imposing person, and his gruff voice with its high degree of lallation could hardly have been attractive; but his gentle personality commanded respect, and his keen intellect inspired disciples. Much of Peano's mathematics is now of historical interest; but his summons to clarity and rigor in mathematics and its teaching continues to be relevant, and few have expressed this call more forcefully.

BIBLIOGRAPHY

I. ORIGINAL WORKS. See Ugo Cassina, ed., *Opere scelte*, 3 vols. (Rome, 1957–1959), which contains half of Peano's articles and a bibliography (in vol. I) that lists approximately 80 percent of Peano's publications. A more complete list is in Hubert C. Kennedy, ed., *Selected Works of Giuseppe Peano* (Toronto, 1972). The fifth ed. of the *Formulario mathematico* has been reprinted in facsimile (Rome, 1960).

II. SECONDARY LITERATURE. The most complete biography is Hubert C. Kennedy, *Giuseppe Peano* (Basel, 1974). Ten articles on the work of Peano are in Ugo Cassina, *Critica dei principî della matematica e questioni di logica* (Rome, 1961) and *Dalla geometria egiziana alla matematica moderna* (Rome, 1961). Also see Alessandro Terracini, ed., *In memoria di Giuseppe Peano* (Cuneo, 1955), which contains articles by eight authors. A list of these and other items is in *Selected Works of Giuseppe Peano*.

HUBERT C. KENNEDY

PEARL, RAYMOND (*b.* Farmington, New Hampshire, 3 June 1879; *d.* Hershey, Pennsylvania, 17 November 1940), *biology, genetics.*

Pearl was the only child of Frank Pearl and Ida May McDuffee. He attended public schools in Farmington and nearby Rochester. In 1899 he earned the A.B. in biology at Dartmouth College and the Ph.D. in 1902 at the University of Michigan, where his dissertation was on the behavior of a flatworm (*Planaria*). He also studied at the University of Leipzig in 1905 and at University College, London, from 1905–1906. In London he studied under Karl Pearson, whose influence led Pearl to apply statistics to population studies.

Pearl was an instructor in zoology at the University of Pennsylvania (1906–1907) until he became chairman of the department of biology at the Maine Agricultural Experiment Station (1907–1918), where he studied the heredity and reproduction of poultry and cattle. As chief of the statistical division of the U.S. Food Administration from 1917 to 1919, he studied the relationship of food to population. Pearl's long association with the Johns Hopkins University began in 1918, when he became professor of biometry and vital statistics in the School of Hygiene and Public Health (1918–1925). He was also professor of biology in the School of Medicine (1923–1940), research professor and director of the Institute of Biological Research (1925–1930), and statistician at the Johns Hopkins Hospital (1919–1935).

A prodigious researcher and a voluminous and articulate writer, Pearl achieved renown as a pioneer in world population changes, birth and death rates, and longevity. He founded and edited the *Quarterly Review of Biology* from 1926 and *Human Biology* from 1929. On 29 June 1903 he married Maud Mary DeWitt, who assisted his researches and writing; the couple had two daughters, Ruth DeWitt and Penelope Mackey.

Pearl attracted public attention in 1920 with a mathematical equation for determining population to the year 2100. His predictions deviated only 3.7 percent in the 1940 census. His other research findings, often controversial, led him to believe that the length of life varied inversely with the tempo or pace of living, that heredity predominated over environment in the length of life and in shaping one's destiny, that moderate drinkers lived longer than total abstainers, and that intellectuals had a better chance to live longer than did manual workers. In one study he analyzed the reproductive histories; the use of contraception; and the social, economic, educational, health, and religious histories of 30,949 mothers.

Pearl received many honorary degrees for his work relating biology to the social sciences. He was president of the International Union for Scientific Investigation of Population Problems (1928–1931), the American Association of Physical Anthropologists (1934–1936), and the American Statistical Association (1939). He was also made a knight (1920) and an officer (1929) of the Crown of Italy.

Obituary accounts called Pearl "a statistician of the human race" and a "biologist-philosopher." H. L. Mencken praised his lucid writing style, his wide knowledge and interests, his scientific creativity, and his delight in playing the French horn.

BIBLIOGRAPHY

I. ORIGINAL WORKS. Pearl's writings include *Modes of Research in Genetics* (New York, 1915); *Diseases of Poultry* (New York, 1915), written with F. M. Surface and M. R. Curtis; *The Nation's Food* (Philadelphia, 1920); *The Biology of Death* (Philadelphia, 1922); *Introduction to Medical Biometry and Statistics* (Philadelphia–London, 1923; 3rd ed. 1940); *Studies in Human Biology* (Baltimore, 1924); *The Biology of Population Growth* (New York, 1925);

Alcohol and Longevity (New York, 1926); *To Begin With* (New York, 1927; rev. 1930); *The Rate of Living* (New York, 1928); *Constitution and Health* (London–New York, 1933); *The Ancestry of the Long-Lived* (Baltimore, 1934), written with Ruth DeWitt Pearl; and *The Natural History of Population* (London–New York, 1939). He was editorial associate of *Biometrika, Journal of Agricultural Research, Genetics, Metron, Biologia generalis,* and *Acta biotheoretica.*

II. SECONDARY LITERATURE. Biographical and obituary accounts are A. W. Freeman, "Raymond Pearl, 1879–1940," in *American Journal of Public Health,* **31,** no. 1 (1941), 81–82; H. S. Jennings, "Raymond Pearl, 1879–1940," in *Biographical Memoirs. National Academy of Sciences,* **22** (1943), 295–347, which includes a full bibliography; H. L. Mencken, in Baltimore *Sun* (24 Nov. 1940); J. R. Miner and J. Berkson, "Raymond Pearl, 1879–1940," in *Scientific Monthly,* **52** (1941), 192–194; "News and Notes," in *American Journal of Sociology,* **16,** no. 4 (1941), 604; and *Dictionary of American Biography,* XXII, supp. 2 (1958), 521–522.

FRANKLIN PARKER

PEARSON, GEORGE (*b.* Rotherham, England, 1751 [baptized 4 September]; *d.* London, England, 9 November 1828), *chemistry.*

Pearson was one of the first chemists in Britain to accept the "antiphlogistic" theories of Lavoisier. He is best known for his role in introducing into Britain the nomenclature devised by Lavoisier and other leading French chemists. He studied medicine at Edinburgh University from 1770 to 1774 and received the M.D. in 1773; he also studied chemistry under Joseph Black. After a brief period at St. Thomas's Hospital in London, Pearson spent about two years in Europe before establishing a medical practice in Doncaster, where he stayed for about six years. He eventually moved to London. In 1787 he became chief physician at St. George's Hospital. He was admitted to the Royal Society in 1791 and for many years served on the council.

On hearing of Edward Jenner's successful inoculation against smallpox, in which he used matter from the pustule of a cowpox patient, Pearson became interested in the subject. He published a number of articles and pamphlets and eventually set up an institution to provide vaccinations. His program, however, delayed, rather than hastened, the general adoption of Jenner's method, for Pearson used a defective vaccine which frequently produced severe eruptions resembling smallpox. Ill feeling thus developed between Jenner and Pearson. Pearson tended to belittle Jenner's achievements and opposed his successful claim for remuneration from the government.

A glimpse of Pearson as a lecturer was afforded by the American chemist Benjamin Silliman, who, when planning his visit to Europe in 1805–1806, had been given a letter of introduction to Pearson as "the greatest chemist in England." Silliman said Pearson lectured on chemistry, materia medica, and therapeutics for two and a quarter hours without a break. "There was no interval for breathing or for a gentle transition to a new subject. This mental repletion was not favorable to intellectual digestion" (see G. P. Fisher, *Life of Benjamin Silliman*, I [New York, 1866], 144–145).

Nevertheless Pearson seems to have been a competent chemist. He investigated the composition of "James's powder," a popular febrifuge which made a fortune for Robert James. He found that it was a mixture of bone ash and antimony oxide. In 1792 he extended the work of Smithson Tennant, who had shown that carbon was obtained when powdered marble was heated with phosphorus (S. Tennant, "On the Decomposition of Fixed Air," in *Philosophical Transactions of the Royal Society*, **81** [1791], 182–184). Pearson showed that sodium carbonate could be similarly decomposed, and he discovered calcium phosphide by heating phosphorus with quicklime. He noted the reaction of calcium phosphide with water and the spontaneous combustion of "phosphoric air" (phosphine). With J. Stodart he investigated the composition of Indian ("wootz") steel (see R. A. Hadfield, *Faraday and His Metallurgical Researches* [London, 1931], pp. 36–37 and *passim*) and made a useful contribution to the history of metallurgy by analyzing some ancient weapons and utensils.

In 1789 the Dutch chemists A. Paete van Troostwijk and J. R. Deiman succeeded in decomposing water by frictional electricity, although they were unable to show conclusively that hydrogen and oxygen were formed. They were assisted by J. Cuthbertson, who constructed the apparatus; Cuthbertson also collaborated with Pearson in a series of experiments over two years in the 1790's in which a more convincing demonstration of the formation of the two constituents of water was effected. The amount of the gases actually obtained was, however, very small; and an entirely successful decomposition of water by electricity was not possible until the invention of the voltaic cell.

Pearson also published a number of papers of mainly medical content. He investigated a number of body tissues and fluids and showed, for example, that the blackening of lung tissue is caused by the absorption of carbon from the atmosphere. These researches were continued in an unpublished Bakerian lecture.

A feature of Lavoisier's *Méthode de nomenclature chimique* (Paris, 1787) had been a large folding sheet which presented, in columns, the names of all known substances, classified according to the tenets of the new chemistry. Lavoisier gave the proposed new names in adjoining columns. It was this sheet that Pearson translated. He included both English and Latin equivalents, an explanatory text, and many additions. Pearson also adopted the term "nitrogen," which was first coined by Chaptal as *nitrogène*. Pearson considered the original French *azote* unsuitable because it was based on a purely negative characteristic.

BIBLIOGRAPHY

I. ORIGINAL WORKS. Pearson's M.D. dissertation was *Disputatio physica inauguralis de putridine animalibus post mortem quam superveniente* (Edinburgh, 1773). His investigation of the waters from the springs in Buxton, conducted while he was living in Doncaster, is embodied in *Observations and Experiments for Investigating the Chymical History of the Tepid Springs of Buxton . . .*, 2 vols. (London, 1784) and in a short pamphlet, *Directions for Impregnating the Buxton Water, With Its Own and Other Gases, and for Composing Artificial Buxton Water* (London, 1785). His most important pamphlets on vaccination are *An Inquiry Concerning the History of the Cow Pox Principally With a View to Supersede and Extinguish the Small Pox* (London, 1789), repr. in E. M. Crookshank, ed., *History and Pathology of Vaccination*, II (London, 1889), 34–91; and *An Examination of the Report of the Committee of the House of Commons on the Claims of Remuneration for the Vaccine Pock Inoculation: Containing a Statement of the Principal Historical Facts of the Vaccina* (London, 1802). He also published *Heads and Notes of a Course of Chemical Lectures* (London, 1806).

Pearson's work on nomenclature is *A Translation of the Table of Chemical Nomenclature, Proposed by De Guyton, Formerly de Morveau, Lavoisier, Berthollet & de Fourcroy; With Additions & Alterations, Prefixed by an Explanation of the Terms, and Some Observations on the New System of Chemistry* (London, 1794). A 2nd, enl. ed. was published in 1799, in which Pearson added tables of chemical affinity; the new symbols of J. H. Hassenfratz and P. A. Adet, which had appeared in the *Méthode de nomenclature chymique*; and symbols used by T. Bergman and C. J. Geoffroy. He also included objections that had been made to the new nomenclature by various chemists.

An incomplete list of Pearson's papers is in the Royal Society *Catalogue of Scientific Papers*, IV, 795. His writings include "Experiments & Observations to Investigate the Composition of James's Powder," in *Philosophical Transactions of the Royal Society*, **81** (1791), 317–367; "Experiments Made With the View of Decompounding Fixed Air, or Carbonic Acid," *ibid.*, **82** (1792), 289–308;

"Experiments to Investigate the Nature of a Kind of Steel, Manufactured at Bombay and There Called Wootz; With Remarks on the Properties and Composition of the Different States of Iron," *ibid.*, **85** (1795), 322–346; "Observations on Some Ancient Metallic Arms & Utensils; With Experiments to Determine Their Composition," *ibid.*, **86** (1796), 395–451; "Experiments & Observations Made With a View of Ascertaining the Nature of the Gas Produced by Passing Electric Discharges Through Water," *ibid.*, **87** (1797), 142–158, full paper in Nicholson's *Journal of Natural Philosophy, Chemistry & the Arts*, **1** (1797), 241–248, 299–305, 349–355; "On the Colouring Matter of the Black Bronchial Glands, and of the Black Spots of the Lungs," in *Philosophical Transactions of the Royal Society*, **103** (1813), 159–170; and "Researches to Discover the Faculties of Pulmonary Absorption, With Respect to Charcoal," MS in the Royal Society Archives, A.P. 13 (1827–1829), no. 21, read 20 Dec. 1827.

II. Secondary Literature. No informative biography of Pearson exists. A short account, with a list of his publications, is in *Gentleman's Magazine*, **99**, pt. 1 (1829), 129–131. A partial account of Pearson's involvement with Jenner is given by D. Fisk, *Dr. Jenner of Berkeley* (London, 1959), 148 and *passim*.

E. L. Scott

PEARSON, KARL (*b.* London, England, 27 March 1857; *d.* Coldharbour, Surrey, England, 27 April 1936), *applied mathematics, biometry, statistics.*

Pearson, founder of the twentieth-century science of statistics, was the younger son and the second of three children of William Pearson, a barrister of the Inner Temple, and his wife, Fanny Smith. Educated at home until the age of nine, he was sent to University College School, London, for seven years. He withdrew in 1873 for reasons of health and spent the next year with a private tutor. He obtained a scholarship at King's College, Cambridge, in 1875, placing second on the list. At Cambridge, Pearson studied mathematics under E. J. Routh, G. G. Stokes, J. C. Maxwell, Arthur Cayley, and William Burnside. He received the B.A. with mathematical honors in 1879 and was third wrangler in the mathematical tripos that year.

Pearson went to Germany after receiving his degree. At Heidelberg he studied physics under G. H. Quincke and metaphysics under Kuno Fischer. At Berlin he attended the lectures of Emil du Bois-Reymond on Darwinism. With his father's profession no doubt in mind, Pearson went up to London, took rooms in the Inner Temple in November 1880, read in Chambers in Lincoln's Inn, and was called to the bar in 1881. He received an LL.B. from Cambridge University in 1881 and an M.A. in 1882, but he never practiced.

Pearson was appointed Goldsmid professor of applied mathematics and mechanics at University College, London, in 1884 and was lecturer in geometry at Gresham College, London, from 1891 to 1894. In 1911 he relinquished the Goldsmid chair to become the first Galton professor of eugenics, a chair that had been offered first to Pearson in keeping with Galton's expressed wish. He retired in 1933 but continued to work in a room at University College until a few months before his death.

Elected a fellow of the Royal Society in 1896, Pearson was awarded its Darwin Medal in 1898. He was awarded many honors by British and foreign anthropological and medical organizations, but never joined and was not honored during his lifetime by the Royal Statistical Society.

In 1890 Pearson married Maria Sharpe, who died in 1928. They had one son, Egon, and two daughters, Sigrid and Helga. In 1929 he married a co-worker in his department, Margaret Victoria Child.

At Cambridge, Pearson's coach under the tripos system was Routh, probably the greatest mathematical coach in the history of the university, who aroused in Pearson a special interest in applied mathematics, mechanics, and the theory of elasticity. Pearson took the Smith's Prize examination, which called for the very best in mathematics. He failed to become a prizeman; but his response to a question set by Isaac Todhunter was found, on Todhunter's death in 1884, to have been incorporated in the manuscript of his unfinished *History of the Theory of Elasticity*, with the comment "This proof is better than De St. Venant's."[1] As a result, in the same year Pearson was appointed by the syndics of the Cambridge University Press to finish and edit the work.

Pearson did not confine himself to mathematics at Cambridge. He read Dante, Goethe, and Rousseau in the original, sat among the divinity students listening to the discourse of the university's regius professor of divinity, and discussed the moral sciences tripos with a fellow student. Before leaving Cambridge he wrote reviews of two books on Spinoza for the *Cambridge Review*, and a paper on Maimonides and Spinoza for *Mind*.

Although intensely interested in the basis, doctrine, and history of religion, Pearson rebelled at attending the regular divinity lectures, compulsory since the founding of King's in 1441, and after a hard fight saw compulsory divinity lectures abolished. He next sought and, with the assistance of his father, obtained release from compulsory attendance at chapel; after which, to the astonishment and pique of the authorities, he continued to attend as the spirit moved him.

Pearson's life in Germany, as at Cambridge, involved much more than university lectures and related study. He became interested in German folklore, in medieval and renaissance German literature, in the history of the Reformation, and in the development of ideas on the position of women. He also came into contact with the ideas of Karl Marx and Ferdinand Lassalle, the two leaders of German socialism. His writings and lectures on his return to England indicate that he had become both a convinced evolutionist and a fervent socialist, and that he had begun to merge these two doctrines into his own rather special variety of social Darwinism. His given name was originally Carl; at about this time he began spelling it with a "K." A King's College fellowship, conferred in 1880 and continued until 1886, gave Pearson financial independence and complete freedom from duties of any sort, and during these years he was frequently in Germany, where he found a quiet spot in the Black Forest to which he often returned.

In 1880 Pearson worked for some weeks in the engineering shops at Cambridge and drew up the schedule in Middle and Ancient High German for the medieval languages tripos. In the same year he published his first book, a literary work entitled *The New Werther*, "by Loki," written in the form of letters from a young man wandering in Germany to his fiancée.

During 1880–1881 Pearson found diversion from his legal studies in lecturing on Martin Luther at Hampstead, and on socialism, Marx, and Lassalle at workingmen's clubs in Soho. In 1882–1884 he gave a number of courses of lectures around London on German social life and thought from the earliest times up to the sixteenth century, and on Luther's influence on the material and intellectual welfare of Germany. In addition he published in the *Academy*, *Athenaeum*, and elsewhere a substantial number of letters, articles, and reviews relating to Luther. Many of these were later republished, together with other lectures delivered between 1885–1887, in his *The Ethic of Freethought* (1888).

During 1880–1884 Pearson's mathematical talent was not entirely dormant. He gave University of London extension lectures on "Heat" and served as a temporary substitute for absent professors of mathematics at King's College and University College, London. At the latter Pearson met Alexander B. W. Kennedy, professor of engineering and mechanical technology, who was instrumental in securing Pearson's appointment to the Goldsmid professorship.

During his first six years in the Goldsmid chair, Pearson demonstrated his great capacity for hard work and extraordinary productivity. His professorial duties included lecturing on statics, dynamics, and mechanics, with demonstrations and proofs based on geometrical and graphical methods, and conducting practical instruction in geometrical drawing and projection. Soon after assuming the professorship, he began preparing for publication the incomplete manuscript of *The Common Sense of the Exact Sciences* left by his penultimate predecessor, William Kingdon Clifford; and it was issued in 1885. The preface, the entire chapter "Position," and considerable portions of the chapters "Quantity" and "Motion" were written by Pearson. A far more difficult and laborious task was the completion and editing of Todhunter's unfinished *History of the Theory of Elasticity*. He wrote about half the final text of the first volume (1886) and was responsible for almost the whole of the second volume, encompassing several hundred memoirs (1893). His editing of these volumes, along with his own papers on related topics published during the same decade, established Pearson's reputation as an applied mathematician.

Somehow Pearson also found the time and energy to plan and deliver the later lectures of *The Ethic of Freethought* series; to complete *Die Fronica* (1887), a historical study that traced the development of the Veronica legend and the history of the Veronica-portraits of Christ, written in German and dedicated to Henry Bradshaw, the Cambridge University Librarian; and to collect the material on the evolution of western Christianity that later formed much of the substance of *The Chances of Death* (1897). In these historical studies Pearson was greatly influenced and guided by Bradshaw, from whom he learned the importance of patience and thoroughness in research. In 1885 Pearson became an active founding member of a small club of men and women dedicated to the discussion of the relationship between the sexes. He gave the opening address on "The Woman's Question," and addressed a later meeting on "Socialism and Sex." Among the members of the group was Maria Sharpe, whom he married in 1890.

In the 1890's the sole duty of the lecturer in geometry at Gresham College seems to have been to give three courses per year of four lectures to an extramural audience on topics of his own choosing. Pearson's aim in applying for the lectureship was apparently to gain an opportunity to present some of his ideas to a fairly general audience. In his first two courses, delivered in March and April 1891 under the general title "The Scope and Concepts of Modern Science," he explored the philosophical foundations of science. These lectures, developed and enlarged, became the first edition of *The Grammar of Science* (1892), a remarkable book that influenced the scientific thought of an entire generation.

Pearson outlined his concept of the nature, scope, function, and method of science in a series of articles in the first chapter of his book. "The material of science," he said, "is coextensive with the whole physical universe, not only . . . as it now exists, but with its past history and the past history of all life therein," while "The function of science" is "the classification of facts, the recognition of their sequence and their relative significance," and "The unity of all science consists alone in its method, not its material . . . It is not the facts themselves which form science, but the method in which they are dealt with." In a summary of the chapter he wrote that the method of science consists of "(a) careful and accurate classification of facts and observation of their correlation and sequence; (b) the discovery of scientific laws by aid of the creative imagination; (c) self-criticism and the final touchstone of equal validity for all normally constituted minds." He emphasized repeatedly that science can only describe the "how" of phenomena and can never explain the "why," and stressed the necessity of eliminating from science all elements over which theology and metaphysics may claim jurisdiction. The *Grammar of Science* also anticipated in many ways the revolutionary changes in scientific thought brought about by Einstein's special theory of relativity. Pearson insisted on the relativity of all motion, completely restated the Newtonian laws of motion in keeping with this primary principle, and developed a system of mechanics logically from them. Recognizing mass to be simply the ratio of the number of units in two accelerations as "expressed briefly by the statement that mutual accelerations are *inversely* as masses" (ch. 8, sec. 9), he ridiculed the current textbook definition of mass as "quantity of matter." Although recognized as a classic in the philosophy of science, the *Grammar of Science* is little read today by scientists and students of science mainly because its literary style has dated it.

Pearson was thus well on the way to a respectable career as a teacher of applied mathematics and philosopher of science when two events occurred that markedly changed the direction of his professional activity and shaped his future career. The first was the publication of Galton's *Natural Inheritance* in 1889; the second, the appointment of W. F. R. Weldon to the Jodrell professorship of zoology at University College, London, in 1890.

Natural Inheritance summed up Galton's work on correlation and regression, concepts and techniques that he had discovered and developed as tools for measuring the influence of heredity;[2] presented all that he contributed to their theory; and clearly reflected his recognition of their applicability and value in studies of all living forms. In the year of its appearance, Pearson read a paper on *Natural Inheritance* before

the aforementioned small discussion club, stressing the light that it threw on the laws of heredity, rather than the mathematics of correlation and regression. Pearson became quite charmed by the concept and implications of Galton's "correlation," which he saw to be a "category broader than causation . . . of which causation was only the limit, and [which] brought psychology, anthropology, medicine and sociology in large parts into the field of mathematical treatment," which opened up the "possibility . . . of reaching knowledge—as valid as physical knowledge was then thought to be—in the field of living forms and above all in the field of human conduct."[3] Almost immediately his life took a new course: he began to lay the foundations of the new science of statistics that he was to develop almost single-handed during the next decade and a half. But it is doubtful whether much of this would have come to pass had it not been for Weldon, who posed the questions that impelled Pearson to make his most significant contributions to statistical theory and methodology.[4]

Weldon, a Cambridge zoologist, had been deeply impressed by Darwin's theory of natural selection and in the 1880's had sought to devise means for deriving concrete support for it from studies of animal and plant populations. Galton's *Natural Inheritance* convinced him that the most promising route was through statistical studies of variation and correlation in those populations. Taking up his appointment at University College early in 1891, Weldon began to apply, extend, and improve Galton's methods of measuring variation and correlation, in pursuit of concrete evidence to support Darwin's "working hypothesis." These undertakings soon brought him face to face with problems outside the realm of the classical theory of errors: How describe asymmetrical, double-humped, and other non-Gaussian frequency distributions? How derive "best"—or at least "good"—values for the parameters of such distributions? What are the "probable errors" of such estimates? What is the effect of selection on one or more of a number of correlated variables? Finding the solution of these problems to be beyond his mathematical capacity, Weldon turned to Pearson for help.

Pearson, in turn, seeing an opportunity to contribute, through his special skills, to the improvement of the understanding of life, characteristically directed his attention to this new area with astonishing energy. The sudden change in his view of statistics, and the early stages of his rapid development of a new science of statistics are evident in the syllabuses of his lectures at Gresham College in 1891–1894 and in G. Udny Yule's summaries of Pearson's two lecture courses on the theory of statistics at University College during the sessions of 1894–1895 and 1895–1896,[5] undoubtedly the first of their kind ever given. Pearson was an enthusiast for graphic presentation; and his Gresham lectures on "Geometry of Statistics" (November 1891–May 1892) were devoted almost entirely to a comprehensive formal treatment of graphical representation of statistical data from the biological, physical, and social sciences, with only brief mention of numerical descriptive statistics. In "Laws of Chance" (November 1892–February 1893) he discussed probability theory and the concept of "correlation," illustrating both by coin-tossing and card-drawing experiments and by observations of natural phenomena. The term "standard deviation" was introduced in the lecture of 31 January 1893, as a convenient substitute for the cumbersome "root mean square error" and the older expressions "error of mean square" and "mean error"; and in the lecture of 1 February, he discussed whether an observed discrepancy between a theoretical standard deviation and an experimentally determined value for it is "sufficiently great to create suspicion." In "The Geometry of Chance" (November 1893–May 1894) he devoted a lecture to "Normal Curves,"[6] one to "Skew Curves," and one to "Compound Curves."

In 1892 Pearson lectured on variation, and in 1893 on correlation, to research students at University College, the material being published as the first four of his *Philosophical Transactions* memoirs on evolution. At this time he worked out his general theory of normal correlation for three, four, and finally n variables. Syllabuses or summaries of these lectures at University College are not available, but much of the substance of the four memoirs is visible in Yule's summaries. Those of the lectures of November 1895 through March 1896 reveal Pearson's early groping toward a general theory of skew correlation and nonlinear regression that was not published until 1905. His summary of Pearson's lecture of 14 May 1896 shows that considerable progress had already been made on both the experimental and theoretical material on errors of judgment, measurement errors, and the variation over time of the "personal equations" of individual observers that constituted Pearson's 1902 memoir on these matters.

These lectures mark the beginning of a new epoch in statistical theory and practice. Pearson communicated some thirty-five papers on statistical matters to the Royal Society during 1893–1901. By 1906 he had published over seventy additional papers embodying further statistical theory and applications. In retrospect, it is clear that Pearson's contributions during this period firmly established statistics as a discipline in its own right. Yet, at the time, "the main purpose of all this work" was not development of statistical theory and techniques for their own sake but, rather, "development and application of statistical methods for the study of problems of heredity and evolution."[7]

In order to place the whole of Pearson's work in proper perspective, it will be helpful to examine his contributions to distinct areas of theory and practice. Consider, for example, his "method of moments" and his system of wonderfully diverse frequency curves. Pearson's aim in developing the method of moments was to provide a general method for determining the values of the parameters of a frequency distribution of some particular form selected to describe a given set of observational or experimental data. This is clear from his basic exposition of the subject in the first (1894) of his series of memoirs entitled "Contributions to the Mathematical Theory of Evolution."[8]

The foundations of the system of Pearson curves were laid in the second memoir of this series, "Skew Variation in Homogeneous Material" (1895). Types I–IV were defined and applied in this memoir; Types V and VI, in a "Supplement . . ." (1901); and Types VII–XII in a "Second Supplement . . ." (1916). The system includes symmetrical and asymmetrical curves of both limited and unlimited range (in either or both directions); most are unimodal, but some are U-, J-, or reverse J-shaped. Pearson's purpose in developing them was to provide a collection of frequency curves of diverse forms to be fitted to data as "*graduation curves*, mathematical constructs to describe more or less accurately what we have observed."[9] Their use was facilitated by the central role played by the method of moments: (1) the appropriate curve type is determined by the values of two dimensionless ratios of centroidal moments,

$$\beta_1 = \frac{\mu_3^2}{\mu_2^3} \quad \text{and} \quad \beta_2 = \frac{\mu_4}{\mu_2^2},$$

defined in the basic memoir (1894); and (2) values of the parameters of the selected types of probability (or frequency) curve are determined by the conditions $\mu_0 = 1$ (or $\mu_0 = N$, the total number of observations), $\mu_1 = 0$, and the observed or otherwise indicated values of $\mu_2 (= \sigma^2)$, β_1, and β_2. The acceptance and use of curves of Pearson's system for this purpose may also have been aided by the fact that all were derived from a single differential equation, to which Pearson had been led by considering the slopes of segments of frequency polygons determined by the ordinates of symmetric and asymmetric binomial and hypergeometric probability distributions. That derivation may well have provided some support to Pearson curves as probability or frequency curves, rather than as purely arbitrary graduation curves. Be that as it may, the fitting of Pearson curves to observational data was extensively practiced by biologists and social scientists in the decades that followed. The results did much to dispel the almost religious acceptance of the normal distribution as the mathematical model of variation of biological, physical, and social phenomena.

Meanwhile, Pearson's system of frequency curves acquired a new and unanticipated importance in statistical theory and practice with the discovery that the sampling distributions of many statistical test functions appropriate to analyses of small samples from normal, binomial, and Poisson distributions—such as χ^2, s^2, t, s_1^2 / s_2^2, and r (when $\rho = 0$)—are represented by particular families of Pearson curves, either directly or through simple transformation. This application of Pearson curves, and their use to approximate percentage points of statistical test functions whose sampling distributions are either untabulated or analytically or numerically intractable, but whose moments are readily evaluated, have now transcended their use as graduation curves; they have also done much to ensure the value of Pearson's comprehensive system of frequency curves in statistical theory and practice. The use of Pearson curves for either purpose would, however, have been gravely handicapped had not Pearson and his co-workers prepared detailed and extensive tables of their ordinates, integrals, and other characteristics, which were published principally in *Biometrika* beginning in 1901, and reprinted, with additions, in his *Tables for Statisticians and Biometricians* (1914; Part II, 1931).

As statistical concepts and techniques of correlation and regression originated with Galton, who devised rudimentary arithmetical and graphical procedures (utilizing certain medians and quartiles of the data in hand) to derive sample values for his "regression" coefficient, or "index of co-relation," r. Galton was also the first, though he had assistance from J. D. Hamilton Dickson, to express the bivariate normal distribution in the "Galtonian form" of the frequency distribution of two correlated variables.[10] Weldon and F. Y. Edgeworth devised alternative means of computation, which, however, were somewhat arbitrary and did not fully utilize all the data. It was Pearson who established, by what would now be termed the method of maximum likelihood, that the "best value of the correlation coefficient" (ρ) of a bivariate normal distribution is given by the sample product-moment coefficient of correlation,

$$r = \frac{\Sigma xy}{N s_x s_y} = \frac{\Sigma xy}{\sqrt{\Sigma(x^2) \cdot \Sigma(y^2)}},$$

where x and y denote the deviations of the measured values of the x and y characteristics of an individual sample object from their respective arithmetic means (m_x and m_y) in the sample, Σ denotes summation over all N individuals in the sample, and s_x and s_y are the sample standard deviations of the measured values of x and y, respectively.[11] The expression "coefficient of correlation" apparently was originated by Edgeworth in 1892,[12] but the value of r defined by the above equation is quite properly known as "Pearson's coefficient of correlation." Its derivation may be found in section 4b. of "Regression, Heredity, and Panmixia" (1896), his first fundamental paper on correlation theory and its application to problems of heredity.

In the same memoir Pearson also showed how the "best value" of r could be evaluated conveniently from the sample standard deviations s_x, s_y and either s_{x-y} or s_{x+y}, thereby avoiding computation of the sample product moment ($\Sigma xy/N$); gave a mistaken expression for the standard deviation of the sampling error[13] of r as a measure of ρ in large samples—which he corrected in "Probable Errors of Frequency Constants . . ." (1898); introduced the term "coefficient of variation" for the ratio of a standard deviation to the corresponding mean expressed as a percentage; expressed explicitly, in his discussion of the trivariate case, what are now called coefficients of "multiple" correlation and "partial" regression in terms of the three "zero-order" coefficients of correlation (r_{12}, r_{13}, r_{23}); gave the partial regression equation for predicting the (population) mean value of trait X_1, say, corresponding to given values of traits X_2 and X_3, the coefficients of X_2 and X_3 being expressed explicitly in terms of r_{12}, r_{13}, r_{23} and the three sample standard deviations (s_1, s_2, s_3); gave the formula for the large-sample standard error of the value of X_1 predicted by this equation; restated Edgeworth's formula (1892) for the trivariate normal distribution in improved determinantal notation; and carried through explicitly the extension to the general case of a p-variate normal correlation surface, expressed in a form that brought the computations within the power of those lacking advanced mathematical training.

In this first fundamental memoir on correlation, Pearson carried the development of the theory of multivariate normal correlation as a practical tool almost to completion. When the joint distribution of a number of traits X_1, X_2, . . ., X_p, ($p \geq 2$) over the individuals of a population is multivariate normal, then the population coefficients of correlation, ρ_{ij}, ($i, j = 1, 2, \ldots, p$; $i \neq j$), completely characterize the degrees of association among these traits in the population—traits X_i and X_j are independent if and only if $\rho_{ij} = 0$ and completely interdependent if and only if ρ_{ij} equals ± 1—and the regression in the population of each one of the traits on any combination of the others is linear. It is clear from footnotes to section 5 of this memoir that Pearson was fully aware that linearity of regressions and this comprehensive feature of population (product-moment) coefficients of correlation do not carry over to multivariate skew frequency distributions, and he recognized "the need of [a] theory of skew correlation" which he proposed to treat "in a memoir on skew correlation."[14] The promised memoir, *On the General Theory of Skew Correlation and Non-Linear Regression*, appeared in 1905.

Pearson there dealt with the properties of the correlation ratio, $\eta(= \eta_{yx})$, a sample measure of correlation that he had introduced in a paper of 1903 to replace the sample correlation coefficient, r, when the observed regression curve of y on x (obtained by plotting the means of the y values, $\bar{y}_{x_i}$, corresponding to the respective x values, $x_1, x_2, \ldots$, as a function of x) exhibits a curvilinear relationship and showed that η is the square root of the fraction of the variability of the N y values about their mean, $\bar{y}$, that is ascribable to the variability of the y means $\bar{y}_{x_i}$ about $\bar{y}$; that $1 - \eta^2$ is the fraction of the total variability of the y values about their mean $\bar{y}$ contributed by the variability of the y values within the respective x arrays about their respective mean values, $\bar{y}_{x_i}$, within these arrays; and that $\eta^2 - r^2$ is the fraction ascribable to the deviations of the points $(\bar{y}_{x_i}, x_i)$ from the straight line of closest fit to these points, indicating the importance of the difference between η and r as an indicator of the departure of regression from linearity.[15] He also gave an expression for the standard deviation of the sampling error of η in large samples that has subsequently been shown to be somewhat inaccurate; classified the different forms of regression curves and the different patterns of within-array variability that may arise when the joint distribution of two traits cannot be represented by the bivariate normal distribution, terming the system "homoscedastic" or "heteroscedastic" according to whether the within-array variability is or is not the same for all arrays, respectively; gave explicit formulas for the coefficients of parabolic, cubic, and quartic regression curves, in terms of $\eta^2 - r^2$ and other moments and product moments of the sample values of x and y; and listed the conditions in terms of $\eta^2 - r^2$ and the other sample moments and product moments that must be satisfied for linear, parabolic, cubic, and quartic regression equations to be adequate representations of the observed regression of y on x.

In a footnote to the section "Cubical Regression," Pearson noted that he had pointed out previously[16]

that when a polynomial of any degree, p $(p \leq n)$, is fit to all of n distinct observational points by the method of moments, the curve determined by "the method of moments becomes identical with that of least squares"; but, he continued, "the retention of the method of moments . . . enables us, without abrupt change of method, to introduce the need for η, and to grasp at once the application of the proper SHEPPARD'S corrections [to the sample moments and product moments of x and y when the measurements of either or both are coarsely grouped]."

Pearson clearly favored his method of moments; but the method of least squares has prevailed. However, use of the method of least squares to fit polynomial regression curves in a bivariate correlation situation involves an extension beyond the original formulation and development of the method of least squares by Legendre, Gauss, Laplace, and their followers in the nineteenth century. In this classical development of the method of least squares, one of the variables—x, for example—was a quantity that could be measured with negligible error, and the other, y, a quantity of interest functionally related to x, the observed values of which for particular values of x, Y_x, were, however, subject to nonnegligible measurement errors. The problem was to determine "best" values for the parameters of the functional relation between y and x despite the measurement errors in the observed values of Y_x. The method of least squares as developed by Gauss gave a demonstrably optimal solution when the functional dependence of y upon x was expressible with negligible error in a form in which the unknown parameters entered linearly—for instance, as a polynomial in x. In the Galton-Pearson correlation situation, in contrast, the traits X and Y may both be measurable with negligible error with respect to any single individual but in some population of individuals have a joint frequency or probability distribution. The regression of y on x is not an expression of a mathematical functional dependence of the trait Y on the trait X but, rather, an expression of the mean of values of Y corresponding to values of $X = x$ as a function of x—for example, as a polynomial in x. In the classical least-squares situation, the aim was to obtain the best possible approximation to the correct functional relation between the variables despite variations introduced by unwanted errors of measurement. In the Galton-Pearson correlation situation, on the other hand, the aim of regression analysis is to describe two important characteristics of the joint variation of the traits concerned. Pearson's development of the theory of skew correlation and nonlinear regression was, therefore, not merely an elaboration on the work of Gauss but a major step in a new direction.

Pearson did not pursue the theory of multiple and partial correlation beyond the point to which he had carried it in his basic memoir on correlation (1896). The general theory of multiple and partial correlation and regression was developed by his mathematical assistant, G. Udny Yule, in two papers published in 1897. Yule was the first to give mathematical expressions for what are now called partial correlation coefficients, which he termed "net correlation coefficients." What Pearson had called coefficients of double regression, Yule renamed net regressions; they are now called partial regression coefficients. The expressions "multiple correlation" and "partial correlation" stem from the paper written with Alice Lee and read to the Royal Society in June 1897.[17]

In order to see whether the correlations found in studies of the heredity of continuously varying physical characteristics held also for the less tractable psychological and mental traits, Pearson made a number of efforts to extend correlation methods to bivariate data coarsely classified into two or more ordered categories with respect to each trait. Thus, in "On the Correlation of Characters Not Quantitatively Measurable" (1900), he introduced the "tetrachoric" coefficient of correlation, r_t, derived on the supposition that the traits concerned were distributed continuously in accordance with a bivariate normal distribution in the population of individuals sampled, though not measured on continuous scales for the individuals in the sample but merely classified into the cells of a fourfold table in terms of more or less arbitrary but precise dichotomous divisions of the two trait scales. The derived value of r_t was the value of the correlation coefficient (ρ) of the bivariate normal distribution with frequencies in four quadrants corresponding to a division of the x, y plane by lines parallel to the coordinate axes that agreed exactly with the four cell frequencies of the fourfold table. Hence the value of r_t calculated from the data of a particular fourfold table was considered to be theoretically the best measure of the intensity of the correlation between the traits concerned. Pearson gave a formula for the standard deviation of the sampling error of r_t in large samples. He corrected two misprints in this formula and gave a simplified approximate formula in a paper of 1913.[18]

To cope with the intermediate case, in which one characteristic of the sample individuals is measured on a continuous scale and the other is merely classified dichotomously, Pearson, in a *Biometrika* paper of 1909, introduced (but did not name) the "biserial" coefficient of correlation, say r_b.

The idea involved in the development of the "tetrachoric" correlation coefficient, r_t, for data classified in a fourfold table was extended by Pearson in 1910 to cover cases in which "one variable is given by alternative and the other by multiple categories." The sample measure of correlation introduced but not named in this paper became known as "biserial η" because of its analogy with the biserial correlation coefficient, r_b, and the fact that it is defined by a special adaptation of the formula for the correlation ratio, η, based on comparatively nonrestrictive assumptions with respect to the joint distribution of the two traits concerned in the population sampled. The numerical evaluation of "biserial η," however, involves the further assumption that the joint variation of the traits is bivariate normal in the population; and its value for a particular sample, say r_n, is taken to be an estimate of the correlation coefficient, ρ, of the assumed bivariate normal distribution of the traits in the population sampled. The sampling variation of r_n as a measure of ρ was unknown until Pearson published an expression for its standard error in large samples from a bivariate normal population in 1917.[19] It is not known how large the sample size N must be for this asymptotic expression to yield a satisfactory approximation.

Meanwhile, Charles Spearman had introduced (1904) his coefficient of rank-order correlation, say r', which, although first defined in terms of the rank differences of the individuals in the sample with respect to the two traits concerned, is equivalent to the product-moment correlation coefficient between the paired ranks themselves. Three years later Pearson, in "On Further Methods of Determining Correlation," gave the now familiar formula, $\hat{\rho} = 2 \sin(\pi r'/6)$, for obtaining an estimate, $\hat{\rho}$, of the coefficient of correlation (ρ) of a bivariate normal population from an observed value of the coefficient of rank-order correlation (r') derived from the rankings of the individuals in a sample therefrom with respect to the two traits concerned; he also presented a formula for the standard error of $\hat{\rho}$ in large samples.

The "tetrachoric" and "biserial" coefficients of correlation and "biserial η" played important parts in the biometric, eugenic, and medical investigations of Pearson and the biometric school during the first two decades of the twentieth century. Pearson was fully aware of the crucial dependence of their interpretation upon the validity of the assumed bivariate normality and was circumspect in their application; his discussions of numerical results are full of caution. (A sample product-moment coefficient of correlation, r, always provides a usable determination of the product-moment coefficient of correlation, ρ, in the population sampled, bivariate normal or otherwise. On the other hand, when the joint distribution of the two traits concerned is continuous but not bivariate normal in the population sampled, exactly what interpretations are to be accorded to observed values of r_t, r_b, and r_n is not at all clear; and if assumed continuity with respect to both variables is not valid, their interpretation is even less clear—they may be virtually meaningless.) The crucial dependence of the interpretation of these measures on the uncheckable assumption of bivariate normality of the joint distribution of the traits concerned in the population sampled, together with their uncritical application and incautious interpretation by some scholars, brought severe criticism; and doubt was cast on the meaning and value of "coefficients of correlation" thus obtained. In particular, Pearson and one of his assistants, David Heron, ultimately became embroiled in a long and bitter argument on the matter with Yule, whose paper embodying a theory and a measure of association of attributes free of any assumption of an underlying continuous distribution Pearson had communicated to the Royal Society in 1899. Despite this skepticism, r_t, r_b, and r_n have survived and are used today as standard statistical tools, mainly by psychologists, in situations where the traits concerned can be logically assumed to have a joint continuous distribution in the population sampled and the at least approximate normality of this distribution is not seriously questioned.

Pearson did not attempt to investigate sampling distributions of r or η in small samples from bivariate normal or other population distributions because he saw no need to do so. He and his co-workers in the 1890's and early 1900's saw their mission to be the advancement of knowledge and understanding of "variation, inheritance, and selection in Animals and Plants" through studies "based upon the examination of *statistically large numbers* of specimens," and the development of statistical theory, tables of mathematical functions, and graphical methods needed in the pursuit of such studies.[20] They were not concerned with the analysis of data from small-scale laboratory experiments or with comparisons of yield from small numbers of plots of land in agricultural field trials. It was the need to interpret values of r obtained from small-scale industrial experiments in the brewing industry that led "Student" (W. S. Gosset) to discover in 1908 that r is symmetrically distributed about 0 in accordance with a Pearson Type II curve in random samples of any size from a bivariate normal distribution when $\rho = 0$; and, when $\rho \neq 0$, its distribution is skew, with the longer tail toward 0, and cannot be represented by any of Pearson's curves.[21]

In another paper published earlier in 1908 ("The Probable Error of a Mean"), "Student" had dis-

covered that the sampling distribution of s^2 (the square of a sample standard deviation), in random samples from a normal distribution, can be represented by a Pearson Type III curve. Although these discoveries stemmed from knowledge and experience that "Student" had gained at Pearson's biometric laboratory in London and were published in the journal that Pearson edited, they seem to have awakened no interest in Pearson or his co-workers in developing statistical theory and techniques appropriate to the analysis of results from small-scale experiments. This indifference may have stemmed from preoccupation with other matters, from recognition that establishment of the small trends or differences for which they were looking required large samples, or from a desire "to discourage the biologist or the medical man from believing that he had been supplied with an easy method of drawing conclusions from scanty data."[22]

In September 1914 Pearson received the manuscript of the paper in which R. A. Fisher derived the general sampling distribution of r in random samples of any size $n \geq 2$ from a bivariate normal population with any degree of correlation, $-1 \leq \rho \leq +1$, and pointed out the extreme skewness of the distribution for large positive or negative values of ρ even for large sample sizes.[23] Pearson responded with enthusiasm, congratulated Fisher "very heartily on getting out the actual distribution form of r," and stated that "if the analysis is correct which seems highly probable, [he] should be delighted to publish the paper in *Biometrika*."[24] A week later he wrote to Fisher: "I have now read your paper fully and think it marks a distinct advance . . . I shall be very glad to publish it . . . [it] shall appear in the next issue [May 1915] . . . I wish you had had the leisure to extend the last pages a little . . . I should like to see some attempt to determine at what value of n and for what values of ρ we may suppose the distribution of r practically normal."[25]

In the "last pages" of the paper, Fisher introduced two transformations of r, $r/\sqrt{1 - r^2}$ and $\tanh^{-1} r$, his aim being to find a function of r whose sampling distribution would have greater stability of form as ρ varied from -1 to $+1$, would be more nearly symmetric, or would have an approximately constant standard deviation, for all values of ρ. The first of these two transformations he considered in detail. Denoting the transformed variable by t, and the corresponding transformation of ρ by τ, he showed that the mean value of t was proportional to τ, the constant of proportionality increasing toward unity with increasing sample size. He also gave exact formulas for $\sigma^2(t)$, $\beta_1(t)$, and $\beta_2(t)$, and tables of their numerical values for selected values of τ^2 from .01 to 100 (that is, ρ from .0995 to .995) and sample sizes n from 8 to 53. Although the distribution of t was, by design, much less asymmetric and of more stable form than the distribution of r—this became unmistakably clear when the corresponding values of $\beta_1(r)$ and $\beta_2(r)$ became known in the "Cooperative Study" (see below)—the transformation was not an unqualified success: its distribution was not close to normal except in the vicinity of $\rho = 0$, and $\sigma^2(t)$ was not approximately constant but nearly proportional to $1/(1 - \rho^2)$. In the final paragraph Fisher dismissed the second transformation for the time being with the comment (with respect to the aims mentioned above): "It is not a little attractive, but so far as I have examined it, it does not tend to simplify the analysis . . . ." (He later found it very much to his liking.)

Reasoning about a function of sample values, such as r, in terms of a transform of it, instead of in terms of the function itself, seems to have been foreign to Pearson's way of thinking. He wrote to Fisher:

> I have rather difficulties over this r and t business—not that I have anything to say about it from the theoretical standpoint—but there appear to me difficulties from the everyday applications with which we as statisticians are most familiar. Let me indicate what I mean.
>
> A man finds a correlation coefficient r from a small sample n of a population; often the material is urgent and an answer on the significance has to be given at once. What he wants to know, say, is whether the true value of $r(\rho)$ is likely to exceed or fall short of his observed value by, say, .10. It may be for instance the correlation between height of firing a gun and the rate of consumption of a time fuse, or between a particular form of treatment of a wound and time of recovery. . . . For example, suppose that $\rho = .30$, and I want to find what is the chance that in 40 observations the resulting r will lie between .20 and .40. Now what we need practically are the β_1 and β_2 for $\rho = .30$ and $n = 40$, and if they are not sufficiently Gaussian for us to use the probability integral, we need the frequency curve of r for $\rho = .30$ and $n = 40$ to help us out. . . . Had I the graph of t I could deduce the graph of r, and mechanically integrate to determine the answer to my problem, but you have not got the ordinates of the t-curve and the practical problem remains it seems to me unsolved. It still seems to me essential (i) to determine β_1 and β_2 accurately for r . . . and (ii) determine a table of frequencies or areas (integral curve) of the r distribution curve for values of ρ and n which do not provide approximately Gaussian results. Of course you may be able to dispose of my practical difficulties, which do not touch your beautiful theory.[26]

Pearson then proposed a specific program of tabulation of the ordinates of the frequency curves for r for selected values of ρ and n to be executed by his trained calculators "unless you really want to do them yourself." The letter in which Fisher is said to have "welcomed the suggestion" that the computations of these ordinates be carried out at the Galton laboratory "seems to have been lost through the disturbance of papers during the 1939–45 war."[27] On the other hand, Fisher seems to have agreed (in this missing, or some other, letter) to undertake the evaluation of the integral of the distribution of r for a selection of values of ρ and n. In a May 1916 letter to Pearson he comments, "I have been very slow about my paper on the probability integral."

When not engaged in war work, Pearson and several members of his staff took on the onerous task of developing reliable formulas for the moments of the distribution of r and calculating tables of its ordinates for ρ from 0.0 to 0.9 and selected values of n. In May 1916, Pearson wrote to Fisher: ". . . the *whole* of the correlation business has come out quite excellently . . . . By [$n =$] 25 my curves [curves of the Pearson system] give the frequency very satisfactorily, but even when $n = 400$, for high values of ρ the normal curve is really not good enough . . . ."[28] It is quite clear from this correspondence between Pearson and Fisher during 1914–1916 that the relationship was entirely friendly, and the implication in some accounts of Fisher's life and work[29] that this venture was carried out without his knowledge is far from correct.

The results of this joint effort of Pearson and his staff were published as ". . . A Cooperative Study" in the May 1917 issue of *Biometrika*. Included were tables of ordinates of the distribution of r for $\rho = 0.0(0.1)0.9$ and $n = 3(1)25$, 50, 100, 400; values of $\beta_1(r)$ and $\beta_2(r)$ for the same ρ when $n = 3, 4, 25, 50, 100, 400$; and of the normal approximation to the ordinates for $n = 100$, $\rho = 0.9$, and $n = 400$, $\rho = 0.7(0.1)0.9$. There were also photographs of seven cardboard models showing, for example, the changes in the distribution of r from U-shaped through J-shaped to skew "cocked hat" forms with increasing sample size for $n = 2(1)25$ for $\rho = 0.6, 0.8$, and illustrating the rate of deviation from normality and increasing skewness with increase of ρ from 0.0 to 0.9 in samples of 25 and 50. This publication represented a truly monumental undertaking. Unfortunately, it had little long-range impact on practical correlation analysis, and it contained material in the section "On the Determination of the 'Most Likely' Value of the Correlation in Sampled Population" that contributed to the widening of the rift that was beginning to develop between Pearson and Fisher.

In his 1915 paper Fisher derived (pp. 520–521), from his general expression for the sampling distribution of r in samples of size n from a bivariate normal population, a two-term approximation,

$$\hat{\rho} = r \Big/ \left(1 + \frac{1 - r^2}{2n}\right),$$

to the "relation between an observed correlation of the sample and the *most probable value* of the correlation of the whole population" [emphasis added]. He referred to his 1912 paper "On an Absolute Criterion for Fitting Frequency Curves" for justification of this procedure.[30] Inasmuch as Pearson had shown in his 1896 memoir that an observed sample from a bivariate normal population is "the most probable" when $\rho = r$ ($\mu_x = m_x$, $\sigma_x = s_x$, $\mu_y = m_y$, and $\sigma_y = s_y$), Fisher's proposed adjustment must have been puzzling to him. The result Fisher obtained is the same as what would be obtained, via the sampling distribution of r, by the method of inverse probability, using Bayes's theorem and an assumed uniform a priori distribution of ρ from -1 to $+1$. This, and Fisher's use of the expression "most probable value," evidently led Pearson, who presumably drafted the text of the "Cooperative Study,"[31] to state mistakenly (pp. 352, 353) that Fisher had assumed such a uniform a priori distribution in deriving his result. Pearson may have been misled also by a "Draft of a Note"[32] that he had received from Fisher in mid-1916, commenting on a paper by Kirstine Smith that had appeared in the May 1916 issue of *Biometrika*, in which Fisher had written: "There is nothing at all 'arbitrary' in the use of the method of moments for the normal curve; as I have shown elsewhere it flows directly from the absolute criterion ($\Sigma \log f$ a maximum) derived from the Principle of Inverse Probability."

Not realizing that Fisher had not only not assumed a uniform a priori distribution of ρ but had also considered his procedure (which he later termed the method of "maximum likelihood") to be completely distinct from "inverse probability" via Bayes's theorem with an assumed a priori distribution, Pearson proceeded to devote over a page of the "Study" to pointing out the absurdity of such an "equal distribution of ignorance" assumption when estimating ρ from an observed r. Several additional pages contain a detailed consideration of alternative forms for the a priori distribution of ρ, showing that with large samples the assumed distribution had little effect on the end result but in small samples could dominate the sample evidence, from which he concluded that "in problems like the present indiscriminate use of Bayes' Theorem is to be deprecated" (p. 359). All of this amounted to flogging a dead horse, so to speak, because Fisher was as fully opposed as Pearson to using Bayes's theorem in such problems. Unfortunate-ly, Fisher probably was totally unaware of this offending section before proofs became available in 1917. Papers such as the "Study" were not readily typed in those days, so that there would have been only a single manuscript of the text and tables prior to typesetting. Had Fisher, who was then teaching mathematics and physics in English public schools, been in closer touch with Pearson, these misunderstandings might have been resolved before publication of the offending passages.

In August 1920 Fisher sent Pearson a copy of his manuscript "On the 'Probable Error' of a Coefficient of Correlation Deduced From a Small Sample," in which he reexamined in detail the $\tanh^{-1} r$ transformation and, denoting the transformed variable by z and the corresponding transformation of ρ by ζ, showed that z can be taken to be approximately normally distributed about a mean of $\zeta + \dfrac{\rho}{2(n-1)}$ with a standard deviation equal to $1/\sqrt{n-3}$, the normal approximation being extraordinarily good even in very small samples—of the order of $n = 10$. This transformation thus made it possible to answer questions of the types that Pearson had raised without recourse to tables of the integral of the distribution of r, and obviated the immediate need for the preparation of such tables. (It was not until 1931 that Pearson suggested to Florence N. David the computation of tables of the integral. Values of the integral obtained by quadrature of the ordinates given in the "Cooperative Study" were completed in 1934. Additional ordinates and values of the integral were calculated to facilitate interpolation. These improved tables, together with four charts for obtaining confidence limits for ρ given r, were published in 1938.[33])

In his discussion of applications, Fisher took pains to point out that the formula he had given in his 1915 paper for what he then "termed the 'most likely value,' which [he] now, for greater precision, term[ed] the 'optimum' value of ρ, for a given observed r" involved in its derivation "no assumption whatsoever as to the probable distribution of ρ," being merely that value of ρ for which the observed r occurs with greatest frequency." He also noted that one is led to exactly the same expression for the optimum value of ρ in terms of an observed r if one seeks the optimum through the z distribution rather than the r distribution and he commented that the derivation of this optimum cannot, therefore, be inferred to depend upon an assumed uniform prior distribution of ζ and upon an assumed uniform prior distribution of ρ, since these two assumptions are mutually inconsistent. Then, "though . . . reluctant to criticize the distinguished statisticians who put their names to the Cooperative

Study," Fisher went on to criticize with a tone of ridicule some of the illustrative examples of the application of Bayes's theorem considered on pp. 357–358 of the "Study," without noting the authors' conclusions from these, and other examples considered, that such "use of Bayes' Theorem is to be deprecated" (p. 359) and when applied to "values observed in a small sample may lead to results very wide from the truth" (p. 360). Fisher concluded his paper with a "Note on the Confusion Between Bayes' Rule and My Method of the Evaluation of the Optimum."

Pearson returned the manuscript to Fisher with the following comment:

> . . . I fear if I could give full attention to your paper, which I cannot at the present time, I should be unlikely to publish it in its present form, or without a reply to your criticisms which would involve also a criticism of your work of 1912—I would prefer you publish elsewhere. Under present printing and financial conditions, I am regretfully compelled to exclude all that I think erroneous on my own judgment, because I cannot afford controversy.[34]

Fisher therefore submitted his paper to *Metron*, a new journal, which published the work in its first volume.[35]

The cross criticism, at cross purposes, conducted by Pearson and Fisher over the use of Bayes's theorem in estimating ρ from r was multiply unfortunate: it was unnecessary and ill-timed; it might have been avoided; and it fostered ill will and fueled the innately contentious temperament of both parties at an early stage of their argument over the relative merits of the method of moments and method of maximum likelihood. This argument was started by Fisher's "Draft of a Note," which Pearson took to be a criticism not only of the minimum chi-square technique that Kirstine Smith had propounded but also of his method of moments, and refused to publish it in both original (1916) and revised (1918) forms on the grounds of its being controversial and liable to provoke a quarrel among contributors.[36] The argument, which grew into a raging controversy, was fed by later developments on various fronts and continued to the end of Pearson's life—and beyond.[37]

In 1922 Fisher found the sampling distribution of η^2 in random samples of any size from a bivariate normal population in which the correlation is zero ($\rho = 0$), and later (1928) derived the distribution of η^2 in samples of any size when the x values are fixed and the y values are normally distributed with a common standard deviation σ about array means $\mu_{y|x}$ which may be different for different values of x, thereby giving rise to a nonzero value of the "population" correlation ratio. In particular, it was found that for any value of the population correlation ratio different from zero, the sampling distribution of η tends in sufficiently large samples to be approximately normal about the population value with standard error given by Pearson's formula; but when the correlation ratio in the population is exactly zero—that is, when sampling from uncorrelated material—the sampling distribution of η does not tend to normality with increasing sample size for any finite number of arrays. This led to formulation of new procedures, since become standard, for testing the statistical significance of an observed value of η and of $\eta^2 - r^2$ as a test for departure from linearity.

In 1926 Pearson showed that the distribution of sample regression coefficients, that is, of the slopes of the sample regression of y on x and of x on y, respectively, is his Type VII distribution symmetrical about the corresponding population regression coefficient. It tends to normality much more rapidly than the distribution of r with increasing sample size, so that the use of Pearson's expressions for the standard error of regression coefficients is therefore valid for lower values of n than in the case of r. It is, however, not of much use in small samples, since it depends upon the unknown values of the population standard deviations and correlation, σ_y, σ_x, and ρ_{xy}. Four years earlier, however, in response to repeated queries from "Student" in correspondence, Fisher had succeeded in showing that in random samples of any size from a general bivariate normal population, the sampling distribution of the ratio $(b - \beta)/s_{b-\beta}$, where β is the population regression coefficient corresponding to the sample coefficient b, and $s_{b-\beta}$ is a particular sample estimate of the standard error of their difference, does not depend upon any of the population parameters other than β and is given by a special form of Pearson's Type VII curve now known as "Student's" t-distribution for $n - 2$ degrees of freedom. Consequently, it is this latter distribution, free of "nuisance parameters," that is customarily employed today in making inferences about a population regression coefficient from an observed value of the corresponding sample coefficient.

Although the final steps of correlation and regression analyses today differ from those originally advanced by Pearson and his co-workers, there can be no question that today's procedures were built upon those earlier ones; and correlation and regression analysis is still very much indebted to those highly original and very difficult steps into the unknown taken by Pearson at the turn of the century.

Derivation of formulas for standard errors in large samples of functions of sample values used to estimate parameters of the population sampled did not, of course, originate with Pearson. It dates from Gauss's derivation (1816) of the standard errors in large samples of the respective functions of successive sample absolute moments that might be used as estimators of the population standard deviation. Another early contribution was Gauss's derivation (1823) of a formula comparable with that derived by Pearson in 1903 for the standard error in large samples of the sample standard deviation as estimator of the standard deviation of an arbitrary population having finite centroidal moments of fourth order or higher. Subsequent writers treated these matters somewhat more fully and made a number of minor extensions, but the first general approach to the problem of standard errors and intercorrelations in large samples of sample functions used to estimate values of population parameters is that given in "On the Probable Errors of Frequency Constants . . . ," written by Pearson and his young French mathematical demonstrator, L. N. G. Filon, and read to the Royal Society in November 1897. In section II there is the first derivation of the now familiar expressions for the asymptotic variances and covariances of sample estimators of a group of population parameters in terms of mathematical expectations of second derivatives of the logarithm of what is now called the "likelihood function," but without recognition of their applicability only to maximum likelihood estimators, a limitation first pointed out by Edgeworth (1908).[38] Today these formulas are usually associated with Fisher's paper "On the Mathematical Foundations of Theoretical Statistics" (1922)—and perhaps rightly so, because, although the expressions derived by Pearson and Filon, and by Fisher, are of identical mathematical form, what they meant to Pearson and Filon in 1897 and continued to mean to Pearson may have been quite different from what they meant to Fisher.[39] (This may have been a major obstacle to their conciliation.)

Specific formulas derived by Pearson and Filon included expressions for the standard error of a coefficient of correlation r; the correlation between the sample means m_x and m_y of two correlated traits; the correlation between the sample standard deviations, s_x and s_y; the correlation between a sample coefficient of correlation r and a sample standard deviation s_x or s_y; the standard errors of regression coefficients, and of partial regression coefficients, for the two- and three-variable cases, respectively; and the correlations between pairs of sample correlation coefficients (r_{12}, r_{13}), (r_{12}, r_{34})—all in the case of large samples from a correlated normal distribution. In the process it was noted that in the case of large samples from a correlated normal distribution, the errors of sample

means are uncorrelated with the errors of sample standard deviations and sample correlation coefficients; and that through failure to recognize the existence of correlation between the errors of sample standard deviations and a sample correlation coefficient, the formula given previously for the large sample standard error of the sample correlation coefficient r was in error, because it was appropriate to the case in which the population standard deviations, σ_x and σ_y, are known exactly. Large sample formulas were found also for the standard errors and correlations between the errors of sample estimates of the parameters of Pearson Type I, III, and IV distributions, making this the first comprehensive study of such matters in the case of skew distributions.

Pearson returned to this subject in a series of three editorials in *Biometrika*, "On the Probable Errors of Frequency Constants," prepared in response to a need expressed by queries from readers. The first (1903) deals with the standard errors of, and correlations between, (i) cell frequencies in a histogram and (ii) sample centroidal moments, in terms of the centroidal moments of a univariate distribution of general form. Some of the results given are exact and some are limiting values for large samples. In some instances a "probable error" ($= 0.6745 \times$ standard error) is given, but the practice is deprecated: "The adoption of the 'probable error' . . . as a measure of . . . exactness must not, however, be taken as equivalent to asserting the validity of the normal law of errors or deviations, but merely as a purely conventional reduction of the standard deviation. It would be equally valid provided it were customary to omit this reduction or indeed to multiply the standard deviation by any other conventional factor" (p. 273).

The extension to samples from a general bivariate distribution was made in "Part II" (1913), reproduced from Pearson's lecture notes. Formulas were given for the correlation of errors in sample means; the correlation of errors in sample standard deviations; the standard error of the correlation coefficient r (in terms of the population coefficient of correlation ρ and the β_2's of the two marginal distributions); the correlation between the random sampling deviations of a sample mean and a sample standard deviation for the same variate; correlation between the random sampling deviations of sample mean of one variate and the standard deviation of a correlated variate; the correlation between a mean and a sample coefficient of correlation; the correlation between the sampling deviations of a sample standard deviation and sample coefficient of correlation; and the standard errors of coefficients of linear regression lines and of the means of arrays. In this paper it is also shown that in the case of all symmetric distributions, there is no correlation between the sample mean and sample standard deviation. "Part III" (1920) deals with the standard errors of, and the correlations between, the sampling variations of the sample median, quartiles, deciles, and other quantiles in random samples from a general univariate distribution. The relative efficiency of estimating the standard deviation of a normal population from the difference between two symmetrical quantiles of a large sample therefrom is discussed, and the "optimum" is found to be the difference between the seventh and ninety-third percentiles.

The results given in these three editorials are derived by a procedure considerably more elementary than that employed in the Pearson-Filon paper. Some of the results given are exact; others are limiting values for large samples; and many have become more or less standard in statistical circles.

The July 1900 issue of *Philosophical Magazine* contained Pearson's paper in which he introduced the criterion

$$\chi^2 = \Sigma \frac{(f_i - F_i)^2}{F_i}$$

as a measure of the agreement between observation and hypothesis overall to be used as a basis for determining the probability with which the differences $f_i - F_i$, $(i = 1, 2, \dots, k)$, collectively might be due solely to the unavoidable fluctuations of random sampling, where f_i denotes the observed frequency (the observed number of observations falling) in the ith of k mutually exclusive categories, and F_i is the corresponding theoretical frequency (the number expected in the ith category in accordance with some particular true or hypothetical frequency distribution), with $\Sigma f_i = \Sigma F_i = N$, the total number of independent observations involved. To this end he derived the sampling distribution of χ^2 in large samples as a function of k, finding it to be a specialized form of the Pearson Type III distribution now known as the "χ^2 distribution for $k-1$ degrees of freedom," the $k-1$ being explained by the remark (in our notation) "only $k-1$ of the k errors are variables; the kth is determined when the first $k-1$ are known"; he also gave a small table of the integral of the distribution for χ^2 from 1 to 70 and k from 3 to 20. Of Pearson's many contributions to statistical theory and practice, this χ^2 text for goodness of fit is certainly one of his greatest; and in its original and extended forms it has remained one of the most useful of all statistical tests.

Four years later, in *On the Theory of Contingency and Its Relation to Association and Normal Correlation*, Pearson extended the application of his χ^2 criterion to the analysis of the cell frequencies in a "contingency table" of r rows and c columns resulting from the partitioning of a sample of N observations into r distinct classes in terms of some particular characteristic, and into c distinct classes with respect to another characteristic; showed how the χ^2 criterion could be used to test the independence of the two classifications; termed $\phi^2 = \chi^2/N$ the "mean square contingency" and

$$C = \sqrt{\frac{\chi^2}{N + \chi^2}}$$

the coefficient of mean square contingency; showed that, if a large sample from a bivariate normal distribution with correlation coefficient ρ is partitioned into the cells of a contingency table, then C^2 will tend to approximate ρ^2 as the number of categories in the table increases, the correct sign of ρ then being determined from the order of the two classifications and the pattern of the cell frequencies within the $r \times c$ table; and that, when $r = c = 2$, ϕ^2 is equal to the square of the product-moment coefficient of correlation computed from the observed frequencies in the fourfold table with purely arbitrary values (for instance, 0, 1) assigned to the two row categories and to the two column categories.

Pearson made much of the fact that the value of χ^2 and of C is unaffected by reordering either or both of the marginal categories, so that χ^2 provides a means of testing the independence of the two characteristics (such as eye color and occupation) in terms of which the marginal classes are defined without, and independently of, any additional assumptions as to the nature of the association, if any. In view of the above-mentioned relation of C to ρ under the indicated circumstances, C would seem to be a generally useful measure of the degree or intensity of the association when a large value of χ^2 leads to rejection of the hypothesis of independence; and Pearson proposed its use for this purpose. It is, however, not a very satisfactory measure of association—for example, the values of C obtained from an $r \times c$ classification and an $r' \times c'$ classification of the same data will usually be different. Also, some fundamental objections have been raised to the use of C, or any other function of χ^2, as a measure of association. Nonetheless, C played an important role in its day in the analysis of data classified into $r \times c$ tables when the categories for both characteristics can be arranged in meaningful orders—if the categories for either characteristic cannot be put into a meaningful order, then there can be no satisfactory measure of the intensity of *the* association; and a large value of χ^2 may simply be an indication of some fault in the sampling procedure.

In a 1911 *Biometrika* paper, Pearson showed how

his χ^2 criterion could be extended to provide a test of the hypothesis that "two independent distributions of frequency [arrayed in a $2 \times c$ table] are really samples from the same population." The theoretical proportions in the respective cells implied by the presumed common population being unknown, they are estimated from the corresponding proportions of the two samples combined. Illustrative examples show that to find P, the probability of a larger value of χ^2, the "Tables for Testing Goodness of Fit" are to be entered with $n' = c$, signifying that there are $c - 1$ "independent variables" ("degrees of freedom") involved, which agrees with present practice. In a *Biometrika* paper, "On the General Theory of Multiple Contingency . . ." (1916), Pearson gave a new derivation of the χ^2 distribution, as the limiting distribution of the class frequencies of a multinomial distribution as the sample size $N \to \infty$; pointed out (pp. 153–155) that if q linear restraints are imposed on the n' cell frequencies in addition to the usual $\Sigma f_i = N$, then to find P one must enter the tables with $n' - q$; and extended the χ^2 technique to testing whether the frequencies arrayed in two ($2 \times c$) contingency tables can be considered random samples from the same bivariate population. In this application of "partial χ^2," Pearson considers the c column totals of each table to be fixed, thereby imposing $2c$ linear restraints on the $4c$ cell frequencies involved. The theoretical proportion, p_{1j}, in the presumed common population, corresponding to the cell in the top row and jth column of either table being unknown, it is taken as equal to the corresponding proportion in this cell of the two tables combined, ($j = 1, 2, \ldots, c$), thereby imposing c additional linear restraints (p_{2j} is, of course, simply $1 - p_{1j}$, [$j = 1, 2, \ldots, c$]). Hence there remain only $4c - 2c - c = c$ "independent variables"; and Pearson notes that the χ^2 tables are to be entered with $n' = c + 1$. These two papers clearly contain the basic elements of a large part of present-day χ^2 technique.

In section 5 of his 1900 paper on χ^2, Pearson pointed out that one must distinguish between a value of χ^2 calculated from theoretical frequencies F_i derived from a theoretical probability distribution completely specified a priori and values of χ_s^2, say, calculated from theoretical frequencies $\tilde{F}_i$ derived from a theoretical probability distribution of specified form but with the values of one or more of its parameters left unspecified so that "best values" for these had to be determined from the data in hand. It was clear that χ_s^2 could never exceed the "true" χ^2. From a brief, cursory analysis Pearson concluded that the difference $\chi^2 - \chi_s^2$ was likely to be negligible. Evidently he did not realize that the difference might depend on the number of constants the values of which were determined from

the sample and that, if k constants were fit, χ_s^2 might be zero.

Ultimately Fisher showed in a series of three papers (1922, 1923, 1924) that when the unknown parameters of the population sampled are efficiently estimated from the data in such a manner as to impose c additional linear restraints on t cell frequencies, then, when the total number of observations N is large, χ_s^2 will be distributed in accordance with a χ^2 distribution for $(t - 1 - c)$ degrees of freedom. Pearson had recognized this in the cases of the particular problems discussed in his 1911 and 1916 papers considered above; but he never accepted Fisher's modification of the value of n' with which the "Tables of Goodness of Fit" were to be entered in the original 1900 problem of testing the agreement of an observed and a theoretical frequency distribution when some parameters of the latter were estimated from the observed data, or in the 1904 problem of testing the independence of the two classifications of an $r \times c$ contingency table.

During Pearson's highly innovative decade and a half, 1891–1906, in addition to laying the foundations of the major contributions to statistical theory and practice reviewed above, he also initiated a number of other topics that later blossomed into important areas of statistics and other disciplines. Brief mention was made above of "On the Mathematical Theory of Errors of Judgment . . ." (1902). This investigation was founded on two series of experiments in which three observers each individually (a) estimated the midpoints of segments of straight lines; and (b), estimated the position on a scale of a bright line moving slowly downward at the moment when a bell sounded. The study revealed that the errors of different observers estimating or measuring the same series of quantities are in general correlated; that the frequency distributions of such errors of estimation or measurement certainly are not always normal; and that the variation over a period of time of the "personal equation" (the pattern of the systematic error or bias of an individual observer) is not explainable solely by the fluctuations of random sampling. The investigation stemmed from Pearson's observation that when three observers individually estimate or measure a series of physical quantities, the actual magnitudes of which may or may not be known or determinable, then, on the assumption of independence of the judgments of the respective observers, it is possible to determine the standard deviations of the distributions of measurement errors of each of the three observers from the observed standard deviations of the differences between their respective measurements of the same quantities. The investigation reported in this memoir is thus the forerunner of the work carried out by Frank E. Grubbs during the 1940's on methods for determining the individual precisions of two, three, four, or more measuring instruments in the presence of product variability.

A second example is provided by Pearson's "Note on Francis Galton's Problem" (August 1902), in which he derived the general expression for the mean value of the difference between the rth and the $(r + 1)$th individuals ranked in order of size in random samples of size n from any continuous distribution. This is one of the earliest general results in the sampling theory of order statistics, a very active subfield of statistics since the 1930's. Pearson later gave general expressions for the variances of, and correlations between, such intervals in random samples from any continuous distribution in a joint paper with his second wife, "On the Mean . . . and Variance of a Ranked Individual, and . . . of the Intervals Between Ranked Individuals, Part I . . ." (1931).

A third example is the theory of "random walk," a term Pearson coined in a brief letter, "The Problem of the Random Walk," published in the 17 July 1905 issue of *Nature*, in which he asked for information on the probability distribution of the walker's distance from the origin after n steps. Lord Rayleigh replied in the issue of 3 August, pointing out that the problem is formally the same as that of "the composition of n isoperiodic vibrations of unit amplitude and of phases distributed at random" (p. 318), which he had considered as early as 1880, and indicated the asymptotic solution as $n \to \infty$. The general solution for finite n was published by J. C. Kluyver in Dutch later the same year and, among other applications, provides the basis for a test of whether a set of orientation or directional data is "random" or tends to exhibit a "preferred direction." With John Blakeman, Pearson published *A Mathematical Theory of Random Migration* (1906), in which various theoretical forms of distribution were derived that would result from random migration from a point of origin under certain ideal conditions and solutions to a number of subsidiary problems were given, results that have found various other applications. Today "random walks" of various kinds, with and without reflecting or absorbing barriers, play important roles not only in the theory of Brownian motion but also in the treatment of random phenomena in astronomy, biology, physics, and communications engineering; in statistics, they are used in the theory of sequential estimation and of sequential tests of statistical hypotheses.

Pearson's involvement in heredity and evolution dates from his first fundamental paper on correlation and regression (1896), in which, to illustrate the value of these new mathematical tools in attacking problems of heredity and evolution, he included evaluations of partial regressions of offspring on each parent for sets of data from Galton's *Record of Family Faculties* (London, 1884) and considerably extended Galton's collateral studies of heredity by considering types of selection, assortative mating, and "panmixia" (suspension of selection and subsequent free interbreeding). Galton's formulation, in *Natural Inheritance* (1889), of his law of ancestral heredity was somewhat ambiguous and imprecise because of his failure to take into account the additional mathematical complexity involved in the joint consideration of more than two mutually correlated characteristics. Pearson supposed him to mean (p. 303) that the coefficients of correlation between offspring and parent, grandparent, and great-grandparent, . . . were to be taken as $r, r^2, r^3, \ldots$. This led him to the paradoxical conclusion that "a knowledge of the ancestry beyond the parents in no way alters our judgment as to the size of organ or degree of characteristic probable in the offspring, nor its variability" (p. 306), a conclusion that he said in a footnote "seems especially noteworthy" inasmuch as it is quite contrary to what "it would seem natural to suppose."

In "On the Reconstruction of the Stature of Prehistoric Races" (1898), Pearson used multiple regression techniques to predict ("reconstruct") average measurements of extinct races from the sizes of existing bones and known correlations among bone lengths in an extant race, as a means of testing the accuracy of predictions in evolutionary problems in the light of certain evolutionary theories.

Meanwhile, Galton had formulated (1897) his "law" more precisely. After some correspondence Pearson, in "On the Law of Ancestral Heredity" (1898), subtitled "A New Year's Greeting to Francis Galton, January 1, 1898," expressed what he christened "Galton's Law of Ancestral Heredity" in the form of a multiple regression equation of offspring on midparental ancestry

$$x_0 = \frac{1}{2}\frac{\sigma_0}{\sigma_1} x_1 + \frac{1}{4}\frac{\sigma_0}{\sigma_2} x_2 + \frac{1}{8}\frac{\sigma_0}{\sigma_3} x_3 + \cdots,$$

where x_0 is the predicted deviation of an individual offspring from the mean of the offspring generation, x_1 is the deviation of the offspring's "midparent" from the mean of the parental generation, x_2 the deviation of the offspring's "midgrandparent" from the mean of the grandparental generation, and so on, and $\sigma_0 \sigma_1 \ldots$ are the standard deviations of the distributions of individuals in the respective generations. In order that this formulation of Galton's law be unambiguous, it was necessary to have a precise definition of "sth midparent." The definition that Pearson adopted "with reservations" was "[If] a father is a first parent, a grandfather a second parent, a great-grandfather a third parent, and so on, [then] the mid sth parent or the sth mid-parent is derived from [is the mean of] all 2^s individual sth parents" (footnote, p. 387).

From this formulation Pearson deduced theoretical values for regression and correlation coefficients between various kin, tested Galton's stature data against these expectations, and suggested generalizing Galton's law by substituting $\gamma\beta$, $\gamma\beta^2$, $\gamma\beta^3$, ... for Galton's geometric series coefficients 1/2, 1/4, 1/8, ... to allow "greater scope for variety of inheritance in different species" (p. 403). In the concluding section Pearson claims: "If either [Galton's Law], or its suggested modification be substantially correct, they embrace the whole theory of heredity. They bring into one simple statement an immense range of facts, thus fulfilling the fundamental purpose of a great law of nature" (p. 411). After noting some difficulties that would have to be met and stating, "We must wait at present for further determinations of hereditary influence, before the actual degree of approximation between law and nature can be appreciated," he concluded with the sweeping statement: "At present I would merely state my opinion that, with all due reservations it seems to me that . . . it is highly probable that [the law of ancestral heredity] is the simple descriptive statement which brings into a single focus all the complex lines of hereditary influence. If Darwinian evolution be natural selection combined with *heredity*, then the single statement which embraces the whole field of heredity must prove almost as epoch-making to the biologist as the law of gravitation to the astronomer" (p. 412).

These claims were obviously too sweeping. Neither the less nor the more general form of the law was founded on any clear conception of the mechanism of heredity. Also, most unfortunately, some of the wording employed—for instance, "I shall now proceed to determine . . . the correlation between an individual and any sth parent from a knowledge of the regression between the individual and his mid-sth parent" (p. 391) —tended to give the erroneous idea that the law expressed a relation between a particular individual and his sth parents, and thus to mislead biologists of the period, who had not become fully conscious that regression equations merely expressed relationships that held on the average between the generic types of "individuals" involved, and not between particular individuals of those types.

During the summer vacations of 1899 and 1900 Pearson, with the aid of many willing friends and colleagues, collected material to test a novel theory of "homotyposis, which if correct would imply that the correlation between offspring of the same parents should on the average be equal to the correlation between undifferentiated like organs of an individual." The volume of data collected and reduced was far greater than Pearson had previously attempted. The result was a joint memoir by Pearson and several members of his staff, "On the Principle of Homotyposis and Its Relation to Heredity . . . Part I. Homotyposis in the Vegetable Kingdom," which was "received" by the Royal Society on 6 October 1900. William Bateson, biologist and pioneer in genetics, who had just become a convert to Mendel's theory, was one of those chosen to referee the memoir, which was "read"—presumably only the five-page abstract[40] and certainly in highly abridged form—at the meeting of 15 November 1900. In the discussion that followed the presentation, Bateson sharply criticized the paper, its thesis being, in his view, mistaken; and other fellows present added criticism of both its length and its content.

The next day (16 November 1900) Weldon wrote to Pearson: "The contention 'that numbers mean nothing and do not exist in Nature' is a very serious thing, which will have to be fought. Most other people have got beyond it, but most biologists have not. Do you think it would be too hopelessly expensive to start a journal of some kind?. . ."[41] Pearson was enthusiastically in favor of the idea—on 13 December 1900 he wrote to Galton that Bateson's adverse criticism "did not apply to this memoir only but to all my work, . . . if the R. S. people send my papers to Bateson, one cannot hope to get them printed. It is a practical notice to quit. This notice applies not only to *my* work, but to most work on similar statistical lines."[42] On 29 November Weldon wrote to him: "Get a better title for this would-be journal than I can think of!"[43] Pearson replied with the suggestion that "the science in future should be called Biometry and its official organ be *Biometrika*."[44]

A circular was sent out during December 1900 to solicit financial support and resulted in a fund sufficient to support the journal for a number of years. Weldon, Pearson, and C. B. Davenport were to be the editors; and Galton agreed to be "consulting editor." The first issue appeared in October 1901, and the editorial "The Scope of *Biometrika*" stated:

> *Biometrika* will include (a) memoirs on variation, inheritance, and selection in Animals and Plants, based upon the examination of statistically large numbers of specimens (this will of course include statistical investigations in anthropometry); (b) those developments of statistical theory which are applicable to biological problems; (c) numerical tables and graphical solutions tending to reduce the labour of

statistical arithmetic; (d) abstracts of memoirs, dealing with these subjects, which are published elsewhere; and (e) notes on current biometric work and unsolved problems.

In the years that followed, *Biometrika* became a major medium for the publication of mathematical tables and other aids to statistical analysis and detailed tables of biological data.

The memoir on homotyposis was not published in the *Philosophical Transactions* until 12 November 1901, and only after a direct appeal by Pearson to the president of the Royal Society on grounds of general principle rather than individual unfairness. Meanwhile, Bateson had prepared detailed adverse criticisms. Under pressure from Bateson, the secretary of the Royal Society put aside protocol and permitted the printing of Bateson's comments and their issuance to the fellows at the meeting of 14 February 1901— before the full memoir by Pearson and his colleagues was in their hands, and even before its authors had been notified whether it had been accepted for publication. Then, with the approval of the Zoological Committee, Bateson's full critique was published in the *Proceedings of the Royal Society* before the memoir criticized had appeared.[45] One can thus appreciate the basis for the acerbity of Pearson's rejoinder, which he chose to publish in *Biometrika*[46] because he had been "officially informed that [he had] a right to a rejoinder, but only to such a one as will not confer on [his] opponent a right to a further reply!" (footnote, p. 321).

This fracas over the homotyposis memoir was but one manifestation of the division that had developed in the 1890's between the biometric "school" of Galton, Weldon, and Pearson and certain biologists— notably Bateson—over the nature of evolution. The biometricians held that evolution of new species was the result of gradual accumulation of the effects of small continuous variations. In 1894 Bateson published a book in which he noted that deviations from normal parental characteristics frequently take the form of discontinuous "jumps" of definite measurable magnitude, and held that discontinuous variation of this kind—evidenced by what we today call sports or mutations—is necessary for the evolution of new species.[47] He was deeply hurt when Weldon took issue with this thesis in an otherwise very favorable review published in *Nature* (10 May 1894).

When Gregor Mendel's long-overlooked paper of 1866 was resurrected in 1900 by three Continental botanists, the particulate nature of Mendel's theory of "dominance" and "segregation" was clearly in keeping with Bateson's views; and he became a totally committed Mendelist, taking it upon himself to convert all English biologists into disciples of Mendel.

Meanwhile, Weldon and Pearson had become deeply committed adherents to Galton's law of ancestral heredity, to which Bateson was antipathetic. There followed a heated controversy between the "ancestrians," led by Pearson and Weldon, and the "Mendelians," led by Bateson. Pearson and Weldon were not, as some supposed, unreceptive to Mendelian ideas but were concerned with the too ready acceptance of Mendelism as a complete gospel without regard to certain incompatibilities they had found between Mendel's laws of "dominance" and "segregation" and other work. Weldon, the naturalist, regarded Mendelism as an unimportant but inconvenient exception to the ancestral law. Pearson, the applied mathematician and philosopher of science, saw that Mendelism was not incompatible with the ancestral law but in some circumstances could lead directly to it; and he sought to bring all heredity into a single system embodying both Mendelian and ancestrian principles, with the latter dominant. To Bateson, Mendel's laws were the truth and all else was heresy. The controversy raged on with much mutual incomprehension, and with great bitterness on both sides, until Weldon's death in April 1906 removed the most committed ancestrian and Bateson's main target.[48] Without the help of Weldon's biologically trained mind, Pearson had no inclination, nor the necessary training, to keep in close touch with the growing complexity of the Mendelian hypothesis, which was coming to depend increasingly on purely biological discoveries for its development; he therefore turned his attention to unfinished business in other areas and to eugenics.

During the succeeding decades Mendelian theory became firmly established—but only after much testing on diverse material, clarification of ideas, explanation of "exceptions," and tying in with cytological discoveries. Mendel's laws have been shown to apply to many kinds of characters in almost all organisms, but this has not entirely eliminated "biometrical" methods. Quite the contrary: multiple regression techniques are still needed to cope with the inheritance of quantitative characters that presumably depend upon so many genes that Mendelian theory cannot be brought to bear in practice. For example, coat color of dairy cows depends upon only a few genes and its Mendelian inheritance is readily verified; but the quantitative trait of milk production capacity is so complex genetically that multiple regression methods are used to predict the average milk-production character of offspring of particular matings, given the relevant ancestral information.

In fact, geneticists today ascribe the reconciliation of the "ancestral" and "Mendelian" positions, and definitive synthesis of the two theories, to Fisher's first genetical paper, "The Correlations to be Expected Between Relatives on the Supposition of Mendelian Inheritance" (1918), in which, in response to new data, he improved upon the kinds of models that Pearson, Weldon, and Yule had been considering 10–20 years before, and showed clearly that the correlations observed between human relatives not only could be interpreted on the supposition of Mendelian inheritance, but also that Mendelian inheritance must lead to precisely the kind of correlations observed.

Weldon's death was not only a tremendous blow to Pearson but also removed a close colleague of high caliber, without whom it was not possible to continue work in biometry along some of the lines that they had developed during the preceding fifteen years. Yet Pearson's productivity hardly faltered. During his remaining thirty years his articles, editorials, memoirs, and books on or related to biometry and statistics numbered over 300; he also produced one in astronomy and four in mechanics and about seventy published letters, reviews, and prefatory and other notes in scientific publications, the last of which was a letter (1935) on the aims of the founders of *Biometrika* and the conditions under which the journal had been published.

Following Weldon's death, Pearson gave increasing attention to eugenics. In 1904 Galton had provided funds for the establishment of a eugenics record office, to be concerned with collecting data for the scientific study of eugenics. Galton kept the office under his control until late in 1906, when, at the age of eighty-four, he turned it over to Pearson. With a change of name to eugenics laboratory, it became a companion to Pearson's biometric laboratory. It was transferred in 1907 to University College and with a small staff carried out studies of the relative importance of heredity and environment in alcoholism, tuberculosis, insanity, and infant mortality.[49] The findings were published as Studies in National Deterioration, nos. 1–11 (1906–1924) and in Eugenics Laboratory Memoirs, nos. 1–29 (1907–1935). Thirteen issues of the latter were devoted to "The Treasury of Human Inheritance" (1909–1933), a vast collection of pedigrees forming the basic material for the discussion of the inheritance of abnormalities, disorders, and other traits.

Pearson's major effort during the period 1906–1914, however, was devoted to developing a postgraduate center in order "to make statistics a branch of applied mathematics with a technique and nomenclature of its own, to train statisticians as men of science . . . and in general to convert statistics in this country from being the playing field of *dilettanti* and controversialists into

a serious branch of science, which no man could attempt to use effectively without adequate training, any more than he could attempt to use the differential calculus, being ignorant of mathematics."[50] At the beginning of this period Pearson was not only head of the department of applied mathematics, but also in charge of the drawing office for engineering students, giving evening classes in astronomy, directing the biometric and eugenics laboratories, and editing their various publications, and *Biometrika*, a tremendous task for one man. In the summer of 1911, however, he was able to cut back somewhat on these diverse activities by relinquishing the Goldsmid chair of applied mathematics to become the first Galton professor of eugenics and head of a new department of applied statistics in which were incorporated the biometric and eugenics laboratories. But he also assumed a new task about the same time: soon after Galton's death in 1911, his relatives had asked Pearson to write his biography. The first volume of *The Life, Letters and Labors of Francis Galton* was published in 1914, the second volume in 1925, and the third volume (in two parts) in 1930. It is an incomparable source of information on Galton, on Pearson himself, and on the early years of biometry. Although the volume of Pearson's output of purely statistical work was somewhat reduced during these years by the task of writing this biography, it was still immense by ordinary standards.

Pearson was the principal editor of *Biometrika* from its founding to his death (vols. 1–28, 1901–1936), and for many years he was the sole editor. Under his guidance it became the world's leading medium of publication of papers on, and mathematical tables relating to, statistical theory and practice. Soon after World War I, during which Pearson's group was deeply involved in war work, he initiated the series Tracts for Computers, nos. 1–20 (1919–1935), many of which became indispensable to computers of the period. In 1925 he founded *Annals of Eugenics* and served as editor of the first five volumes (1925–1933). Some of the tables in *Tables for Statisticians and Biometricians* (pt. I, 1914; pt. II, 1931) appear to be timeless in value; others are no longer used. *The Tables of the Incomplete Beta-Function* (1934), a compilation prepared under his direction over a period of several decades, remains a monument to him and his co-workers.

In July 1932 Pearson advised the college and university that he would resign from the Galton professorship the following summer. The college decided to divide the department of applied statistics into two independent units, a department of eugenics with which the Galton professorship would be associated, and a new department of statistics. In October 1933 Pearson was established in a room placed at his disposal by the zoology department; his son, Egon, was head of the new department of statistics; and R. A. Fisher was named the second Galton professor of eugenics. Pearson continued to edit *Biometrika* and had almost seen the final proofs of the first half of volume 28 through the press when he died on 27 April 1936.

NOTES

1. Quoted by E. S. Pearson in *Karl Pearson: An Appreciation . . .*, p. 4 (*Biometrika*, **28**, 196).
2. Galton discovered the statistical phenomenon of regression around 1875 in the course of experiments with sweet pea seeds to determine the law of inheritance of size. Using 100 parental seeds of each of 7 different selected sizes, he constructed a two-way plot of the diameters of parental and offspring seeds from each parental class. Galton then noticed that the median diameters of the offspring seeds for the respective parental classes fell nearly on a straight line. Furthermore, the median diameters of offspring from the larger-size parental classes were less than those of the parents; and for the smaller-size parental classes, they were greater than those of the parents, indicating a tendency of the "mean" offspring size to "revert" toward what might be described as the average ancestral type. Not realizing that this phenomenon is a characteristic of any two-way plot, he first termed it "reversion" and, later, "regression."

Examining these same data further, Galton noticed that the variation of offspring size within the respective parental arrays (as measured by their respective semi-interquartile ranges) was approximately constant and less than the similarly measured variation of the overall offspring population. From this empirical evidence he then inferred the correct relation, variability of offspring family = $\sqrt{1 - r^2} \times$ variability of overall offspring population, which he announced in symbolic form in an 1877 lecture, calling r the "reversion" coefficient.

A few years later Galton made a two-way plot of the statures of some human parents of unselected statures and their adult children, noting that the respective marginal distributions were approximately Gaussian or "normal," as Adolphe Quetelet had noticed earlier from examination of each of these variables separately, and that the frequency distributions along lines in the plot parallel to either of the variate axes were "apparently" Gaussian distributions of equal variation, which was less than, and in a constant ratio $\sqrt{1 - r^2}$ to, that of the corresponding marginal distributions. To obtain a numerical value for r, Galton expressed the deviations of the individual values of both variates from their respective medians in terms of their respective semi-interquartile ranges as a unit, so that r became the slope of his regression line.

In 1888 Galton made one more great and far-reaching discovery. Applying the techniques that he had evolved for the measurement of the influence of heredity to the problem of measuring the degree of association between the sizes of two different organs of the same individual, he reached the conception of an "index of co-relation" as a measure of the degree of relationship between two such characteristics and recognized r, his measure of "reversion" or "regression," to be such a coefficient of co-relation or correlation, suitable for application to all living forms.

Galton, however, failed to recognize and appreciate the additional mathematical complexity necessarily involved in the joint consideration of more than two mutually correlated characteristics, with the result that his efforts to formulate and implement what became known as his law of ancestral heredity were somewhat confused and imprecise. It remained for Pearson to provide the necessary generalization and precision of formulation in the form of a multiple regression formula.

For fuller details, see Pearson's "Notes on the History of Correlation" (1920).
3. *Speeches . . . at a Dinner . . . in [His] Honour*, pp. 22–23; also quoted by E. S. Pearson, *op. cit.*, p. 19 (*Biometrika*, **28**, 211).
4. An examination of *Letters From W. S. Gosset to R. A. Fisher 1915–1936*, 4 vols. (Dublin, 1962), issued for private circulation only, reveals that Gosset (pen name "Student"), played a similar role with respect to R. A. Fisher. When and how they first came into contact is revealed by the two letters of Sept. 1912 from Gosset to Pearson that are reproduced in E. S. Pearson's "Some Early Correspondence . . ." (1968).
5. E. S. Pearson, *op. cit.*, apps. II and III.
6. Pearson was not the first to use this terminology: "Galton used it, as did also Lexis, and the writer has not found any reference which seems to be its first use" (Helen M. Walker, *Studies . . .*, p. 185). But Pearson's consistent and exclusive use of this term in his epoch-making publications led to its adoption throughout the statistical community.
7. E. S. Pearson, *op. cit.*, p. 26 (*Biometrika*, **28**, 218).
8. The title "Contributions to the Mathematical Theory of Evolution" or "Mathematical Contributions . . ." was used as the general title of 17 memoirs, numbered II through XIX, published in the *Philosophical Transactions* or as Drapers' Company Research Memoirs, and of 8 unnumbered papers published in the *Proceedings of the Royal Society*. "Mathematical" became and remained the initial word from III (1896) on. No. XVII was announced before 1912 as a forthcoming Drapers' . . . Memoir but has not been published to date.
9. From Pearson, "Statistical Tests," in *Nature*, **136** (1935), 296–297, see 296.
10. Pearson, "Notes on the History of Correlation," p. 37 (Pearson and Kendall, p. 197).
11. Pearson did not use different symbols for population parameters (such as μ, σ, ρ) and sample measures of them (m, s, r) as has been done in this article, following the example set by "Student" in his first paper on small-sample theory, "The Probable Error of a Mean" (1908). Use of identical symbols for population parameters and sample measures of them makes Pearson's, and other papers of this period, difficult to follow and, in some instances, led to error.
12. Pearson, "Notes on the History of Correlation," p. 42 (Pearson and Kendall, p. 202).
13. In the rest of the article, the term "standard error" will be used instead of "standard deviation of the sampling error." Pearson consistently gave formulas for, and spoke of the corresponding "probable error" (or "p.e.") defined by,

probable error = 0.674489 . . . × standard error,

the numerical factor being the factor appropriate to the normal distribution, and reserved the term "standard deviation" (and the symbol σ) for description of the variation of individuals in a population or sample.
14. Footnote, p. 274 (*Early . . . Papers*, p. 134).
15. There are always two sample η's, η_{yx} and η_{xy}, corresponding to the regression of y on x and the regression of x on y, respectively, in the sample. When these regressions are both exactly linear, $\eta_{yx} = \eta_{xy} = r$; otherwise η_{yx} and η_{xy} are different.

In this memoir Pearson defines and discusses the correlation ratio, η_{yx}, and its relation to r entirely in terms of a sample of N paired observations, (x_i, y_i), $(i = 1, 2, ..., N)$. The implications of various equalities and inequalities between the correlation ratio of a trait X with respect to a trait Y in some general (nonnormal) bivariate population and ρ, the product-moment coefficient of correlation of X and Y in this population, are discussed, for example, in W. H. Kruskal, "Ordinal Measures of Association," in *Journal of American Statistical Association*, **53** (1958), 814–861.

16. In Pearson, "On the Systematic Fitting of Curves to Observations and Measurements," in *Biometrika*, **1**, no. 3 (Apr. 1902), 264–303, see p. 271.

17. Pearson and Alice Lee, "On the Distribution of Frequency (Variation and Correlation) of the Barometric Height at Diverse Stations," in *Philosophical Transactions of the Royal Society*, **190A** (1898), 423–469, see 456 and footnote to 462, respectively.

18. Pearson, "On the Probable Error of a Coefficient of Correlation as Found From a Fourfold Table," in *Biometrika*, **9**, nos. 1–2 (Mar. 1913), 22–27.

19. Pearson, "On the Probable Error of Biserial η," *ibid.*, **11**, no. 4 (May 1917), 292–302.

20. *Ibid.*, **1**, no. 1 (Oct. 1901), 2. Emphasis added.

21. Student, "Probable Error of a Correlation Coefficient," *ibid.*, **6**, nos. 2–3 (Sept. 1908), 302–310. In a 1915 letter to R. A. Fisher (repro. in E. S. Pearson, "Some Early Correspondence . . .," p. 447, and in Pearson and Kendall, p. 470), Gosset tells "how these things came to be of importance [to him]" and, in particular, says that the work of "the Experimental Brewery which concerns such things as the connection between analysis of malt or hops, and the behaviour of the beer, and which takes a day to each unit of the experiment, thus limiting the numbers, demanded an answer to such questions as 'If with a small number of cases I get a value r, what is the probability that there is really a positive correlation of greater than (say) 25 ?' "

22. E. S. Pearson, "Some Reflexions . . .," pp. 351–352 (Pearson and Kendall, pp. 349–350).

23. R. A. Fisher, "Frequency Distribution of the Values of the Correlation Coefficient in Samples From an Indefinitely Large Population," in *Biometrika*, **10**, no. 4 (May 1915), 507–521.

24. Letter from Pearson to Fisher dated 26 Sept. 1914, repro. in E. S. Pearson, "Some Early Correspondence . . .," p. 448 (Pearson and Kendall, p. 408).

25. Letter from Pearson to Fisher dated 3 Oct. 1914, partly repro. *ibid.*, p. 449 (Pearson and Kendall, p. 409).

26. Letter from Pearson to Fisher dated 30 Jan., 1915, partly repro. *ibid.*, pp. 449–450 (Pearson and Kendall, pp. 409–410).

27. *Ibid.*, p. 450 (Pearson and Kendall, p. 410).

28. Letter from Pearson to Fisher dated 13 May 1916, repro. *ibid.*, p. 451 (Pearson and Kendall, p. 411).

29. J. O. Irwin, in *Journal of the Royal Statistical Society*, **126**, pt. 1 (Mar. 1963), 161; F. Yates and K. Mather, in *Biographical Memoirs of Fellows of the Royal Society*, **9** (Nov. 1963), 98–99; P. C. Mahalanobis, in *Biometrics*, **20**, no. 2 (June 1964), 214.

30. R. A. Fisher, "On an Absolute Criterion for Fitting Frequency Curves," in *Messenger of Mathematics*, **41** (1912), 155–160.

This paper marks Fisher's break away from inverse probability reasoning via Bayes's theorem but, although evident in retrospect, the "break" was not clear-cut: not having yet coined the term "likelihood," he spoke (p. 157) of "the probability of any particular set of θ's" (that is, of the parameters involved) being "proportional to the chance of a given set of observations occurring"—which appears to be equivalent to the proposition in the theory of inverse probability that, assuming a uniform a priori probability distribution of the parameters, the ratio of the a posteriori probability that $\theta = \theta_o + \xi$ to the a posteriori probability that $\theta = \theta_o$ is equal to the ratio of the probability of the observed set of observations when $\theta = \theta_o + \xi$ to their probability when $\theta = \theta_o$. He also described (p. 158) graphical representation of "the inverse probability system." On the other hand, he did stress (p. 160) that only the relative (not the absolute) values of these "probabilities" were meaningful and that it would be "illegitimate" to integrate them over a region in the parameter space.

Fisher introduced the term "likelihood" in his paper "On the Mathematical Foundations of Theoretical Statistics," in *Philosophical Transactions of the Royal Society*, **222A** (19 Apr. 1922), 309–368, in which he made clear for the first time the distinction between the mathematical properties of "likelihoods" and "probabilities," and stated:

> I must plead guilty in my original statement of the Method of Maximum Likelihood to having based my argument upon the principle of inverse probability; in the same paper, it is true, I emphasized the fact that such inverse probabilities were relative only . . . . Upon consideration . . . I perceive that the word probability is wrongly used in such a connection: probability is a ratio of frequencies, and about the frequencies of such [parameter] values we can know nothing whatever (p. 326).

31. E. S. Pearson, "Some Early Correspondence . . .," p. 452 (Pearson and Kendall, p. 412).

32. Repro. *ibid.*, pp. 454–455 (Pearson and Kendall, pp. 414–415).

33. F. N. David, *Tables of the Ordinates and Probability Integral of the Distribution of the Correlation Coefficient in Small Samples* (London, 1938).

34. Letter from Pearson to Fisher dated 21 Aug. 1920, repro. in E. S. Pearson, "Some Early Correspondence . . .," p. 453 (Pearson and Kendall, p. 413).

35. R. A. Fisher, "On the 'Probable Error' of a Coefficient of Correlation Deduced From a Small Sample," in *Metron*, **1**, no. 4 (1921), 1–32.

36. Letters from Pearson to Fisher dated 26 June 1916 and 21 Oct. 1918, repro. in E. S. Pearson, "Some Early Correspondence . . .," pp. 455, 456, respectively (Pearson and Kendall, pp. 415, 416).

37. Pearson, "Method of Moments and Method of Maximum Likelihood," in *Biometrika*, **28**, nos. 1–2 (June 1936), 34–59; R. A. Fisher, "Professor Karl Pearson and the Method of Moments," in *Annals of Eugenics*, **7**, pt. 4 (June 1937), 303–318.

38. F. Y. Edgeworth, "On the Probable Error of Frequency Constants," in *Journal of the Royal Statistical Society*, **71** (1908), 381–397, 499–512, 652–678.

39. The identical mathematical form of expressions derived by the method of maximum likelihood and by the method of inverse probability, if a uniform prior distribution is adopted, has been a source of continuing confusion. Thus, the "standard errors" given by Gauss in his 1816 paper were undeniably derived via the method of inverse probability and, strictly speaking, are the standard deviations of the a posteriori probability distributions of parameters concerned, given the observed values of the particular functions of sample values considered. On the other hand, by virtue of the above-mentioned equivalence of form, Gauss's 1816 formulas can be recognized as giving the "standard errors," that is, the standard deviations of the sampling distributions, of the functions of sample values involved for fixed values of the corresponding population parameters. Consequently, speaking loosely, one is inclined today to attribute to Gauss the original ("first") derivation of these "standard error" formulas, even though he may have had (in 1816) no conception of the "sampling distribution," for fixed values of a population parameter, of a sample function used to estimate the value of this parameter. In contrast, the result given in his 1821 paper almost certainly refers to the sampling

distribution of s, and not to the a posteriori distribution of σ.

Edgeworth's discussion is quite explicitly in terms of inverse probability. Pearson-Filon asymptotic formulas are derived afresh in this context and are said to be applicable only to "solutions" obtained by "the genuine inverse method," the "fluctuation of the *quaesitum*" so determined "being less than that of any other determination" (pp. 506–507).

The correct interpretation of the formulas derived by Pearson and Filon is somewhat obscured by their use of identical symbols for population parameters and the sample functions used to estimate them, and by the fact that their choice of words is such that their various summary statements can be interpreted either way. On the other hand, their derivation starts (p. 231) with consideration of a ratio of probabilities, introduced without explanation but for which the explanation may be the "proposition in the theory of Inverse Probability" mentioned in note 30 above; and Pearson says, in his letter of June 1916 to Fisher (see note 32), "In the first place you have to demonstrate the logic of the Gaussian rule . . . I frankly confess I approved the Gaussian method in 1897 (see *Phil. Trans.* Vol. 191, A, p. 232), but I think it logically at fault now." These facts suggest that Pearson and Filon may have regarded the "probable errors" and "correlations" they derived as describing properties of the joint a posteriori probability distribution of the population parameters, given the observed values of the sample functions used to estimate them.

40. *Proceedings of the Royal Society,* **68** (1900), 1–5.
41. Quoted by Pearson in his memoir on Weldon, in *Biometrika,* **5,** no. 1 (Oct. 1906), 35 (Pearson and Kendall, p. 302).
42. Letter from Pearson to Galton, quoted in Pearson's *Life . . . of Francis Galton,* IIIA, 241.
43. Quoted by Pearson in his memoir on Weldon, in *Biometrika,* **5,** no. 1 (Oct. 1906), 35 (Pearson and Kendall, p. 302).
44. *Ibid.*
45. W. Bateson, "Heredity, Differentiation, and Other Conceptions of Biology: A Consideration of Professor Karl Pearson's Paper 'On the Principle of Homotyposis,' " in *Proceedings of the Royal Society,* **69,** no. 453, 193–205.
46. Pearson, "On the Fundamental Conceptions of Biology," in *Biometrika,* **1,** no. 3 (Apr. 1902), 320–344.
47. W. Bateson, *Materials for the Study of Variation, Treated With Especial Regard to Discontinuity in the Origin of Species* (London, 1894).
48. For fuller details, see either of the articles by P. Froggatt and N. C. Nevin in the bibliography; the first is the more complete.
49. These studies were not without a price for Pearson: he became deeply involved almost at once in a hot controversy over tuberculosis and a fierce dispute on the question of alcoholism. See E. S. Pearson, *Karl Pearson . . . ,* pp. 59–66 (*Biometrika,* **29,** 170–177).
50. From a printed statement entitled *History of the Biometric and Galton Laboratories,* drawn up by Pearson in 1920; quoted in E. S. Pearson, *Karl Pearson . . . ,* p. 53 (*Biometrika,* **29,** 164).

BIBLIOGRAPHY

I. ORIGINAL WORKS. A bibliography of Pearson's research memoirs and his articles and letters in scientific journals that are on applied mathematics, including astronomy, but not statistics, biometry, anthropology, eugenics, or mathematical tables, follows the obituary by L. N. G.

Filon (see below). A bibliography of his major contributions to the latter five areas is at the end of P. C. Mahalanobis, "A Note on the Statistical and Biometric Writings of Karl Pearson" (see below). The individual mathematical tables and collections of such tables to which Pearson made significant contributions in their computation or compilation, or through preparation of explanatory introductory material, are listed and described in Raymond Clare Archibald, *Mathematical Table Makers* (New York, 1948), 65–67.

Preparation of a complete bibliography of Pearson's publications was begun, with his assistance, three years before his death. The aim was to include all of the publications on which his name appeared as sole or part author and all of his publications that were issued anonymously. The result, *A Bibliography of the Statistical and Other Writings of Karl Pearson* (Cambridge, 1939), compiled by G. M. Morant with the assistance of B. L. Welch, lists 648 numbered entries arranged chronologically under five principal headings, with short summaries of the contents of the more important, followed by a sixth section in which a chronological list, "probably incomplete," is given of the syllabuses of courses of lectures and single lectures delivered by Pearson that were printed contemporaneously as brochures or single sheets. The five major categories and the number of entries in each are the following:

I. Theory of statistics and its application to biological, social, and other problems (406);

II. Pure and applied mathematics and physical science (37);

III. Literary and historical (67);

IV. University matters (27);

V. Letters, reviews, prefatory and other notes in scientific publications (111).

Three omissions have been detected: "The Flying to Pieces of a Whirling Ring," in *Nature,* **43,** no. 1117 (26 Mar. 1891), 488; "Note on Professor J. Arthur Harris' Papers on the Limitation in the Applicability of the Contingency Coefficient," in *Journal of the American Statistical Association,* **25,** no. 171 (Sept. 1930), 320–323; and "Postscript," *ibid.,* 327.

The following annotated list of Pearson's most important publications will suffice to reveal the great diversity of his contributions and their impact on the biological, physical, and social sciences. The papers marked with a single asterisk (*) have been repr. in *Karl Pearson's Early Statistical Papers* (Cambridge, 1948) and those with a double asterisk (**), in E. S. Pearson and M. G. Kendall, eds., *Studies in the History of Probability and Statistics* (London–Darien, Conn., 1970), referred to as Pearson and Kendall.

"On the Motion of Spherical and Ellipsoidal Bodies in Fluid Media" (2 pts.), in *Quarterly Journal of Pure and Applied Mathematics,* **20** (1883), 60–80, 184–211; and "On a Certain Atomic Hypothesis" (2 pts.), in *Transactions of the Cambridge Philosophical Society,* **14,** pt. 2 (1887), 71–120, and *Proceedings of the London Mathematical Society,* **20** (1888), 38–63, respectively. These early papers on the motions of a rigid or pulsating atom in an infinite incompressible fluid did much to increase Pearson's stature in applied mathematics at the time.

William Kingdon Clifford, *The Common Sense of the Exact Sciences* (London, 1885; reiss. 1888), which Pearson edited and completed.

Isaac Todhunter, *A History of the Theory of Elasticity and of the Strength of Materials From Galilei to the Present Time*, 2 vols. (Cambridge, 1886–1893; reiss. New York, 1960), edited and completed by Pearson.

The Ethic of Freethought (London, 1888; 2nd ed., 1901), a collection of essays, lectures, and public addresses on free thought, historical research, and socialism.

"On the Flexure of Heavy Beams Subjected to a Continuous Load. Part I," in *Quarterly Journal of Pure and Applied Mathematics*, **24** (1889), 63–110, in which for the first time a now-much-cited exact solution was given for the bending of a beam of circular cross section under its own weight, and extended to elliptic cross sections in ". . . Part II," *ibid.*, **31** (1899), 66–109, written with L. N. G. Filon.

The Grammar of Science (London, 1892; 3rd ed., 1911; reiss. Gloucester, Mass., 1969; 4th ed., E. S. Pearson, ed., London, 1937), a critical survey of the concepts of modern science and his most influential book.

* "Contributions to the Mathematical Theory of Evolution," in *Philosophical Transactions of the Royal Society*, **185A** (1894), 71–110, deals with the dissection of symmetrical and asymmetrical frequency curves into normal (Gaussian) components and marks Pearson's introduction of the method of moments as a means of fitting a theoretical curve to experimental data and of the term "standard deviation" and σ as the symbol for it.

* "Contributions to the Mathematical Theory of Evolution. II. Skew Variation in Homogeneous Material," *ibid.*, **186A** (1895), 343–414, in which the term "mode" is introduced, the foundations of the Pearson system of frequency curves is laid, and Types I–IV are defined and their application exemplified.

* "Mathematical Contributions to the Theory of Evolution. III. Regression, Heredity, and Panmixia," *ibid.*, **187A** (1896), 253–318, Pearson's first fundamental paper on correlation, with special reference to problems of heredity, in which correlation and regression are defined in far greater generality than previously and the theory of multivariate normal correlation is developed as a practical tool to a stage that left little to be added.

The Chances of Death and Other Studies in Evolution, 2 vols. (London, 1897), essays on social and statistical topics, including the earliest adequate study ("Variation in Man and Woman") of anthropological "populations" using scientific measures of variability.

* "Mathematical . . . IV. On the Probable Errors of Frequency Constants and on the Influence of Random Selection on Variation and Correlation," in *Philosophical Transactions of the Royal Society*, **191A** (1898), 229–311, written with L. N. G. Filon, in which were derived the now-familiar expressions for the asymptotic variances and covariances of sample estimators of a group of population parameters in terms of derivatives of the likelihood function (without recognition of their applicability only to maximum likelihood estimators), and a number of particular results deduced therefrom.

* "Mathematical . . . V. On the Reconstruction of the Stature of Prehistoric Races," *ibid.*, **192A** (1898), 169–244, in which multiple regression techniques were used to reconstruct predicted average measurements of extinct races from the sizes of existing bones, given the correlations among bone lengths in an extant race, not merely as a technical exercise but as a means of testing the accuracy of predictions in evolutionary problems in the light of certain evolutionary theories.

"Mathematical . . . On the Law of Ancestral Heredity," in *Proceedings of the Royal Society*, **62** (1898), 386–412, a statistical formulation of Galton's law in the form of a multiple regression of offspring on "midparental" ancestry, with deductions therefrom of theoretical values for various regression and correlation coefficients between kin, and comparisons of such theoretical values with values derived from observational material.

"Mathematical . . . VII. On the Correlation of Characters not Quantitatively Measurable," in *Philosophical Transactions of the Royal Society*, **195A** (1901), 1–47, in which the "tetrachoric" coefficient of correlation r_t was introduced for estimating the coefficient of correlation, ρ, of a bivariate normal distribution from a sample scored dichotomously in both variables.

* "On the Criterion That a Given System of Deviations From the Probable in the Case of a Correlated System of Variables Is Such That It Can Be Reasonably Supposed to Have Arisen From Random Sampling," in *London, Edinburgh and Dublin Philosophical Magazine and Journal of Science*, 5th ser., **50** (1900), 157–175, in which the "χ^2 test of goodness of fit" was introduced, one of Pearson's greatest single contributions to statistical methodology.

"Mathematical . . . IX. On the Principle of Homotyposis and Its Relation to Heredity, to the Variability of the Individual, and to That of Race. Part I. Homotyposis in the Vegetable Kingdom," in *Philosophical Transactions of the Royal Society*, **197A** (1901), 285–379, written with Alice Lee *et al.*, a theoretical discussion of the relation of fraternal correlation to the correlation of "undifferentiated like organs of the individual" (called "homotyposis"), followed by numerous applications; the paper led to a complete schism between the biometric and Mendelian schools and the founding of *Biometrika*.

* "Mathematical . . . X. Supplement to a Memoir on Skew Variation," *ibid.*, 443–459; Pearson curves Type V and VI are developed and their application exemplified.

* "On the Mathematical Theory of Errors of Judgment With Special Reference to the Personal Equation," *ibid.*, **198A** (1902), 235–299, a memoir still of great interest and importance founded on two series of experiments, each with three observers, from which it was learned, among other things, that the "personal equation" (bias pattern of an individual observer) is subject to fluctuations far exceeding random sampling and that the

errors of different observers looking at the same phenomena are in general correlated.

"Note on Francis Galton's Problem," in *Biometrika*, **1**, no. 4 (Aug. 1902), 390–399, in which Pearson found the general expression for the mean value of the difference between the rth and the $(r + 1)$th ranked individuals in random samples from a continuous distribution, one of the earliest results in the sampling theory of order statistics —similar general expressions for the variances of and correlations between such intervals are given in his joint paper of 1931.

"On the Probable Errors of Frequency Constants," in *Biometrika*, **2**, no. 3 (June 1903), 273–281, an editorial that deals with standard errors of, and correlations between, cell frequencies and sample centroidal moments, in terms of the centroidal moments of a univariate distribution of general form. The extension to samples from a general bivariate distribution was made in pt. II, in *Biometrika*, **9**, nos. 1–2 (Mar. 1913), 1–19; and to functions of sample quantiles in pt. III, *ibid.*, **13**, no. 1 (Oct. 1920), 113–132.

* *Mathematical . . . XIII. On the Theory of Contingency and Its Relation to Association and Normal Correlation*, Drapers' Company Research Memoirs, Biometric Series, no. 1 (London, 1904), directed toward measuring the association of two variables when the observational data take the form of frequencies in the cells of an $r \times c$ "contingency table" of qualitative categories not necessarily meaningfully orderable, an adaptation of his χ^2 goodness-of-fit criterion, termed "square contingency," being introduced to provide a test of overall departure from the hypothesis of independence and the basis of a measure of association, the "coefficient of contingency" $c = \sqrt{\chi^2/(\chi^2 + n)}$, which was shown to tend under certain special conditions to the coefficient of correlation of an underlying bivariate normal distribution.

On Some Disregarded Points in the Stability of Masonry Dams, Drapers' Company Research Memoirs, Technical Series, no. 1 (London, 1904), written with L. W. Atcherley, in which it was shown that the assumptions underlying a widely accepted procedure for calculating the stresses in masonry dams are not satisfied at the bottom of the dam, the stresses there being in excess of those so calculated, with consequent risk of rupture near the base—still cited today, this paper and its companion *Experimental Study . . .* (1907) caused great concern at the time, for instance, with reference to the British-built Aswan Dam.

* *Mathematical . . . XIV. On the General Theory of Skew Correlation and Non-Linear Regression*, Drapers' Company Research Memoirs, Biometric Series, no. 2 (London, 1905), dealt with the general conception of skew variation and correlation and the properties of the "correlation ratio" η (introduced in 1903) and showed for the first time the fundamental importance of the expressions $(1 - \eta^2)\, \sigma_y^2$ and $(\eta^2 - r^2)\, \sigma_y^2$ and of the difference between η and r as measures of departure from linearity, as well as those conditions that must be satisfied for linear, parabolic, cubic, and other regression equations to be adequate.

"The Problem of the Random Walk," in *Nature*, **72** (17 July 1905), 294, a brief letter containing the first explicit formulation of a "random walk," a term Pearson coined, and asking for information on the probability distribution of the walker's distance from the origin after n steps—Lord Rayleigh indicated the asymptotic solution as $n \to \infty$ in the issue of 3 Aug., p. 318; and the general solution for finite n was published by J. C. Kluyver in Dutch later the same year.

Mathematical . . . XV. A Mathematical Theory of Random Migration, Drapers' Company Research Memoirs, Biometric Series, no. 3 (London, 1906), written with John Blakeman. Various theoretical forms of distribution were derived that would result from random migration from an origin under certain ideal conditions, and solutions to a number of subsidiary problems were given—results that, while not outstandingly successful in studies of migration, have found various other applications.

** "Walter Frank Raphael Weldon, 1860–1906," in *Biometrika*, **5**, nos. 1–2 (Oct. 1906), 1–52 (repr. as paper no. 21 in Pearson and Kendall), a tribute to the man who posed the questions that impelled Pearson to some of his most important contributions, with additional details on the early years (1890–1905) of the biometric school and the founding of *Biometrika*.

Mathematical . . . XVI. On Further Methods of Determining Correlation, Drapers' Company Research Memoirs, Biometric Series, no. 4 (London 1907), dealt with calculation of the coefficient of correlation, r, from the individual differences $(x - y)$ in a sample and with estimation of the coefficient of correlation, ρ, of a bivariate normal population from the ranks of the individuals in a sample of that population with respect to each of the two traits concerned.

An Experimental Study of the Stresses in Masonry Dams, Drapers' Company Research Memoirs, Technical Series, no. 5 (London, 1907), written with A. F. C. Pollard, C. W. Wheen, and L. F. Richardson, which lent experimental support to the 1904 theoretical findings.

A First Study of the Statistics of Pulmonary Tuberculosis, Drapers' Company Research Memoirs, Studies in National Deterioration, no. 2 (London, 1907), and *A Second Study . . .: Marital Infection, . . .* Technical Series, no. 3 (London, 1908), written with E. G. Pope, the first two of seven publications by Pearson and his co-workers during 1907–1913 on the then-important and controversial subjects of the inheritance and transmission of pulmonary tuberculosis.

"On a New Method of Determining Correlation Between a Measured Character A, and a Character B, of which Only the Percentage of Cases Wherein B Exceeds (or Falls Short of) a Given Intensity Is Recorded for Each Grade of A," in *Biometrika*, **6**, nos. 1 and 2 (July–Oct. 1909), 96–105, in which the formula for the biserial coefficient of correlation, "biserial r," is derived but not named, and its application exemplified.

"On a New Method of Determining Correlation When One Variable Is Given by Alternative and the Other by Multiple Categories," *ibid.*, **7**, no. 3 (Apr. 1910), 248–257, in which the formula for "biserial η" is derived but not named, and its application exemplified.

A First Study of the Influence of Parental Alcoholism on the Physique and Ability of the Offspring, Eugenics Laboratory Memoirs, no. 10 (London, 1910), written with Ethel M. Elderton, gave correlations between drinking habits of the parents and the intelligence and various physical characteristics of the offspring, and examined the effect of parental alcoholism on the infant death rate.

A Second Study . . . Being a Reply to Certain Medical Critics of the First Memoir and an Examination of the Rebutting Evidence Cited by Them, Eugenics Laboratory Memoirs, no. 13 (London, 1910), written with E. M. Elderton.

A Preliminary Study of Extreme Alcoholism in Adults, Eugenics Laboratory Memoirs, no. 14 (London, 1910), written with Amy Barrington and David Heron. The relations of alcoholism to number of convictions, education, religion, prostitution, mental and physical conditions, and death rates were examined, with comparisons between the extreme alcoholic and the general population.

"On the Probability That Two Independent Distributions of Frequency Are Really Samples From the Same Population," in *Biometrika*, **8**, nos. 1–2 (July 1911), 250–254, in which his χ^2 goodness-of-fit criterion is extended to provide a test of the hypothesis that two independent samples arrayed in a $2 \times c$ table are random samples from the same population.

Social Problems: Their Treatment, Past, Present and Future. . ., Questions of the Day and of the Fray, no. 5 (London, 1912), contains a perceptive, eloquent plea for replacement of literary exposition and folklore by measurement, and presents some results of statistical analyses that illustrate the complexity of social problems.

The Life, Letters and Labours of Francis Galton, 3 vols. in 4 pts. (Cambridge, 1914–1930).

Tables for Statisticians and Biometricians (London, 1914; 2nd ed., issued as "Part I," 1924; 3rd ed., 1930), consists of 55 tables, some new, the majority repr. from *Biometrika*, a few from elsewhere, to which Pearson as editor contributed an intro. on their use.

"On the General Theory of Multiple Contingency With Special Reference to Partial Contingency," in *Biometrika*, **11**, no. 3 (May 1916), 145–158, extends the χ^2 method to the comparison of two ($r \times 2$) tables and contains the basic elements of a large part of present-day χ^2 technique.

"Mathematical Contributions . . . XIX. Second Supplement to a Memoir on Skew Variation," in *Philosophical Transactions of the Royal Society*, **216A** (1916), 429–457, in which Pearson curves Types VII–XI are defined and their applications illustrated.

"On the Distribution of the Correlation Coefficient in Small Samples. Appendix II to the Papers of 'Student' and R. A. Fisher. A Cooperative Study," in *Biometrika*, **11**, no. 4 (May 1917), 328–413, written with H. E. Soper, A. W. Young, B. M. Cave, and A. Lee, an exhaustive study of the moments and shape of the distribution of r in samples of size n from a normal population with correlation coefficient ρ as a function of n and ρ, and of its approach to normality as $n \to \infty$, with special attention to determination, via inverse probability, of the "most

likely value" of ρ from an observed value of r—the paper that initiated the rift between Pearson and Fisher.

"De Saint-Venant Solution for the Flexure of Cantilevers of Cross-Sections in the Form of Complete and Curtate Circular Sectors, and the Influence of the Manner of Fixing the Built-in End of the Cantilever on Its Deflection," in *Proceedings of the Royal Society*, **96A** (1919), 211–232, written with Mary Seegar, a basic paper giving the solution regularly cited for cantilevers of such cross sections—Pearson's last paper in mechanics.

** "Notes on the History of Correlation. Being a Paper Read to the Society of Biometricians and Mathematical Statisticians, June 14, 1920," in *Biometrika*, **13**, no. 1 (Oct. 1920), 25–45 (paper no. 14 in Pearson and Kendall), deals with Gauss's and Bravais's treatment of the bivariate normal distribution, Galton's discovery of correlation and regression, and Pearson's involvement in the matter.

Tables of the Incomplete Γ-Function Computed by the Staff of the Department of Applied Statistics, University of London, University College (London, 1922; reiss. 1934), tables prepared under the direction of Pearson, who, as editor, contributed an intro. on their use.

Francis Galton, 1822–1922. A Centenary Appreciation, Questions of the Day and of the Fray, no. 11 (London, 1922).

Charles Darwin, 1809–1922. An Appreciation. . . ., Questions of the Day and of the Fray, no. 12 (London, 1923).

"Historical Note on the Origin of the Normal Curve of Errors," in *Biometrika*, **16**, no. 3 (Dec. 1924), 402–404, announces the discovery of two copies of a long-overlooked pamphlet of De Moivre (1733) which gives to De Moivre priority in utilizing the integral of essentially the normal curve to approximate sums of successive terms of a binomial series, in formulating and using the theorem known as "Stirling's formula," and in enunciating "Bernoulli's theorem" that imprecision of a sample fraction as an estimate of the corresponding population proportion depends on the inverse square root of sample size.

"On the Skull and Portraits of George Buchanan," *ibid.*, **18**, nos. 3–4 (Nov. 1926), 233–256, in which it is shown that the portraits fall into two groups corresponding to distinctly different types of face, and only the type exemplified by the portraits in the possession of the Royal Society conforms to the skull.

"On the Skull and Portraits of Henry Stewart, Lord Darnley, and Their Bearing on the Tragedy of Mary, Queen of Scots," *ibid.*, **20B**, no. 1 (July 1928), 1–104, in which the circumstances of Lord Darnley's death and the history of his remains are discussed, anthropometric characteristics of his skull and femur are described and shown to compare reasonably well with the portraits, and the pitting of the skull is inferred to be of syphilitic origin.

"Laplace, Being Extracts From Lectures Delivered by Karl Pearson," *ibid.*, **21**, nos. 1–4 (Dec. 1929), 202–216, an account of Laplace's ancestry, education, and later life that affords necessary corrections to a number of earlier biographies.

Tables for Statisticians and Biometricians, Part II (London, 1931), tables nearly all repr. from *Biometrika*, with pref. and intro. on use of the tables by Pearson, as editor.

"On the Mean Character and Variance of a Ranked Individual, and on the Mean and Variance of the Intervals Between Ranked Individuals. Part I. Symmetrical Distributions (Normal and Rectangular)," in *Biometrika*, **23**, nos. 3–4 (Dec. 1931), 364–397, and ". . . Part II. Case of Certain Skew Curves," *ibid.*, **24**, nos. 1–2 (May 1932), 203–279, both written with Margaret V. Pearson, in which certain general formulas relating to means, standard deviations, and correlations of ranked individuals in samples of size n from a continuous distribution are developed and applied (in pt. I) to samples from the rectangular and normal distributions, and (in pt. II) to special skew curves (Pearson Types VIII, IX, X, and XI) that admit exact solutions.

Tables of the Incomplete Beta-Function (London, 1934), tables prepared under the direction of and edited by Pearson, with an intro. by Pearson on the methods of computation employed and on the uses of the tables.

"The Wilkinson Head of Oliver Cromwell and Its Relationship to Busts, Masks and Painted Portraits," in *Biometrika*, **26**, nos. 3–4 (Dec. 1934), 269–378, written with G. M. Morant, an extensive analysis involving 107 plates from which it is concluded "that it is a 'moral certainty' drawn from circumstantial evidence that the Wilkinson Head is the genuine head of Oliver Cromwell."

"Old Tripos Days at Cambridge, as Seen From Another Viewpoint," in *Mathematical Gazette*, **20** (1936), 27–36.

Pearson edited two scientific journals, to which he also contributed substantially: *Biometrika*, of which he was one of the three founders, always the principal editor (vols. **1–28**, 1901–1936), and for many years the sole editor; and *Annals of Eugenics*, of which he was the founder and the editor of the first 5 vols. (1925–1933). He also edited three series of Drapers' Company Research Memoirs: Biometric Series, nos. 1–4, 6–12 (London, 1904–1922) (no. 5 was never issued), of which he was sole author of 4 and senior author of the remainder; Studies in National Deterioration, nos. 1–11 (London, 1906–1924), 2 by Pearson alone and as joint author of 3 more; and Technical Series, nos. 1–7 (London, 1904–1918), 1 by Pearson alone, the others with coauthors. To these must be added the Eugenics Laboratory Memoirs, nos. 1–29 (London, 1907–1935), of which Pearson was a coauthor of 4. To many others, including the 13 issues (1909–1933) comprising "The Treasury of Human Inheritance," vols. I and II, he contributed prefatory material; the Eugenics Laboratory Lecture Series, nos. 1–14 (London, 1909–1914), 12 by Pearson alone and 1 joint contribution; Questions of the Day and of the Fray, nos. 1–12 (London, 1910–1923), 9 by Pearson alone and 1 joint contribution; and Tracts for Computers, nos. 1–20 (London, 1919–1935), 2 by Pearson himself, plus a foreword, intro., or prefatory note to 5 others.

Pearson has given a brief account of the persons and early experiences that most strongly influenced his development as a scholar and scientist in his contribution to the volume of *Speeches* . . . (1934) cited below; fuller accounts of his Cambridge undergraduate days, his teachers, his reading, and his departures from the norm of a budding mathematician are in "Old Tripos Days" above. His "Notes on the History of Correlation" (1920) contains a brief account of how he became involved in the development of correlation theory; and he gives many details on the great formative period (1890–1906) in the development of biometry and statistics in his memoir on Weldon (1906) and in vol. IIIA of his *Life . . . of Francis Galton.*

A very large number of letters from all stages of Pearson's life, beginning with his childhood, and many of his MSS, lectures, lecture notes and syllabuses, notebooks, biometric specimens, and data collections have been preserved. A large part of his scientific library was merged, after his death, with the joint library of the departments of eugenics and statistics at University College, London; a smaller portion, with the library of the department of applied mathematics.

Some of Pearson's letters to Galton were published by Pearson, with Galton's replies, in vol. III of his *Life . . . of Francis Galton.* A few letters of special interest from and to Pearson were published, in whole or in part, by his son, E. S. Pearson, in his "Some Incidents in the Early History of Biometry and Statistics" and in "Some Early Correspondence Between W. S. Gosset, R. A. Fisher, and Karl Pearson," cited below; and a selection of others, from and to Pearson, together with syllabuses of some of Pearson's lectures and lecture courses, are in E. S. Pearson, *Karl Pearson: An Appreciation* . . ., cited below.

For the most part Pearson's archival materials are not yet generally available for study or examination. Work in progress for many years on sorting, arranging, annotating, cross-referencing, and indexing these materials, and on typing many of his handwritten items, is nearing completion, however. A first typed copy of the handwritten texts of Pearson's lectures on the history of statistics was completed in 1972; and many dates, quotations, and references have to be checked and some ambiguities resolved before the whole is ready for public view. Hence we may expect the great majority to be available to qualified scholars before very long in the Karl Pearson Archives at University College, London.

II. Secondary Literature. The best biography of Pearson is still *Karl Pearson: An Appreciation of Some Aspects of His Life and Work* (Cambridge, 1938), by his son, Egon Sharpe Pearson, who stresses in his preface that "this book is in no sense a Life of Karl Pearson." It is a reissue in book form of two articles, bearing the same title, published in *Biometrika*, **28** (1936), 193–257, and **29** (1937), 161–248, with two additional apps. (II and III in the book), making six in all. Included in the text are numerous instructive excerpts from Pearson's publications, helpful selections from his correspondence, and an outline of his lectures on the history of statistics in the seventeenth and eighteenth centuries. App. I gives the syllabuses of the 7 public lectures Pearson gave at Gresham

College, London, in 1891, "The Scope and Concepts of Modern Science," from which *The Grammar of Science* (1892) developed; app. II, the syllabuses of 30 lectures on "The Geometry of Statistics," "The Laws of Chance," and 'The Geometry of Chance" that Pearson delivered to general audiences at Gresham College, 1891–1894; app. III, by G. Udny Yule, repr. from *Biometrika*, **30** (1938), 198–203, summarizes the subjects dealt with by Pearson in his lecture courses on "The Theory of Statistics" at University College, London, during the 1894–1895 and 1895–1896 sessions; app. VI provides analogous summaries of his 2 lecture courses on "The Theory of Statistics" for first- and second-year students of statistics at University College during the 1921–1922 session, derived from E. S. Pearson's lecture notes; and apps. IV and V give, respectively, the text of Pearson's report of Nov. 1904 to the Worshipful Company of Drapers on "the great value that the Drapers' Grant [had] been to [his] Department" and an extract from his report to them of Feb. 1918, "War Work of the Biometric Laboratory."

The following publications by E. S. Pearson are useful supps. to this work: "Some Incidents in the Early History of Biometry and Statistics, 1890–94," in *Biometrika*, **52**, pts. 1–2 (June 1965), 3–18 (paper 22 in Pearson and Kendall); "Some Reflexions on Continuity in the Development of Mathematical Statistics, 1885–1920," *ibid.*, **54**, pts. 3–4 (Dec. 1967), 341–355 (paper 23 in Pearson and Kendall); "Some Early Correspondence Between W. S. Gosset, R. A. Fisher, and Karl Pearson, With Notes and Comments," *ibid.*, **55**, no. 3 (Nov. 1968), 445–457 (paper 25 in Pearson and Kendall); *Some Historical Reflections Traced Through the Development of the Use of Frequency Curves*, Southern Methodist University Dept. of Statistics THEMIS Contract Technical Report no. 38 (Dallas, 1969); and "The Department of Statistics, 1971. A Year of Anniversaries . . ." (mimeo., University College, London, 1972).

Of the biographies of Karl Pearson in standard reference works, the most instructive are those by M. Greenwood, in the *Dictionary of National Biography, 1931–1940* (London, 1949), 681–684; and Helen M. Walker, in *International Encyclopedia of the Social Sciences*, XI (New York, 1968), 496–503.

Apart from the above writings of E. S. Pearson, the most complete coverage of Karl Pearson's career from the viewpoint of his contributions to statistics and biometry is provided by the obituaries by G. Udny Yule, in *Obituary Notices of Fellows of the Royal Society of London*, **2**, no. 5 (Dec. 1936), 73–104; and P. C. Mahalanobis, in *Sankhyā*, **2**, pt. 4 (1936), 363–378, and its sequel, "A Note on the Statistical and Biometric Writings of Karl Pearson," *ibid.*, 411–422.

Additional perspective on Pearson's contributions to biometry and statistics, together with personal recollections of Pearson as a man, scientist, teacher, and friend, and other revealing information are in Burton H. Camp, "Karl Pearson and Mathematical Statistics," in *Journal of the American Statistical Association*, **28**, no. 184 (Dec. 1933), 395–401; in the obituaries by Raymond Pearl, *ibid.*,

31, no. 196 (Dec. 1936), 653–664; and G. M. Morant, in *Man*, **36**, no. 118 (June 1936), 89–92; and in Samuel A. Stouffer, "Karl Pearson—An Appreciation on the 100th Anniversary of His Birth," in *Journal of the American Statistical Association*, **53**, no. 281 (Mar. 1958), 23–27. S. S. Wilks, "Karl Pearson: Founder of the Science of Statistics," in *Scientific Monthly*, **53**, no. 2 (Sept. 1941), 249–253; and Helen M. Walker, "The Contributions of Karl Pearson," in *Journal of the American Statistical Association*, **53**, no. 281 (Mar. 1958), 11-22, are also informative and useful as somewhat more distant appraisals. L. N. G. Filon, "Karl Pearson as an Applied Mathematician," in *Obituary Notices of Fellows of the Royal Society of London*, **2**, no. 5 (Dec. 1936), 104–110, seems to provide the only review and estimate of Pearson's contributions to applied mathematics, physics, and astronomy. Pearson's impact on sociology is discussed by S. A. Stouffer in his centenary "Appreciation" cited above; and Pearson's "rather special variety of Social-Darwinism" is treated in some detail by Bernard Semmel in "Karl Pearson: Socialist and Darwinist," in *British Journal of Sociology*, **9**, no. 2 (June 1958), 111–125. M. F. Ashley Montagu, in "Karl Pearson and the Historical Method in Ethnology," in *Isis*, **34**, pt. 3 (Winter 1943), 211–214, suggests that the development of ethnology might have taken a different course had Pearson's suggestions been put into practice.

The great clash at the turn of the century between the "Mendelians," led by Bateson, and the "ancestrians," led by Pearson and Weldon, is described with commendable detachment, and its after-effects assessed, by P. Froggatt and N. C. Nevin in "The 'Law of Ancestral Heredity' and the Mendelian-Ancestrian Controversy in England, 1889–1906," in *Journal of Medical Genetics*, **8**, no. 1 (Mar. 1971), 1–36; and "Galton's 'Law of Ancestral Heredity': Its Influence on the Early Development of Human Genetics," in *History of Science*, **10** (1971), 1–27.

Notable personal tributes to Pearson as a teacher, author, and friend, by three of his most distinguished pupils, L. N. G. Filon, M. Greenwood, and G. Udny Yule, and a noted historian of statistics, Harald Westergaard, have been preserved in *Speeches Delivered at a Dinner Held in University College, London, in Honour of Professor Karl Pearson, 23 April 1934* (London, 1934), together with Pearson's reply in the form of a five-page autobiographical sketch. The centenary lecture by J. B. S. Haldane, "Karl Pearson, 1857–1957," published initially in *Biometrika*, **44**, pts. 3–4 (Dec. 1957), 303–313, is also in *Karl Pearson, 1857–1957. The Centenary Celebration at University College, London, 13 May 1957* (London, 1958), along with the introductory remarks of David Heron, Bradford Hill's toast, and E. S. Pearson's reply.

Other publications cited in the text are Allan Ferguson, "Trends in Modern Physics," in British Association for the Advancement of Science, *Report of the Annual Meeting, 1936*, 27–42; Francis Galton, *Natural Inheritance* (London–New York, 1889; reissued, New York, 1972); R. A. Fisher, "The Correlation Between Relatives on the Supposition of Mendelian Inheritance," in *Transactions of the Royal*

Society of Edinburgh, **52** (1918), 399–433; H. L. Seal, "The Historical Development of the Gauss Linear Model," in *Biometrika*, **54**, pts. 1–2 (June 1967), 1–24 (paper no. 15 in Pearson and Kendall); and Helen M. Walker, *Studies in the History of Statistical Method* (Baltimore, 1931).

CHURCHILL EISENHART

[Contribution of the National Bureau of Standards, not subject to copyright.]

PEASE, FRANCIS GLADHELM (*b*. Cambridge, Massachusetts, 14 January 1881; *d*. Pasadena, California, 7 February 1938), *astronomy*.

Pease, the son of Daniel and Katherine Bangs Pease, received his education in Illinois. He attended high school in Highland Park and the Armour Institute of Technology in Chicago (now part of the Illinois Institute of Technology), where in 1901 he received a B.S. in mechanical engineering. Armour also awarded Pease an honorary M.S. in 1924 and D.Sc. in 1927, and he received another honorary D.Sc. in 1934 from Oglethorpe University. In 1922 he was elected a fellow of the Royal Astronomical Society.

Upon completing his formal education in 1901, Pease became a staff member of the Yerkes Observatory. There, with G. W. Ritchey, he studied problems in optics and instrument design, and carried out astronomical observations with the twenty-four-inch reflector. In 1904 he went to the Mount Wilson Observatory, where he remained as an instrument designer and astronomer until his death. He did, however, spend 1918 as chief draftsman in the engineering section of the National Research Council.

Pease's combination of instrumental expertise and observational experience made him immensely important to the Mount Wilson Observatory, which was embarking upon the construction of several large instruments. He helped design the 60-inch and 100-inch reflectors, the 60-foot and 150-foot towers, and the 20-foot and 50-foot interferometers, as well as much of the auxiliary equipment used with these instruments. He was also responsible for solving many of the design problems of the 200-inch telescope. Aware of the immense potential of larger telescopes, Pease spent considerable time developing plans and publishing papers on the need for, and uses and difficulties of, such instruments.

Pease was associated with A. A. Michelson in the first determination of stellar diameters, using interferometers for the difficult measurement of fringes as a function of mirror separation. He also assisted Michelson and F. Pearson in redetermining the velocity of light and in repeating the Michelson-Morley experiment.

Pease's direct spectrographic study with W. S. Adams and M. L. Humason of nebulae and star clusters enabled him to continue the measurements of rotations and radial velocities of spirals, which V. M. Slipher had begun in 1914 at the Lowell Observatory. In astronomical research Pease made important, although not pioneering, contributions; in instrument design, however, he was a leading figure of the twentieth century.

BIBLIOGRAPHY

I. ORIGINAL WORKS. Pease's key papers include "Radial Velocities of Six Nebulae," in *Publications of the Astronomical Society of the Pacific*, **27** (1915), 239–240; "The Rotation and Radial Velocity of the Spiral Nebula N.G.C. 4594," in *Proceedings of the National Academy of Sciences*, **2** (1916), 517–521; "Photographs of Nebulae With the 60-Inch Reflector 1911–1916," in *Astrophysical Journal*, **46** (1917), 24–55; "Interferometer Observations of Star Diameters," in *Publications of the Astronomical Society of the Pacific*, **34** (1921), 183; "On the Design of Very Large Telescopes," *ibid.*, **38** (1926), 195–207; "The Ball-Bearing Support System for the 100-Inch Mirror," *ibid.*, **44** (1932), 257, 308–312; and "Measurement of the Velocity of Light in a Partial Vacuum," in *Astrophysical Journal*, **82** (1935), 26–61, written with A. A. Michelson and F. Pearson. Some of his correspondence with G. E. Hale about designs for the 200-inch telescope are in the George Ellery Hale papers (1882–1937), Mount Wilson Observatory library, Pasadena, California.

II. SECONDARY LITERATURE. Obituaries of Pease are W. S. Adams, in *Publications of the Astronomical Society of the Pacific*, **50** (1938), 119–121, with portrait; G. Stromberg, in *Popular Astronomy*, **46** (1938), 357–359; and by an anonymous writer in *Monthly Notices of the Royal Astronomical Society*, **99** (1938), 312. For additional, related material see A. Pannekoek, *A History of Astronomy* (London, 1961). Pease's contributions to Mount Wilson are discussed in Helen Wright's biography of Hale, *Explorer of the Universe* (New York, 1966).

RICHARD BERENDZEN
RICHARD HART

PECHAM, JOHN (*b*. Sussex, England, *ca*. 1230–1235; *d*. Mortlake, Surrey, England, 8 December 1292), *optics, cosmology, mathematics*.

Pecham was probably born in the vicinity of Lewes in Sussex, possibly in or near the village of Patcham, and received his elementary education at the priory of Lewes.[1] He later matriculated in the arts faculties at Paris and Oxford, probably in that order. He became a Franciscan in the late 1240's or in the 1250's and was sent to Paris to undertake theological studies between 1257 and 1259.[2] In 1269 he received the doctorate in theology and for the next two years served as regent master in theology. Pecham returned to Oxford in 1271 or 1272 as eleventh lecturer in theology to the Franciscan school, a position he held until his appointment as provincial minister of the order in 1275. Two years later he was called to Italy as master in theology to the papal curia, and in 1279 he was elected archbishop of Canterbury. During his thirteen years as archbishop, Pecham maintained a zealous program of reform. He conscientiously endeavored to improve the administration of his province and persistently fought the practices of plurality and nonresidence; he called two reform councils and opposed, at every opportunity, the spread of "dangerous" philosophical novelties.

Of Pecham's intellectual development we know very little, although the major forces shaping his outlook probably came from within his own order. In the thirteenth century the Franciscan Order was a stronghold of Augustinianism and, consequently, of opposition to the new Aristotelian and Averroist ideas penetrating Europe. It is thus no surprise that Pecham became one of the leaders in the resistance against heterodox Aristotelian, and even more moderate Thomist, innovations.[3] But the Franciscan Order could provide more than antagonism toward philosophical and theological novelties. Among the English Franciscans a tradition of mathematical science had been initiated by Robert Grosseteste (who lectured to the Franciscans at Oxford and probably bequeathed his library to them at his death) and advanced by Roger Bacon. There can be little doubt that this tradition influenced Pecham: there is ample evidence that he and Bacon were personally acquainted and, indeed, resided together in the Franciscan friary at Paris during the period when Bacon was writing his principal scientific works. Nevertheless, this should not be taken to mean that Pecham was Bacon's student or protégé (there is no evidence for either) or that the influences on Pecham were limited to the Franciscan Order; Pecham's optical works, for example, reveal the influence not only of Augustine, Grosseteste, and Bacon but also of Aristotle, Euclid, al-Kindī, Ibn al-Haytham, Moses Maimonides, and perhaps Ptolemy and Witelo; and the primary influence in this instance was not Augustine or Grosseteste or Bacon, but Ibn al-Haytham.

Works. Pecham's indisputably genuine works on natural philosophy and mathematical science are *Tractatus de numeris* (or *Arithmetica mystica*); *Tractatus de perspectiva*; *Perspectiva communis*, extant in both an original and a revised version; and *Tractatus de sphera*. In addition to these, a treatise entitled *Theorica planetarum* is attributed to Pecham in several manuscripts and has commonly been regarded as genuine, although the question of its authenticity has in fact never been explored with care. Material of considerable scientific import is also contained in Pecham's treatises on the soul, *Tractatus de anima* and *Questiones de anima*, and his *Questiones de beatitudine corporis et anime*.[4] Two other scientific treatises have also been attributed to Pecham, *Perspectiva particularis* and *Tractatus de animalibus*, but there is no evidence supporting either attribution.

Of Pecham's scientific works only those on optics have been subjected to serious scrutiny; nevertheless, it is possible to make a few remarks about several of the others. The *Tractatus de sphera* was apparently a rival to, rather than a commentary on, Sacrobosco's *De sphaera*.[5] In this work Pecham presents an elementary discussion of the sphericity (or circularity) of the principal bodies of the world (for instance, the heavens, raindrops, and solar radiation passing through noncircular apertures); the rotation of the heavens; the equality and inequality of days; the climatic zones of the terrestrial sphere; the origin of eclipses; and other topics of a cosmologic nature.

The *Tractatus de numeris* begins with the classification of number into abstract and concrete; concrete number is further subdivided into corporeal and spiritual number, spiritual number is divided into five additional categories, and so on. After further discussion of the elementary properties of numbers (odd and even, equality and inequality) and the perceptibility of number by the external senses, Pecham turns to the mystical properties of numbers: he employs number to elucidate the mysteries of the Trinity and concludes with an analysis of the mystical meanings of the numbers 1 to 30, 36, 40, 50, 100, 200, 300, and 1,000.

The earliest of Pecham's optical works was the *Tractatus de perspectiva*, probably written for the Franciscan schools during Pecham's years as a teacher at Paris or Oxford (1269–1275) or possibly during his provincial ministership (1275–1277). It is a rambling piece of continuous prose, not divided into propositions like the later *Perspectiva communis*, that treats the full range of elementary optical matters. Like the *Tractatus de numeris*, and unlike the *Perspectiva communis*, it is filled with quotations from the Bible and patristic sources, especially Augustine, that give it a theological and devotional flavor. With a few exceptions the *Tractatus de perspectiva* and *Perspectiva communis* are identical in theoretical content, although each includes certain topics that the other omits.

The work on which Pecham's fame has chiefly rested

is the *Perspectiva communis*, probably written between 1277 and 1279 during Pecham's professorship at the papal curia.[6] In the first book Pecham discussed the propagation of light and color, the anatomy and physiology of the eye, the act of visual perception, physical requirements for vision, the psychology of vision, and the errors of direct vision. In book II he discussed vision by reflected rays and presented a careful and sophisticated analysis of image formation by reflection. Book III was devoted to the phenomena of refraction, the rainbow, and the Milky Way.

The central feature of Pecham's optical system and the dominant theme of book I of the *Perspectiva communis* is the theory of direct vision. Here, as elsewhere, Pecham endeavored to reconcile all the available authorities—Aristotle, Euclid, Augustine, al-Kindī, Ibn al-Haytham, Ibn Rushd, Grosseteste, and Bacon. Following Ibn al-Haytham, Pecham argued that the emission of visual rays from the observer's eye is neither necessary nor sufficient as an explanation of sight; the primary agent of sight is therefore the ray coming to the eye from a point on the visible object. But in an attempt to follow Aristotle, al-Kindī, and Grosseteste as well, Pecham argued that visual rays do nevertheless exist and perform the important, but not always necessary, function of moderating the luminous rays from the visible object and making them "commensurate with the visual power." Thus Pecham, like Bacon, resolved the age-old debate between the emission and intromission theories of vision in favor of a twofold radiation, although, to be sure, priority was given to rays issuing from the visible object.

The rays issuing from points on the visible object fall perpendicularly onto the cornea and penetrate without refraction to the sensitive ocular organ, the glacial humor (or crystalline lens); nonperpendicular rays are weakened by refraction and therefore can be largely ignored. Since only one perpendicular ray issues from each point of the visible object and the collection of such perpendicular rays maintains a fixed order between the object and the eye, a one-to-one correspondence is established between points on the object and points on the glacial humor, and unconfused perception of the visual field is thus achieved. Vision is not "completed," however, in the glacial humor. There is a further propagation of the rays (or species) through the vitreous humor and optic nerve to the common nerve, where species from the two eyes combine, and eventually to the anterior part of the brain and the "place of interior judgment."

Pecham's optical system included significantly more than a theory of direct vision. He briefly discussed the doctrine of species; treated at length the propagation of rays; and developed a theory to explain how solar radiation, when passing through noncircular apertures, gives rise to circular images. He expressed the full law of reflection and applied it to image formation by plane, spherical, cylindrical, and conical mirrors; in this analysis he revealed an implicit understanding of the nature of the focal point of a concave mirror. Although he did not possess a mathematical law of refraction, he successfully applied the general qualitative principles of refraction to the images that result from refraction at plane and circular interfaces between transparent media of various densities. In his discussion of the rainbow Pecham again attempted to reconcile different theories. He argued that all three kinds of rays (rectilinear, reflected, and refracted) concur in the generation of the rainbow.

Significance and Influence. Pecham saw himself primarily not as a creative scientific thinker but as an expositor of scientific matters in elementary terms. He remarked at the beginning of the *Tractatus de sphera*:

> In the present opusculum, I intend to explain the number, figure, and motion of the principal bodies of the world (as well as related matters) insofar as is sufficient for an understanding of the words of Holy Scripture. And certain of these matters I have found treated in other works, but because of their difficulty, brevity, and in some cases falsity, they are useless for the elementary students that I intend to serve.[7]

In the *Tractatus de perspectiva* he remarked that he had undertaken to discuss light and number "for the sake of my simpler brothers," and in the preface to the *Perspectiva communis* he indicated that his goal was to "compress into concise summaries the teachings of perspective, which [in existing treatises] are presented with great obscurity."[8] Pecham's significance in the history of science is principally the result of his success in achieving this goal. He is most notable not as one who formulated new theories and interpretations, although on many occasions he did, but as one who skillfully presented scientific knowledge to his contemporaries and posterity by writing elementary textbooks.

Pecham's success was greatest in the case of the *Perspectiva communis*. This text is still extant in more than sixty manuscripts and went through twelve printed editions, including a translation into Italian, between 1482 and 1665. It was used and cited by many medieval and Renaissance natural philosophers, including Dominicus de Clavasio, Henry of Langenstein, Blasius of Parma, Lorenzo Ghiberti, Leonardo da Vinci, Albert Brudzewski, Francesco Maurolico, Giambattista della Porta, Girolamo Fabrici, Johannes Kepler, Willebrord Snellius, and G. B. Riccioli. It was lectured upon, in the late Middle Ages, at the universities of Vienna, Prague, Paris, Leipzig, Cracow, Würzburg, Alcalá, and Salamanca.[9] The *Perspectiva communis* was the most widely used of all optical texts from the early fourteenth until the close of the sixteenth century, and it remains today the best index of what was known to the scientific community in general on the subject.

NOTES

1. The evidence for both claims is a letter written by Pecham in 1285, in which he refers to his "nourishment from childhood" in the vicinity of the priory of Lewes and the comforts and honors he has received from its teachers; see *Registrum epistolarum*, III, 902. Several historians have argued that Pecham was born in Kent rather than Sussex.
2. In assigning the latter dates, I am following Douie, *Archbishop Pecham*, p. 8.
3. On Pecham's position vis-à-vis Averroism and Thomism, see Fernand van Steenberghen, *The Philosophical Movement in the Thirteenth Century* (Edinburgh, 1955), 94–104. Van Steenberghen calls Pecham "the true founder of neo-Augustinianism" (p. 103).
4. Scientific content is especially evident in the *Questiones de beatitudine corporis et anime*, in *Johannis Pechami Quaestiones tractantes de anima*, Hieronymus Spettman, ed., which is *Beiträge zur Geschichte der Philosophie des Mittelalters*, XIX, pts. 5–6 (Münster, 1918), although Pecham's psychology is apparent in all of them. On Pecham's psychology see Sharp, *Franciscan Philosophy*, 185–203; and *Die Psychologie des Johannes Pecham*, Spettman, ed., which is *Beiträge zur Geschichte der Philosophie des Mittelalters*, XX, pt. 6 (Münster, 1919).
5. According to Thorndike, *Sphere of Sacrobosco*, 24–25.
6. The dating of the *Perspectiva communis* is discussed in Lindberg, *Pecham and the Science of Optics*, 14–18; and in Lindberg, "Lines of Influence in Thirteenth-Century Optics: Bacon, Witelo, and Pecham," in *Speculum*, **46** (1971), 77–83.
7. Latin text in Thorndike, *op. cit.*, 445.
8. See Lindberg's eds. of these two treatises for the texts.
9. For a fuller account of the influence of the *Perspectiva communis*, see Lindberg, *Pecham and the Science of Optics*, 29–32.

BIBLIOGRAPHY

I. ORIGINAL WORKS. The *Perspectiva communis* (in both the original and the revised versions) is available in a recent ed. and English trans. by David C. Lindberg, *John Pecham and the Science of Optics* (Madison, Wis., 1970). The known extant MSS and eleven early printed eds. are listed in the intro. to this ed. Pecham's other optical work, the *Tractatus de perspectiva*, is also available in a modern critical version, David C. Lindberg, ed., in Franciscan Institute Publications, Text Ser. no. 16 (St. Bonaventure, N.Y., 1972).

No other complete scientific work of Pecham has been printed. The first five chapters of the *Tractatus de numeris* have been edited from four MSS and published as an appendix to *Tractatus de anima Ioannis Pecham*, Gaudentius Melani, ed. (Florence, 1948), 138–144. Lynn

Thorndike has published the opening paragraphs and incipits of later paragraphs of the *Tractatus de sphera* in *The Sphere of Sacrobosco and Its Commentators* (Chicago, 1949), 445–450; and Pierre Duhem has published the section on pinhole images from this same work in *Le système du monde*, III (Paris, 1915), 524–529. The *Theorica planetarum* is extant only in MS.

For a full listing of Pecham's works, including extant MSS and eds., see Victorinus Doucet, "Notulae bibliographicae de quibusdam operibus Fr. Ioannis Pecham O.F.M.," in *Antonianum*, **8** (1933), 207–228, 425–459; Palémon Glorieux, *Répertoire des maîtres en théologie de Paris au XIIIᵉ siècle*, II (Paris, 1933), 87–98; and *Fratris Johannis Pecham quondam archiepiscopi Cantuariensis Tractatus tres de paupertate*, C. L. Kingsford et al., eds. (Aberdeen, 1910), 1–12.

II. SECONDARY LITERATURE. The best biography of Pecham is Decima L. Douie, *Archbishop Pecham* (Oxford, 1952). Other valuable sources on Pecham's life and thought are David Knowles, "Some Aspects of the Career of Archbishop Pecham," in *English Historical Review*, **57** (1942), 1–18, 178–201; Hieronymus Spettman, "Quellenkritisches zur Biographie des Johannes Pecham," in *Franziskanische Studien*, **2** (1915), 170–207, 266–285; and D. E. Sharp, *Franciscan Philosophy at Oxford in the Thirteenth Century* (Oxford, 1930), 175–207. For a short biographical sketch and additional bibliography, see Lindberg, *Pecham and the Science of Optics*, 3–11.

Pecham's optical work has been most fully analyzed in the following works by David C. Lindberg: *John Pecham and the Science of Optics*; "The *Perspectiva communis* of John Pecham: Its Influence, Sources, and Content," in *Archives internationales d'histoire des sciences*, **18** (1965), 37–53; "Alhazen's Theory of Vision and Its Reception in the West," in *Isis*, **58** (1967), 321–341; and "The Theory of Pinhole Images From Antiquity to the Thirteenth Century," in *Archive for History of Exact Sciences*, **5**, no. 2 (1968), 154–176. Brief descriptions of Pecham's other scientific works are found in *Registrum epistolarum fratris Johannis Peckham archiepiscopi Cantuariensis*, Charles T. Martin, ed., III (London, 1885), lvi–cxlv; and Lynn Thorndike, "A John Peckham Manuscript," in *Archivum Franciscanum Historicum*, **45** (1952), 451–461.

DAVID C. LINDBERG

PECQUET, JEAN (*b.* Dieppe, France, 9 May 1622; *d.* Paris, France, February 1674), *anatomy.*

Pecquet spent his youth in Normandy, first in Dieppe and then in Rouen, where he met Blaise Pascal. In 1642 he went to Paris, where he was a member of the various scientific circles that preceded the Académie des Sciences. He joined the entourage of the Fouquet brothers, François, bishop of Agde, and Nicolas, superintendent of finance. Pecquet enrolled at the Paris Faculty of Medicine around 1646, at the age of twenty-four. Finding the atmosphere unfavorable, he matriculated at Montpellier on 15 July 1651, received his *licence* on 16 February 1652, and defended his doctoral thesis on 23 March 1652.

Pecquet subsequently returned to Paris, where he had both worldly and scientific careers. He was physician to Nicolas Fouquet, as well as to the Marquise de Sévigné, her daughter, and her grandchildren; his name occasionally appears in the marquise's correspondence. Pecquet was also friendly with the Paris scientists Jacques Mentel, Louis Gayant, Adrien Auzout, and Claude Perrault. He probably knew Steno from the time of the latter's visit to Paris (1664–1665), as well as other, less notable foreign physicians, including Martin Bogdan, municipal physician of Bern.

The quantity of Pecquet's scientific production was slight. He participated in experiments on the transfusion of blood performed in 1666–1667 at the Académie des Sciences, as did his friends Gayant (provost of the *communauté* of the surgeons of Paris and consulting surgeon to the royal army) and Perrault.

The *Mémoires de l'Académie royale des sciences* for 1666 to 1669 (**10** [Paris, 1730], 476–477) mentions a note on liver parasites. Pecquet also debated the question of the agent of vision with Mariotte (1669), who contended that it was in the choroid coat; Pecquet believed the retina to be the sensory membrane. Pecquet's only important accomplishment was the discovery of the chyle reservoir, which he called the *receptaculum chyli*—not *cisterna*, a word introduced into anatomical nomenclature by his friend Thomas Bartholin.

To understand the genesis of Pecquet's investigations, it is important to remember that when he began them, the great discovery dividing and preoccupying physicians was that of the circulation of the blood. Harvey had announced it in 1628 and returned to it in 1649 in his two letters to Jean Riolan, dean of the Paris Faculty of Medicine. Rejected by the Paris medical officials, Harvey's discovery was taught at the Jardin du Roi and furnished dissenting physicians with subjects for study, such as the circulation of various body fluids, as well as methodology, *anatomia animata*, the ancestor of experimental physiology. The experimenting physician, who actively examined nature instead of passively contemplating it, was Pecquet's ideal.

Pecquet was probably introduced to the study of the lymphatic system by Mentel, a Harveian physician who had received his doctorate at Paris in 1632. Tradition relates that Mentel had observed human lymphatics around 1629, but it was Aselli's discovery in 1622 of the chyliferous vessels in the dog that drew the attention of researchers to the "white vessels."

Aselli's discovery had also propagated the erroneous idea—accepted by Vesling (1647), among others—that the chyliferous vessels terminate in the liver after traversing the pancreas. Aselli's "pancreas" included both the true pancreas and the groups of ganglia situated behind it in the mesentery.

Harvey believed that the resorption of the chyle occurred in the mesenteric veins and that the liver was the site of hematopoiesis. His chief opponent, Jean Riolan, did not admit the existence of the "white vessels," even though Falloppio had probably seen the lymphatics of the liver and Eustachi had observed the thoracic duct of the horse (*vena alba thoracis*) in 1564. In 1642, the year of Pecquet's arrival in Paris, Johann Georg Wirsung discovered the duct that bears his name; but yet instead of identifying it with the excretory canal of the pancreas, he considered it to be a chyliferous vessel, emerging from the intestine and ending in the pancreas.

It was in these circumstances that Pecquet, while still a student, defied the reigning conceptions and engaged not in the "mute and frozen science" of cadaver anatomy, but in *anatomia animata* on dogs, cattle, pigs, and sheep. Using a dog that was digesting, he showed the following:

1. If the heart has been resected, pressure on the mesenteric root causes the chyle to spurt into the superior vena cava.

2. The chyle is directed toward the subclavian veins by two paravertebral canals that swell when their distal extremities are ligatured.

3. The origin of the ascending chyliferous ducts is situated in a prevertebral and subdiaphragmatic ampulla—"this sought-after sanctuary of the chyle, this reservoir sought with so much difficulty."

4. The posterior part of Aselli's pancreas is composed of lymphatic ganglia.

5. No mesenteric chyliferous vessel goes to the liver (a fact confirmed by Glisson in 1654), and the inferior vena cava, incised above the liver, reveals no trace of chyle.

The human thoracic duct was rediscovered by Thomas Bartholin, Rudbeck, and Gayant. With Perrault and Gayant, Pecquet eventually observed the communications of the human thoracic duct with the lumbar veins.

Pecquet's discovery was received with great interest and provoked sharp debate, particularly with Riolan. It was warmly welcomed by Bartholin, who distinguished the chylous vessels from the other "white vessels," which he called lymphatics, and by Rudbeck. The latter saw the lymphatic system as a new type of vascular system, long unrecognized because it can be made visible only by special preparations. Nevertheless, the significance of the lymphatic system was still far from clear. Lympho-neural anastomoses were described in terms of Cartesian "nerve tubes." Wharton and Glisson thought that the glands received juices excreted by the nerves and that they eliminated them through the lymphatics. Pecquet, like Bartholin, believed that communications existed between the *cisterna chyli* and the urinary tracts; these structures would short-circuit the renal tubule system and would explain the rapid filling of the bladder after a copious intake of liquid.

Pecquet's friend Perrault likened the thoracic duct to a glandular canal, thus showing that he still believed in humors carried by special vessels and not in "juices" (*sucs*) synthesized by the glands from the blood.

BIBLIOGRAPHY

I. ORIGINAL WORKS. Pecquet's major writing, the *Experimenta nova anatomica*, went through several eds. and versions: *Experimenta nova anatomica, quibus incognitum hactenus chyli receptaculum et ab eo per thoracem in ramos usque subclavios vasa lactea deteguntur . . .* (Paris, 1651); a copy of this ed., with illustrations (Harderwijk, n.d.); *Experimenta nova academica . . . Huic secundae editioni . . . accessit de thoracicis lacteis dissertatio in qua Jo. Riolani responsio ad eadem experimenta nova anatomica reputatur . . .* (Paris, 1654); *Experimenta nova anatomica, quibus incognitum hactenus chyli receptaculum et ab eo, per thoracem, in ramos usque subclavios vasa lactea deteguntur. . . . Accedunt clarissimorum virorum epistolae tres ad auctorem,* in J. A. Munierus, *De venis tam lacteis thoracicis quam lymphaticis . . .* (Genoa, 1654); and *Experimenta nova anatomica . . . chyli motu* (Amsterdam, 1661). An English trans. is *New Anatomical Experiments by Which the Hitherto Unknown Receptacle of the Chyle and the Transmission From Thence to the Subclavial Veines by the Now Discovered Lacteal Chanels of the Thorax Is Plainly Made Apear in Brutes . . . Being an Anatomical Historie Publickly Propos'd by Thomas Bartoline to Michael Lysere, Answering* (London, 1653).

Other works are *Brevis destructio, seu litura responsionis Riolani ad ejusdem Pecqueti esperimenta per Hyginum Thalassium* (Paris, 1655; Amsterdam, 1661), which is also found in Siboldus Hemsterhuys, ed., *Messis aurea, seu collectanea anatomica . . .* (Leiden, 1654; Heidelberg, 1659); in Daniel Le Clerc and J. J. Manget, eds., *Bibliotheca anatomica* (Geneva, 1685); and in Thomas Bartholin, *Anatomia . . . tertium ad sanguinis circulationem reformata . . .* (Laon, 1651); "Lettre de M. Pecquet à M. de Carcavi touchant une nouvelle découverte de la communication du canal thoracique avec la veine émulgente," in *Journal des sçavans* (4 Apr. 1667), 53–56; and *Réponse . . . à la lettre de Mr. l'Abbé Mariotte sur une nouvelle découverte touchant la vueüe* (Paris, 1668); and "Lettres écrites par MM. Mariotte, Pecquet et Perrault sur le sujet d'une nouvelle découverte touchant la vueüe faite par M. Mariotte," in *Recueil de plusieurs traitez de mathématiques de l'Académie royale des sciences* (Paris, 1676).

II. SECONDARY LITERATURE. There are unsigned articles on Pecquet in A. L. Bayle and A. J. Thillaye, eds., *Biographie médicale,* II (Paris, 1855), 13–14; J.-E. Dezeimeris, *Dictionnaire historique de la médecine ancienne et moderne,* III (Paris, 1836), 689; *Dictionnaire historique de la médecine ancienne et moderne,* III (Mons, 1778), 507–508; Michaud, ed., *Biographie universelle ancienne et moderne,* XXXIII, 247–249; and *Nouvelle biographie médicale depuis les temps les plus reculés jusqu'au nos jours,* XXXIX (Paris, 1863), 443–444.

Bartholin's fundamental investigations on the human lymphatics in 1652–1653 were completed by those made independently in 1651 by Olof Rudbeck. On this subject see V. Maar, "Thomas Bartholinus," in *Janus,* **21** (1916), 273–301, and Axell Garböe, "Thomas Bartholin," I–II. On Rudbeck see *Annals of Medical History* (1928).

See also Berchon, "Victor Hugo et la découverte de Pecquet," in *Chronique médicale,* **21** (1914), 429–431; A. Chéreau, "Pecquet," in *Dictionnaire encyclopédique des sciences médicales,* XXII (Paris, 1886), 202; J. Delmas, "Pecquet," in *Médecins célèbres* (Paris, 1947), 94; R. Desgenettes, "Pecquet," in *Dictionnaire des sciences médicales—biographie médicale,* VI (Paris, 1824), 384–385; P. Gilis, "Pecquet," in *Bulletin de la Société des sciences médicales et biologiques de Montpellier,* 3 (1921–1922), 32–60, with portrait; in *Montpellier médical,* **43** (1921), 627–628; and *Normandie médicale,* **32** (1922), 141–156, 177–191; E. Hintzsche, "Anatomia animata," in *Revue Ciba,* **64** (1948), 2398–2399; Georges Laux, "Tricentenaire de la thèse de J. Pecquet. L'oeuvre anatomique," in *Séance publique de la section montpelleraine de la Société française d'histoire de la médecine, 31 Mars 1952* (Montpellier, 1952); and "Jean Pecquet. Son oeuvre anatomique," in *Monspelliensis Hippocrates,* no. 37 (1967), 7–12, with portraits and facsimiles; Jean Lucq, "Jean Pecquet. 1622–1674," a thesis at the University of Paris (1925, no. 22); Pagel, "Pecquet," in *Biographisches Lexicon der hervorragenden Ärzte,* IV (Berlin–Vienna, 1932), 543; the anonymous "Jean Pecquet," in *Progrès médical,* ill. supp. no. 5 (1926), 39–40; P. Rabier, "Le centenaire de Pecquet," in *Paris médical,* **46** (supp.) (1922), 171–173; and C. Webster, "The Discovery of Boyle's Law and the Concept of the Elasticity of Air in the Seventeenth Century," in *Archive for History of Exact Sciences,* **2** (1965), 441–502, with illustrations and references.

PIERRE HUARD
MARIE-JOSÉ IMBAULT-HUART

PEIRCE, BENJAMIN (*b.* Salem, Massachusetts, 4 April 1809; *d.* Cambridge, Massachusetts, 6 October 1880), *mathematics, astronomy.*

In an address before the American Mathematical Society during the semicentennial celebration of its founding in 1888 as the New York Mathematical Society, G. D. Birkhoff spoke of Benjamin Peirce as having been "by far the most influential scientific personage in America" and "a kind of father of pure mathematics in our country."

Peirce's background and training were completely American. The family was established in America by John Peirce (Pers), a weaver from Norwich, England, who settled in Watertown, Massachusetts, in 1637. His father, Benjamin Peirce, graduated from Harvard College in 1801, and served for several years as representative from Salem in the Massachusetts legislature; he was Harvard librarian from 1826 until 1831, prepared a printed catalog of the Harvard library (1830–1831), and left a manuscript history of the university from its founding to the period of the American Revolution (published 1833). Peirce's mother, Lydia Ropes Nichols of Salem, was a first cousin of her husband. On 23 July 1833 Peirce married Sarah Hunt Mills, daughter of Harriette Blake and Elijah Hunt Mills of Northampton, Massachusetts. They had a daughter, Helen, and four sons: James Mills Peirce, professor of mathematics and an administrator at Harvard for fifty years; Charles Sanders Peirce, geodesist, mathematician, logician, and philosopher; Benjamin Mills Peirce, a mining engineer who wrote the U.S. government report on mineral resources and conditions in Iceland and Greenland; and Herbert Henry Davis Peirce, a diplomat who served on the staff of the legation in St. Petersburg and who later arranged for the negotiations between Russia and Japan that led to the Treaty of Portsmouth on 5 September 1905.

Peirce attended the Salem Private Grammar School, where Henry Ingersoll Bowditch was a classmate. This relationship influenced the entire course of Peirce's life, since Ingersoll Bowditch's father, Nathaniel Bowditch, discovered Peirce's unusual talent for mathematics. During Peirce's undergraduate career at Harvard College (1825–1829), the elder Bowditch enlisted Peirce's aid in reading the proof-sheets of his translation of Laplace's *Traité de mécanique céleste*. Peirce gave evidence of his own mathematical powers in his revision and correction of Bowditch's translation and commentary on the first four volumes (1829–1839), and also with his proof (in 1832) that there is no odd perfect number that has fewer than four prime factors.

Peirce taught at Bancroft's Round Hill School at Northampton, Massachusetts, from 1829 until 1831, when he was appointed tutor in mathematics at Harvard College; he received his M.A. from that institution in 1833. At Harvard he became University professor of mathematics and natural philosophy (1833–1842), then Perkins professor of astronomy and

mathematics (1842–1880). During the early days of his teaching at Harvard, Peirce published a popular series of textbooks on elementary branches of mathematics.

Peirce's continued interest in the theory of astronomy was apparent in his study of comets. Around 1840 he made observations in the old Harvard College observatory; his 1843 Boston lectures on the great comet of that year stimulated the support that led to the installation of the new telescope at the Harvard Observatory in June 1847. Since 1842 Peirce had also supervised the preparation of the mathematics section of the ten-volume *American Almanac and Repository of Useful Knowledge*, and in 1847 he published therein a list of known orbits of comets. In 1849 Charles Henry Davis, a brother-in-law of Peirce's wife, was appointed superintendent of the newly created *American Ephemeris and Nautical Almanac*, and Peirce was appointed consulting astronomer (1849–1867).

Peirce was not only helpful to Davis in planning the general form of the *Ephemeris*, but he also began a revision of the theory of planets. He had become deeply interested in the work of Le Verrier and John Couch Adams that had permitted Galle's discovery of the planet Neptune on 23 September 1846. In cooperation with Sears Walker, Peirce determined the orbit of Neptune and its perturbation of Uranus. Simon Newcomb wrote in his *Popular Astronomy* (1878) that the investigation of the motion of the new planet was left in the hands of Walker and Peirce for several years, and that Peirce was "the first one to compute the perturbations of Neptune produced by the action of the other planets." Peirce was led to believe that Galle's "happily" discovered Neptune and Le Verrier's calculated theoretical planet were not the same body and that the latter did not exist—an opinion that led to considerable controversy.

In conjunction with his work on the solar system, Peirce became interested in the mathematical theory of the rings of Saturn. In 1850 George Phillips Bond, assistant in the Harvard College observatory, discovered Saturn's dusky ring and on 15 April 1851 announced to a meeting of the American Academy of Arts and Sciences his belief that the rings were fluid, multiple, and variable in number. Peirce published several mathematical papers on the constitution of the rings in which he reached the same conclusion concerning their fluidity. His review of the problem at that time led to a most unfortunate priority dispute.

Peirce also enjoyed a distinguished career in the U.S. Coast Survey. In 1852 he accepted a commission —at the request of Alexander Dallas Bache, who was then superintendent—to work on the determination of longitude for the Survey. This project involved Peirce in a thorough investigation of the question of errors of observation; his article "Criterion for the Rejection of Doubtful Observations" appeared in B. A. Gould's *Astronomical Journal* in July 1852. The criterion was designed to determine the most probable hypothesis whereby a set of observations might be divided into normal and abnormal, when "the greater part is to be regarded as normal and subject to the ordinary law of error adopted in the method of least squares, while a smaller unknown portion is abnormal and subject to some obscure source of error." Some authorities regarded "Peirce's criterion"—which gave good discrimination and acceptable practical results—as one of his most important contributions, although it has since been demonstrated to be invalid.

After Bache's death Peirce became superintendent of the Coast Survey (1867–1874), while maintaining his association with Harvard. He arranged to carry forward Bache's plans for a geodetic system that would extend from the Atlantic to the Gulf. This project laid the foundation for a general map of the country independent of detached local surveys. Peirce's principal contribution to the development of the Survey is thought to have been the initiation of a geodetic connection between the surveys of the Atlantic and Pacific coasts. He superintended the measurement of the arc of the thirty-ninth parallel in order to join the Atlantic and Pacific systems of triangulation.

Peirce also took personal charge of the U.S. expedition that went to Sicily to observe the solar eclipse of 22 December 1870, and, as a member of the transit of Venus commission, sent out two Survey parties— one to Nagasaki and the other to Chatham Island —in 1874. Peirce also played a role in the acquisition of Alaska by the United States in 1867, since in that year he sent out a reconnaissance party, whose reports were important aids to proponents of the purchase of that region. In 1869 he sent parties to observe the eclipse of the sun in Alaska and in the central United States.

Peirce's eminence made him influential in the founding of scientific institutions in the United States. In 1847 the American Academy of Arts and Sciences appointed him to a committee of five in order to draw up a program for the organization of the Smithsonian Institution. From 1855 to 1858 he served with Bache and Joseph Henry on a council to organize the Dudley observatory at Albany, New York, under the direction of B. A. Gould. In 1863 he became one of the fifty incorporators of the National Academy of Sciences.

Despite his many administrative obligations, Peirce continued to do mathematics in the 1860's. He read before the National Academy of Sciences a number of papers on algebra, which had resulted from his interest in Hamilton's calculus of quaternions and finally led to

Peirce's study of possible systems of multiple algebras. In 1870 his *Linear Associative Algebra* appeared as a memoir for the National Academy and was lithographed in one hundred copies for private circulation. The opening sentence states that "Mathematics is the science which draws necessary conclusions." George Bancroft received the fifty-second copy of the work, and in an accompanying letter (preserved in the manuscript division of the New York Public Library) Peirce explained that

> This work undertakes the investigation of all possible single, double, triple, quadruple, and quintuple Algebras which are subject to certain simple and almost indispensable conditions. The conditions are those well-known to algebraists by the terms of *distributive* and *associative* which are defined on p. 21. It also contains the investigation of all sextuple algebras of a certain class, i.e., of those which contain what is called in this treatise an *idempotent* element.

D. E. Smith and J. Ginsburg, in their *History of Mathematics Before 1900*, speak of Peirce's memoir as "one of the few noteworthy achievements in the field of mathematics in America before the last quarter of the century." It was published posthumously in 1881 under the editorship of his son Charles Sanders Peirce (*American Journal of Mathematics*, **4**, no. 2, 97–229).

In *A System of Analytic Mechanics* (1855) Peirce again set forth the principles and methods of the science as a branch of mathematical theory, a subject he developed from the idea of the "potential." The book has been described as the most important mathematical treatise that had been produced in the United States up to that time. Peirce's treatment of mechanics has also been said, by Victor Lenzen, to be "on the highest level of any work in the field in English until the appearance of Whittaker's *Analytical Dynamics*" in 1904. Peirce was widely honored by both American and foreign scholarly and scientific societies.

BIBLIOGRAPHY

I. ORIGINAL WORKS. Peirce's works include *An Elementary Treatise on Sound* (Boston, 1836); *An Elementary Treatise on Algebra* (Boston, 1837), to which are added exponential equations and logarithms; *An Elementary Treatise on Plane and Solid Geometry* (Boston, 1837); *An Elementary Treatise on Plane and Spherical Trigonometry, . . . Particularly Adapted to Explaining the Construction of Bowditch's Navigator and the Nautical Almanac* (Boston, 1840); *An Elementary Treatise on Curves, Functions, and Forces,* 2 vols. (Boston, 1841, 1846); and *Tables of the Moon* (Washington, D.C., 1853) for the *American Ephemeris and Nautical Almanac. Tables of the*

Moon was used in taking the *Ephemeris* up to the volume for 1883 and was constructed from Plana's theory, with Airy's and Longstreth's corrections, Hansen's two inequalities of long period arising from the action of Venus, and Hansen's values of the secular variations of the mean motion and of the motion of the perigee.

Later works are *A System of Analytic Mechanics* (Boston, 1855); *Linear Associative Algebra* (1870), edited by C. S. Peirce, which appeared in *American Journal of Mathematics*, **4** (1881), 97–229, and in a separate vol. (New York, 1882); and James Mills Peirce, ed., *Ideality in the Physical Sciences*, Lowell Institute Lectures of 1879 (Boston, 1881).

Peirce's unpublished letters are in the National Archives, Washington, D. C., and in the Benjamin Peirce and Charles S. Peirce collections of Harvard University.

II. SECONDARY LITERATURE. On Peirce and his work, see reminiscences by Charles W. Eliot, A. Lawrence Lowell, W. E. Byerly, Arnold B. Chace, and a biographical sketch by R. C. Archibald, in *American Mathematical Monthly*, **32** (1925), repr. as a monograph, with four new portraits and addenda (Oberlin, 1925), which contains in sec. 6 a listing with occasional commentary of Peirce's writings and massive references to writings about him. See also Bessie Zaban Jones and Lyle Gifford Boyd, *The Harvard College Observatory* (Cambridge, Mass., 1971), esp. the chap. entitled "The Two Bonds," which gives a detailed description of the unhappy relationship that developed between Peirce and George and William Bond.

See further R. C. Archibald, in *Dictionary of American Biography* (New York, 1934); A. Hunter Dupree, "The Founding of the National Academy of Sciences—A Reinterpretation," in *Proceedings of the American Philosophical Society*, **101**, no. 5 (1957), 434–441; M. King, ed., *Benjamin Peirce . . . A Memorial Collection* (Cambridge, Mass., 1881); Victor Lenzen, *Benjamin Peirce and the United States Coast Survey* (San Francisco, 1968); Simon Newcomb, *Popular Astronomy* (New York, 1878), esp. pp. 350 (on the rings of Saturn), 363 (on the perturbation of Neptune), and 403 (on comets); H. A. Newton, "Benjamin Peirce," in *Proceedings of the American Academy of Arts and Sciences*, 16, n.s., **8**, pt. 2 (1881), 443–454, repr. in *American Journal of Science*, 3rd ser., **22**, no. 129 (1881), 167–178; James Mills Peirce, in *Lamb's Biographical Dictionary of the United States*, VI (Boston, 1903), 198; and Poggendorff, II (1863), 387–388; and III (1858–1883), 1012–1013. See also F. C. Pierce, *Peirce Genealogy* (Worcester, Mass., 1880).

CAROLYN EISELE

PEIRCE, BENJAMIN OSGOOD, II (*b.* Beverly, Massachusetts, 11 February 1854; *d.* Cambridge, Massachusetts, 14 January 1914), *mathematics, physics.*

Peirce's father, who bore the same names, was by 1849 a merchant in the South African trade, having previously been professor of chemistry and natural philosophy at Mercer University, Macon, Georgia. His mother was Mehetable Osgood Seccomb of Salem, Massachusetts. Peirce and his father were close companions, and in 1864 they traveled together to the Cape of Good Hope. They shared a love of music; Peirce's father played the flute and Peirce himself frequently sang in Oratorio and Choral Society performances. Later in his professional career at Harvard, Peirce served as a member of the committee on honors and higher degrees in music.

In 1872, after a two-year apprenticeship as a carpenter (during which he read extensively and perfected the Latin his father had taught him) Peirce was admitted to Harvard College. He became the first research student of John Trowbridge and published, during his junior year, a paper that revealed a "remarkable knowledge of Becquerel, Rowland, Maxwell, and Thomson; a remarkable use of electromagnetic equipment; a remarkable application of mathematics." Under Trowbridge's influence he investigated magnetization; he later developed an interest in problems in heat conduction, and wrote a number of papers on those subjects.

Peirce was graduated in 1876 with highest honors in physics. During the next year, he served as laboratory assistant to Trowbridge and then studied under Wiedemann in Leipzig, where he took the Ph.D. (1879). In 1880 he worked in Helmholtz' laboratory in Berlin, where he met Karl Pearson, who became his lifelong friend. He also met Isabella Turnbull Landreth, a student in the conservatory of music, and they were married in her native Scotland in 1882. They had two daughters.

Peirce's research efforts in Germany were in a sense unrewarding. Edwin Hall wrote of the "unhappy turn of fate" that led Peirce to devote "a year or more of intense labor on gas batteries at a time when physical chemistry was floundering through a bog of experimentation . . . misdirected by the false proposition that the electromotive force of a battery should be calculable from the heat yielded by the chemical operations occurring in it." Peirce exercised the greatest care in testing some 400 batteries, of six different types, and found no data to support this principle, which had been advocated by Wiedemann and by William Thomson. Although he regretfully recorded his findings, he did not openly challenge such authorities, and Wiedemann and Thomson's theorem was only later disproved by J. Willard Gibbs and Helmholtz.

In 1880 Peirce returned to the United States and taught for one year at the Boston Latin School. He began his teaching career at Harvard University as an instructor in 1881, and in 1888, following Lovering's retirement, was appointed Hollis professor of mathematics and natural philosophy. He soon established himself as an able administrator.

In 1883 Peirce was one of the first scientists to study retinal sensitivity by means of the spectrum instead of revolving discs. But his 1889 work, "Perception of Horizontal and of Vertical Lines," was essentially psychological. The full extent of his mathematical talent was first revealed in 1891, in a paper entitled "On Some Theorems Which Connect Together Certain Line and Surface Integrals." His *Short Table of Integrals*, which eventually became an indispensable reference tool for scientists and mathematicians, was first published as a pamphlet in 1889.

Peirce was a member of various American and foreign societies. In 1913 he served as president of the American Physical Society, which he had helped to organize, and as vice-president of the American Mathematical Society. He also served as an editor of the *Physical Review*. He was a cousin, at several removes, of Charles Sanders Peirce.

BIBLIOGRAPHY

I. Original Works. Poggendorff, III, col. 1013; IV, cols. 1128–1129; and V, cols. 952–953, gives a detailed bibliography. Peirce's major works are *Elements of the Theory of the Newtonian Potential Function* (Boston, 1888); *A Short Table of Integrals*, issued as a pamphlet in 1889, but subsequently published in Byerly, ed., *Elements of the Integral Calculus* (Boston, 1889) and enlarged in many later eds.; and *Mathematical and Physical Papers, 1903–1913* (Cambridge, Mass., 1926), which contains 56 papers. Peirce's papers and correspondence are preserved in the archives of Harvard College.

II. Secondary Literature. For works on Peirce and his work, see *American Men of Science*, 2nd ed. (Lancaster, Pa., 1910), p. 364; R. Archibald, in *Dictionary of American Biography*, XIV, 397–398; *Boston Transcript* (14 Jan. 1914); Edwin Hall, *et al.*, "Harvard University Minute on the Life and Services of Professor Benjamin Osgood Peirce," in the university archives, repr. from *Harvard University Gazette* (21 Feb. 1914); Edwin Hall, "Biographical Memoir of Benjamin Osgood Peirce," in *Biographical Memoirs. National Academy of Sciences*, **8** (1919), 437–466, which also contains a complete bibliography of his mathematical and physical papers; *Lamb's Biographical Dictionary of the United States*, VI (Boston, 1903), 198; J. Trowbridge, "Benjamin Osgood Peirce," in *Harvard Grads's Magazine* (Mar. 1914); A. G. Webster, "Benjamin Osgood Peirce," in *Science* (1914), repr. in *Nation* (23 Apr. 1914); and *Who's Who in America, 1912–1913*.

Carolyn Eisele

PEIRCE, CHARLES SANDERS (*b.* Cambridge, Massachusetts, 10 September 1839; *d.* Milford, Pennsylvania, 19 April 1914), *logic, geodesy, mathematics, philosophy, history of science.*

Peirce frequently asserted that he was reared in a laboratory. His father, Benjamin Peirce, was professor of mathematics and natural philosophy at Harvard University at the time of Charles's birth; he personally supervised his son's early education and inculcated in him an analytic and scientific mode of thought. Peirce attended private schools in Cambridge and Boston; he was then sent to the Cambridge High School, and, for a term, to E. S. Dixwell's School, to prepare for Harvard. While at college (1855–1859), Peirce studied Schiller's *Aesthetische Briefe* and Kant's *Kritik der reinen Vernunft*, both of which left an indelible mark on his thought. He took the M.A. at Harvard (1862) and the Sc.B. in chemistry, *summa cum laude*, in the first class to graduate from the Lawrence Scientific School (1863). Despite his father's persistent efforts to encourage him to make a career of science, Peirce preferred the study of methodology and logic.

Upon graduation from Harvard, Peirce felt that he needed more experience in methods of scientific investigation, and he became a temporary aide in the U.S. Coast Survey (1859). For six months during the early 1860's he also studied, under Louis Agassiz, the techniques of classification, a discipline that served him well in his logic research. Like Comte, Peirce later set up a hierarchy of the sciences in which the methods of one science might be adapted to the investigation of those under it on the ladder. Mathematics occupied the top rung, since its independence of the actualities in nature and its concern with the framing of hypotheses and the study of their consequences made its methodology a model for handling the problems of the real world and also supplied model transforms into which such problems might be cast and by means of which they might be resolved.

Peirce was appointed a regular aide in the U.S. Coast Survey on 1 July 1861 and was thereby exempted from military service. On 1 July 1867 he was appointed assistant in the Survey, a title he carried until his resignation on 31 December 1891. In the early days his assignments were diverse. He observed in the field the solar eclipse of 1869 in the United States and selected the site in Sicily from which an American expedition—headed by his father and including both himself and his wife—observed the solar eclipse of 22 December 1870. He was temporarily in charge of the Coast Survey Office in 1872, and on 30 November of that year his father appointed him to "take charge of the Pendulum Experiments of the Coast Survey." Moreover he was to "investigate the law of deviations of the plumb line and of the azimuth from the spheroidal theory of the earth's figure." He was further directed to continue under Winlock the astronomical work that he had begun in 1869, while an assistant at the Harvard College Observatory; his observations, completed in 1875, were published in 1878 in the still important *Photometric Researches*. He was an assistant computer for the nautical almanac in 1873, and a special assistant in gravity research from 1884 to 1891. During the 1880's, however, Peirce found it increasingly difficult, under the changing administration of the Survey, to conform to the instructions issued him; in 1891 he tendered a forced resignation and left government service. (In 1962 a Coast and Geodetic Survey vessel was named for him, in somewhat belated recognition of his many contributions.)

Peirce's astronomical work, which he began in 1867, was characterized as "pioneer" by Solon I. Bailey, director of the Harvard Observatory in 1920. Peirce attempted to reform existing scales of magnitudes with the aid of instrumental photometry, and he investigated the form of the galactic cluster in which the sun is situated, the determination of which was "the chief end of the observations of the magnitude of the stars."

From April 1875 to August 1876 Peirce was in Europe to learn the use of the new convertible pendulum, "to compare it with those of the European measure of a degree and the Swiss Survey," and to compare his "invariable pendulums in the manner which has been usual by swinging them in London and Paris." In England he met Lockyer, Clifford, Stokes, and Airy; and in Berlin, Johann Jacob Baeyer, the director of the Prussian Geodetic Institute, where Peirce compared the two standards of the German instrument and the American one. He was invited to attend the meetings of the European Geodetic Association held in Paris during the summer of 1875, and there made a name as a research geodesist. His discovery of an error in European measurement, which was due to the flexure of the pendulum stand, led to the important twenty-three-page report that Plantamour read for him at Geneva on 27 October 1877. The first Peirce pendulum was invented in June 1878 and superseded the Repsold model used in the Coast and Geodetic Survey. Although the United States did not become a member of the International Geodetic Association until 1889, Peirce's geodetic work was widely recognized. His paper on the value of gravity, read to the French Academy on 14 June 1880, was enthusiastically received, and he was invited to attend a conference on the pendulum of the Bureau des Longitudes.

In 1879 Peirce succeeded in determining the length of the meter from a wavelength of light. Benjamin Peirce described this feat, an adumbration of the work of Michelson, as "the only sure determination of the meter, by which it could be recovered if it were to be lost to science." By 1882 Peirce was engaged in a mathematical study of the relation between the variation of gravity and the figure of the earth. He claimed that "divergencies from a spherical form can at once be detected in the earth's figure by this means," and that "this result puts a new face on the relation of pendulum work to geodesy."

Peirce's mathematical inventiveness was fostered by his researches for the Coast Survey. His theory of conformal map projections grew out of his studies of gravity and resulted in his quincuncial map projection of 1876, which has been revived by the Coast Survey in chart no. 3092 to depict international air routes. This invention represented the first application of elliptic functions and Jacobian elliptic integrals to conformal mapping for geographical purposes. Peirce was further concerned with topological mapping and with the "Geographical Problem of the Four Colors" set forth by A. B. Kempe. The existential graphs that he invented as a means of diagrammatic logical analysis (and which he considered his *chef d'oeuvre*) grew out of his experiments with topological graphic elements. These reflect the influence on his thought of Tait's historic work on knots and the linkage problems of Kempe, as well as his own belief in the efficacy of diagrammatic thinking.

Peirce's interest in the linkage problem is first documented in the report of a meeting of the Scientific Association at the Johns Hopkins University, where Peirce was, from 1879 to 1884, a lecturer in logic and was closely associated with members of the mathematics department directed by J. J. Sylvester. (It was Sylvester who arranged for the posthumous republication, with addenda and notes by Charles Peirce, of Benjamin Peirce's *Linear Associative Algebra*.) Peirce had persuaded his father to write that work, and his father's mathematics influenced his own. J. B. Shaw has pointed out that two other lines of linear associative had been followed besides the direct one of Benjamin Peirce, one by use of the continuous group first announced by Poincaré and the other by use of the matrix theory first noted by Charles Peirce. Peirce was the first to recognize the quadrate linear associative algebras identical with matrices in which the units are letter pairs. He did not, however, regard this combination as a product, as did J. W. Gibbs in his "Elements of Vector Analysis" of 1884. Gibbs's double-dot product, according to Percey F. Smith, "is exactly that of C. S. Peirce's vids, and accordingly the algebra of dyadics based upon the double-dot law of multiplication is precisely the matricular algebra" of Peirce. In his *History of Mathematics*, Florian Cajori wrote that "C. S. Peirce showed that of all linear associative algebras there are only three in which division is unambiguous. These are ordinary single algebra, ordinary double algebra, and quaternions, from which the imaginary scalar is excluded. He showed that his father's algebras are operational and matricular." Peirce's work on nonions was to lead to a priority dispute with Sylvester.

By the time Peirce left the Johns Hopkins University, he had taken up the problem of continuity, a pressing one since his logical analysis and philosophical interpretation required that he deal with the infinite. In his 1881 paper "Logic of Number," Peirce claimed to have "distinguished between finite and infinite collections in substantially the same way that Dedekind did six years later." He admired the logical ingenuity of Fermat's method of "infinite descent" and used it consistently, in combination with an application of De Morgan's syllogism of transposed quantity that does not apply to the multitude of positive integers. Peirce deduced the validity of the "Fermatian method" of reasoning about integers from the idea of correspondence; he also respected Bolzano's work on this subject. He was strongly impressed by Georg Cantor's contributions, especially by Cantor's handling of the infinite in the second volume of the *Acta Mathematica*. Peirce explained that Cantor's "class of *Mächtigkeit* aleph-null is distinguished from other infinite classes in that the *Fermatian inference* is applicable to the former and not to the latter; and that generally, *to any smaller class some mode of reasoning is applicable which is not applicable to a greater one.*" In his development of the concept of the orders of infinity and their aleph representations, Peirce used a binary representation (which he called "secundal notation") of numbers. He eventually developed a complete algorithm for handling fundamental operations on numbers so expressed. His ingenuity as an innovator of symbolic notation is apparent throughout this work.

Peirce's analysis of Cantor's *Menge* and *Mächtigkeit* led him to the concept of a supermultitudinous collection beyond all the alephs—a collection in which the elements are no longer discrete but have become "welded" together to represent a true continuum. In his theory of logical criticism, "the temporal succession of ideas is continuous and not by discrete steps," and the flow of time is similarly continuous in the same sense as the nondiscrete superpostnumeral multitudes. Things that exist form an enumerable collection, while those *in futuro* form a denumerable collection (of multitude aleph-null). The possible different courses of the future have a first abnumeral multitude (two raised to the exponent aleph-null) and the possibilities of such possibilities will be of the second abnumeral multitude (two raised to the exponent "two raised to the exponent aleph-null"). This procedure may be continued to the infinitieth exponential, which is thoroughly potential and retains no relic of the arbitrary existential—the state of true continuity. Peirce's research on continuity led him to make an exhaustive study of topology, especially as it had been developed by Listing.

Peirce's philosophy of mathematics postulated that the study of the substance of hypotheses only reveals other consequences not explicitly stated in the original. Mathematical procedure therefore resolves itself into four parts: (1) the creation of a model that embodies the condition of the premise; (2) the mental modification of the diagram to obtain auxiliary information; (3) mental experimentation on the diagram to bring out a new relation between parts not mentioned in its construction; and (4) repetition of the experiment "to infer inductively, with a degree of probability practically amounting to certainty, that every diagram constructed according to the same precept would present the same relation of parts which has been observed in the diagram experimented upon." The concern of the mathematician is to reach the conclusion, and his interest in the process is merely as a means to reach similar conclusions, whereas the logician desires merely to understand the process by which a result may be obtained. Peirce asserted that mathematics is a study of what is or is not logically possible and that the mathematician need not be concerned with what actually exists. Philosophy, on the other hand, discovers what it can from ordinary everyday experience.

Peirce characterized his work in the following words: "My philosophy may be described as the attempt of a physicist to make such conjecture as to the constitution of the universe as the methods of science may permit. . . . The best that can be done is to supply a hypothesis, not devoid of all likelihood, in the general line of growth of scientific ideas, and capable of being verified or refuted by future observers." Having postulated that every additional improvement of knowledge comes from an exercise of the powers of perception, Peirce held that the observation in a necessary inference is directed to a sort of diagram or image of the facts given in the premises. As in mathematics, it is possible to observe relations between parts of the diagram that were not noticed in its construction. Part of the business of logic is to construct such diagrams. In short, logical truth has the same source as mathematical truth, which is derived from the observation of diagrams. Mathematics uses the language of imagery to trace out results and the language of abstraction to make generalizations. It was Peirce's claim to have opened up the subject of abstraction, where Boole and De Morgan had concentrated on studies of deductive logic.

In 1870 Peirce greatly enlarged Boolean algebra by the introduction of a new kind of abstraction, the dyadic relation called "inclusion"—"the connecting link between the general idea of logical dependence and the idea of sequence of a quantity." The idea of quantity is important in that it is a linear arrangement whereby other linear arrangements (for example, cause and effect and reason and consequent) may be compared. The logic of relatives developed by Peirce treats of "systems" in which objects are brought together by any kind of relations, while ordinary logic deals with "classes" of objects brought together by the relation of similarity. General classes are composed of possibilities that the nominalist calls an abstraction. The influence of Peirce's work in dyadic relations may be seen in Schröder's *Vorlesungen über die Algebra der Logik*, and E. V. Huntington included Peirce's proof of a fundamental theorem in his "Sets of Independent Postulates for the Algebra of Logic" and in *The Continuum* referred to a statement that Peirce had published in the *Monist*. Peirce's contribution to the foundations of lattice theory is widely recognized.

In describing multitudes of systems within successive systems, Peirce reached a multitude so vast that the individuals lose their identity. The zero collection represents germinal possibility; the continuum is concrete-developed possibility; and "The whole universe of true and real possibilities forms a continuum upon which this universe of Actual Existence is a discontinuous mark like a point marked on a line."

The question of nominalism and realism became for Peirce the question of the reality of continua. Nature syllogizes, making inductions and abductions—as, for example, in evolution, which becomes "one vast succession of generalizations by which matter is becoming subjected to ever higher and higher laws." Laws of nature in the present form are products of an evolutionary process and logically require an explanation in such terms. In the light of the logic of relatives, Peirce maintained, the general is seen to be the continuous and coincides with that opinion the medieval Schoolmen called realism. Peirce's Scotistic stance—in opposition to Berkeley's nominalism—caused him to attack the nominalistic positions of Mach, Pearson, and Poincaré. Peirce accused the positivists of confusing psychology with logic in mistaking sense impressions, which are psychological inferences, for logical data. Joseph Jastrow tells of

being introduced by Peirce "to the possibility of an experimental study of a psychological problem," and they published a joint paper, "On Small Differences in Sensation," in the *Memoirs of the National Academy of Sciences* (1884).

William James was responsible for Peirce's worldwide reputation as the father of the philosophical doctrine that he originally called pragmatism, and later pragmaticism. Peirce's famous pragmatic maxim was enunciated in "How to Make Our Ideas Clear," which he wrote (in French) on shipboard before reaching Plymouth on the way to the Stuttgart meetings of the European Geodetic Association in 1877. The paper contains his statement of a laboratory procedure valid in the search for "truth"—"Consider what effects, that might conceivably have practical bearings, we conceive the object of our conception to have. Then, our conception of these effects is the whole of our conception of the object." In a letter to his former student Christine Ladd-Franklin, Peirce emphasized that "the meaning of a *concept* . . . lies in the manner in which it could *conceivably* modify purposive action, and *in this alone*." Moreover "pragmatism is one of the results of my study of the formal laws of signs, a study guided by mathematics and by the familiar facts of everyday experience and by no other science whatever." John Dewey pointed out that reality, in Peirce's system, "means the object of those beliefs which have, after prolonged and cooperative inquiry, become stable, and 'truth,' the quality of these beliefs, is a logical consequence of this position." The maxim underlies Peirce's epistemology, wherein the first procedure is a guess or hypothesis (abductive inference) from which are set up subsidiary conclusions (deductive inference) that can be tested against experimental evidence (inductive inference).

The results of the inductive process are ratios and admit of a probability error, abnormal occurrences corresponding to a ratio of zero. This is valid for infinite classes, but for none larger than the denumeral. Consequently, induction must always admit the possibility of exception to the law, and absolute certainty is unobtainable. Every boundary of a figure that represents a possible experience ought therefore to be blurred, and herein lies the evidence for Peirce's claim to priority in the enunciation of a triadic logic.

Morris Cohen has characterized Peirce's thought as germinal in its initiation of new ideas and in its illumination of his own "groping for a systematic view of reason and nature." Peirce held that chance, law, and continuity are basic to the explanation of the universe. Chance accounts for the origin of fruitful ideas, and if these meet allied ideas in a mind prepared for them, a welding process takes place—a process called the law of association. Peirce considered this to be the one law of intellectual development.

In his educational philosophy Peirce said that the study of mathematics could develop the mind's powers of imagination, abstraction, and generalization. Generalization, "the spilling out of continuous systems of ideas," is the great aim of life. In the early 1890's he was convinced that modern geometry was a rich source of "forms of conception," and for that reason every educated man should have an acquaintance with projective geometry (to aid the power of generalization), topology (to fire the imagination), and the theory of numbers (to develop the power of exact reasoning). He kept these objectives in view in the mathematics textbooks that he wrote after his retirement from the Coast Survey; these works further reflect the influence of Arthur Cayley, A. F. Möbius, and C. F. Klein. Peirce's adoption of Cayley's mathematical "absolute" and his application of it to his metaphysical thought is especially revealing. "The Absolute in metaphysics fulfills the same function as the absolute in geometry. According as we suppose the infinitely distant beginning and end of the universe are *distinct*, *identical*, or *nonexistent*, we have three kinds of philosophy, hyperbolic, parabolic, or elliptic." Again "the first question to be asked about a continuous quantity is whether the two points of its absolute coincide." If not, are they in the real line of the scale? "The answers will have great bearing on philosophical and especially cosmogonical problems." For a time Peirce leaned to a Lobachevskian interpretation of the character of space.

Peirce once wrote to Paul Carus, editor of the *Monist*, "Few philosophers, if any, have gone to their work as well equipped as I, in the study of other systems and in the various branches of science." In 1876, for example, Peirce's thought on the "economy of research" was published in a Coast and Geodetic Survey report. It became a major consideration in his philosophy, for the art of discovery became for him a general problem in economics. It underlay his application of the pragmatic maxim and became an important objective in his approach to problems in political economy, in which his admiration of Ricardo was reflected in his referring to "the peculiar reasoning of political economy" as "Ricardian inference." Peirce's application of the calculus approach of Cournot predated that of Jevons and brought him recognition (according to W. J. Baumol and S. W. Goldfeld) as a "precursor in mathematical economics."

Peirce also sought systems of logical methodology in the history of logic and of the sciences. He became known for his meticulous research in the scientific and logical writings of the ancients and the medieval Schoolmen, although he failed to complete the book on the history of science that he had contracted to write in 1898. For Peirce the history of science was an instance of how the law of growth applied to the human mind. He used his revised version of the Paris manuscript of Ptolemy's catalogue of stars in his astronomical studies, and he included it for modern usage in *Photometric Researches*. He drew upon Galileo—indeed, his abductive inference is identical twin to Galileo's *il lume naturale*—and found evidence of a "gigantic power of right reasoning" in Kepler's work on Mars.

Peirce spent the latter part of his life in comparative isolation with his second wife, Juliette Froissy, in the house they had built near Milford, Pennsylvania, in 1888. (His second marriage, in 1883, followed his divorce from Harriet Melusina Fay, whom he had married in 1862.) He wrote articles and book reviews for newspapers and journals, including the *Monist*, *Open Court*, and the *Nation*. As an editorial contributor to the new *Century Dictionary*, Peirce was responsible for the terms in logic, metaphysics, mathematics, mechanics, astronomy, and weights and measures; he also contributed to the *Dictionary of Philosophy and Psychology*. He translated foreign scientific papers for the Smithsonian publications, served privately as scientific consultant, and prepared numerous papers for the National Academy of Sciences, to which he was elected in 1877 and of which he was a member of the Standing Committee on Weights and Measures. (Earlier, in 1867, he had been elected to the American Academy of Arts and Sciences.) Peirce also lectured occasionally, notably at Harvard (where he spoke on the logic of science in 1865, on British logicians in 1869–1870, and on pragmatism in 1903) and at the Lowell Institute. None of his diverse activities was sufficient to relieve the abject poverty of his last years, however, and his very existence was made possible only by a fund created by a group of friends and admirers and administered by his lifelong friend William James.

BIBLIOGRAPHY

I. Original Works. Bibliographies and works by Peirce include Carolyn Eisele, ed., *The New Elements of Mathematics by Charles S. Peirce*, 4 vols. (The Hague, 1974); Charles Hartshorne and Paul Weiss, eds., *The Collected Papers of Charles Sanders Peirce*, I–VI (Cambridge, Mass., 1931–1935); Arthur W. Burks, ed., VII–VIII (Cambridge, Mass., 1958), with a bibliography in vol. VIII—supp. 1 to this bibliography is by Max Fisch, in Philip Wiener, and Harold Young, eds., *Studies in the Philosophy of Charles Sanders Peirce*, 2nd ser. (1964), 477–485, and supp. 2 is in *Transactions of the Charles S. Peirce Society*, **2**, no. 1 (1966), 51–53. Also see Max Fisch, "A Draft of a Bibliography of Writings About C. S. Peirce," in *Studies*, 2nd ser., 486–514; supp. 1 is in *Transactions of the Charles S. Peirce Society*, **2**, no. 1 (1966), 54–59. Papers in the Houghton Library at Harvard University are listed in Richard S. Robin, *Annotated Catalogue of the Papers of Charles S. Peirce* (Amherst, 1967). In addition, see Richard S. Robin, "The Peirce Papers: A Supplementary Catalogue," in *Transactions of the Charles S. Peirce Society*, **7**, no. 1 (1971), 37–58. Unpublished MSS are in the National Archives, the Library of Congress, the Smithsonian Archives, and in the Houghton Library, Harvard University.

For Peirce's work during 1879–1884, see *Johns Hopkins University Circulars*, esp. "On a Class of Multiple Algebras," **2** (1882), 3–4; "On the Relative Forms of Quaternions," **13** (1882), 179; and "A Communication From Mr. Peirce [On nonions]," **22** (1883), 86–88.

In the period 1870–1885, Peirce published fourteen technical papers as appendices to *Reports of the Superintendent of the United States Coast and Geodetic Survey*. See "Notes on the Theory of Economy of Research," **14** (1876), 197–201, repr. in W. E. Cushen, "C. S. Peirce on Benefit-Cost Analysis of Scientific Activity," in *Operations Research* (July–Aug., 1967), 641–648; and "A Quincuncial Projection of the Sphere," in **15** (1877), published also in *American Journal of Mathematics*, **2** (1879), and in Thomas Craig, *A Treatise on Projections* (1882). See also "Photometric Researches," in *Annals of Harvard College Observatory* (Leipzig, 1878); and preface: "A Theory of Probable Inference"; note A: "Extension of the Aristotelian Syllogistic"; and note B: "The Logic of Relatives," in Peirce, ed., *Studies in Logic. By Members of the Johns Hopkins University* (Boston, 1883).

See also *Charles S. Peirce Über die Klarheit unserer Gedanken* (*How to Make Our Ideas Clear*), ed., trans., and with commentary by Klaus Oehler (Frankfurt am Main, 1968); Edward C. Moore, ed., *Charles S. Peirce: The Essential Writings* (New York, 1972); *Charles S. Peirce Lectures on Pragmatism* (*Vorlesungen über Pragmatismus*), ed., trans., and annotated by Elisabeth Walther (Hamburg, 1973); and Morris R. Cohen, ed., *Chance, Love, and Logic* (New York, 1923).

II. SECONDARY LITERATURE. The *Transactions of the Charles S. Peirce Society* contain a large number of papers on Peirce and his work. There are also interesting biographical notices in a number of standard sources—see esp. those by N. Bosco, in *Enciclopedia filosofica* (Florence, 1967); Murray G. Murphey, in *The Encyclopedia of Philosophy* (New York–London, 1967); Paul Weiss, in *Dictionary of American Biography* (New York, 1934); and Philip P. Wiener, in *International Encyclopedia of the Social Sciences* (New York, 1968). See also *Lamb's Biographical Dictionary of the United States* (Boston, 1903); and *American Men of Science* (1906), which contains Peirce's own list of his fields of research.

Recent books, not necessarily listed in the bibliographies

cited above, include John F. Boler, *Charles S. Peirce and Scholastic Realism* (Seattle, 1963); Hanna Buczynska-Garewicz, *Peirce* (Warsaw, 1965); Douglas Greenlee, *Peirce's Concept of Sign* (The Hague–Paris, 1973); Edward C. Moore and Richard S. Robin, eds., *Studies in the Philosophy of Charles Sanders Peirce*, 2nd ser. (Amherst, 1964); Murray G. Murphey, *The Development of Peirce's Philosophy* (Cambridge, Mass., 1961); Francis E. Reilly, *Charles S. Peirce's Theory of Scientific Method* (New York, 1970); Don D. Roberts, *The Existential Graphs of Charles S. Peirce* (The Hague–Paris, 1973); Elisabeth Walther, *Die Festigung der Überzeugung und andere Schriften* (Baden-Baden, 1965); Hjamer Wennerberg, *The Pragmatism of C. S. Peirce* (Uppsala, 1962); and Philip P. Wiener and Frederic H. Young, eds., *Studies in the Philosophy of Charles Sanders Peirce* (Cambridge, Mass., 1952).

Especially pertinent to this article are J. C. Abbott, *Trends in Lattice Theory* (New York, 1970); Oscar S. Adams, "Elliptic Functions Applied to Conformal World Maps," in *Department of Commerce Special Publication No. 112* (1925); and "The Rhombic Conformal Projection," in *Bulletin géodésique*, **5** (1925), 1–26; Solon I. Bailey, *History and Work of the Harvard College Observatory* (1931); W. J. Baumol and S. M. Goldfeld, *Precursors in Mathematical Economics* (London, 1968); Max Bense and Elisabeth Walther, *Wörterbuch der Semiotik* (Cologne, 1973); Garrett Birkhoff, *Lattice Theory* (New York, 1948); Rudolf Carnap, *Logical Foundations of Probability* (London, 1950); Clarence I. Lewis, *A Survey of Symbolic Logic* (Berkeley, 1918); James Byrnie Shaw, *Synopsis of Linear Associative Algebra* (Washington, D.C., 1907); Percey F. Smith, "Josiah Willard Gibbs," in *Bulletin of the American Mathematical Society* (Oct. 1903), 34–39; and Albert A. Stanley, "Quincuncial Projection," in *Surveying and Mapping* (Jan.–Mar., 1946).

See also the section "Charles Sanders Peirce," in *Journal of Philosophy, Psychology and Scientific Methods*, **13**, no. 26 (1916), 701–737, which includes Morris R. Cohen, "Charles S. Peirce and a Tentative Bibliography of His Published Writings"; John Dewey, "The Pragmatism of Peirce"; Joseph Jastrow, "Charles Peirce as a Teacher"; Christine Ladd-Franklin, "Charles S. Peirce at the Johns Hopkins"; and Josiah Royce and Fergus Kernan, "Peirce as a Philosopher."

More recently published essays by Carolyn Eisele, not necessarily listed above, include "The *Liber abaci* Through the Eyes of Charles S. Peirce," in *Scripta mathematica*, **17** (1951), 236–259; "Charles S. Peirce and the History of Science," in *Yearbook. American Philosophical Society* (Philadelphia, 1955), 353–358; "Charles S. Peirce, American Historian of Science," in *Actes du VIIIᵉ Congrès international d'histoire des sciences* (Florence, 1956), 1196–1200; "The Charles S. Peirce-Simon Newcomb Correspondence," in *Proceedings of the American Philosophical Society*, **101**, no. 5 (1957), 410–433; "The Scientist-Philosopher C. S. Peirce at the Smithsonian," in *Journal of the History of Ideas*, **18**, no. 4 (1957), 537–547; "Some Remarks on the Logic of Science of the Seventeenth

Century as Interpreted by Charles S. Peirce," in *Actes du 2ᵉᵐᵉ Symposium d'histoire des sciences* (Pisa–Vinci, 1958), 55–64; "Charles S. Peirce, Nineteeth-Century Man of Science," in *Scripta mathematica*, **24** (1959), 305–324; "Poincaré's Positivism in the Light of C. S. Peirce's Realism," in *Actes du IXᵉ Congrès international d'histoire des sciences* (Barcelona–Madrid, 1959), 461–465; "The Quincuncial Map-Projection of Charles S. Peirce," in *Proceedings of the 10th International Congress of History of Science* (Ithaca, 1962), 687; and "Charles S. Peirce and the Problem of Map-Projection," in *Proceedings of the American Philosophical Society*, **107**, no. 4 (1963), 299–307.

Other articles by Carolyn Eisele are "Fermatian Inference and De Morgan's Syllogism of Transposed Quantity in Peirce's Logic of Science," in *Physis. Rivista di storia della scienza*, **5**, fasc. 2 (1963), 120–128; "The Influence of Galileo on the Thought of Charles S. Peirce," in *Atti del Simposio su Galileo Galilei nella storia e nella filosofia della scienza* (Florence–Pisa, 1964), 321–328; "Peirce's Philosophy of Education in His Unpublished Mathematics Textbooks," in Edward C. Moore and Richard S. Robin, eds., *Studies in the Philosophy of Charles Sanders Peirce*, 2nd ser., (1964), 51–75; "The Mathematics of Charles S. Peirce," in *Actes du XIᵉ Congrès international d'histoire des sciences* (Warsaw, 1965), 229–234; "C. S. Peirce and the Scientific Philosophy of Ernst Mach," in *Actes du XIIᵉ Congrès international d'histoire des sciences* (Paris, 1968), 33–40; and "Charles S. Peirce and the Mathematics of Economics," in *Actes du XIIIᵉ Congrès international d'histoire des sciences* (Moscow, 1974).

Essays by Max H. Fisch include "Peirce at the Johns Hopkins University," in Philip P. Wiener and Frederic H. Young, eds., *Studies in the Philosophy of Charles Sanders Peirce* (Cambridge, 1952), 277–312, written with Jackson I. Cope; "Alexander Bain and the Genealogy of Pragmatism," in *Journal of the History of Ideas*, **15** (1954), 413–444; "A Chronicle of Pragmaticism, 1865–1897," in *Monist*, **48** (1964), 441–466; "Was There a Metaphysical Club in Cambridge?," in Edward C. Moore and Richard S. Robin, eds., *Studies in the Philosphy of Charles Sanders Peirce*, 2nd ser. (Amherst, 1964), 3–32; "Peirce's Triadic Logic," in *Transactions of the Charles S. Peirce Society*, **2** (1966), 71–86, written with Atwell Turquette; "Peirce's Progress from Nominalism Toward Realism," in *Monist*, **51** (1967), 159–178; and "Peirce's Ariste: The Greek Influence in His Later Philosophy," in *Transactions of the Charles S. Peirce Society*, **7** (1971), 187–210.

Essays by Victor F. Lenzen include "Charles S. Peirce and *Die Europaische Gradmessung*," in *Proceedings of the XIIth International Congress of the History of Science* (Ithaca, 1962), 781–783; "Charles S. Peirce as Astronomer," in Edward C. Moore and Richard S. Robin, eds., *Studies in the Philosophy of Charles Sanders Peirce*, 2nd ser. (Amherst, 1964), 33–50; "The Contributions of Charles S. Peirce to Metrology," in *Proceedings of the American Philosophical Society*, **109**, no. 1 (1965), 29–46; "Development of Gravity Pendulums in the 19th Century,"

in United States Museum Bulletin 240: *Contributions From the Museum of History and Technology*, Smithsonian Institution, paper 44 (Washington, 1965), 301–348, written with Robert P. Multhauf; "Reminiscences of a Mission to Milford, Pennsylvania," in *Transactions of the Charles S. Peirce Society*, **1** (1965), 3–11; "The Role of Science in the Philosophy of C. S. Peirce," in *Akten des XIV Internationalen Kongresses für Philosophie* (Vienna, 1968), 371–376; "An Unpublished Scientific Monograph by C. S. Peirce," in *Transactions of the Charles S. Peirce Society*, **5** (1969), 5–24; "Charles S. Peirce as Mathematical Geodesist," *ibid.*, **8** (1972), 90–105; and "The Contributions of C. S. Peirce to Linear Algebra," in Dale Riepe, ed., *Phenomenology and Natural Existence (Essays in Honor of Martin Farber)* (New York, 1973), 239–254.

C<small>AROLYN</small> E<small>ISELE</small>

PEIRESC, NICOLAS CLAUDE FABRI DE (*b.* Belgentier, Var, France, 1 December 1580; *d.* Aix-en-Provence, France, 24 June 1637), *astronomy, scientific patronage.*

Peiresc was the son of Raynaud de Fabri, sieur de Callas and *conseiller* in the Parlement of Provence, and Marguerite de Bompar de Magnan. Originally from Pisa, the Fabri family had lived in Provence for many years, acquiring property and social standing. The name that Nicolas Claude assumed formally in 1624 was derived from an estate in his mother's dowry, the hamlet of Peiresc high in the Alpes de Provence. Peiresc's education began at Aix and Avignon and continued at the Jesuit *collège* at Tournon, where he made his first contact with astronomy.

In 1599 Peiresc went to Padua, where he met the erudite and generous jurist, numismatist, and antiquarian Giovanni Vincenzo Pinelli (1535–1602). Here also he met Galileo, then a professor at the university. From some time in 1600 he traveled in Italy, Switzerland, and France, visiting galleries and libraries and meeting learned men; he finally settled down to serious legal studies at Montpellier under the rigorous and inspiring teaching of Julius Pacius (1550–1635), a learned Protestant who had taught in Hungary, at Heidelberg, and Sedan before going to Aix, Padua, and Valence. The influences of Pinelli and Pacius stimulated in Peiresc a curiosity about antiquity, the arts and sciences, and the diversity of the natural world; and he viewed these two men as living examples of the Renaissance *virtuoso*: the man of taste and intelligence who communicates his knowledge as he offers his books and instruments for the use and satisfaction of his contemporaries.

Having received his degree in law, Peiresc returned to Aix and was admitted *conseiller* (1604) in the

Parlement of Provence, taking over the seat of an uncle. In 1605 he went to Paris as secretary to Guillaume du Vair, president of the Parlement of Provence, and in 1606 accompanied ambassador Le Fèvre de La Boderie to England, where he met L'Obel, the botanist of James I, and numerous learned amateurs of the arts and sciences, among them William Camden and Henry Savile. He returned to France by way of the Netherlands, meeting other antiquarians and scientists, including L'Écluse, to whom he later sent seeds of thirty-six plants native to Provence and names of others provided by friends in Aix and its environs.

Peiresc's attitude toward natural phenomena was exhibited in early July 1608, when mysterious splashes of red appeared suddenly on walls and trees in and around the city. Popularly attributed to a "rain of blood," the phenomenon was regarded with superstitious awe. Peiresc considered the circumstances and concluded that the red substance had been excreted by the chrysalides of the butterfly *Vanessa*, which was numerous in the summer of that year.

In 1610 Peiresc read Galileo's *Sidereus nuncius* and learned of the latter's discoveries made with the newly developed telescope. Peiresc's patron, du Vair, had already acquired one of the new instruments and with it the astronomer Joseph Gaultier[1] and Peiresc were the first in France (24 and 25 November) to see the four satellites of Jupiter. Galileo named these satellites Sidera Medicea. In 1611 Peiresc observed Venus and Mercury in the morning sky after sunrise, distinguished the crescent phases of Venus, and was the first to see the nebula in the sword of Orion, announced and described by Huygens in 1658.

During these years Peiresc's main interest was the recording of the times of planetary events. The journal he kept from 24 November 1610 to 21 June 1612 preserves a record largely of observations of the relative positions of the satellites of Jupiter, gradually establishing their period of revolution. In this work he had several assistants, the most helpful being Jean Lombard, who made an expedition to Marseilles, Malta, Cyprus, and Tripoli (Lebanon), in each place recording the positions of the satellites in local time. These observations, later collated with time recorded in Aix, permitted Peiresc to calculate terrestrial longitudinal differences. This interest was maintained by Peiresc and in 1635 led finally to a more systematic and successful operation: determining the length of the Mediterranean with a good deal of accuracy.

In 1616 Peiresc again went to Paris in the service of du Vair and remained there for about seven years. Now a mature scholar, he met intellectual circles in Paris on even terms and was soon introduced to the "Cabinet" of the Dupuy brothers, learned librarians and students of law and history, in whose quarters meetings were held weekly for erudite discussions and exchange of news. Through the Dupuys, Peiresc met many men with whom he maintained contact for the rest of his life. Most important for the scientific movement was Mersenne, the Minorite father in whose cell a more specialized group met at frequent intervals. Mersenne and Peiresc regularly exchanged letters, discussing news of books, experiments, observations, and the theories and opinions that were opening fresh perspectives on knowledge of the natural world.[2]

While in Paris, Peiresc made a simple telescopic observation of the comet of 1618; but without mathematical instruments he could take no angular measurements, and he left no record of what motion he had perceived. In the same year Louis XIII granted him the abbacy of a monastic house at Guîtres, north of Bordeaux, the income from which permitted the employment of a priest for ecclesiastical duties and also funds which he could use for the purchase of books. His position as *abbé* was regularized when he took the tonsure in 1624. After du Vair died in 1621, Peiresc remained in Paris until the summer of 1623, when he returned to Provence and remained there for the rest of his life. During his stay in Paris he sponsored or assisted in the publication of important books, representative of his own erudite and scientific interests. These works included the *Epistolae mathematicae de divinatione* (1623) of George of Ragusa (1579–1622), the *Histoire des grands chemins de l'empire romain* (1622) by Nicolas Bergier (1567–1623), as well as the much read satiric novel *Argenis* by John Barclay (1582–1621). One notes that these books were all by men recently deceased or in failing health.

Peiresc's long and fruitful association with Gassendi began about 1624. Gassendi had been teaching in Aix since 1616. When Peiresc returned from Paris he joined Gaultier in urging Gassendi to continue his philosophic writings against Aristotelianism and, later, to develop his discussion of the atomistic philosophy of Epicurus. Peiresc could lay no claim to profound philosophic insight, but he was as discontented as Gassendi with the stagnation of traditional physics. He was fully aware of the changes in intellectual perspective demanded by the accumulation of new facts in every field of human interest. His outlook was that of a collector, rather than of a systematist, who was content to accumulate artifacts and data, books and manuscripts of many kinds, plants and animals, and by correspondence to make his collections and knowledge available to innumerable friends, including many whom he would never meet.

With his associates Peiresc again timed celestial

happenings on the occasion of the lunar eclipse of 20 June 1628, observed in Aix with Gassendi and Gaultier, and in Paris by Mersenne and the mathematician Mydorge. These observations permitted the calculation of the Paris–Aix longitudinal differential with much greater accuracy than had been possible before. Parhelia were observed in 1629 and a solar eclipse in 1631; but the transit of Mercury anticipated by Kepler for 7 November 1631 was missed by Gaultier and Peiresc, who had to admit sheepishly that they had taken too long over Mass and that when they had climbed to the observatory toward noon the sky was clear, the sun spotless, and the transit was over.[3] Thus Gassendi, in Paris, made the only serious observation of the first predicted transit of a planet across the disk of the sun.

From this time on, celestial phenomena were studied with vigor. In 1633 sunspots attracted attention; Gassendi's suggestion that they were actually spots on the solar surface and not small satellites close to the sun was verified. In 1634 an observatory was constructed on the roof of the Hôtel Callas and observations of Jupiter, Mercury, and Saturn were made, mostly by Gassendi. Expeditions to Tycho Brahe's observatory at Uraniborg and to Alexandria had established the meridians of those places, and now a network was ready for larger operations. The lunar eclipse of 28 August 1635 was more widely observed than any other to date, largely as a result of the many priests, merchants, and secretaries of embassies (trained under Gaultier, Peiresc, and Gassendi) who were able to use instruments supplied by Peiresc and to establish more or less effective stations in Rome, Naples, Aleppo, Cairo, and Tunis. Reports from these scattered points, taken with observations made at Aix, Digne, and Paris, permitted reasonably accurate longitudinal distances covering most of the Mediterranean, from Marseilles to the Levant, particularly Aleppo. Results concerning the dimensions of the sea were checked by consultation with experienced pilots in the port of Marseilles.

The work done by Gaultier, Gassendi, and Peiresc in determining the true length of the Mediterranean depended on the development of the telescope, more accurate timekeeping, and the presence of observers capable of using modern instruments at appropriate points on or near the coasts of the sea. The mapping of reference points on the lunar surface and the use of positions of the satellites of Jupiter permitted closer approximations to the true length of about 41°30′ of longitude as opposed to 60° given in the Ptolemaic maps and to the generally exaggerated dimensions of the portolans.

Innumerable personal interests also filled the life of Peiresc. His duties as a member of the sovereign court of Provence, as a *sénateur*, and as a priest of the church, were considerably less exacting than the needs of his gardens and collections, his correspondence, and the call of science as he understood it. He could be deemed a dilettante were it not that the activities he shared or sponsored achieved a degree of success. Besides his work in astronomy, for which Gaultier and Gassendi must be given much credit, Peiresc collected and studied fossils and crystals, as well as ancient coins and medals. He was well aware of the importance of the latter for establishing historical sequences. After Gassendi had sent him Aselli's *De lactibus* (1627), Peiresc sponsored in his house the dissection by local surgeons of a cadaver, finding the chyliferous vessels in the human body as Aselli had found them in other mammals. Similarly, as the fame of Harvey's *De motu cordis et sanguinis* spread abroad, Peiresc planned to trace in the heart the channels in the septum—which Harvey had not found but which a local surgeon, one Payen, claimed to have exhibited to Peiresc and Gassendi.

Peiresc was told of Harvey's *De motu cordis* in early August 1629, a full year after its publication at Frankfurt. In a letter to the Dupuys, 11 August 1629,[4] he told of his interest in the book and on 15 September he thanked them for obtaining a copy for him, asking that it be sent by the post. In the meantime Gassendi had written that he had seen the book before leaving for Germany. He expressed his views in a letter to Mersenne,[5] saying that the circulation through the arteries and veins seems "fort vraysemblable et establye"; but that he finds that Harvey imagines that the blood cannot pass from the right ventricle to the left by way of the septum "là où il me souvient que le Sieur Payen nous a fait voir autrefois qu'il y a non seulement des pores mais des canaux très ouverts."[6]

On 17 January 1630[7] Peiresc wrote to the Dupuys that the book had come; but that he had not been able to read it—"mais à ce peu que j'en ay veu, je le trouve bien agréable." He regretted the death of Payen, the local surgeon whom Gassendi claimed had made a curious observation that Harvey could have used.

Gassendi returned to this subject in the *Vita*,[8] saying that he had informed Peiresc of this excellent new book by outlining its argument and adding that Peiresc had wished to obtain a copy in order to investigate the valves in the veins and to observe other things, including the wanderings (*maeandros*) of the channels of the heart, which Harvey denied but of which "I assured him" (*quos Harvaeus est inficiatus, et de quibus ipse feceram securum*).

There is no reference in either context to anatomical research resulting from the reading of Harvey's book and nothing corresponding to the work on the lymphatics later done under Peiresc's guidance. There is merely a reference, somewhat vague, to a dead local surgeon, who claimed to have discovered certain passages in the septum that Harvey did not find.

In these investigations Peiresc was a sponsor and in some cases the originator of such trials; but the actual work, even on occasion the astronomical observations he recorded, was performed by his staff and associates. There is little reason to believe he himself was sufficiently skilled to perform operations of any delicacy. He was a patron and amateur of science, the arts, and erudition, better equipped to write letters to his friends than to record concisely and effectively the investigations carried out in the Hôtel Callas.

Peiresc's interest in lenses and concave mirrors led him in 1634 to speculate about vision and to study the structure and function of different parts of the eye. With a local surgeon, Cayre, and with his own assistant, Lombard, and occasionally with Gaultier and Gassendi, Peiresc dissected the eyes of a small shark, dolphin, tuna, ox, sheep, owl, and an eagle and eaglet. The results of these investigations are recorded in MS 1877 at the Bibliothèque Inguimbertine, Carpentras. He also recorded personal observations of the behavior of his own eyes, for example, the persistence of afterimages. None of these records were published, although there are references to them in the correspondence; nor did this work lead to theoretical or practical results.[9]

From about 1634 Gassendi lived more or less continuously as a guest of Peiresc while working on the philosophy of Epicurus. Peiresc's health, never robust, declined in early 1637; and it is related that he died on 24 June in the arms of Gassendi, the pattern of whose life was now seriously disturbed. The philosopher sought other refuges and finally turned to the congenial task of writing his widely read and influential book *Viri illustris Nicolai Claudii Fabricii de Peiresc . . . vita*, published in Paris by Cramoisy in 1641 after critical reading by François Luillier, Jean Chapelain, and perhaps others. Through this book Peiresc and his work came to be known to many who had neither visited his collections and library at Belgentier and Aix nor exchanged letters with him. Translated under the title *The Mirrour of True Nobility and Gentility* (1657) by William Rand and dedicated to the English virtuoso John Evelyn, this record of a patron of the sciences takes its place in the literature associated with the rise of organized natural philosophy in England.

An understanding of Peiresc's intellectual position must be derived from his activity taken as a whole rather than from any personal statement. A practical man, he found little reason to think one kind of knowledge superior to another. He believed that an intelligent person can link experience in one discipline with what is learned in another and that cooperation and free communication are the basis on which sound knowledge—that is, science—and therefore human wisdom can advance. It is a mistake to look at merely one aspect of Peiresc's career or to consider it from a special point of view, for in his life of service to learning in all its forms, he exemplified much of what Francis Bacon proposed in his utopian Salomon's House. Peiresc's protest to Cardinal Francesco Barberini (31 January 1635) on behalf of Galileo is typical of his foresight: he saw that in the long run an adverse judgment would profit no man, neither the cause of religion nor the cause of truth, and that Galileo would be a martyr, as Socrates had been, to forces of darkness and ignorance if he were right and to a gospel professing mercy if he were wrong. Like many men of science, Peiresc may be described as a skeptic, which indicates merely that he reserved judgment, awaiting truth as time reveals it. He was a product of the Renaissance in his comprehensiveness, his delight in beauty, and his spontaneous vitality. He took pleasure in old books and coins and in collecting plants and animals.

Peiresc's gardens at Belgentier were in their day the third largest in France, surpassed only by those of the king at Paris and at Montpellier. Peiresc is known to have had jasmine from India, guaiac from South America, Persian lilacs, Egyptian papyrus, varieties of myrtle, ginger, lentiscus, and *polianthes tuberosa*, as well as foreign grapes. He was fond of cats, introducing the Angora cat to Europe, and briefly possessed an elephant and a type of antelope described as an "alzaron."

Gabriel Naudé, Mazarin's bibliophile librarian, who described Peiresc's house at Aix as a "marché très fréquenté," where one could see "des marchandises très précieuses des deux Indes, Éthiopie, Grèce, Allemagne, Italie, Espagne, Angleterre . . . aucun navire n'entrait dans les ports de France sans apporter pour Peiresc des statues, des manuscrits samaritains, coptes, arabes, hébreux, chinois, grecs, les restes de l'antiquité la plus reculée."[10]

Although Peiresc's ideas were often vague and their theoretical basis imprecise, the spontaneity of his reactions to events and observations led to questions that Gassendi, in particular, deemed worthy of consideration; and he often developed these ideas in directions that Peiresc could neither foresee nor exploit. Bloch has suggested that this combination of two very different intellects was fruitful not only in Gassendi's thought but also in the evolution of science in France. It is probable that the organization of the amateurs of science in the house of Habert de Montmor, where Gassendi spent his last years, was a by-product of the extended periods during which Gassendi participated in or witnessed the intense and sometimes ill-coordinated investigations carried out at the Hôtel Callas and at Belgentier.

Perhaps not skillful himself, Peiresc did not withdraw, as some do, into bookish speculation, but rather drew on the talents of the skilled. His work for science was a natural extension of his taste for the arts and erudition. Two very different men summed up his work: soon after Peiresc's death, J.-L. Guez de Balzac wrote: "Dans une fortune médiocre, il avait les pensées d'un grand seigneur"; and at the end of the century, Pierre Bayle stated: "Jamais homme ne rendit plus de services à la République des Lettres que celui-ci."[11]

NOTES

1. P. Humbert, "Joseph Gaultier de la Villette, astronome provençal," in *Revue d'histoire des sciences et de leurs applications*, **1** (1948), 314–342.
2. *Correspondance du P. Marin Mersenne*, Mme Paul Tannery *et al.*, eds., I–VII (Paris, 1932–), contains much well-documented information on Peiresc and his interests.
3. P. Humbert, "A propos du passage de Mercure, 1631," in *Revue d'histoire des sciences et de leurs applications*, **3** (1950), 27 ff., discusses part of the text of a letter of Peiresc to Gassendi, 22 Dec. 1631, that Tamizey de Larroque left unpublished, doubtless as "trop scientifique."
4. *Correspondance du Mersenne*, III, 156.
5. *Correspondance du Mersenne*, II, 132 ff.
6. *Ibid.*, IV, 208.
7. *Correspondance du Mersenne*, III, 216–217.
8. Also in Gassendi, *Opera*, V, 300–301.
9. Cf. P. Humbert, "Les études de Peiresc sur la vision," in *Archives internationales d'histoire des sciences*, **4** (1951), 654–659.
10. Quoted without source by Isaac Uri, *François Guyet* (Paris, 1886), 41.
11. Pierre Bayle, *Dictionnaire historique et critique*, III (Paris, 1720), 2217. Jean-Louis Gues de Balzac to F. Luillier, 15 Aug. 1640, in *Oeuvres*, L. Moreau, ed., I (Paris, 1854), 474–478.

BIBLIOGRAPHY

No published works by Peiresc are known to exist. His correspondence has been collected in *Lettres de Peiresc*, P. Tamizey de Larroque, ed., Documents Inédits sur l'Histoire de France, 7 vols. (Paris, 1888–1898); 10 vols. were originally planned. This ed. is difficult to use because the editor omitted many passages and sometimes whole letters as "trop scientifique"; also, the classification by correspondents does not facilitate the establishment of historical or biographical sequence. Letters received by Peiresc, the originals of which are scattered, appeared in twenty-one separately annotated publications; they have been reprinted in *Les correspondants de Peiresc*, Tamizey

de Larroque, ed., 2 vols. (Geneva, 1972). See also *Correspondants de Peiresc dans les anciens Pays-bas*, R. Lebègue, ed. (Brussels, 1943).

Francis W. Gravit, *The Peiresc Papers*, University of Michigan Contributions in Modern Philology no. 14 (Ann Arbor, Mich., 1950), lists 193 separate items, ten MSS now lost, and sixty-two secondary MSS, mostly copies. It lists neither the 200 or more ancient and medieval MSS nor the 5,000 books in Peiresc's library. Of the MSS that Gravit lists, nos. 18, 47, 65, 76, 113, 129, 132, 133, 145, and 146 seem to be the most valuable for the historians of various sciences. Gravit also wrote a substantial unpublished diss., "Peiresc, Patron of Scholars" (Ph.D. diss., Univ. of Michigan, 1939).

The basis of any biographical study must be Gassendi's *Viri illustris Nicolai Claudii Fabricii de Peiresc . . . vita* (Paris, 1641; The Hague, 1651, 1655), trans. by W. Rand as *The Mirrour of True Nobility and Gentility* (London, 1657); this work also appeared in Gassendi's *Opera omnia*, V (Lyons, 1658) and was abridged unfaithfully by J. B. Requier, *Vie de N. Peiresc, conseiller au Parlement de Provence* (Paris, 1770). Pierre Borel, a physician from Castres, added factual material to Gassendi's *Vita* in *Auctorium ad vitam Peirescii* (The Hague, 1655).

Pierre Humbert, *Un amateur: Peiresc* (Paris, 1933), and G. Cahen-Salvador, *Un grand humaniste: Peiresc* (Paris, 1951), are the most extensive studies in recent times. Each has a bibliography with reference to original documents and to studies of detail.

Olivier René Bloch, in *La philosophie de Gassendi: nominalisme, matérialisme et métaphysique*, International Archives of the History of Ideas no. 38 (The Hague, 1971), remarks on both the importance of Peiresc's cosmopolitan outlook and his emphasis on observation and experiment in the development of Gassendi's thinking. Seymour L. Chapin, "Astronomical Activities of Nicolas Claude Fabri de Peiresc," in *Isis*, **48** (1957), 13–29, is a good survey of its field, based on the printed material but apparently without fresh contact with the MSS.

Other articles are listed by Alexandre Cioranescu in his *Bibliographie de la littérature française du 17e siècle*, III (Paris, 1965–1966), nos. 53.790–53.925.

HARCOURT BROWN

PEKELHARING, CORNELIS ADRIANUS (*b.* Zaandam, Holland, 19 July 1848; *d.* Utrecht, Holland, 18 September 1922), *physiological chemistry, medicine.*

Pekelharing was the son of Cornelis Pekelharing, a physician, and Johanna van Ree. In 1866 he became a medical student at the University of Leiden, where his interests ranged from chemistry and physics to social and religious questions. The well-known physiologist Adriaan Heynsius appointed him his assistant from 1871 to 1876. A skilled and conscientious laboratory worker, Pekelharing became a licensed physician in 1872 and established a practice in Leiden. In 1873 he married Willemina Geertruida Campert; they had five children. Pekelharing received the M.D. degree in 1877 after a masterful defense of his dissertation on the determination of urea in blood and tissues.

Pekelharing returned to the laboratory after his appointment in 1878 as instructor in physiology and anatomy at the School of Veterinary Medicine in Utrecht. Here he developed his research interests, many of which he maintained throughout his life, without neglecting his teaching duties. Protein digestion in the stomach and its end product, which he called pepton, were thoroughly investigated by Pekelharing's group. His many publications on this subject became the center of much controversy in Europe. He also elucidated the protein nature of pepsin. The study of anthrax led him to take up bacteriology. He went to Leipzig to study with Julius Cohnheim, a student of Virchow's, and in 1886 visited Koch in Berlin. In 1881 Pekelharing was appointed professor of pathology and anatomy at the University of Utrecht. In 1888 his assignment was changed to physiological chemistry and histology. With the neurologist C. Winkler and a growing number of medical students, Pekelharing studied the role of leukocytes in inflammation and phagocytosis. He continued his work with anthrax bacilli and spores. Subsequent investigations included the role of calcium in blood clotting, arteriosclerosis, urine pigments, enzyme precursors, intestinal iron absorption, and hemoglobin and glycogen in oysters.

Pekelharing became interested in nutrition in 1886, when he and Winkler were sent to the Dutch East Indies to investigate the cause of beriberi. They were joined by Christiaan Eijkman. In accordance with the general conviction of his time, Pekelharing looked for and found a microorganism that he believed to be the causative agent of beriberi. Nevertheless, he was not totally satisfied with his findings; and upon returning to Holland in 1887, he convinced the Dutch government of the need for a medical research laboratory in Batavia (now Djakarta). Eijkman was appointed its first director. With the assistance of Grijns, Eijkman subsequently discovered the involvement of a dietary factor in the development of beriberi.

In 1905 Pekelharing reported his efforts to maintain mice on a diet of purified nutrients. Only with the addition of milk as a dietary supplement was he able to do so; and he thus concluded that milk contains an unknown substance which, even though in very small amounts, is essential to the diet. Without these substances, he stated, the organism lacks the ability to metabolize the major nutrients. Since his reports were published in Dutch, Pekelharing's findings received little attention. Nevertheless, he became increasingly interested in the new science of nutrition, and in 1908 his monograph on proteins as food appeared. During World War I he focused his attention on problems of mass feeding. He was also instrumental in the founding of the Netherlands Institute of Nutrition.

In 1918 Pekelharing reached retirement age, but he continued studying and writing. An outstanding teacher and scholar, he was active in the Royal Netherlands Association for the Advancement of Medicine, served twice as its president, and was editor of its journal for many years. Pekelharing was in the forefront of the fight against alcoholism. His many honors included membership in the Royal Netherlands Academy of Sciences.

BIBLIOGRAPHY

I. ORIGINAL WORKS. A complete bibliography of Pekelharing's papers and monographs is given in J. M. Baart de la Faille et al., "Leven en werken van Cornelis Adrianus Pekelharing 1848–1922," in N.V. A. Oosthoek's Uitgeversmij (Utrecht, 1948), 211–217. His major works include "Sur le dosage de l'urée," in Archives néerlandaises des sciences exactes et naturelles, 10 (1875), 56; "Recherches sur la nature et la cause du beriberi et sur les moyens de la combattre," in Baillière et Fils (1888), written with Winkler; "Ueber eine neue bereitungsweise des Pepsins," in Zeitschrift physiologische Chemie, 22 (1896), 233; "On the Proteins of the Glandular Thymus," in Proceedings of the Section of Sciences. K. Nederlandse akademie van wetenschappen, 3 (1901), 383; and "Der Eiweiszverbrauch im Tierkorper," in Zentralblatt für die gesamte Physiologie und Pathologie des Stoffwechsels, n.s. 4 (1909), 289.

II. SECONDARY LITERATURE. On Pekelharing and his work, see A. M. Erdman, "Cornelis Adrianus Pekelharing," in Journal of Nutrition, 83 (1964), 1–9; and H. Zwaardemaker, "L'oeuvre de C. A. Pekelharing jusqu'à son septuagenaire," in Archives néerlandaises de physiologie de l'homme et des animaux, 2 (1918), 451–464.

ANNE MARIE ERDMAN

PELETIER, JACQUES (b. Le Mans, France, 25 July 1517; d. Paris, France, July 1582), *mathematics, medicine.*

Peletier was the ninth of fifteen children born to Pierre Peletier, a barrister in Le Mans, and Jeanne le Royer. His family, educated in theology, philosophy, and law, wanted him to pursue these diciplines. He therefore studied philosophy at the Collège de Navarre (Paris) and read law for five years in Le Mans. But when he became secretary in the late 1530's to René du Bellay, bishop of Le Mans, he decided that his interests were not in philosophy or law.

In 1541 Peletier published *L'art poëtique d'Horace, traduit en vers François*, the preface of which pleaded for a national language, thus anticipating the ideas of the later Pléiade. He also studied Greek, mathematics, and later medicine, always as an autodidact. In 1543 he became rector of the Collège de Bayeux in Paris, a post that soon bored him. He therefore left Paris in 1547 and lived as a vagabond. Among the cities he visited were Bordeaux, Poitiers, Lyons, Paris, and Basel. Working alternately as a teacher in mathematics and as a surgeon, he devoted his life to poetry and science. Peletier shared with the Pléiade, a group of seven poets whose leader was Pierre de Ronsard, a desire to create a French literature. He also stated that French was the perfect instrument for the sciences and planned to publish mathematical books in the vernacular. Temporarily, however, he published only in Latin (1557–*ca.* 1572) because no one would accept his somewhat peculiar French orthography. Peletier's poetry had scientific aspects, especially the second part of *L'amour des amours* (1555), in which he published descriptive-lyric verses on nature, natural phenomena, and astronomy which revealed the influence of Lucretius. He also published two minor works on medicine.

In 1545 Peletier published a short comment on Gemma Frisius' *Arithmeticae practicae methodus facilis.* In 1549 the *Arithmétique* appeared. In this work Peletier tried to satisfy both the theoretical requirements and the practical needs of the businessman. This topic had been previously discussed in Latin by C. Tunstall and Gemma Frisius, but Peletier was the first to combine both in a textbook in the vernacular. Peletier wrote *L'algèbre* (1554) in French in his own orthographic style. In this work he adopted several original and ingenious ideas from Stifel's *Arithmetica integra* (1544) and showed himself to have been strongly influenced by Cardano. Peletier's work presented the achievements already reached in Germany and Italy, and he was the first mathematician to see relations between coefficients and roots of equations.

In the *In Euclidis elementa demonstrationum* (1557) Peletier rejected the method of superposition as nongeometric. His arguments for this opinion, however, were used for the contrary view by Petrus Ramus. A long note on the angle of contact—in Peletier's view not a finite quantity and not an angle at all—was the starting point for various disputes, especially with C. Clavius. This work was vehemently criticized by J. Buteo.

Translations into French or Latin and several reprints, especially of the French editions, indicate that Peletier's works were quite successful. His other mathematical publications were devoted to such topics as the measurement of the circle, contact of straight lines and curves with curves, and duplication of the cube. The basic ideas in these publications often originated in Peletier's discussions with Buteo and Clavius.

BIBLIOGRAPHY

I. Original Works. An incomplete bibliography of Peletier's works is given by C. Jugé in *Jacques Peletier du Mans* (Paris, 1907). His major works include *Arithmeticae practicae methodus facilis per Gemmam Frisium, huc accesserunt Peletarii annotationes* (Paris, 1545), subsequent eds. between 1549 and 1557; *L'arithmétique departie en quatre livres* (Poitiers, 1549), with later eds. between 1552 and 1969; *L'algebre departie en deus livres* (Lyons, 1545; 3rd ed., 1620), with a Latin trans. as *De occulta parte numerorum* (Paris, 1560); *In Euclidis elementa geometrica demonstrationum libri sex* (Lyons, 1557; 2nd ed., Geneva, 1610), with a French trans. (Geneva, 1611); *Commentarii tres, primus de dimensione circuli, secundus de contactu linearum, tertius de constitutione horoscopi* (Basel, 1563), an ed. of the second part also appeared (Paris, 1581); *Disquisitiones geometricae* (Lyons, 1567); and *In C. Clavium de contactu linearum apologia* (Paris, 1579).

Peletier's letter *ad Razallium* against Buteo was published at the end of *De occulta parte numerorum.* The *In Euclidis elementa* of 1573, mentioned by Jugé, is not Peletier's work but one of the many eds. "cum praefatione St. Gracilis."

II. Secondary Literature. C. Jugé (see above) provides a biography of Peletier. For works on his poetry, see A. Boulanger, *L'art poétique de Jacques Peletier* (Paris, 1830); *Dictionnaire des lettres françaises, le seizième siècle* (Paris, 1951), 561–563; F. Letessier, "Un humaniste Manceau: Jacques Peletier (1517–1582)," in *Lettres d'humanité. Bulletin de l'Association Guillaume Budé,* supp. 9 (1950), 206–263; H. Staub, *Le curieux désir. Scève et Peletier du Mans poètes de la connaissance* (Geneva, 1967); and D. B. Wilson, "The Discovery of Nature in the Work of Jacques Peletier du Mans," in *Bibliothèque d'humanisme et renaissance,* **16** (1954), 298–311. His contacts with the Pléiade are discussed by H. Chamard in *Histoire de la Pléiade* (Paris, 1961–1963), *passim,* and in L. C. Porter's intro. to the repr. of Peletier's *Dialogue de l'ortografe e prononciation françoese* (Poitiers, 1550; repr. Geneva, 1966).

Peletier's mathematics is discussed by H. Bosmans, "L'algèbre de J. Peletier du Mans," in *Revue des questions scientifiques,* **61** (1907), 117–173, which uses the 1556 ed. of *L'algèbre*; N. Z. Davis, "Sixteenth-century French Arithmetics on the Business Life," in *Journal of the History of Ideas,* **21** (1960), 18–48; V. Thebault, "A French Mathematician of the Sixteenth Century: Jacques Peletier (1517–1582)," in *Mathematics Magazine,* **21** (1948), 147–150; M. Thureau, "J. Peletier, mathématicien manceau au XVIe siècle," in *La province du Maine*, 2nd ser., **15** (1935), 149–160, 187–199; and J. J. Verdonk, *Petrus Ramus en de wiskunde* (Assen, 1966), 264–268; on his contacts with P. Nunez, see L. de Matos, *Les Portugais en France au XVIe siècle* (Coimbra, 1952), 123–125.

J. J. VERDONK

PELL, JOHN (*b.* Southwick, Sussex, England, 1 March 1611; *d.* London, England, 12 December 1685), *mathematics.*

Pell was the son of John Pell, vicar of Southwick, and Mary Holland, who both died when he was a child. In 1624 he left Steyning School in Sussex for Trinity College, Cambridge. He received the B.A. in 1629 and the M.A. in 1630. By the latter year he was assistant master at Collyer's School in Horsham, and then at Samuel Hartlib's short-lived Chichester academy. On 3 July 1632 he married Ithamaria Reginalds, the second daughter of Henry Reginalds of London. In 1638 the Comenian group, of which Hartlib was a leading member, arranged his move to London; and he soon won a reputation for his knowledge of mathematics and languages. The success of the group was thwarted by political developments; not wanting to take a church living, Pell had to emigrate to secure a mathematical post. In December 1643 he became professor of mathematics at Amsterdam and, in 1646, at the newly opened academy in Breda. From 1654 to 1658 he was a Commonwealth agent in Zurich. After the Restoration, Pell became rector of Fobbing in Essex, vicar of Laindon, and then chaplain to Gilbert Sheldon, bishop of London.[1] For a time he lived with a former pupil at Brereton Hall. He died in London in poverty.[2]

Opinions about Pell's significance as a mathematician have always varied, and a full assessment will be impossible until his writings have been collected and analyzed. Houzeau and Lancaster, and others, have suggested that his "Description and Use of the Quadrant" (1628) and other works were printed. His first publication was undoubtedly *Idea of Mathematics*, which appeared anonymously after circulating in manuscript in an early version before 1630. The work was published in Latin and in English in 1638 and republished as part of John Dury's *The Reformed Librarie-Keeper* in 1650. The *Idea* won Pell "a great deal of repute both at home and abroad" and led to his post at Amsterdam. His arguments are clearly very close to those of Bacon, Comenius, and their followers but also have a large personal element. The tract stressed the importance of mathematics and proposed "the writing of a *Consilarius Mathematicus*, the establishment of a public library of all mathematical

books, and the publication of three new treatises." A copy was sent by Pell's patron, Theodore Haak, to P. Mersenne, who circulated the work; Descartes replied approvingly.[3]

At Amsterdam, Pell's fame was enhanced by his *Controversiae de vera circuli mensura* (1647), which attacked C. S. Longomontanus and earned the approbation of Roberval, Hobbes, Cavendish, Cavalieri, Descartes, and others.[4] In 1647 Pell read his *oratio inauguralis* at Breda and was praised by an eyewitness[5] for the excellence of his delivery and his explanation of "the use and dignity" of mathematics.

Most mathematicians know of Pell through his equation[6] $x^2 = 1 + Ay^2$. Some suggest that Euler mistakenly attributed to Pell some work of William Lord Brouncker, but the equivalent equation $x = 12yy - zz$ occurs in Thomas Brancker's 1668 translation, *An Introduction to Algebra*,[7] of J. H. Rahn's *Teutsche Algebra oder algebraische Rechenkunst* (Zurich, 1659). Pell edited the latter part of the translation. Aubrey, however, stated that "Rhonius was Dr. Pell's scholar at Zurich and came to him every Friday night after he had writt his post-lettres" and claimed that the *Algebra* was essentially Pell's work.[8] If this statement is accepted, Pell should also be credited with innovations in symbolism (particularly $\div$) and with setting out equations in three columns (two for identification and one for explanation), otherwise credited to Rahn. Without further evidence, it is best to assume that there was joint responsibility for these innovations and that Pell's contemporary reputation as a mathematician, and particularly as an algebraist, was not unearned.

NOTES

1. His academic reputation is indicated by his D.D. at Lambeth and election as a fellow of the Royal Society in 1663.
2. Some of his books and manuscripts were acquired by Richard Busby, master of Westminster School, which still has some of his books. The MSS came to the British Museum via Thomas Birch; other manuscripts were left at Brereton.
3. Wallis, "An Early Mathematical Manifesto," *passim.*
4. Dijksterhuis, "John Pell," p. 293.
5. Edward Norgate, quoted by D. Langedijk in " ' De illustre schole ende Collegium Auriacum ' te Brede," p. 131.
6. Whitford, *The Pell Equation*, p. 2. Cajori does not accept or even refer to Whitford's argument.
7. *Loc. cit.*, p. 143, no. 34. The relation between the 1659 and 1668 eds. is discussed in more detail in a forthcoming article by C. J. Scriba.
8. Aubrey's biography was partly checked by Pell himself and later supplemented by Haak.

BIBLIOGRAPHY

I. ORIGINAL WORKS. For a 1967 repr. of the 1638 *Idea* and the 1682 and 1809 versions, see Wallis. Two other anonymous works not cited in the text are *Easter Not*

Mistimed (London, 1664) and *Tabula numerorum quadratorum* (London, 1672). See notes for a reference to his many MSS, often mistakenly said to have been published.

II. SECONDARY LITERATURE. Writings on Pell and his work are J. Aubrey's biography of Pell, Bodleian MS 6 f.53, printed in *Brief Lives*, A. Clark, ed., II (Oxford, 1898), 121–131, and in O. L. Dick's 1949–1950 ed.; P. Bayle, in *A General Dictionary, Historical and Critical*, J. P. Bernard et al., eds., VIII (London, 1739), 250–253; T. Birch, *The History of the Royal Society of London*, IV (London, 1757), 444–447; F. Cajori, "Rahn's Algebraic Symbols," in *American Mathematical Monthly*, **31** (1924), 65–71; E. J. Dijksterhuis, "John Pell in zijn strijd over de rectificatie van den cirkel," in *Euclides*, **8** (1932), 286–296; J. C. Houzeau and A. Lancaster, *Bibliographie générale de l'astronomie* (Brussels, 1882–1887, repr., 1964); and D. Langedijk, " 'De illustre schole ende Collegium Auriacum' te Brede," in G. C. A. Juten, ed., *Taxandria: Tijdschrift voor Noordbrabentsche geschiedenis en volkskunde xlii*, III (Bergen op Zoom, 1932), 128–132.

For additional information see C. de Waard's biography of Pell in *Nieuw Nederlandsch biografisch woordenboek*, III (1914), cols. 961–965; and "Wiskundige bijdragen tot de pansophie van Comenius," in *Euclides*, **25** (1950), 278–287; P. J. Wallis, "An Early Mathematical Manifesto —John Pell's *Idea of Mathematics*," in *Durham Research Review*, no. 18 (1967), 139–148; E. E. Whitford, *The Pell Equation* (New York, 1912); and A. Wood, in *Fasti Oxonienses*, P. Bliss, ed., I (London, 1815), cols. 461–464, and in 1967 fasc., repr. (New York–London).

P. J. WALLIS

PELLETIER, BERTRAND (*b.* Bayonne, France, 31 July 1761; *d.* Paris, France, 21 July 1797), *chemistry*.

The son of Bertrand Pelletier, a pharmacist, and Marie Sabatier, Pelletier was apprenticed to his father until 1778. He then continued his pharmaceutical training with Bernard Coubet in Paris, where he was befriended by Jean d'Arcet, an acquaintance of his father, and Pierre Bayen. In 1782 he became d'Arcet's assistant and lecture demonstrator at the Collège de France, and soon published his first paper, an account of the preparation and properties of arsenic acid.

In 1783, on d'Arcet's recommendation, H. M. Rouelle's widow appointed Pelletier manager of her pharmacy in the rue Jacob. He qualified as a master pharmacist in 1784, the year of his marriage to Marguerite Sédillot, and then bought the Rouelle pharmacy (which is still called the Pharmacie Pelletier). Chemical investigations took up much of his time, however, so he assigned the management of the business to his elder brother, Charles, also a master pharmacist. From 1783 Pelletier was registered as a student in the Paris Faculty of Medicine, but he did not graduate there. In 1790, however, he made two journeys to Rheims, where he passed the examinations for his doctorate in medicine. The Paris Académie des Sciences elected Pelletier in 1792, the year before its suppression.

Pelletier was a skillful chemist, concerned more with experiment than with theory. He spent much time checking and extending the researches of others, and therefore made few original contributions to chemistry. His experimental skill was demonstrated in 1784, when, at the suggestion of the crystallographer J.-B. Romé de l'Isle, he prepared crystals of several very soluble or deliquescent salts by using the techniques of slow evaporation and seeding. In 1785 he confirmed C. W. Scheele's discovery that the gas now called chlorine is obtained from the reaction between marine (hydrochloric) acid and manganese calx (dioxide) and, independently of C. L. Berthollet, he came to the incorrect conclusion that it was a compound of marine acid and oxygen. But unlike Berthollet, Pelletier did not yet accept Lavoisier's antiphlogistic theory; and he followed Scheele in describing chlorine as "dephlogisticated marine acid," even though he thought it was a compound containing marine acid. By the action of chlorine on alcohol Pelletier obtained a product that he regarded as marine ether (ethyl chloride), but it must have been chloral. He considered other "ethers"—sulfuric (diethyl ether), nitrous (ethyl nitrite or nitrate), and acetous (ethyl acetate)—to be formed by the action on alcohol of the dephlogisticated air present in the various acids. He continued to call oxygen "dephlogisticated air" until late in 1787; and it seems that, like his mentor d'Arcet, he accepted Lavoisier's theory and the new nomenclature only after some hesitation.

Pelletier's important series of researches on phosphorus (1785–1792) included the preparation, for the first time, of the phosphides of most metals. The slow oxidation of phosphorus over water yielded an acid that he thought was phosphorous acid, but he did not complete his examination of its salts; in 1816 P. L. Dulong showed that it was in fact hypophosphoric acid.

Copper was scarce during the French Revolution, and in 1790 Pelletier devised a process for recovering it from bell metal (an alloy of copper and tin) by oxidation with manganese dioxide, which attacked the tin before the copper; a good yield was obtained, but A. F. Fourcroy's method of atmospheric oxidation proved to be cheaper and was generally preferred. Pelletier became a member of the Bureau de Consultation des Arts et Métiers and of the Commission Temporaire des Arts, and for both organizations he helped to prepare reports on crafts and industries of national importance. The best-known of these was the report recommending Nicolas Leblanc and Michel-Jean Dizé's process for soda manufacture; but Pelletier also contributed to reports on M. E. Janety's malleable platinum, Armand Seguin's method for tanning leather, the production of soap, and the repulping of waste paper.

Pelletier was appointed assistant professor when the École Polytechnique opened in 1794, and he helped Guyton de Morveau with the course on mineral chemistry. In 1795 he was elected to the Institut de France. He served on a commission of the Institut that investigated methods of refining and analyzing saltpeter for gunpowder manufacture, but he was already suffering from pulmonary tuberculosis and died before the work was finished.

BIBLIOGRAPHY

I. ORIGINAL WORKS. Most of Pelletier's publications are listed in Poggendorff, II, col. 392. His reports on the extraction of copper from bell metal, the manufacture of soda, and the production of soap were written jointly with Jean d'Arcet and others; details are given in the bibliography of d'Arcet, in *Dictionary of Scientific Biography*, III, 561. These and other reports were reprinted with all of Pelletier's scientific articles in a collected ed. published by his brother Charles Pelletier and his brother-in-law Jean Sédillot, as *Mémoires et observations de chimie de Bertrand Pelletier*, 2 vols. (Paris, 1798). As a member of various commissions of the Institut de France, Pelletier contributed to several reports that were eventually published in *Procès-verbaux des séances de l'Académie [des Sciences]*, I (Hendaye, 1910), 32–33 (examination of some minerals with d'Arcet and Claude Lelievre); 71–75 (analysis of an alloy, with P. Bayen *et al.*); 228–230 (report on a memoir by N. Deyeux, with L. B. Guyton de Morveau *et al.*); 244–256 (report on the refining and analysis of salpeter, with Guyton *et al.*).

In 1792 Pelletier joined the editorial board of *Annales de chimie*; he was also a coeditor of the short-lived *Journal d'histoire naturelle*, which was founded by Lamarck and others in 1792 and ceased publication in the same year.

II. SECONDARY LITERATURE. See Sédillot, "Éloge de B. Pelletier," in *Mémoires et observations de chimie de Bertrand Pelletier*, I (Paris, 1798), vii–xxvii. Further information, including the correct date of birth, is given by P. Dorveaux, "Bertrand Pelletier," in *Revue d'histoire de la pharmacie*, **6** (1937), 5–24.

W. A. SMEATON

PELLETIER, PIERRE-JOSEPH (*b.* Paris, France, 22 March 1788; *d.* Paris, 19 July 1842), *chemistry, pharmacy.*

Following the example of his distinguished father, Bertrand Pelletier, Pierre-Joseph chose pharmacy and chemistry as his lifework. In 1810 he qualified as a pharmacist after achieving a brilliant scholastic record at the École de Pharmacie. Pelletier earned his *docteur ès sciences* in 1812 and in 1815 was named assistant professor of natural history of drugs at the École de Pharmacie, but he lectured mainly on mineralogy, which he had studied under R. J. Haüy. In 1825 he was promoted to full professor of natural history, succeeding Pierre Robiquet, and in 1832 he became assistant director of the school. In addition to his academic responsibilities and research commitments, Pelletier directed a pharmacy on the rue Jacob and a chemical plant at Clichy.

Pelletier's early scientific efforts, mostly concerned with the analysis of gum resins and coloring matter in plants, culminated in 1817 with a brilliant work on the isolation of emetine in an impure form. His collaborator in this work was François Magendie. The investigation of gum resins, begun by Pelletier in a report on opopanax in 1811, was followed in the next two years by publications on sagapenum, asafetida, bdellium, myrrh, galbanum, and caranna gum. From 1813 to 1817 his articles dealt mainly with natural products (sarcocolla, toad venom, amber, olive gum) and coloring matter contained in red sandalwood, alkanet, and curcuma (written with H. A. Vogel). In 1817 the discovery by Pelletier and Magendie of the "matière vomitive" in ipecac root, named emetine by Pelletier and verified by animal experiments, was announced in a paper read before the Académie des Sciences.

The period from 1817 to 1821 was remarkably productive for Pelletier, who had acquired a new collaborator in Joseph-Bienaimé Caventou, a gifted young pharmacy intern attached to the Saint-Antoine Hospital in Paris. Their keen interest in the chemistry of natural products led them in 1817 to study the action of nitric acid on the nacreous material of human biliary calculi and the green pigment in leaves, which they were the first to name chlorophyll. In 1818 they obtained crotonic acid from croton oil and analyzed carmine in cochineal. Two years later, in 1820, Pelletier and Caventou isolated ambrein from ambergris. But it was their discovery of a number of plant alkaloids that brought them international fame: strychnine (1818); brucine (1819); veratrine (1819), independently of Karl Meissner; cinchonine, first obtained by B. A. Gomes in 1810 but again isolated and more extensively studied by Pelletier and Caventou (1820); quinine, the most important of their discoveries from a therapeutic standpoint (1820); and caffeine (1821), independently of Robiquet and Runge. Pelletier also published his own research on gold compounds (1820), piperine (1821), and various species of cinchona (1821).

For the remaining two decades of his life Pelletier continued his alkaloid and phytochemical investigations. He also studied the decomposition products of pine, resin, amber, and bitumen. In 1823 the results of a combustion analysis of nine alkaloids, undertaken by Pelletier and J.-B. Dumas, provided conclusive evidence for the presence of nitrogen in alkaloids, a fact that Pelletier and Caventou had earlier failed to ascertain. In 1832 Pelletier reported his discovery of narceine, a new opium alkaloid, to the Academy. The following year he published, with J. P. Couerbe, a study of picrotoxin. But relations between the two collaborators became embittered when Couerbe, Pelletier's former student and *chef des travaux* at his chemical plant, refused to support Pelletier's claim to priority in the isolation of thebaine, another opium alkaloid. Instead, Couerbe gave credit for the discovery of thebaine (called paramorphine by Pelletier) to Thiboumery, who had been employed by Pelletier as *directeur des travaux*. A happier association was subsequently established with Philippe Walter. This collaboration led to the publication of a number of interesting papers on oily hydrocarbons obtained from the destructive distillation of amber and bitumen. One of these studies (1837–1838), of an oily by-product of pine resin used in the manufacture of illuminating gas, resulted in their discovery of a substance that they designated as "rétinnaphte," now known as toluene (C_7H_8).

After 1821, Pelletier and Caventou still conducted a few investigations jointly, including further researches on strychnine and procedures for its extraction from nux vomica (1822); chemical examination of upas (1824); the manufacture of quinine sulfate (1827); and the isolation of cahinca acid, the bitter crystalline substance in cahinca root (1830), with André François. Although ably carried out, this work was overshadowed by their earlier discoveries. Among Pelletier's other collaborative efforts were an analysis, undertaken with Corriol, of a species of cinchona (*Cinchona cordifolia*), which enabled them to isolate aricine in 1829; a chemical examination of curare, with Petroz, in 1829; and a posthumous memoir on guaiacum with H. Sainte-Claire Deville, published in 1844.

Pelletier was named a member of the Paris Académie de Médecine in 1820 and was elected to the Académie des Sciences in 1840. In 1827 Pelletier and Caventou were awarded the Montyon Prize of 10,000 francs by the latter academy in recognition of their discovery of quinine. Both men were also honored in 1900 by an impressive statue erected on the boulevard St.-Michel, which was destroyed during the German occupation of Paris in World War II but was replaced by another monument dedicated in 1951. A firm defender of the established political order, Pelletier was, in Caventou's words, "partisan aussi sincère qu'éclairé de nos institutions monarchiques et constitutionnelles."

BIBLIOGRAPHY

I. ORIGINAL WORKS. Pelletier's earlier papers include "Analyse de l'opopanax," in *Annales de chimie*, **79** (1811), 90–99; "Analyse du galbanum," in *Bulletin de pharmacie*, **4** (1812), 97–102; "Réflexions sur le tannin et sur quelques combinaisons nouvelles de l'acide gallique avec des substances végétales," in *Annales de chimie*, **87** (1813), 103–108, 218–219; "Examen chimique de quelques substances colorantes de nature résineuse," in *Bulletin de pharmacie*, **6** (1814), 432–453; "Mémoire sur la gomme d'olivier," in *Journal de Pharmacie*, **2** (1816), 337–343; and "Recherches chimiques et physiologiques sur l'ipécacuanha," in *Annales de chimie et de physique*, **4** (1817), 172–185, written with F. Magendie. For the most important joint publications of Pelletier and Caventou, see Alex Berman, "Caventou," in *Dictionary of Scientific Biography*, III, 160.

Other representative works by Pelletier, written alone or in collaboration, are "Faits pour servir à l'histoire de l'or," in *Annales de chimie et de physique*, **15** (1820), 5–26, 113–127; "Examen chimique du poivre (*Piper nigrum*)," *ibid.*, **16** (1821), 337–351; "Recherches sur la composition élémentaire et sur quelques propriétés caractéristiques des bases salifiables organiques," *ibid.*, **24** (1823), 163–191, written with J.-B. Dumas; "Note sur la caféine," in *Journal de pharmacie*, **12** (1826), 229–233; "Notice sur une nouvelle base salifiable organique venant du Pérou," *ibid.*, **15** (1829), 565–568, written with Corriol; "Examen chimique du curare," in *Annales de chimie et de physique*, **40** (1829), 213–219, written with Petroz; "Nouvelles recherches sur l'opium," *ibid.*, **50** (1832), 240–280; "Nouvelle analyse de la coque du Levant," *ibid.*, **54** (1833), 178–208, written with Couerbe; and "Examen chimique des produits provenant du traitement de la résine pour l'éclairage au gaz," *ibid.*, **67** (1838), 269–303, written with P. Walter. For a more complete listing of Pelletier's articles, see Royal Society *Catalogue of Scientific Papers*, IV, 806–810.

II. SECONDARY LITERATURE. See A. Bussy, "Discours prononcé à la distribution des prix de l'École de pharmacie pour l'année 1842, suivi d'une notice sur feu Pelletier, par A. Bussy, secrétaire de l'École," in *Journal de pharmacie et de chimie*, 3rd ser., **3** (1843), 48–58; J. B. Caventou, "Discours prononcé sur la tombe de M. Pelletier," in *Bulletin de l'Académie royale de médecine*, **7** (1841–1842), 1011–1016; *Centenaire de l'École supérieure de pharmacie, 1803–1903* (Paris, 1904), 264–265, 283–284, 295–297, 354; Marcel Delépine, "Joseph Pelletier and Joseph Caventou," in *Journal of Chemical Education*, **28** (1951), 454–461; J.-B. Dumas, *Discours prononcé aux funérailles de M. Pelletier, le 22 juillet 1842* (Paris, 1842);

M. M. Janot, "Joseph Pelletier, 1788–1842," in *Figures pharmaceutiques françaises* (Paris, 1953), 59–64; J. R. Partington, *A History of Chemistry*, IV (London–New York, 1964), 244–245, 558, and *passim*; and Horst Real and Wolfgang Schneider, "Wer entdeckte Chinin und Cinchonin?" in *Beiträge zur Geschichte der Pharmazie*, **22**, no. 3 (1970), 17–19.

ALEX BERMAN

PELOUZE, THÉOPHILE-JULES (*b.* Valognes, Manche, France, 26 February 1807; *d.* Paris, France, 31 May 1867), *chemistry*.

Pelouze was the son of Edmond Pelouze, whose interests in industrial technology and invention were reflected in many publications. Pelouze decided originally on a career in pharmacy and after serving apprenticeships in pharmacies in La Fère and Paris, he was appointed to a hospital pharmacy internship at the Salpêtrière in Paris. An accidental meeting with Joseph-Louis Gay-Lussac, whose student and laboratory assistant he later became, changed the course of his life. Pelouze, undaunted by financial hardship, so impressed Gay-Lussac by his zeal and talents that Gay-Lussac became a lifelong patron and friend of the young chemist. In 1830 Pelouze secured a post teaching chemistry in Lille and shortly thereafter competed successfully for the position of assayer at the Paris mint. Further recognition and success came rapidly: he was elected to the Académie des Sciences (1837); he taught and was professor of chemistry at the École Polytechnique (1831–1846) and at the Collège de France (1831–1850); he was president of the Commission of the Mint (1848); he was a member of the Paris Municipal Council (1849); and he succeeded Gay-Lussac as consulting chemist at the Saint-Gobain glassworks (1850).

Beginning in 1830, Pelouze quickly established himself as an outstanding analytical and experimental chemist. His early investigations included studies of salicin (1830), with Jules Gay-Lussac; sugar beet (1831); fermentation (1831), with Frédéric Kuhlmann; conversion of hydrocyanic acid into formic acid; and decomposition of ammonium formate into hydrocyanic acid and water (1831). Later he investigated pyrogallic acid (1833); ethyl phosphoric acid (1833); discovered ethyl cyanide (1834); and found the correct formula for potassium dinitrosulfite (1835). In 1836 Pelouze and Liebig, with whom Pelouze had worked in Giessen, published a long memoir dealing with a number of organic substances, including their discovery of oenanthic ester and the corresponding acid. Noteworthy, too, were Pelouze's discovery of nitrocellulose (1838); oxidation of borneol to obtain camphor (1840); synthesis of butyrin (1843), with Amédée Gélis; production of glycerophosphoric acid (1845); work on curare (1850), with Claude Bernard; and investigation of American petroleum (1862–1864), with Auguste Cahours. Interested mainly in empirical facts, Pelouze was, unfortunately, indifferent to the seminal chemical theories of his time.

In Paris, Pelouze founded the most important private laboratory school of chemistry in France. He trained many students and made his laboratory facilities available for the personal research of Bernard and other French and foreign chemists.

BIBLIOGRAPHY

I. ORIGINAL WORKS. Pelouze published at least 90 papers, alone or with other eminent chemists, most of which appeared in *Annales de chimie et de physique* or in *Comptes rendus . . . de l'Académie des sciences* and were repr. in other periodicals. For listings of these articles, see A. Goris *et al.*, *Centenaire de l'internat en pharmacie des hôpitaux et hospices civils de Paris* (Paris, 1920), 531–532; Poggendorff, II, 394–396, and III, 1015; and Royal Society *Catalogue of Scientific Papers*, IV, 810–814, and VIII, 583.

A major work by Pelouze was his *Traité de chimie générale*, 3 vols. and atlas (Paris, 1848–1850), written with E. Frémy. In later eds. the work was expanded, and it also appeared in a number of abridged versions.

II. SECONDARY LITERATURE. On Pelouze and his work, see J.-B. Dumas, *Discours et éloges académiques*, I (Paris, 1885), 127–198; C. von Martius, "Nekrolog auf Th. Julius Pelouze," in *Neues Repertorium für Pharmacie*, **17** (1868), 506–510; J. R. Partington, *A History of Chemistry*, IV (London–New York, 1964), 395 and *passim*; Warren De la Rue, "Proceedings of the Chemical Society," in *Journal of the Chemical Society*, **21** (1868), xxv–xxix; and Marc Tiffeneau, in A. Goris *et al.*, *Centenaire de l'internat en pharmacie des hôpitaux et hospices civils de Paris* (Paris, 1920), 615.

For Pelouze's relations with Bernard, see Joseph Schiller, *Claude Bernard et les problèmes scientifiques de son temps* (Paris, 1967), 63–64.

ALEX BERMAN

PELTIER, JEAN CHARLES ATHANASE (*b.* Ham, France, 22 February 1785; *d.* Paris, France, 27 October 1845), *physics*.

Peltier was born to a poor family; his father earned a living as a shoemaker. A quick intelligence and perseverance were displayed at an early age, as were mechanical skills. His formal education, however, was limited to the local schools. At the age of fifteen he was apprenticed to a German clockmaker named Brown in Saint-Quentin. He was refused permission to study and was generally ill-treated; after two years, in 1802, his father removed him from this position and apprenticed him in Paris to another clockmaker, named Métra, who had worked for A.-L. Bréquet. After an attempt to enter the army, which was prevented by his mother's disapproval, Peltier attracted the attention of Bréquet and entered his employ in 1804. In 1806 Peltier established his own shop and married a Mlle Dufant. The death of his wife's mother in 1815 brought him a modest inheritance, which was sufficient for their needs, and he retired.

Even while working at his trade, Peltier read broadly; when he retired, he devoted his attention to a wide range of studies and began to compose a Latin grammar. He then became interested in the phrenology of Franz Gall and was inspired, at age thirty-six, to study anatomy in order to obtain a more complete knowledge of the structure of the brain. He attended a number of vivisection demonstrations by Magendie, in which electricity was used to stimulate nerves. These demonstrations led Peltier to the study of electricity, which he pursued for the last twenty years of his life.

Peltier's first scientific paper was delivered to the Académie des Sciences in 1830. In it he showed that chemical effects can be obtained from a dry pile if the surface area of the plates is sufficiently large. This work also showed that Peltier had some understanding of the difference between current and voltage, with which electricians were to struggle for another ten years.

Stimulated by the work of Nobili, Peltier constructed a sensitive galvanometer to measure the conductivities of antimony and bismuth for small currents. Peltier's use of small samples of these nonductile materials was fortunate because the anomalous behavior of these materials led him to construct a thermoelectric thermoscope and to measure the temperature distribution along a series of thermocouple circuits. He discovered that a cooling effect can take place at one junction and excessive heating at the other. He then confirmed this discovery by using an air thermometer in place of the thermoscope.

Peltier did not pursue the effect he had discovered, and its importance was not fully recognized until after the thermodynamic work of William Thomson twenty years later. He did, however, write a paper on thermoelectric piles, and he spent some time studying the relations between static and dynamic electricity.

Peltier's remaining scientific endeavors fell into two major categories: microscopy and meteorology. His work in microscopy was an outgrowth of his anatomical and physiological interests; most of his observations were on various animalcules. In meteorology he made numerous measurements of electrical charges in the atmosphere and developed a theory that accounted for various cloud and storm formations on the basis of charge distribution. In 1842 he conducted a field trip to obtain such measurements. A cold resulting from this trip left him in a weakened condition, from which he never recovered.

BIBLIOGRAPHY

I. ORIGINAL WORKS. A bibliography of more than 60 papers by Peltier is contained in the Royal Society *Catalogue of Scientific Papers*, IV, 814–817. His discovery of the "Peltier effect" appears in "Nouvelles expériences sur la caloricité des courants électriques," in *Annales de chimie*, **56** (1834), 371–386.

II. SECONDARY LITERATURE. A memoir by Peltier's son, F. A. Peltier, *Notice sur la vie et les travaux scientifiques de J. C. A. Peltier* (Paris, 1847), was translated by M. L. Wood in *Report of the Board of Regents of the Smithsonian Institution* (1867), 158–202.

BERNARD S. FINN

PEMBERTON, HENRY (*b.* London, England, 1694; *d.* London, 9 March 1771), *physics, mathematics, physiology, medicine.*

Little is known of Pemberton's family or youth beyond the significant fact that he was introduced to mathematics at grammar school. He read, independently, Halley's editions of Apollonius and then traveled to Leiden to study medicine with Boerhaave. In Leiden he was further introduced to the work of Newton, the decisive event of his intellectual life. Pemberton interrupted his stay in Leiden to study anatomy in Paris and then returned to London about 1715 to attend Saint Thomas's Hospital. Although he took his degree at Leiden in 1719, he never practiced medicine extensively because of his delicate health. He did, however, serve for several years as professor of physics at Gresham College.

Pemberton's thesis, on the mechanism by which the eye accommodates to objects at different distances (1719), was his most important independent work. Treating the crystalline lens as a muscle, he argued that it accommodates to vision at varying distances by changes in shape. Students of physiological optics in the eighteenth century knew the work, and Pemberton ranks as one of the precursors of Thomas Young.

Pemberton's work on the mechanism of accommodation was nearly his last independent work, for he was determined to join the circle of Newton's epigones. He attempted, unsuccessfully, to approach the master through John Keill. But Richard Mead, Newton's friend and physician, showed Newton a paper in which Pemberton refuted Leibniz' measure of the force of moving bodies—an obsequious essay larded with references to "the great Sir Isaac Newton." Although the measure of the force of moving bodies was not an issue germane to Newtonian mechanics, Newton was apparently pleased with the attack on Leibniz. He made Pemberton's acquaintance; and Pemberton sought to cement the relation by contributing another obsequious essay on muscular motion, which converted itself into a panegyric on Newtonian method, to Mead's edition of Cowper's *Myotomia reformata*, completed in 1723 and published in 1724. When work on the third edition of Newton's *Principia* began late in 1723, Pemberton was the editor.

Pemberton devoted the major portion of his attention to the edition during the following two and a half years. He was a conscientious editor who carefully attended to the details of style and consistency, but nothing more substantive in the edition bears his stamp. The third edition of the *Principia* (1726) is the primary vehicle by which Pemberton's name has survived. The meagerness of his contribution, in comparison with the promise of his thesis at Leiden, suggests how deadening the role of sycophant can be.

Pemberton had labored assiduously to earn Newton's favor; apparently he intended to make his position near Newton the foundation of a career. Already he was at work on a popularization of Newtonianism for those without mathematics—*A View of Sir Isaac Newton's Philosophy*, which finally appeared in 1728 with prefatory assurances that Newton had read and approved it. He had also announced an English translation of the *Principia* and a commentary on it. In 1728 he received the Gresham position. Other aspiring young men had also courted Newton, however, and they chose to dispute the inheritance. John Machin, secretary of the Royal Society, sponsored and aided Andrew Motte's rival translation, which beat Pemberton's work to the press. Discouraged, he abandoned the commentary and virtually ended his career as a scientist.

Pemberton was thirty-five years old when Motte's translation appeared in 1729. Although he lived more than forty years more, he did almost nothing further to fulfill his earlier promise. During the 1730's, he was drawn into the fringes of the *Analyst* controversy on the foundations of the calculus. In 1739 the College of Physicians engaged him to reedit and translate their pharmacopoeia—*The Dispensatory of the Royal College of Physicians* (1746). He spent the following seven years on the project, attempting, he said, to purge it of the trifles that disgraced it. From the point of view of medical science, the job was undertaken too soon, and it had to be repeated again before the end of the century. At Gresham College he delivered courses of lectures on chemistry and physiology, which his friend James Wilson later published; both were minor works. Toward the end of his life he returned to his early love of mathematics and published four papers in the *Philosophical Transactions of the Royal Society*.

Pemberton was a man of deep friendships and broad learning. His first publication was a mathematical letter addressed to James Wilson, to whom, fifty years later, he left his papers. In his *View of Newton's Philosophy* he published a poem on Newton by a young friend, Richard Glover, whose continuing poetic efforts evoked pamphlets written by Pemberton praising Glover's work with a show of literary erudition. Glover's political connections led Pemberton to write an essay on political philosophy, which remained unpublished. He also wrote on weights and measures. He was known as a lover of music who never missed a performance of a Handel oratorio.

BIBLIOGRAPHY

I. ORIGINAL WORKS. Pemberton's major works include *Dissertatio physica-medica inauguralis de facultate oculi qua ad diversas rerum conspectarum distantias se accommodat* (Leiden, 1719); *Epistola ad amicum de Cotesii inventis, curvarum ratione, quae cum circulo & hyperbola comparationem admittunt* (London, 1722); "Introduction. Concerning the Muscles and Their Action," in William Cowper, *Myotomia reformata*, Richard Mead, ed. (London, 1724); "A Letter to Dr. Mead . . . Concerning an Experiment, Whereby It Has Been Attempted to Shew the Falsity of the Common Opinion, in Relation to the Force of Bodies in Motion," in *Philosophical Transactions of the Royal Society*, **32** (1722), 57; *A View of Sir Isaac Newton's Philosophy* (London, 1728); *Observations on Poetry, Especially the Epic* (London, 1738); *The Dispensatory of the Royal College of Physicians* (London, 1746); *Some Few Reflections on the Tragedy of Boadicia* (London, 1753); *A Course of Chemistry* (London, 1771); and *A Course of Physiology* (London, 1773).

II. SECONDARY LITERATURE. See I. Bernard Cohen, "Pemberton's Translation of Newton's *Principia*, With Notes on Motte's Translation," *Isis*, **54** (1963), 319–351; and *Introduction to Newton's 'Principia'* (Cambridge, Mass., 1971), 265–286; and the biographical sketch published by James Wilson as the preface to Pemberton's *Course of Chemistry*.

RICHARD S. WESTFALL

PENCK, ALBRECHT (*b.* Reuditz [near Leipzig], Germany, 25 September 1858; *d.* Prague, Czechoslovakia, 7 March 1945), *geomorphology, geology, paleoclimatology, hydrology, cartography.*

Born near the outer limit of the maximum southward advance of the Quaternary Scandinavian ice sheet, Penck took a lifelong interest in glacial deposits. In 1875 he entered the University of Leipzig to study natural sciences. In the same year Otto Torell delivered a forceful lecture at Berlin, which persuaded his audience that the boulder clay of the north European plain had been carried by a continental ice sheet and not by floating ice; he thus vindicated and perpetuated the ideas of A. Bernhardi (1832). Shortly thereafter Penck found and wrote about a northern "basalt" erratic embedded in the diluvium near Leipzig.

At Leipzig, Penck studied chemistry under Adolf Kolbe, geology under Hermann Credner, mineralogy and petrography under Ferdinand Zirkel, and botany under August Schenk. In 1877 Credner chose him to assist in a geological survey of Saxony, and Penck mapped on a scale of 1:25,000 the Grimma-Colditz area southeast of Leipzig. In 1879, from the detailed analysis of a sequence of glacial sedimentation (*Geschiebeformation*) that showed alternations of unbedded glacial clay (*Geschiebelehm*) and laminated sands and clays, he postulated at least three main ice advances, or glacial phases, interspersed with two interglacial periods during which rivers had laid down normal, bedded deposits. In the following year Penck worked under the geologist Karl von Zittel at Munich, which was near the outer (northern) limit of the maximum advance of the Alpine ice sheets. Penck's subsequent investigations into Quaternary geology were especially concerned with Alpine glaciation.

In 1882 Penck summarized his local fieldwork in *Die Vergletscherung der deutschen Alpen . . .*, which soon became a standard reference and was his *Habilitationsschrift* as *Privatdozent* in geography at the University of Munich (1883). Two years later Penck was elected to the chair of physical geography at the University of Vienna, where he stayed for nearly twenty years, developing a well-equipped geographical institute and achieving an international reputation. When not lecturing or writing, he collaborated with Eduard Brückner on extensive field studies in the Alpine valleys undertaken with a view to perfecting a chronology of ice sheet advances and retreats. The immediate result was a series of articles on the influence of glaciers on valley development and valley forms; the ultimate result was the classic three-volume *Die Alpen im Eiszeitalter* (1901–1909). During this period Penck traveled to England several times from 1883, to the Pyrenees (1884), and to Norway (1892) to study glacial features and other landform types for a general work on morphology. Reflected in numerous articles dealing with erosion and denudation, these travels culminated in his two-volume *Morphologie der Erdoberfläche* (1894). Penck subsequently made several journeys through Western Europe and visited Canada and the United States in 1898, the Balkans and Australia in 1900, and the United States and Mexico in 1904. Before leaving Vienna, he had taught many German and foreign scholars.

In 1906 Penck succeeded Ferdinand von Richthofen in the chair of geography at the Geographisches Institut of the University of Berlin. His inaugural lecture dealt with the fundamental importance of fieldwork in geographical studies ("Beobachtung als Grundlage der Geographie"), and as director of the institute for the next twenty years he set a fine example. In the winter of 1908–1909 he and his family visited the United States. Penck taught at Columbia University and lectured at Yale and other universities; he also met G. K. Gilbert in California. They returned to Germany via Hawaii, Japan, North China, and Siberia. (In the same scholar exchange program, W. M. Davis lectured on landforms at Berlin.) The last part of *Die Alpen im Eiszeitalter* appeared in 1909; up to this time, and for a few more years, his work at Berlin was virtually an extension of his studies at Vienna.

The outbreak of World War I was a turning point in Penck's thought rather than in his life. Apart from Quaternary problems, which had always interested him, his thinking became more geographical and less geomorphological. Directing more effort to sociopolitical themes, he showed an increasing interest in ethnographic, cultural, and nationalistic topics. In 1917–1918 he served as rector of the University of Berlin; and his inaugural discourse, "Über politische Grenzen," was a study of frontiers, especially European. The best frontiers, he thought, coincided with the living space (*Lebensraum*) indispensable to the life and security of a state. Germany had in part acquired *Lebensraum* but unfortunately had failed to retain the entire mineral basin of Lorraine. Now in 1917 Penck hoped that Germany would keep all the territories currently occupied so far as they were indispensable, and that it would further acquire colonies to furnish essential raw materials.

These and similar views led his friend Davis to write in a review of the *Festband* (1918) that was presented to Penck by his former students on his sixtieth birthday: "He used to be liked as much as admired but during the war some of his statements have lessened the esteem formerly felt for him" (*Geographical Review*, 10 [1920], 249). Penck played a considerable role in the revival of German nationalism after World War I; he was, for example, one of the chief advocates of the foundation of the Berlin *Volkshochschule*. The *Lebensraum* concepts (*Reichboden*, *Sprachboden*, *Volksboden*, and *Kulturboden*) and the ethnographic, cultural, and social surveys fostered and undertaken by Penck and others later proved disastrous but were then highly popular in Germany and had honored antecedents in the work of Friedrich Ratzel. Penck thus enjoyed great national esteem and achieved membership in the Berlin Mittwochsgesellschaft. His success was dimmed when his brilliant son Walther died of cancer in September 1923 at the age of 35. He supervised the publication (1924–1928) of his son's literary remains, including four articles, and *Die morphologische Analyse* (Stuttgart, 1924), an important contribution to the study of landforms.

About this time Penck's interests in oceanography yielded their best results. As director of the Institut für Meereskunde he was responsible for extending the oceanographic museum at the University of Berlin and was involved in the arrangements for the Meteor Expedition (1925), which, under A. Merz, made several sounding traverses in the South Atlantic. In 1926 Penck retired from the chair of geography at Berlin and was succeeded by his former student Norbert Krebs. Penck continued to live in Berlin, however, where he worked on geographical and editorial problems in connection with the geographical institute of the university.

By 1927 much of the wartime breach of friendship with Davis had been healed—largely owing to the death of Walther Penck, whom Davis greatly admired—and Penck spent some time lecturing in the United States, with the University of Arizona as his base. In 1928 he presided with distinction over both the centennial celebrations of the Berlin Gesellschaft für Erdkunde and the meetings of the Oceanic Conference. Most of his biographers consider 1928 "the peak of his career," but from a scientific viewpoint there can be no doubt that he reached his peak in 1909 or 1910. His Austrian work was full of scientific innovations and included his concepts for an international map on the scale of 1:1,000,000; his Berlin work was full of the less scientific branches of geography. In fact, for the last thirty years of his life he was more a regional geographer and demographer than an earth scientist.

The majority of Penck's approximately sixty-five articles and books written after his retirement concern Quaternary chronology, cartography, and population problems. There remained withal more than a hint of *Lebensraum*—evident in his description in 1934 of Krebs's important atlas *Deutsches Lebensraum in Mitteleuropa*, which Penck had initiated, and in his associated interest in political boundaries—as well as a tinge of regional geography (*Länderkunde*). Penck also wrote several competent biographies, including

those of Brückner (1928), Gilbert (1929), J. Partsch (1928), Richthofen (1930, 1933), and F. von Wieser (1929). His last projects involved the study, with a group of students, of the relationship between the potential productivity and possible number of inhabitants per unit area of land mass. During World War II, his house was damaged by bombs and he moved to Prague.

The assessment of Penck's contributions to the earth sciences is complicated by the change in his views. He did not hesitate to accept new theories or to recant his ideas. This development can be illustrated clearly from three facets of his work. First, in his concepts of regional geography he was an early follower of Richthofen. Thus, his "Das deutsche Reich" (1887) superimposed spatial distribution of various phenomena upon a detailed physical base, with the use of new physiographic terms such as *Alpenvorland* (foreland). But after 1914 his regional concepts changed rapidly to unit areas of landscape in which the visible repercussions of the natural and sociocultural environment allowed the establishment of core and fringe areas. Man's activities and his acquired traits and inherited characteristics entered more strongly into the spatial relationships. The concept of *Lebensraum* loomed large with what might be considered a regrettable chauvinistic veneer, and with strong hints at possible expansion and regrets at the noncoincidence of political, social, economic, and cultural distributions. Second, Penck changed his views considerably on the descriptive analysis of landforms. At first his elaborate empirical descriptions lacked any notable sequential development among the individual forms; but under the influence of Davis, Penck recognized the value of a "cyclic" or sequential progress. After 1918, he rejected Davis' theory; and, with his son Walther, he placed the rate and nature of uplift as dominant factors in the analysis of certain landforms. Third, Penck quite early agreed with Suess on the leading principle that secular variations in the relative altitude of land and sea were due to worldwide fluctuations of sea level (eustasism) rather than to crustal movements. By 1900 Penck had modified his views and had accepted independent crustal movement (regional or local) as a concomitant factor in elevating or depressing coastlines.

Assessing his contributions is complicated also by the wide range of geographical topics that he discussed. He published more than 400 books and articles, and many of the latter were issued separately in book form. Yet his chief scientific writings concerned four branches of the natural sciences: Quaternary geology and chronology, geomorphology, hydrology, and cartography.

In his Quaternary studies Penck's early work on the superficial deposits of the north German lowlands and of the Alpine valleys and piedmont plains increased the number of distinct epochs of glaciation to three or four. Prior to Penck's work only two such epochs were commonly accepted in continental Europe. Although James Geikie had enumerated five ice advances and James Croll (on climatic theories) had enumerated seven, Penck's suggestions were the first to be based on firm geological evidence. Following the publication of *Die Alpen im Eiszeitalter* the sedimentation evidence for at least four main ice advances in the Alps was indisputable. They were named Günz, Mindel, Riss, and Würm; the first three being right-bank alpine tributaries of the Danube and the last a tributary of the Isar River near Munich. Penck used for reference the capital letters in a wide-spaced alphabetical sequence, which could, if necessary, incorporate future discoveries of ice advances in a mnemonic order.

For nearly half a century this scheme provided a nomenclature and a time scale for European Pleistocene studies. *Die Alpen im Eiszeitalter* was a milestone in the history of the investigation of the Quaternary; its results, according to Davis (*Geographical Journal*, **34** [1909], 651), formed "an indispensable guide for all future students of the subject, a standard from which all future progress must be measured." The findings revealed the great length of the Riss-Würm interglacial and its mildness as compared with the present, as shown by the plant-bearing Hötting breccia near Innsbruck. The Würm (or last ice advance) had, on moraine evidence, experienced at least three significant pauses or stages of retreat. During glaciation, the permanent snowline of the Alps had advanced 1,200 meters; and its lowering was caused, Penck and Brückner believed, by a moderate decrease in the mean annual temperature and consequent increase in proportion of snowfall to total precipitation, rather than by an increase in the total precipitation.

Penck lived to see significant modifications to his scheme: an older (Donau) advance was subsequently added, which allowed the scheme to conform to postulated variations in insolation; various local terminologies not based on the Alps were adopted for Scandinavian and British ice advances; and the main glaciations, particularly the Würm, were more rigorously divided into stadials and interstadials. Among Penck's other contributions to glacial geology was the term "tillite," which he coined in 1906 for the ancient Dwyka moraines of the Permo-Carboniferous glaciation in South Africa.

Penck's main contributions in geomorphology were to the general classification of landforms, to knowledge of individual landform types, and to the significance of climatic change in landform-analysis. *Morphologie der Erdoberfläche*, the first unified text of geomorphology, followed in the tradition of Suess's *Das Antlitz der Erde* (1883–1909) and Richthofen's *Führer für Forschungsreisende* (1886); Penck acknowledged his debt to each and also to James Dana. Penck's work is divided into three parts. The first part deals mathematically—with the aid of numerous formulas and equations—with general surface morphology and with Penck's concepts of morphography and morphometry. The second part describes in detail the various forms (landforms) that are recognizable upon the surface of the earth and the various processes, endogenous and exogenous, at work in their genesis. Most of the principles stated here were basically familiar to students; but much of the information was new and the presentation was unified, ingenious, and scientific. The third includes the study of oceans, coastlines, and islands. The arrangement of particular sections in this work is similar to Richthofen's *Forschungsreisende*; but the battalion of facts, evidence, and computations more closely resembles Dana's geological manuals. As Charles Lapworth wrote admiringly (*Geographical Journal*, **5** [1895], 580), "the work is an encyclopaedia of facts and conclusions, admirably classified and digested; and affords, at the same time, a complete index to the literature of the subject."

Penck's attempt to construct a unified system of landform analysis and classification was of outstanding importance. He emphasized form or shape in relation to genetic processes rather than to functional processes, and he stated that fundamental types could be formed by many different processes. This Penckian system created or nurtured the German, as distinct from the American (Davisian), system of landform analysis. Penck's system was expounded more widely in 1895 at the Sixth International Geographical Congress in London, with a masterly summary in English. It stated that changes on the earth's surface result from erosion (true erosion and denudation), accumulation, and dislocation, which cause the formation of new surfaces and the destruction and alteration of existing surfaces. Thus the character of the surface relief depends partly on the geological structure, including disturbances and dislocations. These structures may be of a stratified nature (practically horizontal, undulating or warped, intensely folded, fractured) or of an igneous nature (extrusive, or volcanic, and intrusive). Erosion, denudation, and accumulation affect these geological structural types and result in the creation of six fundamental forms: the plain, the escarpment, the valley, the mount, the cup-shaped hollow, and the cavern. The forms are differentiated by their slopes; and the "form-elements" combine to build up fundamental forms, which usually occur in association or groups to compose a special landscape. The form-elements, fundamental forms, and landscape are the three minor morphological elements of the earth's surface. The three higher categories are the extended area of equal elevation (a combination of landscapes); the system (a grouping of such areas); and, finally, the continental block and abyssal deep. Between the surface forms and agencies of change there is one relation: the major forms are due exclusively to dislocations, while the minor forms arise in a variety of ways.

The same fundamental form can arise from either erosion, accumulation, or dislocation; and, with one exception, each process can result in the six fundamental forms. Penck suggested the term "homoplastic" for forms with the same shape and "homogenetic" for those with the same origin. But a uniform and clear terminology, he believed, as well as a knowledge of the genesis of landforms superior to that existing already, had to be acquired. Penck stated that each fundamental form (except the plain) includes three groups of homogenetic features and that each group falls into various subdivisions according to the special kind of erosion, accumulation, or dislocation that has operated. By naming the homogenetic members of each fundamental form according to its genesis, two nouns could express both the plastic and genetic relations (plain of accumulation). The definition could be made more explicit by the addition of adjectives (plain of marine accumulation).

One of the most significant features of geomorphology is the contrast between this system of landform description and the cyclic concept of Davis, who postulated a sequence of development in each landscape and based landform analysis mainly on structure, process, and stage. Penck recognized and used some of Davis' sequential ideas; but as Walther Penck, from 1912 on, became intrigued with the intense folding of the Andes, he and his father increasingly emphasized the importance of rate of uplift on valley-side slopes.

In 1919 Penck published an important article on the summit levels of the Alps, "Die Gipfelflur der Alpen." In direct opposition to Davis' theory that peaks were eroded uplifted peneplains, Penck developed the concept that mechanical disintegration rapidly increases with altitude and that in each region there exists a maximum altitude above which the highest relief will not rise. He explained the existence of mature, or flattened, surfaces at great heights in the interior ranges of the Alps by assuming that the massif was uplifted slowly at first and then more rapidly. The spacing of the valley dissection and the nature of the valley-side slopes reflect this accelerating uplift. At an intermediate stage the sharp ridge crests (where the steep valley-side slopes intersect) will maintain a constant, absolute altitude and constant relief because the rate of upheaval and rate of deepening of the master valleys are balanced. Davis replied at length in "The Cycle of Erosion and the Summit Level of the Alps" (*Journal of Geology*, **31** [1923], 1–41). Although he admitted Penck's exceptional stature as a geographer and the "unquestionably large" value of the "Gipfelflur" essay, he considered it necessary to "correct" Penck's so-called corrections of the Davisian system. Influenced by his German colleagues, Penck moved increasingly away from Davis' cyclic concept, and by 1928 he had already abandoned the idea of the sequential development of landforms in favor of a scheme based on the ratio between rates of erosion and uplift ("Die Geographie unter den erdkundlichen Wissenschaften," in *Naturwissenschaften*, **16** [1928], 33–41).

Penck's chief contributions to knowledge of individual landform types were to glacial forms, especially in *Die Alpen im Eiszeitalter*. In this work, as well as in earlier articles, he stressed the importance of the overdeepening of glacial valleys and the significance of glacial through valleys. He was also instrumental in pointing out the general association between till sheets, terminal moraines, and outwash gravels and sands that develop on bordering lowlands outside the overdeepened piedmont basin at the end of an Alpine valley. This association was later equally applied to the peripheries of continental ice sheets.

To climatic geomorphology, as distinct from paleoclimatology, Penck made two significant contributions. He recognized an areal classification of surface morphology based on correlations with humid, subhumid, semiarid, arid, and nival (glacial) climatic areas. He was one of the first to insist that "we see on the earth's surface not only the features of the present climate but also those of a past climate" (*American Journal of Science*, **19** [1905], 169).

Penck's detailed accounts of the Danube River, "Die Donau" (1891), and the Oder River (1899) were among the earliest scientific analyses of the water budget and the flow regime of Central European rivers. His interest in cartography was responsible for initiating many distribution maps and at least one influential atlas on sociocultural themes, Krebs's *Deutsches Lebensraum in Mitteleuropa*. He advocated the production of Prussian maps on the scale of 1:100,000 for general purposes and of a standard series of global maps on a scale of 1:1,000,000. Penck introduced this idea in 1891 at the Fifth International Geographical Congress in Berne. The matter was raised at each successive congress; and at the eighth congress in Washington (1904), Penck again addressed the delegates and presented maps compiled on that scale by the French, Germans, and British. International conferences were subsequently held in 1908 and 1913 to resolve outstanding problems with regard to standard specifications, spelling, and production of the 1:1,000,000 world sheets (IMW). Of the estimated 840 sheets needed to cover the land areas of the world, only 97 had been published by 1931. Within a few years of Penck's death the greater part of the land areas had been covered by standard IMW maps.

BIBLIOGRAPHY

I. ORIGINAL WORKS. Penck's published works comprise about 410 books and articles. The selective list given here includes works referred to in the text and others that exemplify his contributions to major themes. His works on Pleistocene geology include *Die Vergletscherung der deutschen Alpen . . .* (Leipzig, 1882); *Die Alpen im Eiszeitalter*, 3. vols (Leipzig, 1901–1909), written with E. Brückner; and "Europa im Eiszeitalter," in *Geographische Zeitschrift*, **43** (1937), pt. 1. On geomorphology, see *Morphologie der Erdoberfläche*, 2 vols. (Stuttgart, 1894); "Die Geomorphologie als genetische Wissenschaft," in *Report of the Sixth International Geographical Congress, London, 1895* (1896), 735–757; and "Die Gipfelflur der Alpen," in *Sitzungsberichte der Preussischen Akademie der Wissenschaften*, **17** (1919), 256–263. On hydrography, see "Die Donau," in *Schriften des Vereins zur Verbreitung naturwissenschaftlicher Kenntnisse in Wien*, **31** (1891), 1–101; and "Der Oderstrom," in *Geographische Zeitschrift*, **5** (1899), 19–47, 84–94; and on cartography, "The Construction of a Map of the World on a Scale of 1:1,000,000," in *Geographical Journal*, **1** (1893), 253–261.

Other works on geography include "Das deutsche Reich," in A. Kirchhoff's *Länderkunde von Europa*, I (Leipzig, 1887), 115–596; "Die österreichische Alpengrenze," in *Zeitschrift der Gesellschaft für Erdkunde zu Berlin* (1915), 329–368, 417–448; *Über politische Grenzen* (Berlin, 1917); "Die Stärke der Verbreitung des Menschen," in *Mitteilungen der Geographischen Gesellschaft in Wien* (1942), 241–269; *Beobachtung als Grundlage der Geographie* (Berlin, 1906); and "Geography Among the Earth Sciences," in *Proceedings of the American Philosophical Society*, **66** (1927), 621–644.

II. SECONDARY LITERATURE. The chief biographies and bibliographies of Penck are: *1877–1903: Druckschriften von Albrecht Penck* (Vienna, 1903), a list of 162 items compiled by A. E. Forster; Erich Wunderlich, "Albrecht Penck: Zu seinem 70 Geburtstag am 25. September 1928," in *Geographischer Anzeiger*, **29** (1928), 297–306; *1877–1928. Druckschriften von Albrecht Penck . . .* (Berlin, 1928), with bibliography of 350 items to early 1928; Norbert Krebs, "Nachruf auf Albrecht Penck," in *Jahrbuch der Deutschen Akademie der Wissenschaften zu Berlin* (1946–1949), 202–212; Johann Sölch, "Albrecht Penck," in *Mitteilungen der Geographischen Gesellschaft in Wien*, **89** (1946), Heft 7–12, 88–122; Walter Behrmann, "Albrecht Penck 25.9.1858–7.3.45," in *A. Petermanns Mitteilungen aus J. Perthes Geographischer Anstalt*, **92** (1948), 190–193; H. Spreitzer, "Albrecht Penck," in *Quartär* (1951), 109–139; Edgar Lehmann, "Albrecht Penck," in *Deutsche Akademie der Wissenschaften zu Berlin*, **64** (1959); Herbert Louis, "Albrecht Penck und sein Einfluss auf Geographie und Eiszeitforschung," in *Die Erde*, **89** (1958), Heft 3–4, 161–182 (extends bibliography of *1928 Druckschriften* to a total of 406 items); and G. Englemann, "Bibliographie Albrecht Penck," in *Wissenschaftliche Veröff d. Deutschen Institut für Länderkunde* (1960), 331–447. For controversy over landform analysis between the Pencks and W. M. Davis see R. J. Chorley *et al.*, *The History of the Study of Landforms*, II (London, 1973). For Penck's contributions to cartography see Walter Behrmann, "Die Bedeutung Albrecht Pencks für die Kartographie," in *Blätter d. Dt. Kartogr. Ges.*, no. 2 (1938), 22 pp.

ROBERT P. BECKINSALE

PENCK, WALTHER (*b.* Vienna, Austria, 30 August 1888; *d.* Stuttgart, Germany, 29 September 1923), *geology*.

Penck's interest in natural science developed under the tutelage of both his father, the geologist and geomorphologist Albrecht Penck, and his teacher, Paul Pfurtscheller. When the elder Penck moved to the University of Berlin, Penck began his undergraduate studies there, but these studies were soon interrupted when, in 1908–1909, he accompanied his father to the United States, where the latter was an exchange professor at Columbia University. During this year, he traveled widely with his father and met many geologists, including G. K. Gilbert. After returning to Berlin via Hawaii, Japan, China, and Siberia, Penck enrolled at the University of Heidelberg, from which he graduated; he subsequently continued his studies in Vienna.

In 1912 he was appointed geologist to the Dirección General de Minas in Buenos Aires, where he was responsible for geological surveying and topographic mapping in northwest Argentina. Aided by his mountaineering ability, he mapped some 4,500 square miles of territory in less than two years and made a reconnaissance across the Andes. It was during these years (1912–1914) that Penck formalized his ideas regarding the pattern of tectonic movements. His studies of the Upper Cretaceous and Tertiary sediments flanking the Calchaqui mountains, Sierra de Famatina, and Sierra de Fiambalá in the Puna de Atacama led him, like his father, to posit temporal patterns of uplift much more varied than the pattern of rapid uplift followed by long quiescence, which was accepted by W. M. Davis.

Penck believed that most tectonic movements began and ended slowly, and that the common pattern of such movements involved a slow initial uplift, an accelerated uplift, a deceleration in uplift, and, finally, quiescence. There can be no doubt that much of Penck's geomorphic work was an attempt to provide physiographic support for the general pattern of uplift that he had previously inferred from stratigraphical evidence. The importance that Penck placed on identifying the movements of the source area from the record of sedimentation is clearly stated in the first chapter of his *Die morphologische Analyse.* Few geologists would now attempt more than to suggest the occurrence of some generalized uplift on the sole evidence of the sedimentary record, and even fewer would infer the pattern of uplift in any great detail. In 1917 Joseph Barrell showed that much of the character of the sedimentary record is determined by the subsidence of the basin of sedimentation, as distinct from the behavior of the adjacent source area. Although these behaviors are often so closely linked that it is difficult to distinguish between them, the work of Barrell began to cast doubt on the simple association between the nature of sedimentation and the pattern of uplift of the source area.

The major results of Penck's work in Argentina were not published until the end of World War I. The war broke out while he was in Germany on leave and, although his South American work qualified him for a geological post at the University of Leipzig, he served for a while in the German army in Alsace. At the end of 1915 he was appointed professor of mineralogy and geology at the University of Constantinople. For the next two and a half years he made tectonic observations in Anatolia (where he visited the Bithynian Olympus) and did varied geological work in the region of the Sea of Marmara (where he studied the coal strata of the Dardanelles). He also served as a professor at the Agricultural College of Halkaly. Malaria forced him to return to Germany in the summer of 1918; shortly thereafter he published the two substantial works that summarized his studies in Turkey.

Penck was unable to return to Turkey after the end of the war, and he became an unsalaried professor at the University of Leipzig, where he also held a lectureship in topographical and geological surveying. Refusing, despite straitened financial circumstances, more lucrative posts that would have inhibited his researches, Penck studied the terrain of the German highlands, and in particular that of the Black Forest. In 1921 he recovered some of his Turkish assets. Shortly afterward he died of cancer, survived by his wife and two small sons.

During the last years of his career, Penck developed his most influential ideas on the interpretation of landforms through analysis of the relationships between endogenetic (diastrophic) and exogenetic (erosional) processes. Of the three major publications that embodied his views, only the least important, "Wesen und Grundlagen der morphologischen Analyse" (1920), was published before his death. "Die Piedmontflächen des südlichen Schwarzwaldes" (1925) was based upon two lectures that he gave at Leipzig in December 1921; his book *Die morphologische Analyse* (1924) was only part of a contemplated larger work and was assembled and edited by his father. This last, posthumously published work was not only fragmentary but also hurriedly written, full of obscure terminology, and often unclear. Apart from J. E. Kesseli's mimeographed translation (1940) of an abstract of chapter 6, which discussed the development of slopes, *Die morphologische Analyse* was not translated into English until 1953. Simons, one of Penck's later translators, wrote "I have hardly ever met more difficult and obscure language. Quite often it was difficult to tell whether he said yes or no."

It is unfortunate that, for a period of more than twenty years, the only English interpretation of Penck's geomorphic ideas was that available in a highly critical article published in 1932 by his major opponent, W. M. Davis. Davis concentrated on Penck's Black Forest paper of 1925 and, besides seizing on the obvious difficulties of interpreting topographic discontinuities as the product of continuous crustal uplift, grossly misrepresented Penck's ideas, particularly in attributing to him the postulate of the parallel retreat of one major slope element which leaves beneath itself a surface of less declivity (compare fig. 4 of Davis' 1932 article with fig. 4 of Penck's 1925 publication). By World War II the Davis-Penck controversy, as it was carried out in the English-speaking world, had foundered in a doctrinaire and depressingly semantic morass.

Penck believed that landforms could be interpreted through the ratios that might be expected to occur between exogenetic processes (which he believed to be of uniform type but developed at different rates in different climates) and a wide spectrum of endogenetic processes. He also thought that diastrophic movements were of two major types, which could occur independently or together. He named the first type *Grossfalt* ("great" or "broad" fold) and stated that it was produced by lateral compression with flanking synclines; this fold became narrower with time and was superficially faulted and thrusted in later stages. Penck interpreted "basin and range" structures as belonging to this type. He treated these in detail in *Die morphologische Analyse*, in which he tried unsuccessfully to show that the facies of the sediments derived from these folds do not indicate intermittent uplift. He viewed the whole summit area of such a range as a deformed primary peneplain that was formed during slow initial uplift and correlated with unconformities in the basin.

The second type of movement defined by Penck was regional arching. He stated that this movement was produced by differential uplift, thus generating domes (*Gewölbes*) that progressively expanded their area with time but were not necessarily associated with flanking down-warps. Penck slighted the physiographic results of this type of movement in *Die morphologische Analyse*, but described them in detail in his 1925 paper on the Black Forest. All popular expositions of Penck's geomorphic views were based to some extent on his description of the landforms that might be developed on such a dome, the surface of which forms a series of stepped erosional benches (*Piedmonttreppen*) of differing age.

Where the two types of crustal movements occur together, as in the Alps, Penck thought that a more complex deformation was produced in which the regional doming, often outlasting the *Grossfalt*, was responsible for the general relief. He believed that regional up-doming began with a major phase of waxing development (*aufsteigende Entwicklung*) in which the accelerating uplift rates were generally in excess of stream degradation and the resulting landforms were dominated by the crustal instability. This development was followed by a general decline in the rate of uplift, during which a short period of uniform development (*gleichförmige Entwicklung*), in which the rate of erosion by streams overtook those of uplift, was succeeded by a dominantly waning phase (*absteigende Entwicklung*), during which the rate of uplift decreased, becoming stable as the landscape became progressively dominated by the erosional processes of valley widening. In this model the initially slow uplift would result in the formation and subsequent elevation of a primary peneplain (*Primärrumpf*), with convex valley-side slopes. As the uplift accelerated, the peneplain would be surrounded by a series of *Piedmonttreppen*, each of which had originated as a piedmont flat (*Piedmontfläche*) on the slowly rising dome margin. Penck believed convex breaks of slope (*Knickpunkte*) to form on the radially draining river courses during accelerating uplift, leaving "one convex nick after the other . . ., below each one there begins a narrow, steep course reach with convex valley slopes, above each there is a broader reach with concave slope profiles" ("Die Piedmontflächen des südlichen Schwarzwaldes," p. 90). The concave stream-reaches between the convex nicks are formed in association with the *Piedmonttreppen*; each tends to act as an independent local baselevel for the subsequent valley widening on either side of the stream course. Penck made no clear distinction between continuous acceleration of uplift and continuous but intermittently accelerated uplift; the mechanisms that he evoked for the production of *Piedmonttreppen* and *Knickpunkte* also lacked clarity. Davis made much of these points and the modern geomorphologist can only find it difficult to understand how topographic discontinuities can develop during the waxing phase of Penck's model.

Penck's imaginative work was nonetheless of particular value in repairing the omission of diastrophic causes in much of the classic geomorphic literature.

BIBLIOGRAPHY

I. ORIGINAL WORKS. The more important of Penck's 34 works include *Die tektonischen Grundzüge Westkleinasiens* (Stuttgart, 1918); "Grundzüge der Geologie des Bosporus," in *Veröffentlichungen des Instituts für Meereskunde an dem Universität*, n.s. **4** (1919), 1–71; "Der Südrand der Puna de Atacama (Nordwestargentinien). Ein Beitrag zur Kenntnis des andinen Gebirgstypus und zu der Frage der Gebirgsbildung," in *Abhandlungen der Sächsischen Akademie der Wissenschaften*, Math.-Phys. Kl., **37**, no. 1 (1920), 1–420; "Wesen und Grundlagen der morphologischen Analyse," in *Bericht Sächsischen Akademie der Wissenschaften*, Math.-nat. Kl., **72** (1920), 65–102; "Über die Form Andiner Krustenbewegungen und ihre Beziehung zur Sedimentation," in *Geologische Rundschau*, **14** (1923), 301–315; "Die morphologische Analyse. Ein Kapitel der physikalischen Geologie," in *Geographische Abhandlungen*, 2nd ser., **2** (1924), 1–283; this work was subsequently published separately (Stuttgart, 1924), and trans. by H. Czech and K. C. Boswell as *Morphological Analysis of Landforms* (London, 1953). This ed. contains a short biography of Penck (pp. vii–viii) and a list of his publications (pp. 352–353). See also "Die Piedmontflächen des südlichen Schwarzwaldes," in *Zeitschrift der Gesellschaft für Erdkunde zu Berlin* (1925), 83–108, with mimeographed trans. by M. Simons, "The Piedmont-flats of the Southern Black Forest" (1961).

II. SECONDARY LITERATURE. On Penck and his works, are O. Ampferer, "Walther Penck," in *Verhandlungen der*

Geologischen Bundesanstalt, **4** (1924), 81–82; H. G. Backlund, "Walther Penck," in *Geologiska Foreningins I Stockholm Förhandlinger*, **45**(5) (1923), 445–447; J. Barrell, "Rhythms and the Measurement of Geologic Time," in *Bulletin of the Geological Society of America*, **28** (1917), 745–904; H. Baulig, "Sur les gradins de piedmont," in *Journal of Geomorphology*, **2** (1939), 281–304, a somewhat misguided criticism of Penck's concept of slope development; I. Bowman, "The Analysis of Landforms: W. Penck on the Topographic Cycle," in *Geographical Review*, **16** (1926), 122–132, a critical article on *Die morphologische Analyse* written with the approval and help of Davis; R. J. Chorley, "The Diastrophic Background to Twentieth-Century Geomorphological Thought," in *Bulletin of the Geological Society of America*, **74** (1963), 953–970; R. J. Chorley et al., *The History of the Study of Landforms*, (Methuen–London, 1973), *passim*, which presents the important personal correspondence between Penck and Davis; W. M. Davis, "Piedmont Benchlands and the Primärrumpfe," in *Bulletin of the Geological Society of America*, **43** (1932), 399–440, a detailed attack on Penck's 1925 publication; G. K. Gilbert, "The Convexity of Hilltops," in *Journal of Geology*, **17** (1909), 344–350; and J. E. Kesseli, *The Development of Slopes* (Berkeley, Calif., 1940), mimeographed; F. Kossmat, "Walther Penck," in *Centralblatt für Mineralogie, Geologie und Paläontologie*, **25** (1924), 123–127.

Additional works include H. Lautensach, "Albrecht und Walther Penck," in *Zeitschrift für Geomorphologie*, n.s. **2** (1958), 245–250; A. G. Ogilvie, "Argentine Physiographical Studies: A Review," in *Geographical Review*, **13** (1923), 112–121, a review of "Der Südrand der Puna de Atacama" and other works; A. Penck, "Biography of Walther Penck," Foreword to *Die morphologische Analyse* (1924), VII–XVIII; A. Penck, "Letter Regarding 'Die morphologische Analyse,' " in *Geographical Review*, **16** (1926), 350–352, a reply to Bowman (1926); C. O. Sauer, "Landforms in the Peninsular Range of California as Developed About Warner's Hot Springs and Mesa Grande," in *University of California Publications in Geography*, **3**, no. 4 (1929), 199–290, an attempt to apply Penck's geomorphic notions in North America; M. Simons, "The Morphological Analysis of Landforms: A New Review of the Work of Walther Penck," in *Transactions of the Institute of British Geographers*, no. 31 (1962), 1–14, a penetrating review of many of Penck's ideas; and indispensable in the preparation of this biographical note; H. Spreitzer, "Die Piedmonttreppen in der regionalen Geomorphologie," in *Erdkunde*, **5**, no. 4 (1951), 294–304; Symposium, "Walther Penck's Contribution to Geomorphology," in *Annals of the Association of American Geographers*, **30** (1940), 219–284; Y.-F. Tuan, "The Misleading Antithesis of Penckian and Davisian Concepts of Slope Retreat in Waning Development," in *Proceedings of the Indiana Academy of Science*, **67** (1958), 212–214; and O. D. von Engeln, *Geomorphology* (New York, 1942), 256–268, an exposition based on Davis (1932).

RICHARD CHORLEY

PENNANT, THOMAS (*b.* Downing, near Holywell, Flintshire, Wales, 14 June 1726; *d.* Downing, 16 December 1798), *natural history*.

Pennant was the eldest son of David and Arabella Mytton Pennant. His first schooling was under the Reverend W. Lewis. In 1744 he matriculated at Queen's College, Oxford, but left without an undergraduate degree, probably because he had been active in troubles between undergraduates and faculty. In 1759 he married Elizabeth Falconer; they had a daughter, Arabella, and a son, David. His wife died in 1764, and Pennant married Anne Mostyn in 1777; two children, Thomas and Sarah, were born to them. He subsequently inherited his father's property, where he discovered a rich lead mine.

Calling himself a "moderate Tory," Pennant was active in politics and served as sheriff of Flintshire. He enjoyed excellent health throughout the first seventy years of his life, ascribing it to traveling on horseback and avoiding supper, which he called "the meal of excess." He kept a strict schedule, retiring at ten and rising at seven, and concentrated seriously when he worked. The recognition that he received included election to the Royal Society of Uppsala (1757), the Royal Society of London (1767), and various foreign societies.

Pennant's passion for natural history began in 1738, when he received a copy of Willughby's *Ornithology* as a gift. In 1746, while still at Queen's College, Pennant toured Cornwall and met the geologist William Borlase, who encouraged his interest in minerals and fossils. Pennant's first publication, a description of an earthquake at Downing in 1750, appeared in the *Philosophical Transactions of the Royal Society*. He later admitted a "rage" to become an author.

At Pennant's suggestion Gilbert White began writing the letters that became *The Natural History and Antiquities of Selborne*, and forty-four of the 110 letters in it are addressed to Pennant. Pennant also had a talent for observation and organization. He was able to combine his own observations with information from Thomas Hutchins, Ashton Blackburn, Alexander Garden, Benjamin Smith Barton, and Peter Simon Pallas, and thus to produce his classic work, *Arctic Zoology*. He also corresponded with the leading naturalists of his day.

Although Pennant had little ability for theorizing, he did contribute to organizing, popularizing, and promoting the study of natural history. His writings tended to emphasize the goodness and usefulness of nature, which he considered a reflection of a sanctified creation. In classification he supported the views of his countryman John Ray and, later, those of Linnaeus. Pennant was a representative of the best of the gentleman-naturalists who flourished in the late eighteenth century and who sought to comprehend all of nature.

BIBLIOGRAPHY

I. ORIGINAL WORKS. Pennant's published writings include *The British Zoology. Class 1. Quadrupeds. 2. Birds* (London, 1766), enl. to 4 vols., *British Zoology* (London, 1768–1770), a standard text; *Indian Zoology* (London [?], 1769); *Synopsis of Quadrupeds* (Chester, 1771), with subsequent eds. entitled *History of Quadrupeds*. The first of his travel books, *A Tour in Scotland, 1769* (Chester, 1771), was reissued in 1772, 1774, 1775, and 1790; Pennant also published many travel accounts and guidebooks for the British Isles, but one, the *Tour on the Continent, 1765* (London, 1948), remained unpublished until it was edited by G. P. de Beer for the Ray Society.

Subsequent writings are *Genera of Birds* (Edinburgh, 1773); *Arctic Zoology*, 2 vols. (London, 1784–1785) and its *Supplement* (London, 1787); *Catalogue of My Works* (London, 1786); *The Literary Life of the Late Thomas Pennant, Esq. by Himself* (London, 1793); *The History of the Parishes of Whiteford and Holywell* (London, 1796); *Outlines of the Globe*, 4 vols. (London, 1798–1800). The last title, planned to reach 14 vols., describes imaginary travels to many parts of the world. Several of Pennant's books were translated for foreign-language eds. and many appeared in several English eds.

II. SECONDARY LITERATURE. There is no sufficient biography of Pennant in existence; and his autobiographical work, cited above, is incomplete at best. Information about him can be found in Georges Cuvier, "Thomas Pennant," in *Biographie universelle*, XXXIII (Paris, 1823), 315–318; R. W. T. Gunther, *Early Science in Oxford*, XI (Oxford, 1937), 131–132, for information about Pennant's college experiences; Sir William Jardine, *The Natural History of Humming-Birds*, II (Edinburgh, 1833), 1–39; W. L. McAtee, "The North American Birds of Thomas Pennant," in *Journal of the Society for the Bibliography of Natural History*, **4**, pt. 2 (January 1963), 100–124; W. L. McAtee, "Thomas Pennant," in *Nature Magazine*, **45** (Feb. 1952), 98, 108; John Nichols, *Literary Anecdotes of the Eighteenth Century*, VIII (London, 1815), *passim*; Peter Simon Pallas, *A Naturalist in Russia; Letters From Peter Simon Pallas to Thomas Pennant*, Carol Urness, ed. (Minneapolis, 1967), with a biography of Pennant on 169–175; and Warwick Wroth, "Thomas Pennant," in *Dictionary of National Biography*, XLIX (1895), 320–323.

CAROL URNESS

PENNY, FREDERICK (*b.* London, England, 10 April 1816; *d.* Glasgow, Scotland, 22 November 1869), *analytical chemistry, toxicology.*

The third son of Charles Penny, a wholesale stationer, Penny was educated at schools in Sherborne (Dorset) and Tooting, London. He was then apprenticed (1833–1838) to the pharmacist and analytical chemist Henry Hennell at the Apothecaries' Hall. Penny described himself as a "pupil" at the lectures of W. T. Brande and M. Faraday at the Royal Institution in 1836 and 1837.

In 1839, on Thomas Graham's strong recommendation, Penny suceeded W. Gregory in the unremunerative chair of chemistry at Anderson's College, Glasgow. Classes were small and brought him few fees, and this, together with the rents he assumed for his laboratory and classrooms, forced Penny to exploit his brilliant analytical talents in legal and commercial consultancy. Consequently, he published little and failed to fulfill the scientific promise he had shown in London. He did, however, visit Liebig at the University of Giessen in 1843 and was awarded the Ph.D. there on the basis of his published work.

Penny was dwarfed by a crooked spine caused when a governess threw him to the ground as a child. He married a Miss Perry in 1851 and had one daughter.

Penny's most important paper appeared in 1839. While trying to assay potassium nitrate in crude saltpeter, he found that the actual, as opposed to the theoretical, quantities of potassium chloride that are produced by the reaction of the nitrate with hydrochloric acid are different. Suspecting that the received chemical equivalents were at fault, he undertook a polished reappraisal of the equivalent weights (oxygen = 8) of the key elements: chlorine, nitrogen, potassium, sodium, and silver.

This elegant work, which was highly praised by, and later influential on, J. S. Stas, was of twofold significance. First, for the practical techniques involved: the use of special apparatus and a counterpoised balance, the use of carefully prepared reagents, and the exploitation of the nitrate-chloride and chlorate-chloride conversions. Second, because the results, Penny thought, confirmed those that E. Turner had published in 1833, and implied that "the favourite hypothesis [Prout's], of all equivalents being simple multiples of hydrogen, is no longer tenable" (*Philosophical Transactions*, **129** [1839], 32). Stas came to the same conclusion in 1860. Although Penny was clearly Turner's successor and Stas's predecessor in matters of atomic weight determinations—Penny even suspected the correctness of the published combining weight of carbon—he was unable to pursue these investigations in Scotland.

All of Penny's Scottish publications related to practical problems. In 1850 he introduced a volumetric determination of iron by the reduction of potassium chromate, or bichromate, using potassium ferricyanide as an external indicator. He also extended this method

510

to the estimation of tin and iodine. Although A. W. von Hofmann once professed never to have heard of him, Penny had a high commercial reputation in Scotland; and, undoubtedly, he restored Anderson College's dormant reputation for medical, and especially technical, chemistry. He also became widely known throughout British medical and legal circles for the brilliance and composure of his Crown evidence in murder trials, notably those of the celebrated Madeleine Smith in 1857 (arsenic, nonproven) and Dr. Edward Pritchard in 1865 (aconite, guilty). The last months of Penny's life were made bitter by James Young's tactless endowment of an additional chair of technical chemistry at Anderson College, which appeared to Penny to threaten his livelihood and reputation.

BIBLIOGRAPHY

I. ORIGINAL WORKS. Penny's two most important papers are "On the Application of the Conversion of Chlorates and Nitrates Into Chlorides, and of Chlorides Into Nitrates, to the Determination of Equivalent Numbers," in *Philosophical Transactions of the Royal Society*, **129** (1839), 13–33; and "On a New Method for the Determination of Iron in Clay-band and Black-band Ironstone," in *Chemical Gazette*, **8** (1850), 330–337. Twelve other papers are listed in the Royal Society *Catalogue of Scientific Papers*, IV, 819–820; and VIII, 587. Penny's pamphlets are *Testimonials in Favour of Frederick Penny, Ph.D. . . . Candidate for the Professorship of Chemistry in the University of Edinburgh* [Glasgow, 1843]; *The Public Wells of Glasgow, With Analytical Reports by R. D. Thomson, M.D. and Dr. Penny* (Glasgow, 1848); and *Chemical Report on the Examination of the Water of Loch Katrine* (Glasgow, 1854).

Subsequent works include *Glasgow Water Supply Question* (Glasgow, 1855); *Report on the Experimental Operations at Loch Katrine* (London, 1855); and the important *Dr. Penny's Remonstrance and Appeal Against the Nomination and Appointment of an Additional Professor of Chemistry in Anderson's University* (Glasgow, 1869); and four analyses of Glasgow waters, 1854–1855, in J. Burnet, ed., *History of the Water Supply to Glasgow* (Glasgow, 1869).

Adams (below) mentioned "a large quantity of unfinished manuscripts," but these have not been located. There are several letters at the University of Glasgow and the Andersonian Library at the University of Strathclyde, Glasgow.

II. SECONDARY LITERATURE. Replies to Penny's 1869 pamphlet are *Retraction and Apology to Dr. Penny with Reference to Evidence Given by Mr. Mayer Before a Select Committee of the House of Commons* (Glasgow, 1869); and J. Adams, *Reasons of Protest* (Glasgow, 1869). These pamphlets may be found in Glasgow and Edinburgh libraries.

Obituary notices are James Adams, in *Glasgow Medical Journal*, **2** (1870), 258–270, concerned mainly with defending Penny's reputation; James Bryce, "President's Address," in *Proceedings of the Glasgow Philosophical Society*, **7** (1871), 364–371; A. H. Sexton, *The First Technical College* (London, 1894), 50; and A. W. Williamson, in *Journal of the Chemical Society*, **23** (1870), 301–306.

See also A. J. Berry, "Frederick Penny. A Forgotten Worker on Equivalent Weights," in *Chemistry and Industry*, **51** (1932), 453–454; J. Butt, "James Young, Scottish Industrialist and Philanthropist" (Ph.D. thesis, University of Glasgow, 1964), *passim*; and H. Irvine, "The Centenary of Penny's [Volumetric] Process," in *Science Progress*, **39** (1951), 63–66.

W. H. BROCK

PENSA, ANTONIO (*b.* Milan, Italy, 15 September 1874; *d.* Pavia, Italy, 17 August 1970), *anatomy, histology, embryology.*

For a detailed study of his life and work, see Supplement.

PERCY, JOHN (*b.* Nottingham, England, 23 March 1817; *d.* London, England, 19 June 1889), *metallurgy.*

Percy was the third son of Henry Percy, a solicitor. Persuaded, against his inclination, to prepare for a medical career, he studied in Paris (where he met Gay-Lussac, Thenard, and Jussieu) and Edinburgh, where he graduated M.D. in 1838. His thesis, on the presence of alcohol in the brain, won a gold medal. Although he obtained a hospital post in Birmingham in 1839, he never established a practice; instead, his early interest in chemistry was reawakened by the local metal industries. In the same year he married Grace Piercy, who died in 1880.

In 1846 Percy studied the nature of slags; he later turned to the extraction of silver from its ores by a process dependent upon the solubility of silver chloride in sodium thiosulfate (a phenomenon discovered by Herschel in 1819). He was elected to the Royal Society in 1847. In 1851 he was appointed lecturer at the Metropolitan School of Science (later the Royal School of Mines), which was then under the direction of Sir Henry de la Beche. He subsequently became professor and thus exerted a profound influence on the progress of British metallurgy; many of his pupils achieved great distinction. His teaching was both methodical and innovative; and Percy transformed metallurgy from a repertoire of practices into a scientific discipline. The inventions of his pupils (for example, the Thomas-Gilchrist process for making iron from phosphorus-rich ores) were, however, more important than Percy's own.

Using the results of a large number of chemical analyses, Percy made a survey of the national resources of iron ore. This survey was incorporated into his large, unfinished work on metallurgy; perhaps the first writer since the Renaissance to attempt to achieve the comprehensiveness of Agricola and Ercker. Percy held many official lectureships, including one at the Royal Military Academy in Woolwich, and was called upon for technical advice on many military defense questions. He disapproved of the removal by the government of the Royal School of Mines to South Kensington, and he resigned in 1879.

Percy made two personal collections during his life: one of watercolors and engravings, which was dispersed by sale after his death, and one of metallurgical specimens of historical interest, which has fortunately survived intact and is now in the Science Museum at South Kensington. He was a lifelong student of political and social questions, often forcefully expressing himself in public, both in speech and writing, although he was not always sensitive to the appropriateness of the occasion.

BIBLIOGRAPHY

Percy's major work was *A Treatise on Metallurgy*, 4 vols. (1864–1880). See also J. F. Blake, *Catalogue of the Collection of Metallurgical Specimens Formed by the Late John Percy, Esq.*, . . . (London, 1892).

Obituary notices are found in *Athenaeum*, **1** (1889), 795; *Journal of the Iron and Steel Institute*, **1** (1889), 210; and *Proceedings of the Geological Society*, **46** (1890), 45.

FRANK GREENAWAY

PEREIRA (or **Pererius**), **BENEDICTUS** (*b*. Ruzafa [near Valencia], Spain, 1535; *d*. Rome, Italy, 6 March 1610), *physics, mechanics, astrology.*

Little is known of Pereira's early life before his admission to the Society of Jesus in 1552. After joining the order, Pereira was sent to Sicily, and then Rome, to complete his education. In Rome he taught various disciplines and arts and became known also as an exponent of scripture, on which he left several commentaries.

Pereira's most important work was his treatise on natural philosophy, *De communibus omnium rerum naturalium*, known also as *Physicorum . . . libri*. First published in Rome in 1562, this Aristotelian commen-

tary went through many subsequent European editions and was used as a philosophy textbook in the flourishing Jesuit schools. It was widely read and is cited in several of the writings of the young Galileo. The section on dynamics (book XIV) is staunchly Aristotelian. Although various theories of violent motion were described, most were rejected, particularly the Parisian impetus theory. In his dislike for Parisian dynamics, Pereira belonged to a strong Italian tradition, upheld also by Girolamo Cardano, Gasparo Contarini, Andrea Cesalpino, and Girolamo Borro.

The *De communibus* was quoted frequently in the Renaissance debate on the nature of mathematics. Like some of his fellow Aristotelians, Pereira was reluctant to allow Aristotle's admission that abstract mathematical demonstrations were of the greatest certainty. Pereira took the extreme position that neither mathematics nor any other science could satisfy Aristotle's very strict criteria for certainty.

Pereira's *Adversus fallaces et superstitiosas artes* (1591) was an outright attack on the occult arts, including alchemy and natural magic, the interpretation of dreams, and astrology. Like the *De communibus*, this treatise enjoyed a wide circulation, although for more notorious reasons. In denouncing magic, Pereira began with the paradoxical premise that natural magic did exist, and was indeed the noblest part of physics, mathematics, and medicine. Because of this exalted status, however, natural magic was accessible to only a very few learned and good men. The evil, therefore, lay in the pretensions of the ignorant and wicked to such knowledge. Such pretensions resulted in abuses, deception, and poverty. Despite its intrinsic goodness, Pereira advocated that the pursuit of natural magic, and of alchemy in particular, be banned.

In the section on the interpretation of dreams, Pereira reverted to Aristotle and concluded that dreams ought neither to be heeded nor disregarded to excess. Those who accepted fixed rules in this matter should be denounced as followers of superstition.

The final section, which dealt with astrology, seems to have been inspired by Sixtus V's bull of 1586 condemning judicial astrology. Pereira used arguments from Giovanni Pico della Mirandola and other sources to show that the heavens do not manifest portents and that the rules of astrology are absurd— any fulfillment of predictions was ascribed to the work of demons. Pereira passed over in silence the acceptance of astrology by Thomas Aquinas and Albertus Magnus. In his earlier *De communibus*, however, the Jesuit had cited Aquinas' favorable opinion without adding a condemnation thereof.

PEREIRA (left column)

BIBLIOGRAPHY

I. ORIGINAL WORKS. Pereira's major works are *De communibus omnium rerum naturalium principiis et affectionibus, libri quindecim* (Rome, 1562), later reprinted in Rome (1576, 1585), Venice (1586, 1592, 1609), Paris (1579, 1585, 1589), Lyons (1585, 1588, 1603), Cologne (1595, 1598, 1601, 1603, 1609), and Ingolstadt (1590); and *Adversus fallaces et superstitiosas artes, id est de magia, de observatione somniorum et de divinatione astrologica, libri tres* (Ingolstadt, 1591), later reprinted in Venice (1591, 1592), Lyons (1592, 1602, 1603), Paris (1616), and Cologne (1598, 1612). An English trans. by Percy Enderbie, *The Astrologer Anatomised*, was issued in London in 1661 and again in 1674. Some of Pereira's commentaries on Aristotle's *Physics* are in the Nationalbibliothek, Vienna, MSS 10476, 10478, 10491, and 10509.

II. SECONDARY LITERATURE. Pereira's religious and scientific works are listed in A. De Backer, ed., *Bibliothèque de la Compagnie de Jésus*, VI (Brussels–Paris), 499–507. Pereira is discussed briefly in Pierre Duhem, *Études sur Léonard de Vinci*, III (Paris, 1913), 203–204; Lynn Thorndike, *A History of Magic and Experimental Science*, VI (New York, 1914), 409–413; and Neal W. Gilbert, *Renaissance Concepts of Method* (New York, 1960), 91. For Galileo's citations of Pereira, see Galileo Galilei, *Opere*, A. Favaro, ed., I (Florence, 1890), 24, 35, 145, 318, 411.

PAUL LAWRENCE ROSE

PEREIRA, DUARTE PACHECO

PEREIRA, DUARTE PACHECO (*b*. Santarém [?], Portugal, *ca*. 1460; *d*. Lisbon [?], Portugal, 1533), *navigation*.

Although not all of the voyages that the Portuguese sailor and pilot Pereira made during his lifetime are known, it is known that he did not participate in several expeditions cited by historians. For example, he would have been very young in 1471 to have taken part in the assault on the north African fortress of Arzila. It is generally believed that he was entrusted by King Manuel I with an expedition in 1498 to America, where he supposedly sailed along the coast of Brazil for the first time. But this assertion, based solely on one obscure passage in his book, is doubtful. It is certain, however, that in 1488 Pereira was on Prince's Island, southwest of the Cameroons, when Bartholomeu Dias was returning to Europe. Pereira was very ill, and the discoverer of the Cape of Good Hope brought him back to Lisbon. In 1503 Pereira was in India with Alfonso de Albuquerque. Remaining there to defend the weak king of Cochin against the powerful King Samorim of Calicut, he succeeded in driving back the fierce and repeated attacks of the Samorim against a small band of Portuguese. Pereira thus became a national hero, and the fame of his exploit at Cochin spread throughout Europe.

In 1505 Pereira returned to Lisbon, where he began his *Esmeraldo de situ orbis*, a title that is still unexplained. He never completed the work and it is known only from incomplete copies. He subsequently undertook missions for the king along the coasts of Portugal and North Africa. In 1519 he became governor of the fortress and commercial entrepôt of São Jorge da Mina, in the Gulf of Guinea. Three years later he was arrested and imprisoned in Lisbon, presumably as the result of irregularities he had committed while in office. After regaining the king's confidence, he was freed and was awarded a lifelong pension.

Pereira's *Esmeraldo* may be considered a routier, or collection of sailing directions, with an introduction on contemporary seamanship. It has several novel aspects, and departs from the style of the medieval routiers, for example that by Pierre Garcie. The introduction contains such interesting elements as the "rules of the sun" for determining latitudes and information concerning tides.

BIBLIOGRAPHY

I. ORIGINAL WORKS. The three published editions of the *Esmeraldo de situ orbis* are all based on surviving eighteenth-century copies. The 1st ed. (Lisbon, 1892) was published by Azevedo Bastos, in celebration of the fourth centenary of the discovery of America. The 2nd (Lisbon, 1905) contains philological comments by the editor A. E. Silva Dias. The 3rd ed. (Lisbon, 1954) was sponsored by the Academia Portuguesa de Historia and includes notes by Damião Peres.

II. SECONDARY LITERATURE. J. Barradas de Carvalho has published a series of studies on Pereira and the significance of his book in University of São Paulo, Brazil, *Revista de história* (1966–1970).

LUÍS DE ALBUQUERQUE

PÉRÈS, JOSEPH JEAN CAMILLE

PÉRÈS, JOSEPH JEAN CAMILLE (*b*. Clermont-Ferrand, France, 31 October 1890; *d*. Paris, France, 12 February 1962), *mathematics, mechanics*.

The son and son-in-law of distinguished philosophers, Pérès entered the École Normale Supérieure in 1908, became *agrégé* in mathematics in 1911, and was immediately awarded a scholarship to enable him to earn a doctorate. Introduced by Émile Borel to Vito Volterra, he left for Italy to prepare his dissertation under the latter's supervision. He defended the dissertation *Sur les fonctions permutables de Volterra* in 1915, while teaching *mathématiques spéciales* at the *lycée* of Montpellier. After brief stays at the faculties of Toulouse and Strasbourg, he was from 1921 to 1932 professor of rational and applied mechanics at Marseilles, where in 1930 he founded an institute of fluid mechanics. Called to the Sorbonne in 1932, he devoted his scientific efforts primarily to developing the field of fluid mechanics. But his personal qualities led to his being burdened with ever more numerous and demanding duties. He taught at all the *grandes écoles* and from 1954 to 1961 was dean of the Paris Faculty of Sciences during a difficult time of expansion and profound transformation. Moreover, he fulfilled extensive responsibilities in several major national and international research organizations, notably the Centre National de la Recherche Scientifique and the International Committee of Scientific Unions.

Pérès won prizes from the Académie des Sciences in 1932, 1938, and 1940 and was elected a member in 1942. He was a foreign member of the Accademia Nazionale dei Lincei, Accademia delle Scienze, and the National Academy of Sciences, as well as an active member of the Académie Internationale d'Histoire des Sciences from 1948. Pérès's positions and honors testify to his exceptionally fruitful life, devoted to the combination of teaching and research.

Volterra's initial influence on Pérès and their warm thirty-year friendship account to a large degree for the course of Pérès's research, which was at first oriented toward pure analysis and then toward mechanics. The events of his career simply accentuated a development the outlines of which were determined at the outset.

Pérès's results on integral equations extended those of Volterra, notably regarding composition products of permutable functions with a given function and, later, the composition of functions of arbitrary order. These findings are now considered classical, as is his theory of symbolic calculus, which is more general than Heaviside's. Work of this type in analysis harmonized with the needs of fluid mechanics. In the latter domain, which experienced great progress in France through Pérès's efforts, his work was linked in large part to that of other researchers. Aiming at various applications, especially in aeronautics, Pérès conducted studies on the dynamics of viscous fluids, on the theory of vortices, and on movements with slip streams while refining the method of electrical analogies. In constructing his "wing calculator," as well as analogous devices—for measuring the pressure of lapping waves on jetties, for example— Pérès remained in close contact with those testing the equipment. To his scientific colleagues he remained a circumspect theorist, animator, and promoter.

At the beginning of his career Pérès obtained two results, now bearing his name, that are not connected with the fields mentioned above. One concerned Levi-

Civita parallelism (1919); the other, impact with friction (1924). In the second area he achieved one of the last great successes of rational mechanics. The gift for theoretical speculation manifested in these investigations remained the mainspring of his work and of his influence, and the fruitfulness of both is explained by his openness to new ideas.

BIBLIOGRAPHY

I. Original Works. Pérès's books include *Sur les fonctions permutables de Vito Volterra* (Paris, 1915), his diss.; *Leçons sur la composition et les fonctions permutables* (Paris, 1924); *Les sciences exactes* (Paris, 1930); *Cours dé mécanique des fluides* (Paris, 1936); *Tables numériques pour le calcul de la répartition des charges aérodynamiques suivant l'envergure d'une aile* (Paris, 1936), written with L. Malavard and L. Romani; *Théorie générale des fonctionnelles* (Paris, 1936); *Notice sur les titres et travaux scientifiques* (Paris, 1942), submitted with his candidacy to the Academy; and *Mécanique générale* (Paris, 1953).

Among his memoirs published in the *Comptes rendus* of the Academy are "Actions d'un fluide visqueux sur un obstacle," **188** (1929), 310–312, 440–441; "Sur le mouvement limite d'Oseen," **192** (1931), 210–212; "Sur les analogies électriques en hydrodynamique," **194** (1932), 1314–1316, written with L. Malavard; "Sur le calcul analogique des effets de torsion," **211** (1940), 131–133, written with L. Malavard; "Sur le calcul expérimental," *ibid.*, 275–277; and "Calcul symbolique d'Heaviside et calcul de composition de V. Volterra," **217** (1943), 517–520.

His other noteworthy works include the editing of *Leçons sur les fonctions de lignes de Vito Volterra* (Paris, 1913); "Le parallélisme de M. Levi-Civita et la courbure Riemannienne," in *Rendiconti. R. Accademia dei Lincei* (June 1919); "Choc avec frottement," in *Nouvelles annales de mathématiques*, **2** (1924); Pérès edited this journal, with R. Brocard and H. Villat, from 1923 to 1927; "Une application nouvelle des mathématiques à la biologie, la théorie des associations biologiques," in *Revue générale des sciences* (1927); and "Les divers aspects de la mécanique. Quelques notions concernant son enseignement," in *Mécanique*, no. 322 (Feb. 1944), 27-29.

II. Secondary Literature. On Pérès and his work, see the notices by P. Costabel, in *Archives internationales d'histoire des sciences*, **15** (1962), 137–140; H. Villat, in *Comptes rendus . . . de l'Académie des sciences*, **254** (1962); and M. Zamansky, in *Revue de l'enseignement supérieur*, no. 2 (1962), 95–97.

Pierre Costabel

PÉREZ DE VARGAS, BERNARDO (*b.* Madrid, Spain, *ca.* 1500–1533), *astronomy, biology, metallurgy.*

Few biographical data are known of Pérez de Vargas. His parents were of distinguished lineage, hence the title of "magnífico" which he appended to his name. From Madrid he moved to the province of Málaga; in one of his works he described himself as a resident of Coín, a town of that province. In 1563 he published the *Repertorio perpetuo o fábrica del universo*. There are extant copies of only the second part of this work. Most Spanish bibliographers, including Colmeiro and Navarrete, believed that both parts were published, although Tamayo gave the opinion that the first part remained as a manuscript in folio, the whereabouts of which is unknown. Palau has suggested that the *Sumario de cosas notables*, published in 1560, is the aforementioned first part.

The *Repertorio perpetuo*, as the second half of its title indicates, dealt with the "structure of the universe." It discussed such subjects as the nature of matter, the age of the globe and man, time and its measurements, astrology, the proper times for purges and bloodletting, and lunar and solar eclipses.

Pérez de Vargas' most important work, however, was on metallurgy, *De re metalica*; this work was published in 1568, although it bore a royal license dated 1564. It was composed of nine books, varying from five to twenty-five chapters, and contained thirteen illustrations. Starting from a philosophical discussion of the form and matter of metals, Pérez de Vargas admitted the possibility of alchemy. The work then proceeded to discuss mining and the smelting and development of metals and minerals. Diego de Meneses, who had owned and worked mines in the New World for thirty years, wrote the preface; he recommended the circulation of *De re metalica* among the miners of Peru and in other parts of America, where he had observed that much gold and silver was lost owing to a lack of adequate knowledge concerning refining processes.

Despite Pérez de Vargas' assertion in the introduction that the contents of his book were culled from the works of many famous authors and that the greater part of it had been subjected to experimentation, *De re metalica* was largely copied, with some paragraphs lifted in full, from Vannuccio Biringuccio's more meritorious *Pirotechnia* (1540). Pérez de Vargas referred to some mines in Spain not mentioned by Biringuccio, but his dependence on the latter would explain the absence of any mention of the development of quicksilver and the process of amalgamation, already known in Spain and America; amalgamation was probably of Spanish origin.

Nonetheless, *De re metalica* was useful because it was the first extensive book on metallurgy in Spanish. Although there was a Spanish translation of Glanville's *De proprietatibus rerum* in the fifteenth century, the scope of this work was not as extensive as *De re metalica*.

BIBLIOGRAPHY

I. ORIGINAL WORKS. Pérez de Vargas' works are *Sumario de cosas notables* (Toledo, 1560); *Repertorio perpetuo o fábrica del universo* (Toledo, 1563); *De re metalica* (Madrid, 1568); and "De los edificios y máquinas que pertenecen al arte de laborar los metales," a work (probably a MS) referred to by Pérez de Vargas in one of his works but of which there are no extant copies. There is a two-volume French trans. of *De re metalica* entitled *Traité singulier de métallique* (Paris, 1743).

II. SECONDARY LITERATURE. On Pérez de Vargas and his work, see Eugenio Maffei and Ramón Rua Figueroa, *Apuntes para una biblioteca española*, 2 vols. (Madrid, 1873); and Felipe Picatoste y Rodríquez, *Apuntes para una biblioteca científica española del siglo XVI* (Madrid, 1891).

VICENTE R. PILAPIL

PERKIN, WILLIAM HENRY (*b.* London, England, 12 March 1838; *d.* Sudbury, England, 14 July 1907), *synthetic organic chemistry, physical organic chemistry.*

Perkin was the son of George Fowler Perkin, a builder and contractor. He became interested in chemistry at an early age and in 1851 was sent to the City of London school, where—although science was not part of the curriculum—he was able to attend the weekly lectures on chemistry given by one of the classmasters during the dinner hour. Perkin's father was opposed to his making a career in chemistry, but he was encouraged by his master, Thomas Hall, through whose intercession he was enrolled in the Royal College of Science when he was fifteen. Perkin attended the lectures of the German chemist A. W. von Hofmann and, by the end of his second year at the college, was appointed Hofmann's assistant.

Perkin established his own laboratory at home at about the same time; one of his first pieces of private research was concerned with a coloring material. With Arthur H. Church he began to investigate the reduction products of dinitrobenzene and dinitronaphthalene. From the latter, Perkin and Church obtained a colored substance that they named "nitrosonaphthalene," which proved to be one of the first of the azo-dyes derived from naphthalene to be manufactured. They subsequently patented their process. Perkin's major discovery, that of mauve, the first synthetic dyestuff, occurred shortly thereafter, during the Easter vacation of 1856, when Perkin was only eighteen.

Hofmann had previously remarked to Perkin on the desirability of synthesizing quinine. Taking up the problem Perkin (basing his experiments on the idea, now understood to be unsound, that the structure of a chemical compound could be determined from the molecular formula alone) first treated toluidine with bichromate of potash, then repeated the process with an aniline salt. From the latter he obtained not quinine but a dirty, dark-colored precipitate. Some special instinct caused him to examine this precipitate further, and he discovered it to have coloring properties. From it he succeeded in isolating mauve, or aniline purple, the first dyestuff to be produced commercially from coal-tar. Almost immediately he sent a sample to a firm of dyers in Perth, with the request that they try it for coloring silk. In reply he received a letter that said, "If your discovery does not make the goods too expensive, it is decidedly one of the most valuable that has come out for a long time."

Perkin thus decided to patent his method for manufacturing the new dyestuff. His father agreed to provide financial support, although Hofmann had tried to discourage the venture, and a factory building was begun at Greenford Green in June 1857. Among the initial problems that the manufacturers faced was the refining of suitable raw materials; the eighteen-year-old Perkin had to work out a method of converting nitrobenzene to aniline and to devise not only a new technique but also a new apparatus. Nonetheless Perkin's "Tyrian purple" was being used in London dyehouses within six months, and shortly thereafter other firms in England and France were engaged in its production. Many other procedures for making mauve were soon patented. These represented only slight modifications of Perkin's original process, but fortunately for Perkin none of these newer methods yielded mauve as cheaply as his "bichromate method."

Perkin's discovery gave impetus to a new coal-tar dyestuffs industry. Perkin was able to keep his factory working at a profit in spite of the discovery of a number of other new coloring materials by a number of other chemists; in 1864 he himself introduced a new method for the alkylation of magenta, which allowed him to compete with the manufacturers of other violet dyes.

In 1868 the German chemists Graebe and Liebermann announced that they had synthesized alizarin, the natural coloring matter of madder; their process, however, was too expensive to be of more than scientific interest. Within a year Perkin worked out two new methods to manufacture alizarin more cheaply; both used coal-tar products, one being based upon dichloroanthracene and the other upon the sulfonic acid of anthraquinone. Synthetic alizarin soon replaced rose madder as the prime red dye, both in England and on the Continent. By the end of 1869 Perkin's company had made a ton of alizarin, and by 1871 they were manufacturing 220 tons a year.

Perkin had always hoped to devote himself completely to pure science, and by 1873 he found that his factory and patents could guarantee him the means for a modest retirement. The following year, when he was thirty-six, he sold his factory and turned full time to the research in pure chemistry that he had conducted concurrently with his industrial work. He had already made significant contributions to organic chemistry, even while burdened by commerce; in 1858, a year after his factory had opened, he had discovered that aminoacetic acid could be obtained by heating bromoacetic acid with ammonia. By 1860, in collaboration with B. F. Duppa, he had established the relationships between tartaric, fumaric, and maleic acids and had accomplished the synthesis of cinnamic acid from dibromo succinic acid. About 1867 he began to investigate the action of acetic anhydride on aromatic aldehydes, which led him to the method of synthesizing unsaturated acids by what is now known as "Perkin's synthesis"—a method that he applied, within a year of its discovery, to synthesizing coumarin. This line of investigation culminated, after Perkin's retirement from the dyestuffs industry, in his discovery that cinnamic acid could be synthesized from benzaldehyde—a discovery that made possible the first synthesis of indigo by Baeyer and Caro.

Upon retiring from business Perkin had a new house built at Sudbury and converted the old, adjacent one into a laboratory, where he continued to work almost until the time of his death. In 1881 he became interested in the magnetic rotatory polarization of certain organic compounds and so developed his investigations that the examination of this property became an important tool in considering questions of molecular structure. Perkin devoted the last twenty-five years of his life to this physical aspect of organic chemistry; he was commended for his work by Professor Bruehl, himself one of the pioneers of the application of optical methods to the determination of chemical constitutions, who wrote to him in 1906, "Before you began work there was little, almost nothing, known of this subject, certainly nothing of practical use to the chemist. You created a new branch of science. . . ."

Perkin's personal life was essentially uneventful. His devotion to his work and his family was so complete that, aside from participating in the activities of several scientific societies, he took no part in outside affairs. He was married twice: in 1859 to Jemima Harriet Lissett, who died in 1862, then in 1866 to a Polish girl, Alexandrine Caroline Mollwo, who survived him. He had two sons, both of whom became distinguished professors of chemistry, from his first marriage and one son, Frederick, and four daughters from his second. Perkin was of a retiring disposition and chose to avoid publicity; although colleagues in pure chemistry accorded him considerable recognition for his work, he was less honored by his co-workers in the field of commercial dyestuffs manufacture. In 1906, however, jubilee celebrations were held in England and the United States in commemoration of Perkin's discovery of mauve; distinguished scientists and industrialists from all over the world attended them, and Perkin was knighted upon this occasion. He died of pneumonia, perhaps weakened by the strain attendant upon celebrity, shortly thereafter.

BIBLIOGRAPHY

A complete list of Perkin's work is in Sidney M. Edelstein, "Sir William Henry Perkin," in *American Dyestuff Reporter*, **45** (1956), 598–608.

For further information on Perkin's life and work, see B. Harrow, *Eminent Chemists of Our Times* (New York, 1927); R. Meldola, *Jubilee of the Discovery of Mauve and of the Foundation of Coal-Tar Industry by Sir W. H. Perkin* (London, 1906), and "Obituary Notice," in *Journal of the Chemical Society*, **93** (1908), 2214; and M. Reiman, "On Aniline and Its Derivatives," a treatise on the manufacture of aniline colors, to which is added an appendix, "The Report on the Colouring Matters Derived from Coal Tar," shown at the French Exhibition (1867) by A. W. von Hofmann, Mme G. DeLair, and C. Girard; William Crookes revised and edited the whole work (London, 1868).

SIDNEY EDELSTEIN

PERKIN, WILLIAM HENRY, JR. (*b.* Sudbury, Middlesex, England, 17 June 1860; *d.* Oxford, England, 17 September 1929), *organic chemistry*.

Perkin was the eldest son of William Henry Perkin, the pioneer of synthetic dyestuffs, and Jemima Lissett. He studied at the Royal College of Chemistry in London and then under Johannes Wislicenus at the University of Würzburg (1880–1882) and Adolf von Baeyer at the University of Munich (1882–1886). Soon after his return to Britain, he married, became professor of chemistry at the new Heriot-Watt College in Edinburgh (1887), and was elected a fellow of the Royal Society (1890). In 1892 he succeeded Carl Schorlemmer in the chair of organic chemistry at Owens College in Manchester. Following the retirement (1912) of William Odling from the Waynflete professorship, Perkin moved to Oxford to take charge of an almost moribund department, which, in spite of the stringencies of World War I, he quickly transformed.

Perkin was much influenced by the personality of von Baeyer, and he himself became almost the archetype of a German professor of the best sort—cultured (he was an accomplished musician), fond of walking holidays in the Alps, and devoted to a rather narrow field of research, which nevertheless infused and inspired all his teaching. He was a skilled practical worker, and at no time in his life did he desert the laboratory for long. As a young man in Germany he made the first derivatives of cyclopropane and cyclobutane, thus disproving a widely held opinion that only carbon rings of five or six members could exist. Von Baeyer subsequently used these results in his "strain theory." Perkin's later work was concerned almost entirely with the elucidation of the structures of natural products by degradation and synthesis. He and his students worked on camphor and the terpenes, the natural dyestuffs brazilin and haematoxylin; and a long series of alkaloids, including berberine, harmine, cryptopine, strychnine, and brucine.

When Perkin died complaints were voiced that he had never been given a Nobel Prize. His fundamental shortcoming, however, was that he always applied himself to problems with well-defined solutions, which he studied by established techniques. His solutions, when found, were incorporated into chemistry with little remark. Consequently, he is now less well remembered than his colleagues and brothers-in-law, Lapworth and Kipping, who preferred to break fresh ground.

BIBLIOGRAPHY

I. ORIGINAL WORKS. Perkin wrote more than 200 papers, mostly with collaborators, and a number of textbooks, of which the most successful was *Organic Chemistry* (London, 1894; 2nd ed., 1929), written with F. S. Kipping.

II. SECONDARY LITERATURE. The Chemical Society has published an elaborate obituary entitled *The Life and Work of Professor William Henry Perkin* (London, 1932), which contains a personal memoir by A. J. Greenaway and accounts of Perkin's scientific work by his former colleagues J. F. Thorpe and R. Robinson.

Obituary notices are in *Chemistry and Industry*, **48** (1929), 1008–1012; *Nature*, **124** (1929), 623–627; and *Proceedings of the Royal Society*, **130A** (1930), i–xii. Perkin is also noticed in J. R. H. Weaver, ed., *Dictionary of National Biography 1922–1930* (London, 1967), 665–667.

W. V. FARRAR

PÉRON, FRANÇOIS (*b.* Cérilly, France, 22 August 1775; *d.* Cérilly, 14 December 1810), *zoology, natural history*.

Péron came from a family of modest means. He was intellectually gifted, and began the study of theology in 1791. But he abandoned theology in 1792 and enrolled at the Allier Battalion. He fought in Alsace, where he was wounded and taken prisoner. He was exchanged in 1794 and returned home blind in one eye. Pierre-Lazare Petit-Jean, a notary in Cérilly, financed his studies for three years at the École de Médecine in Paris. Péron was very interested in anthropology, and after learning that an expedition to New Holland (Australia) needed a physician-naturalist, he volunteered for the position. With the support of the naturalists Jussieu and Lacépède, he was accepted as a zoologist.

On 19 October 1800 Péron sailed from Le Havre on the *Géographe*, bound for Tasmania and Australia, with stops scheduled at the Canary Islands, Mauritius, and Timor. Aboard the ship he made the acquaintance of Lesueur and the botanist Leschenault de la Tour. Dysentery broke out on board; and only a few of the scientists and crew survived. The voyage ended at Port Jackson (Sydney Harbor) on 20 June 1802. Péron, Leschenault, and Lesueur had been left behind on King Island (in Bass Strait), when the ship sailed to evade a storm. After twelve days on the island they were rescued by an English vessel.

On 25 March 1804 the expedition arrived at Lorient, France. They returned with about a hundred live animals that had never been seen in Europe, which were intended for the Empress Josephine's château, Malmaison; they also brought plants for her garden and a sizable herbarium. Péron became a frequent guest at Malmaison and was even the empress' reader, which was only a pretext so that he could be supported in his research. Péron, however, was weakened by the voyage, and he did not live long enough to complete his proposed works.

BIBLIOGRAPHY

I. ORIGINAL WORKS. Péron's works are *Histoire générale et particulière de tous les animaux qui composent la famille des médulles* (n.p., n.d.), written with Lesueur; *Mémoire sur le nouveau genre Pyrosoma* (n.p., n.d.); *Mémoire sur quelques faits zoologiques applicables à la théorie du globe, lu à la classe des sciences physiques et mathématiques de l'Institut national* (n.p., n.d.); *Notice sur l'habitation des animaux marins* (n.p., n.d.), written with Lesueur; *Observations sur la dysenterie des pays chauds et sur l'usage du bétel* (n.p., n.d.); *Précis d'un mémoire lu à l'Institut national sur la température des eaux de la mer, soit à sa surface, soit à diverses profondeurs* (Paris, 1816); and *Sur les Méduses du genre Eguorée* (Paris, 1816), 55–99, written with Lesueur.

See also *Voyage de découvertes aux terres australes exécuté sur les corvettes le Géographe, le naturaliste et la goëlette la Casuarina pendant les années 1800–1804 . . .,* I (Paris, 1807), with a preface by Cuvier; *Voyage de découvertes aux terres australes. Historique*, II (Paris, 1816), continued by M. Louis Freycinet; *Voyage de découvertes aux terres australes . . . navigation et géographie . . . par L. Freycinet* (Paris, 1815); *Voyage de découvertes aux terres australes, fait par ordre du gouvernement sur les corvettes le Géographe, le Naturaliste et la goëlette Casuarina pendant les années 1800–1804 rédigé par F. Péron, et continué par Louis de Freycinet*, 2nd ed., 4 vols. (Paris, 1824).

II. SECONDARY LITERATURE. On Péron and his work, see in L. G. Michaud, ed., *Biographie universelle*, new ed. (Paris, 1854–1865), XXXII; and Maurice Girard, *François Péron, naturaliste, voyageur aux terres australes. Sa vie, appréciation de ses travaux, analyse raisonnée de ses recherches sur les animaux vertébrés et invertébrés d'après ses collections déposées au Muséum d'Histoire naturelle . . .* (Paris, 1857), with a portrait.

P. JOVET
J. MALLET

PÉROT, JEAN-BAPTISTE GASPARD GUSTAV ALFRED (*b*. Metz, France, 3 November 1863; *d*. Paris, France, 28 November 1925), *physics.*

Alfred Pérot's most important work involved experiments in optical interferometry and in electricity. He was ingenious with apparatus and as a teacher emphasized the importance of direct contact with experimentation.

Pérot studied at the *lycée* in Nancy and then at the École Polytechnique in Paris. In 1884 he returned to Nancy and worked under Blondlot in the physics laboratory of the university. In 1888 he received the *docteur ès sciences* for measurements of the specific volumes of saturated vapors and for determining the mechanical equivalent of heat. (Pérot's result for the mechanical equivalent was good, but the work was interesting mainly because of the indirect method that Pérot used, which was based on the equation of Clapeyron.)

In 1888 Pérot joined the University of Marseilles as *maître de conférences* and became much involved in problems of electricity. He studied dielectric properties and electromagnetic waves, and he was considered an expert on topics relating to the emerging electrical industry. (In 1894 a special chair in industrial electricity was created for him at the university.) He collaborated with Charles Fabry (1894–1901) in developing and using a new method of optical interferometry. In 1901 Pérot accepted an invitation to be the first director of the *laboratoire d'essais* of the Conservatoire des Arts et Métiers—a difficult administrative task. In 1908 he returned to research at the Meudon Observatory and to teaching at the

École Polytechnique. He studied properties of the solar atmosphere (using the interference and spectroscopic techniques he had developed earlier) and problems associated with the triode and with telegraphy.

The initial inspiration for developing interferometry came when Fabry was asked to help in measuring the distance between metallic surfaces about a micron apart. Fabry thought of using interference between rays of light that have undergone different numbers of reflections between the two surfaces, and he and Pérot began to study the very fine fringes produced by reflections between silvered films. This work led to development of the "Fabry-Pérot interferometer." According to Fabry, he and Pérot complemented each other nicely in this work; Fabry was more theoretically inclined, while Pérot imagined the actual mechanical arrangements that would make the technique succeed. Fabry, Pérot, and Macé de Lepinay (who already in 1885 used optical methods to determine thicknesses) used the new interferometer to determine the mass of a cubic centimeter of water. Later, Fabry and Pérot used the silver-film interferometer as a spectroscopic analyzer and measured the wavelengths of the black lines in the solar spectrum—thus making it possible to correct small errors in Rowland's wavelengths.

Pérot's analysis of solar spectra involved some interesting problems, since small shifts in wavelength are produced by a variety of causes (for example, pressure effects, convection currents, and the Doppler effect due to rotation). Pérot was inspired to separate some of these effects, and from 1920 to 1921 he tried to verify the gravitational red shift of Einstein's general theory of relativity. (Experimental verification of the gravitational red shift is difficult, and conclusive measurements were not made until 1960; see R. H. Dicke, *The Theoretical Significance of Experimental Relativity* [New York, 1964], 25–27.)

BIBLIOGRAPHY

I. ORIGINAL WORKS. Perot's articles include "Sur la mesure du volume spécifique des vapeurs saturées et la détermination de l'équivalent mécanique de la chaleur," in *Journal de physique*, **7** (1888), 129–148; "Les applications industrielles d'électricité," in *Annales de la Faculté des Sciences de Marseille*, **4** (1895); "Mesure de petites épaisseurs en valeur absolue," in *Comptes rendus hebdomadaires des séances de l'Académie des sciences*, **123** (1896), 802–805, written with C. Fabry; "Sur une nouvelle méthode de spectroscopie interférentielle," *ibid.*, **126** (1898), 34–36, written with C. Fabry; and "Mesure de la pression de l'atmosphère solaire dans la couche du magnésium et vérification du principe de relativité," *ibid.*, **172** (1921), 578–581. More of Perot's papers are listed in Royal Society *Catalogue of Scientific Papers*, 4th ser., XVII, 798, and in Poggendorff, IV, 1140–1141; V, 958–959; and VI, 1984.

II. SECONDARY LITERATURE. On Pérot's life and work, see the essays by Charles Fabry in *Bulletin de la Société astronomique de France*, **40** (1926), 40–43 (with the announcement on pp. 2–3), and in *Astrophysical Journal*, **64** (1926), 209–214, which includes information about the initial development of the silver-film interferometer. See also the bibliography to the article on C. Fabry.

SIGALIA DOSTROVSKY

PERRAULT, CLAUDE (*b.* Paris, France, 25 September 1613; *d.* Paris, 11 October 1688), *zoology, medicine, plant and animal physiology, architecture, mechanical engineering.*

Perrault was the son of Pierre Perrault, originally from Tours and an advocate at the Parlement de Paris, and Paquette Leclerc. It was a talented, versatile, and close-knit family; his brothers were the fairy-tale writer Charles Perrault and the hydrologist Pierre Perrault. As boys, the brothers collaborated in such things as writing mock-heroic verse, and in adult life each aided the career of the other. Perrault was educated at the Collège de Beauvais and then trained as a physician; he presented his thesis at the University of Paris in 1639. He then practiced quietly for the next twenty years, acquiring a reputation, but publishing nothing until he was invited to become a founding member of the Académie des Sciences in 1666. He may have owed this invitation, in part, to the influence of his brother Charles, who was then assistant to the chief minister, Colbert, patron of the Academy.

In June 1667 the Academy was invited to dissect a thresher shark and a lion which had died at the royal menagerie. The reports on these dissections were the first of a long series of anatomical descriptions, which ultimately included those of twenty-five species of mammals, seventeen birds, five reptiles, one amphibian, and one fish. These were eventually assembled in 1676 as memoirs toward a natural history of animals and first appeared anonymously. The anatomists worked as a team and every description had to be accepted by all. Nevertheless, Perrault's name has always been attached to the descriptions, and, in the early years at least, he was undoubtedly the leader of the group.

In general the reports followed a traditional pattern: the anatomists first compared the species with the accounts given by the ancient naturalists, then investigated any legends attached to the species, primarily to dispel them. The authors then proceeded to examine the external appearance of the head, the main internal organs, and the skeleton. Although problems of respiration in birds, fish, and aquatic mammals were of interest to them, the Parisian anatomists (like most naturalists of their day) considered the mechanisms of unusual anatomical features to be particularly worthy of investigation. Perrault discussed the structure of bird feathers and their adaptation to flight, and in his examination of ostrich feathers suggested why they were unsuited for this purpose. In the group's initial dissections Perrault stressed the mechanical functions of the spiral intestine of the shark and the mechanism that retracts the claws of the lion.

In the rationalist atmosphere of the day, it was the debunking of old and popular myths that most attracted public attention. The group tested whether salamanders lived in fire, whether pelicans fed their young with their own blood by stabbing their breasts, and whether chameleons could live on air and change their color to match that of their surroundings; in each case they found the old belief false. Perrault and his group did not, however, spend as much time on these points as has been supposed, and Perrault appears to have been prouder of his positive observations, as, for example, his careful description of the protrusion of the tongue of the chameleon (which he falsely attributed to vascular pressure) and the independent swiveling motion of its eyes. Although some of the discoveries on which the Parisians most prided themselves—including the nictitating membrane that Perrault first observed in a cassowary, the external lobation of the kidneys in the bear, and the castoreal glands of the beaver—had been observed earlier, no such detailed and exact descriptions and illustrations had been published before.

The Parisian dissections were made over several years as specimens became available, usually by the death of some animal at the menagerie. During this time, Perrault was certainly thinking about wider problems of comparative anatomy and physiology and botany. He claimed to have conceived independently and expounded to the Academy two theories, which, although subsequently shown to be erroneous, were in his lifetime, and for many years thereafter, highly influential. These theories concerned the circulation of sap in plants and the embryonic growth from preformed germs, which Perrault thought to be present in all parts of the body. He stated that his botanical theory was first proposed to the Academy in January 1667; it was not, however, a strictly circulatory theory. Perrault thought that there were two fluids at work, one conveying nourishment absorbed from the air through the branches and bark of the trunk to the roots, and a second transporting nourishment absorbed from the earth up to the branches through internal channels. His arguments,

which were supported by a number of experiments, had to be reevaluated by later workers, including Hales, who in the eighteenth century refuted this general hypothesis. Perrault's preformation theory, first stated in 1668, was somewhat overshadowed by the similar but more detailed expositions of his contemporaries.

Not until 1680 did Perrault begin to publish an all-embracing natural philosophy which comprehended these theories, together with his other researches in anatomy, various aspects of animal and plant physiology, and acoustics. The influence of Descartes, although scarcely acknowledged, is patent in this work. Accepting the concept of an atmosphere composed of coarser and subtler parts of the air and of a still finer "ethereal body," Perrault claimed that this assumption allowed him to explain the phenomena of elasticity and hardness. These two key ideas then enabled him to account for almost anything else, from metallurgical phenomena to the sounds of different musical instruments. He also thought that peristaltic motion explained the action of arteries and the contraction of muscles.

Perrault's longest essay was devoted to sound (or noise, as he preferred to call it), which he attempted to explain as an agitation of the air. This agitation, however, affects only the ear, which is not touched by wind or other motions of the air. Perrault rejected the concept of sound waves for he thought that sound should be understood as an agitation that occurs in a restricted space and is produced by the impact of particles in a narrow rectilinear beam. He also discussed the comparative anatomy of the organs of hearing in the various animals he had dissected, and discovered that the lower larynx is the organ of sound in birds. In order to establish the difference between sight and hearing, he made similarly detailed comparisons of different organs of vision.

Perrault's basic ideas had probably been developed well before their publication, but he lacked the leisure to write them up. In fact, at the height of his researches in natural history, he was even more active as an architect than as an anatomist. In 1667 he was invited to join the committee that eventually produced a plan for the completion of the Louvre. Much of his time over the next few years must have been devoted to this task (and to the intrigue that went with it), for the colonnade of the Louvre largely follows his plans. In the same year he produced designs for the observatory, which both he and Colbert hoped would be a center for all the activities of the Academy. When it was objected that Perrault's plans were not well suited for astronomical observations, they were modified, but the observatory, when completed, was still mainly his work. He also designed a triumphal arch, built a house for Colbert in Sceaux in 1673, and worked on two Paris churches from 1674 to 1678. The journal of his journey to Bordeaux in the autumn of 1669 contained mainly architectural notes.

In connection with his work on the Louvre, Perrault became interested in the problem of friction in machines. Several of the machines he designed to overcome this problem were used at the Louvre and then, in 1691, at the Invalides. These designs appeared with other inventions, among them a pendulum-controlled water clock and a pulley system to rotate the mirror of a reflecting telescope, in a posthumous collection published by his brother Charles. Perrault also included among his essays one on ancient music, to show its inferiority to that of his own day; but he was also enough of a classicist to translate Vitruvius.

After Colbert's death, the position of the Perrault family declined. Claude Perrault's house was among those torn down to make room for the Place des Victoires and he seems to have spent his last years writing his essays, possibly at his brother's house. But he was a keen academician until his death. He died of an infection received at the dissection of a camel. Although the extraordinary breadth of his interests and his ability to make significant discoveries in so many fields may have prevented him from achieving complete mastery in any one of them, Perrault was nevertheless an original and highly influential figure. Few of his predecessors described so many species in such detail, or with such clarity and precision.

BIBLIOGRAPHY

I. ORIGINAL WORKS. Many of Perrault's reports are included in *Mémoires pour servir à l'histoire naturelle des animaux* (Paris, 1671); for the complex publication history of this work, and of the individual *Descriptions anatomiques* that preceded it, see E. J. Cole, *A History of Comparative Anatomy* (London, 1944), 396–401. Subsequent works are *Essais de physique, ou recueil de plusieurs traites touchant les choses naturelles*, 4 vols. (Paris, 1680, 1688), republished with some minor works as *Oeuvres diverses de physique et de méchanique*, 2 vols. (Leiden, 1721); and *Recueil de plusieurs machines de nouvelle invention* (Paris, 1700).

II. SECONDARY LITERATURE. On Perrault and his work, see Charles Perrault, *Mémoires de ma Vie* (published with Claude Perrault), *Voyage à Bordeaux*, P. Bonnefon, ed. (Paris, 1909) and *Les hommes illustres qui ont paru en France, pendant ce siècle*, I (Paris, 1696), 67–68; J. Colombe, "Portraits d'ancêtres: III. Claude Perrault," in *Hippocrate*, **16**, nos. 4–5 (1949), 1–47; Marquis de Condorcet, *Éloges des academiciens de l'Académie Royal des Sciences* (Paris, 1773), 83–103; and A. Hallays, *Les Perrault* (Paris, 1926).

Perrault's anatomical descriptions are analyzed by E. J. Cole (see above), 393–458; his architectural work is discussed in L. Hautecoeur, *Histoire de l'architecture classique en France*, III (Paris, 1948), 441–461; and the "Essais de physique" are discussed in J. Leibowitz, *Claude Perrault, physiologiste* (Paris, 1930).

The Perrault papers at the Academy are listed in a descriptive catalog (not seen by the author) prepared by Alan Gabbey. A copy is deposited in the Archives.

A. G. KELLER

PERRAULT, PIERRE (*b.* France, 1611; *d.* France, 1680), *natural history.*

Very little is known about the personal life of Pierre Perrault, who was rather overshadowed, at least during his lifetime, by his three younger brothers: Claude (1613–1688), a physician, scientist, and the architect of the Louvre; Nicholas (1624–1662), a noted theologian; and Charles (1628–1703), a critic and the author of the Mother Goose fairy tales. Pierre, following in his father's footsteps, became a lawyer and joined the government service as an administrator. He bought the post of receiver-general of finances for Paris. His timing was rather unfortunate, for Louis XIV soon remitted the *tailles* due for the previous ten years. Perrault, along with other tax collectors, encountered financial difficulties. He borrowed on the current year's (1664) revenue and was caught in the act by Colbert, who was then at the height of his power. He was dismissed and was forced to sell his post at a loss. The affair left him almost penniless.

It is not known how Perrault earned his living after the dismissal. He did, however, make a very poor translation of Alessandro Tassoni's *Secchia rapita.*

The book *De l'origine des fontaines* was published anonymously at Paris in 1674. Its authorship, the subject of considerable controversy in the past, has been variously attributed to André Félibien, Denis Papin, and finally to its true author, Perrault. In it he reviewed the various earlier hypotheses on the origin of springs and proposed an experimental investigation to prove that rainfall alone is sufficient to sustain the flow of springs and rivers throughout the year. Perrault considered the Seine River, from its source to Aynay-le-Duc (now Aignay-le-Duc), determining the total drainage area for that portion and making observations of annual rainfall. Using the average annual rainfall, he estimated the total volume of water that precipitated over the drainage area. The losses due to "feeding the trees, herbs, vapours, [and] extraordinary swellings of the river when it rains" were deducted from this figure to obtain sustained runoff. The total annual flow of the Seine was estimated by comparing its flow with that of the Gobelins River near Versailles, which had been measured previously. Having determined the total annual rainfall over the entire drainage area of the River Seine and the total annual flow of the river itself, Perrault experimentally demonstrated that only one-sixth of the annual rainfall was necessary to sustain the river flow. Thus for the first time it was scientifically proven that rainfall is more than adequate to supply river flow.

But Perrault did not believe in the general infiltration of rainwater and, thereby, recharge of groundwater. He went to great lengths to find evidence of general infiltration, and from his observations he concluded that it was only an occasional and local phenomenon. In the beginning of the second part of his book, Perrault differentiated his own view from that held by Vitruvius, Gassendi, Pallisy, and Jean François, which he referred to as "general opinion." He objected to their concept of infiltration of rainwater into the earth and said that he did not believe that there is enough precipitation for the earth to be soaked with it as much as necessary, and still leave over a sufficient quantity to cause rivers and springs.

Perrault's experimental work on the rainfall and runoff of the upper Seine is a milestone in the history of hydrology. Admittedly his experimental techniques were somewhat crude and his figures could have been more refined, but his reasoning was flawless, his method irrefutable, and his was the first experimentation to prove categorically that rivers originated from rainfall. Edmé Mariotte later used more sophisticated measuring techniques to confirm Perrault's findings. The second half of the concept of the hydrologic cycle, that enough water evaporated from oceans and rivers to come down as rainfall, was experimentally proved by Edmond Halley. Biswas, in his *History of Hydrology*, has suggested that Perrault, Mariotte, and Halley should be considered as cofounders of experimental hydrology. But when it is considered that Mariotte and Halley were familiar with Perrault's work and may have been considerably influenced by it, Perrault's contributions to hydrology become all the more important.

An international symposium on the history of hydrology was held at Paris in 1974, by the International Hydrological Decade, to mark the tricentenary of the publication of Perrault's trailblazing book.

BIBLIOGRAPHY

I. ORIGINAL WORKS. Perrault's major writing is *De l'origine des fontaines* (Paris, 1674), trans. by A. LaRocque as *On the Origin of Springs* (New York, 1967). He also translated Alessandro Tassoni's *La secchia rapita* as *Le seau enlevé* (Paris, 1678),

II. SECONDARY LITERATURE. See Asit K. Biswas, "Beginning of Quantitative Hydrology," in *Journal of the Hydraulics Division, American Society of Civil Engineers*, **94** (1968), 1299–1316; and *History of Hydrology* (Amsterdam, 1970), 208–213; and S. Delorme, "Pierre Perrault," in *Archives internationales d'histoire des sciences*, **27**, no. 3 (1948), 388–394.

MARGARET R. BISWAS
ASIT K. BISWAS

PERRIER, EDMOND (*b.* Tulle, France, 9 May 1844; *d.* Paris, France, 31 July 1921), *zoology*.

The son of a school principal in Tulle, Perrier began his education in that city and completed his secondary education in Paris. In 1864 he scored well on the competitive entrance examinations to both the École Polytechnique and the science section of the École Normale Supérieure. At the suggestion of Pasteur, who was then its director, he chose the latter institution, where his teacher was Lacaze-Duthiers. He earned his *licence ès sciences* in mathematics and physics in 1866, passed the *agrégation* in physics in 1867, and began teaching physics at the *lycée* of Agen. A few months later he returned to Paris where Lacaze-Duthiers had secured his appointment as *aide-naturaliste* at the Muséum d'Histoire Naturelle. He obtained his *licence* in natural science in 1868 and the following year defended a dissertation, "Recherches sur les pédicellaires et les ambulacres des astéries et des oursins," that earned him the *doctorat ès sciences naturelles*. Named *maître de conférences* in zoology at the École Normale Supérieure in 1872, he held similar posts several years later at the *écoles normales* of Sèvres and of St.-Cloud. He was appointed professor-administrator at the Muséum d'Histoire Naturelle in 1876 and in 1900 became its director, a post he held for some twenty years. Elected to the Paris Academy of Sciences in 1892, he became its president in 1913.

The major portion of Perrier's zoological work is devoted to the anatomy, physiology, and taxonomy of the invertebrates. He participated in oceanographic expeditions in the Atlantic in 1881 and in the Mediterranean in 1883 and established the Museum's marine biology laboratory at St.-Vaast-la-Hougue in 1887. He also was called upon to classify the material obtained on several expeditions, notably the starfish collected under the direction of Alexander Agassiz.

Perrier, who declared his acceptance of the theory of evolution in 1879, was always particularly interested in the study of the oligochaetes and echinoderms, since these groups represented the two major types of animal organization: segments arranged in linear series and segments radiating from a center. His richest theoretical work, and perhaps his most original, is *Les colonies animales* (1881). In it he attempted to comprehend the evolutionary formation of groups of organisms, starting with the simplest creatures, which are favored in their evolution by their ability to reproduce by division or budding. Certain of these creatures remained independent, while others, Perrier explained, agglomerated into colonies in which, at first, they preserved their individuality. In a subsequent stage this individuality was eliminated by the effect of a division of physiological labor implying a reciprocal dependence as well as a differentiation of forms. The later transformations of the linear or irregular (simple or coalescent) colonies were, on this view, the origin of the major taxonomic divisions.

At the time of its publication (1902) another work by Perrier, "Tachygenèse" (written in collaboration with Charles Gravier), was also of theoretical interest. In it Perrier sought to explain apparent difficulties of the biogenetic law by the phenomenon of embryogenic acceleration (according to which in a series of organisms, "the higher the given organism is in the series, the more rapid, in general, is the development and the more advanced is the stage of development at which hatching occurs") and by the occurrence of embryonic adaptations that modify the subsequent development of the organism.

Perrier quickly became one of the principal defenders in France of the theory of evolution; but he was never a Darwinian in the strict sense and was one of those mainly responsible for the revival of Lamarckism in France. Perrier was interested in the history of his discipline and wrote, in addition to his book on Lamarck, a long preface to Quatrefage's *Émules de Darwin* and *La philosophie zoologique avant Darwin*, which is still a useful source for the study of biology in the nineteenth century.

The author of a substantial *Traité de zoologie* and several textbooks, Perrier was also director of the *Annales des sciences naturelles* (*zoologie*) from 1900 until his death. His many popular articles appeared mainly in *Revue scientifique* and in the newspaper *Le temps*.

BIBLIOGRAPHY

I. ORIGINAL WORKS. A chronological list of Perrier's scientific publications is at the end of the article by R. Anthony cited below. Perrier himself prepared, on the occasion of his candidacies for the Paris Academy of Sciences, *Notice sur les travaux scientifiques de H. O. Edmond Perrier* (Paris, 1875, 1886, 1892), containing an analysis of his works.

The following works are of particular importance: "Recherches sur les pédicellaires et les ambulacres des astéries et des oursins," in *Annales des sciences naturelles*, 5th ser., **12** (1869), 197–304; **13** (1870), 5–81; "Recherches pour servir à l'histoire des lombriciens terrestres," in *Archives (nouvelles) du Muséum d'histoire naturelle*, **8** (1872), 5–198; "Révision de la collection des stellérides du Muséum d'histoire naturelle," in *Archives de zoologie expérimentale et générale*, **4** (1875), 265–450 and **5** (1876), 1–104, 209–304; "Le transformisme et les sciences physiques," in *Revue scientifique*, **16** (1879), 890–895; "Rôle de l'association dans le regne animal," *ibid.*, **17** (1879), 553–559; *Les colonies animales et la formation des organismes* (Paris, 1881); "Sur l'appareil circulatoire des étoiles de mer," in *Comptes rendus . . . de l'Académie des sciences*, **94** (1882), 658–661, written with J. Poirier; *La philosophie zoologique avant Darwin* (Paris, 1884); *Le transformisme* (Paris, 1888); *Traité de zoologie*, 10 fascs. (Paris, 1893–1932); "La tachygenèse ou accélération embryogénique, son importance dans les modifications des phénomènes embryogéniques, son rôle dans la transformation des organismes," in *Annales des sciences naturelles* (*zoologie*), **16** (1902), 133–374, written with C. Gravier; *La terre avant l'histoire* (Paris, 1921); and *Lamarck* (Paris, 1925).

The bulk of Perrier's MSS are in the archives of the Paris Academy of Sciences and the Muséum National d'Histoire Naturelle.

II. SECONDARY LITERATURE. To date no full study of Perrier's work exists, but the following articles are useful: R. Anthony, "Edmond Perrier, 1844–1921," in *Archives du Muséum national d'histoire naturelle*, 6th ser., **1** (1926), 1–14; C. Gravier, "En souvenir de M. Edmond Perrier," in *Bulletin du Muséum national d'histoire naturelle* (1921), no. 7; and M. Phisalix, "Edmond Perrier (1844–1921)," in *Bulletin de l'Association des élèves de Sèvres* (Jan. 1922).

C. LIMOGES

PERRIER, GEORGES (*b.* Montpellier, France, 28 October 1872; *d.* Paris, France, 16 February 1946), *geodesy.*

Perrier was the son of François Perrier, who revived French geodesy and created the Service Géographique de l'Armée. He graduated from the École Polytechnique in 1894 as an artillery officer, intending to continue his family's military and scientific tradition. For more than half a century his activities centered on geodesy, interrupted only by World War I and certain peacetime requirements of his military career. In addition to achieving important results as an officer in the Service Géographique de l'Armée, he concentrated on two major geodesic tasks.

First, as a young officer he played a major role in preparing and executing a scientific mission sent to Peru and Ecuador to measure an arc of meridian at low latitudes. Lasting from 1901 to 1906, the project was particularly difficult because of the topography and climate of the Andean cordilleras. Perrier was the only geodesist who participated from beginning to end. After returning to France he was placed in charge of evaluating and processing all the measurements and of publishing the results. This overwhelming assignment, delayed by the two world wars, dragged on and eventually diminished in significance as a result of the development of new geodetic techniques.

Second, from 1919 until his death Perrier served as secretary-general of the organization created in 1919 and several years later named the Association Internationale de Géodésie. This body replaced the Association Géodésique Internationale, which had had its headquarters in Potsdam and the activities of which had been interrupted in 1914 by the war. Transforming the general secretariat of the new association into a center of activity in geodesy, Perrier suggested and encouraged many undertakings, improved existing publications, and created new ones.

BIBLIOGRAPHY

I. ORIGINAL WORKS. Perrier produced the following portions of Ministère de l'Instruction Publique, *Mission du Service géographique de l'armée pour la mesure d'un arc de méridien équatorial en Amérique du Sud, sous le contrôle scientifique de l'Académie des sciences (1899–1906)*, pt. B, *Géodésie et astronomie*: II, fasc. 1, *Notices sur les stations (Atlas)* (Paris, 1913); II, fasc. 1, *Notices sur les stations (Atlas). Appendice: Origine, notation et sens des noms géographiques de l'Atlas; vocabulaires espagnol–français et quichua–français"* (Paris, 1918); III, fasc. 1, *Angles azimutaux* (Paris, 1910); III, fasc. 2, *Compensation des angles, calcul des triangles* (Paris, 1912); III, fasc. 7, *Latitudes astronomiques observées aux théodolites à microscopes*, pt. 1, "Considérations générales," preceded by "Introduction historique" (also found in III, fasc. 8, *Latitudes astronomiques observées aux astrolabes à prisme*) (Paris, 1925); and III, fasc. 7, pts. 2 and 3, *Tableaux numériques des observations et conclusions* (Paris, 1911).

His other writings include *Pascal* (Paris, 1901), written with A. Hatzfeld—"Travaux scientifiques," pp. 113–191, is by Perrier; "La figure de la terre, les grandes opérations géodésiques, l'ancienne et la nouvelle mesure de l'arc méridien de Quito," in *Revue annuelle de géographie*, 2nd ser., **2** (108), 201–508; "Les académiciens au Pérou, 1735–1744," in *L'astronomie* (Mar.–Apr. 1911); *La géodésie militaire française, historique et travaux actuels et La géodésie moderne à l'étranger* (Paris, 1912), two lectures given at the Service Géographique de l'Armée; *Union géodésique et géophysique internationale: Première assemblée générale, Rome 1922, section de géodésie* (Toulouse, 1922); *Bibliographie des oeuvres de géographie mathématique publiées en France de 1910 à 1920 inclus, précédé d'un projet de classification et d'indexation pour la géo-*

graphie mathématique, which is **19**, sec. 2, no. 1 of *Bibliographie scientifique française* (1922); *Comptes rendus de la première assemblée générale de la section de géodésie de l'union géodésique et géophysique internationale, réunie à Rome en mai 1922, rédigés et publiés avec 18 annexes par . . . G. Perrier* (Toulouse, 1923)—the appendixes contain, under Perrier's signature, the secretary-general's administrative and financial report (79–83), a note on the junction of the French and Italian triangulations, (95–100), and a note on the electric recording of the oscillations of a pendulum (148–157), written with Gustave Ferrié.

Additional works are "Où en est la géodésie? Les problèmes et les travaux actuels," in *L'astronomie*, **37** (1923), 433–457, 505–526; "La deuxième assemblée générale de l'Union géodésique et géophysique internationale, section de géodésie, Madrid, . . . 1924," in *Bulletin géodésique*, no. 4 (Oct.–Dec. 1924), 241–278; "Les raisons géodésiques de l'isostasie terrestre," in *Annuaire du Bureau des longitudes* for 1926, Sect. B., *Tables de l'ellipsoïde de référence internationale* (Paris, 1928), written with E. Hasse; "La coopération internationale en géodésie et en géophysique. Troisième assemblée générale de l'Union internationale de géodésie et géophysique, Prague, 1927," in *Annuaire du Bureau des longitudes* for 1928, sect. C; "Triangulation de détail des régions andines centrale et septentrionale," in *Géographie*, **49**, nos. 5–6 (May–June 1928), 365–385, and **50**, nos. 1–2 (July–Aug. 1928), 26–49; "L'Académie des sciences, le Bureau des Longitudes et les grandes missions scientifiques," in *Annuaire du Bureau des longitudes* for 1933, Sect. C; and *Petite histoire de la géodésie* (Paris, 1939).

II. SECONDARY LITERATURE. See Élie Cartan, "Information nécrologique . . .," in *Comptes rendus . . . de l'Académie des sciences*, **222**, no. 8 (18 Feb. 1946), 421–423; M. Delhau, "Le général Georges-François Perrier," in *Bulletin des séances. Institut r. colonial belge*, **18**, no. 1 (1947), 127–164, with photograph; "Le général Georges Perrier," in *Bulletin géodésique*, n.s. no. 1 (July 1946), 7–21, with photograph; "Notice nécrologique sur le général Perrier," in *Comptes rendus du Comité National français de géodésie et géophysique* for 1946, 17–21; and *Notice sommaire sur les titres et travaux scientifiques de M. Georges Perrier* (Toulouse, 1926).

A. GOUGENHEIM

PERRIN, JEAN BAPTISTE (*b.* Lille, France, 30 September 1870; *d.* New York, New York, 17 April 1942), *physical chemistry*.

Along with his two sisters, Perrin was raised in modest circumstances by his mother, after his father, an army officer, died of wounds received in the Franco-Prussian War. Perrin obtained his secondary education in Lyons and at the Lycée Janson-de-Sailly in Paris, where his special preparation in mathematics enabled him, in 1891, after serving one year in the army, to gain entrance into the École Normale Supérieure. In 1895 he became *agrégé-préparateur* at the École Normale, and two years later he completed his doctorate.

Perrin's years as a student at the École Normale were exceptionally formative, owing primarily to the influence of his teacher, Marcel Brillouin, who was an outspoken advocate of Boltzmann's "statistical mechanics" and an outspoken adversary of Ostwald's and Mach's "energetics." It is possible to detect Perrin's atomistic biases even in his first paper of 1895, in which he reported experiments demonstrating that cathode rays are negatively charged by collecting them in a "Faraday cup" (an open-ended metal cylinder with appropriate electrical connections). In 1896 Perrin won the Joule Prize of the Royal Society for his experiments on cathode rays and for certain preliminary studies on Röntgen's recently discovered X rays; this formed the basis for his doctoral thesis the following year.

Soon after receiving his degree, Perrin married Henriette Duportal; they had a daughter, Aline, and a son, Francis. Perrin was placed in charge of developing a course in physical chemistry at the Sorbonne, for which he wrote his pro-Boltzmannian *Traité de chimie physique. Les principes* (1903). For Perrin, these years, in general, were years of transition. The focus of his research shifted from cathode rays and X rays, and a general concern with the atomic hypothesis (in 1901 he suggested, for example, that the atom was like a miniature solar system), to experiments on ion transport and the whole problem of how an electrolyte transfers its charge to the walls of a container (*électrisation par contact*). It was out of these studies, in turn, and the stimulation provided by Siedentopf and Zsigmondy's 1903 invention of the "slit ultramicroscope," that Perrin's interest arose in the behavior of colloidal particles and, in particular, in their Brownian motion. By 1906 this problem had already begun to attract his attention, and in 1908 he inaugurated his classic series of experiments on the subject.

It struck Perrin that colloidally suspended particles undergoing Brownian motion (as a result of collisions with the molecules of the surrounding fluid) should distribute themselves vertically in a definite way at equilibrium. Only after finding experimentally that their number decreases exponentially with increasing height, and only after proving that this variation (and hence a definite value of Avogadro's number) follows from kinetic theory, did Perrin learn, through Langevin, of Einstein's and Smoluchowki's 1905–1906 theoretical papers on Brownian motion, and sub-

sequently understand that his work was also consistent with theirs.

In auxiliary experiments Perrin proved that Stokes's law (and hence his calculation of the particle's mass) was valid for particles as small as 0.1 micron. In 1909 Perrin's student Chaudesaigues also demonstrated the accuracy of Einstein's prediction that the mean displacement of a given particle undergoing Brownian motion is proportional to the square root of the time of observation, a result that undercut earlier criticisms of Einstein's work by Svedberg and others. During the same year Perrin continued to refine and extend his experiments (for example, he verified Einstein's formula for rotational Brownian motion). Perrin's work brought him a great deal of formal recognition over the years: in 1909 he was awarded the Prix Gaston Planté; he was appointed to a chair of physical chemistry especially created for him at the Sorbonne, which he held for three decades (1910–1940); in 1911 and 1921 he received invitations to the extremely influential Solvay conferences; in 1923 he was elected to the Académie des Sciences (he became its president in 1938); he was awarded eight honorary degrees, several prizes, and membership in seven foreign academies of science; and in 1926 he received the Nobel Prize for physics. His most fundamental conclusion—that he had finally uncovered irrefutable proof for the real existence of atoms—contrary to the assertions and expectations of Ostwald, Mach, and others—was soon universally accepted and popularized in his book *Les atomes* (1913), which went through many editions and translations.

As an army officer in World War I, Perrin worked on acoustic detection devices for submarines and other military equipment. Between 1918 and 1921 he studied the phenomenon of fluorescence and the interaction between light and matter. He simultaneously demonstrated his insight into current problems of nuclear physics by offering essentially correct, albeit qualitative, speculations on the origin of solar energy and on the nature of nuclear reactions. In subsequent years, as a convinced socialist, Perrin became increasingly involved with the institutional development of science in France. In the late 1930's, for example, he was primarily responsible both for establishing the Centre National de la Recherche Scientifique and for founding the Palais de la Découverte in Paris. In 1940 his well-known and outspoken antifascism made it necessary for him to emigrate from France. He came to the United States, where he helped establish the French University of New York (École Libre des Hautes Études). His son, Francis, was then teaching at Columbia University, where Perrin himself had been an exchange professor in 1913.

Perrin died in New York, but after the war his remains were returned to his homeland and buried in the Panthéon.

BIBLIOGRAPHY

I. ORIGINAL WORKS. Perrin's initial papers were "Nouvelles propriétés des rayons cathodiques," in *Comptes rendus hebdomadaires des séances de l'Académie des sciences*, **121** (1895), 1130; and his doctoral thesis, "Rayons cathodiques et rayons de Roentgen," in *Annales de chimie et de physique*, **11** (1897), 496–554. Two of his early Sorbonne papers were "Mécanisme de l'électrisation de contact et solutions colloïdales," in *Journal de chimie physique*, **2** (1904), 601–651; **3** (1905), 50–110. He offered a summary of his 1908–1909 work (especially as it had appeared earlier in *Comptes rendus*) in "Mouvement Brownien et réalité moléculaire," in *Annales de chimie et de physique*, **18** (1909) 1–114, trans. into English by Frederick Soddy (London, 1910) and into German by J. Donau (Dresden–Leipzig, 1910). Two of Perrin's postwar papers were "La fluorescence," in *Annales de physique*, **10** (1918), 133–159, and "Matière et lumière," *ibid.*, **11** (1919), 1–108. These papers, and later papers directed at institutional concerns, have been collected under the title *Oeuvres scientifiques de Jean Perrin* (Paris, 1950). Perrin's two most important books are *Traité de chimie physique*, I, *Les principes* (Paris, 1903), and *Les atomes* (Paris, 1913).

II. SECONDARY LITERATURE. The most comprehensive study of Perrin's life and work is Mary Jo Nye, *Molecular Reality* (London, 1972), the bibliography of which lists all important secondary sources on Perrin, certain primary source documents not contained in *Oeuvres scientifiques de Jean Perrin*, and other primary source documents, for example, Einstein's papers on Brownian motion.

ROGER H. STUEWER

PERRINE, CHARLES DILLON (*b.* Steubenville, Ohio, 28 July 1867; *d.* Villa General Mitre, Argentina, 21 July 1951), *astronomy*.

After a brief career in business, Perrine, who was skilled in photography, became professionally interested in astronomy. In 1893 he joined the staff at the Lick Observatory as secretary; shortly thereafter he became widely known for his discovery, observation, and calculation of orbits of comets and for his determination of solar parallax from observations of the asteroid Eros. He was made acting astronomer and then astronomer. In 1901 he discovered motion in the nebulosity surrounding a nova in Perseus.

Between 1900 and 1909 Perrine accompanied four eclipse expeditions, directing one in 1901 from the Lick to Sumatra. He also spoke on eclipses at the Interna-

tional Congress of Sciences (1904) in St. Louis. Perrine's most widely acclaimed scientific achievement occurred in 1904 and 1905, when he discovered the sixth and seventh satellites of Jupiter. His subsequent research, initiated by J. A. Keeler, with the Crossley reflector at the Lick was less publicized but of considerable importance; it led to most of the work contained in volume VIII of the *Publications of the Lick Observatory*, which dealt with nebulae and star clusters.

In 1909 Perrine was appointed director of the Argentine National Observatory at Cordoba. He was also responsible for the establishment of the astrophysical station in Bosque Alegre. The sixty-inch reflector at this station made it one of the principal observatories in the Southern Hemisphere. Sixteen volumes of the *Resultades del Observatorio Nacional Argentino* were published during Perrine's directorship.

Despite his scientific achievements, Perrine and his office became a target for nationalist politicians and he was attacked verbally by deputies in the Argentine Congress. In 1931 he was barely missed by a sniper's bullet and in 1933 the Argentine Congress passed legislation removing authority from the director of the observatory. He retired, under duress, in 1936.

Perrine received several honors, including the Lalande Prize from the Paris Academy of Sciences in 1897; the Gold Medal from the Sociedad Astronómica de Mexico; and an honorary Sc.D. from the University of Santa Clara, California, in 1905. He was president of the Astronomical Society of the Pacific in 1907, and a member of various American and foreign societies.

BIBLIOGRAPHY

I. ORIGINAL WORKS. Perrine published nearly 200 papers. His most important articles include "Comet c 1895," in *Publications of the Astronomical Society of the Pacific*, **7** (1895), 342–343; "Preliminary Report of Observations of the Total Solar Eclipse of 1901, May 17, 18," in *Astrophysical Journal*, **14** (1901), 349–359; "Motion of the Faint Nebula Surrounding Nova Persei," *ibid.*, 359–362; "Some Total Eclipse Problems," *ibid.*, **20** (1904), 331–337; "Experimental Determination of the Solar Parallax From Negatives of Eros Made With the Crossley Reflector," in *Publications of the Astronomical Society of the Pacific*, **16** (1904), 267; "Discovery of a Sixth Satellite to Jupiter," *ibid.*, **17** (1905), 22–23; and "The Seventh Satellite of Jupiter," *ibid.*, 62–63.

II. SECONDARY LITERATURE. Biographical information on Perrine is given in Jacques Cattel, ed., *American Men of Science*, 8th ed. (Lancaster, Pa., 1949), 1928; and a brief obituary by Jorge Bobone appears in *Publications of the Astronomical Society of the Pacific*, **63** (1951), 259.

A collection of some of Perrine's correspondence with Hale is contained in "The George Ellery Hale Papers, 1882–1937," microfilm ed., California Institute of Technology (Pasadena, Calif., 1968).

RICHARD BERENDZEN
DANIEL SEELEY

PERRONCITO, EDOARDO (*b.* Viale d'Asti, Italy, 1 March 1847; *d.* Pavia, Italy, 4 November 1936), *parasitology, bacteriology.*

Perroncito studied at the University of Turin and obtained a degree in veterinary medicine in 1867. In 1873 he won a public competition for the chair of veterinary pathological anatomy at Turin. His professorship was confirmed the following year; he was only twenty-seven.

His scientific interests were mainly in parasitology and bacteriology, subjects which although relevant to human pathology had been very little studied. The emphasis of his research shifted from the purely veterinary to the human level. Some of his most important research was on *Echinococcus* and *cysticercosis,* and on other parasitic infections in animals that are easily transmitted to man by infected food. Perroncito extended his interest to the prophylaxis and cure of these infections. He emphasized the importance of hygiene and advocated stricter and more complete supervision of meat and a more practical approach to the construction of slaughterhouses. He also campaigned for the adoption of refrigeration to preserve food products. He carried out important studies on bovine tuberculosis, which he demonstrated to be identical to human tuberculosis; and he was active in making known in Italy Pasteur's studies on the prophylaxis and cure of rabies.

There was almost no aspect of the infective pathology and parasitology of animals (and of some plants) that Perroncito did not carefully investigate, in many cases discovering their etiopathogenetic cause and searching for means of prevention and cures. These activities led to the creation in 1875 of the first chair of parasitology in Italy. The post, established at Turin, was created for Perroncito.

Perroncito's name is especially connected with his efforts to identify the cause of the anemia that was killing large numbers of the miners (mainly Italian) working on the St. Gotthard Tunnel. His research was also relevant to the health of thousands of other workers in mines, furnaces, and similar environments. Perroncito discovered that the fatal illness was caused by the presence in the human body of the worm *Anchylostoma duodenale,* already described by Dubini in 1843. He studied its complete biological cycle and

means of diffusion, and found that it could be eliminated by means of a medicine based on the oil of the male fern.

The priority of Perroncito's discovery was disputed by others involved in the same research. The polemic lasted many years, and Perroncito became very embittered, but his priority was finally acknowledged. In 1932, on the fiftieth anniversary of the completion of the St. Gotthard Tunnel, the Institut de France awarded him the Prix Montyon. His other awards included honorary degrees from academies, universities, and societies throughout the world.

BIBLIOGRAPHY

I. ORIGINAL WORKS. Perroncito's writings include *Sugli echinococchi negli animali domestici* (Turin, 1871); and "La tubercolosi in rapporto alla economia sociale e rurale," in *Annali della Accademia d'agricoltura di Torino,* **18** (1875). See also *L'anemia dei minatori in Ungheria* (Turin, 1886); *Sulla trasmissione della rabbia dalla madre al feto attraverso la placenta e per mezzo del latte* (Turin, 1887); *Studi sull'immunità pel carbonchio* (Turin, 1889); *Sulla utilizzazione delle carni degli animali da macello affetti da tubercolosi* (Turin, 1892); and *La maladie des mineurs . . . une question résolue* (Turin, 1912).

II. SECONDARY LITERATURE. See P. Ghisleni, "Edoardo Perroncito," in *Giornale dell'Accademia di medicina di Torino,* **100** (1937), 39–47, with bibliography; and V. Marzocchi, "Edoardo Perroncito," in *Patologia comparata della tubercolosi,* **3** (1937), 96–98.

CARLO CASTELLANI

PERRONET, JEAN-RODOLPHE (*b.* Suresnes, France, 8 October 1708; *d.* Paris, France, 27 February 1794), *civil engineering.*

Perronet was the son of a Swiss officer in French service. His maternal uncle, the mathematician Crousaz, encouraged his early interest in mathematics; but Perronet gave up his plan to join the Corps du Génie Militaire (he had passed the entrance examinations) when his father died. Instead, at the age of seventeen he entered the office of Debeausire, architect to the city of Paris. He soon carried out assignments of considerable responsibility. About 1735 he was named *sous-ingénieur* of the Corps des Ponts et Chaussées in the administrative district (*généralité*) of Alençon, where he designed roads. Perronet returned to Paris in 1747, when the Corps des Ponts et Chaussées appointed him head of its newly founded Bureau Central des Dessignateurs; this institution was designed mainly as a training center for young engineers and was later renamed École des Ponts et

Chaussées. Henceforth Perronet's engineering activities concentrated on the design and construction of bridges. In 1750 he became inspector general, and in 1763 head, of the Corps des Ponts et Chaussées, with the title *premier ingénieur du roi*. In addition, from 1757 until 1786 he served as inspector general of France's saltworks. He received many honors, and his fame remained undiminished to his death.

Apart from his institutional role as the highest-ranking civil engineer of the French state during the last decades of the *ancien régime*, Perronet's significance is twofold. As director of the École des Ponts et Chaussées, from the school's inception to his death in 1794, he was the founder of one of the world's first engineering schools. He graduated some 350 students, outstanding among whom were Antoine de Chézy, Emiland Marie Gauthey, and Riche de Prony.

In the design of bridges Perronet developed the classical stone arch bridge to its ultimate perfection. He increased the span of the individual arches, reduced the width of the piers, and shaped the arches in curves composed of several circle segments, which combined aesthetic elegance with ease of construction. This design not only minimized the interference of the bridge with the flow pattern of the river below, at normal level and in floods, but it also reduced the weight of the bridge, and hence its load upon the foundations. The best-known bridges—among the thirteen that Perronet designed—are the Pont de Neuilly (completed 1774), the Pont Sainte-Maxence (1785), and the Pont de la Concorde (1791), still standing.

BIBLIOGRAPHY

I. ORIGINAL WORKS. Perronet's chief work is *Description des projets et de la construction des ponts de Neuilly, de Mantes, d'Orléans . . .* 3 vols. (Paris, 1782–1789). He also wrote a number of memoirs, most of which are on civil engineering; a bibliography compiled by W. Hoffmann (see below) lists eleven items.

II. SECONDARY LITERATURE. Biographical works by Perronet's contemporaries are Pierre-Charles Lesage, *Notice pour servir à l'éloge de Perronet* (Paris, 1805); and G.-C.-F.-M. Riche de Prony, *Notice historique sur Jean-Rodolphe Perronet* (Paris, 1829). Useful articles on Perronet are in *Nouvelle biographie générale*, XXXIX (Paris, 1865), cols. 650–652; and, especially, W. Hoffmann, in J. S. Ersch and J. G. Gruber, eds., *Allgemeine Encyklopädie der Wissenschaften und Künste*, pt. 17, sec. 3 (Leipzig, 1842), 272–280. Perronet's bridges are discussed in James Kip Finch, "The Master of the Stone Arch," in *Consulting Engineer* (London), **18**, no. 4 (Apr. 1962), 128–132.

OTTO MAYR

PERROTIN, HENRI JOSEPH ANASTASE (*b.* St. Loup, Tarn-et-Garonne, France, 19 December 1845; *d.* Nice, France, 29 February 1904), *astronomy*.

Perrotin was the son of an employee in the telegraph service. His scholastic ability earned him scholarships to the *lycée* at Pau and the Faculté des Sciences of Toulouse. His professor at the latter, F. Tisserand, invited him to work at the Toulouse observatory (of which he was the director); and in 1873 he appointed Perrotin astronomer there.

During his career Perrotin made many observations, both astrometric (double stars, planets, satellites, asteroids, comets) and astrophysical (sunspots, study of planetary surfaces). He discovered five asteroids between 1874 and 1878 and a sixth in 1885. Perrotin turned to celestial mechanics and in his doctoral dissertation established the first precise theory of the asteroid Vesta (1879). In this work he expanded the perturbing function as far as the eighth order relative to the eccentricities and inclinations, an achievement that has been applied by astronomers to verify recent theories of Vesta.

In 1879 Perrotin was engaged by Raphaël Bischoffsheim, the banker who built the Nice observatory, to become director of the observatory and to install its equipment. Perrotin devoted himself to this task until his death. The most important of the instruments that he put into service was the seventy-six-centimeter refractor (1886), which was then the world's largest. An inspiring leader of men, he obtained a great deal from his collaborators; and the first years of the observatory were marked by important projects, notably in spectroscopy and work on the asteroids. Perrotin's measurements of the speed of light were based on the slotted-wheel method applied to beams sent between the observatory and surrounding hilltops. The value of 299,880 kilometers per second, obtained in 1902 utilizing a combined trajectory of ninety-two kilometers, was considered the best estimate for more than thirty years.

In 1892 Perrotin was elected a corresponding member of the Académie des Sciences, which had twice awarded him a prize; and in 1894 he became a corresponding member of the Bureau des Longitudes.

BIBLIOGRAPHY

I. ORIGINAL WORKS. Perrotin's most important papers are "Théorie de Vesta," in *Annales de l'Observatoire astronomique magnétique et météorologique de Toulouse*, **1** (1880), B1–B90, also in *Annales de l'Observatoire de Nice*, **3** (1890), B1–B118, and **4** (1895), A3–A71; "Détermination des différences de longitudes entre Nice, l'Île Rousse et Ajaccio," in *Annales de l'Observatoire de Nice*,

8 (1904), 3–242, written with P. Hatt and L. Driencourt; and "Détermination de la vitesse de la lumière . . . ," *ibid.*, **11** (1908), A3–A98, written with A. Prim.

Perrotin published his astronomical observations, principally in about fifty "Notes," in *Comptes rendus . . . de l'Académie des sciences* from 1875 to 1903 and, between 1875 and 1889, in *Astronomische Nachrichten*. Also worthy of mention is "Parallaxe solaire déduite des observations d'Éros," in *Bulletin astronomique*, **20** (1903), 161–165.

Perrotin founded the *Annales de l'Observatoire de Nice*, directed the publication of the first 10 vols., and wrote several of them; among the latter are **2** (1887), devoted to various of his astronomical works, and "Description de l'Observatoire de Nice," in **1** (1899), 1–152. With a view toward the establishment of the Nice observatory, Perrotin made an extensive inquiry, the main findings of which he published in *Visite à divers observatoires d'Europe* (Paris, 1881), which describes the equipment of 31 European observatories.

II. Secondary Literature. The most important obituary notices are the unsigned "Todes-Anzeige," in *Astronomische Nachrichten*, **165** (1904), 254–255; and "M. Henri Perrotin," in *Nature*, **69** (1904), 468; and E. Stephan, "J. A. Perrotin," in *Annales de l'Observatoire de Nice*, **8** (1904), i–iv.

Jacques R. Lévy

PERSEUS (*fl.* third century B.C. [?]), *mathematics.*

Perseus is known only from two passages in Proclus. In one passage his name is associated with the investigation of "spiric" curves as that of Apollonius of Perga is with conics, Nicomedes with the conchoids, and Hippias of Elis with the quadratrices.[1] In the second passage, derived from Geminus, Proclus says that Perseus wrote an epigram upon his discovery, "Three lines upon five sections finding, Perseus made offering to the gods therefor."[2]

In another place Proclus says that a spiric surface is thought of as generated by the revolution of a circle standing upright and turning about a fixed point that is not its center; wherefore it comes about that there are three kinds of spiric surface according as the fixed point is on, inside, or outside the circumference.[3] The spiric surface is therefore what is known today as a "tore"; in antiquity Hero of Alexandria gave it the name "spire" or "ring."[4]

These passages throw no light on the provenance of Perseus and leave wide room for conjecture about his dates. He must have lived before Geminus, as Proclus relies on that author; and it is probable that the conic sections were well advanced before the spiric curves were tackled. Perseus therefore probably lived between Euclid and Geminus, say between 300 and 70 B.C., with a preference for the earlier date.

What Perseus actually discovered is also uncertain. In rather more precise language than that of Proclus, a spiric surface may be defined as the surface generated by a circle that revolves about a straight line (the axis of revolution) always remaining in a plane with it. There are three kinds of spiric surfaces, according as the axis of revolution is outside the circle, tangential to it, or inside it (which are called by Proclus the "open," "continuous," and "interlaced"; and by Hero the "open," "continuous," and "self-crossing").

A spiric section on the analogy of a conic section would be a section of a spiric surface by a plane, which it is natural to assume is parallel to the axis in the first place. Proclus says that the sections are three in number corresponding to the three types of surface, but this is difficult to understand or to reconcile with the epigram. G. V. Schiaparelli showed how three different spiric curves could be obtained by a section of an open tore according as the plane of section was more or less distant from the axis of revolution,[5] and Paul Tannery entered upon a closer mathematical analysis that led him to give a novel interpretation to the epigram.[6] If r is the radius of the generating circle, a the distance of its center from the axis, and d the distance of the cutting plane from the axis, in the case of the open tore (for which $a > r$), the following five cases may be distinguished:

$$a + r > d > a \tag{1}$$
$$d = a \tag{2}$$
$$a > d > a - r \tag{3}$$
$$d = a - r \tag{4}$$
$$a - r > d > 0 \tag{5}$$

Of these the curve produced by (4) is Proclus' first spiric curve, the "hippopede" or "horse-fetter," which is like a figure eight and had already been used by Eudoxus in his representation of planetary motion; (1) is Proclus' second, broad in the middle; (3) is his third, narrow in the middle; (2) is a transition from (1) to (3); and (5) produces two symmetrical closed curves. If the tore is "continuous" ("closed" in modern terminology), $a = r$, the forms (1), (2), and (3) remain as for the "open" tore, but (4) and (5) disappear and there is no new curve. If the tore is "interlaced" ("reentrant"), $a < r$, and the forms (4) and (5) do not exist; but there are three new curves corresponding to (1), (2), and (3), each with an oval inside it.

Tannery deduced that what the epigram means is that Perseus found three spiric curves in addition to the five sections. In this deduction he has been followed by most subsequent writers, Loria even finding support in Dante.[7] Although the interpretation is not impossible, it puts a strain upon the Greek. It is simpler to suppose that Tannery has correctly identified the five sections, but that Perseus ignored (2) and (5) as not really giving new curves. Thus he found "three curves in five sections." If we suppose that he took one of his curves from the five sections of the "open" tore, one from the five sections of the "continuous," and one from the five sections of the "interlaced," we could reconcile Proclus' statement also, but it is simpler to suppose that Proclus, writing centuries later, made an error.

NOTES

1. Proclus, *In primum Euclidis*, G. Freidlein, ed. (Leipzig, 1873; repr. Hildesheim, 1967), p. 356.6–12.
2. *Ibid.*, pp. 111.23–112.2.
3. *Ibid.*, p. 119.9–13.
4. Heron, Definitiones 97, in J. L. Heiberg, ed., *Heronis Alexandrini opera quae supersunt omnia*, IV (Leipzig, 1912), pp. 60.24–62.9.
5. G. V. Schiaparelli, *Le sfere omocentriche di Eudosso, di Calippo e di Aristotele* (Milan, 1875), pp. 32–34.
6. Paul Tannery, *Mémoires scientifiques*, II (Toulouse–Paris, 1912), pp. 26–28.
7. Gino Loria, *Le scienze esatte nell'antica Grecia*, 2nd ed. (Milan, 1914), p. 417, n. 2.

BIBLIOGRAPHY

On Perseus or his works, see T. L. Heath, *The Thirteen Books of Euclid's Elements*, 2nd ed. (Cambridge, 1926; repr. New York, 1956), I, 162–164; *A History of Greek Mathematics*, II (Oxford, 1921), 203–206; G. V. Schiaparelli, *Le sfere omocentriche di Eudosso, di Calippo e di Aristotele* (Milan, 1875), 32–34; and Paul Tannery, "Pour l'histoire des lignes et de surfaces courbes dans l'antiquité," in *Bulletin des sciences mathématiques et astronomiques*, 2nd ser., **8** (Paris, 1884), 19–30; repr. in *Mémoires scientifiques*, **2** (Toulouse–Paris, 1912), 18–32.

IVOR BULMER-THOMAS

PERSONNE, JACQUES (*b.* Saulieu, Côte-d'Or, France, 17 October 1816; *d.* Paris, France, 11 December 1880), *chemistry, pharmacy*.

Orphaned at an early age when his father, a lime-burner, died in an accident, Personne experienced much hardship. After completing an apprenticeship in pharmacy, he enrolled in the Paris School of Pharmacy and later competed successfully for an internship in a hospital pharmacy. From 1849 until his death in 1880, Personne served as chief pharmacist in three Paris municipal hospitals: Midi (1849–1857), Pitié (1857–1878), and Charité (1878–1880). From 1843 onward his connection with the Paris School of Pharmacy was continuous, first as *préparateur*, then as *chef des travaux*, and finally in 1877 as instructor of a newly established course in analytical chemistry. In 1875 Personne was admitted to the Academy of

Medicine. In 1877 at the age of sixty-one, he earned his *docteur ès sciences physiques* and in 1878 became a member of the Council on Public Hygiene and Health of the department of the Seine.

Despite his heavy hospital and teaching responsibilities, Personne carried on almost four decades of unremitting research. Among his most important investigations was a long chemical and botanical study of lupulin (1854). Later he produced the first experimental evidence that red phosphorus was safer than and superior to regular phosphorus in the production of hydrobromic and hydriodic acids and their esters (1861). In his researches on chloral hydrate (1869–1870)—which earned him the Barbier Prize of the Academy of Sciences—Personne not only developed standards of identity and purity for chloral hydrate, but also discovered and investigated chloral alcoholate. Personne believed that he had experimentally confirmed Liebreich's view that chloral hydrate owed its hypnotic effect to the release of chloroform in the blood. The Barbier Prize commission shared this belief, although it is now known that the *in vivo* effect is due to the release of trichloroethanol.

Personne's work includes such diverse subjects as acids and oxides of manganese, with Michel Lhermite (1851); fermentation of acetic acid (1853); oxidation of oil of turpentine (1856); chemical analysis of cannabis (1857); compounds formed by the interaction of iodine and tin (1862); and the determination of quinine in urine (1878).

BIBLIOGRAPHY

I. ORIGINAL WORKS. For listings of Personne's publications, see A. Goris *et al.*, *Centenaire de l'internat en pharmacie des hôpitaux et hospices civils de Paris* (Paris, 1920), 536–538; Poggendorff, III, 1024; and Royal Society *Catalogue of Scientific Papers*, IV, 837; VIII, 596; X, 1035.

II. SECONDARY LITERATURE. On Personne and his work, see E. C. Jungfleisch, "Discours prononcé aux obsèques de M. J. Personne," in *Journal de pharmacie et de chimie*, 5th ser., **3** (1881), 109–112; C. Méhu, "Discours prononcé aux obsèques de M. Personne," in *Bulletin de l'Académie de médecine*, **9** (1880), 1320–1322; and A. Villiers, "J. Personne," in *Centenaire de l'École supérieure de pharmacie de l'Université de Paris, 1803–1903* (Paris, 1904), 226–232.

ALEX BERMAN

PERSOON, CHRISTIAAN HENDRIK (*b.* Cape of Good Hope, South Africa, 31 December 1761; *d.* Paris, France, 15 November 1836), *botany, mycology*.

Persoon was the son of Christiaan Daniel Persoon (originally Persohn), a native of the island of Usedom [now Uznam] on the coast of Prussian Pomerania but a Dutch citizen at the time his son was born, and Elisabeth Wilhelmina Groenewald. The belief that his mother was a Hottentot has long since been disproved. Sent to Europe in 1775 for further education, he was orphaned the following year by the death of his father. Since Persoon and his two sisters were minors, their guardianship fell to the orphan masters at the Cape; and Persoon was to receive a sizable sum of money if he continued his studies. This legacy was sufficient to provide him with a modest annual income. Various adverse circumstances, however, caused him to live under the most dire conditions during a considerable period of his later life in Paris. He never accepted a paid position.

After attending the Gymnasium at Lingen, on the River Ems, he studied theology at Halle (1783–1786), medicine for a brief period at Leiden (1786), and medicine and the natural sciences at Göttingen (1787–1802). He never completed his university studies but in 1799 was awarded an honorary Ph.D. by the Kaiserlich-Leopoldinisch-Karolinische Deutsche Akademie der Naturforscher, then at Erlangen. He was elected a foreign or corresponding member of a number of learned societies. Almost nothing is known about his life while he was in Germany. At Halle he met F. W. von Leysser and other botanists, who may have been responsible for his turning to that field. At Göttingen he met J. A. Murray, professor of botany, and, undoubtedly, many young botanists who later became famous. Certainly half a dozen of them contributed important works on mycology. He must have known G. F. Hoffmann, then famous, who introduced Goethe to cryptogamy.

In 1802, for an unknown reason, Persoon moved to Paris, where he resided until his death. During much of this time his financial distress was great. In 1828 the Dutch government granted him a pension in exchange for his botanical collections, which are now in the Rijksherbarium at Leiden. As a gesture of gratitude, at his death Persoon donated his newly accumulated herbarium and library to the Dutch government. He maintained a wide correspondence with many botanists; a very extensive set of letters is now in the possession of the University Library at Leiden. He sought, unsuccessfully, to return to the Cape by invoking the assistance of James E. Smith of London.

Persoon is known in particular for his mycological publications, which culminated in the *Synopsis fungorum* (1801), rightly considered the basis of modern mycology. His classification was later elaborated by E. M. Fries and P. A. Saccardo. A modification of his system of the "macromycetes," now known as the Friesian tradition, still plays an important role in mycology, although it is gradually being replaced by a radically different system based mainly on microscopic characters. The influence of the *Synopsis* during the decades following its publication was enormous, for it made possible an unprecedented growth of the number of described genera and species of fungi. Persoon began a greatly revised version of the *Synopsis* under the title *Mycologia europaea*. Three volumes were published (1822–1826), but it remained incomplete.

At almost the same time the Swedish botanist and mycologist E. M. Fries began a rival work, the *Systema mycologicum* (1821–1832), which soon replaced Persoon's *Synopsis*. The latter has been accepted as the starting point for the nomenclature of the Gasteromycetes, Uredinales, and Ustilaginales; Fries's *Systema* became the starting point for the nomenclature of "fungi caeteri." In France one of Persoon's correspondents, J. B. Mougeot, kept the Persoonian tradition alive; and in the Vosges and the French Jura a flourishing group of mycologists included Lucien Quélet, Émile Boudier, and N. T. Patouillard. The mycological department of the Rijksherbarium publishes *Persoonia. A Mycological Journal*, and he also has been commemorated by a number of generic names, including *Persoonia* J. E. Smith (Proteaceae).

Persoon's importance as a phanerogamist is firmly based on his *Synopsis plantarum* (1805–1807), which sought to describe briefly all the phanerogams then known. Earlier he had reedited Murray's fifteenth edition of Linnaeus' *Systema vegetabilium* (1797). He advised F. W. Junghuhn to go to the Dutch East Indies and was instrumental in obtaining a post for him in the service of the Dutch government.

BIBLIOGRAPHY

I. Original Works. Persoon's *Tentamen dispositionis methodicae fungorum* (Leipzig, 1797) contains the first draft of his classification of fungi. Knowledge of this group was further developed in *Synopsis fungorum* (Göttingen, 1801), which became the basis of mycological taxonomy, and *Mycologia europaea*, 3 vols. (Erlangen, 1822–1826). His fame as a phanerogamist is due mainly to his *Synopsis plantarum* (Paris–Tübingen, 1805–1807).

II. Secondary Literature. An article by A. L. A. Fée on Persoon in *Giornale botanico italiano* (1846), translated into French by M. Rousseau as "Notice sur Persoon," in *Bulletin de la Société royale de botanie belgique*, **30** (1891), 50–60, and into Dutch by C. E. Destrée as "Aanteekeningen betreffende C. H. Persoon," in *Nederlandsch kruidkundig Archief*, **2**, no. 6 (1894), 366–377, is not altogether reliable. Other important publications (listed chronologically) are G. Schmid, "Eine unbekannte mykologische Arbeit Persoons (1793) zugleich ein Beitrag zur Lebensgeschichte des Verfassers," in *Zeitschrift für Pilzkunde*, **12** (1933), 54–60; J. Ramsbottom, "C. H. Persoon and James E. Smith," in *Proceedings of the Linnean Society of London*, **146** (1934), 10–21; and J. L. M. Franken, "Uit die lewe van 'n beroemde Afrikaner, Christiaan Hendrik Persoon," in *Annale van die Universiteit van Stellenbosch*, **15B** (1937), 1–102.

M. A. DONK

PERSOZ, JEAN-FRANÇOIS (*b.* Cortaillod, Neuchâtel, Switzerland, 9 June 1805; *d.* Paris, France, 12 or 18 September 1868), *chemistry.*

After working in several pharmacies in Neuchâtel, Persoz went to Paris, to study under Thenard at the Collège de France. From 1826 to 1832 he was *préparateur* to Thenard, and in 1833 he earned his *docteur ès sciences physiques* from the Paris Faculty of Sciences. Persoz then spent seventeen years (1833–1850) in Strasbourg in scientific, teaching, and administrative posts, including those of professor of chemistry at the Faculty of Sciences, assayer of the Mint, and professor of chemistry and director of the Strasbourg School of Pharmacy. Returning to Paris in 1850, Persoz became a *suppléant* to Dumas, who was then teaching chemistry at the Sorbonne; he was appointed *maître de conférences* at the École Normale Supérieure at about the same time. In 1852 he received a professorship at the Conservatoire des Arts et Métiers, where he lectured on dyeing and printing of textiles.

Among Persoz's most important accomplishments were two collaborative works published in 1833. The first, written with Anselme Payen, reported the isolation of diastase from malt extract; this research revealed that diastase converts starch into sugar. The second work, written with Biot, showed that the partial hydrolysis of starch with mineral acids yields a substance (dextrin) that proved dextrorotatory on the plane of polarized light, and that a similar effect on polarized light can be obtained by boiling cane sugar with dilute acid.

Persoz later published an influential book on the chemistry of molecular combinations, *Introduction à l'étude de la chimie moléculaire* (Paris–Strasbourg, 1839), and a four-volume treatise with an atlas on textile printing, *Traité théorique et pratique de l'impression des tissus* (Paris, 1846). Noteworthy, too, among his numerous investigations were his discovery of the production of methane by heating an acetate with caustic alkali (1839), his method for combining sulfur dioxide and phosphorus pentachloride to obtain thionyl chloride (1849), and his work on tungsten compounds (1863). Many of his publications dealt with analytical chemistry and chemical technology.

BIBLIOGRAPHY

I. ORIGINAL WORKS. In addition to his treatises on the chemistry of molecular combinations (1839) and on the printing of textiles (1846) already mentioned, Persoz published many papers in the *Comptes rendus hebdomadaires des séances de l'Académie des Sciences,* and in leading chemical journals of the day. For listings of Persoz's articles written alone or with others, see Poggendorff, II, 408–410, and III, 1024; and the Royal Society *Catalogue of Scientific Papers*, IV, 838–840, and VIII, 596.

II. SECONDARY LITERATURE. See Fritz Ferchl, *Chemisch-Pharmazeutisches Bio- und Bibliographikon* (Mittenwald, 1937), 404–405; Gabriel Humbert, *Contribution à l'histoire de la pharmacie strasbourgeoise* (Mulhouse, 1938), 217–219; E. V. McCollum, *A History of Nutrition* (Boston, 1957), 13–14, and *passim*; J. R. Partington, *A History of Chemistry*, IV (London–New York, 1964), 429 and *passim*; and René Sartory, "Jean-François Persoz," in *Figures pharmaceutiques françaises* (Paris, 1953), 95–100.

ALEX BERMAN

PETER ABANO. See **Abano, Pietro d'.**

PETER ABELARD. See **Abailard, Pierre.**

PETER OF AILLY. See **Ailly, Pierre d'.**

PETER BONUS. See **Petrus Bonus.**

PETER OF DACIA. See **Peter Philomena of Dacia.**

PETER PEREGRINUS, also known as **Pierre de Maricourt** (*fl. ca.* 1269), *magnetism.*

Other than that he was the author of the first extant treatise on the properties and applications of magnets, virtually nothing is known of Peregrinus. Two sources provide what little data we have: (1) his famous letter, or treatise, on the magnet, *Epistola Petri Peregrini de Maricourt ad Sygerum de Foucaucourt, Militem, De Magnete*, "Letter on the Magnet of Peter Peregrinus of Maricourt to Sygerus of Foucaucourt, Soldier"; and (2) the *Opus tertium* of Roger Bacon.

Only one date in Peregrinus' life is fixed with certainty. At the conclusion of the *Epistola*, he added

"Completed in camp, at the siege of Lucera, in the year of our Lord 1269, eighth day of August."[2] From this account it would appear that Peregrinus was a member of the army of Charles of Anjou, King of Sicily, who was at that time personally directing an assault on Lucera (a city in Apulia, approximately twelve miles west of Foggia). Given Peregrinus' apparent interest in mechanical devices and instruments, Schlund has suggested[3] that he may have served in some technical capacity, perhaps as an engineer.

Peter may have received the appellation "Peregrinus" in connection with one or more of the assaults on Lucera. Under the control of the Hohenstaufens, Lucera had been besieged three times between 1255 and 1269, when it fell for the last time. The Papacy had declared these assaults against the Hohenstaufens and their Saracen allies official crusades. Since during the twelfth and thirteenth centuries the honorific title "Peregrinus" could be awarded not only to those who went on pilgrimages to the Holy Land but also to those who fought in recognized crusades in the Holy Land and elsewhere, Peregrinus may have thus earned it by participating in the siege.[4]

The manuscripts of the *Epistola* indicate that Peregrinus' full name was Petrus de Maharncuria, or Pierre de Maricourt, signifying that he probably came from the town of Méharicourt in Picardy.[5] Although there is evidence that Peregrinus was of noble birth,[6] the suggestion that he was a theologian is unconvincing[7] and the assertion that he was a Franciscan is baseless.[8] The lack of biographical data has even prompted an unsuccessful attempt to determine whether Peregrinus might be identical with one of his better-known thirteenth-century namesakes.[9]

Apart from the little that is revealed by the *Epistola* itself, further knowledge of Peregrinus as a scientist and investigator of natural phenomena depends heavily on the authenticity of certain statements in Roger Bacon's *Opus tertium* and whether in that same treatise Peregrinus is intended in references to a "Master Peter" (*Magister Petrus*). In chapter 11 of that treatise, which was written during 1267,[10] Bacon spoke of the need for good mathematicians and declared that "there are only two perfect mathematicians, Master John of London and Master (*Magister*) Peter de Maharn-curia, a Picard."[11] Since two of the five manuscripts of the *Opus tertium*, including the oldest, carry this statement in the margin, it is possible that it was added by a scribe and subsequently incorporated into the text of other manuscripts.[12] It is therefore difficult to give full credence to the claim that Bacon had Peregrinus[13] in mind when, a few lines below, he stated "Nor can any one

obtain their services [that is, of good mathematicians] unless he be the Pope or another great prince, especially the services of that one who is the best of all of them, of whom I have written in the *Opus minus* and shall write again in [the proper] place."[14] Since Peregrinus is neither mentioned nor alluded to in the single fragmentary manuscript of the *Opus minus*[15] known thus far, the claim is further eroded. Whoever may have been the author of the statement citing Peregrinus as one of two "perfect mathematicians," it is of interest that he referred to him as "Magister," probably signifying that Peregrinus had earned a Master of Arts degree, perhaps at the University of Paris.

In chapter 13 of the *Opus tertium*, Bacon praised a "Magister Petrus" as the only Latin writer to realize that experience rather than argument is the basis of certainty in science.[16] Later in the same chapter, following a discussion of burning mirrors, Bacon declared that "I know of only one person who deserves praise in the works of this science." At this point a marginal notation in one[17] of the five manuscripts used in Brewer's edition of the *Opus tertium* reads: "Notandum de magistro Petro de Maharne Curia" ("It should be noted that this is about Peter of Maharne Curia"). If the glossator is correct, it becomes highly probable that Peregrinus was intended by the earlier reference to "Magister Petrus," and Bacon's laudatory description in the lines that follow must also refer to Peregrinus. Bacon's description would reveal an idealistic and indefatigable scientist:

. . . for he does not trouble about discourses or quarrels over words, but follows the works of wisdom and keeps quietly to them. And so, though others strive blinkingly to see, as a bat in the twilight, the light of the sun, he himself contemplates it in its full splendour, on account of which he is a master of experiments (*dominus experimentorum*) and thus by experience he knows natural, medical, and alchemical things, as well as all things in the heavens and beneath them: indeed he is shamed if any layman, or grandam, or soldier, or country bumpkin knows anything that he himself does not know. Wherefore he has inquired into all operations of metal-founding, and the working of gold and silver and other metals, and of all minerals; and he knows all things pertaining to the army and to arms and the chase: and he has examined all that relates to agriculture, the measurement of land, and the works of farmers; and he has also reflected upon the experiments, devices, and incantations of witches and magicians, and likewise the illusions and tricks of all jugglers; so that nothing is hidden from him which he ought to know, and he knows how to reprobate[18] all things false and magical. And so without him it is impossible that philosophy could be completed, or be treated usefully or with certainty. But just as he cannot be valued with respect to price, so he does not estimate his own worth. For should he wish to stand well with kings and princes, he would find those who would honour him and enrich him. Or, if he were to show in Paris by his works of wisdom all that he knows, the whole world would follow him: yet because either way he would be hindered from the bulk of his experiments in which he most delights, so he neglects all honour and enrichment, the more since he might, whenever he wished it, attain to riches by his wisdom.[19]

On the basis of this extraordinary encomium, written in 1267, Bacon is conjectured to have met, or to have come to know about, Peregrinus during the 1260's. Had Bacon known him earlier, it is likely that he would have mentioned him in the *Communia mathematica*, written in the late 1250's, in which Robert Grosseteste, Adam March, and John Bandoun are singled out as praiseworthy mathematicians.[20]

Despite the paucity of information about Peregrinus, it seems evident that he was greatly, and perhaps primarily, interested in the construction of instruments and devices. According to him the *Epistola* was to form "part of a treatise in which we shall show how to construct physical instruments."[21] Similar interests are reflected in part 2, chapter 2, of the *Epistola*, where Peregrinus declares his intention to explain "how iron is held suspended in air by virtue of the stone"[22] in "the book on the action of mirrors" (*in libro de operibus speculorum*), which he was writing or planned to write.

Although no such work has yet been found, Bacon, immediately following the lengthy passage quoted above and still, presumably, speaking of Peregrinus, stated that "He [that is, Peregrinus] has already labored three years on one burning mirror [set for?] a fixed distance and, by the grace of God will soon complete it. Although we have books on the construction of such mirrors, the Latins are ignorant as to how to build them, nor has any among them attempted it."[23] Twice again in the *Opus tertium* (chaps. 33 and 36)[24] lavish praise is heaped upon the constructor of this same burning mirror (or so it seems) and the mirror itself, now mentioned as actually completed. A treatise on the construction of an astrolabe (*Nova compositio astrolabii particularis*),[25] in which the year 1261 is mentioned, has been attributed to Peregrinus and bears further witness to his overriding interest in the fabrication of instruments.

Scientific Thought. Since the *Epistola* is the sole authentic work attributed to Peregrinus that has been edited and made generally known, it alone must serve for the present as the basis of any evaluation of his scientific achievement. The *Epistola* is a brief treatise in two parts; the first, in ten chapters, describes the properties and effects of the lodestone, while the second, in three chapters, is devoted to the construction of three instruments utilizing the special properties and powers of the magnet.

The scope of the work and the essential prerequisites for conducting an investigation into magnetism are outlined in the first two chapters. Since the *Epistola* was to constitute part of a larger treatise on the construction of instruments, Peregrinus explicitly confined his attention to the manifest properties of the magnet, leaving aside all consideration of its occult powers. An investigator into the properties of magnetism must not only be knowledgeable about nature and the celestial motions, but also be clever in the use of his hands.

Turning to the magnet or lodestone itself, in part 1, chapter 3, Peregrinus named four characteristics: color (it should resemble polished iron exposed to the tarnishing effect of the air); homogeneity (although a magnet is rarely completely homogeneous, the more homogeneous it is, the more efficiently it performs); weight (a function of homogeneity and density—a heavier magnet is a better magnet); and virtue, or power to attract iron. Although the north-south orientation properties of a magnetized needle had been described and utilized in magnetic compasses since the eleventh century (and probably earlier) in China and since the twelfth century in the Latin West,[26] and although it had been known from antiquity that magnets could attract and repel iron, Peregrinus left the first extant account of magnetic polarity and methods for determining the poles of a magnet (pt. 1, chap. 4; Peregrinus may also have been the first to apply the term *polus* to a magnetic pole).[27] Just as the celestial sphere has a north and south pole, so also does every magnet.

A celestial analogy aided Peregrinus in his description of the first of two methods for locating the poles of a magnet. Since the meridian circles of the celestial sphere converge and meet at the poles, the lines drawn on a spherical magnet (called a *terrella* by William Gilbert[28] but perhaps first shaped and used by Peregrinus) will similarly meet at the poles when the investigator adheres to the following procedure:

> Let a needle or elongated piece of iron, slender like a needle, be placed on the stone, and a line be drawn along the length of iron dividing the stone in the middle. Then let the needle or iron be placed in another position on the stone and mark the stone with a line in a similar manner according to that position.[29]

All the lines drawn in this fashion will converge in the two opposite points or poles. The poles may also be found by noting at what point on the spherical magnet a needle or piece of iron clings with the greatest force. To render this method more precise, Peregrinus recommended that a small, oblong needle, or piece of iron, of approximately two finger nails in length, be located on or near the poles until it lies perpendicular to the stone (that is, stands upright). The marks representing these points should lie diametrically opposite. The two methods described here were also employed by Gilbert.[30]

In distinguishing north and south poles (pt. 1, chap. 5), Peregrinus presented a qualitative description of the fundamental law of magnetic polarity. If a lodestone is laid in a plate or cup, which in turn is placed in a vessel filled with water so that "the stone may be like a sailor in a ship"[31]—that is, free to turn in any direction without colliding into the sides of the vessel—then the north pole of the lodestone (*polus septentrionalis lapidis*) will face toward the north celestial pole and the south pole of the stone will face to the south celestial pole. Peregrinus observed that whenever the lodestone is forcibly turned away from its north-south orientation, it will always return to that orientation upon removal of the constraint.

The effect that a hand-held magnet will have upon a floating magnet serves as a paradigm for the general effect that one magnet has upon another (pt. 1, chap. 6). If the north pole of a hand-held magnet is brought in close proximity to the south pole of a floating magnet, the latter will seek to adhere to the former, an effect that will be repeated when the south pole of the hand-held magnet is brought near the north pole of the floating magnet. After formalizing this behavior in a general rule, Peregrinus observed that when the like poles of these magnets are brought close together, "the stone which you hold in your hand will appear to flee the floating stone."[32] To explain attraction and repulsion between the poles of magnets, Peregrinus resorted (pt. 1, chap. 9) to the agent-patient relationship so popular in medieval natural philosophy. He observed that if a magnet is broken in two each part will function as a magnet with north and south poles. If the opposite poles of the parts are then brought together, they will seek to unite and rejoin into a single magnet, since "an active agent strives not only to join its patient to itself but to unite with it, so that out of the agent and the patient there may be made one."[33] Indeed, if the two parts were cemented at the point of contact, the opposite poles would become unified and the resulting magnet would have a north and south pole

and be identical in every way with the original magnet. The union of agent and patient, which involves an attraction and union of opposite poles, is accounted for by a "likeness" or "similitude" (*similitudo*) between them. Peregrinus does not explain how a "similitude" between opposite poles is to be understood. John of St. Amand (*fl.* 1261–1298), a medical commentator and seeming contemporary of Peregrinus, likewise sought to account for the attraction between magnets and between a magnet and iron by saying that "it [that is, the magnet] does it by multiplying its like (*similitudo*) and, without any evaporation, exciting the active power which exists incomplete in iron, which is born to be completed by the form of the magnet, nay is moved towards it."[34]

On the question of which of two mutually attracting magnets is the agent and which the patient Peregrinus provided no answer. Presumably, if one magnet were assumed to be stationary (say, held in the hand) and the other free to move, it would be plausible to expect Peregrinus to designate the former as agent and the latter as patient. Otherwise the choice seems wholly arbitrary. Should the two north (or south) poles be brought into proximity, the two magnets could not be reunited into a single magnet, since the "identity or similitude of the parts would not be conserved."[35] The single magnet formed from the joining of like poles would possess two north (or south) poles and would differ in species from the original magnet, which possessed two opposite poles.

The ability of a magnet to orient itself with the celestial poles in a north-south direction is transmissible to iron upon contact (pt. 1, chap. 7). Let a magnetized iron needle (whether by "iron needle" Peregrinus meant iron or steel is left unspecified; if iron, the needle would have required repeated remagnetization)[36] be placed upon a piece of wood or straw that floats upon water. The end of the needle that had been touched by the region around the north pole of the magnet will turn toward the southern part of the heavens; and, conversely, the end touched by the area around the south pole of the magnet will orient itself toward the north celestial pole (but not the pole star). Since the magnetized needle takes on the polar properties of a magnet, it will behave like a magnet. Consequently, the south pole of the needle will be attracted to the north pole of the magnet and repelled by its south pole; and the north pole of the needle will be attracted to the south pole of the magnet and repelled by its north pole (pt. 1, chap. 8). The polarity of a magnetized needle is reversible, however, when, as Peregrinus (and also John of St. Amand)[37] observed, similar poles of a magnet and magnetized needle are brought into contact. When the north pole of a magnet is made to touch the north pole of a needle, it converts the latter to a south pole. "And the cause of this," Peregrinus explained, "is the impression of the last agent, confounding and changing the virtue of the first."[38] Given the agent-patient relationship discussed in part 1, chapter 9, Peregrinus would undoubtedly have accounted for this as the striving of an agent, the magnet, to unite with its patient, the iron needle. To achieve this objective the agent transforms the patient by altering its north pole to a south pole.

It was almost inevitable that Peregrinus should have inquired about the source of magnetic force (pt. 1, chap. 10). First, he disposed of the popular view that mines of magnetic stone in northern regions were the cause of the north-south orientation of a magnet. To support his position, Peregrinus stated that (1) magnetic stone is found in many parts of the world; (2) the polar regions are uninhabitable and thus could not be the source of magnetic stone; and (3) a magnet, or magnetized iron, orients to the south as well as the north. In rightly rejecting this notion, however, Peregrinus overlooked the fruitful concept, developed later by Gilbert, that the earth itself is a large spherical magnet. Instead, Peregrinus looked to the heavens in the belief that the poles of a magnet receive their virtue from the celestial poles.[39]

Although knowledge of magnetic declination (apparently already known in China in the eleventh century[40]) might have dissuaded Peregrinus from his opinion, there was reasonable evidence in its favor. Peregrinus was convinced that the poles of a magnet orient themselves in the meridian and that all meridians converge at the celestial poles; he was also aware that Polaris, the pole star, does not rest at the celestial north pole, but revolves around it—a fact virtually unknown to astronomers or seamen, which Columbus discovered for himself.[41] From this knowledge Peregrinus concluded that the poles of a magnet, or magnetized needle, always point directly to the celestial poles rather than to the pole star, as commonly believed.[42] From this conclusion it was an easy and perhaps irresistible inference that the poles of a magnet received their power to attract and repel directly from the celestial poles. Indeed, Peregrinus thought that every part of a spherical magnet received its power from the corresponding part of the celestial sphere.[43]

As a test for this claim, he suggested the construction of a spherical magnet with fixed pivots at its poles, which would leave the magnet free to rotate. The sphere should be positioned on the meridian circle "so that it moves in the manner of armillaries in such a way that the elevation and depression of its poles may correspond with the elevation and depression of the poles of the heavens in the region where you may be."[44] If these instructions are followed faithfully, the spherical magnet, receiving magnetic virtue from every part of the celestial sphere, should commence to turn on its axis round the pivots,[45] thus simulating the daily celestial motion and functioning as a perfect clock. Although Peregrinus did not claim to have constructed such a perpetual motion machine, there is the hint that an abortive attempt was made, for he stated that failure of the sphere to perform as described could only be attributed to lack of skill in the contriver rather than deficiency in the theory, which he judged wholly sound. Peregrinus thus insulated his theory from the practical consequences that he himself deduced from it. Both Gilbert, who referred to this passage and mentioned Peregrinus by name,[46] and Galileo[47] rejected such claims.

Magnetic power as a source of perpetual motion is taken up again at the conclusion of the *Epistola* (pt. 2, chap. 3), where Peregrinus described construction of a continually moving toothed wheel powered by an oval magnet. The latter is so positioned that each tooth of the wheel will, in turn, be attracted to the north pole of the magnet. Under the influence of the attraction, the tooth acquires sufficient momentum to move beyond the north pole and into the vicinity of the south pole, by which it is repelled toward the north pole. As each tooth is alternately attracted and repelled, the wheel maintains a perpetual motion. Thus Peregrinus joined Villard de Honnecourt (*fl.* 1225–1250)[48] in proposing perpetual motion wheels in defiance of medieval Scholastic theory, which generally denied the possibility of inexhaustible forces in nature.

If Peregrinus' attempt to apply magnetic force to perpetual motion was misconceived, his use of it in the improvement of the compass was surely not. He described two compasses, one wet and one dry. The first (pt. 2, chap. 1), a floating compass, represents a considerable improvement over those that had been in use: an oval magnet is encapsulated in a wooden case and floated on water in a large rounded vessel. The rim of the vessel is divided into four quadrants according to the cardinal points of the compass. Each quadrant is then subdivided into ninety equal parts. A rule with sighting pins, positioned perpendicularly at each end, is placed on the encapsulated magnet. This rule extends to diametrically opposed points on the graduated rim. With this instrument, perhaps the first mariner's compass with divisions, not only could the direction of a ship be determined, but also the azimuth of the sun, moon, and stars.

Although the Chinese used magnetic compasses with geomantic divisions centuries before Peregrinus,[49] it is not clear whether they used them in the mariner's compass, of which clear mention is made in the eleventh century.[50]

The second compass (pt. 2, chap. 2), dry and pivoted, was deemed by Peregrinus an improvement over the floating compass. A vessel in the shape of a jar (which may be made from any solid material, preferably transparent) is constructed with a transparent lid of glass or crystal on which are marked the cardinal points. After subdividing each quadrant into ninety parts or degrees, a movable rule with perpendicular sights is fastened to the top of the lid. An axis of brass or silver is positioned at the center of the vessel between the bottom side of the lid and the bottom of the vessel. In the center of the axis, and at right angles to it, two needles—one of iron, the other of brass or silver—are inserted perpendicular to each other. Upon magnetizing the iron needle, the vessel, with its lid, is turned until the north-south points of the lid are aligned with the magnetized needle (as an obvious consequence, the silver or brass needle becomes aligned in an east-west direction). Azimuthal readings of the sun and stars may now be taken by rotating the movable rule on the lid. Peregrinus appears to have been the first to describe such a compass.[51]

The *Epistola* ranks as one of the most impressive scientific treatises of the Middle Ages. Although much of what Peregrinus included may have been known and expressed earlier in a vague and incomplete manner, the *Epistola* was the first extant treatise devoted exclusively to magnetism. Not only did Peregrinus bring together virtually all the relevant, contemporary knowledge on magnetism, but he obviously added to it and, of the greatest importance, organized the whole into a science of magnetism. He formulated rules for the determination of magnetic polarity, which then enabled him to enunciate rules for attraction and repulsion, all of which would today form the basis of an introductory lesson on magnetism.[52] As the two magnetic compasses and perpetual motion devices for clock and wheel testify, Peregrinus was also seriously concerned with the practical application of magnetic force. The subsequent influence of his treatise was considerable. The existence of at least thirty-one manuscript versions of it bears witness to its popularity during the Middle Ages. Of greater significance, however, was its eventual impact on Gilbert, who, in his famous *De Magnete* (1600), not only mentioned Peregrinus by name, but also drew upon the *Epistola* to build upon and add to the solid empirical rules on magnetic

polarity and induction formulated by Peregrinus more than three centuries earlier.

NOTES

1. I have cited the title as given in Bertelli's ed., *Bullettino*, I (Rome, 1868), 70. For variant titles, see Bertelli, *ibid.*, 4–7; E. Schlund, "Petrus Peregrinus von Maricourt," in *Archivum Franciscanum historicum*, **5** (1912), 22–39; and S. P. Thompson, "Petrus Peregrinus de Maricourt," in *Proceedings of the British Academy*, **2** (1905–1906), 400–407.
2. From the trans. of the *Epistola* by H. D. Harradon, "Some Early Contributions to the History of Geomagnetism—I," 17. Although the date 1269 is recorded in only three of thirty-one known MSS, it appears in what may be the oldest of them (see Schlund, "Petrus Peregrinus," in *Archivum Franciscanum historicum*, **4** [1911], 450, and **5** [1912], 23.
3. Schlund, *ibid.*, **4**, 455.
4. For details on the crusades against Lucera and the significance of the term "peregrinus," see Schlund, *ibid.*, 450–455.
5. Schlund, *ibid.*, 449.
6. Schlund, *ibid.*, 451; based on a Picard family "de Maricourt" listed in the *Dictionnaire de la Noblesse* by De la Chenaux-Desbois.
7. F. Picavet, *Essais sur l'histoire générale et comparée des théologies et des philosophies médiévales*, 240–242, 252.
8. Stewart Easton, *Roger Bacon and His Search for a Universal Science* (Oxford, 1952), 120–121.
9. Schlund, "Petrus Peregrinus," in *Archivum Franciscanum Historicum*, **4**, 441–448.
10. Bacon himself mentions the year. See 277, 278 of J. S. Brewer's ed. of Bacon's *Opus tertium, Opus minus,* and *Compendium studii philosophie* in *Fr. Rogeri Bacon Opera quaedam hactenus inedita* (Rerum Britannicarum Medii Aevi, no. 15; London, 1859).
11. Brewer, *ibid.*, lxxv and 35.
12. See Schlund, "Petrus Peregrinus," in *Archivum Franciscanum historicum*, **4**, 445–446.
13. Brewer, *Fr. Rogeri Bacon*, xxxvii.
14. My translation from Brewer, *ibid.*, 35. Brewer gives two variant translations on xxxvii and lxxv.
15. Brewer, *ibid.*, xxxvii. Even if an alleged marginal gloss in the *Opus minus* mentioning a "Master Peter" is a correct reading—and this is dubious—there is no good reason to assume that Peregrinus is the "Peter" intended (see Schlund, "Petrus Peregrinus," in *Archivum Franciscanum historicum*, **4**, 446–447).
16. Brewer, *ibid.*, 43.
17. Oxford, Bodleian, "e Musaeo" 155–3705; for the Latin text, see Brewer, *ibid.*, 46.
18. At this point, "Petrus de Maharne Curia" appears as a marginal gloss in British Museum, Cotton MSS, Tiberius C. V.
19. Thompson's trans., 380. I have slightly altered the trans., which was made from Brewer's ed., 46–47.
20. Easton, *Roger Bacon*, 88.
21. Pt. 1, chap. 1, as translated by H. D. Harradon in *Terrestrial Magnetism and Atmospheric Electricity*, **48** (1943), 6.
22. Harradon, *ibid.*, 16. On the claims to suspend iron in air by magnets, see Dorothy Wyckoff's trans., *Albertus Magnus Book of Minerals* (Oxford, 1967), 148 and Bertelli, *Bullettino* I, 87, n. 6.
23. My trans. from Brewer's ed., 47; see also Thompson's trans., 379.
24. Brewer, *Fr. Rogeri Bacon*, 112–116; see also F. Picavet, *Essais sur l'histoire générale et comparée des théologies et des philosophies médiévales*, 247, 252.
25. See Bertelli, *Bullettino*, I, 5, and bibliography, below.
26. Joseph Needham, *Science and Civilisation in China*, IV (Cambridge, 1962), pt. 1, 246, 249–250, and 274.

27. Schlund, "Petrus Peregrinus," in *Archivum Franciscanum historicum*, **4**, 636, n. 5.

28. *De Magnete*, bk. I, chap. 3, in Thompson's English trans., *On the Magnet*, 2nd ed. (New York, 1958; 1st ed., London, 1900), 13.

29. Harradon trans., 7.

30. *De Magnete*, bk. I, chap. 3 (13–14 of Thompson's trans.). Gilbert employed a third method using a versorium, that is, "a piece of iron touched with a loadstone, and placed upon a needle or point firmly fixed on a foot so as to turn freely about" (*ibid.*).

31. Harradon trans., 8.

32. *Ibid.*

33. *Ibid.*, 10. On medieval explanations of the causes of magnetic attraction, see W. James King, "The Natural Philosophy of William Gilbert and His Predecessors," in *Contributions From the Museum of History and Technology*, Smithsonian Institution Bulletin 218 (Washington, D.C., 1959), 125–129, and Harry A. Wolfson, *Crescas' Critique of Aristotle* (Cambridge, Mass., 1929), 90–92.

34. See Lynn Thorndike, "John of St. Amand on the Magnet," in *Isis*, **36** (1945), 156.

35. Harradon trans., 10.

36. E. Gerland, *Geschichte der Physik* (Berlin, 1913), 213.

37. Thorndike, "John of St. Amand," 157.

38. Harradon trans., 9.

39. Gilbert (*De Magnete*, bk. III, ch. 1; Thompson's trans., 116), citing Peregrinus by name, emphatically rejects this explanation.

40. Needham, *Science and Civilisation in China*, IV, pt. 1, 250.

41. See Samuel Eliot Morison, *Admiral of the Ocean Sea, A Life of Christopher Columbus*, 2 vols. (Boston, 1942), I, 271.

42. See Duane H. D. Roller, *The "De Magnete" of William Gilbert*, 36, 39.

43. A similar view was expressed by John of St. Amand; see Thorndike, "John of St. Amand," 156–157.

44. Harradon trans., 11–12.

45. Without mention of either Peregrinus or the title of the treatise, Nicole Oresme, in bk. II, question 3, of his *Questiones super De Celo*, makes a probable reference to this device. See Claudia Kren, "The 'Questiones super De Celo' of Nicole Oresme" (Ph.D. diss., University of Wisconsin, 1965), 474–476.

46. *De Magnete*, bk. VI, chap. 4; Thompson trans., 223.

47. Stillman Drake, trans., *Dialogue Concerning the Two Chief World Systems* (Berkeley, Calif., 1962), 413–414.

48. See Theodore Bowie, *The Sketchbook of Villard de Honnecourt* (Bloomington, Ind., 1959), 134.

49. Needham, *Science and Civilisation in China*, IV, pt. 1, 262–263, 296–297.

50. *Ibid.*, 279–280.

51. Thompson, 388. The Chinese did not learn of the dry, pivoted compass until the sixteenth century (Needham, *Science and Civilisation in China*, IV, pt. 1, 290).

52. E. J. Dijksterhuis, *The Mechanization of the World Picture* (Oxford, 1961), 153.

BIBLIOGRAPHY

I. ORIGINAL WORKS. The most complete list of MSS of the *Epistola* has been compiled by Erhard Schlund, O.F.M., in "Petrus Peregrinus von Maricourt, sein Leben und seine Schriften (ein Beitrag zur Roger Baco-Forschung)," in *Archivum Franciscanum historicum*, **5** (1912), 22–35. Of the 31 extant MSS described, 29 are Latin (for easier identification, the opening and closing lines [that is, *incipits* and *explicits*] are often supplied) and two, located in Vienna, represent two versions of a single Italian trans. made during the Middle Ages or Renaissance. In addition, five Latin MSS that may once have existed but the fate of which are unknown are also briefly cited and discussed. Another list of MSS, not quite as complete as Schlund's but including an English trans., possibly of the late sixteenth or early seventeenth century (in Gonville and Caius College, Cambridge), has been published by Silvanus P. Thompson, F.R.S., "Petrus Peregrinus de Maricourt and his Epistola De Magnete," in *Proceedings of the British Academy*, **2** (1905–1906), 400–404. Included are MSS owned by Thompson as well as five MSS the previous existence of which is plausibly conjectured. In the same article (404–408), Thompson presents the most comprehensive list yet produced of the printed eds. and trans. of the *Epistola* (11 partial and complete versions in all are cited; a useful but less extensive list appears in Schlund's article on 36–40; the original basis of both lists was probably furnished by Baldassare Boncompagni, "Intorno alle edizioni della *Epistola De Magnete* di Pietro Peregrino de Maricourt," in *Bullettino di bibliografia e di storia delle scienze matematiche e fisiche*, IV [Rome, 1871], 332–339).

The first published ed. was that of Achilles P. Gasser, *Petri Peregrini Maricurtensis De Magnete seu Rota perpetui motus libellus . . .* (Augsburg, 1558), which was followed by a few inadequate and truncated versions. Not until 1868 did the first critical text appear. Working from 7 MSS and the 1558 ed., Timoteo Bertelli, a Barnabite monk, published a new ed. of the *Epistola* in "Sulla Epistola di Pietro Peregrino di Maricourt e sopra alcuni trovati e teorie magnetiche del secolo XIII," in *Bullettino di bibliografia e di storia delle scienze matematiche e fisiche*, I (Rome, 1868), 70–89. A few years later, in an article entitled "Intorno a due Codici Vaticani della *Epistola De Magnete* di Pietro Peregrino di Maricourt," in *Bullettino*, IV (Rome, 1871), 303–331, Bertelli listed additional variant readings (see especially, 315–319) to his ed. of 1868. Using Bertelli's ed. and incorporating some of the later variants, G. Hellmann published another ed. of the *Epistola* in his *Rara Magnetica, Neudrucke von Schriften und Karten über Meteorologie und Erdmagnetismus* (Berlin, 1898), no. 10. By collating at least nine additional MSS (seven from Oxford) with printed eds., especially Bertelli's, Silvanus P. Thompson, on 390–398 of his article cited above, subsequently published a large number of additional variants, cuing them to the page and line numbers of Bertelli's 1868 ed. Thus despite five printed Latin eds., as well as a plagiarized version by Joannes Taisnier (1562), a facs. repr. by Bernard Quaritch (1900), and an ed. and English trans. promised by Charles Sanders Peirce (*Prospectus of an Edition of 300 Numbered Copies* [*150 for America*] *of the Earliest Work of Experimental Science: The Epistle of Pierre Pelerin de Maricourt to Sygur de Foucaucourt, Soldier, On the Lodestone* [New York, 1892], 16 pp., of which pp. 12–13 contain a sample Latin text based on Bibliothèque Nationale, fonds Latin, 7378A; see Thompson's article, pp. 406–407 for a full description and *Collected Papers of Charles Sanders Peirce*, VII, VIII, Arthur W. Burks, ed. [Cambridge, Mass., 1966], 280–282, for a lengthy quotation from 1–6 of the *Prospectus*, which Burks dates *ca.* 1893), there is as yet no single definitive Latin ed. based on all or most of the MSS.

Leaving aside two early printed English trans. of 1579 (?) and 1800 (see Thompson, 405), there now exist three major modern English trans. (1) Silvanus P. Thompson, *Epistle of Petrus Peregrinus of Maricourt, to Sygerus of Foucaucourt, Soldier, Concerning the Magnet* (London, 1902), based upon the eds. of Gasser, Bertelli, and Hellmann; (2) *The Letter of Petrus Peregrinus On the Magnet, A.D. 1269*, translated by Brother Arnold [Joseph Charles Mertens] with introductory notice by Brother Potamian [M. F. O'Reilly] (New York, 1904), made from the Gasser ed.; and (3) H. D. Harradon, "Some Early Contributions to the History of Geomagnetism-I," in *Terrestrial Magnetism and Atmospheric Electricity* (now the *Journal of Geophysical Research*), **48** (1943), 3–17. The title of the trans., which actually appears on 6–17, is "The Letter of Peter Peregrinus de Maricourt to Sygerus de Foucaucourt, Soldier, Concerning the Magnet." Although Harradon makes no mention of the ed., or eds., on which his trans. was based, one may conjecture that Hellmann's ed. was used. Included in Harradon's trans. is a prologue consisting solely of chapter titles, which Thompson (384 of the article cited above) believes is a scribal interpolation compiled from the original chapter headings that precede each chapter.

An as yet unexamined and unpublished work on the construction of an astrolabe is assigned to Peregrinus in the title of a treatise in Latin MS codex Vatican Palatine 1392, which reads: *Petri Peregrini Nova Compositio Astrolabii Particularis (Peter Peregrinus' New Composition [or Construction] of a Special Astrolabe)*; no folio numbers are given by T. Bertelli, who mentions the MS in his article "Sopra Pietro Peregrino di Maricourt e la sua *Epistola De Magnete*," in *Bullettino*, I (Rome, 1868), 5. Since reference is made to certain astronomical tables completed by Campanus of Novara in 1261, the treatise was probably written after that date (see Bertelli, *ibid.*, 5, n. 1). A second MS is reported (without folio numbers) in the Library of Genoa ("à la Bibl. de Gênes") by J. G. Houzeau and A. Lancaster, *General Bibliography of Astronomy to the Year 1880*, I, pts. 1 and 2, new ed. with intro. and author index by D. W. Dewhirst (London, 1954), 640, col. 1, nr. 3197. Some suspicion is cast on this reference, however, since the authors cite the very page in Bertelli's memoir where the Vatican MS is listed. Whether they intended to identify a second manuscript "à la Bibl. de Gênes" (that is, Genoa) or merely to report the existence of the Vatican MS, which erroneously became a Genoa MS, is unclear. A possible third MS appears among Schlund's list of MSS of Peregrinus' *Epistola* ("Petrus Peregrinus von Maricourt," **5** [1912], 32, nr. 27). On fol. 20r–22v and 25v–36r of Latin codex Österreichische Nationalbibliothek, Vienna, 5184 (sixteenth century), treatises, or parts of treatises, appear,

titled, respectively, *Tractatus De Compositione Instrumenti Horarum Diei et Noctis (Treatise On the Construction of an Instrument for [Determining] the Hours of the Day and the Night)* and *Tractatus De Compositione Astrolabii (Treatise On the Construction of an Astrolabe)*. Schlund conjectured that both were parts of the *Epistola*, but the second might well be all or part of the *Nova Compositio Astrolabii Particularis*.

II. SECONDARY LITERATURE. The most extensive study of Peregrinus and his *Epistola* consists of two memoirs by Timoteo Bertelli in *Bullettino di bibliografia e di storia delle scienze matematiche e fisiche*, I (Rome, 1868). The first ("memoria prima"), "Sopra Pietro Peregrino di Maricourt e la sua *Epistola De Magnete*," 1–32, is concerned with Peregrinus' life, MSS of the *Epistola*, and contemporary and later authors, down to 1868, who spoke of Peregrinus, used his work, or edited and translated his treatise. The second memoir ("memoria seconda"), "Sulla *Epistola* di Pietro Peregrino di Maricourt e sopra alcuni trovati e teorie magnetiche del secolo XIII," is in three parts. Part 1, 65–89, includes the Latin ed. of the *Epistola* and a description of the MSS used; part 2, 90–99, 101–139, considers other medieval authors who discussed magnetism; and part 3, 319–420, further analyzes the content of the *Epistola* and traces its subsequent influence. A careful reexamination and evaluation of the life and works of Peregrinus, as well as a summary of the contents of the *Epistola* and an attempt to place Peregrinus in the context of scholastic thought, was published by Erhard Schlund, O.F.M., in "Petrus Peregrinus von Maricourt, sein Leben und seine Schriften (ein Beitrag zur Roger Baco-Forschung)," *in Archivum Franciscanum historicum*, **4** (1911), 436–455, 633–643. Peregrinus' life and *Epistola* are sketchily summarized by Silvanus P. Thompson, "Petrus Peregrinus de Maricourt and his *Epistola De Magnete*," in *Proceedings of the British Academy*, **2** (1905–1906), 377–390 (the lists of variants, MSS, eds., and trans. of the *Epistola* mentioned above, follow on 390–408; see also Thompson's *Peregrinus and his Epistola* [London, 1907]). For an examination of Roger Bacon's alleged remarks about Peregrinus, and an attempt to demonstrate that Peregrinus was a theologian, see François Picavet, *Essais sur l'histoire générale et comparée des théologies et des philosophies médiévales* (Paris, 1913), chap. 11 ("Le maitre des expériences, Pierre de Maricourt, l'exégète et le théologien vantés par Roger Bacon"), 233–254.

Among numerous summaries of the *Epistola*, see Park Benjamin, *The Intellectual Rise of Electricity* (London, 1895); Jean Daujat, *Origines et formation de la théorie des phénomènes électriques et magnétiques*, I (Paris, 1945); Paul Fleury Mottelay, *Bibliographical History of Electricity and Magnetism* (London, 1922), 45–54 (bibliography on 54); Duane H. D. Roller, *The "De Magnete" of William Gilbert* (Amsterdam, 1959), 39–42 (see bibliography, 186–190); and George Sarton, *Introduction to the History of Science*, II, pt. 2 (Baltimore, 1927–1948), 1030–1032, with bibliography. On the specific problem of declination, see Heinrich Winter, "Petrus Peregrinus von Maricourt und die magnetische Missweisung," in *Forschungen und Fortschritte*, **11** (1935), 304–306.

EDWARD GRANT

PETER PHILOMENA OF DACIA, also known as **Petrus Dacus, Petrus Danus, Peter Nightingale** (*fl.* 1290–1300), *mathematics, astronomy.*

Originally a canon of the cathedral in Roskilde, Denmark, Peter Nightingale first appears as the recipient of a letter from Hermann of Minden (provincial of the German Dominicans, 1286–1290) thanking him for the gift of some astronomical instruments and proposing to him that he leave Italy for Germany.[1] In 1291–1292 he is listed as a member of the University of Bologna,[2] where he taught mathematics and astronomy to pupils who included the astrologer Magister Romanus.[3] During 1292 Peter went to Paris, where in that and the following year he produced many writings. After that the sources are silent about him until 4 July 1303, when a letter from Pope Boniface VIII shows that he had returned to Denmark, in his former position as a canon of Roskilde.[4] The years of Peter's birth and death are unknown; and since he is not mentioned in the necrology of his cathedral, it is probable that he died abroad. Although he was a canon regular, he has often been considered a Dominican[5] and confused with the Swedish Dominican author of the same name. This mistake was corrected by H. Schück in 1895 but nevertheless persists in more recent literature.[6] His identification with another Petrus de Dacia, who in 1327 was rector of the University of Paris, has also been shown to be incorrect.[7]

A recent survey has revealed that there are more than 200 extant manuscripts of Peter's numerous works.[8] These can be divided into two groups, the first of which comprises the following writings:

Commentarius in Algorismum vulgarum (10 MSS). This commentary to Sacrobosco's well-known text-book of arithmetic was completed on 31 July 1291 at Bologna and is the only work of Peter Nightingale that has been edited and printed.[9] It contains some original contributions, notably a new and better method of extracting cube roots.[10]

Tabula multiplicationis (2 MSS). A multiplication table in the sexagesimal system and, accordingly, destined for use by astronomers.

Declaratio super Compotum (2 MSS). A commentary on the twelfth-century *Compotus metricus manualis* of Gerlandus of Besançon. It has not yet been examined.

Kalendarium with *canones* (56 MSS). This calendar for the period 1292–1369 was computed in Paris as a substitute for the much-used calendar of Robert Grosseteste, which had run out.[11] The appended *canones* give rules for adjusting the calendar for a new seventy-six-year period. Such adjustments were made in 1369 and around 1442. This calendar was intended to give more precise times of the phases of the moon than Grosseteste's work, with which it has often been confused.[12]

Tractatus eclipsorii (2 MSS). This newly found treatise describes the construction and use of a volvelle or equatorium for determining eclipses. It was written in Paris but contains a reference to Roskilde and is presumably the first evidence of Peter's interest in devising astronomical computers. It is followed by:

Tabulae coniunctionum solis et lune, that is, a table of mean conjunctions of the sun and moon;

Tabula temporis diurni, a table giving the length of the day as a function of the declination of the sun, calculated for the middle of the seventh climate (approximately the latitude of Paris);

Tabula diversitatis aspectuum lune ad solem, a table of the lunar parallax in longitude and latitude, for the same latitude as the preceding table, and meant to be used in connection with the *Tractatus eclipsorii*; and

Tabula equacionis dierum, a table of the equation of time as a function of the longitude of the sun.

Tabula lune with *canones* (68 MSS). This was Peter's most popular work. It exists in two versions: a numerical table and a diagram by which the approximate positions of the moon can be rapidly found from its age and the months of the year.

Tabula planetarum with *canones* (8 MSS). A diagram showing the governing planet for each day of the week and each hour of the day.

All the above works are well-authenticated writings by Peter Nightingale, but it is more difficult to ascertain the authorship of the treatises of the second group:

Tractatus de semissis (10 MSS). A long treatise on the construction and use of an equatorium for calculating planetary longitudes, written in Paris in 1293. No specimen of this instrument has survived, but a modern reconstruction based on the text was published in 1967.[13]

Tractatus novi quadrantis (18 MSS). This work was written in 1293 in Paris and describes the "new quadrant" invented some years earlier by Jacob ben Māḥir ibn Tibbon (Profatius Judaeus).[14] Peter's text seems to be a translation from the Hebrew original, provided with a careful introduction explaining the construction of this curious device, in which the astrolabe is transformed into a quadrant. It is not yet clear whether the other later Latin version dating from 1299 and attributed to Armengoud of Montpellier has anything to do with Peter's treatise.

Tractatus eclipsis solis et lune (1 MS). This is a brief treatise on how the problem of computing eclipses can be solved by geometrical construction.

In many manuscripts the three writings of the second group are attributed to a Petrus de Sancto Audomaro, or Peter of St.-Omer. But two manuscripts of the *Tractatus de semissis* are stated to be by Petrus Danus of St. Audomaro, while another simply calls the author Petrus Danus. Internal evidence and a comparison of astronomical parameters prove the three texts to be works by the same author, who accordingly must have been a very competent astronomer working in Paris at exactly the same time as Peter Nightingale. The latter is a definitely historical person, while it has been impossible to find any other records of the former in contemporary sources. Therefore, there are good reasons to agree with the hypothesis, proposed by E. Zinner in 1932, that the two authors are identical. In that case all the works mentioned above must be attributed to Peter Nightingale, whose possible connection with St.-Omer remains to be explained.

Apart from his works in pure mathematics, Peter Nightingale made two important contributions to medieval science. One was his work on astronomical computing instruments, for which he occupies a very important position in the history of astronomical computing machines. He was not the first Latin writer in this field, which in the later Middle Ages increasingly attracted the attention of astronomers. About 1260 the Paris astronomer Campanus of Novara had constructed a set of six equatoria for calculating longitudes.[15] Peter, however, was the first to invent a computer that solved this problem for all the planets with a single instrument. This device reduced the number of graduated circles and facilitated the construction of the instrument, the main principle of which was later adopted by John of Lignères and Chaucer.[16] The *Tractatus de semissis* also contains Peter's efforts to correct traditional astronomical parameters by new observations.

Peter's second achievement was in the field of astronomical tables, in which his calendar remained in constant use for 150 years. This calendar had the peculiar feature that for each day of the year it listed both the declination of the sun and the length of the day. The same features are found in a contemporary calendar by the Paris astronomer Guillaume de St.-Cloud, who seems to have collaborated with Peter Nightingale during the latter's sojourn in Paris.[17] The prehistory of this calendar was put into perspective by A. Otto, who in 1933 drew attention to a passage in the partly extant *Liber daticus* of Roskilde cathedral. It appears that in 1274 an unnamed astronomer belonging to the chapter made a series of observations,

unique for his time, of the altitude of the sun at noon, from which he calculated the length of the day by a *kardagas sinuum* (a trigonometrical diagram replacing a sine table).[18] Both the altitude and the length of the day were tabulated in the now lost calendar of the cathedral. In this respect the Roskilde calendar may be considered the prototype of the calendar calculated by Peter Nightingale in Paris. This is not to say that he was identical with the unknown Roskilde astronomer of 1274; but there is no doubt that it was he who brought the principle from Denmark to France, thus creating a hitherto unknown link between Scandinavian astronomy and European science in general.

NOTES

1. Published in Paul Lehmann, "Skandinaviens Anteil an der lateinischen Literatur und Wissenschaft des Mittelalters," in *Sitzungsberichte der Bayerischen Akademie der Wissenschaften zu München*, Phil.-hist. Abt. (1936), 53–54.
2. Ellen Jørgensen, "Om nogle middelalderlige forfattere der naevnes som hjemmehørende i Dacia," in *Historisk tidsskrift*, 8th ser., **3** (1910–1912), 253–260.
3. Lynn Thorndike, *History of Magic and Experimental Science*, III (New York, 1934), 647–649.
4. A. Krarup, in *Bullarium danicum*, no. 947 (1932), 834–835.
5. J. Quétif and J. Echard, *Scriptores ordinis Praedicatorum*, II (Paris, 1721).
6. H. Schück, *Illustrerad Svensk literaturhistoria*, I (Stockholm, 1895), 343; G. Sarton, *Introduction to the History of Science*, II (Baltimore, 1931), 996–997.
7. C. E. Bulaeus, *Historia Universitatis Parisiensis*, II (Paris, 1668), 210, 982; cf. H. Denifle and A. Chatelain, *Chartularium Universitatis Parisiensis*, II (Paris, 1891), nos. 863, 955.
8. This survey, by Olaf Pedersen, is not yet completed. It supersedes previous inventories by G. Eneström, "Anteckningar om matematikern Petrus de Dacia och hans skrifter," in *Öfversigt af K. Vetenskapsakademiens förhandlingar* (1885), 15–27, 65–70, and (1886), 57–60; and E. Zinner, *Verzeichnis der astronomischen Handschriften des deutschen Kulturgebietes* (Munich, 1925), nos. 2055–2082.
9. Maximilian Curtze, *Petri Philomeni de Dacia in Algorismum vulgarem Johannis de Sacrobosco commentarius una cum algorismo ipso* (Copenhagen, 1897).
10. G. Eneström, "Über die Geschichte der Kubikwurzelausziehung im Mittelalter," in *Bibliotheca mathematica*, 3rd ser., **14** (1914), 83–84; cf. M. Cantor, *Geschichte der Mathematik*, 2nd ed., II (Leipzig, 1899–1900), 90.
11. E. Zinner, "Petrus de Dacia, en middelalderlig dansk astronom," in *Nordisk astronomisk tidsskrift*, **13** (1932), 136–146; German trans. in *Archeion*, **18** (1936), 318–329.
12. First by J. Langebek, in *Scriptores rerum Danicarum*, IV (Copenhagen, 1786), 260 f., where Grosseteste's calendar was edited and attributed to Petrus de Dacia.
13. O. Pedersen, "The Life and Work of Peter Nightingale," in *Vistas in Astronomy*, **9** (1967), 3–10; cf. O. Pedersen, "Peder Nattergal og hans astronomiske regneinstrument," in *Nordisk astronomisk tidsskrift*, **44** (1963), 37–50.
14. This text has been edited in an unpublished thesis by Lydik Garm, "Profatius Judaeus' traktat om kvadranten" (Aarhus, Institute for the History of Science, 1966).
15. F. J. Benjamin and G. J. Toomer, *Campanus of Novara and Medieval Planetary Theory* (Madison, Wis., 1971).

16. D. J. de Solla Price, *The Equatorie of the Planetis* (Cambridge, 1955), 17 f. (Chaucer) and 188 f. (John of Lignères).
17. P. Duhem, *Le système du monde*, new ed., IV (Paris, 1954), 14 f.; cf. Zinner, *loc. cit.*
18. A. Otto, *Liber daticus Roskildensis* (Copenhagen, 1933), 32–33. The importance of the Roskilde astronomer was first pointed out by A. A. Bjørnbo, "Die mathematischen S. Marco-Handschriften in Florenz," in *Bibliotheca mathematica*, 3rd ser., **12** (1912), 116.

OLAF PEDERSEN

PETERS, CARL F. W. (*b.* Pulkovo, Russia, 16 April 1844; *d.* Königsberg, Germany [now Kaliningrad, R.S.F.S.R.], 2 November 1894), *astronomy, geodesy*.

Peters was the son of the astronomer Christian A. F. Peters. Between 1862 and 1866 he studied at Kiel, Berlin, and Munich, became adjunct at the Hamburg observatory in 1867, and received the Ph.D. at Göttingen in 1868. He then became his father's assistant at the Altona observatory. In this post he determined the length of the seconds pendulum for Altona, Berlin, and Königsberg and in 1870–1871 executed new observations with Bessel's pendulum apparatus between Königsberg and Güldenstein, a castle in Holstein. He was appointed observer in 1872 and the following year moved to Kiel, where the Altona observatory had been relocated. Here he became academic lecturer in astronomy in 1876.

After his father's death Peters edited three volumes of the *Astronomische Nachrichten* (**97–99**) during 1880–1881, and in 1882 he became assistant professor of astronomy. A year later he assumed the directorship of the chronometer *Observatorium* of the imperial navy, a post conferred on him because of his extremely careful investigations of the rate of chronometers. He determined that they were influenced not only by temperature but also by humidity and magnetism. He also reduced the existing observations of the double star 61 Cygni, deriving an accurate orbit, and edited the German version of A. N. Sawitsch's *Practical Astronomy*.

In 1888 Peters was appointed professor at the University of Königsberg and director of its observatory, where he began observations with the meridian circle. His early death, after a long illness, prevented any major achievements in this new field. Peters was a man of great kindness and cordiality, and of an unusually humane temperament.

BIBLIOGRAPHY

Peters' writings include *Astronomische Tafeln und Formeln* (Hamburg, 1871); *Entfernung der Erde von der Sonne* (Berlin, 1873); *Beobachtungen mit dem Besselschen Pendelapparat in Königsberg und Güldenstein* (Hamburg, 1874); "Einige Bemerkungen über die Vorbestimmung des Chronometerstandes," in *Annalen der Hydrographie . . .*, **5** (1877), 207–214; *Die Fixsterne*, in the series Wissenschaft der Gegenwart (Leipzig, 1883); "Magnetische Einflüsse auf den Gang der Chronometer," in *Annalen der Hydrographie . . .*, **12** (1884), 316–318; "Bestimmung der Bahn des Doppelsterns 61 Cygni," in *Astronomische Nachrichten*, **113** (1885), 321–340; and "Einfluss der Feuchtigkeit der Luft auf den Gang der Chronometer," in *Annalen der Hydrographie*, **15** (1887), 505–512.

An obituary is J. Franz, in *Vierteljahrsschrift der Astronomischen Gesellschaft* (Leipzig), **30** (1895), 12–16.

H.-CHRIST. FREIESLEBEN

PETERS, CHRISTIAN AUGUST FRIEDRICH (*b.* Hamburg, Germany, 7 September 1806; *d.* Kiel, Germany, 8 May 1880), *astronomy*.

Peters' father, a merchant, saw to it that his son, who did not regularly attend secondary school, obtained a good knowledge of mathematics and astronomy. He was so successful that H. C. Schumacher, the editor of the *Astronomische Nachrichten*, learned of Peters and induced him to study geodesy and astronomy. Peters subsequently entered the University of Königsberg, where he received the Ph.D. under Bessel. From 1834 to 1838, as assistant at the Hamburg observatory Peters observed mainly with the transit instrument. In 1839 he was appointed assistant at the new Pulkovo observatory, where he worked for nearly ten years, finally becoming assistant director under F. G. W. Struve. He observed the polestar, the newly discovered planet Neptune, and parallaxes of fixed stars.

In 1849 Peters returned to Königsberg to become professor of astronomy. This post was not connected with the directorship of the observatory, but he did have access to Bessel's famous heliometer. In 1854 Peters moved to Altona as director of the observatory and editor of the *Astronomische Nachrichten*, of which he edited fifty-eight volumes (**40–97**), from 1855 till the end of his life. In 1872 the Altona observatory was moved to Kiel and reconstructed on a larger scale, a plan that Peters had favored since 1864. In 1874 Peters became ordinary professor at the University of Kiel.

Both a student and a successor of Bessel, Peters sought to ascertain the base of spherical astronomy. His investigations concerning nutation, the proper motion of Sirius, and the parallaxes of fixed stars are his main achievements.

BIBLIOGRAPHY

Peters' writings include *Numerus constans nutationis . . . in specula Dorpatensi annis 1832–1838 observatis deductus* (St. Petersburg, 1842); "Resultate aus den Beobachtungen des Polarsterns an der Pulkowaer Sternwarte," in *Mémoires de l'Académie impériale des sciences de St.-Pétersbourg*, 6th ser., **3** (1844); "Über die eigene Bewegung des Sirius," in *Astronomische Nachrichten*, **32** (1851), 1–58; "Recherches sur la parallaxe des étoiles fixes," in *Mémoires de l'Académie impériale des sciences de St.-Pétersbourg*, 6th ser., **5** (1853); "Über die Länge des einfachen Sekundenpendels auf dem Schlosse Güldenstein," in *Astronomische Nachrichten*, **40** (1855), 1–152; *Bestimmung des Längenunterschiedes Altona–Schwerin* (Altona, 1861); "Ein Repsoldsches Äquatorial zu Altona," in *Astronomische Nachrichten*, **58** (1862), 271–352; *Das Land Swante–Wustrow oder das Fischland* (Wustrow, 1866); and *Bestimmung des Längenunterschiedes Göttingen–Altona* (Kiel, 1880).

An obituary is A. Winnecke, in *Vierteljahrsschrift der Astronomischen Gesellschaft* (Leipzig), **16** (1881), 5–8.

H. C. FREIESLEBEN

PETERS, CHRISTIAN HEINRICH FRIEDRICH (*b*. Coldenbüttel, Schleswig, Denmark [now Schleswig-Holstein, Germany], 19 September 1813; *d*. Clinton, New York, 18 July 1890), *astronomy*.

After attending the Gymnasium in Flensburg Peters studied mathematics and astronomy with Encke at the University of Berlin, where he took the Ph.D. in 1836, then with Gauss at Göttingen. From 1838 to 1843 he worked on a private survey of Mount Etna, then was appointed director of the government trigonometric survey of Sicily. He held this post until 1848, when he was deported for actively supporting the Sicilian revolutionaries. In 1849, following the fall of Palermo, Peters went to Constantinople, where he remained for the next five years. Although political circumstances—including the Crimean War—precluded expeditions, Peters was able to learn Arabic and Turkish.

In 1854, carrying introductions from Humboldt, Peters immigrated to the United States. He was employed by the Coast Survey, and detailed first to the Cloverden Observatory in Cambridge, and then to the Dudley Observatory in Albany. In 1858 he was appointed professor of astronomy and director of the Litchfield Observatory at Hamilton College, Clinton, N.Y. Although funds were short (he often went for months without salary) he remained at Hamilton for the rest of his life.

Peters' primary scientific interest was observational positional astronomy. While in Naples, long before Carrington took up such work, Peters charted the latitudinal and longitudinal proper motions and internal developments of sunspots. At Hamilton College Peters attempted to chart, without photog-

raphy, all the stars down to (and even below) the fourteenth magnitude situated within 30° on either side of the ecliptic. He coincidentally discovered forty-eight asteroids and computed their orbits. In 1869 he organized a party to observe a total eclipse of the sun, and in 1874 he led one of eight U.S. government expeditions to observe the transit of Venus; he was a member of the International Astrophotographic Congress held in Paris in 1887. Drawing on both his linguistic ability and his astronomical knowledge Peters collated the star catalogs in various Continental manuscript copies of Ptolemy's *Almagest*. E. B. Knobel collated the British manuscripts and issued a revised Ptolemaic catalog in 1915, after Peters' death.

Peters was a member or a fellow of a number of scientific societies, including the American Academy of Arts and Sciences (1856), the National Academy of Sciences (1876), the American Philosophical Society (1878), and the Royal Astronomical Society (1879); he received the French Legion of Honor in 1887.

BIBLIOGRAPHY

I. ORIGINAL WORKS. Peters' writings include *De principio minimae actionis dissertatio* (Berlin, 1836); *Report . . . on the Longitude of Elmira* (Albany, 1864); *Report . . . on the Longitude and Latitude of Ogdensburg* (Albany, 1865); and *Celestial Charts Made at the Litchfield Observatory* (Clinton, N.Y., 1882), with 20 charts each covering 5° dec. and 20^m r.a., another 20 were finished, but unpublished, at his death. Posthumous works are E. B. Frost, ed., *Heliographic Positions of Sun-spots Observed at Hamilton College from 1860–1870*, Carnegie Institution of Washington Publication no. 43 (Washington, D.C. 1907); and *Ptolemy's Catalogue of Stars*, Carnegie Institution of Washington Publication no. 86 (Washington, D.C., 1915), written with E. B. Knobel. The Royal Society of London *Catalogue of Scientific Papers* lists 144 papers by Peters; his correspondence with his friend G. P. Bond is at the Harvard College Observatory.

II. SECONDARY LITERATURE. On Peters and his work, see *Christian Henry Frederick Peters, September 19, 1813, July 18, 1890* (Hamilton, N. Y., 1890), a memorial vol. printed for private circulation. Obituary notices are in *Sidereal Messenger*, **9** (1890), 439–442; *Monthly Notices of the Royal Astronomical Society*, **51** (1890–1891), 199–202; and *Astronomische Nachrichten* (Aug. 1890). For Peters' controversy with C. A. Borst over ownership of a research MS, see "Dr. Peters' Star Catalogue," in *Sidereal Messenger*, **8** (1889), 138–139, 455–458; *Utica Morning Herald* (9 Nov. 1889); and Simon Newcomb, *Reminiscences of an Astronomer* (Boston, 1903), 372–381.

DEBORAH JEAN WARNER

PETERSEN, JULIUS (*b.* Sorø, Denmark, 16 June 1839; *d.* Copenhagen, Denmark, 5 August 1910), *mathematics.*

Petersen's interest in mathematics was awakened at school, where his main occupation was solving problems and attempting the trisection of the angle. At the age of seventeen he entered the College of Technology in Copenhagen; but after some years of study he transferred to the University of Copenhagen, from which he graduated in 1866 and received the doctorate in 1871. His dissertation treated equations solvable by square roots with applications to the solution of problems by ruler and compass. During his university years and after graduation Petersen taught in secondary schools. In 1871 he was appointed docent at the College of Technology and, in 1887, professor at the University of Copenhagen, a post he held until the year before his death.

Through his terse, well-written textbooks Petersen has exerted a very strong influence on mathematical education in Denmark. Several of his books were translated into other languages. Worthy of particular mention is his *Methods and Theories for the Solution of Problems of Geometrical Constructions* (Danish, 1866; English, 1879; German, 1879; French, 1880; Italian, 1881; Russian, 1892). His other writings cover a wide range of subjects in algebra, number theory, analysis, geometry, and mechanics. Perhaps his most important contribution is his theory of regular graphs, inspired by a problem in the theory of invariants and published in *Acta mathematica* in 1891.

BIBLIOGRAPHY

Petersen's works are listed in Niels Nielsen, *Matematiken i Danmark 1801–1908* (Copenhagen–Christiania, 1910).

There are obituaries by H. G. Zeuthen, in *Oversigt over det K. Danske Videnskabernes Selskabs Forhandlinger 1910* (1910–1911), I, 73–75; C. Juel and V. Trier, in *Nyt Tidsskrift for Matematik*, *A*, **21** (1910), 73–77, in Danish; and C. Juel, "En dansk Matematiker," in *Matematisk Tidsskrift*, A (1923), 85–95.

BØRGE JESSEN

PETERSON, KARL MIKHAILOVICH (*b.* Riga, Russia [now Latvian S.S.R.], 25 May 1828; *d.* Moscow, Russia, 19 April 1881), *mathematics.*

Peterson was the son of a Latvian worker, a former serf named Mikhail Peterson, and his wife, Maria Mangelson. In 1847 he graduated from the Riga Gymnasium and enrolled at the University of Dorpat. The lectures of his scientific tutor Ferdinand Minding provided an occasion for Peterson's writing his thesis "Über die Biegung der Flächen" (1853), for which he received the degree of bachelor of mathematics.

Later Peterson moved to Moscow where he worked first as a private teacher then, from 1865 until his death, as a mathematics teacher at the German Peter and Paul School. Becoming intimately acquainted with scientists close to N. D. Brashman and A. Y. Davidov, Peterson took an active part in the organization of the Moscow Mathematical Society and in its work. He published almost all of his writings in *Matematicheskii sbornik*, issued by the society.

In 1879 the Novorossiiskii University of Odessa awarded Peterson an honorary doctorate in pure mathematics for his studies on the theory of characteristics of partial differential equations, in which, by means of a uniform general method, he deduced nearly all the devices known at that time for finding general solutions of different classes of equations. These studies were to a certain extent close to the works of Davidov (1866) and N. Y. Sonin (1874). However, Peterson's principal discoveries are connected with differential geometry.

In the first part of his thesis Peterson established certain new properties of curves on surfaces and in the second part he continued Gauss's and Minding's works on the bending of surfaces. Here he for the first time obtained equations equivalent to three fundamental equations of Mainardi (1856) and Codazzi (1867–1869), which involve six coefficients of the first and the second quadratic differential forms of a surface. Peterson also proved—in different expression—the theorem usually bearing the name of Bonnet (1867): the geometrical form of the surface is wholly determined if the coefficients of both quadratic forms are given. Minding found the thesis excellent, but these results were not published during Peterson's lifetime and found no development in his articles which were printed after 1866. Brief information on Peterson's thesis was first given by P. Stäckel in 1901; a complete Russian translation of the manuscript, written in German and preserved in the archives of the University of Tartu, was published in 1952.

In his works Peterson elaborated new methods in the differential geometry of surfaces. Thus, he introduced the notion of bending on a principal basis, namely, bending under which a certain conjugate congruence of curves on the surface remains conjugate; such congruence is called the principal basis of a surface. Peterson established numerous general properties of conjugate congruences and studied in depth the bending on a principal basis of surfaces of second order, surfaces of revolution, minimal and translation surfaces. All these surfaces and some others constitute a class of surfaces, quite interesting in its properties, named after Peterson.

Although Peterson did not teach at the university, his ideas initiated the studies of B. K. Mlodzeevsky and, later, of his disciples Egorov, S. P. Finikov, and S. S. Bushgens. Peterson's discoveries also found a somewhat belated reputation and extension in other countries, for example, in the works of Darboux and Bianchi. Outside the Soviet Union, however, his remarkable studies on the theory of surfaces are still mentioned but rarely in the literature on the history of mathematics.

BIBLIOGRAPHY

I. ORIGINAL WORKS. Peterson's writings include "Ob otnosheniakh i srodstvakh mezhdu krivymi poverkhnostyami" ("On Relationships and Kinships Between Surfaces"), in *Matematicheskii sbornik*, **1** (1866), 391–438; "O krivykh na poverkhnostiakh" ("On Curves on Surfaces"), *ibid.*, **2** (1867), 17–44; *Über Kurven und Flächen* (Moscow–Leipzig, 1868); "Ob integrirovanii uravnenii s chastnymi proizvodnymi" ("On the Integration of Partial Differential Equations"), in *Matematicheskii sbornik*, **8** (1877), 291–361; **9** (1878), 137–192; **10** (1882), 169–223; and *Ob integrirovanii uravnenii s chastnymi proizvodnymi po dvum nezavisimym peremennym* ("On the Integration of Partial Differential Equations With Two Independent Variables"; Moscow, 1878). For a French trans. of Peterson's works, see *Annales de la Faculté des sciences de l'Université de Toulouse*, 2nd ser., **7** (1905), 5–263. See also "Ob izgibanii poverkhnostei" ("On the Bending of Surfaces"), his dissertation, in *Istoriko-matematicheskie issledovaniya*, **5** (1952), 87–112, with commentary by S. D. Rossinsky, pp. 113–133.

II. SECONDARY LITERATURE. On Peterson and his work, see (listed chronologically) P. Stäckel, "Karl Peterson," in *Bibliotheca mathematica*, 3rd ser., **2** (1901), 122–132; B. K. Mlodzeevsky, "Karl Mikhailovich Peterson i ego geometricheskie raboty" ("Karl Mikhailovich Peterson and His Geometrical Works"), in *Matematicheskii sbornik*, **24** (1903), 1–21; D. F. Egorov, "Raboty K. M. Petersona po teorii uravnenii s chastnymi proizvodnymi" ("Peterson's Works on Partial Differential Equations"), *ibid.*, 22–29—the last two appear in French trans. in *Annales de la Faculté des sciences de l'Université de Toulouse*, 2nd ser., **5** (1903), 459–479; D. J. Struik, "Outline of a History of Differential Geometry," in *Isis*, **19** (1933), 92–120; **20** (1933), 161–191; S. D. Rossinsky, "Karl Mikhailovich Peterson," in *Uspekhi matematicheskikh nauk*, **4**, no. 5 (1949), 3–13; I. Y. Depman, "Karl Mikhailovich Peterson i ego kandidatskaya dissertatsia" ("Peterson and His Candidature Dissertation"), in *Istoriko-matematicheskie issledovaniya*, **5** (1952), 134–164; I. Z. Shtokalo, ed., *Istoria otechestvennoy matematiki* ("History of Native Mathematics"), II (Kiev, 1967); and A. P. Youschkevitch, *Istoria matematiki v Rossii do 1917 goda* ("A History of Mathematics in Russia to 1917"; Moscow, 1968).

A. P. YOUSCHKEVITCH
A. T. GRIGORIAN

PETIT, ALEXIS THÉRÈSE (*b.* Vesoul, France, 2 October 1791; *d.* Paris, France, 21 June 1820), *physics.*

Petit was an outstanding pupil at the École Centrale in Besançon and later at a private school in Paris that was staffed by teachers from the École Polytechnique. He had fulfilled the entrance requirements for the École Polytechnique by the time he was ten-and-a-half and he enrolled there in 1807, when he was sixteen, the minimum age for entry. He was first in his entering class; when he graduated, in 1809, he was placed *hors de ligne*, and the next student in the year was designated "first." Petit was immediately taken onto the staff as a teaching assistant.

In 1810 Petit also became professor of physics at the Lycée Bonaparte in Paris. As a teacher he was both popular and successful, and when he succeeded to J.-H. Hassenfratz's chair of physics at the École Polytechnique in 1815, after a year as assistant professor, he extended and improved the courses in his subject. His last years, however, were clouded by grief and illness; shortly after the death of his young wife, in 1817, he contracted tuberculosis, the disease from which he died. He was a member of the Société Philomatique from February 1818 but was never elected to the Académie des Sciences.

Petit's most important work was done in collaboration with his close friend Pierre Dulong. (This collaborative work is discussed in detail in the article on Dulong.) Their association began in 1815, probably in response to the prize competition on thermometry and the laws of cooling that was then set by the first class of the Institute. By 1818, when the prize was awarded to them, Petit and Dulong had conducted a classic experimental investigation, which established the gas thermometer as the only reliable standard and put the approximate nature of Newton's law of cooling beyond all doubt. It was after a further year of intense activity, devoted mainly to the measurement of the specific heats of solids, that Petit and Dulong discovered their law of atomic heats. Since the discovery was made, suddenly and quite by chance, only one week before it was announced to the Académie des Sciences on 12 April 1819, it is not surprising that the evidence for their categorical statement, "the atoms of all elementary substances have exactly the same capacity for heat," was inadequate. In fact the exactness of the law was in doubt from the start and was never to be established.

Petit's comments on theoretical issues were characterized by his receptiveness to new ideas. He received a thoroughly conventional education in physics at the École Polytechnique, where the customary emphasis was placed on such doctrines as the corpuscular theory of light, the caloric theory of heat, and the other theories of imponderable fluids. Thus, not surprisingly, when he himself began to teach there, his teaching was completely orthodox, as may be seen in some manuscript notes of the lectures that he gave in the winter of 1814–1815. But in December 1815, as a result of some experiments on the refraction of light in gases—which he had performed with his brother-in-law Dominique Arago—Petit openly rejected the corpuscular theory and became one of the earliest supporters of the wave theory, which had just been revived in France by Fresnel.

The Petit-Dulong paper of April 1819 on atomic heats was likewise marked by a skepticism toward established doctrine. In it Petit and Dulong rejected the caloric theory and, almost certainly under the influence of Dulong's close friend Berzelius, substituted for it the electrical explanation of heats of chemical reaction. The 1819 paper also contained a statement of support for the chemical atomic theory, which, owing largely to the opposition of Berthollet and his followers, had made little headway in France.

Although he is best known for his experimental work, Petit had an equal, if not greater, talent for mathematics. Evidence of this is found in his brilliant doctoral thesis of 1811 on the theory of capillary action (treated in the manner of Laplace) and in a paper on the theory of machines written in 1818.

BIBLIOGRAPHY

I. ORIGINAL WORKS. In the absence of an ed. of Petit's collected works, his papers have to be consulted in the journals in which they originally appeared. The *Annales de chimie et de physique* between 1816 and 1819 is the most useful source. A partial bibliography is given in Poggendorff, II, 415–416.

II. SECONDARY LITERATURE. The standard biographical sketch of Petit is the obituary notice by J.-B. Biot, published in *Annales de chimie et de physique*, **16** (1821), 327–335, and *Journal de physique, de chimie, d'histoire naturelle et des arts*, **92** (1821), 241–248. On his work with Dulong, see R. Fox, "The Background to the Discovery of Dulong and Petit's Law," in *British Journal for the History of Science*, **4** (1968–1969), 1–22; J. Jamin, "Études sur la chaleur statique. Dulong et Petit," in *Revue des deux mondes*, 2nd ser., **11** (1855), 375–412; and J. W. van Spronsen, "The History and Prehistory of the Law of Dulong and Petit as Applied to the Determination of Atomic Weights," in *Chymia*, **12** (1967), 157–169. See also R. Fox, *The Caloric Theory of Gases From Lavoisier to Regnault* (Oxford, 1971), especially pp. 227–248. Petit's paper on the history of machines is discussed in C. C. Gillispie, *Lazare Carnot savant* (Princeton, 1971), 107–111.

ROBERT FOX

PETIT, PIERRE (*b.* Montluçon, France, 8 December 1594 or 31 December 1598; *d.* Lagny-sur-Marne, France, 20 August 1677), *physics, astronomy.*

The son of a minor provincial official, Petit spent his early adult life as *contrôleur de l'election* in Montluçon. In 1633 he traveled to Paris and was appointed Commissaire Provincial de l'Artillerie by Richelieu; he became Intendant Général des Fortifications in 1649. Petit's governmental career was complemented by an active role in French science for more than four decades.

A member of the group of savants meeting at Marin Mersenne's lodgings in the Place Royale, he exemplified those investigators who, in contrast to the increasingly doctrinaire Cartesians, emphasized the importance of accurate experimental observation in validating scientific theories. Petit criticized the lack of adequate astronomical facilities, which he thought had prevented the French from keeping abreast of observations made elsewhere in Europe, and urged the establishment of a royal observatory. His private collection of telescopes and instruments was among the best in Paris and included a number of his own inventions, most notably a perfected filar micrometer later used by Cassini I.

Petit worked with or knew many of the major scientists of the period. In 1646 he collaborated with Blaise Pascal in Rouen and repeated Torricelli's experiment on the barometric vacuum. A regular correspondent of Henry Oldenburg, Petit was keenly interested in the scientific studies pursued in England and played a central role in facilitating the exchange of ideas and inventions between the two national communities. His *Dissertation sur la nature des comètes* (1665) was praised in England and on the Continent for the accuracy and completeness of its observations and discussion; his studies on magnetic declination were equally well-praised. A leading member of the Montmor Academy, Petit was a forceful advocate for the creation of an official science organization. He was, however, ignored by Colbert in the initial selection of members of the Académie Royale des Sciences in

1666; this surprising disappointment was partially compensated for by Petit's election as one of the first foreign fellows of the Royal Society of London in April 1667.

BIBLIOGRAPHY

I. ORIGINAL WORKS. Petit's major scientific writings include *L'usage ou le moyen de pratiquer par une règle toutes les opérations du compas de proportion* (Paris, 1634); *Dissertation sur la nature des comètes . . . avec un discours sur les prognostiques des éclipses et autres matières curieuses* (Paris, 1665); *Dissertations académiques sur la nature du froid et du chaud . . . avec un discours sur la construction et l'usage d'un cylindre arithmétique, inventé par le même autheur* (Paris, 1671).

Petit gave a model account of his and Pascal's experiments in a letter to Pierre Chanut (French Ambassador to Sweden) dated 26 November 1646; the letter is reprinted in Blaise Pascal, *Oeuvres complètes*, Léon Brunschvicg and Pierre Boutroux, eds., I (Paris, 1908), 325–345. The account was published the following year as *Observation touchant le vuide faite pour la première fois en France* (Paris, 1647).

Petit gave an account of his filar micrometer, in which he acknowledged the simultaneous development of the same instrument by Auzout and Picard, in "Extrait d'une Lettre de M. Petit Intendant des Fortifications . . . touchant une nouvelle machine pour mesurer exactement les diamètres des astres. Du 12 Mars 1667," in *Journal des sçavans*, no. 9 (16 May 1667). Petit's complete bibliography is somewhat confused, since a number of his works have been attributed by some to another Pierre Petit of Paris, a prolific medical writer and historian as well as a contemporary of Petit. Thus Petit's *Observationes aliquot eclipsium solis et lunae, cum dissertationibus de latitudine Lutetiae, et declinatione magnetis, necnon de novo systemate mundi quod anonymus dudum proposuit*, published with Jean-Baptiste Du Hamel's *Astronomia physica* (Paris, 1660), is incorrectly attributed by the British Museum *Catalogue* to Petit the medical writer and historian. Finally, Petit's letters to Oldenburg are reprinted in A. Rupert Hall and Marie Boas Hall, eds., *The Correspondence of Henry Oldenburg* (Madison, 1965–), *passim*.

II. SECONDARY LITERATURE. Details concerning Petit's life and work are given in *Biographie universelle*, J. Michaud, ed., XXXII (repr. Graz, 1968), 588–589; and Jean Pierre Nicéron, *Mémoires pour servir à l'histoire des hommes illustres dans la république des lettres*, **42** (Paris, 1741), 191–195. On Petit's collaboration with Pascal, see Pierre Humbert, *L'oeuvre scientifique de Blaise Pascal* (Paris, 1947), pp. 73 ff. A useful account of Petit's activities in Parisian scientific circles is given by Harcourt Brown, *Scientific Organizations in Seventeenth Century France* (Baltimore, 1934), *passim*.

MARTIN FICHMAN

PETOSIRIS, PSEUDO- (*fl.* Egypt, second and first centuries B.C.), *astrology.*

During antiquity several texts relating to divination and astrology circulated under the names Petosiris and Nechepso. Nechepso is the name of a king whom Manetho included in the twenty-sixth Egyptian dynasty (*ca.* 600 B.C.); and the most famous Petosiris was the high priest of Thoth (*ca.* 300 B.C. [?]),[1] although many others bore this name signifying "Gift of Osiris." Whether the author of the works circulating under their names had these two individuals, or some others, in mind we cannot know.

The fragments of these works, which were collected by E. Riess,[2] fall into four main groups: (1) those using astral omens as developed by the Egyptians in the Achemenid and Ptolemaic periods from Mesopotamian prototypes to give general indications; (2) those derived from a revelation-text in which Nechepso the king, guided by Petosiris, sees a vision that grants him a knowledge of horoscopic truth; (3) a treatise on astrological botany for medical purposes and another on decanic medicine; and (4) treatises on numerology.

(1) The fragments of texts employing astral omina are largely from authors of late antiquity: Hephaestio of Thebes (*fl. ca.* 415), Proclus (410–485), and John Lydus (*fl. ca.* 560). As preserved to us, the fragments represent radical reworkings of the original texts. It is those fragments, and especially fragment 6 (Riess), which C. Bezold and F. Boll[3] saw to be related to Mesopotamian texts and that allowed Kroll[4] to date the original to the second century B.C. The fragments belonging to this text[5] use as omens eclipses, the heliacal rising of Sirius, and comets. Fragment 6[6] uses as omens the color of the eclipsed body; the simultaneous occurrence of winds blowing from the several directions and of shooting stars, halos, lightning, and rain; and the presence of the eclipsed body in each of the signs of the zodiac (a substitution for Egyptian months). Fragment 6 also divides the day or night into four periods, each of which has three seasonal hours. Most of these elements are found in the demotic papyrus published by R. A. Parker,[7] and many of them in the relevant tablets of the Sin and Shamash sections of the Babylonian astral omen series *Enūma Anu Enlil*.

Fragment 8[8] summarizes a similar treatment of eclipse omens from Campestrius, "who follows the Petosirian traditions." Fragment 7,[9] also on eclipse omens, seems to be from another but still ancient source in which the scheme of geographical references was rather strictly limited to Egypt and its neighbors in contrast to fragment 6, where the eclipses affect the whole Eurasian continent.

Fragment 12[10] gives annual predictions based on the situation at the heliacal rising of Sirius, including the positions of the planets and the color of the star and direction of the winds; it is to be compared to the demotic papyrus published by G. R. Hughes[11] and also with "Eudoxius"[12] and Pseudo-Zoroaster.[13] In the middle of Hephaestio, I, 23, is a description of the manner in which the effective force of the planets is transmitted through the spheres to the sublunar sphere. This passage presupposes both Aristotelian physical theories and a planetary system based on epicycles, eccentrics, or both. If the passage is a genuine quotation from a text written in the second century B.C., it is of the greatest interest as providing the earliest evidence known to us of a theory of astral influence. The fragment contains other elements of interest to a historian of horoscopy—for example, a categorization of the planets as malefic or benefic and the use of aspects. But these elements may have been added by Hephaestio or some unknown predecessor, or the whole chapter may have nothing to do with the work published under the names of Nechepso and Petosiris.

Very doubtful indeed is the attribution to that work of fragments 9,[14] 10,[15] and 11.[16] The ominous bodies are the comets, of which there was originally one type associated with each of the planets. Such comets of the planets are found also in early Sanskrit astral omen texts (for example, in the *Gargasaṃhitā*), but we have as yet no cuneiform tablets that would give us a common source. In any case, there is little reason to assign these specific fragments to Nechepso and Petosiris.

Perhaps also forming a part of the astral omen texts are two other sets of fragments dealing with problems that interested the earliest men who attempted to convert general omens into ones significant for individuals and who used Babylonian techniques. These two problems are the date of a native's conception[17] and the computation of the length of his life based on the rising times between the ascendent and the nonagesimal.[18]

(2) The horoscopic text includes all of the passages from Valens' *Anthologies* (I give the references to the edition by W. Kroll [Berlin, 1908]) and some from Firmicus Maternus. In it Nechepso saw a vision,[19] which included a perception of the motions of the planets that is redolent of pre-Ptolemaic astronomy. He described what he had learned from this revelation in at least thirteen books of very obscure iambic senarii. As we know the ideas there expressed only through the dim intellect of Vettius Valens, we are not surprised to find the "mysteries" largely either self-

contradictory or too fragmentary to be comprehended fully. Some passages in Valens[20] indicate that he knew of a separate work of Petosiris (entitled *Definitions*) in addition to that of Nechepso, to whom he usually refers as "the king," although in another place[21] he speaks of "the king and Petosiris" together. Several passages[22] contain quotations from "the king's" thirteenth book.

Among the principal astrological doctrines discussed by Nechepso and Petosiris in the poetic work (or works) available to Valens are the computation of the length of life of the native;[23] the calculation of the Lot of Fortune, which is also used in computing the length of life;[24] the determination of good and bad times during the native's life, based on various methods of continuous horoscopy (the planetary periods, the lord of the year, and the revolution of the years of nativities);[25] dangerous or climacteric times;[26] and various aspects of the native's life: travel,[27] injury,[28] children,[29] and death.[30] It is probable that Firmicus Maternus drew upon this same collection for his references to Petosiris' and Nechepso's geniture of the universe,[31] his statement that Petosiris only lightly touched upon the doctrine of the decans,[32] and his denial that Petosiris and Nechepso dealt with the *Sphaera barbarica*. Add also the discussion of initiatives in Julian.[33]

(3) Nechepso is known as an authority on materia medica (plants and stones) under astral influence.[34]

(4) The numerological treatises are of two sorts, both explained in a letter of Petosiris to King Nechepso, which is extant in numerous recensions. The simpler form utilizes only the numerical equivalent of the Greek letters in the querist's name; the second form utilizes the day of the lunar month and the "Circle of Petosiris."[35] Another numerological text, which is based on the zodiacal signs, occurs in a letter addressed to Nechepso.[36]

The significance of Pseudo-Petosiris' works (esp. 1 and 2) is their illumination of—although in a very fragmentary form—two important processes of Ptolemaic science: the development of the astral omens that the Egyptians of the Achemenid period had derived from Mesopotamia, and the invention of a new science of astrology based on Greek astronomy and physics in conjunction with Hellenistic mysticism and Egypto-Babylonian divination from astral omens. The effect of their teachings on their successors was profound, although the primitiveness of their methods meant that only their heirs of a mystic (Valens) or antiquarian (Hephaestio and Lydus) bent cite them in detail. That influence is acknowledged not only in the fragments mentioned above, but also at various places in the important *Epitome Parisina*.[37]

NOTES

1. G. Lefebvre, *Le tombeau de Petosiris*, 3 vols. (Cairo, 1923–1924).
2. E. Riess, "Nechepsonis et Petosiridis fragmenta magica," in *Philologus*, Supplementband **6** (1892), 327–394, to which many more fragments could be added.
3. C. Bezold and F. Boll, *Reflexe astrologischer Keilinschriften bei griechischen Schriftstellern* (Heidelberg, 1911).
4. W. Kroll, "Aus der Geschichte der Astrologie," in *Neue Jahrbücher für das Klassische Altertum, Geschichte und Deutsche Literatur*, **7** (1901), 559–577, esp. 573–577.
5. Frs. 6–12 in Riess, some of which are very dubious.
6. Hephaestio, I, 21, who attributes the material to the ancient Egyptians; another version, using Roman months rather than zodiacal signs, was published by F. Boll, in *Catalogus Codicum Astrologorum Graecorum*, VII (Brussels, 1908), 129–151.
7. R. A. Parker, *A Vienna Demotic Papyrus on Eclipse and lunar-omina* (Providence, 1959).
8. Lydus, *De ostentis*, 9.
9. Hephaestio, I, 22.
10. Hephaestio, I, 23, who attributes it to the ancient, wise Egyptians; cf. *Catalogus Codicum Astrologorum Graecorum*, V, pt. 1 (Brussels, 1904), 204.
11. G. R. Hughes, "A Demotic Astrological Text," in *Journal of Near Eastern Studies*, **10** (1951), 256–264.
12. *Catalogus Codicum Astrologorum Graecorum*, VII, 181–187.
13. *Geoponica*, I, 8 and I, 10 = fr. 0,40; and fr. 0,41 in J. Bidez and F. Cumont, *Les mages hellénisés*, II (Paris, 1938), 178–183.
14. John Lydus, *De ostentis*, 11–15, from Campestrius.
15. Hephaestio, I, 24.
16. Servius, *In Aeneidem*, X, 272, who follows Avienus, but also mentions Campestris (sic!) and Petosiris.
17. Fr. 14; cf. Achinapolus in Vitruvius, *De architectura*, IX, 6,2; Pseudo-Zoroaster, fr. 0,14 Bidez-Cumont, II, 161–162; and A. Sachs, in *Journal of Cuneiform Studies*, **6** (1952), 58–60.
18. Frs. 16 and 17 and also fr. 5 (Valens, III, 16) and Valens, III, 3, and VIII, 6; cf. Berosus, frs. 32 and 33 in P. Schnabel, *Berossos und die babylonisch-hellenistische Literatur* (Leipzig–Berlin, 1923), 264. Also see Hephaestio, II, 18, 72 (this quotation does not include the important fragment of the *Salmeschoeniaca*, II, 18, 74–75), and Pliny's report of their computation of the distances of the planetary spheres (fr. 2). This last may belong to 2.
19. Fr. 1; Valens, VI, preface.
20. Valens, II, 3; VIII, 5; IX, 1.
21. *Ibid.*, VII, 5; cf. III, 10.
22. *Ibid.*, II, 3; III, 14; IX, preface; IX, 1.
23. *Ibid.*, III, 10 = fr. 18, which gives a computation based on a point computed similarly to a Lot and entirely different from the method employed in the passages we have assigned to 1.
24. This is given in Nechepso's thirteenth book and in Petosiris, *Definitions*; Valens, II, 3; III, 14 = fr. 19; IX, 1.
25. Valens, V, 6 = fr. 20 and VII, 5 = fr. 21; cf. III, 14; VI, 1.
26. *Ibid.*, III, 11 = fr. 23.
27. *Ibid.*, II, 28.
28. *Ibid.*, II, 36; cf. fr. 27 from Firmicus.
29. *Ibid.*, II, 39.
30. *Ibid.*, II, 41 = fr. 24.
31. Fr. 25, where they are correctly stated to be drawing on an Hermetic source; cf. test. 6.
32. Fr. 13, but cf. fr. 28.
33. *Catalogus Codicum Astrologorum Graecorum*, I (Brussels, 1898), 138. (I doubt the authenticity of the brief statement about quartile and trine aspect published in *Catalogus Codicum Astrologorum Graecorum*, VI [Brussels, 1903], 62.)
34. Frs. 28–32 and 35–36; the latter two, drawn from the work of Thessalus, should now be consulted in the edition of H.-V. Friedrich (Meisenheim am Glan, 1968); cf. also *Catalogus Codicum Astrologorum Graecorum*, I, 126.
35. Frs. 37–42; see also *Catalogus Codicum Astrologorum Graecorum*, I, 128; IV (Brussels, 1903), 120–121; XI, pt. 2 (Brussels, 1934), 152–154, 163–164; Pseudo-Bede in *Patrologia Latina*, XC, cols. 963–966; and cf. Psellus in a letter published in *Catalogus Codicum Astrologorum Graecorum*, VIII, pt. 1 (Brussels, 1929), 131.
36. *Catalogus Codicum Astrologorum Graecorum*, VII, 161–162.
37. *Ibid.*, VIII, pt. 3 (Brussels, 1912), 91–119.

BIBLIOGRAPHY

Aside from Riess's collection of fragments, the main study of Pseudo-Petosiris is C. Darmstadt, *De Nechepsonis-Petosiridis Isagoge quaestiones selectae* (Leipzig, 1916); unfortunately, he attributes to Nechepso-Petosiris far more than the evidence of the fragments warrants. Rather unsatisfactory articles are W. Kroll in Pauly-Wissowa's *Real-Encyclopädie der classischen Altertumswissenschaft*, **16** (1935), cols. 2160–2167; **19** (1938), col. 1165; and W. Gundel and H. G. Gundel, *Astrologumena* (Wiesbaden, 1966), 27–36.

DAVID PINGREE

PETRIE, (WILLIAM MATTHEW) FLINDERS (*b.* Charlton, Kent, England, 3 June 1853; *d.* Jerusalem, Palestine [now Israel], 28 July 1942), *Egyptology, archaeology.*

Petrie's delicate health in childhood prevented him from going to school or university. He was taught at home by his parents and developed a keen interest in antiquities and surveying. His father encouraged him in particular to make surveys of British earthworks, which led to his interest in measurement. Petrie's first book, *Inductive Metrology*, appeared in 1877, and three years later he published a field survey of Stonehenge.

In 1881 Petrie's father, inspired by the notions of Charles Piazzi Smyth regarding the pyramids, planned a trip to Egypt with his son; but in the end, Petrie went alone to survey them. He published *The Pyramids and Temples of Gizeh* in 1883, following two years' work. In this book Petrie disproved and abandoned Smyth's esoteric theories. In 1883 the Egypt Exploration Fund (later Society) was founded, and Petrie was appointed its first field director. He wrote to Miss Edwards, the secretary of the Fund, in 1883 that "The prospect of excavating in Egypt is a most fascinating one to me, and I hope that the results may justify my undertaking such a work." This hope was brilliantly realized. Petrie began work at Tanis in 1884 but subsequently quarreled with the Fund. In 1894 he founded the Egyptian Research Account, renamed the British

School of Archaeology in Egypt in 1905. He directed this until 1926, when, disillusioned by Egypt, he transferred his attention to Palestine, where he worked until his death.

For a period of ten years (1896–1906) Petrie worked again with the Egypt Exploration Society, but on the whole his career was devoted to his own excavations and publications. His annual excavations were followed by immediate publications and exhibitions in London. In 1892 he was elected professor of Egyptology at the University of London, a post he held until 1933. He was also elected a fellow of both the Royal Society (1902) and the British Academy (1912) and was knighted in 1923. Petrie was essentially an individualist and a free-lance worker; he was an authoritarian who brooked no opposition or criticism, and, as Woolley has stated, he had "a dogmatic assurance of his own rightness." During his lifetime, he trained at least two generations of Egyptologists and Near Eastern archaeologists.

Among the most remarkable of his finds were the early royal tombs at Abydos; the Tell el-Amarna correspondence and the numerous relics at Tell el-Amarna itself; the discoveries of Mycenaean and Pre-Mycenaean pottery at Ghurob and Kahun; and the discovery of the predynastic cultures of Egypt, particularly those of Nakada and Ballas (which he examined in 1894–1895) and at Diospolis Parva (in 1898–1899). Nakada was revealed to be a prehistoric cemetery of more than 2,000 graves, and gave its name to the Nakada period. The British Museum declined Petrie's offer of the type series from this cemetery on the ground that they had been advised it was "unhistoric rather than prehistoric." In his memoir *Diospolis Parva* (1901) Petrie systematically arranged the predynastic Egyptian material for the first time and invented the technique of sequence-dating, which he further described in *Methods and Aims in Archaeology* (1904).

When he began working in Egypt, Petrie was sharply critical of the methods of his predecessors, and wrote that "The true line lies as much in the careful noting and comparison of small details as in more wholesale and off-hand clearance." The advances and developments in techniques and methods that he made, as well as his actual discoveries of dynastic and predynastic Egypt, made the last quarter of the nineteenth century the "heroic age" of Egyptian archaeology. In 1892 he published *Ten Years' Diggings*, a remarkable record of his work. He continued to dig in Egypt for more than thirty years, and then in Palestine for nearly twenty years. His fieldwork, diggings, and devotion to archaeology were later chronicled in his autobiography, *Seventy Years in Archaeology* (London, 1931).

In 1889, at Ghurob, Petrie found Mycenaean pottery among the remains of the late eighteenth dynasty; he also found what he called Proto-Greek or Aegean pottery. The following year, at Kahun, he found painted Aegean or Proto-Greek pottery mixed with that of the twelfth dynasty. No pottery of this Proto-Greek style had hitherto been found in the Aegean. Petrie, however, was not content to regard the Kahun pottery as "foreign" ware; he unhesitatingly cataloged it as Aegean, a splendid example of skilled guesswork. In 1891 he visited Mycenae to verify the dating of the Ghurob and Kahun sites. He recognized examples of Egyptian influence and actual imports of Egyptian objects in Mycenae that dated to the eighteenth dynasty period. He thus established two synchronisms; one between the Aegean or Proto-Greek ware and the twelfth dynasty of Egypt, and the second between Mycenae and the eighteenth dynasty. On this basis Petrie declared that an Aegean civilization had begun about 2500 B.C. and that the dates of the late Mycenaean civilization were between 1500 and 1000 B.C. He dated the Mycenaean "treasuries" between 1400 and 1200 B.C., the Vaphio cups at about 1200 B.C., and the shaft graves at 1150 B.C. It was a remarkably fine use of cross-dating and one of the first demonstrations of this method of extending historical chronology to primitive regions.

Ernest Gardner, then director of the British School of Archaeology in Athens, writing of Petrie's chronological structuring, said that he had "done more in a week than the Germans had done in ten years to clear up the matter from an Egyptian basis." Petrie himself, writing in 1931 and looking back to his early conclusions on Greek chronology, said "there seems little to alter in the outline reached then, though forty years have since passed."

Petrie's contributions to the development of archaeology included not only his substantive work in Egypt and Palestine, but also his revolutionary techniques, which are of paramount importance to the study of antiquity.

BIBLIOGRAPHY

Petrie's major works are cited above. See also Margaret Murray, *My First Hundred Years* (London, 1966); Sidney Smith, obituary notice in *Proceedings of the British Academy*, **28** (1942), 307–324; Leonard Woolley, in *Dictionary of National Biography 1941–1950* (London, 1959), 666–667; J. D. Wortham, *The Genesis of British Egyptology 1549–1906* (Norman, Okla., 1971), 115–126; and W. R. Dawson and E. P. Uphill, *Who Was Who in Egyptology* (London, 1972), 228–230, which has a complete bibliography.

GLYN DANIEL

PETROV, NIKOLAY PAVLOVICH (*b.* Trubchevsk, Orlovskaya Oblast, Russia, 25 May 1836; *d.* Tuapse, U.S.S.R., 15 January 1920), *mechanics, engineering.*

The son of a military man, Petrov graduated in 1855 from the Konstantinovsky Military School in St. Petersburg with the rank of ensign. He immediately enrolled at the Nikolaevskaya Engineering Academy, where Vyshnegradsky guided his studies in applied mechanics and where he was especially influenced by Ostrogradsky. After graduating in 1858, Petrov was retained in the mathematics department, where he worked under Ostrogradsky. On the latter's death in 1862 Petrov began teaching a course in higher mathematics at the Academy, while from 1866 he taught applied mechanics at the St. Petersburg Technological Institute. In 1867 he became adjunct professor of applied mechanics at the Engineering Academy.

In 1876 Petrov was invited to the U.S. Centennial Exposition in Philadelphia. On the basis of material collected during this trip, he published a work in 1882 on mechanical equipment for ports and cargo deposits at railroad stations; it presented methods for designing elevators and mechanical devices used in shipping grain and coal. In a paper published in 1878 on continuous braking systems of trains, he was the first to arrive at equations for the motion of wheels in the presence and absence of braking, as well as an equation for the motion of the center of gravity of a train during braking. As a result of his theoretical investigations, he found the true maximum speed for any possible braking system.

In 1888 Petrov was elected an honorary member of the Moscow Polytechnical Society and was awarded the gold medal of the Russian Technical Society for inventing an instrument to determine the internal and external friction of liquids. As chairman of the Department of State Railroads (1888–1892) he was active in the construction of the Trans-Siberian Railroad. In 1892 he became chairman of the Engineering Council of the Ministry of Means of Communication, and from 1893 to 1900 he was deputy minister of means of communication. In 1894 Petrov became an honorary member of the St. Petersburg Academy of Sciences, and from 1896 to 1905 he was chairman of the Russian Technical Society.

Petrov's most important work was in the hydrodynamic theory of lubricants. His investigations were characterized by a masterful command of mathematical method and an outstanding gift for experiment. Petrov's results were based on broad experimental study of friction in liquids and machines, the most important part of which he conducted himself. Petrov accurately formulated the physical laws that might provide a basis for calculating elementary frictional forces. He demonstrated that the frictional force developed within a viscous liquid is proportional to the velocity of relative motion and to the surface area of contact; it does not depend on pressure, and the coefficient of proportionality depends only on the properties of the liquid.

Petrov also confirmed experimentally Newton's formula for the force of resistance of a viscous liquid with one layer in motion relative to another layer, $F = \mu(\partial v/\partial n)$, where v is the velocity, n is the distance between layers along the normal to the surface of constant velocity, and μ is the coefficient of viscosity. He determined that the coefficient of internal friction of a liquid varies significantly with temperature; this relationship was experimentally determined for each type of lubricant.

Petrov also studied the effects of friction in a bearing in which the lubricating layer fills the intermediate space between two cylinders having a common geometrical axis. During rotation friction causes the shaft to carry along with it the nearest adjacent layer of lubricant. This layer moves more slowly than the shaft, since it is impeded by friction with the next adjacent layer of lubricant. The last layer, carried along by friction with the penultimate layer, is in turn retarded by friction with the surface of the bearing. Using this model, Petrov examined bearings that operate with only a thin layer of lubricant. Computing the equations of motion of a viscous liquid, integrating them, and using Newton's formula presented above, he discovered the law of friction that bears his name.

Petrov's works have formed the basis of the hydrodynamic theory of friction in the presence of lubrication and provided an impetus for the further development of theoretical and experimental research in this field.

BIBLIOGRAPHY

I. ORIGINAL WORKS. The basic ideas of Petrov's hydrodynamic theory of lubricants were stated in the following works: "Trenie v mashinakh i vlianie na nego smazyvayushchey zhidkosti" ("Friction in Machines and the Influence of a Lubricating Liquid on It"), in *Inzhenernyi zhurnal*, **24** (1883), no. 1, 71–140; no. 2, 227–279; no. 3, 377–436; no. 4, 535–641; also published separately (St. Petersburg, 1883); *Opisanie i rezultaty opytov nad treniem zhidkostey i mashin* ("Description and Results of Experiments on the Friction of Liquids and Machines"; St. Petersburg, 1886); "Prakticheskie rezultaty opytov" ("Practical Results of Experiments"), in *Inzhenernyi zhurnal*, **26** (1887), also published separately; and "Frottement dans les machines," in *Zapiski Imperatorskoi akademii nauk*, **10**, no. 4 (1900), 1–84.

His other writings include "Ochertanie zubtsov kruglykh tsilindricheskikh koles dugami kruga" ("Configuration of the Teeth of Round Cylindrical Wheels With Circular Arcs"), in *Inzhenernyi zhurnal*, **12** (1871), which was his first scientific paper; *O nepreryvnykh tormoznykh sistemakh* ("On Continuous Braking Systems"; St. Petersburg, 1878); *Peregruzka i khranenie khlebnogo zerna. Peregruzka kamennogo ugla* ("Shipment and Storage of Cereal Grain. Shipment of Coal"; St. Petersburg, 1882); *Résultats les plus marquants de l'étude théorique et expérimentale sur le frottement médiat* (St. Petersburg, 1889); "Sur le frottement des liquides," in *Izvestiya Imperatorskoi akademii nauk*, **5** (1896), 365–373; *Un moyen de déterminer les déformations du rail soutenu par des supports mobiles sous la pression d'une roue usée en mouvement* (St. Petersburg, 1910); and *Davlenie koles na relsy. Prochnost relsov i ustoychivost puti* ("The Pressure of Wheels on Rails. Strength of the Rails and Stability of the Track"; St. Petersburg, 1915), a summary of his investigations.

Petrov's writings are also included in L. S. Leybenzon, ed., *Gidrodinamicheskaya teoria smazki* ("The Hydrodynamic Theory of Lubricants"; Moscow–Leningrad, 1934); and L. S. Leybenzon, ed., *Gidrodinamicheskaya teoria smazki*, in the series Klassiki Nauki (Moscow, 1948), an anthology.

II. SECONDARY LITERATURE. On Petrov and his work, see A. S. Akhmatov, "Nikolay Pavlovich Petrov," in *Lyudi russkoy nauki. Tekhnika* ("Men of Russian Science"; Moscow, 1965), 240–246; A. T. Grigorian, *Ocherki istorii mekhaniki v Rossii* ("Sketches of the History of Mechanics in Russia"; Moscow, 1961), 213–217; V. M. Kostomarov and A. G. Burgvits, *Osnovopolozhnik teorii gidrodinamicheskogo trenia v mashinakh N. P. Petrov* ("Petrov, the Founder of the Theory of Hydrodynamic Friction in Machines"; Moscow, 1952); and L. S. Leybenzon and N. I. Glagolev, "Vydayushchysya ucheny i inzhener N. P. Petrov" ("The Outstanding Scientist and Engineer N. P. Petrov"), in *Izvestiya Akademii nauk SSSR*, no. 7 (1946), 929–933.

A. T. GRIGORIAN

PETROV, VASILY VLADIMIROVICH (*b*. Oboyan, Russia, 19 July 1761; *d*. St. Petersburg, Russia, 15 August 1834), *physics, chemistry.*

The son of a parish priest, Petrov graduated from the Kharkov Collegium in 1785 and studied at the Teacher's Gymnasium in St. Petersburg. He taught physics, mathematics, Latin, and Russian at the mining school of Barnaul (Altay) from 1788 to 1791, then taught in St. Petersburg at the Izmaylov Cadets School (1791–1797) and the Main Medical School. In 1795 Petrov became extraordinary professor and, in 1800, professor at the Medical-Surgical Academy. There he created a first-class *cabinet de physique* and

at the beginning of the nineteenth century did basic research in physical chemistry, electrostatics, and galvanism.

From 1802 Petrov was corresponding member, from 1809 extraordinary, and from 1815 ordinary academician of the St. Petersburg Academy of Sciences. He was elected honorary member of the Erlangen Physics-Medical Society (1810) and the University of Vilna (1829).

Petrov was an active follower of Lavoisier not only in the promotion and application of the oxygen theory of combustion but also in the treatment of heat and light as chemical elements, in which he included electrical and galvanic fluids.

In *Sobranie fiziko-khimicheskikh novykh opytov i nablyudeny* ("Collection of New Physical-Chemical Experiments and Observations," 1801) and in a series of articles later published in *Umozritelnye issledovania Sankt-Peterburgskoy Akademii nauk* ("Speculative Research of the St. Petersburg Academy of Sciences") Petrov described his experiments on the possibility of burning organic and inorganic substances in a vacuum and in some gases that do not sustain combustion (carbon dioxide gas, hydrogen chloride, sulfur dioxide). He showed that even in the absence of air, substances containing oxygen can burn, whereas the transformation of metals into oxides is impossible.

Petrov also examined various forms of phosphorescence from the viewpoint of the oxygen theory of combustion, showing that luminescence of rotten wood can occur only in the presence of oxygen and is a "very slow form of combustion." By demonstrating that the phosphorescence of minerals does not depend on the presence of oxygen, he distinguished photoluminescence from chemiluminescence. He also investigated the relationship of the luminescence of crystal phosphorus to temperature.

In *Izvestie o galvani-voltovskikh opytakh* ("News of Galvanic-Voltaic Experiments," 1803) Petrov described experiments carried out in the spring of 1802 with a battery of 2,100 copper-zinc elements. He also related its structure and principles of operation—the use of sealing wax and wax to insulate the wires, chemical indicators for observing the oxidation-reduction processes at the electrodes, and methods for eliminating oxidization on the surfaces of the metal disks. Of great importance is the description of the stable arc discharge and the indication of its possible use in artificial lighting, melting metals, obtaining pure metallic oxides, and reduction of metals from oxides mixed with powdered carbon and oils.

Petrov observed discharges at low pressures and in particular described a decomposing discharge. He investigated the relation of electrolysis of various substances to temperature and electromotive force, and used parallel tubes filled with electrolytes to observe the relation of the current to the cross section of the conductor.

In *Novye elektricheskie opyty* ("New Electrical Experiments," 1804) Petrov described experiments that showed the possibility of electrifying metals by friction. He used the bell glass of an air pump for studying electrostatic discharges in a vacuum, in hydrogen, in nitrogen, and in carbon dioxide.

After his election to the Academy of Sciences, Petrov made meteorological observations in St. Petersburg and also processed the observations sent from other Russian cities. He conducted a special study of the relation of velocity of vaporization of ice and snow to atmospheric pressure, temperature, and wind force.

The decline in Petrov's scientific activity during the last twenty-five years of his life was caused by financial difficulties related to the War of 1812 and later by his impaired health.

BIBLIOGRAPHY

Petrov's "Izvestie o galvani-voltovskikh opytakh" ("News of Galvanic-Voltaic Experiments") was reprinted in *Sbornik k stoletiyu so dnya smerti pervogo russkogo electrotekhnika akademika Vasilia Vladimirovicha Petrova* ("Collection on the Centenary of the Death of the First Russian Electrotechnician Academician Vasily Vladimirovich Petrov"; Moscow–Leningrad, 1936), i–viii, 1–194.

There is an annotated bibliography of his works in S. I. Vavilov, ed., *K istorii fiziki i khimii v Rossii v nachale XIX v.* ("Toward a History of Physics and Chemistry in Russia at the Beginning of the Nineteenth Century"; Moscow–Leningrad, 1940), 193–210. Other works on Petrov's life and work are A. A. Eliseev, *Vasily Vladimirovich Petrov* (Moscow–Leningrad, 1949), with bibliography on pp. 172–179; O. A. Lezhneva, "Die Entwicklung der Physik in Russland in der ersten Hälfte des 19. Jahrhunderts," in *Beiträge zur Geschichte der Naturwissenschaften* (1960), 203–225; and Y. A. Shneyberg, "O bataree V. V. Petrova i ego opytakh s elektricheskoy dugoy i razryadom v vakuume" ("On Petrov's Battery and His Experiments With the Electric Arc and Discharge in a Vacuum"), in *Elektrichestvo*, no. 11 (1953), 72–75.

OLGA A. LEZHNEVA

PETROVSKY, IVAN GEORGIEVICH (*b.* Sevsk, Orlov guberniya, Russia, 18 January 1901; *d.* Moscow, U.S.S.R., 15 January 1973), *mathematics.*

Petrovsky's major works dealt with the theory of partial differential equations, the topology of algebraic curves and surfaces, and the theory of probability. After graduating from the technical high school in Sevsk in 1917, he worked in various Soviet institutions until 1922, when he entered Moscow University. He graduated from the division of physics and mathematics in 1927 and remained at Moscow until 1930 as a graduate student of D. F. Egorov.

From 1929 to 1933 Petrovsky was assistant professor and *dozent* at Moscow. In 1933 he became professor and, in 1935, doctor of physical-mathematical sciences. From 1951 he was head of the department of differential equations. During World War II he was dean of the faculty of mechanics and mathematics; and from 1951 until his death he was rector of the university.

Petrovsky combined his work at the university with activity at various scientific and teaching institutions. From 1943 he worked at the V. A. Steklov Institute of Mathematics at the Academy of Sciences, of which he was vice-director from 1947 to 1949. For many years he was editor-in-chief of *Matematicheskii sbornik*.

In 1943 Petrovsky was elected corresponding member and, in 1946, full member of the Soviet Academy of Sciences. From 1949 to 1951 he was academician-secretary of the division of physical and mathematical sciences of the Academy, and from 1953 until his death he was a member of the Presidium of the Academy. He was twice awarded the State Prize of the U.S.S.R., and he received the title of Hero of Socialist Labor. He was also a member of the Soviet Committee for the Defense of Peace and vice-president of the Institute of Soviet-American Relations.

Petrovsky's first research dealt with the investigation of the Dirichlet problem for Laplace's equation (1928) and the theory of functions of a real variable (1929). In the early 1930's he began research on the topology of algebraic curves and surfaces in which he achieved fundamental results and methods. In 1933 he proved Hilbert's hypothesis that a curve of the sixth order cannot consist of eleven ovals lying outside each other. The method that Petrovsky devised for this proof was useful in solving the more general problem of embedding components of algebraic curves of any order in a projective plane. In 1949 he generalized certain of his results to include algebraic surfaces in n-dimensional space.

The results of Petrovsky's work (1934) on the solvability of the first boundary-value problem for the heat equation were widely applied in the theory of probability, especially in research connected with the Khinchin-Kolmogorov law of the iterated logarithm. Petrovsky's article on the theory of random processes (1934) considerably influenced an investigation of limit laws for the sum of a large number of random variables with the aid of the transition to random processes with continuous time. The work also contains the so-called method of upper and lower sums, which became the basic analytical method of research in the field.

A second work, also published in 1934, examined the behavior, near the origin of the coordinates of integral curves, of a system of equations of the form

$$\frac{dx_i}{dt} = \sum_{k=1}^{n} \alpha_{ik} x_k + \phi_i(x_1, \cdots, x_n).$$

This work was, essentially, the first full investigation of a neighborhood of a singular point in the three-dimensional case.

In 1937–1938 Petrovsky distinguished and studied classes of systems of partial differential equations, which he first identified as either elliptical, hyperbolic, or parabolic. In 1937 he published his proof that the Cauchy problem for nonlinear systems of differential equations, which Petrovsky called hyperbolic, is well-posed. In a work on the Cauchy problem for systems of linear partial differential equations in nonanalytic functions (1938) Petrovsky studied systems for which the Cauchy problem is uniformly well-posed relative to the variation of the surface, for which the original data are given. Petrovsky introduced the concept of parabolic systems and investigated the problem of the analyticity of the solution of such systems in space dimensions. In 1937 he introduced his famous notion of elliptical systems and showed that when the functions are analytic, all sufficiently smooth solutions will be analytic, thereby giving a more complete solution of Hilbert's nineteenth problem. Petrovsky's results were the starting point for numerous investigations, including those of J. Leray and L. Gårding; and they determined the basic direction of the development of the theory of systems of partial differential equations.

In widely known works on the qualitative theory theory of hyperbolic equations (1943–1945) Petrovsky introduced the concept of lacunae and obtained necessary and sufficient conditions for the existence of stable lacunae for uniform hyperbolic equations with constant coefficients. He also solved completely the question of lacunae for linear hyperbolic systems with variable coefficients in the case of two independent variables.

In 1945 Petrovsky investigated the extent of the discontinuitites of the derivatives of the displacements on the surface of a nonuniform elastic body that is free from the influence of external forces; and in 1954 he examined the character of lines and surfaces of a discontinuity of solutions of the wave equations.

Many well-known specialists in the theory of differential equations were students of Petrovsky, whose seminar (the Petrovsky seminar) is a leading center for the study of the theory of partial differential equations. His course texts are widely known.

BIBLIOGRAPHY

I. ORIGINAL WORKS. Petrovsky's major works are "Über das Irrfahrtproblem," in *Mathematische Annalen*, **109** (1934), 425–444; "Ueber das Verhalten der Integralcurven eines Systemes gewöhnlicher Differentialgleichungen in der Nahe lines singularen Punktes," in *Matematicheskii sbornik*, **41** (1934), 107–156; "Zur ersten Randwertaufgabe der Warmeleitungsgleichung," in *Compositia Mathematica*, **1** (1935), 383–419; "Über das Cauchysche Problem für Systeme von partiellen Differentialgleichungen," in *Matematicheskii sbornik*, **2** (1937), 815–870; "On the Topology of Real Plane Algebraic Curves," in *Annals of Mathematics*, **39**, no. 1 (1938), 197–209; "Sur l'analyticité des solutions des systèmes d'équations différentielles," in *Matematicheskii sbornik*, **5** (1939), 3–70; *Lektsii po teorii obyknovennykh differentsialnykh uravneny* ("Lectures on the Theory of Ordinary Differential Equations"; Moscow–Leningrad, 1939); "On the Diffusion of Waves and the Lacunas for Hyperbolic Equations," in *Matematicheskii sbornik*, **17** (1945), 289–370; *Lektsii po teorii integralnykh uravneny* (Moscow–Leningrad, 1948), trans. into German as *Vorlesungen über die Theorie der Integralgleichungen* (Würzburg, 1953); and *Lektsii ob uravneniakh s chastnymi proizvodnymi* (Moscow–Leningrad, 1948), trans. into English as *Lectures in Partial Differential Equations* (New York, 1954) and into German as *Vorlesungen über partielle Differentialgleichungen* (Leipzig, 1955).

II. SECONDARY LITERATURE. On Petrovsky's work and its influence, see P. S. Aleksandrov *et al.*, "Ivan Georgievich Petrovsky," in *Uspekhi matematicheskikh nauk*, **26**, no. 2 (1971), 3–22, with bibliography, pp. 22–24; *Matematika v SSSR za 40 let* ("Mathematics in the U.S.S.R. for the Last Forty Years"), II (Moscow, 1959), 538–540, for a bibliography of 51 of his publications; and *Matematika v SSSR za 50 let* ("Mathematics in the U. S. S. R. for the Last Fifty Years"), II, pt. 2 (Moscow, 1970), 1035.

S. DEMIDOV

PETRUS. See also **Peter.**

PETRUS BONUS, also known as **Bonus Lombardus** or **Buono Lombardo of Ferrara** (*fl. ca.* 1323–1330), *alchemy.*

Petrus Bonus is known through the extant texts of his alchemical work. He has been differentiated from the Petrus Bonus who was doctor of laws in the

University of Ferrara (1396–1402), and from Petrus Bonus Advogarius, who taught astronomy or astrology at Ferrara and issued astrological predictions in the late fifteenth century.[1] According to the explicit of his alchemical treatise, Master Petrus Bonus, *phisicus*, or doctor of medicine, in 1323 discussed a *quaestio* on alchemy in Traù, Dalmatia.[2] In 1330 (1338, 1339, or 1350), in Pola, Istria, he composed *The Precious New Pearl*,[3] a scholastic exposition of the arguments, with the names of appropriate authorities, for and against the validity of the alchemical art.

Since Petrus Bonus approached the problem of the transmutation of baser metals into gold "with a pen in his hand rather than an alembic and with volumes of the past literature . . . rather than metals and chemicals,"[4] his accomplishment is significant not for any new chemical or scientific data but, rather, for the light that it sheds on current practices, theories, and authorities in alchemy and in other areas of natural science in the early fourteenth century. Like his earlier contemporaries, principally Arnald of Villanova, Ramón Lull, Roger Bacon, and Albertus Magnus, to whom alchemical writings of about the same era are attributed, but whose names Petrus Bonus did not mention,[5] he believed that the adept alchemist could produce gold from baser metals with the use of the philosophers' stone. He held that the substance and material cause of this stone was quicksilver alone. In this view Petrus Bonus agreed with Arnald of Villanova, whom he probably knew through the *Lilium*, one of the few works of Latin origin that he cited.[6]

He rejected the alternative view advanced in other writings that both quicksilver and sulfur are essential, that is, that quicksilver is the matter of, and sulfur is the active agent that shapes and forms, the philosophers' stone. According to Petrus Bonus, gold, the most perfect of metals, had been purified of sulfur. It had thus attained in nature the stage of perfection toward which the baser metals are striving.[7] Therefore, according to Petrus Bonus, the process of transmutation consists principally in the separation from the baser metals of the sulfur that blackens, corrodes, or discolors the metals. This separation goes on at a slow and protracted rate in nature in the bowels of the earth. The skilled operator, who is conversant with the literature of the past and adept in the use of the philosophers' stone, can greatly hasten the separation in the laboratory. The form of gold can be introduced in the twinkling of an eye, but only with divine assistance.[8]

Although Petrus Bonus insisted upon an acquaintance with the past literature of alchemy—chiefly that by authors of Greek and Arabic or Muslim origin,

such as Aristotle, Hermes, Morienus, Jabir ibn Hayyān (Geber), Rasis (probably al-Razī), Ibn Rushd, Ibn Sīnā, and the authors of the *Turba philosophorum* —and also upon the need to check speculative thought by practice and experience,[9] he nonetheless was finally obliged to admit that he had not been able to penetrate into the secret of the philosophers' stone and that he had to fall back upon the mystery of the divine will. Petrus Bonus accepted "alchemy as possessing a divine as well as natural character." He held that "sufficient natural reasons for the philosophers' stone" could not be given. One must believe it, as one believes in "the miracles of Christianity." To him the "art is a divine secret transcending both natural reason and experience."[10] Thus *The Precious New Pearl* lucidly portrays the direction that alchemists were to take in the fourteenth century and thereafter.

Petrus Bonus shed light not only on the practices and perplexities of the alchemists but also on other items of natural interest in his time. In seeking analogies to the transmutation of metals, he set forth the belief of his contemporaries in the spontaneous generation of frogs, ants, and flies from dust and clouds or refuse. He insisted that animals so generated were the same as those generated in the usual fashion.[11] Hence he affirmed that gold, which would stand up to various tests, was the same as gold generated in nature. Further, he revealed that it was current knowledge that in Aristotle's time there was opposition to the geocentric theory, with alternative views that, like the planets, the earth moved in circular motion.[12] He mentioned the discovery of gold in the silver mines of Serbia and noted the existence of silver mines in Germany and alum mines in the vicinity of Constantinople.[13]

Although *The Precious New Pearl* is an extremely detailed and even repetitious work, it is nonetheless very informative. This accounts for the interest in it of its first editor, Janus Lacinius, and the frequency of its publication in the sixteenth century and thereafter.

NOTES

1. Lynn Thorndike, *History of Magic and Experimental Science*, III (New York, 1934), 147 ff.
2. *Ibid.* Thorndike has quoted the citation by Tiraboschi, *Storia della letteratura italiana*, V (Milan, 1823), 332, of the Este MS, "Quaestio . . . per Magistrum Bonum Ferrariensem physicum sub MCCCXXIII anno . . . tunc temporis salariatum in civitate Traguriae de provincia Dalmatiae." Other MSS that contain similar citations regarding the *quaestio* in 1323 are British Museum, Harley 672, XV cent., f. 169; Orléans 289 (243), XV cent., f. 187v; and 290 (244), XVI cent., f. 96.
3. MS, British Museum, Harley 672, XV cent., f. 169, "Explicit Preciosa novella margarita edita a magistro Bono

Lombardo de Ferraria phisico introducens ad artem alkimie. Composita 1330 in civitate Polle in provincia Istrie"; similarly MSS Orléans 289 (243), XV cent., f. 187v, with the date 1338; Orléans 290 (244), XVI cent., ff. 1–96, with the date 1350. Of the printed eds., that of Zetzner, *Theatrum chemicum*, V (1660), has the dates 1330 and 1339, as does Manget, *Bibliotheca chemica curiosa*, II (1702), 1–80.

4. Thorndike, III, 153.
5. Thorndike, III, 150–151; for these authors see Thorndike, II and III, *passim*.
6. *Ibid.*, III, 160; Zetzner, V, 546, 559, 568. For Arnald of Villanova and the *Lilium*, see Thorndike, III, 62 ff.
7. Thorndike, III, 160; Zetzner, V, 508–509, 546, 567–568, 580.
8. Thorndike, III, 158 ff.; Zetzner, V, 550 ff., 632 ff.
9. Zetzner, V, 568 ff.; for the numerous authors cited, see esp. Julius Ruska, "L'alchimie à l'époque de Dante," in *Annales Guébhard-Séverine*, **10** (1934), 410–417, esp. pp. 415–416, where some twenty authors are counted without those of the *Turba philosophorum*.
10. Thorndike, III, 159; Zetzner, V, 580–588, caps. 6–8.
11. Thorndike, III, 162; Zetzner, V, 647.
12. Thorndike, III, 161–162; Zetzner, V, 642.
13. Thorndike, III, pp. 160–161; Zetzner V, 681, 682, also 549.

BIBLIOGRAPHY

I. ORIGINAL WORKS. For MS texts, see British Museum, Harley 672, XV cent., ff. 1–169 (D. W. Singer, *Catalogue of Latin and Vernacular Alchemical Manuscripts in Great Britain and Ireland Dating From Before the XVI Century*, I [Brussels, 1928], no. 276); Orléans 289 (243), XV cent., ff. 1–187v (J. Corbett, *Catalogue des manuscrits alchimiques latins: II. Manuscrits des bibliothèques publiques des départements français* [Brussels, 1951], no. 39); Orléans 290 (244), XVI cent., ff. 1–96 (Corbett, II, no. 40); Bodleian, Ashmole 1426, XV cent., ff. 103–115, a gloss or commentary on *The Precious New Pearl* (Singer, I, no. 277); and Paris, Bibliothèque nationale 14006, XV cent., ff. 44r–45v, an abridgment of *The Precious New Pearl* (J. Corbett, *Catalogue des manuscrits alchimiques latins: I. Manuscrits des bibliothèques publiques de Paris* [Brussels, 1939], no 53).

The earliest printed ed. of *The Precious New Pearl* is Janus Lacinius, ed., *Pretiosa margarita, novella de thesauro, ac pretiosissimo philosophorum lapide (Petro Bono Ferrariensi autore) Artis huius diuinae typus, et methodus: collectanea ex Arnaldo, Rhaymundo, Rhasi, Alberto, et Michaele Scoto . . . apud Aldi filios* (Venice, 1546). For the above and other eds. of the 16th and early 17th centuries see Thorndike, III, 148, 151, notes 8 and 18.

The full text is in Eberhard Zetzner, *Theatrum chemicum praecipuos . . . tractatus de chemiae et lapidis philosophici antiquitate, veritate jure, praestantia et operationibus continens*, V (Strasbourg, 1660), 507–713; and J. J. Manget, *Bibliotheca chemica curiosa*, I (Geneva, 1702), 1–80. The Janus Lacinius ed. was translated into German by W. G. Stollen, *Pretiosa margarita, oder Neu-erfundene köstliche Perle, von dem unvergleichlichen Schatz und höchst-kostbahren Stein der Weisen . . .* (Leipzig, 1714); and into English, in abridged form, by A. E. Waite, *The New Pearl of Great Price: A Treatise Concerning the Treasure and Most Precious Stone of the Philosophers, or the Method and Procedure of This Divine Art* (London, 1894; 1963), 49–184.

II. SECONDARY LITERATURE. The major critical study on Petrus Bonus is Lynn Thorndike, *History of Magic and Experimental Science*, III (New York, 1934), Ch. 9. Briefer accounts are Robert Multhauf, *The Origins of Chemistry* (London, 1966), 191–193; Julius Ruska, "L'alchimie à l'époque du Dante," in *Annales Guébhard-Séverine*, **10** (1934), 410–417 (translated by A. Kuenzi); George Sarton, *Introduction to the History of Science*, III (Baltimore, 1927–1948), 750–752; and J. M. Stillman, "Petrus Bonus and Supposed Chemical Forgeries," in *Scientific Monthly*, **16** (1923), 318–325.

PEARL KIBRE

PETTENKOFER, MAX JOSEF VON (*b.* Lichtenheim [near Neuburg], Germany, 3 December 1818; *d.* Munich, Germany, 10 February 1901), *chemistry, hygiene, epidemiology.*

Although Pettenkofer initiated advances in many fields of science, his fame rests chiefly upon his pioneering accomplishments in experimental hygiene, a discipline that he founded. He was the fifth of eight children born in a solitary, converted custom house at a former border crossing in the Danubian marshes of lower Bavaria. His father, Johann Baptist Pettenkofer, the youngest of four sons of a customs official who had bought the property, farmed the peat bog unsuccessfully. His industrious mother, nineteen years her husband's junior, was of Oberpfalz peasant stock.

A parental uncle, the pharmacist Franz Xaver Pettenkofer, became court apothecary to Ludwig I of Bavaria in 1823. As his marriage was childless, he helped to educate four of his brother's children, who went successively to Munich to live in their uncle's official apartment in the royal residence; Max arrived there in 1827. While yearning for country-life simplicities, he gradually overcame the limits of his early parish schooling, made prizewinning progress through Latin school, and in 1837 matriculated with distinction from the humanistic Gymnasium. He entered the University of Munich with a predilection for philology, but accepted his uncle's insistence upon two years in philosophy and natural sciences, followed by apprenticeship at the court pharmacy.

On completing the prescribed university courses, of which he liked chemistry most, Pettenkofer worked diligently under tutelage, and in one year (instead of the usual three) was appointed assistant. But his uncle's strict regimen and demanding nature provoked the high-spirited youth to abandon his post and leave Munich. Under the pseudonym "Tenkof" he took minor parts at the Augsburg theater. Neither uncomplimentary reviews nor emissaries from the scandalized apothecary altered his course. He became captivated, however, by Helene Pettenkofer, the daughter of another uncle, Josef Pettenkofer, and she consented to marry Max, but only if he resumed steady ways. Accordingly, he left the stage, became engaged to Helene, and received a prodigal's welcome from his Munich uncle, who nevertheless forbade employment in the court pharmacy, advising that the medical profession was more suited to a former actor. In 1841 he returned to university studies and by June 1843 passed with honors the state qualifying examinations for both pharmacist and physician. His doctoral dissertation, "Ueber Mikania Guaco," concerned a plant of the *Eupatorium* genus, native to Mexico and Colombia, the sap of which reputedly had medicinal value in snakebite, rabies, and cholera. Self-experiments with a resin chemically extracted from the leaves induced vomiting, quickened pulse, and profuse sweating.

Pettenkofer was unwilling to practice either profession. While still an undergraduate, he had improved the sensitivity and specificity of Marsh's test for arsenic. The mineralogist Johann von Fuchs now advised additional training in medical chemistry, foreseeing a chair in this specialty at Munich. With Fuchs's influence Pettenkofer secured a bursary to attend the 1843–1844 winter semester at the University of Würzburg under Josef Scherer, a former pupil of Justus Liebig. There he detected large amounts of hippuric acid in the urine of a child whose diet consisted of only bread and apples—a notable example of the influence of diet upon urinary composition—and he developed the specific color reaction for bile, a test which still carries his name. He spent the summer at the University of Giessen, where he became an enthusiastic disciple of Liebig, who was then at the zenith of his powers and fame. Assigned to investigate the chemistry of meat, Pettenkofer discovered in human urine a new amino acid, creatinine. But a lack of funds ended this brief interlude.

At Munich, ministerial indifference dashed his hopes for a university post in medical chemistry. Unemployed and frustrated, he turned to poetry, composing romantic poems (published over forty years later as *Chemische Sonette*) glorifying chemistry and its adepts, from Roger Bacon to Liebig. In 1845 an appointment as assistant at the Royal Mint sufficiently relieved his financial problems, and he at last married his cousin Helene. Pettenkofer's duties, official and unofficial, agreeably challenged his resourcefulness. The costs of Bavarian currency conversion were minimized by retrieving precious metals from the old silver thalers.

The gold that was separated during refining contained about 3 percent silver, which was tenaciously combined with small amounts of platinum. Pettenkofer devised methods for separating the gold from the silver and recovering the platinum. By a slow-cooling process in the mint ovens he reproduced the beautiful bloodred ("haematinon") coloration of a specimen of *porporino antico* that was possessed by the king. He also reported the presence of sulfocyanic acid in human saliva. In 1846 he was elected an extraordinary member of the Bavarian Academy of Sciences. In the following year a ministerial change reopened the possibility of a chair in medical chemistry at Munich. On Fuchs's urging, Pettenkofer became a candidate. With royal support he was appointed extraordinary professor in November 1847, four months before the king abdicated.

His lecture course was developed slowly, with frequent changes of title and content. Pathologic chemistry was lightly treated, but the applications of chemistry to nutrition, public health, sanitation, and forensic medicine were emphasized. Another component, at first unformulated, concerned the role of chemistry in analyzing man's personal environment. His first lectures were given in 1853 under the title "Dietetic Physical-Chemistry," and not until 1865, when a new chair of hygiene was created for him, did he adopt the title "Lectures on Hygiene." In 1850 a remarkable address to the Royal Academy of Sciences, "Ueber die regelmässigen Abstände der Aequivalentzahlen der sogenannten einfachen Radicale," revealed his reflective mastery of chemical principles and presaged the periodic law of the elements. As verification of the alleged mathematical relationships between certain elements depended upon accurate atomic weights, Pettenkofer sought vainly for modest support from the Academy to make the necessary precise determinations. His classic report, published in an obscure journal, was reprinted in Liebig's *Annalen der Chemie und Pharmacie* (1858) when his priority was threatened. In 1899 the German Chemical Society awarded him a gold medal commemorating the fiftieth anniversary of the historic address.

Pettenkofer's versatility in solving practical problems was nearly inexhaustible. He observed that German hydraulic lime equaled English Portland cement in hardening properties if the calcining temperature of the marl was reduced. He also discovered means of improving the illuminating power of wood gas, so that (until coal became cheaper) several German cities and the Munich railway station were lit thereby. Such accomplishments enhanced his widespread reputation for chemical inventiveness and excited new demands. In the early 1860's his reports on the restoration of oil paintings in the Alte Pinakothek emphasized proper heating of art galleries to prevent the dampness that opacified many varnishes. He was also recognized professionally, being nominated to the Chief Medical Commission (Obermedizinalausschuss) in 1849. Upon his uncle's death (1850), he was appointed part-time director of the royal pharmacy, with tenure of the apartment in which his earlier years were spent. His brother Michael became court apothecary and managed the operating details. Under their administration, a model profitable institution developed.

When the new king, Maximilian II, informed the Commission about the uncomfortable dryness and possible health hazards from heating the palace by circulated hot air instead of stoves, Pettenkofer was delegated to resolve the problem. His investigations disclosed that the dryness was caused by the faster-flowing heated air desiccating the room walls. This project showed how such vague expressions as "salubrity of dwellings" could be substantiated by explicit data; the project was also his starting point for the new science of experimental hygiene. He realized that determinations of the physical properties of building materials were extensible to adjacent soil, personal clothing, and more remote factors concerning human health.

In 1852 he helped the king arrange Liebig's appointment to the chair of chemistry at Munich. Although Pettenkofer had become ordinary professor of medical chemistry (1852), he never competed with the acknowledged master, but instead attained preeminence in the discipline created by himself. At Pettenkofer's request, Liebig permitted his name to be attached to the well-known meat extract that Pettenkofer was manufacturing in the court pharmacy.

In 1857 better accommodation became available in the new Physiological Institute. Pettenkofer investigated air exchange in Munich hospitals and studied artificial ventilation in Paris. A simplified method of carbon dioxide assay was used to evolve standards of atmospheric purity for occupied rooms. He cast new light on air permeation through room walls, on the composition of ground air and its penetrability into dwellings, and on the vitiation of air by heating and lighting arrangements. Other studies were facilitated after 1860 by an airtight metallic respiratory apparatus, invented by himself and paid for by the king, who patronized science as his father had patronized the arts. This unique structure comfortably housed a human subject or large experimental animal for a given period while the gaseous exchange and all bodily gains or losses were measured exactly. Thus, in collaboration with Carl Voit, one of his earliest pupils, Pettenkofer established many basic nutritional facts,

such as the dietetic requirements of normal people at rest and in various activities, the vital necessity of adequate protein intake, the protein-sparing properties of carbohydrate and fat during starvation, and the need of the diabetic for extra protein and fat to replace unused carbohydrate.

These advances captured international attention. Voit became director of the Physiological Institute in 1863. Two years later Pettenkofer was made ordinary professor of hygiene and elected university rector at Munich. During an audience with the young King Ludwig II, Pettenkofer promoted hygiene so effectively that chairs were created at the universities of Würzburg and Erlangen, and the subject was made compulsory in state medical examinations. The new discipline had taken firm root. In 1865, with Voit and two associates, Pettenkofer founded and for eighteen years coedited the *Zeitschrift für Biologie*, which published many of his reports. The collaborative studies on nutrition continued until Pettenkofer moved into his own institute. His special interest in the hygienic importance of air focused on its relationship to clothing and particularly to soil. He discussed the functions of clothing in the first volume of the *Zeitschrift*; and in 1872, in three popular lectures, he dealt with air in relation to clothing, dwelling, and soil.

Pettenkofer believed that soil had fundamental sanitary relationships, for "an impurity cleaves longest and most tenaciously to the soil, which suffers no change of place, like air and water." An unexpected, late offshoot of his work on soil aeration was his observation of coal gas poisoning that resulted from seepage into houses from leaking mains (1883). But his initial and continuing preoccupation with this field stemmed mainly from his determination to explain recurrent cholera epidemics—the grimmest challenge to hygiene in the nineteenth century. His introduction to cholera came as member of a commission which had been appointed to review scientifically the 1854 epidemic in Bavaria. He studied ten outbreaks, including one in detail in Munich, where he and his young daughter contracted the disease and their cook died of it. As cholera was neither purely contagious (like smallpox) nor purely miasmatic (like malaria), Pettenkofer concluded that it must be contagio-miasmatic. He developed the hypothesis that choleraic excreta embodied a contagious factor, the dissemination of which required soils of a particular constitution: moist, porous, and polluted. Penetrating into such terrain, "the cholera germ-bearing excrements . . . modify the existing process of decay and decomposition," so that, besides normal putrefactive gases, "a specific Cholera-Miasma is developed, which is then spread along with other exhalations into the houses" (1855). From his survey in Munich, Pettenkofer concluded that drinking water did not cause the outbreak. This conclusion was then generalized and extended to typhoid fever (highly endemic in Munich). Thus his epidemiologic doctrines were directly opposed to those of John Snow and William Budd in England.

He then investigated the varied regional incidence of cholera in Bavaria. Its recurrence along certain river valleys was attributed to their being areas of natural soil drainage rather than routes of travel; and he deduced that the decisive factor in the genesis of cholera was the moisture content of the local soil, which was indicated by the groundwater level. When the water table fell, as in summer, a larger soil volume became available for production of the toxic miasma. This hypothesis of the mode of spread of cholera became an *idée fixe*. Pettenkofer expounded his theory in the *Zeitschrift*, and his pupils L. Buhl and L. Seidel each discussed the etiology of typhoid fever from similar theoretic standpoints (1865). Their position was a compromise between the "contagionist" view of Snow and Budd, which stated that the intestines of cholera and typhoid patients were the primary origin of the specific infective agents, and the extreme "localist" concept developed by James Cuningham and his Anglo-Indian associates in Calcutta, which held that cholera epidemics arose because of properties of the localities concerned. Pettenkofer's localist leanings did not diminish when disinfection of excreta failed to halt the 1866 cholera outbreak in Germany. Moreover, his travels in 1868 revealed that the comparative immunity of Lyons to cholera, and the recent outbreaks in Malta and Gibraltar, were all explicable by the nature of their underlying terrain. In an extensive review, *Boden und Grundwasser in ihren Beziehungen zu Cholera und Typhus* (1869), he proposed that an "x" factor, dependent on human intercourse, and a "y" factor, derived from soil, were essential for production of the true cholera poison "z." The reaction of the germ and the soil factor might occur in the soil itself, in the air of the dwelling, or perhaps in the human body. But the germ alone could no more cause cholera than swallowing yeast cells could produce intoxication.

Despite denials that cholera or typhoid might be waterborne, Pettenkofer's hygienic philosophy required that the water supply of a city be free from impurities. Between 1867 and 1883 he initiated measures whereby the drinking water supply of Munich became one of the finest in Europe. Further, since cholera tends to rage where the greatest filth prevails, he set about providing the city with good drainage and sewerage. After the 1854 epidemic, the possibility was mooted of replacing the unsanitary night cartage of excreta with float-canalization (*Schwemmkanalisation*), in which all excreta and household wastes were piped into the natural streamlets and canals traversing Munich and thence into the swift-flowing Isar River. This system, initiated in 1858, publicly backed in 1870, and completed in 1892, testified to Pettenkofer's vision, persistence, scientific authority, and persuasiveness.

Munich acknowledged these contributions to its cleanliness by granting him honorary citizenship in 1872. Two public lectures entitled "Ueber den Werth der Gesundheit für eine Stadt" (1873) illustrated well his talent for inspiring further hygienic advances. These advances were evident from the essay "Munich a Healthy Town" (1889) and from the changes reported to the Epidemiological Society of London by C. Childs, an English physician, in "The History of Typhoid Fever in Munich" (1898).

A flattering call to Vienna in 1872 was rejected by Pettenkofer after the German government assured him that a hygienic institute would be erected for him in Munich. In 1876 he also refused Chancellor Bismarck's invitation to direct the new *Reichsgesundheitsamt* (Imperial Health Office). He was honorary president of the second International Congress of Hygiene and Demography, held in 1878 in Paris. In 1879 the first Institute of Hygiene, with abundant space and equipment for teaching and research, was formally opened under his direction. In 1882, with H. W. von Ziemssen's collaboration, a *Handbuch der Hygiene* appeared; and with two colleagues Pettenkofer founded and coedited the *Archiv für Hygiene* in 1883. In that year he was granted hereditary nobility.

When Koch first announced his isolation of the "comma bacillus" from cholera cases (1883), Pettenkofer readily accepted this vibrio as his "x" factor, but refused to modify his views on the paramountcy of the telluric "y" factor. Perhaps his attitude hardened because he was not invited to the first cholera conference in Berlin in 1884, organized by the *Reichsgesundheitsamt*, of which he was an extraordinary member. Koch visited him at Munich later that year, but there was no rapprochement. Pettenkofer attended the second cholera conference (1885), but Koch seemed unaware or disdainful of Pettenkofer's thirty years of careful epidemiologic enquiries and of his major role at earlier cholera conferences in Weimar (1867), Berlin (1873), and Vienna (1874). Koch and Carl Flügge now founded and coedited the *Zeitschrift für Hygiene* (1885), while Pettenkofer reiterated and amplified his doctrines in the *Archiv für Hygiene* (1886–1887). The two schools of inflexible proponents and loyal adherents polarized their irreconcilable opinions in Munich and Berlin. In 1892, after a classic waterborne epidemic killed some 8,000 inhabitants of Hamburg within three months, the seventy-four-year-old Pettenkofer defiantly drank a cubic centimeter of culture of a recently isolated *Vibrio cholerae*. His colleague R. Emmerich subsequently repeated the experiment. They both developed diarrhea and excreted cholera vibrios for several days. These were proclaimed negative reactions and hence dramatic vindications of Pettenkofer's doctrine. The possibilities of immunity from previous exposure to the infecting agent or of the low virulence of the culture, however, were not raised. But the tide of evidence and opinion was not reversed, and little more was heard (outside the Munich school) of the localist or groundwater theory.

Honors and weariness now descended upon the intrepid hygienist. His seventieth birthday celebrations were highlighted by an address signed by over 100 artists, and by Munich and Leipzig jointly creating a Pettenkofer Foundation to provide prizes for scientific accomplishments in hygiene. For his doctoral jubilee in 1893, a *Festschrift* and a volume of *Archiv für Hygiene* were dedicated to him; Munich presented its golden Citizen's Medal, and many other German and foreign honors were bestowed. In 1896 he was granted the title *Excellenz*, and in 1897 received the Harben Medal from the Royal Institute of Public Health in England as "founder of scientific hygiene." Honorary doctorates from universities and honorary memberships in foreign medical and hygienic associations were very numerous. After his last public address, "Ueber Selbstreinigung der Flüsse" (1891), he continued academic lectures for another three years. In 1894 he became professor emeritus, and within the next two years resigned his editorial duties and retired from the court pharmacy. In 1899 he terminated a decade as president of the Bavarian Academy of Sciences.

Pettenkofer retained his apartment in the royal residence for winter living, but was happiest in his country home at Seeshaupt on the Starnberger See. He restored the land, pruned trees, planted crops, and rowed on the lake. His only contacts with hygiene were through occasional visitors and lively correspondence with former students and disciples, many of whom now held chairs of hygiene in Germany and other countries. Although physically strong and mentally alert, he complained of tiredness, loss of memory, and inability to concentrate. His wife had died in 1890; and of their five children, two sons and a daughter had predeceased her. Pettenkofer especially mourned the loss of his gifted, eldest son, a medical student, who died from tuberculosis in 1869. Despite the care and concern of surviving relatives, he feared for his reason and threatened suicide. At the end of January 1901, a septic throat caused him much pain and insomnia, aggravating his depression. He bought a revolver and one night, two hours after being put to bed by his daughter-in-law, shot himself in the head. He was buried in South Munich cemetery. A seated statue of him was erected in a main public square. In 1944 the Hygienic Institute was destroyed by bombs and fire, but a new "Max v. Pettenkofer-Institut für Hygiene und Medizinische Microbiologie" was completed on a neighboring site in 1961. An adjacent street still bears his name.

Pettenkofer was genial and sociable, carrying his culture and honors lightly, yet fully aware of the significance of his theories. A leonine countenance, self-confident bearing, and skillful delivery helped to make his lectures unforgettable. He worked prodigiously, rising early and often retiring late. His character was truly benevolent and without pettiness or spite, but he could be scornful of pretentiousness, angry at injustice, and stubborn in self-defense. His disciples revered him as father-figure and wise visionary. As an investigator the mark of genius appeared in the discrimination with which he selected mundane phenomena for delicate observation, and in the unexcelled virtuosity applied to determining their cause. Although his approach was highly original, he firmly believed in the practical aims of scientific hygiene, and all his research and exhortative efforts were directed toward promoting public health in its broadest sense. Indirectly, by elevating hygiene to an accepted discipline in medical training, he stimulated a new social outlook that encouraged the physician to provide not only relief from disease, but counsel and leadership toward healthful living.

A lenient view may be taken of Pettenkofer's misconceptions about cholera and enteric infections. Although often biased in the selection of data supporting his contentions, the sincerity of his motives was never impugned. His deeply rooted obsession with soil as the major source of certain ailments yielded great benefits to Munich when its soil was cleansed by the introduction of effective drainage and sewerage. If the hubristic tendencies of some early bacteriologists were tempered by his skepticism, he was not antagonistic to their emerging science. At the 1885 conference, he magnanimously termed Koch's discovery "a great enrichment of our pathologic knowledge about cholera." His attitude might have been less obdurate against a more tactful adversary. After all, Koch was his junior by a quarter-century, and likewise even Pasteur by four years.

In honor of his eighty-first birthday, the citizens of Munich presented another gold medal "as a sign of unlimited veneration, gratitude and love," to "the High Priest of Hygiene . . . the remover of pernicious diseases from the home soil."

BIBLIOGRAPHY

I. ORIGINAL WORKS. Pettenkofer wrote over 20 monographs and more than 200 separate articles in German scientific and medical journals between 1842 and 1898. There is no collected ed. E. E. Hume's biographical review (see below) contains a bibliography of 227 items, which is fairly complete but sprinkled with inaccuracies.

Among Pettenkofer's reports on hygienic topics available in English are "Ueber den Respirations- und Perspirations-Apparat im physiologischen Institute zu München," in Erdmann's *Journal für praktische Chemie*, **82** (1861), 40–50, trans. by A. Ten Brook as "Description of Apparatus for Testing the Results of Perspiration and Respiration in the Physiological Institute of Munich," in *Smithsonian Report for 1864*, (Washington, 1865), pp. 235–239; *Beziehungen der Luft zu Kleidung, Wohnung, und Boden* (Brunswick, 1872), 3 lectures, trans. by A. Hess as *The Relations of the Air to the Clothes We Wear, the House We Live in, and the Soil We Dwell On* (London, 1873); *Ueber den Werth der Gesundheit für eine Stadt* (Brunswick, 1873), 2 lectures, trans. by H. E. Sigerist as *The Value of Health to a City* (Baltimore, 1941), repr. from *Bulletin of the History of Medicine*, **10** (1941), 473–503, 593–613; and "Der Boden und sein Zusammenhang mit der Gesundheit des Menschen," in *Deutsche Rundschau*, **29** (1881), 217–234, trans. as "Sanitary Relations of the Soil," in *Popular Science Monthly*, **20** (1882), 332–340; and "Munich a Healthy Town" (Munich, 1889), written with H. W. von Ziemssen.

English trans. or expressions of Pettenkofer's views on cholera include "Observations on Dr. Buchanan's Lecture on Professor von Pettenkofer's Theory of the Propagation of Cholera and Enteric Fever," in *Medical Times and Gazette*, **1** (1870), 629–632, 661–663, 687–689; "On the Recent Outbreak of Cholera in. Munich," *ibid.*, **1** (1874), 582–583; "On the Probability of an Invasion of Cholera in Europe," in *Sanitary Record*, n.s. **5** (1883–1884), 47–51; "Professor Max von Pettenkofer on Cholera Afloat," in *Lancet* (1884), **2**, 338–340; and "Cholera," *ibid.*, 769–771, 816–819, 861–864, 904–905, 992–994, 1042–1043, 1086–1088. His contributions to the 1874 Conférence Sanitaire Internationale in Vienna were freely translated by T. W. Hime as *Cholera: How to Prevent and Resist It* (London, 1875; 2nd ed. 1883).

Other such works are *Künftige Prophylaxis gegen Cholera* . . . (Munich, 1875), with trans. and abstr. by A. Rabaglioti as "Artificial Prophylaxis Against Cholera," in *Sanitary Record*, **3** (1875), 35–39; "Die Choleraepidemie in der königlichen bayerischen Gefangenenanstalt Laufen an der Salzach," in *Bericht der Choleracommission für das Deutsche Reich* (Berlin, 1875), with trans. as *Outbreak of Cholera Among Convicts* . . . (London, 1876); "Die Cholera in Syrien und die Choleraprophylaxe in Europa," in *Zeitschrift für Biologie*, **12** (1876), 102–128, with trans.

as "The Cholera in Syria and the Prophylaxis of Cholera in Europe," in *Practitioner*, **16** (1876), 401–415; "Neun ätiologische und prophylaktische Sätze aus den amtlichen Berichten über die Choleraepidemien in Ostindien und Nordamerica," in *Deutsche Vierteljahrsschrift für öffentliche Gesundheitspflege*, **9** (1877), 177–224, with trans. as "Nine Propositions Bearing on the Aetiology and Prophylaxis of Cholera, Deduced From the Official Reports of the Cholera-Epidemic in East India and North America," in *Practitioner*, **18** (1877), 135–160, 204–240; *Zum gegenwärtigen Stand der Cholerafrage* (Munich, 1887), repr. from *Archiv für Hygiene*, **4** (1886), 249–354, 397–546; **5** (1886), 353–445; **6** (1887), 1–84, 129–233, 303–358, 373–441; **7** (1887), 1–81, with abstr. and trans. by H. Koplik as "The Present Aspect of the Cholera Question," in *Lancet* (1886), **2**, 29–30, 89–91; and "Ueber Cholera mit Berücksichtigung der jüngsten Cholera-Epidemie in Hamburg," in *Münchener medizinische Wochenschrift*, **39** (1892), 807–817, discussion 826–828, with trans. and abstr. as "On Cholera, With Reference to the Recent Epidemic at Hamburg," in *Lancet* (1892), **2**, 1182–1185.

His monographs or booklets include *Ueber Chemie in ihrem Verhältnisse zur Physiologie und Pathologie* (Munich, 1848); *Ueber Oelfarbe und Conservirung der Gemälde durch das Regenerations-Verfahren* (Brunswick, 1850); *Untersuchungen und Beobachtungen über die Verbreitungsart der Cholera* . . . (Munich, 1855); *Ueber den Luftwechsel in Wohngebäuden* (Munich, 1858); *Ueber die Verlegung der Gottesäcker in Basel* (Basel, 1864); *Die Cholera vom Jahre 1866 in Weimar* (Weimar, 1867); *Ueber die Ursachen und Gegenwirkung von Cholera-Epidemien in Erfurt* (Erfurt, 1867); *Boden und Grundwasser in ihren Beziehungen zu Cholera und Typhus* (Munich, 1869), repr. from *Zeitschrift für Biologie*, **5** (1869), 171–310; *Das Canal- oder Siel-System in München* (Munich, 1869); *Verbreitungsart der Cholera in Indien* (Brunswick, 1871); *Ueber die Aetiologie des Typhus* (Munich, 1872); *Ueber den gegenwärtigen Stand der Cholera-Frage* . . . (Munich, 1873); *Vorträge über Canalisation und Abfuhr* (Munich, 1876); *Populäre Vorträge* (Munich, 1877); *Die Cholera* (Breslau, 1884); *Chemische Sonette* (Munich, 1886); *Der epidemiologische Theil des Berichtes über die Thätigkeit der zur Erforschung der Cholera im Jahre 1883 nach Aegypten und Indien entsandten deutschen Commission* (Munich, 1888); and *Die Verunreinigung der Isar durch das Schwemmsystem von München* (Munich, 1890). He was coeditor, with H. W. von Ziemssen, of *Handbuch der Hygiene* . . . (Leipzig, 1882). He also wrote several obituaries and commemorative tributes, of which the most important is *Dr. Justus Freiherrn von Liebig zum Gedächtnis* (Munich, 1874).

Characteristic chemical reports are "Sichere und einfache Methode das Arsenik mittelst des Marsh'schen Apparates entwickelt von allen andern ähnlichen Erscheinungen augenfällig zu unterscheiden," in *Repertorium für die Pharmacie*, **76** (1842), 289–307; "Nachtrag zur Arsenik-probe . . ." *ibid.*, **83** (1844), 328–336; "Ueber Mikania Guaco," *ibid.*, **86** (1844), 289–323, his inaugural diss. at the University of Munich (1844); "Ueber das Vorkommen einer grossen Menge Hippursäure im Menschenharne," in Liebig's *Annalen der Chemie und Pharmacie*, **52** (1844), 86–90; "Notiz über eine neue Reaction auf Galle und Zucker," *ibid.*, 90–96; "Vorläufige Notiz über einen neuen stickstoffhaltigen Körper im Harne," *ibid.*, 97–100; "Ueber die Affinirung des Goldes und über die grosse Verbreitung des Platins," in *Münchner gelehrte Anzeiger*, **24** (1847), 589–598; "Bemerkungen zu Hopfgartner's Analyse eines englischen und eines deutschen hydraulischen Kalkes," in Dingler's *Polytechnisches Journal*, **113** (1849), 357–371; "Ueber die regelmässigen Abstände der Aequivalenzahlen der sogenannten einfachen Radicale," in *Münchner gelehrte Anzeiger*, **30** (1850), 261–272; and "Ueber das Haematinon der Alten und über Aventuringlas," in Erdmann's *Journal für praktische Chemie*, **72** (1857), 50–53.

Works on various aspects of hygiene include "Ueber den Unterschied zwischen Luftheizung und Ofenheizung in ihrer Einwirkung auf die Zusammensetzung der Luft der beheizten Räume," in Dingler's *Polytechnisches Journal*, **119** (1851), 40–51, 282–290; "Ueber die wichtigsten Grundsätze der Bereitung und Benützung des Holzleuchtgases," in Erdmann's *Journal für praktische Chemie*, **71** (1857), 385–393; "Berichte über Ventilations-Apparate," in *Abhandlungen der naturwissenschaftlich-technischen Commission bei der königlichen baierischen Akademie*, **2** (1858), 19–68; "Besprechung allgemeiner auf die Ventilation bezüglicher Fragen," *ibid.*, 69–126; "Ueber die Bestimmung der freien Kohlensäure im Trinkwasser," in Erdmann's *Journal für praktische Chemie*, **82** (1861), 32–40; "Ueber eine Methode die Kohlensäure in der atmosphärischen Luft zu bestimmen," *ibid.*, **85** (1862), 165–184; "Ueber die Respiration," in Liebig's *Annalen der Chemie und Pharmacie*, supp. 2 (1862–1863), 1–52; "Untersuchungen über die Respiration," *ibid.*, 52–70, written with C. Voit; "Ueber die Wahl der Begräbnissplätze," in *Zeitschrift für Biologie*, **1** (1865), 45–68; "Ueber die Funktion der Kleider," *ibid.*, 180–194; "Ueber Kohlensäureausscheidung und Sauerstoffaufnahme während des Wachens und Schlafens beim gesunden und kranken Menschen," in Liebig's *Annalen der Chemie und Pharmacie*, **141** (1867), 295–322; "Ueber Kohlensäuregehalt der Luft im Boden (Grundluft) von München in verschiedenen Tiefen und zu verschiedenen Zeiten," in *Zeitschrift für Biologie*, **7** (1871), 395–417; **9** (1873), 250–257; "Beleuchtung des königliche Residenztheaters in München mit Gas und mit elektrischem Licht," in *Archiv für Hygiene*, **1** (1883), 384–388; "Ueber Vergiftung mit Leuchtgas," in *Festschrift des aerztlichen Vereins München . . .* (Munich, 1883), pp. 68–74; "Der hygienische Unterricht an Universitäten und technischen Hochschulen," opening speech, *VI. International Congress for Hygiene and Demography* (Vienna, 1887); and "Ueber Selbstreinigung der Flüsse," in *Deutsche medizinische Wochenschrift*, **17** (1891), 1277–1281.

Researches on the physiology of nutrition include "Ueber die Produkte der Respiration des Hundes bei Fleischnahrung, und über die Gleichung der Einnahmen und Ausgaben des Körpers dabei," in Liebig's *Annalen der Chemie und Pharmacie*, supp. 2 (1862–1863), 361–377; "Untersuchungen über den Stoffverbrauch des normalen Menschen," in *Zeitschrift für Biologie*, **2** (1866), 459–573; "Ueber den Stoffverbrauch bei der Zuckerharnruhr," *ibid.*, **3** (1867), 380–444; "Respirationsversuche am Hunde bei Hunger und ausschliesslicher Fettzufuhr," *ibid.*, **5** (1869), 369–392; and "Ueber die Zersetzungsvorgänge im Thierkörper bei Fütterung mit Fleisch und Fett," *ibid.*, **9** (1873), 1–40, all written with C. Voit. Pettenkofer's report on Liebig's meat extract is "Ueber Nahrungsmittel im Allgemeinen und über den Werth des Fleischextracts als Bestandtheil der menschlichen Nahrung insbesonders," in Liebig's *Annalen der Chemie und Pharmacie*, **167** (1873), 271–292.

His views on the etiology and epidemiology of cholera and typhoid fever are illustrated further in "Die Bewegung des Grundwassers in München von März 1856 bis März 1862," in *Sitzungsberichte der königlichen baierischen Akademie der Wissenschaften zu München*, **1** (1862), 272–290; "Ueber die Verbreitungsart der Cholera," in *Zeitschrift für Biologie*, **1** (1865), 322–374; "Ueber den gegenwärtigen Stand des Grundwassers in München," *ibid.*, 375–377; "Die sächsische Choleraepidemie des Jahres 1865," *ibid.*, **2** (1866), 78–144; "Ueber die Schwankungen der Typhussterblichkeit in München von 1850 bis 1867," *ibid.*, **4** (1868), 1–39; "Die Immunität von Lyon gegen Cholera und das Vorkommen der Cholera auf Seeschiffen," *ibid.*, 400–490; "Prof. Dr. Hallier über den Einfluss des Trinkwassers auf dem Darmtyphus in München," *ibid.*, 512–530; "Die Choleraepidemie des Jahres 1865 in Gibraltar," *ibid.*, **6** (1870), 95–119; "Die Choleraepidemien auf Malta und Gozo," *ibid.*, 143–203; "Typhus und Cholera und Grundwasser in Zürich," *ibid.*, **7** (1871), 86–103; and "Ueber Cholera auf Schiffen und den Zweck der Quarantänen," *ibid.*, **8** (1872), 1–70.

Additional writings include "Auszug aus den Untersuchungen von Dr. Douglas Cunningham in Ostindien, über die Verbreitungsart der Cholera," *ibid.*, 251–293; "Ist das Trinkwasser Quelle von Typhusepidemien?", *ibid.*, **10** (1874), 439–526; "Aetiologie des Abdominal-Typhus," in *Archiv für öffentliche Gesundheitspflege*, **9** (1884), 92–100; "Ueber Desinfection der ostindischen Post als Schutzmittel gegen Einschleppung der Cholera in Europa," in *Archiv für Hygiene*, **2** (1884), 35–45; "Die Cholera in Indien," *ibid.*, 129–146; "Rudolf Virchow's Choleratheorie," in *Berliner klinische Wochenschrift*, **21** (1884), 488–490, with Virchow's reply, *ibid.*, 490–491; "Die Trinkwassertheorie und die Cholera-Immunität des Forts William in Calcutta," *ibid.*, **3** (1885), 147–182; "M. Kirchner, Ueber Cholera mit Berücksichtigung der jüngsten Choleraepidemie in Hamburg," in *Centralblatt für Bakteriologie*, **12** (1892), 898–904, in response to Kirchner's review, *ibid.*, 828–836; "Ueber die Cholera von 1892 in Hamburg und über Schutzmaassregeln," in *Archiv für Hygiene*, **18** (1893), 94–132; and "Choleraexplosionen und Trinkwasser," in *Münchener medizinische Wochenschrift*, **48** (1894), 221–224, 248–251.

A small collection of his reprints and decorations, and a fine oil portrait, survive in the rebuilt Max v.

Pettenkofer Institute of the University of Munich. The bulk of his papers are in the Bavarian State Museum in Munich.

II. SECONDARY LITERATURE. Obituaries in German include "Nachruf Max von Pettenkofer gewidmet," in *Archiv für Hygiene*, **39** (1901), 313–320; R. Emmerich, "Erinnerungen an Max v. Pettenkofer," in *Deutsche Revue*, **27** (1902), 81–92; F. Erismann, "Max von Pettenkofer," in *Deutsche medizinische Wochenschrift*, **27** (1901), 209–211, 253–255, 285–287, 299–302, 323–327; M. Gruber, "Max v. Pettenkofer (1818–1901)," in *Wiener klinische Wochenschrift*, **14** (1901), 213–218; G. W. A. Kahlbaum, "Worte des Gedenkens an Max von Pettenkofer," in *Abhandlungen der Naturforschenden Gesellschaft zu Basel*, **13** (1901), 326–337; K. B. Lehmann, "Max von Pettenkofer," in *Münchener medizinische Wochenschrift*, **48** (1901), 464–473; L. Pfeiffer, "Zum Gedächtniss für Max von Pettenkofer," in *Hygienische Rundschau*, **11** (1901), 717–732; M. Rubner, "Zum Andenken an Max v. Pettenkofer," in *Berliner klinische Wochenschrift*, **38** (1901), 268–270, 301–303, 321–326; C. Voit, "Max von Pettenkofer, dem Physiologen, zum Gedächtnis," in *Zeitschrift für Biologie*, **41**, n.s. **23** (1901), I–VIII, and *Max von Pettenkofer zum Gedächtniss* (Munich, 1902).

Obituaries in English are by C. Childs, "Geheimrath Max von Pettenkofer, of Munich," in *Transactions of the Epidemiological Society*, n.s. **20** (1901), 118–125; J. S. Haldane, "The Work of Max von Pettenkofer," in *Journal of Hygiene*, **1** (1901), 289–294; and an editorial, with brief additional tributes by Sir John Simon and W. H. C. Corfield, "Max Josef von Pettenkofer, M.D.," in *British Medical Journal* (1901), **1**, 489–490.

Other German references bearing on Pettenkofer's life and work are L. Buhl, "Ein Beitrag zur Aetiologie des Typhus," in *Zeitschrift für Biologie*, **1** (1865), 1–25; E. Ebstein, "Max Pettenkofer als junger Professor—und Komödiant," in *Deutsche medizinische Wochenschrift*, **54** (1928), 1813–1814; R. Emmerich, "Max von Pettenkofer," in *Centralblatt für allgemeine Gesundheitspflege*, **12** (1893), 207–217, and *Max Pettenkofer's Bodenlehre der Cholera Indica* (Munich, 1910); H. Eyer, *100 Jahre Lehrstuhl für Hygiene an der Ludwig-Maximilians-Universität München* (Munich, 1965); K. M. Finkelnburg *et al.*, *Festschrift des niederrheinischen Vereins für öffentliche Gesundheitspflege und des Centralblattes für allgemeine Gesundheitspflege, zur Feier des 50jährigen Doctor-Jubiläums Max von Pettenkofers am 30. Juni 1893* (Bonn, 1893); I. Fischer, "Max von Pettenkofer," in *Biographisches Lexikon der hervorragender Aerzte*, 2nd ed., IV (1932), 576–577; *Jubelband dem Herrn Geh. Rath Prof. Dr. M. von Pettenkofer zu seinem 50jährigen Doctor-Jubiläum gewidmet von seinen Schülern* (*Archiv für Hygiene*, *17*) (1893); K. Kisskalt, "Max von Pettenkofer," in *Grosse Naturforscher*, H. W. Frickhinger, ed. (Stuttgart, 1948); A. Kohut, "Ein Gedenkblatt zu seinem 80. Geburtstage (3. Dezember)," in *Pharmazeutische Zeitung*, **43** (1898), 853–855; K. B. Lehmann, "Max v. Pettenkofer und seine Verdienste um die wissenschaftliche und praktische Hygiene," in *Deutsche Vierteljahrsschrift für öffentliche Gesundheitspflege*, **25** (1893), 361–385; O. Neustatter, "Max Pettenkofer," in M. Neuberger, ed., *Meister der Heilkunde*, VII (Vienna, 1925), 1–89; "Die Pettenkofer-Feier," in *Münchener medizinische Wochenschrift*, **40** (1893), 536–538; E. Roth, "Von Pettenkofer als populärer Schriftsteller," in *Deutsche Vierteljahrsschrift für öffentliche Gesundheitspflege*, **25** (1893), 386–396; L. Seidel, "Ueber den numerischen Zusammenhang, welcher zwischen der Häufigkeit der Typhus-Erkrankungen und dem Stande des Grundwassers während der letzten 9 Jahre in München hervorgetreten ist," in *Zeitschrift für Biologie*, **1** (1865), 221–236; H. E. Sigerist, "Max Pettenkofer (1818–1901)," *Grosse Aerzte* (Munich, 1932), pp. 288–292; G. Sticker, *Abhandlungen aus der Seuchengeschichte und Seuchenlehre, II. Die Cholera* (Giessen, 1912), pp. 133–150, 290–299; J. Soyka, "Zur Aetiologie des Abdominal Typhus," in *Archiv für Hygiene*, **6** (1887), 257–302; and R. Virchow, "Erwiderung an Herrn von Pettenkofer," in *Berliner klinische Wochenschrift*, **21** (1884), 490–491.

Among English references to Pettenkofer's theories are G. Buchanan, "On Prof. Pettenkofer's Theory of the Propagation of Cholera," in *Medical Times and Gazette*, **1** (1870), 283–285; W. Budd, *Typhoid Fever . . .* (London, 1874; repr. New York, 1931); C. Childs, "The History of Typhoid Fever in Munich," in *Lancet* (1898), **1**, 348–354; J. M. Cuningham, "Recent Experience of Cholera in India," *ibid.* (1874), **1**, 477–479; H. M. Dietz, "The Activity of the Hygienist F. Erismann in Moscow (Unpublished Documents and Letters to M. v. Pettenkofer)," in *Clio Medica*, **4** (1969), 203–210; E. E. Hume, *Max von Pettenkofer . . .* (New York, 1927); E. McClellan, "A Reply to an Address of Prof. Max von Pettenkofer of Munich . . .," in *Practitioner*, **19** (1877), 61–78, 148–160; C.-E. A. Winslow, "Pettenkofer—The Last Stand," in *The Conquest of Epidemic Disease* (Princeton, N.J., 1944), chap. 15, pp. 311–336.

CLAUDE E. DOLMAN

PETTERSSON, HANS (*b.* Kälhuvudet, Marstrand, Bohuslän, Sweden, 26 August 1888; *d.* Göteborg, Sweden, 25 January 1966), *oceanography*.

Like his father, Pettersson became one of the most outstanding oceanographers of his period. After matriculating in Stockholm, and graduating at Uppsala, he studied physics under K. Ångstrom and Sir William Ramsay, working on problems in optics and radioactivity. In 1913 he was appointed to the staff of the Svenska Hydrografiska-Biologiska Kommissionen and was soon publishing papers on the tides and currents of the Kattegat. Like his father, he was particularly interested in the differences of flow in stratified water, waves on internal boundary surfaces, and improved methods of measuring water density and flow. Throughout this work he had a compelling interest in changes of sea level brought about by meteorological factors and in the effect of oceans on climate. He shared his father's urge to demonstrate that the dominant meteorological features of northwest Europe are determined to a large extent by the heat capacity and water transport of the North Atlantic Ocean. Following up his earlier interests he studied radioactivity in seawater and sediments, and penetration of light into the sea.

In general, he seemed to prefer spectacular explanations for oceanic phenomena, invoking, for example, a cosmic origin rather than more disciplined terrestrial sources to explain the relatively high content of nickel in some deep sea sediments. He offered a catastrophe of a volcanic nature as an alternative to turbidity-current deposition to explain the presence of organic material on the equational West Atlantic plain. He held tenaciously to the idea that abyssal plains were formed by vast outpourings of lava. One of his aims was to promote discussion and rouse interest; in this he was very successful. He was a lecturer at the Göteborgs Högskola from 1914 to 1930, when he was appointed professor. He was largely responsible for persuading wealthy businessmen to finance the Oceanografiska Institutet in 1939, and was director of this laboratory until 1956.

He is best known for his round-the-world, Swedish deep-sea expedition in the *Albatross* (1946–1948), for which he again obtained the funds and loan of the vessel from a Swedish shipping combine and private donors. One of the main achievements was the sampling of deep-sea sediments with a new piston core-sampler, developed largely by his colleague Dr. Kullenberg. Radioactivity and optical studies were also prominent. Within four years of the return of the expedition he was honored by many universities and learned societies, mainly in Europe, but also in the United States. In 1956 he was elected a foreign member of the Royal Society of London.

After his retirement in 1956 he held a research professorship in geophysics at the University of Hawaii, and he continued as a prominent figure in oceanography and geophysics until his death in 1966.

BIBLIOGRAPHY

See M. Sears, ed., *Progress in Oceanography*, III (Elmsford, 1965), which commemorated his seventy-fifth birthday; it contains an appreciation of his work by one of his former pupils and a full bibliography of some 180 publications covering fifty-one years. His semipopular book *Westward Ho With the Albatross* (London–New York, 1953) covered much of his life story and many of his interests.

G. E. R. Deacon

PETTY, WILLIAM (*b.* Romsey, Hampshire, England, 26 May 1623; *d.* London, England, 16 December 1687), *economics, demography, geography.*

Petty was a prominent virtuoso in an age of the many-sided genius. His investigations ranged over anatomy, geodesy, the design of ships, and the application of mathematics to diverse natural and practical problems. His major contributions were in what he called "political arithmetic."

Petty was the eldest surviving child of Anthony Petty, a cloth worker and tailor who owned his home and probably some farm land, and Francesca Denby Petty. Petty's chief childhood amusement, he later told John Aubrey, was "looking on the artificiers, e.g. smyths, the watchmakers, carpenters, joiners, etc." After the usual education in Latin, Greek, and arithmetic, he became at the age of thirteen a cabin boy on a merchant ship. He studied navigation while aboard, although he was extremely nearsighted. After ten months at sea he broke his leg and was set ashore near Caen.

There he impressed the Jesuit fathers, who admitted him to their college. More than a year later he returned to England and joined the navy. He left after the outbreak of civil war but always retained an interest in ships and the sea. In 1643 Petty went to the Netherlands to study medicine at Utrecht, Leiden, and Amsterdam. In 1645 he continued on to Paris and studied anatomy with Hobbes, who introduced him to Mersenne and his famous circle of friends who studied natural philosophy.

In 1646 Petty returned to England and met Samuel Hartlib, who persuaded Petty to write a tract on education. The result was *The Advice of W.P. to Mr. S. Hartlib for the Advancement of Some Particular Parts of Learning* (1648). Following Bacon's teachings, Petty recommended the establishment of a college "for the advancement of all mechanical arts and manufactures," where practical and theoretical questions would be investigated and a history of the trades would be written.

Petty resumed his anatomical studies, and by 1649 he was at Oxford University. In that year John Wilkins and other members of the university formed a club for experimental philosophy, which was an antecedent to the Royal Society of London. Because of the proximity to an apothecary shop, the club soon began holding its meetings in Petty's lodgings.

Petty's professional standing advanced rapidly. In 1650 he received the doctorate of physic from Oxford and became a candidate at the College of Physicians in London. He was soon appointed professor of anatomy and vice-principal of Brasenose College, Oxford, and then professor of music at Gresham College, London.

Nevertheless, in 1652 he left these positions to become physician-general to Cromwell's army in Ireland. Having found it necessary to pay the troops with land from the defeated Irish, Cromwell needed a land survey. The appointed supervisor proved inept, and in 1655 Petty volunteered to carry out the survey in thirteen months. His proposal was accepted, and he engaged about a thousand men for the task. In March 1656 he completed the survey as scheduled. Although it was an outstanding achievement, there were errors of underestimation of 10–15 percent, which correspondingly lessened his pay.

As a supplement to the Down Survey, Petty also undertook the complete mapping of Ireland. A general map and thirty-five county and barony maps were printed around 1685—the most detailed maps ever published for a whole country. Even more detailed maps, some of which have since been destroyed by fire, remained unpublished. Another supplement to the survey was the first census of Ireland, which was taken around 1659; the extent of Petty's involvement is unknown. The only copy of the results was among his papers, but he never made use of it in his writings.

Petty's payment for his survey enabled him to buy cheaply forfeited and mortgaged lands, thus acquiring considerable property, which he continued to augment throughout his life. Having acquired his wealth from other men's misfortunes, Petty endured hostility and litigation for the rest of his life.

Petty abandoned the practice of medicine and henceforth devoted a major part of his time and thought to managing his property. He was a friend of the Cromwells, both before and after the collapse of the Commonwealth; but he acquiesced in the Restoration, and Charles II knighted him in April 1661. Petty aspired to, but never received, an important government office. One of his hopes was to be placed in charge of an Irish statistical office. He was also on good terms with James II, although disappointed in his support of the Irish Catholics.

In 1667 Petty married Elizabeth Fenton, the attractive and intelligent widow of Sir Maurice Fenton. She was the daughter of Sir Hardress Waller, a prominent Irish Protestant, who had provided strong support for Petty's land survey. Two sons and a daughter survived infancy. Although Petty twice declined a baronetcy, James II made his widow Baroness Shelburn in 1688.

By the end of 1659 Petty had returned from Ireland to London, where he rejoined those members of the philosophical club who had moved back from Oxford and had begun meeting at Gresham College. When this group became incorporated in 1662 as the Royal Society of London for Promoting Natural Knowledge,

Petty was a charter member of its council. In 1673 he was elected vice-president. His interest in the society never waned, but his participation was curtailed by his becoming nearly blind in 1670 and by his being in Ireland managing his property from 1666 to 1673 and from 1676 to 1685.

A thoroughgoing Baconian, Petty emphasized the collection of information and the practical application of scientific principles and knowledge. Before the Royal Society he read instructions concerning the technical processes that were involved in his father's trade of cloth making and dyeing. In a discourse read before the Royal Society in 1674, he expressed interests in the physical sciences that were typical for his time. He urged the study of number, weight, and measurement; and he provided diverse examples, such as the relationship between scale and strength of structures; calculations of the distance that sounds, odors, and light travel in relation to the magnitude of the source; and formulas to predict prices and human longevity. He also suggested an explanation of elasticity and an atomic theory of matter. Atoms, he believed, were tiny magnets of different sexes.

Petty's most notable application of physical principles to a practical problem was in the development of his famous twin-hulled ships. He designed and constructed three of them between 1662 and 1664 and another in 1684. The first two ships were rather successful, but the third sank in a storm with all hands aboard, and the fourth was a complete failure. His concept was nevertheless valid and is exemplified in the modern catamaran.

Petty's writings that are relevant to the social sciences were his most enduring achievement. The time spent managing his Irish holdings undoubtedly reduced the time he could devote to scholarly writings. On the other hand, those holdings provided the incentive and orientation for his writings on political arithmetic.

Inseparable from Petty's writings is John Graunt's important *Natural and Political Observations Mentioned in a Following Index, and Made Upon the Bills of Mortality*; published in January 1662, it started the sciences of demography and statistics. In spite of Graunt's name on the title page and his election to the Royal Society on the book's merits, seven contemporaries referred to Petty as the author. The available evidence does not establish their claim. Petty and Graunt became friends around 1650 and remained so until Graunt's death. It seems likely that Petty discussed with Graunt the analysis of the London bills of mortality, and perhaps the book would not have been published without Petty's assistance and encouragement.

Petty's writings most comparable to Graunt's *Observations* are ten brief essays (1682–1687) on the population of London, Dublin, Paris, Rome, and other cities. These essays reveal Petty's appreciation of the importance of population as an economic factor. Because there were few vital statistics for any city except London, he relied upon unreliable indexes of population, such as the number of chimneys.

Although his figures were sometimes questionable, Petty was the first economic theorist to make a significant attempt to base economic policy upon statistical data. His *Treatise of Taxes and Contributions* (1662), possibly his best work, discussed the economy of Ireland and England and attempted to formulate sound policies for promoting wealth and collecting taxes. He was the first to emphasize the value of labor as a part of national wealth, and he also provided an important analysis of rents. His short *Verbum sapienti*, written about 1665 and published in 1691, is more quantitative and contains the first estimate of national incomes and the first discussion of the velocity of money. *The Political Anatomy of Ireland*, written about 1672 and published in 1691, also on economic policy, is supported by economic geography. In *Political Arithmetick*, written 1671–1676 and published in 1690, Petty extended his discussion to a comparison of the wealth and economic policies of England and France. He argued the benefits of a division of labor and the gains from foreign trade in *Another Essay in Political Arithmetick Concerning the Growth of the City of London* (1683). He also left other manuscripts on the Irish and English economy that have been published only recently. These include *A Treatise of Ireland* (1899), written in 1687 as advice for James II—advice neither requested nor heeded.

Petty's writings were, nevertheless, influential in England, and as an economic theorist he was not surpassed before 1750.

BIBLIOGRAPHY

I. ORIGINAL WORKS. Excellent detailed bibliographies of Petty's published writings and some of his MSS are Charles Henry Hull, ed., *The Economic Writings of Sir William Petty Together With the Observations Upon the Bills of Mortality, More Probably by Captain John Graunt*, II (Cambridge, 1899; facs. ed., New York, 1963), 633–657; Yann Morvran Goblet [pseudonym for Louis Tréguiz], *La transformation de la géographie politique de l'Irelande au XVIIᵉ Siècle dans les cartes et essais anthropogéographiques de Sir William Petty*, I (Paris, 1930), ix–xxiii; and Geoffrey Keynes, *A Bibliography of Sir William Petty F.R.S. and Observations on the Bills of Mortality by John Graunt F.R.S.* (Oxford, 1971).

Twelve of Petty's treatises have been reprinted with introductions and notes by Henry Hull, in the work mentioned above. Other works by Petty include *The History of the Survey of Ireland, Commonly Called the Down Survey, A.D. 1655–6*, Thomas Aiskew Larcom, ed. (Dublin, 1851; facs. ed., New York, 1967); and *A Census of Ireland, circa 1659*, Séamus Pender, ed. (Dublin, 1939). Lord Lansdowne has edited three important collections of Petty's MSS: *The Petty Papers: Some Unpublished Writings of Sir William Petty*, 2 vols. (London–Boston, 1927; facs. ed., New York, 1966); *The Petty-Southwell Correspondence, 1676–1687* (London, 1928; facs. ed., New York, 1967); and *The Double Bottom or Twin-Hulled Ship* (Oxford, 1931).

II. SECONDARY LITERATURE. The most important contemporary accounts of Petty are by John Aubrey and John Evelyn; both are reprinted in Keynes' *Bibliography*, 85–95. The most detailed, and still essential, biography is Edmund George Petty Fitzmaurice, *The Life of Sir William Petty, 1623–1687* (London, 1895). Fitzmaurice also wrote the account in the *The Dictionary of National Biography*, new ed., XV, 999–1005. A very interesting recent biography is Eric Strauss, *Sir William Petty, Portrait of a Genius* (London–Glencoe, Ill., 1954), which includes a discussion of Petty's work.

Bacon and Hartlib's influence on Petty is admirably discussed in Walter E. Houghton, "The History of Trades: Its Relation to Seventeenth-Century Thought, as Seen in Bacon, Petty, Evelyn, and Boyle," in *Journal of the History of Ideas*, 2 (1941), 33–60, repr. in Philip P. Wiener and Aaron Noland, eds., *Roots of Scientific Thought, a Cultural Perspective* (New York, 1957), 354–381.

On Petty's participation in the beginnings of the Royal Society, see Thomas Sprat, *The History of the Royal-Society of London, for the Improving of Natural Knowledge* (London, 1667), facs. ed., Jackson I. Cope and Harold Whitmore Jones, eds. (St. Louis–London, 1958); Thomas Birch, *A History of the Royal Society for Improving of Natural Knowledge, From Its First Rise*, I (London, 1756); Irvine Masson and A. J. Youngson, "Sir William Petty, F.R.S. (1623–1687)," in *The Royal Society, Its Origins and Founders*, Harold Hartley, ed., (London, 1960), 79–90; and Margery Purver, *The Royal Society: Concept and Creation* (Cambridge, Mass., 1967).

On Petty's *Discourse Made Before the Royal Society the 26. of November 1674. Concerning the Use of Duplicate Proportion in Sundry Important Particulars: Together With a New Hypothesis of Springing or Elastique Motions*, see A. Wolf, F. Dannemann, A. Armitage, and Douglas McKie, *A History of Science, Technology and Philosophy in the 16th & 17th Centuries*, 2nd ed. (New York, 1950), 484; and Robert H. Kargon, "William Petty's Mechanical Philosophy," in *Isis*, 56 (1965), 63–66. On Petty's ships, see Lord Lansdowne's intro. to *The Double Bottom or Twin-Hulled Ship of Sir William Petty* (Oxford, 1931). On the relationship between science and technology in Petty's work, Hessen's famous arguments concerning Newton would for the most part apply; see Boris M. Hessen, "The Social and Economic Roots of Newton's 'Principia,'" in *Science at the Cross Roads: Papers Presented to the International Congress of the History of Science and Technology in London From June 20th to July 3rd, 1931 by the Delegates of the U.S.S.R.* (London, 1931), 151–176; repr. as separate book (New York, 1971).

On the Down Survey, see Petty's account mentioned above. On the census, see Pender's intro. to the volume cited above. The Down Survey, the maps, Petty's contributions to geography, and his career in Ireland are thoroughly and admirably discussed by Goblet (Tréguiz), *La transformation de la géographie politique.* See also his *A Topographical Index of the Parishes and Townlands of Ireland in Sir William Petty's MSS. Barony Maps* (*c. 1655–9*) (*Bibliothèque Nationale de Paris, fonds anglais, nos. 1 & 2*) *and Hiberniae Delineatio* (*c. 1672*) (Dublin, 1932); and Séan O'Domhnaill, "The Maps of the Down Survey," in *Irish Historical Studies*, 3 (1943), 381–392.

The authorship of Graunt's *Natural and Political Observations* has been discussed in C. H. Hull, ed., *Economic Writings of Sir William Petty*, I (Cambridge, 1899), xxxix–liv; Wilson Lloyd Bevan, "Sir William Petty. A Study in English Economic Literature," in *Publications of the American Economic Association*, 9, no. 4, (1894), 42–46; Lansdowne, *The Petty Papers*, II, 273–284, and *The Petty-Southwell Correspondence*, xxiii–xxxii; Major Greenwood, *Medical Statistics From Graunt to Farr* (Cambridge, 1948), 36–39; D. V. Glass, "John Graunt and His *Natural and Political Observations*," in *Notes and Records. Royal Society of London*, 19 (1964), 78–89, 97–100; P. D. Groenewegen, "Authorship of the *Natural and Political Observations Upon the Bills of Mortality*," in *Journal of the History of Ideas*, 28 (1967), 601–602; and Geoffrey Keynes, *A Bibliography of Sir William Petty* (Oxford, 1971), 75–77.

On Petty's contributions to demography and statistics, see Harald Westergaard, *Contributions to the History of Statistics* (London, 1932; facs. ed., New York, 1968), 28–31; Greenwood, *Medical Statistics*, 2–27; Wolf *et al.*, *A History of Science*, 429–430, 598–602; Tréguiz, *La transformation*, II, bk. 7; James Bonar, *Theories of Population From Raleigh to Arthur Young* (London, 1931; facs. ed., London, 1966), ch. 3; and Charles F. Mullett, "Sir William Petty on the Plague," in *Isis*, 28 (1938), 18–25. Petty's interest in the application of his demographic ideas in the United States is discussed in James H. Cassedy, *Demography in Early America: Beginnings of the Statistical Mind* (Cambridge, Mass., 1969).

On Petty's contributions to economics, see Bevan, *Sir William Petty*; Phyllis Deane, "William Petty," in *International Encyclopedia of the Social Sciences*, XII (1968), 66–68; William Letwin, *The Origins of Scientific Economics* (London, 1963; Garden City, N.Y., 1964), ch. 5; Walter Müller, *Sir William Petty als politischer Arithmetiker: Eine soziologisch-statistische Studie* (Gelnhausen, 1932); Maurice Pasquier, *Sir William Petty, ses idées économiques* (Paris, 1903); and Eric Roll, *A History of Economic Thought*, 2nd ed. (New York, 1942), 99–114.

FRANK N. EGERTON III

PEUERBACH, GEORG VON (*b.* Purbach, Austria, 30 May 1423; *d.* Vienna, Austria, 8 April 1461), *mathematics, astronomy.*

For a detailed study of his life and work, see Supplement.

PEYER, JOHANN CONRAD (*b.* Schaffhausen, Switzerland, 26 December 1653; *d.* Schaffhausen, 29 February 1712), *physiology.*

Born into a patrician family, Peyer studied medicine in Basel before becoming the pupil of J. Guichard du Verney at Paris and later of Vieussens at Montpellier. He then returned to his native Schaffhausen, where, with his teacher Johann Jakob Wepfer and the latter's son-in-law Johann Conrad Brunner, he formed the "Schaffhausen trio," whose important contributions to the new methodology of medical research were the explanation of symptoms by connecting them with the lesion in the body, considered as the site of the disease, and experimentation on animals (*anatomia animata*) to study either the functioning of organs or the effects of medicines on the organism. It is not always easy to determine the individual contribution of each member of the trio from their joint publications. In any case, after a ten-year collaboration through the 1680's Peyer quarreled with Wepfer and Brunner and spent the rest of his life as professor of logic, rhetoric, and medicine at the local Gymnasium.

A member of the Academia Naturae Curiosorum Sacra, Peyer sent, under the pseudonym Pythagoras, many letters to the Academy on the antiperistaltic movements of the intestine, cinchona bark, and other subjects.

The iatrochemical theories that were then dominant oriented scientists toward the study of digestion and the digestive system. Hence in 1682 Peyer described the lymphatic nodules and masses located in the walls of the ileum that now bear his name (or sometimes that of Johannes Nicolaus Pechlin, who in 1672 had described them in a work on the anatomy of the intestinal tract). According to William Cole, Severino had observed follicular regions in the small intestine of animals (1645).

Adenography was then in fashion, but the interpretation of the dissections is somewhat confusing today. In fact, the chemical phenomena of digestion were unknown, and the theory of the lymphatic system had barely been outlined. It was thought that the excretory canal of the pancreas was a chyliferous vessel originating in the intestine and entering the gland (Moritz Hofmann, 1641; J. G. Wirsung, 1642). C. Brunner attributed to the duodenal glands that now bear his name a role in the secretion of lymph. Thus it is not astonishing that Peyer supposed the ileal follicles to be glands excreting the digestive juices (E. Hintzsche, pp. 2401–2402).

Peyer also studied the stomach of ruminants in his *Merycologia* (1685) and the anatomy of normal and abnormal fetuses. He probably assisted Brunner in his pancreatectomies on dogs. These operations resulted in diabetes, but neither Peyer nor Brunner could interpret the results obtained (1683).

Wepfer—apparently the leader of the Schaffhausen trio—had written the first book on experimental toxicology, *Cicutae aquaticae historia et noxae commentario illustrata* (1679). He had been led to believe that the activity of the heart could be explained only by its special structure. Peyer attempted to confirm this hypothesis, either with his Schaffhausen friends or with his Basel friend J. J. Harder. In 1681 he succeeded in making the hearts of dead animals—and even of human beings who had been hanged—beat by blowing air into the veins or by utilizing other stimuli. Despite his imperfect technique he achieved an artificial cardiac activity lasting several hours. These experiments were repeated in 1702 by Baglivi, who studied the tonicity of the *fibra motrix*. He concluded from them that the heart died not from lack of nervous fluid but from lack of blood (M. D. Grmek, pp. 313–314). Later, supporters of the doctrine of irritability investigated this problem, taken up by Bidder. In his letters to Harder, Peyer revealed some of his other discoveries: hermaphroditism of the pulmonate snail and an epizootic disease that may have been foot-and-mouth disease.

BIBLIOGRAPHY

I. ORIGINAL WORKS. Peyer's writings include *Exercitatio anatomico-medica de glandulis intestinorum, earumque usu et affectionibus. Cui subjungitur anatome ventriculi gallinacei* (Schaffhausen, 1677); *Methodus historiarum anatomico-medicarum exemplo ascitis vitalium organorum vitio ex pericardii coalitu cum corde nato illustrata* (Paris, 1678); *Meditatio de valetudine humana* (Basel, 1681); *Parerga anatomica et medica septem* (Geneva, 1681); *Paeonis et Pythagorae exercitationes anatomicae et medicae familiares bis quinquaginta, Hecatombe non Hecatae sed illustri Academiae naturae curiosorum sacra* (Basel, 1682), 100 letters dated 12 Jan. 1677 to 8 July 1681 written by Peyer (Pythagoras) and Harder (Paeonis); *Merycologia sive de ruminantibus et ruminatione commentarius* (Basel, 1685); and *Observatio circa urachum in foetu humano pervium*, edited by his son Johan Jacob Peyer (Lyons, 1721).

II. SECONDARY LITERATURE. See E.-H. Ackerknecht, *Grands médecins suises de 1500 à 1900, Conférence du*

Palais de la Découverte D109 (Paris, 1966); Conrad Brunner and Wilhelm von Muralt, *Aus den Briefen hervorragender schweizer Ärzte des 17. Jahrhunderts* (Basel, 1919), 153–226; M. D. Grmek, "La notion de fibre vivante chez les médecins de l'école iatrophysique," in *Clio medica*, **5**, no. 4 (Dec. 1970), 297–318; E. Hintzsche, "Anatomia animata," in *Revue Ciba*, **69** (1948), 2395–2412; *Recherches, découvertes et inventions des médecins suisses* (Basel, n.d.); Robert Lang, *Das Collegium humanitatis in Schaffhausen*, I, *1648–1727* (Leipzig, 1893), 29 ff.; F. V. Mandach, "Über das klassische Werk des schweizer Arztes Joh. Conr. Peyer *De glandulis intestinorum*," in *Korrespondenzblatt für schweizer Ärzte*, **33** (1903), 445–450, 479–482; Bernhard Peyer and Heinrich Peyer, "Bildnis und Siegel des Arztes Johann Conrad Peyer," supp. to *Veröffentlichungen der Schweizerischen Gesellschaft für Geschichte der Medizin . . .*, **13** (1943); Bernhard Peyer-Amsler, "Johann Conrad Peyer 1653–1712," in Reinhard Frauenfelder, ed., *Geschichte der Familie Peyer mit den Wecken 1410–1932* (Zurich, 1932), 299–346—notes 1–7, pp. 333 f., list all the works dealing with Peyer's life and there is a facs. of a letter by Peyer on p. 323 (note [I] on Peyer also appeared as a supp. to *Veröffentlichungen der Schweizerischen Gesellschaft für Geschichte der Medizin . . .*, **8** [1932]); and H. E. Sigerist, "Die Verdienste zweier Schaffhauser Ärzte (J. C. Peyer und J. C. Brunner) um die Erforschung der Darmdrüsen," in *Verhandlungen der Schweizerischen naturforschenden Gesellschaft*, **102** (1921), 153 f.

PIERRE HUARD
M. J. IMBAULT-HUART

PEYSSONNEL, JEAN ANDRÉ (*b*. Marseilles, France, 19 June 1694; *d*. Guadeloupe, 24 December 1759), *botany, zoology*.

The eighth child of a physician at the Hôtel-Dieu in Marseilles, Peyssonnel visited the Antilles at the age of fifteen and Egypt three years later. He studied medicine at the University of Aix, where he defended his dissertation before a jury headed by his father. He began practice in Marseilles, which in 1720 suffered a severe epidemic of plague; Peyssonnel's efforts on behalf of the stricken were rewarded by a royal pension. During his year in Marseilles, Peyssonnel and some friends founded an academy devoted to belles lettres, in the tradition of the "ancient academy" of Marseilles.

A naturalist by inclination, Peyssonnel was interested in marine natural history. He observed the Mediterranean currents and studied corals, confirming the "flowering" established twenty years earlier by Count Luigi Marsigli. How the plant produced the red, stony portion, however, remained a mystery. Peyssonnel informed the president of the Paris Academy of Sciences, the Abbé Jean-Paul Bignon, of the progress of his research. In 1723 he became a correspondent of the Academy, to which he presented a paper on coral, which he then considered to be a flowering plant, in 1724.

Sent by the king to the Barbary Coast "to make discoveries in natural history" and to visit the country around Tunis and Algiers, Peyssonnel described his travels in letters to Bignon and in 1726 sent him two papers concerning his research on madrepores and other corals. The essence of his findings was that corals are not plants, but animals. The so-called flowers retract on contact with air but reappear when returned to the sea. It is animal matter, soft and milky, that covers the organism's stony parts. Further, Peyssonnel believed that "insects," such as the sea anemone, are also corals and madrepores. Peyssonnel's text, transmitted by Bignon to Réaumur, was read at the Academy on 8 and 28 June and 3 July 1726. Réaumur did not mention the author's name for fear of subjecting a distinguished person to ridicule: the idea seemed unacceptable to everyone, as Peyssonnel was informed in letters from Réaumur and Bernard de Jussieu.

Undaunted, Peyssonnel continued his studies in marine natural history. His pamphlet of 1726, *Mémoire sur les courans de la Méditerranée*, was the first work written on the Mediterranean currents. Distributed by the municipal magistrates of Marseilles to ship captains, it stimulated them to communicate their own observations.

In 1727 Peyssonnel departed for Guadeloupe as "royal botanist to the American islands." He spent the rest of his life on that island, where he married and fathered a son and several daughters. Although prevented by administrative difficulties from mining the sulfur of the Grande Soufrière volcano, which he had explored, he continued his research on marine life. His results provided him with complete confirmation of his earlier assertions, a fact he communicated in a letter of 1733 to Antoine de Jussieu.

In 1740 Trembley discovered the green hydra that Réaumur called a polyp, and the analogy with "marine plants" was cited. Guettard and Bernard de Jussieu confirmed, on the French coast, Peyssonnel's findings, and Réaumur admitted his own error (*Mémoires pour servir à l'histoire naturelle des insectes*, VI [1742], preface). Although he regained the esteem of the Academy, of which he was a corresponding member, it was to the Royal Society of London that Peyssonnel sent a manuscript on coral (in French). A résumé of it was presented to the Society on 7 May 1752 by W. Watson, who stressed the high quality of Peyssonnel's work (*Philosophical Transactions* [1753]). In 1756 Peyssonnel published in London a translation of Watson's article, supplemented by various writings on a plan to establish an annual prize at the Academy of Marseilles, to be awarded for the best paper on a subject in marine natural history. From 1756 until his death in 1759 he presented ten further articles recording his scientific observations to the Royal Society.

BIBLIOGRAPHY

I. ORIGINAL WORKS. Peyssonnel's published works are *La contagion de la peste expliquée et les moyens de s'en préserver, par le S***, Docteur en Médecine* (Marseilles, 1723); *Mémoire sur les courans de la Méditerranée* (Marseilles, 1726), 600 copies of which were printed at the expense of the Chambre de Commerce de Marseille, repr. in the 1756 collection under the title "Essai de physique ou conjectures fondées sur quelques observations qui peuvent conduire à la connaissance et à l'explication des courans de la mer Méditerranée"; and *Traduction d'un article des Transactions Philosophiques sur le Corail—Projet proposé à l'Académie de Marseille pour l'établissement d'un Prix . . . et réponse de l'Académie. Diverses observations sur les courants de la Mer, faites en différents endroits* (London, 1756).

II. SECONDARY LITERATURE. For the coral controversy see *Registre de l'Académie des sciences*, 8 and 28 June and 3 July 1725; "Sur le corail," in *Histoire de l'Académie royale des sciences* (1727), 37–39; Réaumur, "Observations sur la formation du corail et des autres productions appelées plantes pierreuses," in *Mémoires de l'Académie royale des sciences* (1727), 269–281; Bernard de Jussieu, "Examen de quelques productions marines qui ont été mises au nombre des plantes et qui sont l'ouvrage d'une sorte d'insectes de mer," *ibid.*, (1742), 290–302; Pierre Flourens, "Analyse d'un ouvrage manuscrit intitulé Traité du Corail," in *Annales Sc. nat. Zoologie*, ser. 2, **9** (1838), 334; and "Analyse d'un ouvrage manuscrit intitulé Traité du Corail par le Sieur de Peyssonnel," in *Journal des Savants* (Feb. 1838). See also Dureau de la Malle, Peyssonnel, and Desfontaines, *Voyages dans les Régences de Tunis et d'Alger* (Paris, 1838); Alfred Lacroix, "Notice historique sur les cinq de Jussieu," in *Mémoires de l'Institut*, **63** (1941), 24; and Noël Duval, "La solution d'une énigme: les Voyageurs Peyssonnel et Giménez à Sbeitla en 1724," in *Bull. Soc. Nat. Antiquaires France* (2 June 1965).

LUCIEN PLANTEFOL

PEZARD, ALBERT (*b.* Neuflize, Ardennes, France, 1 April 1875; *d.* Paris, France, 21 November 1927), *endocrinology.*

Pezard's parents were farmers. He studied at the École Normale of Charleville, then won admission to the École Normale of St.-Cloud. Several professors from the Sorbonne who taught at St.-Cloud soon found that Pezard was one of their most brilliant science students. He obtained his master's degree from the University of Paris with honors in both physical and natural sciences. His success in the difficult natural sciences *agrégation* made him eligible for a professorship at two renowned Paris *collèges*: Colbert and Jean-Baptiste Say. Pezard's teaching duties were time-consuming but he fulfilled them even after 1908, when he was active in biological investigation. His attraction to research was noticed by one of his former teachers at St.-Cloud, Charles Gravier, professor of zoology at the Muséum d'Histoire Naturelle, who recommended him to Émile Gley, professor at the Collège de France, one of the founders of endocrinology. Gley directed the Station Physiologique du Collège de France, and Pezard was soon elected associate director of the station, where he worked for nearly twenty years.

Pezard first studied the physiological conditioning of the secondary sexual characters in birds. Full publication of his findings, in his doctoral dissertation, was delayed until 1918 by his military duties during World War I. The dissertation contained many new results, such as Pezard's establishment of the true secondary sexual characters in the male bird. He showed their strict dependence upon an endocrine secretion, since castration brings their immediate regression, and gave a simple but accurate algebraic expression of this regression. He also deduced from the effects of total castration of females that the ovary normally secretes a substance that inhibits the evolution of plumage and the development of spurs. This was the first demonstration of the inhibitory action of an endocrine secretion.

In his pioneer study on the experimental production of sexual inversion and hermaphroditism Pezard defined the conditions required for the grafting of testicular transplants. With this procedure he showed that a minimal, or threshold, amount of the specific hormone must be secreted in order to elicit a given secondary sexual character, each character responding to a different threshold amount. Thus Pezard introduced into endocrinology the "all or none" law, classical in other domains of physiology. In 1922 Pezard began the most active years of his scientific life, working closely with Fernand Caridroit and with Knud Sand of Copenhagen. Their papers, treating the experimental production of gynandromorphic hens, demonstrate the important implication of their results for genetics. They concluded that hormones obviously do not interfere with the fundamental genotypic complex, but act as regulators of dominances. These hormones operate, as in sex, not as creating agents but as exteriorization factors.

They neither destroy existing genes nor provide new genes.

Pezard's work, which exerted a marked influence on biologists, found artistic expression in his creation of strange and beautiful birds, such as hens decorated with a cock's brilliant feathers and proud comb. His reputation was great outside France, which failed to give him a university professorship and left him to teach high school pupils.

BIBLIOGRAPHY

Pezard's writings include "Sur la détermination des caractères sexuels secondaires chez les Gallinacés," in *Comptes rendus hebdomadaires des séances de l'Académie des sciences*, **153** (1911), 1027–1030; "Sur la détermination des caractères sexuels secondaires chez les Gallinacés, greffe de testicule et castration post-pubérale," *ibid.*, **154** (1912), 1183–1186; "Développement expérimental des ergots et croissance de la crête chez les femelles des Gallinacés," *ibid.*, **158** (1914), 513–516; "Transformation expérimentale des caractères sexuels secondaires chez les femelles des Gallinacés," *ibid.*, **160** (1915), 260–263; "Loi numérique de la régression des organes érectiles consécutive à la castration post-pubérale," *ibid.*, **164** (1917), 234–236; *Le conditionnement physiologique des caractères sexuels secondaires chez les Oiseaux* (Paris 1918); Édition du Bulletin Biologique de la France et de la Belgique; "Facteur modificateur de la croissance normale et loi de compensation," in *Comptes rendus hebdomadaires des séances de l'Académie des sciences*, **169** (1919), 997-1000; "Castration alimentaire chez les Coqs soumis au régime carné exclusif," *ibid.*, 1177–1180; "Secondary Sexual Characteristics and Endocrinology," in *Endocrinology*, **4** (1920), 527–541; "Castration intrapubéale et généralisation de la loi parabolique de régression," in *Comptes rendus hebdomadaires des séances de l'Académie des sciences*, **171** (1920), 1081–1084; "Loi du 'tout ou rien' ou de constance fonctionelle du testicule considéré comme glande à sécrétion interne," *ibid.*, **172** (1921), 89–91; and "Temps de latence dans les expériences de transplantation testiculaire et loi du 'tout ou rien,'" *ibid.*, 176–179.

See also "Numerical Law of Regression of Certain Secondary Sex Characters," in *Journal of General Physiology*, **9** (1921), 271–283; "Notion de 'seuil différentiel' et explication humorale du gynandromorphisme des Oiseaux bipartis," in *Comptes rendus hebdomadaires des séances de l'Académie des sciences*, **174** (1922), 1573–1576; "Notion de seuil différentiel et masculinisation progressive de certaines femelles d'oiseaux," *ibid.*, **175** (1922), 236–239; "Interpénétration testiculaire chez les Coqs castrés incomplètement," *ibid.*, 284–287, written with Caridroit; "L'hérédité sex-linked chez les Gallinacés. Interprétation fondée sur l'existence de la forme neutre et sur les propriétés de l'hormone ovarienne," *ibid.*, 910–913, written with Caridroit; "L'action de l'hormone testiculaire sur la valence relative des facteurs allélomorphes chez les Ovins," *ibid.*, 1099–1102, written with Caridroit; "La loi du 'tout ou rien.' Exposé général," in *Journal de physiologie et de pathologie générale*, **20** (1922), 200–211; "La loi du 'tout ou rien' et le gynandromorphisme endocrinien," *ibid.*, 495–508; "Caractères sexuels secondaires et tissus interstitiels," in *Comptes rendus de la Société de biologie*, **88** (1923), 245–248; "Critique de la théorie de Bouin et Ancel," *ibid.*, 333–336; "Féminisation d'un Coq adulte Leghorn doré," *ibid.*, **89** (1923), 947–950, written with Sand and Caridroit; "Le gynandromorphisme biparti experimental," *ibid.*, 1103–1106, written with Sand and Caridroit; and "Gynandromorphisme biparti fragmentaire d'origine mâle," *ibid.*, 1271–1274, written with Sand and Caridroit.

See also "Productions expérimentales du gynandromorphisme biparti chez les Oiseaux," in *Comptes rendus hebdomadaires des séances de l'Académie des sciences*, **176** (1923), 615–618, written with Sand and Caridroit; "Les modalités du gynandromorphisme chez les Oiseaux," *ibid.*, **177** (1923), 76–79, written with Caridroit; "Modifications raciales par greffe ovarienne chez les Coqs," in *Comptes rendus de la Société de biologie*, **40** (1924), 737–740, written with Sand and Caridroit; "Poecilandrie d'origine endocrinienne chez les Gallinacés," *ibid.*, **90** (1924), 676–679, written with Sand and Caridroit; "Potentialités homologues et potentialités hétérologues chez la Poule domestique," *ibid.*, 737–740; "Les effets de la castration sur le plumage du Coq domestique," *ibid.*, 677–680; "Remarques au sujet de l'hérédité sex-linked chez les Gallinacés," *ibid.*, 935–938, written with Caridroit; "Survie d'un transplant testiculaire actif en présence d'un ovaire producteur d'oeufs mûrs chez la Poule domestique," *ibid.*, 1459–1462; "Évolution et fonction d'un transplant ovarien chez un Coq adulte Leghorn doré," *ibid.*, **91** (1924), 1075–1078, written with Sand and Caridroit; and "Le gynandromorphisme en mosaïque et les dysharmonies endocriniennes chez les Gallinacés," *ibid.*, 1116–1119, written with Sand and Caridroit.

See also "Modifications hormono-sexuelles chez les Gallinacés adultes et théorie de la forme spécifique," in *Comptes rendus hebdomadaires des séances de l'Académie des sciences*, **178** (1924), 2011–2014, written with Sand and Caridroit; "Le gynandromorphisme biparti expérimental. Récurrences raciales dictées par la mue automnale et caractéres transitoires de certaines modifications pigmentaires," *ibid.*, **177** (1924), 1087–1090, written with Sand and Caridroit; "Le gynandromorphisme expérimental et le non antagonisme des glandes sexuelles chez les Gallinacés adultes," in *Comptes rendus de la Société de biologie*, **92** (1925), 427–430, written with Sand and Caridroit; "L'évolution des potentialités chez la Poulette," *ibid.*, 495–498; "Une notion nouvelle, l'existence d'un seuil différentiel racial dans certains complexes hybrides des Gallinacés," *ibid.*, 566–569, written with Sand and Caridroit; "Le gynandromorphisme périodique chez un Coq adulte," *ibid.*, 1034–1037, written with Sand and Caridroit; "Inversion sexuelle du plumage observées chez nos sujets lors de la récente mue et notion du seuil hormonique," *ibid.*, **93** (1925), 1094–1096, written with Sand and

Caridroit; "Quelques faits nouveaux concernant les greffes d'ovaires effectuées sur le Coq domestique," *ibid.*, **94** (1926), 520–523, written with Sand and Caridroit; "Analyse de quelques déviations sexuelles secondaires chez les Gallinacés," *ibid.*, 741–744, written with Caridroit; "La bipartition longitudinale de la plume, faits nouveaux concernant le gynandromorphisme élémentaire," *ibid.*, 1074–1078, written with Caridroit; and "La présence de l'hormone testiculaire dans le sang d'un Coq normal. Démonstration directe fondée sur la greffe autoplastique de crétillons," *ibid.*, **95** (1926), 296–300, written with Caridroit.

See further "Les hormones sexuelles et le gynandromorphisme chez les Gallinacés," in *Archives de biologie*, 36 (1927), 541–647, written with Sand and Caridroit; "Les caractères sexuels secondaires," in Masson's *Traité de physiologie*, XI (Paris, 1927), 125–163; "Inversion sexuelle autonome d'une Cane de Rouen," in *Comptes rendus de la Société de biologie*, **96** (1927), 1295–1298, written with Caridroit; "Classement des seuils différentiels du plumage chez la poule domestique," *ibid.*, 1372–1375, written with Caridroit; "Remarques concernant la loi du 'tout ou rien,' " *ibid.*, **97** (1927), 442–446; "État actuel de la théorie de l'interstitielle," *ibid.*, 620–623; "Die Bestimmung des Geschlechtsfunktion bei den Hühnern," in *Ergebnisse der Physiologie*, 27 (1928), 552–656; and *La détermination de la fonction sexuelle chez les Gallinacés*, Masson, ed. (Paris, 1930).

A. M. MONNIER

PEZENAS, ESPRIT (*b.* Avignon, France, 28 November 1692; *d.* Avignon, 4 February 1776), *hydrography, astronomy, physics.*

Pezenas was the son of E. F. Pezenas, a notary and court clerk, and Gabrielle de Rivières. He entered the Jesuit *collège* in Avignon at the age of ten and began his novitiate when he was seventeen. At the conclusion of his studies he taught first in Lyons and then at the Jesuit *collège* in Aix. (He taught physics in 1724 and 1726, logic in 1725, and metaphysics in 1727.) In 1728 Pezenas was named professor of hydrography at the École Royale d'Hydrographie at Marseilles and was assigned to teach the galley officers. He held this post until the school was closed in 1749, when he was appointed director of the Observatoire Ste.-Croix in Marseilles, a Jesuit establishment that later became Observatoire Royal de la Marine. In 1763, upon the suppression of the Jesuit order in France, Pezenas retired to Avignon, where he died at the age of eighty-three. He was a member of the Académie de Marine and, from 1750, a corresponding member of the Académie Royale des Sciences.

Besides giving highly regarded lectures, Pezenas published a number of works on hydrography and sailing. Notable among these were treatises on piloting, a work on gauging barrels and ships, and several treatises on nautical astronomy in which he set forth innovations in the use of such instruments as the vernier, the azimuth compass, and the octant. His interest in the determination of longitudes led to several papers on the subject. Assigned to design and estimate the cost of a canal that would supply Marseilles with water taken from the Durance River, he conducted the necessary surveying. Meanwhile, he had also become increasingly interested in astronomical observation. He paid for some of his observatory equipment, and in 1749 the king granted him the services of two associate astronomers, both Jesuits. He presented his first observations (including the determination of the latitude of Marseilles) in 1731 in the *Mémoires de Trévoux* (*Mémoires pour servir à l'histoire des sciences et des beaux arts*); the others appeared in *Histoire de l'Académie Royale des Sciences*.

Pezenas played a major role in the diffusion in France of important works by English scientists, especially in mathematics and optics. Although his scientific achievements were modest, Pezenas was an effective popularizer who made skillful use of the scientific and technical knowledge of his time.

BIBLIOGRAPHY

I. ORIGINAL WORKS. Pezenas's main publications are listed in J. M. Quérard, *La France littéraire*, VII (Paris, 1835), 111–112; Poggendorff, II, 422–423; and A. de Backer, A. de Backer, and C. S. Sommervogel, *Bibliothèque de la Compagnie de Jésus*, VI (Brussels–Paris, 1845), 647.

His principal works are *Éléments de pilotage* (Marseilles, 1733); *Pratique du pilotage* (Marseilles, 1741); *La théorie et la pratique du jaugeage* (Avignon, 1749); *Astronomie des marins* . . . (Avignon, 1766); and *Histoire critique de ia découverte des longitudes* (Avignon, 1775). In addition, several of his papers are in *Mémoires de mathématique et de physique rédigés à l'Observatoire de Marseille*, 2 vols. (Avignon, 1755–1756).

Among the most important translations by Pezenas are C. Maclaurin's *Traité des fluxions*, 2 vols. (Paris, 1749), and *Éléments d'algèbre* (Paris, 1750); J. T. Desaguliers's *Cours de physique expérimentale*, 2 vols. (Paris, 1751); H. Baker's *Traité du microscope* (Paris, 1754); John Ward's *Guide des jeunes mathématiciens* (Paris, 1756); J. Harrison's *Principes de la montre* . . . (Avignon, 1767); R. Smith's *Cours complet d'optique*, 2 vols. (Avignon, 1767); and W. Gardiner's *Tables de logarithmes* (Avignon, 1770).

II. SECONDARY LITERATURE. Besides the bibliographical articles cited above, the principal studies of Pezenas's life and work are the following, listed chronologically:

J. Lalande, "Éloge du P. Pezenas," in *Journal des sçavans* (1779), 569–571, repr. in *Bibliographie astronomique* (Paris, 1803), see index; J. B. Delambre, in *Biographie universelle*, XXXIII (1823), 563–565, also in new ed., XXXII (1861), 663–664; P. Levot, in F. Hoefer, ed., *Nouvelle biographie générale*, XXXIX (1862), cols. 791–792; and B. Aoust, in *Mémoires de l'Académie des sciences, lettres et beaux-arts de Marseille*, ser. 2, **20** (1870), 1–16. Details concerning various aspects of Pezenas's work can be found in R. Taton, ed., *Enseignement et diffusion des sciences en France au XVIIIe siècle* (Paris, 1964), see index.

JULIETTE TATON

PFAFF, JOHANN FRIEDRICH (*b.* Stuttgart, Germany, 22 December 1765; *d.* Halle, Germany, 21 April 1825), *mathematics*.

Pfaff came from a distinguished family of Württemberg civil servants. His father, Burkhard Pfaff, was chief financial councillor and his mother was the only daughter of a member of the consistory and of the exchequer; Johann Friedrich was the second of their seven sons.

The sixth son, Christoph Heinrich (1773–1852), did work of considerable merit in chemistry, medicine, and pharmacy. He also investigated "animal electricity" with Volta, Humboldt, and others. Pfaff's youngest brother, Johann Wilhelm Andreas (1774–1835), distinguished himself in several areas of science, especially in mathematics, and became professor of mathematics at the universities of Würzburg and Erlangen; but the rapid changes in his scientific interests prevented him from attaining the importance of Johann Friedrich.

As the son of a family serving the government of Württemberg, Pfaff went to the Hohe Karlsschule in Stuttgart at the age of nine. The school, which was well-administered but subject to a harsh military discipline, served chiefly to train Württemberg's government officials and superior officers. Pfaff completed his legal studies there in the fall of 1785.

On the basis of mathematical knowledge that he acquired by himself, Pfaff soon progressed to reading Euler's *Introductio in analysin infinitorum*. In the fall of 1785, at the urging of Karl Eugen, the duke of Württemberg, he began a journey to increase his scientific knowledge. He remained at the University of Göttingen for about two years, studying mathematics with A. G. Kaestner and physics with G. C. Lichtenberg. In the summer of 1787 he traveled to Berlin, in order to improve his skill in practical astronomy with J. E. Bode. While in Berlin, on the recommendation of Lichtenberg, Pfaff was admitted to the circle of followers of the Enlightenment around Friedrich Nicolai. In the spring of 1788 he traveled to Vienna by way of Halle, Jena, Helmstedt, Gotha, Dresden, and Prague.

Through the recommendation of Lichtenberg, Pfaff was appointed full professor of mathematics at the University of Helmstedt as a replacement for Klügel, who had been called to Halle. Pfaff assumed the rather poorly paid post with the approval of the duke of Württemberg.

At first Pfaff directed all his attention to teaching, with evident success: the number of mathematics students grew considerably. Gauss, after completing his studies at Göttingen (1795–1798), attended Pfaff's lectures and, in 1798, lived in Pfaff's house. Pfaff recommended Gauss's doctoral dissertation and, when necessary, greatly assisted him; Gauss always retained a friendly memory of Pfaff both as a teacher and as a man.

While in Helmstedt, Pfaff aided students whose talents he recognized. For example, he was a supporter of Humboldt following his visit to Helmstedt and he recommended him to professors at Göttingen. During this period he also formed an enduring friendship with the historian G. G. Bredow. Their plan to edit all the fragments of Pappus of Alexandria progressed no further than a partial edition (Book 4 of the *Collectio*) done by Bredow alone.

In 1803 Pfaff married Caroline Brand, a maternal cousin. Their first son died young; the second, Carl, who edited a portion of his father's correspondence, became an historian, but his career was abbreviated by illness.

A serious threat to Pfaff's academic career emerged at the end of the eighteenth century, when plans were discussed for closing the University of Helmstedt. This economy measure was postponed—in no small degree as a result of Pfaff's interesting essay "Über die Vorteile, welche eine Universität einem Lande gewährt" (Häberlins *Staatsarchiv* [1796], no. 2)—but in 1810 the university was in the end closed. The faculty members were transferred to Göttingen, Halle, and Breslau. Pfaff went to Halle at his own request, again as professor of mathematics. After Klügel's death in 1812 he also took over the direction of the observatory there.

Pfaff's early work was strongly marked by Euler's influence. In his *Versuch einer neuen Summationsmethode . . .* (1788) he uncritically employed divergent series in his treatment of Fourier expansions. In editing Euler's posthumous writings (1792) and in the inaugural essay traditionally presented by new professors at Helmstedt—"programma inaugurale, in quo peculiaris differentialis investigandi ratio

ex theoria functionum deducitur" (1788)—as well as in 1795, Pfaff investigated series of the form

$$\sum_{k=1}^{n} \arctan \frac{f(k+1) - f(k)}{1 + f(k) \cdot f(k+1)}.$$

A friend of K. F. Hindenburg, the leader of the German combinatorial school, Pfaff prepared a series of articles between 1794 and 1800 for *Archiv der reinen und angewandten Mathematik* and *Sammlung combinatorisch-analytischer Abhandlungen*, which were edited by Hindenburg. The articles consistently reflect the long-winded way of thinking and expression of Hindenburg's school, with the single exception of "Analysis einer wichtigen Aufgabe des Herrn La Grange" (1794), which sought to free the Taylor expansion (with the remainder in Lagrange's form) from the tradition that embedded it in the theory of combinations and instead to present it as a primary component of analysis.

In 1797 Pfaff published at Helmstedt the first and only volume of an introductory treatise on analysis written in the spirit of Euler: *Disquisitiones analyticae maxime ad calculum integralem et doctrinam serierum pertinentes*. In 1810 he participated in the solution of a problem originating with Gauss that concerned the ellipse of greatest area that can be inscribed in a given quadrilateral. This led him to investigate conic pencils of rays.

Pfaff presented his most important mathematical achievement, the theory of Pfaffian forms, in "Methodus generalis, aequationes differentiarum partialium, necnon aequationes differentiales vulgares, utrasque primi ordinis, inter quotcunque variabiles, complete integrandi," which he submitted to the Berlin Academy on 11 May 1815. Although it was printed in the *Abhandlungen* of the Berlin Academy (1814–1815) and received an exceedingly favorable review by Gauss, the work did not become widely known. Its importance was not appreciated until 1827, when it appeared with a paper by Jacobi, "Über Pfaff's Methode, eine gewöhnliche lineare Differentialgleichung zwischen 2 n Variabeln durch ein System von n Gleichungen zu integrieren" (*Journal für die reine und angewandte Mathematik*, **2**, 347 ff.).

Pfaff's "Methodus" constituted the starting point of a basic theory of integration of partial differential equations which, through the work of Jacobi, Lie, and others, has developed into the modern Cartan calculus of extreme differential forms. (On this subject see, for example, C. Carathéodory, *Variationsrechnung und partielle Differentialgleichungen 1. Ordnung*, I [Leipzig, 1956].)

The core of the method that Pfaff made available

can be described as follows: In the title of the "Methodus" the expression "aequationes differentialis vulgares" appears; by this Pfaff meant equations of the form

$$\sum_{i=1}^{n} \varphi_i(x_1, x_2, \cdots, x_n)\, dx_i = 0,$$

the left side of which, in modern terminology, is a differential form in n variables (Pfaffian form). The equation itself is called a Pfaffian equation. Now, by means of a first-order partial differential equation in $n+1$ variables,

$$F(x_1, x_2, \cdots, x_n; z; p_1, p_2, \cdots, p_n) = 0,$$

where the partial derivatives

$$p_i = \frac{\partial z}{\partial x_i}, \qquad i = 1, 2, \cdots, n,$$

one can easily transform the equation

$$dz - \sum_{i=1}^{n} p_i\, dx_i = 0$$

into a Pfaffian equation in $2n$ variables by eliminating dz.

The significance of the reduction of a partial differential equation to a Pfaffian equation had previously been recognized by Euler and Lagrange. The reduction could not be exploited, however, for lack of an integration theory of the Pfaffian forms which would be valid for all n; it was this deficiency that Pfaff's "Methodus" in large measure remedied. Gauss justifiably emphasized this aspect of Pfaff's work in his review in *Göttingische gelehrte Anzeigen* (1815).

Pfaff's theory is based on a transformation theorem that in current terminology, and going a little beyond Pfaff, can be stated in the following manner: A Pfaffian form $\sum_{i=1}^{n} \varphi_i\, dx_i$ with an even number of variables can be transformed, by means of a factor $\rho(x_1, x_2, \cdots, x_n)$ into a Pfaffian form of $n-1$ variables. Moreover, for the case $n=2$, ρ is simply the Euler multiplier or integrating factor of the differential equation $\varphi_1\, dx_1 + \varphi_2\, dx_2 = 0$. For $\sum_{i=1}^{4} \varphi_i\, dx_i$, therefore, there is a multiplier ρ, so that $\rho \sum_{i=1}^{4} \varphi_i\, dx_i$ can be written in the form $\sum_{i=1}^{3} \psi_i(y_1, y_2, y_3)\, dy_i$ and the y_i's are independent functions of $x_1, \cdots, x_4$.

For a Pfaffian form with an odd number of variables there is in general no corresponding multiplier that will enable one to reduce the number of variables.

In the 1827 article cited above, Jacobi later provided a suitable method of reduction: a Pfaffian form $\sum_{i=1}^{n} \varphi_i\, dx_i$ with an odd number of variables can, through subtraction of a differential dw, which is always reducible by means of the transformation $x_i = f_i(y_1, y_2, \cdots, y_{n-1}, t)$ $i = 1, 2, \cdots, n$, be brought to the form $\sum_{i=1}^{n-1} \psi_i\, dy_i$, where the ψ_i's are functions of the y_i's.

Through alternately employing transformation (following Pfaff) and reduction (following Jacobi) one can finally bring every Pfaffian form with arbitrary number of variables into a canonical form: for $n = 2p$, into the form $z_1\, dz_2 + z_3\, dz_4 + \cdots + dz_{2p-1}\, dz_{2p}$; and for $n = 2p + 1$, into the form $dz_1 + dz_2, dz_3 + \cdots + z_{2p}\, dz_{2p+1}$.

Lie later gave the relationship between partial differential equations and Pfaffian forms a geometrical interpretation that possessed a greater intuitive clarity than the analytic approach.

BIBLIOGRAPHY

I. ORIGINAL WORKS. There is a list of Pfaff's writings in Poggendorff, II, cols. 424–425. They include *Versuch einer neuen Summationsmethode nebst anderen damit zusammenhängenden analytischen Bemerkungen* (Berlin, 1788); "Analysis einer wichtigen Aufgabe des Herrn La Grange," in Hindenburg's *Archiv der reinen und angewandten Mathematik*, **1** (1794), 81–84; *Disquisitiones analyticae maxime ad calculum integralem et doctrinam serierum pertinentes* (Helmstedt, 1797); "Methodus generalis, aequationes differentiarum partialium, necnon aequationes differentiales vulgares, utrasque primi ordinis, inter quotcunque variabiles complete integrandi," in *Abhandlungen der Preussischen Akademie der Wissenschaften* (1814–1815), 76–135, also translated into German by G. Kowalewski as no. 129 in Ostwald's Klassiker der exakten Wissenschaften (Leipzig, 1902); and *Sammlung von Briefen, gewechselt zwischen Johann Friedrich Pfaff...*, Carl Pfaff, ed. (Leipzig, 1853).

II. SECONDARY LITERATURE. See G. Kowalewski, *Grosse Mathematiker*, 2nd ed. (Munich–Berlin, 1939), 228–247; and Carl Pfaff's biographical introduction to his ed. of his father's correspondence, pp. 1–35. Also see articles on Pfaff in *Neuer Nekrolog der Deutschen*, **3** (1825), 1415–1418; and *Allgemeine deutsche Biographie*, XXV (Leipzig, 1887), 592–593.

H. WUSSING

PFEFFER, WILHELM FRIEDRICH PHILIPP (*b.* Grebenstein, near Kassel, Germany, 9 March 1845; *d.* Leipzig, Germany, 31 January 1920), *botany, chemistry.*

Pfeffer was the son of Wilhelm Pfeffer, an apothecary in Grebenstein, and Luise Theobald, whose family was associated with the clergy. His parents intended him to be the third successor to the apothecary shop founded by his great-grandfather; and even after several years of university study, Pfeffer still planned to enter the profession of pharmacy. He thus made sure of a strong background in chemistry, physics, and botany; and his theoretical studies and practical experience in preparation for such a career provided him with broad insight as well as techniques that would become useful in fine experimentation when he turned his full attention to botany, and especially to plant physiology.

Pfeffer attended the grammar school in Grebenstein until he was twelve; then, after additional private instruction, he entered the electoral Gymnasium near Kassel. Three years later (before he had completed his Gymnasium studies) his father took him into the apothecary shop as an apprentice. Pfeffer's father, a man of broad scientific interests, had a large herbarium and had gathered extensive collections in many fields of the natural sciences; he also wrote a textbook (unpublished) of pharmaceutical chemistry and corresponded with scientists in Germany and abroad. He supplemented his son's education in many ways and imbued him with his own enthusiasm for the study of nature. Pfeffer received an early introduction to botany by accompanying his father on expeditions into the nearby countryside, and at the age of six he was pressing flowers and collecting specimens for several of his own collections. The scope of Pfeffer's explorations was considerably widened when, at the age of twelve, he began to make excursions into the high Alps with his uncle Gottfried Theobald, whose geological and botanical trips kindled the boy's enthusiasms still further while also developing his ability as an alpinist. Pfeffer was fearless about searching in difficult locations for certain mosses and rare plant specimens, and he became one of the earliest to climb the Matterhorn. After his marriage (1884) to Henrika Volk, Pfeffer avoided such hazardous mountaineering, although visiting the Alps was always his favorite vacation.

As an apprentice to his father, Pfeffer prepared plants and herbs and ground ingredients, made up chemicals and medicinal preparations, and was responsible for various analyses. He also maintained the shop, which dispensed not only pharmaceutical chemicals but sold homemade candies, cleansers, and even shoe polish prepared on the premises. Pfeffer also used his father's microscope to examine the fine structure of various specimens of seeds, fibers, and starches; these observations were aided by texts on the microscope and Mohl's *Grundzüge der Anatomie und Physiologie der vegetabilischen Zelle.* After passing the examination for apothecary's assistant, Pfeffer entered the University of Göttingen to study chemistry and prepare for a career in pharmacy.

At Göttingen Pfeffer attended lectures in physics, chemistry, zoology, and botany; and although his atypical preparation for the university had left deficiencies which he now strove to remedy, he was able to begin a dissertation in chemistry shortly after his matriculation at the age of eighteen. He submitted this work, "Über einige Derivative des Glyzerins und dessen Überführung in Allylen," and received his doctorate in chemistry and botany in early February 1865, having spent barely four semesters at Göttingen.

In the summer of the same year, at Marburg, Pfeffer continued his pharmaceutical studies and for the time being set aside consideration of an academic career, thus following his father's wishes. He then received an assistantship at an apothecary in Augsburg and later in Chur, where his uncle still taught in the canton school. Pfeffer resumed alpine climbing with his uncle and gathered the mosses that were to be the subjects of his first papers. He subsequently returned to the University of Marburg and in December 1868 passed the examination qualifying him for the profession of apothecary, as his father had desired. He now became more certain, however, of his preference for an academic career in botany. Encouraged by the botanist Albert Wigand, Pfeffer studied the development of blossoms; he then went to Berlin at the end of the next summer and obtained a much sought-after place in Pringsheim's private laboratory, where the activity centered about investigations of the developmental history of plants. Here Pfeffer began his studies of the germination of *Selaginella.* He continued this work in Würzburg under the plant physiologist Julius von Sachs, who encouraged Pfeffer to direct his researches to problems in plant physiology. He thus studied the effects of light from different parts of the spectrum on the decomposition of carbon dioxide in plants and analyzed some of the effects of external stimuli on the growth of plants. The chemistry and physics he had previously studied were already of great help to Pfeffer, and he presented some of this work for his habilitation at Marburg.

In March 1871 Pfeffer was appointed *Privatdozent* at Marburg, where he investigated protein metabolism in plants and was especially concerned with the formation and diffusion of asparagine. He also began extensive researches, which continued for many years, on irritability in plants, studying movements due to irritability in the "sensitive plant," *Mimosa pudica,* and the staminal filaments of Cynareae. From his observations of irritability phenomena and his understanding of their broad implications, Pfeffer undertook his classic investigations of osmosis, with a view toward explaining the basic causes and mechanisms of such manifestations. Pfeffer's osmotic investigations were first pursued at Marburg and continued at the University of Bonn, where, in 1873, he was appointed professor extraordinarius of pharmacy and botany. He made the first direct measurements of osmotic pressures in plants during these studies, which, published in his *Osmotische Untersuchungen* (Leipzig, 1877), were to provide van't Hoff with the values for his calculations. Thus Pfeffer's work was invaluable in the development of the theory of solution, itself a landmark in the history of physical chemistry.

At Bonn, where he was also custodian of the Botanical Institute, Pfeffer's various researches included studies of the periodic movements of leaf organs. In 1877 he was appointed professor of botany at the University of Basel, but in the fall of 1878 he accepted a post at the University of Tübingen. During nine years here he investigated plant irritability and respiration. His work on chemotaxis, which evolved from this period, demonstrated the attraction of certain specific substances for the small, free-swimming organisms he was studying: it appeared that malic acid drew the spermatozoids of ferns and *Selaginella* to the archegonium, for they were as readily drawn to the capillary tubes that Pfeffer filled with this solution. In certain mosses Pfeffer discovered that a similar stimulus was exerted by a cane-sugar solution. He also found chemotropism in bacteria, flagellates, and various other organisms.

In 1881 Pfeffer published his comprehensive *Pflanzenphysiologie*, which became a well-known reference work. It presented not only a mine of information but also a view of Pfeffer's aims and philosophy as a physiologist studying fundamental life processes with plants as his subjects. His investigations probed all implications indefatigably, and he was ingenious at devising apparatus for acute measurements and various laboratory experiments. Pfeffer followed specific phenomena in his search for ultimate causes. He was convinced that changes in energy underlay the processes of plant life and that the phenomena of life, if penetrated, would be understood "as the natural consequences of given conditions." Yet he stressed the complexities of life processes: Within each cell there were constellations of still finer organizations and chains of interrelated reactions, and within each organ there were intricately correlated relationships. In the living organism there was a cooperation and self-regulation of the whole; following disturbances, this relationship tended to restore the previous equilibrium or establish a new state.

Students from both Germany and abroad entered Pfeffer's botanical laboratory at Tübingen, where they found a unique combination in his personal stimulus to their researches and the chance to work with a teacher whose knowledge of physics and chemistry had enabled him to pursue a range of microchemical and other investigations and to construct fine physical apparatus. Pfeffer was unmatched in setting up instrumentation to measure plant movements, growth, and osmotic pressure, and to pursue other observations toward the solution of complex problems of plant physiology. He had a penchant for theorizing, for exploring the range of possibilities, and for exactitude. His students' papers and some of his own appeared in the *Untersuchungen aus dem botanischen Institut zu Tübingen* (1881–1888).

In 1887 Pfeffer was appointed professor of botany at the University of Leipzig, where he was again active in teaching and busy with administrative duties and was the director of the Botanical Institute. His responsibilities were increased in 1895 when, following the death of Pringsheim, he became coeditor with Eduard Strasburger of the *Jahrbuch für wissenschaftliche Botanik*.

Pfeffer was a member of many leading societies, both German and foreign; and his honors included degrees from the universities of Halle, Königsberg, and Oslo. Cambridge University awarded him the honorary degree of doctor in science in 1898.

At Leipzig the number of Pfeffer's students grew; they came from many countries, and many were from the United States. A stimulating teacher in the laboratory, he enlivened his lectures with demonstrations and made use of projection apparatus. In a container for the purpose, students placed slips with questions he would answer at botanical club meetings, and surreptitiously Pfeffer added challenging questions of his own. In 1915, at the age of seventy, a *Festschrift* of the *Jahrbücher für wissenschaftliche Botanik* was dedicated to Pfeffer. (Among his former students named in the volume were Carl Correns and Wilhelm Johannsen.) In the same year a special issue of *Naturwissenschaften* commemorated Pfeffer's scientific contributions.

The last years of Pfeffer's life, however, were deeply troubled and unhappy: He had become increasingly affected by feelings of depression; the brutality of the war haunted him, and he was apprehensive about the political and social changes he witnessed in Germany. His only son was killed less than two months before the armistice.

Many of Pfeffer's investigations were basic to plant physiology. His work on the role of asparagine was controversial but nevertheless an advance in the study of plant metabolism when viewed in a historical context. He made extensive contributions to the study of irritability in plants by investigating the movements of leaves, the opening and closing of flowers, the influences of variations of light and of temperature, the effects of tactile stimuli, and the physiology of transmission in irritability phenomena. He also studied the sleep movements of plants. Using aniline dyes, he pioneered the method of vital staining and followed the assimilation and accumulation of various dyes within the living cell.

Abbé Nollet, in 1748, was the first to explain osmosis; and as Pfeffer noted, the phenomenon had been "rediscovered" several times. Moritz Traube had even constructed semipermeable precipitation membranes and used them in studying the cell. While searching for the causes of the extremely high osmotic pressures he had observed in plants, Pfeffer improved upon Traube's membranes. After trying methods that similarly produced membranes that were too fragile and burst under pressure, Pfeffer devised his *Pfeffer-Zelle*, his "pepper pots." Using unglazed, porous porcelain cells, he precipitated membranes of copper ferrocyanide within them. Tightly supported by the walls of the cells, they withstood increased pressures; and Pfeffer was able to make direct measurements of solutions of various substances at different concentrations and temperatures. Pfeffer considered this cell a model of the plant cell, or in his terms, the protoplast with its surrounding membranes. His results showed proportionate relationships between the concentrations of the solutions in the cells and the osmotic pressures, and temperature likewise proved to be directly related to osmotic pressure.

Pfeffer, then teaching at Bonn, communicated his findings to the physicist Clausius. The values for the pressures within a plant cell seemed inordinately high at first, and Pfeffer later recalled that Clausius had thought that such pressures must be impossible and was convinced of their accuracy only when Pfeffer gave him further proof. Pfeffer acknowledged, however, that Clausius did not examine the question closely at the time.

Some time afterward, at Amsterdam, the botanist De Vries, who was engaged in researches related to osmotic pressures, met van't Hoff and told him of the values for osmotic pressures that Pfeffer had published in *Osmotische Untersuchungen*. Van't Hoff then referred to Pfeffer's work and drew his broad analogies between osmotic pressures and gas pressures. Thus Pfeffer's determinations were the values on which van't Hoff based his theoretical considerations. In his classic paper of 1887 van't Hoff outlined the experimental method that Pfeffer had used in obtaining his determinations. Pfeffer's technical achievement in making these measurements proved difficult to match.

Pfeffer suggested in *Osmotische Untersuchungen* that the "threads" he had permitted to fall might be a point of departure for the physicist; later he described his work to Clausius. He recalled, "I repeatedly expressed in conversations with him that some kind of connection had to exist between the osmotic effect on one hand and the size and number of the molecules on the other hand" (E. Cohen, p. 119). Pfeffer was therefore aware of the wider implications of his measurements, even though he never pursued them. Nevertheless, the development of the theory of solution has assured Pfeffer an enduring role in the history of physical chemistry. He was one of the triumvirate who guided German botany in their time; the obituary in *Nature* stated, "With his death the three outstanding figures of the older German botany —Sachs, Strasburger, and Pfeffer—have all passed away."

BIBLIOGRAPHY

I. ORIGINAL WORKS. Pfeffer's major works are *Osmotische Untersuchungen. Studien zur Zellmechanik* (Leipzig, 1877) and *Pflanzenphysiologie. Ein Handbuch des Stoffwechsels und Kraftwechsels in der Pflanze*, 2 vols. (Leipzig, 1881; 2nd ed., 1897–1904), with English trans. by A. J. Ewart as *The Physiology of Plants, a Treatise Upon the Metabolism and Sources of Energy in Plants*, 3 vols. (Oxford, 1900–1906). A complete bibliography of 100 titles is given in Fitting (see below).

II. SECONDARY LITERATURE. A biographical sketch by G. Haberlandt, "Wilhelm Pfeffer," in *Naturwissenschaften*, 3 (1915), 115–118, is followed by contributions describing various aspects of Pfeffer's work: Ernst Cohen, "Wilhelm Pfeffer und die physikalische Chemie," pp. 118–120; Friedrich Czapek, "Die Bedeutung von W. Pfeffer's physicalischen Forschungen für die Pflanzenphysiologie," pp. 120–124; L. Jost, "Die Bedeutung Wilhelm Pfeffers für die pflanzenphysiologische Technik und Methodik," pp. 129–131; H. Kniep, "Wilhelm Pfeffer's Bedeutung für die Reizphysiologie," pp. 124–129.

See also Albert Charles Chibnall, *Protein Metabolism in Plants* (New Haven–London–Oxford, 1939), 6–34, 37, 42–45, 65, 122, 170–171, for Pfeffer's views on asparagine and his work on protein metabolism in plants; and Harry Clay Jones, trans. and ed., *The Modern Theory of Solution. Memoirs by Pfeffer, van't Hoff, Arrhenius and Raoult* (New York–London, 1899), pp. v–vi, 3–10, 14–16, with excerpts from *Osmotische Untersuchungen* and from van't Hoff's paper and its reference to Pfeffer's determinations of osmotic pressure.

For biographical material see Frank M. Andrews, "Wilhelm Pfeffer," in *Plant Physiology*, 4 (1929), 285–288; Hans Fitting, "Wilhelm Friedrich Philipp Pfeffer," in

Deutsches Biographisches Jahrbuch, II (1917–1920), 578–582, 750–751, and "Wilhelm Pfeffer," in *Berichte der Deutschen botanischen Gesellschaft*, **38** (1920), 30–63, with a comprehensive bibliography; Wilhelm Ostwald, "Wilhelm Pfeffer," in *Chemiker-Zeitung*, **44** (1920), 145; G. J. P. [George James Peirce], "Wilhelm Pfeffer," in *Science*, n.s. **51** (1920), 291–292; Hans and Ernst G. Pringsheim, "Wilhelm Pfeffer," in *Berichte der Deutschen chemischen Gesellschaft*, **53A** (1920), 36–39; V. H. R., "Prof. Wilhelm Pfeffer, For. Mem. R. S.," in *Nature*, **105** (1920), 302; and Wilhelm Ruhland, "Wilhelm Pfeffer," in *Berichte über die Verhandlungen der Sächsischen Akademie der Wissenschaften zu Leipzig. Math.–Phys. Kl.*, **75** (1923), 107–124.

GLORIA ROBINSON

PFEIFFER, PAUL (*b.* Elberfeld [now Wuppertal], Germany, 21 April 1875; *d.* Bonn, Germany, 4 March 1951), *chemistry*.

Pfeiffer was the son of Hermann Pfeiffer, a head clerk and later factory owner, and Emilie Willmund. He studied for two semesters at the University of Bonn under Kekulé and Anschütz before entering the University of Zurich (1894), where he became Werner's best-known student, protégé, and eventually "chief of staff." After receiving his doctorate in 1898, for a paper "Molekülverbindungen der Halogenide des 4-wertigen Zinns und der Zinnalkyle" (published with Werner as coauthor in *Zeitschrift für anorganische Chemie*, **17** [1898], 82–110), he studied for one semester each with Ostwald at Leipzig and Hantzsch at Würzburg. On 14 August 1901 he married his cousin Julie Hüttenhoff. In the same year, with the acceptance of his *Habilitationsschrift*, "Beitrag zur Chemie der Molekülverbindungen," he became *Privatdozent* at the University of Zurich and in 1908 associate professor of theoretical chemistry. In 1916, as a result of personal and political conflicts with Werner, Pfeiffer left Zurich for the University of Rostock, even though Werner was ill at the time and Pfeiffer was certain to be appointed his successor. In 1919 Pfeiffer moved to the Technische Hochschule in Karlsruhe. Three years later he was appointed to the directorship of the chemical institute at the University of Bonn, Kekulé's old chair, where he remained until his retirement in 1947.

Pfeiffer's work encompassed both inorganic and organic chemistry as well as the borderland between these disciplines. As the intellectual—but not academic—successor to Werner, Pfeiffer's main interest was in coordination compounds, particularly those of chromium. He investigated their constitution, configuration, isomerism, acid-base and hydrolysis reactions, and their relationships to double salts and salt hydrates. He was the first to apply Werner's coordina-

tion theory to crystals. He also studied both inorganic and organic tin compounds, inner complexes, metal organic compounds, and the chemistry of dyes. He was a pioneer in the field of halochromism—the formation of colored substances from colorless organic bases by the addition of acids or solvents. His contributions to pure organic chemistry include studies of cyclic compounds, quinhydrones, stilbene compounds, unsaturated acids, and the relationship of ethylene compounds to ethane and acetylene compounds.

BIBLIOGRAPHY

I. ORIGINAL WORKS. Most of Pfeiffer's work appeared in *Berichte der Deutschen chemischen Gesellschaft* and *Zeitschrift für anorganische Chemie*. His monograph *Organische Molekülverbindungen* (Stuttgart, 1922) was reprinted in 1927. A detailed bibliography is given in Poggendorff, VIIA, 552–553.

II. SECONDARY LITERATURE. A summary of Pfeiffer's early career appeared in the *Festschrift* compiled for the opening of the chemical institute of the University of Zurich, *75 Jahre chemischer Forschung an der Universität Zürich* (Zurich, 1909). There are biographical data and evaluations of Pfeiffer's work by his former student R. Wizinger, "P. Pfeiffers Beitrag zur Entwicklung der Komplexchemie," in *Angewandte Chemie*, **62A** (1950), 201–205; and "In memoriam Paul Pfeiffer, 1875–1951," in *Helvetica chimica acta*, **36** (1953), 2032–2037. An unpublished autobiography, "Mein Lebenslauf" (1947), is available at the University of Bonn. *Angewandte Chemie*, **62**, nos. 9–10 (20 May 1950), was devoted to Pfeiffer on the occasion of his seventy-fifth birthday. Biographical data can be found in G. B. Kauffman, "Crystals as Molecular Compounds: Paul Pfeiffer's Application of Coordination Theory to Crystallography," in *Journal of Chemical Education*, **47** (1970), 277–278; and R. E. Oesper, "Paul Pfeiffer," *ibid.*, **28** (1951), 62.

GEORGE B. KAUFFMAN

PFLÜGER, EDUARD FRIEDRICH WILHELM (*b.* Hanau, Germany, 7 June 1829; *d.* Bonn, Germany, 16 March 1910), *physiology*.

Pflüger's father, Johann Georg Pflüger, began his career as a businessman and commercial traveler. Later he became a passionate politician and leader of the democrats in Hanau. He was a combative person and repeatedly came into conflict with government agencies; in the period 1841–1843 he became involved in a high treason trial. In 1848 he was active in the Frankfurt *Vorparlament*. He studied law in his later years in order to participate in political proceedings, and in 1848 he founded his own political journal. His wife, Charlotte Wilhemine Richter, died in 1855. On his mother's side Pflüger was descended from

Huguenots who had immigrated to Hanau from Dauphiné. He married Christine Marc of Wiesbaden in 1869. They had three daughters, Anna (who later married the chemist Richard Anschütz), Rosa, and Hildegard.

Pflüger, who usually signed his name simply as Eduard, spent his childhood years in Hanau and attended the Gymnasium there. His youth was overshadowed by political developments. He himself became a passionate democrat in 1848, but only for a short time. When he was arrested with rebellious Heidelberg students in 1849, he abandoned politics and law, which he had been studying at Heidelberg since the summer term of 1849, and took up the study of medicine.

In the summer term of 1850 he became a medical student at Marburg, and in 1851 he continued his medical studies at Berlin. There he became an admirer and student of Johannes Müller. In his student years he worked in Müller's laboratory and attended lectures given by Müller and Emil du Bois-Reymond. He once witnessed a demonstration of the inhibitory effect of the vagus nerve on the heart in Müller's laboratory. As a result he had the auspicious idea of seeking similar inhibitory effects on the intestine, which he discovered in the rabbit. On the basis of this work he received the M.D. under Müller in 1855. He had already earned such a degree in 1851 at Giessen for a dissertation, dedicated to Müller, dealing with the reflex and psychical capacities of the spinal cord of the frog. This work, written at the age of twenty-two, was his first scientific publication. Pflüger studied this question several more times during his career.

Pflüger's work on electrotonus qualified him as a university lecturer under du Bois-Reymond at the end of 1858, a few months after Müller's death. Pflüger worked mostly at his own residence, although under the supervision of du Bois-Reymond, the founder of scientific electrophysiology. Electrotonus was, methodologically considered, a very difficult topic. Pflüger was able to determine the basic laws of the changes in sensitivity that take place in a section of nerve subjected to a direct current from a cathode and from an anode which, due to polarization, spreads "extrapolarly." The laws proved to be dependent on the polarity, the direction, and the strength of the direct current. This finding, known as Pflüger's law of convulsion, was required learning for German medical students until the middle of the twentieth century. The principles of the diagnostic and therapeutic applications of the galvanic current in medicine are based on it.

Pflüger's early researches revealed his exceptional sagacity, perseverance, and experimental exactness.

Because of these qualities, on 28 February 1859 he received the chair of physiology at Bonn, succeeding Helmholtz. Helmholtz had recommended him to the Bonn faculty by stating: "Concerning physiology, among the younger pure physiologists, Pflüger in Berlin appears to me to be the most talented and promising." In his new post Pflüger was given little in the way of space or resources. Helmholtz had been responsible for both anatomy and physiology, but Pflüger assumed only the physiological duties. He used not the old anatomy building in the Hofgarten (built in 1824) but the so-called pavilion, a cramped building in the northeast corner of the university, where a provisional laboratory was constructed for his use. The initially modest facilities caused Pflüger to direct his research to histology. He studied the embryonal development of the ovary (1861–1863), the nerve endings in the salivary glands (1866), and the gas exchange in the blood and in the cells. He developed a gas evacuation pump for this purpose (1864–1865).

In his investigation of the ovary Pflüger also studied the question of whether the egg cells originate by division or "in free cell formation." Pflüger saw the embryonal ovary built up from hollow tubular sacs ("Pflüger's Tubes"), in the lumina of which were closely packed, bright vesicles, which were probably cells. In these sacs he thought the oogonia could be seen. The endings of secretory nerves, he believed, entered directly into the secreting cells.

Pflüger's studies of gas exchange continued for many years and encountered extraordinarily great methodological difficulties. Before Pflüger's time it had not been established whether the oxidizing processes of combustion take place in the lungs (Lavoisier), in the blood (Müller), or in the cells. He succeeded in demonstrating that cellular activity, or the energy requirement of the cell, determines the magnitude of the oxygen consumption; the blood respires comparatively little. In related work, Pflüger's experiment on the "table-salt frog" became famous: a frog in which the blood was replaced by a physiological salt solution displayed no significant decrease in gas exchange.

The concept of the "respiratory quotient" was also developed by Pflüger. He conducted new studies to show that the exchange of gas in the lungs and tissues results exclusively from the fall in partial pressure of the gases and cannot be considered as a secretion. That the respiratory action is stimulated by a surplus of carbon dioxide and a lack of oxygen was another definitive result of his work. His famous work, "Über die physiologische Verbrennung in den lebenden Organismen" (Pflüger's *Archiv*, **10** [1875], 251–367), consolidated these studies, which subsequently led Pflüger to consider the maintenance of heat in cold surroundings. He found that cold was the most effective stimulus to the increase of metabolism. He localized this process—through the application of curare—in the musculature. This finding also remains valid today.

Another field that claimed Pflüger's attention for several decades was the metabolism of the nutritive substances: protein, fat, and carbohydrates. He published more than sixty works on glycogen alone. Yet, despite the greatest exactitude in his methods, his determination of nitrogen-bearing substances had no unqualified success. He erroneously saw in protein alone the "source of the muscular force," and he considered protein in general to be the only nourishing substance. In fact he held this position on the basis of the hypothesis that the secret of living matter lies in the molecular structure of protein. His finding that the quantity of protein ingested determines the amount of decomposition of protein in the body has proved to be correct. Thus he did not believe that glycogen could be produced from protein. He became involved in violent controversies over this matter, especially with Voit's school in Munich. Shortly before his death, however, he became convinced of his error.

Pflüger expended much time, energy, and inventiveness on the improvement of methods for determining glycogen. In opposition to most other researchers, he believed that pancreatic diabetes was a nervous disturbance. In a letter (1896) to his daughter we find the complaint: "Glycogen is still the dream of my days and nights. It's dreadful." The result of this work was a large book, *Das Glykogen und seine Beziehungen zur Zuckerkrankheit* (2nd ed., 1905). Containing over five hundred pages, it included a review of the entire world literature on this subject, which was cited and utilized precisely. He died of a liver carcinoma at the age of eighty-one.

Pflüger was only of medium stature but powerfully built. His large beard gave him a commanding appearance. He was humane, rather reticent, and even shy when away from the Institute or his family. Pflüger attended few congresses, but he exercised a strong influence on his contemporaries while serving as editor of *Archiv für die gesamte Physiologie des Menschen und der Tiere* from 1868. Few people went as far as Pflüger in public criticism of the works of others, and he was the most feared critic of his time. His remarks could even degenerate into personal abuse; and when it was a matter of eliminating errors, he knew no restraint. He demanded the highest standards of diligence, exactness, and conclusiveness in his demonstrations. His polemic against Voit, Hermann Munk, Hermann Senator, and others was caustic beyond all measure. "Criticism is the most important motive of progress;

for that reason I practice it," he stated (see *Archiv*, **222** [1929], 561). His lectures were original and stimulating but not easy.

Pflüger loved his family above all else. He enjoyed taking long hikes with his wife and daughters and was exceedingly concerned about his health and theirs. He was a Christian but did not belong to any church. He claimed countless animals for experimental purposes —156 dogs in the last year of his life alone. Despite his respect for living creatures, the desire for knowledge took precedence. His wife once sighingly remarked that she had constantly had a very powerful rival, science.

As much as Pflüger regarded hypotheses as necessary in his discipline and sometimes even made far-reaching use of them, to that same degree he confined his work to physiology and to the questions of the life sciences that are open to experiment. He viewed the living being as a great unity, full of both teleology and mechanism (*Archiv*, **15** [1877], 57–103). He reserved his greatest reverence for Aristotle, whose likeness hung over his desk. Pflüger attributed the unifying forces in the organism to the nervous system. He thus rejected the neuron theory and upheld the "continuity theory" of the nervous system. In his article "Über den elementaren Bau des Nervensystems" (*Archiv*, **112** [1906], 1–40) he expressed himself emphatically on this point. His articles constantly demonstrated an intensive study of the literature and even a careful study of original sources already historical in his day. For this reason his works are frequently useful reading even today.

Pflüger was strongly opinionated. He called himself a student of Müller, but not of du Bois-Reymond, with whom he had worked the longest. His relations with du Bois-Reymond were not always untroubled. He seems to have had no friend among the physiologists, and his only lifelong friend was the botanist N. Pringsheim.

Pflüger was a member of the Leopoldina and honorary member of many foreign academies; he also was awarded the order *Pour le mérite*. He was rector at Bonn in the academic year 1889–1890.

BIBLIOGRAPHY

I. ORIGINAL WORKS. Pflüger's works include "De functionibus medullae oblongatae et spinalis psychicis" (M.D. diss., Giessen University, 1851); *Die sensorischen Funktionen des Rückenmarks der Wirbeltiere nebst einer neuen Lehre von den Leitungsgesetzen der Reflexionen* (Berlin, 1853); "De nervorum planchnicorum functione" (M.D. diss., University of Berlin, 1855); *Das Hemmungsnervensystem für die peristaltische Bewegung der Gedärme* (Berlin, 1857); *Untersuchungen über die Physiologie des Elektrotonus* (Berlin, 1859); *Über die Eierstöcke der*

Säugethiere und des Menschen (Leipzig, 1863); *Über die Kohlensäure des Blutes* (Bonn, 1864); "Beschreibung meiner Gaspumpe," in *Untersuchung aus dem physiologischen Laboratorium zu Bonn* (Berlin, 1865), 183–188; *Die Endigungen der Absonderungsnerven in den Speicheldrüsen* (Bonn, 1866); "Uber die physiologische Verbrennung in den lebenden Organismen," in *Pflügers Archiv für die gesamte Physiologie des Menschen und der Tiere*, **10** (1875), 251–367.

Subsequent writings are "Die teleologische Mechanik der lebendigen Natur," in *Pflügers Archiv für die gesamte Physiologie des Menschen und der Tiere*, **15** (1877), 57–103; "Die Physiologie und ihre Zukunft," *ibid.*, 361–365; "Wesen und Aufgaben der Physiologie," *ibid.*, **18** (1878), 427–442, the inaugural address at the Physiological Institute at Bonn–Poppelsdorf, 9 Nov. 1878; *Die allgemeinen Lebenserscheinungen* (Bonn, 1889), his rectorial address at Bonn; *Über die Kunst der Verlängerung des menschlichen Lebens* (Bonn, 1890), oration delivered on the Kaiser's birthday; "Das Glykogen und seine Beziehungen zur Zuckerkrankheit," in *Pflügers Archiv für die gesamte Physiologie des Menschen und der Tiere*, **96** (1903), 1–398, published as a book (Bonn, 1905); and "Über den elementaren Bau des Nervensystems," in *Pflügers Archiv für die gesamte Physiologie des Menschen und der Tiere*, **112** (1906), 1–40.

II. SECONDARY LITERATURE. On Pflüger and his work see A. Bethe, "E. Pflüger als Begründer dieses Archives," in *Pflügers Archiv für die gesamte Physiologie des Menschen und der Tiere*, **222** (1929), 569–572; W. Bleibtreu, "Pflügers Persönlichkeit," *ibid.*, 562–568; W. Haberling and S. Pagel, "Pflüger, Ed. Fr. W.," in *Biographisches Lexikon der hervorragenden Ärzte aller Zeiten und Völker*, 2nd ed., IV (Berlin–Vienna, 1932), 586–587; E. Heischkel, "Eduard Pflüger (1829–1910). Physiologe," in *Lebensbilder aus Kurhessen und Waldeck, 1830–1930*, I. Schnack, ed., IV (Marburg, 1950), 253–263—*Lebensbilder . . .* is no. 20 of Veröffentlichungen der Historischen Kommission für Hessen und Waldeck; M. Nussbaum, *E. F. W. Pflüger als Naturforscher* (Bonn, 1909), with partial bibliography; R. Rosemann, "Pflügers Lebenswerk," in *Pflügers Archiv für die gesamte Physiologie des Menschen und der Tiere*, **222** (1929), 548–562; K. E. Rothschuh, *Entwicklungsgeschichte physiologischer Entdeckungen in Tabellenform* (Munich, 1952), nos. 137, 140, 221, 225, 227, 250, 603, 640, 677, 680, 721, 724, 748, 782, 941, 1000, 1032, 1317, 1392; and *Geschichte der Physiologie* (Berlin, 1953), esp. 133–134; F. Runkel, "Eduard Pflügers Vorfahren und Jugendzeit," in *Pflügers Archiv für die gesamte Physiologie des Menschen und der Tiere*, **222** (1929), 572–574; and K. Schmiz, *Die medizinische Fakultät der Universität Bonn 1818–1918. Ein Beitrag zur Geschichte der Medizin* (Bonn, 1920), 26–29.

Obituaries are by René du Bois-Reymond in *Berliner klinische Wochenschrift*, **47** (1910), 658–659; H. Boruttau in *Deutsche medizinische Wochenschrift*, **36** (1910), 851–852; E. von Cyon in *Pflügers Archiv für die gesamte Physiologie des Menschen und der Tiere*, **132** (1910), 1–19; J. A. F. Dastre in *Comptes rendus des séances de la Société de biologie*, **68** (1910), 648–650; H. Leo in *Münchener medizinische Wochenschrift*, **57** (1910), 1128–1129; F. Schenck in *Naturwissenschaftliche Rundschau* (1910), 340; and A. D. Waller in *Nature*, **83** (1910), 314.

Additional material may be found in the archives of the Institut für Geschichte der Medizin, Münster University.

K. E. ROTHSCHUH

PHILINUS OF COS (*b.* Cos; *fl. ca.* 250 B.C.), *medicine.*

Philinus of Cos, about whom very little information has survived (we do not know the titles of any of his works), played an interesting role in the beginnings of the empirical school of medicine and of medical skepticism. As a native of Cos he certainly was acquainted with the Hippocratic tradition. He studied under Herophilus, who originally belonged to the Coan school of physicians. It is not known whether, like his teacher, Philinus spent time in Alexandria; but it is known that by severing relations with Herophilus he helped to establish the empirical school of medicine (see Deichgräber, fr. 6), which had close contacts with the philosophy of skepticism. Since Herophilus also had such contacts (see F. Kudlien, "Herophilos und der Beginn der medizinischen Skepsis," in *Gesnerus*, **21** [1964], 1–13), the difference between him and his pupil may not be evident. The answer is that Philinus was fundamentally more rigorous than his teacher. He evidently transformed the latter's etiological skepticism (the chief causes of disease are not known) into an etiological nihilism (it is impossible to know the causes). This transformation had consequences in medical diagnostics: in opposition to his teacher, Philinus denied the utility of reading the pulse and "thereby shut medicine's diagnostic eyes" (see Deichgräber, fr. 77). On this point at least, Philinus' medical ideas emerge more clearly than H. Diller supposed; but beyond it nothing can be affirmed concerning Philinus.

BIBLIOGRAPHY

Accounts of Philinus are collected in K. Deichgräber, *Die griechische Empirikerschule*, 2nd enlarged ed. (Berlin–Zurich, 1965). See also H. Diller's short article "Philinos no. 9," in Pauly-Wissowa, *Real-Encyclopädie der classischen Altertumswissenschaft*, XIX (Stuttgart, 1938), cols. 2193–2194.

FRIDOLF KUDLIEN

PHILIP, ALEXANDER PHILIPS WILSON (*b.* Shieldhall, Scotland, 15 October 1770; *d.* Boulogne, France, 1851 [?]), *medicine, physiology.*

Wilson Philip was christened Alexander Philips Wilson but in 1811 changed his name to Alexander

Philips Wilson Philip; his writings that were published before 1807 bear the name of A. P. Wilson. He received his early education in Edinburgh and studied medicine at the medical school of the University of Edinburgh, under William Gregory, Alexander Monro (Secundus), Joseph Black, and William Cullen; he graduated M.D. on 25 June 1792 with a thesis entitled "De dyspepsia." After studying in London he returned to Edinburgh and was admitted a fellow of the Royal College of Physicians of Edinburgh on 3 February 1795. Probably for reasons of health, he left Edinburgh. In 1798 he was appointed physician to the Winchester County Hospital and in 1802 to the Worcester General Infirmary. On account of friction with local colleagues, he resigned the latter position in 1818 and in 1820 went to London, where he soon became a leading physician.

Wilson Philip was made a licentiate of the Royal College of Physicians of London on 22 December 1820, a fellow on 25 June 1834, and on 11 May 1826 a fellow of the Royal Society. Meantime he built up a large and lucrative practice, especially among the aristocracy who lived near his large home in fashionable Cavendish Square. About 1842 Wilson Philip retired from practice, and in 1843 or 1844 he moved to Boulogne (it has been said, to avoid imprisonment for insolvency). Nothing is known of this episode, and although it appears that he died in France, the precise date of his death is unknown. It has been suggested that W. M. Thackeray based his character Dr. Brand Firmin in *The Adventures of Philip* on Wilson Philip, but McMenemy thinks this unlikely.

Wilson Philip was a man of great energy and diligence, and of kindliness toward his patients. Although he himself possessed a critical outlook, he was temperamentally unable to tolerate criticism from others. He was frequently involved in vitriolic polemics and violent arguments concerning his clinical and experimental work, but he eschewed medical politics. Although he wrote profusely, his literary style is a difficult and tedious one, and he is often guilty of repetition and self-glorification.

In addition to a busy medical practice, Wilson Philip also undertook physiological research. Concerning clinical medicine he wrote on urinary gravel (1792), fevers (1799–1804, 1807), indigestion (1821, 1824), and on many other topics. From these works he may be seen to have been a critical and accurate observer of disease, but his reasoning—like that of many of his contemporaries— was based on unproven hypotheses and relics of the eighteenth-century systems of disease. No doubt his therapeutic advice, although mostly ill-founded, was often valuable, but his many publications contributed little or nothing to the advancement of internal medicine as a science. Nevertheless, his works were popular in their time, and the four-volume *Treatise on Febrile Diseases* (1799–1804), for example, went through four editions and was translated into German and French.

Wilson Philip investigated experimentally the action of opium (1795), mercury (1805), galvanism (1817), and Malvern waters (1805). His book on indigestion (1821), a condition that interested him throughout his career, was well received by the profession—unlike some of his later publications, including that *On the More Obscure Diseases of the Brain* (1835), which was described, according to McMenemy, as "the mixture as before" or a "shameless piece of self-exaltation."

In his early years Wilson Philip carried out important physiological research on the nervous system and capillary circulation, and today his reputation rests upon the results of this research. He was one of a small group of British physicians who contributed to the field of physiology, which at that time was dominated by the French and Germans. His book *An Experimental Enquiry Into the Laws of the Vital Functions* (1817) is especially important. In some famous experiments he showed that digestion ceased with section of the vagus nerve, that gastric secretion could be decreased by damage or removal of parts of the brain or spinal cord, and that movement of the gut could be independent of brain control. These results stimulated a great deal of further research.

Wilson Philip's studies of nervous influences on the cardiovascular system were equally significant. Albrecht von Haller maintained that the capillaries were unable to contract, but Wilson Philip, along with others, refuted this conclusion and went on to demonstrate that cardiac acceleration and inhibition were produced by stimulation of the nervous system. He also showed that although the heart and blood vessels act independently of the brain and spinal cord, as Haller and the French physiologist J. J. C. Legallois had maintained, they could be affected by drugs that acted on the nervous system, since they are centrally regulated (but not primarily centrally controlled). In his experiments Wilson Philip used the microscope to detect changes in the caliber of blood vessels. This marked a very early use of this instrument in physiological research in England.

BIBLIOGRAPHY

I. ORIGINAL WORKS. Pettigrew (1840, see below) lists many of Wilson Philip's publications, including several in journals; and McMenemy (1958, see below) cites the important works.

Works published before 1807 appear under the style "A. P. Wilson"; these include *An Inquiry Into the Remote Causes of Urinary Gravel* (Edinburgh, 1792; German trans., 1795); *An Experimental Essay on the Manner in Which Opium Acts on the Living Animal Body* (Edinburgh, 1795); *Treatise on Febrile Diseases*, 4 vols. (Winchester, 1799–1804; 4th ed., London, 1820; German trans., Leipzig, 1804–1812; and French trans., Paris, 1819); *Observations on the Use and Abuse of Mercury* (Winchester, 1805); *An Analysis of the Malvern Waters* (Worcester, 1805); and *An Essay on the Nature of Fever* (Worcester, 1807).

Works published after 1807 under the name "A. P. W. Philip," or "A. P. Wilson Philip" are *Treatise on Indigestion and Its Consequences* (London, 1821; 7th ed., 1833; German trans., Leipzig, 1823; and Dutch trans., Amsterdam, 1823; 8th ed. as *A Treatise on Protracted Indigestion and Its Consequences, etc.* [London, 1842]). His most important work is *An Experimental Inquiry Into the Laws of the Vital Functions* (London, 1817; 2nd ed., 1818; 3rd. ed., 1826; and 4th ed., 1839; with German trans., Stuttgart, 1828; and Italian trans., in F. Tantini, *Opusculi scientifici*, II [Pisa, 1822]).

II. SECONDARY LITERATURE. The best account of Wilson Philip and his work is by W. H. McMenemy, "Alexander Philips Wilson Philip (1770–1847), Physiologist and Physician," in *Journal of the History of Medicine and Allied Sciences*, **13** (1958), 289–328, with portrait. McMenemy adds useful details to the official accounts, such as those of W. Munk, *The Roll of the Royal College of Physicians of London*, III (London, 1878), 227–238; and J. F. Payne in *Dictionary of National Biography*, XV (London, 1921–1922), 1041–1042.

A contemporary assessment is that of T. J. Pettigrew, in *Medical Portrait Gallery. Biographical Memoirs of the Most Celebrated Physicians, Surgeons, etc.*, III (London, 1840), 16, with portrait. Wilson Philip's work in the context of the history of neurophysiology is discussed by M. Neuburger, in *Die historische Entwicklung der experimentellen Gehirn- und Rückenmarksphysiologie vor Flourens* (Stuttgart, 1897), 225, 251–255, 266–267, 270–271, 275. *Extracts From an Experimental Inquiry* (1817) is included in J. F. Fulton and L. G. Wilson, *Selected Readings in the History of Physiology*, 2nd ed. (Springfield, Ill., 1966), 82–85.

EDWIN CLARKE

PHILLIPS, JOHN (*b.* Marden, Wiltshire, England, 25 December 1800; *d.* Oxford, England, 24 April 1874), *geology, paleontology.*

Phillips was the son of John Phillips of Blaen-y-Ddol, Carmarthenshire, an excise officer, and Elizabeth Smith, daughter of John Smith of Churchill, Oxfordshire. He remained unmarried, and for many years at York and at Oxford his sister Anne was hostess at his home. Phillips was left an orphan at an early age and entered into the care of his maternal uncle, the geologist and land surveyor William Smith. He was educated at a school near Bath and also spent a year in the house, and under the instruction, of the Reverend Benjamin Richardson of Farleigh Hungerford; but his formal education ended before he reached the age of fifteen when he returned to live with his uncle in London. There, after Smith's fossil collection had been bought for the nation in 1815, Phillips assisted in preparing a catalog and in arranging the specimens "according to Linnaeus" before their delivery to the British Museum.

One of the few to practice the art of lithography in England, Phillips was entrusted by Smith with copying and lithographing some of his reports. For the next nine years he acted as assistant and amanuensis to his uncle and was almost constantly his companion. During this time, apart from professional assignments, they were occupied in compiling the series of county geological maps; and both together and independently they made many geological traverses throughout the north of England.

In 1824, following an invitation to Smith to lecture to the Yorkshire Philosophical Society, Phillips was engaged to arrange the fossil collections at the museum at York. Shortly afterward he was appointed curator of the society's museum, a post he held until the end of 1840.

In 1831 Phillips played a leading part in organizing at York the general meeting of British scientists that became the British Association for the Advancement of Science. This society was founded "to give a stronger impulse and a more systematic direction to scientific inquiry; to promote the intercourse of those who cultivate science in different parts of the British empire with one another, and with foreign philosophers; to obtain a more general attention to the objects of science, and a removal of any disadvantages of a public kind which impede its progress." He was the executive officer of the Association until 1859, and throughout this period he arranged the venue for its annual assembly, maintained close links with leading British scientists, edited the society's annual reports and, through his efficiency and cordial relationships, was a major contributor to its success.

Phillips was an accomplished lecturer and teacher and gave courses in geology and zoology in many towns in the north of England under the auspices of the local scientific and philosophical societies. In 1831 he began similar courses in London, and in 1834 he was elected a fellow of the Royal Society and was appointed professor of geology at King's College, London. He gave up this post in 1840, when he joined the Geological Survey under De la Beche. In 1844 he became professor of geology at Trinity College, Dublin. But an expected appointment to a senior position in the Irish branch of the Geological Survey, which could have been held concurrently, did not materialize; and the following year he relinquished his Dublin post. Phillips' assignment with the Geological Survey involved work in Southwest England and detailed geological mapping around the Malvern Hills and in South Wales.

In 1853 Phillips was appointed deputy reader in geology at Oxford, and on the death of William Buckland in 1856 he became reader and subsequently professor. He also played an important part in the building of the new University Museum and was its keeper until his death, which resulted from a fall.

By his early training and by inclination, Phillips was a practical field geologist, skilled in the making of geological maps; and his most important contributions to stratigraphical geology were descriptive. In his volumes on the geology of Yorkshire he recorded the stratigraphy and structure of the "Mountain" (Carboniferous) Limestone and the Jurassic and Cretaceous strata of a large area of the north of England. He also introduced the term "Yoredale series" (1836, p. 37) for sediments showing a rhythmic succession of shales, sandstones, and limestones, together constituting a special facies of the uppermost zone of the Carboniferous Limestone series in this region. He traced the changes in these sediments when followed laterally and interpreted them as due to changes in the depositional environment.

In his work on the fossils of Southwest England (1841, p. 160), Phillips introduced the term "Mesozoic" to identify the geological era between the Paleozoic and Cenozoic and to include the "New Red" (Triassic), "Oolitic" (Jurassic), and Cretaceous periods. This book was an essential supplement to De la Beche's first official Geological Survey memoir, *Report on the Geology of Cornwall, Devon, and West Somerset* (1839). A similar style of presentation was continued in Phillips' volume on the geology of the Paleozoic rocks in the vicinity of the Malvern Hills. By these descriptions and illustrations of the stratigraphy and characteristic fossils of particular formations, Phillips contributed notably to the background of knowledge by which progress in stratigraphical classification and correlation was made possible.

In 1852 John Phillips brought mature geological experience to his own personal observation of the physical features of the surface of the moon, using at first the great telescope belonging to the Earl of Rosse. These investigations arose out of the appointment of an ad hoc committee by the British Association charged with the task of procuring a new series of drawings or surveys of selected parts of the lunar disk. The drawings were to be made under a set of standard conditions of representation and on a uniform scale. Since few observers were willing to undertake the investigations, it was left to Phillips to pursue, virtually alone, the queries enumerated in the committee's prospectus. By 1853 he was recording his observations photographically on collodion plates and employing his great artistic skill in accurate and detailed drawings. After he reached Oxford there was an interval of several years before he resumed the study using an up-to-date telescope provided by the Royal Society.

Phillips emphasized the need for continuous observation of selected areas and the recording of each one at different times of the lunar day so that the configurations could be accurately determined. In a summary of his findings published in 1868, Phillips drew vivid analogies between many of the features seen on the surface of the moon and those known to him intimately by observation and measurement of the earth.

BIBLIOGRAPHY

I. Original Works. A complete bibliography of Phillips' works is given in *Proceedings of the Yorkshire Geological Society* (see below). Works on regional geology include *Illustrations of the Geology of Yorkshire*, I (York, 1829; 2nd ed., London, 1835; 3rd ed., London, 1875), II (London, 1836); *Figures and Descriptions of the Palaeozoic Fossils of Cornwall, Devon, and West Somerset* (London, 1841); and *Geology of Oxford and the Valley of the Thames* (Oxford, 1871). His lunar work, submitted in papers to the Royal Society, is summarized in "Notices of Some Parts of the Surface of the Moon," in *Philosophical Transactions of the Royal Society*, **158** (1868), 333–346. Other astronomical researches are mentioned in "The Planet Mars," in *Quarterly Journal of Science*, **2** (1865), 369–381. Phillips included certain autobiographical material in his *Memoirs of William Smith* (London, 1844).

II. Secondary Literature. A number of obituary notices are mentioned in T. Sheppard, "John Phillips," in *Proceedings of the Yorkshire Geological Society*, **22** (1933), 153–187, which contains a full bibliography of Phillips' scientific papers and a number of portraits with the location of the originals.

J. M. Edmonds

PHILLIPS, THEODORE EVELYN REECE (*b.* Kibworth, Leicestershire, England, 28 March 1868; *d.* Headley, Surrey, England, 13 May 1942), *astronomy*.

Phillips was the son of the Reverend Abel Phillips, formerly of Barbados and a missionary in West Africa. He was educated at Yeovil Grammar School and in 1891 graduated B.A. from St. Edmund Hall, Oxford. He was ordained in the same year and became curate at the Church of the Holy Trinity in Taunton.

In 1896, while curate at Hendford (near Yeovil), Phillips began systematic observation of the planets, especially Jupiter and Mars, with a nine-and-a-quarter-inch altazimuth reflector. He continued his observations, with that instrument when he moved to Croydon and later, in Ashstead, when he acquired a twelve-and-a-quarter-inch equatorial reflector. From 1911 he used an eight-inch reflector loaned by the Royal Astronomical Society; and when he became rector of Headley in 1916, he used an eighteen-inch reflector loaned by the British Astronomical Association, of which he had been president from 1914 to 1916.

Phillips directed the Jupiter section of the association from 1900 to 1933 and the Saturn section from 1935 to 1940. From 1896 to 1941 he submitted more than 400 drawings to the Mars section.

Phillips' work on Jupiter followed that of A. S. Williams, W. F. Denning, and others who had observed the drift of the surface markings of Jupiter in different latitudes. These markings were charted by timing their passage over the central meridian; the *Memoirs of the British Astronomical Association* (1897–1898) included Phillips' tables with deduced rotation periods for different latitudes. The *Memoirs* for 1932–1933, which were not published until 1939, recorded his last observations.

The observations published under Phillips' care are perhaps the only satisfactory continuous records of the movements of Jupiter during his career. They include a complete history of the appearance and movement of the red spot and the south tropical disturbance, which was first recorded in 1901, and of disturbances heralding the return (1920, 1928) of the south equatorial belt and other south tropical characteristics. Phillips is known to have recorded more than 30,000 spot transits.

Following a suggestion by H. H. Turner, Phillips conducted a harmonic analysis of the light curves of about eighty stars; and he made protracted observations of double stars. He was the president of the International Astronomical Union, Commission Sixteen; and he represented the Church of England at Geneva in 1922, when it was proposed that Easter become a fixed, rather than a movable, feast. He was president of the Royal Astronomical Society from 1927 to 1929. Among his many observational records is a continuous set of rainfall records for Headley that covers twenty-five years; and he made a harmonic analysis of annual temperature curves for several places in Great Britain. Phillips was also an amateur botanist and a university extension lecturer for many years. He received an honorary D.Sc. from Oxford University shortly before his death. In 1906 he married Mellicent Kynaston of Croydon. Their only son, the Reverend John E. T. Phillips, became an amateur astronomer.

BIBLIOGRAPHY

Phillips was a regular contributor to the publications of the British Astronomical Association. He also contributed the articles "Jupiter," "Mercury," "Neptune" (in part), "Saturn," and "Venus," in the 14th ed. of the *Encyclopaedia Britannica* (1929); revised R. S. Ball's *A Popular Guide to the Heavens*, 4th ed. (London, 1925); and collaborated with W. H. Steavenson in editing *Hutchinson's Splendour of the Heavens*, 2 vols. (London, 1923–1926).

For brief accounts of his life, see the obituary by B. M. Peek in *Journal of the British Astronomical Association*, **52** (1942), 203–208. See also M. Davidson, "Honour for Rev. T. E. R. Phillips," in *Observatory*, **64** (1942), 228–231, written shortly before Phillips' death.

J. D. NORTH

PHILLIPS, WILLIAM (*b.* London, England, 10 May 1775; *d.* London, 2 April 1828), *geology.*

Phillips inherited his father's printing and bookselling business in London but also devoted much leisure time to studying the natural sciences. In this pursuit he found a kindred spirit in his younger brother Richard (1778–1851), who became a successful chemist. They were the grandsons of Catherine Phillips, a noted Quaker, and were lifelong members of the Society of Friends.

Phillips became increasingly interested in geology and in November 1807 was one of the founding members of the London Geological Society. He subsequently spent most of his spare time on mineralogy and stratigraphy. In 1825 a crystal of the zeolite family—a hydrated aluminosilicate of calcium, potassium, and sodium—was named "phillipsite" after him. He was elected a fellow of the Royal Society in 1827.

Phillips contributed about twenty-seven papers, mainly on mineralogy and with an emphasis on Cornish minerals, to the *Transactions of the Geological Society of London* and to other scientific journals. He also published three influential, standard textbooks, two on mineralogy and one mainly on stratigraphy, that enjoyed a great popularity. His *Outlines of Mineralogy and Geology* (1815) had gone into a fourth edition by 1826, and his *Elementary Introduction to the Knowledge of Mineralogy* (1816) was largely rewritten and reissued as a fifth edition in 1852. This work is illustrated with numerous woodcuts of crystals. In 1829 the *Quarterly Journal of the Geological Society of London* stated that:

> It was after the invention of Dr. Wollaston's reflective Goniometer, that his [Phillips'] assiduity and success in the use of that beautiful instrument enabled him to produce his most valuable Crystallographic Memoirs; and the third edition of his elaborate work on Mineralogy [*An Elementary Introduction to Mineralogy* (London, 1823)] contains perhaps the most remarkable results ever yet produced in Crystallography, from the application of goniometric measurement, without the aid of mathematics.

Phillips' most influential work was that on the stratigraphy of England and Wales, which began as a digest of English geology, entitled *A Selection of Facts From the Best Authorities, Arranged so as to Form an Outline of the Geology of England and Wales* (London, 1818). Phillips then collaborated with Conybeare on an enlarged version, *Outlines of the Geology of England and Wales, With an Introductory Compendium of the General Principles of That Science, and Comparative Views of the Structure of Foreign Countries* (London, 1822). In this work Phillips incorporated some of his own fieldwork—for example, his study of the chalk cliffs on each side of the Strait of Dover. The book was received with great enthusiasm. Almost a century later (*Encyclopaedia Britannica*, 11th ed. [1910], XXI, 408) it was still extolled "as a model of careful original observation, of judicious compilation, of succinct description, and of luminous arrangement, it has been of the utmost service in the development of geology in Britain."

The stratigraphical information presented in this work actually depended largely on the ideas of William Smith. The book publicized Smith's concepts and methods and showed convincingly that a secure foundation for the comparative study of sedimentary strata can be obtained only with the assistance of fossil content. The clear geological cross sections and the fairly complete exposition of the contemporary geological knowledge of sedimentary rocks were based, with certain modifications, on Smith's terminology and stratigraphy.

Not surprisingly, this classic work had a marked influence on British geology, and the stratigraphical framework popularized in it became of worldwide significance. The book was highly praised in the United States, in an anonymous review, probably by Benjamin Silliman; it was, however, weak in its geomorphological concepts. Although the authors derided Wernerian theories, they still believed that valleys were formed by violent currents when the landmass was upheaved from beneath the sea.

BIBLIOGRAPHY

There is an obituary notice in *Quarterly Journal of the Geological Society of London, Proceedings*, **1** (1829), 113. Conybeare and Phillips' textbook is reviewed anonymously in *American Journal of Science*, **7** (1824), 203–240.

See also R. J. Chorley *et al.*, *The History of the Study of Landforms*, I (London, 1964), *passim*; and H. B. Woodward, *A History of the Geological Society of London* (London, 1907), *passim*.

ROBERT P. BECKINSALE

PHILO OF BYZANTIUM (*fl. ca.* 250 B.C.), *physics, mechanics, pneumatics.*

Little is known of Philo's life. Vitruvius includes him, with Archytas, Archimedes, Ctesibius, and others, in a list of inventors,[1] while Hero of Alexandria mentions a work on an automatic theater by him[2] and Eutocius cites his work on the duplication of the cube.[3] These constitute the only references to Philo in antiquity; what else is known of him must be inferred from the hints that exist in his few extant writings. These writings are fragments of a large book on mechanics, Philo's only known work. From references to the bronze-spring catapult, recently invented by Ctesibius (*fl. ca.* 270 B.C.), it is possible to reach an approximate date for Philo's career. It is also clear that Philo was able to travel to Rhodes and Alexandria to study catapults, which suggests that he may have been wealthy, or have had a wealthy patron—perhaps his friend Ariston, to whom each of the surviving books of the larger mechanics is dedicated. (Nothing else is known of Ariston, who would seem to have been a man of position and of some mathematical sophistication; in Arabic versions of the text his name is rendered as Māristūn.)[4] Diels states that, like Hero, Philo was a mere artisan, but he gives no reason for his opinion.[5]

Philo chose to write his textbook on mechanics, the Σύνταξις τῆς μηχανικῆς in κοινή, the vernacular common to the whole Greek-speaking world of the time. Certainly, this straightforward language is better suited to his practical purpose than is the intricate Attic literary prose; the book is full of technical detail that would be of service to an architect, contractor, or—in its sections on war machines and fortifications—a general, and perhaps Ariston was one of these.

It is possible, through studying the extant parts of Philo's *Mechanics*, to surmise what the contents of the whole work must have been, especially since Philo often refers both to what he has already written and to what he intends to write. One can thus reconstruct a list of nine books:

1. Introduction

Of these, book 4 (the *Belopoeica*), book 5 (the *Pneumatica*), book 7 (the *Paraskeuastica*), and book 8 (the *Poliorcetica*) are extant. The Greek text exists for the *Belopoeica* and for parts of the *Paraskeuastica* and *Poliorcetica*; the *Pneumatica* was for many years known only through a Latin translation of an Arabic version of the first sixteen chapters. At the beginning of the twentieth century, however, B. Carra de Vaux found three manuscripts (one in the Bodleian Library and two in the library of Hagia Sophia), which provided a fuller Arabic text; previous to this discovery, the *Paraskeuastica* and the *Poliorcetica* were together known as book 5.

Book 4, the *Belopoeica*, is concerned with the construction of catapults. It is from this book that Philo's travels may be discovered. In chapter 3, he remarks that his application of mathematics to the building of these weapons resulted from the interest that the Alexandrian kings took in the technical arts. (This would indicate that he was in Alexandria in the time of the first Ptolemies.) In chapter 4, Philo states that he has talked with catapult experts in Alexandria, and has examined catapults in Rhodes; in chapter 39, he goes on to mention that although he himself has not seen Ctesibius' bronze-spring catapult, it has been described to him in detail by people who have. He displays a great interest in experimentation, and would seem to have invented improved catapults himself.

Philo gives the rules for constructing a catapult from a module derived from either the length of the arrow or the weight of the projectile, a method first worked out by Alexandrian technicians. Philo then approaches the problem of designing a catapult that will deliver a missile of twice the weight of one launched by another catapult; in establishing the module by which such a catapult should be constructed it is necessary for him to double the cube, since the respective weights of the two missiles are in the proportion of the cubes of their diameters.

This cannot be done by a Euclidean construction with ruler and compass alone; the method is to find two mean proportionals. Philo writes (chapter 7):[6] "the reduplication of the cube, which I have explained in the first Book, but which I do not hesitate to write

here also" (see fig. 1). "Let there then be given a certain straight line A, for which, for example, we have to find the double cube; I then place the double of it, B, at right angles to it, and from the other end of B I draw at right angles a straight line of indefinite length

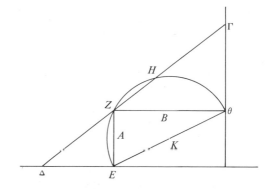

FIGURE 1. Philo's figure for the reduplication of the cube.

towards Γ ⟨and from the end of A I draw at right angles a straight line of indefinite length towards Δ⟩; from the angle marked Θ ⟨to the angle marked E⟩ I draw the straight line K, and divide it in two, and let the middle be the point K, and with K as centre and $K\Theta$ as radius I draw a half circle, which goes also through the point Z. Then I take an accurately fashioned ruler and place it so that it cuts both the straight lines, taking care that one point of it touches the angle (Z), and turning it till I get the part of the ruler from the intersection marked Γ to the part that falls on the intersection with the circle, marked $H[Z]$, to be equal to the length from the intersection marked to that which falls on the angle marked Z. And then ΔE is the double of the cube of EZ, $\Theta\Gamma$ of that of $E\Delta$, ΘZ of that of $\Theta\Gamma$. The diameter of the circle which has to take the spring is found in this way." Additions to the text have been made by August Brinkmann, and they are so obvious that it is possible that Philo himself omitted them, since this is just an example, an application, of the proof given in the first book.

Eutocius (in his commentary on Archimedes, *De sphaera*, Book 2)[7] reviews the different ways of reduplicating the cube. He gives Hero's solution, and then proceeds to Philo's solution, using Philo's figure, but with lettering of his own and adding two lines from Hero's figure, from K to Δ and Z (see fig. 2).

The construction is the same as that of Philo, but Eutocius uses fewer words. When he has placed the ruler, he writes: "Let it then be assumed that the ruler has the position taken by ΔBEZ, where, as stated, ΔB is equal to EZ. I say then that $A\Delta$ and ΓZ are middle proportions to AB and $B\Gamma$."

He then gives the proof in this way: "Let us assume

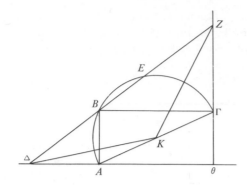

FIGURE 2. Eudocius' figure for Philo's reduplication of the cube.

that ΔA and $Z\Gamma$ are prolonged and intersect at Θ; then it is evident that, since BA and $Z\Theta$ are parallel, the angle at Θ is right, and that the half-circle $AE\Gamma$ if it is filled out also will go through Θ. Now since ΔB and EZ are equal, $E\Delta$ by EB will be equal BZ by BE. But $E\Delta$ by ΔB is equal to ΘA by ΔA, for both are equal to the square of the tangent from Δ; but BZ by ZE is equal to ΘZ by $Z\Gamma$, for both are equal to the tangent from Z; so also $\Theta\Delta$ by ΔA is equal to ΘZ by $Z\Gamma$, and from this it follows that $\Delta\Theta$ to ΘZ is equal to $B\Gamma$ to ΔA. But as $\Delta\Theta$ is to ΘZ, so is both $B\Gamma$ to ΓZ and ΔA to AB, for in the triangle $\Delta\Theta Z$ $B\Gamma$ is parallel to $\Delta\Theta$, and BA is parallel to ΘZ. So then, as $B\Gamma$ to ΓZ, so ΓZ to ΔA and ΔA to AB, which was to be proved."

This construction is almost the same as that of Hero; for the $B\Theta$ parallelogram is the same as that assumed in Hero's construction, and also the prolonged sides ΘA and $\Theta\Gamma$, and the ruler turned on the point B. The only difference is that (in Hero) we move the ruler around B until the lines from the middle of $A\Gamma$, that is K, become equal as they are intersected by it where they reach $\Theta\Delta$ and ΘZ, as $K\Delta$ and KZ, but here (in Philo) till ΔB becomes equal to EZ. In either construction the same thing follows, but the latter is more easy in practice, for to see that ΔB and EZ are equal can be done if the ruler is divided into equal parts, and very much more easily than by trying to find out by compasses from K if the lines from K to Δ and to Z are equal."

It appears that the first part of this construction was written by Eutocius in his own way, but the middle part, the proof, may be copied from Philo. The comparison of the two constructions is Eutocius' own contribution; when the figures are drawn, Hero's method is easier.

Philo goes on to describe a method of improving catapults by using wedges to tighten the sinews. He also gives a design for a catapult with bronze springs,

which he notes was inspired by the report that Ctesibius had made such a machine. Philo did not know the details of Ctesibius' catapult at the time he devised his own, and when he was able to compare the two weapons, he discovered that they were different in several respects. Philo also describes Ctesibius' air-driven catapult, and discusses an automatic catapult invented at Rhodes by a man named Dionysius, about whom nothing else is known. None of these devices is mentioned by either Vitruvius (in 25 B.C.) or Hero (in A.D. 62).

Philo's fifth book, the *Pneumatica*, begins with a series of introductory chapters that incorporate a number of experiments almost certainly taken from Ctesibius, the founder of the science of pneumatics. These chapters were copied by Hero. The rest of the book (like Hero's work on the same subject) consists of descriptions of pneumatic toys—trick jars, inexhaustible bowls, and other apparatus for parlor magic. Many of these were probably reconstructed or reinvented by Hero and others.[8] All the chapters are illustrated in the extant Arabic manuscripts, but the illustrations have never been published.

The surviving parts of books 7 and 8, the *Paraskeuastica* and the *Poliorcetica*, indicate that each book consisted of a large number of short chapters. These were considered together as one book in earlier editions of Philo's work, and may be divided into four sections, of which the first two constitute the *Paraskeuastica*, and the second two the *Poliorcetica*. The first section contains eighty-seven chapters devoted to the techniques of fortifying a town—constructing walls and towers, digging moats, setting up palisades, and placing catapults. The second section consists of fifty-seven chapters on provisioning a town against siege. In it Philo describes the proper construction of storerooms and lists the foodstuffs to be kept therein, together with methods for keeping stored foods fresh. He gives several recipes for "iron rations" for the besieged and recommends poisoning supplies that might otherwise be used by the enemy. He promises a full treatment of poisons in a later book (presumably one of the lost chapters of book 8). Philo also gives a list of materials and tools to be prepared or procured against a siege, and describes an optical telegraph, which employs a clepsydra as a mechanism, for maintaining communications with allies beyond the perimeter of the besieging forces.

Section 3 has seventy-five chapters, primarily devoted to a number of different ways of defending town walls against attack and to the means of defense against an attack from the sea. Philo also discusses the importance of the availability of good doctors during time of war, and states that invalids should be made certain of pensions, that the dead should be buried with honor, and that widows should be provided for.

The last section is 111 chapters long; it deals with how to lay siege to a town, how to use catapults, testudos, and other engines of war, and how to capture a town through starvation or bribery. There are also discussions of secret messages (Philo promises a more detailed discussion of this subject in a following book that is now lost) and cryptography, and an account of how to attack a town from the sea. Philo again mentions his longer treatment of poisons, this time as something that he has already written; it may therefore be assumed that this chapter is one of the missing fragments of book 8. He further states that he has drawn figures to illustrate all of the kinds of fortifications that he has discussed,[9] but these drawings have also been lost.

Since only fragments remain, it is impossible to judge Philo's textbook on mechanics as a whole. His thoroughness and attention to detail, however, are evident in every part that remains. He is not identical with a later Philo of Byzantium who wrote a work on the seven wonders of the world.

NOTES

1. Vitruvius, *De architectura*, VII, intro., 14.
2. Hero, *Automata*, XX, 1 and 3. *Heronis Alexandrini Opera quae supersunt omnia*, W. Schmidt, ed., I (Leipzig 1899).
3. Eutocius, in *Archimedis Opera omnia cum commentariis Eutocii*, J. L. Heiberg, ed., 2nd ed., III (Leipzig, 1915), 60.
4. B. Carra de Vaux, "L'invention de l'hydraulis," in *Revue des études grecques*, **21** (1908), 332–340.
5. Hermann Diels, "Über das physikalische System des Straton," in *Sitzungsberichte der Preussischen Akademie der Wissenschaften zu Berlin*, **9** (1893), 110, n. 3.
6. Philo, *Belopoeica*, VII.
7. Eutocius, *loc. cit.*, n. 3 above.
8. A. G. Drachmann, *Ktesibios, Philon and Heron*, no. 4 in the series Acta Historica Scientiarum Naturalium et Medicinalium (Copenhagen, 1948).
9. Philo, *Mechanics*, 7–8, sec. 1, ch. 87.

BIBLIOGRAPHY

Editions of Philo's works are the Greek texts of the *Belopoeica* and the *Poliorcetica*, both edited by R. Schoene: *Philonis mechanicae syntaxis libri IV et V* (Berlin 1892), where IV is the *Belopoeica* and V the *Poliorcetica*, later known as bks. 7–8.

A later ed. of the *Belopoeica* is Philon's *Belopoiika* (*4. Buch der Mechanik*), H. Diels and E. Schramm, eds., in *Abhandlungen der Preussischen Akademie der Wissenschaften* for 1918, Phil.-hist. Kl., no. 16 (Berlin 1919), with the Greek text, the MS figures, a German trans., and reconstructions of all the engines.

The book on *Pneumatics*, found in Arabic trans. only, is edited by Carra de Vaux: "Le livre des appareils pneumatiques et des machines hydrauliques, par Philon de Byzance," in *Notices et extraits des manuscrits de la Bibliothèque nationale*, **38** (1903), 27–235; here is the Arabic text and a French trans., with intro. (all figures redrawn by the editor).

A Latin trans. of an Arabic trans. of the first 16 chs. of the *Pneumatics* is edited by V. Rose, in *Anecdota graeca et graecolatina*, no. 2 (Berlin, 1870), 297–314, with 13 figs. copied from the MS. This ed. is reprinted in *Heronis Alexandrini Opera quae supersunt omnia*, I (Leipzig, 1899), 458–489, with a German trans. The original of the Latin trans. is slightly different from the Arabic text edited by Carra de Vaux.

The *Paraskeuastica* and *Poliorcetica* have been published as *Exzerpte aus Philons Mechanik B. VII und VIII* (*vulgo fünftes Buch*), Greek text with German trans. by H. Diels and E. Schramm, in *Abhandlungen der preussischen Akademie der Wissenschaften* for 1919 (1920), Phil.-hist. Kl., no. 12; with drawings by the editors.

A. G. DRACHMANN

PHILOLAUS OF CROTONA (*fl.* second half of fifth century B.C.), *philosophy, astronomy, medicine.*

Like the majority of the Pythagoreans living in the Pythagorean centers of Crotona and Metapontum in the middle of the fifth century B.C., Philolaus fled after the oubreak of the democratic rebellion, during which the meeting houses of the Pythagoreans were burned down. He first went to Thebes but later settled in Tarentum, the only remaining center of Pythagorean political activity in southern Italy. There he is said to have taught the mathematician Archytas.

The ancient tradition concerning Philolaus' writings and doctrine is so confused and contradictory that some modern scholars have questioned his very existence, others have doubted that he ever wrote or published anything, and still others have tried to show that none of the fragments that have come down to us under his name are genuine. His existence, however, is established beyond reasonable doubt by Plato's *Phaedo* (61e). That there existed at least one genuine work by Philolaus is attested by Menon, a disciple of Aristotle and a conscientious historian who lived only about a century later than Philolaus. In his history of medicine, of which fragments have been discovered on a papyrus, Menon quotes Philolaus' medical doctrines.

According to a widespread ancient tradition, Philolaus had written, but did not publish, a comprehensive work of Pythagorean doctrine, the manuscript of which was purchased by Plato at a very high price and then copied. Thus Philolaus' work became public. After the book had become famous, other books, not written by Philolaus, appear to have been published under his name. Since all later Pythagoreanism was strongly influenced by Plato, however, it is possible to distinguish between pre-Platonic and post-Platonic Pythagorean literature. This criterion has been used especially by W. Burkert to separate the probably genuine from the spurious fragments of Philolaus' work.

According to this criterion, the fragments that can be considered genuine contain many rather abstruse speculations concerning the relation between certain numbers and certain gods of traditional Greek mythology, as well as speculations about numbers, places, and things that were more noble or more deserving of honor ($\tau\iota\mu\iota\acute{\omega}\tau\epsilon\rho\alpha$) than others. The fragments also reveal a tendency to combine elements of various doctrines that were prevalent in the second half of the fifth century–although not all were specifically Pythagorean—into a rather muddled whole. This approach is hardly "scientific," and there would be little reason to mention Philolaus in the context of the history of science if it were not for the considerable influence of his astronomical system on the development of astronomy, even after Copernicus.

Knowledge of this system has evolved from three sources: Aetius, a late Greek doxographer; Achilles, a late Greek commentator on the *Phaenomena* of Aratus; and Aristotle. The first two, who differ from each other in some details, especially in the explanation of the light emanating from the sun, mention Philolaus by name. Aristotle, describing essentially the same system, does not mention Philolaus by name but attributes the system to "some of the Pythagoreans, who had lived in Southern Italy," Aristotle's reason for this attribution may be that, according to one tradition, Philolaus' system was further elaborated by a certain Hicetas.

Contrary to all earlier astronomical systems, and also to those accepted later by Plato and Aristotle, Philolaus' system states that the center of the universe is occupied not by the earth but by a central fire (not identical with the sun), around which the earth moves at considerable speed. That we do not see this central fire is explained by assuming that the earth always turns the same side to the central fire and that we live on the opposite side. A "counter-earth," or "anti-earth" ($\dot{\alpha}\nu\tau\acute{\iota}\chi\theta\omega\nu$), exists on the opposite side of the central fire but at a lesser distance. The "anti-earth" revolves around the central fire simultaneously with the earth, which is why we can never see it. Above the earth and at greater distances from the central fire the other heavenly bodies likewise revolve around the central fire—first the moon, then the sun, and then the five planets: Mercury, Venus, Mars, Jupiter, and Saturn. Outermost is the fiery sphere of the fixed stars. The sun, according to Aetius, is a hollow mirror collecting the light from below (the central fire?) and reflecting and focusing it toward the earth. According to Achilles, it is, on the contrary, similar to a convex lens, collecting the light that emanates from the outer sphere and likewise focusing it in the direction of the earth.

To understand the position of this strange system within the history of astronomy, the following factors must be considered. From the early fifth century B.C. Greek philosophers and cosmologists were puzzled by the apparently irregular motions of certain heavenly bodies. Anaxagoras, among others, tried to explain the movements of the stars by adopting mechanics as an analogue. Others, like the early Pythagoreans, considered the heavenly bodies as living beings endowed with a higher reason than humans. These philosophers thought it unworthy of such divine beings to move as irregularly as animals on this earth, rather than moving with a constant speed in the most beautiful and simple curve—the circle. Plato, who adopted this view, asked the famous mathematician Eudoxus of Cnidus if the apparent movements of the celestial bodies could be explained on the assumption that they were combinations of circular movements with constant velocity. Eudoxus actually succeeded in constructing a model of twenty-seven spheres, one within the other and each moving at a constant speed. The inner spheres were directed by the outer spheres, which moved in different directions. Thus the apparent movements of the celestial bodies could be approximately accounted for. Because of careful observations, some disagreements remained; and the number of spheres within this system was later increased to thirty-three by the astronomer Callippus. Aristotle increased the number to fifty-five. Within all these systems, however, the earth remained in the center of the universe.

By removing the earth from the center of the universe, Philolaus anticipated modern astronomical theory and, specifically, the Copernican system. It is natural to assume that Philolaus must have tried also to account mathematically for the apparent movements of the heavenly bodies, although it is difficult to see what the assumption of an invisible central fire and an invisible anti-earth could have contributed to such an explanation. Since the system, as reported by both Aetius and Achilles, did not present such an account, B. L. Van der Waerden suspected that Philolaus' system must have differed from that described by ancient tradition. He states that either the most important step in the development of early Greek astronomy was taken by a muddleheaded speculator (*ein Wirrkopf*) or Philolaus' system must have been different.

Van der Waerden, in a most ingenious fashion, constructed a Philolaic system, accounting to some extent for the observed phenomena. Aristotle, however, when speaking of the Pythagoreans of southern Italy, who invented the system otherwise ascribed to Philolaus, states expressly that they did not try to account for the observed phenomena by means of mathematical constructions. Instead, they removed the earth from the center of the universe for the sole reason that only fire, the most noble (τιμιώτατον) of the elements, was worthy of occupying that place. The anti-earth was added to bring the number of the celestial bodies to ten, because ten was the "perfect number." If this is so—and Aristotle, after all, is not a contemptible witness—one will have to admit that it was an unscientific, muddleheaded speculator and not a great mathematician or astronomer who first suggested, against all appearances, that the earth is not in the center of the universe and that it is not at rest but moving along at great speed. This speculator also encouraged the inventors of the heliocentric system, Aristarchus of Samos and Copernicus, who greatly admired Philolaus.

BIBLIOGRAPHY

On Philolaus and his influence, see A. Boeckh, *Philolaus des Pythagoreers Lehren nebst den Bruchstücken seines Werkes* (Berlin, 1819); W. Burkert, *Weisheit und Wissenschaft* (Nuremburg, 1962); H. Diels, "Über die Excerpte von Menons Iatrica in dem Londoner Papyrus 137," in *Hermes*, **28** (1893), 428–434; K. von Fritz, *Grundprobleme der Geschichte der antiken Wissenschaften* (Berlin, 1970), 157–166; R. Mondolfo, "Sui frammenti di Filolao. Contribuzione a una revisione del processo di falsità," in *Rivista di filologia e di istruzione classica*, n.s. **15** (1937), 225–245; B. L. Van der Waerden, "Die Astronomie der Pythagoreer," in *Verhandlingen der K. nederlandsche akademie van wetenschappen*. Afdeeling natuurkunde, **20**, pt. 1 (1951), 1–136; and K. von Fritz, "Philolaos" in Pauly-Wissowa, supp. XIII (1974), 453–483.

KURT VON FRITZ

PHILOPONUS. See **John Philoponus.**

PIANESE, GIUSEPPE (*b.* Civitanova del Sannio, Campobasso, Italy, 19 March 1864; *d.* Naples, Italy, 22 March 1933), *pathological anatomy*.

For a detailed study of his life and work, see Supplement.

PIAZZI, GIUSEPPE (*b.* Ponte in Valtellina, Italy [now Switzerland], 16 July 1746; *d.* Naples, Italy, 22 July 1826), *astronomy*.

As a young man, Piazzi entered the Theatine Order in Milan. He completed his studies there and in Rome, obtaining the doctorate in philosophy and mathematics. From 1769 until 1779 Piazzi taught mathematics in a number of Italian cities; in 1780 he was summoned by the prince of Caramanico, Bourbon viceroy of Sicily, to fill the chair of higher mathematics at the Academy of Palermo. The viceroy encouraged Piazzi in his wish to establish an astronomical observatory in Palermo, and toward the end of the 1780's Piazzi went to England in order to obtain the best possible equipment.

In England, Piazzi met Maskelyne, William Herschel, and Ramsden. He investigated Herschel's large telescopes (indeed, he fell and broke his arm while examining one of them that was mounted outdoors) and, with Maskelyne, observed at Greenwich the solar eclipse of 3 June 1788. His first astronomical work, a study of the difference in longitude between various observatories, based on that of Greenwich, was published in the *Philosophical Transactions of the Royal Society* in 1789. The most important result of Piazzi's English visit, however, was the great five-foot vertical circle, a masterpiece of eighteenth-century technology, that he commissioned from Ramsden. It was installed in the new observatory in the Santa Ninfa tower of the royal palace of Palermo in 1789, and is still preserved there. The Palermo observatory opened in 1790, and Piazzi was appointed its director, a post that he retained for most of the rest of his life.

Having returned to Palermo, Piazzi took up the problem of the precise determination of the astronomical coordinates (direct ascension and declination) of the principal stars. Palermo was then the southernmost European observatory, and the favorable climatic conditions that it provided allowed him to study more stars than had been previously cataloged, with a greater degree of accuracy. In the course of his regular observations Piazzi, on the night of 1 January 1801, was searching a region in Taurus in which he hoped to see a star of the seventh magnitude, listed in Lacaille's catalog, which he had previously observed. Before that star appeared, however, he noticed the passage of a somewhat fainter body that Lacaille had not listed. Piazzi continued to observe the new body on the following evenings and ascertained from its movement that it must be a planet or comet. He watched it regularly until 11 February 1801, during which period its retrograde motion ceased and it began to advance, until it had moved near enough to the sun that it could not be seen at its passage to the meridian. It was therefore necessary to calculate its orbit around the sun to find it again.

Piazzi communicated his discovery almost immediately to his friend Barnaba Oriani, director of the Brera observatory in Milan, and to J. E. Bode, director of the Berlin observatory. As early as 24 January 1801, he wrote to Oriani:

> I have announced this star as a comet, but since it is not accompanied by any nebulosity and, further, since its movement is so slow and rather uniform, it has occurred to me several times that it might be something better than a comet. But I have been careful not to advance this supposition to the public. I will try to calculate its elements when I have made more observations.

In his reply to Piazzi, Oriani wrote, "I congratulate you on your splendid discovery of this new star. I do not think that others have noticed it, and because of its smallness, it is unlikely that many astronomers will see it."

Piazzi had made observations for a period of forty-one days, over a geocentric arc of only 3°. He published his observations in 1801 as *Risultati delle osservazioni della nuova stella scoperta il 1° gennaio 1801 nell'Osservatorio di Palermo*. Other astronomers were eager to rediscover the new body; if it were a planet, it should be possible, on the example of Uranus, to compute from Piazzi's observations a circular orbit, even if the arc of the presumably elliptical orbit were to prove short. In December 1801 Gauss calculated both such an orbit and an ephemeris for the new body. He communicated his calculations to F. X. von Zach, director of the Gotha observatory, who employed them to rediscover the body in almost exactly the position that Gauss had predicted. It was thus apparent that it was a planet, and in a publication of 1802, *Della scoperta del nuovo pianeta "Cerere Ferdinandea,"* Piazzi named it for Ceres, the patron goddess of Sicily.

Piazzi's discovery involved him in a genteel polemic with William Herschel; on 22 May 1802, following Olbers' discovery of Pallas, Herschel wrote to Piazzi from Slough to argue that these new planets could not be so called in the same sense as the planets within the solar system. He proposed that Ceres and Pallas be called "asteroids," since they are intermingled with, and similar to, the small fixed stars. He further suggested that these bodies were not worthy of the name of planets, since they did not occupy the space betweeen Mars and Jupiter "with sufficient dignity." Herschel went on to advocate three forms of celestial bodies—planets, asteroids, and comets—a hierarchy

that led Piazzi to gloss his letter with the remark, "Soon we shall also be seeing counts, dukes, and marquesses in the sky!" (In the course of time, the question has been resolved in Piazzi's favor, since "asteroid" has fallen into disuse, while the term "small planet" has become standard.)

In 1792 Piazzi returned to making precise determinations of the coordinates of the fixed stars. After ten years of intense and fatiguing work, he published at Palermo, in 1803, a catalog of the medial positions of 6,748 stars, under the title *Praecipuarum stellarum inerrantium positiones mediae ineunte saeculo decimonono ex observationibus habitis in specula panoromitana ab anno 1792 ad annum 1802*. This catalog was more accurate than any of its predecessors; Zach pronounced it epochal, and the Institut de France awarded it the Lalande prize for the best astronomical work published in 1803.

Piazzi then carried his work a step further. Doubting the value of the precession of the equinoxes used at that time, Piazzi undertook to determine the right ascension of a number of basic stars, relating them directly to the sun, in order to improve on earlier observations (including those made at Greenwich). Since he was at that time in poor health, he enlisted the aid of Niccolò Cacciatore as his collaborator. Piazzi's *Praecipuarum stellarum inerrantium positiones mediae ineunte saeculo decimonono ex observationibus habitis in specula panormitana ab anno 1792 ad annum 1813*, published in Palermo in 1813, cataloged the mean position of 7,646 stars. It was widely esteemed among astronomers, and the Institut de France again awarded Piazzi a prize.

In 1817 Piazzi published (again at Palermo) the two-volume *Lezioni elementari di astronomia*, which he sent to Oriani, who discussed it appreciatively. Oriani was also anxious to persuade Piazzi to republish his earlier observations, but he did not do so. (In 1845 L. von Littrow incorporated Piazzi's observations of 1792 to 1795 in *Annalen der K. K. Sternwarte in Wien*.)

In March 1817 Piazzi was summoned to Naples by King Ferdinand I, who wished him to supervise the completion of the observatory already under construction on the hill at Capodimonte. The building had been begun under the direction of Joachim Murat, but had remained unfinished because of the unstable political circumstances of the kingdom. Although he received an enthusiastic reception, Piazzi was reluctant to leave Palermo. He stated his feelings in a letter to Oriani: "I shall never yield to the invitations and kindnesses that are showered upon me so that I might remain in Naples. I would thus stain the last years of my life with the vilest ingratitude." The king nevertheless appointed him director general of the observatories of both Sicily and Naples, with the freedom to remain in whichever of the two kingdoms that he preferred, and Piazzi subsequently divided his time between the two. He took considerable pains in the building and equipping of the Naples observatory, and, on Oriani's recommendation, secured Carlo Brioschi, of the Istituto Geografico Militare Lombardo, as its director. Brioschi gratified Piazzi by publishing, in 1824, *Comentari astronomici della specola reale di Napoli.*

Piazzi returned to settle in Naples in 1824, his health weakened. The king had commissioned him to reform the system of weights and measures, and he had been elected president of the Neapolitan Academy of Sciences. He died in Naples of an acute disease.

BIBLIOGRAPHY

I. ORIGINAL WORKS. Piazzi's major works are cited in the text. In addition, a partial bibliography—beginning with his first publication, "Results of Calculations of the Observations Made at Various Places of the Eclipse of the Sun . . . on June 3, 1788," in *Philosophical Transactions of the Royal Society,* **79** (1789), 55–61—is in the Royal Society *Catalogue of Scientific Papers,* IV, 897.

II. SECONDARY LITERATURE. See G. Abetti, *Storia dell'astronomia* (Florence, 1963); F. Angelitti, "Per il centenario della morte dell'astronomo Giuseppe Piazzi," in *Memorie della Società astronomica italiana,* **3** (1925), 369–395; A. Bemporad, "Giuseppe Piazzi—commemorazione tenuta nella R. Università di Napoli," *ibid.,* 396–413; and Rudolf Wolf, *Biographien zur Kulturgeschichte der Schweiz,* IV (Zurich, 1862), 275–292.

GIORGIO ABETTI

PICARD, CHARLES ÉMILE (*b.* Paris, France, 24 July 1856; *d.* Paris, 11 December 1941), *mathematics.*

Picard's father, the director of a silk factory, was of Burgundian origin; his mother was the daughter of a doctor from northern France. At the death of her husband, during the siege of Paris in 1870, she was obliged to seek employment in order to care for her two sons. Picard was a brilliant student at the Lycée Henri IV and was especially interested in literature, Greek, Latin, and history. An avid reader with a remarkable memory, he acquired a rare erudition. For many years he retained a liking for physical exercise—gymnastics and mountain climbing—and an interest in carefully planned travel. He chose his vocation after reading a book on algebra at the end of his secondary studies. In 1874, after only one year of preparation, he was accepted as first candidate by the École Normale Supérieure and as second candidate by the École Polytechnique. After a famous interview with Pasteur, he chose the former, where he would be permitted to devote himself entirely to research. He placed first in the competition for the *agrégation* in 1877 but had already made several important discoveries and had received the degree of *docteur ès sciences.*

From 1877 to 1878 Picard was retained as an assistant at the École Normale Supérieure. Appointed professor at the University of Toulouse in 1879, he returned to Paris in 1881 as lecturer in physical and experimental mechanics at the Sorbonne and as lecturer in mechanics and astronomy at the École Normale Supérieure. Although he accepted these teaching posts outside his preferred field, Picard continued his work in analysis, and the first of the two famous theorems that bear his name dates from 1879, when he was twenty-three. In 1885 he was unanimously elected to the chair of differential and integral calculus at the Sorbonne, where he served as his own *suppléant* before reaching the prescribed age of thirty for the post. In 1897, at his own request, he exchanged this chair for that of analysis and higher algebra, where he was able to train students for research.

Nominated in 1881 by the section of geometry for election to the Académie des Sciences, he was elected in 1889. In 1886 he received the Prix Poncelet and in 1888 the Grand Prix des Sciences Mathématiques for a memoir that was greatly admired by Poincaré. Picard's mathematical activity during the period 1878–1888 resulted in more than 100 articles and notes. A member of the Académie Française (1924), he received the Grande Croix de la Légion d'Honneur in 1932 and the Mittag-Leffler Gold Medal from the Swedish Academy of Sciences in 1937. He received an honorary doctorate from five foreign universities and was a member of thirty-seven academies and learned societies.

Picard was chairman of numerous commissions, including the Bureau des Longitudes; and his administrative abilities and his sincere and resolute character earned him great prestige. As permanent secretary of the Académie des Sciences from 1917 to his death in 1941, he wrote an annual notice on either a scientist or a subject of current interest. He also wrote many prefaces to mathematical books and participated in the publication of works of C. Hermite and G.-H. Halphen.

An outstanding teacher, Picard was devoted to the young, and from 1894 to 1937 he trained more than 10,000 engineers at the École Centrale des Arts et Manufactures. He was responsible, with extraordinary success, for choosing pupil-teachers at the École Normale Supérieure de Jeunes Filles de Sèvres (1900–1927). He was director of the Société des Amis des Sciences, founded by Pasteur to look after needy scholars and their families.

In 1881 Picard married the daughter of his mentor and friend Charles Hermite. His life of uninterrupted professional success was clouded by the death of his daughter and two sons in World War I. His grandsons were wounded and captured in World War II, and the invasion and occupation of France darkened the last two years of his life. He died in the Palais de l'Institut, where he lived as *secrétaire perpétuel* of the Academy.

Picard's works were mostly in mathematical analysis and algebraic geometry. As early as 1878 he had studied the integrals of differential equations by making successive substitutions with equations having suitable partial derivatives. The following year he discovered the first of the two well-known theorems that bear his name. The first states: Let $f(z)$ be an entire function. If there exist two values of A for which the equation $f(z) = A$ does not have a finite root, then $f(z)$ is a constant. From this theorem it follows that if $f(z)$ is an entire function that is not a constant, there cannot be more than one value of A for which $f(z) = A$ has no solution.

Picard's second theorem, which extended a result stated by Weierstrass, states: Let $f(z)$ be a function, analytic everywhere except at a, where it has an essential isolated singularity; the equation $f(z) = A$ has in general an infinity of roots in any neighborhood of a. Although the equation can fail for certain exceptional values of the constant A, there cannot be more than two such values (1880). This result led to a classification of regular analytic functions; and it was the origin of important work carried out especially by Émile Borel and Otto von Blumenthal. The latter established generalizations that he called Picard's little theorem and Picard's big theorem. Picard's theorems revealed the fruitfulness of the idea of introducing, in the terms of a problem, a restriction bearing on the case of an exception that can be shown to be unique.

From 1883 to 1888 Picard extended Poincaré's investigations on automorphic functions to functions of two complex variables, which he called hypergeometric and hyperfuchsian (1883, 1885). These functions led Picard to the study of algebraic surfaces (1901). Setting himself the task of studying the analogies between the theory of linear differential equations and the theory of algebraic equations, Picard took up Galois's theory and obtained for a

linear differential equation a group of transformations now called the Picard group.

Picard's method for demonstrating the existence of the integrals of differential equations by successive approximations at first appears very simple. The introduction of n functions $u_1, u_2, \ldots, u_n$ reestablishes the system

$$\frac{du_i}{dx} = f_i(x, u_1, u_2, \cdots, u_n), \qquad i = 1, 2, \cdots, n,$$

with the initial conditions $x = x_0$ gives $u_i = a_i$. There is then resolved by n quadratures the system

$$\frac{dv_i}{dx} = f_i(x, a_1, a_2, \cdots, a_n),$$

the v_i satisfying the initial conditions and the same being true of

$$\frac{dw_i}{dx} = f_i(x, v_1, v_2, \cdots, v_n)$$

and so forth. It remains to prove—and this is the essential point—that under certain conditions (identified by Cauchy) the functions that are successively introduced tend toward limits that are precisely the desired integrals in the neighborhood of x_0. Picard himself extended his method to numerous cases, particularly to the equations of complex variables and also to integral equations. He, as well as his successors, thus demonstrated the preeminence of his method. Integral equations became of considerable importance in mathematical physics, with much of the genuine progress due to Fredholm. By completing the earlier works, Picard made more precise the necessary conditions for the existence of the various types of equations.

These works, as well as many dispersed results found in notes, were assembled in Picard's three-volume *Traité d'analyse*, which immediately became a classic and was revised with each subsequent edition. The work was accessible to many students through its range of subjects, clear exposition, and lucid style. Picard examined several specific cases before discussing his general theory.

In theoretical physics Picard applied analysis to theories of elasticity, heat, and electricity. He was particularly successful in achieving an elegant solution to the problem of the propagation of electrical impulses along cables (*équation des télégraphiques*). This research was to have been collected in a fourth volume of his treatise on analysis; but it appeared instead in four fascicles of *Cahiers scientifiques*.

After 1900 Picard published several historical and philosophical reflections, in particular *La science moderne et son état actuel* (1905), and speeches and reports. When he was more than eighty years old he presented considerations on the questions of homogeneity and similarity encountered by physicists and engineers.

Throughout his life Picard supported the innovations of other mathematicians, including the early work of Lebesgue. With Poincaré he was the most distinguished French mathematician of his generation.

BIBLIOGRAPHY

I. ORIGINAL WORKS. Picard's writings include "Sur la forme des équations différentielles du second ordre dans le voisinage de certains points critiques," in *Comptes rendus hebdomadaires des séances de l'Académie des sciences*, **87** (1878), 430–432, 743–746; "Mémoire sur les fonctions entières," in *Annales scientifiques de l'École normale supérieure*, 2nd ser., **9** (1880), 145–166; "Sur la réduction du nombre des périodes des intégrales abéliennes," in *Bulletin de la Société mathématique de France*, **11** (1883), 25–53; "Sur les fonctions hyperfuchsiennes provenant des séries hypergéométriques de deux variables," in *Annales scientifiques de l'École normale supérieure*, 3rd ser., **2** (1885), 357–384; "Mémoire sur la théorie des fonctions algébriques de deux variables indépendantes," in *Journal de mathématiques pures et appliquées*, 4th ser., **5** (1889), 135–319; *Traité d'analyse*, 3 vols. (Paris, 1891–1896); and *Théorie des fonctions algébriques de deux variables indépendantes*, 2 vols. (Paris, 1897–1906), written with Georges Simart.

Subsequent writings include "Sur la résolution de certaines équations à deux variables," in *Bulletin de la Société mathématique de France*, **25** (1901); *Sur le développement de l'analyse et ses rapports avec diverses sciences* (Paris, 1905); *La science moderne et son état actuel* (Paris, 1905); *L'histoire des sciences et les prétentions de la science allemande* (Paris, 1916); *Les sciences mathématiques en France depuis un demi-siècle* (Paris, 1917); *Discours et mélanges* (Paris, 1922); and *Mélange de mathématiques et de physique* (Paris, 1924).

His later writings are "Leçons sur quelques types simples d'équations aux dérivées partielles avec des applications à la physique mathématique," in *Cahiers scientifiques*, fasc. 1 (1925); "Leçons sur quelques équations fonctionnelles avec des applications à divers problèmes d'analyse et de physique mathématique," *ibid.*, fasc. 3 (1928); "Leçons sur quelques problèmes aux limites de la théorie des équations différentielles," *ibid.*, fasc. 5 (1930); "Leçons sur quelques équations fonctionnelles," *ibid.*, fasc. 6 (1930); *Un coup d'oeil sur l'histoire des sciences et des théories physiques* (Paris, 1930); "Quelques applications analytiques de la théorie des courbes et des surfaces algébriques," in *Cahiers scientifiques*, fasc. 9 (1931); and *Discours et notices* (Paris, 1936).

II. SECONDARY LITERATURE. An early biography of Picard is Ernest Lebon, *Émile Picard, biographie, bibliographie* (Paris, 1910), which has details of 256 of his works. See also René Garnier, ed., *Centenaire de la nais-*

sance d'Émile Picard (Paris, 1957), which has reports of speeches by colleagues and pupils.

His mathematical discoveries are discussed in Émile Borel, *Leçons sur les fonctions méromorphes* (Paris, 1903), ch. 3; and Otto Blumenthal, *Principes de la théorie des fonctions entières d'ordre infini* (Paris, 1910), ch. 7.

LUCIENNE FÉLIX

PICARD, JEAN (*b*. La Flèche, France, 21 July 1620; *d*. Paris, France, 12 October 1682), *astronomy, geodesy*.

Nothing is known about Picard's youth. According to Esprit Pezenas in *Histoire critique de la découverte des longitudes* (1775), it was the astronomer Jacques de Valois who led Picard, a gardener for the duke of Créqui, to make astronomical observations and who may also have encouraged him to enter a seminary, where he seems to have taken religious orders; at the end of his life Picard may have been prior of the abbey of Rillé in Anjou. On 21 August 1645 Picard assisted Gassendi in the observation of a solar eclipse and remained with him for some time. Some biographers have thought that he substituted for and then replaced Gassendi in his chair at the Collège Royal, but archival evidence contradicts this hypothesis.

In 1666 Picard was named a founding member of the Académie Royale des Sciences and, even before its opening, participated in several astronomical observations. In collaboration with Adrien Auzout he perfected the movable-wire micrometer and utilized it to measure the diameters of the sun, the moon, and the planets. During the summer of 1667 he applied the astronomical telescope to the instruments used in making angular measurements—quadrants and sectors—and was aware that this innovation greatly expanded the possibilities of astronomical observation. The making of meridian observations by the method of corresponding heights, which he suggested in 1669, was not put into practice until after his death. Yet when the Academy decided to remeasure an arc of meridian in order to obtain a more accurate figure for the earth's radius, Picard was placed in charge of the operation. He employed the method of skeleton triangulation devised by Snell (1617) but greatly improved the associated observational techniques.

Picard decided to measure the distance between two localities at approximately the same meridian (Sourdon, near Amiens, and Malvoisine, near Corbeil-Essonnes), to determine the difference in their latitudes, and to deduce from these results the length of a degree of meridian. The project lasted from 1668 to 1670. The base he selected was very long (5,663 toises, as against the 168 used by Snell) and his triangulation consisted of thirteen triangles. But it was primarily through the use of instruments fitted with telescopes, quadrants, and sectors for angular measurements that Picard attained a precision thirty to forty times greater than that achieved previously. Consequently, from his measurements of the various distances and angles, Picard was able to obtain the notable result of 57,060 toises for the terrestrial degree (Lacaille in 1740 and Delambre in 1798 obtained 57,074 toises). This increased precision made possible a great advance in the determination of geographical coordinates and in cartography, and enabled Newton in 1684 to arrive at a striking confirmation of the accuracy of his principle of gravitation.

The results of this undertaking were scarcely published in Picard's *Mesure de la terre* (1671) when he undertook another project that he had proposed to the Academy in 1669: to determine the coordinates of Uraniborg in order to compare the important observations that Tycho Brahe had made there between 1576 and 1597 with those that would be obtained at the Paris observatory. During eight months in Denmark in 1671–1672, Picard, aided by one assistant and a young Danish astronomer, Ole Römer—whose outstanding ability he recognized—obtained the data he was seeking. He convinced Römer to return with him to France, and Römer carried out brilliant work at Paris until 1681. In compiling his registers of observations, Picard noted an annual displacement of the polestar that was later explained by the combination of aberration and nutation; he also brought back a copy of Tycho Brahe's registers of observations.

In 1673 Picard moved into the Paris observatory and collaborated with Cassini, Römer, and, later, Philippe de La Hire on the institution's regular program of observations. He also joined many missions away from the observatory. The first of these enabled him to provide more precise data on the coordinates of various French cities (1672–1674); others, conducted from 1679 to 1681 with La Hire, had the purpose of establishing the bases of the principal triangulation of a new map of France. The results of these geodesic observations were published in 1693 by La Hire. The new map that was drawn from them contained corrections of as much as 150 kilometers' longitude and 50 kilometers' latitude.

Meanwhile, in 1674–1675 Picard played a very active role in the important surveying operations undertaken by the Academy to supply the châteaux of Marly and Versailles with water. He perfected the existing methods, notably through use of the telescope level, and prepared a treatise on this subject published by La Hire in 1684. Picard was not able to put the finishing touches on the book; for, although he was still making observations on 12 September 1682, he died on 12 October after a brief illness.

Picard was also responsible for many improvements in procedures and instruments and for observations that stimulated later discoveries. For example, he pointed out the phenomenon of "barometric glow," the first observation of electric discharge in a rarefied gas. He was also one of the first to observe the fixed stars in full daylight. In addition, he noted the influence of temperature on atmospheric refraction and participated in the measurement of the parallax of Mars in 1672. But it was not he who published the first volumes of *Connaissance des temps* (1679–1684), as has been supposed, but Joachim Dalencé, who obtained the royal privilege for them.

Considered in his time a scientist of the first rank, Picard has been eclipsed by several of his contemporaries—for instance, Cassini. Nevertheless, he helped to advance several branches of science, exhibiting a remarkable flair for observation and a very refined sense of the practical.

BIBLIOGRAPHY

I. ORIGINAL WORKS. Picard wrote two books, *Mesure de la terre* and *Traité du nivellement* (see below), and a number of memoirs that appeared in the following compendia published by the Académie Royale des Sciences: *Recueil de plusieurs traitez de mathématiques* . . . (Paris, 1676), abbrev. as *Recueil de plusieurs traitez*; *Divers ouvrages de mathématiques et de physique* . . . (Paris, 1693), 337–422: "Divers ouvrages de M. Picard," P. de La Hire, ed., abbrev. as *Divers ouvrages*; *Recueil d'observations faites en plusieurs voyages par ordre de sa majesté pour perfectionner l'astronomie et la géographie avec divers traitez astronomiques* . . . (Paris, 1693), no. 3, P. de La Hire, ed., abbrev. as *Recueil*; *Mémoires de l'Académie royale des sciences depuis 1666 jusqu'en 1699*, VI (Paris, 1730), 479–707, "Divers ouvrages de M. Picard," abbrev. as *Mémoires*, VI; *Mémoires de l'Académie royale des sciences depuis 1666 jusqu'en 1699*, VII (Paris, 1729), 191–411, abbrev. as *Mémoires*, VII.

Mesure de la terre (Paris, 1671) was repr. without change in 1676 (*Recueil de plusieurs traitez*, no. 2) and repub. in 1729 (*Mémoires*, VII, 133–190) and in 1740 (in *Degré du méridien entre Paris et Amiens déterminé par la mesure de M. Picard et par les observations de MM. de Maupertuis, Clairaut, Camus, Le Monnier* [Paris, 1740], 1–106).

Traité du nivellement . . . avec une relation de quelques nivellements faits par ordre du roy et un abrégé de la Mesure de la terre . . . (Paris, 1684), which included additional material supplied by the editor, P. de La Hire, was repub.

in 1728, 1730 (*Mémoires*, VI, 631–707), and 1780; it was also trans. into Italian (Florence, 1723) and German (Berlin, 1749).

Picard's other writings were published in 1693 by P. de La Hire—generally on the basis of MSS, some of which were incomplete—and were brought out again in 1729–1730 in vols. VI and VII of the *Mémoires*. These include "De la pratique des grands cadrans par le calcul" (*Divers ouvrages*, 341–365; *Mémoires*, VI, 481–531); "De mensuris" (*Divers ouvrages*, 366–368; *Mémoires*, VI, 532–537); "De mensura liquidorum & aridorum" (*Divers ouvrages*, 370–374; *Mémoires*, VI, 540–549); "Fragmens de dioptrique" (*Divers ouvrages*, 375–412; *Mémoires*, VI, 550–627); "Voyage d'Uranibourg ou observations astronomiques faites au Danemarck" (*Recueil*, 1–29; *Mémoires*, VII, 191–230)—the title page of the first version of this work seems to indicate that it was published separately in 1680; "Observations astronomiques faites en divers endroits du royaume en 1672, 1673, 1674" (*Recueil*, 33–46; *Mémoires*, VII, 327–347); "Observations faites à Brest et Nantes en 1679," written with La Hire (*Recueil*, 47–56; *Mémoires*, VII, 377–390); "Observations faites à Bayonne, Bordeaux et Royan en 1680," written with La Hire (*Recueil*, 57–64; *Mémoires*, VII, 391–398); and "Observations faites aux côtes septentrionales de France en 1681," written with La Hire (*Recueil*, 65–76; *Mémoires*, VII, 399–411).

Picard's astronomical observations made at Paris between 1666 and 11 Sept. 1682 were incorporated by P. C. Le Monnier in his *Histoire céleste . . .* (Paris, 1741), 1–263. The registers that Picard kept of his observations are at the Paris observatory.

II. SECONDARY LITERATURE. The few biographical accounts devoted to Picard are quite short: J. A. N. de Concordet, in *Éloges des académiciens . . .* (Paris, 1773), 36–48; J. B. Delambre, in Michaud, ed., *Biographie universelle*, XXXIV (Paris, 1823), 253–256, and new ed., XXXIII (Paris, 1861), 173–175; F. Arago, in *Notices biographiques*, III (Paris, 1854), 313–314; E.-M., in F. Hoefer, ed., *Nouvelle biographie générale* (Paris, 1862), cols. 48–49; E. Doublet, in *Revue générale des sciences . . .*, **31** (1920), 561–564; F. Boquet, in *Histoire de l'astronomie* (Paris, 1925), 362–364; and E. Armitage, in *Endeavour*, **13**, no. 49 (1954), 17–21.

More precise details are in Fontenelle, *Histoire de l'Académie royale des sciences*, I (Paris, 1733), see secs. on "Astronomie" for 1666–1682, and II (1733), 202, 222–223, 353–354; and C. Wolf, *Histoire de l'observatoire de Paris de sa fondation à 1793* (Paris, 1902), see index. Picard's astronomical and geodesic work is analyzed in some detail by J.-S. Bailly in *Histoire de l'astronomie moderne*, II (Paris, 1779), 335–354; J. de Lalande, in *Bibliographie astronomique* (Paris, 1803), see index; J. B. Delambre, in *Histoire de l'astronomie moderne*, II (Paris, 1821), 597–632; and G. Bigourdan, *L'astronomie . . .* (Paris, 1916), see index. His work in cartography was treated by L. Gallois, "L'Académie des sciences et les origines de la carte de Cassini," in *Annales de géographie*, **18** (1909), 193–204.

Picard's collaboration with Auzout is discussed in a dissertation by R. M. McKeon, "Établissement de l'astronomie de précision et oeuvre d'Adrien Auzout" (Paris, 1965), see index.

JULIETTE TATON
RENÉ TATON

PICCARD, AUGUSTE (*b*. Basel, Switzerland, 28 January 1884; *d*. Lausanne, Switzerland, 24 March 1962), *physics*.

With his twin brother, Jean Félix (*d*. Minneapolis, Minnesota, 23 January 1960), Auguste Piccard achieved fame and distinction as a scientist and explorer of the stratosphere and the ocean depths. Sons of Jules and Hélène Haltenhoff Piccard, the Piccards were members of a prominent Vaudois family: their grandfather was *commissaire général* of the canton; their father, head of the chemistry department at the University of Basel; and their uncle Paul, designer of the first Niagara Falls–type turbines, which he manufactured and sold through the Piccard-Pictet Company he founded in Geneva. They attended the local *Oberrealschule* before entering the Federal Institute of Technology in Zurich, from which Auguste received a degree in mechanical, and Jean Félix in chemical engineering. Obtaining doctorates in their respective fields, the brothers served for many years as university professors, Auguste in Zurich and Brussels, Jean Félix at Munich (where he was assistant to Adolph von Baeyer), Lausanne, Chicago, the Massachusetts Institute of Technology, and the University of Minnesota. Jean also held positions with the Hercules Powder Company in Delaware and the Bartol Foundation of the Franklin Institute, Philadelphia; he became a U.S. citizen in 1931.

Auguste Piccard attracted world attention when, on 27 May 1931, ascending with Paul Kipfer from Augsburg, Germany, in a free balloon, he achieved a new altitude record of 51,775 feet. The sixteen-hour flight, which ended on an Austrian glacier, marked the first use of a pressurized cabin for manned flight. It was followed on 18 August 1932 by an ascent with Max Cosyns from Zurich that attained 53,153 feet and ended near Lake Garda, Italy. After his last flight, in 1937, Piccard devoted himself for the better part of ten years to studies aimed at realizing his youthful dream to "plunge into the sea deeper than any man before." Although interrupted by World War II, his research resulted in 1948 in an unsuccessful first trial of his bathyscaphe (from the Greek for "deep" and "boat")—a self-propelled, untethered metal sphere designed on balloon principles and intended to withstand pressures of 12,000 pounds per square inch at a depth of 12,000 feet, off the Cape Verde Islands. Despite this failure, a second model in 1953 carried Auguste and his son Jacques to a depth of 10,168 feet, thereby trebling the 1934 record of William Beebe off the Bermuda coast. Piccard and his son built a third bathyscaphe, *Trieste*, which he sold to the U.S. navy in the late 1950's. He lived to see his son, with Lt. Don Walsh, USN, set a new world record of 35,800 feet with the *Trieste* in the Marianas Trench of the Pacific Ocean on 23 January 1960. Father and son were working on a new ship called a mesoscaphe at the time of Piccard's death.

BIBLIOGRAPHY

I. ORIGINAL WORKS. Piccard wrote three books: *Audessus des nuages* (Paris, 1933); *Entre ciel et terre* (Lausanne, 1946); and *Au fond des mers en bathyscaphe* (Paris, 1954), the last published simultaneously in German as *Über den Wolken. Unter den Wellen* (Wiesbaden, 1954). A bibliography of his articles is in Latil and Rivoire (below).

II. SECONDARY LITERATURE. Works on Piccard are Adelaide Field, *Auguste Piccard, Captain of Space, Admiral of the Abyss* (Boston, 1969); Alan Honour, *Ten Miles High, Two Miles Deep; The Adventures of the Piccards* (New York, 1957); Pierre de Latil and Jean Rivoire, *Le professeur Auguste Piccard* (Paris, 1962); Alida Malkus, *Exploring the Sky and Sea; Auguste and Jacques Piccard* (Chicago, 1961); and Kurt R. Stehling and William Beller, "The First Space-Gondola Flight," in *Skyhooks* (New York, 1962), ch. 13.

MARVIN W. MCFARLAND

PICCOLOMINI, ARCANGELO (*b.* Ferrara, Italy, 1525; *d.* Rome, Italy, 19 October 1586), *medicine, anatomy, physiology.*

Little is known of Piccolomini's early life. He received his doctorate in philosophy and medicine at Ferrara, probably in the late 1540's, and then taught philosophy at the University of Bordeaux. In 1556 he published at Paris a commentary on Galen's *De humoribus*; Piccolomini dedicated the work to Bishop Michele della Torre, the papal nuncio in France. Under the latter's patronage Piccolomini went to Rome, where he was eventually named physician to Pope Pius IV (1559–1565). He retained this office until his death, serving in turn Pius V, Gregory XIII, and Sixtus V. In 1575 he was given the chair in medical practice at the Sapienza, where he also lectured on anatomy. In 1582 he became general *protomedicus* for the Papal States.

In 1586 Piccolomini published his course of anatomical lectures, *Anatomicae praelectiones*, to forestall an unauthorized edition based on the notes of students. The course itself was supplemented by a series of anatomical demonstrations by the prosector Leonardo Biondini. This collaboration may explain why Piccolomini did not stress thorough morphological description in his own lectures, except in individual instances where he regarded the descriptions of earlier anatomists as faulty. Among his more noteworthy descriptions were those of the abdominal muscles, the termination of the acoustic nerve, the anastomoses of the fetal heart, and the differences between the male and female pelvis. He was the first anatomist after Salomon Alberti (1585) to describe the venous valves as a general phenomenon, although, like Alberti, Piccolomini probably learned of the valves from Fabrici, who had publicly announced the discovery at Padua in 1578 or 1579. Piccolomini also related a number of interesting pathological observations.

On the whole, though, the element of descriptive anatomy in the *Praelectiones* is quite subordinate to the discussion of highly abstract questions of psychology and physiology. In its theoretical orientation the work resembles the "Physiologia" (1542) of Jean Fernel, who was the one contemporary to receive Piccolomini's unqualified praise. Piccolomini followed Fernel in maintaining a strongly Neoplatonist view of the soul and in stressing the importance of "supra-elementary" powers as causes of vital phenomena. He thought, for example, that the formative powers of animal semen were due to three supraelementary powers derived from the parents, namely celestial heat, celestial spirit, and the vegetative soul—"instructed and taught by the most wise God." But these powers could only begin the process of generation, the completion of which required the direct infusion of a substantial form from the heavenly bodies for each new creature.

While Piccolomini derived much of his physiology from Aristotle and Galen, his system had many characteristic features of its own. Most notably, where Aristotle regarded the heart as the one ruling organ of the body and Galen emphasized the independence of the brain and heart in controlling different aspects of bodily function, Piccolomini upheld the supreme hegemony of the brain, on which even the heart depends for its vivifying and pulsatile faculties. Piccolomini also rejected other Aristotelian and Galenic doctrines in favor of supposedly Hippocratic views: that the semen of both parents is drawn from all parts of their bodies, that the heart is a muscle, and that the peculiar "celestial heat" of animals is not innate but is inhaled together with the air. On numerous other points of detail Piccolomini introduced his own functional doctrines, most of them derived speculatively; and his opposition to several of Colombo's physiological theories included a lengthy refutation of the pulmonary circulation. *Anatomicae praelectiones* was not reprinted after 1586, but it left a number of discernible marks on the detailed texture of physiological thought during the late sixteenth and early seventeenth centuries.

BIBLIOGRAPHY

I. ORIGINAL WORKS. Piccolomini's works include *In librum Galeni de humoribus commentarii*, with Greek and Latin texts (Paris, 1556; Venice, 1556); and *Anatomicae praelectiones . . . explicantes mirificam corporis humani fabricam: et quae animae vires, quibus corporis partibus, tanquam instrumentis, ad suas obeundas actiones, utantur; sicuti tota anima, toto corpore* (Rome, 1586).

II. SECONDARY LITERATURE. On Piccolomini and his work, see Francesco Pierro, *Arcangelo Piccolomini Ferrarese (1525–1586) e la sua importanza nell'anatomia postvesaliana*, which is Quaderni di storia della scienza e della medicina, no. 6 (Ferrara, 1965).

JEROME J. BYLEBYL

PICKERING, EDWARD CHARLES (*b*. Boston, Massachusetts, 19 July 1846; *d*. Cambridge, Massachusetts, 3 February 1919), *astronomy*.

Pickering, the elder son of Edward Pickering and Charlotte Hammond, was a descendant of one of New England's oldest and most distinguished families. John Pickering, his first American ancestor, had emigrated from Yorkshire and settled in Salem, Massachusetts, in 1636, bringing with him the family coat of arms (a lion rampant) and the motto *Nil desperandum*. Timothy Pickering, Edward's great-grandfather, served in the cabinets of Washington and John Adams.

Pickering attended the Boston Latin School for five years, where he "studied little and learnt less." Forced to memorize long passages of such works as Xenophon's *Anabasis*, he acquired a great distaste for the classics. He did, however, find time to read mathematical works on his own, for example Charles Davies' *Legendre's Elements of Geometry and Trigonometry*. Finding these more to his liking, he proposed entering the Lawrence Scientific School at Harvard, only to be informed by his schoolmaster that the "only requisite would be to know enough to come in when it rained."

Pickering entered the chemical department of the Lawrence Scientific School in 1862, largely on the advice of Charles William Eliot, then assistant professor of mathematics and chemistry. There he "found studies hard but delightful and enjoyed work exceedingly." That spring, although offered a position as assistant instructor, he declined it on Eliot's advice and entered the engineering department. He graduated *summa cum laude* in 1865, on his nineteenth birthday.

After two years as assistant instructor of mathematics at the Lawrence Scientific School, Pickering was appointed assistant professor of physics at the recently founded Massachusetts Institute of Technology. During his ten years there, he revolutionized the teaching of physics. With the encouragement of the Institute's founder and president, William Barton Rogers, Pickering established the first physical laboratory in America specifically designed for student instruction. He devised a series of experiments on the construction and use of apparatus, the properties of gases, and the mechanics of solids, and wrote instructions to enable students to perform them. The students were further encouraged to design experiments and to publish their original research. Pickering later compiled the instructions he had written and published them as *Elements of Physical Manipulation* (2 vols. [Boston, 1873–1876]), thereby producing the first American laboratory manual of physics.

On 10 October 1876 Eliot, who had been elected president of Harvard in 1869, appointed Pickering director of the Harvard College Observatory. Pickering and his wife, Elizabeth Wadsworth Sparks (the daughter of Jared Sparks, a noted historian and former Harvard president), moved to Observatory Hill on 1 February 1877; and he began work that very day. Eliot's selection of a physicist for the post rather than an observational astronomer evoked considerable criticism. Eliot, however, had sound reasons for his appointment: he had known Pickering both as an undergraduate at the Lawrence Scientific School and as a colleague on the MIT faculty, and was thoroughly familiar with his unusual scientific and administrative abilities. It is also possible that Eliot was aware that the direction of astronomical research was undergoing a crucial change.

Pickering realized at once that the greatest opportunities in astronomical research lay in the new field of astrophysics rather than in the astronomy of position and motion, which had occupied the chief place in the programs of other observatories. This is not to say that he ignored the "old" astronomy—several members of the observatory staff spent twenty years in preparing each of the two Harvard zones of the Astronomische Gesellschaft's star catalog—but the astrophysical work accomplished under his directorship was of incomparably greater volume and importance. He was a pioneer in three main fields of astronomical research: visual photometry, stellar spectroscopy, and stellar photography.

Before Pickering began his photometric measurements, he made two important decisions: (1) he adopted the magnitude scale suggested by Norman Pogson in 1854, whereby a change of one magnitude represents a change of a factor of 2.512 in brightness, and (2) he chose α Ursae Minoris (Polaris), then thought to be of constant brightness, as the standard and arbitrarily assigned a magnitude of 2.1 to it. Working in close cooperation with George B. Clark, Pickering designed and had the firm of Alvan Clark and Sons construct several new models of photometers. This culminated in the development of a revolutionary new instrument, the meridian photometer, in which the image of a star crossing the meridian is brought alongside the image of Polaris by suitable arrangement of mirrors and prisms. Thus each star could be measured at its point of highest visibility.

This photometric work continued for nearly a quarter of a century. Pickering never tired of the routine work involved and made more than 1.5 million photometric readings. The brightness of every visible star was measured and remeasured to obtain the greatest possible accuracy. The photometric studies culminated in 1908 with the publication of the *Revised Harvard Photometry*. Printed as volumes 50 and 54 of the *Annals of Harvard College Observatory*, it lists the magnitudes of more than 45,000 stars brighter than the seventh magnitude and remained the standard reference until photographic methods largely supplanted visual ones.

Pickering's researches in stellar spectroscopy were made possible largely through the establishment of the Henry Draper Fund in 1886. Under the terms of this fund, Mrs. Draper supplied money to the Harvard observatory for Pickering and his assistants to photograph, measure, and classify the spectra of the stars and to publish the resulting catalog in the *Annals* as a memorial volume to Henry Draper. The program consisted of three main parts: a general survey of stellar spectra for all stars north of −25° and brighter than the sixth magnitude; a study of the spectra of the fainter stars; and a detailed investigation of the spectra of the brighter stars.

The spectra were produced by placing a large prism in front of the telescope's objective. While this did not give the definition attainable by use of a spectroscopic slit, it allowed a large number of spectra to be photographed on a single plate and gave sufficient definition. The principal investigators on the project were Williamina P. Fleming, Annie Jump Cannon, Antonia C. Maury (Henry Draper's niece), and a large corps of women computers. This led some contempo-

rary wags to refer to the Harvard team as "Pickering and his harem."

These investigations culminated with the publication of *The Henry Draper Catalogue*, printed between 1918 and 1924 as volumes 91–99 of the *Annals*. In this work nearly a quarter of a million stellar spectra were measured by Annie Jump Cannon and placed into one of twelve main spectral classes (P, O, B, A, F, G, K, M, R, N, Continuous, and Peculiar). This system was unanimously adopted by the International Union for Cooperation in Solar Research but was later modified slightly by the Committee of the International Astronomical Union on Spectral Classification.

The third principal field of Pickering's research was stellar photography. As early as 1883 he decided to chart all of the visible stars by means of photography. At the International Astrophotographic Congress organized in 1887 at Paris, however, it was decided that several observatories would participate in preparing a photographic atlas of the sky. Although the Congress intended to publish a map of the heavens in about five years, progress was so slow that Pickering maintained his desire to issue his own photographic map of the sky (the *Carte du ciel* is still incomplete). The acquisition of a substantial fund enabled him to carry out his plan. In 1889 Catherine Wolf Bruce, responding to a circular Pickering had issued, donated money for a large photographic telescope. The Bruce telescope, employing a photographic doublet with a twenty-four-inch aperture ground by the Clarks, was completed in 1893; and after a year and a half of testing, it was shipped to Harvard's Boyden Station at Arequipa, Peru, where it was used routinely in photographing the heavens.

In 1903 Pickering issued a *Photographic Map of the Entire Sky*, the first such map ever published, but it was not made with the Bruce telescope. Instead, two 2.5-inch doublets were used in Cambridge and Arequipa to map stars down to the twelfth magnitude on fifty-five plates. In addition, Pickering's habit of routinely photographing as large a portion of the visible sky as possible on every clear night resulted in the Harvard Photographic Library, which provides a photographic history, on some 300,000 glass plates, of all stars down to the eleventh magnitude. This record, duplicated nowhere else, is heavily relied on today by astronomers everywhere.

Other investigations that Pickering undertook were in photographic photometry. This was one of the chief interests of his later years, and an increasing part of the work of the observatory was devoted to establishing a standard system of stellar photographic magnitudes. The study of variable stars was also a marked feature of the observatory's work during his administration, and Pickering was instrumental in the founding of the American Association of Variable Star Observers. In 1889 he discovered that the brighter component of ζ Ursae Majoris (Mizar) was a spectroscopic binary—that is, a double star that is not resolvable in the telescope but which can be detected by the periodic doubling of its spectral lines. In 1886 he observed three systems of lines in ζ Puppis, the third of which formed a series closely resembling the Balmer lines of hydrogen. Pickering thought they represented hydrogen under some unknown conditions of temperature or pressure; Niels Bohr later showed that the "Pickering series" was actually due to ionized helium.

Pickering thoroughly believed in the advantages of broad associations in astronomy. One of his most cherished hopes was to organize a centralized institution to distribute funds to astronomers of all nations. He published several pamphlets on this subject, but his plan met with little success. For a short period Pickering was enabled to administer $500 gifts to American and European astronomers through another donation from Catherine Wolf Bruce. The establishment of the Carnegie Institution in 1902 raised his hopes, but he became bitterly disappointed when its executive committee made it clear that it preferred to support established observatories and other enterprises of its own creation rather than individual scientists. In 1906 he approached the Rockefeller Foundation for funds to implement another of his plans, the establishment of an international southern telescope at some favorable site, preferably in South Africa. Again he met with no success.

During his lifetime Pickering received numerous awards and honors. Six American and two European universities bestowed honorary doctorates upon him, and he was made a knight of the Prussian Ordre Pour le Mérite. Besides being a member of the American scientific societies, he was either a member or a foreign associate of the royal or national societies of England, France, Germany, Italy, Ireland, Sweden, Mexico, and Russia. He was awarded the Henry Draper Gold Medal of the National Academy of Sciences, the Rumford Gold Medal of the American Academy of Arts and Sciences, the Bruce Gold Medal of the Astronomical Society of the Pacific, and the gold medal of the Royal Astronomical Society on two occasions.

In all of his astronomical investigations, Pickering was not a speculator or theorizer but was content to be, in his words, "a collector of astronomical facts." Whereas theoretical reasoning not based on well-established data had little attraction for him, the posthumous value of the work of William Herschel and Friedrich Argelander appealed strongly to him.

Recognizing that the best service he could render to astronomy was the accumulation of facts, he instituted great research projects, often of a considerably routine nature, so that a sufficient basis in fact could be established for the solution of stellar problems by future astronomers.

When Pickering died in 1919, the Harvard College Observatory had been in operation for eighty years and he had been its director for forty-two of those years. Such a vast network of correspondence was established with observatories and astronomers throughout the world that the Harvard observatory under Pickering became the major distributing house of astronomical news. There was virtually no astronomer active during this period who did not benefit in one way or another from Pickering's interest and assistance. Indeed, many of his fellow astronomers thought of him as "the dean of American science."

BIBLIOGRAPHY

I. ORIGINAL WORKS. An extensive bibliography of Pickering's works numbering 266 items, prepared by Jenka Mohr, is appended to Solon I. Bailey, "Biographical Memoir of Edward Charles Pickering," in *Biographical Memoirs. National Academy of Sciences*, **15** (1934), 169–178. This bibliography does not include Pickering's contributions to the *Bulletin. Astronomical Observatory, Harvard College* or to *Circular. Astronomical Observatory of Harvard College* (many of which are unsigned), nor does it include the annual *Report. Astronomical Observatory of Harvard College*.

Pickering's papers are in the Harvard University Archives. The collection, which totals sixty-eight linear feet, includes personal and official correspondence, an autobiography, an autobiographical and personal notebook, and other notebooks and scrapbooks.

II. SECONDARY LITERATURE. There is as yet no full-length biography of Pickering. Bailey's "Memoir" cited above is taken, with only slight alterations, from his *History and Work of the Harvard Observatory* (New York, 1931). A recent and extremely valuable account of Pickering's observatory directorship can be found in Bessie Zaban Jones and Lyle Gifford Boyd, *The Harvard College Observatory. The First Four Directorships, 1839–1919* (Cambridge, Mass., 1971), more than half of which is devoted to the Pickering years.

HOWARD PLOTKIN

PICKERING, WILLIAM HENRY (*b.* Boston, Massachusetts, 15 February 1858; *d.* Mandeville, Jamaica, 16 January 1938), *astronomy*.

The younger brother of the astronomer E. C. Pickering, William graduated from Massachusetts

Institute of Technology in 1879. He taught there for a time and was appointed an assistant professor at Harvard observatory in 1887. In 1891 he set up Harvard's Boyden Station at Arequipa, Peru. Around 1900 he led expeditions to Jamaica, and from 1911 he was in charge of a permanent Harvard observing station there. Upon his retirement in 1924 the station became Pickering's private observatory.

Pickering was a pioneer in dry-plate celestial photography, and the Harvard photographic sky survey was undertaken at his suggestion. He took some of the earliest photographs of Mars (1888), and the lunar photographs he obtained in Jamaica (1900) were long the finest and most complete.

In 1899 Pickering discovered Phoebe on photographic plates taken, at his request, for possible new satellites of Saturn and demonstrated that it has a retrograde orbit. Saturn was the first planet known to possess both direct and retrograde satellites.

Pickering also made extensive visual observations of the planets and their satellites, discovering the "oases" on Mars (1892), recording apparent changes on the lunar surface (which he attributed to hoarfrost and vegetation), and claiming short rotation periods (now known to be incorrect) for Jupiter's Galilean satellites.

From 1907 Pickering paid considerable attention to predicting the location of trans-Neptunian planets; and after Pluto was discovered, faint images of it were located on plates taken for him in 1919. Percival Lowell, for whom Pickering had helped set up the observatory near Flagstaff, Arizona, in 1894, is generally accorded greater credit for the discovery, although Pickering's prediction was quite independent and more accurate in many respects; in any case, it has since become clear that the discovery was completely accidental.

BIBLIOGRAPHY

I. ORIGINAL WORKS. Among Pickering's principal writings are "Investigations in Astronomical Photography," in *Annals of Harvard College Observatory*, **32** (1895), 1–115; *The Moon* (New York, 1903); "The Ninth Satellite of Saturn," in *Annals of Harvard College Observatory*, **53** (1905), 45–73; "Researches of the Boyden Department," *ibid.*, **61** (1908), 1–103; "A Search for a Planet Beyond Neptune," *ibid.*, **61** (1909), 113–373; "Reports on Mars," nos. 1–44, in *Popular Astronomy*, **22–38** (1914–1930); *Mars* (Boston, 1921); and "Early Observations of the Elliptical Disks of Jupiter's Satellites," in *Annals of Harvard College Observatory*, **82** (1924), 61–74.

II. SECONDARY LITERATURE. Obituary notices are L. Campbell, in *Publications of the Astronomical Society of the Pacific*, **50** (1938), 122–125; and E. P. Martz, in *Popular Astronomy*, **46** (1938), 299–310. For a comparison of the conclusions by Lowell and Pickering concerning Mars, see W. W. Campbell, "The Problems of Mars," in *Publications of the Astronomical Society of the Pacific*, **30** (1918), 133–146. On Pickering's study of the Galilean satellites, see J. Ashbrook, "W. H. Pickering and the Satellites of Jupiter," in *Sky and Telescope*, **26** (1963), 335–336. On the nonpredictability of Pluto, see E. W. Brown, "On a Criterion for the Prediction of an Unknown Planet," in *Monthly Notices of the Royal Astronomical Society*, **92** (1931), 80–101.

BRIAN G. MARSDEN

PICTET, MARC-AUGUSTE (*b.* Geneva, Switzerland, 23 July 1752; *d.* Geneva, 19 April 1825), *physics.*

The son of Charles Pictet and Marie Dunant, Pictet came of an old and respected Genevan family. After a private education he studied at the Law Faculty of the Academy of Geneva, and it was only after qualifying as a lawyer in 1774 that he turned his attention seriously to science. His first mentor was the astronomer J. A. Mallet-Favre; but the greatest influence on him during his early years was that of H. B. de Saussure, who fostered Pictet's interest in physics and meteorology and secured his appointment to the chair of philosophy at the Academy of Geneva when age and ill health brought about his own retirement in 1786.

Pictet was always prominent in public life. At the time of Geneva's annexation to France in 1798, he did much to protect the interests of his city and of the Protestant religion, to which he ardently subscribed. Respected by Napoleon and a frequent visitor to Paris during the Consulate and Empire, he served as a member of the Tribunate from 1802 until 1807 and as one of the inspectors of the Imperial University from 1808 to 1815. He was prominent also in the scientific circles of Paris at this time; Berthollet and other French scientists were among his closest friends, and he often attended meetings of the first class of the Institut de France, of which he became a nonresident associate in 1802 and a corresponding member in 1803. His many other honors included membership of the Legion of Honor (1804) and fellowships of the Royal Society of London and of Edinburgh (1791 and 1796, respectively). By his marriage to Susanne Françoise Turrettini, which lasted from 1776 until her death in 1811, he had three daughters.

Pictet's most important research, a series of experiments on heat and hygrometry, was described in his *Essai sur le feu* (1790). Although widely read and even translated into English and German, the *Essai* broke little new ground. For example, his demonstration that radiant heat is reflected in the same way as light merely confirmed a conclusion already reached by J. H. Lambert and Saussure. And his experiments on the refraction and velocity of radiant heat, which could have led to results of great interest, were inconclusive. Although Pictet's research was mainly experimental, he was not uninterested in theory. In the *Essai*, for instance, he discussed the competing views of the nature of heat at some length and, although unwilling to commit himself, declared a slight preference for the material theory in the form given by Lavoisier. Hence he chose to consider heat as the fluid caloric rather than as a vibration either of the ordinary particles of matter or, in the manner of several Swiss scientists, of an all-pervading subtle fluid. He also opposed many of his compatriots by taking up Lavoisier's cause in the struggle for the acceptance of the new chemistry, and it was in a series of lectures given by Pictet in 1790 that Lavoisier's views were first given public support in Geneva.

Although Pictet earned a considerable reputation by his own research, which embraced geology, geodesy, astronomy, and meteorology as well as physics, he was even better known for his help and encouragement to others. In Geneva he worked tirelessly as a leading member of the Société des Arts, the Société de Physique et d'Histoire Naturelle, and the Société Helvétique des Sciences Naturelles; and he made what were probably his most important contributions to science as the joint founder and editor of two scientific journals: the *Journal de Genève* (published by the Société des Arts from 1787 to 1791) and the *Bibliothèque britannique*, founded in 1796 in collaboration with his younger brother Charles and his friend F. G. Maurice. Established originally to inform Continental readers of British publications and research, the *Bibliothèque britannique* was especially important in the maintenance of communications between Britain and the Continent during the Napoleonic Wars. After 1815, when it abandoned its special concern for British science and was renamed the *Bibliothèque universelle*, the journal continued to serve as a source of information that took little account of national barriers, although after 1815 Swiss contributions increased in number and importance.

Through his extensive international correspondence and his travels—mainly in France, Italy, and Britain—Pictet won many friends. As a zealous worker for science, a discerning editor, a patriot who showed no trace of chauvinism, and a man of great gentleness and modesty, he fully deserved the high esteem in which he was held throughout his life.

BIBLIOGRAPHY

I. ORIGINAL WORKS. Pictet's *Essai sur le feu* (Geneva, 1790), trans. into English by W. B[elcombe] as *An Essay on Fire* (London, 1791), was intended to be the first volume in a work entitled *Essais de physique*, but no further volumes were published. His *Voyage de trois mois en Angleterre, en Écosse, et en Irlande pendant l'été de l'an IX (1801 v. st.)* (Geneva, an XI [1802]), first published as a series of letters to the *Bibliothèque britannique*, is a very interesting account. His numerous contributions to the *Bibliothèque britannique* and the *Bibliothèque universelle* are listed in the Royal Society *Catalogue of Scientific Papers*, IV, 902–903; but his articles in the *Mémoires de la Société des arts* and the *Mémoires de la Société de physique et d'histoire naturelle de Genève* are not mentioned. Some of Pictet's correspondence with other Genevans is preserved at the Bibliothèque Publique et Universitaire of Geneva, but most of his personal papers and other correspondence are in the possession of the Rilliet family of Geneva. A copy, by Edmond Pictet, of a diary kept by Pictet while in Paris between 1802 and 1804 has been published as "Journal d'un genevois à Paris," in *Mémoires et documents publiés par la Société d'histoire et d'archéologie de Genève*, 2nd ser., 5 (1893–1901), 98–133.

II. SECONDARY LITERATURE. The standard biographical source is the obituary by J. P. Vaucher, in *Bibliothèque universelle*, sec. "Sciences et Arts," 29 (1825), 65–88. Other useful sketches are R. Wolf, *Biographien zur Kulturgeschichte der Schweiz*, III (Zurich, 1860), 373–394; Michaud, ed., *Biographie universelle*, new ed., XXXIII, 208–210; and A. de Montet, *Dictionnaire biographique des genevois et des vaudois*, II (Lausanne, 1878), 296–298. A MS of Edmond Pictet's "Dates des principales fonctions publiques, distinctions scientifiques et autres, dans la vie de Marc-Auguste Pictet," in the Bibliothèque Publique et Universitaire in Geneva, contains useful information not available elsewhere. Accounts of Pictet's connections with Mme de Staël and of his part in the introduction of Lavoisier's ideas in Geneva appear in P. Kohler, *Madame de Staël et la Suisse* (Lausanne–Paris, 1916), 408–412; and J. Deshusses, "Le physicien Marc-Auguste Pictet et l'adoption de la doctrine chimique de Lavoisier par les savants genevois," in *Bulletin de l'Institut national genevois*, 61 (1961), 100–112. His work for the *Bibliothèque britannique* is discussed in D. M. Bickerton, "A Scientific and Literary Periodical, the *Bibliothèque britannique* (1796–1815): Its Foundation and Early Development," in *Revue de littérature comparée*, 4 (1972), 527–547.

ROBERT FOX

PICTET, RAOUL-PIERRE (*b.* Geneva, Switzerland, 4 April 1846; *d.* Paris, France, 27 July 1929), *low-temperature physics.*

Pictet, son of Auguste Pictet-de Bock, a military

officer in various foreign services, was descended from a prominent Geneva family. After studying physics and chemistry in Geneva and Paris (1868–1870), he returned to his native city and devoted himself to experimentation in the physics of low temperatures, with an eye to the fast-growing and lucrative refrigeration industry. A compression refrigeration system that he developed, with sulfur dioxide as its cooling medium, functioned at a much lower pressure than competing systems; contact with water, however, often turned the refrigerant into corrosive sulfurous acid. This system, protected by a number of patents, was marketed with some success.

It was Pictet's researches that led to a scientific achievement which at once made him internationally famous. In December 1877, when Louis Paul Cailletet was about to report his liquefaction of oxygen to the Paris Academy of Sciences, Pictet cabled from Geneva that he had achieved the same feat. Cailletet and Pictet had worked independently and by different methods. While Cailletet's method had been to compress, cool, and expand the gas to be liquefied, Pictet had employed the "cascade" process, in which the refrigeration cycles of three different cooling media with successively lower critical temperatures were arranged in series, so that the gas liquefied first would act as a coolant in the liquefaction of the next. Pictet used sulfur dioxide in the first cycle, carbon dioxide in the second, and oxygen in the last. Although Cailletet could establish a priority of a few weeks, Pictet has been allowed to share the credit for the first liquefaction of an atmospheric gas. His claim also to have liquefied hydrogen was later shown to be based on error (Carl Linde, *Aus meinem Leben und von meiner Arbeit* [Munich, n.d. (1916?)], 68–72; Kurt Mendelssohn, *The Quest for Absolute Zero* [London, 1966], 41–42).

In 1879 Pictet was given a chair of "industrial physics" at the University of Geneva, which he held for seven years. In 1886 he left academic life to establish an industrial research laboratory in Berlin and to market his inventions. The chief feature of his refrigeration system now became a patented refrigerant, *liquide Pictet* (sulfur dioxide plus carbon dioxide), which involved him in controversy because he had claimed it to be exempt from the second law of thermodynamics. Although, as before, his machines were prone to disintegrate because of corrosion unless carefully shielded from moisture, he enjoyed some commercial success. During the later part of his life, spent in Paris, he continued to publish scientific papers; but his death in 1929' went virtually unnoticed.

BIBLIOGRAPHY

I. ORIGINAL WORKS. Pictet described his 1877 experiment in *Mémoire sur la liquéfaction de l'oxygène et la liquéfaction et solidification de l'hydrogène* (Geneva, 1878). An extensive bibliography of his works is in Poggendorff, III, 1040; IV, 1163; V, 975; and VI, 2014.

II. SECONDARY LITERATURE. Biographical data are found in an obituary by C.-E. Guye, in *Comptes rendus des séances de la Société de physique et d'histoire naturelle de Genève*, **47** (1930), 18–20; and in *Dictionnaire historique et biographique de la Suisse*, V (Neuchâtel, 1930). For discussions of his work see, besides Linde and Mendelssohn (cited in text), Ferdinand Rosenberger, *Geschichte der Physik*, III (Brunswick, 1887–1890), 416, 652–653; and W. R. Woolrich, *The Men Who Created Cold* (New York, 1967), 171–173.

OTTO MAYR

PIERCE, GEORGE WASHINGTON (*b.* Webberville, Texas, 11 January 1872; *d.* Franklin, New Hampshire, 25 August 1956), *applied physics*.

Pierce was the second of three sons of G. W. Pierce, a farmer and cattleman; his mother was Mary Gill Pierce. Academic talent manifested itself early: despite the limitations of rural schools in central Texas, he entered the University of Texas at eighteen with sufficiently advanced standing to graduate in three years. His first publication was written with his professor, Alexander Macfarlane, during his senior year. Pierce then taught in secondary schools and held various odd jobs for four years. In 1898 he won a fellowship to Harvard, where he remained for the rest of his scientific career. In 1900 he received the Ph.D. with a thesis on measurements of short radio waves.

After a postdoctoral year spent partly in Ludwig Boltzmann's laboratory at Leipzig, Pierce was appointed assistant in physics at Harvard and progressed steadily to a full professorship (1917); in 1921 he succeeded E. H. Hall as Rumford professor of physics. During these years he worked out much of the scientific underpinnings of electrical communications. He wrote basic papers of great lucidity on the resonant circuits and crystal detectors used in early radiotelegraphy, extended the use of semiconductor crystals to electroacoustics, and showed how mercury-vapor discharge tubes could be used for current control and sound recording.

In 1912 Pierce collaborated with A. E. Kennelly on measurements of the electric characteristics of telephone receivers, in the course of which work they discovered the concept of motional impedance. Pierce's work on submarine detection during World War I led to his offering the first postgraduate course anywhere on underwater sound signaling, to which the U.S. Navy for many years sent an annual contingent of student officers. Together with undergraduate courses on the applications of electromagnetic phenomena, it led to Harvard's pioneering position in radio communications, a position Pierce consolidated by writing the two classic American textbooks on the subject and by becoming the first director of Harvard's famed Cruft Laboratory in 1914. At Cruft he was associated for thirty years with E. L. Chaffee, who succeeded him as director.

Pierce is best remembered for bridging the gap between phenomenological knowledge and technological application of two similar physical effects: piezoelectricity and magnetostriction. The first effect led to the development of the quartz-crystal "Pierce oscillator" used in circuits that control the frequency of radio transmitters, standards, and meters; the second, to generators of underwater sound used in sonar and ultrasonic devices. The elucidation of physical phenomena by a professor, the elaboration of the principles of their applications by his doctoral students, and the technological utilization of the principles (and sometimes patents) outside the university—the sequence that came to characterize postgraduate education at the best American schools of engineering and applied science—thus had its inception at the Cruft Laboratory under Pierce and Chaffee. Less typically, Pierce became wealthy through his patents, some of which he exploited vigorously, and usually successfully, in the face of interference suits by large corporations. He was an exceedingly warm and droll individual, much revered by his students.

Pierce's work in ultrasound led to his later interests in sound generation by bats and insects, which persisted past his retirement in 1940 and led to a book published when he was seventy-six. His many honors included election to the National Academy of Sciences in 1920, the Medal of Honor of the Institute of Radio Engineers (of which he was president in 1918 and 1919) in 1929, and the Franklin Medal in 1943.

BIBLIOGRAPHY

I. ORIGINAL WORKS. Pierce's books are *Principles of Wireless Telegraphy* (New York, 1910); *Electric Oscillators and Electric Waves* (New York, 1919); and *The Song of Insects* (Cambridge, Mass., 1948). He also wrote or was coauthor of some 30 scientific papers and received 53 patents.

II. SECONDARY LITERATURE. The article by Frederick A. Saunders and Frederick V. Hunt in *Biographical Memoirs. National Academy of Sciences*, **33** (1959), 351–380, includes a complete list of Pierce's publications and American patents. A memoir by David Rines, his patent attorney, in the form of a letter addressed to F. V. Hunt, is in the archives of Harvard University, together with some of Pierce's notebooks and correspondence. For a glimpse of Pierce's influence on his contemporaries, see B. F. Miessner, *On the Early History of Radio Guidance* (San Francisco, 1964), 14, 24–25.

CHARLES SÜSSKIND

PIERI, MARIO (*b.* Lucca, Italy, 22 June 1860; *d.* Sant' Andrea di Còmpito (Lucca), Italy, 1 March 1913), *projective geometry, foundations of geometry.*

Pieri's father, Pellegrino Pieri, was a lawyer; his mother was Erminia Luporini. He began his university studies in 1880 at Bologna, where Salvatore Pincherle was among the first to recognize his talent; but he obtained a scholarship to the Scuola Normale Superiore of Pisa in November 1881 and completed his university studies there, receiving his degree on 27 June 1884. After teaching briefly at the technical secondary school in Pisa he became professor of projective geometry at the military academy in Turin and also, in 1888, assistant in projective geometry at the University of Turin, holding both posts until 1900. He became *libero docente* at the university in 1891 and for several years taught an elective course in projective geometry there.

On 30 January 1900, following a competition, he was named extraordinary professor of projective and descriptive geometry at the University of Catania. In 1908 he transferred to Parma, where in the winter of 1911 he began to complain of fatigue. His fatal illness, cancer, was diagnosed a few months later.

For ten years following his first publication in 1884, Pieri worked primarily in projective geometry. From 1895 he studied the foundations of mathematics, especially the axiomatic treatment of geometry. Pieri had made a thorough study of Christian von Staudt's geometry of position, but he was also influenced by his colleagues at the military academy and the university, Giuseppe Peano and Cesare Burali-Forti. He learned symbolic logic from the latter, and Peano's axiom systems for arithmetic and ordinary geometry furnished models for Pieri's axiomatic study of projective geometry.

In 1895 Pieri constructed ordinary projective geometry on three undefined terms: point, line, and segment. The same undefined terms were used in 1896 in an axiom system for the projective geometry of hyperspaces, and in 1897 he showed that all of the geometry of position can be based on only two undefined terms: projective point and the join of two projective points. In the memoir "I principii della geometria di posizione composti in un sistema logico-deduttivo" (1898) Pieri combined the results reached thus far into a more organic whole. Here the same two undefined terms were used to construct projective geometry as a logical-deductive system based on nineteen sequentially independent axioms—each independent of the preceding ones—which are introduced one by one as they are needed in the development, thus allowing the reader to determine on which axioms a given theorem depends. Of this paper Bertrand Russell wrote: "This is, in my opinion, the best work on the present subject" (*Principles of Mathematics*, 2nd ed. [New York, 1964], 382), a judgment that Peano echoed in his report in 1903 to the judging committee for the Lobachevsky Award of the Société Physico-Mathématique de Kasan. (Pieri received honorable mention, the prize going to David Hilbert.)

In their axiom systems for ordinary geometry, Pasch had used four undefined terms, and Peano three. With Pieri's memoir of 1899, "Della geometria elementare come sistema ipotetico-deduttivo," the number was reduced to two—point and motion—the latter understood as the transformation of one point into another. Pieri continued to apply the axiomatic method to the study of geometry, and in several subsequent publications he investigated the possibility of using different sets of undefined terms to construct various geometries. In "Nuovi principii di geometria proiettiva complessa" (1905) he gave the first axiom system for complex projective geometry that is not constructed on real projective geometry.

Two brief notes published in 1906–1907 on the foundations of arithmetic are notable. In "Sur la compatibilité des axiomes de l'arithmétique" he gave an interpretation of the notion of whole number in the context of the logic of classes; and in "Sopra gli assiomi aritmetici" he selected as primitive notions "number" and "successor of a number," and characterized them with a system of axioms that from a logical point of view simplified Peano's theory. In 1911 Pieri may have been on the point of beginning a new phase of his scientific activity. He was then attracted by the vectorial calculus of Burali-Forti and Roberto Marcolongo, but he left only three notes on this subject.

Pieri became one of the strongest admirers of symbolic logic; and although most of his works are published in more ordinary mathematical language, the statements of colleagues and his own statements show that Pieri considered the use of Peano's symbolism of the greatest help not only in obtaining rigor but also in deriving new results.

Pieri was among the first to promote the idea of geometry as a hypothetical-deductive system. His address at the First International Congress of Philosophy in 1900 had the highly significant title "Sur la géométrie envisagée comme un système purement logique." Bertrand Russell wrote in 1903: "The true founder of non-quantitative Geometry is von Staudt. . . . But there remained one further step, before projective Geometry could be considered complete, and this step was taken by Pieri. . . . Thus at last the long process by which projective Geometry has purified itself from every metrical taint is completed" (*Principles of Mathematics*, 2nd ed. [New York, 1964], 421).

BIBLIOGRAPHY

I. Original Works. A chronological list of Pieri's publications appears in Beppo Levi, "Mario Pieri," in *Bullettino di bibliografia e storia delle scienze matematiche*, 15 (1913), 65–74, with additions and corrections in 16 (1914), 32. The list includes 57 articles, a textbook of projective geometry for students at the military academy, a translation of Christian von Staudt's *Geometrie der Lage*, and four book reviews.

II. Secondary Literature. Besides the obituary by Beppo Levi (cited above), see Guido Castelnuovo, "Mario Pieri," in *Bollettino della mathesis*, 5 (1913), 40–41; and [Giuseppe Peano], "Mario Pieri," in *Academia pro Interlingua, Discussiones*, 4 (1913), 31–35. On the centennial of Pieri's birth Fulvia Skof published "Sull'opera scientifica di Mario Pieri," in *Bollettino dell' Unione matematica italiana*, 3rd ser., 15 (1960), 63–68.

Hubert C. Kennedy

PIERO DELLA FRANCESCA. See **Francesca, Piero della.**

PIERRE. See **Peter.**

PIETTE, LOUIS-ÉDOUARD-STANISLAS (*b*. Aubigny, Ardennes, France, 1827; *d*. 1906), *archaeology, paleontology.*

Although trained as a lawyer and active as a magistrate, Piette is best known for his archaeological and paleontological research. He made major contributions to Paleolithic archaeology by his own discoveries, his championship of Paleolithic art, his special study of Paleolithic portable art, and his ideas on the classification of the Paleolithic. He discovered Gourdan, Lortet, Mas-d'Azil and Brassempouy, all sites of Paleolithic art, and excavated prehistoric barrows at Avezac-Prat, Bartres, Osun, and La Halliade, near Lourdes.

Mortillet's proposal for classifying the Paleolithic into Chellean, Mousterian, Solutrean, and Magdalenian was later modified by inserting the Acheulean between Chellean and Mousterian. Piette's scheme divided the Paleolithic into the Amygdalithic, Niphetic, and Glyptic periods. The Amygdalithic was characterized by hand axes and comprised the Chellean and Acheulean. The Niphetic was Mortillet's Mousterian. The Glyptic, or "âge des beaux-arts," was characterized by the presence of art. Piette divided it into three stages: Papalian or Eburnian, characterized by sculpture in relief and in the round; Gordanian, characterized by engravings and of a time when animals now extinct still existed; and Lorthetian, also characterized by engravings, particularly on reindeer bone, but not associated with any extinct fauna. Piette's scheme was never adopted; but his collection of portable art, now at the Musée des Antiquités Nationales at St.-Germain-en-Laye, is one of the most important collections of Paleolithic art in existence. His *L'art pendant l'âge du renne* (1907) was beautifully illustrated with 100 plates by J. Pilloy. Accepting the authenticity of the Altamira paintings, which had been disputed since their discovery in 1875, Piette claimed that they were Magdalenian in date and described them as authentic in his *Équides de la période quaternaire d'après les gravures de ce temps* (1887).

In 1887 Piette began digging at Mas-d'Azil (Ariège) in the foothills of the Pyrenees, about forty miles southwest of Toulouse. Here the Arise River tunnels through the rock for over a quarter of a mile; and in this great tunnel, on both banks of the river, Piette excavated two rock shelters and found, above a rich Magdalenian deposit, a thick layer containing flat harpoons of staghorn, and pebbles painted with red ochre mixed with bones of red deer and wild boar. To this post-Magdalenian industry Piette gave the name Azilian. He believed that the pebbles represented an early form of alphabetic writing.

In 1879 still another amateur archaeologist and lawyer, Edmond Vielle, found an industry of post-Paleolithic character in the Aisne, which he labeled the Tardenoisian. The Azilian and the Tardenoisian were the first industries of what is now called the Mesolithic. Piette established this period between Paleolithic and Neolithic but called it the Metabatic Age, or Age of Transition. Like his other names, it was not widely adopted.

BIBLIOGRAPHY

See *Collection Piette: art mobilier préhistorique* (Paris, 1964), with a preface by Henri Breuil, introduction by André Varagnac, and a catalogue by Marthe Chollot. See also G. E. Daniel, *A Hundred Years of Archaeology* (London, 1950), 122–126, 131–132, 232.

GLYN DANIEL

PIGOTT, EDWARD (*b.* 1753; *d.* Bath, England, 1825), and **PIGOTT, NATHANIEL** (*b.* Whitton, Middlesex, England; *d.* 1804), *astronomy*.

Although there is little personal data extant concerning the lives of the gentleman astronomers Nathaniel and Edward Pigott, their careers cast interesting light on the early development of stellar astronomy in Great Britain. Nathaniel Pigott was the son of Ralph Pigott and his wife Alathea, the daughter of William, eighth Viscount Fairfax of Gilling Castle; while in France he married, at an unknown date, Anna Mathurina de Beriol. Edward Pigott was their second son, the first to survive infancy.

Nathaniel Pigott was a surveyor and landed proprietor as well as an amateur astronomer. He spent much of his life on the Continent, settling for a while at Caen. The *Philosophical Transactions of the Royal Society* for 1767 contains an account of his observations there of the solar eclipse of 16 August 1765. He also recorded observations of the transit of Venus of 1769, made a series of meteorological and longitudinal measurements in the Low Countries (between 1770 and 1778), and observed the transit of Mercury of 1786 from Louvain. He was elected to the Royal Society on 16 June 1772; to the Brussels Academy in 1773; and became a corresponding member of the Paris Academy of Sciences in 1776.

In September 1771 the Pigott family left Caen to return to England. They lived at Frampton, Glamorganshire for ten years, then moved to Bootham, Yorkshire, where they improvised an astronomical observatory in the garden. Edward Pigott had already become actively engaged in astronomy—he assisted his father in the observation of 1769—and at Bootham he made his first discovery, that of a nebula in the constellation Coma Berenices. In 1783 he discovered a new comet, an accomplishment later mistakenly ascribed to his father, along with a number of others. (A possible source of this confusion lies in the fact that although Edward Pigott kept a diary—much of it in French—comprising his work from 1770 until 1782, he failed to put his name to it.)

In about 1783 Edward Pigott struck up a friendship with John Goodricke, who had himself the year before, when he was eighteen, discovered the periodic variability of Algol. Not to be outdone, Edward Pigott noted that the star η Aquilae is periodically variable; he made his discovery on 10 September 1784, apparently the same night upon which Goodricke discovered the variability of yet another star, β Lyrae. Within the week, Goodricke had also determined the variability of δ Cephei. The happy partnership ended prematurely in April 1786, when Goodricke died, at the age of twenty-one, probably from pneumonia that he contracted while making observations. Edward Pigott's reaction to this loss must be left to conjecture, since his diary ceased before that time.

Having, in the latter part of 1786, accompanied his father to Louvain to observe the transit of Mercury, Edward Pigott may have extended his stay there. At any rate, he did not report any new variables until 1795, when, having returned to England and settled at Bath, he announced the variability of R Scuti and R Coronae Borealis. (These stars were later recognized as prototypes of certain classes of irregular variables; the cause of their variability is as yet uncertain.) He subsequently discovered another variable star in Scutum and two more comets, as well as determining the proper motions of several stars. Edward Pigott was a frequent contributor to the *Philosophical Transactions of the Royal Society*; his works published therein include a number of important papers on the method of observing stars with a transit instrument.

Following the treaty of Amiens in 1802, Edward Pigott took the first opportunity to return to the Continent. When hostilities again broke out in 1803, he was arrested and detained at Fontainebleau. He wrote to William Herschel of his melancholy at "being separated from my journals, books and instruments"; after a time, however, doubtless through the good offices of his friends in the French scientific community, he was supplied with materials to continue his work. A treatise that he wrote while in detention was published by the Royal Society in 1803; Sir Joseph Banks, president of that body, exerted his influence on Edward Pigott's behalf, and secured his release in 1806. In the meantime, Nathaniel Pigott had died while traveling abroad.

In 1807 Edward Pigott observed the great comet of that year; at this time he was at his home in Belvedere, Bath. The last record of him is a letter from John Herschel, dated from Slough, 8 May 1821. Herschel

asked Edward Pigott if he and his father might propose him for membership in the recently formed London (later Royal) Astronomical Society; although Pigott could not have been unaware of the honor that such a proposal implied, and although he endorsed Herschel's letter as an invitation, there is no indication that he replied to it. He was sixty-eight, and his interest in the subject may have faded—or perhaps he was disappointed that his lifework had not received recognition from another quarter. At any rate, he was not elected, and nothing else is known of him until his death.

BIBLIOGRAPHY

The following works by Pigott appeared in *Philosophical Transactions of the Royal Society*: "Account of a Nebula in Comâ Berenices," **71** (1781), 82; "On the Discovery of a Comet in 1783," **74** (1784), 20; "Observations on the Comet in 1783," *ibid.*, 460; "Observations of a New Variable Star," **75** (1785), 127; "On Those Stars Which the Astronomer of the Last Century Suspected to be Changeable," **76** (1786), 189; "On the Transit of Mercury Over the Sun, Made at Louvain, in the Netherlands," *ibid.*, 389; "The Latitude and Longitude of York Determined From Astronomical Observations, With the Method of Determining the Longitudes of Places by Observation of the Moon's Transit Over the Meridian," *ibid.*, 409; "An Account of Some Luminous Arches," **80** (1790), 47; "Determination of the Longitudes and Latitudes of Some Remarkable Places Near the Severn," *ibid.*, 385; "On the Periodical Changes of Brightness of Two Fixed Stars," **87** (1797), 133; "On the Changes in the Variable Star in Sobieski's Shield, From Five Years Observations; With Conjectures Respecting Unenlightened Heavenly Bodies," **95** (1805), 131; "Observations on the Eclipse of the Sun, Aug. 11, 1765, at Caen in Normandy," **57** (1767), 402; "Observations on the Transit of Venus, Jan. 3, 1769, at Caen," **60** (1770), 257; "Meteorological Observations at Caen for 1765–69," **61** (1771), 274; "Astronomical Observations in the Austrian Netherlands," **66** (1776), 182; "Discovery of Double Stars in 1779, at Frampton House in Glamorganshire," **71** (1781), 84; "Astronomical Observations," *ibid.*, 347; "An Observation of the Meteor of August 18th, 1783, Made on Hewitt Common, Near York," **74** (1784), 457; "Observations of the Transit of Mercury Over the Sun's Disc, Made at Louvain, May 3, 1786," **76** (1786), 384.

ZDENĚK KOPAL

PILATRE DE ROZIER, JEAN FRANÇOIS (*b*. Metz, France, 30 March 1754; *d*. Wimille, near Boulogne, France, 15 June 1785), *education, aeronautics.*

The son of Mathurin Pilastre du Rosier, an innkeeper, and Madeleine Willemart, Pilatre was baptized

François but later added the name Jean and modified his surname. (He never used the form Pilâtre.) After studying pharmacy for three years in Metz, he attended scientific courses at Paris. About 1776 he taught a physics course in Paris and for a short time was professor of chemistry at the Société d'Émulation of Rheims. He returned to Paris about 1780 as keeper of the physics and natural history cabinets of the Comte de Provence, brother of Louis XVI.

Under his patronage Pilatre founded the Musée, a private institution for higher education that opened in 1781 on the rue St.-Avoye but soon moved to the rue de Valois. By 1785 it had 700 members, including the academicians Condorcet, Fourcroy, and Vicq d'Azyr, who gave their encouragement, as well as many ladies and gentlemen of society who attended lectures on a wide range of literary and scientific subjects.

Pilatre was skilled at arranging lecture demonstrations, but the research that he attempted was of little merit. Hoping to be elected to the Académie des Sciences, he submitted chemical and physical memoirs on several occasions between 1781 and 1784 but was never proposed as a candidate. His one useful invention was a respirator that enabled a man working in the noxious atmosphere of a deep well or cesspit to breathe fresh air, which was supplied by a flexible hose from the surface; and he courageously demonstrated it himself. It was praised in 1783 by the Société Royale de Médecine but was not generally adopted.

After being present at Versailles on 19 September 1783, when Étienne Montgolfier's hot-air balloon safely carried a sheep, a cock, and a duck for two miles, Pilatre took part in the trials of a new balloon constructed by Montgolfier in the garden of J. B. Réveillon, a paper manufacturer. This balloon had room for two in a gallery around the base, from which a brazier suspended under the opening of the balloon could be fed with fuel. On 15 October Pilatre rose to eighty feet in the tethered balloon, and he soon learned how to vary the altitude by controlling the fire. Accompanied by Marquis François Laurent d'Arlandes, an infantry major, he made the first human flight on 21 November 1783, taking off from the Château de la Muette, west of Paris, and traveling nearly six miles across the city in about twenty-five minutes, at about 3,000 feet. Pilatre made several other hot-air ascents, notably with Joseph Montgolfier and five others at Lyons on 19 January 1784 and with the chemist J. L. Proust on 23 June 1784, when they reached a height of about 11,000 feet above Versailles.

Pilatre hoped to make the first aerial crossing of the English Channel, and early in January 1785 he was at Boulogne. The wind was unfavorable, however, and the honor went to J. P. Blanchard and John Jeffries, who flew from Dover to Calais on 7 January. Pilatre accompanied Blanchard to Paris and made him a member of the Musée. He subsequently visited England, where he was present at ascents by Blanchard on 21 May and 3 June.

Pilatre attempted his own crossing from Boulogne on 15 June 1785, accompanied by Pierre Ange Romain, one of the constructors of the balloon, which was of a new type designed by Pilatre. Hot air being denser than hydrogen, a hot-air balloon had to be larger than a hydrogen balloon in order to carry the same weight; but its altitude could easily be changed by varying the size of the fire. Hoping to combine the advantages of both types, Pilatre attached a hydrogen balloon to the top of a small cylindrical hot-air balloon, apparently assuming that escaping hydrogen would rise and that there would be no danger of ignition from the fire below. Tragically, he was proved wrong. The balloon caught fire at about 1,700 feet and crashed near Boulogne, killing both occupants.

After Pilatre's death the Musée was reorganized and called the Lycée. Under its later names, Lycée Républicain (1792) and Athénée de Paris (1802), it played an important part in the scientific and cultural life of Paris until the 1840's.

BIBLIOGRAPHY

I. ORIGINAL WORKS. Seven memoirs by Pilatre were published in *Observations sur la physique* . . . between 1780 and 1782, and are listed in the collective index, *ibid.*, **29** (1786), 468–469. Some other writings were published posthumously by A. Tournon de la Chapelle (see below). Pilatre's only separate publication was *Première expérience de la montgolfière construite par ordre du roi* . . . (Paris, 1784), a description of his flight on 23 June 1784.

II. SECONDARY LITERATURE. There are a number of incorrect dates in Pilatre's first biography, Tournon de la Chapelle, *La vie et les mémoires de Pilatre de Rozier* (Paris, 1786). Later accounts of value are Léon Babinet, *Notice sur Pilatre de Rozier* (Metz, 1865); P. Dorveaux, "Pilatre de Rozier," in *Bulletin de la Société d'histoire de la pharmacie* (1920), 209–220, 249–258; and "Pilatre de Rozier et l'Académie des sciences," in *Cahiers lorrains*, **8**, (1929), 162–166, 182–185; and W. A. Smeaton, "Jean François Pilatre de Rozier, the First Aeronaut," in *Annals of Science*, **11** (1955), 349–355. Some dates in Smeaton's account are corrected in a review by A. Birembaut in *Archives internationales d'histoire des sciences*, **11** (1958), 100–101; further details of Pilatre's flights correcting statements by earlier authors are given by W. A. Smeaton, "The First and Last Balloon Ascents of Pilatre de Rozier," *ibid.*, 263–269.

For accounts of the early history of the Musée (after 1785, the Lycée), see C. Cabanes, "Histoire du premier musée autorisé par le gouvernement," in *Nature* (Paris), **65** (1937), pt. 2, 577–583; and W. A. Smeaton, "The Early Years of the Lycée and the Lycée des Arts: A Chapter in the Lives of A. L. Lavoisier and A. F. de Fourcroy. I. The Lycée of the Rue de Valois," in *Annals of Science*, **11** (1955), 257–267.

Pilatre's early balloon flights are described by B. Faujas de Saint-Fond, *Description des expériences de la machine aérostatique de MM. de Montgolfier* . . . (Paris, 1783; 2nd ed., 1784) and *Première suite de la description* . . . (Paris, 1784), of which no further volumes were published.

W. A. SMEATON

PINCHERLE, SALVATORE (*b.* Trieste, Austria [now Italy], 11 March 1853; *d.* Bologna, Italy, 10 July 1936), *mathematics*.

Born of a Jewish business family, Pincherle completed his preuniversity studies in Marseilles, where his family had migrated. The unusually sophisticated teaching of science there seems to have been a decisive factor in diverting his interest from the humanities to mathematics; and by 1869, when he entered the University of Pisa, the decision to study mathematics had already matured. His teachers at Pisa included Betti and Dini; Pincherle was greatly affected by both of them. After graduating in 1874, Pincherle became a teacher at a *liceo* in Pavia. A scholarship for study abroad enabled him to spend the academic year 1877–1878 in Berlin, where he met Weierstrass, who influenced all his subsequent work. In 1880 Pincherle became professor of infinitesimal analysis at the University of Palermo. He remained there only a few months, having been appointed to a chair at the University of Bologna. He retired in 1928.

Pincherle greatly improved the level of mathematics at the University of Bologna, which had badly deteriorated during the final years of papal domination. The university later acknowledged his contribution by naming the mathematics institute for him during his lifetime. In Bologna, Pincherle also founded (1922) the Italian Mathematical Union, of which he was the first president. At the Third International Congress of Mathematicians, held at Bologna in 1928, of which he was president, Pincherle restored the truly international character of international mathematical congresses by reopening participation to German and other mathematicians who had been excluded since World War I.

Pincherle's contributions to mathematics were mainly in the field of functional analysis, of which he was one of the principal founders, together

with Volterra. Remaining faithful to the ideas of Weierstrass, he did not take the topological approach that later proved to be the most successful, but tried to start from a series of powers of the D derivation symbol. Although his efforts did not prove very fruitful, he was able to study in depth the Laplace transformation, iteration problems, and series of generalized factors. He was the author of several textbooks, notably for secondary schools, at which he had had direct practical experience.

Pincherle was a member of the Accademia Nazionale dei Lincei and the Bayerische Akademie der Wissenschaften, which, despite the rise of Nazism, sent him a warm message on his eightieth birthday in 1934. In 1954 the city of Trieste held a solemn celebration of the centenary of his birth.

BIBLIOGRAPHY

There is an accurate bibliography of Pincherle's writings from 1874 to 1936, with 245 references, by Ettore Bortolotti, in *Bollettino dell'Unione matematica italiana*, **16** (1937), 37–60. On his life and work, see the notices by Ugo Amaldi, in *Annali di matematica pura ed applicata*, 4th ser., **17** (1938), 1–21; and Leonida Tonelli, in *Annali della Scuola normale superiore*, 2nd ser., **6** (1937), 1–10; and F. G. Tricomi, *Salvatore Pincherle nel centenario della nascità*, Pubblicazioni della Facoltà di scienze e d'ingegneria, Università di Trieste, ser. A, **60** (1954).

F. G. TRICOMI

PINCUS, GREGORY GOODWIN (*b.* Woodbine, New Jersey, 9 April 1903; *d.* Boston, Massachusetts, 22 August 1967), *endocrinology*.

Pincus is best known for his work with his associates in the development of the birth control pill. He received the B.S. degree at Cornell University in 1924 and a master's and doctorate in science at Harvard in 1927, working under the geneticist W. E. Castle and the animal physiologist W. J. Crozier. Pincus lived in Europe from 1929 to 1930, studying at Cambridge with F. H. A. Marshall and John Hammond, both pioneers in reproductive biology, and then at the Kaiser Wilhelm Institute with the geneticist R. B. Goldschmidt. In 1930 he returned to Harvard and was appointed an assistant professor in 1931. His pioneer work, *The Eggs of Mammals*, was published in 1936. He was at the University of Cambridge in 1937 and became a visiting professor in 1938 at Clark University, Worcester, Massachusetts.

Pincus conducted research on stress for the U.S. navy and air force during World War II. In

1944 he and Hudson Hoagland established the Worcester Foundation for Experimental Biology, which soon became internationally known as a center for the study of steroid hormones and mammalian reproduction. Pincus became a professor at Tufts Medical School in 1945 and at Boston University in 1951. In 1944 he organized the annual Laurentian Hormone Conference and edited the first twenty-three volumes of its proceedings, *Recent Progress in Hormone Research* (1946–1967).

Encouraged by Margaret Sanger, in 1951 Pincus and M. C. Chang started their studies on the effects of various newly synthesized hormones on reproduction in laboratory animals and found that several progestational compounds administered orally could prevent pregnancy, mainly by inhibition of ovulation. In collaboration with J. Rock and C. R. Garcia, Pincus immediately extended these studies to humans and perfected the oral contraceptive pill.

With his associates Pincus published about 350 papers on tropism in rats, genetics of mice, fatherless rabbits, fertilization and transplantation of eggs, diabetes, cancer, schizophrenia, adrenal hormones, and aging. He made significant contributions to knowledge of the effects, metabolism, and biosynthesis of steroid hormones. Pincus was coeditor of *The Hormones*, volumes 1–5, and his book, *Control of Fertility*, was published in 1965. He died of myeloid metaplasia, probably due to his early work with organic solvents.

Pincus was prominent in the study of mammalian reproductive physiology and endocrinology for more than thirty-five years. Some of his contributions in the early 1930's concerned processes involved in mammalian fertilization and development. With increasing knowledge of steroid hormones in the early 1940's, his attention became increasingly focused on the roles of these substances in general physiology and especially in reproduction. In the early 1950's, when powerful, orally active, synthetic hormonelike compounds were produced, Pincus and his associates seized the opportunity to develop an oral contraceptive. Their success was such that they produced that pharmaceutical rarity, a chemical agent that is virtually 100 percent effective. More important, the work of Pincus and his colleagues has transformed family planning in all the parts of the world in which it is systematically employed.

BIBLIOGRAPHY

Pincus' works include *The Eggs of Mammals* (New York, 1936); "The Comparative Behavior of Mammalian Eggs in vivo and in vitro," in *Proceedings of the American Philosophical Society*, **83** (1940), 631–646, written with H. Shapiro; "Studies of the Biological Activity of Certain 19-Nor Steroids in Female Animals," in *Endocrinology*, **59** (1956), 695–707, written with M. C. Chang *et al.*; *The Control of Fertility* (New York, 1965); and "Control of Conception by Hormonal Steroids," in *Science*, **153** (1966), 493–550.

M. C. CHANG

PINEL, PHILIPPE (*b*. Jonquières, near Castres, France, 20 April 1745; *d*. Paris, France, 25 October 1826), *medicine.*

Pinel was the son of a master surgeon who practiced in St.-Paul-Cap-de-Joux, a village between Castres and Toulouse. His mother, Élisabeth Dupuy, came from a family that had since the seventeenth century produced a number of physicians, apothecaries, and surgeons. Despite this medical heritage, Pinel's early education, first at the Collège de Lavaur and then at the Collège de l'Esquille in Toulouse, was an essentially literary one; he was greatly influenced by the Encyclopedists, particularly Rousseau. Having decided upon a career in religion, he enrolled in the Faculty of Theology at Toulouse in July 1767; in April 1770, however, he left it for the Faculty of Medicine, from which he received the M.D. on 21 December 1773. Simultaneously with his medical training, Pinel studied mathematics, an interest that is apparent in his medical writings.

In 1774 Pinel went to Montpellier, where for four years he frequented the medical school and hospitals. He there began to formulate and to practice the principles that he later recommended to his students: "Take written notes at the sickbed and record the entire course of a severe illness." He supported himself by giving mathematics lessons, conducting a private anatomy course, and writing theses for rich students. He also met Chaptal, who later acknowledged Pinel's influence upon his intellectual development. In 1777 Pinel presented two iatromechanical papers, on the application of mathematics to human anatomy, to the Société Royale des Sciences de Montpellier; he was named a corresponding member in July of that year.

In 1778 Pinel went to Paris. He carried with him letters of recommendation to the geometer Jacques Cousin, who advised him to give up medicine and devote himself to the exact sciences. He visited libraries and hospitals (particularly P. J. Desault's service at the Hôtel-Dieu) and frequented the *salon* of Mme Helvétius, into which he had been introduced by Cabanis, and where he met Franklin. Mme Helvétius's house in Auteuil was a gathering place for the school later called *idéologues*, and Pinel became acquainted with the sensationalist doctrines of Locke and

Condillac, which strongly influenced his work. As a graduate of Toulouse, however, he was unable to practice medicine in the capital.

In 1784 Pinel became editor of the *Gazette de santé*, in which he published a number of articles chiefly concerned with hygiene and mental disorders, a subject in which he had interested himself following the illness of a friend in 1783. In 1785 he translated William Cullen's *First Lines of the Practice of Physic* and three volumes of the *Philosophical Transactions of the Royal Society* into French. He also wrote articles on medicine for the daily *Journal de Paris* and, in 1788, published a new edition of Baglivi's *Opera omnia*.

Pinel took no active political role during the Revolution, but devoted himself to attempting to aid those who had been proscribed, among them Condorcet. On 25 August 1793 he was appointed, at the instance of his friends Cabanis and Jacques Thouret, *médecin des infirmeries* of the Hospice de Bicêtre, where he was able to begin implementing his ideas on the humane treatment of the insane. (He had previously been a frequent visitor at the Belhomme nursing home for the mentally ill, but had been unable to convince the director—who was primarily concerned with making a profit—to accept his therapeutic notions.) At the Bicêtre Pinel had the chains removed from his patients, an event commemorated in both paintings and popular prints. On 13 May 1795 he became chief physician of the Hospice de la Salpêtrière, a post that he retained for the rest of his life. Here he was in charge of 5,000 pensioners, aged women, and chronically ill patients; there was a 600-bed ward for the mentally ill, a 250-bed infirmary for acutely ill patients, and, at first, a small infirmary for sick orphans. Pinel was eventually assisted in his work by A. J. Landré-Beauvais, J. E. D. Esquirol, and C. J. A. Schwilgué.

On 4 December 1794 the Convention Nationale (three years after the dissolution of the medical guilds and faculties by the Legislative Assembly) established three *écoles de santé*, and Pinel, upon the recommendation of Fourcroy and Thouret, was named adjunct professor of medical physics at the school in Paris. In 1795 he became professor of medical pathology, a chair that he held for twenty years; he was briefly dismissed from this position in 1822, with ten other professors suspected of political liberalism, but reinstated as an honorary professor shortly thereafter. Pinel was elected to the Académie des Sciences in 1804 and was a member of the Academy of Medicine from its founding in 1820. In addition to working in hospitals and teaching, Pinel often served as a consulting physician, although he did not have the rich and influential patients that Corvisart or Portal did.

The difficult beginning and slow progress of his career neither discouraged nor embittered Pinel, and his eventual success did not diminish his modesty. Although he is properly considered one of the founders of psychiatry, Pinel's contemporaries regarded him as a master of internal medicine, a reputation based upon the authoritative classification of diseases that he set out in his *Nosographie philosophique*, published in 1798.

Pinel's nosological work should be viewed in the context of the great eighteenth-century concern with classification, of which the works of Linnaeus are exemplary. Specifically medical classifications had been offered by William Cullen and David McBride, in 1769 and 1787, respectively, while Erasmus Darwin's *Zoonomia* appeared in 1794–1796. Pinel was aware of the difficulties that his predecessors had faced, but he approached his task cheerfully, secure in his belief that a disease was "an indivisible whole from its commencement to its conclusion, a regular ensemble of characteristic symptoms." Since these symptoms could be observed and analyzed, a classification of disease was possible.

Pinel thus divided diseases into five classes—fevers, phlegmasias, hemorrhages, neuroses, and diseases caused by organic lesions. Nearly one third of the *Nosographie* is devoted to the first class, fevers, which Pinel subdivided into angiotenic, meningogastric, adenomeningic, adynamic, ataxic, and adenoneural forms, corresponding respectively to the inflammatory, bilious, mucous, putrid, malignant, and pestilential fevers of the ancient authors. Pinel subsequently added the order of hectic fevers, which had been described in 1803 by his then disciple Broussais; these six classes were further subdivided into eight genera and a number of species.

Pinel classified phlegmasias by the structure of the affected membranes (or tissues). He thus arrived at five orders: cutaneous phlegmasias, including eruptive fevers and dermatological diseases; mucous phlegmasias, classified by location, and including opthalmia, quinsy, gastritis, and enteritis; serous phlegmasias, including phrenitis, pleurisy, and peritonitis; parenchymatous and cellular phlegmasias; and phlegmasias of the muscle, fibrous, and synovial tissues. In his *Traité des membranes* of 1800, Bichat acknowledged the influence of Pinel's book on his own work.

Among Pinel's third class of diseases, hemorrhage, only those of the mucous membranes (epistaxis, hemoptysis, hematemesis, hemorrhoid, and metrorrhagia) seemed to him to have been studied sufficiently. Among the fourth class, neuroses, Pinel included not only psychiatric illnesses, but also diseases of the sense organs, spasmodic visceral disorders, and dysfunctions of the genital organs. His fifth class, which in the first edition of the *Nosographie* he called "diseases of which the seat is in the lymphatic system," comprised more generally systemic diseases, scurvy, syphilis, and cancer among them, as well as heart disease, dropsy, and kidney stone.

Pinel composed the *Nosographie* as a textbook. It went through several editions, among which important variations may be found. In the first, for example, Pinel refused to acknowledge the distinguishing features of scarlet fever and puerperal fever, although he later classified scarlet fever among the eruptive fevers, and remarked on the occurrence in the same epidemic of both simple quinsy and true scarlet fever. He continued to deny the existence of puerperal fever as an entity (as he continued to deny the existence of fevers concomitant to any stage of reproduction), and it was only in the last edition of his book that he recognized it as a special form of peritonitis. Although the *Nosographie* was a notable success among Pinel's students and disciplines, it also provoked a number of criticisms. Broussais, in particular, attacked Pinel's ideas on idiopathic fevers. Pinel chose to ignore his critics, however, and even forbade his followers to respond to them.

Pinel's other medical writings, from his first communications to the Montpellier Société Royale des Sciences, give evidence of his mathematical training. He drew up precise "tables synoptiques" to determine the frequency of occurrence of certain illnesses, together with their modes of development and their prognoses. He conducted rigorous experiments to measure the effectiveness of various medicines, and devised a numerical method of evaluation. His own therapy was conservative; he contented himself with a pharmacopoeia of only fifty-five vegetable substances and thirty-nine "chemical products," which he used sparingly. He recorded his "extreme distaste" for polypharmacy, objected to the use of bloodletting and purges, and proscribed the use of quinine (even for malaria) and opiates (even for severe pain). Nonetheless, Pinel easily accepted new discoveries, including Corvisart's technique of sounding by percussion and the use of the stethoscope for mediate auscultation, introduced by Laennec. Pinel created an inoculation clinic in his service at the Salpêtrière in 1799 and the first vaccination in Paris was given there in April 1800.

Pinel's psychiatric work effectively transformed the prison for the insane into a hospital. He did not merely initiate better treatment for the mentally ill, however, but rather concerned himself with establishing psychiatry as a discrete branch of medicine. He published a number of articles on the subject, beginning in 1784, then synthesized his findings in "Recherches et observations sur le traitement moral des aliénés" (1799) and *Traité medico-philosophique de l'aliénation mentale* (1801), to which his 1807 communication to the Institut de France is an important supplement.

Pinel's classification of mental diseases retained the old divisions of such illnesses as manic, melancholic, demented, and idiotic. He presented these classes (with a disclaimer—it was necessary to retain them "for the time being," since medicine was not advanced enough for subtler distinctions) as late as 1812. He nevertheless made finer distinctions, isolating mania from delirium, and pointing out that in this state the intellectual functions might be intact, and, in his description of idiocy, citing stupor, the first stage of some types of mental disease. Pinel recognized the relationship between periodic mania and melancholy and hypochondria and stressed the danger of suicide by the melancholic patient. He also mentioned the possibility of altruistic homicide.

In establishing the cause of mental illness, Pinel was wary of "metaphysical discussions or certain ideological ramblings," and he categorically rejected the notion of demonic possession or sorcery. Faithful to the doctrines of Locke and Condillac, he considered emotional disorders to be the primary factor in precipitating intellectual dysfunctions; he also took into account heredity, morbid predisposition, and what he called individual sensitivity.

Pinel's psychiatric therapeutics, his "traitement moral," represented the first attempt at individual psychotherapy. His treatment was marked by gentleness, understanding, and goodwill. He was opposed to violent methods—although he did not hesitate to employ the straitjacket or force-feeding when necessary. He recommended close medical attendance during convalescence, and he emphasized the need of hygiene, physical exercise, and a program of purposeful work for the patient. A number of Pinel's therapeutic procedures, including ergotherapy and the placement of the patient in a family group, anticipate modern psychiatric care.

Pinel was also concerned with the proper training of infirmary personnel and with the proper administration of an institution for the mentally ill. A generation of specialists in mental diseases, led by Esquirol, was educated at the Salpêtrière and disseminated Pinel's ideas throughout Europe.

Pinel was married in 1792 to Jeanne Vincent; of their three sons, one, Scipion, became a specialist in mental illness. Having been widowed in 1811, Pinel was married again, in 1815, to Marie-Madeleine Jacquelin-Lavallée.

BIBLIOGRAPHY

I. ORIGINAL WORKS. Pinel's writings include *Nosographie philosophique ou méthode de l'analyse appliquée à la médecine* (Paris, an VII [1798]; 6th ed., 1818); "Recherches et observations sur le traitement moral des aliénés," in *Mémoires de la Société médicale d émulation de Paris*, **2** (an VII [1799]), 215–255; *Traité médico-philosophique sur l'aliénation mentale ou la manie* (Paris, an IX [1801]; 2nd ed., 1809); *La médecine rendue plus précise et plus exacte par l'application de l'analyse* (Paris, 1802; 3rd ed., 1815); and "Resultats d'observations et construction de tables pour servir à déterminer le degré de probabilité de la guérison des aliénés," in *Mémoires de la classe des sciences mathématiques et physiques de l'Institut* (1807), 169–205.

II. SECONDARY LITERATURE. See E. H. Ackerknecht, *Medicine at the Paris Hospital 1794–1848* (Baltimore, 1967); H. Baruk, *La psychiatrie française de Pinel à nos jours* (Paris, 1967); F. J. V. Broussais, *Examen de la doctrine médicale généralement adoptée et des systèmes modernes de nosologie* (Paris, 1816); P. Chabbert, "Philippe Pinel à Paris (jusqu'à sa nomination à Bicêtre)," in *Comptes rendus du XIXe Congrès international de l'histoire de la médecine* (Basel, 1966), 589–595; M. Foucault, *Histoire de la folie à l'âge classique* (Paris, 1961); and *Naissance de la clinique, une archéologie du regard médical* (Paris, 1963); W. H. Lechler, *Philippe Pinel. Seine Familie, seine Jugend- und Studienjahre* (Munich, 1960); W. Riese, "Philippe Pinel (1745–1826), His Views on Human Nature and Disease, His Medical Thought," in *Journal of Nervous and Mental Disease*, **114**, no. 4 (Oct. 1951), 313–323; and "An Outline of a History of Ideas in Psychotherapy," in *Bulletin of the History of Medicine*, **25**, no. 5 (Sept.–Oct. 1951), 442–456; R. Sémelaigne, *Aliénistes et philanthropes, les Pinel et les Tuke* (Paris, 1912); and J. Vinchon, "Philippe Pinel," in *Commentaires sur dix grands livres de la médecine française* (Paris, 1968), 89–106.

PIERRE CHABBERT

PINGRÉ, ALEXANDRE-GUI (*b.* Paris, France, 4 September 1711; *d.* Paris, 1 May 1796), *astronomy*.

There seem to be few details of Pingré's early life, but he is said to have been a somewhat precocious child with a great desire for knowledge. He was educated by the Congregation of Ste. Geneviève and in 1727, at the age of sixteen, entered the religious order of Ste. Geneviève de Senlis. There is no doubt of his intellectual abilities, for in 1735, when he was only twenty-four, he became professor of theology at the University of Ste. Geneviève. Like many French Roman Catholic clerics, Pingré followed the rather independent Augustinian opinions of the seventeenth-century bishop Cornelis Jansen; and when action was taken against the Jansenists in 1745, he was deprived of his chair and sent by his order to teach Latin in the schools outside Paris. Accused more than once of corrupting the minds of his young pupils, he was obliged to move from one place to another until the eminent surgeon Claude Le Cat decided to help him. In 1744 Le Cat had founded an academy of sciences in Rouen; and since the academy was still without an astronomer in 1749, he invited Pingré, who had recently moved to that city, to accept the post. It proved to be the turning point of Pingré's career. He was later recalled to Paris, where he settled permanently as an astronomer but with literature, history, music and, in later life, botany as his hobbies. Contemporaries spoke of him with affection, and he seems to have been a pious, kindly, and tolerant man.

Pingré was thirty-eight when he began a serious study of astronomy, but within a year he was able to calculate the lunar eclipse of 23 December 1749 well enough for his results to be submitted to the Académie des Sciences in Paris. Certain writers of Pingré's obituary notices state that through these calculations he found an error in the figures for the eclipse that Lacaille had prepared; but the evidence for this, and for the strong friendship between the two men, appears doubtful. Pingré's rapidly growing abilities as an astronomer need not be questioned, however; and after he had made observations at Rouen of the transit of Mercury across the sun's disk in 1753, his reputation was sufficient for the Academy to elect him a *correspondant*. Soon afterward his order recalled him to Paris and established a small observatory for him on the roof of the Abbey of Ste. Geneviève.

Also during 1753 Pingré began working with P. C. Le Monnier, who greatly encouraged him and whom he helped prepare *État du ciel à l'usage de la marine*, a nautical almanac giving hour angles of the moon for the purpose of determining longitude at sea by use of a method devised by Le Monnier. Although the work, which was complementary to the *Connaissance des temps*, did not find favor with mariners and appeared only for the years 1754 to 1757, it greatly enhanced Pingré's reputation as a computer.

Indeed, Pingré was becoming well-known as an astronomer; and in 1755 he was appointed a member of the commission established that year to examine the measurement of an arc of the meridian made some eighty years before by Jean Picard. In 1756 the Academy honored Pingré by electing him *associé libre*, the highest rank of membership open to a cleric. Also about this time he was invited by the provost of the Paris guilds to design a sundial for the corn market that would display the entry of the sun into the various zodiacal signs; this involved Pingré in an observing program as well as much computation, and he did not complete the commission until 1764.

Under the leadership of Delisle, the French took a great interest in the transit of Venus that was to occur in 1761, and Pingré became involved in the international arrangements made to ensure that observations of a phenomenon allowing the sun's distance to be precisely determined were carried out from points as widely scattered as possible. Commissioned by the Academy to observe from Rodriguez Island in the Indian Ocean, he left France early in January 1761.

This was during the Seven Years War; and since British naval supremacy might possibly present difficulties, Pingré armed himself with instructions from the British authorities commanding that he be unmolested and allowed to proceed without delay. His outward journey was uneventful until his ship met a damaged French vessel, the commander of which ordered Pingré's ship to stay with him. Only Pingré's dogged persistence got him and his assistant Denis Thuillier transshipped at last, and they arrived at Rodriguez with little time left to establish their observatory. At the transit on 6 June there was rain and cloud for a great part of the time, so that only a few observations could be made. The island was later sacked three times by the British; and the expedition's ship was attacked and boarded on the way home, despite Pingré's British instructions. Therefore, when the vessel reached Lisbon, Pingré decided to journey overland, reaching Paris late in May 1762. The expedition was not unsuccessful, for besides a few useful transit observations, Pingré had many longitude determinations, some of which led to a replotting of the charted position of the Cape Verde Islands. His analysis of the observations led him to the rather large value of 10.6 seconds of arc for the solar parallax, a figure that he later modified.

On his return Pingré also became engaged in preparing a second edition of Lacaille's *L'art de vérifier les dates*, originally designed to give sufficient details of eclipses during the previous 1,800 years to serve as a guide for dating historical events. He checked all the calculations and added additional eclipses up to A.D. 1900. The new edition appeared in 1770; but Pingré continued to work on the subject, computing eclipses back to 1000 B.C. and publishing the results in the *Mémoires de mathématique et physique* . . . of the French Academy. He also took a leading part in the preparations for observing the 1769 transit of Venus, and in 1766 and 1767 he presented two reports to the Academy about suitable observing stations. Undaunted by his previous experiences—the war was now over—Pingré set forth on voyages in 1767, 1768, and 1771. They were primarily intended to check chronometers by Ferdinand Berthoud and

Leroy, but on the 1768 voyage he visited Haiti, where he observed the 1769 transit. Later he recomputed the solar parallax from the complete observations; and in 1772 he announced a value of 8.8 seconds of arc, a figure extremely close to the present figure of 8.794.

Having become astronomer-geographer to the navy, Pingré in 1769 was appointed chancellor of his old university. In 1772 he became librarian at Ste. Geneviève; and although in his sixties, he continued with his computing and began to take an increasing interest in old observations. Pingré put his immense classical knowledge to use in translating and editing the *Astronomica* of Marcus Manilius and the earlier *Phaenomena* of Aratus of Soli, and especially in preparing his most important work, the two-volume *Cométographie ou traité historique et théorique des comètes* (1783–1784). This monumental work was divided into four parts, the first of which was a history of astronomy from Babylonian and Egyptian times, with particular reference to ideas about comets. The second part was a catalog of all comets observed since antiquity, with the orbital elements of 166 for which paths had been computed, 50 of them by Pingré himself. The third section discussed cometary returns, theories about the nature of comets, and the physical effects likely to ensue from their close approach to the earth. The fourth part concerned cometary orbits and methods for computing them. The high reputation of the *Cométographie* was deserved, and as recently as 1950 it was officially recommended as a source book of cometary information.

Pingré's other great book, the purely historical *Annales célestes du dix-septième siècle*, took him thirty years to complete and contained carefully checked and edited astronomical observations from the seventeenth century, both published and unpublished. In 1791 Le Monnier and Lalande persuaded the Academy to vote a large sum for its publication; but the printer was slow, and Pingré's death in 1796, coupled with devaluation the preceding year, led the printer to abandon the project and to sell the printed sheets as wastepaper. Worse still, the manuscript was lost. Almost a century later, however, a Parisian bibliophile found in a country town what turned out to be Le Monnier's set of sheets; and the remainder of the manuscript was discovered in the archives of the Paris observatory. In 1898, at the instigation of C. G. Bigourdain, the Academy again decided to publish; and the volume appeared in 1901. There is still a voluminous collection of Pingré's unedited manuscripts at the library of Ste. Geneviève. They do not seem to be astronomical, however, but to cover his other interests, ranging from translations of Spanish voyages, history and historical criticism, and literary sketches to liturgical hymns, musical satires, and a vast amount of French and Latin poetry. It is as an astronomer, however, that Pingré is remembered.

BIBLIOGRAPHY

I. ORIGINAL WORKS. Pingré's main works were *Cométographie ou traité historique et théorique des comètes*, 2 vols. (Paris, 1783–1784); and *Annales célestes du dix-septième siècle*, C. G. Bigourdain, ed. (Paris, 1901).

II. SECONDARY LITERATURE. The most complete biographical note is G. Riche de Prony, "Notice sur la vie et les ouvrages d'Alexandre-Gui Pingré," in *Mémoires de l'Institut national des sciences et arts. Sciences mathématiques et physiques* (an VI [1798]), **1**, xxvi–xlvi. There is also a reasonably full note on his astronomy, with some strictures on his accuracy as an observer, by J. B. Delambre in his *Histoire de l'astronomie du dix-huitième siècle* (Paris, 1827), 664–687. For a résumé of his work in connection with the transits of Venus, see H. Woolf, *The Transits of Venus* (Princeton, 1959), esp. 98–115.

COLIN A. RONAN

PIRES, TOMÉ (*b.* Portugal, *ca.* 1470; *d.* China, *ca.* 1540), *pharmacology.*

Little is known of Pires' life before his arrival in India in 1511. He was the son of a royal apothecary and was himself "apothecary of prince D. Alfonso," perhaps the son of João II, king of Portugal. Pires was undoubtedly attracted to India by the prospect of the good career that apothecaries (frequently mentioned in documents of the period) could expect to make for themselves there. In 1511, aboard a fleet commanded by Garcia de Noronha, he went to Cochin, where it may be assumed that he practiced his trade. From a letter signed by Pires it can be deduced that he held the post of "factor of drugs."

In 1513 Pires was chosen to go to Malacca to help the factor put an end to troubles arising from trade duties. He was subsequently named registrar and checker of the Portuguese entrepôt, as well as factor. Profiting from his stay in Malacca, he took a position as clerk in a fleet bound for Java, where he visited the northern coast.

When Pires returned to Cochin in 1515, the first Portugese voyage to China was being organized; and Lopo Soares d'Albergaria, successor to Afonso de Albuquerque in the Portuguese government of India, chose him to be ambassador to China. Pires departed in February 1516 aboard a fleet of five ships under the command of Fernão Peres de Andrade. A year later he arrived in Canton but had to remain there for three years before reaching the court of the emperor in Peking. He was rejected by the Chinese nobles, and thus returned, disillusioned, to Canton, where he and three or four companions were imprisoned. Pires was later freed but was never able to leave China.

Pires' only known work is *Suma oriental*, a masterpiece on the geography, ethnography, and commerce of the Orient at the beginning of the sixteenth century.

BIBLIOGRAPHY

I. ORIGINAL WORKS. Two different MS copies of *Suma oriental* have been preserved: at the National Library in Lisbon (MS 299), and at the library of the Chamber of Deputies in Paris. The first ed., an Italian trans. by G. B. Ramusio from a MS similar to the one in Paris, was *Sommario di tutti le regni, citta, & populi orientali, con li traffichi & mercantie, che iui si trovano, comenciando dal mar Rosso fino alli populi della China* (Venice, 1550). In 1944 Armando Cortesão prepared the Paris MS for publication, providing an English trans. and detailed intro., *The Suma Oriental of Tomé Pires, an Account of the East, From the Red Sea to Japan . . . Written in Malacca and India in 1512–1515 . . .*, 2 vols. (London, 1944).

II. SECONDARY LITERATURE. On Pires and his work, see A. Cortesão, *A primeira embaixada portuguesa à China* (Lisbon, 1945); and "A propósito do ilustre boticário Tomé Pires," in *Revista portuguesa de farmácia*, **13** (1963). See also T'ien-Tse Chang, "Malacca and the Failure of the First Portuguese Embassy to Peking," in *Journal of Southeast Asian History*, **3** (1962).

LUÍS DE ALBUQUERQUE

PIRĪ RAIS (or Re'is), MUḤYĪ AL-DĪN (*b.* Gelibolu [Gallipoli], Turkey, 1470; *d.* Egypt, 1554), *geography, cartography.*

Pirī Rais was the son of Hajjī Muḥammad Rais and the nephew of Kemal Rais, a famous Turkish admiral. From 1487 to 1493 he served in the Turkish navy and fought in several battles under the supervision of his uncle. After the death of his uncle in 1511, he left the navy and began work on his first map. Subsequently he entered the service of the Algerian corsair Khair al-Din Barbarossa (*ca.* 1483–1546).

In 1516–1517 Pirī was given command of several vessels that were involved in the Ottoman campaign against Egypt. He conquered Alexandria, a feat that enabled him to meet Sultan Selim I (1512–1520), to whom he presented the map of 1513, completed at Gelibolu.

After Egypt was joined to the Ottoman Empire, Pirī returned to Gelibolu and began to write his *Kitab-i Bahriye*. Because of the conflict in Egypt, he was appointed as a guide to Ibrahim Pasha of Parga

(1493–1536). On the way to Egypt, a storm forced the fleet to take refuge at Rhodes for a month. Pirī's frequent references to his records attracted the attention of Ibrahim Pasha, who encouraged him to complete his book so that it could be presented to the sultan. In 1526 Pirī was appointed admiral of the South Seas. His last official post was admiral of the Red and Arabian seas.

In 1929 a fragment of a map was discovered in the Topkapi Palace Museum (Figure 1). It depicts the Iberian Peninsula, the western bulge of North Africa, the Atlantic Ocean, and the coast and the islands of America. It is drawn with great care on gazelle hide and includes colored pictures and marginal notes about the countries, peoples, animals, and plants. The signature reveals that this is the map drawn by Pirī Rais in 1513 and presented to Sultan Selim I in 1517.

The map is a portolano chart, a design that was thought to be simple and to have no mathematical basis. There are no markings for latitude and longitude; instead there are lines radiating from centers. The assumption regarding mathematics is erroneous. The existence of a mathematical basis for Pirī's map was initially suggested by the five projection centers in the Atlantic Ocean. It was then easy to convert the portolano to modern coordinates of latitude and longitude. One can see two compass roses, one in the north and one in the south. Each is divided into thirty-two parts, and the division lines extend beyond the rose frames.

In one of the marginal notes, Pirī states that he used some twenty maps in constructing his own. Eight of these were of the world, drawn in the days of Alexander the Great; four were by Portuguese explorers and recorded the discoveries made before 1508 on the South American coast by Vespucci, Vicente Yáñez Pinzón (commander of the *Niña* in 1492–1493), and Juan Díaz de Solis (d. 1516); one by an Indian; and one, the most important, that had belonged to Columbus. The latter may have come into Pirī's possession during the fight against the Spanish in the western basin of the Mediterranean in 1501.

Pirī's map has all the important information that was on Columbus' map. For instance, Trinidad is spelled "Kalerot," which probably was derived from a point on the island that was named Galera by Columbus. Puerto Rico is called San Juan Bautista. The drawing of islands on the South American coast opposite Trinidad shows the influence of Columbus, who believed the newly discovered continent to be a group of islands. Haiti was called Hispaniola by Columbus and the Island of Spain by Pirī. The Antilles and Cuba are shown on the map as a continent, as they were believed to be by Columbus. Hence Pirī called Central America "the coast of Antillia."

The fifth marginal note about America and its discovery states:

> These coasts are named the shores of Antillia. They were discovered in the year 896 of Hijra. It is reported that a Genoese infidel named Colombo discovered these places. A book fell into the hands of Colombo; and he found in it that at the end of the western side [of the world], there were coasts and islands and all sorts of metals and precious stones. Having studied this book thoroughly, Colombo explained these matters to the great of Genoa and said, "Give me two ships. Let me go and find these places." They said, "Can an end or a limit be found to the Western Sea? Its vapor is full of darkness." Colombo saw that no help was forthcoming from the Genoese. He went to the king of Spain and told his story in detail. The answer was that of the Genoese. Colombo petitioned for a long time, until finally the king of Spain gave him two ships, saw that they were well equipped, and said, "Colombo, if it happens as you say, we will make you an Admiral."

Cities and citadels are indicated on the map by red lines. Mountains are drawn in outline and rivers are marked with thick lines; rocky regions are indicated in black; shoals and shallow waters by reddish dots; and rocky areas in the sea by crosses. One of the remarkable aspects of Pirī's map is that the features on the Atlantic coast of Africa bear Turkish names: Babadağ (Father Mountain); Akburun (White Cape), now Cape Blanco; Yeşil Burun (Green Cape), now Cape Verde; this map is an original work based on various maps and the personal experience of Pirī Rais and his friends.

In 1528, in Gelibolu, Pirī Rais drew a second map (Figure 2). The upper left corner shows the northern part of the Atlantic Ocean and newly discovered regions of North and Central America. Greenland is in the north and the Azores in the south. The Azores include San Mikal, Santa Maria, Buriko, and San Jorjo. Two large pieces of land are depicted. The one in the north is called Baccolao; the other, Terra Nova. Pirī says that both were discovered by Portuguese. Terra Nova had not yet been fully explored, and only the known parts are shown on the map. He calls Florida "San Juan Bautisto," the name given to Puerto Rico on the 1513 map. Cuba, Haiti, the Bahamas, and the Antilles are drawn accurately.

In the notes near Labrador, Pirī says, "This is Baccolao; the Portuguese infidels discovered it. The coasts of Terra Nova were discovered by the Portuguese explorer Carlos Real in 1500, and his brother Miguel Real discovered Labrador a year later."

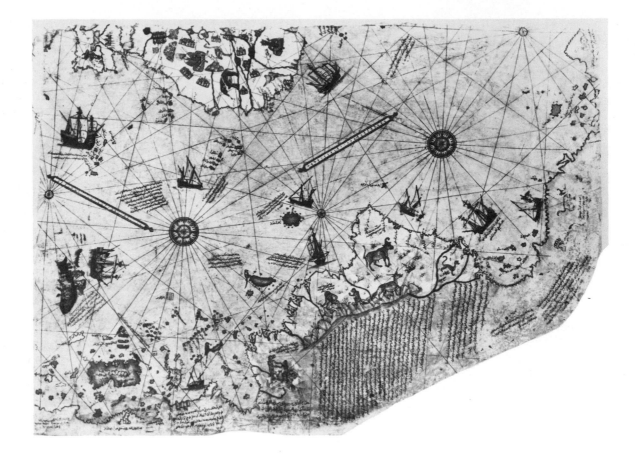

FIGURE 1.   The map of 1513 (above).

FIGURE 2.   The map of 1528 (below).

FIGURE 3.   Map from *Kitab-ī Bahriye*, 1521 (right).

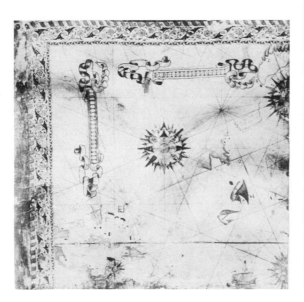

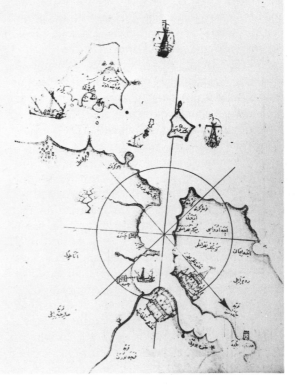

Pirī cites an explorer who planned to travel overland to reach the ocean. It is quite possible that he meant Balboa, who crossed the Isthmus of Panama and reached the Pacific Ocean in 1513.

By comparison of these two maps one can easily deduce that Pirī Rais continued to follow the new discoveries with great care. He showed only the parts of the world that had been discovered and left the unexplored areas blank. When Vespucci declared that South America was a new continent, that land drew the attention of the geographers. Consequently various maps of the new continent were drawn, and Pirī was the most important of the cartographers involved.

To make available all his own observations and all previous information that he could not fit onto the maps, Pirī collected them as *Kitab-ī Bahriye* ("On Navigation"; 1521). It is basically a naval guidebook with essential data on the most important coastal routes and large maps and detailed charts in different colors (Figure 3). The main portion of the book is devoted to the Mediterranean coast and islands.

The book is composed of twenty-one chapters. Pirī first gives historical and geographical information and then discusses the necessary practical navigational data. The accuracy of many of his statements is indisputable. In chapters 1 and 2 Pirī explains his aim in writing the book and describes his life at sea with Kemal Rais. In chapters 3–5 he gives information about storms, winds, and the compass. Chapters 6 and 7 concern maps and emblematic signs on maps. In chapter 8 Pirī discusses the continents and the seas. Chapter 9 is devoted to the geographic discoveries of the Portuguese. In chapter 21 Pirī mentions the Atlantic Ocean and tells the reader of a new continent, Antiliā, the mountains of which contain rich gold ores and in the seas, pearls. He says that it was discovered by sailors and gives information about the inhabitants, frightful creatures having flat faces and eyes a full span apart. The chapter on the Western Sea contains all that was known about the discovery of America at the time.

BIBLIOGRAPHY

Pirī Rais's only published work is *Kitab-ī Bahriye*, Şerafettin Yaltkaya, ed. (Istanbul, 1935).

Secondary literature includes A. Adnan Adivar, *Osmanli Türklerinde Ilim* (Istanbul, 1943); Afet I'nan, "Bir Türk amirali; XVI. astin büyük ceografi: Pirī Reis (Un amiral-géographe turc du XVI siècle—Pirī Reis, auteur de la plus ancienne carte de l'Amérique)," in *Belleten*, 1, no. 2 (1937), 333–348; *America's Oldest Map Made by a Turkish Admiral: Pirī Reis*, trans. by Leman Yolaç (Ankara, 1950); and *Pirī Reis' in Amerika Haritasi, 1513–1528*

(Ankara, 1950); Yusuf Akçura, "Map Drawn by Pirī Reis," in *Illustrated London News* (23 July 1923); and "Pirī Reis haritasi hakkinda izahname (Die Karte des Pirī Reis. Pirī Reis Map. Carte de Pirī Reis)," in *Türk tarih karamu* (Istanbul, 1935); H. Alpagut, F. Kurtoğlu, "Mukaddime I-LV: Pirī Reis: *Kitab-ī Bahriye*," *ibid.*, no. 2 (Istanbul, 1935); W. Y. Callien, "The Evolution of the Map of the Earth (Dünya haritasinin evrimi)," in *Ankara üniversitesi Dil ve tarih-coğrafya fakültesi dergisi*, 8, no. 1 (1949), 149–153; H. Deismann, *Forschungen und Funde im Serai* (Berlin–Leipzig, 1933), 111–122; and Charles H. Hapgood, "Ancient Knowledge of America and Antarctica," in *Actes du dixième Congrès international d'histoire des sciences* (Ithaca, N.Y., 1962), 479–485.

See also P. Kahle, *Pirī Reis, Bahriye, Das türkisches Segelhandbuch für das mittelländische Meer von Jahre 1521*, 2 vols. (Berlin–Leipzig, 1926); "Importe colombiane in una carta turco del 1513," in *Cultura*, 1, fasc. 10 (Milan-Rome, 1931), 1–13; *Die verscholtene Columbus Karte non 1498 in einer Türkisen Weltkarte von 1513* (Berlin-Leipzig, 1933), with trans. as "The Lost Columbus Map of 1498 Discovered in a Turkish Map of the World of 1513," in *Aligarh Muslim University Journal* (1935); Hans von Mžik, "Pirī Reis und seine *Bahriye*," in *Beiträge zur historischen Geographie* (Leipzig–Vienna, 1929), 60–76; Ibrahim Hakki Konyali, *Topkapi Sarayinda deri üzerine yapilmiş eski haritalar* (Istanbul, 1936); K. Kretchmer, *Die Entwicklung der Kartographie von America* (Gotha, 1891); Eugen Oberhummer, "Eine Turkische Karte zur Entdeckung Americas," in *Anzeiger der Akademie der Wissenschaften, Wien* (1931), 18–27; and "Eine Karte des Colombus in Türkische Überlieferung," in *Mitteilungen der Geographischen Gesellschaft, Wien*, 78 (1934), 115.

Additional works are Sadi Selen, "Pirī Reis' in Şimali Amerika Haritasi . . .," in *Belleten*, 1, no. 2 (1937), 515–523; and Huseyin Yurdaydin, "*Kitab-ī Bahriye*'nin telif meselesi," in *Ankara üniversitesi Dil ve tarih-coğrafya fakultesi dergisi*, 10, pts. 1–2 (1952), 143–146.

SEVİM TEKELİ

PIROGOV, NIKOLAY IVANOVICH (*b*. Moscow, Russia, 25 November 1810; *d*. Vishnya, Ukraine, Russia, 5 December 1881), *surgery, anatomy.*

The son of a major in the commissary service, Pirogov grew up in fairly cultured surroundings, learned to read early, and was fluent in foreign languages as a child. In 1824 the family was left without means and the father died suddenly. Pirogov might have become a civil servant; but Efrem Mukhin, the family physician, who was professor of surgery and anatomy at Moscow University, arranged for him to be admitted to the Medical Faculty at Moscow, even though Pirogov was then only fourteen and the entrance age was sixteen.

Pirogov chose surgery as his specialty; but during his four years at the university he was present at only two operations and did not perform any himself. Nevertheless, he received a good general theoretical preparation. After graduating in 1828, he was sent, with Mukhin's advice and help, for a teaching career at Dorpat (now Tartu) University, where the professorial institute was being established. He studied surgery and anatomy under the direction of J. F. Moier and in 1832 defended his doctoral dissertation, on the ligation of the ventral aorta. In this important work, which was soon published in a German translation, Pirogov tried not only to improve the technical procedure of the operation but also to explain how the body reacts to it.

From 1833 to 1835 Pirogov visited the leading German clinics and observed the existing state of surgery. He became convinced that without special study of anatomy and physiology, surgery—even with the most advanced technique—could never rise to the level of a science but would remain an art. Upon his return to Russia, Pirogov found that the chair of surgery at Moscow University that he himself had hoped to win was occupied; thus, in 1836, he accepted the post of professor of surgery at Dorpat. Although he was only twenty-six, his reputation was already substantial. A work published the following year laid the foundation of surgical anatomy.

From 1841 to 1856 Pirogov headed the department of surgery and the surgical clinic, founded on his initiative, at the 1,000-bed hospital of the St. Petersburg Medical-Surgical Academy. He also taught pathological anatomy and founded a museum of anatomical pathology at the Academy. Working in an unheated, poorly lit basement that was the anatomical theater of the Academy, Pirogov lectured and performed countless operations and 12,000 dissections in anatomical pathology. During this time he spent about three years in military service, organizing and providing medical aid to the wounded. In 1847 he developed a theory of the action and use of anesthetic and, before using it on a patient, tested it on himself. He was the first to introduce anesthetic through the rectum, and in his clinic choloroform was first used in Russia. He also originated the intravenous administration of anesthetic ether. Pirogov was the first to use ether under battle conditions (1847); and in 1854–1855, during the siege of Sevastopol, he introduced the mass use of anesthetic in surgical operations at the front.

Pirogov's work on topographical anatomy (1851–1859) laid a firm foundation for that field as a special area of science having great practical significance for surgery. The work was followed by his discovery of new methods of anatomical research: the study of the forms and relative positions of the organs by dissecting frozen cadavers and removing organs from them. Both these extremely simple methods opened previously unknown possibilities for precisely determining the forms and positions of organs and tissues. Pirogov's work comprised four volumes of drawings of organs and tissues in their natural relative positions and an explanatory text. It immediately received widespread recognition and enhanced his reputation as a distinguished surgeon and anatomist.

During the Crimean War, Pirogov organized medical aid and developed the basic principles of field surgery. The first to use plaster casts, he conceived the technique in 1851 while observing the work of a sculptor. His experiences in field surgery, published in German in 1864, became a standard reference.

In 1856 Pirogov returned to St. Petersburg. Irritated by conditions at the Medical-Surgical Academy, he retired permanently from teaching and hospital work. In the same year Pirogov published a paper on the problems of pedagogy, which produced a great impression. He condemned the restrictions on education for the poor and for non-Russians and supported education for women. He also came out against early specialization and advocated the development of secondary schools. After the death of Nicholas I, Pirogov was appointed director of school affairs for the south of Russia. He came into conflict with the governor-general of Odessa and in 1858 was transferred to the same post in Kiev. He was forced to retire three years later and settled on his estate in the southern Ukraine. In 1862 he was named director of a group of young Russian scientists sent abroad to prepare for professorships. After Garibaldi had been severely wounded in the leg in August 1862 during the battle of Aspromonte, Pirogov attended him and recommended a successful method of cure. After his return to Russia in 1866, Pirogov lived almost exclusively on his estate, which he left for prolonged periods only twice: in 1870, when he traveled to the battlefields of the Franco-Prussian War as a representative of the Russian Red Cross; and in 1877, when he served as a surgeon in the Russo-Turkish War for the independence of Bulgaria.

Pirogov's other achievements include a procedure for amputation of the shin that retained the calcaneal bone; improved methods of tying the major blood vessels for hemostasis; a classic description of shock; the use—before the introduction of antisepsis—of spirit of camphor, aqueous solution of chlorine, or tincture of iodine to combat the festering of wounds;

and the demonstration of the importance of diet in treating the wounded.

Pirogov is considered a founder of contemporary surgery and topographical anatomy, and I. P. Pavlov credited him with placing surgery on a scientific basis.

BIBLIOGRAPHY

I. ORIGINAL WORKS. Recent collections of Pirogov's writings are *Izbrannye pedagogicheskie sochinenia* ("Selected Pedagogical Works"; Moscow, 1953); and *Sobranie sochiney* ("Collected Works"), 8 vols. (Moscow, 1957–1962). Important works published during his lifetime are *Anatomia topographica. . .* , 4 vols. (Petropoli, 1851–1859); and *Grundzüge der allgemeinen Kriegschirurgie* (Leipzig, 1864), translated into Russian as *Nachala obshchey voennopolevoy khirurgii* ("The Principles of General Military Field Surgery"), 2 vols. (Dresden, 1865–1866).

II. SECONDARY LITERATURE. See N. N. Burdenko, "N. I. Pirogov—osnovopolozhnik voenno-polevoy khirurgii" ("N. I. Pirogov—Founder of Military Field Surgery"), in Pirogov's *Nachala obshchey voenno-polevoy khirurgii* ("Beginnings of General Military Field Surgery"), I (Moscow, 1941), 9–42; A. M. Geselevich and Y. I. Smirnov, *N. I. Pirogov* (Moscow, 1960); A. N. Maksimenkov, *N. I. Pirogov* (Leningrad, 1961); and I. G. Rufanov, *N. I. Pirogov—veliky russky khirurg i ucheny* ("N. I. Pirogov—Great Russian Surgeon and Scientist"; Moscow, 1956).

S. R. MIKULINSKY

PISANO. See **Fibonacci, Leonardo.**

PISO, WILLEM (*b.* Leiden, Netherlands, *ca.* 1611; *d.* Amsterdam, Netherlands, November 1678), *medicine, pharmacy.*

Piso was the son of Hermannus Piso van Cleef; his mother's name is unknown.[1] He matriculated as a medical student at the University of Leiden in 1623, at the age of twelve. He received the M.D. degree at Caen[2] on 4 July 1633 and subsequently established a practice in Amsterdam.

Piso's fame rests on his work as physician of the Dutch settlement in Brazil (1636–1644), which had Johan Maurits van Nassau as governor.[3] In Brazil he gathered the data for the books that made him famous.

Although he already had the M.D. degree, Piso matriculated at Leiden again on 3 March 1645, after his return from Brazil. He must soon have rejoined his former chief, however, for a letter dated September 1645 was sent by Piso to his friend Caspar van Baerle, professor of philosophy at the Amsterdam Athenaeum, from the "camp of Maurits van Nassau."[4]

Later Piso settled in Amsterdam, and on 1 September 1648 he married Constantia Spranger. He became a leading physician there, serving as *decanus* of the Collegium Medicum from 1656 to 1660 and again in 1670. His name is mentioned as a consultant in the works of Nicolaas Tulp (1593–1674) and Job van Meekren (*ca.* 1611–1666). Piso is remembered for his work in tropical medicine and pharmacy, but his chief contribution was perhaps his scientific approach to his work. Although he could not free himself from the Hippocratic and Galenic doctrines he had studied at the university and he explained some of his observations in terms of them, he studied the medical lore of the Brazilian natives very closely and felt free to adopt and recommend their methods if they proved effective. He was the first to point out that the health of Europeans in the tropics is best preserved by adopting the way in which the natives live. During the first decades of their settling in the tropics, the Dutch lived as they had at home. They built their houses of brick; they wore heavy, dark clothing; they swaddled their infants. These practices caused diseases, and the infant mortality was enormous. Piso told his compatriots to beware of the cool nights in Brazil; not to drink too much, especially sour beverages; and to take plenty of exercise. Piso recorded what he had learned in Brazil in *Historia naturalis Brasiliae*, a folio volume in twelve books, the first four of which are by Piso while the others, which deal chiefly with natural history, were written by Georg Markgraaff.[5] The latter was probably an assistant to Piso, for Piso says in several places that he ordered Markgraaff to make drawings or perform other chores in his free time. In a later edition, *De Indiae utriusque re naturali et medica*, the subject matter of the book is more consolidated, and in the process the distinction between contributions of the two authors has become somewhat vague; consequently, Piso has sometimes been accused of plagiarism. That Piso did not intend to take credit for what was not his is clear from the first edition, where the line is sharply drawn. His editing of *De Indiae* was done because the work was intended to be a handbook of tropical medicine, pharmacology, and natural history. His share covered the Americas, while the East Indies were represented by adding the complete works of Jacobus Bontius.[6]

Piso was the first to distinguish yaws, which he called *bubas*, from venereal disease, and he recommended the treatment used by the natives. He stated that defective nutrition was the cause of hemeralopia (day blindness),[7] fully discussed tropical intestinal disorders, and distinguished their various forms. Dysentery ("fluxus cum febre et sanguine") in particular was well researched; Piso recommended the native root ipecacuanha to cure this disease, advice followed for centuries. His description of the chigoe (*Pulex penetrans* or *Tunga penetrans*), the troubles it causes, and the treatment of these troubles has never been surpassed. Here again, he needed the experience of the Brazilian natives. On numerous expeditions into the back country, Piso searched for medicinal herbs. He was the first to bring ipecacuanha to the attention of the Western medical world and also discussed such American specifics as *Radix Chinae* (*Smilax Pseudo China* L.), sarsaparilla (*Smilax sarsaparilla* L.), *Radix mechoacan* (*Convolvulus brasiliensis* L.), sassafras (*Laurus sassafras* L.), and guaiacum (*Guaiacum officinale*). For these and other contributions, Piso deserves to be remembered as one of the pioneers of tropical medicine.

NOTES

1. Van Andel (intro. to "Capita") and Baumann state that the family name originally was Pies, while von Römer states that it was Lepois. A French physician, Charles Lepois (1563–1633), was also known as Carolus Piso. But Willem Piso's father was called "van Cleef," which indicates a German origin.
2. Not at Leiden in 1630, as von Römer states.
3. Johan Maurits van Nassau (1604–1679) served in the army of the States-General from 1621.
4. According to van Andel (intro. to "Capita"). This can be only Johan Maurits van Nassau; there was no Maurits van Nassau alive at the time. Upon his return from Brazil, Johan Maurits van Nassau became lieutenant general of the cavalry of the States-General (24 Oct. 1644) and commander of the fortress at Wesel (3 Nov. 1644). Hence this letter was probably sent from Wesel. See F. J. G. ten Raa and F. de Bas, *Het Staatsche leger*, IV (Breda, 1918), 332, 342.
5. Markgraaff appears to be unknown in the biographical literature. There is no M.D. after his name on the title page of the *Historia naturalis Brasiliae*. After his name is "de Liebstadt, Misnici Germani." Both Liebstadt and Misnia (Meissen) are in Saxony. According to van Andel ("Willem Piso"), Markgraaff died in 1643 on the coast of Guinea. Several variants of the name are found: Marcgraaf, Marggraaf, Marcgrav.
6. Jacobus Bontius (1592–1631), physician to the Dutch East India Company in Batavia, 1627–1631. See *Opuscula selecta Neerlandicorum de arte medica*, X (Amsterdam, 1931).
7. Not night blindness, as van Andel ("Willem Piso") states. See Vos, where a translation of Piso's remarks on tropical eye diseases is given.

BIBLIOGRAPHY

I. Original Works. *Historia naturalis Brasiliae . . . in qua non tantum plantae et animalia, sed indigenarum morbi, ingenia mores describuntur et iconibus supra quingentas illustrantur* (Amsterdam, 1648) consists of 12 books, of which the first 4, by Piso, have the general title *De medicina Brasiliensi*. They are *De aere, aquis et locis*; *De morbis endemiis*; *De venenatis et antidotis*; *De facultatibus*

simplicium. The remaining 8 were written by Markgraaff under the general title *Historiae rerum naturalium Brasiliae*. These are *De plantis* (3 bks.); *De piscibus*; *De avibus*; *De quadripedibus et serpentibus*; *De insectis*; *De ipsa regione et illius incolis cum appendice de Tapuyis et de Chilensibus*.

In *De Indiae utriusque re naturali et medica* (Amsterdam, 1658), the subject matter is organized somewhat differently. Piso contributed *Historiae naturalis et medicinae Indiae Occidentalis libri quinque* and *Mantissa aromatica, sive de aromatum cardinalibus quator et plantis aliquot Indices in medicinum receptis, relatio nova*; Markgraaff wrote *Tractatus topographicus et meteorologicus Brasiliae, cum observatione eclipsis solaris, quibus additi sunt illius et aliorum commentarii de Brasiliensium et Chilensum indole et lingua*. This book also contains the complete works of Jacobus Bontius with some editing by Piso.

Oost- en West Indische warande. Vervattende aldaar de leef- en geneeskonst. Met een verhaal van de specerijen, boom- en aard gewassen, dieren, etc. Door Jac. Bontius, Gul. Piso en Geo. Markgraef (Amsterdam, 1694; 2nd ed. 1734) is not a trans. but an abstract of the writings of Bontius, Piso, and Markgraaff compiled for the use of naval and tropical surgeons.

A later Latin ed. of part of his main work is *Historia medica Brasiliae, novam editionem curavit et praefatus est Josephus Eques de Vering . . .* (Vienna, 1817); a Portuguese version is *Historia natural do Brasil illustrada. Edição comemorativa do primeiro cinquentenário du Museu Paulista* (São Paulo, 1948).

In the library of the University of Leiden are three letters by Piso: to J. van Wullen, a Lutheran minister in Amsterdam; to Nicolaas Heinsius (1620–1681), a Latin poet and diplomat; and to Caspar van Baerle (1584–1648), the author of *Rerum per octennium in Brasilia et alibi nuper gestarum* (Amsterdam, 1647, 1660, 1698; German trans., Kleve, 1659).

II. Secondary Literature. See M. A. van Andel, "Willem Piso, een baanbreker der tropische geneeskunde," in *Bijdragen tot de geschiedenis der geneeskunde*, **4** (1924), 239–254; "Bontius en Piso over de dysenterie in de beide Indiën," *ibid.*, **11** (1931), 285–292; and intro. to "Capita nonnula de ventris fluxibus, de dysteneria, de lue indica, di ipecacuanha," in *Opuscula selecta Neerlandicorum de arte medica*, XIV (Amsterdam, 1937), xii–xxxviii, the best study on Piso, in Dutch and English, with extracts from Piso's works in the original language (Latin or Dutch) with English trans.; E. D. Baumann, *Uit drie eeuwen Nederlandsche geneeskunde* (Amsterdam, 1951), 102–104; L. S. A. M. von Römer, "Dr. Willem Piso," in *Nieuw Nederlandsch biografisch woordenboek*, IX (1933), 805–806, unreliable; J. van den Vondel, "Behoude reis aen Willem Pizo, Graef Maurits van Nassaus doctor, staende op sijn vertreck naer Brezijl," in H. Diferee, ed., *De volledige werken van Joost van den Vondel*, II (Utrecht, 1929), 375–376; and J. A. Vos, "De geneeskunde, in het bijzonder de oogheelkunde, bij Willem Piso," in *Bijdragen tot de geschiedenis der geneeskunde*, **39** (1959), 7–11.

PETER W. VAN DER PAS

Dictionary
of Scientific
Biography
cSs